Fodor's

D0901144

SPAIN

**Where to Stay and Eat
for All Budgets**

**Must-See Sights
and Local Secrets**

Ratings You Can Trust

Fodor's Travel Publications   New York, Toronto, London, Sydney, Auckland
www.fodors.com

FODOR'S SPAIN

Editors: Debbie Harmsen and John D. Rambow

Editorial Production: Bethany Cassin Beckerlegge
Editorial Contributors: Ben Curtis, Ignacio Gómez, Michael Kessler, Jared Lubarsky, Mary McLean, Norman Renouf, George Semler, Stephen "Kip" Tobin
Maps: David Lindroth, *cartographer*; Rebecca Baer and Bob Blake, *map editors*
Design: Fabrizio La Rocca, *creative director*; Guido Caroti, *art director*; Melanie Marin, *senior picture editor*
Production/Manufacturing: Colleen Ziemba
Cover Photo (The Corrida, San Fermin Festival, Pamplona): Alan Copson/age fotostock

SPECIAL SALES

This book is available for special discounts for bulk purchases for sales promotions or premiums. Special editions, including personalized covers, excerpts of existing books, and corporate imprints, can be created in large quantities for special needs. For more information, write to Special Markets/Premium Sales, 1745 Broadway, MD 6-2, New York, NY 10019, or e-mail specialmarkets@randomhouse.com.

AN IMPORTANT TIP & AN INVITATION

Although all prices, opening times, and other details in this book are based on information supplied to us at press time, changes occur all the time in the travel world, and Fodor's cannot accept responsibility for facts that become outdated or for inadvertent errors or omissions. So **always confirm information when it matters,** especially if you're making a detour to visit a specific place. Your experiences—positive and negative—matter to us. If we have missed or misstated something, **please write to us.** We follow up on all suggestions. Contact the Spain editor at editors@fodors.com or c/o Fodor's at 1745 Broadway, New York, NY 10019.

THIS 2007 EDITION PRINTED IN THE UNITED STATES OF AMERICA

10 9 8 7 6 5 4 3 2 1

Be a Fodor's Correspondent

Your opinion matters. It matters to us. It matters to your fellow Fodor's travelers, too. And we'd like to hear it. In fact, we *need* to hear it.

When you share your experiences and opinions, you become an active member of the Fodor's community. That means we'll not only use your feedback to make our books better, but we'll publish your names and comments whenever possible. Throughout our guides, look for "Word of Mouth," excerpts of your unvarnished feedback.

Here's how you can help improve Fodor's for all of us.

Tell us when we're right. We rely on local writers to give you an insider's perspective. But our writers and staff editors—who are the best in the business—depend on you. Your positive feedback is a vote to renew our recommendations for the next edition.

Tell us when we're wrong. We're proud that we update most of our guides every year. But we're not perfect. Things change. Hotels cut services. Museums change hours. Charming cafés lose charm. If our writer didn't quite capture the essence of a place, tell us how you'd do it differently. If any of our descriptions are inaccurate or inadequate, we'll incorporate your changes in the next edition and will correct factual errors at fodors.com *immediately*.

Tell us what to include. You probably have had fantastic travel experiences that aren't yet in Fodor's. Why not share them with a community of like-minded travelers? Maybe you chanced upon a beach or bistro or B&B that you don't want to keep to yourself. Tell us why we should include it. And share your discoveries and experiences with everyone directly at fodors.com. Your input may lead us to add a new listing or highlight a place we cover with a "Highly Recommended" star or with our highest rating, "Fodor's Choice."

Give us your opinion instantly at our feedback center at www.fodors.com/feedback. You may also e-mail editors@fodors.com with the subject line "Spain Editor." Or send your nominations, comments, and complaints by mail to Spain Editor, Fodor's, 1745 Broadway, New York, NY 10019.

You and travelers like you are the heart of the Fodor's community. Make our community richer by sharing your experiences. Be a Fodor's correspondent.

¡Buen Viaje!

Tim Jarrell, Publisher

CONTENTS

CONTENTS

ABOUT THIS BOOK

Our Ratings

Sometimes you find terrific travel experiences and sometimes they just find you. But usually the burden is on you to select the right combination of experiences. That's where our ratings come in.

As travelers we've all discovered a place so wonderful that its worthiness is obvious. And sometimes that place is so experiential that superlatives don't do it justice: you just have to be there to know. These sights, properties, and experiences get our highest rating, **Fodor's Choice,** indicated by orange stars throughout this book.

Black stars highlight sights and properties we deem **Highly Recommended,** places that our writers, editors, and readers praise again and again for consistency and excellence.

By default, there's another category: any place we include in this book is by definition worth your time, unless we say otherwise. And we will.

Disagree with any of our choices? Care to nominate a place or suggest that we rate one more highly? Visit our feedback center at www. fodors.com/feedback.

Budget Well

Hotel and restaurant price categories from ¢ to $$$$ are defined in the opening pages of each chapter. For attractions, we always give standard adult admission fees; reductions are usually available for children, students, and senior citizens. Want to pay with plastic? **AE, D, DC, MC, V** after restaurant and hotel listings indicate if American Express, Discover, Diner's Club, MasterCard, and Visa are accepted.

Restaurants

Unless we state otherwise, restaurants are open for lunch and dinner daily. We mention dress only when there's a specific requirement and reservations only when they're essential or not accepted—it's always best to book ahead.

Hotels

Hotels have private bath, phone, TV, and air-conditioning and operate on the European Plan (aka EP, meaning without meals), unless we specify that they use the Continental Plan (CP, with a continental breakfast), Breakfast Plan (BP, with a full breakfast), or Modified American Plan (MAP, with breakfast and dinner) or are all-inclusive (including all meals and most activities). We always

list facilities but not whether you'll be charged an extra fee to use them, so when pricing accommodations, find out what's included.

Many Listings
- ★ Fodor's Choice
- ★ Highly recommended
- ⊠ Physical address
- ↔ Directions
- ⌖ Mailing address
- ☎ Telephone
- 🖷 Fax
- ⊕ On the Web
- ✉ E-mail
- 🖃 Admission fee
- ☉ Open/closed times
- ▶ Start of walk/itinerary
- Ⓜ Metro stations
- ▭ Credit cards

Hotels & Restaurants
- 🏨 Hotel
- 🛏 Number of rooms
- ⌂ Facilities
- ⑩ Meal plans
- ✗ Restaurant
- ⌂ Reservations
- ⌂ Dress code
- ↘ Smoking
- ⅋ BYOB
- ✗🏨 Hotel with restaurant that warrants a visit

Outdoors
- ⅄ Golf
- ⚠ Camping

Other
- ☺ Family-friendly
- 🔂 Contact information
- ⇨ See also
- ⊠ Branch address
- ☞ Take note

WHAT'S WHERE

Spain's diverse geographical and cultural elements give you a rich variety of experience within a relatively small area (312,965 sq mi), with each player contributing a different style, strength, and personality. Along the northern coast, the wet, green Asturias, Galicia, Cantabria, and Euskadi (the Basque Country) are an Iberian Ireland, whereas southern Andalusia juxtaposes North African tastes, sounds, and architecture with some surprisingly green Arcadian pockets of its own. On the northeast border, the Pyrenees draw winter-sports fans, whereas the Mediterranean coast and Balearic Islands delight sun-seekers. Spain's mountain ranges—Sierra Nevada, Picos de Europa, Guadarrama, Sierra de la Demanda, to name just a few—contrast with La Mancha, Castile's central plain, a dramatically dry high steppe wherein Madrid lies. In bustling Barcelona, colorful Moderniste architecture stands out from Spain's most characteristic architectural style, the exposed brick Mudejar hybrid of Moorish and Christian elements.

MADRID

Madrid's bright blue skies and boundless energy make every sight and sound seem larger than life. Although you expect royal palaces to be grand, Madrid's Palacio Real has 2,800 rooms. The Prado, Reina Sofía, and Thyssen-Bornemisza museums pack 9,000 Spanish and other European masterworks into an art-saturated half mile. Sunday's flea market in El Rastro is as thick with overpriced oddities as it is with crowds. The cafés in the Plaza Mayor, one of Europe's grandest squares, and the wine bars in the nearby Cava Baja are perpetually abuzz, and nightlife stretches into the wee hours around Plaza Santa Ana in a neighborhood that once teemed with actors, poets, and playwrights during Spain's 16th-century Golden Age. Late-night action provides the heartbeat of Madrid, distracting you from the thought of sleep.

OLD & NEW CASTILE

Despite what you may have heard about the rain in Spain falling mainly on the plain, the Spanish *meseta* is actually an arid reach of windy skies and wide vistas. Cut with rocky gorges and fringed with gaunt mountains, this vast plateau is severe, melancholic, and mysterious. It was here that Don Quijote tilted at windmills, and somber Ávila, ringed by its original 11th-century wall, was the locale for the mystical ecstasies of Santa Teresa. Toledo, sitting calmly on a battlement-topped granite cliff, inspired El Greco's moody canvases; golden Segovia, with the Roman aqueduct leading to the walled city on a shelf

of rock, is a feast for all the senses. The sight of Cuenca can be startling: how can 500-year-old houses cling to the sides of a precipice? Salamanca dazzles with Renaissance architecture, including one of Spain's largest and most graceful public squares. Northern Castile, easily dismissable as a barren wasteland, is the site of Valladolid's National Museum of Sculpture, the largest and finest collection of polychrome wood pieces in the world, as well as medieval Burgos, a traditional religious and military center and home of El Cid, the Christian Reconquest's legendary hero. Prosperous León hums with student activity but is best known for its cathedral's 125 stained-glass windows.

CANTABRIA, THE BASQUE COUNTRY, NAVARRA & LA RIOJA

Northern Spain breaks all the favorite stereotypes about Iberia: there's little Arab influence, and it's not flat or arid. Greener, cloudier, and stubbornly independent in spirit, part of the north is, of course, Basque, a country within a country, with its own language and culture as well as its own coastline on the Bay of Biscay, one of the peninsula's wildest and toughest shores. San Sebastián, near the French border, and the Cantabrian resort Santander, to the west, are seaside showpieces. Navarra stretches from snowcapped Pyrenees in the northwest, through stunningly great valleys, to the lunar aridity of the Bardenas Reales in its southeast corner. La Rioja, a mixture of highlands, plains, and vineyards in and around the Ebro River basin, produces some of Spain's finest wines. Bilbao has experienced a cultural renaissance that began with Frank Gehry's titanium-skinned Guggenheim Museum. Already endowed with an excellent Museum of Fine Arts, renowned Basque restaurants, a vigorous musical tradition, and an Old Quarter filled with architectural treasures, Bilbao has now become a design and art destination as well, with an inherited hard-nosed steelmaking, coal-mining, and shipbuilding spirit that shows no sign of disappearing.

GALICIA & ASTURIAS

On the way to Santiago de Compostela to pay homage to St. James, Christian pilgrims once crossed Europe to a corner of Spain so remote it was called *finis terrae* (end of the earth), Europe's westernmost point and, until 1492, as far as anyone knew, the world's. Santiago still resonates with mystic importance, especially in and around its magnificent cathedral, and on July 25, the feast of St. James. The ancient pilgrimage—the Camino de Santiago—regained popularity as the second

WHAT'S WHERE

millennium drew to a close; today's pilgrims come from around the world to walk the final weeks from the Pyrenees to Santiago. *Enxebre,* the local word for fine Galician dining, covers a multitude of delicious items, from oysters in Vigo, to the seafood and Albariño and Ribeiro wines throughout the region. In the more mountainous Asturias, towns are among green hills in the highlands, and sandy beaches stretch out along the Atlantic. Scattered sets of stilted *hórreos* (granaries) with Christian and Celtic symbols seem like tiny chapels, and the jagged Picos de Europa tower massively to the south. Restaurants and taverns there serve the best beans and rice pudding in all of Spain, and the strong, tangy blue cheeses of the Picos de Europa make all but the best of Manchego cheese seem dull by comparison.

THE PYRENEES

Until the early 20th century, the mountain range separating the Iberian Peninsula from the rest of Europe was a world of its own, with a dozen highland cultures and languages. Valleys were isolated from each other and from the world below and beyond. Spain's natural border with France has also been seen as a nexus where medieval peoples took refuge and exchanged culture and learning. Cut by some 23 steep north–south valleys on the Spanish side alone, with four independent geographical entities—the valleys of Camprodón, Cerdanya, Aran, and Baztán—the Pyrenees has a wealth of areas to explore. A haven from the 8th-century Moorish invasion, the Pyrenees became an unlikely repository of Romanesque art and architecture, as well as a natural preserve of wildlife and terrain. Ordesa National Park, Spain's Grand Canyon, is a day's hike of great natural beauty.

BARCELONA & NORTHERN CATALONIA

The poet Federico García Lorca called Barcelona's Rambla the only street in the world he wished would never end. A mass of strollers, market goers, artists, street entertainers, vendors, scammers, and vamps, this flow of humanity prepares your eye and imagination for Barcelona's startling and occasionally bizarre architectural landmarks. Antoni Gaudí's sinuous Casa Milà and emphatically unique Sagrada Família church took the late-19th- and early-20th-centuries' Art Nouveau movement into the heart of natural form and design, and the intricate Art Nouveau Palau de la Música takes aesthetic whimsy to the limit. Outside Barcelona are less-explored Catalan towns such as medieval Girona, with its important Jewish quarter,

and the whitewashed village of Cadaqués on the Costa Brava, a rocky shore shaded with pines and lapped by a lustrous sea.

SOUTHERN CATALONIA & THE LEVANTE

The sun rises (*se levanta*) from the Mediterranean to give the citrus-scented, mountain-backed plain near Valencia its name and lend a glow to the city's Christian and Moorish landmarks. The sea yields ingredients for Valencia's emblematic paella and makes a dramatic backdrop for the Roman ruins of cosmopolitan Tarragona. Where the Mediterranean meets the Ebro River, 200,000 birds wallow in the wetlands of the Delta de l'Ebre Natural Park. Farther inland, castles, fortresses, and the mountains of the Sierra de Beceite lure you into some of the peninsula's most unspoiled landscapes.

THE SOUTHEAST

Not unlike the time when Don Quijote moved from one exploit to another across the vast tracts of La Mancha, there's still plenty of drama in this empty landscape, which seems to change with every turn of the road. Rice paddies and fragrant orange groves give way to the palm-fringed port city of Alicante, the fertile plains and dry hills of Murcia, and the craggy lunar landscapes of Almería. Along the way, ceramics are handcrafted from the local white clay in towns such as Alicante and rural Albacete; and saffron, red peppers, and dates flavor the region's rice-based cuisine. Modern resorts, overcrowded and to be avoided in August, line the Costa Blanca; inland festivities include Alcoy's annual Moros y Cristianos pageant, which reenacts the Christians' recapture of Alcoy from the Moors in the 13th century. Still, the scenery steals the show, especially on the crowd-free coast of the Cabo de Gata in the off-season, a haven for rare wildlife and anyone in search of an unspoiled beach.

THE BALEARIC ISLANDS

Halfway between France and Africa, these once-remote landfalls off Spain's eastern coast are a playground for northern Europeans. Britain occupied Minorca in the 18th century, and Germany seems to have established an unofficial 21st-century colony on Majorca. Ibiza blasts to life nightly with the anything-goes heat that comes with modern tourism—but even this dance-crazed isle, with its summer clubbers, has its quiet coves and lonely seasons. Majorca combines tourist-clogged pockets with undiscovered corners: rugged mountains, abandoned monasteries, and a smattering of Christian and Moorish monuments such as the Arab baths in the Balearic capital, Palma. Minorca offers explorations of the ancient cities of Ciu-

WHAT'S
WHERE

tadella and Mahón, a plethora of ancient megalithic menhirs and talayots, and trips to usually deserted beaches (try to stay away in August, when they're crowded). Formentera, the most purely pastoral of the Balearic Islands, retains a wild beauty.

THE COSTA DEL SOL

At the very worst of Spain's overdeveloped seaside resorts, sun-seekers from Europe's bleaker climes fill every cranny of this famous strip. More than 320 days of sunshine a year and end-less beaches have made the Costa del Sol like Miami Beach—high-rise hotels lining the shores, ample golf courses, and all. Málaga, the provincial capital and a busy cosmopolitan sea-port, has a recently opened Picasso Museum. Marbella, a longtime glitterati favorite, also has a pristine Andalusian old quarter. For more of the same, head into the mountains, where villages such as Casares seem immune to the goings-on along the coast (even as it shimmers below), and the ancient town of Ronda straddles a giant river gorge. East toward Granada, Nerja combines a cliff-bound, gray-sand beach with enor-mous caves full of natural spires.

GRANADA, CÓRDOBA & EASTERN ANDALUSIA

Al-Andalus, the Moorish empire on the Iberia Peninsula, held on until 1492 in this corner of their caliphate. Granada's Al-hambra is a marvel of patios, arches, and intricate carvings, with the lush Generalife palace gardens next door, and across the Darro river gorge is the Moors' old neighborhood, the Al-baicín, a cluster of flower-festooned, white villas tumbling down a hillside. South of Granada, on the slopes of the Sierra Nevada, lie the villages of the Alpujarras, where descendants of transplanted Galicians craft rugs, blankets, baskets, and pot-tery. Córdoba's Mezquita—a mosque with a cathedral in the middle—is sublime, its 850 columns topped with red-and-white arches. Near the mosque is the only surviving syna-gogue in Andalusia, nestled among the thick-walled homes of the medieval Jewish Quarter with intimate, flower-choked in-terior courtyards. South of Córdoba, the Subbética region is rich in natural parks and historical and archaeological sites. The historic mining town of Guadix is peppered with caves scooped out of the sandstone mountains, many of them still inhabited. In Jaén, the parched landscape is interrupted by islets of green, such as the *Parque de Cazorla,* Spain's largest na-tional park, and by Renaissance towns such as Úbeda and Baeza, filed with splendid mansions and churches. Also, olive groves stretch through the province.

SEVILLE & WESTERN ANDALUSIA	Seafaring heroism and high adventure reverberate in the Guadalquivir River's swampy Atlantic delta. Since 1100 BC Cádiz has been port of call for Phoenicians, Carthaginians, and Romans working trade routes at the western end of the Mediterranean. It was from Huelva that Columbus set out to discover the New World and at Sanlúcar de Barrameda that Magellan's expedition, with Juan Sebastián Elkano in command, completed the first circumnavigation of the globe. And then there's Seville, most colorful during its Holy Week festival, but brimming with romance year-round. The city's Giralda minaret–turned–bell tower, massive cathedral, and sumptuous Alcázar palace recall Moorish caliphs and Christian kings. In the rustic tapas bars, your bill gets marked up in chalk on the wooden counter. Farther south, the fishing town of Sanlúcar de Barrameda serves unbeatable *langostinos* (jumbo shrimp) and manzanilla, the local sherrylike wine. In the vast vineyards around Jerez de la Frontera, more than a half million barrels of sherry are maturing at any given time, and the flamenco tradition provides passionate song and dance. Puerto de Santa María is famous for its prawns, and the Cádiz, Sanlucar, Jerez triangle is considered the birthplace and sanctuary of the Spanish tapas tradition.
EXTREMADURA	You'll need a taste for the remote and rustic before heading to Spain's far west, the outer *(extrema)* Río Duero *(dura)* borderland with Portugal. The Castilian *dehesa* (range land), meadows studded with live oak trees, provides habitat for the Iberian black pig, descended from the wild boar, that produces one of Spain's—and the world's—great delicacies: *jamón ibérico de bellota* (Iberian acorn-fed cured ham). A journey through the wooded valleys and ocher farmlands of this western region feels a bit like time travel. The land is hushed and haunting. Even in prosperous Cáceres, nothing modern disrupts the Old Quarter, packed with medieval and Renaissance churches and palaces; and in Trujillo, the nearly deserted streets are lined with mansions of Spain's imperial age. Ancient Mérida, founded in 25 BC, is Spain's richest trove of Roman remains. Out in the mountains, dramatic vantage points are the Jerte Valley—which turns white in late March with the blossoming of its 1 million cherry trees—and the monastery of Our Lady of Guadalupe, in the town with the same name.

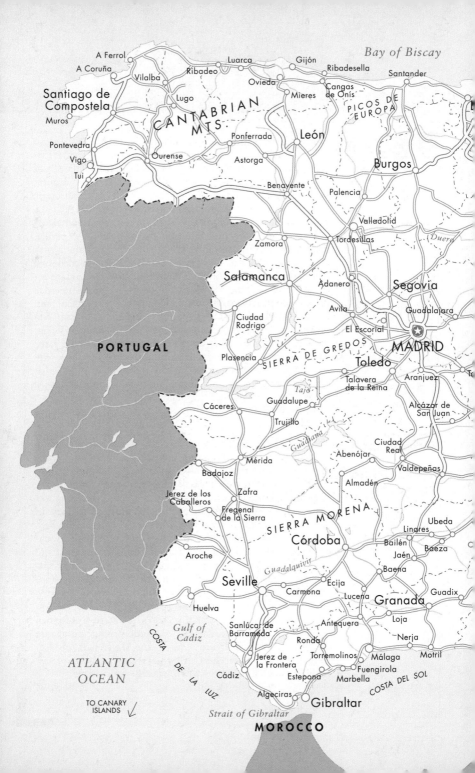

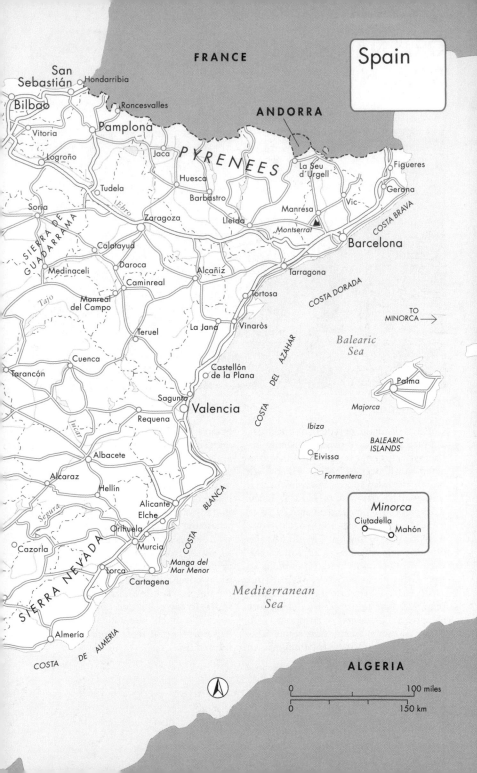

QUINTESSENTIAL SPAIN

El Desayuno

Coffee is the main ingredient at breakfast, although toast or croissants usually accompany this important event—the occasional draft beer or coffee spiked with brandy may also appear. Spanish workers, be they hard hats or suits, show up in the workplace by 8 or 9 and emerge by 10 or so ready for a substantial snack to get them through to lunch at 2. Bars and cafés offer specials on juice, coffee, and a sandwich or roll of some kind. *Café solo* is an espresso, except in Barcelona, where it's just a *café*. *Un café solo corto* is even more concentrated. *Café solo doble* is a double dose of espresso. *Café cortado* is an espresso with a drop or two of cream. *Café con leche* is closer to half and half. A *carajillo* is an espresso with a hit of cognac.

El Tapeo

Spain's primary contribution to world dining customs, tapas work best in climates and societies where movement, improvisation, and variety are seen as preferable to stasis, prior planning, and predictability. Tapas are generally thought to have originated in Andalusia and spread north, where the Basques embraced the concept with enthusiasm: the Catalans took longer to adjust from their francophilia-generated *aperitiu* (aperitif) tradition. Tapas today cover a vast range of morsels, from the simplest *patata brava* (potatoes in hot sauce) to *foie con reducción de Modena y solomillo* (duck liver with a reduction of balsamic vinegar from Modena sauce on fillet of beef).

Spain is composed of many distinct entities and elements, but some of the rituals of daily life have transcended regional idiosyncrasy and become universal.

La Siesta

The unabashed Spanish pursuit of pleasure and the unswerving devotion to establishing a healthy balance between work and play is nowhere more apparent than in this midday shutdown. However, as air-conditioning, fitness clubs, and other distractions gain ascendancy in modern Spain, and Mom-cooked lunches, once a universal ritual, become all but extinct in the two-salary, 21st-century Spanish family, the siesta question is increasingly debated. Although the classic midday snooze described by novelist Camilo Jose Cela as *"de padrenuestro y pijama"* (with a prayer and pajamas) is rarely practiced these days, the fact remains that most stores and businesses close from 1:30 to 4:30 or later, and whether they're sleeping, feasting, exercising, or canoodling, one thing is certain: they're not working.

El Fútbol

The Spanish National Fútbol (soccer) League and the *tortilla de patata* (potato omelet) have been described as the only widely shared phenomena that bind the nation together. In the case of the league, the tie that binds often resembles tribal warfare, as bitter rivalries centuries old are played out on the field. Some of these, such as the Real Sociedad (San Sebastián)–Athletic de Bilbao feud, are fraternal in nature, brother Basques battling for boasting rights, but others, such as the Madrid–Barcelona standoff, are as basic to Spanish history as Moros y Cristianos, a reenactment of the battle between the Moors and the Christians. The beauty of the game is best appreciated in the stadiums, but local sports bars, many of them official fan clubs of local teams, are a chance to see *fútbol* passions at their wildest.

IF YOU LIKE

Art

During the Spanish Golden Age (1580–1680), the empire's wealth flowed to the imperial capital of Madrid, and Spanish monarchs used it not only for defense and civil projects but to finance the arts. Painters from El Greco to Rubens, and writers from Lope de Vega to Cervantes, were drawn to the luminous (and solvent) royal court. For the first time in Europe, the collecting of art became an important symbol of national wealth and power.

- **Centro de Arte Reina Sofía,** Madrid. The modern collection focuses on Spain's three great modern masters—Pablo Picasso, Salvador Dalí, and Joan Miró. It houses Picasso's *Guernica*.

- **Museo de Bellas Artes,** Seville. Among the fabulous works are those of Murillo, Zurbarán, Valdés Leal, and El Greco; examples of Seville Gothic art; baroque religious sculptures; and Sevillian art of the 19th and 20th centuries.

- **Prado,** Madrid. One of the world's greatest museums, it holds masterpieces by Italian and Flemish painters, but its jewels are the works of Spaniards: Goya, Velázquez, and El Greco.

- **Thyssen-Bornemisza Museum,** Madrid. An ambitious collection of 800 paintings traces the development of Western humanism as no other in the world.

- **Museo Guggenheim,** Bilbao. The world-famous mesmerizing building houses works from the Venetian and the New York Guggenheim collections, but also from big-name Spanish modern artists.

Beaches

Nearly surrounded by bays, oceans, gulfs, straits, and seas, Spain is a beach-lover's dream come true. August beaches are overcrowded and to be avoided, whereas winter beaches offer solitude and sunshine without heat. Castelldefels, 20 minutes south of Barcelona, and Sitges, another 15 minutes south, allow you to watch the sun set into the Mediterranean from November to April. In San Sebastián, La Concha's midtown ocher arch is a favorite for winter walking and jogging.

Beaches on the Costa del Sol from Málaga to Gibraltar are warm enough for swimming year-round, though the overdeveloped high-rise apartments that have replaced charming fishing villages along this strip are ugly and depressing. The Costa Cálida on either side of Cartagena features a 106-square-mi saltwater lagoon separated from the sea by La Manga del Mar Menor, a 14-mi strip of land.

Known for its warm-water temperatures and the healing properties of its brine and iodine content, the Mar Menor offers year-round beaches and bathing. Matalascañas, at the western end of the Andalusian coast, and La Antilla, west of Huelva, are fine beaches except when late July and August crowds make them a nightmare. South of Huelva are Cadiz's Atlantic wild and very windy beaches, quite appreciated by watersports fans and by locals fleeing from the Mediterranean crowds and chaos. Spain's northern beaches, from the French border at the Bidasoa River at Hondarribia to the border with Portugal at the Río Miño, are the best, offering a wide variety of urban beaches and remote strands. Finally, Spain's Balearic archipelagoes offer year-round beach options, although they can be too cold for swimming from November to May.

Exploring the Outdoors

Crisscrossed with mountain ranges, Spain has areas that are ideal for walking, mountain biking, and backpacking. The Pyrenees offer superior hiking and trekking on well-marked trails from the Atlantic Bay of Biscay to the Mediterranean, among them the 40- to 45-day GR-11 trail that runs from the Atlantic Ocean to the Mediterranean Sea. The Sierra de Gredos, west of Ávila, and the Sierra de Guadarrama, north of Madrid, are also popular for climbing and trekking. Hiking is also excellent in the interior of Spain, in the Alpujarra mountains southeast of Granada, and in the numerous national parks, from the marshy Doñana wetlands in the south to the mountainous Picos de Europa in the north. Still in vogue after hundreds of years is the Pilgrimage Road to Santiago de Compostela; it traverses the north of Spain from either Roncesvalles in Navarra or the Aragonian Pyrennees to Galicia. Mountain streams in the Pyrenees and other ranges throughout Spain offer trout- and salmon-fishing opportunities that can combine nicely with hiking and camping expeditions. Perhaps the best part of Spain's outdoor space and activities is that they often bring you nearer to some of the finest architecture and cuisine Iberia has to offer.

- **Doñana National Park,** Western Andalusia. One of Europe's last tracts of true wilderness includes wetlands, beaches, shifting sand dunes, marshes, 150 species of rare birds, and countless kinds of wildlife, including the endangered imperial eagle and lynx.

- **Ordesa and Monte Perdido National Park,** the Pyrenees. Hike in Spain's version of the Grand Canyon. The 57,000-acre park features waterfalls, caves, forests, meadows, and more.

Food

Spanish cooking has come into its own over the last 20 years. The Mediterranean diet, with its emphasis on olive oil, fish, vegetables, garlic, onions, and red wine, is now understood to be not only delicious but a healthful way to eat. Innovative chefs, including Ferran Adrià and Pedro Subijana, and such masters as Juan Mari Arzak and Santi Santamaría, are making Spain's regional cuisines famous throughout the world, and new stars—Martin Berasategui, Sergi Arola, Fermí Puig, and Carme Ruscalleda Puig—are filling the firmament with new aromas and textures.

- **Arzak,** San Sebastián. The traditional Basque food at this extremely popular, internationally famous spot is jazzed up by the owner's innovations.

- **El Bullí,** Girona, Costa Brava. Call months ahead for a chair at this seaside getaway with a 12-course menu. It's open only half the year.

- **El Celler de Can Roca,** Girona, Costa Brava. The best restaurant in town is also one of Catalonia's top six food destinations, perhaps for its oddball blendings.

- **El Chaflán,** Madrid. Come for the annual white-truffle sampler week, but expect new and sophisticated dishes anytime.

- **La Broche,** Madrid. El Bulli's Ferran Adrià's best disciple plays with texture and temperature, drawing on his Catalonian roots but also turning his back on them when inspiration calls.

- **El Racó de Can Fabes,** Sant Celoni. One of Spain's top four restaurants, it's well worth the 45-minute train ride from Barcelona.

GREAT ITINERARIES

MADRID, ANDALUSIA & BARCELONA— THE THREE MAIN IBERIAN CULTURES

Days 1–5: Madrid

The elegant Plaza Mayor is the perfect jumping-off point for a tour of Spain's capital. To the west, see the Plaza de la Villa, Royal Palace, and opera house; to the south wander around the maze of streets of La Latina and the Rastro; to the east visit the Plaza Santa Ana and theater district. Madrid's Paseo del Arte (Art Walk) takes in three major museums, including the Prado. Toledo and Segovia make excellent side trips.

Logistics: A car in Madrid is a liability, given the city's traffic gridlocks. Even taxis are frustrating. Consider either walking, taking the metro, or using the usually fluid bus transport up and down the Paseo de la Castellana, the city's central artery. Segovia, Toledo, and El Escorial are all easily reachable by train or bus (which is usually the better means). The high-speed train (AVE) to Córdoba and Seville, a smooth and scenic delight, is the only way to go.

Day 6: Córdoba & Its Mosque

This capital of both Roman and Moorish Spain was a center of Western art and culture between the 8th and 11th century. Córdoba's sprawling mosque (now a cathedral) bears witness to the city's brilliant past. The medieval Jewish Quarter unfolds in tiny, beckoning alleyways, and the dozen *iglesias fernandinas,* Mudejar churches built over mosques after the Reconquest, are, in themselves, lovely and a perfect way to help guide you around the city. The paintings by Julio Romero de Torres are the icing on the cake.

Logistics: After you arrive by AVE, a taxi to the center of town and another out to the Umayyad summer palace at Medina Azahara are all you need in Córdoba, beyond a good pair of shoes. Another short breather on the train the next morning brings you to Seville.

Days 7–8: Seville & Andalusia

Seville's Giralda tower, cathedral, bull-ring, and Barrio de Santa Cruz are visual feasts. Forty minutes south you can sip the world-famous sherries of Jerez de la Frontera, then munch jumbo shrimp on the beach at Sanlúcar de Barrameda.

Logistics: From Seville's AVE station, take a taxi to your hotel. After that, walking and hailing the occasional taxi are the best plans for exploring El Barrio de Santa Cruz, Triana, and the Barrio de la Macarena. The Seville-to-Granada leg of this trip is best accomplished by renting a car. However, the Sevilla-to-Granada trains (four daily, just over three hours, costing less than €20) are an alternative if you'd rather not face the perils and unpredictabilities of the road.

Days 9–10: Granada & the Alhambra

The hilltop Alhambra palace was conceived by the Moorish caliphs as heaven on earth and still strikes many as exactly that. The nearby Generalife palace has lush, formal gardens. Down in the city, see the Royal Chapel, with the tombs of Ferdinand and Isabella; the cathedral; and the magnificent Albaicín, the ancient Moorish quarter.

Logistics: A car is useless in Granada proper. However, you may wish to consider taking a half-day or full-day tour of the villages of the Alpujarra. From there you can retrace your steps to Granada or head on to the coastal freeway. Either way it's an 800-km (500-mi) drive to Barcelona. Otherwise, an overnight train or a one-hour flight from Granada to Barcelona will painlessly position you for the last portion of this whirlwind tour.

Days 11–15: Barcelona & Catalonia

Key walks in 2,000-year-old Barcelona are the Gothic Quarter and La Ribera; the Eixample, with Art Nouveau buildings by Gaudí and others; and Gaudí's Güell Park and the massive, unfinished Sagrada Família church. A stroll on the Rambla and a trip to the Boqueria market are musts, along with the church of Santa Maria del Mar, the Museu Picasso, and the flamboyant Palau de la Música.

Logistics: A car in Barcelona is a nuisance. The FGC train and metro service close early: taxis are generally the best way to get back to your hotel after dinner.

TIPS

❶ Spain's modern freeways are as good as any in the world—with the exception of the signs, which have writing that's often too small to decipher while comfortably traveling at the routine speed of 120 km/h (74 mph).

❷ Tolls on Spanish highways are astronomically high. Between gasoline prices and tolls, traveling by car is economical only for two or more passengers. A diesel rental car will nearly double your mileage.

❸ Madrid is within six hours of anywhere, and the scenery is relentlessly, well, scenic, because no billboards are permitted on Spanish highways and deforestation allows for panoramic views wherever you drive. Overnight trains (some of which can even transport your car) from Barcelona to Málaga or Seville make sense, but the Barcelona-to-Bilbao drive is now well under five hours. Domestic flights are another option.

GREAT ITINERARIES

THE NORTH: THE BASQUE COUNTRY, CANTABRIA, ASTURIAS & GALICIA

Days 1–2: San Sebastián

San Sebastián is one of Spain's most beautiful—and delicious—cities. Belle Epoque buildings nearly encircle the tiny bay, and tapas bars flourish in the old quarter. Visiting San Sebastián without a look at Pasajes de San Juan is a mistake. Likewise, an excursion to Hondarribia is a must. The cider mills in Astigarraga are another important off–San Sebastián visit.

Logistics: Whether you arrive by plane, train, or car, you'll need a car to explore the Basque Country properly. Although there is no need for a car in San Sebastián proper, the visits to cider houses in Astigarraga, Chillida Leku on the outskirts of town, and many of the finest restaurants around San Sebastián, are possible only by car. (Of course, if you go by taxi, you won't have to worry about getting lost.) The freeway west to Bilbao is beautiful and fast, but the coastal road through Orio, Zarautz, Guetaria, and Zumaia is recommended at least as far as Zumaia.

Days 3–4: The Basque Coast

The Basque coast between San Sebastián and Bilbao is lined with beaches, rocky cliffs, and picture-perfect fishing ports. The wide beach at Zarautz, the fishermen's village of Guetaria, the Zuloaga Museum in Zumaia, Mundaka's famous left-breaking surfing wave, and Bermeo's port and fishing museum should all be near the top of your list.

Logistics: To see the Basque coast, forget about time and wind along the coastal roads that twist through places such as

Elantxobe, Bakio, Mundaka, and San Juan Gaztelugatxe. From Bilbao there is a train, the Euskotren, that runs from the Atxuri station through the Urdaibai wetlands and the Ría de Gernika to Mundaka.

Days 5–6: Bilbao

Bilbao's Guggenheim Museum is worth a trip for the building itself, and the Museum of Fine Arts has an impressive collection of Basque and Spanish paintings. Restaurants and tapas bars are famously good in Bilbao, and the city's cultural offerings, from opera to jazz to bullfights in August, has always been first-rate.

Logistics: In Bilbao, use the subway or the Euskotram, which runs up and down the Nervión estuary.

Days 7–9: Santander & Cantabria

The elegant beach town Santander has a summer university and an excellent summer music festival. Santillana del Mar is one of Spain's best Renaissance towns, and the Altamira cave museum offers famous prehistoric cave paintings. Exploring the Picos de Europa will take you through some the peninsula's wildest reaches, and the port towns along the coast provide some of Spain's wildest and purest beaches.

Logistics: Santander stretches for several miles along its Sardinero beachfront and there is little enough traffic, except in mid-August, but parking is expensive and scarce, so it's better to make use of the bus service. For explorations into the towns and hills of Cantabria, an automobile is indispensable.

Days 10–12: Oviedo & Asturias

The coast road through Ribadesella and cider capital Villaviciosa to Oviedo is a scenic tour punctuated with numerous tempting beaches. Oviedo, its cathedral, and its pre-Romanesque churches are worlds away from Córdoba's Mezquita and Granada's Alhambra. Gijón is a fishing and freight port, summer resort, and university town, and the villages along the coast such as Cudillero and Luarca remain quite unspoiled and serve famous fish and seafood.

Logistics: The A8 coastal freeway gets you quickly and comfortably from points east to Oviedo and just beyond. From there west into Galicia the two-lane N634 and the coastal N632 are the slow but scenic routes to Santiago de Compostela.

Days 13–15: Santiago de Compostela & Galicia

Spain's northwest corner, with Santiago de Compostela at its spiritual and geographic center, is a green land of bagpipes and apple orchards. Lugo, Ourense, A Coruña, and Vigo are the major cities, and the Albariño wine country, along the Río Miño border with Portugal, and the rías (estuaries), full of delicious seafood, will keep you steeped in *enxebre,* Gallego for local specialties and atmosphere.

Logistics: Once in Galicia, the four-lane freeways AP9 and A6 whisk you from Lugo and Castro to Santiago de Compostela and down into the Rias Baixas. Cars are the only way to tour Galicia, and the slower the better. The AC552 route around the upper northwest corner and the Rías Altas turns into the AC550 coming back into Santiago.

TIP

Languages across the north of Spain go from Basque or Euskera in the eastern Basque Country; to Castilian Spanish in Santander and Cantabria; to Bable, a local dialect, in Asturias; and Gallego, a Portuguese-like romance language, in Galicia. Be prepared for bilingual traffic signs and local spellings that do not match your map, which probably adheres to the "traditional" Castilian spelling.

WHEN TO GO

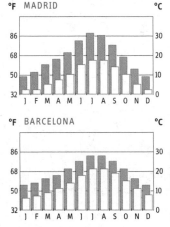

May and October are the optimal times to visit Spain, as the weather is generally warm and dry and the air refreshing. May gives you more hours of daylight, and October offers a chance to enjoy the harvest season, which is especially colorful in the wine regions.

In April you'll see spectacular fiestas, particularly Seville's *Semana Santa* (Holy Week) followed by the *Feria de Abril* (April Fair), showcasing horses, bulls, and flamenco. By then the weather in southern Spain is warm but still cool enough to make sightseeing comfortable.

Spain is the number-one destination for European travelers. **To avoid crowds and the heat, avoid coming in July or August.** Summer overcrowding is at its worst along the coasts, because the Mediterranean and the Atlantic are too cold for swimming the rest of the year. In August, major cities empty, with Spaniards migrating to the beach—expect huge traffic jams August 1 and 31—and small shops and some restaurants shut down; most museums remain open.

Climate

During summer in Spain, temperatures frequently hit 100°F (38°C). Although air-conditioning is the norm in hotels and museums (and on some Barcelona, and all Madrid, subways—except when the system is broken, which happens frequently), walking and general exploring can be uncomfortable. Locals fight the heat with lots of iced drinks, *terrazas* (Spanish culture of outdoor drinking and dining), and even a lunchtime dip in the sea in the coastal cities. Winters are mild and rainy along the coasts and bitterly cold elsewhere. Snow is infrequent except in the mountains, where you can ski December through March in the Pyrenees and at resorts near Granada, Madrid, and Burgos.

🛈 **Forecasts Weather Channel Connection** (☎ 900/932-8437 95¢ per minute ⊕ www.weather.com). Spain's National Weather Service **Instituto Nacional de Metereología** (⊕ www.inm.es) also offers seven-day forecasts for more than 8,000 local sites.

ON THE CALENDAR

WINTER	
January	**Epiphany** (January 6) is when youngsters leave their shoes on the doorstep to be filled with gifts from the Three Kings.
February	**Carnival** dances through Spain just before Lent, most flamboyantly in Cádiz, Sitges, Santa Cruz de Tenerife, and Las Palmas de Gran Canaria. Reserve lodging far in advance.
March	In Valencia, giant papier-mâché figures are torched for **Las Fallas**. **Semana Santa** (Holy Week) is the most spectacular feast of all, with Seville staging the most elaborate processions.
SPRING	
April	Horseback parades make Seville's **Feria de Abril** photogenic. Roses for the women and books for the men celebrate Barcelona's April 23 **Festa de Sant Jordi**, lovers' day, the city's best day of the year.
May	The **Jerez Horse Fair** is a pageant of equestrian events. Barcelona is fragrant on **Sant Ponç** (May 11), when farmers and herbalists take over the city to sell natural products and herbal remedies. In Madrid, **San Isidro** (May 15) kicks off two weeks of the best bullfighting in Spain.
June	From mid-June to mid-July, Granada's **International Festival of Music and Dance** brings orchestras, opera companies, and ballet corps to the grounds of the Alhambra.
SUMMER	
July	The **Fiesta de San Fermín** and the accompanying running of the bulls (July 6–13) through Pamplona's streets unleash wine, bravado, and merriment. Late in the month, Villajoyosa's **Moros y Cristianos** finds Valencians reenacting ancient battles in medieval costume.
August	**El Místeri** (August 11–15), in Elche, is Europe's oldest Christian mystery play. A **Tomato Battle** reddens the town of Buñol, near Valencia, on the last Wednesday of the month. Consuegra, near Toledo, turns another color for the **Saffron Rose Festival**.
FALL	
September	Jerez celebrates harvesttime with **Fiestas de Otoño** (Autumn Festivals). On and around September 24, Barcelona celebrates **La Mercè** with concerts, fireworks, *gegants* (giants) and *caps grossos* (big heads), parades in which people wear giant papier-mâché heads.
October	**El Pilar** (October 12), celebrates Virgen del Pilar, patron saint of Spain and of Hispanic culture worldwide. The festivities bring representatives from the Spanish-speaking world around the globe.

Madrid

WORD OF MOUTH

"Madrid is definitely the kind of place to enjoy the buzz on the street—wandering around from place to place, people-watching from your seat at an outdoor café after a hard day of studying great works of art or a big stroll through Retiro Park. Keep in mind that a lot of the 'buzz' starts after the sun sets and runs late. And you certainly don't have to be out clubbing . . . to enjoy late-night Madrid. If the weather is right, you can sit outside in, say, the Santa Ana area, have a great conversation . . . while nursing a drink and enjoying the commotion all around you . . . ."

—Molloy95

By Ignacio
Gómez

SWASHBUCKLING MADRID CELEBRATES itself and life in general around the clock. After spending much of the 20th century at the center of a totalitarian regime, the first democratic elections after Francisco Franco's death in 1975 and the ensuing and enduring wave of political and social freedom had Madrid bursting back onto the world stage with an energy redolent of its 16th-century golden age, when painters and playwrights swarmed to the flame of Spain's brilliant royal court. A vibrant crossroads for Iberia and the world's Hispanic peoples and cultures, the Spanish capital has an infectious appetite for art, music, and epicurean pleasure.

After the first gulp of icy mountain air, the next thing likely to strike you is the vast, cerulean, cumulus-clouded sky immortalized in the paintings of Velázquez. *"De Madrid al cielo"* ("from Madrid to heaven") goes the saying, and the heavens seem just overhead at the center of the 2,120-foot-high Castilian plateau. "High, wide, and handsome" might aptly describe this sprawling conglomeration of ancient red-tile rooftops punctuated by redbrick Mudejar churches and gray-slate roofs and spires left by the 16th-century Habsburg monarchs who made Madrid the capital of Spain in 1561.

Then there are the paintings, the artistic legacy of one of the greatest global empires ever assembled. King Carlos I (1500–58), who later became emperor Carlos V, inherited most of Europe between 1516 and 1519, and amassed art from all corners of his empire—which is how the early masters of the Flemish, Dutch, Italian, French, German, and Spanish schools found their way to Spain's palaces. The collection was eventually placed in the Prado Museum, part of the grand Madrid built in the 18th century by the Bourbon king Carlos III—known as the Rey-Alcalde, or King-Mayor, for his preoccupation with municipal (rather than global) projects such as the Royal Palace, the Parque del Buen Retiro, and the Paseo del Prado. Among the Prado, the contemporary Reina Sofía museum, the eclectic Thyssen-Bornemisza collection, and Madrid's smaller artistic repositories—the Real Academia de Bellas Artes de San Fernando, the Convento de las Descalzas Reales, the Sorolla Museum, the Lázaro Galdiano Museum, and still others—there are more paintings in Madrid than anyone can hope to contemplate in a lifetime.

Modern-day Madrid spreads eastward into the 19th-century grid of the Barrio de Salamanca and sprawls northward through the neighborhoods of Chamberí and Chamartín. But the Madrid to explore carefully on foot is right in the center: the oldest one, between the Royal Palace and Madrid's midtown forest, the Parque del Buen Retiro. These neighborhoods will introduce you to the city's finest resources—its people and their electricity, whether at play in bars or at work in finance or the media and film industries, all in what Madrid's Oscar Wilde, Ramón Gomez de la Serna, called *"la rompeolas de las Españas,"* the breakwater of Spain's many peoples and cultures.

Long accused of growing chaotically, and of fixating on its past splendor, Madrid nowadays tries to balance its fondness for tradition—one of its biggest charms for the visitors—with the requirements of a major

GREAT ITINERARIES

1

IF YOU HAVE 2 DAYS
On the first morning, see the masterworks in the **Museo del Prado** ㉒ and tour the Paseo del Prado between **Estación de Atocha** ㉕ and **Plaza Colón** ㊶, past the fountains at **Fuente de Neptuno** ㉑ and the **Plaza de la Cibeles** ㉟. Have lunch in or near **Plaza Santa Ana** ㊹. Then cut through the **Puerta del Sol** ❺ to see Madrid's Times Square–where locals in Madrid gather to ring in the New Year–on your way to the **Plaza Mayor** ❶. Cut behind the glass-and-iron Mercado de San Miguel and through tiny Calle Puñonrostro to **Plaza de la Villa** ⑲ on your way to the church of **San Nícolas de los Servitas** ⑱ and then the **Plaza de Oriente** ❽, where you can tour the **Palacio Real** ❾ and the **Teatro Real** ⑩. If it's summer, take in the sunset from a terrace table at El Ventorrillo at the south end of Calle Bailén's Viaducto. Later, visit the tapas bars along Cava de San Miguel and end by having a drink on **Plaza de la Paja** ❷ or at the Café Marula terrace under the Puente de Segovia.

On Day 2, see Picasso's *Guernica* and other works at the **Centro de Arte Reina Sofía** ㉖. Have lunch on **Cava Baja** ❹, in La Latina, and visit the nearby **Basílica de San Francisco el Grande** ❸. If you have room for more art, explore the **Museo Thyssen-Bornemisza** ㉓, and take a stroll at sunset or earlier in the **Parque del Buen Retiro** ㉙ before dinner.

IF YOU HAVE 4 OR MORE DAYS
Follow the itinerary above, then on Day 3 go to either Toledo or Segovia to spend the day. On Day 4, take a break from museums and wander along the castizo neighborhoods: the literary neighborhood around **Plaza Santa Ana** ㊹, Chueca (with some good lunch stopovers on Calle Libertad and Calle Barbieri), and Malasaña, walking from **Centrode Conde Duque** ㊲ to the **Templo de Debod** ⑯, in Parque del Oeste, to catch the last glimpse of the sunset. Finish off the day sipping a drink on any of the terraces on Calle Rosales, near the Templo, before dinner. If it's summer, say goodbye to the city by having an after-dinner drink at one of the *terrazas* on Castellana.

If you happen to have a few more days, take in the 16th-century **Convento de las Descalzas Reales** ❻, the **Convento de la Encarnación** ❼, and the **Real Academia de Bellas Artes de San Fernando** ⑳, and put aside some time to visit **Museo Sorolla** ㊷, the **Museo Lázaro Galdiano** ㊸, the **Real Fábrica de Tapices** ㉘, and Goya's frescos at **Ermita San Antonio de la Florida** ⑫. Use one afternoon to do some shopping in the Salamanca neighborhood or on Calles Fuencarral and Hortaleza. Make room for some flamenco at any of the listed tablaos, listen to recorded flamenco and make your own moves on the dance floor at any of the hangouts on Calle Echegaray (such as Cardamomo, El Burladero, or Los Gabrieles), or, if it's summer, see if there are any concerts at the magnificent main plaza of the **Centro de Conde Duque** ㊲.

Numbered bullets refer to the Madrid map on pages 36–37.

urban center. In line with some other cities, Madrid is expanding (mostly northward) and drawing some of the world's best architects in her bid to ensure that its tourist attractions extend beyond its well-known baroque landmarks. This is the case with Jacques Herzog and Pierre de Meuron, who are set to build a new arts center (Caixa Forum) across from the Botanical Garden, as well as the major renovations by Rafael Moneo and Jean Nouvel of the Museo del Prado and the Centro Reina Sofía. Other projects include the massive but stylish new airport terminal (already nicknamed "the slingshot"), which began operating in early 2006, and the daring renovation project of the whole area of Paseo del Prado that's been entrusted to Portuguese architect Alvaro Siza. These major enhancements, as well as a growing influx of immigrants, are bringing new shades to a city that already had an eye-catching palette and knows how to bewitch its visitors.

As the highest capital in Europe, Madrid is hot in summer and freezing in winter, with temperate springs and autumns. Especially in winter—when steamy café windows beckon you inside for a hot *caldo* (broth) and the blue skies are particularly bright—Madrid *is* the next best place to heaven. Moreover, it's ideally placed for cherished getaways to dozens of Castilian hamlets and to Toledo, Segovia, and El Escorial.

About the Restaurants

Madrid has attracted generations of courtiers, diplomats, and tradesmen, all of whom have brought tastes and styles from other parts of the Iberian peninsula and the world. The city's best restaurants have traditionally specialized in Basque cooking, though contemporary Mediterranean interpretations from Catalonia (namely by Ferran Adrià's disciples) and even Asian-fusion restaurants have begun to rock the city's culinary canons. Madrid's many seafood specialists capitalize on the abundant fresh produce trucked in nightly from the Atlantic and the Mediterranean coasts.

Madrid's cuisine is based on the roasts and thick soups and stews of Castile, Spain's high central *meseta* (plain). Roast suckling pig and lamb are standard Madrid feasts, as are baby goat and chunks of beef from Ávila and the Sierra de Guadarrama. *Cocido madrileño* and *callos a la madrileña* are local specialties. The white and green asparagus, formerly grown by the kings in Aranjuez and now coming from other regions, are also favorites. Cocido is a hearty winter meal of broth, garbanzo beans, vegetables, potatoes, sausages, pork, and hen. The best cocidos are simmered in earthenware crocks over coals and served in three courses: broth, beans, and meat. Cocido anchors the midday winter menu in the most elegant restaurants as well as the humblest holes-in-the-wall. Callos are a simpler concoction of veal tripe stewed with tomatoes, onions, hot paprika, and garlic. *Jamón serrano* (cured ham)—a specialty from the livestock lands of Teruel, Extremadura, and Andalusia—has become a Madrid staple; wanderers are likely to come across a *museo del jamón* (literally, "ham museum"), where legs of the dried delicacy dangle in store windows or in bars. For top-quality free-range, acorn-fed, native Iberian ham ask for *jamón ibérico de bellota*. For faster dining, try *pincho de tortilla* (a portion of potato omelet served with some bread on

IF YOU LIKE

ART MUSEUMS

Madrid's greatest daytime attractions are its three magnificient art museums, the Prado, the Reina Sofía, and the Thyssen-Bornemisza, all within 1 km (½ mi) of one another along the leafy Paseo del Prado, sometimes called the Paseo del Arte. The Prado has the world's foremost collections of Goya, El Greco, and Velázquez, topping off hundreds of other 14th- to 19th-century masterpieces. The Reina Sofía focuses on modern art, especially Dalí, Miró, and Picasso, whose famous *Guernica* hangs here; it also shows contemporary Spanish artists, such as Jorge Oteiza, Eduardo Chillida, Antoni Tàpies, and Antonio Lopez, as well as postmodern temporary exhibits. The Thyssen-Bornemisza encompasses the entire history of Western art, with collections of impressionist and German expressionist works.

BULLFIGHTING

Bullfighting is an artistic spectacle, not to be confused with sport. For those not squeamish about the sight of six dying bulls, it offers all the excitement of a major stadium event, held every Sunday afternoon from April to early November. Nowhere in the world is bullfighting better than at Madrid's Las Ventas on Calle Alcalá in Salamanca. The sophisticated audience follows the happenings closely, and the uninitiated might be baffled by their reactions: cheers and hoots can be hard to distinguish, and it can take years to understand what prompts the wrath of such a hard-to-please crowd. Tickets can be purchased at the ring or, for a 20% surcharge, at one of the agencies on Calle Victoria, just off the Puerta del Sol. Most *corridas* start in late afternoon, and the best fights of all—the world's top displays of bullfighting—come during the three weeks of consecutive daily events that mark the feast of San Isidro, in May. Tickets can be tough to get through normal channels but are always available from scalpers on Calle Victoria and at the stadium. You can bargain, but even Spaniards pay prices of perhaps 10 times the face value—up to €120 or more.

MUSIC

Madrid's music ranges from Bach organ recitals in the Catedral de la Almudena to flamenco performances with dinner at Casa Patas, summer concerts at the Centro de Conde Duque's main courtyard, or jazz jam sessions at Café Berlín or Café Populart. In between there are renowned groups playing in intimate chapels, churches, and convents, the Auditorio Nacional, the Teatro Real opera house, the auditorium at the Academia Real de Bellas Artes de San Fernando, and other venues. The Juan March Foundation organizes ongoing classical series. Architecture is never better appreciated than when accompanied by music; check listings for musical events held in spaces you wouldn't otherwise be able to glimpse (such as old churches and palatial homes).

the side) or a *cazuelita* (small earthenware bowl) of anything from wild mushrooms to *riñones al jerez* (lamb or veal kidneys stewed in sherry).

The house wine in basic Madrid restaurants is often a sturdy, uncomplicated Valdepeñas from La Mancha. Serious dining is normally accompanied by a Rioja or a more powerful, complex Ribera de Duero, the latter from northern Castile. Ask your waiter's advice; a smooth Rioja, for example, may not be up to the task of accompanying a cocido or a roast suckling pig. After dinner, try the anise-flavor liqueur (*anís*) produced outside the nearby village of Chinchón.

WHAT IT COSTS In Euros				
	$$$$	$$$	$$	$	¢
AT DINNER	over €25	€18–€25	€12–€18	€8–€12	under €8

Prices are per person for a main course at dinner.

About the Hotels

Try bargaining at the pricier properties: weekend and August discounts of up to 30% or more are widely available. You can also find *hostal* rooms, often on the upper floors of apartment buildings with shared or private baths, for €40 or less. Because these cheap lodgings are often full and don't take reservations, only a few are listed here—you simply have to try your luck door-to-door. Many are in the old city between the Prado and the Puerta del Sol; start your quest around Plaza Santa Ana.

WHAT IT COSTS In Euros				
	$$$$	$$$	$$	$	¢
FOR 2 PEOPLE	over €225	€150–€225	€80–€150	€50–€80	under €50

Prices are for two people in a standard double room in high season, excluding tax.

EXPLORING MADRID

The real Madrid is not to be found along its major arteries such as Gran Vía and the Paseo de la Castellana. To find the quiet, intimate streets and squares that give the city its true character, duck into the warren of villagelike byways in the downtown area 2½ km (1½ mi) square extending from the Royal Palace to the Parque del Buen Retiro and from Plaza de Lavapiés to the Glorieta de Bilbao. Broad *avenidas,* twisting medieval alleys, grand museums, stately gardens, and tiny, tile taverns are all jumbled together, creating an urban texture so rich that walking is really the only way to soak it in. Sadly, petty street crime is a serious problem in Madrid, and tourists are frequent targets. Be on your guard, and try to blend in: keep cameras concealed, avoid obvious map reading, and secure bags and purses, especially on the buses and subway and outside restaurants and cafés. The Japanese embassy has told Madrid authorities that tourists who appear East Asian seem to be at particular risk.

Numbers in the text correspond to numbers in the margin and on the Madrid, Side Trips from Madrid, and El Escorial maps.

Old Madrid

The narrow streets of old Madrid wind back through the city's history to its beginnings as an Arab fortress. Madrid's historic quarters are not so readily apparent as the ancient neighborhoods of Toledo and Segovia, nor are they so grand, but make time to explore their quiet alleys.

A GOOD WALK

Start in the **Plaza Mayor ❶** ▶. Looking up at the playfully erotic mural on the Casa de la Panadería, which now houses the city tourist information center, exit under the arch to the far left and walk down Ciudad Rodrigo, and turn left. Across the street is the restored San Miguel market. As Cava de San Miguel becomes Calle Cuchilleros, look to the left for Botín, Madrid's oldest restaurant and a onetime Hemingway haunt.

The plaza with the bright murals at the intersection of Calle Segovia is called **Puerta Cerrada**, or Closed Gate, for the (always closed) city gate that once stood here. The mural up to the left reads, "*Fui sobre agua edificada; mis muros de fuego son*" ("I was built on water; my walls are made of fire"), a reference to the city's origins as a fortress with abundant springs and its ramparts, made of the kind of flint that creates sparks.

Nuncio widens, and on your left at No. 17 is the Taberna de Cien Vinos; sample some Spanish wine here. Opposite is the church of San Pedro el Viejo (St. Peter the Elder), one of Madrid's oldest, with a Mudejar tower. Bear right and walk the narrow and short Calle Príncipe Anglona to come to **Plaza de la Paja ❷**. Down on the right is the ramped Costanilla de San Andrés, which leads to Calle Segovia and a view of the viaduct above. Look farther down Príncipe Anglona to see the Mudejar tower on San Pedro church; was reportedly built in 1354 after the Christian Reconquest of Algeciras, near Gibraltar.

At the top of Plaza de la Paja is the church of San Andrés and to the left of its entrance the Museo de San Isidro, a small municipal museum. Past the church, turn right after Plaza de los Carros into Plaza Puerta de Moros, then down Carrera San Francisco to visit the **Basílica de San Francisco el Grande ❸**. Backtrack and turn left after San Andrés down **Cava Baja ❹**, packed with bars and restaurants. Casa Lucio, at No. 35, is said to be a favorite of King Juan

IGNACIO'S TOP 5

- The bars in the Cava Baja in the La Latina neighborhood, for their wide variety of local wines and sophisticated tapas.

- The Plaza Mayor on any late night, when it's silent and almost empty.

- The Retiro gardens and especially the surroundings of its biggest lake, where passersby, jugglers, and musicians gather every morning on the weekend.

- The Prado Museum, for its impressive display of art, which is both captivating and overwhelming.

- The contagious, kinetic night vibe of two adjoining, young, and bustling neighborhoods, Malasaña and Chueca.

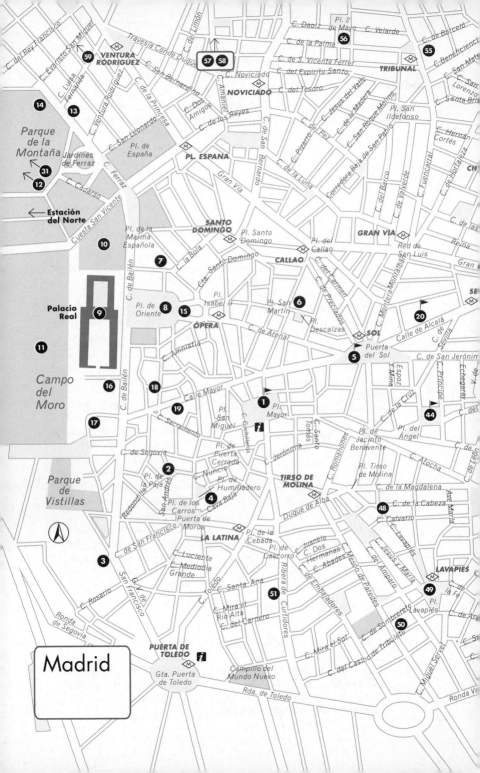

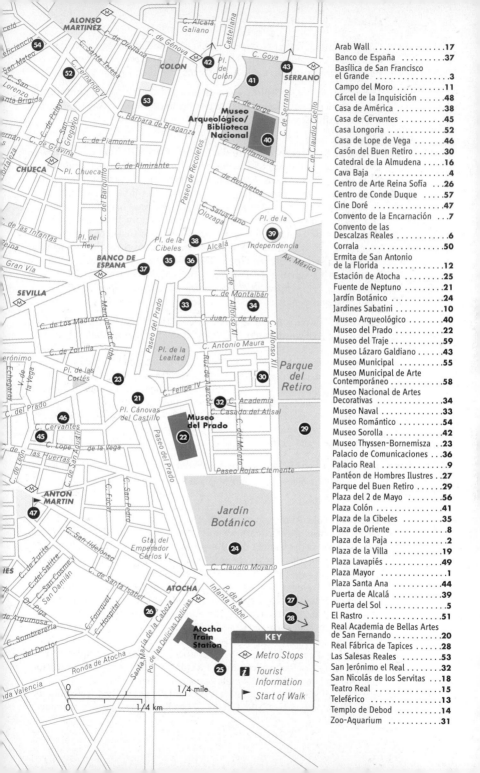

Carlos I; Casa Lucas at No. 30 is a great place to have imaginative tapas; and Julián de Tolosa at No. 18 has fine Basque fare. Continue across Puerta Cerrada and up Calle Cuchilleros to return to Plaza Mayor.

TIMING This two-hour walk requires some short uphill climbs. Allow ample time for stops—especially in summer, when heat will be a factor—to absorb some café and terrace life.

What to See

❸ Basílica de San Francisco el Grande. In 1760 Carlos III built this impressive basilica on the site of a Franciscan convent, allegedly founded by St. Francis of Assisi in 1217. The dome, 108 feet in diameter, is the largest in Spain, even larger than that of St. Paul's in London. The seven main doors were carved of American walnut by Casa Juan Guas. Three chapels adjoin the circular church, the most famous being that of **San Bernardino de Siena,** which contains a Goya masterpiece depicting a preaching San Bernardino. The figure standing on the right, not looking up, is a self-portrait of Goya. The 16th-century Gothic choir stalls came from La Cartuja del Paular, in rural Segovia province. ⊠ *Pl. de San Francisco, La Latina* ☎ *91/365–3800* ⌨ €3 *guided tour* ☉ *Tues.–Fri. 11–12:30 and 4–6:30 (5–7:30 June–Sept.), Sat. 11–noon.*

★ **❹ Cava Baja.** The narrow, old streets south of Plaza Mayor and across Calle Segovia are well worth exploring: from Plaza Mayor, walk to Plaza Puerta Cerrada where Calle Segovia begins and cross over to Cava Baja. Stroll down Cava Baja, the epicenter of the fashionable and historic La Latina neighborhood, crowded with a variety of excellent tapas bars (such as Casa Lucas, La Chata, and El Tempranillo), traditional restaurants (Julián de Tolosa, Casa Lucio), and even a low-key flamenco night bar with live performances (La Soleá). The lively atmosphere of the Cava Baja spills over into nearby streets and squares, including Almendro, Cava Alta, Plaza del Humilladero, and Plaza de la Paja. ⊠ *Across Calle Segovia, La Latina.*

┏━━━━━
┃ **NEED A BREAK?**   With its backdrop of classical music, **Café del Nuncio** (on Costanilla del Nuncio s/n, in Plaza Mayor) **is a relaxing place for a coffee or beer.**

❷ Plaza de la Paja. At the top of the hill, on Costanilla San Andrés, the Plaza de la Paja was the most important square in medieval Madrid. The plaza's jewel is the **Capilla del Obispo** (Bishop's Chapel), built between 1520 and 1530; this was where peasants deposited their tithes, called *diezmas*—literally, one-tenth of their crop. The stacks of wheat on the chapel's ceramic tiles refer to this tradition. Architecturally, the chapel marks a transition from the blockish Gothic period, which gave the structure its basic shape, to the Renaissance, the source of the decorations. Go inside to see the intricately carved polychrome altarpiece by Francisco Giralta, with scenes from the life of Christ. Opening hours are erratic; try to visit during Mass or on feast days. The chapel is part of the complex of the domed church of **San Andrés,** one of Madrid's oldest, which for centuries held the remains of Madrid's male patron saint, San Isidro Labrador (they are now safeguarded, together with his wife's, at the Real Colegiata de San Isidro, on nearby Calle Toledo). The church was severely damaged during the civil war. St. Isidore the Laborer was a peasant who worked fields belonging to the Vargas family. The 16th-century **Vargas palace** forms the eastern side of the Plaza de la Paja. According to legend, St. Isidro worked little but had the best-tended fields thanks to many hours of prayer. When Señor Vargas came out to investigate the phenomenon, Isidro made a spring of sweet water spurt from the ground to quench his master's thirst. A hermitage (Ermita de San Isidro), now on Paseo de la Ermita del Santo, west of the Manzanares river, was built next to the spring in 1528. Every May 15 there's a procession followed by festivities in the meadow next to the hermitage. Because St. Isidro's power had to do with water, his remains were traditionally paraded through the city in times of drought. The **Museo de San Isidro**, on Plaza de San Andrés and next to San André's entrance, is on what was a 16th-century palace and supposedly the saint's home four centuries earlier. Among other interesting items related to the saint and the city's history, the museum features a model of the San Andrés church before all of its artistic treasures were destroyed. ⊠ *Plaza de la Paja, Centro.*

➤ ❶ **Plaza Mayor.** Austere, grand, and often surprisingly quiet compared with the rest of Madrid, this arcaded public square—one of the largest in Europe—has seen it all: autos-de-fé (trials of faith, i.e., public burnings of heretics); the canonization of saints; criminal executions; royal marriages, such as that of Princess María and the King of Hungary in 1629; bullfights (until 1847); masked balls; fireworks; and all manner of other events. It is still the site of fairs, bazaars, and performances.

This space was once occupied by a city market, and many of the surrounding streets retain the names of the trades and foods once headquartered there. Nearby are Calle de Cuchilleros (Knifemakers' Street), Calle de Lechuga (Lettuce Street), Calle de Fresa (Strawberry Street), and Calle de Botoneros (Buttonmakers' Street). The plaza's oldest building is the one with the brightly painted murals and the gray spires, called Casa de la Panadería (Bakery House) in honor of the bread shop over which it was built; it is now the tourist office. Opposite is the Casa de la Carnicería (Butcher Shop), now a police station.

The plaza is closed to motorized traffic, making it a pleasant place to sit at one of the sidewalk cafés, watching alfresco artists, street musicians, and Madrileños from all walks of life. Sunday morning brings a stamp and coin market. Around Christmas the plaza fills with stalls selling trees, ornaments, and nativity scenes, as well as all types of practical jokes and tricks for December 28, Día de los Inocentes—a Spanish version of April Fools' Day. ⊠ *Plaza Mayor, Centro.*

Central Madrid

The 1-km (½-mi) stretch between the Royal Palace and the Puerta del Sol is loaded with historic sites.

▌ **A GOOD WALK**

Begin at the **Puerta del Sol ❺** ➤, the center of Madrid. If you stand with your back to the clock, Calle Arenal is the second street from the far left leaving the plaza: walk down Arenal and turn right into Plaza Celenque. Up on your left, at the corner with Calle Misericordia, is the

Convento de las Descalzas Reales ❻. Follow Misericordia and turn left into the charming Plaza de San Martín. At No. 1 is the **Fundación Caja Madrid,** called *Casa de las Alhajas* (House of the Jewels). The exhibitions housed here, often done in collaboration with the Thyssen Museum, can be visited for free. Return from there to Calle Arenal, turn right and walk to Plaza Isabel II; then cross the plaza to your right and walk down the short Calle de Arrieta; at the end sits **Convento de la Encarnación** ❼. Turn left here onto Calle Pavia (off Calle San Quintin) to enter the **Plaza de Oriente** ❽.

Here you have a choice of going directly to the **Palacio Real** ❾, to your right, or visiting its gardens (1 km [½ mi] farther on) and/or taking a cable-car ride. For the latter, cross Calle Bailén and walk to the right: from here you can look across the formal **Jardines Sabatini** ❿ to the Casa de Campo park and the Guadarrama Mountains. Walk up Bailén, avoiding the overpass, and turn left down Cuesta de San Vicente, then left into Paseo Virgen del Puerto for the entrance to the gardens and the **Campo del Moro** ⓫. Exit the gardens through the same entrance and get Paseo de la Florida from the roundabout at Príncipe Pío. (Optional: From that roundabout you can take Bus 33 to the **Zoo–Aquarium** ㉛.) Next, walk for about 10 minutes down Paseo de la Florida until you arrive at **Ermita de San Antonio de la Florida** ⓬, the small church with Goya's frescoes. Across from the church you can find Casa Mingo, an inexpensive, traditional, and popular Asturian restaurant that's famous for its roasted chicken and great cider. Walk to the back of the church and get the overpass crossing the railway; you'll find yourself at Parque del Oeste. Once you get to the end of the overpass, turn right and take Calle Francisco y Jacinto Alcántara to the left and up. You'll pass the **Escuela Nacional de Cerámica** and the Floridablanca cemetery. Forty-three of the people who died in the events of May 2, 1808 (*see* The Events of May 2 box, *below*) are buried in it. Once you get to the top of the street, if you walk east, you'll reach the Rosaleda, the Parque del Oeste's rose garden, which every May and June holds an International Rose contest. Otherwise walk northward and uphill until you reach the **Teleférico** ⓭ (cable car) to the Casa de Campo, which grants panoramic views of Madrid. To see the Egyptian **Templo de Debod** ⓮, skirt the park to the right along Calle Rosales.

Opposite the Royal Palace on the Plaza de Oriente is the **Teatro Real** ⓯. Walking down Bailén with the palace on your right, you can enter its huge courtyard and admire the view from atop the escarpment in front of it. Alongside the palace is the **Catedral de la Almudena** ⓰. Walk past the cathedral and turn right onto Calle Mayor: on your left, on Cuesta de la Vega, are the remains of Madrid's **Arab Wall** ⓱. Walk back east up Calle Mayor, crossing Bailén. Turn left onto Calle San Nicolás to see the church of **San Nicolás de los Servitas** ⓲. Return to Calle Mayor and press ahead: on your right you'll see the **Plaza de la Villa** ⓳ Madrid's city hall. Farther up Mayor, bear right on Plaza Morenas and enter the **Plaza Mayor** ❶ through the arch. The Andalusian Torre de Oro bar on the left displays gory pictures of bullfights. On the far side, at No. 33, is the restaurant El Soportal, which gives out the plaza's best free tapas with each drink order. (Watch out for inflated prices at the other restaurants, especially if you sit outside.) Exit the plaza to the left of El Soportal and head down Calle de Postas and back to the Puerta del Sol. Proceed up the right side of the square, past the headquarters of the regional government; in winter consider having a traditional *caldo* (broth) in the charming old shop at the restaurant Lhardy on Carrera de San Jerónimo.

TIMING Without side trips to the palace gardens, the Goya's frescoes, or the cable car, you can cover this ground in three hours. Set aside an additional morning or afternoon to visit the Royal Palace.

What to See

⑰ Arab Wall. The remains of the Moorish military outpost that became the city of Madrid are visible on Calle Cuesta de la Vega. The sections of wall here protected a fortress built in the 9th century by Emir Mohammed I. In addition to being an excellent defensive position, the site had plentiful water and was called *Mayrit,* Arabic for "source of life" (this is the likely origin of the city's name). All that remains of the *medina*—the old Arab city that formed within the walls of the fortress—is the neighborhood's crazy quilt of streets and plazas, which probably follow the same layout they followed more than 1,100 years ago. The park **Emir Mohammed I,** alongside the wall, is the site of concerts and plays in summer. ⊠ *C. Cuesta de la Vega, Centro.*

⑪ Campo del Moro (Moors' Field). Below the Sabatini Gardens, but accessible only by an entrance on the far side, is the Campo del Moro. Enjoy the clusters of shady trees, winding paths, and the long lawn leading up to the Royal Palace. Even without considering the riches inside, the palace's immense size (it's twice as large as Buckingham Palace) inspires awe. Also inside the gardens is a **Museo de Carruajes** (Carriage Museum), displaying royal carriages and equestrian paraphernalia from the 16th through 20th century. ⊠ *Paseo Virgen del Puerto s/n, Centro.*

⑯ Catedral de la Almudena. The first stone of the cathedral (which adjoins the Royal Palace to the south) was laid in 1883 by King Alfonso XII, and the result was consecrated by Pope John Paul II in 1993. (It was built on the site where the old church of Santa María de la Almudena stood. Santa María, demolished in 1868, was Madrid's oldest registered church and was thought to be the city's main mosque during the Arab's rule.) The new cathedral was intended to be Gothic in style, with needles and spires, but funds ran low, so the design was simplified by Fernando Chueca Goltia into the existing, more austere classical form. The cathedral has a wooden statue of Madrid's female patron saint, the Virgin of Almudena, reportedly discovered after the 1085 Christian Reconquest of Madrid. Legend has it that when the Arabs invaded Spain, the local Christian population hid the statue of the Virgin in a vault carved in the old Roman wall that encircled the city. When Christians reconquered Madrid in 1085, they looked for it, and after nine days of intensive praying—others say it was after a procession honoring the Virgin—the wall opened up to show the statue framed by two lighted candles. Its name is derived from the place where it was found: the wall of the old citadel (in Arabic, *almudeyna*). ⊠ *C. Bailén 10, Centro* ☎ *91/542–2200* ⊠ *Free* ☾ *Daily 9–9.*

❼ Convento de la Encarnación (Convent of the Incarnation). Once connected to the Royal Palace by an underground passageway, this Augustinian convent was founded in 1611 by the wife of Felipe III. It has several artistic treasures, including a reliquary. Among the reliquary's sacred bones is a vial containing the dried blood of St. Pantaleón, which is said to liquefy every year on July 27. The ornate church has superb acoustics for medieval and Renaissance choral music; check city listings for concerts. A €6 ticket allows for a combined visit of both this and the Convento de las Descalzas Reales. ⊠ *Plaza de la Encarnación 1, Ópera* ☎ *91/454–8800 tourist information office* ☜ *€3.60* ⊙ *Tues.–Thurs. and Sat. 10:30–12:45 and 4–5:45, Fri. 10:30–12:45, Sun. 11–1:45.*

❻ Convento de las Descalzas Reales (Convent of the Royal Discalced, or Barefoot, Nuns). This 16th-century building was restricted for 200 years to women of royal blood. Its plain, brick-and-stone facade hides paintings by Zurbarán, Titian, and Brueghel the Elder—all part of the dowry the novices had to provide when they joined the monastery—as well as a hall of sumptuous tapestries crafted from drawings by Peter Paul Rubens. The convent was founded in 1559 by Juana of Austria, one of Felipe II's sisters, who ruled Spain while he was in England and the Netherlands. It houses 33 different chapels—the age of Christ when he died and the maximum number of nuns allowed to live at the monastery at the same time—and more than 100 sculptures of Jesus as a baby. About 30 nuns (not necessarily of royal blood) still live here, cultivating their own vegetables in the convent's garden. The tour (required) is conducted in Spanish only. ⊠ *Plaza de las Descalzas Reales 3, Centro* ☎ *91/454–8800* ☜ *€5* ⊙ *Tues.–Thurs. and Sat. 10:30–12:30 and 4–5:30, Fri. 10:30–12:30, Sun. 11–1:30.*

⓬ Ermita de San Antonio de la Florida (Goya's tomb). Built from 1792 to 1798 by the Italian architect Francisco Fontana, this neoclassical church was financed by King Carlos IV, who also commissioned Goya to paint the vaults and the main dome. The painter, who by that time was already deaf, took 120 days to complete his assignment. He painted them alone with the help of a little boy who would stir the pigments for him. This gave him absolute freedom to depict events of the 13th century (Saint Anthony of Padua resurrecting a death man) as if they had happened five centuries later, and using naturalistic images never used before to paint religious scenes. Opposite the image of the frightening dead man on the main dome Goya painted himself as a man covered with a blackish cloak. The frescoes' third-restoration phase ended in 2005, and now visitors can admire them in their full splendor. The painter, who died in Bordeaux in 1828, is buried here (without his head, since it was stolen in France), under an unadorned gravestone.

San Antonio is the patron saint of young maidens, and every June 13 there is a festival in which marriageable women congregate at the church to request a husband. They throw 13 hairpins in a basin and press a hand firmly against them. The number of hairpins that stick to it determines the number of boyfriends they'll have that year. ⊠ *Glorieta de San Antonio de la Florida 5 Príncipe Pío* ☎ *91/542–0722* ☜ *Free* ⊙ *Tues.–Fri. 9:30–8, Sun. 10–2.*

⑩ Jardines Sabatini (Sabatini Gardens). The formal gardens to the north of the Royal Palace are crawling with stray cats—but are nonetheless a pleasant place to rest or watch the sun set. ✉ *C. Bailén s/n, Centro.*

⑨ Palacio Real. The Royal Palace was commissioned in the early 18th century by the first of Spain's Bourbon rulers, Felipe V, on the same strategic site where Madrid's first Alcázar (Moorish fortress) was built in the 9th century. Before you enter, admire the classical French architecture on the graceful **Patio de Armas.** King Felipe was obviously inspired by his childhood days at Versailles with his grandfather Louis XIV. Look for the stone statues of Inca prince Atahualpa and Aztec king Montezuma, perhaps the only tributes in Spain to these pre-Columbian American rulers. Notice how the steep bluff drops westward to the Manzanares River—on a clear day, this vantage point also commands a view of the mountain passes leading into Madrid from Old Castile; thus it's easy to see why the Moors picked this particular spot for a fortress.

*Fodor's*Choice
★

Inside, 2,800 rooms compete with each other for over-the-top opulence. A nearly two-hour guided tour in English winds a mile-long path through the palace. Highlights include the **Salón de Gasparini,** King Carlos III's private apartments, with swirling, inlaid floors and curlicued, stucco wall and ceiling decoration, all glistening in the light of a 2-ton crystal chandelier; the **Salón del Trono,** a grand throne room with the royal seats of King Juan Carlos and Queen Sofía; and the **banquet hall,** the palace's largest room, which seats up to 140 people for state dinners. No monarch has lived here since 1931, when Alfonso XIII was deposed after a republican electoral victory. The current king and queen live in the far simpler Zarzuela Palace on the outskirts of Madrid, using this palace only for official occasions.

Also visit the **Museo de Música** (Music Museum), where five stringed instruments by Stradivarius form the world's largest such collection; the **Painting Gallery** (Music Museum), which displays works by Spanish, Flemish, and Italian artists from the 15th century onward; the **Armería Real** (Royal Armory), with historic suits of armor and frightening medieval torture implements; and the **Real Oficina de Farmacía** (Royal Pharmacy), with vials and flasks used to mix the king's medicines. The palace also has the **Biblioteca Real** (Royal Library), with a first edition of Cervantes's *Don Quijote,* which for now remains off-limits to visitors. When planning a visit here, note that the Royal Palace is closed during official receptions. ✉ *C. Bailén s/n, Centro* ☎ *91/454–8800* 🎟 *€8, guided tour €9; Royal Armory only €3.40* ◷ *Apr.–Sept., Mon.–Sat. 9–6, Sun. 9–3; Oct.–Mar., Mon.–Sat. 9:30–5, Sun. 9–2.*

⑧ Plaza de Oriente. The stately plaza in front of the Royal Palace is surrounded by massive stone statues of various Spanish monarchs from Ataulfo to Fernando VI. These sculptures were meant to be mounted on the railing on top of the palace, but Queen Isabel of Farnesio, one of the first royals to live in the palace, had them removed because she was afraid their enormous weight would bring the roof down. (Well, that's what she *said.* . . . According to palace insiders, the queen wanted the statues removed because her own likeness had not been placed front and center.)For most Madrileños, the Plaza de Oriente is forever linked with Francisco Franco. The *generalísimo* liked to speak from the roof of the Royal Palace to his followers as they crammed into the plaza below. Even now, on the November anniversary of Franco's death, the plaza fills with supporters, most of whom are old-timers, though the event occasionally has drawn swastika-waving skinheads from other European countries in a fascist tribute. ⊠ *Plaza de Oriente, Centro.*

19 Plaza de la Villa. Madrid's town council has met in this medieval-looking complex since the Middle Ages, and it's now the city hall (plans are afoot to move the city hall headquarters to the post office building at Plaza Cibeles). The oldest building is the **Casa de los Lujanes,** on the east side—it's the one with the Mudejar tower. Built as a private home in the late 15th century, the house carries the Lujanes crest over the main doorway. Also on the plaza's east end is the brick-and-stone **Casa de la Villa,** built in 1629, a classic example of Madrid design with clean lines and spire-topped corner towers. Connected by an overhead walkway, the **Casa de Cisneros** was commissioned in 1537 by the nephew of Cardinal Cisneros. It's one of Madrid's rare examples of the flamboyant plateresque style, which has been likened to splashed water. ⊠ *C. Mayor, Centro* ⊙ *Closed to the public except for free guided tour in Spanish Mon. at 5.*

▶ 5 Puerta del Sol. Crowded with people and exhaust, Sol is the nerve center of Madrid's traffic. The city's main subway interchange is below, and buses fan out from here. A brass plaque in the sidewalk on the south side of the plaza marks Kilometer 0, the spot from which all distances in Spain are measured. The restored 1756 French-neoclassical building near the marker now houses the offices of the regional government, but during Franco's reign it was the headquarters of his secret police, and it's still known folklorically as the Casa de los Gritos (House of Screams). Across the square is a bronze statue of Madrid's official symbol, a bear with a *madroño* (strawberry tree), and a statue of King-Mayor Carlos III on horseback. ⊠ *Puerta del Sol, Centro.*

18 San Nicolás de los Servitas (Church of St. Nicholas of the Servitas). This church tower is one of the oldest buildings in Madrid. There's some debate over whether it once formed part of an Arab mosque. It was more likely built after the Christian Reconquest of Madrid in 1085, but the brickwork and the horseshoe arches are evidence that it was crafted by either Mudejars (Moorish workers) or Spaniards well versed in the style. Inside, exhibits detail the Islamic history of early Madrid. ⊠ *Near Plaza de San Nicolás, Centro* ☎ *91/559-4064* 🎟 *Donation suggested* ⊙ *Tues.–Sat. 8:30 AM–9:30 AM and 6:30–9 PM, Sun. and Mon. 8:30–2 and 6–9; groups by appointment.*

15 Teatro Real (Royal Theater). Built in 1850, this neoclassical theater was long a cultural center for Madrileño society. A major restoration project has left it filled with golden balconies, plush seats, and state-of-the-art stage equipment for operas and ballets. Upstairs there's an elegant restaurant that's worth a look. ⊠ *Plaza de Isabel II, Centro* ☎ *91/516–0660* ⊕ *www.teatro-real.com.*

⓭ Teleférico. Kids love this cable car, which takes you from the Rosaleda gardens in the Parque del Oeste to the center of Casa de Campo. The walk from where the cable car drops you off to the zoo and theme park is at least 2 km (1 mi), and you'll probably have to ask for directions; it's easier to ride out, turn around, and come back. ⊠ *Estación Terminal Teleférico, Paseo de Pintor Rosales, at C. Marques de Urquijo, Centro* ☎ *91/541–7450* ⊠ *€3.50 one-way, €4.80 round-trip* ☼ *Apr.–Sept., daily noon–dusk; Oct.–Mar., weekends noon–dusk.*

⓮ Templo de Debod. This authentic 4th-century BC Egyptian temple was donated to Spain in gratitude for its technical assistance with the construction of the Aswan Dam. It's near the site of the former Montaña barracks, where Madrileños bloodily crushed the beginnings of a military uprising in 1936. The western side of the small park around the temple is the best place to watch Madrid's outstanding sunset. ⊠ *Hill in Parque de la Montaña, near Estación del Norte, Centro* ☎ *91/765–1008* ⊠ *Free* ☼ *Oct.–Mar., Tues.–Fri. 9:45–1:45 and 4:15–6:15, weekends 10–2; Apr.–Sept., Tues.–Fri. 10–2 and 6–8, weekends 10–2; free guided tour Sat. at 11:30 and 12:30.*

㉛ Zoo-Aquarium. One of the most comprehensive zoological parks in Europe, Madrid's zoo houses a large variety of animals (including rarities such as an albino tiger) that are grouped according to their geographical origin. It also has a dolphinarium and a wild bird reservoir that hold entertaining exhibitions twice a day on weekdays, and several more on weekends. To get a good seat, arrive a few minutes before the show begins, especially on the weekend. Give yourself at least three to four hours to stroll through the entire park. To enjoy the outdoors and save a little time, bring your own food and eat at one of the picnic zones. It is in the Casa de Campo, a large park right outside the western part of the city. The best way to get here is by subway to Príncipe Pío and then Bus 33 to the zoo. ⊠ ☎ *91/512–3770* ⊕ *www.zoomadrid.com* ⊠ *Adults, €14.90; children 3–7, €12.20; younger children, free* ☼ *Winter, daily 11–6; summer, daily 10:30–7:30 (sometimes until 8 or 9 PM).*

The Art Walk

Madrid's three art museums are all within walking distance of one another via the Paseo del Prado. The Paseo was designed by King-Mayor Carlos III as a leafy nature walk with glorious fountains and a botanical garden for respite in scorching summers. As you walk east down Carrera de San Jerónimo toward the Paseo del Prado, consider that this was the route followed by Ferdinand and Isabella more than 500 years ago toward the church of San Jerónimo el Real. The *Paseo del Arte* (art pass) allows you to visit the three museums for €12. You can buy it at any of the three museums, and you don't have to visit all on the same day.

▌ A GOOD WALK Exit the Puerta del Sol onto Calle de Alcalá, and you'll find on your left the **Real Academia de Bellas Artes de San Fernando ㉕** ▶. Take the next right, past the elegant bank buildings, onto Calle Sevilla and turn left at Plaza Canalejas—where La Violeta, at No. 6, sells violet-flavor sweets—onto Carrera de San Jerónimo. (If you cross the plaza onto Calle

Príncipe, you'll reach the Plaza Santa Ana tapas area.) Walk down San Jerónimo to Plaza de las Cortés.

The granite building on the left, its stairs guarded by bronze lions, is the Congreso, lower house of Las Cortes, Spain's parliament. Walk past the landmark Westin Palace on the right to the **Fuente de Neptuno** ㉑ in the wide Paseo del Prado—the **Museo del Prado** ㉒ is across the boulevard to the right. On your left is the **Museo Thyssen-Bornemisza** ㉓, and across the plaza on the left is the elegant Ritz hotel, alongside the obelisk dedicated to all those who have died for Spain. Either tackle one or both of these museums now, or continue strolling.

Turning right and walking south on Paseo del Prado, you can see the **Jardín Botánico** ㉔ on the left and eventually **Estación de Atocha** ㉕, a railway station said to resemble the overturned hull of a ship. It's worth a quick visit for its humid indoor park, which has tropical trees, benches, paths, and a restaurant. Across the traffic circle, the immense pile of painted tiles and winged statues houses Spain's Ministry of Agriculture. The **Centro de Arte Reina Sofía** ㉖, site of Picasso's *Guernica,* is in the building with the exterior glass elevators, best accessed by walking up Calle Atocha from the station and taking the first left. If you walk between the front entrance of the Ministry of Agriculture and the Atocha station (which will be on your right), you'll reach a gas station, after which the street splits. Take the street to your right, Avenida de la Ciudad de Barcelona. On the left hand side of the street is a church, Nuestra Señora de Atocha. Once you pass it, you'll come to Calle Julián Gayarre, which crosses to the left. Turn onto this street and a few yards later, on your left hand side, will be the main entrance to the **Panteón de Hombres Ilustres** ㉗. On the corner of Julián Gayarre and Calle Fuenterrabía is a big brick building, the **Real Fábrica de Tapices** ㉘. Retrace your steps, and a block before the Ministry of Agriculture, make a right on Calle Alfonso XII, which puts the Anthropology Museum on your left. Calle Alfonso XII runs along the west side of the vast **Parque del Buen Retiro** ㉙. Straight ahead, on your left, is the **Casón del Buen Retiro** ㉚. Behind the Casón, you can find the the the church of **San Jerónimo el Real** ㉜ on the street running south. If you walk down the street, which ends at the back of the Casón del Buen Retiro, you can get back to the Plaza Cánovas del Castillo and the Fuente de Neptuno.

Back at the fountain, turn right and walk up the right side of Paseo del Prado (or, even better, the leafy central promenade). After passing the **Museo Naval** ㉝, cross Calle Montalbán, where the **Museo Nacional de Artes Decorativas** ㉞ is located. Finally, you'll reach the **Plaza de la Cibeles** ㉟, surrounded by the **Palacio de Comunicaciones** ㊱, the **Banco de España** ㊲, and the **Casa de América** ㊳. Turn right at Cibeles, walk up Calle Alcalá, and you can see Madrid's unofficial symbol, the **Puerta de Alcalá** ㊴, and, again, the Parque del Buen Retiro. About 100 yards north of Cibeles, on the Paseo de Recoletos, you can see a grand yellow mansion on the right—now a bank headquarters, this was once the home of the Marquis of Salamanca, who at the turn of the 20th century built the exclusive shopping and residential neighborhood (northeast of here) that bears his name. Continue north for the **Museo**

Arqueológico ⑩, which adjoins the National Library, and the **Plaza Colón** ⑪. If you're an art buff, press on to the **Museo Sorolla** ⑫ and **Museo Lázaro Galdiano** ⑬.

TIMING With a visit to the Reina Sofía and the Parque del Buen Retiro, you can do this walk in four to five hours. Set aside a morning or an afternoon *each* to return to the Prado and Thyssen-Bornemisza.

What to See

㊲ **Banco de España.** This massive 1884 building, Spain's central bank, takes up an entire block. It's said that part of the nation's gold reserves are held in great vaults that stretch under the Plaza de la Cibeles traffic circle all the way to the fountain. (Some reserves are also stored in Fort Knox, in the United States.) The bank is not open to visitors, but if you can dodge traffic well enough to reach the median strip in front of it, you can take a fine photo of the fountain and the palaces with the Puerta de Alcalá arch in the background. ⊠ *Paseo del Prado s/n, at Plaza de la Cibeles, Centro.*

㊳ **Casa de América.** A cultural center and art gallery focusing on Latin America, the Casa is in the allegedly haunted Palacio de Linares, built by a man who made his fortune in the Americas and returned to a life of incestuous love and strange deaths. ⊠ *Paseo de Recoletos 2, Centro* ☎ *91/595–4800* ⊕ *www.casamerica.es* ⊠ *Free* ☉ *Sept.–July, Tues.–Sat. 11–2 and 5–8, Sun. 11–2.*

㉚ **Casón del Buen Retiro.** This Prado annex is a five-minute walk from the museum and is free with a Prado ticket. The building, once a ballroom, and the formal gardens in the Retiro are all that remain of Madrid's second royal complex—at one time it filled the entire neighborhood. On display are 19th-century Spanish paintings and sculpture, including works by Sorolla and Rusiñol. A regal restoration of the complex will yield brand-new halls devoted to 17th- and 19th-century Spanish art. At this writing, the halls were closed for renovation, but scheduled to open by or in 2007. ⊠ *C. Alfonso XII s/n, Retiro* ☎ *91/330–2867* ☉ *Tues.–Sat. 9–7, Sun. 9–2.*

㉖ **Centro de Arte Reina Sofía** (Queen Sofía Art Center). Madrid's museum of modern art is in a converted hospital, the classical granite austerity of which is somewhat relieved (or ruined, depending on your point of view) by the playful pair of glass elevator shafts on its facade. Three separate buildings joined by a common vault were added to the original complex in a renovation that was finally inaugurated by the end of 2005. The first contains an art bookshop and a public library, the second a center for contemporary exhibitions, and the third an auditorium and restaurant/cafeteria managed by Sergi Arola of La Broche. This latter, although expensive, makes an excellent stop for a refreshment, be it a cup of tea or coffee, a snack, or even a cocktail.

FodorśChoice
★

The collection focuses on Spain's three great modern masters—Pablo Picasso, Salvador Dalí, and Joan Miró—and has contributions from Juan Gris, Jorge Oteiza, Pablo Gargallo, Julio Gonzalez, Eduardo Chillida, and Antoni Tàpies. Take the elevator to the second floor to see the heavy hitters, then to the fourth floor for the rest of the permanent collection, which includes both Spanish and international artists. The other floors have traveling exhibits. The exhibition rooms are numbered 1 to 45, beginning chronologically with the turn-of-the-20th-century birth of Spain's modern movement on the second floor and continuing to contemporary artists such as Eduardo Chillida in Rooms 42 and 43 on the fourth floor. The free English-language guide-booklet is excellent, as are the plastic-covered notes available at each display.

The museum's showpiece is Picasso's *Guernica,* in the center hall on the second floor. The huge black-and-white canvas depicts the horror of the Nazi Condor Legion's bombing of the ancient Basque town of Gernika in 1937, during the Spanish civil war. The work—in tone and structure a 20th-century version of Goya's *The 3rd of May*—is something of a national shrine. *Guernica* did not reach Madrid until 1981, as Picasso had stipulated in his will that the painting return to Spain only after democracy was restored.

The room in front of *Guernica* has surrealist works, with six canvases by Miró. Room 10 belongs to Salvador Dalí, hung in three *ámbitos* (areas). The first has the young artist experimenting with different styles, as in his cubist self-portrait and his classical landscape *Paisaje de Cadaqués;* the second shows the evolving painter of the Buñuel portrait and portraits of the artist's sister; and the third includes the full-blown surrealist work for which Dalí is best known, *The Great Masturbator* (1929) and *The Enigma of Hitler* (1939), with its ghostly umbrella and broken, dripping telephone.

The rest of the museum is devoted to more recent art, including the massive sculpture *Toki Egin,* by Eduardo Chillida (who died in 2002), considered among Spain's greatest sculptors, and five paintings by Barcelona artist Antoni Tàpies, whose works use such materials as wrinkled sheets and straw. ⊠ *Santa Isabel 52, Atocha* ☎ *91/467–5062* ⊕ *http://museoreinasofia.mcu.es* ⊡ *€6, free Sat. after 2:30 and all day Sun.* ⊘ *Mon. and Wed.–Sat. 10–9, Sun. 10–2:30.*

㉕ Estación de Atocha. Madrid's Atocha railroad station, a steel-and-glass hangar, was built in the late 19th century by Alberto Palacio Elissague, the same architect who became famous for his work with Ricardo Velázquez in the creation of the Palacio de Cristal (Crystal Palace) in Madrid's Retiro park. The immense space was filled in the late 20th century with a tropical rain forest. Closed for many years, and nearly torn down during the '70s, Atocha was restored and refurbished by Spain's internationally acclaimed architect Rafael Moneo and has reopened. ⊠ *Paseo de Atocha s/n, Retiro* ☎ *91/420–9875.*

㉑ Fuente de Neptuno (Neptune's Fountain). At Plaza Canovas del Castillo, midway between the Palace and Ritz hotels and the Prado and Thyssen-Bornemisza museums, this fountain is at the hub of Madrid's Paseo del Arte. It was a rallying point for Atlético de Madrid soccer triumphs (counterpoint to Real Madrid's celebrations at the Fuente de la Cibeles up the street). It's been quiet here for the past few years, with Atlético mired in second division (a concept comparable to the New York Yankees slipping down to the minors). With Atlético's return to first division in spring of 2002, the Fuente de Neptuno is waiting to revive its pivotal role in Madrid life. ⊠ *Plaza Canovas del Castillo, Centro.*

㉔ Jardín Botánico (Botanical Garden). Just south of the Prado Museum, the gardens provide a pleasant place to stroll or sit under the trees. True to the wishes of King Carlos III, they hold many plants, flowers, and cacti from around the world. ⊠ *Plaza de Murillo 2, Retiro* ☎ *91/420–3017* ⊕ *www.rjb.csic.es* ▨ *€2* ⊙ *Nov.–Feb., daily 10–6; Mar. and Oct., daily 10–7; Apr. and Sept., daily 10–8; May–Aug., daily 10–9.*

㊵ Museo Arqueológico (Museum of Archaeology). The museum shares its neoclassical building with the **Biblioteca Nacional** (National Library). The biggest attraction here is a replica of the prehistoric cave paintings in Altamira, Cantabria, underground in the garden. (Access to the real thing is highly restricted.) Inside the museum, look for *La Dama de Elche,* a bust of a wealthy, 5th-century BC Iberian woman, and notice that her headgear is a rough precursor to the mantillas and hair combs still associated with traditional Spanish dress. The ancient Visigothic votive crowns are another highlight; discovered in 1859 near Toledo, they are believed to date back to the 8th century. ⊠ *C. Serrano 13, Salamanca* ☎ *91/577–7912* ⊕ *http://man.mcu.es* ▨ *€3, free Sat. after 2:30 and all day Sun.* ⊙ *Museum Tues.–Sat. 9:30–8:30, Sun. 9:30–2:30. Library weekdays 9–9, Sat. 9–2* ☎ *91/580–7823 library.*

㉒ Museo del Prado (Prado Museum). When the Prado was commissioned
Fodor'sChoice by King-Mayor Carlos III, in 1785, it was meant to be a natural-science
★ museum. The king wanted the museum, the adjoining botanical gardens, and the elegant Paseo del Prado to serve as a center of scientific enlightenment. By the time the building was completed in 1819, its purpose had changed to exhibiting the art gathered by Spanish royalty since the time of Ferdinand and Isabella. The museum is adding a massive new wing, designed by Rafael Moneo, that will resurrect long-hidden works by Zurbarán and Pereda and more than double the number of paintings on display from the permanent collection. (At this writing, and after quarrels between the current and the former government over the renovations' ever-increasing budget, the wing was still undergoing work; it is expected to be completed by 2007.)

The Prado's jewels are its works by the nation's three great masters: Francisco Goya, Diego Velázquez, and El Greco. The museum also holds masterpieces by Flemish, Dutch, German, French, and Italian artists, collected when their lands were part of the Spanish Empire. The museum benefited greatly from the anticlerical laws of 1836, which forced monasteries, convents, and churches to forfeit many of their artworks for public display.

Enter the Prado via the Goya entrance, with steps opposite the Ritz hotel, or by the less-crowded Murillo door opposite the Jardín Botánico. The layout varies (grab a floor plan), but the first halls on the left, coming from the Goya entrance (7A to 11 on the second floor, or *planta primera*), are usually devoted to **17th-century Flemish painters,** including Peter Paul Rubens (1577–1640), Jacob Jordaens (1593–1678), and Antony van Dyck (1599–1641).

Room 12 introduces you to the meticulous brushwork of **Velázquez** (1599–1660) in his numerous portraits of kings and queens. Look for the magnificent *Las Hilanderas (The Spinners)*, evidence of the artist's talent for painting light. The Prado's most famous canvas, Velázquez's *Las Meninas (The Maids of Honor)*, combines a self-portrait of the artist at work with a mirror reflection of the king and queen in a revolutionary interplay of space and perspectives. Picasso was obsessed with this work and painted several copies of it in his own abstract style, now on display in the Picasso Museum in Barcelona.

The south ends of the second and top floors (*planta primera* and *planta segunda*) are reserved for **Goya** (1746–1828), whose works span a staggering range of tone, from bucolic to horrific. Among his early masterpieces are portraits of the family of King Carlos IV, for whom he was court painter—one glance at their unflattering and imbecilic expressions, especially in the painting *The Family of Carlos IV*, reveals the loathing Goya developed for these self-indulgent, reactionary rulers. His famous side-by-side canvases, *The Clothed Maja* and *The Nude Maja*, may represent the young duchess of Alba, whom Goya adored and frequently painted. No one knows whether she ever returned his affection. The adjacent rooms house a series of idyllic scenes of Spaniards at play, painted as designs for tapestries.

Goya's paintings took on political purpose starting in 1808, when the population of Madrid rose up against occupying French troops. *The 2nd of May* portrays the insurrection at the Puerta del Sol, and its even more terrifying companion piece, *The 3rd of May,* depicts the nighttime executions of patriots who had rebelled the day before. The garish light effects in this work typify the romantic style, which favors drama over detail, and make it one of the most powerful indictments of violence ever committed to canvas.

Goya's "black paintings" are dark, disturbing works, completed late in his life, that reflect his inner turmoil after losing his hearing and his deep embitterment over the bloody War of Independence. These are copies of the monstrous hallucinatory paintings Goya made with marvelously free brushstrokes on the walls of his house by southern Madrid's Manzanares River, popularly known as *La Quinta del Sordo* (the deaf one's villa). Having grown gravely ill in his old age, Goya was deaf, lonely, bitter, and despairing; his terrifying *Saturn Devouring One of His Sons* (which Goya displayed in his dining room!) communicates the ravages of age and time.

Near the Goya entrance, the Prado's ground floor (*planta baja*) is filled with 15th- and 16th-century Flemish paintings, including the bizarre proto-surrealist masterpiece *Garden of Earthly Delights,* by Hieronymus Bosch (circa 1450–1516). Next come Rooms 60A, 61A, and 62A, filled with the passionately spiritual works of **El Greco** (Doménikos Theotokópoulos, 1541–1614), the Greek-born artist who lived and worked in Toledo. El Greco is known for his mystical, elongated forms and faces—a style that was shocking to a public accustomed to strictly representational images. Two of his greatest paintings, *The Resurrec-*

tion and *The Adoration of the Shepherds,* are on view here. Before you leave, stop in the 14th- to 16th-century Italian rooms to see Titian's *Portrait of Emperor Charles V* and Raphael's exquisite *Portrait of a Cardinal.* ⊠ *Paseo del Prado s/n, Retiro* ☎ *91/330–2800* ⊕ *http://museoprado.mcu.es* ▱ *€6, free Sun.* ☉ *Tues.–Sun. 9–8.*

**NEED A
BREAK?** **La Dolores** (⊠ **Plaza de Jesús 4, Santa Ana** ☎ **91/429–2243) is an atmospheric old ceramic-tile bar that's the perfect place for a beer or glass of wine and a plate of olives. It's a great alternative to the Prado's basement cafeteria and is just across the Paseo, then one block up on Calle Lope de Vega.**

㊹ Museo Lázaro Galdiano. A 10-minute walk across the Castellana from the Museo Sorolla, the stately mansion of writer and editor José Lázaro Galdiano (1862–1947) has both decorative items and paintings by Bosch, El Greco, Murillo, and Goya, among others; this is a remarkable collection comprising five centuries of Spanish, Flemish, English, and Italian art. Bosch's *St. John the Baptist* and the many Goyas are the stars of the show, with El Greco's *San Francisco de Asisi* and Zurbarán's *San Diego de Alcalá* close behind. It was completely renovated in 2005. ⊠*Serrano 122, Salamanca* ⊕*www.flg.es* ☎*91/ _____ 561–6084* ▱ *€4* ☉ *Wed.–Mon. 10–4:30.*

㊷ Museo Sorolla. Spain's most famous impressionist painter, Joaquín Sorolla (1863–1923), lived and worked here for most of his life. Entering this diminutive but cozy domain is a little like stepping into a Sorolla painting, because it's filled with the artist's best-known works, most of which shimmer with the bright Mediterranean light and color of his native Valencia.

Goya, whose late-in-life works were dark and disturbing, displayed his vivid *Saturn Devouring One of His Sons* in his dining room. Bon appetit!

Because the house and garden were also designed by Sorolla, you leave with an impression of the world as seen through this painter's exceptional eye. ⊠ *General Martinez Campos 37, Chamberí* ⊕ *http://museosorolla.mcu.es* ☎ *91/310–1584* ▱ *€2.40, free Sun.* ☉ *Tues.–Sat. 9:30–3, Sun. 10–3.*

㉓ Museo Thyssen-Bornemisza. The newest of Madrid's three major art centers, the "Thyssen" occupies spacious galleries washed in salmon pink and filled with natural light in the late-18th-century Villahermosa Palace, finished in 1771. This ambitious collection of 800 paintings traces the history of Western art with examples from every important movement, from the 13th-century Italian Gothic through 20th-century American pop art. The works were gathered from the 1920s to the 1980s by Swiss industrialist Baron Hans Heinrich Thyssen-Bornemisza and his father. At the urging of his wife, Carmen Cervera (a former Miss Spain), the baron donated the entire collection to Spain in 1993. A renovation in 2004 increased the number of paintings on display to include the baron's wife's personal collection. Critics have described the museum's paintings as the minor works of major artists and the major works of minor artists, but, be that as it may, the collection traces the development of Western humanism as no other in the world.

**Fodor'sChoice
★**

One of the high points here is Hans Holbein's *Portrait of Henry VIII* (purchased from the late Princess Diana's grandfather, who used the money to buy a new Bugatti sports car). American artists are also well represented; look for the Gilbert Stuart portrait of George Washington's cook, and note how closely the composition and rendering resemble the artist's famous painting of the Founding Father himself. Two halls are devoted to the impressionists and postimpressionists, including many works by Pissarro and a few each by Renoir, Monet, Degas, Van Gogh, and Cézanne. Find Pissarro's *Saint-Honoré Street in the Afternoon, Effect of Rain* for a jolt of mortality, or Renoir's *Woman with a Parasol in a Garden* for a sense of bucolic beauty lost. Picasso's *Harlequin with a Mirror* is a self-portrait of a spurned lover, and Dalí's *Dream Caused by the Flight of a Bee Around a Pomegranate a Second before Awakening* will take you back to Hieronymus Bosch's *Garden of Earthly Delights*, 300 yards and 500 years away in the Prado.

Within 20th-century art, the collection is strong on dynamic and colorful German expressionism, with some works by Georgia O'Keeffe and Andrew Wyeth along with Hoppers, Bacons, Rauschenbergs, and Lichtensteins. The temporary exhibits are often fascinating. ⊠ *Paseo del Prado 8, Centro* 🖰 *91/369–0151* ⊕ *www.museothyssen.org* 🖾 *Permanent collection € 6, temporary exhibition € 5, combined € 9* ⊙ *Tues.–Sun. 10–7.*

㊱ Palacio de Comunicaciones. This ornate building on the southeast side of Plaza de la Cibeles, built at the start of the 20th century, is Madrid's main post office, a massive stone compound of French, Viennese, and traditional Spanish influences. Even if you aren't planning on mailing any postcards, it's worth visiting its main hall. ⊠ *Plaza de Cibeles, Centro* 🖰 *902/197197* ⊙ *Weekdays 8:30 AM–9:30 PM, Sat. 8:30–2.*

㉙ Parque del Buen Retiro (literally, "the Retreat"). Once the private playground of royalty, Madrid's crowning park is a vast expanse of green encompassing formal gardens, fountains, lakes, exhibition halls, children's play areas, outdoor cafés, and a **Puppet Theater** featuring free slapstick routines that even non–Spanish speakers will enjoy. Shows take place on Saturday at 1 and on Sunday at 1, 6, and 7. The park is especially lively on weekends, when it fills with street musicians, jugglers, clowns, gypsy fortune-tellers, and sidewalk painters along with hundreds of Spanish families out for a walk. The park holds a book fair in May and occasional flamenco concerts in summer. From the entrance at the Puerta de Alcalá, head straight toward the center and you can find the **Estanque** (lake), presided over by a grandiose equestrian statue of King Alfonso XII, erected by his mother. Just behind the lake, north of the statue, is one of the best of the park's many cafés. If you're feeling nautical, you can rent a boat and work up an appetite rowing.

The 19th-century **Palacio de Cristal** (Crystal Palace), southeast of the Estanque, was built to house exotic plants from the Philippines, a Spanish possession at the time. This airy marvel of steel and glass sits on a base of decorative tile. Next door is a small lake with ducks and swans. At the south end of the park, along the Paseo del Uruguay, is the **Ros-**

aleda (rose garden), an English garden bursting with color and heavy with floral scents for most of the summer. West of the Rosaleda, look for a statue called the **Ángel Caído** (Fallen Angel), which Madrileños claim is the only one in the world depicting the prince of darkness before (during, actually) his fall from grace. ⊠ *Puerta de Alcalá, Retiro.*

④ **Plaza Colón.** Named for Christopher Columbus, this plaza has a statue of the explorer (identical to the one in Barcelona's port) looking west from a high tower in the middle of the square. Beneath the plaza is the **Centro Cultural de la Villa** (☎ 91/480–0300), a performing-arts facility. Behind Plaza Colón is **Calle Serrano,** the city's premier shopping street (think Gucci, Prada, and Loewe). Stroll in either direction on Serrano for some window-shopping. ⊠ *Plaza Colón, Centro.*

NEED A BREAK?

El Espejo (⊠ Paseo de Recoletos 31, Centro ☎ 91/308–2347) comprises two classy bars near the Plaza Colón–one in a Belle Epoque setting on a side street, the other in a pavilion of glass and wrought iron in the middle of the Paseo de Recoletos. Sit on the shady terrace or in the air-conditioned, stained-glass bar and rest your feet while sipping a coffee or a beer.

㉟ **Plaza de la Cibeles.** A tree-lined walkway runs down the center of Paseo del Prado to the grand Plaza de la Cibeles, where the famous Fuente de la Cibeles (Fountain of Cybele) depicts the nature goddess driving a chariot drawn by lions. Even more than the officially designated bear and arbutus tree, this monument, beautifully lighted at night, has come to symbolize Madrid—so much so that during the civil war, patriotic Madrileños risked life and limb to sandbag it as Nationalist aircraft bombed the city. ⊠ *Plaza de la Cibeles, Centro.*

㊳ **Puerta de Alcalá.** This triumphal arch was built by Carlos III in 1778 to mark the site of one of the ancient city gates. You can still see the bomb damage inflicted on the arch during the civil war. ⊠ *C. de Alcalá s/n, Retiro.*

▶ ⑳ **Real Academia de Bellas Artes de San Fernando** (St. Ferdinand Royal Academy of Fine Arts). Designed by Churriguera in the waning baroque years of the early 18th century, this museum showcases 500 years of Spanish painting, from Ribera and Murillo to Sorolla and Zuloaga. The tapestries along the stairways are stunning. Because of a lack of personnel, now they show only the first floor, which displays paintings up to the 18th century, including Goya. The same building houses the **Instituto de Calcografía** (Prints Institute), which sells limited-edition prints from original plates engraved by Spanish artists, including Goya. Check listings for classical and contemporary concerts in the small upstairs concert hall. ⊠ *Alcalá 13, Sol* ☎ *91/524–0864* 🖅 *€2.40, free Wed.* ⊙ *Tues.–Fri. 9–7, Sat.–Mon. 9–2:30; free guided tour Wed. 5–7.*

㉜ **San Jerónimo el Real.** Ferdinand and Isabella used this church and cloister as a *retiro,* or place of meditation—hence the name of the nearby park. The building was devastated in the Napoleonic Wars, then rebuilt in the late 19th century. ⊠ *Moreto 4, behind Prado museum, Retiro* ☎ *91/ 420–3578* ⊙ *Daily 10–1 and 5–8:30.*

28 **Real Fábrica de Tapices.** Tired of the previous monarchs' dependency on the Belgium and Flemish thread mills and craftsmen, King Philip V decided to establish the Royal Tapestry factory in Madrid in 1721. It was originally housed near Alonso Martínez, and moved to its current location in 1889. From early on some of Europe's best artists collaborated in the factory's tapestry designs. The most famous was Goya, who produced 63 cartoons (rough plans), some of which can be seen at the Prado Museum. It's said that he originally put so much detail into them that the craftsmen complained about him making their work miserable.

The factory, still in operation, applies traditional weaving techniques from the 18th and 19th centuries to modern and classic designs—including Goya's. Carpets are available for sale (you can suggest your own design), at skyrocketing prices (€840 a square meter [10-¾ square feet] for carpets, €9,000–€12,000 a square meter for tapestries). Since 1998 the factory has also run a training center that teaches traditional weaving techniques to unemployed teenagers, who later become craftspeople. ⊠ *Fuenterrabía 2, Atocha* ☎ *91/434-0550* ☉ *Weekdays 9–2; guided tour every 45 mins starting at 9.*

27 **Panteón de Hombres Ilustres.** Originally created in 1892–99 as a cloister to a great basilica that was never built, this Byzantine-style building now houses the mausoleums and sepulchres of seven of Spain's most illustrious 19th- and early-20th-century politicians. Three of them—Antonio Cánovas del Castillo (killed in 1897), José Canalejas (1912), and Eduardo Dato e Iradier (1921)—were prime ministers, and all were murdered, which points to the violence and convolutions of the period's politics. ⊠ *Julián Gayarre 3, Atocha* ☎ *91/454-8800* ☒ *Free* ☉ *Oct.–Mar., Mon.–Sat. 9:30–6, Sun. 9–3; Apr.–Sept., Mon.–Sat. 9–7, Sun. 9–4.*

33 **Museo Naval.** Jack Aubrey, the character Russell Crowe played in *Master and Commander,* would be bouncing off the walls experiencing the 500 years of Spanish naval history displayed in this museum. The collection, which includes documents, maps, weaponry, paintings, and hundreds of ship models of different sizes, is best enjoyed by those who speak some Spanish. Beginning with Queen Isabella and King Ferdinand's reign and the expeditions led by Christopher Columbus and the conquistadors, exhibits also reveal how Spain built a naval empire that battled Turkish, Algerian, French, Portuguese, and English armies and commanded the oceans and the shipping routes for a century and a half. Moving to the present day, the museum covers Spain's more recent shipyard and naval construction accomplishments. ⊠ *Paseo del Prado 5, Cibeles* ☎ *91/3523-8789* ⊕ *www.museonavalmadrid.com* ☒ *Free* ☉ *Tues.–Sun. 10–2. Guided tour, in Spanish only, weekends at 11:30.*

34 **Museo Nacional de Artes Decorativas.** This palatial building showcases 60,000 textiles, pieces of furniture—including some installed in reconstructed period rooms—jewelry, ceramics, glass, crystal, and metalwork items. The collection, displayed in chronological order, starts with medieval and Renaissance items on the first floor and ends with the 18th- and 19th-century pieces on the top floor. The ground floor is taken up by temporary exhibitions and some avant-garde works. ⊠ *Montalbán*

12, Cibeles ☎ *91/532–6499* ⊕ *http://mnartesdecorativas.mcu.es*
✉ *€2.40, free Sun.* ⊘ *Tues.–Sat. 9:30–3, Sun. 10–3. Guided tour, in
Spanish only, Sun. at 11:30.*

The Barrio de las Letras

The Spanish word *castizo* means "authentic," and *los Madrileños castizos* are the Spanish equivalent of London's cockneys. However, the castizos are now in retreat, their place increasingly taken up by a growing number of immigrants and young Spanish professionals willing to withstand the chaos of living within these lively and creative enclaves. Castizo Madrid is made up of several neighborhoods, and here we suggest three different itineraries, starting with the neighborhood that's in the center, *Barrio de las Letras* (the Writers' Neighborhood), and that neighborhood's heart, Plaza de Santa Ana. From there you can continue on to two other nearby neighborhoods. Within all three neighborhoods are a growing number of immigrants as well as problems that come with unemployment. Purse snatching and petty crime are not uncommon, so think twice about this walk if you don't feel streetwise. However, the streets surrounding the Plaza Santa Ana are more interesting after dark, as they pack some of Madrid's best tapas bars and nightspots.

Long favored by tourists for its clean-cut looks and its many places for fun, the Barrio de las Letras was named for the many important writers and playwrights who set up house within a few blocks of Plaza de Santa Ana. The City Hall's recent decisions to restrict the traffic to residents only and to close Calle Huertas (full of bars and clubs) to vehicle traffic have added to the charm of walking and socializing in this neighborhood.

⌐ A GOOD WALK

Begin at the **Plaza Santa Ana** ㊹ ⟩, hub of the theater district in the 17th century and now a center of nocturnal activity, not all of it desirable. The plaza's notable buildings include, at the lower end, the Teatro Español. Walk up to the sunny Plaza del Ángel (next to the Reina Victoria hotel) and turn down Calle de Las Huertas, past the ancient olive tree and plant nursery behind the San Sebastián church—once the church cemetery, this was the final resting place of Lope de Vega, whose sepulchre is displayed inside the church. Walk down Huertas to No. 18, Casa Alberto, an ancient (though still excellent) bar and restaurant as well as the house where Miguel de Cervantes was living when he finished some of his most important works, including the second part of *Don Quijote.* Continue to Calle León, named for a lion kept here long ago by a resident Moor. A short walk to your left brings you to the corner of Calle Cervantes. As the plaque on the wall overhead attests, *Don Quijote's* author died on April 23, 1616, in what is now called the **Casa de Cervantes** ㊺. Down the street, at No. 11, is the **Casa de Lope de Vega** ㊻, where the "Spanish Shakespeare," Fray Lope Félix de la Vega Carpio, lived and worked.

A right from Calle Cervantes onto Calle Quevedo takes you past the Basque *sidrería* (cider house) Zerain—where you can catch cider in your glass as it spurts directly from the barrel—down to the corner across from the convent and church of the Trinitarias Descalzas (Discalced, or Barefoot, Trinitarians, a cloistered order of nuns). Just before the corner, on the wall to your left, is a plaque honoring Quevedo, the 17th-century poet who gives the street its name, and who lived in a building that was once on this site. (Credited with having the best command of the Spanish language ever, Quevedo acquired the building and ousted a tenant who couldn't pay his bills because of his gambling debts. This tenant just happened to be another famous poet, Góngora, with whom Quevedo sustained a poetry rivalry that had lasted for decades.)

Miguel de Cervantes was buried inside the Trinitarias Descalzas with his wife and one of Lope de Vega's daughters, who remained cloistered in that convent for more than 60 years. When Lope de Vega died, they made the funeral procession parade in front of the convent so that his daughter could have a last glimpse of her father. Cervantes' remains, on the other hand, were misplaced at the end of the 17th century when the convent was renovated, and haven't been found since.

TIMING   Allow one and a half hours for the Barrio de las Letras walk.

What to See

45 Casa de Cervantes. A plaque marks the private home where Miguel de Cervantes Saavedra, author of *Don Quijote de la Mancha,* committed his final words to paper: *"Puesto ya el pie en el estribo, con ansias de la muerte . . ."* ("One foot already in the stirrup and yearning for death . . ."). The Western world's first runaway best seller, and still one of the most widely translated and read books in the world, Cervantes' spoof of a knightly novel playfully but profoundly satirized Spain's rise and decline while portraying man's dual nature in the pragmatic Sancho Panza and the idealistic Don Quijote, ever in search of wrongs to right. ⊠ *C. Cervantes and C. León, Santa Ana.*

46 Casa de Lope de Vega. Considered the Shakespeare of Spanish literature, Fray Lope Félix de la Vega Carpio (1562–1635) is best known as Lope de Vega. A contemporary and adversary of Cervantes, he wrote some 1,800 plays and enjoyed great success during his lifetime. His former home is now a museum with period furnishings; it's an intimate look into a bygone era: everything here, from the whale-oil lamps and candles to the well in the tiny garden and the pans used to warm the bedsheets, brings you closer to the great dramatist. Don't miss the Latin inscription over the door: PARVA PROPIA MAGNA / MAGNA ALIENA PARVA (small but mine big / big but someone else's small). ⊠ *C. Cervantes 11, Santa Ana* 🕾 *91/429–9216* 🎫 *€2, free Sat.* ☉ *Sept.–July, Tues.–Fri. 9:30–2, Sat. 10–2.*

▶ **44 Plaza Santa Ana.** This plaza was the heart of the theater district in the 17th century—the golden age of Spanish literature—and is now the center of Madrid's thumping nightlife. A statue of 17th-century playwright Pedro Calderón de la Barca faces the **Teatro Español.** Rebuilt in 1980 after a fire, the theater stands on the site of the old Teatro Príncipe, founded in 1583. The original theater was first reconstructed in the 17th century to adapt to the Italian-style stage requirements, and then destroyed by another fire in 1812. It got its current name in 1849. Playwrights such as Lope de Vega, Tirso de Molina, Calderón de la Barca, and Valle Inclán released some of their plays there. Opposite the theater, the **Villa Rosa**, with a facade of ceramic tile, is a popular nightspot. The **Gran Hotel Reina Victoria,** which was not always so upscale, has been a favorite of bullfighters, including the famed Manolete. Off to the side of the hotel is the diminutive **Plaza del Ángel,** with one of Madrid's best jazz clubs, the Café Central. Back on Plaza Santa Ana is one of Madrid's most famous cafés, the former Ernest Hemingway hangout **Cervecería Alemana,** still catnip to writers, poets, and beer drinkers. ⊠ *Plaza de Santa Ana s/n, Centro.*

Lavapiés & the Rastro

The Lavapiés neighborhood has the highest concentration of immigrants—mostly Chinese and North African—in Madrid. This has resulted in plenty of ethnic markets and inexpensive restaurants in the area, and a bustling amount of crowds and culture, especially at the Plaza de Lavapíes. City Hall's new project is to turn Plaza Tirso de Molina, near the Rastro, into a flower market—the related construction makes Lavapiés currently look more rundown than the other parts of Castizo Madrid, which were rehabilitated earlier.

A GOOD WALK

From Plaza de Santa Ana walk a block south of Calle Príncipe onto Calle Huertas. Make a left on that street and then take the third street to the right, Calle Amor de Dios. Walk to its end, the busy Calle Atocha; across the street is the church of San Nicolás. The predecessor of this plain, modern church was burned in 1936, but the site is historic: like many churches during that turbulent period, the original building fell to the wrath of working-class crowds who felt victimized by centuries of clerical oppression. To the left of the church, walk down Pasaje Doré, where, if it's early in the day, you can pass through the colorful Anton Martín market.

Turn right on Calle Santa Isabel, by the **Cine Doré** ㊼ ▶, and take your first left on Calle de la Rosa, which after a jog to the right becomes Calle de la Cabeza. Pass the restaurant Casa Lastra. On the southwest corner with Calle Lavapiés is the site of the **Cárcel de la Inquisición** ㊽. Turn left here: this is the beginning of the Barrio Lavapiés, an old 16th-century quarter that was first inhabited mostly by Jewish and Arab people who had converted to Christianity. Some have suggested that this was the site of the old Judería (Jewish Quarter), but medieval documents confirm that the quarter was not on the outskirts of town but in the old city center, where the Almudena Cathedral currently stands. Jewish inhabitants were first persecuted in Spain at the end of the 14th century, and as a result of the ensuing violence, many converted to Christianity. Arabs faced the same fate, and although for centuries they were allowed to hold on to their beliefs, in 1507 King Ferdinand and Queen Isabella forced them to either convert or exile. Known as Lavapiés (literally, "wash-feet") after the medieval custom of bathing one's feet before entering the *aljama* (ghetto), this hillside neighborhood is a quintessentially grassroots working-class Madrid barrio, full of artists, immigrants, students, and aspiring actors, though gentrification is beginning to creep in—the streets have been recobbled, and lighting has been improved. Still, hold on to your belongings tightly and keep your camera out of sight. Explore the side streets off Calle Lavapiés; then continue down and south until you reach the heart of the neighborhood, **Plaza Lavapiés ㊽**. Café Barbieri, on the plaza's northeastern corner is more than 100 years old; it's a good option if you need a break.

Leave the plaza heading west on Calle Sombrerete. After two blocks you'll reach the intersection of Calle Mesón de Paredes, on the corner of which you can see a beautifully preserved example of a popular Madrid architecture style, the **Corrala ㊿**. Life in this type of balconied apartment building is very public, with laundry flapping in the breeze, babies crying, and old women gossiping over the railings. Neighbors once shared common kitchen and bath facilities on the patio. Work your way west, crossing Calle de Embajadores into the neighborhood known as **El Rastro ㉛**, with streets of small family stores selling furniture, antiques, and a cornucopia of used junk (some of it greatly overpriced). On Sunday, El Rastro becomes a flea market, and Calle de Ribera de Curtidores, the steep main drag, is closed to traffic and jammed with outdoor booths, shoppers, and pickpockets.

TIMING Allow one and a half hours for this walk. The Anton Martín market comes to life every weekday morning. El Rastro can be saved for a Sunday morning if you decide to join the milling throng at the flea market—you'll want to spend at least an hour or so there. After the market, you can head toward La Latina and its many restaurants for lunch.

What to See

㊽ **Cárcel de la Inquisición** (Inquisition Jail). Unmarked by any historical plaque, the former jail is now a large tapas bar, the **Taberna de Lavapiés**, named for the old Jewish Quarter. Here Jews, Moors, and others designated unrepentant heathens or sinners bent to the inquisitors' whims; the prison later became a Cárcel de la Corona (Crown Prison) for the incarceration of wayward soldiers, priests, and nuns. Ask a bartender if you can see the original, two-story medieval patio out back—it's tiny, but highly evocative. ⊠ *Southeast corner of C. Cabeza and C. Lavapiés, Lavapiés* ☎ *91/369–3218* ☉ *Daily 9 AM–2 AM.*

㊼ **Cine Doré.** A rare example of Art Nouveau architecture in Madrid, the hip Cine Doré shows movies from the Spanish National Film Archives and eclectic foreign films for €2.50 per session. Show times are listed in newspapers under *"Filmoteca."* The lobby, trimmed with smart pink neon, has a sleek café-bar and a good bookshop. ⊠ *C. Santa Isabel 3, Lavapiés* ☎ *91/369–1125* ☉ *Tues.–Sun.; 4 shows daily, 1st starting at 5:30 PM.*

㊿ **Corrala.** This structure is not unlike the rowdy outdoor areas, known as *corrales*, used as Madrid's early makeshift theaters; they were usually installed in a vacant lot between two apartment buildings, and families with balconies overlooking the action rented out seats to wealthy patrons of the arts. There's a plaque here to remind you that the setting for the famous 19th-century *zarzuela* (light opera) *La Revoltosa* was a corrala like this one. City-sponsored musical-theater events are occasionally held here in summer. The ruins across the street were once the **Escolapíos de San Fernando,** one of several churches and parochial schools that fell victim to anti-Catholic sentiments during the civil war. ⊠ *C. Mesón de Paredes and C. Sombrerete, Lavapiés.*

51 El Rastro. Named for the *arrastre* (dragging) of animals in and out of the slaughterhouse that once stood here and, specifically, the *rastro* (blood trail) left behind, this site explodes into a rollicking flea market every Sunday from 10 to 2. For serious browsing and bargaining, any *other* morning is a better time to turn up treasures such as old iron grill-work, a marble tabletop, or a gilt picture frame, but Sunday brings out truly bizarre bric-a-brac ranging from stolen earrings to sent postcards to thrown-out love letters. Even so, people-watching is the best part. ⊠ *Ribera de los Curtidores s/n, Centro.*

49 Plaza Lavapiés. The heart of the historic Jewish barrio, this plaza remains a neighborhood hub. To the left is the Calle de la Fe (Street of Faith), which was called Calle Sinagoga until the expulsion of the Jews in 1492. The church of **San Lorenzo** at the end was built on the site of the razed synagogue. Legend has it that Jews and Moors who chose baptism over exile were forced to walk up this street barefoot to the ceremony to demonstrate their new faith. ⊠ *Top of C. de la Fe, Lavapiés.*

NEED A BREAK? Drop into **Taberna de Antonio Sánchez** (⊠ Mesón de Paredes 13, Lavapiés ☎ 91/ 539–7826), Madrid's oldest tavern, for a glass of wine and some tapas. The dark walls (lined with bullfighting paintings), zinc bar, and pulley system used to lift casks of wine from the cellar look much the same as they did when the place first opened in 1830. Meals are also served in a back dining room. Specialties include *rabo de buey* (oxtail stew) and *morcillo al horno* (beef stew).

Chueca & Malasaña

Once known primarily for its nightlife and mostly unsafe streets, these two neighborhoods are the ones in Madrid to have changed the most in the past decade. Money from City Hall and from private investors has helped renovate buildings and public zones, and have drawn prosperous businesses and many professional and young inhabitants who are giving them (especially Chueca, totally transformed by the gay community) an eyebrow-raising face-lift. They both now make for pleasant walks, and have many good nightclubs and inexpensive restaurants for the young and stylish.

A GOOD WALK This walk combines well with that of Plaza de Santa Ana and the Barrio de las Letras. Or you can head straight here. In that case, the best option would be to take the subway to Plaza Chueca and start the walk from there. Otherwise, start from Santa Ana and walk north past the Teatro Español onto Calle Príncipe. At the end of this street you will find Plaza de Canalejas. Keep straight, on Calle Sevilla, and cross Alcalá to Calle Virgen de los Peligros. On the corner of Virgen de los Peligros is Starbucks, and next to it is Faborit, a great café at which to stop for fresh juice or a cup of coffee. Calle Virgen de los Peligros ends on Gran Vía. Walk across it and get onto Calle Clavel, a narrow street that will lead you to Plaza Vázquez de Mella. Make a right on Calle Infantas and then walk to the plaza at the end of the street, Plaza del Rey. The building bearing number one at the Plaza is called the House of the Seven Chimneys, and was built in 1577 by Juan de Herrera, who was also the Monasterio de El Escorial's architect.

Make a left on the southern edge of the plaza, on Calle Barquillo, and then take the first street to the left, Calle San Marcos, and then the third to the right, Calle Barbieri. This and the previous street down, Calle Libertad, are two of Chueca's most attractive hangouts, with plenty of affordable bars and restaurants where you can grab a bite and refuel. Continue along Barbieri and after crossing Calle Augusto Figueroa (popular for its shops that sell samples of name-brand, high-quality shoes) you reach Plaza de Chueca, the heart of the neighborhood. The plaza, once a hangout for drug addicts and other underworld types, is now an oasis, with heaps of bars and summer terraces. Don't leave without having a beer at Bodegas Angel Sierra, on the northern side of the plaza, one of Madrid's oldest bars. Make a left on the street that runs along the Bodegas' main entrance, Calle Barbieri, and then turn right on Calle Pelayo. The street ends on Calle Fernando VI.

Right before getting to this street, on your left, is a modernist building of intricate design—the **Casa Longoria** ⓾, Spain's headquarters for its national performance rights organization. If you have time, make a right on Fernando VI and walk four blocks up to Plaza de las Salesas. On the far side of the plaza are stairs to **Las Salesas Reales** ⓾, also called the church of Santa Bárbara. Retrace your steps and keep walking along Fernando VI. Make a left two blocks after Casa Longoria, on Calle San Mateo. Halfway down the street is the **Museo Romántico** ⓾. That street ends on Calle Fuencarral, which marks the border between Chueca and Malasaña. Make a right at the corner. Two blocks later you come across a redbrick building with an ornate front entrance: the **Museo Municipal** ⓾. Inside is an incredibly accurate old model of Madrid that shouldn't be missed.

Take the street beginning on the left across from the museum, San Vicente Ferrer, one of Malasaña's arteries. During the 1980s Malasaña was a center for the cultural movement called *la movida* that turned the city upside down and help Madrid gain fame as a nightlife paradise. The movement brought together people from various scenes, such as rockers, mods, punks, artists, anarchists, and squatters—the filmmaker Pedro Almodóvar was one of its most visible spokespeople. Malasaña, now a hot spot for people of all ages, has many renovated buildings and lots of small, creative businesses that have sweetened the neighborhood's looks and enhanced its charm. Walk down San Vicente Ferrer— to your left is another popular café, Café Manuela. Continue along and make a right when you see a beautifully tiled pharmacy on the right side of the street. After turning right at the pharmacy walk down two blocks to reach the **Plaza del 2 de Mayo** ⓾, an animated enclave where the Spanish War of Independence erupted in 1808. Take the street on the western side of the plaza, Calle Daoiz—named after one of the heroes who lost his life on that day—onto San Bernardo. Cross the street and head down the first street to the right, Calle Quiñones, which borders the southern wall of the Convent of Monsterrat, used from 1842 to 1914 as a female prison. Calle Quiñones ends on Plaza de las Comendadoras, which bears this name because of the convent—now a primary school—and the church that flanks the northern side of the plaza. Cross Calle Amaniel, and take the narrow Calle Cristo, where there are some good summer terraces. The street ends on Plaza Guardias de Corps, across from the massive museum and art center **Centro de Conde Duque** ⑤⑦.

This partially renovated building houses the **Museo Municipal de Arte Contemporáneo** ⑤⑧, the historical library, and a few more exhibition spaces. From there you can make a left on Calle de Conde Duque up to Plaza de Cristino Martos. On the left-hand corner is El Jardín de las Delicias, a cozy and well-hidden café. The stairs south of the plaza will take you onto Princesa, a few yards away from Plaza de España. From there you can take Bus 133 toward the **Museo del Traje** ⑤⑨ (aka Costume Museum). Or you may opt to take the street to the left of Plaza Cristino Martos, Calle San Bernardino, which will lead you to Calle Reyes and back to Calle San Bernardo. Take the street across from San Bernardo, Calle Pez, another of the Malasaña's must-sees. At the end of the street you find a big brick building, the Iglesia de San Antonio de los Alemanes, which first carried the name San Antonio de los Portugueses, for it was built when Phillip II was both king of Spain and Portugal. The church has some interesting frescoes by Carreño and Lucas Jordán. From Pez make a left on Calle Corredera Baja de San Pablo, and once you get to Plaza de San Ildefonso, take any of the streets facing eastward, which will bring you back on Fuencarral. Make a right and indulge in some shopping in the numerous shops that line Fuencarral between Tribunal and Gran Vía.

TIMING   Allow three hours for a walk through Chueca and Malasañ. The areas are always packed with people, especially on the weekends.

What to See

⑤② **Casa Longoria.** A modernist palace commissioned in 1902 by the businessman and politician Javier González Longoria, the Casa Longoria was built by José Grases Riera, a Catalan architect who was also a disciple of Gaudí. The winding shapes, the plant motifs, and the wrought-iron balconies are reminiscent of Gaudí's works in Barcelona. The building's jewel, however, is its main iron, bronze, and marble staircase. This is off-limits to tourists, however, because the building is now in private hands. ✉ *Fernando VI, 4, Chueca.*

⑤⑦ **Centro de Conde Duque.** Built by Pedro de Ribera in 1717–30 to accommodate the Regiment of the Royal Guard, this building of gigantic proportions (its facade is 250 yards long) was used as a military academy and an astronomical observatory in the 19th century. A fire damaged the upper floors in 1869, and after some decay it was partially renovated and turned into a cultural and arts center (this is the north patio and the impressive main plaza, which highly contrasts with the southern edge, still in dire straits). The center features temporary art exhibitions in different spaces, including the *sala de bóvedas* (Hall of the

Vaults), right across from the big courtyard, and public and historical libraries. In summer outdoor concerts are held in the main plaza. ⊠ *Conde Duque 9 and 11, Malasaña* ☉ *Tues.–Sat. 10–9, Sun. 11–2:30 exhibitions only.*

⌐ NEED A BREAK?

While on San Bernardo and before crossing over to the Convent of Monsterrat on Calle Quiñones, stop for an ice-cream break at what is probably Madrid's tastiest, most fashionable, and priciest ice-cream parlor, **Giangrossi** (⊠ Alberto Aguilera 1, Malasaña ☎ 900/555–009). Although the name sounds Italian, Giangrossi is an Argentine ice-cream chain with three locations. In addition to the one on Alberto Aguilera, branches are on the corner of Hermosilla and Velazquez, and near Santiago Bernabeau. Creative flavors include *dulce de leche* (a very sweet caramel spread well known in South America), mascarpone, or *turrón* (a type of candy eaten at Christmas, usually with dried fruit in it) as well as pink grapefruit, pineapple, and melon sorbets. What's with the funny-looking, triangular scoops? That's the way they serve a cone in Argentina.

59 Museo del Traje. Opened in 2004, the Museum of Costume traces the evolution of dress in Spain, from the old burial garments worn by kings and nobles (very few pieces of which have withstood the erosion of time) and the introduction of French fashion by Phillip V, to the 20th-century creations of couturiers such as Balenciaga and Pertegaz. The 18th century claims the largest number of pieces. The explanatory notes are, for once, also in English. The museum has a superb restaurant. To get here, take Bus 46 from Moncloa or walk along the northeastern edge of Parque del Oeste, also from Moncloa. ⊠ *Av. Juan de Herrera 2, Ciudad Universitaria* ☎ *91/549–7150* ⊕ *http://museodeltraje.mcu.es* ⊠ *€3; free Tues. after 2:30 and Sun.* ☉ *Tues.–Sat. 9:30–7, Sun. 10–3.*

55 Museo Municipal. Founded in 1929 on what was formerly a hospice built in the late 17th century, the museum displays paintings, drawings, pictures, ceramics, furniture, and other objects that help visitors understand the history of Madrid. There is a good exhibition on Madrid that will be best enjoyed by those who speak Spanish and who already know a bit about the city's history. However, two exhibits—the ornamented facade, a baroque jewel by Pedro de Ribera, and the painstakingly precise, nearly 18-foot model of Madrid, a project coordinated by León Gil de Palacio in 1830—are highlights almost everyone can enjoy. Part of the permanent collection is not on display because of renovation work. ⊠ *Fuencarral, Malasaña* ☎ *91/532–6499* ⊠ *Free* ☉ *Tues.–Fri. 9:30–8; weekends 10–2.*

58 Museo Municipal de Arte Contemporáneo. To reach this museum inside the Centro de Conde Duque, take the door to your right after the entrance and walk up the stairs. Founded in 2001, the Municipal Museum displays on two floors 200 modern artworks acquired by City Hall since 1980. The paintings, graphic artwork, sculpture, and photography are mostly by local artists. ⊠ *Conde Duque 9 and 11, Malasaña* ☎ *91/588–5928* ⊠ *Free* ☉ *Tues.–Sat. 10–9, Sun. 11–2:30.*

54 **Museo Romántico.** The Marquis de la Vega-Inclán founded this small museum in 1924. It displays Spanish art, furniture, documents, and decorative artifacts from the Romantic era. With the exception of a Goya on display in the chapel, the museum does not have incredibly valuable pieces, but what it does have is charming. As of this writing it was closed for renovation but expected to be open in 2007—no guarantees, though. ⊠ *San Mateo, 13, Chueca* ☎ *91/448-1071.*

56 **Plaza del 2 de Mayo.** On this unassuming square stood the Monteleón Artillery barracks, where some brave Spanish soldiers and citizens fought Napóleon's invading troops on May 2, 1808. The arch that now stands in the middle of the plaza was once at the entrance of the old barracks, and the sculpture under the arch represents captains Daoiz and Velarde. All the surrounding streets carry the names of that day's heroes. The plaza, now filled with spring and summer terraces, makes a good place to stop for a drink. One of the most popular cafés, Pepe Botella, carries the demeaning nickname the people of Madrid gave to Joseph Bonaparte, Napóleon's brother, who ruled Spain 1808–13: Botella ("bottle" in English) is a reference to his alleged—but false— fondness for drink. ⊠ *Plaza del 2 de mayo, Malasaña.*

53 **Las Salesas Reales.** Bárbara de Braganza, daughter of the king and the queen of Portugal and married to Spanish king Fernando VI, encouraged the construction of a religious complex (a church and a monastery) that reached what's now Calle Génova. Las Salesas Reales was the first Madrid outpost for the Salesians, a religious order based in France. After the revolution of 1868 the nuns were ousted from the monastery, but the church remains standing, holding some interesting paintings, and Barbara de Braganza and Fernando VI's sepulchres. ⊠ *Plaza de las Salesas, Chueca* ☉ *Open during Mass.*

TAPAS BARS & CAFÉS

The best tapas areas are in La Latina, Chueca, Sol, Santa Ana, Salamanca, and Lavapiés. La Latina is arguably Madrid's trendiest neighborhood and has a large concentration of good tapas bars, especially in Plaza de la Paja and on Cava Baja, Cava Alta, and Almendro streets. Chueca is sophisticated, colorful, and lively. In Santa Ana, a touristy enclave, avoid the bars in the main plaza, which are always crowded and usually pricier, and get into the ones on the side streets. The bars in the Salamanca neighborhood are more sober and traditional, but the food is often excellent.

Tapas Bars

Bodega de la Ardosa. Big wooden barrels serve as tables at this charming tavern with more than 100 years of history. There's great vermouth and draft beer, along with specialties such as *salmorejo* (thick, cold tomato soup that's similar to gazpacho), a very juicy tortilla *de patatas* (Spanish omelette) made by the owner's mother, and croquetas, including varieties with béchamel and prawns (*carabineros*) as well as aromatic

The Events of May 2nd

IN 1808 SPAIN WAS RULED BY CARLOS IV, a king more interested in hunting than in the duties attached to government. The king delegated power to his wife, María Luisa, and she to the chief minister, Godoy, one of the country's most despised statesmen of all time. He succeeded in tripling the country's debt in 20 years, and signed the secret Convention of Fontainebleau with Napoléon, which allowed the French troops to freely cross Spain on their way to Portugal. Napoléon's plans were different—he intended to use the convention as an excuse to annex Spain to his vast domains. While the French troops entered Spain, the Spanish people, tired of the inept king and the greedy Godoy, revolted against the French in Aranjuez on March 17, 1808, hoping Napoléon would hand the throne over to the king's elder son, Prince Ferdinand. In the following days Carlos IV abdicated, and his son was proclaimed the new king, Fernando VII. Napoléon had already chosen a person for that job, though—one of his brothers, José Bonaparte. The shrewd French emperor managed to attract the Spanish royal family to France and had Carlos IV, his wife, and Ferdinand VII imprisoned in Bayona, France, and his brother placed on the Spanish throne.

When French General Murat arrived in Madrid a few days later, on March 23, 1808, with 10,000 men (leaving 20,000 more camped outside the city) following Napoléon's orders, Madrid's Captain General Francisco Javier Negrete ordered the Spanish troops to remain in their military quarters, arguing that resistance was futile. On the morning of May 2, a raging group of civilians revolted in front of the Palacio Real, fearing the French troops intended to send Francisco de Paula, King Carlos IV's youngest son, to Bayona with his brother and father. Gunfire ensued, and word of the events spread all over the city. People rose up, fighting the mightier French troops with whatever they could use as weapons. Two captains, Daoiz and Velarde, and a lieutenant, Ruiz, disobeyed Negrete's orders and quartered at the Monteleón Artillery barracks, which stretched from what is now Plaza de 2 de mayo to Calle Carranza. Helped by a small group of soldiers and some brave citizens who had marched to the barracks from the Royal Palace, the group resisted the French for three hours, doing so with very little ammunition, since they couldn't access the armory.

Daoiz and Velarde died in the bloody fight. Ruiz managed to escape, only to die from his wounds later. Murat's forces executed soldiers and civilians throughout the city, including the Casa de Campo, captured by Goya in one of his two famous paintings of the executions. The events marked the beginning of the five-year War of Independence against the French. The remains of the three military heroes, together with those who were executed at Paseo del Prado, are now held in an obelisk-mausoleum at Plaza de la Lealtad, across from the Ritz hotel.

Paradoxically, José Bonaparte proved to be a good ruler, implementing some wise renovations in the then quite congested and unhygienic city. He built new squares, enlarged key streets, and moved some of the cemeteries outside the city.

cheese (*Cabrales*). By the way, you'll always hear a good selection of jazz here. ⊠ *Colon 13, Malasaña* ☎ *91/521–4979.*

Casa Lucas. Some of the favorites at this small, cozy bar with a short but creative selection of homemade tapas include the *Carinena* (grilled pork sirloin with caramelized onion), *Madrid* (scrambled eggs with onion, *morcilla* (blood pudding) and pine nuts in a tomato base), and *huevos a la Macarena* (puff pastry with mushrooms, fried artichokes, fried ham, béchamel, and pine nuts). ⊠ *Cava Baja 30, La Latina* ☎ *91/365–0804* ⊗ *No lunch Wed.*

El Abuelo. This rusticly decorated place, which has barely changed since it was founded at the beginning of the 20th century, is famous for serving only two tapas (grilled shrimp and shrimp sautéed with garlic), usually accompanied by the house's homemade red wine, and for doing them better than anyone. ⊠ *Victoria 12, Sol* ☎ *91/521–2319.*

El Almendro. Getting a weekend seat in this rustic-looking old favorite is quite a feat. Drop by there any other time and you'll be served great *roscas* (round hot bread filled with various types of cured meats), *huevos rotos* (fried eggs with potatoes), *pistos* (sautéed vegetables with a tomato base), or *revueltos* (a favorite is the *habanero,* scrambled eggs with fava beans and *morcilla* (blood pudding). Note that drinks and food need to be ordered separately (a bell rings when your food is ready). ⊠ *Almendro 13, La Latina* ☎ *91/365–4252.*

★ **El Bocaíto.** This place has three dining areas and more than 130 tapas on the menu, including 15 to 20 types of *tostas* (toast topped with prawns, egg and garlic, pâté with caviar, cockles, and so on), and surely the best *pescaito frito* (deep-fried whitebait) in the city. ⊠ *Libertad 6, Chueca* ☎ *91/532–1219* ⊗ *Closed Sun. and Aug.*

El Cervantes. Clean, comfortable and very popular among locals, this place serves plenty of hot and cold tapas. A good choice here is the *pulpo a la gallega* (octopus with potatoes, olive oil, and paprika). You may also want to go for the tapas sampler. ⊠ *Plaza de Jesús 7, Santa Ana* ☎ *91/429–6093.*

El Santander. Don't be fooled by its drab decor: this bar serves a generous and delightful array of inexpensive and simple tapas. If you can make your way to the always-busy counter, try the quiche lorraine, the *empanadillas,* (small empanadas)—which are usually filled with tuna and look like giant pirogis—or any of the fried stuff on display at the counter, with a glass of vermouth. ⊠ *Augusto Figueroa 25, Chueca* ☎ *91/522–4910* ⊗ *Closed Sun. and Aug.*

★ **Estay.** A two-story bar and restaurant with functional furnishings, this place has quickly become a landmark among the city's posh crowd. The tapas menu is plentiful and diverse. Specialties include the *tortilla Espanola con atun y lechuga* (Spanish omelet with tuna fish and lettuce), and the *rabas* (fried calamari). They have a dish of the day for €12, and a few tapas samplers. ⊠ *Hermosilla 46, Salamanca* ☎ *91/578–0470* ⊗ *Closed Sun.*

★ **Juana la Loca.** This tempting spot serves sophisticated and unusual tapas that can be as pricey as they are delightful (don't miss the tortilla de patatas). If you drop by the bar during the weekend, go early: the tapas will be at their freshest. On weekdays, order by the menu. ⊠ *Plaza Puerta de Moros 4, La Latina* ☎ *91/364–0525* ⊗ *Closed Mon.*

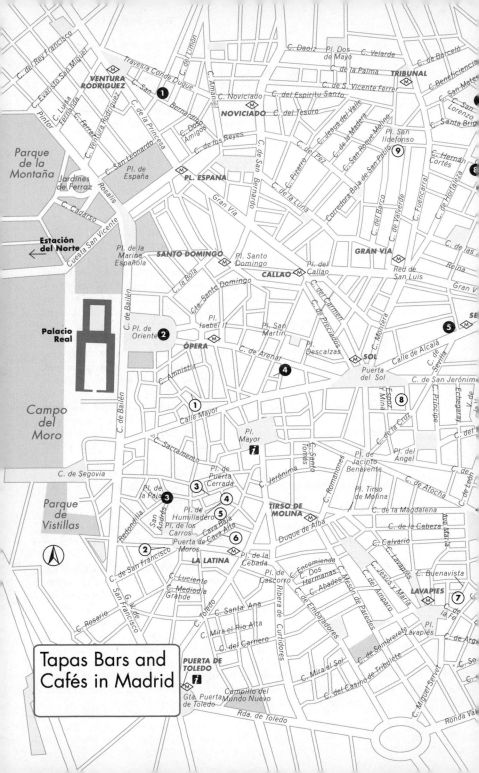

Tapas Bars and Cafés in Madrid

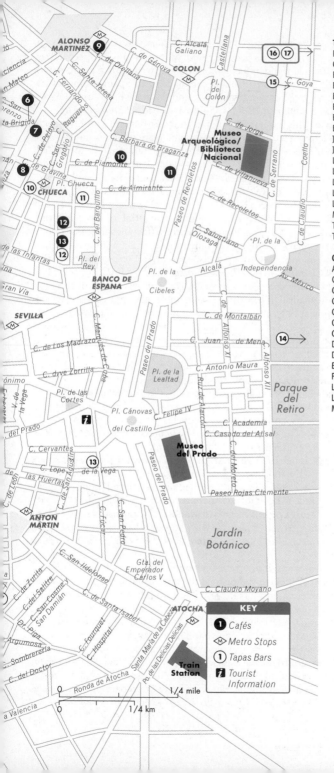

Jurucha. If you're shopping in the Serrano area, this is the place to go for a quick bite. There's a long bar with all the food on display; tapas highlights include the *gambas con allioli* (prawns with a garlic-mayo sauce), fried *empanadillas,* (small empanada) and Spanish omelets. A small seating space has wooden stools, and there are tables at the back. ⊠ *Ayala 19, Salamanca* ☎ *91/575–0098* ☉ *Closed Sun and Aug.*

La Bardemcilla. This homey bar belongs to Javier Bardem's family—note the actor's family pictures on the walls. There are plenty of tables, and there's a good selection of wines and tapas. Highlights include the grilled vegetables, *huevos estrellados,* (fried eggs with potatoes and sausage) and the *croquetas* (béchamel and meat—usually chicken or ham—with a fried bread-crumb crust). There's a fixed-price lunch for less than €10. ⊠ *Augusto Figueroa 47, Chueca* ☎ *91/521–4256* ☉ *Sun. No lunch Sat.*

La Biotza. This trendy place with a slightly industrial look is a favorite among Madrileños working and living in the Salamanca neighborhood. Expect an inexpensive fixed-price lunch menu and a good assortment of tapas and raciones. Show up early, around 1:30 PM, or be prepared to wait. ⊠ *Claudio Coello 27, Salamanca* ☎ *91/781–0313.*

La Dolores. Usually crowded and noisy, this bar serves one of the best draft beers in Madrid. It has also a decent selection of pricey tapas, which you can enjoy at one of the few tables in the back. ⊠ *Plaza de Jesús 4, Santa Ana* ☎ *91/429–2243.*

★ **Laredo.** The nine tables here are some of the most sought after in the city—you need to reserve two or three days in advance—but you can also order at the bar. Variety and quality walk hand in hand here: Laredo serves fresh and simple food (asparagus, some seafood, such as prawns and clams), as well as more scrumptous and elaborate dishes, such as the superb mushroom risotto with duck liver, rice with chicken, small rabbit chops, and mushroom croquetas. The exhaustive menu will tire out your eyes (it's better to follow the waiters' advice). ⊠ *Menorca 14, Retiro* ☎ *91/573–3061* ☉ *Closed Sun and Aug.*

Matritum. This is one of those Spanish places where the wine list is three times the size of the food menu. Matritum is also quieter and cozier than most of the other places in this bar-filled neighborhood. Some of their star tapas include the *patatas a los cinco quesos* (five-cheese potatoes), the *vieiras gratinadas* (grilled grated scallops), or the *delicias de berenjena* (eggplant in three textures with sun-dried tomatoes and goat cheese). ⊠ *Cava Alta 17, La Latina* ☎ *91/365–8237* ☉ *No lunch weekdays.*

Taberna de Cien Vinos. If you're a wine buff, don't leave La Latina without stopping here. Have the dish of the day (usually beans or *marmitako*—a thick tuna-and-potato soup—in winter and a cold soup in summer) with one of the many Spanish wines available by the glass. Nuncio 17, La Latina ☎ *91/365–4704* ☉ Closed Mon. No dinner Sun.

★ **Taberneros.** This museumlike wine bar has wine racks and decanters exhibited all over the tavern, and a menu that includes both local specialties (croquetas, grilled mussels, duck sirloin, fresh liver) and Asian-inspired ones (tuna burger, sirloin in soy sauce). A tapas sampler and a weekly lunch menu are also available. Show up early or prepare to wait awhile by the bar. ⊠ *Santiago 9, Ópera* ☎ *91/542–2460* ☉ *Closed Mon.*

Tapas: A Moveable Feast

1

NEXT TO PAINTINGS, MADRID'S TAPAS may be the city's most creative and irresistible attraction. Originally a lid used to *tapar* (cover or close) a glass of wine, a *tapa* is a kind of hors d'oeuvre that often comes free with a drink. (The term supposedly came from pieces of ham or cheese laid across glasses of wine—to keep flies out and to keep stagecoach drivers sober.) The history of tapas goes back to the 7th- to 15th-century Moorish presence on the Iberian Peninsula. The Moors brought with them exotic ingredients, such as saffron, almonds, and peppers. They introduced sweets and pastries, and created refreshingly cold almond- and vegetable-based soups. The Moorish taste for small and varied delicacies has in fact become Spain's best-known culinary innovation.

Often miniature versions of classic Spanish dishes, tapas (which may be served as individual servings, called pinchos or tapas, or in *raciones,* which usually feed a few) allow you to sample different kinds of food and wine with minimal alcohol poisoning, especially on a *tapeo,* the Spanish version of a pub crawl: you walk off your wine and tapas as you move from bar to bar. Most restaurants have tapas bars where you can test the food without committing to a sit-down meal. Here are a few standards to watch for: *croquetas* (béchamel and meat with a fried bread-crumb crust), *tortilla de patata* (Spanish potato omelet), chorizo (hard pork sausage), *gambas* (shrimp grilled or cooked in parsley, oil, and garlic), *patatas bravas* (potatoes in spicy sauce), and *boquerones en vinagre* (fresh anchovies marinated in salt and vinegar). The best place to start a tapas tour is in and around Plaza Santa Ana or Cava Baja in the La Latina neighborhood.

Cafés

Areia. An old pub converted into a lounge, Areia is furnished with North African and Asian knickknacks and furniture. Cushioned seating in many forms (there's even an Asian-looking wood canopy bed in the back), very low lighting, and lots of nooks make this a cozy place to share a drink. Best to go in the afternoon or early at night to be sure you get a cushion of your own. ⊠ *Hotaleza 92, Chueca* ☎ *91/310–0307.*
Cacao Sampaka. Heaven on earth for any chocolate lover, the café-shop sells cute little paninis, tantalizing blends of fresh juices, a great selection of pastries, and, of course, chocolate in just about every form and flavor imaginable. ⊠ *Orellana 4, Alonso Martínez* ☎ *91/319–5840* ۞ *Closed Sun. except 1st Sun. of month.*
Café de Oriente. This landmark has a magnificent view of the Royal Palace and its front yard. Divided into two sections—the left one serves tapas and raciones and the right one serves more elaborate food—the café also has a splendid terrace that's open when the sun is out. ⊠ *Plaza de Oriente 2, Centro* ☎ *91/547–1564.*
Café del Círculo (La Pecera). Spacious and elegant with large velvet curtains, marble columns, hardwood floors, painted ceilings, and sculptures

scattered throughout, this eatery inside the famous art center, Círculo de Bellas Artes, feels more like a private club than a café; expect a bustling, intellectual crowd. ⊠ *Marqués de Casa Riera 2, Centro* ☎ 91/522–5092.

Café Gijón. Madrid's most famous literary café has hosted highbrow *tertulias* (discussion groups that meet regularly to hash out the political and artistic issues of the day) since the 19th century. ⊠ *Paseo de Recoletos 21, Chamberí* ☎ 91/521–5425.

Café Libertad. More than just a café, this Madrid staple is a music and poetry venue—almost every famous songwriter, musician, and poet has passed through this decadent and charming, evenings-only hangout. ⊠ *C. de la Libertad 8, Chueca* ☎ 91/532–1150 ⊕ *www.libertad8cafe.com.*

Chocolatería San Ginés. Gastronomical historians suggest that the practice of dipping explains the reason for Spaniard's lasting fondness for hot, thick chocolate. Only a few of the old places where this hot drink was served exclusively (with crisp churros), such as this *chocolaterí*, remain standing. Open from 6 PM to 7 AM, it also has the privilege of being the last stop of the bleary-eyed after a night out. ⊠ *Pasadizo de San Ginés, enter by Arenal 11, Sol* ☎ 91/365–6546 ⊙ *Closed Mon.*

Delic. This warm and inviting café is a hangout for Madrid's trendy crowd. Besides the *patatitas con mousse de parmesano* (potatoes with a Parmesan-cheese mousse) and zucchini cake, homesick travelers will find carrot cake, brownies, and pumpkin pie among the selections. ⊠ *Costanilla de San Andrés 14, Plaza de la Paja, La Latina* ☎ 91/364–5450 ⊙ *Closed Mon. and Aug. 1–15.*

Diurno. A Chueca landmark, this café, DVD rental stop, and takeout is the type of place where you'd expect to run into your yoga teacher. Spacious, with large windows facing the street, sleek white chairs and couches, and lots of plants, Diurno serves healthful snacks and sandwiches as well as indulgent coffee-shop desserts. ⊠ *San Marcos 37, Chueca* ☎ 91/522–0009.

El Jardin Secreto. This place has a romantic and exotic setting, with eclectic furniture and lamps (both for sale), savory chocolates, and a generous selection of tasty pastries. It's the perfect place to sip infusions and unwind. ⊠ *Conde Duque 2, Centro* ☎ 91/364–5450.

Faborit. A chain store bold enough to open next door to Starbucks better serve some great coffee and for less money. Faborit does, and offers a warm, high-tech environment (a hanging screen displays the variety of coffees and teas and their prices) to boot. Whether your feet hurt and the sun is blazing, or it's chilly out and you're tired of shivering, indulge in the mug cappuccino with cream or the chai cappuccino—you'll still be able to splurge later. The café is two blocks away from the neighborhood Sol. ⊠ *Alcalá 21, Huertas* ☎ 91/521–8616.

Laan Café. Always packed with a fashionable local crowd, this split-level café is on a busy street. The inside has a subdued European glamour: dark-wood floors, red-leather couches, and painted panels. ⊠ *C. Pelayo 28, Chueca* ☎ 91/522–6861 ⊙ *Closed Mon. morning.*

La Sueca. Light plays an important role in the Scandinavian-esque decor of this inviting space, where there are stripped wood floors, leather stools in primary colors, and large, white-wood tables. Besides the savory Bai-

leys Irish Cream and chocolate cakes, La Sueca also carries baked po-tatoes with different toppings. ✉ *Hortaleza 67, Chueca* ☎ *91/319–0487.*
Maison Blanche. In front is a gourmet shop selling bagels as well as other breads, rice, pastas, and accessories, and in back is a restaurant-café with white-marble floors and iron columns painted white. On offer here are international dishes such as crepes, couscous, pastas, and salads. For those with a sweet tooth, don't miss the tiramisu or the chocolate cake. ✉ *C. Piamonte 10, Chueca* ☎ *91/522–8217* ◷ *Closed Sun. nights.*

WHERE TO EAT

Madrileños tend to eat their meals even later than people in other parts of Spain, and that's saying something. Restaurants open for lunch at 1:30 and fill up by 3, during which time most offer a *menú del día* (fixed menu) that includes a main course, dessert, wine, and coffee. Dinner-time begins at 9, but reservations for 11 are common, and a meal can be a lengthy (up to three hours) affair. If you face hunger meltdown sev-eral hours before dinner, make the most of the early-evening tapas hour. Dress in most Madrid restaurants and tapas bars is casual but stylish. Compared with Barcelona, the pricier places are a bit more formal; men often wear jackets and ties, and women often wear skirts.

Chamartín

$$$$
Fodor'sChoice
★
✗ **El Chaflán.** Juan Pablo Felipe has converted what was once a venue for traditional Cantabrian cuisine into a temple of sophistication. The sooth-ing pastel tones, indirect colored lighting, and minimalist atmosphere evoke comfort and style. The open kitchen gives you a view of the master chef at work. The dishes and the sampler menu change constantly to reflect the chef's innovative style. The seasonal highlights include the a unique gazpacho (a transparent golden gelatin obtained from a mix of tomato water, olive oil, and vinegar, with cumin bread, pepper, and ham on top), an exceptionally creamy mushroom risotto, and savory red-tuna dishes. ✉ *Av. de Pio XII 34, Chamartín* ☎ *91/345–0450* ▭ *AE, DC, MC, V* ◷ *Closed Sun., Easter, and 2 wks in Aug. No lunch Sat.*

★ **$$$–$$$$**
✗ **Casa Benigno.** Owner-creator Don Norberto takes gracious care at what he does by providing a carefully edited menu and some painstakingly se-lected wines and olive oils to enthusiastic customers. Inside a casual and understated hideaway, the few tables breathe craftsmanship in every corner. Enriching the experience are ceramic plates from Talavera, great Danish herring, the best rice in the city (cooked with extra-flat paella pans made especially for the restaurant), and a chef with an astounding knowl-edge of food, who markets his own brand of tuna and generously talks with all his guests without ever looking at his watch. ✉ *Benigno Soto 9, Chamartín* ☎ *91/416–9357* ⌖ *Reservations essential* ▭ *AE, DC, MC, V* ◷ *No dinner Sun. in Aug. Closed Christmas and Easter wks.*

$$$
✗ **Sacha.** Playful sketches decorate the walls of this French bistrolike restaurant filled with oversize antique furniture. The cuisine is provin-cial Spanish—with a touch of imagination. The *lasaña de changurro* (large-crab lasagna), *arroz con setas y perdiz* (rice with mushrooms and partridge), and *emperador suculento* (swordfish on a fried tomato base) are some of the house specialties. ✉ *Juan Hurtado de Mendoza 11,*

Chamartín ☎ *91/345–5952* ⚇ *Reservations essential* ▤ *AE, DC, MC, V* ⊘ *Closed Sun. and Aug.*

Chueca & Malasaña

$$$$
Fodor'sChoice
★

✕ Asiana. Young chef Renedo and his friend Takeshi surprise even the most jaded palates in a unique setting—Renedo's mother's antique Asian-furniture store, which used to be a ham-drying shed. They bring to their job a bursting and contagious enthusiasm for cooking and experimentation as well as painstaking attention to detail. Sit among a Vietnamese bed, a life-size Buddha, and other merchandise for sale while enjoying the perfectly balanced and eclectic 10-dish fixed menu. Using traditional Spanish cooking as his base, Renedo also uses as inspiration his years in Italy, Japan, and the United States. The menu can be altered to meet special dietary needs. ⊠ *Travesía de San Mateo 4, Chueca* ☎ *91/310–4020 or 91/310–0965* ⚇ *Reservations essential* ▤ *MC, V* ⊘ *Closed Sun. and Mon. No lunch.*

$$
✕ Taberna Carmencita. One of Chueca's charms is that next to a stylish fusion noodle restaurant you can find traditional places like this one, where time and customers seems to run on a different pace. This old Madrid favorite retains much of the atmosphere it had in the mid-20th century, when Carmencita herself cared for customers as though they were long-lost children. Try the *chipirones en su tinta* (squid in its ink) the *albóndigas castizas* (meatballs with tripe and chickpeas), or go for the €23 sampler menu. The ceramic-tile tavern is just north of the Gran Vía–Calle Alcalá intersection. ⊠ *Libertad 16, Centro* ☎ *91/531–6612* ▤ *AE, DC, MC, V* ⊘ *Closed Sun. No lunch Sat.*

$–$$
✕ Nina. One of the first local restaurants to bring sophistication and refinement to a neighborhood best known for its wild and unrestricted spirit, Nina is in an airy loftlike interior with high ceilings, iron columns, exposed brick-and-alabaster walls, and dark hardwood floors. Waiters dressed in black serve the creative Mediterranean cuisine with an Eastern touch to a mostly young and hip crowd. Highlights include the goat cheese *milhojas* (pastry puffs), glazed codfish, *bacalao* (salt cod) with honey sauce and the venison and mango in a mushroom sauce. It has a good weekday fixed-price lunch menu and serves brunch on the weekends. ⊠ *Manuela Malasaña 10, Malasaña* ☎ *91/591–0046* ⊘ *AE, DC, MC, V.*

★ $
✕ Arabia. After you cross the heavy wool rug hanging at this restaurant's entrance, you may feel as if you've entered a warm Aladdin's cave, decorated with adobe, wood, brass work, whitewashed walls, and lavish palms. Full of young boisterous Madrileños, it's a great place to go to get elaborate Moroccan dishes such as the stewed lamb with honey and dry fruits or a vegetarian favorite such as couscous with milk and pumpkin. To start, try the best falafel anywhere outside of Morocco or the yogurt cucumber salad. Request a table or cushioned floor seating, and be sure to make a reservation if you want to eat here on the weekend. ⊠ *Piamonte 12, Chueca* ☎ *91/532–5321* ⊘ *Closed Mon. No lunch Tues.–Fri.*

¢–$
✕ Bazaar. Owners of La Finca de Susana opened up another restaurant in Chueca, one that resembles an old-fashioned convenience store. Done in tones of white, Bazaar serves low-price and creative Mediterranean

food of reasonable quality in a trendy environment. The square-shape upper floor has big windows facing the street, high ceilings, columns, and hardwood floors; the downstairs is bigger although less interesting. While watching the young passersby through the large windows, order the tuna *rosbif* (tuna roasted and sliced thinly like beef) with mango chutney, or the tender ox with Parmesan and arugula. For dessert, a popular choice is the *chocolatísimo* (chocolate soufflé). To get a table, arrive by 1 for lunch and by 8:30 for dinner. ⊠ *C. Libertad 21, Chueca* ☎ *91/523–3905* ⌲ *Reservations not accepted* ▤ *MC, V.*

¢–$ ✕ **Pulcinella.** Tired of not being able to find a true Italian restaurant in the city, owner Enrico opened up this homey trattoria, filled with memorabilia of Italian artists. It seems like a direct transplant from Naples. Superb pastas and the best pizzas in the city cooked in a brick oven are the stars here. ⊠ *Regueros 7, Chueca* ☎ *91/319–7363* ⌲ *Reservations essential* ▤ *AE, MC, V, DC.*

Huertas, Santa Ana & Sol

★ $$$$ ✕ **La Terraza—Casino de Madrid.** This rooftop terrace just off Puerta del Sol is in one of Madrid's oldest, most exclusive clubs (the *casino* is a club for gentlemen, not gamblers). The food is inspired and overseen by Ferran Adrià, who runs his own famous restaurant, El Bullí, near Roses in Catalonia. Francisco Roncero's creations closely follow Adrià's trademarks: try any of the light and tasty mousses, foams, and jellies, or indulge in the unique tapas—experiments of flavor, texture, and temperature. There's also a sampler menu. ⊠ *Alcalá 15, Sol* ☎ *91/521–8700* ⌲ *Reservations essential* ▤ *AE, DC, MC, V* ⊙ *Closed Sun. and Aug. No lunch Sat.*

$$$$ ✕ **Lhardy.** Serving Madrid specialties for more than 150 years, Lhardy looks about the same as it must have on day one, with dark-wood paneling, brass chandeliers, and red-velvet chairs. Most people come for the traditional *cocido a la madrileña* (a hearty meal of broth, meat, and garbanzo beans) and *callos a la madrileña (veal tripe stewed with onions and tomatoes)*. Game, sea bass, and soufflés are also available. Dining rooms are upstairs; the ground-floor entry doubles as a delicatessen and stand-up coffee bar that fills on chilly winter mornings with shivering souls sipping steaming-hot *caldo* (broth) from silver urns. ⊠ *Carrera de San Jerónimo 8, Sol* ☎ *91/522–2207* ▤ *AE, DC, MC, V* ⊙ *Closed Aug. No dinner Sun.*

$$$ ✕ **Come Prima.** There are fancier and surely more expensive Italian restaurants in the city, but none as warm or authentic. Decorated with black-and-white photos of Italian actors and movie scenes, the restaurant is divided into three nooks. The bistrolike front with the green-and-white checkered tablecloths is the most charming. The portions are large, eye-catching, and tastefully presented; diners love risottos such as the Milanesa with lobster and the porcini. The menu also offers great dry and fresh pasta dishes and surprises such as liver- or pumpkin-filled ravioli, and the timbale *Come Prima* (a molded pasta cake filled with vegetables). ⊠ *C. Echegaray 27, Santa Ana* ☎ *91/420–3042* ⌲ *Reservations essential* ▤ *MC, V* ⊙ *No lunch Sun. and Mon.*

$$–$$$ ✕ **La Ancha.** The traditional Spanish menu includes some of the best lentils, meat cutlets, and croquettes in Madrid, as well as more elaborate dishes,

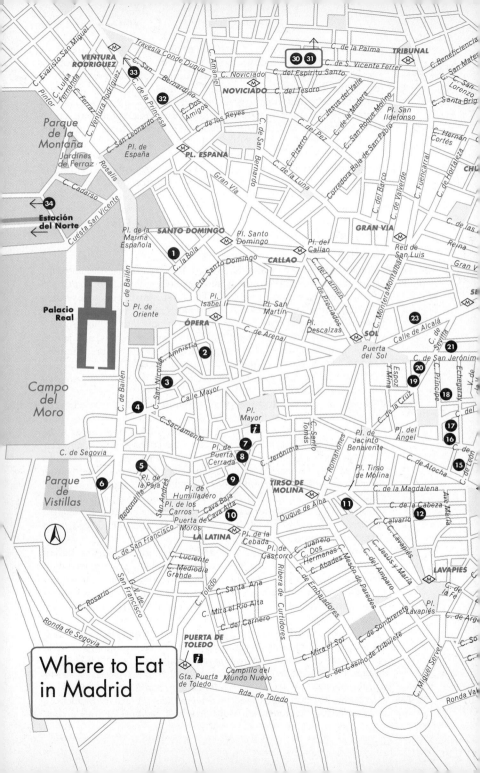

Where to Eat in Madrid

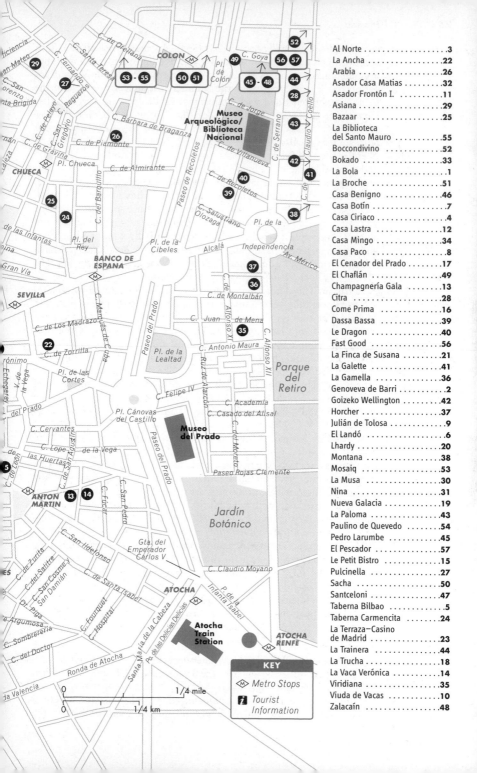

such as the juicy *tortilla con almejas* (Spanish omelet with clams). Both locations belong to the same family and are unpretentious inside but are outstanding in terms of quality. The original Prícipe de Vergara location has a tented patio for the summer; the newer one behind the Congress is often filled with politicians. ✉ *Príncipe de Vergara 204, Chamartín* ☎ *91/563–8977* ✉ *Zorrilla 7, Centro* ☎ *91/429–8186* 🖃 *AE, DC, MC, V* ☉ *Closed Sun. and 1 wk in Aug.; Zorrilla branch closed 3 wks in Aug.*

★ $$ ✕ **El Cenador del Prado.** The name means "The Prado Dining Room," and the settings include a boldly painted dining area and plant-filled conservatory, as well as a separate baroque salon (a sitting area, mainly occupied by large groups). The innovative menu has French and Asian touches, as well as exotic Spanish dishes. The house specialty is *patatas a la importancia* (sliced potatoes fried in a sauce of garlic, parsley, and clams); other options include black rice with baby squid and prawns, and sirloin on a pear pastry puff. For dessert try the *bartolillos* (custard-filled pastries). ✉ *C. del Prado 4, Retiro* ☎ *91/429–1561* 🖃 *AE, DC, MC, V* ☉ *Closed 1 wk in Aug. No dinner Sun.*

$–$$ ✕ **La Trucha.** This Andalusian deep-fry specialist, decorated with hang-
FodorsChoice ing hams, ceramic plates, and garlic, is one of the happiest places in
★ Madrid. The staff is jovial, and the house specialty, *trucha a la truchana* (trout stuffed with ham and ample garlic), is a work of art. Other star entrées are *chopitos* (baby squid), *pollo al ajillo* (chunks of chicken in crisped garlic), and *espárragos trigueros* (wild asparagus). *Jarras* (pitchers) of chilled Valdepeñas seem to function like laughing gas in this magic little bistro. The Nuñez de Arce branch, near the Hotel Reina Victoria, is usually less crowded. ✉ *Manuel Fernandez y Gonzalez 3, Santa Ana* ☎ *91/429–5833* ✉ *Nuñez de Arce 6, Santa Ana* ☎ *91/532–0890* 🖃 *AE, MC, V* ☉ *Nuñez de Arce branch closed Sun., Mon., and Aug.*

¢–$ ✕ **La Finca de Susana.** A huge, diverse crowd comes here in search of grilled vegetables, oven-cooked *bacalao* (salt cod) with spinach, and caramelized duck. Not irrelevant is the fact that this is one of the best bargains in the city. The loftlike interior comes with hardwood floors and is decorated with warm tones. At the end of the dining room is a huge bookcase lined with wine bottles. Arrive by 1 for lunch and 8:30 for dinner or be prepared to wait. ✉ *C. Arlabán 4, Centro* ☎ *91/369–3557* ⌕ *Reservations not accepted* 🖃 *MC, V.*

¢ ✕ **Nueva Galicia.** This small family-run bar and restaurant has long been one of the best values in the center of Madrid—it's two blocks from the Puerta del Sol. You can eat inside or at tables on the pedestrian-only side street. A starter, main course, dessert, and a full bottle of wine can be had for a ridiculously low €7.50; or you can choose to share some of the larger portions (*raciones*). ✉ *Cruz 6, Sol* ☎ *91/522–5289* 🖃 *No credit cards* ☉ *Closed Sun. and Aug.*

La Latina

$$$–$$$$ ✕ **Julián de Tolosa.** This rustic, designer-decorated spot is famous for *alubias rojas* (red kidney beans) from the Basque town of Tolosa. The *ibérico* (acorn-fed) ham here is fine sliced and juicy, and the two-person *chuletón* (T-bone steak) is excellent. The *pimientos de piquillo* (roasted sweet red peppers) come to the table sizzling and may just be the best in the

world. Try a Basque *txakolí* (tart, young white wine) with your first course and a Ribera de Duero later. Let maître d' and owner Angela talk you into a small flask of *pacharán*, the famous Basque sloe-berry liqueur, served over coffee. ✉ *Cava Baja 18, La Latina* ☎ *91/365–8210* ⚭ *Reservations essential* ▭ *DC, MC, V* ⊘ *No dinner Sun.*

$$$
Fodor'sChoice
★
✕ **Casa Botín.** The *Guinness Book of Records* calls this the world's oldest restaurant (1725), and Hemingway called it the best. The latter claim may be a bit over the top, but the restaurant *is* excellent and extremely charming (and so successful that the owners opened a "branch" in Miami, Florida). There are four floors of tile and wood-beam dining rooms, and, if you're seated upstairs, you'll pass ovens dating back centuries. Musical groups called *tunas* often drop in to meander among the hordes. Specialties are *cochinillo* (roast pig) and *cordero* (roast lamb). It's rumored Goya washed dishes here before he made it as a painter. ✉ *Cuchilleros 17, off Plaza Mayor, La Latina* ☎ *91/366–4217* ▭ *AE, DC, MC, V.*

★ $$$
✕ **Casa Paco.** This Castilian tavern wouldn't have looked out of place two or three centuries ago. Squeeze past the old, zinc-top bar, crowded with Madrileños downing shots of Valdepeñas red wine, and into the tile dining rooms. Feast on thick slabs of red meat, sizzling on plates so hot that the meat continues to cook at your table. The Spanish consider overcooking a sin, so expect looks of dismay if you ask for your meat well done (*bien hecho*). You order by weight, so remember that a *medio kilo* is more than a pound. To start, try the *pisto manchego* (La Mancha version of ratatouille) or the Castilian *sopa de ajo* (garlic soup). ✉ *Puerta Cerrada 11, La Latina* ☎ *91/366–3166* ⚭ *Reservations essential* ▭ *DC, MC, V* ⊘ *Closed Sun. and Aug.*

★ $$$
✕ **El Landó.** This castizo restaurant with dark-wood-panel walls and lined with bottles of wine serves classic Spanish food. On the staircase that leads to the main dining area are pictures of famous celebrities who have eaten at this typically noisy landmark. Specialties of the house are *huevos estrellados* (fried eggs with potatoes and sausage), grilled meats, a good selection of fish (sea bass, haddock, grouper) with many different sauces, and steak tartare. As you sit down for your meal, you'll immediately be served a plate of bread with tomato, a salad, and Spanish ham. ✉ *Plaza Gabriel Miró 8, La Latina* ☎ *91/366–7681* ⚭ *Reservations essential* ▭ *AE, DC, MC, V* ⊘ *Closed Sun. and Aug.*

$$
Fodor'sChoice
★
✕ **Casa Ciriaco.** At Madrid's most traditional restaurant—host to a long list of Spain's illustrious, from royalty to philosophers and painters to bullfighters—expect simple home cooking in an unpretentious environment. You can get a flask of Valdepeñas or a split of a Rioja reserve to accompany the *perdiz con judiones* (partridge with broad beans). The *pepitoria de gallina* (hen in an almond sauce) is another favorite. ✉ *C. Mayor 84, La Latina* ☎ *91/559–5066* ▭ *AE, MC, V* ⊘ *Closed Wed. and Aug.*

★ $–$$
✕ **Taberna Bilbao.** Run by a couple, this popular tavern—highly praised by local restaurant owners and restaurant goers—is somewhere between a tapas bar and a restaurant. It has three small dining areas, floor and walls of red Italian marble, plain wooden furniture, and a menu that is representative of Basque cuisine. Try any of the fish or mushroom

revueltos (scrambled eggs), the *habas* (fava beans), or the *bacalao* (cod). And order a glass of *txakolí* (tart, young Basque white wine). ✉ *Costanilla de San Andrés 8, Plaza de la Paja, La Latina* ☎ *91/365–6125* ⓐ *Reservations essential* ⊟ *DC, MC, V* ⊘ *Closed 1st 2 wks of Sept. and Feb. No lunch Mon.*

$ ✗ Viuda de Vacas. This rustic, two-story restaurant—in a building that's more than 200 years old—is one of the pioneers that helped made La Latina neighborhood a gastronomic destination. Simplicity is key, from the furnishings, which still preserve some of the old tiles, to the traditional, high-quality food—cooked in a coal kitchen. This place is a perennial favorite for all ages. Highlights include *calabacines gratinados* (grilled zucchini), *rabo de toro* (bull's tail), and *bacalao dorado a la portuguesa* (cod with fried onions and fries). Owners have discussed closing it for renovations, so call ahead to make sure it's open during your visit. ✉ *Cava Alta 23, La Latina* ☎ *91/366–5847* ⊟ *DC, MC, V* ⊘ *Closed Thurs. and 10 days in Sept. No dinner Sun.*

Lavapiés & Antón Martín

$$$ ✗ Asador Frontón I. Fine meat and fish are the headliners here. Uptown's Asador Frontón II is swankier, but this downtown original is more charming. Appetizers include *anchoas frescas* (fresh grilled anchovies) and *pimientos rellenos con bacalao* (peppers stuffed with cod). The huge *chuletón* (T-bone steak), seared over charcoal and sprinkled with sea salt, is for two or more; order *cogollo de lechuga* (lettuce hearts) to accompany. The *cogotes de merluza* (hake jowls) are supremely light and aromatic. ✉ *Tirso de Molina 7, entrance on Jesus y Maria, 1, Lavapiés* ☎ *91/369–1617* ⓐ *Reservations essential* ⊟ *AE, DC, MC, V* ⊘ *Closed 1 wk in Aug. No dinner Sun.*

$$ ✗ Casa Lastra. Established in 1926, this Asturian tavern is popular with Lavapiés locals. The rustic, half-tile walls are strung with relics from the Asturian countryside, including wooden clogs, cow bells, sausages, and garlic. Specialties include *fabada* (Asturian white beans stewed with sausage), *fabes con almejas* (white beans with clams), and *queso de cabrales,* aromatic cheese made in the Picos de Europa. Great hunks of crisp bread and hard Asturian cider complement a hearty meal; desserts include tangy baked apples. There's an inexpensive fixed-price lunch menu on weekdays. ✉ *Olivar 3, Lavapiés* ☎ *91/369–0837* ⊟ *MC, V* ⊘ *Closed Wed. and July. No dinner Sun.*

$$ ✗ Champagnería Gala. Hidden on a back street not far from Calle Atocha and the Reina Sofía museum, this cheerful Mediterranean restaurant is usually packed, thanks to the choice of paellas, *fideuás* (paellas with noodles instead of rice), risottos, and hearty bean and chickpea stews—all served with salad, dessert, and a wine jar. The same type of rice must be ordered for tables of four and fewer. The front dining area is modern and festive; the back room incorporates trees and plants in a glassed-in patio. ✉ *Moratín 22, Antón Martín* ☎ *91/429–2562* ⓐ *Reservations essential* ⊟ *No credit cards.*

$$ ✗ La Vaca Verónica. In the golden-age literary quarter, this romantic little hideaway gathers a following for its *carne a la plancha* (grilled meat with potatoes and peppers), *pescado a la sal* (fish cooked in a shell of salt), homemade pastas with various seafood dressings, and terrific salads. The pasta *a los carabineros* (with scarlet shrimp) is seductive. ⊠ *Moratín 38, Antón Martín* ☎ *91/429–7827* ☰ *AE, DC, MC, V* ⊗ *No lunch Sat.*

$$ ✕ **Le Petit Bistro.** Carlos and his wife, Frederique, took on a great challenge to convert what was once a bullfighting-themed tavern into a Parisian bistro. Although some elements, such as the long brass copper bar, hint at its castizo origins, there's much that's truly French here, including the service, a superb Sunday brunch, and the wine and cocktails (Kir Royal, pastis). Specialties include Brie *croquetas* (Brie cheese in a breadcrumb crust and deep fried), the assortment of oysters, and the Chateaubriand steak with butter, tarragon, and white vinegar. ⊠ *Plaza de Matute 5, Antón Martín* ☎ *91/429–6265* ☰ *AE, MC, V* ⊗ *Closed Mon. No lunch Sun.*

Moncloa

$$$–$$$$ ✕ **Bokado.** Chefs Mikel and Jesús Santamaría, best known for breaking ground in the world of tapas in both Navarra and the Basque Country, have brought their talent to Madrid. Away from the bustling city center and five minutes from Moncloa, the restaurant, a spacious, elegant, and design-rich setting, is part of the Museo del Traje's building. There's even a terrace and garden that's ideal for summer dining. The menu is a modern example of the fancy combinations that make Basque cuisine renowned, including stews, fish and seafood dishes (oysters, monkfish, haddock), mushroom delicacies, and savory game dishes. ⊠ *Av. Juan de Herrera 2 Moncloa* ☎ *91/549–0041* ☰ *AE, MC, V* ⊗ *No dinner Sun. and Mon.*

¢ ✕ **Casa Mingo.** This bustling place, built into a stone wall beneath the Estación del Norte (across the street from the hermitage of San Antonio de la Florida), resembles an Asturian cider tavern. Expect to share long tables with other diners; the only items on the menu are succulent roast chicken, cheese, salad, and sausages, all to be taken with *sidra* (hard cider). Small tables are set up on the sidewalk in summer. If you don't come early (1 for lunch, 8:30 for dinner), you may have to wait for a table. ⊠ *Paseo de la Florida 34, Moncloa* ☎ *91/547–7918* ⚒ *Reservations not accepted* ☰ *No credit cards.*

Ópera & Palacio Real

$$$ ✕ **Asador Casa Matias.** Like Julián de Tolosa, its kin, this restaurant a block off Plaza de España draws crowds for its juicy meats (you can see the hearty portions of meat being grilled in the exposed kitchen) and its tender red peppers. The extensive menu includes other good options, too, such as the thick stews or the whitefish dishes. The interior makes extensive use of wood and slate, and huge barrels full of cider are scattered around the two floors. The apple-green and deep-yellow walls and ceilings help subdue this rustic look a bit. ⊠ *C. San Leonardo 12, Plaza España* ☎ *91/541–7683 or 91/541–1046* ⚒ *Reservations essential* ☰ *AE, DC, MC, V* ⊗ *No dinner Sun.*

$$–$$$ ✕ **Al Norte.** In the colonnade of a bland brick building that looks completely out of place in the neighborhood, and near one of the oldest churches in Madrid, this sophisticated restaurant specializes in Atlantic, especially Asturian and Galician, dishes. This allows for a great variety of soups, stews, and meats (such as roasted piglet, wild boar, or venison) in winter; a good selection of salads and fish in summer; and regional staples such as *tortas*, the Austurian corn-and-wheat fried cakes, year-round. Other features include an elaborate and unusual ice-cream menu and a terrace for summer dining. ⊠ *San Nicolas 8, Palacio Real* ☎ *91/547–2222 or 91/559–3604* ⚐ *Reservations essential* ▭ *AE, DC, V, MC* ⊙ *No dinner Sun.*

$$ ✗ **Genoveva de Barri.** A few blocks from Palacio Real, this charming restaurant is on a *callejuela* (small street) that's easy to miss. Young chef and sommelier Gonzalo Lara broke away from his father (owner and chef of the acclaimed Laray) to experiment on his own. The result is a bare space with a handful of tables and a few baroque touches: white-and-gold wallpaper, fringed mirrors, and a hanging crystal lamp. The short menu is full of surprises: duck tartare; scrambled eggs with lobster, asparagus, and mushrooms; and an unconventional, although expert, selection of wines. ⊠ *Espejo 10, Ópera* ☎ *91/547–8014* ⚐ *Reservations essential* ▭ *AE, V* ⊙ *No dinner Sun. and Mon.*

$$ ✗ **La Bola.** First opened as a *botellería* (wine shop) in 1802, La Bola developed slowly into a tapas bar and eventually into a full-fledged restaurant. The traditional setting is the draw: the bar is original, and the dining nooks, decorated with polished wood, Spanish tile, and lace curtains, are charming. The restaurant still belongs to the founding family, with the seventh generation currently in training. The house specialty is *cocido a la madrileña* (a hearty meal of broth, garbanzo beans, vegetables, potatoes, and pork). ⊠ *Bola 5, Ópera* ☎ *91/547–6930* ▭ *No credit cards* ⊙ *No dinner Sun. Closed Sun. in Aug. No dinner Sat. in Aug.*

Retiro

$$$$ ✗ **Horcher.** Once Madrid's best restaurant, Horcher is now widely considered little more than an overpriced reminder of its former glory. Nevertheless, the faithful continue to fill this shrine to fine dining. Wild boar, venison, hare, partridge, and wild duck are standard fare. Fish and meat stroganoff, pork chops with sauerkraut, and *baumkuchen* (a chocolate-covered fruit-and-cake dessert) reflect the restaurant's Germanic roots. The dining room is decorated with rust-color brocade and antique Austrian porcelain; an ample selection of French and German wines rounds out the menu. ⊠ *Alfonso XII 6, Retiro* ☎ *91/522–0731* ⚐ *Reservations essential* 🏛 *Jacket and tie* ▭ *AE, DC, MC, V* ⊙ *Closed Sun. and Aug. No lunch Sat.*

$$$$ ✗ **Viridiana.** This place has a relaxed, somewhat cramped bistro feel, its black-and-white scheme punctuated by prints from Luis Buñuel's classic anticlerical film, the restaurant's namesake. Iconoclast chef Abraham Garcia says "market-based" is too narrow a description for his creative menu, which changes every two weeks. Some standard dishes include *foie de pato con chutney de rosas* (duck foie with rose chutney) and *huevos sobre mousse de hongos* (eggs on a mushroom mousse). Or try the superb duck pâté drizzled with sherry and served with Sauternes or Tokay wine. ⊠ *Juan de Mena 14, Retiro* ☎ *91/531–1039* ⚐ *Reservations essential* ▭ *AE, MC, V* ⊙ *Closed Sun. and Holy Week.*

★ $$$ ✗ **La Gamella.** Some of the American-born former chef Dick Stephens's dishes—Caesar salad, hamburger, steak tartare—are still on the reasonably priced menu at this perennially popular dinner spot. The new selections are a fusion of Mediterranean and American dishes. The sophisticated rust-red dining room, batik tablecloths, oversize plates, and attentive service remain the same. The lunchtime menú del día is a great value. ⊠ *Alfonso XII 4, Retiro* ☎ *91/532–4509* ▤ *AE, DC, MC, V* ☉ *Closed Sun. No lunch Sat.*

Salamanca & Chamberí

★ **$$$$** ✕ **Goizeko Wellington.** Aware of the more sophisticated palate of Spain's new generation of diners, the owners of the Madrilenean traditional dreamland that is Goizeko Kabi have opened a new restaurant that share the virtues of its kin, but none of its stuffiness. The menu delivers the same quality of *bacalaos* (codfish), *kokotxas de merluza* (hake jowls), and *chipirones encebollados* (baby squid sauteed in onions), and also includes pastas, risottos, and carpaccios. The decor blends citrus-yellow walls and indirect, intimate lighting with elements such as lattices and screens to help make things look warm and modern. ⊠ *Villanueva 34, Salamanca* ☎ *91/577–6026* ⚖ *Reservations essential* ▤ *AE, DC, MC, V* ☉ *Closed Sun. No lunch Sat. in July and Aug.*

★ **$$$$** ✕ **La Biblioteca del Santo Mauro.** After restoring the El Amparo restaurant to its former self, Vasque chef Carlos Posadas has brought his talent to this simply decorated restaurant in the former library of the Duke of Santo Mauro, inside the hotel of the same name. Here he delves into the realms of Mediterranean and classic Spanish cuisine to produce light and reinterpreted seasonal dishes using meat (pigeon, venison, veal) and fish (sea bass, hake, turbot). Diners are surrounded by tall antique wood bookshelves that contain some of the original volumes and still distill a noble aroma; on the weekends extra tables are set in the old dance room, and in summer clients are encouraged to dine in the garden, which has some of the city's oldest chestnut trees. ⊠ *C. Zurbano 36, Chamberí* ☎ *91/319–6900* ⚖ *Reservations essential* ▤ *AE, DC, MC, V.*

$$$$ ✕ **La Broche.** Sergi Arola, a Ferran Adrià disciple, has vaulted directly

Fodor'sChoice to the top of Madrid dining. The minimalist dining room allows you

★ to concentrate on the hot-cold, surf-turf counterpoints of the seasonal menu. (Surf-turf has become a hallmark of the chef's style; playing with food temperature is also a distinctive trait.) The *menú de degustación* (sampler menu) permits Sergi and his staff to run you through contrasts, generally progressing from light to dark, fish to foie, seafood to tenderloin. ⊠ *Miguel Angel 29, Chamberí* ☎ *91/399–3437* ⚖ *Reservations essential* ▤ *AE, DC, MC, V* ☉ *Closed weekends, Easter wk, and Aug.*

$$$$ ✕ **Santceloni.** Santi Santamaría's Madrid branch of his Racó de Can Fabes

Fodor'sChoice (near Barcelona) has proved an immediate and major success in the Span-

★ ish capital. One of the reigning troika of Spanish chefs—along with Juan Mari Arzak and Ferran Adrià—Santamaría may be the best of all. Lighter and more original than Arzak, less playful and bizarre than Adrià, Santamaría serves exquisite combinations of Mediterranean ingredients accompanied by a comprehensive and daring wine list. ⊠ *Paseo de la Castellana 57, Chamberí* ☎ *91/210–8840* ⚖ *Reservations essential* ▤ *AE, DC, MC, V* ☉ *Closed Sun. and Aug. No lunch Sat.*

$$$$ ✕ **Zalacaín.** This place introduced nouvelle Basque cuisine to Spain in
Fodor'sChoice   the 1970s and has since become a Madrid classic. It's particularly
★   known for using the best and freshest seasonal products available, as
well as for having the best service in town. From the variety of fungi
and game meat to the hard-to-find seafood served, the food here tends
to be unusual—you won't find many of these sorts of ingredients, or
dishes, elsewhere. The restaurant has a deep-apricot color scheme that
is made more dramatic by dark wood and gleaming silver. Inside, you'll
feel like you're in an exclusive villa. ⊠ *Alvarez de Baena 4, Salamanca*
☎ *91/561–4840* ⌂ *Reservations essential* 🏛 *Jacket and tie* ☰ *AE,
DC, V* ⊘ *Closed Sun., Aug., and 1 wk at Easter. No lunch Sat.*

$$$–$$$$ ✕ **El Pescador.** Cross the rustic front door, and you'll forget you're in a
city without a sea. Fishnets, anchors, and other fishing paraphernalia
line the walls, but it's the smell that hints that this restaurant belongs
to the best fish market in town. The owner is so proud of the freshness
of his superb sole, turbot, grouper, and sea bass that the fish (oven-cooked,
grilled, or with salsa) all come plain. The starters, an encyclopedia of
seafood, include barnacles, crayfish, oysters, shrimp, and more. Quench
your thirst with the Albariño white wine specially made for the house.
⊠ *C. J. Ortega y Gasset 75, Salamanca* ☎ *91/402–1290 or 91/402–
2304* ⌂ *Reservations essential* ☰ *MC, V* ⊘ *Closed Sun.*

$$$–$$$$ ✕ **La Paloma.** With a soft and elegant interior with light blue walls, marble floors, linen tablecloths, and upholstered armchairs, this spot perfectly fits into its bourgeois environment. In this split-level restaurant,
chef Segundo Alonso pays great attention to detail, taking care that his
modern Spanish dishes can compete with any in Madrid's priciest restaurants. It's best known for game meats and a variety of mushrooms in
season. Other dishes to try include *erizos de mar gratinados* (toasted
sea urchins with quail eggs) and *ensalada templada de carabineros*
(warm artichoke and scarlet shrimp salad). ⊠ *Jorge Juan 39, Salamanca* ☎ *91/576–8692* ☰ *AE, DC, MC, V* ⊘ *Closed Sun. and Aug.*

$$$–$$$$ ✕ **La Trainera.** With its nautical theme and maze of little dining rooms,
this informal restaurant is all about fresh seafood—the best that money
can buy. Crab, lobster, shrimp, mussels, and a dozen other types of shellfish are served by weight in *raciones* (large portions). Although many Spanish diners share several plates of these shellfish as their entire meal, either
the grilled hake, sole, or turbot makes an unbeatable second course. To
accompany the legendary *carabineros* (giant scarlet shrimp), skip the listless house wine and go for a bottle of Albariño, from the southern Galician coast. ⊠ *Lagasca 60, Salamanca* ☎ *91/576–8035* ☰ *AE, DC, MC,
V* ⊘ *Closed Sun. and Aug.*

$$$–$$$$ ✕ **Pedro Larumbe.** This restaurant is literally the pinnacle of the ABC shopping center between Paseo de la Castellana and Calle Serrano. Dining
quarters include a summer roof terrace (that turns into a lively bar after
dinner) and an Andalusian patio. Chef-owner Pedro Larumbe is known
for presentations of such contemporary dishes as diced sirloin with
Swiss-chard ravioli and truffled cauliflower, or codfish with a spider-
crab stew and a roasted-pepper soup. The dessert buffet is an art exhibit. A good wine list complements the fare. ⊠ *Paseo de la Castellana*

34, at C. Serrano 61, Salamanca ☎ *91/575–1112* ▭ *AE, DC, MC, V* ⊗ *Closed Sun. and Easter wk. No lunch Sat.*

$$$ ✗ **Citra.** Young cooking wizard Elís Murciano understands that today's youngsters can be tomorrow's customers. That's why his sober yet elegant restaurant is separated into two well-defined areas. The bar and the tables next to the entrance allow for casual dining: customers are offered a selection of sophisticated tapas (smaller portions of the regular courses), and a six-tapas sampler for €25. The upper floor is where the daring but balanced creations of the young Venezuelan chef, trained in top-notch Spanish and French restaurants, achieve their greatest splendor: highlights include the salmon tartare, the fig carpaccio, the mushroom risotto, the superb venison steak, and the delicious scallops over caramelized mushroom. For dessert, don't miss the chocolate soufflé. ⊠ *C. Castelló, 18, Salamanca* ☎ *91/575–2866* ⌂ *Reservations essential* ▭ *AE, DC, MC, V* ⊗ *Closed Sun.*

★ **$$$** ✗ **Dassa Bassa.** What look like stairs leading you into a disco actually open up into an old underground coal bunker, now a trendy restaurant. The young chef Darrio Barrio (the cook contenders battle in what it is now the Spanish version of *Beat the Chef*) combines conventional recipes with more adventuresome creations inspired by his stints with Adriá, Larumbe, and Subijana. The menu changes according to what's available in the market. Some recent highlights were the half-grilled salmon with miso foam and wasabi gelatin, bull's tail with red wine, and caramelized suckling pig. ⊠ *C. Villalar 7, Salamanca* ☎ *91/576–7397* ⌂ *Reservations essential* ▭ *AE, DC, MC, V* ⊗ *Closed Sun. and Mon.*

★ **$$–$$$** ✗ **Boccondivino.** After years of low-quality Italian restaurants, Madrileños are witnessing the resurrection of Transalpine gastronomy, thanks to a handful of star-studded newcomers. The one surely at the top of everybody's list is this Sardinian restaurant, decorated in gray and blue tones, whose menu is a feast for both the eye and the stomach. From plates such as *malloreddus* (a small shell-shape wheat pasta)—either with sheep's-milk cheese and black truffle or with eggplant and curd cheese—to the Carneroli rice risottos to the dishes made with spicy Italian pork sausages, or the painstakingly selected homemade cheeses, everything here feels a good notch more authentic than what you're used to. It also has a good selection of savory and fruity wines from Sardinia and sweet delicacies such as the *seada,* a pastry filled with milk-based curd and a special honey made with truffles. ⊠ *C. Castelló 81, Salamanca* ☎ *91/575–7947* ▭ *AE, DC, MC, V* ⊗ *Closed Sun.*

$$–$$$ ✗ **Montana.** Montana has two spaces with a small number of tables and an all-white minimalist décor warmed by such touches as a rich red-velvet curtain that leads to a patio in the main dining room, an exposed kitchen, and the wine racks at the entrance. The owners of this family-run restaurant bring most of their meat (baby goat, home-bred pigeon) and vegetables from their *finca* (farm) in Ávila. Other specialties include *huevos estrellados* (fried eggs) over potatoes and carmelized onions, and a marinated sardine salad. For dessert, there's chocolate soufflé. The Spanish wine list is carefully selected. ⊠ *C. Lagasca 5, Salamanca* ☎ *91/435–9901* ⌂ *Reservations essential* ▭ *AE, DC, MC, V* ⊗ *Closed Sun.*

$$ ✕ La Galette. This quaint place will satisfy both vegetarians and non-vegetarians. In the evening it's candlelighted, and baroque music plays in the background. Specialties include apple *croquetas* (béchamel and apple mixed in a bread-crumb crust and then deep-fried), spinach with tofu, onion soup, and zucchini soup. ⊠ *C. Conde de Aranda 11, Salamanca* ☎ *91/576–0641* ▤ *AE, DC, MC, V.*

$$ ✕ Le Dragon. A more humble competitor to other big-shot Chinese restaurants such as Asia Gallery and Tse-Yang, Le Dragon attracts a younger, less stuffy crowd because of its tasteful combination of food (Chinese with a Japanese influence) and décor. Creatively using screens, panels, and lighting, the restaurant sets up an intimate and distinctive atmosphere between its many tables. The regulars go for the crispy duck, crispy rice with shrimp, and dim sum. Another option is the extensive sampler menu for two or more people (€24 each). ⊠ *C. Gil de Santivañes 2, Salamanca* ☎ *91/435–6668 or 91/435–6669* ⚑ *Reservations essential* ▤ *AE, DC, MC, V.*

$$ ✕ Paulino de Quevedo. What appears to be a completely refurbished barn serves as the dining room for a big-name chef in traditional Spanish cooking, who opened this second restaurant aimed at a more sophisticated crowd. The menu takes traditional dishes on a detour to create stars such as the grilled squid stuffed with vegetables or the caramelized foie with a passion-fruit vinaigrette. Some of the best tapas in Madrid (main courses in miniature plus original creations) are served in the front casual dining area. The tablecloths and cutlery are both reminders of the owner's own castizo origins. ⊠ *C. Jordán 7, Chamberí* ☎ *91/591–3929* ⚑ *Reservations essential* ▤ *AE, DC, MC, V* ⊘ *Closed Sun. and Aug.*

$–$$ ✕ Mosaiq. At this sumptuous restaurant, made fashionable by its trendy young crowd, the enclosed patio and its ceramic-tile and wrought-iron furniture are perfect for lunch or summer dining. Below it is an intimate dining area with transparent fabric used as partitions, cushioned seating, small leather stools, and large brass plates as tables. The top floor has a curtained area with colorful rolls of fabric that make you feel like you're having lunch in a textile market, plus another, more conventional dining area. The menu is traditional Moroccan with some not-so-risqué options to accommodate the Spanish taste; go for the sampler starter and any of the tagine dishes. ⊠ *C. Caracas 21, Salamanca* ☎ *91/308–4446* ⚑ *Reservations essential* ▤ *AE, MC, V.*

¢ ✕ Fast Good. At the first location, the food was neither fast nor exceptionally good. With the opening of the second restaurant, the Ferran Adrià–sponsored project for healthful, creative, fresh fast food has improved, making this a great alternative dining and take-out option. The menu, divided into cold and hot choices, includes an interesting combination of gourmet salads with their own particular dressings, *bocatines* (finger sandwiches), hamburgers, paninis, fries fried in olive oil that is changed on a daily basis, fresh juice combinations such as red peach with azahar (orange blossom) essence, and two rich flavors of flan: chocolate and coconut. The decor is lively and meant to accommodate groups or those dining alone. ⊠ *C. Juan Bravo 3, Salamanca* ☎ *91/577–4151.*

WHERE TO STAY

From the beginning of the new millennium, Madrid has added more than 15,000 new hotel rooms. The increase in the offer has raised competition between hotels, especially in the four-star range. This and the variable pricing systems now used by most of the establishments makes it easy for visitors to come across considerable fluctuations in prices, even with hotels of the same category belonging to the same chain. Most hotels also offer special weekend plans and special prices for the month of August (usually the slowest of the year). If you do not have a well-defined preference, requesting fares from a few hotels within the same quality range will likely save you a few bucks.

Two chains, Catalonia and Vincci, opened up two new hotels on Calle Prado—an unbeatable location for tourists visiting Madrid—in early 2006, complementing their already-in-place Catalonia Moratín and Vincci Centrum.

$$$$
Fodor'sChoice
★
AC Palacio del Retiro. An early-20th-century restored palatial building owned by a noble family with extravagant habits (the elevator carried the horses up and down from the exercise ring on the roof), this spectacular hotel closely follows the Santo Mauro's template: tasteful, modern decor in a historical building. Palacio preserves even more of its grandiose past: baseboards and fountains covered with ceramics from Talavera, original Parisian stained-glass windows, marble floors and columns, and original moldings. All rooms have superb views of the nearby Retiro Park. The double superior rooms' bathroom doors are full-size Lichtenstein silk-screen prints. ⊠ *Alfonso XII 14, Retiro, 28014* 🕾 *91/523–7460* 🖷 *91/523–7461* ⊕ *www.ac-hotels.com* ⟿ *51 rooms* ♿ *Restaurant, in-room safes, cable TV, Wi-Fi, exercise equipment, bar, 3 meeting rooms, parking (fee)* ⊟ *AE, DC, MC, V.*

$$$$
Fodor'sChoice
★
AC Santo Mauro. Once the Canadian embassy, this turn-of-the-20th-century mansion is now an intimate luxury hotel, an oasis of calm a short walk from the city center. The neoclassical architecture is accented by contemporary furniture in white, gray, eggplant, and black hues. Some of the rooms in the main building still maintain the original details and fixtures. The top-notch restaurant is in what used to be the mansion's library. Views vary; request a room with a terrace overlooking the gardens. ⊠ *Zurbano 36, Chamberí, 28010* 🕾 *91/319–6900* 🖷 *91/308–5477* ⊕ *www.ac-hotels.com* ⟿ *51 rooms* ♿ *Restaurant, coffee shop, cable TV, in-room VCRs, Wi-Fi, pool, gym, sauna, bar, meeting room, parking (fee)* ⊟ *AE, DC, MC, V.*

$$$$
Gran Meliá Fénix. An impressive lobby with marble floors and columns decorated with antique furniture, and a blue stained-glass dome ceiling define the style of this completely refurbished Madrid institution. The hotel overlooks Plaza de Colón on the Castellana and is a mere hop from the posh shops of Calle Serrano. Its spacious rooms are decorated in reds and golds and are amply furnished; flowers abound. Ask for a room facing the Plaza de Colón; otherwise, the view is rather dreary. ⊠ *Hermosilla 2, Salamanca, 28001* 🕾 *91/431–6700* 🖷 *91/576–0661* ⊕ *www. solmelia.com* ⟿ *216 rooms, 9 suites* ♿ *3 restaurants, café, cable TV,*

in-room data ports, Wi-Fi, health club, spa, piano bar, babysitting, parking (fee) ⊟ *AE, DC, MC, V.*

$$$$ 🏨 **Hesperia Madrid.** Although a bit farther from the historic area but still in the commercial center, Hesperia welcomes visitors with a long, remarkably sophisticated lobby decorated by renowned designer Pasqua Ortega. Designed using materials such as limestone and light woods, it provides a soothing contrast to the bustling Castellana street outside and ends in a *patio de luces* (atrium) surrounded by the open restaurant La Manzana and common spaces, which have live harp and piano music in the afternoons. Carpeted rooms, though less impressive in terms of size and decor, have all sorts of facilities, including a pillow menu to make sure you feel at home. ⊠ *Paseo de la Castellana 57, Salamanca, 28046* 🕾 *91/210–8800* 🖷 *91/210–8899* ⊕ *www.hesperia-madrid.com* ➴ *139 rooms, 32 suites* ⟁ *2 restaurants, cable TV, in-room data ports, gym, bar, concierge, Wi-Fi, in-room Internet access (broadband data ports or DSL), parking (fee)* ⊟ *AE, DC, MC, V.*

★ $$$$ 🏨 **Hotel Urban.** Owned by Catalan entrepreneur and renowned art collector Jordi Clos, this hotel stylishly mixes the ancient (tall New Guinea carvings in the lobby, the small Egyptian museum, and the antique Chinese or Burmese statues in every room) with some daring sophistication: the tall alabaster column that majestically stands in the lobby's atrium, the main staircase's walls, covered in tiles with gold inlay, and the sleek cocktail bar. Rooms, done in dark hues, with lots of dark wood and leather, are less flamboyant, and some are small. The hotel also has a super restaurant and great views from the swimming pool and summer bar on the roof terrace. ⊠ *Carrera de San Jerónimo 34, Sevilla, 28014* 🕾 *91/787–7770* 🖷 *91/787–7799* ⊕ *www.derbyhotels.com* ➴ *96 rooms, 3 junior suites, 4 suites* ⟁ *2 restaurants, in-room safes, cable TV, Wi-Fi, pool, health club, bar, meeting room, parking (fee)* ⊟ *AE, DC, MC, V.*

$$$$ 🏨 **Orfila.** This elegant 1886 town house, hidden away on a leafy little
Fodor'sChoice residential street not far from Plaza Colón, has every comfort of a larger
★ hotel, but more intimate, personalized surroundings. Originally the intown residence of the literary and aristocratic Gomez-Acebo family, Orfila 6 was an address famous for theater performances in the late 19th and early 20th centuries. The restaurant, garden (superb for summer dining), and tearoom have period furniture; guest rooms are draped with striped and floral silks. ⊠ *Orfila 6, Chamberí, 28010* 🕾 *91/702–7770* 🖷 *91/702–7772* ⊕ *www.hotelorfila.com* ➴ *20 rooms, 12 suites* ⟁ *Restaurant, cable TV, in-room data ports, Wi-Fi, health club, bar, meeting room, parking (fee)* ⊟ *AE, DC, MC, V.*

$$$$ 🏨 **Ritz.** Alfonso XIII, about to marry Queen Victoria's granddaughter, encouraged the construction of this hotel, the most exclusive in Spain, for his royal guests. Opened in 1910 by the king himself (who personally supervised construction), the Ritz is a monument to the Belle Epoque, its salons furnished with rare antiques, hand-embroidered linens, and handwoven carpets. All of the rooms have canopy beds, and some have views of the Prado. The famous and pricey restaurant, Goya, serves a Sunday brunch feast that is accompanied by the soothing strains of harp music; from February to May, you'll enjoy chamber music during weekend tea and supper. ⊠ *Plaza de la Lealtad 5, Prado, 28014* 🕾 *91/*

701–6767 🖷 91/701–6776 ⊕ *www.ritzmadrid.com* ⇥ *167 rooms* ᐸ *Restaurant, in-room fax, cable TV, in-room data ports, health club, hair salon, massage, bar, parking (fee)* ▤ *AE, DC, MC, V.*

★ **$$$$** ▦ **Tryp Ambassador.** On an old street between Gran Vía and the Royal Palace, the Ambassador occupies the renovated 19th-century palace of the Dukes of Granada. A magnificent front door and a graceful three-story staircase recall the building's aristocratic past; the rest has been transformed into elegant, somewhat soulless lodgings favored by executives. Large guest rooms have sitting areas and mahogany furnishings, and floral fabrics. The greenhouse restaurant, filled with plants and songbirds, is especially pleasant on cold days. ⊠ *Cuesta Santo Domingo 5 and 7, Ópera, 28013* ☎91/541–6700 🖷91/559–1040 ⊕*www.solmelia. com* ⇥ *182 rooms, 24 suites* ᐸ *Restaurant, cable TV, bar, business services, airport shuttle, parking (fee)* ▤ *AE, DC, MC, V.*

$$$$ ▦ **Villa Magna.** The concrete facade here gives way to an interior furnished with 18th-century antiques. Prices are very high, but it's hard to find flourishes such as a champagne bar and—in the largest suite in Madrid—a white baby-grand piano. All rooms have large desks, and the suites' bathrooms have fresh flowers. Its French-inspired Restaurante del Hotel (formerly Le Divellec) has walnut paneling and the feel of an English library, and you can dine on its garden terrace in season. The other restaurant, the Tse-Yang, is Madrid's fanciest Chinese restaurant. ⊠ *Paseo de la Castellana 22, Salamanca, 28046* ☎ *91/587–1234* 🖷 *91/431–2286* ⊕*www. madrid.hyatt.com* ⇥ *164 rooms, 18 suites* ᐸ *2 restaurants, cable TV, in-room data ports, Wi-Fi, health club, hair salon, massage, 2 bars, babysitting, business services, car rental, parking (fee)* ▤ *AE, DC, MC, V.*

★ **$$$$** ▦ **Villa Real.** For a medium-size hotel that combines elegance, modern amenities, friendly service, *and* a great location, look no further: the Villa Real faces Spain's parliament and is convenient to almost everything, particularly the Prado and Thyssen-Bornemisza museums. The simulated 19th-century facade gives way to an intimate lobby with modern furnishings. Many rooms are split level, with a small sitting area. Some suites have whirlpool baths. ⊠ *Plaza de las Cortés 10, Prado, 28014* ☎ *91/420–3767* 🖷*91/420–2547* ⊕*www.derbyhotels.es* ⇥ *94 rooms, 20 suites* ᐸ *Restaurant, cable TV, in-room data ports, Wi-Fi, hair salon, sauna, bar, meeting room, parking (fee)* ▤ *AE, DC, MC, V.*

★ **$$$$** ▦ **Westin Palace.** Built in 1912, Madrid's most famous grand hotel is a Belle Epoque creation of Alfonso XIII and has hosted the likes of Salvador Dalí, Marlon Brando, Rita Hayworth, and Madonna. Guest rooms are high-tech and generally impeccable; banquet halls and lobbies have been beautified, and the facade has been restored. The Art Nouveau stained-glass dome over the lounge remains exquisitely original, and guest room windows are double-glazed against street noise. The suites are no less luxurious than the opulent public spaces with Bang & Olufsen CD players, spacious bathrooms, double sinks, hot tubs, and separate shower stalls. It now hosts the very popular Asia Gallery restaurant. ⊠ *Plaza de las Cortés 7, Prado, 28014* ☎ *91/360–8000* 🖷*91/ 360–8100* ⊕ *www.palacemadrid.com* ⇥ *465 rooms, 45 suites* ᐸ *2 restaurants, café, cable TV, in-room data ports, Wi-Fi, gym, sauna, bar, business services, meeting room, parking (fee)* ▤ *AE, DC, MC, V.*

$$$–$$$$ ▦ **De Las Letras.** This hotel inspired by literature (it even has a book cat-
alog in every room) is a seamless mix of modern pop interior design that
respects and accents the original details of the 1917 structure (glazed
tiles, canopies, original wood-and-iron elevator, wooden staircase, and
stone carvings). Rooms are painted in tones of ocher, orange, or bur-
gundy, with high ceilings, wooden floors, indirect lighting, and over-the-
top modern bathrooms. The junior suites have a terrace with a whirlpool
bath. Enjoying a meal or a cocktail in the restaurant and lounge with
large windows facing the street, you would never think you're around
the corner from the bustling Gran Vía. ⊠ *Gran Vía 11, Centro, 28013*
☎ *91/523–7980* ☎ *91/523–7981* ⊕ *www.hoteldelasletras.com* ⬩ *103
rooms, 1 suite, 6 junior suites* ⚲ *Restaurant, cable TV, in-room DVD
& CD players, in-room data ports, Wi-Fi, health club, bar, library,
meeting room, parking (fee), Internet* ⊟ *AE, DC, MC, V.*

$$$–$$$$ ▦ **Hotel Bauzá.** With a balanced combination of modern style and ele-
gance, this hotel has dark-wood floors, stereos in every room, and other
details, such as the environmentally friendly bikes with motors for guests,
that make it a good alternative to the higher-end hotels. The rooms have
functional yet distinctive furniture (each room is decorated with an orig-
inal photograph signed by the artist), and the bathrooms are beautifully
tiled. The restaurant serves Mediterranean-fusion food and has great views
of one of Madrid's great shopping streets, Calle Goya. ⊠ *Goya 79,
Salamanca, 28001* ☎ *91/435–7545* ☎ *91/431–0943* ⊕ *www.hotelbauza.
com* ⬩ *167 rooms, 3 suites, 7 apartments* ⚲ *Restaurant, cable TV, in-
room data ports, Wi-Fi, health club, bar, library, DSL or in-room broad-
band, meeting room, parking (fee)* ⊟ *AE, DC, MC, V.*

$$$–$$$$ ▦ **Vincci Soho.** Faithful to its surname, this hotel seems as if it had been
transplanted from London or New York into one of Madrid's busiest
neighborhoods. Everything on its ground floor—the lamps, the mustard
color circular divan that sits in front of the reception desk, the meeting
lounges with velvet armchairs and silk screens, the steel butterfly cutouts
on the restaurant walls—highlights elegance and imagination. There are
no two rooms alike in shape—the hotel is made of five old private
houses—but they're all comfortable and bright—even the interior ones,
thanks to a large open courtyard that which keeps the street noise out
and lets the sun in. ⊠ *Prado 18, Santa Ana, 28014* ☎ *91/141–4100*
☎ *91/141–4100* ⊕ *www.vinccihoteles.com* ⬩ *167 rooms* ⚲ *Bar, restau-
rant, cable TV, Wi-Fi, safe box, parking (fee)* ⊟ *AE, DC, MC, V.*

$$$ ▦ **Catalonia Moratín.** The aristocratic corridor leading to the registration
desk, the atrium (where the walls are still partly made of original gran-
ite blocks), and the magnificent main wooden staircase, presided over
by a lion statue—these are the elements that best reveal this building's
18th-century origins. The other common areas, including a reading room
with a small library and the restaurant, have less character. Guest rooms
are comfortable, with functional wooden furniture and striped curtains
and bedspreads. Bathrooms have cream-color tiles and green marble sinks.
⊠ *C. Atocha 23, Sol, 28012* ☎ *91/369–7171* ☎ *91/360–1231* ⊕ *www.
hoteles-catalonia.es* ⬩ *63 rooms* ⚲ *Restaurant, in-room safes, cable
TV, in-room data ports, bar, library* ⊟ *AE, DC, MC, V.*

★ **$$$** ▣ **Gran Hotel Canarias.** Once the residence of a count, this fully restored hotel, a block away from the Prado Museum, is a reasonable yet luxurious alternative to the five-star hotels that populate the area. In the lobby and common areas you can find odd combinations such as a brown-leather couch and period chairs, but guest rooms are spacious, with hand-painted Canarian motifs, bold-color carpets from the Royal Factory of Tapestries, and wooden furniture. Bathrooms are tiled in green marble with huge mirrors and showers. The cafeteria, open to the public, is a magnet for the passersby. ⊠ *Plaza Cánovas del Castillo 4, Prado, 28014* ☎ *91/330–2400* 🖷 *91/360–0798* ⊕ *www.granhotelcanarias.com* 🖈 *114 rooms, 5 suites* ⌂ *Restaurant, cafeteria, in-room safes, cable TV, in-room broadband, Wi-Fi, gym, meeting room, parking (fee)* ⊟ *AE, DC, MC, V.*

$$$ ▣ **Meliá Reina Victoria.** A great loss for many Madrileños—it was formerly the dive where all bullfighters would convene and get dressed before heading off towards the Las Ventas arena—this new hotel will nonetheless lure many tourists fond of cutting-edge technology. The bull heads once displayed in the former lobby will make way for hip shops, rooms with iPod outlets, safe boxes for laptops, a home theater system, and bathrooms with hydromassage showers. It will also have a terrace/bar on the rooftop that with its view of Plaza Santa Ana will surely become a hot spot. ⊠ *Plaza Santa Ana 14, Santa Ana, 28014* ☎ *91/531–4500* 🖷 *91/522–0307* ⊕ *www.solmelia.com* 🖈 *192 rooms, 5 suites* ⌂ *Bar, restaurant, cable TV, Wi-Fi, safe box, laundry, parking (fee)* ⊟ *AE, DC, MC, V.*

$$$ ▣ **Hotel Catalonia Las Cortes.** A late 18th-century palace formerly owned by the Duke of Noblejas, this hotel retains a good shred of its noble past: a gorgeous wooden staircase, some of the old moldings, and stained windows, and has a classic feel without being ostentatious or overwhelming. Rooms are elegant and wallpapered in greyish tones, whereas bathrooms—with more bland decor—are quite decent in size for the city's standards. Better still, it's just a few yards away from Plaza Santa Ana. ⊠ *Prado 6, Santa Ana, 28014* ☎ *91/389–6051* 🖷 *91/389–6052* ⊕ *www.hoteles-catalonia.com* 🖈 *55 rooms, 8 junior suites, 2 suites* ⌂ *Bar, restaurant, cable TV, Wi-Fi, safe box, laundry, parking (fee)* ⊟ *AE, DC, MC, V.*

$$$ ▣ **Hotel Intur Palacio San Martín.** In an unbeatable location across from one of Madrid's most celebrated monuments (the Convent of Descalzas), **Fodor's Choice** this hotel, once the old U.S. embassy and later a luxurious residential ★ building crowded with noblemen, still exudes a kind of glory. The entrance leads to a glass-dome atrium that serves as a tranquil sitting area. The hotel has preserved an antique elevator, and many of the ceilings are carved and ornate. The rooms are spacious and carpeted; request one facing the big plaza. ⊠ *Plaza de San Martín 5, Centro, 28013* ☎ *91/701–5000* 🖷 *91/701–5010* ⊕ *www.intur.com* 🖈 *93 rooms, 8 suites* ⌂ *Restaurant, café, cable TV, in-room data ports, Wi-Fi, gym, sauna, meeting rooms, parking (fee)* ⊟ *AE, DC, MC, V.*

$$$ ▣ **Hotel Preciados.** In a 19th-century building on the quieter edge of one of Madrid's main shopping areas, this hotel is both charming and convenient. The rooms are modern and sophisticated, with hardwood floors and opaque glass closets. Some of the "double superiors" (slightly more expensive) have slanted ceilings and skylights in the bathrooms. ⊠ *C.*

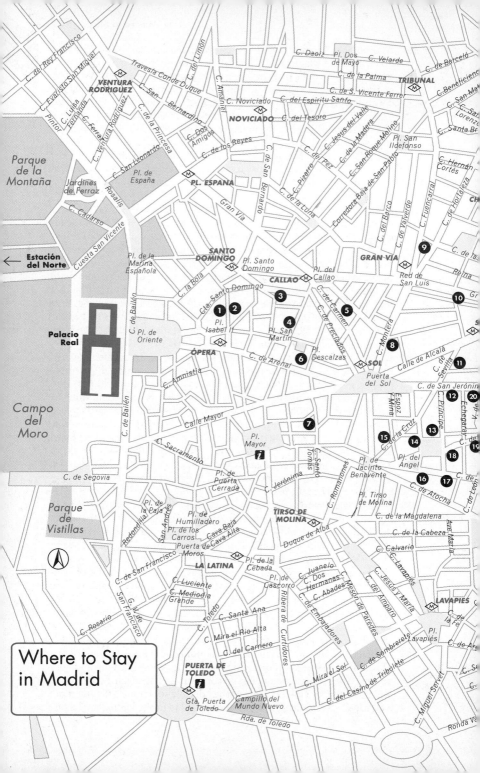

Where to Stay in Madrid

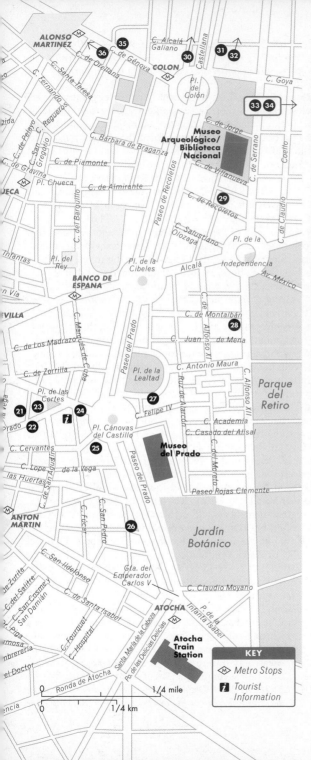

Preciados 37, Centro, 28013 ☎ *91/454–4400* 📠 *91/454–4401* ⊕ *www. preciadoshotel.com* ↪ *73 rooms, 5 suites* ⚬ *Restaurant, café, cable TV, in-room data ports, Wi-Fi, massage, bar, meeting room, parking (fee)* ⊟ *AE, DC, MC, V.*

$$$ ⊞ **Jardín de Recoletos.** This sleek apartment hotel offers great value on a quiet street close to Plaza Colón and upmarket Calle Serrano. The large lobby has marble floors and a stained-glass ceiling, and adjoins a café, restaurant, and the hotel's restful private garden. The large rooms, with light-wood trim and beige-and-yellow furnishings, include sitting and dining areas. "Superior" rooms and suites have hydromassage baths and large terraces. Book well in advance. ✉ *Gil de Santivañes 6, Salamanca, 28001* ☎ *91/781–1640* 📠 *91/781–1641* ↪ *36 rooms, 7 suites* ⚬ *Restaurant, café, room service, kitchenettes, cable TV, in-room VCRs, in-room data ports, Wi-Fi, parking (fee)* ⊟ *AE, DC, MC, V* ⑩ *BP.*

$$$ ⊞ **NH Lagasca.** In the heart of the elegant Salamanca neighborhood, this newish hotel combines large, brightly decorated rooms with an unbeatable location two blocks from Madrid's main shopping street, Calle Serrano. The marble lobbies border on the coldly functional, but they're fine as a meeting place. ✉ *Lagasca 64, Salamanca, 28001* ☎ *91/575–4606* 📠 *91/575–1694* ⊕ *www.nh-hotels.com* ↪ *100 rooms* ⚬ *Restaurant, cable TV, bar, meeting room, parking (fee)* ⊟ *AE, DC, MC, V.*

$$$ ⊞ **Petit Palace Arenal.** Near the bustling tourist area Sol, this fairly new and popular hotel maintains some of its location's original characteristics, including a wood staircase, some wooden beams, and the vaulted exposed-brick walls in the meeting and breakfast rooms downstairs. The rooms, tastefully done with deep-purple ceilings, and outfitted with modern light fixtures and tempered-glass sinks, already show some wear and tear. This chain boutique hotel has two nearby locations with similar features: the Petit Palace Puerta del Sol on the same street but closer to Sol, and the Posada del Peine at C. Postas 17. ✉ *Arenal 16, Sol, 28013* ☎ *91/564–4355* 📠 *91/564–0854* ⊕ *www.hthoteles.com* ↪ *64 rooms* ⚬ *Cafeteria, in-room safes, cable TV, in-room broadband, business services, meeting room* ⊟ *AE, DC, MC, V.*

$$$ ⊞ **Petit Palace Ducal.** At the core of Madrid's most youthful shopping district, this former hostel is now a modern high-tech hotel that preserves some of the original elements (such as the wrought-iron elevator and staircase). The rooms have dark-wood floors and headboards and track lighting; some have bunk beds and can house up to five people. The café, open to the public, has large windows that face the street. ✉ *Hortaleza 3, Chueca, 28004* ☎ *91/521–1043* 📠 *91/521–5064* ⊕ *www.hthoteles. com* ↪ *58 rooms* ⚬ *Café, in-room safes, cable TV, in-room broadband, business services, meeting room* ⊟ *AE, DC, MC, V.*

$$$ ⊞ **Quo Puerta del Sol.** Between Santa Ana and Sol, this modern and design-oriented boutique hotel has rooms with views of the city center that are equipped with cutting-edge technology, dark hardwood floors, and modern touches such as the stainless-steel-and-glass sinks in the bathrooms. Common areas may not be ample in size but are nonetheless charming, trendy, and full of character. ✉ *C. Sevilla 4, Centro, 28014* ☎ *91/532–9049* 📠 *91/531–2834* ⊕ *www.hotelesquo.com* ↪ *61 rooms, 1 junior suite* ⚬ *Café, cable TV, in-room data ports, Wi-Fi, parking (fee)* ⊟ *AE, DC, MC, V.*

1

$$–$$$ ⊞ **Suite Prado.** Popular with Americans on short stays, this stylish apartment hotel is near the Prado, the Thyssen-Bornemisza, and the Plaza Santa Ana tapas area. The attractive attic studios on the fourth floor have sloped ceilings with wood beams; there are larger suites downstairs. All apartments are brightly decorated and have marble baths and basic kitchens. Breakfast is served daily, on request, by a friendly staff. Triple rooms are a great deal. ⊠ *Manuel Fernández y González 10, Santa Ana, 28014* ☏ *91/420–2318* 🖷 *91/420–0559* ⊕ *www.suiteprado.com* ↩ *18 suites* ☖ *Kitchenettes, cable TV, in-room data ports, Wi-Fi, parking (fee)* ⊟ *AE, DC, MC, V.*

$$ ⊞ **Alicia Room Mate.** The all-white lobby, with curvatious walls, ceiling and lamps sets the mood for the mostly young urbanite visitors of this former trench coat factory that now, as a hotel, sells style at affordable prices. Carpeted rooms abound in modern features, although they're not spectacular in size—the black slate bathrooms, all with showers, are in the bedroom separated only by a glass door. Just a few more euros will upgrade you to an executive, with a small terrace, or a *minisuite,* with very large windows that will turn you into a privileged observer of everything that's going on in Plaza Santa Ana. ⊠ *Prado 2, Santa Ana, 28014* ☏ *91/389– 6095* 🖷 *91/369–4795* ⊕ *www.room-matehoteles.com* ↩ *34 rooms, 3 suites* ☖ *Bar, cable TV, Wi-Fi, parking (fee)* ⊟ *AE, DC, MC, V.*

$$ ⊞ **Ateneo Hotel.** This hotel is in the restored 18th-century building that once housed the Ateneo, a club founded in 1835 to promote freedom of thought. The spacious rooms are done in cream-and-light-wood tones with parquet flooring and red-and-gold-striped spreads on the bed. Exterior rooms have balconies overlooking the crowded street, except those on the fourth floor, which have sloped ceilings and a skylight above the bed. ⊠ *Montera 22, Sol, 28013* ☏ *91/521–2012* 🖷 *91/523–3136* ⊕ *www.hotel-ateneo.com* ↩ *38 rooms, 6 junior suites* ☖ *Cable TV, in-room data ports, meeting room* ⊟ *AE, DC, MC, V* ⏍ *BP.*

$$ ⊞ **Inglés.** Virginia Woolf was among the first luminaries to discover this place, in the middle of the old city's bar-and-restaurant district. Since Woolf's time, the Inglés has attracted more than its share of less-celebrated artists and writers. Half of the rooms were tiled and painted in 2005, and new bathrooms were installed, but the decor still resembles the ornate and outdated lobby. The suites, which are double rooms with a salon, are nonetheless a bargain. You get twice the space for what you'd pay for a standard double elsewhere. Also, if your room faces Calle Echegaray, you can get an unusual aerial view of the medieval quarter, which is all red tiles and ramshackle gables. ⊠ *Echegaray 8, Santa Ana, 28014* ☏ *91/429–6551* 🖷 *91/420–2423* ↩ *58 rooms* ☖ *Cafeteria, cable TV, gym, bar, parking (fee); no a/c in some rooms* ⊟ *AE, DC, MC, V.*

$$ ⊞ **Liabeny.** Although unassuming in style and a bit outdated, this 1960s hotel near a plaza (and several department stores) between Gran Vía and Puerta del Sol has large and comfortable rooms with floral fabrics and big windows. Interior and top-floor rooms are the quietest. ⊠ *Salud 3, Centro, 28013* ☏ *91/531–9000* 🖷 *91/532–7421* ⊕ *www.liabeny.es* ↩ *220 rooms* ☖ *Restaurant, café, cable TV, in-room data ports, Wi-Fi, health club, bar, meeting room, parking (fee)* ⊟ *AE, DC, MC, V.*

$$ ⊞ **Room Mate Mario.** More than just a good deal, this modern and stylish hotel is in the city center, steps away from the major sites and nightlife. Although somewhat small and limited in services, its bold modern style—reflected in original silk printed headboards and combinations of white, gray, and black tones—and friendly service are a breath of fresh air among the traditional and neoclassic hotel options in Madrid. ✉ *Campomanes 4, Centro, 28013* 🕾 *91/548–8548* 🖷 *91/559–1288* ⊕ *www.room-matehoteles.com* ⬚ *54 rooms, 3 suites* ♨ *Café, cable TV, in-room data ports, Wi-Fi, laundry facilities* ☰ *AE, DC, MC, V* ⦿l *CP.*

$–$$ ▦ **7 Colors.** Primarily but not exclusively gay, this is the perfect place for those who love design but don't plan on spending too much time in their rooms. Based on the concept of color therapy, each room is decorated in a specific color with integrated bathrooms; you can play with the intensity of light to suit your mood. The yellow, red, and orange rooms have balconies and face the street. Get more space with the double superior room for a little extra. The rectangular white table at the entrance serves as a meeting and breakfast room. Reserve rooms in advance. ✉ *Huertas 14, 2nd exterior left, Santa Ana, 28012* 🕾 *91/429–6935* 🖷 *91/ 429–6935* ⊕ *www.7colorsrooms.com* ⬚ *10 rooms* ♨ *Cable TV, meeting room, public Internet* ☰ *AE, DC, MC, V* ⦿l *CP.*

★ **$** ▦ **Hostal Adriano.** Tucked away on a street with dozens of bland competitors and a couple of blocks away from Sol, this option stands out for its price and quality. The rooms, although not especially big, are charming and far from the standard hostal fare. Brightly colored walls and comforter covers (changed every three days) with furniture and accessories collected over the years by its two friendly Argentine owners make each room unique. The best of the lot has been wallpapered with some old María Callas pictures and the musical score from *Tosca.* ✉ *De la Cruz 26, 4th fl., Santa Ana, 28012* 🕾 *91/521–1339* ⊕ *www.hostaladriano. com* ⬚ *22 rooms* ♨ *In-room safes, cable TV, Internet room* ☰ *MC, V.*

$ ▦ **Mora.** You'll find this cheery hotel with a sparkling, faux-marble lobby and bright, carpeted hallways across the Paseo del Prado from the Botanical Garden. Guest rooms are modestly decorated (those on the fourth floor are newer) but large and comfortable; those on the street side have great views of the gardens and the Prado, and double-pane windows keep them fairly quiet. For breakfast and lunch, the attached café is excellent, affordable, and popular with locals. ✉ *Paseo del Prado 32, Centro, 28014* 🕾 *91/420–1569* 🖷 *91/420–0564* ⊕ *www.hotelmora. com* ⬚ *62 rooms* ♨ *Café, cable TV* ☰ *AE, DC, MC, V.*

¢ ▦ **Hostal Santa Cruz.** On a quiet plaza steps from the eastern entrance to Plaza Mayor, this budget hotel, fully renovated in 2004, has tidy rooms painted in cream colors, simple but sometimes surprising furniture (some of the rooms have white-leather headboards), and clean tile bathrooms, which may come with a shower or with a small bathtub. All rooms face the street, but numbers 6, 7, and 8 have balconies overlooking the plaza. If the Santa Cruz is fully booked, the upstairs floor houses another commendable hostal, Cruz Sol, which has similar prices and features. ✉ *Plaza de Santa Cruz 6, 2nd fl., Sol, 28012* 🕾 *91/522–2441* 🖷 *91/523–7088* ⊕ *www.hostalsantacruz.com* ⬚ *16 rooms* ♨ *Meeting room* ☰ *AE, DC, MC, V.*

¢ ▦ **Hostal Villar.** Rooms, which go from single to quadruple and with or without bathrooms (those facing the busy Calle Príncipe are among the ones without baths), are reasonably large, clean, and comfortably decorated, with matching bedspreads and curtains. However, the bathrooms are rather small. The service here is friendly and attentive. ⊠ *Príncipe 18, Santa Ana, 28012* ☎ *91/531–6600* 🖶 *91/521–5073* ⊕ *www.villar.es* ➳ *40 rooms, 27 with bath* ▭ *MC, V.*

NIGHTLIFE & THE ARTS

The Arts

As Madrid's reputation as a vibrant, contemporary arts center has grown, artists and performers have arrived in droves. Consult the weekly *Guía del Ocio* (published Friday) or daily listings in any of the leading newspapers—*El País, El Mundo,* or *ABC,* all of which are understandable even if you don't read much Spanish. The Festival de Otoño (Autumn Festival), from late September to late November, blankets the city with pop concerts, poetry readings, flamenco, and ballet and theater from world-renowned companies. Other annual events include outstanding bonanzas of film, contemporary art, and jazz, salsa, rock, and African music, all at reasonable prices. Seats for the classical performing arts are best purchased through your hotel concierge, on the Internet, or at the hall itself. **El Corte Inglés** (☎ 902/400222 ⊕ www.elcorteingles.es/entradas) sells tickets for major concerts. **FNAC** (⊠ Preciados 28, Sol ☎ 91/595–6100) sells tickets to musical events. **Tele-Entradas** (☎ 902/101212) and **Entradas.com** (☎ 902/221622) are ticket brokers.

Concerts & Dance

Convento de la Encarnación and the Real Academia de Bellas Artes de San Fernando hold concerts. The modern **Auditorio Nacional de Música** (⊠ Príncipe de Vergara 146, Salamanca ☎ 91/337–0100 ⊕ www.auditorionacional.mcu.es) is Madrid's main concert hall, with spaces for both symphonic and chamber music. The resplendent **Teatro Real** (⊠ Plaza de Isabel II, Ópera ☎ 91/516–0660 ⊕ www.teatro-real.com) is the site of opera and dance performances.

The subterranean **Centro Cultural de la Villa** (⊠ Plaza de Colón, Salamanca ☎ 91/480–0300 information, 902/101212 tickets—cost of call is shared by both parties) has an eclectic program ranging from gospel and blues to flamenco and Celtic dance. The **Fundación Juan March** (⊠ Castello 77, Salamanca ☎ 91/435–4240) offers chamber music Monday and Saturday at noon, and Wednesday at 7:30 PM.

The **Círculo de Bellas Artes** (⊠ Marqués de Casa Riera 2, Centro ☎ 902/422442 ⊕ www.circulobellasartes.com), at the junction between Gran Vía and Alcalá, has concerts, theater, dance performances, art exhibitions, and other arts events. The **Centro de Conde Duque** (⊠ Conde Duque 11, Centro ☎ 91/588–5834) is best known for its summer live music concerts (flamenco, jazz, pop), but it also has free and often interesting exhibitions. **La Casa Encendida** (⊠ Ronda de Valencia 2, Lavapiés ☎ 91/506–3875 ⊕ www.lacasaencendida.com) is an exhibition space with movie festivals, art shows, dance performances, and weekend events for children.

Film

Of Madrid's 60 movie theaters, only 12 show foreign films, generally in English, with original sound tracks and Spanish subtitles. These are listed in newspapers and in the *Guía de Ocio* under "v. o."—*versión original,* that is, undubbed. Your best bet for catching a new release is the **Ideal Yelmo Cineplex** (✉ Doctor Cortezo 6, Centro ☎ 902/220922). The excellent, classic v. o. films at the **Filmoteca Cine Doré** (✉ Santa Isabel 3, Lavapiés ☎ 91/369–1125) change daily. However, there are also good theaters around the Plaza de España. **Alphaville** (✉ Martín de los Heros 14, Plaza de España ☎ 91/559–3836) is a leading v. o. theater a block off Plaza de España. **Renoir Plaza de España** (✉ Martín de los Heros 12, Plaza de España ☎ 91/541–4100) offers v. o. films. **Princesa** (✉ Princesa 3, Plaza de España ☎ 91/541–4100) is a good option for original-version films. **Renoir Princesa** (✉ Princesa 5, Plaza de España ☎ 91/541–4100) has two theaters in the underpass below what's popularly known as Plaza de los Cubos. **Luna** (✉ Luna 2, Centro ☎ 91/522–4752) is an old staple a block off Gran Vía. The latest multiplex that opened in the city is **Verdi** (✉ Bravo Murillo 28, Quevedo ☎ 91/447–3930).

Flamenco

The best flamenco in Madrid is found at Café de Chinitas, whereas Café Central is the city's best-known jazz venue. For salsa, it's Azúcar.

Spain's best flamenco habitat is Andalusia, but if you won't be traveling south, here are a few possibilities. Note that tablaos charge around €25 to €32 for the show only (with a complimentary drink included). You can save money by dining elsewhere and arriving in time for the show. But if you want to dine at the *tablaos* anyway, note that three of them, Carboneras, Corral de la Moreriá, and Café de Chinitas, also offer a show and fixed-menu option that's worth considering.

Café de Chinitas. It's expensive, but the flamenco here is the best in Madrid. Reserve in advance; shows often sell out. There are ongoing performances starting at 10:30 PM Monday through Saturday. ✉ *Torrija 7, Ópera* ☎ *91/559–5135* ☉ *Closed Sun.*

Casa Patas. Along with tapas, this well-known space offers good, relatively authentic (according to the performers) flamenco. Prices are more reasonable than elsewhere. Shows are at 10:30 PM Monday through Thursday, and at 9 PM and midnight on Friday and Saturday. ✉ *Canizares 10, Lavapiés* ☎ *91/369–0496* ☉ *Closed Sun.*

Corral de la Morería. Dinner à la carte and well-known visiting flamenco stars accompany the resident dance troupe. Since Morería opened its doors in 1956, celebrities such as Frank Sinatra and Ava Gardner have left their autographed photos for the walls. Shows are nightly at 10 PM and midnight. ✉ *Morería 17, on C. Bailén; cross bridge over C. Segovia and turn right, Centro* ☎ *91/365–8446.*

Las Carboneras. One of Madrid's prime flamenco showcases, it rivals Casa Patas as the best option in terms of quality and price. Performing here are young and less commercial artists as well as more established stars on tour. Shows are staged at 9 PM and 10:30 PM Monday through Thursday and at 8:30 PM and 11 PM on Friday and Saturday. ✉ *Plaza del Conde de Miranda 1, Centro* ☎ *91/542–8677* ☉ *Closed Sun.*

Theater

English-language plays are rare. When they do come to town, they're staged at any of a dozen venues. One theater you won't need Spanish for is the **Teatro de la Zarzuela** (⊠ Jovellanos 4, Centro ☏ 91/524–5400), which specializes in the traditional Spanish operetta known as *zarzuela,* a kind of bawdy comedy. Calle Gran Vía has become a small reproduction of the West End and Broadway, and there you'll find popular musicals adapted for the Spanish audience, as well as some local productions. The **Teatro Español** (⊠ Príncipe 25, Santa Ana ☏ 91/360–1480) brings big leading companies from all over the world and often performs Spanish classics. The **Compañía Nacional de Teatro Clásico** (⊠ Teatro Pavón, Embajadores 9, Tirso de Molina ☏ 91/528–2819) keeps 17th-century Spanish classics alive.

Nightlife

Nightlife—or *la marcha*—reaches legendary heights in Madrid. It has been said that Madrileños rarely sleep, largely because they spend so much time in bars—not drunk, but socializing in the easy, sophisticated way that's unique to this city. This is true of old as well as young, and it's not uncommon for children to play on the sidewalks past midnight while multigenerational families and friends convene over coffee or cocktails at an outdoor café. The streets best known for their social scenes, however, do attract a younger clientele; these include Huertas, Moratín, Segovia, Victoria, and the areas around the Plaza Santa Ana and the Plaza de Anton Martín. The adventurous may want to explore the scruffier bar district around the Plaza Dos de Mayo, in the Malasaña area, where trendy, smoke-filled hangouts line both sides of Calle San Vicente Ferrer and of Calle La Palma. A few blocks east are the haunts of Chueca, where tattoo studios and street-chic boutiques break up the endless alleys of gay and lesbian bars, techno discos, and after-hours clubs.

Cabaret

Berlin Cabaret (⊠ Costanilla de San Pedro 11, Centro ☏ 91/366–2034 ☉ Closed Sun.) professes to provide cabaret as it was performed in Berlin in the '30s. Combining magic, chorus girls, and ribaldry, it draws an eccentric crowd for vintage café theater. On Friday and Saturday the fun lasts until daybreak.

Discos

Madrid's oldest and one of the hippest discos for all-night dancing to an international music mix is **El Sol** (⊠ C. Jardines 3, Centro ☏ 91/532–6490), open until 5:30 AM. There's live music around midnight Thursday through Saturday. **Joy Eslava** (⊠ C. Arenal 11, Sol ☏ 91/366–3733), a downtown disco in a converted theater, is an old standby. **Palacio de Gaviria** (⊠ Arenal 9, Sol ☏ 91/526–6069), a maze of rooms turned into a disco, is mainly for foreigners.

Pachá (⊠ Barceló 11, Centro ☏ 91/447–0128 ☉ Closed Mon.–Wed.) is always energetic. **Fortuny** (⊠ Fortuny 34, Chamberí ☏ 91/319–0588) attracts a celebrity crowd, especially in summer, when the lush outdoor patio opens. Put on your best dancing shoes: the door is ultraselective.

Salsa has become a fixture in Madrid; check out the most spectacular moves at **Azúcar** (✉ Paseo Reina Cristina 7, Atocha ☎ 91/501–6107). **Clamores** (✉ Albuquerque 14, Chamberí ☎ 91/445–7938 ☉ Closed after 11 PM Sun.) plays live music until 2:30 AM. Attracting a sophisticated crowd, **Moma** (✉ José Abascal 56, Chamberí ☎ 91/399–4830 ☉ Closed Sun.–Tues.) is a modern, chic disco decorated in lots of red and white. Dress accordingly. **Golden Boite** (✉ Duque de Sesto 54, Retiro ☎ 91/573–8775) is always hot from midnight on. For funky rhythms, try **Stella** (✉ C. Arlabán 7, Centro ☎ 91/531–6378 ☉ Closed Sun.–Wed.). On Thursday it's called Mondo (electronic and house music); on Friday and Saturday it's the Room—a wilder scene. Show up late. **Shabay** (✉ C. Miguel Ángel, 3, Chamberí ☎ 91/319—7692) rides on the ethnic wave that pervades the city, with lots of fusion music and Indian and South Asian remixes. The elegant, spacious setting is furnished with wicker seats, low tables, and plenty of candles. Flamboyant crowds show up late. Popular for its quiet summer terrace under the Puente de Segovia arches and its unbeatable electro-funk mixes, **Marula Café** (✉ C. Caños Viejos, 3, Palacio Real ⊕ www.marulacafe.com ☎ 91/366–1596) is a cleverly designed narrow space with lots of illuminated wall art.

Five minutes away from Plaza de Castilla **Liberata** (✉ C. Alberto Alcocer, 43, Chamartín ☎ No phone ☉ Closed Mon.) is the latest venue for those who like to see and be seen. With a very strict door policy, it's got two big bars, Japanese-inspired fountains, and a platform where the DJ remixes mainstream classics.

Bars & Nightclubs

Jazz, rock, flamenco, and classical music are all popular in Madrid's many small clubs.

Bar Cock. Resembling a room at some very exclusive club (with all the waiters in suits), this bar with a dark-wood interior, cathedral-like ceilings, a big chimney, two engraved columns, and large leather chairs at every table serves about 20 different cocktails (hence the name). It caters to an older, more classic crowd. ✉ *C. Reina 16, Chueca* ☎ *91/532–2826.*
Café Belén. The handful of tables here are rarely empty on the weekends, thanks to the candlelight and cozy atmosphere—it attracts a young, mixed, post-dinner crowd in the area and in search of the first drink of the night. Weekdays are mellower. ✉ *C. Belen 5, Chueca* ☎ *91/308–2747.*
Café Central. Madrid's best-known jazz venue is chic, and the musicians are often internationally known. Performances are usually from 10 PM to midnight. ✉ *Plaza de Ángel 10, Santa Ana* ☎ *91/369–4143.*
Café de la Palma. With a bar in the front, a music venue for intimate concerts, and a chill-out room in the back, and a café in the center room, this is a must if you're in the Malasaña neighborhood. ✉ *La Palma 62, Malasaña* ☎ *91/522–5031.*
Café Jazz Populart. Blues, jazz, Brazilian music, reggae, and salsa start at 11 PM. ✉ *Huertas 22, Santa Ana* ☎ *91/429–8407.*
Calle 54. It strives to unite two concepts hard to mix: good Latin jazz and good food. And although it is still working on the latter, its spa-

Summer Terraces

1

MADRID IS BLAZING hot in the late spring and summer, and Madrileños seem to have a nearly relentless yearning for nightlife. As a result, the city allows nearly 2,000 bars and restaurants to create outdoor spaces for enjoying the cool, dry summer nighttime air while sipping a beer.

For formal summer dining, we recommend some of the good hotel restaurants, most of which have private and peaceful gardens or roof terraces that avoid the street noise. Possibilities include the Ritz hotel, La Biblioteca del Santo Mauro, El Jardín de Orfila (the restaurant at the Hotel Orfila), or the roof terrace at the Hotel Urban. Two midrange restaurants with good terraces are Sacha and Pedro Larumbe—the latter's rooftop restaurant turns into one of Madrid's

most fashionable terraces at night.

If you just want to grab a bite or an early-evening drink, drop by the La Latina neighborhood, especially Plaza de la Paja or Plaza de San Andrés, across from the Church of San Andrés, or sit on any of the terraces at Plaza de Olavide, an enclave favored mostly by locals, near Malasaña and the Bilbao subway stop. Plaza Santa Ana is a pricier, more touristy alternative. Plaza Chueca, in the neighborhood of the same name, and the Mercado de Fuencarral (halfway between Gran Vía and Tribunal), the Plaza de 2 de Mayo, and the Plaza de las Comendadoras in the Malasaña neighborhood are always bustling and crowded with younger people.

The best nightlife is along the terraces on Castellana.

---

cious bottom floor is one of the best places in the north of the city to stop for a gin fizz and for good live music (concerts usually begin at 11:30 PM and are usually free). ☒ *Paseo de la Habana, 3, Chamartín* ☎ *91/214-1412* ⊕ *www.calle54.net* ☉ *Closed Sun.*

Costello. A multispace locale that combines a café and a lounge, Costello caters to a more relaxed and conversational crowd, with a bottom floor suited to partygoers with the latest in live and club music. On weekdays, it also features theater and stand-up comedy. ☒ *Caballero de Gracia 10, Sol* ☎ *91/522-1815.*

Del Diego. Arguably Madrid's trendiest cocktail bar, it's frequented by a variety of crowds from movie directors to moviegoers. ☒ *Calle de la Reina 12, Centro* ☎ *91/523-3106* ☉ *Closed Sun.*

El Barbú. The dimly lighted interior is what results when designers use rich fabrics to create a Gothic atmosphere with fetish undertones. The two levels of three different spaces covered in exposed brick and walls in earth tones can get really packed. However, there are always little nooks with small chairs with velvety embroidered cushions to escape and enjoy a refreshing cocktail. ☒ *C. Santiago 3, Ópera* ☎ *91/542-5698* ☉ *Closed Sun.*

El Clandestino. This bar-café is a hidden hot spot with a local following. Jam sessions on the bottom floor (open only from Thursday to Saturday night) alternate mellow jazz with house and ambient music. ☒ *Barquillo 34, Centro* ☎ *91/521-5563* ☉ *Closed Sun.*

El Junco. Owners turned what was just another bar into a very happening jazz venue. The live music is a plus, but what really gets the crowd going and coming back for more are the DJs that mix into the night. ⊠ *Plaza Santa Bárbara 10, Alonso Martínez* ⊕ *www.eljunco.com* ☎ *91/ 319–2081* ⊘ *Closed Sun. and Mon.*

El Viajero. The name of this trilevel café, bar, and restaurant, the top of which is an irresistible and popular terrace, means "The Traveler." It's decorated with antique knickknacks from around the world, and is painted in striking colors. ⊠ *Plaza de la Cebada 11, La Latina* ☎ *91/366–9064* ⊘ *Closed Sun. night and Mon.*

Glass Bar Urban Hotel. Madrileños finally have a place where they can have oysters and caviar at 2 AM. The bar and stools are of gray leather and set on illuminated glass floors. The M2 (Japanese melon liqueur Midori and lime syrup) is the highlight of the extensive cocktail menu. ⊠ *Carrera de San Jerónimo 34, Sol* ☎ *91/787–7770.*

Honky Tonk. This bar has live performances and is open daily 9–5 (no, not *that* 9–5). The classic night scene attracts people of all ages. ⊠ *Covarrubias 24, Chamberí* ☎ *91/445–6886.*

Jazzanova. Spacious and with a live DJ, this bar and restaurant in the Colon area is a perfect place for a professional and sophisticated crowd to go for the first drink of the night. At this relaxed lounge, you won't have to put up with a noisy crowd or elbow your way up to the bar. ⊠ *Paseo de la Castellana 8, Colon* ☎ *91/578–3487* ⊘ *No dinner Sun.*

Larios Café. Cuban restaurant, bar, and disco, this art-deco scene is a great place to sip a mojito any day of the week. The dance floor is open Thursday through Saturday night. ⊠ *Silva 4, Centro* ☎ *91/547–9394.*

Los Gabrieles. This building has remarkable tile walls—advertisements from the turn of the 20th century, when this was a high-class brothel. On the same street are other night hangouts worth a look. ⊠ *Echegaray 17, Santa Ana* ☎ *91/429–6261.*

Museo Chicote. Another landmark, recently refurbished and regaining popularity, this cocktail bar and lounge is also said to have been one of Hemingway's haunts. ⊠ *Gran Vía 12, Centro* ☎ *91/532–6737* ⊘ *Closed Sun.*

Oliver. Here you can find two bars in one: daily there's an upstairs lounge and restaurant; late at night there's a full-fledged Chueca disco in the brick-lined basement cavern. ⊠ *Almirante 12, Centro* ☎ *91/ 521–7379* ⊘ *Closed Sun. and Mon.*

Torero. Come if you think you can get in—the bouncer allows only those judged to be *gente guapa* (beautiful people) to enter. The bottom floor, open only from Thursday to Saturday night, is a huge exposed-brick, vaulted room. The upper floor is open Tuesday through Saturday. ⊠ *Cruz 26, Santa Ana* ☎ *91/523–1129* ⊘ *Closed Sun. and Mon.*

Viuda Negra. When diners at the trendy restaurant Viuda Blanca are ready to begin the night, they need not leave the premises to have a cocktail. A block from Ópera (subway stop), this bar puts interesting, sometimes avant-garde, projections on its walls and also employs a live DJ for an early-thirties crowd. ⊠ *Campomanes 6, Ópera* ☎ *91/548–7529* ⊘ *Closed Sun.*

Why not?. Long and narrow and always packed with a very local (mostly gay) crowd from the neighborhood, this is a great place to hear '70s and

'80s Spanish and American pop music. When it closes, the throng of people moves over to the even wilder Polana on C. Barbieri, which has the same owner. ✉ *C. San Bartolomé 6, Chueca* ☎ *91/523–0581.*

SPORTS & THE OUTDOORS

Bicycling

Though bicycling in the city can be a risky option because of the heavy traffic and Madrileños' disregard for regulations, the city parks and the surroundings towns are good for enjoyable rides. **Bravo Bike** (✉ Montera 25–27, Sol ☎ 91/559–5523 or 607/448440, ask for Kaspar ⊕ www. bravobike.com) is a trustworthy company that's been organizing one-day or multiday biking tours around Madrid (Toledo, Aranjuez, Chinchón, Segovia) and Spain (the pilgrimage to Santiago, the Andalucía route, and others) since 1999. They also have a guided city tour (€25) and rent bikes (€15 a day) if you're brave enough to head out on your own. The best way to contact them is by e-mail (info@bravobike.com). Another company that rents bicycles and organizes guided tours (in Madrid and all over Spain) is **Bike Spain** (✉ Carmen 17, Sol ☎ 91/522–3899, 677/ 356586, ask for Pablo ⊕ www.bikespain.info). The company charges between €15 a day for bike rentals and €75 for one-day guided trips including meals. Bike Spain also organizes the **Discover Madrid** (☎ 91/ 588–2906 Patronato de Turismo) bike tours for city hall. These take place every Saturday and are a real bargain at €9 (includes rental fee).

To go out on your own, two good alternatives are the Retiro Park and the Casa de Campo. To get to the latter, you can take your bike on the subway, but only on weekends and holidays. You must ride in the first car, and you must enter at a station where attendants are present. Get off at the Casa de Campo subway stop. There you will find a map to the *anillo verde* (green ring), a special circuit for bicycles that runs along Casa de Campo and some other nearby parks.

Another pleasant option is to get off at Lago (near the park's biggest lake), and either make your own path or go to the **Centro de Información de la Casa de Campo** (open Sun. 10 AM–2 PM, and Tues.–Sat. 10 AM–2 PM and 4 to 5, 6, 7, or 8 PM, depending on time of year). The information center, next to the lake's dock, can provide you with park and trail information.

Golf

Eleven golf courses surround Madrid, and more are on the way. The successes of Seve Ballesteros, José María Olazabal, and Sergio García have created a new surge of interest in golf in Spain. Most golf clubs require proof of club membership. **Golf Olivar de la Hinojosa** (✉ Av. Dublín s/n, Barajas ☎ 91/721–1889 ⊕ www.golfolivar.com), in Campo de las Naciones outside town, is open to the public, with two courses (one 18 holes, one 9) and golf lessons. They have a fixed all-week greens fee of €42.50. Reservations, essential on weekends, can be made up to one week in advance. **La Herrería Club** (✉ Ctra. Robledo de Chavela s/n, Escorial ☎ 91/890–5111 ⊕ www.golflaherreria.com), in San Lorenzo de Escorial, is open to the public. Their greens fee is €62.50 during the week and €108 on weekends. However, weekend spots are usually reserved for members. Playing golf at La Herrería Club's 18-hole course, in the shadow of the monolithic Monastery of San Lorenzo del Escorial, is one of Spain's great golfing experiences.

Hiking

The northern section of the region around Madrid region is lined by a mountain range, the Sierra de Guadarrama. Also running into some parts of Ávila and Segovia, the range is on its way to becoming Spain's 14th national park. Long favored by naturalists, writers (including John Dos Passos), painters, poets, and historians, it also attracts sporty Madrileños looking to distance themselves from the chaos of the capital. The Sierra's eastern border lies at Puerto de Somosierra, west of the A1 highway heading to Burgos; the little town of Robledo de Chavela, southwest of El Escorial, marks the park's western edge. Near the middle of this long stretch sprouts another branch to the northeast, giving the Sierra de Guadarrama the shape of a fork, with the Valle de Lozoya in between the fork's tines. Hiking options are nearly limitless, but two destinations stand out because of their geological importance: the Parque de la Pedriza, a massive, orangish, fancifully shaped granite landscape in the Cuenca Alta del Manzanares, and the Peñalara's alpine cirques (basins) and lakes. The Peñalara is the park's highest peak—a holdover from the ice age that created the entire range.

Aventúrate (⊠ Monte Esquinza 41, Chamberí ☎ 91/845–0931 ⊕ www. aventurate.com) specializes in organizing hikes in the Sierra de Guadarrama area and beyond. There are one-day hikes to nearby spots in the Sierra de Guadarrama every Saturday and Sunday for around €25, as well as more extensive excursions (including mountain climbing) to some of Spain's highest and more challenging peaks.

The **Arawak Viajes Madrid** (⊠ Peñuelas 12, Atocha ☎ 91/474–2524 ⊕ www.arawakviajes.com) travel agency offers three or four different one-day trips every weekend to different spots in the Madrid Sierra (and to Guadalajara or Sierra de Gredos), plus a weekend trek every month. Prices to the Sierra de Guadarrama are usually around €20 to €25. You must reserve in advance and pay within one day of making the reservation. Buses depart from Estación de Autobuses Ruiz on Ronda de Atocha 12.

Running

Your best bet for having a run is the Parque del Buen Retiro, where a path circles the park and others weave under trees and through formal gardens. The Casa de Campo is crisscrossed by numerous, sunnier trails.

Swimming

Madrid has an antidote to the dry, sometimes intense heat of the summer months—a superb system of clean, popular, well-run municipal swimming pools (admission about €4). A good option in summer is **Piscina Canal Isabel II** (⊠ Plaza Juan Zorrilla, entrance off Av. de Filipinas, Chamberí ☎ 91/533–1791). It has grass, diving boards, and a wading pool for kids.

Tennis

There are public courts at the **Instalación Deportiva Municipal Casa de Campo** (⊠ Casa de Campo s/n, Casa de Campo ☎ 91/464–9617). To get there, take the subway, the 10 line, to Lago and then walk for about five minutes. Make sure you keep the big lake on your right. There are tennis courts at **Centro de Vírgen del Puerto** (⊠ Paseo Bajo de la Vírgen del Puerto, Centro ☎ 91/366–2840), another public sports complex behind the Palacio Real. The courts are a 10- to 15-minute walk from the subway stop at Príncipe Pío.

Soccer

Fútbol is Spain's number-one sport. Madrid has four teams, Real Madrid, Atlético Madrid, Rayo Vallecano, and Getafe. The two major teams are Real Madrid and Atlético Madrid. For tickets, either call a week in advance to reserve and pick them up at the stadium or stand in line at the stadium of your choice. The **Estadio Santiago Bernabeu** (⊠ Paseo de la Castellana 140, Chamartín ☎ 91/398–4300 ⊕ www.realmadrid.es), which seats 75,000, is home to Real Madrid, winner of a staggering nine European Champion's Cups, the first in 1956. Atlético Madrid plays at the **Estadio Vicente Calderón** (⊠ Virgen del Puerto 67, Arganzuela ☎ 91/366–4707 or 91/364–0888 ⊕ www.clubatleticodemadrid.com), on the edge of the Manzanares river south of town.

Ballooning

Globos y Dirigibles Boreal (⊠ General Zabala 21, Chamartín ☎ 91/561–3968 ⊕ www.globosboreal.com) organizes one-hour balloon trips over the Madrid and Segovia regions. Trips for groups of five people or more cost €150 each: you can schedule a date and time. Otherwise, you can join one of their scheduled flights, which usually take place on weekends. Departure points are outside the city, but the company can give you a ride if you have no means of transportation. Flights last about an hour, and you need to pay in advance, either at their office or through a money transfer. Reserve ahead, because spots fill up quickly.

SHOPPING

Spain has become one of the world's centers for design of every kind. You'll have no trouble finding traditional crafts, such as ceramics, guitars, and leather goods (albeit not at countryside prices), but, at this point, the city is more like Rodeo Drive than the bargain bin. Known for contemporary furniture and decorative items as well as chic clothing, shoes, and jewelry, Spain's capital has become stiff competition for Barcelona. Keep in mind that many shops, especially those that are small and family run, close during lunch hours, on Sunday, and on Saturday afternoon. Shops generally accept most major credit cards.

Department Stores

El Corte Inglés. Spain's largest department store carries the best selection of everything, from auto parts to groceries, electronics, lingerie, and designer fashions. They also sell tickets for major sports and arts events, have their own travel agency, a restaurant (usually the building's top floor), and a great gourmet store. Madrid's biggest branch is the one on the corner of Calle Raimundo Fernández Villaverde and Castellana, which is not a central location. Try instead the one at Sol-Callao (split into three separate buildings), or the ones at Serrano or Goya (these are also in two independent buildings). ✉ *Preciados 1, 2, and 3, Sol* ☎ *91/ 379–8000, 901/122122 general information, 902/400222 ticket sales* ⊕ *www.elcorteingles.es* ✉ *Callao 2, Centro* ☎ *91/379–8000* ✉ *Goya 76 and 85, Salamanca* ☎ *91/432–9300* ✉ *Princesa 41, 47, and 56, Centro* ☎ *91/454–6000* ✉ *Serrano 47 and 52, Salamanca* ☎ *91/432– 5490* ✉ *Raimundo Fernández Villaverde 79, Chamartín* ☎ *91/418–8800.*

Mango. The Turkish brothers Isaac and Nahman Andic opened their first store in Barcelona in 1984. Two decades later Mango has stores all over the world, and the brand rivals Zara as Spain's healthiest fashion venture. Mango's target customer is the young, modern, and urban woman. In comparison with Zara, Mango has fewer formal options. ✉ *Fuencarral 70, Malasãa* ☎ *91/523–0412* ⊕ *www.mango.com* ✉ *Fuencarral 140, Bilbao* ☎ *91/445–7811* ✉ *Goya 83, Salamanca* ☎ *91/435– 3958* ✉ *Hermosilla 22, Salamanca* ☎ *91/576–8303.*

Zara. For those with young, functional, and designy tastes but slim wallets (picture hip clothes that won't last you more than one or two seasons), Zara—whose minimalist window displays are hard to miss—carries the latest looks for men, women, and children. Zara is self-made entrepreneur Amancio Ortega's textile empire flagship, which you will find all over the city. In 2003 it launched a new line, Zara Home, that sells design products for the house. Zara's clothes are considerably cheaper in Spain than in the United States or the United Kingdom. Zara has two outlet stores in Madrid—in the Gran Vía store and in Calle Carretas; the latter branch is called Lefties. If you choose to try your luck at the outlets, keep in mind that Monday and Thursday is when new deliveries arrive—and therefore the days when you have the best chance of finding good stuff. ✉ *Centro Comercial ABC, Serrano 61, Salamanca* ☎ *91/ 575–6334* ✉ *Gran Vía 34, Centro* ☎ *91/521–1283* ✉ *Velázquez 49, Salamanca* ☎ *91/575–1476* ✉ *Carretas 6, Sol* ☎ *91/522–6945* ✉ *Princesa 63, Centro* ☎ *91/543–2415* ✉ *Conde de Peñalver 4, Salamanca* ☎ *91/435–4135.*

Shopping Districts

Madrid has three main shopping areas. The first, the area that stretches from Callao to Puerta del Sol (Calle Preciados, Gran Vía on both sides of Callao, and the streets around the Puerta del Sol), includes the major department stores (El Corte Inglés and the French music-and-book chain FNAC), and popular brands such as H&M and Zara.

The second area, far more elegant and expensive, is in the eastern Salamanca district, bounded roughly by Serrano, Juan Bravo, Jorge Juan (and its blind alleys), and Velázquez; the shops on Goya extend as far as Alcalá. The streets just off the Plaza de Colón, particularly Calle Serrano and Calle Ortega y Gasset, have the widest selection of designer fashions—think Prada, Loewe, Armani, or Louis Vuitton—as well as other mainstream and popular local designers (Purificación García, Pedro del Hierro, Adolfo Domínguez, or Roberto Verino). Hidden within Calle Jorge Juan, Calle Lagasca, and Calle Claudio Coello is the widest selection of smart boutiques from renowned young Spanish designers, such as Sybilla, Josep Font, Amaya Arzuaga, and Victorio & Lucchino.

Finally, for hipper clothes, Chueca is your best stop. Calle Fuencarral, from Gran Vía to Tribunal, is the street with the most shops in this area. On Fuencarral you can find name brands such as Diesel, Gas, and Billabong, but also local brands such as Homeless, Adolfo Domínguez U (selling the Galician designer's younger collection), and Custo, as well as some makeup stores (Madame B and Mac). Less mainstream and sometimes more exciting is the selection you can find on nearby Calles Hortaleza, Almirante, and Piamonte.

Madrid's newest mall is a four-decker: the **Centro Comercial ABC** (⊠ Paseo de la Castellana 34, at Serrano 61, Salamanca), named for the daily newspaper founded on the premises in the 19th century. The building has an ornate tile facade; inside, a large café is surrounded by shops, including leather stores and hairdressers. The fourth-floor restaurant has a rooftop terrace. **El Jardín de Serrano** (⊠ Goya 6–8, next to Prada, Salamanca), is a smaller mall with an exclusive selection of high-end brands that include jewelry, fashions for men and women, and shoes.

Flea Market

On Sunday morning, Calle de Ribera de Curtidores is closed to traffic and jammed with outdoor booths selling everything under the sun—the weekly transformation into **El Rastro**. The crowds grow so thick that it takes awhile just to advance a few feet amid the hawkers and gawkers. Pickpockets abound here. Hang on to your purse and wallet, and be especially careful if you choose to bring a camera. The flea market sprawls into most of the surrounding streets, with certain areas specializing in particular products. Many of the goods are wildly overpriced. But what goods! The Rastro has everything from antique furniture to exotic parrots and cuddly puppies; from pirated cassette tapes of flamenco music to key chains emblazoned with symbols of the CNT, Spain's old anarchist trade union. Practice your Spanish by bargaining with the vendors over paintings, colorful Gypsy oxen yokes, heraldic iron gates, new and used clothes, and even hashish pipes. They may not lower their prices, but sometimes they'll throw in a handmade bracelet or a stack of postcards to sweeten the deal.

Plaza General Vara del Rey has some of the Rastro's best antiques, and the streets beyond—Calles Mira el Río Alta and Mira el Río Baja—have some truly magnificent junk and bric-a-brac. The market shuts down shortly after 2 PM, in time for a street party to start in the area known as La Latina, centered on the bar El Viajero in Plaza Humilladero.

Off the Ribera are two *galerías,* courtyards with higher-quality, higher-price antiques shops. All the shops (except for the street vendors) are open during the week.

┌── **NEED A**
│ **BREAK?** If you find yourself anywhere near the top of the Rastro, you can stop into **Bar Santurce** at C. Amazonas 14 in the neighborhood of Lavapiés. It's small, and you'll have to push your way to the counter, but it has speedy and friendly service and great sardines, spicy green peppers, and calamari.

Specialty Stores

Books

Casa del Libro (✉ Maestro Victoria 3, Centro ☎ 91/521–4898), not far from the Puerta del Sol, has an impressive collection of English-language books, including city guides and translated Spanish classics. It's also a good source for maps, cookbooks, and gifts. Its discount store around the corner, on Calle Salud 17, sells English classics. **Booksellers** (✉ José Abascal 48, Chamberí ☎ 91/442–8104), just off the upper Castellana near the Hotel Miguel Angel, has a large selection of books in English. **J&J** (✉ Espíritu Santo 47, Centro ☎ 91/521–8576), a block off San Bernardo, is a charming café and bookstore run by a woman from Alabama and her Spanish husband. The store stocks a good selection of used books in English. For travel books, including English-language books about Madrid, seek out **Deviaje** (✉ Serrano 41, Salamanca ☎ 91/577–9899 ⊕ www.deviaje.com), just blocks away from the intersection of Goya and Serrano. Established in 1950, **La Tienda Verde** (✉ Maudes 23 and 38, Chamberí ☎ 91/535–3810 ⊕ www.tiendaverde.es) is perfect for outdoor enthusiasts planning hikes, mountain-climbing expeditions, spelunking trips, and so forth; they have detailed maps and Spanish-language guidebooks.

Boutiques & Fashion

The free magazine *InfoShopping* (in English and Spanish), distributed at tourist offices and upscale hotels, is a good resource, and provides detailed lists of both young and established Spanish fashion designers, as well as major international stores.

The area with the most concentrated local fashion offering is the **Salamanca** neighborhood, especially Calles Claudio Coello, Lagasca, and the first few blocks of Serrano. There you can find a good mix of mainstream designers, small-scale exclusive boutiques, and multibrand stores. Most mainstream designer stores are located on Calle Serrano. **Adolfo Domínguez** (✉ Serrano 18 and 96, Salamanca ☎ 91/576–7053 ⊕ www.adolfodominguez.com) is a Galician designer with simple, sober, and elegant lines for both men and women. Of his eight other locations in the city, the one at Calle Fuencarral 5, a block away from Gran Vía, is geared toward a younger crowd, with more affordable and colorful clothes. Also popular is the Madrileño designer **Pedro del Hierro** (✉ Serrano 24 and 63, Salamanca ☎ 91/575–6906 ⊕ www.pedrodelhierro.com), who has built himself a good reputation for his sophisticated but uncomplicated clothes for both sexes.

Purificación García (✉ Serrano 28 and 92, Salamanca ☎ 91/435–8013 ⊕ www.purificaciongarcia.es) is also a good choice for women searching for contemporary all-day wear. The three young female designers working for **Homeless** (✉ Serrano 16, Salamanca ☎ 91/781–0612

✉ Fuencarral 16, Chueca ☎ 91/524–1728 ⊕ www.hosshomeless.com) and their hip and fashionable clothes are gaining a growing acceptance with younger crowds. **Trucco** (✉ Claudio Coello 46, Salamanca ☎ 91/575–7997 ✉ Goya 75, Salamanca ☎ 91/432–0208 ✉ Serrano 61, ABC Serrano, Salamanca ☎ 91/576–8449 ⊕ www.trucco.es) caters to the young with seductive outfits at very reasonable prices.

The top stores for non-Spanish fashions are mostly scattered along Ortega y Gasset, between Nuñez de Balboa and Serrano, but if you want the more exclusive of the local brands, head to the smaller designer shops unfolding along Calles Claudio Coello, Jorge Juan, and Lagasca. Start the tour on Calle Jorge Juan and its alleys, and then move northward along Claudio Coello and Lagasca toward the core of the Salamanca district. **Sybilla** (✉ Jorge Juan 12, at end of one of the two cul-de-sacs, Salamanca ☎ 91/578–1322) is the studio of Spain's best-known female designer. Her fluid dresses and hand-knit sweaters have made her a favorite with Danish supermodel Helena Christensen. Next to Sybilla is **Jocomomola** (✉ Jorge Juan 12, Salamanca ☎ 91/575–0005 ⊕ www. jocomomola.com), which happens to be Sybilla's younger and more affordable second brand. There you will find plenty of informal and provocative colorful pieces as well as some accessories. Across from Sybilla is **Roberto Torretta** (✉ Jorge Juan 12, at the end of one of the two cul-de-sacs, Salamanca ☎ 91/435–7989), another designer with a celebrity following and a great talent for mixing materials.

Alma Aguilar (✉ Jorge Juan 12, Salamanca ☎ 91/577–6698) is known for using natural and prime fabrics (silks, cashmere, wool, crepe), and for her small dresses and romantic and feminine coats. For shoes to excite even the most jaded, drop by the small **Columela** (✉ Columela 6, Salamanca ☎ 91/435–1925). You won't find Jimmy Choos or Manolo Blahniks here, but rather a more personal selection: Italy's Trans-parents, France's L'Autre Chose, America's Marc Jacobs, local brands such as Juan Antonio López and Maloles, and shoes made in Italy expressly for the store.

Young designers **Carmen March y Juanjo Oliva** (✉ Nuñez de Balboa 9, 1st fl. right, Salamanca ☎ 91/426–1433) have a unique business model for their showroom and workshop. They have a good selection of draperies, silks, gauzes, tulles, and printed fabrics that they cut to perfectly fit the customer's figure. They also carry a certain number of shoes, including the famous Laetitia's ballerina-style slippers.

Drapes, lines, ribbons, and polka dots are some of the trademarks of **Amaya Arzuaga** (✉Lagasca 50, Salamanca ☎91/426–2815) and its highly elaborate—yet simple-looking—glamorous party dresses. A men's collection is downstairs. **Ángel Schlesser** (✉ Don Ramón de la Cruz 2, Salamanca ☎ 91/575–5574 ✉ Claudio Coello 46, Salamanca ☎ 91/435–4869) sells both casual wear and formal wear with a great attention to detail—his clothes usually have gathers, or small flounces—and with colors aimed at urban women in their thirties and forties. His store on Claudio Coello is an outlet where you can find items from former collections at a reduced price.

Young and highly praised Catalonian designer **Josep Font** (⊠ Don Ramón de la Cruz 51, Salamanca ☎ 91/575–9716) sells his seductive clothes a few blocks from the customary shopping route in the Salamanca neighborhood. Worth the detour, his clothes are distinctive and colorful, with original shapes and small, subtle touches such as ribbons or flounces that act as the designer's signature. The Gallician designer **Kina Fernández** (⊠ Claudio Coello 75, Salamanca ☎ 91/426–2420) has built a name for herself during the last three decades for clothes that are multipurpose, feminine, and very figure conscious. At **Victorio & Lucchino** (⊠ Lagasca 75, Salamanca ☎ 91/431–8786 ⊕ www.victorioylucchino. com) you can find sophisticated party dresses (many with characteristic Spanish features) in materials such as gauze, silk, or velvet, as well as more casual wear and a popular line of jewelry and accessories.

Brothers Custodio and David Dalmau are the creative force behind the success of **Custo** (⊠ Claudio Coello 91, Salamanca ☎ 91/578–1322 ⊠ Fuencarral 29, Chueca ⊕ www.custo-barcelona.com ☎ 91/360–4636), whose eye-catching T-shirts can be found in the closets of showbiz stars such as Madonna or Julia Roberts. They have expanded their collection to incorporate pants, dresses, and accessories, never relinquishing the traits that have made them famous: bold colors and striking graphic designs.

If you're on a tight schedule, dropping by some of the multibrand fashion shops in the neighborhood may save you from a headache. **Nac** (⊠ Génova 17, Alonso Martínez ☎ 91/310–6050 ⊠ Conde de Aranda 6, Salamanca ☎ 91/431–2515) has a good selection of Spanish designer brands (Antonio Miró, Homeless, Josep Font, Jocomomola, and Ailanto). The store on Calle Génova is the biggest among the four they have in Madrid. **A quemarropa** (⊠ Lagasca 58, Salamanca ☎ 91/435–7264) sells very informal clothes for young and modern women from French and Italian designers such as Patrizia Pepe or Et-Vous, and from some Spanish ones such as Masscob. **Bazaar** (⊠ Claudio Coello 88, Salamanca ☎ 91/426–0585) is a charming store that specializes in French and Italian designers and caters to a romantic and casual yet sophisticated woman. Some of the brands they sell are Etoile, Paul & Joe, Antik Batik, and Vanessa Bruno.

Another area that can provide a greatly satisfying shopping experience is **Chueca,** the trapezoidal neighborhood that's roughly contained by Calles Génova and Sagasta to the north, Fuencarral on the west, Gran Vía and Alcalá to the south, and Paseo de Recoletos to the east. Chueca shelters some local name brands (Homeless, Adolfo Domínguez, and Mango) on Calle Fuencarral, and also has a multifloor and multistore market (Mercado de Fuencarral) selling modern outfits for younger crowds at No. 45 on the same street. Prominent designer **Jesús del Pozo** (⊠ Almirante 9, Salamanca ☎ 91/531–3646 ⊕ www.jesusdelpozo.com) has clothes for both sexes. It's an excellent, if pricey, place to try on some classic Spanish style. Chueca's trademark are its multibrand boutiques and the small multibrand fashion shops, often managed by eccentric and outspoken characters. A good example of this is **H.A.N.D** (⊠ Hortaleza 26, Chueca ☎ 91/521–5152), a cozy, tasteful store owned by two

Frenchmen, Stephan and Thierry. They specialize in feminine, colorful, and young French prêt-à-porter designers (Stella Forest, La Petite, Tara Jarmon). The highly energetic owner of **Próxima Parada** (✉ Piamonte 25, Chueca ☎ 91/310–3421) enthusiastically digs into racks looking for daring garments from Spanish designers in her quest to quickly redefine and modernize her customers' look. The store also sells some original clothespins made by art-school students. **Momo** (✉ Almirante 8, Chueca ☎ 91/521–5876 ✉ Jorge Juan 14, Salamanca ☎ 91/577–0704) sells daily wear and fancier nighttime outfits from Spanish and other European designers. **Uno de 50** (✉ Barquillo 41, Chueca ☎ 91/308–2953) carries original, youngish, and inexpensive (all pieces less than €200) costume jewelry (mostly made in leather and a silver-plated tin alloy) and accessories by Spanish designer Concha Díaz del Río. **L'Habilleur** (✉ Plaza de Chueca 8, Chueca ☎ 91/531–3222) is a fancy outlet selling samples and end-of-season designer clothes at a large discount. At **Ensánchez** (✉ Argensola 12, Chueca ☎ 91/319–5850) sister-owners Nuria and Marta Sánchez sell highly original and unique accessories, especially handbags, scarves, and jewelry, from local and international designers. A block west of Calle Fuencarral, on a narrow short street, is **The Deli Room** (✉ Santa Bárbara 4, Malasaña ☎ 91/521–1983), a boutique with funky clothes from young Spanish designers (Josep Font, Ailanto, Miriam Orcaiz, and others).

The area around **Sol** is more mainstream. However, there are some interesting isolated stops such as **Seseña** (✉ De la Cruz 23, Sol ☎ 91/531–6840), which since the turn of the 20th century has outfitted international celebrities in wool and velvet capes, some lined with red satin.

Ceramics

Antigua Casa Talavera (✉ Isabel la Católica 2, Centro ☎ 91/547–3417) is the best of Madrid's many ceramics shops. Despite the name, the finest ware sold here is from Manises, near Valencia, but the blue-and-yellow Talavera ceramics are also excellent. **Cántaro** (✉ Flor Baja 8, Centro ☎ 91/547–9514) sells traditional handmade ceramics and pottery. **Cerámica El Alfar** (✉ Claudio Coello 112, Salamanca ☎ 91/411–3587) has pottery from around Spain. **Sagardelos** (✉ Zurbano 46, Chamberí ☎ 91/310–4830), specializing in modern Spanish ceramics from Galicia, has breakfast sets, coffeepots, and objets d'art.

Crafts & Design

Casa Julia (✉ Almirante 1, Centro ☎ 91/522–0270) is an artistic showcase, with two floors of tasteful antiques, paintings by up-and-coming artists, and furniture in experimental designs. It's a great place to hunt for nontraditional souvenirs. **El Arco** (✉ Plaza Mayor 9, Centro ☎ 91/365–2680) has contemporary handicrafts from all over Spain, including modern ceramics, handblown glassware, jewelry, and leather items.

Fans

Casa de Diego (✉ Puerta del Sol 12, Sol ☎ 91/522–6643 ⊕ www.casadediego.net), established in 1853, manufactures fans, umbrellas, and classic Spanish walking sticks with ornamented silver handles and also sells traditional Spanish ornamental combs, mantillas, and castanets. The

British royal family buys autograph fans here—white kidskin fans for signing on special occasions.

Food & Wine

The Club Gourmet sections in stores sell Spanish wines, olive oils, and food. In the middle of Salamanca's shopping area you can find **Mantequerías Bravo** (✉ C. Ayala 24, Salamanca ☎ 91/576–7641), which has Spanish wines, olive oils, cheeses, and hams. You can find more than 120 different cheeses from all over Spain as well as almost 300 others from nearby countries such as France, Portugal, Italy, or Holland at **Poncelet** (✉ Argensola 27, Alonso Martínez ☎ 91/308–0221 ⊕ www.poncelet. es). Marmalades, utensils, wines, and other items to help you savor your cheese are also available. **Lavinia** (✉ José Ortega y Gasset 16, Salamanca ☎ 91/426–0604 ⊕ www.lavinia.es) claims to be the largest wine store in Europe. It has a large selection of bottles, books, and bar accessories. The upscale chain **Mallorca** (✉ Velázquez 59, Salamanca ☎ 91/431–9909 ✉ Serrano 6, Salamanca ☎ 91/577–1859 ✉ Centro Comercial, Goya 6, Salamanca ☎ 91/431–5555) sells prepared meals, cocktail canapés, chocolates, and wines, and has tapas counters.

Just across from Los Gabrieles, behind Plaza Santa Ana, **Mariano Aguado** (✉ C. Echegaray 19, Santa Ana ☎ 91/429–6088) is a charming 150-year-old wine store with a broad range of wines and fine spirits. The traditional food store **Gonzalez** (✉ León 12, Santa Ana ☎ 91/4295618) holds a secret in back: a cozy and well-hidden bar where you can sample most of the fare they sell: canned asparagus; olive oil; honey; cold cuts; smoked anchovies, salmon, and other fish; and a good selection of Spanish cheeses and local wines. They also serve good, inexpensive breakfasts. Named after the current owner, the liquor store **David Cabello** (✉ Cervantes 6, Santa Ana ☎ 91/4295230) has been in the family for more than 100 years. It's rustic and a bit dusty, and looks like a warehouse rather than a shop, but David knows what he's selling. Head here for a good selection of Rioja wines (some dating as far back as 1920) and local liqueurs, including anisettes and pacharan, a fruity liquor made with sloes.

Hats

Founded in 1894, **Casa Yustas** (✉ Plaza Mayor 30, Sol ☎ 91/366–5084) has headgear ranging from the old three-corner, patent-leather hats of the Guardia Civil to fashionable ladies' hats to Basque berets to black Andalusian *sombreros de mayoral*. Designed as hands-free umbrellas for the rainy Cantabrian coast, Basque berets are much wider than those worn by the French and make excellent gifts.

Leather Goods

On a street full of bargain shoe stores (*muestrarios*), **Caligae** (✉ Augusto Figueroa 18 and 27, Chueca ☎ 91/531–5343) is probably the best of the bunch. Posh **Loewe** (✉ Serrano 26 and 34, Salamanca ☎ 91/577–6056 ✉ Gran Vía 8, Centro ☎ 91/532–7024 ✉ Westin Palace Hotel, Centro ☎ 91/429–8530 ⊕ www.loewe.es) carries high-quality designer purses, accessories, and clothing made of butter-soft leather in dyed, jewel-like colors. The store on Serrano 26 displays the women's collection; items for men are a block away, on Serrano 34. Prices can hit the stratosphere. The owners of **Boxcalf** (✉ Jorge Juan 34, Salamanca ☎ 91/531–5343), on the corner of one of Calle Jorge Juan's alleys, sell exclusive suede, nappa, and leather coats for women, as well as accessories, made in Majorca.

Music

José Ramírez (✉ C. de la Paz 8, Centro ☎ 91/531–4229) has provided Spain and the rest of the world with guitars since 1882, and his store includes a museum of antique instruments. Prices for new ones start at €103 for children and €125 for adults, though some of their top concert models easily break the €10,000 mark. **Percusión Campos** (✉ Olivar 36, Lavapiés ☎ 91/539–2178) is an easy-to-miss percussion shop/workshop where the young Canarian Pedro Navarro crafts his own *cajones flamencos* or flamenco box drums that are greatly appreciated among professionals. Prices range between €120 and €250 and vary according to the quality of woods used. **Real Música** (✉ Carlos III 1, Centro ☎ 91/540–1672), around the corner from the Teatro Real, is a music lover's dream, with books, CDs, sheet music, memorabilia, guitars, and a knowledgeable staff.

SIDE TRIPS

El Escorial

⑥⓪ *50 km (31 mi) northwest of Madrid.*

Felipe II was one of history's most deeply religious and forbidding monarchs—not to mention one of its most powerful—and the great granite monastery that he had constructed in a remarkable 21 years (1563–84) is an enduring testament to his character. Outside Madrid in the foothills of the Sierra de Guadarrama, the **Real Monasterio de San Lorenzo de El Escorial** (Royal Monastery of St. Lawrence of Escorial) is severe, rectilinear, and unforgiving—one of the most gigantic yet simple architectural monuments on the Iberian Peninsula.

Felipe built the monastery in the village of San Lorenzo de El Escorial to commemorate Spain's crushing victory over the French at Saint-Quentin on August 10, 1557, and as a final resting place for his all-powerful father, the Holy Roman Emperor Carlos V. He filled the place with treasures as he ruled the largest empire the world has ever seen, knowing all the while that a marble coffin awaited him in the pantheon deep below. The building's vast rectangle, encompassing 16 courts, is modeled on the red-hot grille upon which St. Lawrence was martyred—appropriate enough, since August 10 was that saint's day. (It's also said that Felipe's troops accidentally destroyed a church dedicated to St. Lawrence during the battle and sought to make amends).

El Escorial is easily reached by car, train, bus, or organized tour from Madrid. If you plan on taking public transportation, the bus is probably the best alternative. Herranz's Lines 661 (through Galapagar) and 664 (through Guadarrama) depart a few times every hour (they run less frequently on the weekends) from bay number 3 at the *Intercambiador*

Side Trips
from Madrid

(station) at Moncloa. The 50-minute ride leaves you within a five-minute walk of the monastery.

You can also take the *cercanías C-8a* (commuter train C-8a) from either Atocha or Chamartín. However, trains run less frequently than the buses and stop at the town of El Escorial, from where you must either take Bus L-4 (also run by Herranz) to San Lorenzo de El Escorial (where the monastery is) or take a strenuous, long walk uphill. To get to the **local tourist office** (⌧ Calle Grimaldi 2 ☎ 91/890–5313), cross the arch that's across from the visitors' entrance to the monastery. The building and its adjuncts—a palace, museum, church, and more—can take hours or even days to tour. Easter Sunday's candlelight midnight Mass draws crowds, as does the summer tourist season.

The monastery was begun by Juan Bautista de Toledo but finished in 1584 by Juan de Herrera, who would eventually give his name to a major Spanish architectural school. It was completed just in time for Felipe to die here, gangrenous and tortured by the gout that had plagued him for years, in the tiny, sparsely furnished bedroom that resembled a monk's cell more than the resting place of a great monarch. It's in this bedroom—which looks out, through a private entrance, into the royal chapel—that you most appreciate the man's spartan nature. Spain's later Bourbon kings, such as Carlos III and Carlos IV, had clearly different tastes, and their apartments, connected to Felipe's by the Hall of Battles, and which can be visited only with an appointment, are far more luxurious.

Perhaps the most interesting part of the entire Escorial is the **Panteón de los Reyes** (Royal Pantheon), a baroque construction room from the 17th century that contains the body of every king since Carlos I except three—Felipe V (buried at La Granja), Ferdinand VI (in Madrid), and Amadeus of Savoy (in Italy). The body of Alfonso XIII, who died in Rome in 1941, was brought to El Escorial in January 1980. The rulers' bodies lie in 26 sumptuous marble-and-bronze sarcophagi that line the walls (three of which are empty, awaiting future rulers). Only those queens who bore sons later crowned lie in the same crypt; the others, along with royal sons and daughters who never ruled, lie nearby, in the **Panteón de los Infantes** built during the reign of Elizabeth II in the third quarter of the 19th century. Many of the royal children are in a single circular tomb made of Carrara marble.

Another highlight is the monastery's surprisingly lavish and colorful **library,** with ceiling paintings by Michelangelo disciple Pellegrino Tibaldi (1527–96). The imposing austerity of El Escorial's facades makes this chromatic explosion especially powerful; try to save it for last. The library houses 50,000 rare manuscripts, codices, and ancient books, including the diary of St. Teresa of Ávila and the gold-lettered, illuminated Codex Aureus. Tapestries woven from cartoons by Goya, Rubens, and El Greco cover almost every inch of wall space in huge sections of the building, and extraordinary canvases by Velázquez, El Greco, David, Ribera, Tintoretto, Rubens, and other masters, collected from around the monastery, are displayed in the **Museos Nuevos** (New Museums). In the **basilica,** don't miss the fresco above the choir, depicting heaven, or Titian's fresco *The Martyrdom of St. Lawrence,* which shows the saint being roasted alive. ⊠ *San Lorenzo de El Escorial* ☎ *91/890–5904 or 91/890–5905* ⌨ *General admission €8; without Panteón, or after 4:30 €7; with guided tour €9* ☉ *Apr.–Sept., Tues.–Sun. 10–6; Oct.–Mar., Tues.–Sun. 10–5.*

Where to Eat

$$$–$$$$　✕ **Charolés.** Some go to El Escorial for the monastery, and others go for Charolés. It's a landmark that attracts a crowd of its own for its noble bearing (thick stone walls and vaulted ceilings, wooden beams and floors, stuffy service), its summer terrace a block from the monastery, and its succulent dishes such as the heavy beans with clams or mushrooms, and the red and game meats served grilled or in stews. It has an extensive wine menu generous in Riojas and Riberas del Duero, and serves a four-course mammoth *cocido* (broth, chickpeas, meats, and in this case, also a salad) on Wednesday and Friday that tests the endurance of even those with the heartiest appetite. ⊠ *Floridablanca 24* ☎ *91/890–5975* ▤ *AE, DC, MC, V.*

$$　✕ **La Cañada Real.** After visiting the massive monastery, this little restaurant is welcoming and cozy. It has fewer than 10 tables with sketches of bullfighters on the walls, antique furniture, and a laid-back crowd. The menu includes a good selection of wines, grilled meats, salads, and hearty

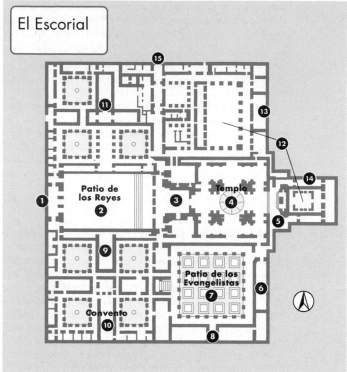

stews. The apple tart is a must for rounding off any meal. ⊠ *Floridablanca 30* ☎ *91/890–2703* ▤ *MC, V* ⊘ *No dinner Sun. and Mon.*

$$ ✕ **La Horizontal.** Away from town and surrounded by trees in what used to be a mountain cabin, this family-oriented restaurant is coveted by Madrileños who come here to enjoy the terrace in the summer and the cozy bar area with a fireplace in the winter. It has a good selection of fish and rice dishes, but the meats and seasonal plates are what draw the large following. Take Paseo Juan de Borbón, which surrounds the monastery, exit through the arches, and pass the *casita del infante* (Prince's Quarters) on your way up to the Monte Abantos, or get a cab at the taxi station on Calle Floridablanca. ⊠ *Camino Horizontal s/n* ☎ *91/890–3811* ▤ *AE, MC, V* ⊘ *No dinner Mon.–Wed. Nov.–Mar.*

Valle de los Caídos

61   *13 km (8 mi) north of El Escorial on C600.*

Ranked as a not-to-be-missed visit until the death of Generalísimo Francisco Franco in 1975, this massive monument to fascism's victory over democracy (religion's victory over communism to some) in the 1936–39 Spanish civil war has become something of an anachronism in the modern democratic Spain of today. Now relegated to a rallying point for the extreme right on key dates, such as the July 18 commemoration of the military uprising of 1936 or the November 20 death of Franco, the Valley of the Fallen is just a few minutes north of El Escorial. A lovely pine forest leads up to a massive basilica carved out of a solid granite mountain. Topped with a cross nearly 500 feet high (accessible by elevator), the basilica holds the tombs of both General Franco and José Antonio Primo de Rivera, founder of the fascist Spanish Falange, but also the bodies of nearly 34,000 Spaniards (of both sides) who died during the civil war, and whose remains were removed from communal graves and buried there between 1959 and 1983.

The monument was built with the forced labor of postwar Republican prisoners and dedicated, rather disingenuously, to all who died in the three-year conflict. Tapestries of the Apocalypse add to the terrifying air inside as every footstep resounds off the polished marble floors and stone walls. An eerie midnight Mass is held here on Easter Sunday, the granite peak lighted by candlelight.

To get here by public transportation, take the 3:15 PM bus from the Herranz station at San Lorenzo de El Escorial. The bus makes a return drive at 5:30 (the bus plus the visit is €8). If you go by car, note that the adjacent Benedictine monastery has a *hospedería* (guesthouse) and a restaurant serving good, inexpensive food. ☎ *91/890–5611* ✉ *Basilica €5; combined with a guided tour of El Escorial €10; without a guided tour €8.50* ⊙ *Apr.–Sept., Tues.–Sun. 10–6; Oct.–Mar., Tues.–Sun. 10–5.*

Chinchón

🔟 *54 km (33 mi) southeast of Madrid, A-3 on M-311.*

A true Castilian town, the village of Chinchón seems a good four centuries removed. It makes an ideal day trip, especially if you save time for lunch at one of its many rustic restaurants; the only problem is that swarms of Madrileños have the same idea, so it's often hard to get a table at lunchtime on weekends.

The high point of Chinchón is its charming **Plaza Mayor,** an uneven circle of ancient three- and four-story houses embellished with wooden balconies resting on granite columns. It's something like an open-air Elizabethan theater, but with a Spanish flavor—in fact, the entire plaza is converted to a bullring from time to time, with temporary bleachers erected in the center and seats on the privately owned balconies rented out for splendid views. (Tickets for these rare fights are hard to come by.)

The commanding **Iglesia de la Asunción** (Church of the Assumption), overlooking the plaza, is known for its Goya mural, *The Assumption of the Virgin.*

Along the M300 near the A-3 highway, you'll pass through the **Valle del Jarama,** scene of one of the bloodiest battles of the Spanish civil war. American volunteers in the Abraham Lincoln Brigade, which fought with the democratically elected Spanish Republican government against Franco's military insurgency, were mauled here in a baptism of fire. Folk singer Pete Seeger immortalized the battle with "There's a valley in Spain called Jarama . . ." The trenches are still visible, and bits of rusty military hardware can still be found in the fields.

Where to Eat

The town's arcaded plaza is ringed by charming balconied restaurants serving hearty Castilian fare, particularly roasts and charcoal-grilled meat. Wherever you dine, try the local *anís,* a licorice-flavor spirit; and if you come to Chinchón in April, look for merriment occasioned by the Fiesta del Anís y del Vino (Anise and Wine Festival). On winter weekends, Madrileños come in droves for the superb cocido, garlic soup, suckling pig, and roasted lamb at the **Parador de Chinchón** (⊠ Av. Generalísimo 1 ☎ 91/894–0836). Expect to pay €50 or more for a full meal, although there is also a €28 fixed-price menu (wine not included). **Mesón de la Virreina** (⊠ Plaza Mayor 28 ☎ 91/894–0015), on the square's northeast corner, is a perfect perch for sipping gazpacho or a glass of Chinchón anís. A meal runs about €20 to €30. Call ahead for a table at **Café de la Iberia** (⊠ Plaza Mayor 17 ☎ 91/894–0998), which has a much-in-demand balcony overlooking the plaza as well as a cozy interior. For around €30 to €35 you can order two dishes, dessert, and water (or the house wine). **Mesón Las Cuevas del Vino** (⊠ Benito Hortelano 13 ☎ 91/894–0285) is a rambling tavern with roaring fireplaces and immense antique wine and olive oil amphoras scattered around a giant olive press. A complete meal (two dishes, dessert, plus water or the house wine) is around €30 to €35. An affordable option is **El Rincón de Pedro** (⊠ Jose Antonio 30 ☎ 91/893–5002), which has an inexpensive daily fixed-price lunch menu, and also serves tapas and sandwiches.

Monasterio de El Paular & Lozoya Valley

63 *100 km (62 mi) north of Madrid.*

Rising from Spain's great central *meseta* (plain), the Sierra de Guadarrama looms northwest of Madrid like a dark, jagged shield separating Old and New Castile. Snowcapped for much of the year, the mountains are indeed rough hewn in many spots, particularly on their northern face, but there is a dramatic exception—the Lozoya Valley.

About 100 km (62 mi) north of the capital, this valley of pines, poplars, and babbling brooks is a cool, green retreat from the often searing heat of the plain. Madrileños come here for a picnic or a simple drive, rarely sharing the space with foreign travelers, to whom the area is virtually unknown.

You need a car to make this trip, and the drive is a pleasant one. Take the A6 northwest from Madrid and exit at signs for the Navacerrada Pass on the N601. As you climb toward the 6,100-foot mountain pass, you come to a road bearing to the left toward Cercedilla. (This little village, a popular base for hikes, is also accessible by train.) Just above Cercedilla, an old Roman road leads up to the ridge of the Guadarrama, where an ancient fountain, known as Fuenfría, for a long time produced the spring water that fed the Roman aqueduct of Segovia. The path traced by this cobble road is very close to the route Hemingway has his hero Robert Jordan take in *For Whom the Bell Tolls* and eventually takes you near the bridge that Jordan blows up in the novel. On the right is the exit for Navacerrada, a mountain village with a nice main plaza whose terraces get crowded during summer weekends with locals sipping beer and having tapas.

If you continue past the Cercedilla road, you come to a ski resort at the highest point of the Navacerrada Pass. Take a right here on M604 and follow the ridge of the mountains for a few miles before descending into the **Lozoya Valley**. The valley is filled with picnic spots along the Lozoya River, including several campgrounds. Across the road from the monastery is the **Centro de Educación Ambiental Puente del Perdón** (☎ 91/869–1757 ☾ Daily 10–6), which provides information on the area, including some lodging and eating options in Rascafría and nearby villages, and suggestions for interesting treks—one of the most beautiful is a route that takes you to La cascada del Purgatorio, Purgatory Falls. Next to the center there's an arboretum, El arboreto Giner de los Ríos, worth visiting. To end the excursion, take M604 north a few miles to Rascafría, and then turn right on a smaller road marked as Miraflores de la Sierra. In that town turn right again, following signs for Colmenar Viejo, and then pick up a short expressway back to Madrid.

Built by King Juan I in 1390, **Monasterio de El Paular** (☎ 91/869–1425) was the first Carthusian monastery in Castile, but was plundered five centuries later with the Disentailment of 1836, when the religious organizations' art treasures were taken by the state and its terrains and constructions auctioned. The state repurchased the monastery (at a much higher price) in two phases, one in 1874 and the other one in 1936, right before the beginning of the civil war. The winner of this last conflict, Francisco Franco, himself a devout Catholic, decided in 1948 to have a Benedictine monastery in Madrid, and nine years later (and 119 years after the last Carthusian left the building) the first monks arrived in El Paular. Nowadays fewer than a dozen Benedictine monks still live here, living and praying exactly as their predecessors did centuries ago. Tours (in Spanish only and conducted by one of the monks) are given Monday to Saturday at noon, 1, and 5 (on Thursday there's no 5 PM tour); Sunday tours are at 1, 4, and 5 from October through April and at 1, 5, and 6 from May through September. If you happen to get there on a Sunday, don't miss the noon Mass. You'll have the privilege of listening to the monks' Gregorian chants. The monastery is on your left as you approach the floor of the Lozoya Valley.

Attached to the monastery, the **Hotel Santa María de El Paular** (☎ 91/ 869–1011 ☏ 91/869–1006 ⊕ www.hotelsantamariapaular.com) is a cozy mountain hotel run by the same Westin chain that owns Madrid's Palace Hotel. The hotel has two good restaurants: Dom Lope, open daily and specializing in traditional Spanish food, and Trastámara, open weekends at lunch for great roasted lamb and suckling pig.

MADRID ESSENTIALS

To research prices, get advice from other travelers, and book travel arrangements, visit www.fodors.com.

Transportation

BY AIR

Madrid is served by Madrid Barajas Airport, 12 km (7 mi) east of the city.

Several major airlines have regular flights from the United States, and others serve London and other European capitals daily. In February 2006, the culmination of a 10-year project produced a fourth terminal (T-4), almost doubling the airport's capacity to 70 million passengers a year. This terminal handles flights from 32 companies, including Aer Lingus, American Airlines, British Airways, Iberia, and Virgin Express. All other American or British airlines depart from and arrive at Terminal 1. The four terminals are connected by a bus service *lanzadera,* which departs every three minutes and gets from Terminal 1 to Terminal 4 in 10 minutes. With the exception of those connecting in Madrid and Barcelona, local flights tend to be expensive. There are four airlines covering this route (Iberia, Air Europa, Spanair, and Vueling), and if you buy a ticket in advance, you can fly to Barcelona for almost the same price as the train or even the bus—there are also sometimes good last-minute air deals.

Spanair usually has the best discounts. Internet flight aggregators such as ⊕ www.edreams.com or ⊕ www.terminala.com can help you get the best price for local flights. Note that some of the local carriers have strict carry-on luggage limits. Shopping among Madrid travel agencies will probably get you a lower fare than those available abroad, especially to and from Great Britain.

AIRPORT TRANSFERS The fastest transfer way to get to terminals 1, 2, and 3 is the subway line number 8 (*Línea 8*). Terminal 4 will not be connected by subway before spring 2007. At the time of this writing, to get to T-4, take subway Line 8 to Barajas (the town, not the airport), and from there take the special bus service to the terminal. The metro runs every few minutes (daily from 6:30 AM to 1 AM) between Nuevos Ministerios (where you can check your luggage) and Barajas Airport; it costs €1 and takes about 15 to 20 minutes.

For a mere €1 there's a convenient bus to Avenida de América, where you can catch the subway or a taxi to your hotel. From Avenida de América you can also take Bus 204, which takes you straight to T-4, and Bus 200, which takes you to the other three terminals. Buses leave every 15 minutes between 5:20 AM and 11:30 PM (slightly less often very early or late in the day).

In bad traffic, the 15-minute taxi ride to Madrid can take the better part of an hour, but it makes sense if you have a lot of luggage. Taxis normally wait outside the airport terminal near the clearly marked bus stop; expect to pay up to €22, more in heavy traffic (and more from Terminal 4, which is farther out), including a surcharge that goes up each year

1

(was €4.50 in 2006). Make sure the driver is on the meter—off-the-meter "deals" will surely cost you more. Finally, some hotels offer shuttle service in vans; check with yours when you reserve.

⑦ Aeropuerto de Madrid Barajas ☎ 902/353570 ⊕ www.aena.es.

⑦ Carriers Air Europa ☎ 902/401501 ⊕ www.air-europa.com. **Iberia** ☎ 902/400500 ⊕ www.iberia.com. **Spanair** ☎ 902/131415 ⊕ www.spanair.es. **Vueling** ☎ 902/333933 ⊕ www.vueling.com.

BY BIKE

Bicycle travel in Madrid is notably absent, perhaps because traffic is too intense or because bicycles don't make enough noise to stand out from the rest of the din. In any case, it's not a good idea.

BY BUS

Madrid has no central bus station; buses are generally less popular than trains (though they can be faster). Most of southern and eastern Spain (including Toledo) is served by the Estación del Sur. From the Estación de Avenida de América two companies, Continental Auto and Alsa (which also has buses departing from the south station), serve mostly the north and the east, respectively. Alsa, for instance, runs two buses to Barcelona daily from Estación del Sur, and almost 20 from Avenida de América. Buses for much of the rest of the peninsula, including Cuenca, Extremadura, Salamanca, and Valencia, depart from the Auto Res station.

Estación de Avenida de América and Estación del Sur have subway stops (Avenida de América and Méndez Álvaro) that leave you right at the station. The Auto Res station is within a two-minute walk of the closer subway stop. If you intend to go to Segovia, take the subway to the Príncipe Pío stop, get the Paseo de la Florida exit and walk on the left-hand side of the street until you get to La Sepulvedana. There are several smaller stations, however, so inquire at travel agencies for the one serving your destination.

The La Sepulvedana bus company serves Segovia, Ávila (the Larrea bus company, with buses that depart from the Estación del Sur, also serves this destination), and La Granja. Herranz goes to El Escorial (it leaves from the Intercambiador de Moncloa; that is, the Moncloa bus station) and from there to the Valle de los Caídos. La Veloz has service to Chinchón, and Aisa goes to Aranjuez and from there to Chinchón.

Red city buses run from about 6 AM to 11:30 PM and cost €1 per ride. After midnight, buses called *búhos* ("night owls") run out to the suburbs from Plaza de Cibeles for the same price. Signs at every stop list all other stops by street name, but they're hard to comprehend if you don't know the city well. Pick up a free route map from the transportation authority's (EMT) kiosks on the Plaza de Cibeles or the Puerta del Sol, where you can also buy a 10-ride ticket called a Metrobus (€6.15) that's also valid for the subway. If you speak Spanish, call for information (☎ 902/507850). Drivers will generally make change for anything up to a €10 note. If you've bought a 10-ride ticket, step just behind the driver and insert it in the ticket-punching machine until the mechanism rings.

▶ Bus Companies **Aisa** ✉ Estación Sur ☎ 902/198788 Ⓜ Méndez Álvaro. **Alsa** ✉ Av. de América 9, Salamanca ☎ 902/422242 ⊕ www.alsa.es Ⓜ Avenida de América. **Continental Auto** ✉ Av. de América 9, Salamanca ☎ 91/745-6300 ⊕ www.continental-auto.es Ⓜ Avenida de América. **Herranz** ✉ Intercambiador de Moncloa, Moncloa ☎ 91/896-9028 Ⓜ Moncloa. **La Sepulvedana** ✉ Paseo de la Florida 11, near Estación del Norte, Moncloa ☎ 91/559-8955 ⊕ www.lasepulvedana.es Ⓜ Príncipe Pío. **La Veloz** ✉ Mediterraneo 49, Atocha ☎ 91/409-7602 Ⓜ Conde de Casal.

▶ Bus Stations **Auto Res** ✉ Fernández Shaw 1, Atocha ☎ 902/020999 ⊕ www.auto-res.net Ⓜ Conde de Casal. **Estación del Sur** ✉ Méndez Álvaro s/n, Atocha ☎ 91/468-4200 ⊕ www.estaciondeautobuses.com Ⓜ Méndez Álvaro.

BY CAR

Felipe II made Madrid the capital of Spain because it was at the very center of his peninsular domains, and to this day many of the nation's highways radiate from Madrid like the spokes of a wheel. Originating at Kilometer 0—marked by a brass plaque on the sidewalk of the Puerta del Sol—these highways include the A6 (Segovia, Salamanca, Galicia); A1 (Burgos and the Basque Country); the A2 (Guadalajara, Barcelona, France); the A3 (Cuenca, Valencia, the Mediterranean coast); the A4 (Aranjuez, La Mancha, Granada, Seville); the A42 (Toledo); and the A5 (Talavera de la Reina, Portugal). The city is surrounded by the M30 (the inner ring road), and the M40 and M50 (the outer ring roads), from which most of these highways are easily picked up. To fight the heavy traffic leaving and getting into Madrid, the government set up an infrastructure plan that includes radial toll highways (marked R1, R2, R3, R4, and R5) that bypass the major highways by 50 to 60 km (31 to 37 mi), as well as the A41, a new toll highway connecting Madrid and Toledo. These options are worth considering, especially if you're driving on a summer weekend or a holiday.

Driving in Madrid is best avoided. Parking is nightmarish, traffic is heavy almost all the time, and the city's daredevil drivers can be frightening. August is an exception; the streets are then largely emptied by the mass exodus of Madrileños on vacation.

If you want to rent a car, nearly every international agency is represented in Madrid, whether in town or at Barajas Airport. It's best to reserve a car before you arrive in Spain; *see* Car Rental *in* Smart Travel Tips for toll-free numbers both at home and in Spain.

BY SUBWAY

The metro is quick, frequent, and, at €1 no matter how far you travel, cheap. Even cheaper is the 10-ride Metrobus ticket, or *billete de diez,* which costs €6.15—it is also valid for buses and is accepted by automatic turnstiles (lines at ticket booths can be long). The system is open from 6 AM to 1:30 AM, though a few entrances close earlier. There are 12 metro lines, and system maps in stations detail their color-coded routes. Note the end station of the line you need, and follow signs to the correct corridor. Exits are marked SALIDA.

▶ Metro Information ☎ 902/444403 ⊕ www.metromadrid.es.

BY TAXI

Taxis are a good deal in Madrid. They work under three different tariff schemes. Tariff 1 is valid in the city center from 6 AM to 10 PM; meters start at €1.75. Supplemental charges include €4.50 to or from the airport, and €2.40 from bus and train stations. Tariff 2 is from 10 PM to 6 AM in the city center (and from 6 AM to 10 PM in the suburbs). During this period the meter runs faster and charges more per kilometer. Tariff 3 runs at night beyond the city limits. You'll find all tariffs listed on the taxi window.

Taxi stands are numerous, and taxis are easily hailed in the street—except when it rains, at which point they're exceedingly hard to come by. Available cabs display a LIBRE sign during the day, a green light at night. Spaniards do not tip cabbies, but if you're inspired, €0.50 is about right for shorter rides; you can go as high as 10% for a trip to the airport. You can call a cab through Tele-Taxi, Radioteléfono Taxi, or Radio Taxi Gremial.

⏻ Taxi Services Radio Taxi Gremial ☎ 91/447-5180. **Radioteléfono Taxi** ☎ 91/547-8200. **Tele-Taxi** ☎ 91/371-2131.

BY TRAIN

Traveling by train is comfortable and safe, but for some lines, especially the regional ones, it's sometimes better to take the bus. This holds true for Segovia (the train runs half as frequently and takes twice the time, and the train station is farther from the city center than the bus station) and Toledo (buses run every 30 minutes, but trains leave only every two hours). If you're planning to reach Barcelona, be sure to check air rates being offered by Iberia, Air Europa, and Spanair.

For train schedules and reservations, go to any of Madrid's major train stations, visit a travel agent, go to the RENFE office on Alcalá 44 across from the Círculo de Bellas Artes, or call the RENFE number—they will transfer you to an English-speaking representative who can guide you through the procedure. If you use the phone to reserve a ticket, RENFE will hold your ticket for the next 72 hours, providing you go buy your ticket at least one day before departure—otherwise your reservation will be canceled. You can get the ticket from an automated machine at the station, if you pay with credit card, or at the service counter—you will have to take a number and stand in line.

The best option, however, is the RENFE Web site (www.renfe.es), which has an English-language section. Click on TIKNET, RENFE's online ticket sales service. You can buy regional destination tickets up to 15 days before departure, but long-distance and the fast-speed train tickets can be bought up to two months in advance.

Unfortunately, at this writing, not all train tickets are available online. This restriction applies to the *cercanías* (commuter trains), international trains, night trains, and some regional trains—for instance, you can buy a ticket online to go from Madrid to Granada or Salamanca, but not one for Madrid to Segovia, Toledo, El Escorial, or Paris.

To buy a ticket online, you must register and provide credit-card information. Also, note that you cannot buy a ticket online within 24 hours of departure. There's a 15% cancellation fee if you cancel more than two hours after making the purchase—if you wish to reschedule your ticket after buying it, you must do so at the counters at the train station. After you buy the ticket, you will be given a car and seat assignment and a *localizador* (localizer). You can then choose to print the ticket and the reservations page or write these three pieces of information (car number, seat number, localizer) down and bring them with you.

If it's the first time you've bought a ticket online through this service, you won't be able to print out the ticket. Instead you'll have to retrieve the tickets at the *venta anticipada* (advance sale) counter. Take a number and stand in line. **Be sure to bring the credit card you used when buying the ticket,** a form of ID, and the localizer. If you've bought tickets online before, you may bypass the counter and instead go directly to your assigned seat on the train. When the conductor comes around, show him the printed ticket or give him the localizer and he will issue the ticket on the spot. You will need your passport and, in most cases, the credit card with which you made the reservation.

The AVE trains work a little differently. If it's the first time you're buying, whether by phone or on the Internet, you'll have to retrieve the tickets at the sale counters; otherwise, you'll find a check-in gate before you get to the platform. There you can show the localizer and be issued a ticket, or you can proceed to the train if you have a printed ticket.

Commuter trains, which travel to El Escorial, Aranjuez, and Alcalá de Henares, run frequently throughout the day. The best way to get a ticket for such trains is to use one of the automated reservation terminals at the station (they're in the *cercanías* area). To purchase tickets for the regional lines that run less frequently but go to popular destinations such as Segovia or Toledo, you need to use the phone reservation system, the ticket counters at the station or in RENFE offices, or the automated reservations terminals at the main train stations.

TRAIN STATIONS Madrid has three main train stations: Chamartín, Atocha, and Norte, the last primarily for commuter trains. Remember to confirm which station you need when arranging a trip. Generally speaking, Chamartín, near the northern tip of Paseo de la Castellana, serves destinations north and west, including San Sebastián, Burgos, León, Oviedo, La Coruña, and Salamanca, as well as France and Portugal and the night train to Barcelona. Atocha, at the southern end of Paseo del Prado, serves towns near Madrid, including El Escorial, Segovia, and Toledo, and southern and eastern cities such as Seville, Málaga, Córdoba, Valencia, and Castellón, and the daily trains to Barcelona. Atocha also sends AVE (high-speed) trains to Córdoba, Seville, Zaragosa, Toledo, Huesca, and Lleida. For some destinations, however, you can depart from either Atocha or Chamartín (this is the case for Toledo, Segovia, El Escorial, and Alcalá de Henares).

🚆 Train Information **Estación de Atocha** ☎ 91/528–4630. **Estación Chamartín** ☎ 91/315–9976. RENFE ☎ 902/240202 ⊕ www.renfe.es.

Contacts & Resources

1

BANKS & EXCHANGING SERVICES

Currently there are more than 2,200 bank branches in Madrid, not including savings-and-loans branches. This number includes local branches of the most important foreign banks, such as Barclays or Citibank, as well as Spain's four major banks, BSCH (Banco Santander Central Hispano), BBVA (Banco Bilbao Vizcaya), Banesto, and Banco Popular. However, the financial entity you are most likely to bump into is Caja Madrid, the region's most important savings-and-loans bank.

Banks usually are open from 8:30 AM to 2:30 PM during the week and from 8:30 AM to 1 PM on Saturday. However, from May to September they're open only on the weekdays. Savings-and-loans banks have a different schedule—for instance, Caja Madrid is open weekdays from 8:15 AM to 2 PM and Saturday from 11 AM to 1:30 PM, although the latter may vary slightly depending on the office size and location. Caja Madrid also has special offices that are open continuously every day until 7 PM or 7:45 PM, in some of the city's key locations: train stations, airport terminals, and the city center (they've got one on Gran Vía 44).

You'll find no trouble exchanging foreign currency into euros, especially in tourist areas (Puerta del Sol, Callao, Gran Ví), and always providing you intend to exchange reasonable amounts.

CHILDREN IN MADRID

If you have children who can sit still long enough for a performance, Madrid has a few good picks. The Teatro de Títeres en el Retiro (Puppet Theater in the Retiro) plays in the Retiro Park from October to May on weekends and holidays (usually at noon). Teatro Pradillo and Sala Tarambana (two of the city's theaters) stage plays for children. The Museo Nacional Centro de Arte Reina Sofía has workshops for children usually related to their temporary or permanent exhibitions. Because of the reduced size of the workshops, you'll have to book a seat in advance. Fundación Mapfre Vida is another art institution that offers workshops for children. *See* Zoo-Aquarium *in* Exploring Central Madrid.
🏠 **Fundación Mapfre Vida** ✉ General Perón 40, Chamartín ☎ 91/581–1596. **Julià Tours** ✉ Gran Vía 68, Centro ☎ 91/559–9605 ⊕ www.juliatours.es. **Museo Nacional Centro de Arte Reina Sofía** ✉ Santa Isabel 52, Atocha ☎ 91/467–5062. **Sala Tarambana** ✉ Dolores Armengot 31, Carabanchel ☎ 91/461–8334. **Teatro Pradillo** ✉ Pradillo, 12, Chamartín ☎ 91/416–9011. **Teleférico** ✉ Paseo Pintor Rosales s/n, Centro ☎ 91/541–7450 ☉ Oct.–Mar., weekends noon–8; Apr.–Sept., daily noon–8.

DISCOUNTS & DEALS

For €36, €46, or €56 for one, two, or three days, respectively, you can get the Madrid Card, which gives you entry to 40 museums (with no standing in lines to buy tickets) and monuments, a tourist bus called Madrid Visión, all the guided visits in the Discover Madrid program (*see* Tour Options, *above*), and admission to Faunia (a thematic zoo outside the city), as well as discounts in stores, movies, theaters, restaurants, and parks. You can buy the card at the municipal and regional tourist offices, on Madrid Visión buses, and at its kiosk next to the Prado Museum on Felipe IV, at Viajes Brújula at Atocha and Chamartín train stations, and at Sol Pentour on Puerta del Sol 6. It's also available through the Madrid Card Web site. In 2006 the city launched a second card, Madrid Card Cultura, with a narrower range of services (but including the entry to the museums and the Discover Madrid guided visits) for €22, €26, or €30 for one, two, or three days, respectively. There's also an *abono turístico* (tourist pass) that allows visitors unlimited use of public buses and subway for a period of one to seven days. Purchase it at any tourist office or subway station, or at select newsstands and tobacco shops. The price ranges from €3.50 for the one-day pass to €18.40 for the seven-day pass.

Madrid Shopping Tours runs a bus around town for determined shoppers. Tuesday through Thursday. For €25, you can see the city's retail districts and nearby factory outlets on a guided tour, and get discounts to boot. You must reserve a spot at least one day in advance. The tour runs from 10 to 6; call for pickup locations.

🛈 **Madrid Municipal Tourist Office** ⊠ Plaza Mayor 3 ☎ 91/588-1636 ⊕ www.munimadrid.es. **Madrid Regional Tourist Office** ⊠ Duque de Medinaceli 2 ☎ 91/429-4951 ⊕ www.madridcard.com. **Madrid Shopping Tour** ☎ 91/316-0657 🖶 91/316-0842 ⊕ www.madridshoppingtour.com.

EMERGENCIES

In any emergency, call 112; an operator will redirect you to the appropriate number. Emergency pharmacies are required to be open 24 hours a day on a rotating basis; pharmacy windows and the major daily newspapers list pharmacies open round-the-clock that day. If you need to go to the hospital, remember that if you have a British (or European Union) passport the public centers will give you free emergency care as they would to any Spanish national. Because there's no bilateral agreement between Spain and the United States, American citizens who receive medical care are subject to medical charges. Be sure to inquire with your health insurance company about its policies.

For English-speaking doctor referrals try Unidad Medica Angloamericana, a private medical center.

The Madrid police run a special phone service in several languages for tourists who are the victims of crimes; call 902/102112. Your complaint will be sent to the police station nearest to where the crime took place, and you will have two days to drop by the station and sign the report.

🛈 **Doctors & Dentists Unidad Médica Angloamericana** ⊠ Conde de Aranda 1, Salamanca ☎ 91/435-1823.

🛈 **Emergency Services Ambulancias Cruz Roja** (Red Cross Ambulances) ☎ 91/522-2222 are on call 24 hours a day. **Ambulancias SAMUR** (Red Cross Ambulances) ☎ 112 are always available.

🛈 **Public Hospitals Hospital La Paz** ⊠ Paseo de la Castellana 261, Chamartín ☎ 91/358-2600. **Hospital Universitario de la Princesa** ⊠ Diego de León, 62, Salamanca ☎ 91/520-2200. **Hospital Universitario Gregorio Marañón** ⊠ C. Doctor Esquerdo, 46, Moncloa ☎ 91/586-8000. **Hospital Universitario San Carlos** ⊠ Profesor Martín Lagos s/n, Moncloa ☎ 91/330-3000.

INTERNET, MAIL & SHIPPING

Madrid's main post office, the Palacio de Comunicaciones, is at the intersection of Paseo de Recoletos and Calle de Alcalá, just one long block north of the Prado Museum. A variety of Internet cafés and services exists throughout the city, especially in the Puerta del Sol neighborhood. Cyber Acceso, BBIGG, Cyberfutura, La Casa de Internet, and EasyInternetCafé are five of the largest ones. Shopkeepers and bartenders are good sources for finding the nearest place to get on to the Internet. Work Center, which has several locations around the city, offers high-quality printing, scanning, faxing, digital printing, and other office services on a 24/7 basis. Wi-Fi is slowly but surely finding its way into the city. Most hotels offer wireless connections, and you can find hot spots in some of the city's trendiest cafés, such as Diurno, Faborit (only after 7 PM), La Pecera at Círculo de Bellas Artes, Laan Café, at the small and also commendable Café Panini on Calle Campomanes near metro Ópera, at the art space La Dinamo on Calle Mira el Sol 2 (between the Rastro and Lavapiés), and at most Starbucks locations—these latter at a hefty cost. The city tourist office on Plaza Mayor also has a hot spot, as does the Barajas airport, both in the VIP rooms and the restaurant areas.

🖂 Post Office **Palacio de Comunicaciones** ⊠ Plaza de Cibeles s/n, Centro ☎ 902/197197 ⊙ Weekdays 8:30 AM–10 PM, Sat. 8:30–8 (after 2 PM, enter by C. Monteleón), Sun. 10–1. 🖂 Internet Cafés **Cyber Acceso** ⊠ Espoz y Mina 17, Sol ☎ 91/532–2622 ⊙ Mon.–Sat. 9 AM–11 PM, Sun. 11–11. **BBIGG** ⊠ Mayor 1, Sol ⊙ Weekdays 10 AM–midnight, weekends 10 AM–2 AM. **La Casa de Internet** ⊠ Luchana 20, Bilbao ☎ 91/594–4200 ⊙ Daily 9 AM–12:30 AM. **Cyberfutura** ⊠ Montera 43, Sol ☎ 91/521–7119 ⊙ Mon.–Sat. 9 AM–1 AM, Sun. 10 AM–1 AM. **EasyInternetCafé** ⊠ Alberto Aguilera 27, Moncloa ⊙ Mon.–Sat. 9 AM–10 PM, Sun. 9 AM–9 PM. **Work Center** ⊠ Alberto Aguilera 1, Plaza de San Bernardo, Centro ☎ 91/121–7600.

MEDIA

The *International Herald Tribune* is available at dawn in Madrid, as are major British dailies. *The Broadsheet,* a magazine you can find at any newsstand, and *In Madrid* (⊕ www.in-madrid.com), a free local newspaper found in shops, the tourist office, pubs, and bars around the city, are filled with listings and suggestions about what to do and where to go for English-speaking residents and visitors.

TOUR OPTIONS

Most medium- to upper-range hotels can arrange standard city tours in either English or Spanish; most offer Madrid Artístico (including the Royal Palace and the Prado), Madrid Panorámico (a basic half-day tour), Madrid de Noche (including a flamenco or nightclub show), and the Sunday-only Panorámico y Toros (a brief city overview followed by a bullfight during the season).

The Plaza Mayor tourist office leads tours of Madrid's old quarters in English every Saturday morning, departing from the office at 10. The same office has a leaflet detailing the popular Spanish- and English-language bus, cycling (there's a €6 bicycle-rental fee), and walking tours run by the *ayuntamiento* (city hall) under the rubric "Descubre Madrid/ Discover Madrid"; you can buy tickets at the Patronato de Turismo or

by calling 902/221622 (a phone ticket service). There's a tour every day of the week, and several on the weekends, with departure points depending on the tour selected. Theme options include Modern Madrid, Madrid of the Hapsburgs, Medieval Madrid, and Madrid of the Bourbons. Tickets run from €3.20 for walking tours to €6.20 if a bus is needed.

For half-day and one-day trips to sites outside Madrid, including Toledo, El Escorial, and Segovia, contact Julià Tours.

The Madrid Visión tourist buses make three different 45-minute to 1½-hour circuits of the city (Historic Madrid, Modern Madrid, and Monumental Madrid) with recorded commentary in English. No reservation is needed; just show up at Puerta del Sol 5, Puerta de Alcalá (Plaza de la Independencia 3), Plaza de Cibeles (Paseo de Recoletos 2) or in front of the Prado Museum. Buses depart every 20 minutes, starting at 10 (9:30 in summer). The one-day and two-day passes, which allow you to get on and off at various attractions, cost €14.50 and €19, and you get better deals if you buy and print the tickets through their Web site. Contact the Asociación Profesional de Informadores to hire a personal guide.

🗷 Tour Operators **Asociacion Profesional de Guias de Turismo** ⊠ C. Ferraz 82, Moncloa ☎ 91/542–1214 🖶 91/541–1221 ⊕ www.apit.es. **Ayuntamiento** ⊠ City Hall, C. Mayor 69, Centro ☎ 91/588–1000. **Julià Tours** ⊠ Gran Vía 68, Centro ☎ 91/559–9605 ⊕ www.juliatours.es. **Madrid Visión** ☎ 91/765–1016 ⊕ www.madridvision.es. **Patronato de Turismo** ⊠ C. Mayor 69, Centro ☎ 91/588–2906. **Plaza Mayor tourist office** ⊠ Plaza Mayor 27, Centro ☎ 91/588–2906 (this number is specially for the Descubre [Discover] Madrid Tours).

VISITOR INFORMATION

Madrid has four regional tourist offices. The best is at Duque de Medinaceli 2 (near the Westin Palace), open Monday through Saturday 8 to 8 and Sunday 9 to 3. The others are at Barajas Airport, open daily 8 to 8; the Chamartín train station, open Monday through Saturday 8 to 8 and Sunday 9 to 3; and the Atocha train station, open daily 9 to 9.

There is also a completely revamped (as of 2005) city tourist office with Wi-Fi access on the Plaza Mayor, across from its former location; it's open daily 9:30 to 8:30 and has six computer stations that give you access to Madrid's largest official tourist database (in Spanish and English): www.esmadrid.es. Additionally, there are four information kiosks in some of the city's most crowded locations: the Plaza de Callao, the Plaza Cibeles, the Plaza de Felipe II, and the airport's new terminal. Though these kiosks don't have as much information as the other offices, they might come in handy if you're in the area. They are open daily 9:30 to 8:30.

🗷 City Tourist Office **Plaza Mayor 27** ☎ 91/588–1636 ⊕ www.munimadrid.es (general information) or www.esmadrid.com (tourist information).

🗷 Regional Tourist Offices **Atocha** ☎ 902/100–007. **Barajas** ☎ 91/305–8656. **Chamartín** ☎ 91/315–9976. **Duque de Medinaceli 2** ☎ 91/429–4951.

Old & New Castile

WORD OF MOUTH

"One of the highlights of Segovia was a walk over to the Knights of St. John Basilica—Vera Cruz. [It was a really] cool place and uncrowded too. As a bonus, it was a local holiday the nights we were in town—for St. Pedro. Live music everywhere, including dozens of brass bands battling for attention. A procession and dancing in the moonlight. Segovia was definitely one of the highlights of our trip."

—winnie

"I loved Cuenca. We stayed in a hotel which was an old convent, which had rooms over the gorge . . . . Absolutely amazing. In my opinion it is more than worth the detour."

—marigross

By Michael
Jacobs

Updated by
Kip Tobin

2

FOR ALL THE VARIETY IN THE TOWNS AND COUNTRYSIDE around Madrid, there's an underlying unity in Castile—the high, wide *meseta* (plain) of gray, bronze, and (briefly) green, split by the Guadarrama mountains just north of the capital. This central Spanish steppe is divided into Old and New Castile, the former (Castilla y León) north of Madrid, the latter (Castilla–La Mancha) south—known as "New" because it was captured from the Moors a bit later. Castilians have historically been a fierce people with a sense that the unification of the Iberian Peninsula was their birthright. The very name Castilla refers to the great east–west line of castles and fortified towns built in the 12th century between Salamanca and Soria. Segovia's Alcázar, Ávila's fully intact city walls, and other bastions and strongholds are among Castile's greatest monuments. Many have been converted into splendid hotels.

Stone, a dominant element in the Castilian countryside, gives the region much of its character. Gaunt mountain ranges frame the horizons; gorges and rocky outcrops break up flat expanses; and the fields around Ávila and Segovia are littered with giant boulders. Castilian villages are built predominantly of granite, and their solid, formidable look contrasts markedly with the whitewashed walls of most of southern Spain. Over the centuries, poets—most notably Antonio Machado, whose experiences at Soria in the early 20th century inspired his haunting *Campos de Castilla* (*Fields of Castile*)—and others have characterized Castile as austere and melancholy. There is a distinct, chilly beauty in the stark lines and soothing colors of these breezy expanses.

Faced with the austerity of the Castilian environment, some inhabitants have taken refuge in the spirit and imagination. Ávila is associated with two renowned mystics—St. Teresa and her disciple St. John of the Cross—and Toledo was the main home of one of the most spiritual of all Western painters, El Greco. Escape into fantasy is best illustrated by Cervantes's hero Don Quijote, in whose imagination even the dreary expanse of La Mancha became magical. Many of the region's architects were similarly fanciful: Castile in the 15th and 16th centuries was the center of the plateresque, an ornamental stone-carving style of extraordinary intricacy, named for its resemblance to silver-plate work. Developed in Toledo and Valladolid, it reached its climax in the university town of Salamanca.

Burgos was the 11th-century capital of Castile and the native city of El Cid ("Lord Conqueror"), Spain's legendary hero of the Christian Reconquest. Francisco Franco's wartime headquarters were established at Burgos during the Spanish civil war (1936–39), possibly as much for symbolic as for strategic reasons. Even today the army and the clergy seem to set the tone in this somber city. León is a provincial capital and prestigious university town. Northwest of León, the medieval Camino de Santiago (Way of St. James) leads Christian pilgrims out of Castile and into Galicia as they wend their way toward Santiago de Compostela.

About the Restaurants

Castilian food is hearty stuff. Classic Castilian dishes are *cordero* (lamb) and *cochinillo* (suckling pig) roasted in a wood oven. Throughout Castile, prize dishes include *perdiz en escabeche,* the marinated partridge of Soria, and *perdiz estofada a la Toledana,* the stewed partridge of Toledo. Castile's most complex and exotic cuisine is perhaps that of Cuenca; here a Moorish influence appears in such dishes as *gazpacho pastor,* a hot terrine made with a mix of game, topped with grapes.

The mountainous districts of Salamanca, particularly the villages of Guijuelo and Candelario, are renowned for their hams and sausages. As the Spanish saying goes, *"Del cerdo se aprovecha todo"* ("All parts of the pig are there to be enjoyed"), a philosophy embraced by many Castilian restaurants. A typical dish in the area of El Bierzo, near León, is *botillo*—pig's tail, ribs, and cheeks stuffed into pig's stomach. Bean dishes are specialties of the villages El Barco (Ávila) and La Granja (Segovia), and *trucha* (trout) and *cangrejos de río* (river crab) are common in Guadalajara.

Among the region's sweets are the *yemas* (sugared egg yolks) of Ávila, *almendras garrapiñadas* (candied almonds) of Alcalá de Henares, *mazapán* (marzipan) of Toledo, and *ponche Segovia* (Segovian egg toddy). *Manchego* cheeses (from La Mancha) are staples throughout Spain, and Aranjuez is known for its strawberries and asparagus.

Most of Spain's everyday table wine has traditionally come from Castilla—La Mancha's Valdepeñas region, the largest vineyard in the world. New winemakers such as Adolfo Muñoz, Carlos Falcó (Marqués de Griñón), and others have been cultivating new grape varietals such as Syrah and Petit Verdot along with the traditional Cencibel (Tempranillo) and cabernet sauvignon vines, with spectacular results. In Castilla–León in the Duero Valley around Valladolid and Peñafiel, look for Vega Sicilia, Mauro, Pingus, Protos, Pesquera, Abadía Retuerta, and Pago de Carraovejas. The Rueda wine-growing region centered around Medina del Campo southwest of Valladolid produces fine white wines with the Verdejo varietal. Cuenca's very sweet Castilian liqueur *resolí,* made from aquavit, coffee, vanilla, orange peel, and sugar, is often sold in bottles in the shape of Cuenca's Casas Colgadas (Hanging Houses). It competes with neighboring Chinchon's age-old Anis del Mono liqueur, an extremely sweet liqueur brewed from herbs and anise.

WHAT IT COSTS In Euros				
$$$$	**$$$**	**$$**	**$**	**¢**
AT DINNER over €20	€15–€20	€10–€15	€6–€10	under €6

Prices are per person for a main course at dinner.

About the Hotels

Many of Spain's paradors are carefully restored castles and palaces. Most of the oldest and most attractive Castilian paradors are in quieter towns

GREAT ITINERARIES

It's possible (but not ideal) to see Aranjuez, Ávila, Segovia, and Toledo on day trips from Madrid. If you have a car, spend at least four days in this area, staying in Toledo, Segovia, and Salamanca, and passing through Ávila. To see the region's main sights requires another four to six days, with overnight stays in Cuenca, Sigüenza, Soria, Zamora, Burgos, and León.

IF YOU HAVE 4 DAYS

Start in ▦ **Toledo** ❶–❻, Spain's intellectual and spiritual capital. Spend a full day visiting El Greco's former stomping grounds; then spend the night; move east the next day to **Aranjuez** ❻, the summer retreat of the Bourbon monarchy. Farther south, check out Don Quijote's windmills at **Consuegra** ❼ and the medieval town of ▦ **Almagro** ❽, with its unique 16th-century theater. Consider spending a night in Almagro's 17th-century parador; then, hit Madrid's ring roads by 10 AM to avoid the rush hour and head north of

Madrid on the NVl to sublime ▦ **Segovia** ❸❶–❹❶, spending a night there. On your fourth day, catch the fountain display in the gardens of the **Palacio Real de la Granja** ❹❷ (The Royal Palace of La Granja de San Ildefonso) before returning to Madrid via the spectacular Navacerrada mountain pass.

IF YOU HAVE 6 DAYS

Spend a day wandering around ▦ **Toledo** ❶–❻, and spend the night; then head north to ▦ **Segovia** ❸❶–❹❶ for the second day and night. See the medieval **Castillo de Coca** ❹❺ on your way to **Ávila** ❹❻. Continue on to ▦ **Salamanca** ❺⓿–❻❷ for the third night and spend the next day soaking up the architecture. Head north to ▦ **Burgos** ❻❼–❼❷ for the night and the next day. See the monastery at Santo Domingo de Silos, or the closer San Pedro de Cardeña, and spend the night in one of the two. Finally, take the Camino de Santiago pilgrimage route and linger in ▦ **León** ❼❾–❽❼.

such as Almagro, Ávila, Chinchón, Cuenca, León, and Sigüenza. Those in Toledo, Segovia, Salamanca, and Soria are modern buildings with magnificent views and, in the case of Segovia, wonderful indoor and outdoor swimming pools. Of course, there are pleasant alternatives to paradors, such as Ávila's Palacio de Valderrábanos (a 15th-century palace next to the cathedral), Segovia's Infanta Isabel, Salamanca's Rector, and Cuenca's Posada San José, a 16th-century convent.

WHAT IT COSTS In Euros				
$$$$	**$$$**	**$$**	**$**	**¢**
FOR 2 PEOPLE over €180	€100–€180	€60–€100	€40–€60	under €40

Prices are for two people in a standard double room in high season, excluding tax.

Exploring Old & New Castile

Castile is a large chunk of Spain, and the region could occupy any traveler for weeks. Old Castile lies to the north and west of Madrid; New Castile to the south and east of Madrid. South of Madrid is ancient Toledo, once home to El Greco, and Aranjuez, with its impressive Royal Palace. Farther south is Consuegra, dominated by hilltop windmills, and the elegant city of Almagro. In southeast Castile, the Huécar and Júcar rivers cut through a rugged countryside, out of which rises Cuenca, built into craggy cliffs. North of Madrid is medieval Segovia with its famed Roman aqueduct, its Alcázar palace, and farther north the fairy-tale-like Castillo de Coca. Northwest of Madrid are the spectacular peaks of the Sierra de Gredos and the walled city of Ávila. Farther northwest is Salamanca, dominated by luminescent sandstone buildings and home to one of Spain's oldest universities. In the northern reaches of Castile are the ancient Castilian capitals of Burgos and León, each with inspiring Gothic cathedrals. If you're driving, Old Castile can be combined with later ventures to the Basque Country or Galicia, and New Castile can lead you on to Extremadura, Andalusia, or the Mediterranean coast.

Numbers in the text correspond to numbers in the margin and on the Toledo, Old & New Castile, Segovia, Salamanca, Burgos, and León maps.

Timing

The best months to tour central Spain are May and October, when the weather is sunny but relatively cool. July and August can be brutally hot, especially south of Madrid. November through February can get bitterly cold, especially in the Sierra de Guadarrama, north and west of Madrid. During the pre-Lenten Carnival, León and nearby La Bañeza are popular party centers. The last week of April, in the cloister at León's San Isidoro, the town councillors and ecclesiastical authorities bow to each other to recall an ancient dispute over the distribution of power between the clergy and the civil authorities.

KIP'S TOP 5

- Climbing the 156 steps to the top of Segovia's Alcázar and admiring the endless perimeter.

- Catching a sunset from Salamanca's Roman bridge as it melts into the trees on the horizon.

- Taking a meditative walk through Leon's cathedral with its mesmerizing, kaleidoscopic windows.

- Staying a night in Cuenca's Parador, which straddles the sublime views of the hanging houses and Huecar river gorge.

- The in-itself joy of getting lost in Toledo's labyrinthine streets.

TOLEDO TO CIUDAD REAL

The contrast between the towns of Toledo and nearby Aranjuez could hardly be more marked. Toledo is a study in austerity, its introverted, gold-tone houses daring you to know them better. Here you can explore the mighty Gothic cathedral and the Sinagoga del Tránsito; contemplate El Greco's most famous painting, *El entierro del Conde de Orgaz (The Burial of Count Orgaz)*; or just roam the winding lanes. Aranjuez has the sumptuous Palacio Real. Consuegra, present in any picture of Don Quijote's windmills, is also the saffron capital of La Mancha. Farther south is historic Almagro, a hub during La Mancha's Age of Chivalry.

Toledo

①–**⑮** *71 km (44 mi) southwest of Madrid.*

Long the spiritual capital of Spain, Toledo perches atop a rocky mount with steep ocher hills rising on either side. The rock on which Toledo stands, bounded on three sides by the Río Tajo (River Tagus), was inhabited in prehistoric times, and there was an important Iberian settlement here when the Romans came in 192 BC. The Romans fortified the highest point of the rock, where you now see the Alcázar, the dominant building in Toledo's skyline. This stronghold was later remodeled by the Visigoths, who transformed the town into their capital by the middle of the 6th century AD. In the early 8th century, the Moors arrived.

The Moors strengthened Toledo's reputation as a great center of religion and learning. Unusual tolerance was extended to those who continued to practice Christianity (the so-called Mozarabs), as well as to the town's exceptionally large Jewish population. Today the Moorish legacy is evident in Toledo's strong crafts tradition, the mazelike arrangement of the streets, and the predominance of brick rather than stone. For the Moors, beauty was a quality to be savored within rather than displayed on the surface, and it's significant that even Toledo's cathedral—one of the most richly endowed in Spain—is hard to see from the outside, largely obscured by the warren of houses around it. Long after the departure of the Moors, Toledo remained secretive.

Alfonso VI, aided by El Cid, captured the city in 1085 and styled himself emperor of Toledo. Under the Christians, the town's strong intellectual life was maintained, and Toledo became famous for its school of translators, who spread to the West a knowledge of Arab medicine, law, culture, and philosophy. Religious tolerance continued, and during the rule of Peter the Cruel (so named because he allegedly had members of his own family murdered to advance himself), a Jewish banker, Samuel Levi, became the royal treasurer and one of the wealthiest and most important men in town. By the early 15th century, however, hostility toward both Jews and Arabs had grown as Toledo developed more and more into a bastion of the Catholic Church.

As Florence had the Medici and Rome the papacy, so Toledo had its long line of cardinals, most notably Mendoza, Tavera, and Cisneros. Under these patrons of the arts, Renaissance Toledo emerged as a center of humanism. Economically and politically, however, Toledo began to decline in the 16th century. The expulsion of the Jews from Spain in 1492, as part of the Spanish Inquisition, had serious economic consequences for Toledo. When Madrid became the permanent center of the Spanish court in 1561, Toledo's political importance eroded, and the expulsion from Spain of the converted Arabs (Moriscos) in 1601 led to the departure of most of Toledo's artisan community. The years the painter El Greco spent in Toledo—from 1572 to his death in 1614—were those of the town's decline. Its transformation into a major tourist center began in the late 19th century, when the works of El Greco came to be widely appreciated after years of neglect. Today, Toledo is prosperous and expensive, as well as conservative, and, therefore, silent at night. Yet Spain has no other town of this size with such a concentration of monuments and works of art.

⌐ A GOOD WALK

The eastern end of the Tagus gorge, along Calle de Circunvalación, is a good place to park your car (except in the middle of the day, when buses line up) and look down over almost all of historic Toledo. For quicker access to your car after a long day's walk, drive into the city and park by the Alcázar.

A complete tour starts at the **Puente de Alcántara** ❶ ⌐. If you skirt the city walls traveling northwest, a long walk past the Puerta de Bisagra on Calle Cardenal Tavera brings you to the **Hospital de Tavera** ❷. If you enter the city wall, walk west and pass the **Museo de la Santa Cruz** ❸ to emerge in the **Plaza de Zocodover** ❹. Due south of here, on Calle Cuesta de Carlos V, is the **Alcázar** ❺; a short walk northwest on Calle Nueva brings you to the **Mezquita del Cristo de la Luz** ❻. From the southwestern corner of the Alcázar, a series of alleys descends to the east end of the **cathedral** ❼. Make your way around the southern side of the building, passing the mid-15th-century Puerta de los Leones. Emerging into the small square in front of the cathedral's west facade, you'll see the stately *ayuntamiento* (town hall) to your right.

Near the Museo de los Concilios, on Calle de San Clemente, take in the richly sculpted portal by Covarrubias on the Convento de San Clemente; across the street is the church of **San Román** ❽. Almost every wall in this part of town belongs to a convent, and the empty streets make for contemplative walks. This was a district loved by the Romantic poet Gustavo Adolfo Bécquer, author of *Rimas* (*Rhymes*), the most popular collection of Spanish verse before García Lorca's *Romancero Gitano*. Bécquer's favorite corner was the tiny square in front of the 16th-century convent church of **Santo Domingo** ❾, a few minutes' walk north of San Román, below the Plazuela de Padilla.

Backtrack, following Calle de San Clemente through the Plaza de Valdecaleros to Calle de Santo Tomé, to get to the church of **Santo Tomé** ❿. Downhill from Santo Tomé, off Calle de San Juan de Díos, is the **Casa de El Greco** ⓫. (Follow the signs, because this is a tricky labyrinth to navigate.) Next door to the Casa de El Greco is the 14th-century **Sinagoga del Tránsito** ⓬, financed by Samuel Levi, and the accompanying Museo Sefardí. From the synagogue, turn right up Calle de Reyes Católicos. A few steps past the town's other synagogue, **Santa María la Blanca** ⓭, is the late-15th-century church of **San Juan de los Reyes** ⓮. The town's western extremity is the **Puente de San Martín** ⓯.

TIMING Toledo's winding streets and steep hills can be exasperating, especially when you're looking for a specific sight. Take the entire day to absorb the town's medieval trappings, and expect to get a little lost.

What to See

❺ **Alcázar.** Closed for renovations until sometime in 2007, the Alcázar ("fortress" in Arabic) was originally a Moorish citadel that stood here from the 10th century to the Reconquest. A tour around the exterior

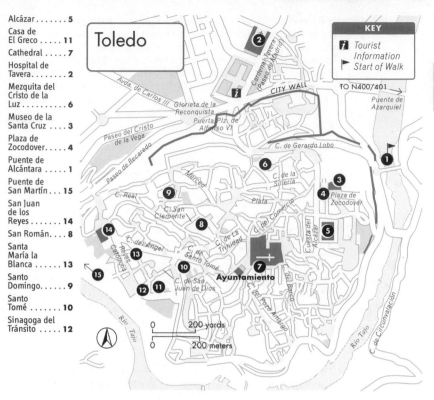

will reveal the south facade, the building's most severe—the work of Juan de Herrera, of El Escorial fame. The east facade incorporates a large section of battlements. The finest facade is the northern, one of many Toledan works by Alonso de Covarrubias, who did more than any other architect to introduce the Renaissance style here. When the renovations are finished, the Alcázar will be the new site for the Museo del Ejercito (Military Museum), formerly in Madrid. The Alcázar's architectural highlight is Covarrubias's Italianate courtyard, which, like most other parts of the building, was largely rebuilt after the civil war, when the Alcázar was besieged by the Republicans. Though the Nationalists' ranks were depleted, they managed to hold on to the building. Franco later turned the Alcázar into a monument to Nationalist bravery; the office of the Nationalist general who defended the building, General Moscardó, has been left exactly as it was after the war, complete with peeling ceiling paper and mortar holes. Also visit the dark cellars, which evoke living conditions at the time of the siege. More cheerful is a ground-floor room full of beautifully crafted swords, a Toledo specialty introduced by Moorish silversmiths. At the top of the grand staircase are rooms displaying a vast collection of toy soldiers. ⊠ *Cuesta Carlos V s/n* ☎ *925/221673* ▨ *€5* ☉ *Tues.–Sun. 9:30–2.*

⑪ Casa de El Greco (El Greco's House). This house is on the property that belonged to Peter the Cruel's treasurer, Samuel Levi. El Greco once lived in a house owned by Levi, but it's pure conjecture that the artist lived here. The interior, decorated in the late 19th century to resemble a "typical" house of El Greco's time, is a fake, albeit a pleasant one. The museum next door has a few of El Greco's paintings, including a panorama of Toledo with the Hospital of Tavera in the foreground. ⊠ *Samuel Levi s/n* ☎ *925/224046* ⌗ *€2.50, free Sat. afternoon and Sun. morning* ⊙ *Tues.–Sat. 10–2 and 4–6, Sun. 10–2.*

❼ Cathedral. Jorge Manuel Theotokópoulos was responsible for the cathedral's Mozarabic chapel, the elongated dome of which crowns the right-hand side of the west facade. The rest of this facade is mainly early 15th century and has a depiction of Mary presenting her robe to Toledo's patron saint, the Visigothic Ildefonsus. Enter the cathedral from the 14th-century cloisters to the left of the west facade. The primarily 13th-century architecture was inspired by Chartres and other Gothic cathedrals in France, but the squat proportions give it a Spanish feel, as do the wealth and weight of the furnishings and the location of the elaborate choir in the center of the nave. Immediately to your right as you enter the building is a beautifully carved plateresque doorway by Covarrubias, marking the entrance to the Treasury. The latter houses a small Crucifixion by the Italian painter Cimabue and an extraordinarily intricate late-15th-century monstrance by Juan del Arfe, a silversmith of German descent; the ceiling is an excellent example of Mudejar (11th-to-16th-century Moorish-influenced) workmanship.

From here, walk around to the ambulatory, off to the right side of which is a chapter house with a strange and quintessentially Spanish mixture of Italianate frescoes by Juan de Borgoña. In the middle of the ambulatory is an example of baroque illusionism by Narciso Tomé, known as the *Transparente,* a blend of painting, stucco, and sculpture. Finally, off the northern end of the ambulatory, you'll come to the sacristy and several El Grecos, including *El Espolio* (Christ Being Stripped of His Raiment). One of El Greco's earliest works in Toledo, it offended the Inquisition, which accused the artist of putting Christ on a lower level than some of the onlookers. El Greco was thrown into prison, where his career might have ended had he not by this time formed friendships with some of Toledo's more moderate clergy. Before leaving the sacristy, look up at the colorful and spirited late-baroque ceiling painting by the Italian Luca Giordano. ⊠ *Arco de Palacio 2* ☎ *925/222241* ⌗ *€6* ⊙ *Mon.–Sat. 10–6:30, Sun. 2–6.*

❷ Hospital de Tavera. You can find this hospital, Covarrubias's last work, outside the walls beyond Toledo's main northern gate, Covarrubias's imposing Puerta de Bisagra. Unlike the former Hospital of Santa Cruz, this complex is unfinished and slightly dilapidated, but it is nonetheless full of character and has the evocatively ramshackle **Museo de Duque de Lema** in its southern wing. The most important work in the museum's miscellaneous collection is a painting by the 17th-century artist José Ribera. The hospital's monumental chapel holds El Greco's *Baptism of Christ* and the exquisitely carved marble tomb of Cardinal Tavera, the last work of Alonso de Berruguete. Descend into the crypt to experience some bizarre acoustical effects. ✉ *Cardenal Tavera 2* ☎ *925/220451* 💶 *€3.25* 🕙 *Daily 10–1:30 and 3:30–5:30.*

⑥ Mezquita del Cristo de la Luz (Mosque of Christ of the Light). A gardener will open the gate and show you around this mosque-chapel, in a park above the northern ramparts; if the gardener's not around, ask at the house opposite. Originally a tiny Visigothic church, the chapel was transformed into a mosque during the Moorish occupation; the Islamic arches and vaulting survived, making this the most important relic of Moorish Toledo. The chapel got its name when the horse of Alfonso VI, riding into Toledo in triumph in 1085, fell to its knees out front (a white stone marks the spot); it was then discovered that a candle had burned continuously behind the masonry throughout the time that the Muslims had been in power. Allegedly, the first Mass of the Reconquest was held here, and later a Mudejar apse was added (now shielded by glass). After you've seen the chapel, the gardener will take you across the ramparts to climb to the top of the Puerta del Sol, a 12th-century Mudéjar gatehouse. ✉ *Cuesta de los Carmelitas Descalzos 10* ☎ *925/ 254191* 💶 *€1.90* 🕙 *Daily 10–2 and 3:30–5:40. Closed Mon.*

③ Museo de la Santa Cruz. This museum is in a beautiful Renaissance hospital with a stunning classical-plateresque facade; unlike Toledo's other sights, it's open all day without a break. The light and elegant interior has changed little since the 16th century, the main difference being that works of art have replaced the hospital beds; among the displays is El Greco's *Assumption* of 1613, the artist's last known work. A small **Museo de Arqueología** (Museum of Archaeology) is in and around the hospital's delightful cloister, off which is a beautifully decorated staircase by Alonso de Covarrubias. ✉ *Cervantes 3* ☎ *925/221036* 💶 *€2* 🕙 *Mon.–Sat. 10–6:30, Sun. 10–2.*

④ Plaza de Zocodover. Toledo's main square was built in the early 17th century as part of an unsuccessful attempt to impose a rigid geometry on the chaotic Moorish ground plan. Nearby, you can find **Calle del Comercio,** the town's narrow and lively pedestrian thoroughfare, lined with bars and shops and shaded in summer by awnings.

▶ **① Puente de Alcántara.** Here is the town's oldest bridge, Roman in origin. Next to the bridge is a heavily restored castle built after the Christian capture of 1085 and, above this, a vast and depressingly severe military academy, a typical example of Fascist architecture under Franco. The bridge is off the city's eastern peripheral road, just north of the Puente Nuevo.

⑮ Puente de San Martín. This pedestrian bridge on the western edge of the town dates from 1203 and has splendid horseshoe arches.

⑭ San Juan de los Reyes. This convent church in western Toledo was erected by Ferdinand and Isabella to commemorate their victory at the Battle of Toro in 1476 and was intended to be their burial place. The building is largely the work of architect Juan Guas, who considered it his masterpiece and asked to be buried here himself. In true plateresque fashion, the white interior is covered with inscriptions and heraldic motifs. ⊠ *Reyes Católicos 17* ☎ *925/223802* ⊒ *€1.90* ☉ *Apr.–Oct., daily 10–7; Nov.–Mar., daily 10–6.*

❽ San Román. A virtually unspoiled part of Toledo hides this early-13th-century Mudéjar church with extensive remains of frescoes inside. It has been deconsecrated and is now the **Museo de los Concilios y de la Cultura Visigótica,** and has statuary, manuscript illustrations, and jewelry. ⊠ *C. de San Clemente s/n* ☎ *925/227872* ⊒ *Free* ☉ *Tues.–Sat. 10–2 and 3:30–6, Sun. 10:15–1:45.*

┏ NEED A BREAK? If the convolutions of Toledo's maze exhaust you, unwind at **Palacio Sancara** (⊠ **Alfonso X El Sabio 6**). Around the corner from the church of San Román, off Plaza Juan de Mariana, this Arabian café-bar has plush couches, low tables, soothing classical music, and colorful tapestries.

⑬ Santa María la Blanca. Founded in 1203, Toledo's second synagogue is nearly two centuries older than the more elaborate Tránsito. The white interior has a forest of columns supporting capitals of enchanting filigree workmanship. Stormed in the early 15th century by a Christian mob, the synagogue was later used as a carpenter's workshop, a store, a barracks, and a refuge for reformed prostitutes. ⊠ *Reyes Católicos 4* ☎ *925/227257* ⊒ *€1.90* ☉ *Apr.–Sept. daily 10–6:45, Oct.–Mar. daily 10–5:45.*

❾ Santo Domingo. A few minutes' walk north of San Román is this 16th-century convent church, where you'll find the earliest of El Greco's Toledo paintings as well as the crypt where the artist is believed to be buried. The friendly nuns at the convent will show you around an odd little museum that includes documents bearing El Greco's signature. ⊠ *Pl. Santo Domingo el Antiguo s/n* ☎ *925/222930* ⊒ *€1.50* ☉ *Mon.–Sat. 11–1:30 and 4–7, Sun. 4–7.*

❿ Santo Tomé. Topped with a Mudéjar tower, this chapel was specially built to house El Greco's most famous painting, *The Burial of Count Orgaz,* and remains devoted to that purpose. The painting portrays the benefactor of the church being buried with the posthumous assistance of St. Augustine and St. Stephen, who have miraculously appeared at the funeral to thank him for all the money he gave to religious institutions named after them. Though the count's burial took place in the 14th century, El Greco painted the onlookers in contemporary costumes and included people he knew; the boy in the foreground is one of El Greco's sons, and the sixth figure on the left is said to be the artist himself. To avoid crowds in summer, try to come here as soon as the building opens. ⊠ *Pl. del Conde 4* ☎ *925/256098* ⊕ *www.santotome.org* ⊒ *€1.90* ☉ *Mar.–mid-Oct., daily 10–6:45; mid-Oct.–Feb., daily 10–5:45.*

⑫ Sinagoga del Tránsito. Financed by Samuel Levi, this 14th-century rectangular synagogue is plain on the outside, but the inside walls are covered with intricate Mudéjar decoration, as well as Hebraic inscriptions glorifying God, Peter the Cruel, and Levi himself. It's said that Levi imported cedars from Lebanon for the building's construction, à la Solomon when he built the First Temple in Jerusalem. Adjoining the main hall is the **Museo Sefardí,** a small museum of Jewish culture in Spain. ⊠ *Samuel Levi s/n*

2

☎ *925/223665* ✉ *€2.50, free Sat. afternoon and Sun.* ⊙ *Mar.–Nov., Tues.–Sat. 10–2 and 4–9, Sun. and holidays 10–2; Dec.–Feb., Tues.–Sat. 10–2 and 4–6, Sun. and holidays 10–2.*

Ⓒ If you're traveling with children, look to Toledo's **Tren Imperial**, a fun little tourist train that chugs past many of the sights to see. The train departs from the Plaza de Zocodover. ☎ *925/142274* ✉ *€3.80 for adults, €2 for kids* ⊙ *Tours daily 11–11.*

Where to Stay & Eat

$$$–$$$$ ✕ **Asador Adolfo.** Steps from the cathedral but discreetly hidden away, this restaurant has an intimate interior with a coffered ceiling painted in the 14th century. Game, fresh produce, and traditional Toledan recipes are prepared in innovative ways. The *tempura de flor de calabacín* (fried zucchini blossoms in saffron sauce) is a tasty starter; King Juan Carlos I has declared Adolfo's partridge stew the best in Spain. Finish with a Toledan specialty, *delicias de mazapán* (marzipan delights). ✉ *La Granada 6* ☎ *925/227321* ⊕ *www.adolfo-toledo.com* ⌕ *Reservations essential* ▤ *AE, DC, MC, V* ⊙ *Closed Mon. No dinner Sun.*

$$–$$$$ ✕ **Casón de los López de Toledo.** A vaulted foyer leads to a patio with marble statues, twittering caged birds, a fountain, and abstract religious paintings; in the dining room, carved wood abounds. The market-based Castilian and continental menu might include garlic-ravioli soup, braised rabbit with sesame sauce and mashed potatoes, or cod with manchego cheese, onions, and olive oil. Try the almond *mazapán* (marzipan) cake topped with cream cheese. It's wise to make reservations. ✉ *Sillería 3* ☎ *902/198344* 🖷 *925/257282* ⊕ *www.casontoledo.com* ▤ *AE, DC, MC, V* ⊙ *No dinner Sun.*

$–$$$ ✕ **Enebro Tapas Bar.** Very popular with the locals, here the motto is, "Don't drink if you're not going to eat." Every drink ordered comes with an ample serving of *patatas bravas* (roast potatoes) and some combination of pizza, olives, and *croquetas* (croquettes). An enormous terrace offers gas lamps and umbrellas to provide heat in the winter and shade in the summer. It's more of a place to take a break than have a full meal, though two people could share a *ración* (larger tapas plate) for a meal if need be. ✉ *Pl. Santiago de los Caballeros 1* ☎ *No phone* ⊕ *www.barenebro. com* ▤ *No credit cards* ⊙ *Closed on major holidays.*

$–$$$ ✕ **Restaurante Maravilla.** Partridge or quail and seafood dishes stand out at this homey and modestly priced spot, though the roast leg of lamb is hard to resist. ✉ *Pl. Barrio Rey 7* ☎ *925/228582* ⊕ *www.hotelmaravilla. com* ▤ *AE, DC, MC, V.*

$$$ ✕🖭 **Parador de Toledo.** This modern building on Toledo's outskirts has an unbeatable panorama of the town. The architecture and furnishings nod to the traditional Toledan style, emphasizing brick and wood. The restaurant ($$$–$$$$) is stately and traditional, with top-quality regional wines and products. ✉ *Cerro del Emperador s/n, 45002* ☎ *925/ 221850* 🖷 *925/225166* ⊕ *www.parador.es* ⇱ *76 rooms* ⌂ *Pool* ▤ *AE, DC, MC, V.*

★ **$$–$$$** ✕🖭 **Hostal del Cardenal.** Built in the 18th century as a summer palace for Cardinal Lorenzana, this quiet and beautiful hotel has rooms with antique furniture. Some rooms overlook the hotel's enchanting wooded garden, which lies at the foot of the town's walls. The restaurant, popular with tourists, has a long-standing reputation; the dishes are mainly local, and in season you can find delicious asparagus and strawberries from Aranjuez. ⊠ *Paseo de Recaredo 24, 45004* ☏ *925/224900* 🖷 *925/ 222991* ⊕ *www.hostaldelcardenal.com* ⟿ *27 rooms* ⚘ *Restaurant, parking (no fee)* ⊟ *AE, DC, MC, V.*

$$-$$$ ⊡ **Hotel Alfonso VI.** Besides being smack in the middle of the historic district, this hotel has great views of the city from its summer terrace. The rooms are modern, clean, and inviting; the restaurant is done in the ubiquitous Mudéjar style and serves good food. ⊠ *General Moscardó 2, 45001* ☏ *925/222600* 🖷 *925/214458* ⊕ *www.hotelalfonsovi.com* ⟿ *83 rooms* ⚘ *Restaurant* ⊟ *AE, DC, MC, V.*

$$-$$$ ⊡ **Hotel Pintor El Greco.** Next door to the painter's house, this friendly hotel occupies what was once a 17th-century bakery. The modern interior is warm and clean, with tawny colors and antique touches, such as exposed-brick vaulting. ⊠ *Alamillos del Tránsito 13, 45002* ☏ *925/ 285191* 🖷 *925/215819* ⊕ *www.hotel-pintorelgreco.com* ⟿ *33 rooms* ⊟ *AE, DC, MC, V.*

Shopping

The Moors established silver work, damascene (metalwork inlaid with gold or silver), pottery, embroidery, and marzipan traditions here, and next to Toledo's church of San Juan de los Reyes a turn-of-the-20th-century art school keeps these crafts alive. For inexpensive pottery, try to stop at the large roadside emporia on the outskirts of town, on the main road to Madrid. Most of the Toledo region's pottery is made in Talavera la Reina, 76 km (47 mi) west of Toledo. Stop at **Museo Ruiz de Luna** (⊠ Pl. de San Agustín ☏ 925/800149 🖾 Museum €0.60, weekends free ☉ Tues.–Sat. 10–2 and 4–6:30, Sun. 10–2) to watch artisans throw local clay, and to trace the development of Talavera's world-famous ceramics—chronicled through 1,500 tiles, bowls, vases, and plates dating back to the 15th century.

Aranjuez

⑯ *47 km (29 mi) south of Madrid, 35 km (22 mi) northwest of Toledo.*

Founded where the rivers Tagus and Jarama meet, Aranjuez was for centuries the spring quarters of the Hapsburg and Bourbon kings. Felipe V, the first of the Bourbon line, decided to transform the impressive Royal Palace, first built by Hapsburg's Felipe II in 1561, to meet the French aesthetic requirements of his time, and gave a boost to the construction of the impressive gardens and parks that surround the palace. Prohibiting people from settling near his lands (a prohibition carried over well into the mid-1700s by other monarchs), Felipe II helped make Aranjuez a privileged green royal oasis praised by travelers visiting the court.

The Aranjuez of today is a medium-size town that still retains the splendor of its palace, gardens, and *sotos*—magnificent avenues in the northern part of the city with groves of trees. Try to visit Aranjuez in the spring or fall, when nature is showing off its brightest colors. And to see the quiet town liven up, plan to visit in May or June when the first of two local festivals celebrates ancient music with an array of concerts in the royal gardens. All concerts are performed from their respective periods with the original instruments used to create each style of music. T

Commuter trains (*tren de cercanías*) to Aranjuez leave often from Madrid's Atocha station; the ride is 50 minutes.

A 10-minute walk along the narrow avenue of Palacio Real will lead you onto the southeastern corner of the **Royal Palace** (🕿 918/910740 📧 Guided tour €5; special tour with access to royal family's rooms €6 ☉ Oct.–Mar., Tues.–Sun. 10–5:15; Apr.–Sept., Tues.–Sun. 10–6:15). The palace dates back to the year 1561, when Felipe II entrusted its design and construction to architect Juan Bautista de Toledo. The work was continued by Bautista's disciple, Juan de Herrera, but it was the Bourbon kings and architects (especially Giacomo Bonavia, who also built the facade) who decided to part with the austerity of the former dynasty, enlarging the palace to adapt it to the ostentatious baroque period and to the increasing number of members of the court. The inside of the palace reflects the taste of the last monarch who inhabited it (Elizabeth II, in the mid-1800s). East and north of the palace extend two gardens: the Parterre, designed during the Bourbon period, and the Island, originally designed by Herrera and mixing Spanish, Flemish, and Italian elements. A tourist train departs from the palace, making an hour tour of the city. Narration is done in several languages.

The city's most impressive garden is the **Jardín del Príncipe,** which spreads between the Tagus course and Calle de la Reina. Designed at the end of the 18th century, it's divided into a dozen distinctive sections. In the northwestern corner of the garden is the old royal jetty and the **Museo de Falúas** (Felucca Museum), home to seven impressive gondolas used by Spanish royalty for festive outings on the Tagus and other Spanish rivers. On the eighth garden to the east of Jardín del Príncipe is **La casita del Labrador** (🕿 91/891–0304) built by Carlos IV as a rustic escape from palace activity. During its construction, however, the king got carried away, creating an ostentatious small palace with all the sumptuous decorative arts of the period on display. The **Royal Laborer's House** can be visited only via a guided tour, conducted in Spanish. Make a reservation in advance. When you've finished your tour, the best way to get back to town is to walk the path parallel to the Calle de la Reina, inside the park.

The **tourist office,** on the eastern side of Plaza San Antonio under the colonnade, can provide more information on other interesting sites, including ones along the avenues filled with elms, ash trees, poplars, linden, and oaks. In spring and summer you can find street vendors selling strawberries with whipped cream by the riverbank near the palace—you can also get them at the city's food market, a restored building from the 1900s that's across from city hall. The city's most renowned restaurant is **Casa Pablo** (✉ Calle Almíbar 42 🕿 918/911–451), decorated with bullfighting paraphernalia. In the front bar, you can get some tapas as well as something to quench your thirst.

From the beginning of April to mid-June the **Tren de la Fresa** (Strawberry Train), with a steam locomotive and wooden wagons, departs on weekends from Atocha at 10:05 AM. After a 90-minute trip, you reach Aranjuez, where you get a guided tour of the city. On the way, train staff, dressed in outfits from the 19th century, serve you strawberries, one of the region's best-known products. Round-trip fare is €24 for adults and €12 for children ages 2 to 12.

To get to Chinchón from Aranjuez, you can take the AISA bus on Calle Infantas 16 (902/19–8788) toward Villarejo. The trip takes about 40 minutes, with buses departing seven times a day on weekdays, twice on Saturday, and once on Sunday.

Consuegra

17 *78 km (48 mi) south of Aranjuez, 125 km (78 mi) south of Madrid (Km 119 on A4).*

This small, historic town is dominated by a spectacular hilltop castle and 11 white **windmills.** You can drive straight up to the first windmill, **El Bolero** (restored to house the local tourist office), and walk upstairs to see the intricate 16th-century machinery. In October, the fields all around Consuegra are purple with **saffron crocuses.** These flowers appear overnight, and the three female stigmas must be handpicked from each one immediately—each flower produces only once. The stamens are then dried over braziers in private homes to become "red gold" worth €1,800 per kilogram. The process—which requires 4,000 crocuses to make 2 grams (0.7 ounce) of saffron—has been used for 700 years. Consuegra's **Fiesta de la Rosa del Azafrán** (Saffron Festival), complete with competitions and saffron-based foods, is held here the last week of October.

Moors and Christians once did battle for the 10th-century **Castillo de Consuegra,** and during the second week in August the town reenacts their medieval conflict twice a day. In the 12th century the castle housed the Knights of St. John of Jerusalem, and here you can imagine that most notorious knight of all, Don Quijote, tilting at the windmills. The ramparts have classic views of the plains of La Mancha, with the town and saffron fields below. ⊕ *www.consuegra.es* ☎ *925/475731 tourist office and castle* ☒ *€2* ☉ *Nov.–Mar., weekdays 9–2 and 3:30–6, weekends 10:30–2 and 3:30–6; Apr.–Oct., weekdays 9–2 and 4:30–7, Sat. 10–2 and 4:30–7, Sun. 10:30–2 and 4:30–7.*

EN ROUTE

Return to the A4 and take the Daimiel exit and bypass to visit **Las Tablas de Daimiel,** a wetland wildlife reserve threatened by drought and farm irrigation. In addition to its rare flora and fauna, the park attracts migrating birds in March, April, October, and November. The longest of the three marked walks takes an hour, and observation towers aid in viewing; residents include red-crested pochards, broad-billed shoveler ducks, great crested glebes, purple herons, and marsh harriers. ☒ *N430 toward Ciudad Real, 12 km (8 mi) west of Daimiel* ☎ *926/693118* ⊕ *www.mma.es/parques/lared/tablas* ☒ *Free* ☉ *Park and visitor center daily 8:30–dusk.*

Almagro

18 *190 km (118 mi) south of Madrid, 65 km (40 mi) south of Consuegra.*

2

The center of this noble town contains the only preserved medieval theater in Europe. The theater stands beside the ancient **Plaza Mayor**, where 85 Roman columns form two facing colonnades supporting green-frame 16th-century buildings. Near the plaza are granite mansions embellished with the heraldic shields of their former owners and a splendid parador in a restored 17th-century convent.

★ The **Corral de Comedias** theater stands almost as it did in the 16th century, when it was built, with wooden balconies on four sides and the stage at one end of the open central patio. During the golden age of Spanish theater—the time of playwrights Calderón de la Barca, Cervantes, and Lope de Vega—touring actors came to Almagro, which then prospered from mercury mines and lace making. The Corral is the site of an international theater festival each July. ⊠ *Pl. Mayor 18* ☎ *926/861539* ✆ *€1.80* ⊕ *www.corraldecomedias.com* ☉ *Tues.–Fri. 10–2 and 4–7 (6–9 July and Aug.), Sat. 10–2 and 4–6 (6–8 July and Aug.), Sun. 11–2 and 4–6 (6–8 July and Aug.)* ☞ *Festival tickets: by credit card, Tele-Entrada, 902/101212; with cash, after mid-May, Palacio de los Medrano, San Agustín 7.*

The **Museo Nacional del Teatro** displays models of the Roman amphitheaters in Mérida (Extremadura) and Sagunto (near Valencia), both still in use, as well as costumes, pictures, and documents relating to the history of Spanish theater. ⊠ *Gran Maestre 2* ☎ *926/261014* ⊕ *http://museoteatro.mcu.es* ☉ *Tues.–Fri. 10–2 and 4–7 (6–9 July), Sat. 11–2 and 4–6 (6–8 July), Sun. 11–2.*

Where to Stay & Eat

$$–$$$ ✗**El Corregidor.** Several old houses stuffed with antiques make up this fine restaurant and tapas bar. The menu centers on rich local fare, including game, fish, and spicy Almagro eggplant, a local delicacy. The €25 *menú de degustación* (house menu) yields seven savory tapas, and the €45 *menu Manchego menu gastronómico* showcases regional specialties, including *pisto manchego,* a La Mancha–style vegetable ratatouille, and *ravioli de cordero* (lamb-stuffed ravioli). ⊠ *Plaza Fray Fernando de Córdoba 2* ☎ *926/860648* ⊟ *AE, DC, MC, V* ☉ *Closed Mon. (except July).*

★ $$$–$$$$ ✗▣**Parador de Almagro.** With cells, cloisters, and patios, this parador ($$$) is a finely restored 17th-century Franciscan convent. Some rooms still resemble monks' cells, albeit with lots of modern conveniences. The restaurant serves fabulous *pisto manchego* (a La Mancha equivalent of ratatouille) and *migas,* fried spiced bread crumbs with chopped pork. There's also a bodega-style wine bar. ⊠ *Ronda San Francisco 31, Almagro 13270* ☎ *926/860100* ⊟ *926/860150* ⊕ *www.parador.es* ➥ *54 rooms* ☖ *Restaurant, pool, bar, meeting rooms* ⊟ *AE, DC, MC, V.*

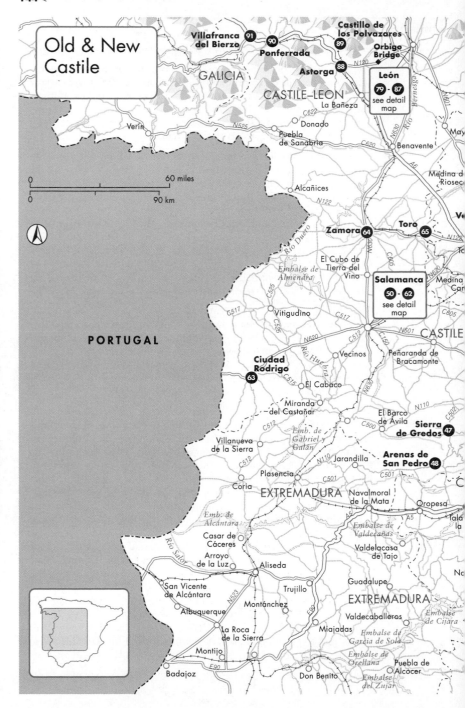

Old & New Castile

Villafranca del Bierzo 91 90 **Ponferrada**

Castillo de los Polvazares 89

Orbigo Bridge

Astorga 88

GALICIA

N120

León 79 - 87 see detail map

CASTILE-LEON

Río Bernesga

La Bañeza

Verín

C622

Donado

N525

Puebla de Sanabria

C620

Benavente

A6

Mayo

Medina d Rioseco

Alcañices

N122

60 miles

90 km

Río Duero

Embalse de Almendra

C525

C517

Zamora 64

Toro 75

Ve

N122

To

El Cubo de Tierra del Vino

C605

N630

Salamanca 50 - 62 see detail map

Medina Car

PORTUGAL

C517

Vitigudino

C526

N620

C517

Río Huebra

Vecinos

C612

C510

N501

C605

CASTILE

Peñaranda de Bracamonte

Ciudad Rodrigo 63

C515

El Cabaco

N630

Miranda del Castañar

C512

Emb. de Gabriel y Galán

N110

El Barco de Ávila

C500

C502

N110

Sierra de Gredos 47

Villanueva de la Sierra

C512

Jarandilla

Arenas de San Pedro 48

Plasencia

C501

Coria

EXTREMADURA

Navalmoral de la Mata

Oropesa

C

Emb. de Alcántara

Río Salor

A5

Embalse de Valdecañas

Tala la

Casar de Cáceres

Valdelacasa de Tajo

Arroyo de la Luz

Aliseda

Guadalupe

No

San Vicente de Alcántara

N523

Trujillo

EXTREMADURA

Albuquerque

Montánchez

E90

Valdecaballeros

Embalse de Cijara

La Roca de la Sierra

Miajadas

Embalse de García de Sola

Montijo

E90

Embalse de Orellana

Puebla de Alcocer

Badajoz

Don Benito

Embalse del Zujar

Ciudad Real

 22 km (14 mi) southwest of Almagro, 116 km (72 mi) south of Toledo.

Alfonso the Wise founded this university town, now the capital of its province, as Villa Real in 1255, and in 1420 Juan II decreed it a bonafide *ciudad* (city). Since then it has become progressively less regal. Only one of its original gate arches, the **Puerta de Toledo**—built in 1328—remains, and the extensive city wall has disappeared altogether. The cathedral, **Santa María del Prado,** (Paseo del Prado s/n) does have a magnificent baroque altarpiece by Giraldo de Merlo. Ciudad Real's present claim to fame is that it's one of the few stops on Spain's first high-speed train, the **AVE**, between Madrid and Seville.

SOUTHEAST OF MADRID

Dramatic landscapes are the draw here: the rocky countryside and magnificent gorges of the Huécar and Júcar rivers make for spectacular views. Cuenca has an impressive museum devoted to abstract art. Nearby towns such as Ciudad Encantada, with its rock formations, and Alarcón, which has a medieval castle, make pleasant excursions.

Cuenca

 167 km (104 mi) southeast of Madrid.

The delightful old town of Cuenca is one of the strangest in Spain. It's built on a sloping, curling finger of rock whose precipitous sides plunge down to the gorges of the Huécar and Júcar rivers. Because the town ran out of room to expand, some medieval houses hang right over the abyss and are now a unique architectural attraction: the Casas Colgadas (Hanging Houses). The old town's dramatic setting grants spectacular gorge views, and its cobblestone streets, cathedral, churches, bars, and taverns contrast starkly with the modern town, which sprawls beyond the river gorges. Though somewhat isolated, Cuenca makes a good overnight stop if you're traveling between Madrid and Valencia. The lower half of the old town is a maze of tiny streets, any of which will take you up to the Plaza del Carmen. From here the town narrows and a single street, Calle Alfonso VIII, continues the ascent to the Plaza Mayor, which you reach after passing under the arch of the town hall. Calle San Pedro shoots off from the northern side of Plaza Mayor; just off Calle San Pedro, clinging to the western edge of Cuenca, is the tiny **Plaza San Nicolás,** a pleasingly dilapidated square. Nearby, the unpaved Ronda del Júcar hovers over the Júcar gorge and commands remarkable views of the mountainous landscape.

The best views are from the square in front of a **small palace** at the very top of Cuenca, where the town tapers out to the narrowest of ledges. Here, gorges are on either side of you, and old houses sweep down toward a distant plateau in front. The palace itself, which has a staid but erroneous history about Alfonso VII's wife, is now a hotel named after her, Hotel Leonora de Aquitania. ⊠ *C. San Pedro 60* ☏ *969/231000.*

The **Museo Diocesano de Arte Sacro** (Diocesan Museum of Sacred Art) is in what were once the cellars of the Bishop's Palace. The beautifully clear display includes a jewel-encrusted, Byzantine diptych of the 13th century; a Crucifixion by the 15th-century Flemish artist Gerard David; and two small El Grecos. From the Plaza Mayor, take Calle Obispo Valero and follow signs toward the Casas Colgadas. ✉ *Obispo Valero 3* ☎ *969/ 224210* ✆ *€2* ☉ *Oct.–May, Tues.–Sat. 11–2 and 4–6, Sun. 11–2; June–Sept., Tues.–Sat. 11–2 and 5–8, Sun. 11–2.*

★ Cuenca's most famous buildings, the **Casas Colgadas** (Hanging Houses), form one of Spain's finest and most curious museums, the **Museo de Arte Abstracto Español** (Museum of Spanish Abstract Art). Projecting over the town's eastern precipice, these houses originally formed a 15th-century palace, which later served as a town hall before falling into disrepair in the 19th century. In 1927 the cantilevered balconies that had once hung over the gorge were rebuilt, and finally, in 1966, the painter Fernando Zóbel decided to create inside the houses the world's first museum devoted exclusively to abstract art. The works he gathered are almost all by the remarkable generation of Spanish artists who grew up in the 1950s and were essentially forced to live abroad during the Franco regime: the major names include Carlos Saura, Eduardo Chillida, Lucio Muñoz, Manuel Millares, Antoni Tàpies, and Zóbel himself. ✉ *Canónigos s/n* ☎ *969/212983* ⊕ *www.march.es/arte/cuenca/index. asp* ✆ *€3* ☉ *Tues.–Fri. 11–2 and 4–6, Sat. 11–2 and 4–8, Sun. 11–2:30.*

The **Puente de San Pablo,** an iron footbridge over the Huécar gorge, was built in 1903 for the convenience of the Dominican monks of San Pablo, who live on the other side. If you don't have a fear of heights, cross the narrow bridge to take in the vertiginous view of the river below and the equally thrilling panorama of the Casas Colgadas. A path from the bridge descends to the bottom of the gorge, landing you by the bridge that you crossed to enter the old town.

Where to Stay & Eat

$$–$$$ ✕ **El Figón de Pedro.** Owner Pedro Torres Pacheco, one of Spain's most
Fodor'sChoice famous restaurateurs, has done much to promote the excellence of Cuenca's
★ cuisine. This pleasantly low-key spot in the lively heart of the modern town serves such local specialties as *ajoarriero,* a paste of pounded salt cod, garlic, and peppers served on toast, and *morteruelo,* a warm pâté made from the livers of game (including rabbit and partridge) and served with garlic bread. For dessert, try the *alaju,* a Moorish sweet made with honey, bread crumbs, almonds, and orange water. Wash down your meal with *resolí,* Cuenca's liqueur made from orange, coffee, and spices. ✉ *Cervantes 13* ☎ *969/226821* ☐ *AE, DC, MC, V* ☉ *No dinner Sun. Closed Mon.*

$–$$ ✕ **La Ponderosa.** Famous around Spain for fine tapas and raciones, both to take home and consume on the premises, this place is always filled to the gills and booming. It is a completely nonsmoking bar. ✉ *San Francisco 20* ☎ *969/213214* ☐ *DC, MC, V* ☉ *Closed Sun. in June and July.*

$–$$ ✕ **Las Brasas.** Meats cooked over wood coals and hearty bean concoctions excel here, with the kitchen and fire visible from the bar of this cozy, oak-floor Castilian enclave. The owners use vegetables from their own garden to make a delicious *pucherete* (white-bean soup). ⊠ *Alfonso VIII 105* ☏ *969/213821* ⊟ *DC, MC, V* ⊙ *Closed Wed. and July.*

$$$ ⌑ **Parador de Cuenca.** In the gorge beneath the Casas Colgadas is this exquisitely restored 16th-century monastery. Rooms are furnished in a lighter and more luxurious style than the norm for Castilian houses of this vintage. ⊠ *Subida a San Pablo s/n, 16001* ☏ *969/232320* 🖷 *969/ 232534* ⊕ *www.parador.es* ⇆ *63 rooms* ⌂ *Restaurant, tennis court, pool, bar* ⊟ *AE, DC, MC, V.*

$$–$$$ ⌑ **Cueva del Fraile.** Seven kilometers (4½ mi) out of town on the Buenache road, this luxurious hotel occupies a 16th-century building surrounded by dramatic landscapes. The rooms have reproduction traditional furniture, stone floors, and, in some cases, wood ceilings. ⊠ *Ctra. Cuenca–Buenache, Km 7, 16001* ☏*969/211571* 🖷*969/256047* ⊕*www. hotelcuevadelfraile.com* ⇆ *75 rooms* ⌂ *Restaurant, tennis court, pool, meeting room* ⊟ *AE, DC, MC, V* ⊙ *Closed Jan.* ⋔ *BP.*

★ $–$$$ ⌑ **Posada San José.** Installed in a 17th-century convent in Cuenca's old town, the *posada* (inn) clings to the top of the Huécar gorge. Furnishings are traditional, and the mood is informal and friendly. ⊠ *Julián Romero 4, 16001* ☏*969/211300* 🖷*969/230365* ⊕*www.posadasanjose. com* ⇆ *29 rooms* ⌂ *Cafeteria, bar; no a/c, no TV in some rooms* ⊟ *AE, DC, MC, V.*

$ ⌑ **Hostal Cánovas.** Near Plaza España, in the heart of the new town, this is one of Cuenca's best bargains. The lobby's not impressive, but the inviting rooms more than compensate with hardwood floors, gold-trim burgundy fabrics, and decorative white moldings. Brothers Edilio and Paulino, the owners, spent more than two years restoring the run-down 1878 building. ⊠ *Fray Luis de León 38, 16001* ☏ *969/213973* ⊕ *www. hostalcanovas.com* ⇆ *17 rooms* ⊟ *AE, MC, V.*

Ciudad Encantada

㉑ *35 km (22 mi) north of Cuenca.*

The "Enchanted City," which is not really a city at all, comprises a series of large and fantastic mushroomlike rock formations erupting in a landscape of pines. This commanding spectacle, deemed "site of national interest," was formed over many millennia by the forces of water and wind on limestone rocks. A footpath can guide you through striking outcrops with names such as El Tobagón (The Toboggan) and Mar de Piedras (Sea of Stones).

Alarcón

㉒ *69 km (43 mi) south of Cuenca.*

This fortified village on the edge of the great plains of La Mancha stands on a high spur of land encircled almost entirely by a bend of the Júcar River. Alarcón's **castle** dates from the 8th century, and in the 14th century it came into the hands of the *infante* (child prince) Don Juan Manuel, who wrote a collection of classic moral tales. Today the castle is one of Spain's finest paradors. If you're not driving, a bus to Motilla will leave you a short taxi ride away (call 969/331797 for a cab). ⊠ *Av. Amigos de los Castillos 3.*

Where to Stay & Eat

$$$–$$$$ ✕⃞ **Parador de Alarcón.** This 8th- to 12th-century gorge-top castle ($$$$) is a fantasy come true, a fortress of Moorish origin decorated in a military motif. The turret room is the best and biggest; the rooms in the corner towers have arrow slit windows, and others have window niches where women did needlework. Dinner is served in an arched baronial hall complete with shields, armor, and a gigantic fireplace. ⊠ *Av. Amigos de los Castillos 3, 16213* ☏ *969/330315* ☏ *969/330303* ⊕ *www.parador.es* ⊲ *14 rooms* ♿ *Restaurant* ▭ *AE, DC, MC, V.*

NORTHEAST OF MADRID

They're off the main tourist tracks, but the provinces of Guadalajara and Soria have a lot to offer and are easily accessible by train. The rail from Madrid to Zaragoza passes through every town in this section, allowing a manageable excursion of two to three days. If you have a car, you can extend this trip with a countryside detour.

Alcalá de Henares

㉓ *30 km (19 mi) east of Madrid, off A2.*

A Roman town (Complutum) in the 1st century AD, and an Arab one (al-Qala ibn Salam, hence its current name) in the 8th century, Alcalá was the site of the first meeting between Christopher Columbus and Isabella, and was also Cervantes' birthplace. By the early 1500s, it had become a major university town, attracting talented people from all over the country and beyond. A few centuries later, after some ups and downs, it remains a bustling gathering point for national and international students, a city that preserves many of its Renaissance architectural riches and is well worth a visit of half of or all of the day.

The best way to get to Alcalá is by a 40-minute commuter train ride from Madrid's Atocha station. From the station to the northern corner of the university's law school, which marks the beginning of the old quarter, it is only a 10-minute walk along Paseo de la Estación.

The city's most significant building is **Colegio Mayor San Ildefonso** (⊠ Plaza San Diego s/n ☏ 91/885–6487), a part of Alcala de Henares' university and now the current university president's office. The university was founded by Cardinal Cisneros in 1499 to teach law, art, and theology; in 1514, medicine was added. Cisneros, Isabella's confessor, was a powerful and wise man who greatly influenced the politics and culture of his time. He coordinated the works that produced the first polyglot Bible (a translation of the holy scriptures in Latin, Greek, Hebrew, and Aramean). After a few centuries of glory, the university closed down in 1836 after the state began confiscating the Catholic Church's assets. Later the university was bought back by a group of citizens in 1850. The group's successors started renting the premises to the state in 1977 for the symbolic amount of 1 peseta a year, so that the university could reopen. The building has four patios and a magnificent chapel, done in a mix of Gothic, plateresque, and Mudejar styles, which houses

Cisneros's highly ornamented sepulchre (his remains are safeguarded beneath Alcalá's cathedral's presbytery), carved in Carrara marble. The beautiful main lecture hall, the students' graduation exam room in the 16th and 17th centuries, is where Juan Carlos I, Spain's present-day king, awards the annual Premio Cervantes, the most distinguished literature award in the Spanish language. Students offer guided tours of the building several times a day—call in advance for one in English.

On the southern part of Plaza Cervantes, the city's main square, is the **Corral de Comedias** (⊠ Plaza de Cervantes 15). This theater was built in 1602 to accommodate student performances. Reconstructed several times, it became a cinema in the second quarter of the 20th century, and a municipal storage room years later. Thanks to the research efforts of three young students, who located and unveiled the remains of the old theater in the early '80s, it was superbly restored and reopened in 2001. Also significant, more for its historical than for its artistic value, is the **Museo Casa Natal de Cervantes** (⊠ Calle Mayor 48 ☎ 91/889–9654 ⊕ www.museo-casa-natal-cervantes.org), a rehabilitated building in what was originally Cervantes' father's house. His father worked nearby at Calle Mayor 46, **Antezana Hospital** (☎ 91/889–9654), now run by nuns who care for old women. The austere, 15th-century courtyard is open to the public. The simple hospital is more impressive and significant than the perfectly refurbished house.

Also worth visiting is the **Museo Arqueológico Regional,** on Plaza de las Bernardas (☎ 91/879–6666). The Regional Archaeological Museum traces the history and evolution of life and human beings in Madrid from the Palaeozoic era, when Madrid was covered by the sea, to the 17th and 18th centuries. On Plaza del Santos Niños is the **Catedral Magistral,** built in the late-Gothic style and still preserving some valuable elements despite a fire that severely damaged it in 1936. Across from the Catedral Magistral, also on Plaza de los Santos Niños, is one of the city's two **tourist offices**—the other is near the southeastern edge of the Colegio Mayor San Ildefonso's building, on Callejón Santa María 1 (91/889–2694). If you're part of a group, you may want to buy guided tours in English (for a total price of €115 to €125) from **Promoción Turística de Alcalá** (⊠ Plaza de los Irlandeses 1 ☎ 91/882–1354 ⊕ www.alcalaturismo.com). The best place to eat in town, as much for its location, on the south side of the Colegio Mayor San Ildefonso, as for its food (great suckling pig, lamb, and venison, and other regional delicacies), is the **Hostería del Estudiante** (⊠ Calle Colegios 3 ☎ 91/8880330), run by Spain's parador system.

Guadalajara

㉔ *17 km (10 mi) northeast of Alcalá, 55 km (34 mi) northeast of Madrid.*

This quiet, affluent provincial capital is popular with Madrid commuters, who own many of the villas with terra-cotta roofs that sprawl down its slopes. Guadalajara was severely damaged in the civil war, but its **Palacio del Infantado** (Palace of the Prince's Territory) still stands and is one of the most important Spanish palaces of its period. Built between 1461 and 1492 by Juan Guas, the palace is a bizarre and potent mixture of Gothic, classical, and Mudéjar influences. The main facade is rich; the lower floors are studded with diamond shapes; and the whole is crowned by a complex Gothic gallery supported on a frieze pitted with intricate Moorish cellular work (the honeycomb motif). Inside is a fanciful and exciting courtyard. The ground floor holds the Museo de Bellas Artes, a modest provincial art gallery. ✉ *Pl. de los Caídos 1* ☎ *949/ 213301* 🖃 *Palacio visit and Museo de Bellas Artes free* ☉ *Weekdays 9–9:30, Sat. 9–2:30 and 4–7:30, Sun. 10–2:30 and 5–7:30.*

EN ROUTE   East of Guadalajara extends the Alcarria, a high plateau crossed by rivers forming verdant valleys. It was made famous in the 1950s by one of the great classics of Spanish travel literature, Camilo José Cela's *Journey to the Alcarria*, in which Cela evoked the backwardness and remoteness of an area barely an hour from Madrid. Even today you can feel far removed from the modern world here.

Pastrana

25 *46 km (28 mi) southeast of Guadalajara, 101 km (61 mi) east of Madrid.*

Heading southeast from Guadalajara on route N320 and taking the CM 2006 fork to the right after 18 km (11 mi), you'll reach Pastrana, where its narrow hilltop lanes merge into the landscape. This pretty village of Roman origin was once the capital of a small duchy. The tiny museum attached to Pastrana's **Colegiata** (collegiate church) displays a glorious series of Gothic tapestries; to see it, stop into the tourist office and they'll send someone to unlock the door for you. *Tourist office* ✉ *Plaza de La Hora* ☎ *949/370672* 🖃 *€2.50* ☉ *Daily 11:30–2 and 4:30–7.*

Even more of a gem is Pastrana's **Museo de Recuerdos de Santa Teresa de Avila y de San Juan de la Cruz and its Museo de Ciencias Naturales.** A unique combination of mysticism, science, and art set in a stunning 16th-to-17th-century convent, the museum's treasures include medieval wood carvings, paintings by masters Luca Giordano and Sebastiano Ricci, memorabilia from the lives and works of Santa Teresa and St. John of the Cross, and an unusual display of shells, woods, and birds from the Philippines brought back by missionary monks. *Convento del Carmen* ✉ *Crtra. de Almonacid de Zorita Km 2* ☎ *949/370057* 🖃 *€2.40* ☉ *Tues.–Sun. 11:30–2 and 3–6.*

Sigüenza

26 *86 km (53 mi) northeast of Guadalajara.*

Sigüenza has splendid architecture and one of the most beautifully preserved cathedrals in Castile. Begun around 1150 and not completed until the early 16th century, Sigüenza's remarkable **cathedral** combines aspects of Spanish architecture from the Romanesque period to the Renaissance. The sturdy western front is forbidding, but hides a wealth of ornamental and artistic masterpieces. Go directly to the sacristan (the sacristy is at the north end of the ambulatory) for a guided tour, which is obligatory when visiting the cathedral. The late-Gothic cloister leads to a room lined with 17th-century Flemish tapestries. In the north transept is the late-15th-century plateresque sepulchre of Dom Fadrique of Portugal. The Chapel of the Doncel (to the right of the sanctuary) contains the tomb of Don Martín Vázquez de Arca, commissioned by Queen Isabella, to whom Don Martín served as *doncel* (page) before dying young (25) at the gates of Granada in 1486. ⊠ *Pl. Mayor* ▣ *€3* ⊙ *Tues.–Sun. 9:30–1:30 and 4:30–7. Guided tours Tues.–Sat. at 11, noon, 4:30, and 5:30, and Sun. at noon and 5:30.*

In a refurbished early-19th-century house next to the cathedral's west facade, the **Museo Diocesano de Arte Sacro** (Diocesan Museum of Sacred Art) contains a prehistoric section and much religious art from the 12th to 18th century. ⊠ *Pl. Mayor* ▣ *€3* ⊙ *Tues.–Sun. 11–2 and 4–7.*

The south side of the cathedral overlooks the arcaded **Plaza Mayor**, a harmonious Renaissance square commissioned by Cardinal Mendoza. The small palaces and cobbled alleys here mark the virtually intact old quarter. Along Calle Mayor you'll find the palace that belonged to the doncel's family. An enchanting **castle,** overlooking wild, hilly countryside from above Sigüenza, is now a parador. Founded by the Romans but rebuilt at various later periods, most of the structure went up in the 14th century, when it became a residence for the queen of Castile, Doña Blanca de Borbón, who was banished here by her husband, Peter the Cruel. ⊠ *C. Mayor.*

Where to Stay & Eat

★ **$$$** ✕▥ **Parador de Sigüenza.** This mighty 12th-century fortress has hosted royalty for centuries, from Ferdinand and Isabella right up to the present king, Juan Carlos. Some rooms have four-poster beds and balconies overlooking the wild landscape. The excellent dining room ($$$–$$$$) makes a leisurely lunch essential; your choices might include roast kid, pheasant, or cod with truffles and cheese. ⊠ *Pl. del Castillo s/n, 19250* 🕾 *949/390100* 🖷 *949/391364* ⊕ *www.parador.es* 🛏 *81 rooms* ♧ *Restaurant, meeting room, parking (fee)* ⊟ *AE, DC, MC, V.*

Medinaceli

㉗ *32 km (20 mi) northeast of Sigüenza.*

The preserved village of Medinaceli—literally "city in the sky"—commands exhilarating views from the top of a long, steep ridge. Dominating the skyline is a Roman triumphal arch from the 2nd or 3rd century AD, the only surviving triple archway of this period in Spain (the arch's silhouette is featured on road signs to national monuments throughout the country). The surrounding village, once the seat of one of Spain's most powerful dukes, was virtually abandoned by the end of the 19th century, and if you come here during the week, you can find yourself in a near ghost town. Madrileños have weekend houses here, as do several Americans. The town is archaic and beautiful, with houses overgrown by shrubs and trees, and unpaved lanes into wild countryside.

Where to Stay & Eat

★ **$–$$** ✕▥ **La Cerámica.** Rustic and relaxed, this country inn near the center of Medinaceli serves fine Castilian cuisine ranging from roasts to thick soups and stews. The rooms are cozy and romantic, with wooden beams and slanted ceilings. Halfway between Zaragoza and Madrid, this is a lucky find for travelers with sufficient time. ☒ *Santa Isabel 2, 42240* ☎ *975/326381* 🖨 *975/326381* 📞 *12 rooms* ⚐ *Restaurant; no a/c, no room TVs* ▤ *AE, DC, MC, V.*

Soria

28 *74 km (46 mi) north of Medinaceli, 234 km (145 mi) northeast of Madrid.*

Prosperous for centuries as a sheep farming center during the 15th-century European wool monopoly that laid the groundwork for Spain's Golden Age, this provincial capital, marred by modern development, is often hit by the cold, biting winds of the Castilian meseta. Still, the Duero valley is splendid, as is the Romanesque touches that remain in Soria.

Soria has strong connections with Spain's finest 20th-century poet Antonio Machado (1875–1939). The Seville-born poet lived a bohemian life in Paris for many years before returning, at the age of 34, to teach French in Soria from 1909 to 1911. An oversize bronze head of Machado by sculptor Pablo Serrano is displayed outside the **school** where he taught, and his former classroom contains a tiny collection of memorabilia. It was in Soria that Machado fell in love with and married his landlady's 16-year-old daughter, Leonor. When his young bride died only two years later, he felt he could no longer stay in a town so full of tragic memories. He moved on to Baeza, in his native Andalusia, and then to Segovia, where he spent his last years in Spain. Machado died in 1939 just after the end of the Spanish civil war in a refugee concentration camp in Collioure after escaping fascist forces as they entered Catalonia. His most successful work, *Campos de Castilla*, was greatly inspired by Soria and Leonor; both the town and the woman haunted him until his death.

Nearly all roads to Soria converge onto the wide, modern promenade El Espolón, the location of the **Museo Numantino** (Museum of Numancia). Founded in 1919, the museum contains archaeological finds rich in prehistoric and Iberian items. One section on the top floor is dedicated to the important Iberian settlement at nearby Numancia that became famous in Spanish legend for its heroic resistance to invading Roman forces in 133 BC. As historical evidence has confirmed, Numancia resisted a lengthy siege, the few survivors choosing to take their own lives rather than fall into Roman hands. Even today, an ultradefensive soccer or political strategy is invariably described as *una defensa numantina*. ☒ *Paseo de El Espolón 8* ☎ *975/221428* 💶 *€1.20, free weekends* ☉ *July–Sept., Tues.–Sat. 10–2 and 5–8, Sun. 10–2; Oct.–May, Tues.–Sat. 10–2 and 4–7, Sun. 10–2.*

The late-12th-century church of **Santo Domingo** (☒ C. Aduana Vieja) has a richly carved, Romanesque west facade. The imposing, 16th-century **Palacio de los Condes de Gomara** (Palace of the Counts of Gomara; ☒ C. Estudios) is now a law court. Dominating the hill just south of the River Duero is Soria's **parador** (☒ Parque del Castillo), which shares a park with the ruins of the town's castle. Calle de Santiago, which leads to the parador, passes the church and cemetery of El Espino, where

Machado's wife, Leonor, is buried. Just before the Dueron River is the **cathedral** (⊠ Santa Apolonia).

Across the River Duero from Soria is the deconsecrated church of **San Juan de Duero,** once the property of the Knights Hospitalers. Outside the church are the curious ruins of a Romanesque cloister, with a rare Spanish example of interlaced arching. The church itself, now maintained by the Museo Numantino, is a small museum of Romanesque art and architecture. ⊠ *Piso de las Ánimas s/n* ☎ *975/230218* ☑ *€0.60* ⊙ *Oct.–June, Tues.–Sat. 10–2 and 4–7, Sun. 10–2; July–Sept. Tues.–Sat. 10–2 and 5–8, Sun. 10–2.*

Take an evocative, half-hour walk along the Duero to the **Ermita de San Saturio;** you'll follow a path (accessible by car) lined by poplars. The hermitage was built in the 18th century above a cave where the Anchorite St. Saturio fasted and prayed. You can climb up to the building through the cave. ☎ *975/180703* ☑ *Free* ⊙ *Tues.–Sat. 10:30–2 and 4:30–6:30 (7:30 in May and June, 8:30 in July and Aug.), Sun. 10:30–2.*

Where to Stay & Eat

$$$$ ✕ **Mesón Castellano.** The most traditional restaurant in town, this cozy establishment has a large, open fire over which succulent *chuletón de ternera* (veal chops) are cooked. Another house specialty is *migas pastoriles* (soaked bread crumbs fried with peppers and bacon), a local dish. ⊠ *Pl. Mayor 2* ☎ *975/213045* ☰ *AE, DC, MC, V.*

$$$ ☷ **Parador de Soria.** On a hilltop surrounded by trees and parkland, this modern parador has excellent views of the hilly Duero Valley. Antonio Machado came often to this site for inspiration. ⊠ *Parque del Castillo s/n, 42005* ☎ *975/240800* 🖷 *975/240803* ⊕ *www.parador. es* ⮑ *67 rooms* ⚭ *Restaurant, pool, bar, meeting rooms, parking (fee)* ☰ *AE, DC, MC, V.*

Numancia

㉙ *7 km (4½ mi) north of Soria.*

The bleak hilltop ruins of Numancia, an important Iberian settlement, are just a few minutes by car from Soria. Viciously besieged by the Romans in 135–134 BC, Numancia's inhabitants chose death rather than surrender. Most of the foundations that have been unearthed date from the Roman occupation. ☑ *€1* ⊙ *Oct.–May, Tues.–Sat. 10–2 and 4–6, Sun. 10–2; June–Sept., Tues.–Sat. 10–2 and 5–9, Sun. 10–2.*

El Burgo de Osma

㉚ *56 km (35 mi) west of Soria.*

El Burgo de Osma is an enticing medieval and Renaissance town dominated by a Gothic cathedral and a baroque bell tower. Many of its historic buildings have been elegantly restored.

Where to Stay & Eat

★ **$$–$$$** ✕ **Virrey Palafox.** The white walls, wood-beam ceiling, and furnishings here are traditional Castilian, and the long dining room has a no-smoking section, a rarity in Spain. Produce is fresh and seasonal, vegetables are homegrown, and excellent local game is served year-round. The house specialty is fish, in particular *merluza Virrey* (hake stuffed with eels and salmon). Every Saturday and Sunday, starting on the last weekend in January and continuing through February and March, a pig is slaughtered and a feast ensues (€39, reservations required). ⊠ *Universidad 7* 📞 *975/340222* 🍴 *AE, DC, MC, V* ✪ *Closed Mon. and late Dec.–mid-Jan. No dinner Sun.*

$$ 🏨 **II Virrey.** Under the same management as the Virrey Palafox, this pleasant hotel adjoins the 16th-century Convent of San Agustín. Constructed with traditional materials, rooms overlook the plaza and have marble floors, stone walls, and elegant decor. ⊠ *C. Mayor 2, 42300* 📞 *975/ 341311* 🖶 *975/340855* ⊕ *www.virreypalafox.com* 🛏 *52 rooms* ⚭ *Dining room, meeting room* 🍴 *AE, DC, MC, V.*

SEGOVIA & ITS PROVINCE

The area north of Madrid prides itself with a rich and varied history, from the Roman aqueduct in Segovia to the 16th-century village of Pedraza de la Sierra, both good places to spend the night. Other towns to visit include Sepúlveda and Castillo de Coca, for their medieval monuments, and La Granja, where the impressive San Ildefonso gardens grow even more spectacular when the fountains are turned on, creating an effect to rival that of Versailles.

Segovia

③–④ *87 km (54 mi) north of Madrid.*

Fodor'sChoice
★

Breathtaking Segovia—on a ridge in the middle of a gorgeously stark, undulating plain—is defined by its Roman and medieval monuments, its excellent cuisine, its embroideries and textiles, and its sense of well-being. An important military town in Roman times, Segovia was later established by the Moors as a major textile center. Captured by the Christians in 1085, it was enriched by a royal residence, and in 1474 the half sister of Henry IV, Isabella the Catholic (married to Ferdinand of Aragón), was crowned queen of Castile here. By that time Segovia was a bustling city of about 60,000 (there are 53,000 today), but its importance soon diminished as a result of its taking the (losing) side of the Comuneros in the popular revolt against the emperor Carlos V. Though the construction in the 18th century of a royal palace in nearby La Granja revived the town's fortunes somewhat, it never recovered its former vitality. Early in the 20th century, Segovia's sleepy charm came to be appreciated by artists and writers, among them painter Ignacio Zuloaga and poet Antonio Machado. Today the streets swarm with tourists from Madrid; you may want to think twice about trying to experience Segovia in summer.

If you approach Segovia on N603, the first building you see is the cathedral, which seems to rise directly from the fields. Between you and Segovia lies, in fact, a steep and narrow valley, which shields the old town from view. Only when you descend into the valley do you begin to see the old town's spectacular position, rising on top of a narrow rock ledge shaped like a ship. As soon as you reach the modern outskirts, turn left onto the Paseo E. González and follow the road marked **Ruta Panorámica**—you'll soon descend on the narrow and winding Cuesta de los Hoyos, which takes you to the bottom of the wooded valley that dips to the south of the old town. Above, you can see the Romanesque church of San Martín to the right; the cathedral in the middle; and on the far left, where the rock ledge tapers, the turrets, spires, and battlements of Segovia's castle, known as the Alcázar.

A GOOD WALK

Driving and parking are problematic on the narrow streets of old Segovia, so it's best to leave the car behind. Beginning at the church of **San Millán** ㉛ ➤, go up Avenida de Fernández Ladreda until you come to the Plaza del Azoguejo, once the town center and marketplace. Directly in front of you are the arches of the grand **Acueducto Romano** ㉜. Turn away from the aqueduct, exit the plaza from the northwest corner, and head up the pedestrian shopping street Calle Cervantes. Continue up the same street, now called Calle de Juan Bravo, and veer off to the left onto Herrería for a look at the late-Gothic **Palacio de Aspiroz/Palacio de los Condes de Alpuente** ㉝, covered with Segovian *esgrafiado* plasterwork (incised with regular patterns). Back on Calle Juan Bravo and farther ahead, you'll come to the Plaza Martín, on which rises another Romanesque church, **San Martín** ㉞. Just to the west of the church is the Biblioteca y Archivo Histórical (Library and Historical Archive), housed in a 17th-century stone structure that served as Segovia's jail until 1933. Off to the left of Juan Bravo, across from the Plaza Martín, is the refreshing Paseo de Salón, a small promenade at the foot of the town's southern walls. This walk was very popular with Spain's 19th-century queen, Isabel II.

At the Plaza del Corpus, where Juan Bravo splits into Calle de La Judería Vieja and Isabel la Católica, a right turn leads directly to the Plaza Mayor. A left turn leads up Calle de La Judería Vieja into the former Jewish quarter, where Segovia's Jews lived as early as the 13th century. Turn right on Calle de San Frutos, which runs along the east side of the cathedral; from here a short alley leads to the lively Plaza Mayor, an ideal place for lunch or an early evening drink. Facing the arcaded square are the 17th-century **ayuntamiento** ㉟ (town hall) and the eastern corner of the **cathedral** ㊱, its flying buttresses a favorite vantage point for storks. From the plaza, take Calle de Valdeláguila to the church of **San Estéban** ㊲. Touristy Calle de Los Leones slopes down from San Estéban toward the western extremity of the old town's ridge. At the western end of the square is the famous **Alcázar,** ㊳ from which you can see the church of **Vera Cruz** ㊴ and **Casa de la Moneda** (former Mint) ㊵. A walk along the city's peripheral road, Paseo de Santo Domingo de Guzmán, leads to the **Monasterio de la Santa Cruz** ㊶.

TIMING   This walk can be done in a few hours, depending on linger time.

What to See

㉜ **Acueducto Romano.** Segovia's Roman aqueduct ranks with the Pont du Gard in France as one of the greatest surviving examples of Roman engineering. Spanning the dip that stretches from the walls of the old town

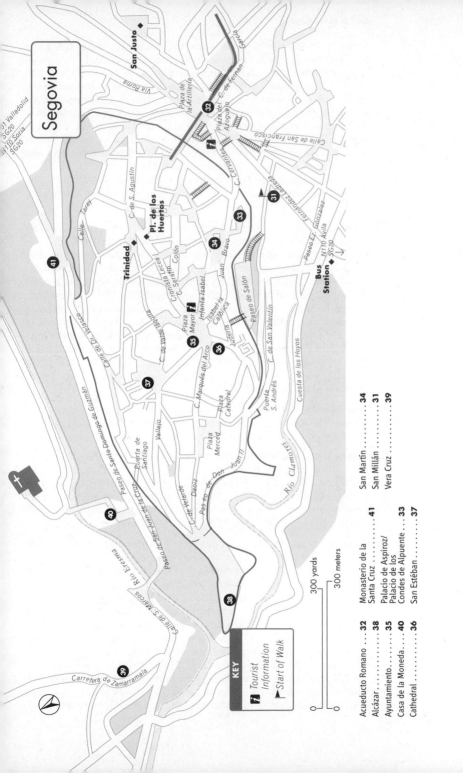

Segovia

San Justo ◆

Plaza de la Artillería

N601 Valladolid
SG20
N110 Soria
SG20

Vía Roma

Calle de la Artillería

Plaza del C. de Ferrari

Gascó

32

Plaza del Azoguejo

i

C. de S. Agustín

Pl. de los Huertos

Trinidad ◆

C. de S. Agustín

Calle Taray

Calle

Cronista Lecea

C. Serafín Colón

Infanta Isabel

Isabel la Católica

Juan Bravo

C. Cervantes

Calle de San Francisco

Fernández Ladreda

Paseo E. G. González

N110 Ávila
SG20

Bus Station ◆

31

33

34

41

Calle de D.I. Velasco

Paseo de Santo Domingo de Guzmán

Río Eresma

Rio de S. Marcos

Calle de San Juan de la Cruz

Puerta de Santiago

Vallejo

C. de Velarde

Paseo de Don Juan II

C. Marqués de Arco

Plaza Mayor

i

35

36

37

Plaza Merced

Plaza Catedral

Puerta S. Andrés

C. de San Valentín

Paseo de Salón

Cuesta de los Hoyos

Río Clamores

38

40

39

Carretera de Zamarramala

✝

KEY

i *Tourist Information*

▲ *Start of Walk*

0 ———— 300 yards
0 ———— 300 meters

Acueducto Romano ...**32**
Alcázar **38**
Ayuntamiento.........**35**
Casa de la Moneda...**40**
Cathedral............**36**

Monasterio de la
Santa Cruz **41**
Palacio de Aspiroz/
Palacio de los
Condes de Alpuente...**33**
San Estéban **37**

San Martín **34**
San Millán **31**
Vera Cruz **39**

to the lower slopes of the Sierra de Guadarrama, it's about 2,952 feet long and rises in two tiers—above what is now the Plaza del Azoguejo, whose name means "highest point"—to a height of 115 feet. The raised section of stonework in the center originally carried an inscription, of which only the holes for the bronze letters remain. The massive granite blocks are held together by neither mortar nor clamps, but the aqueduct has been standing since the end of the first century AD. The only damage it has suffered is the demolition of 35 of its arches by the Moors, and these were later replaced on the orders of Ferdinand and Isabella. Steps at the side of the aqueduct lead up to the walls of the old town. Because pollution from the freeway that passes through the aqueduct has weakened the structure, the road underneath has been closed to traffic. ⊠ *Pl. del Azoguejo.*

㊳ Alcázar. Possibly dating from Roman times, this castle was considerably expanded in the 14th century, remodeled in the 15th, altered again toward the end of the 16th, and completely redone after being gutted by a fire in 1862, when it was used as an artillery school. The exterior, especially when seen from the Ruta Panorámica, is certainly imposing, but the castle is now little more than a pseudomedieval sham. The last remnant of the original structure is the guard tower through which you enter. Crowned by crenellated towers that seem to have been carved out of icing, the rampart can be climbed for superb views; the rest of the interior is a bit disappointing. ⊠ *Pl. de la Reina Victoria Eugenia* ☎ *921/ 460759* ⊕ *www.alcazardesegovia.com* ⊠ *€3.50, plus €1.50 extra to climb the tower* ☉ *Apr.–Sept., daily 10–7; Oct.–Mar., Mon.–Thurs. 10–6, Fri.–Sun. 10–7.*

㉟ Ayuntamiento. The 17th-century town hall stands on the active **Plaza Mayor**. It's closed to the public, but it's a great place to sit and watch the world go by. ⊠ *Pl. Mayor.*

㊵ Casa de la Moneda (Mint). All Spanish coinage was struck here from 1455 to 1730. The mint, scheduled for reconstruction work, offers guided tours every first and third Saturday of the month, with English-language guides available by prior arrangement. Call the number below or e-mail info@segoviamint.org to reserve a tour. ⊠ *C. de la Moneda s/n, just south of River Eresma* ☎ *921/420921* ⊕ *www.segoviamint.org* ⊠ *Free.*

㊱ Cathedral. Begun in 1525 and completed 65 years later, the cathedral was intended to replace an earlier one near the Alcázar, destroyed during the revolt of the Comuneros against Carlos V. It's one of the country's last great examples of the Gothic style. The designs were drawn up by the leading late-Gothicist Juan Gil de Hontañón but executed by his son Rodrigo, in whose work can be seen a transition from the Gothic to the Renaissance style. The interior, illuminated by 16th-century Flemish windows, is light and uncluttered, the one distracting detail being the wooden, neoclassical choir. You enter through the north transept, which is marked MUSEO; turn right, and the first chapel on your right has a lamentation group in wood by the baroque sculptor Gregorio Fernández. Across from the entrance, on the southern transept, is a door opening into the late-Gothic cloister—this and the elaborate door leading into it were transported from the old cathedral and are the work of architect Juan Guas. Under the pavement immediately inside the cloisters are the tombs of Juan and Rodrigo Gil de Hontañón; that these two lie in a space designed by Guas is appropriate, for the three men together dominated the last phase of the Gothic style in Spain. Off the cloister, a small museum of religious art, installed partly in the first-floor chapter house, has a white-and-gold 17th-century ceiling, a late example of Mudéjar *artesonado* work. ⊠ *Plaza Mayor s/n* ☎ *921/462205* ⊞ *Cathedral free, cloister and museum* €2 ⊙ *Apr.–Oct., Mon.–Sat. 9–6:30, Sun. 9–2:30; Nov.–Mar., Mon.–Sat. 9–5:30, Sun. 9–2:30.*

㊶ Monasterio de la Santa Cruz. Built in the 13th century, this church was established by St. Dominick of Guzmán, founder of the Dominican order, and rebuilt in the 15th century by Ferdinand and Isabella. Now it's a private university, La Universidad Sec, and during the academic year, you can see the Gothic interior with plateresque and Renaissance touches. ⊠ *Cardenal Zúñiga s/n* ☎ *921/471997.*

㉝ Palacio de Aspiroz/Palacio de los Condes de Alpuente (Palace of the Counts of Alpuente). This late-Gothic palace is covered with a type of plasterwork known as *esgrafiado,* incised with regular patterns; the style was most likely introduced by the Moors and is characteristic of Segovian architecture. The building is now used for city administrative offices and is no longer open to the public. ⊠ *Pl. del Platero Oquendo.*

㊲ San Estéban. Though the interior has a baroque facing, the exterior has kept some splendid capitals, as well as an exceptionally tall and attractive tower. Due east of the church square is the **Capilla de San Juan de Dios,** next to which is the former pension where the poet Antonio Machado spent his last years in Spain. The family who looked after Machado still owns the building and will show you the poet's room on request, with its kerosene stove, iron bed, and round table. The church is open for mass only. ⊠ *Pl. de San Estéban* ⊙ *Mass daily 8–10* AM *and 7–9* PM.

㉞ San Martín. This unavoidable and elevated Romanesque church, on the main street between the aqueduct and cathedral, stands in a little plaza of the same name. ⊠ *Pl. San Martín* ☎ *921/443402* ⊙ *Open for mass only, daily 8–10* AM *and 7–9* PM.

▶ **㉛ San Millán.** A perfect example of the Segovian Romanesque, this 12th-century church is perhaps the finest in town apart from the cathedral. The exterior is notable for its arcaded porch, where church meetings were once held. The virtually untouched Romanesque interior is dominated by massive columns, whose capitals carry such carved scenes as the Flight into Egypt and the Adoration of the Magi. The vaulting on the crossing shows the Moorish influence on Spanish medieval architecture. ⊠ *Av. Fernández Ladreda 26, 5-min walk outside town walls* ⊙ *Open for mass only, daily 8–10* AM *and 7–9* PM.

㊴ Vera Cruz. Made of the local warm-orange stone, this isolated Romanesque church was built in 1208 for the Knights Templar. Like other buildings associated with this order, it has 12 sides, inspired by the Church of the Holy Sepulchre in Jerusalem. Your trip pays off in full when you climb the bell tower and see all of Segovia profiled against the Sierra de Guadarrama, capped with snow in winter. ⊠ *Ctra. de Zamarramala s/n, on northern outskirts of town, off Cuestra de los Hoyos* ☎ *921/431475* ⊠ *€1.50* ⊘ *May–Sept., Tues.–Sun. 10:30–1:30 and 3:30–7; Oct. and Dec.–Apr., Tues.–Sun. 10:30–1:30 and 3:30–6:30.*

Where to Stay & Eat

★ **$$$$** ✕ **Mesón de José María.** With a lively bar, this Mesón (traditional tavern-restaurant) is hospitable, and its passionately dedicated owner is devoted to maintaining traditional Castilian specialties while concocting innovations of his own. The menu changes constantly according to what's in season. The large, old-style, brightly lighted dining room is often packed, and the waiters are uncommonly friendly. Although it's a bit touristy, it's equally popular with locals. ⊠ *Cronista Lecea 11* ☎ *921/461111* ⊕ *www.rtejosemaria.com* ⊟ *AE, DC, MC, V.*

$$$–$$$$ ✕ **Casa Duque.** Founded in 1895 and still in the family, this restaurant, the oldest in Segovia, has an intimate interior, with homey wood beams and a plethora of fascinating *objetos*. Roasts are the specialty, but the *judiones de La Granja Duque*—enormous white beans from nearby La Granja, served with sausages—are also excellent. ⊠ *Cervantes 12* ☎ *921/462487* ⊕ *www.restauranteduque.es* ⚱ *Reservations essential* ⊟ *AE, DC, MC, V.*

★ **$$–$$$$** ✕ **Mesón de Cándido.** Cándido began life as an inn near the end of the 18th century, and was declared a national monument in 1941. Tucked beside the aqueduct, it has a medley of small, irregular dining rooms decorated with memorabilia. Amid the dark-wood beams and Castilian knickknacks hang photos of the celebrities who have dined here, from Ernest Hemingway to Princess Grace of Monaco. Cándido's son now runs the place. If it's your first time here, the *cochinillo* (piglet), roasted in a wood-fire oven, is a great choice. The partridge stew or roast lamb are also memorable, especially on a freezing winter afternoon with sunlight lighting up the bright ocher aqueduct. ⊠ *Pl. de Azoguejo 5* ☎ *921/425911* ⊕ *www.mesondecandido.es* ⚱ *Reservations essential* ⊟ *AE, DC, MC, V.*

$$$–$$$$ ✕⊞ **Parador de Segovia.** Architecturally one of the most interesting of Spain's modern paradors (if you like naked concrete), this low building is set on a hill overlooking the city; it's a very long walk to the city center. The rooms ($$$) are cold in appearance, but from the large windows the panorama of Segovia and its aqueduct are spectacular. (The ground floors have views of hedges, so request a room with a view if you want one.) The restaurant serves Segovian and international dishes, such as *lomo de merluza al aroma de estragón* (hake fillet with tarragon and shrimp). ⊠ *Ctra. de Valladolid s/n, 2 km (1 mi) from Segovia, 40003* ☎ *921/443737* 🖶 *921/437362* ⊕ *www.parador.es* ⇲ *113 rooms* ⚘ *Restaurant, 2 pools (1 indoor), gym, sauna, meeting room, parking (fee)* ⊟ *AE, DC, MC, V.*

$$–$$$ ⊞ **Infanta Isabel.** You'll get great views of the cathedral from this hotel, perched on the Plaza Mayor—with an entrance on a charming, if congested, pedestrian shopping street. Rooms are light and feminine, with wrought-iron beds and little round tables; those on the plaza have floor-length shutters and small verandas. ⊠ *Pl. Mayor 12, 40001* ☎ *921/*

Step into 14th-century Spain at Majorca's Bellver Castle.

(top left) Wine makers roll barrels of sherry in Cádiz, (top right) an Asturian house is tucked away in the region's verdant countryside, and (bottom) whimsical, scaly creatures adorn Gaudí's Casa Battlló.

(top) Valencia's City of Arts & Sciences complex abuts the Turia River. (bottom) Alcazaba is the original fortress of Granada's Moorish marvel, Alhambra.

(top left) Viura grapes are harvested for white wine in the Rueda region, (top right) candles reflect pilgrims' devotion at Montserrat's monastery, (bottom) and a Moroccan Barbary Ape sits atop a cannon in Gilbraltar.

An architectural triumph of titanium, the Guggenheim Museum is Bilbao's top attraction.

(top left) Galicia's Celtic roots pop up near Torre de Hercules in its modern port city of A Coruña, (top right) Tapas entice in Jerez de la Frontera. (bottom) In Olite, the parador originated as a French-style castle.

(top) Guernica at the Queen Sofía Art Center is one of Picasso's works not to be missed in Madrid. (bottom) Men dressed with cow bells try to scare off evil spirits during La Endiablada in Cuenca.

(top) Horses carry festive pilgrims in El Rocío to the Virgin of the Dew site. (bottom) Yachts in Marina Bay transport vacationers around the Rock.

461300 🖶 *921/462217* ⊕ *www.hotelinfantaisabel.com* 🛏 *37 rooms* ⟁ *Restaurant* 🗖 *AE, DC, MC, V.*

$$ ▦ **Las Sirenas.** If you stay here, not only will you be just steps from the Plaza Mayor, above Segovia's nicest shops, but you'll have the benefit of a prime downtown location, a pillared marble lobby, and, from the best rooms, splendid balcony views of the church of San Millán. Sensuous and classical accents include statues of mermaids at the foot of a curving staircase and Greek vases on antique bedside tables. Drawbacks are the tiny showers and slightly faded furnishings, but it's a hard value to beat. ⊠ *C. Juan Bravo 30, 40001* ☎ *921/462663* ⊕ *www.hotelsirenas. com* 🖶 *921/462657* 🛏 *39 rooms* ⟁ *Bar* 🗖 *AE, DC, MC, V.*

Shopping

After Toledo, the province of Segovia is Castile's most important for crafts. Glass and crystal are specialties of La Granja, and ironwork, lace, and embroidery are famous in Segovia itself. You can buy good lace from the Gypsies in Segovia's Plaza del Alcázar, but be prepared for some strenuous bargaining, and never offer more than half the opening price. For genuine crafts, go to **San Martín 4** (⊠ Pl. San Martín 4), an excellent antiques shop. **Calle Daiza,** leading to the Alcázar, overflows with touristy ceramic, textile, and gift shops.

La Granja de San Ildefonso

42 *11 km (7 mi) southeast of Segovia on N601.*

The major attraction in Segovia's immediate vicinity, the Royal Palace of La Granja stands in the town of La Granja de San Ildefonso, on the northern slopes of the Sierra de Guadarrama. (*Granja* means "farm.") Its site was once occupied by a hunting lodge and a shrine to San Ildefonso, administered by Hieronymite monks from the Segovian monastery of El Parral. Commissioned by the Bourbon king Felipe V in 1719, the palace has been described as the first great building of the Spanish Bourbon dynasty. The Italian architects who finished it in 1739—Juvarra and Sachetti—were responsible for the imposing garden facade, a late-baroque masterpiece anchored throughout its length by a giant order of columns. The interior has been badly gutted by fire; the highlight is the collection of 15th- to 18th-century tapestries in a special museum. It's the **gardens** that are most notable—terraces, ornamental ponds, lakes, classical statuary, woods, and baroque fountains dot the mountainside. On Wednesday, Saturday, and Sunday evenings in the summer (6–7 PM May–September), the fountains are turned on, one by one, creating an exciting spectacle. The starting time has been known to change on a whim; call ahead. ☎ *921/470020* ⊕ *www.patrimonionacional.es* ▧ *Palace €5, gardens free* ☉ *Palace Oct.–Mar., Tues.–Sat. 10–1:30 and 3–5, Sun. 10–2; Apr.–Sept., Tues.–Sun. 10–6. Garden daily 10–sunset.*

Pedraza de la Sierra

43 *30 km (19 mi) northeast of Segovia.*

Though somewhat commercialized and overdone, Pedraza is still a striking 16th-century village. Crowning a rocky outcrop and completely encircled by its walls, it's perfectly preserved, with wonderful views of the Guadarrama mountains. In the center of the village is the frail, irregularly shaped Plaza Mayor, lined with rustic wooden porticoes and dominated by a Romanesque bell tower. Pedraza's romance peaks on the first two Saturdays of July for the **Conciertos de las Velas** (Candle Concerts), when the artificial lights in Pedraza are switched off and the entire town is bathed in the flickering glow of more than 35,000 candles, placed along the streets and in the Plaza Mayor. In the evening (at 10 PM) classical-music concerts take place in the Plaza Mayor and the castle. Concert tickets must be bought at least a month in advance. Contact the **Fundación Villa de Pedraza** or the Segovia tourist office for tickets to the Candle Concerts in July. ⊠ *C. Real 15, Pedraza 40172* ☎ *921/ 509960* ☉ *Tues. and Wed. 10–3:15.*

At the top of Pedraza de la Sierra is the Renaissance **Castillo Pedraza de la Sierra,** a 14th-century stone castle that the painter Ignacio Zuloaga bought as a private home in the early 20th century. Two sons of the French king Francis I were held hostage here after the Battle of Pavia, together with their majordomo, the father of the Renaissance poet Pierre de Ronsard. Note that visiting times are valid except when Zuloaga's heirs are in residence. ☎ *921/509825* 🎟 *€4* ☉ *Wed.–Sun. 11–2 and 4–6.*

Where to Stay & Eat

$$$$ ✕ **El Yantar de Pedraza.** This traditional restaurant on the main square has wooden tables and beam ceilings. Famous for its roast meats, it's the place to come for that most celebrated Pedraza specialty, *corderito lechal en horno de leña* (baby lamb roasted in a wood oven). Dinner is served only for large groups and must be reserved in advance. ⊠*Pl. Mayor* ☎ *921/509842* ▭ *AE, DC, MC, V* ☉ *Closed Mon.*

$$–$$$ 🏨 **El Hotel de La Villa.** Heavy wooden beams everywhere, a roaring fire in the salon, and an elegant dining room make this Pedraza's chicest place to spend the night. A medieval Moorish oven for roasting lamb is in a corner of the restaurant. The bedrooms are an exquisite combination of heavy Castilian rustic and light postmodern design. ⊠ *C. Calzada 5, 40172* ☎ *921/508651* 🖷 *921/508653* ⊕ *www.elhoteldelavilla.com* ➥ *36 rooms, 2 suites* ⚘ *Restaurant, minibars, cable TV, bar, meeting rooms* ▭ *AE, DC, MC, V.*

$$ 🏨 **La Posada de Don Mariano.** Originally a farmer's home, this antique and elegant building has intimate guest rooms filled with rustic furniture and antiques. The restaurant, Enebro, serves cochinillo and a good selection of red meat. ⊠ *C. Mayor 14, 40172* ☎ *921/509886* 🖷 *921/ 509887* ⊕ *www.hoteldonmariano.com* ➥ *18 rooms* ⚘ *Restaurant, bar* ▭ *AE, DC, MC, V.*

Sepúlveda

44 *24 km (15 mi) north of Pedraza de la Sierra, 60 km (37 mi) northeast of Segovia.*

A walled village with a commanding position, Sepúlveda has a charming main square, but its main attraction is the 11th-century **El Salvador,** the oldest Romanesque church in Segovia's province. It has a crude but amusing example of the porches found in later Segovian buildings: the carvings on its capitals, probably by a Moorish convert, are quite fantastical. ⊠ *Cerro de Somosierra.*

Castillo de Coca

45 *52 km (32 mi) northwest of Segovia.*

Perhaps the most famous medieval sight near Segovia—worth a detour between Segovia and Ávila or Valladolid—is the Castillo de Coca. Built in the 15th century for Archbishop Alonso de Fonseca I, the castle is a turreted structure of plaster and red brick, surrounded by a deep moat. It looks like a stage set for a fairy tale, and indeed, it was intended not as a defense but as a place for the notoriously pleasure-loving Archbishop Fonseca to hold riotous parties. The interior, now occupied by a forestry school, has been modernized, with only fragments of the original decoration preserved. Note that opening hours are erratic; call ahead if possible. The restaurant is closed the first Tuesday of every month. ☎ *921/ 586622* 🖃 *€2.50* ☉ *May–Aug., weekdays 10:30–1 and 4:30–7, weekends 11–1 and 4–6; Sept.–Apr., weekdays 10:30–1 and 4:30–6, weekends 11–1 and 4–6. Closed 1st Tues. of every month.*

ÁVILA & SIERRA DE GREDOS

The mountains of the Sierra de Gredos are a fitting backdrop and counterpoint for Ávila's spectacular medieval walls. In Ávila you can trace the history of the mystic and musical St. Teresa, who lived much of her life here in the Gredos mountains, where you can hike and ski. Other sights include the quiet and often overlooked villages near Arenas de San Pedro and the ancient stone bulls of San Martín de Valdeiglesias.

Ávila

46 *107 km (66 mi) northwest of Madrid.*

In the middle of a windy plateau littered with giant boulders, Ávila can look wild and sinister. Modern development on its outskirts partially obscures Ávila's surrounding **walls,** which, restored in parts, look as they did in the Middle Ages. Begun in 1090, shortly after the town was reclaimed from the Moors, the walls were completed in only nine years—accomplished by the daily employment of an estimated 1,900 men. With 9 gates and 88 cylindrical towers bunched together, they are unique to Spain in form, unlike the Moorish defense architecture that the Christians adapted elsewhere. They're most striking when seen from outside town; for the best view on foot, cross the Adaja River, turn right on the Carretera de Salamanca, and walk uphill about 250 yards to a monument of four pilasters surrounding a cross.

The walls reflect Ávila's importance during the Middle Ages. Populated by Alfonso VI mainly with Christians from Asturias, the town came to be known as Ávila of the Knights because of its many nobles. Decline set in at the beginning of the 15th century, with the gradual departure of the nobility to the court of Carlos V in Toledo. Ávila's fame later on was largely because of St. Teresa. Born here in 1515 to a noble family of Jewish origin, Teresa spent much of her life in Ávila, leaving a legacy of convents and the ubiquitous *yemas* (candied egg yolks), originally distributed free to the poor but now sold for high prices to tourists. Ávila is well preserved, but the mood is slightly sad, austere, and desolate. The quietude is dispelled during Fiestas de la Santa Teresa, beginning October 8. The weeklong celebration includes lighted decorations, parades, singing in the streets, and religious observances.

The battlement apse of the **cathedral** forms the most impressive part of the walls. The apse was built mainly in the late 12th century, but the construction of the rest of the cathedral continued until the 18th century. Entering the town gate to the right of the apse, you can reach the sculpted north portal (originally the west portal, until it was moved in 1455 by the architect Juan Guas) by turning left and walking a few steps. The present west portal, flanked by 18th-century towers, is notable for the crude carvings of hairy male figures on each side; known as "wild men," these figures appear in many Castilian palaces of this period.

The Transitional Gothic interior, with its granite nave, is heavy and severe. The Lisbon earthquake of 1755 deprived the building of its Flemish stained glass, so the main note of color appears in the beautiful mottled stone in the apse, tinted yellow and red. Elaborate, plateresque choir stalls built in 1547 complement the powerful high altar of circa 1504 by painters Juan de Borgoña and Pedro Berruguete. On the wall of the ambulatory, look for the early-16th-century marble sepulchre of Bishop Alonso de Madrigal, a remarkably lifelike representation of the bishop seated at his writing table. Known as "El Tostado" (the Toasted One) for his swarthy complexion, the bishop was a tiny man of enormous intellect, the author of 54 books. When on one occasion Pope Eugenius IV ordered him to stand—mistakenly thinking him to still be on his knees—the bishop indicated the space between his eyebrows and hairline, retorting, "A man's stature is to be measured from here to here!" ✉ *Pl. de la Catedral s/n* ☎ *920/211641* ✑ *€4* ☉ *June–Aug., weekdays 10–7, Sat. 10–6:30, Sun. noon–6; Sept.–May, weekdays 10–5, Sat. 10–6, Sun. noon–6.*

The 15th-century **Mansión de los Deanes** (Deans' Mansion) houses the cheerful **Museo de Ávila**, a provincial museum full of local archaeology and folklore. It's a few minutes' walk east of the cathedral apse. ✉ *Pl. de Nalvillos 3* ☎ *920/211003* ✑ *€1.20, free weekends* ☉ *Tues.–Sat. 10–2 and 5–8, Sun. 10–2.* In the **Convento de San José** (de Las Madres), four blocks east of the cathedral on Calle Duque de Alba, is the **Museo Teresiano**, with musical instruments used by St. Teresa and her nuns. ✉ *Las Madres 4* ☎ *920/222127* ✑ *€1* ☉ *Apr.–Oct., daily 10–1:30 and 4–7; Nov.–Mar., daily 10–1:30 and 3–6.*

North of Ávila's cathedral, on Plaza de San Vincente, is the much-venerated Romanesque **Basílica de San Vicente** (Basilica of St. Vincent), founded on the supposed site where St. Vincent was martyred in 303 with his sisters Sts. Sabina and Cristeta. The west front, shielded by a vestibule, has damaged but expressive Romanesque carvings depicting the death of Lazarus and the parable of the rich man's table. The sarcophagus of St. Vincent forms the centerpiece of the basilica's Romanesque interior; the extraordinary, Asian-looking canopy above the sarcophagus is a 15th-century addition. ⊠ *Pl. de San Vicente s/n* ☎ *920/ 255230* ☒ *€1.40* ⊗ *Daily 10–1:30 and 4–6:30.*

The elegant chapel of **Mosen Rubi** (circa 1516) is illuminated by Renaissance stained glass by Nicolás de Holanda. Try to persuade the nuns in the adjoining convent to let you inside. ⊠ *C. de Lopez Nuñez.*

At the west end of the town walls, next to the river in a farmyard nearly hidden by poplars, is the small Romanesque **Ermita de San Segundo** (Hermitage of St. Secundus). Founded on the site where the remains of St. Secundus (a follower of St. Peter) were reputedly discovered, the hermitage has a realistic marble monument to the saint, carved by Juan de Juni. You may have to ask for the key in the adjoining house. ⊠ *Av. de Madrid s/n, toward Salamanca* ☒ *€0.60* ⊗ *Summer, daily 10–1 and 3:30–6; fall–spring, daily 11–1 and 4–5.*

Inside the south wall on Calle Dama, the **Convento de Santa Teresa** was founded in the 17th century on the site of the saint's birthplace. Teresa's famous written account of an ecstatic vision in which an angel pierced her heart influenced many baroque artists, most famously the Italian sculptor Giovanni Bernini. The convent has a small museum with relics—including one of Teresa's fingers; you can also see the small and rather gloomy garden where she played as a child. The restaurant is closed Monday from October through Easter. ⊠ *Pl. de la Santa s/n* ☎ *920/211030* ☒ *Museum €2* ⊗ *May–Sept., weekdays 10–1:30 and 3:30–5:30, Sat. 10–1 and 4–6; Apr.–Oct., weekdays 10–2 and 4–7, Sat. 10–1 and 4–6.*

The **Museo del Convento de la Encarnación** is where St. Teresa first took orders and was then based for more than 30 years. Its museum has an interesting drawing of the Crucifixion by her disciple St. John of the Cross, as well as a reconstruction of the cell she used when she was a prioress here. The convent is outside the walls in the northern part of town. ⊠ *Paseo de la Encarnación s/n* ☎ *920/211212* ☒ *€1.05* ⊗ *May–Oct. weekdays, 9:30–1 and 4–7; Nov.–Apr., weekdays 9:30–1:30 and 3:30–6; weekends 10–1 and 4–6 all year.*

The most interesting architectural monument on Ávila's outskirts is the **Monasterio de Santo Tomás.** A good 10-minute walk from the walls among housing projects, it's not where you would expect to find one of the most important religious institutions in Castile. The monastery was founded by Ferdinand and Isabella with the financial assistance of the notorious Inquisitor-General Tomás de Torquemada, who is buried in the sacristy. Further funds were provided by the confiscated property of converted Jews who ran afoul of the Inquisition. Three decorated cloisters lead to the church; inside, a masterly high altar (circa 1506) by Pedro Berruguete overlooks a serene marble tomb by the Italian artist Domenico Fancelli. One of the earliest examples of the Italian Renaissance style in Spain, this influential work was built for Prince Juan, the only son of Ferdinand and Isabella, who died at 19 while a student at the University of Salamanca. After Juan's burial here, his heartbroken parents found themselves unable to return; in happier times, they had often attended mass here, seated in the upper choir behind a balustrade exquis-itely carved with their coats of arms. ⊠ *Pl. de Granada 1* ☎ *920/220400* 🎫 *€3* ☉ *Tues.–Sun. 10–1 and 4–8.*

Where to Stay & Eat

★ **$$–$$$** ✗ **El Molino de la Losa.** Nearly straddling the serene Adaja River, with one of the best views of the town walls, El Molino is in a 15th-century mill, the working mechanism of which has been well preserved and pro-vides much distraction for those seated in the animated bar. Lamb is roasted in a medieval wood oven, and the beans from nearby El Barco (*judías de El Barco*) are famous. The garden has a small playground for children. ⊠ *Bajada de la Losa 12* ☎ *920/211101 or 920/211102* 🝔 *AE, MC, V* ☉ *Closed Mon.*

$$ ✗ **Mesón del Rastro.** In a wing of the medieval Palacio Abrantes, this restau-rant has a bucolic Castilian interior with exposed stone walls and beams, low lighting, and dark-wood furniture. Try the lamb and El Barco beans; also worthwhile is the *caldereta de cabrito* (goat stew). The place suffers somewhat from its popularity with tour buses, and service is some-times slow and impersonal. ⊠ *Pl. Rastro 1* ☎ *920/211218* ⊕ *www.mesondelrastro.com* 🝔 *AE, DC, MC, V.*

$–$$ ✗🛏 **Las Cancelas.** Locals flock to this little tavern for the €12 *menú del día* (fixed-price special). Push your way through the loud tapas bar to the dining room, where wooden tables are heaped with combination plat-ters of roast chicken, french fries, sunny-side-up eggs, and chunks of home-baked bread. The local T-bone steak, *chuletón de Ávila,* is enormous. The succulent cochinillo, much ordered by the regulars, bursts with fla-vor. Rooms are simple, slightly ramshackle arrangements. ⊠ *Cruz Vieja 6* ☎ *920/212249* 🝩 *920/212230* ⊕ *www.lascancelas.com* 🔑 *14 rooms* ☍ *Restaurant, bar* 🝔 *AE, DC, MC, V* ☉ *Closed Jan. 7–Feb. 3.*

$$$ 🛏 **Parador de Ávila.** A largely rebuilt medieval castle attached to the town walls, Ávila's parador has the advantage of a garden, from which you can sometimes climb up onto the ramparts. The interior is unusually warm, done mostly in tawny tones, and the public rooms are convivial. Guest rooms have terra-cotta tile floors and leather chairs, and their bath-rooms are spacious, gleamingly modern, and fashionably designed. ⊠ *Marqués de Canales de Chozas 2, 05001* ☎ *920/211340* 🝩 *920/226166* ⊕ *www.parador.es* 🔑 *61 rooms* ☍ *Restaurant, café, bar, meet-ing room* 🝔 *AE, DC, MC, V.*

★ **$$–$$$** 🛏 **Palacio de los Velada.** Ávila's top hotel occupies a beautifully restored 16th-century palace in the heart of the city, right beside the cathedral. (It's ideal if you like to relax between sightseeing jaunts.) Upscale locals gather in the bar and the lovely Mediterranean courtyard, and the restaurant is acclaimed. Rooms are modern and comfortable. ⊠ *Pl. de la Catedral 10, 05001* ☎ *920/255100* 🝩 *920/254900* ⊕ *www.veladahoteles.com* 🔑 *145 rooms* ☍ *Restaurant, bar, pub, meeting room* 🝔 *AE, DC, MC, V.*

Sierra de Gredos

47 *79 km (49 mi) southwest of Ávila.*

The C502 from Ávila follows a road dating from Roman times, when it was used to transport oil and flour from Ávila in exchange for potatoes and wood. In winter, the **Sierra de Gredos** (4,435 feet) gives the region a majestic, snowy backdrop. You can enjoy extensive views from the peak; soon after descending you'll see a perfectly preserved stretch of the Roman road, zigzagging down into the valley and crossing the modern road now and then. Today it's used by hikers, as well as by shepherds transporting their flocks to lower pastures in early December.

Where to Stay

$$–$$$ 🏨 **Parador de Gredos.** Built in 1926 on a site chosen by Alfonso XIII, this was the first parador in Spain. The stone architecture has a sturdy look and blends well with the magnificent surroundings. Rooms are standard parador, with heavy, dark furniture and light walls, and more than half have excellent views of the Sierra. An ideal base for hiking or climbing, the framers of Spain's Constitution met here in 1976 to draft the charter for today's constitutional monarchy. ⊠ *Ctra. Barraco–Béjar, Km 42, 05635 Navarredonda de Gredos* ☎ *920/348048* 🖷 *920/348205* ⊕ *www.parador.es* 🛏 *74 rooms* ⚒ *Restaurant, tennis court, bar* ▭ *AE, DC, MC, V.*

Sports & the Outdoors

HIKING &   The Sierra de Gredos is Castile's best area for hiking and mountaineer-
MOUNTAIN   ing. You can base yourself at the parador or at one of six mountain huts
CLIMBING   with limited accommodations and facilities. For information contact **FEDME (Federación Española de Deportes de Montaña y Escalada—Spanish Mountaineering and Climbing Federation)** (⊠ C. Floridablanca 84 ☎ 93/426–4267 🖷 93/426–2575 ⊕ www.fedme.es) in Barcelona.

HORSEBACK   Near the Gredos Parador, **Turactiv Gredos** (⊠ Barajas ☎ 608/920892) of-
RIDING   fers gear and guides for horseback riding, canoeing, fishing, and archery. You can go riding at **Hípica de Bohoyo** (⊠ Bohoyo ☎ 920/341118).

SKIING   Skiing is popular in both the Sierra de Gredos and the Guadarrama resorts of La Pinilla (Segovia), Navacerrada (Madrid), Valdesqui (Madrid), and Valcotos (Madrid). You can call **ATUDEM** (☎ 91/350–2020) for conditions, but it's better to call the slope you're considering. Call the **Federación Madrileña de Deportes de Invierno** (Madrid Federation of Winter Sports; ☎ 91/547–0101) for Sierra de Gredos skiing information.

Arenas de San Pedro

48   *143 km (89 mi) southwest of Madrid.*

This medieval town is surrounded by pretty villages, such as Mombeltrán, Guisando, and Candeleda, where wooden balconies are decorated with flowers. A colorful sight in Candeleda are wicker baskets filled with pimientos for sale. Guisando, incidentally, has nothing to do with the famous stone bulls of that name, 60 km (37 mi) to the east.

San Martín de Valdeiglesias

49   *73 km (45 mi) west of Madrid.*

Just 6 km (4 mi) before San Martín, on the right side of the road, is a stone inscription in front of a hedge; this marks the site where, in 1468,

Isabella the Catholic was acknowledged by the assembled Castilian nobility as rightful successor to Henry IV. The **Toros de Guisando,** or stone bulls, dating from the 6th century BC, are thought to have been used as territorial border markers for a Celtiberian tribe. Just three of many such bulls once scattered around the Castilian countryside (they take their name from the nearby Cerro Guisando, or Guisando Hill), they're now a symbol of the Spanish Tourist Board. To see these taurine effigies, head back east from Arenas on the C501; it's a pleasant drive through countryside bordered to the north by the Gredos range. ⊠ *Near Cerro Guisando, 6 km (4 mi) before San Martín, on right side of road, on other side of hedge with stone inscription.*

SALAMANCA & CIUDAD RODRIGO

Salamanca's radiant sandstone buildings, immense Plaza Mayor, and hilltop riverside perch make it one of the most attractive and beloved cities in Spain. Today, as it did centuries ago, the university predominates, providing an intellectual flavor, a stimulating arts scene, and nightlife to match. About an hour from here are the preserved medieval walls of Ciudad Rodrigo, an interesting town with fewer tourists.

Salamanca

50–62 *205 km (127 mi) northwest of Madrid.*

Fodor'sChoice
★ If you approach from Madrid or Ávila, you'll first see Salamanca rising on the northern banks of the wide and winding River Tormes. In the foreground is its sturdy, 15-arch Roman bridge; above this soars the combined bulk of the old and new cathedrals. Piercing the skyline to the right is the Renaissance monastery and church of San Estéban. Behind San Estéban and the cathedrals, and largely out of sight from the river, extends a stunning series of palaces, convents, and university buildings that culminates in the Plaza Mayor. Despite considerable damage over the centuries, Salamanca remains one of Spain's greatest cities architecturally, a showpiece of the Spanish Renaissance. It is the warmth of golden sandstone, which seems to glow throughout the city, that you will remember above all things.

Already an important settlement in Iberian times, Salamanca was captured by Hannibal in 217 BC and later flourished as a major Roman station on the road between Mérida and Astorga. Converted to Christianity by the end of the 6th century at the latest, it later passed back and forth between Christians and Moors and began to experience prolonged stability only after the Reconquest of Toledo in 1085. The town's later importance was largely because of its university, which grew out of a college founded around 1220 by Alfonso IV of León.

Salamanca thrived in the 15th and early 16th centuries, and the number of students at its university rose to almost 10,000. Its greatest royal benefactor was Isabella, who generously financed both the magnificent New Cathedral and the rebuilding of the university. A dual portrait of Isabella and Ferdinand was incorporated into the facade of the main university building to commemorate her patronage. Nearly all of Salamanca's other outstanding Renaissance buildings bear the five-star crest of the all-powerful and ostentatious Fonseca family. The most famous Fonseca, Alonso de Fonseca I, was the archbishop of Santiago and then of Seville; he was also a notorious womanizer and one of the patrons of the Spanish Renaissance.

Both Salamanca and its university began to decline in the early 17th century, corrupted by extreme clericalism and devastated by a flood in 1626. Some of the town's former glory was recovered in the 18th century, with the construction of the Plaza Mayor by the native Churriguera brothers, who were among the most influential architects of the Spanish baroque. The town suffered in the Peninsular War of the early 19th century and was marred by modern development initiated by Franco after the civil war, but the university has regained its status as one of the most prestigious in Europe. Come on a weekend to witness the social scene.

Salamanca was elected as a European City of Culture for 2002 by the European Union, and the ambitious €60 million project spawned several properties, listed below.

A major theater complex, the **Centro de Artes Escénicas** (⊠ Av. de la Aldehuela s/n, Prosperidad) has a capacity for 1,400. The **Centro de Arte de Salamanca** (⊠ Av. de la Aldehuela, Prosperidad) is a 4,600-square-foot modern art gallery. An indoor stadium, **Edificio Multiusos** (⊠ Av. de los Cipreses, Garrido), holds 6,000 spectators for sporting events or concerts. A museum and research center, **Museo de Historia de la Automoción** (⊠ Pl. del Mercado Viejo s/n ☎ 923/260293 ⊙ Tues.–Fri. 11–2 and 4:30–8, weekends 10–8), focuses on motorized vehicles and displays the library and vintage car collection of Demetrio Gómez Planche.

Parque Arqueológico de San Vicente (⊠ Cerro de San Vicente, City Center) is an archaeological museum based on the ruins of the 10th-to-13th-century San Vicente Convent, in the ancient center of the city. The **Sala de Exposiciones de Santa Domingo** (⊠ Pl. de Concilio de Trento, by Convento de San Estéban) is a 350-square-foot municipal art gallery with a garden for sculpture. The 732-seat theater, **Teatro Liceo** (⊠ Pl. del Liceo, City Center), 40 yards from Plaza Mayor, has been renovated.

A GOOD WALK

In terms of both chronology and parking space, the well-preserved **Puente Romano** 🗓 ☞ makes a good starting point. This is a quiet part of town with a strong rural character; in the summer, Gypsies camp here, picnicking and playing music while they exercise their horses. After crossing the bridge, bear to the right and look for the Moderniste building Casa Lis, which serves as the **Museo Art Nouveau y Art Deco** 🗓. Afterward, make your way up to the old and new **cathedrals** 🗓, built side by side. Across the Plaza Anaya is the neoclassical Colegio de Anaya. If you face the New Cathedral from the plaza, the back of the main building of the **universidad** 🗓 is ahead and to your right, facing the cathedral's west facade. Walk between the two down Calle Cardenal Plá y Deniel, turn right on Calle de Calderón de la Barca, then right again on Calle de Los Libreros, and you'll come into the enchanting quadrangle known as the Patio de Las Escuelas. The main university building (Escuelas May-

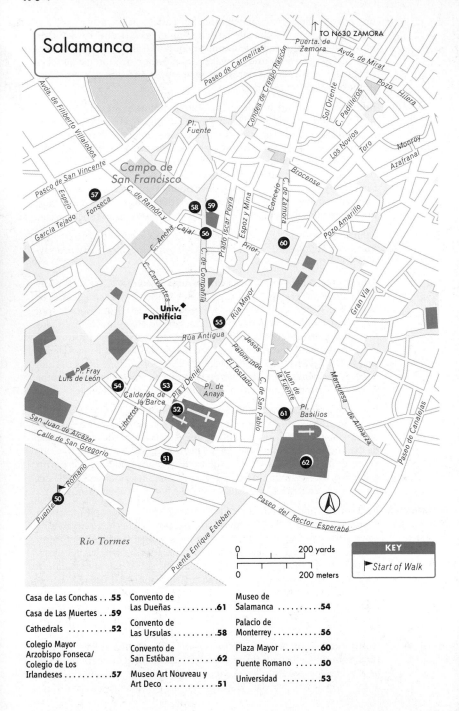

Salamanca

ores) is to your right, and surrounding the square is the Escuelas Menores, built in the early 16th century as a secondary school. In the middle of the square is a statue of the 16th-century poet and philosopher Fray Luis de León, one of the greatest teachers in the history of the university. On the far side of the Patio is the entrance to the **Museo de Salamanca** ⑤④.

If you walk north from the Patio de Las Escuelas on Calle de Los Libreros, then bear right onto Rua Antigua, you can't miss the **Casa de Las Conchas** ⑤⑤. Turn left at Calle de Compañía toward the **Palacio de Monterrey** ⑤⑥. To the left of the palace, follow Calle de Ramón y Cajal to the **Colegio Mayor Arzobispo Fonseca** ⑤⑦. Walk back east through the Campo de San Francisco. On the corner of Calle Las Ursulas and Calle Bordadores is the **Convento de Las Ursulas** ⑤⑧. Farther ahead on Calle Bordadores is the bizarre **Casa de Las Muertes** ⑤⑨. Walk east along Calle del Prior to the **Plaza Mayor** ⑥⓪, the center of town. South of the plaza, on Calle de San Pablo, is the Torre del Clavero, a late-15th-century tower topped by fantastic battlements built for the *clavero* (key warden) of the order of Alcántara. Farther down, the Palacio de La Salina is another Fonseca palace designed by Rodrigo Gil de Hontañón. Try to pop inside for a glimpse of the courtyard, where a projecting gallery is supported by wooden consoles carved with expressive nudes and other dynamic forms. Walking south on Calle de San Pablo and bearing left, you'll circle the Dominican **Convento de Las Dueñas** ⑥①. Facing the Dueñas, up a monumental flight of steps, is the **Convento de San Estéban** ⑥②.

TIMING   Allow at least half a day for this walk.

What to See

⑤⑤ **Casa de Las Conchas** (House of Shells). This house was built around 1500 for Dr. Rodrigo Maldonado de Talavera, a professor of medicine at the university and a doctor at the court of Isabella. The scallop motif was a reference to Talavera's status as chancellor of the Order of St. James (Santiago), whose symbol is the shell. Among the playful plateresque details are the lions over the main entrance, engaged in a fearful tug-of-war with the Talavera crest. The interior has been converted into a public library. Duck into the charming courtyard, which has an upper balustrade carved with virtuoso intricacy in imitation of basketwork. ✉ *Compañía 2* ☎ *923/269317* 💳 *Free* ☺ *Weekdays 9–9, Sat. 9–2 and 4–7, Sun. 10–2 and 4–7.*

⑤⑨ **Casa de Las Muertes** (House of the Dead). Built in about 1513 for the majordomo of Alonso de Fonseca II, the house takes its name from the four tiny skulls that adorn its top two windows. Alonso de Fonseca II commissioned them to commemorate his deceased uncle, the licentious archbishop who lies in the Convento de Las Ursulas, across the street. For the same reason, the facade also bears the archbishop's portrait. The small square in front of the house was a favorite haunt of the poet, philosopher, and university rector Miguel de Unamuno, whose statue stands here. Unamuno supported the Nationalists under Franco at the outbreak of the civil war, but he later turned against them. Placed under virtual house arrest, Unamuno died in the house next door in 1938. During the Franco period, students often daubed his statue red to suggest that his heart still bled for Spain. ✉ *C. Bordadores 6.*

52 For a complete exterior tour of the old and new **Cathedrals,** take a 10-minute walk around the complex, circling counterclockwise. Nearest the river stands the **Catedral Vieja** (Old Cathedral), built in the late 12th century, one of the most interesting examples of the Spanish Romanesque. Because the dome of the crossing tower has strange, plumelike ribbing, it's known as the Torre del Gallo (Rooster's Tower). The much larger **Catedral Nueva** (New Cathedral) dates mainly from the 16th century, though some parts, including the dome over the crossing and the bell tower attached to the west facade, had to be rebuilt after the Lisbon earthquake of 1755. Work began in 1513 under the direction of the distinguished late-Gothic architect Juan Gil de Hontañón, and as at Segovia's cathedral, Juan's son Rodrigo took over the work after his father's death in 1526. The New Cathedral's north facade (which contains the main entrance) is ornamental enough, but the west facade is dazzling in its sculptural complexity. Try to come here in late afternoon, when the sun shines on it.

The interior of the New Cathedral is as light and harmonious as that of Segovia's cathedral, but larger. It's a triumphant baroque effusion designed by the Churrigueras. The wooden choir seems almost alive with anxiously active cherubim and saints. From a door in the south aisle, steps descend into the Old Cathedral, where boldly carved capitals supporting the vaulting are accented by foliage, strange animals, and touches of pure fantasy. Then comes the dome, which seems to owe much to Byzantine architecture; it's a remarkably light structure raised on two tiers of arcaded openings. Not the least of the Old Cathedral's attractions are its furnishings, including sepulchres from the 12th and 13th centuries and a magnificent, curved high altar comprising 53 colorful and delicate scenes by the mid-15th-century artist Nicolás Florentino. In the apse above, Florentino painted an astonishingly fresh Last Judgment fresco.

From the south transept of the Old Cathedral, a door leads into the cloister, begun in 1177. From about 1230 until the construction of the main university building in the early 15th century, the chapels around the cloister served as classrooms for the university students. In the Chapel of St. Barbara, on the eastern side, theology students answered the grueling questions meted out by their doctoral examiners. The chair in which they sat is still there, in front of a recumbent effigy of Bishop Juan Lucero, on whose head the students would place their feet for inspiration. Also attached to the cloister is a small cathedral museum with a 15th-century triptych of St. Catherine by Salamanca's greatest native artist, Fernando Gallego. ✉ *Plá y Deniel s/n* ☎ *923/217476* 🏛 *New Cathedral free, Old Cathedral €3.50* ⊙ *Both cathedrals, Apr.–Sept., daily 10–7:30; Mar.–Oct., daily 10–1 and 4–6.*

57 **Colegio Mayor Arzobispo Fonseca/Colegio de Los Irlandeses** (Irish College). This small college was founded by Alonso de Fonseca II in 1521 to train young Irish priests. It's now a residence hall for guest lecturers at the university. This part of town was the most severely damaged during the Peninsular War of the early 19th century and still has a slightly derelict character. The interior, however, is a treat. To the right immediately inside the college is a late-Gothic chapel, and beyond it lies one of the most classical and genuinely Italianate of Salamanca's many courtyards. ✉ *Fonseca 4* ☎ *923/294570* 🎫 *Free* ☉ *Daily 10–2 and 4–7.*

61 **Convento de Las Dueñas** (Convent of the Dames). Founded in 1419, this convent hides a 16th-century cloister that is the most fantastically decorated in Salamanca, if not in the whole of Spain. The capitals of its two superimposed Salamantine arcades are crowded with a baffling profusion of grotesques that can absorb you for hours. As you're wandering through, take a moment to look down. The interlocking diamond pattern on the ground floor of the cloister is decorated with the knobby vertebrae of goats and sheep. It's an eerie yet perfect accompaniment to all the grinning disfigured heads sprouting from the capitals looming above you. There's another reason to come here: the nuns make and sell excellent sweets. ✉ *Pl. Concilio de Trento* ☎ *923/215442* 🎫 *€1.50* ☉ *Apr.–Oct., Mon.–Sat. 10:30–1 and 4:30–6, Sun. 11–12:45 and 4:30–6:45; Nov.–Mar., Mon.–Sat. 10:30–1 and 4:30–5:45, Sun. 11–12:45 and 4:30–5:45.*

58 **Convento de Las Ursulas** (Convent of the Ursulines). Archbishop Alonso de Fonseca I lies here, in a splendid marble tomb created by Diego de Siloe during the first half of the 16th century. ✉ *Las Ursulas 2* ☎ *923/ 219877* 🎫 *€2* ☉ *Daily 11–1 and 4:30–6. Closed last Sun. of every month.*

NEED A BREAK?

Unwind at **La Regenta** (✉ Espoz y Mina 19–20 ☎ 923/123230), a warm, plush, baroque-style café-bar that shines like a beacon of (flickering candle) light in the thronged heart of town. Heavy green-and-gold curtains block most of the street noise, making the Plaza Mayor, a half a block off, a distant memory. Try a *café al caramelo* (coffee with caramel). In the evening you can order potent cocktails with names like "Kiss Me Boy" and "Sangre de Toro" (Bull's Blood).

62 **Convento de San Estéban** (Convent of St. Stephen). The convent's monks, among the most enlightened teachers at the university, were the first to take Columbus's ideas seriously and helped him gain his introduction to Isabella (hence his statue in the nearby Plaza de Colón, back toward Calle de San Pablo). The complex was designed by one of San Estéban's monks, Juan de Alava. The door to the right of the west facade leads you into a gloomy cloister with Gothic arcading, interrupted by tall, spindly columns adorned with classical motifs. From the cloister, you enter the church at its eastern end. The interior is unified and uncluttered but also dark and severe. The one note of color is provided by the ornate and gilded high altar of 1692, a baroque masterpiece by José Churriguera. The most exciting part of San Estéban, though, is the massive west facade, a thrilling plateresque work in which sculpted figures and ornamentation are piled up to a height of more than 98 feet. ✉ *Pl. Concilio de Trento* ☎ *923/215000* 🎫 *€2* ☉ *Apr.–Sept., daily 10–2 and 4–8; Oct.–Mar., daily 10–2 and 4–7.*

51 **Museo Art Nouveau y Art Deco.** The museum is in the Casa Lis, a modernist building from the end of the 19th century. On display are 19th-century paintings and glass, as well as French and German china dolls, Viennese bronze statues, furniture, jewelry, enamels, and jars. ✉ *Gibraltar 14* ☎ *923/121425* ⊕ *www.museocasalis.org* 🎫 *€2.50* ☉ *Tues.–Fri. 11–2 and 4–7, weekends and holidays 11–8.*

54 **Museo de Salamanca** (Museo de Bellas Artes). Consisting mainly of minor 17th- and 18th-century paintings, this museum, also known as the Museo de Bellas Artes (Museum of Fine Arts), is interesting for its 15th-century building, which belonged to Isabella's physician, Alvárez Abarca. ⊠ *Patio de Escuelas Menores 2* ☎ *923/212235* 🎫 *€1.20, free weekends* ⊙ *Oct.–June, Tues.–Sat. 10–2 and 4–7, Sun. 10–2; July–Sept., Tues.–Sat. 10–2 and 5–8, Sun. 10–2.*

56 **Palacio de Monterrey.** Built after 1538 by Rodrigo Gil de Hontañón, the Monterrey Palace was meant for an illegitimate son of Alonso de Fonseca I. As in Rodrigo's other local palaces, the building is flanked by towers and has an open arcaded gallery running the whole length of the upper level. Such galleries—which in Italy you would expect to see on the ground floor—are common in Spanish Renaissance palaces and were intended to provide privacy for the women of the house and cool the floor below during the summer. The palace is privately owned and not open to visitors, but you can stroll the grounds around it. ⊠ *Compañía s/n.*

60 **Plaza Mayor.** Built in the 1730s by Alberto and Nicolás Churriguera, Salamanca's Plaza Mayor is one of the largest squares in Spain, and many find it the most beautiful. Its northern side is dominated by the lavishly elegant, pinkish **ayuntamiento** (city hall). The square and its arcades are popular gathering spots for most of Salamancan society, and the many surrounding cafés make this the perfect spot for a coffee break. At night, the plaza swarms with students meeting "under the clock" on the plaza's north side. *Tunas* (strolling musicians in traditional garb) often meander among the cafés and crowds, playing for smiles and applause rather than tips.

▶ **50** **Puente Romano** (Roman Bridge). Next to the bridge is an Iberian stone bull, and opposite the bull is a statue commemorating Lazarillo de Tormes, the young hero of the eponymous (but anonymous) 16th-century work that is one of the masterpieces of Spanish literature.

53 **Universidad.** Parts of the university's walls, like those of the cathedral and other structures in Salamanca, are covered with large, ocher lettering recording the names of famous university graduates. The earliest names are said to have been written in the blood of the bulls killed to celebrate the successful completion of a doctorate.

The **Escuelas Mayores** (Major Schools) dates to 1415, but it was not until more than 100 years later that an unknown architect provided the building with its gloriously elaborate facade. Immediately above the main door is the famous double portrait of Isabella and Ferdinand, surrounded by ornamentation that plays on the yoke-and-arrow heraldic motifs of the two monarchs. The double-eagle crest of Carlos V, flanked by portraits of the emperor and empress in classical guise, dominates the middle layer of the frontispiece. Perhaps the most famous rite of passage for new students is to find the carved frog that squats atop a skull at the very top left-hand corner. Legend has it that if you spot the frog on your first try, you'll pass all your exams and have a successful university career; for this reason, it's affectionately called *la rana de la suerte* (the lucky frog). It can be hard to pin down the elusive amphibian; if you're not having any luck, pop inside to the ticket booth, where they've kindly posted a detail of the frontispiece for precisely this purpose. You can then see the beloved frog all over town, on sweatshirts, magnets, pins, jewelry, and postcards.

The interior of the Escuelas Mayores, drastically restored in parts, comes as a slight disappointment after the splendor of the facade. But the *aula* (lecture hall) of Fray Luis de León, where Cervantes, Calderón de la Barca, and numerous other luminaries of Spain's golden age once sat, is of particular interest. Cervantes carved his name on one of the wooden pews up front. After five years' imprisonment for having translated the *Song of Songs* into Spanish, Fray Luis returned to this hall and began his lecture, "As I was saying yesterday . . ."

Your ticket to the Escuelas Mayores also admits you to the nearby **Escuelas Menores** (Minor Schools), built in the early 16th century as a secondary school preparing candidates for the university proper. Passing through a gate crowned with the double-eagle crest of Charles V, you'll come to a green, on the other side of which is a modern building with a fascinating ceiling fresco of the zodiac, originally in the library of the Escuelas Mayores. A fragment of a much larger whole, this painting is generally attributed to Fernando Gallego. ☎ *923/294550 or 923/294400* 🖱 *€4, free Mon. 9–2* ⊙ *Weekdays 9–2 and 4–7, Sat. 9–2 and 4–6:30, Sun. 10–1.*

Where to Stay & Eat

$$$$ ✕ **Chez Víctor.** Try this chic restaurant for a break from traditional Castilian food. Chef-owner Victoriano Salvador learned his trade in France and adapts French cuisine to Spanish taste, with whimsical touches all his own. Sample the traditional *carrillada de buey braseada con jengibre* (cheek of beef braised in ginger) or the more continental *hojaldre de verduras y foie con salsa de trufas* (puff pastry filled with leeks and julienned carrots in a truffle sauce). Desserts are outstanding, especially the chocolate ones. ⊠ *Espoz y Mina 26* ☎ *923/213123* 🗖 *AE, DC, MC, V* ⊙ *Closed Mon. and Aug. No dinner Sun.*

$$$$ ✕ **Río de la Plata.** Off Calle de San Pablo, this tiny basement restaurant has been in business since 1958 and retains an old-fashioned character. The gilded yet quiet interior is a pleasant change of scenery, and the fireplace and local crowd provide warmth. The food is simple but carefully prepared, with good-quality fish and meat. ⊠ *Pl. Peso 1* ☎ *923/219005* 🗖 *AE, MC, V* ⊙ *Closed Mon. and July.*

$$$–$$$$ ✕ **La Hoja Charra.** The restaurant, off Plaza Mayor, has a glass facade, high ceilings, butter-yellow walls, and minimalist art—all signs of a very different kind of Castilian dining experience. Young chef-owner Alberto López Oliva prepares an innovative menu of traditional fare with a twist. *Manitas, manzana, y langostinas al aroma de Módena* are pig trotters with prawns and apple slices, all in Módena vinegar; *perdiz al chocolate con berza* is partridge cooked in chocolate and served with cabbage. ⊠ *Pasaje Coliseum 19* ☎ *923/264028* 🗖 *AE, MC, V* ⊙ *Closed Mon. and last 2 wks of Feb. and Aug. No dinner Sun.*

$$–$$$$ ✕ **El Candil Viejo.** Beloved by locals for its superb, no-nonsense Castilian fare, this tavern is an old favorite with professors in pinstripes and students on dates. Aside from a simple salad, the menu consists of meat, meat, and more meat, including pork, lamb, kid, sausage, and fantastic *marucha* (short ribs) steak. The homemade sausages are especially good. For tapas, try the *farinato* sausage, made from pork, onion, eggs, and bread crumbs, or the *picadillo,* similar but spicier with pepper, garlic, and tomato. ✉ *Ventura Ruiz Aguilera 14–16* ☎ *923/217239* 🖃 *AE, DC, MC, V* ☉ *Closed 3 wks in Jan.*

$–$$ ✕ **El Grillo Azul.** A rare sight in Spain, this vegetarian restaurant—the only one in Salamanca—has an adventurous menu of heaping dishes that easily trump any of the limp salads and veggie options you'll find elsewhere. Dig into the *arroz basmati con calabacín, zanahorias, y piñones* (basmati rice topped with zucchini, carrots, and pine nuts) or an omelet stuffed with almonds and mushrooms. ✉ *C. El Grillo 1* ☎ *923/219233* 🖃 *AE, DC, MC, V* ☉ *Closed Mon. No dinner Sun.*

¢–$$ ✕ **Bambú.** At peak times, it's standing-room only at this jovial basement tapas bar that caters to students on a budget. The floor may be littered with napkins (usually a good sign) and you might have to shout to be heard, but it's the generous tapas and big sloppy *bocadillos* (sandwiches) that draw the crowds. Although paella is usually the exclusive domain of pricey paella restaurants, here (during lunch) you can enjoy a *ración* of paella, ladled out from a large *caldero* (shallow pan). Another bonus: even if you just order a drink, you'll be served a liberal helping of the "tapa of the day." ✉ *C. Prior 4* ☎ *923/260092* ⊕ *www.cafeteriabambu.com* 🖃 *MC, V.*

$$$ ⊞ **AC Palacio de San Estéban.** Near the cathedrals, this fancy hotel is in a former part of the 17th-century Convento de San Estéban. The rooms are modern, finished in cream and white with dark-wood trim. ✉ *Arroyo de Santo Domingo 3, 37001* ☎ *923/262296* 🖥 *917/268872* ⊕ *www.ac-hoteles.com* ⟿ *51 rooms* ⚘ *Restaurant, coffee shop, gym, bar, laundry service, business services, meeting room, parking (fee), no-smoking rooms* 🖃 *AE, DC, MC, V.*

★ $$$ ⊞ **Rector.** From the stately entrance to the high-ceiling guest rooms, this lovely hotel is a true European experience. The sitting areas, hallways, and breakfast room are all spotless, spacious, warm, and quiet, and the owners and staff are very helpful, and can tell you all about Salamanca. ✉ *Paseo Rector Esperabé 10* ☎ *923/218482* 🖥 *923/214008* ⊕ *www.hotelrector.com* ⟿ *14 rooms* ⚘ *Bar* 🖃 *AE, DC, MC, V.*

$$–$$$ ⊞ **NH Palacio de Castellanos.** In an immaculately restored 15th-century palace, this hotel has an exquisite interior patio and an equally beautiful restaurant, as well as a lovely terrace overlooking San Estéban. Rooms are done in peach and white, with wooden bed frames, and have modern, white-tile bathrooms. ✉ *San Pablo 58 y 64, 37008* ☎ *923/261818* 🖥 *923/261819* ⊕ *www.nh-hoteles.com* ⟿ *62 rooms* ⚘ *Restaurant* 🖃 *AE, DC, MC, V.*

$$ ⊞ **San Polo.** Built on the foundations of the old Romanesque church by the same name—the ruins of which you can see through windows in the foyer and hall—the hotel is near the city center and has a friendly staff. The smallish rooms have light ocher tones, with white curtains. ✉ *Arroyo de Santo Domingo 2, 37008* ☎ *923/211177* 🖥 *923/211154*

⊕ *www.hotelsanpolo.com* 🛏 *37 rooms, 1 suite* ♿ *Restaurant, bar, parking (fee)* ▭ *AE, DC, MC, V.*

$ 🏨 **Hostal Plaza Mayor.** You can't beat the location of this great little *hostal*, just steps from the Plaza Mayor. Rooms are small but modern; the only drawback is the noise level on weekends (bring earplugs), when student *tunas* (musicians) sing ballads at the plaza's crowded cafés until the wee hours. Reservations are advisable, as rooms fill up fast. ⊠ *Pl. del Corrillo 20, 37008* ☎ *923/262020* 🖷 *923/217548* 🛏 *19 rooms* ♿ *Restaurant* ▭ *MC, V.*

Nightlife

Particularly in summer, Salamanca sees perhaps the greatest influx of foreign students of any city in Spain—by day they study Spanish, and by night they fill Salamanca's bars and clubs to capacity. **Mesón Cervantes** (⊠ Entrance on southeast corner of Plaza Mayor), an upstairs tapas bar, draws crowds to its balcony for a drink and an unparalleled view of the action. Bask in the romantic glow emanating from stained-glass lamps in the baroque-style **Posada de las Almas** (⊠ Plaza San Boal s/n), the preferred cocktail-and-conversation nightspot for stylish students. Wrought-iron chandeliers hang from the high wood-beam ceilings, harp-strumming angels top elegant pillars, and one entire wall of shelves showcases colorful doll's houses. After 11, a well-dressed twenty- and thirtysomething crowd comes to dance at **Camelot** (⊠ Rua Bordadores 3), an ancient stone-wall warehouse in one corner of the 16th-century Convento de Las Ursulas. For good wine, heaping portions of tapas, and live music, try the **Café Principal** (⊠ Rua Mayor 9). An unusual disco is in a boat on the river, **Barco Ciudad de Salamanca Gogó** (⊠ Paseo Fluvial, beside Enrique Estéban bridge). After-hours types end (if not spend) the night at **Café Moderno** (⊠ Gran Vía 75), tucking into *chocolate con churros* at daybreak. Try your luck at the **Casino Salamanca,** housed in a glitzily refurbished turn-of-the-20th-century factory on the Tormes River, near the Puente Romano. You'll need your passport to enter. ⊠ *C. La Pesca 5* ☎ *923/281628* ⊕ *www.grupocomar.com (listed under Casino Del Tormes)* ⊗ *Sun.–Thurs. 4 PM–4 AM; Fri. and Sat. 4 PM–5 AM.*

Shopping

On Sunday mornings, the **Rastro** flea market is held in Avenida de Aldehuela. Special buses leave from Plaza de España. For unusual gifts, including pottery, ironwork, paintings, and hand-stitched linens, browse through **Indiana** (⊠ Meléndez 2–4 ☎ 923/264243). The husband-and-wife team in tiny **Artesanía Duende** (⊠ C. San Pablo 29 ☎ 923/213622) have been creating and selling unique wooden crafts for decades. Their music boxes, thimbles, photo frames, and other items are beautifully carved or stenciled with local themes, from the *bailes charros*, Salamanca's regional dance, to the floral designs embroidered on the hems of provincial dresses.

Sports & the Outdoors

GOLF There are two golf courses near Salamanca. **Campo de Golf de Salamanca** (⊠ Monte de Zarapicos, Zarapicos ☎ 923/329102 🖷 923/329105 ⊕ www.golfysol.com) is 18 km (12 mi) from Salamanca on the C517 and is more of a country club, with swimming pools, horseback riding, tennis, a gym, and a social club and bar. Three kilometers (2 mi) from

Salamanca is **Golf Villa Mayor** (✉ Villamayor ☎ 923/337011 🖷 923/337007 ⊕ www.villamayorgolf.com).

Ciudad Rodrigo

63 *88 km (54 mi) southwest of Salamanca.*

Surveying the fertile valley of the River Agueda, the small town of Ciudad Rodrigo has numerous well-preserved palaces and churches and makes an excellent overnight stop on the way from Spain to Portugal. The **cathedral** combines the Romanesque and transitional Gothic styles and has a great deal of fine sculpture. Look closely at the early-16th-century choir stalls, elaborately carved with entertaining grotesques by Rodrigo Alemán. The cloister has carved capitals, and the cypresses in its center lend tranquillity. The cathedral's outer walls are still scarred by cannonballs fired during the Peninsular War. ✉ *Pl. de Herrasti* ☎ *923/481424* 🖭 *Cathedral free, museum €2.50* ☉ *Daily 10–1 and 4–6.*

A major Salamanca monument is its fortified medieval **castle,** part of which has been turned into a parador. From here you can climb onto the town's battlements. ✉ *Pl. del Castillo.*

Where to Stay & Eat

$–$$ ✕ **Mayton.** Backed with wood beams and bursting with a wonderfully eccentric collection of antiques ranging from mortars and pestles to Portuguese yokes and old typewriters, this restaurant's interior is charming. In contrast to the busy furnishings, the cooking is simple; specialties include fish, seafood, goat, and lamb. The wine list is surprisingly distinguished, with a broad range of savvy selections ranging in price from €7 to €150. ✉ *La Colada 7* ☎ *923/460720* ⊕ *www.ciudadrodrigo. net/mayton* ▤ *AE, DC, MC, V* ☉ *No dinner Mon.*

$$$ 🏨 **Parador de Ciudad Rodrigo.** The parador's stately entrance is topped by a beautifully preserved medieval stone arch, part of a castle built by Enrique II of Trastamara to stand guard over the Agueda Valley. Room 10 is particularly special: it has original vaulting. Some rooms, as well as the restaurant, overlook a beautiful garden that runs down to the River Agueda. ✉ *Pl. Castillo 1, 37500* ☎ *923/460150* 🖷 *923/460404* ⊕ *www. parador.es* ⬤ *35 rooms* ⚭ *Restaurant, bar* ▤ *AE, DC, MC, V.*

ZAMORA & CITY OF VALLADOLID

Zamora is a densely fertile province divided by the River Duero into two distinct zones: the "land of bread," to the north, and the "land of wine," to the south. The area is most interesting for its Romanesque churches, the finest of which are in Zamora and Toro. The city of Valladolid, in contrast, is less scenic, but it has the National Museum of Sculpture and plenty of interesting history.

Zamora

64 *248 km (154 mi) northwest of Madrid.*

Zamora, on a bluff above the Duero, is not conventionally beautiful, as its many attractive monuments are isolated from one another by ramshackle 19th- and 20th-century development. The town does have a lively, old-fashioned character, making it a pleasant place to pause. In Zamora's medieval town center is the Romanesque church of **San Juan** (⊠ South side of Pl. Mayor ⊙ Open for mass only), remarkable for its elaborate rose window. At the end of Calle Reina is one of Zamora's surviving medieval gates, and near here is the Romanesque church of **Santa María.** ⊠ *North of Pl. Mayor.*

Zamora is famous for its Holy Week celebrations. The **Museo de Semana Santa** (Holy Week Museum) houses the sculptures paraded around the streets in processions during that time. Of relatively recent vintage, these works have an appealing provincial quality—for instance, a Crucifixion group filled with what appears to be the contents of a hardware store, including bales of rope, a saw, a spade, and numerous nails. The museum is in an unsightly modern building next to the church of Santa María. ⊠ *Pl. de Santa María la Nueva* ☎ *980/532295* 🎫 *€3* ⊙ *Tues.–Sat. 10–2 and 5–8, Sun. 10–2.*

Zamora's **cathedral** is in a hauntingly beautiful square at the highest and westernmost point of the old town. Most of the building is Romanesque, but the exterior is most remarkable for its dome, which is flanked by turrets, articulated by spiny ribs, and covered in overlapping stones. The interior is notable for its early-16th-century carved choir stalls. The austere, late-16th-century cloister has a small museum, with an intricate *custodia* (monstrance, or receptacle for the Host) by Juan de Arce and some badly displayed but intriguing Flemish tapestries from the 15th and 16th centuries. ☎ *980/530644* ⊠ *Pl. Catedral* 🎫 *Cathedral free, museum €3* ⊙ *Mar.–Sept., Tues.–Sun. 10–2 and 5–8; Oct.–Feb., Tues.–Sun. 10–2 and 4:30–6:30.*

Surrounding Zamora's cathedral to the north is a sizable park incorporating the heavily restored **castle,** begun in the 11th century. Now a municipal school, it's open to visitors only when classes are in session. Calle Trascastillo, descending south from the cathedral to the river, allows for views of the fertile countryside to the south and the town's old **Roman bridge.** ⊠ *C. Trascastillo.*

Where to Stay & Eat

$$$–$$$$ ✕ **El Rincón de Antonio.** Zamora's finest *cocina de autor* (original cuisine) comes off the burners from behind this stone facade, decorated in sleek contemporary lines. Local upland ingredients and seafood dishes from the Iberian coasts balance a constantly changing menu rich in creativity. ⊠ *Rúa de los Francos 6* ☎ *980/535370* ▭ *AE, DC, MC, V* ⊙ *No dinner Sun.*

$$$ 🏨 **Parador de Zamora.** This restored 15th-century palace is central yet quiet, with a distinctive patio courtyard adorned with coats of arms and classical medallions of historical and mythological figures. The views are excellent, and the staff is friendly and resourceful. ⊠ *Pl. de Viriato 5, 49001* ☎ *980/514497* 🖨 *980/530063* ⊕ *www.parador.es* 🛏 *52 rooms* ⅄ *Restaurant, pool, bar* ▭ *AE, DC, MC, V.*

Toro

 33 km (20 mi) east of Zamora, 272 km (169 mi) northwest of Madrid.

Above a loop of the River Duero and commanding extensive views over the vast plain to the south, Toro was once a provincial capital. In 1833 it was absorbed into the province of Zamora—a loss of status that worked in some ways to its advantage. Zamora developed into a thriving modern town, but Toro slumbered and preserved its old appearance. The town is crowded with Romanesque churches, of which the most important is the **Colegiata,** begun in 1160. The protected west portal, or Portico de La Gloria, has colorfully painted, perfectly preserved statuary from the early 13th century. The Serbian-Byzantine dome is also prominent. In the sacristy is an anonymous 15th-century painting of the Virgin, a moving work in the so-called Hispano-Flemish style titled *La Virgen de la Mosca* (The Virgin of the Fly) for the fly painted on the Virgin's robe. ⊠ *Pl. de la Colegiata* 🖼 *€1* 🕾 *Tourist office 980/694747* ⊕ *www. toroayto.es* ⊘ *Mar.–Nov., daily 10–2 and 4:30–6:30; Dec.–Feb. daily 10:30–2 and 5–7:30; Mon. open for mass only.*

Valladolid

 96 km (60 mi) east of Zamora, 193 km (120 mi) northwest of Madrid.

Modern Valladolid, capital of Castile–León, is a sprawling industrial center in the middle of a flat stretch of Castilian terrain. The surrounding countryside has a desolate, wintry sort of beauty, its vast, brittle fields unfolding grandly toward the horizon, punctuated here and there with swaths of green. The city has an important place in Spain's history: Ferdinand and Isabella were married here, Felipe II was born and baptized here, and Felipe III made Valladolid the capital of Spain for six years.

Fodor'sChoice
★
From the bus station, train station, or wherever you park your car, hop a taxi to the **Museo Nacional de Escultura** (National Museum of Sculpture), at the northernmost point in the old town. The late-15th-century Colegio de San Gregorio, in which the main museum is housed, is a masterpiece with playful, naturalistic detail. The facade is especially fantastic, with ribs in the form of cut-back trees, sprouting branches, and—to complete the forest motif—a row of wild men bearing mighty clubs. Across the walkway from the main museum is a Renaissance palace that houses temporary exhibitions. The main museum is arranged in rooms off an elaborate, arcaded courtyard. Its collections do for Spanish sculpture what those in the Prado do for Spanish painting—the only difference is that most people have heard of Velázquez, El Greco, and Goya, but fewer are familiar with Alonso de Berruguete, Juan de Juni, and Gregorio Fernández, the three artists represented here.

Attendants and directional cues encourage you to tour the museum in chronological order. Begin on the ground floor, with Alonso de Berruguete's remarkable sculptures from the dismantled high altar in Valladolid's church of San Benito (1532). Berruguete, who trained in Italy under Michelangelo, is the most widely appreciated of Spain's postmedieval sculptors. He strove for pathos rather than realism, and his works have an extraordinarily expressive quality. The San Benito altar was the most important commission of his life, and the fragments here allow you to scrutinize his powerfully emotional art. In the museum's elegant chapel (which you normally see at the end of the tour) is a Berruguete retable from 1526, his first known work; on either side kneel gilded bronze figures by the Italian-born Pompeo Leoni.

Many critics of Spanish sculpture think that decline set in with the late-16th-century artist Juan de Juni, who used glass for eyes and pearls for tears. Juni's many admirers, however, find his works intensely exciting, and they are in any case the highlights of the museum's upper floor. Dominating Castilian sculpture of the 17th century was the Galician-born Gregorio Fernández, in whose works the dividing line between sculpture and theater becomes tenuous. Respect for Fernández has been diminished by the number of vulgar imitators his work has spawned, but at Valladolid you can see his art at its best. The enormous, dramatic, and moving sculptural groups assembled in the last series of rooms form a suitably spectacular climax to this fine collection. ⊠ *Cadenas de San Gregorio 1–3* ☎ *983/250375* ⊕ *http://museoescultura.mcu.es* 🎟 *€2.40, free Sat. 4–6 and Sun. 10–2* ⊙ *Sept. 21–Mar. 20, Tues.–Sat. 10–2 and 4–6, Mar. 21–Sept. 20, Tues.–Sat. 10–2 and 4–9, Sun. 10–2.*

At the corner of Calle Angustias is a brick mansion, the **birthplace of Felipe II**. The late-15th-century church of **San Pablo** (⊠ Pl. de San Pablo) has an overwhelmingly elaborate facade. Though the foundations of Valladolid's **cathedral** were laid in late-Gothic times, the building owes much of its appearance to designs executed in the late 16th century by Juan de Herrera, the architect of the Escorial. Further work was carried out by Alberto de Churriguera in the early 18th century. The Juni altarpiece is the one bit of color in an otherwise visually chilly place. ⊠ *Pl. de la Universidad 1* ☎ *983/304362* 🎟 *Cathedral free, museum €2.50* ⊙ *Tues.–Fri. 10–1:30 and 4:30–7, weekends 10–2.*

The main **university building** (⊠ Pl. de la Universidad) sits opposite the garden just south of the cathedral. The exuberant and dynamic late-baroque frontispiece is by Narciso Tomé, creator of the remarkable *Transparente* in Toledo's cathedral. Valladolid's Calle Librería leads south from the main building to the magnificent **Colegio de Santa Cruz** (⊠ Pl. Colegio de Santa Cruz), a large university college begun in 1487 in the Gothic style and completed in 1491 by Lorenzo Vázquez in a tentative, pioneering Renaissance mode. Inside is a harmonious courtyard. The house where Christopher Columbus died in 1506 is now the **Museo de Colón** (Columbus Museum) with a well-arranged collection of objects and explanatory panels illuminating the explorer's life. ⊠ *Colón s/n* ☎ *983/291353* 🎟 *Free* ⊙ *Tues.–Sat. 10–2 and 5–7, Sun. 10–2.*

An interesting remnant of Spain's golden age is the tiny house where the writer Miguel de Cervantes lived from 1603 to 1606. A haven of peace set back from a noisy thoroughfare, **Casa de Cervantes** (Cervantes's House) is best reached by taxi. It was furnished in the early 20th century in a pseudo-Renaissance style by the Marquis of Valle-Inclan—the creator of the El Greco Museum in Toledo. ⊠ *Rastro 7* ☎ *983/308810* 🎟 *€2.40, free Sun.* ⊙ *Tues.–Sat. 9:30–3, Sun. 10–3.*

Where to Stay & Eat

$$$$ ✕ **La Parrilla de San Lorenzo.** Named for St. Lawrence, who was roasted to death over a grill (*parrilla*)—this onetime 16th-century monastery, where nobles sent their children for proper upbringing, serves Castilian fare starring *lechazo* (young, milk-fed lamb) cooked in an *horno de leña* (wood oven). Seafood dishes include *bonito a la forma convento* ("convent-style" tuna marinated in coarse sea salt and olive oil). Each dining room is more opulent than the last—stone arches span several, and walls are adorned with gilded mirrors, iron shields, and backlighted stained-glass religious images. ⊠ *Pedro Niño 1* ☎ *983/335088* ▤ *AE, MC, V* ☾ *No dinner Sun. Closed Mon. in Aug.*

$$$–$$$$ ✕ **La Dovela.** Valladolid's most famous and stylish restaurant counts members of the Spanish royal family among its guests. Specialties include meat roasted in a wood oven and *rape Castellano Gran Mesón* (breaded monkfish with clams and peppers). The daily five-course *menú de degustación* (tasting menu) at €25 is an excellent value, and the cozy downstairs bar serves a creditable *vino de la casa* (house wine) and a great selection of tapas. ⊠ *Paseo Zorrilla 10* ☎ *983/338785* ▤ *AE, DC, MC, V.*

$$–$$$ ▦ **Olid Meliá.** This hotel sits on a modern block amid one of Valladolid's oldest and most attractive districts. The building was erected in the early 1970s, and the rooms have blond-wood furniture. For a splurge, book a room with a sauna or hot tub. The first two floors have a pristine, marble elegance. ⊠ *Pl. de San Miguel 10, 47003* ☎ *983/357200* ▧ *983/ 336828* ⊕ *www.solmelia.com* ⤳ *211 rooms* ⚐ *Restaurant, cafeteria, some in-room hot tubs, bar, meeting room* ▤ *AE, DC, MC, V.*

Nightlife

Valladolid is a university town with a dynamic nightlife. The cafés on the Plaza Mayor are the best places to people-watch as evening falls. Tapas are good in the Zona Santa María la Antigua and on the adjacent Calle Marqués and Calle Paraíso. The modern Zona Paco Suárez is popular with students. More fashionable and less rowdy are the Zona Cantarranas and hidden hot spots around the Plaza del Salvador. For tasty Castilian tapas, make for the boisterous **Bar El Corcho** (⊠ Correo 2 ☎ 983/330861), just off the Plaza Mayor. It has exposed brick walls, sawdust scattered liberally on the floor, and pig haunches and copper pots hanging over the marble-top bar; it's standing room only every night of the week. The house specialty is *tostada de gambas,* toasted French bread heaped with shrimp and drizzled with olive oil. The perennially popular **Disco Bagur** (⊠ C. de la Pasión 13), off Plaza Mayor, is a hopping dance spot.

▌ OFF THE
BEATEN
PATH

MUSEO DEL VINO (Wine Museum) – Valladolid is close to two famous winegrowing regions, **Rueda** for whites and **Ribera del Duero** for *tintos* (reds). Wine buffs can enjoy an easy day's excursion from Valladolid, visiting bodegas and the **Museo del Vino** in the splendid 220-yard-long 11th-century castle at **Peñafiel.** The wine museum is open from October 1 until Easter, Tuesday through Sunday 11:30 to 2 and 4 to 7; in the summer starting after Easter until September 30, Tuesday through Sunday 11 to 2:30 and 4:30 to 8:30. Admission to the castle and museum is €5; €12 includes a tasting. Leave the city heading east to

Renedo and follow the country road via Villabáñez and Valbueno (the famous **Vega Sicilia** bodega, Sir Winston Churchill's favorite) along the Río Duero to Peñafiel. Return by the N122. ☎ *983/881199* ⊕ *www. museodelvinodevalladolid.es.*

BURGOS, LEÓN & CAMINO DE SANTIAGO

Burgos and León are ancient Castilian capitals with lively centers and two of the grandest Gothic cathedrals in Spain. West of Burgos, the N120 to León crosses the ancient Way of St. James, occasionally revealing lovely old churches, tiny hermitages, ruined monasteries, and medieval villages in rolling fields. The snowcapped peaks of the Picos de Europa mark the northwestern horizon. West of León, you can actually follow the well-worn Camino as it approaches Galicia and the very last stops on a pilgrimage route that began all the way back in France or Portugal. Making its way toward the giant cathedral in Santiago de Compostela, this Castilian leg of the Camino passes through medieval towns and quiet valleys as the terrain gets greener, wetter, and hillier.

Burgos

67–72 *240 km (149 mi) north of Madrid.*

On the banks of the Arlanzón River is this small city with some of Spain's most outstanding medieval architecture. The first signs of Burgos, if you approach on the A1 from Madrid, are the spiky twin spires of its cathedral, rising above the main bridge. Burgos's second glory is its heritage as the city of El Cid, the part-historical, part-mythical hero of the Christian Reconquest of Spain. The city has been known for centuries as a center of both militarism and religion, and even today you can see more nuns on its streets than almost anywhere else in Spain. Burgos was born as a military camp in 884—a fortress built on the orders of the Christian king Alfonso III, who was having a hard time defending the upper reaches of Old Castile from the constant forays of the Arabs. It quickly became vital in the defense of Christian Spain, and its identity as an early outpost of Christianity was sealed with the founding of the Royal Convent of Las Huelgas, in 1187. Burgos also became an important station on the Camino de Santiago and thus a place of rest and sustenance for Christian pilgrims throughout the Middle Ages.

★ **67** Start your walk at the **cathedral,** the city's high point, which contains such a wealth of art and other treasures that the local burghers actually lynched their civil governor in 1869 for trying to take an inventory of it. The proud Burgalese apparently feared that the man was angling to remove the treasures. Most of the outside of the cathedral is sculpted in the Flamboyant Gothic style. The cornerstone was laid in 1221, and the two 275-foot towers were completed by the middle of the 14th century, though the final chapel was not finished until 1731. There are 13 chapels, the most elaborate of which is the hexagonal Condestable Chapel. You'll find the **tomb of El Cid** (1026–99) and his wife, Ximena, under the transept. El Cid (whose real name was Rodrigo Díaz de Vivar) was a feudal warlord revered for his victories over the Moors; the medieval *Song of My Cid* transformed him into a Spanish national hero.

At the other end of the cathedral, high above the West Door, is the **Reloj de Papamoscas** (Flycatcher Clock), so named for the sculptured bird that opens its mouth as the mechanism marks each hour. The grilles around the choir have some of the finest wrought-iron work in central Spain, and the choir itself has 103 delicately carved walnut stalls, no two alike. The 13th-century stained-glass windows that once shed a beautiful, filtered light were destroyed in 1813, one of many cultural casualties of Napoléon's retreating troops. ⊠ *Between Pl. del Rey San Fernando and Pl. de Santa María* ☎ *947/204712* ⊕ *www.catedraldeburgos.es* ⊠ *Museum and cloister €4* ☉ *Mar. 19–June 30 and Oct., daily 9:30–1:15 and 4–7; July–Sept. 30, daily 9:30–7:15; Nov. 1–Mar. 18, daily 10–1:15 and 4–6:45.*

68 Across the Plaza del Rey San Fernando from the cathedral is the city's main gate, the **Arco de Santa María**; walk through toward the river and look above the arch at the 16th-century statues of the first Castilian judges; El Cid; Spain's patron saint James; and King Carlos I.

69 The Arco de Santa María fronts the city's loveliest promenade, the **Espolón**. The walkway follows the riverbank and is shaded with luxuri-
70 ant black poplars. The **Casa del Cordón**, a 15th-century palace, is where the Catholic Monarchs received Columbus after his second voyage to the New World. It's now a bank. ⊠ *Pl. de Calvo Sotel.*

71 Founded in 1441, the **Cartuja de Miraflores** is a florid Gothic charter house; its Isabelline church has an altarpiece by Gil de Siloe, said to be gilded with the first gold brought back from the Americas. To get there, follow signs from the city's main gate. ⊠ *3 km (2 mi) east of Burgos, at end of a poplar- and elm-lined rd.* ⊕ *www.cartuja.org* ⊠ *Free* ☉ *Church open for mass Mon.–Sat. 9 AM, Sun. 7:30 and 10:15 AM; main building Mon.–Sat. 10:15–3 and 4–6, Sun. 11–3 and 4–6.*

72 On the western edge of town—a long walk—is the **Monasterio de Las Huelgas Reales,** still run by nuns. Founded in 1187 by King Alfonso VIII, the convent has a royal mausoleum. All but one of the royal coffins were desecrated by Napoléon's soldiers; the one that survived contained clothes that form the basis of the convent's textile museum. ⊠ *1½ km (1 mi) southwest of town, along Paseo de la Isla and left across Malatos Bridge* ☎ *947/201630* ⊕ *www3.planalfa.es/lashuelgas* ⊠ *€5, free Wed. for European Union citizens* ☉ *Tues.–Sat. 10–1 and 3:45–5:30, Sun. 10:30–2.*

Where to Stay & Eat

★ **$$–$$$** ✕ **Casa Ojeda.** Across from the Casa del Cordón, this popular restaurant is known for inspired renditions of Burgos classics, especially roast lamb. ⊠ *C. Vitoria 5* ☎ *947/209052* ⊕ *www.grupojeda.com* ⊟ *AE, DC, MC, V* ☉ *Closed Sun.*

$$$–$$$$ ✕⬚ **Mesón del Cid.** Once a 15th-century printing press, this family-run hotel and restaurant has been hosting travelers and serving Burgalese food for four generations. Guest rooms face the cathedral and are done in traditional Castilian style. The dining rooms have hand-hewn beams and views of the cathedral. The *pimientos rellenos* (peppers stuffed with meat) are excellent, as is the *sopa de Doña Jimena* (garlic soup with

Burgos

bread and egg). ✉ *Pl. Santa María 8, 09003* ☎ *947/208715* 🖷 *947/ 269460* ⊕ *www.mesondelcid.es* ⇆ *56 rooms* ☕ *Restaurant, cafeteria, bar, free parking* ⊟ *AE, DC, MC, V.*

Nightlife

Thanks to a university student population, Burgos has a lively *vida nocturna* (nightlife). House wines and *cañas* (small glasses of beer) flow freely at the crowded tapas bars along Calles Laín Calvo and San Juan, near the Plaza Mayor. Calle Puebla, a small, dark street off Calle San Juan, also gets constant revelers, who pop into Café Principal, La Rebotica, and Spils Cervecería for a quick drink and morsel before moving on to the next hangout. When you order a drink at any Burgos bar, the bartender plunks down a free *pinchito* (small tapa)—a long-standing tradition. The late-night bar scene centers on **Las Llanas,** two interconnected squares near the cathedral.

Shopping

A good buy is a few bottles of local Ribera de Duero *tinto* wines, now strong rivals to those of Rioja-Alta. Burgos is also known for its cheeses. **Casa Quintanilla** (✉ C. Paloma 17) is a good spot to pick up some *queso de Burgos,* a fresh ricottalike cheese.

EN ROUTE For a sojourn with those masters of the Gregorian chant, the double-platinum monks of *Chant* fame, stop at the **Monastery of Santo Domingo de Silos** (☎ 947/390068), 58 km (36 mi) southeast of Burgos. Single men can stay here for up to eight days. Guests are expected to be present for breakfast, lunch, and dinner but are otherwise left to their own devices. If the monastery is full, try to drop in for a vespers service. Quite close to Burgosto the southeast (10 km [6 mi]) is the **Monastery of San Pedro de Cardeña** (☎ 947/290033), a lodging that allows couples and even families—possibly thanks to the monastery's importance in the story of El Cid, the medieval Spanish hero who left his wife and children there when banished into exile.

Sasamón

73 *25 km (16 mi) west of Burgos.*

Turn right off the highway and soon you'll be in the village where the 15th-century hilltop church of Santa María la Real, with a magnificent carved portico, stands beside a tree-lined plaza with a tinkling fountain. You can visit on weekdays, 11 to 2 and 4 to 6. Pick up keys to the church in the nearby Bar Gloria. On the north side of the village is the tiny Ermita de San Isidro Hermitage. If the hermitage is closed, peer through the small window in the door to see, right in the middle of the aisle, its surreal, 20-foot-tall 16th-century Gothic cross. Carved of stone, it depicts the expulsion of Adam and Eve from paradise.

Castrojeriz

74 *20 km (12 mi) southwest of Sasamón.*

From Sasamón, return to the N120 and cross it to reach Olmillas de Sasamón. After passing a castle on your right, continue south, following the CAMINO DE SANTIAGO signs. A few miles after Hontanas, the road passes under an arch of the ruined monastery of **San Anton,** now a farm building. Here you can see two niches by the road where food was once left out for pilgrims. As you approach Castrojeriz, its ruined hilltop **castle** is visible. To see the three local **churches** you may have to call the caretaker, Vicente (☎ 947/377034).

2

Where to Stay & Eat

$–$$ ✕⛏ **La Cachava.** This charming, ancient farmhouse's lovely rooms are painstakingly decorated in original rustic patterns and look out on flowery patios. The food at the restaurant ($–$$$) is as authentic as the decor. ⊠ *Real 93* ☎ *947/378547* ⊕ *www.lacachava.com* ⊅ *8 rooms* ▤ *MC, V* ⊗ *Closed Mon.*

¢ ✕⛏ **La Taberna.** Antonio and María Jesús have restored this 18th-century timber building as a small tavern and inn with good home cooking, including flavorful *sopa de ajo* (garlic soup). They also operate as a basic budget hotel. ⊠ *Real de Oriente 43* ☎ *947/377610* ✉ *lataberna1998@mixmail.com* ⊅ *3 rooms and 1 (separate) rural house with 6 large rooms* ▤ *MC, V* ⊗ *Closed Mon.*

Frómista

75 *54 km (33 mi) northwest of Castrojeriz.*

Take the small road south from Castrojeriz to Itero de la Vega and Boadillo del Camino to reach Frómista. Just before you arrive, the road crosses the Canal de Castilla, begun in 1753 with the dubious idea of linking Salamanca with the port of Santander—and never completed. The town of Frómista has four hospices for present-day pilgrims, and its architectural gem is the 1066 church of San Martín. Richly sculpted inside, it was part of a monastery in the 11th century, which might explain the geographical breathing room it still enjoys.

Where to Eat

$$$–$$$$ ✕ **Hostería de los Palmeros.** Here in a 17th-century pilgrims' hospital, the kitchen serves good fish, game in season, and baby lamb. Dine on an outdoor terrace or in the rather formal upstairs dining room, with a view of the storks' nests on the church of San Telmo, across the highway. ⊠ *Pl. San Telmo 4* ☎ *979/810067* ▤ *AE, DC, MC, V.*

Villalcázar de Sirga

76 *13 km (8 mi) west of Frómista.*

Driving toward Carrión de los Condes, turn right into the village of Villalcázar. The Templar church of Santa María la Blanca has a towering double-arch entrance and the polychrome 13th-century tombs of Felipe, brother of Alfonso X the Learned, and Leonor, his wife.

Carrión de los Condes

77 *7 km (4½ mi) west of Villalcázar de Sirga.*

Drive through this busy town and cross the River Carrión to reach the Real Monasterio San Zoilo on the left. Begun in the 10th century, this former Benedictine monastery has magnificent 16th-century Gothic-Renaissance cloisters and the elaborate tombs of the *condes* (counts) of Carrión. You can visit on weekdays 10:30 to 2 (plus 4 to 8 June through August) and on weekends 10:30 to 2 and 4 to 8 year-round.

Where to Stay

★ $$–$$$ **Hotel Real Monasterio San Zoilo.** This former Benedictine monastery dates back to the 10th century, and its spectacular entrance leads to impressive public rooms with exposed bricks and timbers. The vast refectory can seat 330. One floor up is the restaurant Las Vigas ($$$$), which serves decent Castilian fare at tables set below a forest of medieval beams (*vigas*). The large rooms are well furnished, and the "Habitación del Conde" suite is especially grand. ⊠ *Carrión de los Condes, Palencia 34120* ☎ *979/880050* 🖷 *979/881090* ⊕ *www.sanzoilo.com* 🛏 *45 rooms, 5 suites* ⏷ *Restaurant, bar, meeting room* ⊟ *AE, DC, MC, V.*

Sahagún

78 *44 km (27 mi) west of Carrió de los Condes, 63 km (39 mi) east of León.*

The road winds into Sahagún past rolling fields of wheat. The town was allegedly founded by Charlemagne after he conquered the Moors by the nearby River Cea, and Sahagún is in fact a center of Mudéjar craftsmanship, as evidenced in the brick bell towers and trilobed apses of the 12th-century churches of San Tirso and San Lorenzo. Nuns in the Monasterio de Santa Cruz usually allow visitors to see the treasures, which include a beautifully carved medieval silver casket.

Where to Eat

$$–$$$ ✕ **Luis.** With a long bar overlooking the narrow Plaza Mayor, this popular, family-run restaurant cooks local produce with flair. At €10, the *puerros de Sahagún rellenos de mariscos* (Sahagún leeks stuffed with shellfish) are highly recommended, and there's a good selection of salads. Breakfast, lunch, and dinner are served daily. ⊠ *Pl. Mayor 4* ☎ *987/781085* ⊟ *AE, MC, V.*

León

 333 km (207 mi) northwest of Madrid, 216 km (134 mi) west of Burgos.

The ancient capital of the group of provinces known as Castilla y León (Castile and León) sits on the banks of the Bernesga River in the high plains of Old Castile. Historians say that the name of the city, which was founded as a permanent camp for the Roman legions in AD 70, has nothing to do with the proud lion that has been its emblem for centuries but is instead a corruption of the Roman word *legio* (legion).

The capital of Christian Spain was moved to León from Oviedo in 914 as the Reconquest spread southward, launching the city's richest era. Walls went up around the old Roman town, and you can still see parts of the 6-foot-thick ramparts in the middle of the modern city. Today, León is a wealthy provincial capital and prestigious university town. The wide avenues of western León are lined with boutiques, and the twisting alleys of the half-timbered old town hide the bars, bookstores, and *chocolaterías* most popular with students. As you're wandering the old town, look down occasionally and you just might notice small brass scallop shells set into the street. The scallop is the symbol of St. James; the shells were installed by the town government to mark the path for modern-day pilgrims.

★ ⑦ León is proudest of its soaring Gothic **cathedral,** on the Plaza de Regla, whose soaring upper reaches are built with more windows than stone. Flanked by two aggressively square towers, the facade has three arched, weatherworn doorways, the middle one adorned with slender statues of the apostles. Begun in 1205, the cathedral has 125 long, slender stained-glass windows; dozens of decorative small ones; and three giant, spectacular rose windows. On sunny days, the glass casts bejeweled shafts of light on the beautifully spare, pale-sandstone interior; the windows themselves depict abstract floral patterns as well as various biblical and medieval scenes. A glass door to the choir gives an unobstructed view of nave windows and the painted altarpiece, framed with gold leaf. The cathedral also contains the sculpted tomb of King Ordoño II, who moved the capital of Christian Spain to León. The **museum** has giant medieval hymnals, textiles, sculptures, wood carvings, and paintings. Look for the carved-wood Mudéjar archive, with a letter of the alphabet above each door: it's one of the world's oldest file cabinets. ⊠ *Pl. de Regla* ☎ *987/875770* ⊕ *www.catedraldeleon.org* 🖾 *Cathedral free (€1.70 with guide), museum €3.50, cloister €1* ☉ *Cathedral, Oct.–June, Mon.–Sat. 8:30–1:30 and 4–7, Sun. 8:30–2:30 and 5–7; July–Sept., Mon.–Sat. 8:30–1:30 and 4–8, Sun. 8:30–2:30 and 5–8. Museum, Oct.–May, weekdays 9:30–1:30 and 4–7, Sat. 9:30–1:30; June–Sept., weekdays 9:30–2 and 4–7:30, Sat. 9:30–2 and 4–7.*

⑧⓪ Hidden away just north of the cathedral is the **Fundación Vela Zanetti,** a contemporary, wood-and-windows art museum inside a 15th-century mansion. Zanetti was a 20th-century Castilian artist with a fondness for warm tones and a special interest in human rights. Some of his portraits recall El Greco. Art lovers will find this widely unknown museum a pleasant surprise. ⊠ *C. Pablo Flórez s/n* ☎ *987/244121* 🖾 *Free* ☉ *Tues.–Fri. 10–1:30 and 5–8, weekends 5–8.*

⑧① The arcaded **Plaza Mayor,** in the heart of the old town, is surrounded by simple half-timber houses. On Wednesday and Saturday, the plaza bustles with farmers selling produce and cheeses. Many farmers still wear wooden shoes called *madreñas,* which are raised on three heels, two in front and one in back. They were designed to walk on mud in this usually wet part of Spain.

⑧② Most of León's tapas bars are in the 12th-century **Plaza San Martín.** This area is called the Barrio Húmedo, or Wet Neighborhood, for the large amount of wine spilled here late at night.

⑧③ Southwest of the Plaza San Martín is the **Plaza de Santa María del Camino,** which, as the plaque here points out, used to be called Plaza del Grano (Grain Square) and hosted the local corn and bread market. Also here is the church of **Santa María del Camino,** where pilgrims stop on their way west to Santiago de Compostela. The strange allegorical

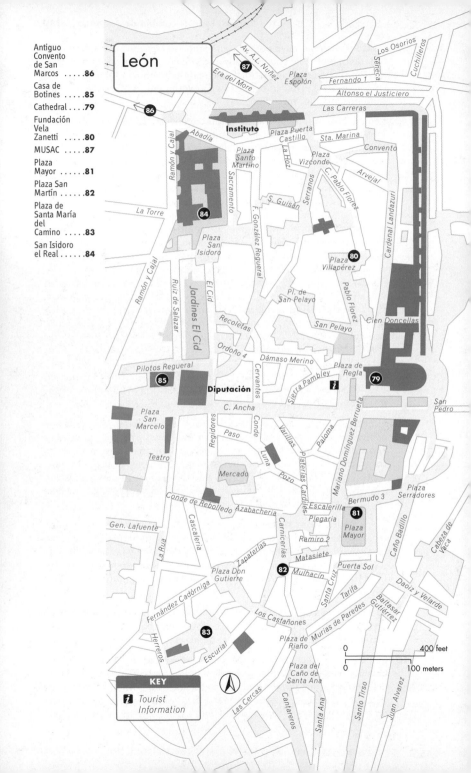

León

KEY

🛈 *Tourist Information*

fountain in the middle depicts two chubby angels clutching a pillar, symbolizing León's two rivers and the capital.

★ ⑧④ The sandstone basilica of **San Isidoro el Real**, on Calle Cid, was built into the side of the city wall in 1063 and rebuilt in the 12th century. The **Panteón de los Reyes** (Royal Pantheon), adjoining the basilica, has been called the Sistine Chapel of Romanesque art for the vibrant 12th-century frescoes on its pillars and ceiling. The pantheon was the first building in Spain to be decorated with scenes from the New Testament. Look for the agricultural calendar painted on one archway, showing which farming task should be performed each month. Twenty-three kings and queens were once buried here, but their tombs were destroyed by French troops during the Napoleonic Wars. Treasures in the adjacent **Museo de San Isidoro** include a jewel-encrusted agate chalice, a richly illustrated handwritten Bible, and many polychrome wood statues of the Virgin Mary. ✉ *Pl. de San Isidoro 4* ☎ *987/876161* ✇ *Basilica free, Royal Pantheon and museum €3.50* ◷ *July and Aug., Mon.–Sat. 9–8, Sun. 9–2; Sept.–June, Mon.–Sat. 9–1:30 and 4–7, Sun. 10–2.*

⑧⑤ Just south of the old town is the **Casa de Botines**, a multigabled, turreted, granite behemoth designed in the late 1800s by that controversial Catalan Antoni Gaudí. It now houses a bank. ✉ *Off Ruiz de Salazar.*

⑧⑥ Fronted by a large, airy pedestrian plaza, the sumptuous **Antiguo Convento de San Marcos** is now a luxury hotel, the Parador Hostal San Marcos. Originally a home for knights of the Order of St. James, who patrolled the Camino de Santiago, and a pit stop for weary pilgrims, the monastery you see today was begun in 1513 by the head of the order, King Ferdinand, who thought that knights deserved something better. Finished at the height of the Renaissance, the plateresque facade is a majestic swath of small sculptures (many depicting knights and lords) and careful ornaments. Inside are an elegant staircase and a cloister full of medieval statues. Have a drink in the bar—its tiny windows are the original defensive slits. The building also houses León's **Museo Arqueológico**, famous for its 11th-century ivory Carrizo crucifix. ✉ *Pl. de San Marcos* ☎ *987/245061* ✇ *Museum €2.50* ◷ *Mon. 10–2, Tues.–Sat. 10–2 and 5–8:30.*

☺ Traveling with children? León has a long **park** on the banks of the Bernesga River, with playground equipment every 100 feet or so.

⑧⑦ Completed in early 2005, **MUSAC, Museum of Modern Art of Castillo y León** reflects the modern León while paying homage to its history with its own cluster of buildings whose exteriors are cascaded with rectangular stained glass, like its cathedral. This "Museum of the Present" brings art to the people by offering varied workshops and activities for children amid exhibiting modern creations from all over the globe. Films and concerts are also put on throughout the year. ✉ *Av. de Los Reyes Leoneses, 24* ☎ *987/090000* ✇ *Free* ◷ *Tues.–Sun. 10–3 and 4–9.*

Bars & Cafés

Most of León's liveliest hangouts are clustered in Plaza Mayor and Plaza San Martín, with the former drawing couples and families and the latter a university crowd. The streets are packed with tapas bars.

In the Plaza Mayor, you might want to start your crawl at **Universal, Mesón de Don Quijote, Casa Benito,** or **Bar La Plaza Mayor.** In the Plaza San Martín, the **Latino Bar at No. 10** serves a glass of house wine and your choice of one of four generous tapas. Cozy **Prada a Tope** serves the local Bierzo wine out of a big barrel.

Where to Stay & Eat

$$–$$$$ ✕ **Nuevo Racimo de Oro.** Upstairs in a ramshackle 12th-century tavern in the heart of the old town, this rustic restaurant, once a hostel and hospital for weary pilgrims, now specializes in roast lamb cooked in a wood-fire clay oven. The spicy *sopa de ajo leonese* (garlic soup) is a classic, and *solomillo Racimo al hojaldre* (veal in puff pastry) makes a tasty entrée. Worth trying is *Tarta de San Marcos*, a lemon cake served with whipped cream. ⌖ *Pl. San Martín 8* ☎ *987/214767 or 987/260146* ⊕ *www.racimodeoro.com* ⊟ *AE, DC, MC, V* ☉ *Closed Sun. June–Sept. No dinner Tues. Closed Wed. Oct.–May.*

$–$$$ ✕ **Adonías.** Enter the bar and go up one flight to this green, softly lighted dining room, furnished with rustic tables and colorful ceramics. The cuisine is based on such regional foodstuffs as cured hams, roast peppers, and chorizo. Try the grilled sea bream or the roast suckling pig, and, if you have room, the banana pudding with chocolate sauce. ⌖ *Santa Nonia 16* ☎ *987/206768* ⊟ *AE, DC, MC, V* ☉ *Closed Sun.*

$–$$$ ✕ **Casa Pozo.** This longtime favorite is across from City Hall on the historic Plaza de San Marcelo. Past the small bar, the bright dining rooms are furnished with heavy Castilian furniture. Owner Gabriel del Pozo Alvarez—called Pin—supervises the busy kitchen while his son, also called Pin, is maître d'. Specialties include roast lamb, river crabs with clams, cod with pimiento and olive oil, and deep-fried hake. ⌖ *Pl. de San Marcelo 15* ☎ *987/223039* ⊟ *AE, DC, MC, V* ☉ *No dinner Sun.*

$$$ ✕▯ **Parador de León.** The magnificent Parador Hotel San Marcos occupies a restored 16th-century monastery built by King Ferdinand to shelter pilgrims walking the Camino de Santiago; the bridge beside it has helped pilgrims cross the Río Bernesga for centuries. The huge, ornamental, plateresque facade also fronts a church and museum of archaeology (which is in the Antiguo Monasterio de San Marcos). Hallways and guest rooms have antiques, high-quality reproductions, and some nice contemporary art. One wing is modern; if you want a more medieval look, ask for a room in the old section. The elegant dining room ($$–$$$$) offers 10 hot and cold regional appetizers for €13, and main dishes from €14 to €32. ⌖ *Pl. de San Marcos 7, 24001* ☎ *987/237300* 🖷 *987/233458* ⊕ *www.parador.es* ⇥ *230 rooms* ⚒ *2 restaurants, pool, hair salon, bar, parking (fee)* ⊟ *AE, DC, MC, V.*

FodorsChoice
★

$$ ▯ **Hotel Paris.** Rooms here are comfortable, and the classic basement *mesón* (tavern) snuggles up to the stone of a Roman wall. The hotel is on the modern thoroughfare heading east from Plaza Santo Domingo, halfway between the cathedral and the new town. ⌖ *Ancha 18, 24003* ☎ *987/238600* 🖷 *987/271572* ⊕ *www.hotelparisleon.com* ⇥ *55 rooms* ⚒ *Restaurant, café, bar, meeting rooms* ⊟ *AE, DC, MC, V.*

Shopping

FOOD Tasty regional treats include roasted red peppers, potent brandy-soaked cherries, and candied chestnuts. You can buy these in food shops all over the city. You can shop while having tapas at **Prada a Tope** (⊠ Pl. San Martín 1), where they're packaged by the house. The shop **Cuesta Castañón** (⊠ Castoñones 2), near Plaza San Martín, has a great selection of wines, cured meats, cookies, preserves, and bottled delicacies, not to mention books on related topics. Friendly owner José María González lets you sample the stock.

At **Hojaldres Alonso** (⊠ Ancha 7), near the cathedral, you can browse through the shelves of local goodies (candied nuts, preserves), all produced at their factory in nearby Astorga, and then head to the café in the back. The focus here is on the baked goods, particularly the *hojaldres* (puff pastries) and *torrijas,* a Castilian version of French toast. The café is a favorite among locals who come for their early evening *merienda* (usually between 6 and 8), Spain's answer to the afternoon tea.

FURNITURE & CRAFTS For fine, funky gifts, visit **Tricosis** (⊠ C. Mulhacín 3 ☎ 987/202953), a gallery opened by art students from the universities of León and Gijón, where colorful papier-mâché and experimental media form outstanding lamps, candleholders, vases, and frames.

EN ROUTE Leaving León, follow signs to the N120 and head southwest. Stop to admire the 13th-century **Orbigo Bridge,** 23 km (14 mi) outside the city, where the knight Quiñones made his stand. Legend has it that Quiñones was the toughest *hombre* on the Camino; in 1434, he staked out his turf on this 24-arch bridge and for a month challenged every other knight who policed the route. You are now on the Way of St. James itself, marked with large scallop signs for drivers and small ones for those who make the journey on foot or bicycle.

Astorga

88 *46 km (29 mi) southwest of León.*

Astorga, where the pilgrimage roads from France and Portugal merge, once had 22 hospitals to lodge and care for ailing travelers. The only one left today is next to the cathedral. The **cathedral** itself is a huge 15th-century building with four statues of St. James. The **Museo de la Catedral** displays 10th- and 12th-century chests, religious silverware, and paintings and sculptures by various Astorgans. ⊠ *Pl. de la Catedral* ☎ *987/615429* ☜ *€2.50* ☉ *Oct.–Dec. and Feb., daily 11–2 and 3:30–6:30; Mar.–Sept., daily 10–2 and 4–8.*

Fodor'sChoice ★ Just opposite Astorga's cathedral is the fairy-tale, neo-Gothic **Palacio Episcopal** (Archbishop's Palace), designed for a Catalan cleric by Antoni Gaudí in 1889. Visiting the palace the last week of August, during Astorga's Fiesta de Santa María, is a treat for the senses; fireworks explode in the sky, casting rainbows of light over Gaudí's ornate, mystical towers. No expense was spared in creating this building, site of the **Museo del Camino** (Museum of the Way). The collection has folk items, such as the standard pilgrim costume—heavy black cloak, staff hung with gourds, and wide-brimmed hat bedecked with scallop shells—as well as contemporary Spanish art. ⊠ *Adjacent to Astorga cathedral* ☎ 987/616882 🖼 €2.50 ◷ *Mar. 20–Sept. 20, Tues.–Sat. 10–2 and 4–8, Sun. 10–2 (and 4–8 in Aug.); Sept. 21–Mar. 19, Tues.–Sat. 11–2 and 4–6, Sun. 11–2.*

Where to Stay & Eat

$–$$$ ✕ **Restaurante Serrano.** Popular with locals, and occasionally serving the likes of game, wild mushrooms, and pork during special gastronomic weeks, this mesón serves both contemporary cuisine and traditional roasts of baby lamb. ⊠ *Portería 2* ☎ *987/617866* ▤ *AE, MC, V* ◷ *Closed last 2 wks in June. No dinner Mon.*

$$–$$$$ ✕▣ **La Peseta.** Family-run since 1871, this place persists in good home cooking, especially the four-dish marathon *cocido maragato*, a kind of country stew. The 18-room inn ($–$$) upstairs offers decent and economical rooms. ⊠ *Pl. de San Bartolomé 3* ☎ *987/617275* ▤ *987/615300* ⬅ *18 rooms* ▤ *AE, DC, MC, V* ◷ *Closed last 2 wks in Oct. and Jan. No dinner Sun. or Tues.*

$$ ▣ **Astur Plaza.** This gleaming, well-run hotel is near Astorga's city hall. The yellow guest rooms have dark-brown furnishings, and ample light shines in from large windows. The lounge is glassed in; the large bar and Los Hornos restaurant have beam ceilings and exposed brick walls. ⊠ *Pl. de España 2 y 3, 24700* ☎ *987/618900* ▤ *987/618949* ⊕ *www.asturplaza.com* ⬅ *32 rooms, 5 suites* ♿ *Restaurant, bar, parking (fee)* ▤ *AE, MC, V.*

Castillo de los Polvazares

89 *51 km (32 mi) west of León, 5 km (3 mi) northwest of Astorga.*

A 15-minute drive from Astorga is Castillo de los Polvazares, a 17th-century village built on the site of a fortified Roman settlement. The city's 30-odd residents live in stone houses emblazoned with crests above their green doorways. Walk down the stone streets and look for storks' nests on top of the village church. Castillo de los Polvazares is in León's Maragatería region, whose people are believed to be a mixture of the ancient Celts and Phoenicians. These traders resisted the Roman invasion of the Iberian Peninsula and reached the height of their prowess as muleteers in the 18th and 19th centuries (hence the wide doorways around town), transporting gold from the Americas to the royal court in Madrid.

Ponferrada

90 *115 km (71 mi) west of León, 64 km (40 mi) west of Astorga on NVI.*

In a hilly region with fertile valleys, Ponferrada is a mining and industrial center that gets its name from an iron toll bridge built by a local bishop in the 1100s. The tall, slim turrets of the 13th-century **Castillo de los Templarios** (Templars' Castle) on the western edge of town has sweeping views of the countryside and may once have been used by the Knights of the Order of St. James to police the route. Restoration is in progress. ⊠ *Florez Osorio 4* ☎ *987/414141* 🖼 *€2.50* ◷ *Apr. and May, Tues.–Sat. 10–2 and 4:30–8, Sun. 10–2; June–mid-Sept., Tues.–Sun. 10:30–2 and 5–9; mid-Sept.–Mar., Tues.–Sat. 10:30–2 and 4–7, Sun. 11–2.*

OFF THE BEATEN PATH

LAS MEDULAS – Leave Ponferrada heading west on the A6 (toward A Coruña), and take the Las Médulas–Puente de Domingo exit to the N536 toward Carucedo. Turning right here, you can either follow the signs to a viewpoint at Orellán or go to the village of **Las Medulas.** From the latter, you can explore the Roman gold mines 21 km (13 mi) west of Ponferrada, where jagged red cliffs rise out of oak and chestnut woods, and great pits lead to deep tunnels, canals, and caves. Bring a flashlight.

Villafranca del Bierzo

⑨ *135 km (84 mi) west of León, 20 km (12 mi) west of Ponferrada.*

After crossing León's grape-growing region, where the complex and full-bodied Bierzo wines are produced, you'll arrive in this medieval village, dominated by a massive and still-inhabited feudal fortress. Villafranca was a destination in itself for some of Santiago's pilgrims: visit the Romanesque church of Santiago to see the Puerta del Perdón (Door of Pardon), a sort of spiritual consolation prize for exhausted worshippers who couldn't make it over the mountains. Stroll the streets and seek out the onetime home of the infamous Grand Inquisitor Torquemada. On the way out, you can buy wine at any of three local bodegas.

Where to Stay & Eat

$$–$$$ ✕🏨 **Parador de Villafranca del Bierzo.** This modern, two-story hotel overlooks the Bierzo valley. Rooms have heavy wood furniture, shuttered windows, and large baths. At the parador's restaurant ($$$$) dine on fresh Bierzo trout, *surtido de verduras naturales* (mixed fresh vegetables), or *tournedo con higos agridulces* (a plump, juicy steak wrapped in bacon and served with marinated figs and wild mushrooms). Try the local Bierzo wine, made primarily from the Mencía grape. ⌂ *Av. de Calvo Sotelo 28, 24500* 🕾 *987/540175* 🖷 *987/540010* ⊕ *www.parador.es* 🛏 *38 rooms* ⚬ *Restaurant, bar, meeting room* 🗀 *AE, DC, MC, V.*

OLD & NEW CASTILE ESSENTIALS

To research prices, get advice from other travelers, and book travel arrangements, visit www.fodors.com.

Transportation

BY AIR

The only international airport in Castile is Madrid's Barajas. Salamanca, León, and Valladolid have domestic airports.

🎦 **Aeropuertos Españoles y Navegación Aérea (AENA)** 🕾 902/404704 ⊕ www. aena.es–this is a central operations center providing information about flights and airports throughout Spain. Operators can speak English.

BY BIKE

Taking bikes on Spanish intercity trains is restricted to overnight trains (on which bikes go under your bunk). Short-range daytime trains normally accept bicycles, though the conductor may decide that the train's too crowded and bump you and your bike. The very expensive alternative is to courier them. Most of Old and New Castile covers the central Spanish meseta, which, though bisected by mountain ranges, is generally flat (if dangerously torrid in summer). Cycling on freeways is against the law. For bike rentals, contact local tourist offices or check with rural hotels.

BY BUS

Bus connections between Madrid and Castile are excellent. There are several stations and stops; buses to **Toledo** (1 hour) leave every half hour from the Estación del Sur, and buses to **Segovia** (1½ hours) leave every hour from La Sepulvedana's headquarters, which are near Príncipe Pío. Larrea sends buses to **Ávila** from the Méndez Alvaro Metro stop. Alsa travels to **León** (4½ hours) and **Valladolid** (2¼ hours), and Auto Res serves **Cuenca** (2¾ hours) and **Salamanca** (3 hours). Buses to **Soria** (3 hours), **El Burgo de Osma** (2½ hours), and **Burgos** (3½ hours) are run by Continental Auto.

From Burgos, buses head north to the Basque Country; from León, you can press on to Asturias. Services *between* towns are not as frequent as those to and from Madrid—if you're traveling between, say, Cuenca and Toledo, you'll find it quicker to return to Madrid and make your way from there. Reservations are rarely necessary; if demand exceeds supply, additional buses are usually called into service.

🚌 Bus Companies **Alsa** ☎ 902/422242 ⊕ www.alsa.es. **Auto Res** ✉ Pl. Conde de Casal 6, Madrid ☎ 902/020999. **Continental Auto** ✉ Intercambiador Autobuses, Av. de América, Madrid ☎ 91/745-6300. **La Sepulvedana/Larrea** ✉ Paseo de la Florida 11, Madrid ☎ 902/222282.

🚌 Bus Stations **Madrid: Estación del Sur** ✉ Méndez Alvaro s/n ☎ 91/468-4200. **Burgos** ✉ C. Miranda s/n ☎ 947/262017. **León** ✉ Paseo Ingeniero Saenz de Miera s/n ☎ 987/211000.

BY CAR

Major divided highways—the A1 through A6—radiate out from Madrid, making Spain's farthest corners no more than five- to six-hour drives. The capital's outlying towns are only minutes away. If possible, avoid returning to Madrid on major highways at the end of a weekend or a public holiday. The beginning and end of August are notorious for traffic jams, as is Easter week, which starts on Palm Sunday and ends on Easter Sunday. Side roads vary in quality but provide one of the great pleasures of driving around the Castilian countryside—surprise encounters with architectural monuments and wild and spectacular vistas.

Car-rental prices are generally more reasonable outside of Toledo and Madrid. You can find outlets in Toledo, Ciudad Real, Segovia, Ávila, Salamanca, Valladolid, Burgos, and León. You'll likely save money if you arrange your rental before leaving home. Spain's leading car-rental agency is Atesa, which works in tandem with National.

🚗 Major National Agencies **Avis** ☎ 902/135531 ⊕ www.avis.com. **Europcar** ☎ 902/105030 ⊕ www.europcar.es. **Hertz** ☎ 902/402405 ⊕ www.hertz.es. **National/Atesa** ☎ 902/100101 ⊕ www.atesa.com.

2

BY TAXI

All cities and most towns have public taxi services, sometimes several. They must show a license number, and at the rear of the vehicle are the letters "SP" (*Servicio Público*). They usually have a sign on the roof reading TAXI and a sign on the windshield that reads either LIBRE in green or OCUPADO in red. If a green light on the roof is lighted, this means the car is for hire (libre). Taxis operate on meters within designated urban centers, and fees are negotiable for farther distances. The meter starts at a set figure, about €1.50, but should not be turned on until you start your journey. Drivers may charge more for extra luggage, for night and holiday services, and for going to and coming from airports or train stations. Give a tip based on service, with a minimum of €0.50.

BY TRAIN

Though it's often faster to travel by bus, all the main towns in Old and New Castile are accessible by train from Madrid. Several make feasible day trips: there are commuter trains from Madrid to Segovia (2 hours), Alcalá de Henares (45 minutes), Guadalajara (1 hour), and Toledo (1½ hours). Trains to Toledo depart from Madrid's Atocha station; trains to Salamanca, Burgos, and León depart from Chamartín; and both stations serve Ávila, Segovia, El Escorial, and Sigüenza, though Chamartín may have more frequent service. The one important town that's accessible only by train is Sigüenza. Trains from Segovia go only to Madrid, but you can change at Villalba for Ávila and Salamanca.

⁊ Train Information RENFE ☎ 902/240202 ⊕ www.renfe.es.

Contacts & Resources

EMERGENCIES

⁊ Emergency Services Emergencies: Fire, Police or Ambulance ☎ 112. **Guardia Civil** ☎ 062. **Información Toxicológica** (Poisoning) ☎ 915/620420. **Insalud** (Public health service) ☎ 061. **Policía Local** (Local police) ☎ 092. **Policía Nacional** (National police) ☎ 091. **Servicio Marítimo** (Air–Sea Rescue) ☎ 902/202202.

LODGING

APARTMENT & VILLA RENTALS Although short-term city rentals are rare, rural tourism feeds a healthy rental market. Madrid and Beyond is a good British-run agency offering packages for individual visitors. The tourist offices in Salamanca and Toledo also have lodging information.

⁊ Local Agents Madrid and Beyond ✉ Gran Via 59, Madrid 28013 ☎ 91/758-0063 🖷 91/542-4391 ⊕ www.madridandbeyond.com.

INTERNET, MAIL & SHIPPING

Most towns have at least one cybercafé, and most hotels have either Wi-Fi or a high-speed connection. The only risk of being without Internet access is if you stumble onto a sparsely populated pueblo and are not staying the night there.

TOURS

Local tourist offices can advise you on city tours and private guides. Be wary of local guides in Ávila and Toledo, however—they can be ruthless in trying to impose their services. If you hire one, do not buy goods in the shops he takes you to—the prices are likely inflated, because the guide often gets a kickback. In summer the tourist offices of Segovia, Toledo, and Aranjuez organize Trénes Turísticos (miniature tourist trains) that glide past all the major sights; contact the local tourist office for schedules, or call 925/142274 for information. Prospect Music & Art Tours Ltd. leads a special art tour of Castile. The best of Britain's cultural-tour specialists is Martin Randall, whose excellent five-day trip includes Madrid and Toledo. Equiberia leads horseback tours ranging from 1 to 10 days, a unique way to experience the gorges, fields, and forests of the Sierra de Guadarrama. ⌘ Tour Operators **Equiberia** ☎ 920/348338. **Martin Randall Travel** ✉ 10 Barley Mow Passage, Chiswick, London W4 4PH, U.K. ☎ 020/8742-3355 🖶 020/8742-7766. **Prospect Music & Art Tours Ltd.** ✉ 36 Manchester St., London W1M 5PE, U.K. ☎ 020/7486-5704 🖶 020/7486-5868.

VISITOR INFORMATION

The central Castilian tourist office is in Madrid, near Plaza de las Cortes. Salamanca has a regional office for Old Castile (Castile–León), and Toledo's only tourist office covers New Castile (Castile–La Mancha). Local tourist offices have town maps.

⌘ Tourist Information **Madrid** ✉ Duque de Medinaceli 2 ☎ 91/429-4951. **Salamanca** ✉ Casa de las Conchas, Rúa Mayor s/n ☎ 923/268571. **Toledo** ✉ Puerta de Bisagra s/n ☎ 925/220843.

⌘ Local Tourist Offices **Alcalá de Henares** ✉ Callejón de Santa María ☎ 91/889-2694. **Almagro** ✉ Bernardas 2 ☎ 926/860717. **Aranjuez** ✉ Pl. San Antonio 9 ☎ 91/891-0427. **Astorga** ✉ Glorieta Eduardo de Castro 5 ☎ 987/618222. **Ávila** ✉ Pl. de la Catedral 4 ☎ 920/211387. **Burgos** ✉ Pl. Alonso Martínez 7 ☎ 947/203125. **Ciudad Real** ✉ Av. Alarcos 31 ☎ 926/216486. **Ciudad Rodrigo** ✉ Puerta de Amayuelas 5 ☎ 923/460561. **Consuegra** ✉ Molino de Viento/Bolero Windmill ☎ 925/475731. **Cuenca** ✉ Pl. Mayor 1 ☎ 969/241050. **Guadalajara** ✉ Pl. de los Caídos 6 ☎ 949/211626. **León** ✉ Pl. de Regla 3 ☎ 987/424236. **Ponferrada** ✉ Gil y Carrasco 4, next to castle ☎ 987/424236. **Salamanca** ✉ Pl. Mayor 14 ☎ 923/218342. **Segovia** ✉ Pl. Mayor 10 ☎ 921/460334. **Sigüenza** ✉ Paseo de la Alameda s/n ☎ 949/347007. **Soria** ✉ Pl. Ramón y Cajal s/n ☎ 975/212052. **Toledo** ✉ Puerta de Bisagra s/n ☎ 925/220843. **Valladolid** ✉ Acera de Recoletos s/n ☎ 983/219310. **Zamora** ✉ C. Santa Clara 20 ☎ 980/531845.

Cantabria, the Basque Country, Navarra & La Rioja

WORD OF MOUTH

"If you are ever in the vicinity of [San Juan de Gaztelugatxe], GO THERE!!! Stunning! . . .. Even if you decide to skip the climbing, the view from the bottom is wonderful. But since good things happen to people that make the extra effort while on vacation—the view down is even better!"

—marigross

"If you love the Modernist movement, then you must visit [El Capricho]. El Capricho is now a restaurant and you will have to dine there to see the interior, but for fans of Gaudí, and I am definitely one, it is worth a visit just to see the exterior."

—OReilly

By George
Semler

NORTHERN SPAIN IS A MISTY land of green hills, low russet rooflines, and colorful fishing villages. Santander, once the main seaport for Old Castile on the Bay of Biscay, is in a mountainous zone wedged between the Basque Country and, to the west, Asturias. Santander and the entire Cantabrian region are cool summer refuges for Madrileños, with sandy beaches, high sierra (including part of the Picos de Europa mountains), and tiny highland towns. The semiautonomous Basque Country, with its steady drizzle (onomatopoetically called the *sirimiri*), damp verdant landscape, and rugged coastline, is a distinct national and cultural entity within the Spanish state. Navarra is considered Basque in the Pyrenees and just Navarran in its southern reaches, along the Ebro River. La Rioja, tucked between the Sierra de la Demanda (a small-to-midsize mountain range that separates La Rioja from the central Castilian steppe) and the Ebro River, is Spain's premier wine country.

Called the País Vasco in Castilian Spanish, and Euskadi in the linguistically mysterious, non-Indo-European Basque language called Euskera, the Basque region is more a country within a country, or a nation within a state (the semantics are much debated). The Basques are known to love competition—it has been said that they will bet on anything that has numbers on it and moves (horses, dogs, runners, weight lifters—anything). Such traditional rural sports as chopping mammoth tree trunks, lifting boulders, and scything grass reflect the Basques' attachment to the land and to farm life as well as an ingrained enthusiasm for feats of strength and endurance. Even poetry and gastronomy become contests in Euskadi, as *bertsolaris* (amateur poets) improvise duels of sharp-witted verse, and male-only gastronomic societies compete in cooking contests to see who can make the best *sopa de ajo* (garlic soup) or *marmitako* (tuna stew).

The Basque Country has longtime connections with both Britain and the United States. Bilbao and its province, Vizcaya, provided iron for Britain's industrial revolution, and Elko, Nevada, is a longtime hub for emigrant Basque shepherds. An agricultural and fishing region before industry made it a center of productivity, the Basque Country has long sent waves of immigrants to the Americas.

The much-reported Basque independence movement is made up of a small but radical sector of the political spectrum. The underground organization known as ETA, or Euskadi Ta Askatasuna (Basque Homeland and Liberty), has killed nearly 900 people in more than 35 years of terrorist activity. Conflict has waxed and waned over the years, though it has never affected travelers. As of April 2006, ETA had declared a "permanent cease-fire," and Basque terrorism seems almost certain to have become a thing of the past.

About the Beaches

Santander has excellent sandy beaches, and the beach at Laredo, between Santander and Bilbao, is one of Spain's best and least known. Between Bilbao and San Sebastián, the beach at Lequeitio is particularly beautiful, and the smaller beaches at Zumaya, Getaria, and Zarauz are usually quiet. San Sebastián's best beach, La Concha, which curves around

GREAT ITINERARIES

IF YOU HAVE 3 DAYS

If you're coming from Madrid or Burgos, drive through the Picos de Europa to **Santander ②**🖼 . Pop over to **Santillana del Mar ❸** to see the museum on the paintings in the nearby Altamira Caves. The next day, follow the Basque coast to **Bilbao ❽-⓰** for a morning visit to the Guggenheim; move on to 🖼 **San Sebastián ㉘** and lunch in the fishing port of **Getaria ㉗**. Drive through **Pamplona ㉛** and Navarra on your third day, approaching from the north if you're continuing across Spain, from the west (and then north) if you're France bound.

IF YOU HAVE 6 DAYS

Coming from Madrid or Burgos, drive through the mountains on your way to the coast. Stop in **Santillana del Mar ❸** and then detour west to **Comillas ❹** and **San Vicente de la Barquera ❺**. In 🖼 **Santander ②**, check out the beach scene and wander around the Plaza Porticada. On Day 2, explore 🖼 **Laredo ❻** and **Castro-Urdiales ❼**. Stop in **Bilbao ❽-⓰** to see the Guggenheim Museum and other top sights. Devote your third day to the Basque coast from Bilbao to San Sebastián, picking and choosing among **Bermeo ⓳**, **Elantxobe ㉓**, **Lekeitio ㉔**, **Ondárroa ㉕**, and **Getaria ㉗**, each of which outdoes the other in activity, color, and cuisine. Spend Day 4 in sybaritic 🖼 **San Sebastián ㉘**. Spend your fifth day in 🖼 **Pamplona ㉛** and the province of Navarra, from which you can continue through southern Navarra to the Basque capital, 🖼 **Vitoria ㉟**. Tour La Rioja on Day 6: drive through **Laguardia ㊱** and **Haro ㊳** to the provincial capital, 🖼 **Logroño ㊲**.

the bay along with the city itself, is scenic and clean, but packed in summer; Ondarreta, at the western end of La Concha, is often less crowded. Surfers gather at Zurriola on the northern side of the Urumea River. Hondarribia, the last stop before the French border, has a vast expanse of fine sand along the Bidasoa estuary.

About the Restaurants

Basque food in and around San Sebastián and Bilbao combines the fish of the Atlantic with a love of sauces that's rare south of the Pyrenees—a result, no doubt, of Euskadi's proximity to France. The now 30-year-old *nueva cocina vasca* (new Basque cooking), originally inspired by the Basque Country's neighbors to the north, invented lightened, streamlined versions of classic Basque dishes such as marmitako (tuna and potato stew). Traditional San Sebastián specialties include *chuleta de buey* (garlicky beefsteak grilled over coals), and firm, flaky *besugo a la parrilla* (sea bream grilled over coals), also wallowing in golden chips of crisped garlic. Around Bilbao, *bacalao al pil-pil* is ubiquitous—cod-flank fillets cooked in a boiled emulsion of garlic and gelatin from the cod itself, so that the oil makes a popping noise ("pil-pil") and a white sauce is created. Other favorites are *kokotxas* (nuggets of cod jaw) and *pimientos de piquillo* (sweet red peppers stuffed with tuna or cod).

Cantabria's cooking is part mountain fare, such as roast kid and lamb or *cocidos* (bean stews) in the highlands, and part seafood on the coast. *Soropotun* is Santander's stew of bonito, potatoes, and vegetables. Navarra is famous for beef, lamb, and vegetable dishes, including *menestra de verduras* (a stew of artichokes, green beans, peas, lettuce, potatoes, onion, and chunks of cured ham). La Rioja has meaty stews and roasts in the mountains and vegetable dishes in the Ebro River basin.

The local Basque wine, *txakolí,* is young and white, made from tart green grapes. It is a refreshing accompaniment to both seafood and meats. La Rioja, south of the Basque Country, produces many of the finest wines in Spain; purists insisting on Basque wine with their Basque cuisine could choose a Rioja Alavesa, from the north side of the Ebro. Navarra also produces some fine vintages, especially rosés and reds—and in such quantity that some churches in Allo, Peralta, and other towns were actually built with a mortar mixed with wine instead of water.

Food isn't cheap in the Basque Country, but some of Europe's finest cuisine is served here in settings that range from the traditional hewn beams and stone walls of old farmhouses to contemporary international restaurants. Don't miss any chance to go to a *sidrería,* a cider house (in Astigarraga, near San Sebastián, there are no fewer than 17) where *tortilla de bacalao* (cod omelet) and thick *chuletas de buey* (beef chops) provide the traditional ballast for copious drinks of hard apple cider.

WHAT IT COSTS In Euros				
$$$$	**$$$**	**$$**	**$**	**¢**
AT DINNER over €20	€15–€20	€10–€15	€6–€10	under €6

Prices are per person for a main course at dinner.

About the Hotels

The largely industrial and well-to-do north is an expensive part of Spain, which is reflected in room rates. San Sebastián is particularly pricey, and Pamplona rates double or triple during the San Fermín fiesta in July. Reserve ahead for Bilbao, where the Guggenheim Museum is filling hotels, and nearly everywhere else in summer. Another lodging option is the Agroturismo lodging network, which often offers rooms in a Basque *caserío* (farmhouse). Check with local tourist offices for details.

WHAT IT COSTS In Euros				
$$$$	**$$$**	**$$**	**$**	**¢**
FOR 2 PEOPLE over €180	€100–€180	€60–€100	€40–€60	under €40

Prices are for two people in a standard double room in high season, excluding tax.

Exploring the Regions

Northern Spain's Bay of Biscay area, at the western end of the Pyrenees and the border with France, is where the Cantabrian Cordillera and the Pyrenees nearly meet. The moist green foothills of the Basque Country

IF YOU LIKE

FIESTAS

Pamplona's feast of **San Fermín** (July 6–14) was made famous by Ernest Hemingway in *The Sun Also Rises* and remains best known for its running of the bulls. Bilbao's **Semana Grande** (Grand Week), in early August, is notorious for the largest bulls of the season and a fine series of street concerts. The coastal town of Lequeitio, east of Bilbao, is famous for its unusual **Fiestas de San Antolín,** in which men dangle (on September 5) from the necks of dead geese strung on a cable over the inlet. Closer to San Sebastián, in the first week of August, the fishing village of **Getaria** celebrates Juan Sebastián Elkano's completion of Magellan's voyage around the world every other year. San Sebastián holds a renowned **international film festival** in late September and celebrates its saint's day January 19 to 20 with **La Tamborrada,** when 100-odd platoons of chefs and Napoléonic soldiers parade hilariously through the streets. Vitoria's weeklong **Fiesta de la Virgen Blanca** (Festival of the White Virgin) celebrates the city's patron saint with bullfights and more beginning on August 4.

HIKING

Well-marked footpaths wend from the Cordillera Cantábrica to the Pyrenees and along the Basque coast, connecting towns, scaling mountains, and ambling from one fishing village to another. The air, color, and scenery far exceed anything you'll experience in a car. Try the walks around Zumaya, or the walk over Jaizkibel between San Sebastián and the French border.

The GR-11 trail crosses the Pyrenees of Navarra, and the Camino de Santiago pilgrimage route crosses Navarra and La Rioja on its way west.

SPORTS

Basques are as passionate about sports as they are about food, and you need not participate to catch the action. If you do want to get up and about, there's excellent sailing, surfing, windsurfing, and trout or Atlantic-salmon fishing in various parts of this rich terrain. Pelota—any number of ball games played against a wall—is the Basque national sport. Most towns have a local *frontón* (backboard or wall), where games normally start at 4 or 4:30 PM. Other Basque rural sports (*herrikirolak*) include the tug-of-war and log-chopping, ram-butting, and scything competitions. The most idiosyncratic contest is the *harrijasotazailes*, the raising of huge rocks by practiced stone lifters. You can also find jai alai (a generic term for ball games from handball to *cesta punta*, played with wicker gloves), *trainera* (whale-boat regattas), and horse races. Athletic de Bilbao has traditionally been the Basque *fútbol* (soccer) giant, with San Sebastián's Real Sociedad just behind, though recently roles have been reversed. Pamplona, Vitoria, and Santander also field first-division soccer teams.

3

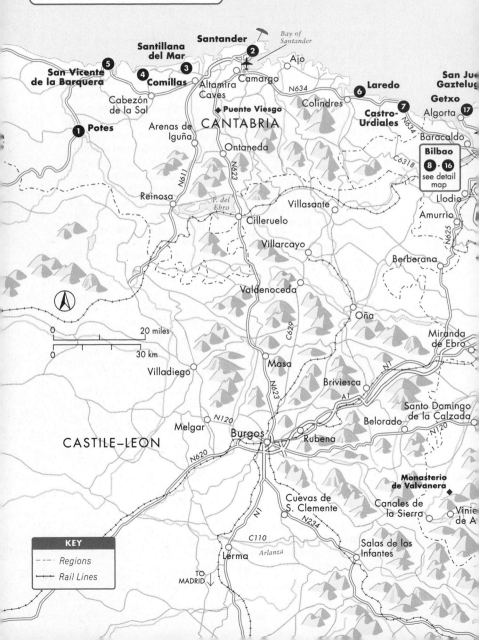

Cantabria, the Basque Country, Navarra & La Rioja

Bay of Biscay

San Jua Gaztelug

Getxo
Algorta ⑰

Baracaldo

Bilbao
⑧ - ⑯
see detail map

Santander

Bay of Santander

Ajo

Santillana del Mar

Camargo

San Vicente de la Barquera ⑤

④ **Comillas**

③

Altamira Caves

N634

Laredo ⑥

Colindres

Castro-Urdiales ⑦

N634

Cabezón de la Sal

◆ **Puente Viesgo**

CANTABRIA

Arenas de Iguña

① **Potes**

Ontaneda

C6318

Llodio

Amurrio

N625

Reinosa

P. del Ebro

Villasante

Cilleruelo

Berberana

Villarcayo

Valdenoceda

Oña

Miranda de Ebro

C629

N611

N623

N1

Masa

Briviesca

A1

Santo Domingo de la Calzada

CASTILE-LEON

Villadiego

N623

N120

Melgar

Rubena

Belorado

N120

Burgos

N620

N1

Cuevas de S. Clemente

Monasterio de Valvanera ◆

Canales de la Sierra

Vinie de A

N234

Salas de los Infantes

C110

Arlanza

Lerma

TO MADRID ↓

0 ————— 20 miles

0 ————— 30 km

KEY

--- Regions

—+— Rail Lines

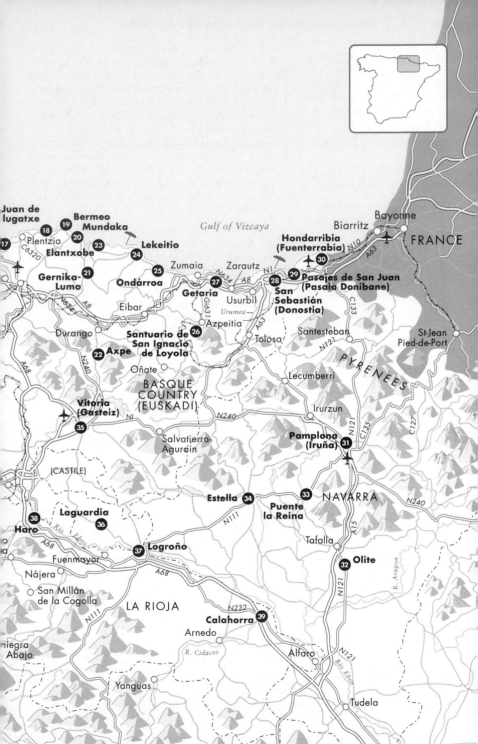

GEORGE'S TOP 5

- Bilbao's two art and architecture gems: el Museo de Bellas Artes and the Guggenheim.

- Mundaka, for the longest left-breaking surfing wave in Europe.

- San Sebastián's Parte Vieja for tapas and tascas (taverns).

- Basque sculptor Eduardo Chillida's Chillida Leku outside of San Sebastín.

- The upper Najerilla river's Virgen de la Valvanera monastery for peace and quiet.

and, to the west, Cantabria, gently fill this space between the otherwise unbroken chain of mountains that rises from the Iberian Peninsula's easternmost point at northern Catalonia's Cap de Creus and ends at western Galicia's Fisterra, or Finisterre, land's end. Navarra—part Basque and part Castilian-speaking Navarrese—lies just southeast and inland of the Basque Country, with the backdrop of the Pyrenees rising up to the north. La Rioja, below Navarra, nestles in the Ebro River valley under the Sierra de la Demanda to the south, and stretches east and downriver to Calahorra and the edge of Spain's central *meseta* (plains).

Numbers in the text correspond to numbers in the margin and on the Cantabria, Basque Country, Navarra & La Rioja, and Bilbao maps.

Timing

May, June, September, and October are the best times to enjoy good weather and avoid the tourist crush, which peaks in August. The Basque Country is rainy, especially in winter; summer is temperate.

CANTABRIA

Historically part of Old Castile, the province of Cantabria was called Santander until 1984, when it became an Autonomous Community. The most direct route from Burgos to Santander is the slow but scenic N623 through the Cordillera Cantábrica, past the Ebro reservoir. For a memorable glimpse of Cantabria's section of the Picos de Europa mountains, however, drive through La Liébana valley via Palencia and Potes, reaching the coast at San Vicente de la Barquera.

Potes

❶ *51 km (31 mi) south of San Vicente de la Barquera, 115 km (69 mi) west of Santander, 173 km (104 mi) north of Palencia.*

Known for its fine cheeses made of milk from cows, goats, and sheep, La Liébana is a highland domain well worth exploring. Named for and sprinkled with ancient bridges, the town of Potes surrounds you with the stunning 9th-century **monasteries** of Santo Toribio de Liébana, Lebeña, and Piasca. The gorges of the Desfiladero de la Hermida pass are 3 km (2 mi) north, and the rustic town of Mogrovejo is on the way to the vertiginous cable car at Fuente Dé, 25 km (15 mi) west of Potes. As you approach **Fuente Dé** by car or foot, you'll see a wall of gray stone rising 6,560 feet straight into the air. Visible at the top is the tiniest of huts: your destination. Get there via a little red-and-white funicular (€8 round-trip). Once at the top, you're hiking along the Ávila Mountain pasturelands, rich in native wildlife, between the central and eastern massifs of the Picos. There's an official entrance to Picos de Europa National Park up here.

Where to Stay & Eat

$–$$$ ✕ **El Bodegón.** Simple, friendly, and cozy, a surprisingly contemporary space awaits behind an ancient stone facade. Here you can find a fine *cocido montañes* (mountain stew of sausage, garbanzo beans, and vegetables) at rock-bottom prices. The €8 lunch menu here is one of the best values for miles around. ⊠ *San Roque 4* ☎ *942/730247* ✉ *AE, DC, MC, V* ☉ *Closed Mon.*

$–$$ ✕▣ **Valdecoro.** You literally can't miss this family-run mountain house, which faces the main road through town. Rooms with modern appointments and an efficient staff make for a pleasant stay. The restaurant ($–$$$) is a town favorite for simple and authentic highland products and recipes prepared with care and wisdom. In winter, try the *cocido lebaniego*, a powerful mountain soup made of broth, beans, pork, chard, and chicken. ⊠ *Roscabado 5, 39570* ☎ *942/730025* ✉ *942/ 730315* ⇴ *41 rooms* ⚷ *Restaurant, free parking* ✉ *AE, DC, MC, V.*

Santander

★ ❷ *390 km (242 mi) north of Madrid, 154 km (96 mi) north of Burgos, 116 km (72 mi) west of Bilbao.*

Santander is one of the great ports on the Bay of Biscay. It's surrounded by beaches that are by no means isolated, but lack the sardinelike package-tour feel of so many Mediterranean resorts. A fire destroyed most of the old town in 1941, so the rebuilt city looks relatively modern, and although it has traditionally been a conservative stronghold loyal to the Spanish state (in contrast to its Basque neighbors), Santander is lively, especially in summer, when its university and music-and-dance festival fill the city with students and performers from abroad. Portus Victoriae, as Santander was then called, was a major port in the 1st- to 4th-century Roman Hispania Ulterior (and even earlier under the aboriginal Cántabros). Commercial life accelerated between the 13th and 16th century, but the waning of Spain's naval power and a series of plagues during the reign of Felipe II caused Santander's fortunes to plummet in the late 16th century. Its economy revived after 1778, when Seville's monopoly on trade with the Americas was revoked and Santander entered fully into commerce with the New World. In 1910 the Palacio de la Magdalena was built by popular subscription as a gift to Alfonso XIII and his queen, Victoria Eugenia, lending Santander prestige as one of Spain's royal watering spots.

Santander benefits from promenades and gardens, most of them facing the bay. Walk east along the Paseo de Pereda, the main boulevard, to the Puerto Chico, a small yacht harbor. Past the Puerto Chico, follow Avenida Reina Victoria, and you'll come to the tree-lined park paths above the first of the city's beaches, Playa de la Magdalena. Walk onto the Península de la Magdalena to the Palacio de la Magdalena, today the summer seat of the University of Menéndez y Pelayo, which conducts Spanish-language and Spanish-culture courses for foreigners. Beyond the Magdalena Peninsula, wealthy locals have built mansions facing the long stretch of shoreline known as El Sardinero, Santander's best beach. The heart of El Sardinero is the Belle Epoque **Gran Casino del Sardinero**, an elegant casino and restaurant worth a quick visit even if gaming tables hold no charms for you. A white building fronted with red awnings and set in a park among sycamores, the casino lies at the center of the vacationer's Santander, surrounded by expensive hotels and several fine restaurants. ✉ *Plaza de Italia s/n* ☎ *942/276054* 💳 *€3* ⊙ *Daily 8 PM–4 AM; slot machines open at 5 PM.*

In the old city, the center of life is the **Plaza Porticada,** officially called the Plaza Velarde. In August this unassuming little square is the seat of Santander's star event, the outdoor International Festival of Music and Dance. The blockish **Catedral de Santander** marks the transition between Romanesque and Gothic. Though largely rebuilt in the neo-Gothic style after serious damage in the 1941 fire, the cathedral retained its 12th-century crypt. The chief attraction here is the tomb of Marcelino Menéndez y Pelayo (1856–1912), Santander's most famous literary figure. The cathedral is across Avenida de Calvo Sotelo from the Plaza Porticada. ✉ *Somorrostro s/n* ☎ *942/226024* 💳 *Free* ⊙ *Weekdays 10–1 and 4–7:30, weekends 8–2 and 4:30–8.*

The **Museo Municipal de Bellas Artes** (Municipal Museum of Fine Arts) has works by Flemish, Italian, and Spanish artists. Goya's portrait of absolutist king Fernando VII is worth seeking out; the smirking face of the lion at the king's feet clues you in to Goya's feelings toward his patron. The same building holds the **Biblioteca Menéndez y Pelayo** (☎ 942/234534), a library with some 50,000 volumes, and the writer's study, kept as it was in his day. ✉ *C. Rubio s/n* ☎ *942/239485* 💳 *Free* ⊙ *Museum Tues.–Fri. 10–1 and 5–8, Sat. 10–1. Library weekdays 9–2 and 4–9:30, Sat. 9–1:30.*

Where to Stay & Eat

$$–$$$$ ✗ **Zacarías.** Whether you want tapas or dinner in full, try out this popular place, known for northern Spanish specialties. Owner and chef Zacarías Puente-Herboso is a well-known food writer and an authority on Cantabrian recipes. Sample the *maganos encebollados* (calamari and caramelized onion) or the *alubias rojas estofadas* (red beans stewed with sausage). ✉ *General Mola 41* ☎ *942/212333* 🍴 *AE, DC, MC, V.*

$$–$$$ ✗ **Bodega del Riojano.** The paintings on wine-barrel ends that decorate this restaurant have given it the sobriquet Museo Redondo (Round Museum). The building dates back to the 16th century, when it was a wine cellar, and this incarnation lives on in dark-wood beams and tables. The menu changes daily and seasonally, but the fish of the day is a sure bet. Desserts are homemade. ✉ *Río de la Pila 5* ☎ *942/216750* 🍴 *AE, DC, MC, V* ⊙ *Closed Mon. No dinner Sun. Oct.–May.*

★ $$–$$$$ 🏨 **Bahía.** Classical decor filled with state-of-the-art equipment and technology all make this Santander's finest hotel, with a front-and-center placement overlooking the Bay of Santander. Rooms are spacious and filled with gauzy drapes and noble pieces of furniture and first-rate wood and stone. ✉ *Av. Alfonso XIII-6, 39000* ☎ *942/205000* 🖷 *942/205001* ⊕ *www.hotelbahia.com* ⇌ *188 rooms* ⌂ *Bar, restaurant, meeting rooms, parking (fee)* 🍴 *AE, DC, MC, V.*

$$–$$$ 🏨 **Las Brisas.** Jesús García and his wife, Teresa, run this 80-year-old mansion as an upscale, cottage-style hotel by the sea. Each room or apartment is different, from dollhouse alcoves to an odd but attractive family duplex apartment. The basement bar and breakfast room are especially cozy. You're a short walk from the beach, and many of the rooms have fine views out to sea. ⊠ *C. la Braña 14, 39005* ☎ *942/270991 or 942/275011* 🖶 *942/281173* ⊕ *www.hotellasbrisas.net* 🛏 *13 rooms, 12 apartments* ⚹ *Bar* ⊟ *AE, DC, MC, V.*

Nightlife & the Arts

Santander's big event is its International Festival of Music and Dance, which attracts leading artists, throughout August. Many festival concerts are staged in the Plaza Porticada; others are held in monasteries, palaces, and churches. To learn of current offerings, collect information at at box offices in the Plaza Porticada and the Jardines de Pereda park. Santander's **Teatro Coliseum** (⊠ Plaza de los Remedios 1 ☎ 942/211460) is a movie theater that becomes a theater proper in summer.

Shopping

Santander's ceramics emporium **La Muralla** (⊠ Calle Arrabal 17 ☎ 942/160301) is known as the best in town. For footwear, **Loocky** (⊠ Lealtad 6 ☎ 942/211368) is tops. Men's fashions rule at **Golf** (⊠ Plaza del Príncipe ☎ 942/312975). Fine foods, including the Santanderino specialty *dulces pasiegos* (light and sugary cakes), can be tried and purchased at **Mantequerís Cántabras** (⊠ Plaza de Italia s/n ☎ 942/272899).

Santillana del Mar

❸ *29 km (18 mi) west of Santander.*

Fodor'sChoice
★

This stunning ensemble of 15th- to 17th-century stone houses is one of Spain's greatest troves of medieval and Renaissance architecture. The town is built around the **Colegiata,** Cantabria's finest Romanesque structure, with a 17th-century altarpiece, the tomb of local martyr Santa Juliana, and sculpted capitals depicting biblical scenes. The adjoining Regina Coeli convent has a **Museo Diocesano** (☎ 942/598105) with liturgical art. ⊠ *Av. Le Dorat 2* ☎ *942/818004* 🎫 *Combined ticket for Colegiata and museum* €*3* ☉ *Daily 10–1 and 4–7; closed Mon. Oct.–May.*

The world-famous **Altamira Caves,** 3 km (2 mi) southwest of Santillana del Mar, have been called the Sistine Chapel of Prehistoric Art for the beauty of their drawings, believed to be some 20,000 years old. First uncovered in 1875, the caves are a testament to early man's admiration of aesthetic beauty and his surprising technical skill in representing it— especially in the use of rock forms to accentuate perspective. The caves are closed to visitors, but the reproduction in the **museum** is open to all. ⊠ *Museo de Altamira, 39330 Santillana del Mar, Cantabria* ☎ *942/818005* 🎫 €*2.50* ☉ *Daily 10–1 and 4–7; closed Mon. Oct.–May.*

Where to Stay & Eat

$$$ ✕🖼 **Parador de Santillana Gil Blas.** Built in the 16th century, this lovely
Fodor'sChoice   parador is in the erstwhile summer home of the Barreda-Bracho fam-
★   ily. Rooms are baronial, with rich drapes and antique furnishings. The dining hall ($$–$$$$) serves good local fare. ⊠ *Pl. Ramón Pelayo 8, 39330* ☎ *942/818000* 🖶 *942/818391* 🛏 *55 rooms, 1 suite* ⚹ *Restaurant, bar, parking (fee)* ⊟ *AE, DC, MC, V.*

$$ ⚅ **Casa del Organista.** A cozy 18th-century house with comfortable and tastefully appointed whitewashed rooms with lovely stone and wood details, this intimate hideaway offers a countrified base for exploring Spain's finest Renaissance town. ✉ *Los Hornos 4, 39330* ☎ *942/ 840352* 🖷 *942/840191* ⊕ *www.casadelorganista.com* 🛏 *14 rooms* ♨ *Breakfast room* ☰ *AE, DC, MC, V* ⊗ *Closed Dec. 15–Jan. 15.*

▌▌ **PUENTE VIESGO –** In 1903 this 16th-century hamlet in the Pas Valley ex-
⌐ OFF THE
BEATEN
PATH

cavated four caves under the 1,150-foot peak of Monte del Castillo, one of which—the Cueva del Castillo—is open to the public. Bison, deer, bulls, and even humanoid stick figures are depicted; the oldest designs are thought to be 35,000 years old. Most arresting are the paintings of 44 (curiously, 35 of them left) hands, reaching out through time. The painters are thought to have blown red pigment around their hands through a hollow bone, leaving the negative image. ✉ *Ctra. N623, Km 28, from Santander* ☎ *942/598425* 🎫 *€4* ⊗ *Apr.–Oct., Tues.–Sun. 9–noon and 3–6:30; Nov.–Mar., Wed.–Sun. 9–2.*

Comillas

❹ *49 km (30 mi) west of Santander.*

This astounding pocket of Catalan Art Nouveau architecture in the green hills of Cantabria will make you rub your eyes in disbelief. Why is it here? The Marqués de Comillas, a Catalan named Antonio López y López (1817–83)—the wealthiest and most influential shipping magnate of his time—was a fervent patron of the arts who encouraged the great Moderniste architects to use his native village as a laboratory. Antonio Gaudí's 1883–89 green-and-yellow-tile villa, El Capricho (a direct cousin of his Casa Vicens in Barcelona), is the main attraction. The town cemetery is filled with Art Nouveau markers and monuments, most notably an immense angel by eminent Catalan sculptor Josep Llimona). **Palacio Sobrellano,** once the home of the Marqués de Comillas, this stately mansion has surprising Art Nouveau ornamentation and furnishings designed by a young Gaudí. ☎ *942/720339* ⊗ *Wed.–Sun. 10–2 and 4–7 Oct.–May; daily 10–2 and 4–7 June–Sept.*

Where to Eat

$$–$$$$ ✕ **El Capricho de Gaudí.** A chance to dine in a Gaudí creation is all but an obligation, especially if the visual rush is accompanied by fresh turbot with young garlic or roast lamb from the moist Cantabrian hills. This unique spot is overpriced, and the usual local warmth is conspicuously absent, but even for a cup of coffee or a bowl of soup it's an unforgettable and unique opportunity to break bread in the same space where the great Moderniste broke all the rules. ✉ *Barrio de Sobrellano* ☎ *942/720365* ☰ *AE, DC, MC, V* ⊗ *Closed Jan. 15–Feb. 15, and Mon. Oct.–May. No dinner Sun.*

San Vicente de la Barquera

❺ *64 km (40 mi) west of Santander, 15 km (9 mi) west of Comillas.*

Important as a Roman port long before many other larger, modern shipping centers (such as Santander) were, San Vicente de la Barquera is one of the oldest and most beautiful maritime settlements in northern Spain. The 28 arches of the ancient bridge **Puente de la Maza,** which spans the *ría* (fjord), welcome you to town. Thanks to its exceptional Romanesque portals, the 15th-century church of **Nuestra Señora de los Angeles** (Our Lady of the Angels) is among San Vicente's most memorable sights. Make sure you check out the arcaded porticoes of the **Plaza Mayor** and the view over the town from the Unquera road (N634) just inland. San Vicente celebrates **La Folía** in late April (the name translates roughly as "folly," and the exact date depends not only on Easter but on the high tide) with a magnificent maritime procession: the town's colorful fishing fleet accompanies the figure of La Virgen de la Barquera as she is transported (in part) by boat from her sanctuary outside town to the village church, where she is honored with folk dances and songs before being returned to her hermitage.

Where to Stay & Eat

$–$$ ✕▤ **Boga-Boga.** This relatively modern building is surrounded by some of San Vicente's most ancient structures, in the center of the *casco viejo* (old town). Rooms are comfortable and unpretentious, although not especially charming. The restaurant ($–$$$) specializes in seafood, such as *merluza al boga-boga* (stewed cod) and *cabracho* (red scorpion fish). ✉ *Pl. José Antonio 9, 39540* ☎ *942/710135* 🖷 *942/710151* 🛏 *18 rooms* ⚗ *Restaurant, café, bar* ▭ *AE, DC, MC, V* ⊘ *Restaurant closed Tues. Oct.–May.*

Laredo

❻ *49 km (30 mi) southeast of Santander, N635 southeast, N634 east.*

You would hardly know it today, but Laredo was a home port of the Spanish Armada and remained Spain's chief northern harbor until the French sacked it in the 18th century and Santander became the regional capital. This little town was thus visited by the Spanish royals, including Isabella the Catholic and Charles I, better known as the Holy Roman Emperor Carlos V. When Charles—the most powerful monarch in European history—stopped by in the mid-16th century, he donated two brass choir desks in the shape of eagles. Charles I's brass choir desks are on display in the parish church of **La Asunción** (Church of the Assumption), in the center of the town's tiny old quarter, which you may want to walk through to see mansions with heraldic coats of arms.

Where to Stay & Eat

$$ ✕▤ **El Risco.** *Risco* is Spanish for "cliff," which is appropriate for a hotel built into the craggy slope overlooking Laredo. The food at the restaurant ($$–$$$$) combines classical and contemporary Cantabrian fare; try the *pimientos rellenos de cangrejo y de buey de mar* (peppers stuffed with crab and fish). Every room has a spectacular view of the town and cove below. Hotel reservations are essential in summer. ✉ *La Arenosa 2, 39770* ☎ *942/605030* 🖷 *942/605055* ⊕ *www.hotelrisco.com* 🛏 *25 rooms* ⚗ *Restaurant, bar* ▭ *AE, DC, MC, V.*

Castro-Urdiales

❼ *34 km (21 mi) northwest of Bilbao.*

Behind Laredo, the N634 winds up into the hills, with views of the Bay of Santoña over your shoulder. A short drive, parts of it within sight of the coast, takes you into the fishing village of Castro-Urdiales, believed to be the oldest settlement on the Cantabrian coast. Castro-Urdiales (*castro* was the Celtiberian word for a fortified village) was the region's leading whaling port in the 13th and 14th centuries, when it had almost three times today's 13,000 residents. Now it's known mainly for its seafood. Overlooking the town is the mammoth, rose-color jumble of roofs and buttresses of the Gothic **Santa María** church. Behind the Santa María church is the medieval **castle**, to which a modern lighthouse has been appended. Aside from its arcaded **Plaza del Ayuntamiento** and the narrow streets of its **old quarter** (much of which burned on May 11, 1813), the main things to see in Castro-Urdiales are the Santa María church, looming Gothically over the town, the ruins of the fortress converted into a lighthouse beside it, and the harbor-front promenade flanked by a row of glass-gallery houses.

⌐ EN ROUTE The 45-minute drive on the N634 from Castro-Urdiales to Bilbao takes you through some of the sprawling industrial development that mars much of Vizcaya (Bizkaia, in Euskera, the Basque language), the westernmost of the three Basque provinces. The A8 freeway will get you to Bilbao in just 15 minutes. A tempting stop is **Santurtzi**, whose **Hogar del Pescador** in the port is a popular spot for sardines.

Where to Eat

$$–$$$$ ✕ **Mesón Marinero.** Local fishermen rub elbows with visiting elites at this pearl of a tavern and restaurant. The tapas on the bar will tempt you to forgo the main meal; if you manage not to *tapear* away the dinner hour, you're in for a treat in the second-floor dining room overlooking Castro's weathered fishing port. *Besugo* (sea bream) is unbeatable here. ✉ *La Correría 23* ☎ *942/860005* 🞸 *AE, DC, MC, V.*

BILBAO & THE BASQUE COAST TO GETARIA

Starring Frank Gehry's titanium meteorite—the Museo Guggenheim Bilbao—Bilbao has established itself as one of Spain's 21st-century darlings. The loop around the coast of Vizcaya and east into neighboring Guipúzcoa province to Getaria and San Sebastián is a succession of colorful ports, ocher beaches, and green hills.

Bilbao

❽–⓰ *34 km (21 mi) southeast of Castro-Urdiales, 116 km (72 mi) east of Santander, 397 km (247 mi) north of Madrid.*

Time in Bilbao (Bilbo, in Euskera) may soon need to be identified as BG or AG (Before Guggenheim, After Guggenheim). Never has a single monument of art and architecture so radically changed a city—or, for that matter, a nation, and in this case two: Spain and Euskadi. Frank Gehry's stunning museum, Norman Foster's sleek subway system, and the glass Santiago Calatrava footbridge have all helped foment a cultural revolution in the commercial capital of the Basque Country. Greater Bilbao encompasses almost 1 million inhabitants, nearly half the total population of the Basque Country and the fourth-largest urban population in Spain. Founded in 1300 by Vizcayan noble Diego López de Haro, Bilbao became an industrial center in the mid-19th century, largely because of the abundance of minerals in the surrounding hills. An affluent industrial class grew up here, as did the working-class suburbs (such as Portugalete and Baracaldo) that line the Margen Izquierda (Left Bank) of the Nervión estuary.

Bilbao's new attractions get more press, but the city's old treasures still quietly line the banks of the rust-color Nervión River. The Casco Viejo (old quarter)—also known as Siete Calles (Seven Streets)—is a charming jumble of shops, bars, and restaurants on the river's Right Bank, near the Puente del Arenal bridge. Throughout the old quarter are ancient mansions emblazoned with family coats of arms, noble wooden doors, and fine ironwork balconies. Carefully restored after devastating floods in August 1983, this is an upscale shopping district replete with excellent taverns, restaurants, and nightlife. The most interesting square is the 64-arch Plaza Nueva, where an outdoor market is pitched every Sunday morning. On the Left Bank, the wide, late-19th-century boulevards of the Ensanche neighborhood, such as Gran Vía (the main shopping artery) and Alameda Mazarredo, are the city's more formal face. Bilbao's cultural institutions include, along with the Guggenheim, a major museum of fine arts, and an opera society (ABAO: Asociacion Bilbaina de Amigos de la Opera) with 7,000 members from all over Spain and parts of southern France. In addition, epicureans have long ranked Bilbao's culinary offerings among the best in Spain. Don't miss a chance to ride the speedy and quiet trolley line, the Euskotram, for a trip along the river from Atxuri station to the San Mames soccer stadium in Basurto.

❽ The **Casco Viejo** is folded into an elbow of the Nervión River behind Bilbao's grand, elaborately restored theater. While exploring, don't miss the colossal food market **El Mercado de la Ribera** at the edge of the river, the **Palacio Yohn** at the corner of Sant Maria and Perro, and the **Biblioteca Municipal Bidebarrieta** at Calle Bidebarrieta 4. Inaugurated in 1890, **Teatro Arriaga** was a symbol of Bilbao's industrial might and cultural vibrancy by the time it burned nearly to the ground in 1914. Styled after the Paris Opéra, the theater defies easy classification: although its symmetry and formal repetition suggest neoclassicism, its ornamentation defines the Belle Epoque style. Walk around to see the stained-glass windows in the back. ⊠ *Plaza Arriaga 1* ☎ *94/479–2036* Ⓜ *Casco Viejo.*

❾ Stop at Calle Esperanza 6 and take the elevator to the **Basílica de Begoña** overlooking the city. The church's Gothic hulk was begun in 1519 on a spot where the Virgin Mary had supposedly appeared long before.

❿ Near the Ayuntamiento Bridge is the riverside *ayuntamiento* (city hall), built in 1892. Ⓜ *Casco Viejo.*

⓫ Don't let the Guggenheim eclipse the **Museo de Bellas Artes** (Museum of Fine Arts). Depending on your tastes, you may find the art here more satisfying. The museum's fine collection of Flemish, French, Italian,

Fodor'sChoice ★

and Spanish paintings includes works by El Greco, Goya, Velázquez, Zurbarán, Ribera, and Gauguin. One large and excellent section traces developments in 20th-century Spanish and Basque art alongside those of their better-known European contemporaries, such as Léger and Bacon. The building sits on the rim of the pretty Doña Casilda park, about a 30-minute walk from the old quarter. ⊠ *Plaza del Museo 2* ☎ *94/ 439–6060* ⬛ *€5.50, free Wed.; combined ticket with Guggenheim (valid 1 yr) €12 plus €2 additional on admittance to 2nd museum* ☉ *Tues.–Sat. 10–1:30 and 4–7:30, Sun. 10–2* Ⓜ *Moyúa.*

▌NEED A BREAK?   **El Kiosko del Arenal** (⊠ Paseo del Arenal s/n, under the bandstand in Paseo del Arenal Ⓜ Casco Viejo) is an excellent place for coffee, beer, or tapas. Terrace tables offer views of the river in summer, and underneath the bandstand is a paradigmatic clean, well-lighted place in winter.

⓬ **Fodor's**Choice ★   Covered with a dazzling 30,000 sheets of titanium, the **Museo Guggenheim Bilbao** opened in October 1997 and became Bilbao's main attraction overnight. The enormous atrium, more than 150 feet high, is connected to the 19 galleries by a system of suspended metal walkways and glass elevators. The ground floor is dedicated to large installations. ☎ *94/435–9080* ⬛ *€11; €12.50 for special exhibits; combined ticket with Museo de Bellas Artes (valid 1 yr) €12 plus €2 additional on admittance to 2nd museum* ☉ *July and Aug., daily 10–8; Sept.–June, Tues.–Sun. 10–8* Ⓜ *Moyúa.*

⓭   Dubbed Bilbao's Eiffel Tower (albeit a horizontal version) down the Nervión is the **Puente de Vizcaya**—commonly called the Puente Colgante (Hanging Bridge). This transporter hung from cables takes cars and passengers across the Nervión, uniting two distinct worlds: exclusive, quiet Las Arenas and Portugalete, a much older, working-class town that spawned Dolores Ibarruri, the famous Republican orator of the Spanish civil war, known as La Pasionaria for her ardor. Portugalete is a 15-minute walk from Santurce, where the quayside Hogar del Pescador serves simple and ample fish specialties. *Besugo* (sea bream) is the traditional choice, but the fresh grilled sardines are hard to surpass. To reach the bridge, take the subway to Areeta, or drive across the Puente de Deusto, turn left on Avenida Lehendakari Aguirre, and follow signs for Las Arenas. ☎ *94/480–1012* ⊕ *www.puente-colgante.org* ⬛ *€0.30 for a crossing; €1.10 for an automobile; €4 for visit to observation deck* Ⓜ *Areeta.*

⓮   **Catedral de Santiago** (St. James's Cathedral). Bilbao's earliest church, this was a pilgrimage stop on the coastal route to Santiago de Compostela. Work on the structure began in 1379, but fire destroyed most of it in 1571; it has a notable outdoor arcade. ⊠ *Plaza de Santiago* Ⓜ *Casco Viejo.* The **Museo Arqueológico, Etnográfico e Histórico Vasco** (Museum of Basque Archaeology, Ethnology, and History) is in a stunning 16th-century convent. The collection centers on Basque fishing, crafts, and agriculture. ⊠ *C. Cruz 4* ☎ *94/415–5423* ⬛ *€4, free Thurs.* ☉ *Tues.–Sat. 10:30–1:30 and 4–7, Sun. 10:30–1* Ⓜ *Casco Viejo.* The **Museo Diocesano de Arte Sacro** (Diocesan Museum of Sacred Art) occupies a carefully restored 16th-century cloister. The inner patio alone, ancient and intimate, is worth the visit. On display are religious silver works, litur-

The Guggenheim Bilbao

IF PICASSO'S *GUERNICA* **WAS** the 20th century's most famous and embattled painting, Bilbao's Guggenheim may be the most celebrated building of all time. Described by Spanish novelist Manuel Vazquez Montalban as a "meteorite," this eruption of light and titanium paradoxically stationed in Bilbao's muscular industrial context has reinvented this city.

Perennially chided as the *barrio industrial* (industrial quarter) in contrast to San Sebastián's *barrio jardín* (garden quarter), Bilbao has long been perceived as a polluted steel and shipbuilding center by the foul-smelling Nervión estuary.

The Guggenheim has changed all that. Frank Gehry's gleaming brainchild, alternately hailed as "the greatest building of our time" (architect Philip Johnson), "the best building of the 20th century" (Spain's King Juan Carlos), and "a miracle" (Herbert Muschamp, *New York Times*), has sparked a renaissance in the Basque Country. In its first year, the Guggenheim attracted 1.4 million visitors, three times the number expected and more than what both Guggenheim museums in New York received together that same period. Revenue in the first year alone exceeded the original investment. Incredibly, the Guggenheim already holds the Spanish record for single-day visits to a museum (9,300), and the crowds are not diminishing.

The museum itself is as superlative as the hoopla suggests. Gehry's quasi-mechanical tour de force provides an ideal context for the postmodern and futuristic artworks it contains. The smoothly rounded, asymmetrical,

ship's-prow-like amalgam of limestone, glass, and titanium ingeniously recalls Bilbao's shipbuilding and steel-manufacturing past while using transparency and reflective materials to create a shimmering, futuristic luminosity. The final section of the Nervión's La Salve bridge is almost part of the structure, rendering the Guggenheim the virtual doorway to Bilbao.

The collection, described by director Thomas Krens as "a daring history of the art of the 20th century," consists of 242 works, 186 from New York's Guggenheim and 50 acquired by the Basque government. Artists whose names are synonymous with the 20th century (Kandinsky, Picasso, Ernst, Braque, Miró, Calder, Malevich) and particularly artists of the '50s and '60s (Pollock, Rothko, De Kooning, Chillida, Tàpies, Iglesias) are joined by contemporary figures (Nauman, Muñoz, Schnabel, Badiola, Barceló, Basquiat). The ground floor is dedicated to large-format and installation work, some of which—such as Richard Serra's *Serpent*—was created specifically for the space it occupies. Claes Oldenburg's *Knife Ship*, Robert Morris's walk-in *Labyrinth*, and pieces by Beuys, Boltansky, Long, Holzer, and others round out the heavyweight division in and around what is now the largest gallery in the world.

3

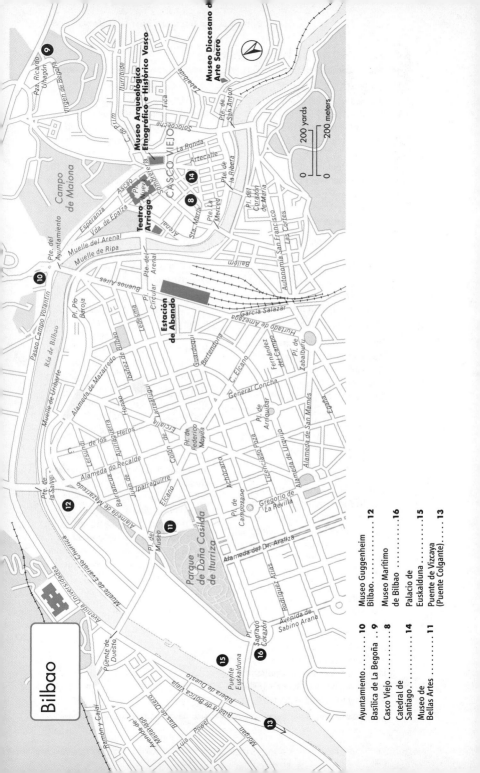

Bilbao

gical garments, sculptures, and paintings dating back to the 12th century. ✉ *Pl. de la Encarnación 9* ☎ *94/432–0125* 🎫 *€2* Ⓜ *Casco Viejo.*

⑮ Palacio de Euskalduna. In homage to the Astilleros Euskalduna (Basque Country shipbuilders) who operated shipyards here beside the Euskalduna bridge into the mid-'80s, this music venue and convention hall resembles a rusting ship. Designed by Federico Soriano, Euskalduna opened in 1999 and is Bilbao's main opera venue and home of the Bilbao Symphony Orchestra. The auditorium has a 2,200-person capacity and 71-stop organ, Spain's largest, offering a different tune and a big turnaround from the pitched battles waged here between workers, Basque nationalists, management, and police as the shipyards laid off thousands. ✉ *Abandoibarra 4, El Ensanche* ☎ *94/403–5000* 🖷 *94/403–5001 (Departamento Comercial)* ⊕ *www.euskalduna.net* 🎫 *Tour €2.50* ☉ *Office weekdays 9–2 and 4–7; box office Mon.–Sat. noon–2 and 5–8:30, Sun. noon–2; guided tours Sat. at noon or by fax appointment* Ⓜ *San Mamés.*

⑯ Museo Marítimo de Bilbao (Maritime Museum of Bilbao). This interesting nautical museum on the left bank of the Ría de Bilbao reconstructs the history of the Bilbao waterfront and shipbuilding industry, beginning with medieval times. Temporary exhibits range from visits by extraordinary seacraft such as tall ships or traditional fishing vessels to thematic displays on 17th- and 18th-century clipper ships or the sinking of the *Titanic.* ✉ *Muelle Ramón de la Sota* ☎ *902/131000* ⊕ *www. museomaritimobilbao.org* 🎫 *€4* ☉ *Tues.–Sun. 10–8* Ⓜ *San Mamés.*

Where to Stay & Eat

\$\$\$–\$\$\$\$ ✕ **Aizian.** Euskera for "in the wind," the Sheraton Bilbao restaurant—under the direction of chef José Miguel Olazabalaga—has in record time become one of the city's most respected dining establishments. Typically Bilbaino culinary classicism doesn't keep Mr. Olazabalaga from creating surprising reductions and contemporary interpretations of traditional dishes such as *la marmita de chipirón,* a stew of sautéed cuttlefish with a topping of whipped potatoes covering the sauce of squid ink. ✉ *C. Lehendakari Leizaola 29, El Ensanche* ☎ *94/428–0035* ▭ *AE, DC, MC, V* ☉ *Closed Sun. and Aug. 1–15* Ⓜ *San Mamés.*

\$\$\$–\$\$\$\$ ✕ **Casa Rufo.** This spot tucked into the back of a delicatessen is famous for *txuleta de buey* (beef chops). Let the affable owners size you up and bring on what you need and desire; these people are into food and like to share it with you. Try the house wine—an excellent *crianza* (two years in oak, one in bottle) from La Rioja—or choose from the wine list, which has top wines from Ribera de Duero, Somantano, and El Priorat. ✉ *Calle Hurtado de Amézaga 5, El Ensanche* ☎ *94/443–2172* 🍴 *Reservations essential* ▭ *AE, DC, MC, V* ☉ *Closed Sun.* Ⓜ *Abando.*

\$\$\$–\$\$\$\$ ✕ **El Perro Chico.** This refuge was named for the bridge below Bilbao's Mercado de la Ribera, where a *perro chico* (colloquial name for an ancient coin) was once charged as a toll. From owner Santiago Diez Ponzoa to chef Rafael García Rossi, everyone has a great time here, where innovative and thoughtful cuisine is prepared without pretense. Try the *pato a la naranja* (duck à l'orange) or the *bacalao con berenjena* (salt cod with eggplant). ✉ *Aretxaga 2* ☎ *94/415–0519* ▭ *AE, DC, MC, V* ☉ *Closed Sun. No lunch Mon.* Ⓜ *Casco Viejo.*

$$$–$$$$ ✕ **Etxanobe.** This luminous corner of the Euskalduna palace overlooks the Nervión river, the hills of Artxanda above, and Bilbao. The panoramic elevator up to the restaurant is guaranteed to jump-start appetite-enhancing adrenaline. Fernando Canales creates sleek, contemporary cuisine on a par with the Basque Country's finest with seasonal offerings ranging from truffles in cream of potato and egg in winter to a superb crab salad in summer. ✉ *Av. de Abandoibarra 4* ☎ *94/442–1071* ▤ *AE, DC, MC, V* ☉ *Closed Sun., Easter wk, and Aug. 1–20* Ⓜ *San Mamés.*

$$$–$$$$ ✕ **Guggenheim Bilbao.** The museum's restaurant-in-residence has a lot to live up to, and easily succeeds. Famous for his eponymous restaurant outside San Sebastián, Martín Berasategui (or his staff) will install you at a table overlooking the Nervión and the green heights of Artxanda, then feed you such exciting creations as *pichón de Bresse* (wild pigeon) and *ensalada de bogavante* (lobster salad). ✉ *Av. Abandoibarra 2* ☎ *94/ 423–9333* ⬦ *Reservations essential* ▤ *AE, DC, MC, V* ☉ *Closed Mon. and Jan. 1–19. No dinner Sun. or Tues.* Ⓜ *Moyúa.*

★ **$$$–$$$$** ✕ **Guria.** The late, great Genaro Pildain, born in what he called "the smallest village in Vizcaya province," was the hands-down dean of Bilbao chefs, a genius of charm and simplicity. Having learned cooking from his mother, Don Genaro presided over one of Bilbao's finest tables for two decades. His business partner Carlos del Rey and chef Tomás Razquin carry on Don Genaro's tradition of generosity and hospitality. Everything's impeccable here, from the *crema de puerros con patatas* (cream of potato-and-leek soup) to the *perretxikos de Orduña* (small, wild spring mushrooms). ✉ *Gran Vía 66* ☎ *94/441–5780* ▤ *AE, DC, MC, V* ☉ *No dinner Sun.* Ⓜ *San Mamés.*

$$$–$$$$ ✕ **Jolastoki.** Housed inside a graceful mansion, this fine restaurant is 20 minutes from downtown (and then a seven-minute walk) on the city's pride-and-joy Norman Foster subway. Wild salmon, from the River Cares; dark, red Bresse pigeon roasted in balsamic vinegar; *lubina al vapor* (steamed sea bass) as light as a soufflé; and encyclopedic salads are done to perfection. The red fruit dessert includes 11 varieties with sorbet in raspberry coulis. ✉ *Los Chopos 24, Getxo* ☎ *94/491–2031* ⬦ *Reservations essential* ▤ *AE, DC, MC, V* ☉ *Closed Mon. No dinner Sun. or Tues.* Ⓜ *Getxo.*

$$–$$$ ✕ **Berton.** Dinner is served until 11:30 in this sleek, contemporary bistro in the Casco Viejo. Fresh wood tables with a green-tint polyethylene finish and exposed ventilation pipes give the dining room a designer look, and the classic cuisine ranges from Iberian ham to smoked salmon, foie gras, cod, beef, and lamb. ✉ *Jardines 11* ☎ *94/416–7035* ▤ *AE, DC, MC, V* ☉ *No dinner Sun. and holidays* Ⓜ *Casco Viejo.*

$–$$$ ✕ **La Deliciosa.** For carefully prepared fare at friendly prices, this is one of the best values in the Casco Viejo. The *crema de puerros* (cream of leeks) is as good as any in town, and the *dorada al horno* (roast gilt-head bream) is fresh from the nearby La Ribera market. ✉ *Jardines 1* ☎ *94/415–0944* ▤ *AE, DC, MC, V* Ⓜ *Casco Viejo.*

$–$$$ ✕ **Victor Montes.** A hot point for the daily *tapeo* (tapas tour), this place is always crowded with congenial grazers. The well-stocked counter might offer anything from wild mushrooms to *txistorra* (spicy sausages) to *Idiazabal* (Basque smoked cheese) or, for the adventurous, *huevas de merluza* (hake roe), all taken with splashes of Rioja, txakolí, or cider. ✉ *Pl.*

Nueva 8 ☎ *94/415–7067* ⚱ *Reservations essential* ☉ *Closed Sun. and Aug. 1–15* Ⓜ *Casco Viejo.*

$–$$ ✕ **Arriaga.** The cider-house experience is a must in the Basque Country. Cider *al txotx* (straight from the barrel), sausage stewed in apple cider, codfish omelets, *txuleton de buey* (beefsteaks), and Idiazabal cheese with quince jelly are the classic fare. Reserving a table is a good idea, especially on weekends. ✉ *Santa Maria 13* ☎ *94/416–5670* 🖃 *AE, DC, MC, V* ☉ *No dinner Sun.* Ⓜ *Casco Viejo.*

$–$$ ✕ **Kiskia.** A modern version of the traditional cider house, this rambling
Fodor'sChoice tavern near the San Mamés soccer stadium serves the classical *sidrería*
★ menu of chorizo sausage cooked in cider, codfish omelet, txuleta de buey, Idiazabal cheese with quince jelly and nuts, and as much cider as you can drink, all for €28. Actors, sculptors, writers, soccer stars, and Bilbao's (and Spain's) who's who frequent this boisterous marvel. ✉ *Pérez Galdós 51, San Mamés* ☎ *94/442–0032* 🖃 *AE, DC, MC, V* ☉ *No dinner Sun.–Tues.* Ⓜ *San Mamés.*

¢–$ ✕ **Xukela.** Amid bright lighting and a vivid palette of greens and crimsons, chef Santiago Ruíz Bombin creates some of the tastiest and most eye-watering *pintxos* (morsels on toothpicks) in all of tapas-dom. ✉ *El Perro 2* ☎ *94/415–9772* 🖃 *AE, DC, MC, V* Ⓜ *Casco Viejo.*

★ **$$–$$$$** ✕▥ **Lopez de Haro.** Because it's just five minutes from the Guggenheim, Bilbao's top hotel has become quite a scene. The converted 19th-century building has an English feel and all the comforts your heart's desires. Club Náutico, a handy alternative on one of Bilbao's many rainy evenings, serves modern and classical Basque dishes ($$–$$$$), ranging from a simple *besugo* (sea bream) or one of the city's famous *bacalao* (codfish) preparations to sleek, contemporary interpretations of traditional favorites. ✉ *Obispo Orueta 2, 48009* ☎ *94/423–5500* 📠 *94/423–4500* ⊕ *www.hotellopezdeharo.com* ⇆ *49 rooms, 4 suites* ⚲ *Restaurant, cafeteria, cable TV, in-room data ports, bar, meeting rooms, parking (fee)* 🖃 *AE, DC, MC, V* Ⓜ *Moyúa.*

$$$$ ▥ **Sheraton Bilbao Hotel.** This colossus, built over what was once the nerve center of Bilbao's shipbuilding industry, feels like a futuristic ocean liner. Designed by architect Ricardo Legorreta and inspired by the work of Basque sculptor Eduardo Chillida (1920–2002), the hotel is filled with contemporary art and models of Spanish ships. Rooms are high, wide, and handsome, with glass, steel, stone, and wood trimmings. The comforts and the views from upper floors are superb. The Chillida café and the restaurant, Aizian, are both excellent. ✉ *C. Lehendakari Leizaola 29, El Ensanche, 48001* ☎ *94/428–0000* 📠 *94/428–0001* ⊕ *www.sheraton-bilbao.com/esp* ⇆ *199 rooms, 12 suites* ⚲ *2 restaurants, minibars, cable TV, in-room data ports, gym, bar, meeting rooms, parking (fee)* 🖃 *AE, DC, MC, V* Ⓜ *San Mamés.*

★ **$$$–$$$$** ▥ **Carlton.** Luminaries who have trod the halls of this grande dame include Orson Welles, Ava Gardner, Ernest Hemingway, Lauren Bacall, and most of Spain's great bullfighters. During the civil war it was the seat of the Republican Basque government; later it housed a number of Nationalist generals. It remains elegant, well attended, and central. ✉ *Pl. Federico Moyúa 2, El Ensanche, 48009* ☎ *94/416–2200* 📠 *94/416–4628* ⊕ *www.aranzazu-hoteles.com* ⇆ *137 rooms, 7 suites*

⌕ *Restaurant, minibars, cable TV, in-room data ports, bar, meeting rooms, parking (fee)* ☰ *AE, DC, MC, V* Ⓜ *Moyúa.*

★ $$$–$$$$ ⚏ **Gran Hotel Domine Bilbao.** As much modern design festival as hotel, this member of the Silken chain, directly across the street from the Guggenheim, showcases the conceptual wit of Javier Mariscal, creator of Barcelona's 1992 Olympic mascot Cobi, and the structural know-how of Bilbao architect Iñaki Aurreroextea. With adjustable window-panes reflecting Gehry's titanium leviathan and every lamp and piece of furniture reflecting Mariscal's playful whimsy, this is the brightest star in Bilbao's design constellation. Comprehensively equipped and comfortable, it's the next best thing to moving into the Guggenheim. ✉ *Alameda de Mazarredo 61, El Ensanche, 48009* ☎ *94/425–3300* 📠 *94/ 425–3301* ⊕ *www.granhoteldominebilbao.com* ⇆ *139 rooms, 6 suites* ⌕ *Restaurant, cafeteria, minibars, cable TV, in-room data ports, bar, meeting rooms, parking (fee)* ☰ *AE, DC, MC, V* Ⓜ *Moyúa.*

$$–$$$$ ⚏ **Petit Palace Arana.** Next to the Teatro Arriaga in the Casco Viejo, this hotel has a blended style. Centenary limestone blocks, exposed brickwork, hand-hewn beams, and spiral wooden staircases are juxtaposed with clean surfaces of glass and steel. The rooms and the showers are a tight fit, and the street below can be noisy on weekends, depending on the location of your room. Ask for a room overlooking the Arriaga theater and the Nervión, for the view and for less night racket. Fifteen executive rooms have exercise bikes and computers. ✉ *Bidebarrieta 2, Casco Viejo, 48005* ☎ *94/415–6411* 📠 *94/416–1205* ⊕ *www.hthotels. com* ⇆ *64 rooms* ⌕ *Minibars, cable TV, in-room data ports, hot tubs, bar, meeting room* ☰ *AE, DC, MC, V* Ⓜ *Casco Viejo.*

$$$
Fodor'sChoice
★   ⚏ **Miró Hotel.** Across from the Guggenheim and one block away from Bilbao's Museo de Bellas Artes, this boutique hotel, refurbished by Barcelona fashion designer Toni Miró, is extremely comfortable and daringly innovative. Rooms are quiet, spacious, and contemporary, with high-tech touches. Public rooms are done in blacks and beiges and are simple and unpretentious; the hip downstairs bar is punctuated with canary-yellow walls. Expect a free drink when you arrive, excellent service throughout your stay, and, if you opt for it, a lavish breakfast with fresh-squeezed orange juice, bacon, eggs, and more—enough to keep you full all day. There's also a CD and DVD library, in addition to plenty of books. ✉ *Alameda de Mazarredo 77, El Ensanche, 48001* ☎ *94/661– 1880* 📠 *94/425–5182* ⊕ *www.mirohotelbilbao.com* ⇆ *45 rooms, 5 suites* ⌕ *Restaurant, room service, minibars, cable TV, in-room data ports, gym, spa, bar, lounge, library, laundry service, meeting rooms, airport shuttle, parking (fee).* ☰ *AE, DC, MC, V* Ⓜ *Moyúa.*

$$–$$$ ⚏ **Hotel Ercilla.** This modern hotel fills with bullfighting crowds during Bilbao's Semana Grande in early August, both because it's near the bull-ring and because it has taken over from the Carlton as the place to see and be seen—it's not the spot for a quiet getaway. Impeccable rooms, amenities, and service underscore its reputation. ✉ *C. Ercilla 37, El Ensanche, 48009* ☎ *94/470–5700* 📠 *94/443–9335* ⊕ *www.hotelercilla. es* ⇆ *335 rooms, 10 suites* ⌕ *Restaurant, cafeteria, minibars, cable TV, in-room data ports, bar, parking (fee)* ☰ *AE, DC, MC, V* Ⓜ *Moyúa.*

$–$$ ⚏ **Iturrienea Ostatua.** Euskara (Basque) for "Hostal of the Fountain," this traditional Basque town house in Bilbao's old quarter has overhead wooden beams, stone floors, and ethnographical and historical objects adorning the walls. Management and staff are invariably smart, polite, and helpful. The only caveat is nocturnal noise on the front side, especially in summer. Try for a room in the back, or bring earplugs. ⊠ *Santa María Kalea 14, Casco Viejo, 48005* ☏ *94/416–1500* 🖶 *94/415–8929* ⊕ *www.iturrieneaostatua.com* ⟿ *21 rooms* ♿ *No a/c* ═ *AE, DC, MC, V* Ⓜ *Casco Viejo.*

Cafés

Bilbao's many coffeehouses and bistros have long provided refuge from the sirimiri and steel mills outside.

Bar los Fueros (⊠ C. de los Fueros 4, Casco Viejo), as much a watering hole as a café, is one of Bilbao's most authentic enclaves, perfect for an *aperitivo* or a nightcap. The **Café Bulevard** (⊠ C. Arenal 3, Casco Viejo) dates back to 1871. Refuel at the enormous **Café Iruña** (⊠ Jardines de Albia, El Ensanche), a turn-of-the-20th-century classic. Founded in 1926, **Café La Granja** (⊠ Pl. Circular 3, El Ensanche), near the Puente del Arenal, is a Bilbao classic for coffee, beer, and *tortilla de patata* (potato omelet). **Café El Tilo** (⊠ C. Arenal 1, Casco Viejo) may be the best in Bilbao, with wooden tables and original frescoes by Basque painter Juan de Aranoa (1901–73). It's open weekdays only. **Café y Té** (⊠ Pl. Federico Moyúa 1, El Ensanche) has a pleasant marble counter and a rural-urban aesthetic.

Nightlife & the Arts

Bilbao holds a music festival in August; inquire at the main tourist office on Paseo de Arenal (☏ 94/479–5770), as venues change. The city's abundant nightlife breaks neatly down into ages and zones. Students and anyone else who can pass for being thirty-ish and under amass on and around Calle Licenciado Poza (known as Pozas, two blocks east of Gran Vía) and the Casco Viejo, where serious *poteo* (tippling) continues until late. Folk dancing sometimes breaks out in the streets. Barring holidays, the first half of the week is quieter. The historic **Teatro Arriaga** (⊠ Pl. Arriaga s/n, Casco Viejo ☏ 94/416–3244) still draws the world's top performers in ballet, theater, concerts, opera, and *zarzuela* (comic opera). The bright **Palacio Euskalduna** (⊠ Abandoibarra 4, El Ensanche ☏ 944/308372), home of the Orquesta Sinfónica de Bilbao, has all but replaced the Arriaga as Bilbao's prime performing-arts venue. All ages meet for drinks at designer Javier Mariscal's playful **Splash & Crash** (⊠ Alameda Mazarredo 61, El Ensanche) cocktail lounge and pub in the Hotel Gran Domine. **Flash** (⊠ C. Telesforo Aranzadi 4, Near Hotel Carlton, El Ensanche) has dinner, dancing, and cocktails. **Magic** (⊠ C. Colón de Larreátegui 80, El Ensanche) is known for '60s music and clients of roughly the same vintage.

Shopping

Basque *txapelas* (berets) make charming gifts. Best when waterproof, these berets keep you remarkably warm in rain and mist. Look for Elosegui, the best-known brand of txapelas, in the old quarter's **Sombreros Gorostiaga** (⊠ C. Victor 9 ☏ 94/416–1276). **Basandere** (⊠ C. Iparaguirre 4 ☏ 94/423–6386), near the Guggenheim, has artisanal Basque crafts and foods. **Olañeta** (⊠ C. Correo 12 ☏ 94/415–1618), in the Casco Viejo, lovingly restored in stone, wood beams, and brick by antiquer Xabier Olañeta, sells charming ladies' wear.

EN ROUTE

From Bilbao, drive west down the Nervión to Neguri and Getxo and follow the coast road around through Baquio, Bermeo, and Mundaka to Gernika before proceeding east. Depending on stops for lunch or sprawling on a breezy beach, this can be a two- to six-hour drive, all of it spectacularly scenic.

Getxo

17 *13 km (8 mi) northwest of Bilbao, 10 km (6 mi) southwest of Plentzia.*

Getxo, an early watering spot for the elite Bilbao industrial classes, has rambling mansions, five beaches, and an ancient fishing port. Restaurants and hotels along the beaches here make good hideaways—only a 20-minute ride from the center of Bilbao, on the British architect Norman Foster's designer subway line from Bilbao.

San Juan de Gaztelugatxe

18 *12 km (7 mi) west of Bermeo.*

"A walk around the Romanesque chapel bell tower is said to cure nightmares and insomnia, as well as to make wishes come true."

This tiny, gemlike hermitage clinging to its rocky promontory over the Bay of Biscay is exactly 231 steps up along a narrow corridor built into the top of a rocky ledge connecting what would otherwise be an island to the mainland. A favorite pilgrimage for Bilbainos on holidays, the Romanesque chapel is said to have been used as a fortress by the Templars in the 14th century. A walk around the bell tower is alleged to cure nightmares and insomnia, as well as to make wishes come true.

Where to Stay & Eat

$-$$ ✕🖳 **Ostatua Gaztelubegi.** The views from this little hotel and restaurant overlooking the hermitage of San Juan de Gaztelugatxe are some of the most vertiginous of the Basque coast. The bar is always booming; the food is simple Basque cooking, from *alubias* to *besugo* (beans to sea bream). ✉ *Ctra. BI–3101, Km 3, from Bakio, 48130* ☎ *94/619–4924* ⊕ *www.bakio.com* ↪ *7 rooms* ⚑ *Restaurant, bar, free parking; no a/c* ▤ *AE, DC, MC, V.*

Bermeo

19 *30 km (18 mi) east of Plentzia, 3 km (2 mi) west of Mundaka.*

Bermeo is easy to miss if you don't park and walk through the old part of town to the port. (On your way, inspect the lovely Udaletxea, or town hall, to check out its sundials in almost perpetual shadow above the fountains, which are dated 1745 at the building's eastern corner.) With the largest fishing fleet in Spain—some 60 long-distance tuna freezer ships of more than 150 tons, and nearly 100 smaller craft that specialize in hake, sea bream, gilthead, and other local species—Bermeo was long famous as a whaling port. In the 16th century, local whalers reportedly were obliged to donate the tongue of every whale to raise money for the church. Bermeo has one of only two wooden-boat shipyards on the northern coast, and the boats in its harbor make a colorful picture. Drive to the top of the windswept hill, where a cemetery overlooks the crashing waves below. Townspeople tend to family tombs at sunset.

Bermeo's **Museo del Pescador** is the only museum in the world dedicated to the craft and history of fishermen and the fishing industry, from whales to anchovies. The tower was built by native son Alonso de Ercilla y Zuñiga (1533–94), poet and eminent soldier. Ercilla's "La Araucana," an account of the conquest of Arauco (Chile), is considered one of the best Spanish epic poems. ⊠ *Torre de Ercilla* 🕾 *946/881171* 🎟 *Free* ⊙ *Tues.–Sat. 10–1:30 and 4–7:30, Sun. 10–1:30.*

Where to Eat

$$–$$$ ✕ **Jokin.** You'll have a good view of the *puerto viejo* (old port) from this cheerful, strategically located restaurant. The fish served comes directly off the boats in the harbor below. Try the *rape Jokin* (anglerfish in a clam and crayfish sauce) or *chipirones en su tinta* (small squid in its own ink) and, for dessert, the *tarta de naranja* (orange cake). ⊠ *Eupeme Deuna 13* 🕾 *94/688–4089* ⊟ *AE, DC, MC, V* ⊙ *No dinner Sun.*

Mundaka

⑳ *45 km (28 mi) northeast of Bilbao.*

Tiny Mundaka, famous with surfers all over the world for its left-breaking roller at the mouth of the Ría de Guernica, has been in crisis since its wave mysteriously disappeared in 2004. October was prime time for Europe's longest wave until a 2003 dredging displaced the sandbar that created it. In 2005, studies were elaborated to determine where the wave has gone and how to get it back. As of early 2006, the wave was better, but not fully recovered, though signs are hopeful that it will be. Meanwhile, the town's elegant summer homes and stately houses bearing coats of arms compete for pride of place with the hermitage on the Santa Catalina peninsula and the parish church's Renaissance door.

Where to Stay & Eat

$$–$$$$ ✕ **Casino José Mari.** Built in 1818 as an auction house for the local fishermen's guild, this building, with wonderful views of Mundaka's beach, is now an eating club. The public is welcome, and it's a prime lunch stop in summer, when you can sit in the glassed-in, upper-floor porch. Very much a local haunt, the club serves excellent fish caught, more often than not, by members. ⊠ *Parque Atalaya, center of town* 🕾 *94/687–6005* ⊟ *AE, MC, V.*

$$–$$$ 🏨 **Atalaya.** This 1911 landmark 37 km (22 mi) from Bilbao was converted very tastefully from a private house to a hotel, and has become a big favorite for quick railroad-getaway overnights from Bilbao and the Guggenheim. (The train ride out is spectacular.) Guest rooms are charming and comfortable; those upstairs have balconies with marvelous views. Room No. 12 is the best in the house. The breakfast

room is cheerful and light. ⊠ *Paseo de Txorrokopunta 2, 48360* ☎ *94/617-7000* 🖶 *94/687-6899* ⊕ *www.hotel-atalaya-mundaka.com* ↩ *11 rooms* ⌂ *Restaurant, bar* ⊟ *AE, DC, MC, V.*

▌EN ROUTE From Mundaka, follow signs for Gernika, stopping at the Mirador de Portuondo—a roadside lookout on the left as you leave town (BI–635, Km 43)—for an excellent view of the estuary.

Gernika-Lumo (Guernica y Lumo)

㉑ *15 km (9 mi) east of Bilbao.*

On Monday, April 26, 1937—market day—Gernika, the Guernica of the Picasso painting, suffered history's second terror bombing against a civilian population. (The first, much less famous, was against neighboring Durango, about a month earlier.) The planes of the Nazi Luftwaffe were sent with the blessings of General Francisco Franco to experiment with saturation bombing of civilian targets and to decimate the traditional seat of Basque autonomy. Since the Middle Ages, Spanish sovereigns had sworn under the ancient **oak tree of Gernika** to respect Basque *fueros* (special local rights—the kind of local autonomy that was anathema to the *generalísimo*'s Madrid-centered "National Movement," which promoted Spanish unity over local identity). More than 1,000 people were killed in the bombing, and today Gernika remains a symbol of independence in the heart of every Basque, known to the world through Picasso's famous canvas *Guernica* (now in Madrid's Centro de Arte Reina Sofía). The city was destroyed—though an oak tree miraculously emerged unscathed—and has been rebuilt as a modern, architecturally uninteresting town. The **Museo de la Paz** offers a closer look at the bombing heard around the world (thanks to the Picasso painting), and the **Museo de Euskalerria** provides insights into Basque culture, history, and ethnology. The stump of the sacred oak, which at last died several decades ago, can be found in the courtyard of the **Casa de Juntas** (a new oak has been planted alongside the old one)—the object of many a pilgrimage. Nearby is the stunning estuary of the **Ría de Gernika**, a stone's throw from some of the area's most colorful fishing towns.

Where to Stay & Eat

$$–$$$$ ✕ **Baserri Maitea.** In the village of Forua 1 km (½ mi) northwest of Gernika, Basseri Maitea is in a stunning 250-year-old Basque caserío. Strings of red peppers and garlic hang from wooden beams in the cathedral-like interior. Entrées include the *pescado del día* (fish of the day) and *cordero de leche asado al horno de leña* (milk-fed lamb roasted in a wood-burning oven). ⊠ *BI–635 to Bermeo, Km 2* ☎ *94/625–3408* ⊟ *AE, DC, MC, V* ☾ *No dinner Sun.–Thurs. Oct.–May.*

$–$$ ▦ **Boliña.** Not far from the famous oak site in downtown Gernika, the Boliña is pleasant and modern, a good base for exploring the Vizcayan coast. Rooms are small but comfortable. ⊠ *Barrenkale 3, 48300* ☎ *94/625–0300* 🖶 *94/625–0304* ↩ *16 rooms* ⌂ *Restaurant, bar* ⊟ *AE, DC, MC, V.*

Embattled Gernika

WHEN SPAIN'S SECOND REPUBLIC COMMISSIONED PICASSO to create a work for the Paris 1937 International Exposition, little did he imagine that his grim canvas protesting the bombing of a Basque village would become one of the most famous paintings in history.

The rural market town of Gernika has been one of the keys to the Basque identity since the 14th century. General Francisco Franco knew the strike would be a blow to Basque nationalism. When the Tuesday, April 26 raid ended, more than 1,000 civilians lay dead or dying in the ruins. Not until the 60th anniversary of the event did Germany officially apologize for the bombing.

Picasso's painting had its own struggle. The Spanish Pavilion in the 1937 International Exposition in Paris nearly substituted a more upbeat work, using *Guernica* as a backdrop. In 1939, Picasso ceded *Guernica* to New York's Museum of Modern Art on behalf of the democratically elected government of Spain—stipulating that the painting should return only to a democratic Spain. Over the next 30 years, as Picasso's fame grew, so did *Guernica*'s—as a work of art and symbol of Spain's captivity.

When Franco died in 1975, two years after Picasso, negotiations with Picasso's heirs for the painting's return to Spain were already under way. Now on display at Madrid's Centro de Arte Reina Sofía, *Guernica* is home for good.

OFF THE BEATEN PATH

CUEVAS DE SANTIMAMIÑE – On the Kortezubi road 5 km (3 mi) from Gernika, the Cuevas de Santimamiñe, also known as Santimamiñe Caverns, have important prehistoric cave paintings. Guided visits are offered weekdays at 10:30, noon, 4, and 5:30, except holidays. On your way out, look for signs for the nearby **Bosque Pintado,** rows of trees vividly painted by Basque artist Agustín Ibarrola, a striking and successful marriage of art and nature. ⊠ *Barrio Basondo, Kortezubi* ☎ *94/625–2975.*

EN ROUTE

For the Santimamiñe caves, continue northeast from Gernika toward Kortezubi on the BI–638. For Elanchove (Elantxobe, in Euskera), turn left at Arteaga and follow the BI–3237 around the east side of the Ría de Gernika and the Urdaibai natural preserve. From there, the coast road through Ea and Ipaster leads to Lekeitio, one of the prettiest ports on the Basque coast. But if you long for a taste of Arcadian highlands 30 minutes inland, drive up to Axpe and see Amboto, Vizcaya's mythical limestone mountain.

Axpe

㉒ *47 km (28 mi) east of Bilbao, 46 km (27 mi) southeast of Gernika.*

The village of Axpe, in the valley of Atxondo, nestles under the limestone heights of 4,777-foot Amboto—one of the highest peaks in the

Basque Country outside of the Pyrenees. Home of the legendary Basque mother of nature, Mari Urrika or Mari Anbotokodama (María, Our Lady of Amboto), Amboto, with its spectral gray rock face, is a sharp contrast to the soft green meadows running up to the very foot of the mountain. According to Basque scholar and ethnologist José María de Barandiarán in his *Mitología Vasca* (Basque Mythology), Mari was "a beautiful woman, well constructed in all ways except for one foot, which was like that of a goat." Her sons, Mikelatz and Atagorri, are, in Basque mythology, representations of good and evil.

To reach Axpe from Bilbao, drive east on A8/E70 freeway toward San Sebastián. From Gernika, drive south on the BI–635 to A6/E70 freeway and turn east for San Sebastián. Get off at the Durango exit 40 km (24 mi) from Bilbao and take the BI–632 road for Elorrio. At Apatamonasterio turn right onto the BI–3313 and continue to Axpe.

Where to Stay & Eat

$$$–$$$$
Fodor'sChoice
★

✕ **Etxebarri.** All the rage around the Iberian Peninsula these days, Víctor Arguinzoniz has introduced cooking over coals to haute cuisine, tailoring woods and coals for different products and improvising equipment such as the pan to char-grill *angulas* (baby eels). Everything from clams and fish to the meats and even the rice with langoustines is healthful, taste-filled, and exciting. ☒ *Plaza San Juan 1* ☎ *94/658–3042* ⊟ *AE, DC, MC, V* ⊘ *Closed Mon. No dinner Sun.*

$$–$$$
Fodor'sChoice
★

✕⛫ **Mendigoikoa.** This handsome group of hillside farmhouses is among the province of Vizcaya's most exquisite hideaways. The lower farmhouse, Mendibekoa (lower mountain), has stunning rooms, an elegant breakfast room, and a glassed-in terrace overlooking the valley. At Mendigoikoa (upper mountain), the restaurant ($$–$$$$), heavy beams loom overhead and a fire usually crackles in the far corner. The *pichón de Navaz a la parrilla* (Navaz pigeon cooked over coals) or the txuleta de buey (great chunks of beef on the bone) are memorable. ☒ *Barrio San Juan 33, 48290* ☎ *94/682–0833* ⛫ *94/682–1136* ⊕ *www.mendigoikoa.com* ⇱ *12 rooms* ⚏ *Restaurant* ⊟ *AE, DC, MC, V* ⊘ *Closed Dec. 22–Jan. 17. Restaurant closed Mon. No dinner Sun.*

Elantxobe

㉓ *27 km (17 mi) from Bermeo.*

The tiny fishing village of Elantxobe (Elanchove, in Spanish) is surrounded by huge, steep cliffs, with a small breakwater that protects its fleet from the storms of the Bay of Biscay. The view of the port from the upper village is breathtaking. The lower fork in the road leads to the port.

Where to Stay & Eat

$–$$

✕⛫ **Casa Rural Arboliz.** On a bluff overlooking the Bay of Biscay about 2 km (1 mi) outside Elantxobe on the road to Lequeitio, this rustic inn is removed from the harborside bustle, offering a breath of the country life on the Basque coast. The modern rooms are simple and have balconies overlooking the sea. The restaurant serves simple Basque specialties with an emphasis on fresh fish and seafood. The *besugo la donostiarra* (sea bream covered in a garlic, oil, and vinegar sauce) is exceptional.

✉ *Arboliz 12, Ibarranguelua 48311* ☎ *94/627–6283* ⊕ *www.euskalnet. net/arboliz* ⇄ *6 rooms* ⌂ *Restaurant* ▤ *AE, DC, MC, V.*

¢–$ ✕▥ **Itsasmin.** In the upper village of Elantxobe, this place rents simple, cheery rooms and serves home-cooked meals in its diminutive dining room ($–$$). ✉ *Nagusia 32* ☎ *94/627–6174* ▤ *94/627–6293* ⇄ *15 rooms* ⌂ *Restaurant* ▤ *AE, DC, MC, V* ⊙ *Closed Dec. 15–Jan. 15.*

Lekeitio

㉔ *59 km (37 mi) east of Bilbao, 61 km (38 mi) west of San Sebastián.*

This bright little town is similar to Bermeo but has two wide, sandy beaches right by its harbor. Soaring over the Gothic church of Santa María (open for mass only) is a graceful set of flying buttresses. Lequeitio is famous for its fiestas (September 1–18), which include a gruesome event in which men dangle for as long as they can from the necks of dead geese tied to a cable over the inlet while the cable is whipped in and out of the water by crowds of burly men at either end.

Ondárroa

㉕ *61 km (38 mi) east of Bilbao, 49 km (30 mi) west of San Sebastián.*

Farther east along the coast from Lekeitio, Ondárroa is a gem of a fishing town. Like its neighbors, it has a major fishing fleet painted various combinations of red, green, and white, the colors of the Ikurriña, the Basque national flag.

EN ROUTE Continuing along the coastal road through Motrico and Deva, you'll approach some of the Basque Country's most colorful fishing ports and finest quayside restaurants. As you enter Zumaia, you'll see the turnoff for Azpeitia and the sanctuary of one of Spain's greatest religious figures, St. Ignatius of Loyola. A half-hour trip up the GI–631 takes you to this colossal structure.

Santuario de San Ignacio de Loyola

㉖ *Cestona: 34 km (21 mi) southwest of San Sebastián.*

The Sanctuary of St. Ignatius of Loyola was erected in honor of Iñigo Lopez de Oñaz y Loyola (1491–1556) after he was sainted as Ignacio de Loyola in 1622 for his defense of the Catholic Church against the tides of Martin Luther's Reformation. The future founder of the Jesuit Order left his life as a courtier to join the army at the age of 26, but after being badly wounded in an intra-Basque battle he returned to his family's ancestral home, underwent a spiritual conversion, and took up theological studies. Almost two centuries later, Roman architect Carlos Fontana designed the basilica that would memorialize the saint. The exuberant baroque structure contrasts with the austere ways of Saint Ignatius himself, who took vows of poverty and chastity after his conversion. The interior is endowed with polychrome marble, ornate altarwork, and a huge but delicate dome. The fortresslike tower house has the room where Ignatius (Iñigo, in Euskera) experienced conversion while recovering from his wound. His teachings emphasized mystical union with

God, the imitation of Christ, human initiative, foreign missionary work, and, especially, the education of youth. Back on the coastal road is **Zumaia,** a cozy little port and summer resort with the estuary of the Urola River flowing (back and forth, according to the tide) through town. The **Museo Zuloaga** (☎ 943/862341), on N634 at the eastern edge of town, has an extraordinary collection of paintings by Goya, El Greco, Zurbarán, and others, in addition to works by the Basque impressionist Ignacio Zuloaga himself. The museum is open from Easter to September 15, Wednesday through Sunday 4 to 8 PM. The rest of the year, it's open by prior arrangement only. Admission is €5.

Where to Stay & Eat

$–$$ ✕ **Bedua.** Locals access this rustic hideaway by boat in the summer. A specialist in *tortilla de patatas con pimientos verdes de la huerta* (potato omelet with homegrown green peppers), Bedua is also known for tortilla de bacalao (codfish omelet), txuleta de buey (beefsteak), and fish of all kinds such as besugo (sea bream). ⊠ *Cestona, Barrio Bedua, 3 km (2 mi) up Urola from Zumaia* ☎ *943/860551* ▤ *MC, V.*

$$ ⊞ **Landarte.** For a taste of life in a Basque caserio (farmhouse), try this restored 16th-century country manor house an hour away in Getaria. The walk over will prime you for the pleasures of Basque dining; the walk back will prepare you for more. Stone walls, hand-hewn beams, sea views, and happy and helpful hosts make this a top choice. ⊠ *Crtra. de Artadi 1, Zumaia 20750* ☎ *943/865358* 🖶 *943/865358* ⊕ *www. landarte.net* ⤳ *6 rooms* ⚲ *Free parking; no a/c* ▤ *AE, DC, MC, V.*

$–$$ ⊞ **Arocena.** This is one of the many spa hotels to which Europeans flocked at the end of the 19th century. The hotel has free bus service to the nearby springs, whose medicinal waters are still used to treat liver-related diseases. Rooms facing away from the road have especially fine views of the mountains. The common rooms, including the restaurant and lobby, retain the hotel's Belle Epoque flavor. ⊠ *San Juan 12, 10 min from sanctuary, 20740 Cestona* ☎ *943/147040* 🖶 *943/147978* ⊕ *www. hotelarocena.com* ⤳ *109 rooms* ⚲ *Restaurant, cable TV, tennis court, pool, health club, bar, playground* ▤ *AE, DC, MC, V.*

Getaria

㉗ *22 km (14 mi) west of San Sebastián.*

From Zumaia, the coast road and several good footpaths lead to Getaria (Guetaria, in Spanish), known as *la cocina de guipúzcoa*, the kitchen of Guipúzcoa province, for its many restaurants and taverns. Getaria was the birthplace of Juan Sebastián Elcano (1460–1526), the first circumnavigator of the globe and Spain's most emblematic naval hero. Elcano took over and completed Magellan's voyage after the latter was killed in the Philippines in 1521. The town's galleonlike **church** has sloping wooden floors resembling a ship's deck. **Zarautz,** the next town, has a wide beach and many taverns and cafés.

Where to Stay & Eat

★ **$$$–$$$$**   ✕ **Kaia Kaipe.** Suspended over Getaria's colorful fishing port and looking past Zarautz and San Sebastián all the way to Biarritz, this spectacular place puts together exquisite fish soups and serves fresh fish right off the boats—you can watch them being unloaded below. The town is the home of Txomin Etxaniz, the premier txakolí (tart young Basque white wine), and this is the place to drink it. ⊠ *General Arnao 4* ☎ *943/ 140500* ⊟ *AE, DC, MC, V* ⊘ *Closed Mar. 1–15 and Oct. 15–31.*

$ ✕▥ **Iribar.** Iribar has been grilling fish and beef over coals for more than half a century. Just uphill from Getaria's singular church, the restaurant stands out for value, family-friendliness, and delicious fish and beef ($–$$$). The four rooms are impeccable, inexpensive, and the only berths available in the heart of this schoonerlike historic village. ⊠ *Kale Nagusia 34* ☎ *943/140406* 🖶 *943/140953* ⊕ *www.iribarjatetxea.com* 🛏 *4 rooms* ⚘ *Restaurant, bar* ⊟ *AE, DC, MC, V* ⊘ *Closed Thurs. and Oct. 1–15, Apr. 1–15. No dinner Wed.*

▌**OFF THE BEATEN PATH** For a look at an authentic Basque farmhouse, or caserio, where the Urdapilleta family farms pigs, sheep, cattle, goats, chickens, and ducks, take a detour up to the village of Bidegoian (8 km [5 mi] short of Tolosa on the Azpeitia–Tolosa road). Pello Urdapilleta (which means "pile of pigs" in Euskara) sells artisanal cheeses and sausages and will show you how upland Basques have traditionally lived and farmed. ⊠ *Elola Azpikoa Baserria, Bidegoian* ☎ *943/681006.*

SAN SEBASTIÁN TO HONDARRIBIA

Graceful, chic San Sebastián invites you to slow down. Stroll the beach, or wander the streets. East of the city is Pasajes, where Lafayette set off to help the colonial forces in the American Revolution, and where Victor Hugo spent a winter writing. Just shy of the French border, you'll hit Hondarribia, a brightly painted, flower-festooned port town.

San Sebastián

㉘ *100 km (62 mi) east of Bilbao.*

Fodor's Choice San Sebastián (Donostia, in Euskera) is an unusually sophisticated city ★ arched around one of the finest urban beaches in the world, **La Concha** (The Shell), so named for its almost perfect resemblance to the shape of a scallop shell. The best way to see San Sebastián is to walk around: promenades and pathways lead up the hills that surround the city. The first records of San Sebastián date from the 11th century. A backwater for centuries, the city had the good fortune in 1845 to attract Queen Isabella II, who was seeking relief from a skin ailment in the icy Atlantic waters. Isabella was followed by much of the aristocracy of the time, and San Sebastián became a favored summer retreat for Madrid's well-to-do. The city is laid out with wide streets on a grid pattern, thanks mainly to the 12 different times it has been all but destroyed by fire. The last conflagration came after the French were expelled in 1813; English–Portuguese forces occupied the city, abused the population, and torched the place. Today, San Sebastián is a seaside resort on a par with Nice and Monte Carlo. It becomes one of Spain's most expensive cities in the summer, when French vacationers descend in droves. It is also, like Bilbao, a center of Basque nationalism.

Every corner of Spain champions its culinary identity, but San Sebastián's refined fare is in a league of its own. Many of the city's restaurants—along with scores of private, all-male eating societies—are in the **Parte Vieja** (old quarter), on the east end of the bay beyond the elegant **Casa Consistorial** (City Hall) and formal **Alderdi Eder** gardens. City Hall began as a casino in 1887; after gambling was outlawed early in the 20th century, the town council moved here from the Plaza de la Constitución, the old quarter's main square. The tiny **Isla de Santa Clara,** right in the entrance to the bay, protects the city from Bay of Biscay storms; this makes La Concha one of the calmest beaches on Spain's entire northern coast. A large hill dramatically dominates each side of the entrance to the bay, too. A visit to **Monte Igueldo,** on the western side of the bay, is a must. (You can drive up for a toll of €1 per person or take the funicular—cable car—for the same amount round-trip; it runs 10 to 8 in summer, 11 to 6 in winter, with departures every 15 minutes.) From the top, you get the remarkable panorama for which San Sebastián is famous: gardens, parks, wide tree-lined boulevards, Belle Epoque buildings, and, of course, the bay itself.

Designed by the world-renowned Spanish architect Rafael Moneo, and situated at the mouth of the Urumea River, the **Kursaal** is San Sebastián's postmodern concert hall, film society, and convention center. The gleaming cubes of glass that make up this bright, rationalist complex were conceived as a perpetuation of the site's natural geography, an attempt to "underline the harmony between the natural and the artificial" and to create a visual stepping-stone between the heights of Monte Urgull and Monte Ulía. It has two auditoriums, a gargantuan banquet hall, meeting rooms, exhibition space, and a sibling set of terraces overlooking the estuary. Martín Berasategui, director of his own restaurant in nearby Lasarte, is the creative force (and financier) behind the Kursaal dining room. ✉ *Av. de la Zurriola, Gros* ☎ *943/003000* ⊕ *www.kursaal.org* 🎫 *€2.50* ⊘ *Guided tours daily at 1:30. For guided tours in English make arrangements in advance.*

Just in from the harbor, in the shadow of Monte Urgull, is the baroque church of **Santa María,** with a stunning carved facade of an arrow-riddled St. Sebastian. The interior is strikingly restful; note the ship above St. Sebastian high on the altar. Looking straight south from the front of Santa María, you can see the facade and spires of the **Catedral Buen Pastor** (Cathedral of the Good Shepherd) across town.

NEED A BREAK?   Steps from the facade of Santa María, in the heart of the old quarter, have a *chocolate con nata*–thick, dark hot chocolate with whipped cream–at the tiny café **Kantoi** (✉ C. Mayor 10, Parte Vieja).

The **Museo de San Telmo** is in a 16th-century monastery behind the Parte Vieja, to the right of the church of Santa María. The former chapel, now a lecture hall, was painted by José María Sert (1876–1945), author of notable works in Barcelona's city hall, London's Tate Gallery, and New York's Waldorf-Astoria hotel. Here, Sert's characteristic tones of gray, gold, violet, and earthy russets enhance the sculptural power of his work, which portrays events from Basque history. The museum displays Basque ethnographic items, such as prehistoric steles once used as grave markers, and paintings by Zuloaga, Ribera, and El Greco. ⊠ *Pl. de Ignacio Zuloaga s/n, Parte Vieja* ☏ *943/424970* ⊠ *Free* ◷ *Tues.–Sat. 10:30–1:30 and 4–8, Sun. 10:30–2.*

San Sebastián is divided by the **Urumea River,** which is crossed by three bridges inspired by late-19th-century French architecture. At the mouth of the Urumea, the incoming surf smashes the rocks with such force that white foam erupts, and the noise is wild and Wagnerian.

OFF THE BEATEN PATH
CHILLIDA LEKU – In the Jáuregui section of Hernani, 10 minutes south of San Sebastián (suggestively close to both Martín Bersategui's restaurant in Lasarte *and* the cider houses of Astigarraga), the Eduardo Chillida Sculpture Garden and Museum, in a 16th-century farmhouse, is a treat for anyone interested in contemporary art. ⊠ *Caserío Zabalaga, Barrio Jáuregui 66, Lasarte* ☏ *943/336006* ⊕ *www.museochillidaleku.com* ⊠ *€8* ◷ *Closed Tues. except July and Aug. and during Holy Week.*

Where to Stay & Eat

$$$$
✗ **Akelaŕe.** On the far side of Monte Igueldo presides Chef Pedro Subijana, one of the most respected and creative chefs in the Basque Country. Prepare for tastes of all kinds, from Pop Rocks in blood sausage to mustard ice cream on tangerine peels. His "straight" dishes are impeccable: try the venison with apple and smoked chestnuts or the *lubina* (sea bass) with goose barnacles. ⊠ *Barrio de Igueldo, Igueldo* ☏ *943/212052 or 943/214086* ⚉ *Reservations essential* ⊟ *AE, DC, MC, V* ◷ *Closed Feb., Oct. 1–15, Tues. Jan.–June, and Mon. except holidays and evenings preceding holidays. No dinner Sun.*

$$$$
FodoŕsChoice
★
✗ **Arzak.** Renowned chef Juan Mari Arzak's little house at the crest of Alto de Miracruz on the eastern outskirts of San Sebastián is internationally famous, so reserve well in advance. Traditional Basque preparations are enhanced by Arzakian innovations designed to bring out the best in the natural products. The ongoing culinary dialogue between Juan Mari and his daughter Elena is one of the most endearing attractions here. They may not always agree, but it's all in the family, and the food just gets better and better. The sauces are perfect and every dish looks beautiful, but the prices (even of appetizers) are astronomical. Treat yourself to a remarkable dessert of chocolate with pine nuts. ⊠ *Alto de Miracruz 21, Alto de Miracruz* ☏ *943/278465* ☏ *943/272753* ⚉ *Reservations essential* ⊟ *AE, DC, MC, V* ◷ *Closed Mon., last 2 wks in June, and Nov. 5–29. No dinner Sun.*

$$$$
FodoŕsChoice
★
✗ **Martín Berasategui.** A sure bet here is the *lubina asada con jugo de habas, vainas, cebolletas y tallarines de chipirón* (roast sea bass with juice of fava beans, green beans, baby onions, and cuttlefish shavings), but go with whatever Martín suggests, especially if it's woodcock, *pichón de Bresse* (Bresse wood pigeon), or any other kind of game. The site of San Sebastián's racetrack, Lasarte is 8 km (5 mi) south of San Sebastián. ⊠ *Loidi Kalea 4, Lasarte* ☏ *943/366471* ⊟ *AE, DC, MC, V* ◷ *Closed Mon., Tues., and mid-Dec.–mid-Jan. No lunch Sat. No dinner Sun.*

$$$$ ✕ **Mugaritz.** This farmhouse in the hills above Errentería 8 km (5 mi)
Fodor'sChoice northeast of San Sebastián is surrounded by spices and herbs tended by
★ boy-genius chef Andoni Luis Aduriz and his crew. In a rustic setting with
, a modern, open feeling, Aduriz demonstrates his mastery over vegetables, foie, and combining seafood with products of the nearby fields and
forest. If you can resist the tasting menu and order carefully à la carte,
Aduriz's inventive, contemporary cuisine is within reach of the non-tycoon budget at about €65 a head. ⊠ *Aldura Aldea 20-Otzazulueta Baserria, Errenteria* ☎ *943/518343* ▤ *AE, DC, MC, V* ⊗ *Closed Mon., Holy
wk, and Dec. 15–Jan. 15. No dinner Sun. No lunch Tues.*

★ **$$$$** ✕ **Urepel.** The cuisine balances classic and contemporary elements in a
felicitous way. The *chicharro al escama dorada* (a skinned, deboned mackerel served under a layer of golden-brown sliced potatoes) is a typical
Urepel invention, as is the unbeatable and unusual dish of foie gras
wrapped with veal. The appetizer of finely carmelized scallops with caviar
is also excellent. There's no head chef; the kitchen staff works as a team,
in prototypically Basque egalitarian fashion. ⊠ *Paseo de Salamanca 3,
Parte Vieja* ☎ *943/424040* ▤ *AE, DC, MC, V* ⊗ *Closed Sun., Tues.,
Christmas and Easter wks, and three wks in July.*

$$$$ ✕ **Zuberoa.** Working in a 15th-century Basque farmhouse 9½ km (6 mi)
Fodor'sChoice northeast of San Sebastián just outside the village of Oiartzun, Hilario
★ Arbelaitz has long been one of San Sebastián's most celebrated chefs.
His original yet simple management of prime raw materials such as spring
cuttlefish or woodcock has earned him a spot as one of Spain's top half
dozen culinary stars. ⊠ *Plaza Bekosoro 1, Oiartzun* ☎ *943/491228*
▤ *AE, DC, MC, V* ⊗ *Closed Sun., Wed., Dec. 1–15, Apr. 21–May 5,
and Oct. 15–30.*

$$$–$$$$ ✕ **Kursaal.** This bright, minimalist space, part of Rafael Moneo's dazzling Palacio de Congresos between the Urumea River and the Zurriola
beach, serves a lighter, less complex version of traditional Basque dishes
along with original creations by chef Raúl Cabrega. Martín Berasategui
is the guiding culinary force behind this establishment, as he is in Bilbao's Guggenheim restaurant. Day or night, the corner table over the
crashing surf is a fine spot for inventive creations such as a postmodern interpretation of marmitako (tuna stew) featuring tiger prawns in
a pipérade of ricotta, shallots, zucchini, Iberian bacon bits, and chicken
broth. The dark pichón de Bresse (Bresse pigeon) is superb, as is the chestnut soup. ⊠ *Zurriola Pasealekua 1, Gros* ☎ *943/003162* ▤ *AE, DC,
MC, V* ⊗ *Closed Mon. and Dec. 20–Jan. 10. No dinner Sun.*

$–$$$ ✕ **Sidrería Petritegui.** For hearty dining and a certain amount of splashing around in hard cider, make this short excursion east of San Sebastián.
Gigantic wooden barrels line the walls, and tables are piled with tortilla de bacalao (codfish omelet), txuleta de buey (thick chunks of beef),
the smoky local sheep's-milk cheese from the town of Idiazabal, and,
for dessert, walnuts and *membrillo* (quince jelly). ⊠ *Ctra. San
Sebastián–Hernani, Km 7, Astigarraga* ☎ *943/457188* ▤ *No credit
cards* ⊗ *No lunch weekdays.*

★ **$$$$** ▦ **Hotel María Cristina.** The graceful beauty of the Belle Epoque is embodied in San Sebastián's most luxurious hotel, which sits on the elegant west bank of the Urumea River. The grandeur continues in salons filled with Oriental rugs, potted palms, and Carrara marble columns, and in bedrooms to match—with gold fixtures and wood wardrobes. Marble bathrooms add still more style. A piano player pounds out an eclectic medley of tunes nightly at the bar. ⊠ *Okendo 1, Centro, 20004* ☎ *943/437600* 🖷 *943/437676* ⊕ *www.westin.com* 🖙 *108 rooms, 28 suites ₺ Restaurant, room service, in-room safes, minibars, cable TV, in-room data ports, massage, bar, piano, babysitting, laundry service, business services, meeting rooms, parking (fee), no-smoking rooms* ⊟ *AE, DC, MC, V.*

$$$-$$$$ 🏨 **Londres y de Inglaterra.** On the promenade above La Concha, this stately hotel has an old-world aesthetic that informs the bright, formal lobby and continues throughout the hotel. The bar and restaurant face the bay, and the guest rooms with views out to sea are the best in town. ⊠ *Zubieta 2, La Concha, 20007* ☎ *943/440770* 🖷 *943/440491* ⊕ *www.hlondres.com* 🖙 *139 rooms, 9 suites ₺ Restaurant, tea shop, minibars, cable TV, bar, casino, meeting rooms, parking (fee)* ⊟ *AE, DC, MC, V.*

$$$ 🏨 **Europa.** A block from the beach and a 15-minute walk around La Concha from the booming Parte Vieja, this small Donosti hotel is staffed by savvy professionals eager to help you make the most of your time in town. Rooms are of moderate size but impeccably equipped and comfortable. ⊠ *San Martín 52, Centro, 20007* ☎ *943/470880* 🖷 *943/471730* 🖙 *68 rooms ₺ Restaurant, minibars, cable TV, bar, parking (fee)* ⊟ *AE, DC, MC, V.*

$$-$$$ 🏨 **Hotel Parma.** Overlooking the Kursaal and the Zurriola beach at the mouth of the Urumea River, this small but shiny modern hotel is also at the edge of the Parte Vieja, San Sebastián's prime grazing area for tapas and vinos. Some of the cheerfully decorated rooms (though not all) have views northeast out to sea. ⊠ *Salamanca Pasealekua 10, Parte Vieja, 20003* ☎ *943/428893* 🖷 *943/424082* ⊕ *www.hotelparma.com* 🖙 *27 rooms ₺ Bar* ⊟ *AE, DC, MC, V.*

$ 🏨 **Aristondo.** A 15-minute drive above San Sebastián on Monte Igueldo, this comfortable farmhouse is a scenic and economical place to stay. Other nearby rural lodging options include farmhouses Izen Eder and Pilotegui. ⊠ *Camino de Pilotegui 70, Igueldo, 20007* ☎ *943/215558* ⊕ *www.nekatur.net* 🖙 *16 rooms ₺ Breakfast room, garden, free parking* ⊟ *No credit cards.*

Tapas Bars

Aloña Berri Bar. Perennial winner of tapa championships, this place across the Urumea River in Gros is well worth the walk. José Ramon Elizondo's miniature creations, from *contraste de pato* (duck à l'orange) to his Moorish-based *bastela de pichón* (pigeon pie), are merely stupendous. Order the excellent crisp asparagus coated with burnt garlic. ⊠ *C. Bermingham 24, Gros* ☎ *943/290818.*

Astelena. On the northeast corner of Plaza de la Constitución, this *bar de toda la vida* (lifetime favorite bar) is famous for its *pastel de pescado* (fish pudding). ⊠ *C. Iñigo 1, Parte Vieja* ☎ *943/425245.*

Bar Ganbara. Near Plaza de la Constitución, morsels here range from shrimp and asparagus to *jamón ibérico* (Iberian acorn-fed ham) on croissants to anchovies, sea urchins, and wild mushrooms in season. ⊠ *C. San Jerónimo 21, Parte Vieja* ☎ *943/422575.*

Bar Gorriti. Next to La Brecha market, this traditional little pintxos bar is a classic, filled with good cheer and delicious tapas. ⊠ *C. San Juan 3, Parte Vieja* ☎ *943/428353.*

Bar Ormazabal. You may not have *thought* you were starving, but when you catch a glimpse of the multicolor, polytextured display that goes up on the Ormazabal bar at midday, hunger pangs will really kick in. ⊠ *C. 31 de Agosto 22, Parte Vieja* ☎ *943/429907.*

Bergara Bar. Just down the street from Aloñ Berri Bar, on the corner of Artexte and Bermingham, you'll find a good selection of tasty pintxos. ⊠ *Artexte 8, Gros.*

Bernardo Etxea. This hangout for locals during the week and everyone else on weekends serves excellent morsels: fried peppers, octopus, salmon with salsa, and especially fine pimientos with anchovies. ⊠ *C. Puerto 7, Parte Vieja* ☎ *943/422055.*

Casa Vallés. Freshly prepared creations go up on the bar at midday and again in the early evening. Beloved by locals, the bar combines great value with excellent food. ⊠ *Reyes Católicos 10, Amara* ☎ *943/452210.*

Casa Vergara. This cozy bar, in front of the Santa María del Coro church, is always filled with reverent tapas devotees; the counter is always piled high with morsels. ⊠ *C. Mayor 21, Parte Vieja* ☎ *943/431073.*

La Cepa. This booming and boisterous tavern is one of the all-time standards. Everything from the Iberian ham to the little olive, pepper, and anchovy combos called "penalties" will whet your appetite. ⊠ *C. 31 de Agosto 7, Parte Vieja* ☎ *943/426394.*

Nightlife & the Arts

Glitterati descend on San Sebastián for its international film festival in the second half of September. Exact dates vary; ask the tourist office on Calle Fueros (☎ 943/426282) or read the local press for details. The same goes for the late-July jazz festival, which draws many of the world's top performers. At night, look for *copas* or *potes* (both "drinks"), and general cruising in and around the Parte Vieja. The **Kursaal** (⊠ Av. de la Zurriola ☎ 943/003000) houses the Orquesta Sinfónica de Euskadi and is the favored venue for ballet, opera, theater, and jazz. There are varied programs of theater, dance, and more at **Teatro Victoria Eugenia** (⊠ Reina Regente s/n, Centro ☎ 943/481155 or 943/481160).

Filled with couples and night owls, **Bideluze** (⊠ Pl. de Guipúzcoa 14, Centro ☎ 943/460219) is always alive. **Akerbeltz** (⊠ Mari Kalea 10, Parte Vieja ☎ 943/460934), at the corner over the port to the left of Santa María del Coro and the Gaztelubide eating society, is a cozy late-night refuge. San Sebastián's top disco is **Bataplan** (⊠ Paseo de la Concha s/n, Centro ☎ 943/460439), near the western end of La Concha. **La Rotonda** (⊠ Paseo de la Concha 6, Centro ☎ 943/429095), across the street from Bataplan, below Miraconcha, is a top nightspot. **Kabutzia** (⊠ Paseo del Muelle s/n, Centro ☎ 943/429725), above the Club Nautico seaward from the Casino, is a busy night haunt. **Discóbolo** (⊠ Blvd. Zumardía 27, Centro ☎ 943/217678), near the Parte Vieja, gets pretty incandescent. **Ku** (⊠ Ctra. Monte Igueldo s/n, Igueldo ☎ 943/212050), up on the hill, has been going strong for three decades.

Shopping

San Sebastián is nonpareil for stylish home furnishings and clothing. Wander Calle San Martín and the surrounding pedestrian-only streets to see what's in the windows. **Ponsol** (⊠ C. Narrica 4, Parte Vieja ☎ 943/420876) is the best place to buy Basque berets (called *boinas* in Spanish and txapelas in Basque); the Leclerq family has been hatting (and clothing) Donostiarras for three generations. **Bilintx** (⊠ C. Fermín Calbetón 21, Parte Vieja ☎ 943/420080) is one of Donosti's best bookstores. Stop into **Maitiena** (⊠ Av. Libertad 32, Centro ☎ 943/424721) for a fabulous selection of chocolates.

3

Pasajes de San Juan

㉙ *10 km (6 mi) east of San Sebastián.*

Generally marked as Pasaia Donibane, in Euskera, there are actually three towns around the commercial port of Rentería: **Pasajes Ancho,** an industrial port; **Pasajes de San Pedro,** a large fishing harbor; and historic **Pasajes de San Juan,** a colorful cluster of 18th- and 19th-century buildings along the channel to the sea. Best reached by driving into Pasajes de San Pedro, on the San Sebastián side of the strait, and catching a launch across the mouth of the harbor (about €0.50, depending on the time of day), this is too sweet a side trip to pass up. In 1777, at the age of 20, General Lafayette set out from Pasajes de San Juan to aid the American Revolution. Victor Hugo spent the summer of 1843 here writing his *Voyage aux Pyrenees.* The **Victor Hugo House** is the home of the tourist office and has an exhibit of traditional village dress. **Ontziola,** a research center for traditional wooden boat design, is directed by Xavier Agote, who taught boat-building in Rockland, Maine. Pasajes de San Juan can be reached via Pasajes de San Pedro from San Sebastián by cab or bus; if you prefer to go on foot, follow the red-and-white-blazed GR trail that begins at the east end of the Zurriola beach—you're in for a spectacular three-hour hike along the rocky coast. By car, take N1 for France and, after passing Juan Mari Arzak's landmark restaurant at Alto de Miracruz, look for a marked left turn into Pasaia or Pasajes de San Pedro.

Where to Eat

$$$–$$$$ ✕ **Casa Cámara.** Four generations ago, Pablo Cámara turned this old fishing wharf on the narrows into a first-class restaurant. The dining room has lovely views and a central tank from which live lobsters and crayfish are hauled up for your inspection. Try *cangrejo del mar* (spider crab with vegetable sauce) or the superb *merluza con salsa verde* (hake in green sauce). ⊠ *Pasajes de San Juan* ☎ 943/523699 ⚲ *Reservations essential* ▤ *AE, DC, MC, V* ☉ *Closed Mon. No dinner Sun.*

$$–$$$ ✕ **Txulotxo.** Cozy and friendly, this exceptional restaurant sits on stilts
Fodor'sChoice at the edge of the Rentería ship passage, perpetually perched in the shadow
★ of the occasional freighter passing only a dozen yards away. The *sopa de pescado* (fish soup), thick and piping hot, is nonpareil, as are the fresh grilled sole and monkfish and the pimiento-wrapped bacalao (codfish). Make sure you leave some time to stroll around town. ⊠ *Pasajes de San*

Juan ☎ 943/523952 🖷 943/519601 🖎 *Reservations essential* ▤ *AE,*
DC, MC, V ☉ *Closed Tues. and Dec. 23–Jan. 15. No dinner Sun.*

Hondarribia

㉚ *12 km (7 mi) east of Pasajes.*

Hondarribia (Fuenterrabía, in Castilian Spanish) is the last fishing port
before the French border. Lined with fishermen's homes and small fishing boats, the harbor is a beautiful but touristy spot. If you have a taste
for history, follow signs up the hill to the medieval bastion and onetime
castle of Carlos V, now a parador.

Where to Stay & Eat

$$$$ ✕ **Alameda.** Hot young Hondarribia star chef Gorka Txapartegi opened
this restaurant in 1997 after working with, among others, Martín Berasategui. The elegantly restored house in upper Hondarribia is a delight,
as are the seasonally rotated combinations of carefully chosen ingredients, from duck to foie gras to vegetables. ⊠ *Minasoroeta 1* ☎ 943/642789
▤ *AE, DC, MC, V* ☉ *Closed Mon., Dec. 24–Jan. 6, June 12–18, and*
Oct. 16–22. No dinner Sun.

$$$$ ✕ **Ramón Roteta.** In a beautiful old villa with an informal garden, this
restaurant serves excellent food and is an easy choice for anyone staying at the parador. Sample the homemade garlic and shrimp pastries
or the rice with vegetables and clams. ⊠ *Villa Ainara, C. Irún 2* ☎ *943/*
641693 ▤ *AE, DC, MC, V* ☉ *Closed Tues., Nov. 15–30, and Feb.*
15–28. No dinner Sun.

$$–$$$ ✕ **La Hermandad de Pescadores.** This "brotherhood" is owned by the local
fishermen's guild and serves simple, hearty fare at reasonable prices. Try
the sopa de pescado or the *almejas a la marinera* (clams in a thick, garlicky sauce). If you come outside of peak hours (2–4 and 9–11), you'll
find space at the long, communal boards. ⊠ *C. Zuloaga s/n* ☎ *943/*
642738 ▤ *AE, DC, MC, V* ☉ *Closed Wed. No dinner Tues.*

$$$–$$$$ ▥ **Parador de Hondarribia.** Replete with suits of armor and other chival-
ric bric-a-brac, this Parador El Emperador is in a superb medieval bas-
tion that dates from the 10th century and housed Spain's founding
Emperor Carlos V in the 16th century. Many rooms have views of the
Bidasoa River and estuary, rife with colorful fishing boats. Reserve ahead
and ask for one of the three "special" rooms, with canopy beds and ba-
ronial appointments; they're worth the extra expense. ⊠ *Pl. de Armas 14,*
20005 ☎ *943/645500* 🖷 *943/642153* ⊕ *www.parador.es* ↝ *36 rooms*
⋔ *Restaurant, minibars, cable TV, bar, meeting rooms, parking (fee)*
▤ *AE, DC, MC, V.*

¢–$ ▥ **Caserío "Artzu."** This family barn and house, with its classic low, wide
roofline, has been here in one form or another for some 800 years. Just
west of the hermitage of Nuestra Señora de Guadalupe, 5 km (3 mi)
above Hondarribia, Artzu offers modernized accommodations in an an-
cient caserío overlooking the junction of the Bidasoa estuary and the
Atlantic. Better hosts than this warm, friendly clan are hard to find.
⊠ *Barrio Montaña, 20280* ☎ *943/640530* ⊕ *www.euskalnet.net/*
casartzu ↝ *6 rooms, 1 with bath* ⋔ *Restaurant, bar; no a/c, no room*
TVs ▤ *No credit cards.*

PAMPLONA & SOUTHERN NAVARRA

Bordering the French Pyrenees and populated largely by Basques, Navarra grows progressively less Basque toward its southern and eastern edges. Pamplona, the ancient Navarran capital, draws crowds with its annual feast of San Fermín, but medieval Vitoria, in the Basque province of Alava, is largely undiscovered by tourists. Olite, south of Pamplona, has a storybook castle, and the towns of Puente la Reina and Estella are visually indelible stops on the Camino de Santiago.

3

Pamplona

 *79 km (47 mi) southeast of San Sebastián.*

Pamplona (Iruña, in Euskera) is known worldwide for its running of the bulls, made famous by Ernest Hemingway in his 1926 novel *The Sun Also Rises*. The occasion is the festival of San Fermín, July 6 to 14, when Pamplona's population triples (along with hotel rates), so reserve rooms months in advance. Tickets to the bullfights (*corridas*), as opposed to the running (*encierro,* meaning "enclosing"), to which access is free, can be difficult to get. Every morning at 7 sharp a skyrocket is shot off, and the bulls kept overnight in the corrals at the edge of town are run through a series of closed-off streets leading to the bullring, a 902-yard dash. Running before them are Spaniards and foreigners feeling festive enough to risk a goring, most wearing the traditional white shirts and trousers with red neckerchiefs and carrying rolled-up newspapers. If all goes well—no bulls separated from the pack, no mayhem—the bulls arrive in the ring in 2½ minutes. The degree of peril in the encierro is difficult to gauge. Serious injuries occur nearly every day; deaths are rare but always a possibility. What's certain is the sense of danger, the mob hysteria, and the exhilaration.

Founded by the Roman emperor Pompey as Pompaelo, or Pameiopolis, Pamplona was successively taken by the Franks, the Goths, and the Moors. In 750, the Pamplonicas put themselves under the protection of Charlemagne and managed to expel the Arabs temporarily. But the foreign commander took advantage of this trust to destroy the city walls, so that when he was driven out once more by the Moors, the Navarrese took their revenge, ambushing and slaughtering the retreating Frankish army as it fled over the Pyrenees through the mountain pass of Roncesvalles in 778. This is the episode depicted in the 11th-century *Song of Roland,* although the French author chose to cast the aggressors as Moors. For centuries after that, Pamplona remained three argumentative towns until they were forcibly incorporated into one city by Carlos III (the Noble, 1387–1425) of Navarra.

Pamplona's **cathedral,** set near the portion of the ancient walls rebuilt in the 17th century, is one of the most important religious buildings in northern Spain, thanks to the fragile grace and gabled Gothic arches of its cloister. Inside are the tombs of Carlos III and his wife, marked by an alabaster sculpture. The **Museo Diocesano** (Diocesan Museum) houses religious art from the Middle Ages and the Renaissance. ⊠ C.

Running with the Bulls

IN *THE SUN ALSO RISES,* Hemingway describes the Pamplona *encierro* (enclosing) in anything but romantic terms. Jake Barnes hears the rocket, steps out on his balcony, and watches the crowd run by: men in white with red sashes and neckerchiefs, those behind running faster, then the bulls. "One man fell, rolled to the gutter, and lay quiet." A textbook move, and first-rate observation and reporting. An experienced runner who falls remains motionless (bulls respond to movement.) In the next encierro in the novel, a man is gored through and through and dies. The waiter at the Iruña café mutters, "You hear? Muerto. Dead. He's dead. With a horn through him. All for morning fun. . . . "

Despite this, generations of young Americans and other internationals have turned this barnyard bull-management maneuver into the Western world's most famous rite of passage. The idea is simple: 6 fighting bulls are guided through the streets by 8 to 10 *cabestros,* or steers (also known as *mansos,* meaning "tame"). The bulls are herded through the bullring to the holding pens from which they will emerge to be fought that afternoon. The course covers 924 yards. The Cuesta de Santo Domingo down to the corrals is the most dangerous part of the run, high in terror and low in elapsed time. The walls are sheer, and the bulls pass quickly. The fear here is that of a bull—as a result of some personal issue or idiosyncrasy—hooking along the wall of the Military Hospital on his way up the hill, forcing runners out in front of the speeding pack in a classic hammer and anvil movement. Mercaderes is

next, cutting left for about 100 yards by the town hall, then right up Calle Estafeta. The outside of each turn and the centrifugal force of 10,000 kilos (22,000 pounds) of bulls and steers are to be avoided here.

Calle Estafeta is the bread and butter of the run, the longest (about 400 yards), straightest, and least complicated part of the course. The classic run, a perfect blend of form and function, is to remain ahead of the horns for as long as possible, fading to the side when overtaken. The long gallop up Calle Estafeta is the place to try to do it. The trickiest part of running with the bulls is splitting your vision so that with one eye you keep track of the bulls behind you and with the other you keep from falling over runners ahead of you.

At the end of Estafeta the course descends left through the *callejón,* the narrow tunnel, into the bullring. The bulls move more slowly here, uncertain of their weak forelegs, allowing runners to stay close and even to touch them as they glide down into the tunnel. The only uncertainty is whether there will be a pileup, in the tunnel. The most dramatic photographs of the encierro have been taken here, as the galloping pack slams through what occasionally turns into a solid wall of humanity. If all goes well—no bulls separated from the pack, no mayhem—the bulls will have arrived in the ring in less than three minutes.

The cardinal crime, punishable by a $1,000 fine, is to attempt to attract the bull, thus removing him from the pack and creating a deadly danger. There were 13 deaths during the 20th century, the last one on July 13, 1995.

Curia s/n ☎ *948/210827* ✉ *€4.50* ⊙ *Museum Weekdays 10–1:30 and 4–7, Sat. 10–1:30.*

On Calle Santo Domingo, in a 16th-century building once used as a hospital for pilgrims on their way to Santiago de Compostela, is the **Museo de Navarra,** with a collection of regional archaeological artifacts and historical costumes. ⊠ *C. Jaranta s/n* ☎ *848/426492* ✉ *€3.50* ⊙ *Tues.–Sat. 9–2 and 5–7, Sun. 9–2.*

Pamplona's most remarkable civil building is the ornate, 18th-century **ayuntamiento,** on the Plaza Consistorial, which over the years has acquired a blackish color that sets off its gilded balconies. Stop in to see the wood-and-marble interior.

3

NEED A BREAK?

Pamplona's gentry has been flocking to the ornate, French-style **Café Iruña** (⊠ Pl. del Castillo 44) since 1888. Beyond the stand-up bar is a bingo hall (you must be 18 to play). The café is open daily 5 PM to 3 AM.

One of Pamplona's greatest charms is the warren of small streets near the **Plaza del Castillo** (especially Calle San Nicolás), which are filled with restaurants, taverns, and bars. Pamplonicas are hardy sorts, well known for their eagerness and capacity to eat and drink. The central **Ciudadela,** an ancient fortress, is a parkland of promenades and pools. Walk through in late afternoon, the time of the *paseo* (traditional stroll), for a taste of everyday life here.

Edificio Baluarte. The Palacio de Congresos y Auditorio de Navarra, built in 2003 by local architectural star Patxi Mangado, is a sleek assemblage of black Zimbabwean granite with a concert hall of exquisite acoustical perfection made of beechwood from Navarra's famed Irati *haya* (beech) forest. Performances and concerts from opera to ballet are held in this modern venue built on the remains of one of the five bastions of Pamplona's 16th-century Ciudadela. ⊠ *Plaza del Baluarte* ☎ *948/066066* ⊕ *www.baluarte.com.*

OFF THE BEATEN PATH

FUNDACIÓN–MUSEO JORGE OTEIZA – Just 8 km (5 mi) northeast of Pamplona on the road toward France, this museum dedicated to the father of modern Basque art is a must-visit. Jorge Oteiza (1908–2003), in his seminal treatise *Quosque Tandem,* called for Basque artists to find an aesthetic of their own, instead of attempting to become part of the rich Spanish canon. Rejecting ornamentation in favor of essential form and a noninvasive use of space, Oteiza created a school of artists—of which Eduardo Chillida (1924–2002) was the most famous sculptor. ⊠ *Alzuza, Ctra. N150, Km 8, from Pamplona* ☎ *948/332074* ⊕ *www.museooteiza.org* ✉ *€4* ⊙ *Tues.–Fri. 10–3, weekends 11–7.*

Where to Stay & Eat

$$$–$$$$ ✕ **Hartza.** Archaic and elegant, this rustic place serves some of the most creative cuisine in Pamplona. Try the *oca con jugo de trufa y manzana* (goose with apple and truffle sauce). ⊠ *Juan de Labrit 19* ☎ *948/224568* ▤ *AE, DC, MC, V* ⊙ *Closed Mon., late July–late Aug., and late Dec.–early Jan. No dinner Sun.*

$$$-$$$$ ✕ **Josetxo.** This warm, elegant family-run restaurant is one of Pamplona's finest. Specialties include *hojaldre de marisco* (shellfish pastry), an *ensalada de langosta* (lobster salad) appetizer, and *muslo de pichón relleno de trufa y foie* (pigeon stuffed with truffles and foie gras). ✉ *Príncipe de Viana 1* ☎ *948/222097* ▭ *AE, DC, MC, V* ⊙ *Closed Sun. except during San Fermín, and Aug.*

$-$$$ ✕ **Erburu.** In the heart of the nightlife district, this dark, wood-beam restaurant is a true find, frequented by Pamplonans in the know. Come here to dine or just to sample tapas at the bar. Standouts are the Basque classic merluza con salsa verde (hake in green sauce) and any of the dishes made with *alcochofas* (artichokes). ✉ *San Lorenzo 19–21* ☎ *948/225169* ▭ *AE, DC, MC, V* ⊙ *Closed Mon. and last 2 wks in July.*

$$ ✕▣ **Casa Otano.** This friendly, tumultuous hotel and restaurant is simple and well placed, right in the middle of the tapas-and-wine circuit and just a few paces from Pamplona's main square. The restaurant downstairs ($-$$$) serves hearty Basque fare. The general energy level is consistent with the madness that will be raging in the street if you come during San Fermín. ✉ *San Nicolás 5, 31001* ☎ *948/225095* 🖷 *948/212012* ⊕ *www.casaotano.com* ➮ *15 rooms* ⚑ *Restaurant, bar; no a/c* ▭ *AE, DC, MC, V* ⊙ *Closed last 2 wks in July.*

$$$-$$$$ ▣ **Los Tres Reyes.** Named for the three kings of Navarra, Aragón, and Castile—who, it was said, could meet at La Mesa de los Tres Reyes, in the Pyrenees, without stepping out of their respective realms—this modern glass-and-stone refuge operates on the same principle: Come to Pamplona and find all the comforts of home. ✉ *C. de la Taconera s/n, 31001* ☎ *948/226600* 🖷 *948/222930* ⊕ *www.hotel3reyes.com* ➮ *152 rooms, 8 suites* ⚑ *Restaurant, cafeteria, minibars, cable TV, pool, health club, hair salon, bar, piano bar, meeting rooms, car rental, parking (fee)* ▭ *AE, DC, MC, V.*

Nightlife & the Arts

The city has a thumping student life year-round, especially along the length of Calle San Nicolas. For an ultra-postmodern nightspot, try **Dodo Club** (✉ San Roque 7 ☎ 948/198989), where breakfast, lunch, free Wi-Fi Internet connection, and, finally, DJs keep things lively around the clock. **El Otro** (✉ Paulino Caballero 52 ☎ 948/132543) is perfect for a quiet libation, and known for its see-out bathrooms with one-way glass. In August, the **Festivales de Navarra** bring theater and other events to Pamplona. A varied summer program of concerts, ballet, and zarzuela is always in the offing; contact the **Teatro Gayarre** (✉ Av. Carlos III Noble 1 ☎ 948/220139) for information.

Shopping

Botas are the wineskins from which Basques typically drink at bullfights or during fiestas. The art lies in drinking a stream of wine from a bota held at arm's length—without spilling a drop, if you want to maintain your honor (not to mention your shirt). The neckerchiefs worn for the running of the bulls are sold in various shops, as are *gerrikos*, the wide belts worn by Basque sportsmen during contests of strength, to hold in overstressed organs. You can buy botas in any Basque town, but Pamplona's **Anel** (✉ C. Comedías 7) sells the best brand, Las Tres Zetas—

"The Three Zs," written as ZZZ. For sweets, try **Salcedo** (⊠ C. Estafeta 37), open since 1800, which invented and still sells almond-based *mantecadas* (powder cakes), as well as *coronillas* (delightful almond-and-cream concoctions). **Hijas de C. Lozano** (⊠ C. Zapatería 11) sells *café y leche* (coffee and milk) toffees that are prized all over Spain.

Olite

③ *41 km (25 mi) south of Pamplona.*

A storybook castle marooned on the plains of Navarra, Olite is an unforgettable glimpse into the life of Spain in the Middle Ages. The 11th-century church of **San Pedro** is interesting for its finely worked Romanesque cloisters and portal. The town's parador is part of a **castle** restored by Carlos III in the French style—ramparts, crenellated battlements, and watchtowers. You can walk the ramparts in the section not occupied by the parador. ⊡ €3 ⊙ *Daily 10–2 and 4–5.*

Where to Stay & Eat

$$$ ✕⊡ **Parador Príncipe de Viana.** This castle parador is a flight of fancy,
Fodor'sChoice named for the grandson of Carlos III, who spent his life here. It's housed
★   in part of Olite's castle complex, and the chivalric tone is well preserved, with grand salons, secret stairways, heraldic tapestries, and the odd suit of armor. ⊠ *Pl. de los Teobaldos 2, 31390* ☎ *948/740000* 🖷 *948/740201* ⊕ *www.parador.es* ⤳ *43 rooms* ⚭ *Restaurant, minibars, bar, meeting rooms* 🖃 *AE, DC, MC, V.*

Puente la Reina

③ *31 km (19 mi) west of Olite, 24 km (15 mi) south of Pamplona.*

Puente la Reina (Gares, in Euskera) is an important nexus on the Camino de Santiago: the junction of the two pilgrimage routes from northern Europe, one passing through Somport and Jaca and the other through Roncesvalles and Pamplona. A bronze sculpture of a pilgrim marks the spot. The graceful medieval bridge over the river Arga was built for pilgrims by Navarran King Sancho VII el Fuerte (the Strong) in the 11th century. The streets, particularly Calle Mayor, are lined with tiny, ancient houses. The church of **Santiago** (St. James; ⊠ C. Mayor) is known for its gold sculpture of the saint. The **Iglesia del Crucifijo** (Church of the Crucifix; ⊠ Ctra. de Pamplona s/n) has a notably expressive wooden sculpture of Christ on a Y-shape cross, gift of a 14th-century pilgrim. The octagonal church of **Santa María de Eunate** (⊠ 5 km [3 mi] east of Puente la Reina) was once used as a burial place for pilgrims who didn't make it. The church of **San Román** (⊠ 6 km [4 mi] west of Puente la Reina), in the restored village of Cirauqui, has an extraordinarily beautiful carved portal.

Where to Stay & Eat

$$$–$$$$ ✕⊡ **Hotel El Peregrino.** A time-honored haven for weary pilgrims on sound budgets, this handsome stone house north of town is hard to pass up. The rooms are small but charming. Roasts, *menestra de verduras* (Navarran vegetable stew), rack of suckling pig, and hearty bean-and-sausage-based soups are among the star offerings at the restaurant ($$–$$$$). ⊠ *Ctra. Pamplona–Logroño, Km 23, 31100* ☎ *948/340075* 🖷 *948/ 341190* ⊕ *www.hotelelperegrino.com* ⟿ *10 rooms, 3 junior suites* ⚹ *Restaurant, minibars, pool, bar* ▤ *AE, DC, MC, V.*

Estella

㉞ *19 km (12 mi) south of Puente la Reina, 48 km (30 mi) north of Logroño.*

Once the seat of the Royal Court of Navarra, Estella (Lizarra, in Euskera) is an inspiring stop on the Camino de Santiago. Its heart is the arcaded Plaza San Martín, its chief civic monument the 12th-century **Palacio de los Reyes de Navarra** (Palace of the Kings of Navarra). **San Pedro de la Rúa** (⊠ C. San Nicolás s/n) has a beautiful cloister and a stunning carved portal. Across the River Ega from San Pedro, the doorway to the church of **San Miguel** has fantastic relief sculptures of St. Michael the Archangel battling a dragon. The **Iglesia del Santo Sepulcro** (Church of the Holy Sepulchre; ⊠ C. Curtidores s/n) has a beautiful fluted portal. **Santa María Jus del Castillo** (⊠ C. Curtidores s/n), converted from a synagogue in 1145, is the only vestige of Estella's medieval Jewish quarter. The **Monasterio de Irache** (⊠ Ctra. de Logroño, Km 3) dates from the 10th century but was later converted by Cistercian monks to a pilgrims' hospital; next door is the famous brass faucet that supplies pilgrims with free-flowing holy wine.

VITORIA & THE RIOJA ALAVESA

Medieval Vitoria, in the Basque province of Alava, is largely undiscovered by tourists, and the Rioja Alavesa and, in particular, Laguardia, rank among the Basque Country's most unforgettable destinations.

Vitoria

㉟ *93 km (56 mi) west of Pamplona, 115 km (71 mi) southwest of San Sebastián, 64 km (40 mi) southeast of Bilbao.*

Vitoria's standard of living has been rated the highest in Spain, based on such criteria as square meters of green space per inhabitant (14), sports and cultural facilities, and pedestrian-only zones. Capital of the Basque Country, and its second-largest city after Bilbao, Vitoria (Gasteiz, in Euskera) is in many ways Euskadi's least Basque city. Neither a maritime nor a mountain enclave, Vitoria occupies the steppelike *meseta de Alava* (Alava plain) and functions as a modern industrial center with a surprisingly medieval *casco antiguo* (old quarter). Founded by Sancho el Sabio (the Wise) in 1181, the city was built largely of granite rather than sandstone, so Vitoria's oldest streets and squares seem especially dark, weathered, and ancient.

Plaza de la Virgen Blanca, in the southwest corner of old Vitoria, is ringed by noble houses with covered arches and white-trim glass galleries. The monument in the center commemorates the Duke of Wellington's defeat of Napoléon's army here in 1813. For lunch, coffee, or tapas, look to the plaza's top left-hand corner for the Cafeteria de la Virgen

Blanca, replete with giant wooden floorboards. The **Plaza de España**, across Virgen Blanca past the monument and the handsome El Victoria café, is an arcaded neoclassical square with the austere elegance typical of formal 19th-century squares all over Spain. The **Plaza del Machete**, overlooking Plaza de España, is named for the sword used by medieval nobility to swear allegiance to the local fueros, or special Basque rights and privileges. A jasper niche in the lateral facade of the Gothic church of **San Miguel** (⊠ Plaza del Machete) contains the Virgen Blanca (White Virgin), Vitoria's patron saint.

The **Palacio de los Alava Esquivel** (⊠ C. de la Soledad) is reached from the Plaza de la Virgen Blanca along Calle de Herrería, which follows the egg-shape outline along the west side of the old city walls. House **No. 27** (⊠ Across from Cantón Anorbin) has elaborately sculpted engravings over the door and a giant coat of arms on the far corner. The house is past the church of San Pedro Apostol. The 15th-century **Torre de Doña Otxanda** (⊠ Before C. de las Carnicerías) houses Vitoria's Museo de Ciencias Naturales (Museum of Natural Sciences).

El Portalón (⊠ C. de la Correría 151), the ancient brick-and-wood house at the corner across from the museum, a hostelry for 500 years, is an excellent restaurant and wine cellar. The **Museo de la Arqueología** (⊠ C. de la Correría) has paleolithic dolmens, Roman art and artifacts, medieval objects, and the famous *stele del jinete* (stele of the horseback rider), an early Basque tombstone. Look at the door nearest the corner in the ocher house at **No. 14** (⊠ At C. Correría and Cantón Apaizgaitegi): its elaborate coat of arms depicts lions and castles, once painted gold and purple. Equally faded trim spirals around the corners of the house, and conch shells appear under scrolls below the windows.

The Torre de los Hurtado de Anda is across from the exquisitely sculpted Gothic doorway on the western facade of the **Catedral de Santa María** (⊠ C. Fray Zacarías Martinez s/n). Go into the courtyard on the west side of this square; in the far right corner, you'll find the sculpted head of a fish protruding from the grass in front of an intensely sculpted door. Walk through Calle Txikitxoa and up Cantón de Santa María behind the cathedral, noting the tiny accretions that have been added to the back of the apse over the centuries, clinging across corners and filling odd spaces. The lovely plateresque facade of the 16th-century **Palacio de Escoriaza-Esquibel** (⊠ C. Fray Zacarías Martinez) overlooks an open space. Don't miss the austere **Palacio Villa Suso** (⊠ C. Fray Zacarías Martinez), built in 1538. It's down toward the Plaza del Machete, across from the church of San Miguel. The **Casa del Cordón** (⊠ C. Cuchillería), a 15th-century structure with a 13th-century tower, stands at No. 24, identifiable by the Franciscan *cordón* (rope) decorating one of the pointed arches on the facade.

★ The 1525 Palacio de Bendaña is home to one of Vitoria's main attractions, the **Museo Fournier de Naipes** (Playing-Card Museum). In 1868 Don Heraclio Fournier founded a playing-card factory, started amassing cards, and eventually found himself with 15,000 sets, the largest and finest such collection in the world. As you survey rooms of hand-painted cards, the distinction between artwork and game piece quickly gets scrambled. The oldest sets date from the 12th century, making them older than the building, and the story parallels the history of printing. The most unusual and finely painted sets come from Japan, India (the Indian cards are round), and the international practice of tarot. One German set has musical bars that can be combined to form hundreds of different waltzes. By the time you reach the 20th-century rooms, contemporary designs have been debunked as unoriginal. You'll never look at cards the same way again. ⊠ *C. Cuchillería 54* ☎ *945/255555* 🖭 *Free* ☉ *Tues.–Fri. 10–2 and 4–6:30, Sat. 10–2, Sun. 11–2.*

Parque de la Florida (⊠ South of Plaza de la Virgen Blanca) is nice respite during a tour of Vitoria. The **Museo Provincial de Armería** (Provincial Arms Museum; ⊠ Paseo Fray Francisco de Vitoria) has prehistoric hatchets, 20th-century pistols, and a sand-table reproduction of the 1813 battle between the Duke of Wellington and the French. The museum is south of the Parque de la Florida. The **Museo de Bellas Artes** (Museum of Fine Arts; ⊠ Paseo Fray Francisco de Vitoria) has paintings by Ribera, Picasso, and the Basque painter Zuloaga. Next door is the Palacio Ajuria-Enea, seat of the Basque government.

OFF THE BEATEN PATH

ARTIUM – Officially titled Centro-Museo Vasco de Arte Contemporáneo, this former bus station as opened in 2002 by King Juan Carlos I, who called it "the third leg of the Basque art triangle, along with the Bilbao Guggenheim and San Sebastián's Chillida Leku." The museum's permanent collection—including 20th- and 21st-century paintings and sculptures by Jorge Oteiza, Eduardo Chillida, Agustín Ibarrola, and Nestor Basterretxea, among many others—makes it one of Spain's finest treasuries of contemporary art. ⊠ *Calle de Francia 24* ☎ *945/209020* ⊕ *www.artium.org* 🖭 €5 ☉ *Tues.–Sun. 11–8.*

Where to Stay & Eat

★ $$$–$$$$ ✕ **El Portalón.** Between the dark, creaky wood floors and staircases and the ancient beams, pillars, and coats of arms, this famous 15th-century inn turns out classical Castillian and Basque specialties that reflect Vitoria's geography and social history. Try the *lomo de cebón asado en su jugo con puré de manzanas* (filet mignon with apple puree) or any of the *merluza* (hake) preparations. ⊠ *C. Correría 151* ☎ *945/142755* ▤ *AE, DC, MC, V* ☉ *Closed Sun., last 3 wks in Aug., Holy Week, and Dec. 24–Jan. 4.*

$$$–$$$$ ✕ **Zaldiarán.** Vitoria's most recent culinary star serves contemporary interpretations of classics and daring combinations of prime ingredients from black truffles to foie (duck or goose liver) to lobster in a sleek and minimalist environment. ⊠ *Av. Gasteiz 21* ☎ *945/134822* ▤ *AE, DC, MC, V* ☉ *Closed Sun. No dinner Tues.*

★ $$$ ✕🛏 **Parador de Argómaniz.** Some 15 minutes east of Vitoria off the N104 road toward Pamplona, this 17th-century palace has panoramic views over the Alava plains and retains a powerful sense of mystery and romance, with long stone hallways punctuated by imposing antiques. Rooms have polished wood floors and huge, terra-cotta-floor bathrooms; some have glass-enclosed sitting areas and/or hot tubs. The wood-beam dining room ($$–$$$$) on the third floor makes each meal feel like a baronial feast. ⊠ *N-I, Km 363, Argómaniz 01192* ☎ *945/*

293200 🖶 *945/293287* 🌐 *www.parador.es* 🛏 *53 rooms* ⚂ *Restaurant, minibars, cable TV, bar, free parking* ▤ *AE, DC, MC, V.*

$–$$$ 🖵 **Canciller Ayala.** This modern structure is handy for in-town comfort, two minutes from the old quarter next to the lush Parque de la Florida. Rooms are bright, streamlined, and beyond reproach, if unremarkable. Standard double rooms may be available at bargain rates in the off-season. ✉ *C. Ramón y Cajal 5, 01007* 🕾 *945/130000* 🖶 *945/133505* 🌐 *www.nh-hotels.com* 🛏 *184 rooms, 1 suite* ⚂ *Restaurant, minibars, bar, meeting rooms, parking (fee)* ▤ *AE, DC, MC, V.*

EN ROUTE Between Vitoria and Logroño, on the north bank of the Ebro River, is the wine-growing Rioja Alavesa region. Either sweep comfortably around on the Madrid road and approach from the west via Haro, Briones (with a lovely medieval bridge), and San Vicente de la Sonsierra, *or* drive south on the slower, curvier A2124 through the Puerto de Herrera pass to the Balcón de La Rioja for a view of the Ebro Valley.

Laguardia

 66 km (40 mi) southeast of Vitoria, 17 km (10 mi) west of Logroño.

Founded in 908 to stand guard, as its name suggests, over Navarra's southwestern flank, Laguardia is on a lofty promontory overlooking the Ebro River and the vineyards of the Rioja Alavesa—La Rioja wine country north of the Ebro in the Basque province of Alava. Flanked by the Sierra de Cantabria, the town rises shiplike, its prow headed north, over the savory sea of surrounding vineyards. Ringed with walls, Laguardia's dense cluster of emblazoned noble facades and stunning patios may have no equal in Spain. Relish the some 50 houses with coats of arms and medieval or Renaissance masonry. The wine cellars and taverns serve excellent local reds, both *vinos del año* (young wines of the year) and *crianzas* (aged three years).

Starting from the 15th-century Puerta de Carnicerías, or Puerta Nueva, the central portal off the parking area on the east side of town, the first landmark is the 16th-century **ayuntamiento,** with its imperial shield of Carlos V. Farther into the square is the current town hall, built in the 19th century. A right down **Calle Santa Engracia** takes you past impressive facades—the floor inside the portal at No. 25 is a lovely stone mosaic, and a walk behind the triple-emblazoned 17th-century facade of No. 19 reveals a stagecoach, floor mosaics, wood beams, an inner porch, and, if you're lucky, the aroma of potato-and-leek soup. Nos. 15 and 9 both have interesting reliefs and masonry. The Puerta de Santa Engracia, with an image of the saint in an overhead niche, opens out to the right, and on the left, at the entrance to Calle Víctor Tapia, house No. 17 bears a coat of arms with the Latin LAUS TIBI (Praise Be to Thee). Laguardia's crown architectural jewel is Spain's only Gothic polychrome portal, on the church of **Santa María de los Reyes.** Protected by a posterior Renaissance facade, the door centers on a lovely, lifelike effigy of La Virgen de los Reyes (Virgin of the Kings), sculpted in the 14th century and painted in the 17th by Juan Francisco de Ribera. Flanking the Virgin are the apostles and biblical scenes.

To the north of the ornate castle and hotel El Collado is the monument to the famous Laguardia composer of fables, Felix María Samaniego (1745–1801), heir to the tradition of Aesop and Lafontaine. Walk around the small, grassy park to the Puerta de Páganos and look right—you can see Laguardia's oldest civil structure, the late-14th-century **Casa de la Primicia,** at Calle Páganos 78 (so named as the place where fresh fruit was sold). If you walk left of the Casa de la Primicia, past several emblazoned houses to Calle Páganos 13, you can see the bodega (wine cellar) at the Posada Mayor de Migueloa, which is usually in full cry. Go through the corridor to the Posada's Calle Mayor entryway and walk up to the **Juanjo San Pedro** gallery at Calle Mayor 1, filled with antiques and artwork.

Where to Stay & Eat

$$–$$$ ✕🏠 **Posada Mayor de Migueloa.** With a tavern at Calle Páganos 13 and
Fodor'sChoice a passageway leading to the stone reception area on Mayor de Migue-
★ loa, this 17th-century palace is a beauty. At the tavern ($$–$$$$), try *patatas a la riojana* (potatoes with chorizo) or *pochas con chorizo y costilla* (beans with sausage and lamb chop). Dinner ranges from beef with foie gras to *mollejas de cordero* (lamb sweetbreads) to *venado con miel y pomelo* (venison with a honey-and-grapefruit sauce). Guest rooms have beautiful, original, rough-hewn ceiling beams. ⊠ *C. Mayor de Migueloa 20, 01300* ☎ *945/621175* 🖷 *945/621022* ⊕ *www.mayordemigueloa.com* 🛏 *8 rooms* ⚐ *Restaurant, bar* ⊟ *AE, DC, MC, V* ☾ *Closed mid-Dec.–mid-Jan.*

$$ ✕🏠 **Marixa.** Aficionados travel great distances to dine in Marixa's lovely restaurant, known for its excellent roasts, views, and value. The heavy, wooden interior is ancient and intimate, and the cuisine ($$–$$$$) is Vasco-Riojano, combining the best of both worlds. Try the *menestra de riojana verduras,* a mixed-vegetable dish, or the *cordero asado a la parrilla,* lamb roasted over coals. Guest rooms are modern, cheery, and carpeted, with views over the medieval walls of Laguardia to the Ebro Valley beyond. ⊠ *C. Sancho Abarca 8, 01300* ☎ *945/600165* 🖷 *945/600202* ⊕ *www.hotelmarixa.com* 🛏 *10 rooms* ⚐ *Restaurant, bar* ⊟ *AE, DC, MC, V* ☾ *Closed mid-Dec.–mid-Jan.*

▌ **HEREDEROS DE MARQUÉS DE RISCAL –** The village of Elciego 6 km (4 mi)
OFF THE southeast of Laguardia is the site of a new Frank Gehry–designed wine-
BEATEN tasting room, restaurant, hotel, and visitor center. Tours of the vineyards—
PATH one of the most historic in La Rioja—as well as the cellars are conducted in various languages, including English. ⊠ *C. Torrea 1, Elciego* ☎ *945/606000* ⊕ *www.marquesderiscal.com* 🖾 *€6* ☾ *Tours Mon.–Sat. 10, noon, and 4.*

LA RIOJA

A natural compendium of highlands, plains, vineyards, and the Ebro River basin, La Rioja has historically produced Spain's finest wines. The area's quarter of a million inhabitants live mainly along the Ebro, in the cities of Logroño, Haro, and Calahorra, but many of its treasures are in the mountains and river valleys. La Rioja's culture and wines both

combine Atlantic and Mediterranean influences, as well as Basque over-
tones and the arid continental ruggedness of Iberia's central meseta.
Drained by the Rivers Oja (hence the name *río oja*), Najerilla, Iregua,
Leza, and Cidacos, La Rioja is composed of the Rioja Alta (Upper
Rioja), the moist and mountainous western end, and the Rioja Baja (Lower
Rioja), the flatter and dryer eastern end, more Mediterranean in climate.
Logroño, the capital, lies between the two.

Logroño

③ *92 km (55 mi) southwest of Pamplona on N-III.*

A busy city of 130,000 and a modern industrial center, Logroño retains
a lovely old quarter between its two bridges, bordered by the Ebro and
the medieval walls. Breton de los Herreros and Muro Francisco de la
Mata are the quarter's most characteristic streets. An important wine-
and tapas-tasting center, **Calle Laurel** and the neighboring streets are collectively known as *el sendero de los elefantes* (the path of the elephants)—an allusion to *trompas* (trunks), Spanish for a snootful. Each
bar is known for a specialty: Bar Soriano for *"champis"* (*champiñones*,
mushrooms), Blanco y Negro for *sepia* (cuttlefish), Casa Lucio for *migas
de pastor* (bread crumbs with garlic and chorizo) and *embuchados*
(crisped, sliced lamb tripe), and La Travesía for *tortillas de patatas* (potato omelets). Order crianza and they'll break out the crystal. A *cosechero*,
wine of the year, is served in small shot glasses, and *reserva* (made with
specially selected grapes aged three years or more in oak and bottle) will
elicit snifters for proper swirling, smelling, and tasting.

Near Logroño, the Roman bridge and the *mirador* (lookout) at **Viguera**
are the main sights in the lower Iregua Valley. Santiago (St. James), according to legend, helped the Christians defeat the Moors at the **Castillo
de Clavijo,** another panoramic spot. The **Leza (Cañon) del Río Leza** is La
Rioja's most dramatic canyon.

Logroño's dominant landmarks are the finest sacred structures in Rioja.
The 11th-century church of the **Imperial de Santa María del Palacio** (✉ C.
Ruavieja s/n) is known as La Aguja (The Needle) for its pyramid-shape,
45-yard Romanesque-Gothic tower. The church of **Santiago el Real**
(Royal St. James; ✉ Plaza de Santiago s/n), reconstructed in the 16th
century, is noted for its equestrian statue of the saint (also known as
Santiago Matamoros—St. James the Moorslayer), which presides over
the main door. **San Bartolomé** (✉ C. San Bartolomé s/n) is a 13th- to 14th-
century French Gothic church with an 11th-century Mudejar tower
and an elaborately sculpted 14th-century Gothic doorway. The **Catedral
de Santa María de La Redonda** (✉ Plaza de los Portales s/n) is a landmark
for its twin baroque towers. Many of Logroño's monuments, such as
the elegant **Puente de Piedra** (Stone Bridge), were built as part of the
Camino de Santiago pilgrimage route.

Where to Stay & Eat

$$–$$$$ ✕ **Asador Emilio.** The Castilian rustic decor here includes a coffered
wood ceiling, which merits a long look. Roast lamb cooked over wood
coals is the specialty, but *aluvias* (kidney beans) and *migas de pastor* (bread

crumbs with garlic and sausage) are hard to resist. ✉ *Republica Argentina 8* ☎ *941/233141* ▭ *AE, DC, MC, V* ☉ *Closed Sun. June–Apr. and Aug.*

$$–$$$ ✕ **El Cachetero.** Local fare based on vegetables is the rule here, but you can also tuck into roast goat or lamb. The cuisine is homespun, its raw materials fresh and seasonally appealing. ✉ *C. Laurel 3* ☎ *941/228463* ▭ *AE, DC, MC, V* ☉ *Closed Sun. and last wk in Aug. No dinner Wed.*

★ $–$$$ ✕ **La Rueda.** Cándida Calleja's upstairs perch over the Calle and Travesía del Laurel tapas-grazing scene is close enough to the action below but removed enough for a breath of fresh air. Memorable dishes include acorn-fed ham or *revuelto de gambas y puntas de espárragos trigueros* (eggs scrambled with shrimp and wild asparagus tips). The downstairs bar serves excellent sepia (cuttlefish) with chilling hits of Rojanda, La Rueda's own fresh young white wine. ✉ *Travesía del Laurel 1* ☎ *941/ 227986* ▭ *AE, DC, MC, V* ☉ *Closed Sun. and Aug.*

$$–$$$ ⊞ **Herencia Rioja.** This modern hotel near the old quarter has contemporary and comfortable rooms, first-rate plumbing, well-trained staff, a fine restaurant, and a healthy, businesslike buzz about it. The halls and corridors are somewhat somber and over-lavish with fabrics, but the functionality of the place makes up for its aesthetic shortcomings. ✉ *Marqués de Murrieta 14, 26005* ☎ *941/210222* 🖷 *941/210206* ⊕ *www.nh-hotels.com* ⤳ *81 rooms, 2 suites* ⌂ *Restaurant, cafeteria, gym, bar* ▭ *AE, DC, MC, V.*

$$–$$$ ⊞ **Marqués de Vallejo.** This family-run hotel is close to, but not overwhelmed by, the food- and wine-tasting frenzy of Calle del Laurel. Rooms are small but intimate, and the best historic sights are nearby. Stash your car in the garage beneath the nearby Plaza del Espolón. ✉ *Marqués de Vallejo 8, 26005* ☎ *941/248333* 🖷 *941/240288* ⊕ *www. hotelmarquesdevallejo.com* ⤳ *30 rooms* ⌂ *Cafeteria, bar, meeting rooms* ▭ *AE, DC, MC, V.*

La Rioja Alta

The Upper Rioja, the most prosperous part of La Rioja's wine country, extends from the Ebro River to the Sierra de la Demanda. La Rioja Alta has the most fertile soil, the best vineyards and agriculture, the most impressive castles and monasteries, a ski resort at Ezcaray, and the historical economic advantage of being on the Camino de Santiago. From Logroño, drive 12 km (7 mi) west on N120 to **Navarrete** to see its noble houses and the baroque altarpiece in Asunción church.

Nájera, 15 km (9 mi) west of Navarrete, was the court of the kings of Navarra and capital of Navarra and La Rioja until 1076, when La Rioja became part of Castile and the residence of the Castilian royal family. The monastery of **Santa María la Real** (☎ *941/363650*), "pantheon of kings," is distinguished by its 16th-century Claustro de los Caballeros (Cavaliers' Cloister), a flamboyant Gothic structure with 24 lacy plateresque Renaissance arches overlooking a grassy patio. The sculpted 12th-century tomb of Doña Blanca de Navarra is the monastery's best-known sarcophagus, and the 67 Flamboyant Gothic choir stalls, dating from 1495, are some of Spain's best.

Santo Domingo de la Calzada, 20 km (12 mi) west of Nájera on the N120, has always been a key stop on the Camino. Santo Domingo was an 11th-century saint who built roads and bridges for pilgrims and founded the hospital that is now the town's parador. The cathedral is a Romanesque-Gothic pile containing the saint's tomb, choir murals, and a walnut altarpiece carved by Damià Forment in 1541. The live hen and rooster in a plateresque stone chicken coop commemorate a legendary local miracle in which a pair of roasted fowl came back to life to protest the innocence of a pilgrim hanged for theft. Be sure to stroll through the town's beautifully preserved medieval quarter.

Enter the **Sierra de la Demanda** by heading south 14 km (8½ mi) on LO–810. Your first stop is the town of **Ezcaray,** with its aristocratic houses emblazoned with family crests, of which the **Palacio del Conde de Torremúzquiz** (Palace of the Count of Torremúzquiz) is the most distinguished. Good excursions from here are the Valdezcaray winter-sports center; the source of the River Oja at Llano de la Casa; La Rioja's highest point, at the 7,494-foot Pico de San Lorenzo; and the Romanesque church of Tres Fuentes, at Valgañón. The town of **San Millán de la Cogolla** is southeast of Santo Domingo de la Calzada. Take LO–809 southeast through Berceo to the Monasterio de Yuso, where a 10th-century manuscript on St. Augustine's *Glosas Emilianenses* has notes in what is considered the earliest example of the Spanish language, the vernacular Latin dialect known as Roman paladino. The nearby Visigothic Monasterio de Suso is where Gonzalo de Berceo, recognized as the first Castilian poet, wrote and recited his 13th-century verse in the Castilian tongue, now the language of more than 300 million people.

Where to Stay & Eat

$$ ✕▦ **Echaurren.** This rambling roadhouse in Ezcaray, 61 km (37 mi) south-
Fodor's Choice west of Logroño, is 7 km (4 mi) below Valdezcaray, La Rioja's prime
★ ski resort. Echaurren is famous for fine traditional cuisine ($$–$$$$) engineered by Marisa Sanchez and the original creations by her son, wunderkind Francis Paniego. Marisa's *patatas a la riojana* (potatoes stewed with peppers and chorizo) are as good as they get, and Francis, a youthful master chef with an immense future in the forefront of Spanish culinary art, experiments with wood coals and aromas. The rooms ($$) are comfortable and contemporary, and the staff and owners warm and engaging. ⊠ *Héroes del Alcázar 2, Ezcaray 26280* ☎ *941/354047* 🖷 *941/ 427133* ⊕ *www.echaurren.com* ⇆ *25 rooms* ⌂ *Restaurant, bar, parking (fee)* ▤ *AE, DC, MC, V.*

Haro

38 *20 km (12 mi) west of Nájera on the N120, 49 km (29 mi) west of Logroño.*

Haro is the wine capital of La Rioja. Its **old quarter** and best taverns are concentrated in the loop known as La Herradura (The Horseshoe), with Santo Tomás at its curve, and the feet leading down San Martín and Santo Tomás to the open space at the upper left-hand (northeast) corner of Plaza de la Paz. Up the left side of the horseshoe, Bar La Esquina, on the left, is the first of many top-notch tapas bars. Bar Los Caños, behind a stone archway at San Martín 5, is built into the vaults and arches of the former church of San Martín. The bar serves an excellent Bikaña crianza and a memorable pintxo of quail egg, anchovy, jalapeño-like pepper, and olive. Haro's century-old **bodegas** (wineries) have been headquartered in the *barrio de la estación* (train-station district) ever since the railroad opened in 1863. Guided tours and tastings, some in English, can be arranged at the facilities themselves or through the tourist office. Haro's June 29 Batalla del Vino (Wine Battle) is an epically wet and alcoholic brawl.

The architectural highlight is the Flamboyant Gothic church of **Santo Tomás,** a single-nave church, with an intricately sculpted, reddish-tinge portal on the south side. The richly gilded 60-foot-high organ facade above the choir loft is stunning.

Where to Stay & Eat

$$–$$$ ✕ **Terete.** A favorite with locals, this rustic place has been roasting lamb in wood ovens since 1877 and serves a hearty *minestra de verduras* (vegetables stewed with bits of ham). The wine cellar is stocked with some of the Rioja's best. ⊠ *C. Lucrecia Arana 17* ☎ *941/310023* ⊟ *AE, DC, MC, V* ☉ *Closed Mon., 1st 2 wks in July, and last 2 wks in Aug.*

★ $$$ 🏨 **Hostería del Monasterio de San Millán.** Declared a World Heritage Site by UNESCO, this magnificent inn occupies a wing of the Monasterio de Yuso. Guest rooms are elegant and somewhat austere, but it has the comforts you need. ⊠ *Monasterio de Yuso San Millan de la Cogolla 26326* ☎ *941/373277* 🖷 *941/373266* ⊕ *www.sanmillan.com* ⇦ *22 rooms, 3 suites* ⌕ *Restaurant, cafeteria, minibars, bar* ⊟ *AE, DC, MC, V.*

$$–$$$ 🏨 **Los Agustinos.** Haro's best hotel is built into a 14th-century monastery whose cloister (now a pleasant patio) is considered one of the best in La Rioja. Arches, a great hall, and tapestries complete the medieval look. ⊠ *San Agustín 2, 26200* ☎ *941/311308* 🖷 *941/303148* ⊕ *www. hotellosagustinos.com* ⇦ *60 rooms* ⌕ *Restaurant, cafeteria, minibars, bar, meeting rooms, parking (fee)* ⊟ *AE, DC, MC, V.*

The Highlands

The rivers forming the seven main valleys of the Ebro basin originate in the Sierra de la Demanda, Sierra de Cameros, and Sierra de Alcarama. **Ezcaray** is La Rioja's skiing capital in the **valley of the Rio Oja** just below the slopes at Valdezcaray in the Sierra de la Demanda. The upper **Najerilla Valley** is La Rioja's mountain sanctuary and wildest corner, an excellent hunting and fishing preserve. The Najerilla River, a rich, weed-choked chalk stream, is one of Spain's best trout rivers. Look for the Puente de Hiedra (Ivy Bridge), its heavy curtain of ivy falling to the surface of the water above Anguiano. The **Monasterio de Valvanera,** off C113 near Anguiano, is the sanctuary of the Virgen de Valvanera, a 12th-century Romanesque-Byzantine wood carving of the Virgin and child. **Anguiano** is renowned for its Danza de los Zancos (Dance of the Stilts), held July 22, when dancers on wooden stilts run downhill into the arms of the crowd in the main square.

The upper **Iregua Valley,** off N111, has the prehistoric Gruta de la Paz caves at Ortigosa. The artisans of **Villoslada del Cameros** make the region's patch-

Spain's Wine Country

THE EBRO RIVER BASIN HAS BEEN AN IDEAL HABITAT for grapevines since pre-Roman times. Rioja wines were first recognized in official documents in 1102, and exports to Europe flourished over the next several centuries. With its rich and uneroded soil, river microclimates, ocean moisture, and sun, La Rioja is ideal for high-quality grapes. Shielded from the arid cold of the Iberian *meseta* (plain) by the Sierra de la Demanda and from the bitter Atlantic weather by the Sierra de Cantabria, Spain's prime wine country covers an area 150 km (93 mi) long and 50 km (31 mi) wide along the banks of the Ebro. The lighter limestone soils in the 50,000 acres of the Rioja Alta (Upper Rioja) produce the region's finest wines; the vineyards in the 44,000-acre Rioja Baja (Lower Rioja) are composed of alluvial and floodplain clay in a warmer climate, ideal for the production of great volume.

The main grape of the Upper Rioja is the Tempranillo—so named for its early (*temprano*) ripening in mid-September—a dark, thick-skinned grape known for power, stability, and fragrance. Other varieties include the Mazuelo, used for longevity and tannin; and the Graciano, which lends aroma and freshness and makes high-quality wine. The Garnacha, the main grape of the Lower Rioja, is an ideal complement to the more acidic Tempranillo. The Viura, the principal white variety, is fresh and fragrant; Malvasía grapes stabilize wines that will age in oak barrels.

Rioja wines are categorized by age. Garantía de Origen is the lowest rank, assuring that the wine comes from

where it purports to come from and has been aged for at least a year. A Crianza wine has aged at least three years, with at least one spent in oak. A Reserva is a more carefully selected wine also aged three years, at least one in oak. Gran Reserva is the top category, reserved for extraordinary harvests aged for at least two years in oak and three in the bottle.

Wine and ritual overlap everywhere in La Rioja. The first wine of the year is offered to and blessed by the Virgin of Valvanera on the riverbank at the Espolón de Logroño. Haro's Batalla del Vino (Wine Battle) festival is famous throughout Spain. Everything from the harvest and the trimming of the vines to the digging of fermentation pools and the making of baskets, barrels, and *botas* (wineskins)—even the glassblowing in bottle manufacture—takes on a magical, almost religious significance.

For a tour of vineyards and wine cellars, start with **Haro,** filled with *bodegas* (wineries) and noble architecture. Haro's *barrio de la estación* (train-station district) has all of La Rioja's oldest and most famous bodegas. Call the **Carlos Serres winery** (San Agustín s/n 941/ 311308) for a tour of the process. The **Muga bodega** (941/310498) welcomes tasters at just about any hour. Other visits in the Upper Rioja could include **Fuenmayor,** a wine-making center with an old quarter; **Cenicero,** with several ancient bodegas; **Briones,** a perfectly preserved Renaissance town; **Ollauri,** with a cave bodega, "the Sistine Chapel of the Rioja"; and **Briñas,** with a wine exhibit.

work quilts, *almazuelas*. Climb to **Pico Cebollera** for a superb view of the valley. Work back toward the Ebro along the River Leza, through Laguna de Cameros and San Román de Cameros (known for its basket weavers), to complete a tour of the Sierra del Cameros. The upper **Cidacos Valley** leads to the **Parque Jurásico** (Jurassic Park) at Enciso, famous for its dinosaur tracks. The main village in the upper **Alhama Valley** is **Cervera del Rio Alhama**, a center for handmade *alpargatas* (rope-sole shoes).

Where to Stay & Eat

$–$$$ ✗ **La Herradura.** High over the ancient bridge of Anguiano, this is an excellent place to try the local specialty, *caparrones colorados de Anguiano con sus sacramentos* (small, red kidney beans stewed with sausage and fatback). Unpretentious and family run, it's usually filled to the gills with Riojanos and fishermen. The house wine is an impressive Uruñuela *cosechero* (young wine of the year) from the Najerilla Valley. ⊠ *Ctra. de Lerma, Km 14, Anguiano* ☎ *941/377151* ☰ *MC, V.*

$ ✗⌂ **Hospedería Abadía de Valvanera.** Built into the former monks' quarters of a 16th-century monastery that was itself built over a 9th-century hermitage, this is an ideal base for hiking and getting away from it all. The church's 12th-century wood carving of the Virgin of Valvanera is the object of an overnight pilgrimage from Logroño every October 15 in celebration of the harvest. A crucial factor in Rioja's grape harvest, the Virgin is portrayed with a pomegranate (symbolizing fertility) and surrounded by vines. The infant in the Virgin's arms is said to have turned away in embarrassment when a barren couple seeking fertility decided to improve their chances by performing the procreative act on the spot. Rooms are simple (bordering on monastic) but comfortable and spotless, and the cuisine ($–$$), though undistinguished, offers local products and dishes at unbeatable prices. ⊠ *Monasterio de Valvanera s/n, 5 km (3 mi) west of LR113, 26323* ☎ *941/377044* 🖶 *941/377194* ⊕ *www.abadiavalvanera.com* 🛏 *28 rooms* ♿ *Restaurant, cafeteria; no a/c, no room TVs* ☰ *AE, DC, MC, V.*

¢–$ ✗⌂ **Venta de Goyo.** A favorite with anglers and hunters in season, this cheery spot across from the mouth of the Urbión River (where it meets the Najerilla) has wood-trim bedrooms with red-check bedspreads and an excellent restaurant ($–$$$$) specializing in venison, wild boar, partridge, woodcock, and game of all kinds. Juan Carlos Jiménez and his nephew, chef Juan Carlos Esteban, serve some of the best *caparrones* (pygmy red beans grown nearby in Anguiano) in La Rioja. ⊠ *Ctra. LR113, Km 24.6, Viniegra de Abajo 26323* ☎ *941/378007* 🖶 *941/ 378048* 🛏 *22 rooms* ♿ *Restaurant, cafeteria, bar* ☰ *AE, DC, MC, V.*

La Rioja Baja

La Rioja's eastern area is more Mediterranean than Atlantic or Castilian in climate and vegetation, bordering the plains of Navarra, Soria, and Aragón. Its main river, the Cidacos, joins the Ebro at Calahorra (population 20,000), the region's largest city.

Lower Rioja has a number of key sights, including **Alfaro**'s medieval houses and church of San Miguel; **Arnedo**'s Monasterio de Vico; **Cornago**'s castle, with its four towers (three conical, one rectangular); **Igea**'s

Palacio del Marqués de Casa Torre; and **Enciso**'s Parque Jurásico (Jurassic Park), with dinosaur tracks 150 million years old. Ten kilometers (6 mi) from Calahorra, there are castle ruins at **Quel**. **Autol** is the site of rock formations known as El Picuezo y La Picueza (roughly, Mr. and Mrs. Rockpile) for their resemblance to man and wife.

Calahorra

③⑨ *46 km (27½ mi) southeast of Logroño, 109 km (65½ mi) northwest of Zaragoza.*

The birthplace of Roman orator and rhetorician Quintilian (teacher of Tacitus), Calahorra was founded by the Romans 2,000 years ago. You can explore the town's Roman and medieval remains by following the tour posted near Calahorra's **ayuntamiento** (town hall)—it covers the Quintilian monument, the Jewish quarter, and the medieval quarter along with the churches of San Andrés, Santiago, and San Celedonio. Ask for a map inside.

Where to Eat

$$–$$$$ ✕ **La Taberna de la Cuarta Esquina.** This simple provincial tavern exemplifies the best of Spain: excellent and unpretentious food and service in a family environment. Roasts and *menestra de verduras* (vegetable stewed with bits of ham) are irresistible here, especially in the dining room with the fireplace. ✉ *Cuatro Esquinas 16* ☎ *941/134355* 🖃 *AE, DC, MC, V* ☉ *Closed Tues. and last 2 wks of July.*

CANTABRIA, BASQUE COUNTRY, NAVARRA & LA RIOJA ESSENTIALS

To research prices, get advice from other travelers, and book travel arrangements, visit www.fodors.com.

Transportation

BY AIR

Bilbao's airport is 12 km (7 mi) outside the city. Iberia has regular connections from here to Madrid, Barcelona, the United Kingdom, France, and Belgium. There are smaller airports at Santander, Hondarribia (serving San Sebastián), Vitoria, Logrono, and Pamplona, with twice-daily service to Madrid and Barcelona.

🏴 Airports **Aeropuerto de Bilbao (Sondika)** ☎ 94/486–9694. **Aeropuerto de Logroño-Agoncillo** ☎ 941/277400. **Aeropuerto de Pamplona** ☎ 948/168700. **Aeropuerto de San Sebastián** ☎ 943/643464 Hondarribia. **Aeropuerto de Santander** ☎ 942/202100. **Aeropuerto de Vitoria** ☎ 945/163500.

BY BIKE

Bicycle travel in the Basque Country and across the north of Spain is hilly and often wet, but for the iron-hearted, -lunged, -legged, and -bottomed, this is a scenic way to travel and terrific exercise, albeit somewhat perilous on narrow roads often tight for passing motorists.

🏴 Bike Maps **Bici Rent Donosti** ✉ Paseo de la Zurriola 22, San Sebastián ☎ 943/279260. **Ciclos Larreki** ✉ Av. de Guipúzcoa s/n, Pamplona ☎ 948/150645. **Comet**

✉ Av. de la Libertad 6, San Sebastián ☎ 943/422351. **Fonfría** ✉ General Dávila 206, Santander ☎ 942/376563.

BY BOAT & FERRY

Santander is linked year-round to Plymouth, England, by a twice-weekly car ferry run by Brittany Ferries. Travel agencies in Spain and England have details; book at least six weeks in advance in summer, as boats fill up fast. Another such option is the twice-weekly ferry between Bilbao and Portsmouth run by Ferries Golfo de Vizcaya. The trip takes about 24 hours. For ferries out to Vigo and points west, Vapores Suardiaz runs carriers during the summer.

🚢 Boat & Ferry Information **Brittany Ferries** ✉ Paseo de Pereda 27, 39002 Santander ☎ 942/220000 or 942/214500 ✉ Millbay Docks, Plymouth PL1 3EW England ☎ 0990/360360. **Ferries Golfo de Vizcaya** ✉ Cosme Etxevarrieta 1, 48009 Bilbao ☎ 94/423–4477. **Vapores Suardiaz** ✉ Colon de Larreategui 30, 48009 Bilbao ☎ 94/423–4300.

BY BUS

Daily bus service connects the major cities to Madrid; call the bus company Continental Auto for details, or go right to the station at Calle Alenza 20. Bus service between cities and smaller towns is comprehensive, but few have central bus stations; most have numerous bus lines leaving from various points in town.

🚌 Bus Company **Continental Auto** ✉ C. Alenza 20, Madrid ☎ 91/533–0400.
🚌 Bus Stations **Bilbao** ✉ Gurtubay 1 ☎ 94/439–5077. **Logroño** ✉ Av. España 1 ☎ 941/235983. **Pamplona** ✉ C. Conde Oliveto 8 ☎ 948/223854. **San Sebastián** ✉ C. Sancho el Sabio 33 ☎ 943/463974. **Santander** ✉ C. Navas de Tolosa s/n ☎ 942/211995. **Vitoria** ✉ C. de los Herran 27 ☎ 945/258400.

BY CAR

Driving is the best way to see this part of Spain, since rural landscapes and small towns are some of the main attractions. Even the remotest points are an easy one-day drive from Madrid, and the north is superbly covered by freeways. From the capital, it's 240 km (149 mi) on the N1 or the A1 toll road to Burgos, after which you can take the N623 to complete the 390 km (242 mi) to Santander. The drive from Madrid to Bilbao is 397 km (247 mi); follow the N1 or A1 past Burgos to Miranda del Ebro, where you pick up the A68.

Car rentals are available in the major cities: Bilbao, Pamplona, San Sebastián, Santander, and Vitoria. Cars can also be rented at Hondarribia, the San Sebastián airport.

🚗 Rental Agencies **Alquibilbo** ✉ General Eguía 20, Bilbao ☎ 94/441–2012. **A-Rental** ✉ C. Pérez Galdos 24, Bilbao ☎ 94/427–0781. **Avis** ✉ C. Monasterio de la Oliva 29, Pamplona ☎ 948/170036 ✉ Aeropuerto de Pamplona ☎ 948/168763 ✉ Triunfo 2, San Sebastián ☎ 943/461527 ✉ Nicolás Salmerón 3, Santander ☎ 942/227025. **Europcar** ✉ Av. Pio XII 43, Pamplona ☎ 948/172523 ✉ Aeropuerto de Pamplona ☎ 948/312798 ✉ Aeropuerto de Fuenterrabía (Hondarribia), San Sebastián ☎ 943/668530 ✉ Aeropuerto de Santander, Santander ☎ 942/262546.

BY TAXI

Taxis normally can be hailed on the street, though from remoter spots, such as Pedro Subijana's Akelaŕe restaurant on Igueldo above San Sebastián, the maître d' will need to call a taxi for you. A taxi stand is called a *parada de taxis*; taxis charge extra for airport drop-offs and pick-ups as well as for baggage; tipping is entirely optional.

BY TRAIN

Santander, Bilbao, San Sebastián, Pamplona, Vitoria, and Logroño are served by direct trains from Madrid's Chamartín Station and, with a transfer or two, virtually every major city in Spain. Trains are not the ideal way to travel within this region, but many cities are connected by RENFE trains. Also, the regional company FEVE runs a delightful nar-row-gauge train that winds through stunning landscapes. From San Se-bastián, lines west to Bilbao and east to Hendaye depart from Estación de Amara; most long-distance trains use Estación del Norte.

🚆 Railway Companies **Euskotren** ✉ Estación de Atxuri, north of Mercado de la Rib-era, Bilbao ☎ 94/433-8007. **FEVE** ☎ 902/100818. **RENFE** ☎ 902/240202 general in-formation ✉ San Sebastián office ✉ C. Camino 1 ☎ 943/426430 ✉ Santander office ✉ Paseo de Pereda 25 ☎ 942/212387 or 942/218567.

🚆 Train Stations **Bilbao** ✉ Estación del Abando, C. Hurtado de Amezaga ☎ 94/423-8623 or 94/423-8636. **Logroño** ✉ Plaza de Europa ☎ 941/240202. **Pamplona** ✉ On road to San Sebastián ☎ 948/130202. **San Sebastián** ✉ Estación de Amara, Plaza Easo 9 ☎ 943/450131 or 943/471852 ✉ Estación del Norte, Av. de Francia ☎ 943/283089 or 943/283599. **Santander** ✉ C. Rodríguez s/n ☎ 942/210211.

Contacts & Resources

EMERGENCIES

Dial 091 for the police.

INTERNET, MAIL & SHIPPING

Cybercafés are easily found in the main cities (as well as most of the smaller towns) of Cantabria, the Basque Country, and La Rioja. Most hotels have free Internet connections for guests. Hotel staff will direct you to the nearest post office branch.

FedEx and DHL serve major metropolitan areas such as Santander, Bil-bao, Pamplona, and San Sebastian through smaller courier branches that arrange pickups. MRW and SEUR are local courier services operating in Spanish cities and towns.

MEDIA

Newspapers in the north of Spain range from the more cosmopolitan Basque Country editions of *El País* to local papers such as *Gara* (in Eu-skara) or, in Bilbao, *El Correo Español*. In San Sebastián, *El Diario Vasco* is the local standard, and in Pamplona it's the *Diario de Navarra*. In Logroño and La Rioja the local daily is the *El Diario de la Rioja*.

TOUR OPTIONS

Travel agents and tourist offices in major cities can suggest tours led by local guides. Bilbao Paso a Paso conducts fine tours of Bilbao.

🚆 Tour Operators **Bilbao Paso a Paso** ✉ Cocherito de Bilbao 20, Ofic. 5 ☎ 94/473-0078.

VISITOR INFORMATION

Information on the three Basque provinces (Alava, Vizcaya, and Guipúzcoa) is available at the government building in Vitoria and the tourist office in San Sebastián.

🚩 Regional Tourist Offices **Bilbao** ✉ Gran Vía 441 Izquierda ☏ 94/424-2277. **San Sebastián** ✉ C. Fueros 1 ☏ 943/426282. **Vitoria** ✉ Parque de la Florida ☏ 945/131321. 🚩 Local Tourist Offices **Bilbao** ✉ Paseo de Arenal 1 ☏ 94/479-5760 or 94/416-5761. **Comillas** ✉ Aldea 6 ☏ 942/720768. **Gernika** ✉ Artekale 5 ☏ 946/255892. **Getaria** ✉ Parque Aldamar 2 ☏ 943/140957. **Haro** ✉ Pl. Monseñor Florentino Rodriguez ☏ 941/303366. **Hondarribia** Fuenterrabía ✉ Javier Ugarte 6 ☏ 943/645458. **Laguardia** ✉ Pl. San Juan ☏ 945/600845. **Logroño** ✉ C. Miguel Villanueva 10 ☏ 941/291260. **Mundaka** ✉ Txorrokopunta 2 ☏ 946/177201. **Pamplona** ✉ C. Duque de Ahumada 3 ☏ 848/420420. **Potes** ✉ Independencia 30 ☏ 942/730787. **San Sebastián** ✉ C. Reina Regente s/n ☏ 943/481166. **Santander** ✉ Jardines de Pereda ☏ 942/216120 ✉ Plaza de Velarde 5 ☏ 942/310708. **San Vicente de la Barquera** ✉ Generalísimo 20 ☏ 942/710797. **Vitoria** ✉ Edificio Europa, Av. Gasteiz ☏ 945/161598. **Zumaia** ✉ Playa de Itzurun s/n ☏ 943/143396.

Galicia & Asturias

WORD OF MOUTH

"I had read wonderful reviews of the Picos de Europa and was prepared to be underwhelmed. I wasn't. This area is divine and almost deserted, so see it before the tourist hordes descend upon it."

—OReilly

"I was very lucky to stay for two nights at the parador in Cangas de Onìs, and of all the hotels/paradores we stayed in, this was my favorite. A very special place."

—cruiseluv

Updated by
Ben Curtis

SPAIN'S MOST ATLANTIC region is en route to nowhere, an end in itself. Stretching northwest from the lonesome Castilian plains to the rocky seacoast, Asturias and Galicia incorporate verdant hills and vineyards, gorgeous *rías* (estuaries), and the country's wildest mountains, the Picos de Europa. Northwestern Spain is a series of rainy landscapes, stretching from your feet to the horizon. Ancient granite buildings wear a blanket of moss, and even the stone *horreos* (granaries) are built on stilts above the damp ground. Swirling fog and heavy mist help keep local folktales of the supernatural alive. The guitar is replaced by the *gaita* (bagpipe), legacy of the Celts' settlements here in the 5th and 6th centuries BC.

Though Galicia and Asturias are off the beaten track for many foreigners, they are not undiscovered: Spanish families flock to these cool northern beaches and mountains each summer. Santiago de Compostela, where a cathedral holds the remains of the apostle James, has drawn pilgrims over the same roads for 900 years, leaving northwestern Spain covered with churches, shrines, and former hospitals. Asturias, north of the main pilgrim trail, has always maintained a separate identity, isolated by the rocky Picos de Europa. This and the Basque Country are the only parts of Spain never conquered by the Moors, so Asturian architecture shows little Moorish influence. It was from a mountain base at Covadonga that the Christians won their first decisive battle against the Moors and launched the Reconquest of Spain, which, though it took some 700 years, made Spain one of the world's most uniformly Catholic countries.

In the Gallego language, the Castilian Spanish *plaza* (town square) is *praza* and the Castilian *playa* (beach) is *praia*. Closer to Portuguese than to Castilian Spanish, Gallego is the language of choice for nearly all road signs in Galicia.

Exploring Galicia & Asturias

Santiago de Compostela holds center stage in Spain's northwest corner, along with the final stages of the Camino de Santiago. To the south are the Rías Baixas, and to the west are the beaches along the Atlantic coast north of the Río Miño and the border with Portugal. Farther north is the thriving port of A Coruña; the Bay of Biscay lies east, along the coasts of Asturias. Oviedo is just inland, backed by the lofty Picos de Europa to the south. Be prepared to fall in love with these magical, remote regions. In Gallego they call the feeling *morriña,* a powerful longing for a person or place you've left behind.

Numbers in the text correspond to numbers in the margin and on the Galicia & Asturias and the Santiago de Compostela maps.

About the Beaches

Galicia's tourist industry is booming, and so is its fishing sector. The Spanish government and the Galician *Xunta* (local government) are vigorously promoting its northern beaches.

Galician and Asturian beaches include urban strands with all the amenities of big-city life a few steps from the sand as well as remote expanses

GREAT ITINERARIES

IF YOU HAVE 3 DAYS

Fly into ⚏ **Santiago de Compostela ❺ - ❿** and spend the first day exploring the town's cathedral and plazas. Head south early on Day 2, driving down the C550 to **Cambados ⓫**, stopping at fishing villages along the Ría de Arousa on the way. Stick with the coast road all the way to ⚏ **Pontevedra ⓰**, where you can spend a night exploring the medieval streets and tapas bars. On your last day drive down to **Vigo ⓳** for a lunch of oysters on Rúa Pescadería, then continue south, arriving before dark at one of Spain's most spectacular hotels, the parador in ⚏ **Baiona ㉑**.

IF YOU HAVE 5 DAYS

Start in ⚏ **Santiago de Compostela ❺ - ❿** and spend a day and a half on the cathedral and old town. Drive north the second afternoon to ⚏ **A Coruña ㉓** and devote Day 3 to admiring the glass galleries on the harbor, exploring the old town, and visiting the Torre de Hercules. On Day 4, head north for some of Spain's loveliest beaches and stroll around coastal **Viveiro ㉗**. Crossing into Asturias, spend the fourth night in **Luarca ㉙**, a village in a cove, or the lively coastal city of **Gijón ㉛**. Finally, on Day 5, drive south to ⚏ **Oviedo ㉚**, to wander around the peaceful provincial capital.

4

that rarely become as crowded as the beaches of the Mediterranean. When the sun comes out, you can relax on the sand on the Asturian beaches of, from east to west, Llanes, Ribadesella, Cudillero, Santa Ana (by Cadavedo), Luarca, and Tapia de Casariego, among many others. In Galicia, the beaches of Muros, Noya, O Grove, the Islas Cíes, Boa, and Testal are the top sun-and-sand destinations. For surfers, Galicia's Montalvo, Foxos, and Canelas beaches, near Pontevedra, are tops. Near Cangas, look for Nerga and Punto de Couso. Farther south, near the estuary of the Miño river, are El Vilar, Balieros, Rio Sieira, and Os Castros. For surf reports, check out www.lanzadera.com/surf.

About the Restaurants

Galicia and Asturias are justly famous for seafood. The quality of the fish is so high that chefs frown on drowning inherent flavors in heavy sauces or pungent seasonings; expect simplicity rather than spice. Fish specialties are *merluza a la gallega,* steamed hake with sweet paprika sauce (Galicia), and *merluza a la sidra,* steamed hake in a tangy Asturian cider sauce (Asturias). Salmon and trout from Asturian rivers are additional treats. The scallop, a symbol of the pilgrimage to Santiago, is popular in Galicia, where you can also find bars serving nothing but wine and *pulpo a feira* (boiled and broiled octopus) or *berberechos* (cockles). Cheeses are delicious all over northwestern Spain: try the tangy *queso Cabrales* (Asturian blue cheese), the sharp Asturian *afuega'l pitu* (literally, "chokes the rooster," because it's so sharp and so thick), and the Galician *queixo tetilla* (a semisoft cheese in the form of a woman's breast), a delicious dessert when served with *membrillo* (quince jelly). Valdeón cheese, from the Picos de Europa village of the same name, is one of the

SPORTS & THE OUTDOORS

With so much rugged wilderness, Spain's northwest has become the country's main outdoor-adventure region. The Picos de Europa and the green hills of Galicia beg to be hiked, trekked, climbed, or simply walked; other open-air diversions include horseback riding, canyon rappelling, bungee jumping, and spelunking. Ribadesella, Asturias, is Spain's white-water capital, with an international kayak race held in August on the Sella River from Arriondas to Ribadesella. Atlantic salmon, sea trout, and trout angling provides an excellent pretext for getting to know some of green Spain's finest river valleys and countryside.

BALLOONING
Stable weather conditions and outstanding mountain landscapes make the Picos de Europa ideal for year-round ballooning. Flights cost from €120 for a 30-minute introduction to €520 for a three-hour trip (prices are per person).

Contacts: Globoastur (✉ Gijón, Asturias ☎ 985/355818 ⊕ www.globoastur.com).

GOLF
Asturias has golf courses in Llanes, Gijón, and Siero. Galician courses include Monte la Zapateira, near A Coruña; Domaio, in Pontevedra province; La Toja, on the island of the same name near O Grove; and Padrón. Santiago's links are near the airport, at Labacolla. Call the club a day in advance to reserve equipment.

Contacts: Campo de Golf del Aero Club Labacolla (✉ Lugar de Mourena, Santiago de Compostela ☎ 981/888276). **Club de Golf La**

Cuesta (✉ 3 km [2 mi] east of Llanes, near Cué ☎ 985/403319). **Club de Golf de Castiello** (✉ Ctra. N632, 5 km [3 mi] from Gijón toward Santander ☎ 985/366313). **Campo Municipal la Llorea** (✉ Ctra. N632, Km 62, La Llorea, Gijón ☎ 985/333191). **Campo Municipal de Golf de las Caldas** (✉ La Premaña s/n, Las Caldas, Oviedo ☎ 985/798132). **Domaio** (✉ Pontevedra ☎ 986/327050). **La Barganiza** (✉ San Martí de Anes-Siero, 12 km [7 mi] from Oviedo and 14 km [9 mi] from Gijón ☎ 985/742468). **La Toja** (✉ Isla de la Toja ☎ 986/730158). **Monte la Zapateira** (✉ C. Zapateira s/n, A Coruña ☎ 981/285200). **Padrón** (☎ 981/453910).

HIKING
The tourist offices in Oviedo and Cangas de Onís can help you organize a Picos de Europa trek. The Picos visitor center in Cangas provides general information, route maps, and a useful scale model of the range. In summer, another reception center opens between Lakes Enol and Ercina, on the mountain road from Covadonga. The Centro de Aventuro Monteverde can organize canoeing, canyon rappelling, bungee jumping, spelunking, horseback riding, and jeep trips. Turismo y Aventura Viesca offers rafting, canoeing, jet skiing, climbing, trekking, bungee jumping, and archery. In A Coruña, Nortrek is a one-stop source for information and equipment pertaining to hiking, rock climbing, skiing, and bungee jumping.

Contacts: Centro de Aventuro Monteverde (✉ Sargento Provisional 5, Cangas de Onís

☎ 985/848079), closed November through March. **Nortrek** (✉ Inés de Castro 7, bajo A Coruña ☎ 981/151674). **Picos de Europa visitor center** (✉ Casa Dago, Av. Covadonga 43, Cangas de Onís ☎ 985/848614). **Turismo y Aventura Viesca** (✉ Av. del Puente Romano 1, Cangas de Onís ☎ 985/357369 ⊕ www.aventuraviesca.com).

HORSEBACK RIDING

Trastur leads wilderness trips on horseback through the remote valleys of western Asturias. The 5- to 10-day outings are designed for both beginners and experienced cowboys; mountain cabins provide shelter along the trail. Tours begin and end in Oviedo and cost about €108 a day, all-inclusive. The Centro Hípico de Turismo Ecuestre y de Aventuras/"Granjo O Castelo" conducts horseback rides along the pilgrimage routes to Santiago from O Cebreiro and Braga (Portugal). **Federación Hípica Gallega** has a list of all riding facilities in Galicia.

Contacts: Centro Hípico de Turismo Ecuestre y de Aventuras/"Granja O Castelo" (✉ Rúa Urzáiz 91-5D, Vigo ☎ 986/425937 ⊕ www.galicianet.com/castelo). **Federación Hípica Gallega** (✉ Fotografo Luis Ksado 17, Edificio Federaciones Deportivas, Vigo ☎ 986/213800 🖷 986/201461 ⊕ www.fhgallega.com). **Trastur** (✉ Muñalen-Cal Teso, Tineo, Asturias ☎ 985/806036 or 985/806310).

SKIING

The region's three small ski areas cater mostly to local families. The largest is San Isidro, in the Cantabrian Mountains, with 4 chairlifts, 8 drag lifts, and more

than 22½ km (14 mi) of slopes. Just east of here is Valgrande Pajares, with two chairlifts, eight slopes, and cross-country trails. West of Ourense, in Galicia, Mazaneda has 2 chairlifts, 17 slopes, and 1 cross-country trail.

Contacts: Mazaneda (☎ 988/309747). **San Isidro** (☎ 987/731115). **Valgrande Pajares** (☎ 985/496123 or 985/957123).

WATER SPORTS

In Santiago, contact diving experts Turisnorte for information on scuba lessons, equipment rental, guided dives, windsurfing, and parasailing. Courageous and experienced sailors might find yachting a spectacular way to discover hidden coastal sights; Yatesport Coruña (also in Santiago) rents private yachts and can arrange sailing lessons.

Contacts: Turisnorte (✉ Raxoeira 14, Milladoiro, A Coruña ☎ 981/530009 or 902/162172). **Yatesport Coruña** (✉ Puerto Deportivo, Marina Sada, Sada, A Coruña ☎ 981/620624).

4

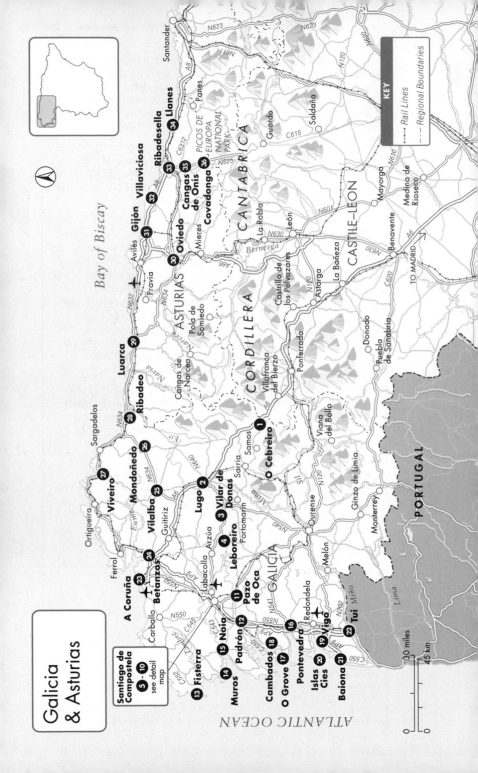

Galicia & Asturias

Santiago de Compostela
see detail map
5 – 10

KEY
- Rail Lines
- Regional Boundaries

Bay of Biscay

ATLANTIC OCEAN

1 O Cebreiro
2 Lugo
3 Vilar de Donas
4 Leboreiro
5–10 Santiago de Compostela
11 Pazo de Oca
12 Padrón
13 Fisterra
14 Muros
15 Noia
16 Redondela
17 Pontevedra
18 Cambados
19 O Grove
20 Islas Cíes
21 Baiona
22 Tui
23 A Coruña
24 Betanzos
25 Vilalba
26 Mondoñedo
27 Viveiro
28 Ribadeo
29 Luarca
30 Oviedo
31 Gijón
32 Villaviciosa
33 Ribadesella
34 Llanes
35 Cangas de Onís
36 Covadonga

ASTURIAS

CANTABRICA

CASTILE-LEON

PORTUGAL

GALICIA

CORDILLERA

PICOS DE EUROPA NATIONAL PARK

TO MADRID

0   30 miles
0   45 km

world's finest blue cheeses, made from cow's milk and fat, then "perfumed." This damp region is also known for hearty stews—in Asturias try *fabada* (butter beans and sausage), and in Galicia *caldo gallego* (white beans, turnip greens, chickpeas, cabbage, and potatoes). Those savory fish or meat pies called *empanadas* are native to Galicia, as is the famous *lacón con grelos* (cured ham with turnips and chorizo sausage). Asturians enjoy *entrecôte con queso Cabrales,* steak topped with a sauce made of the local blue cheese.

The best Galician wine is the fruity, full-bodied, white Albariño, perfect with seafood and more and more popular abroad. The acidic Ribeiro wine is often served in a ceramic bowl rather than a glass. Brandy buffs should try Galicia's *queimada* (which superstitious locals claim is a witches' brew), made of potent, grappalike *orujo* mixed with lemon peel, coffee beans, and sugar in an earthenware bowl, then set aflame and stirred until the desired amount of alcohol is burned off. Asturias is known for its *sidra* (hard cider), served either carbonated or still. Traditionally, cider is poured from overhead and tossed back *immediately* for full enjoyment of its effervescent flavor. Cider houses generally insist that either you or your waiter pour cider correctly (that is, from overhead to a glass held at knee level) to aerate the cider. This process is called the *escancio* (pouring), a much-valued skill around which entire tournaments are held. Give it a try: spilling is allowed.

WHAT IT COSTS In Euros				
$$$$	**$$$**	**$$**	**$**	**¢**
AT DINNER over €20	€15–€20	€10–€15	€6–€10	under €6

Prices are for per person for a main course at dinner.

About the Hotels

The state-run parador chain has nine charming lodgings in Galicia alone: three in elegant mansions, two in ancient fortresses, and one in a former convent at Ribas de Sil, near Ourense. The Rusticae chain is giving the paradores a run for their money with a series of graceful and affordable *pazos* (manor houses). Reservations are important between May and October, and a good idea the rest of the year. Some monasteries provide economical lodging.

WHAT IT COSTS In Euros				
$$$$	**$$$**	**$$**	**$**	**¢**
FOR 2 PEOPLE over €180	€100–€180	€60–€100	€40–€60	under €40

Prices are for two people in a standard double room in high season, excluding tax.

Timing

Summer is best for swimming and enjoying water sports. Spring and fall may be the ideal time to explore, as the weather is reasonable and crowds are few. Winter can be rainy to the point of saturation: Not for nothing is this region called Green Spain.

THE CAMINO DE SANTIAGO

Santiago de Compostela, alleged final resting place for the apostle St. James, was one of the most important Christian sites in the world in the Middle Ages. Making the difficult pilgrimage to this remote corner of Spain all but ensured the faithful a place in heaven—perhaps not least because the route was crowded with highway robbers, gallant pilgrim-protecting knights, and innkeepers prospering in the pilgrim trade. There were also souvenir hawkers, providing the scallop shells that pilgrims wore as a symbol of St. James, a fisherman and the brother of St. John the Evangelist. The main pilgrimage route, the *camino francés,* crosses the Pyrenees from France and heads west across northern Spain, marked by scallop-shell signs. If you drive into Galicia on the A6 expressway from Castile–León, you enter what might be called the homestretch.

O Cebreiro

❶ *32 km (20 mi) northwest of Villafranca del Bierzo.*

From the N-IV at Puerto de Piedrafita, the Camino de Santiago veers left. Climb the steep, narrow road to O Cebreiro, one of the most unusual mountaintop hamlets in Spain. Deserted and haunting outside high season (and often fogged in or snowy to boot), O Cebreiro is a stark settlement built around a 9th-century church. Known for its round, thatched-roof stone huts called **pallozas,** the village has been perfectly preserved and is now an open-air museum showing what life was like in these mountains in the Middle Ages and, indeed, up until a few decades ago. One hut is now a **museum** of the region's Celtic heritage. Higher up, at 3,648 feet, you can visit a rustic 9th-century **sanctuary.**

Where to Stay

¢ 🏨 **Hostal San Giraldo de Aurillac.** This rural budget hotel next to the church provides home cooking and a good base for walking the mountains. The Santuario do Cebreiro next door is run by the same establishment. ⊠ *O Cebreiro, Pedrafita do Cebreiro 27670* ☎ *982/367125* 🖷 *982/ 367115* 📭 *16 rooms* ⚒ *Restaurant, bar; no a/c* ▤ *MC, V.*

Lugo

❷ *31 km (19 mi) north of Sarria on LU546, 26 km (16 mi) north of Portomarín on LU612.*

Just off the A6 freeway, Galicia's oldest provincial capital is most notable for its 2½-km (1½-mi) **Roman wall.** Built in the year 260, these beautifully preserved ramparts completely surround the hidden granite streets of the old town. The walkway on top has good views. The baroque *ayuntamiento* (city hall) has a magnificent rococo facade overlooking the tree-lined Praza Maior (Plaza Mayor). There's a good view of the Río Miño valley from the **Parque Rosalía de Castro,** outside the Roman walls near the cathedral. Lugo's **cathedral,** open daily 8 AM to 8:30 PM, is a mixture of the Romanesque, Gothic, baroque, and neoclassical styles. The **Museo Provincial** (⊠ Pl. de la Soledad ☎ 982/242112 ⊕ www.museolugo.org 🎫 Free ☉ July and Aug., weekdays 11–2 and 5–8, Sat. 10–2; Oct.–June,

---

BEN'S TOP 5

- Watching the oyster hawkers at work while lunching in Vigo's Rúa Pescadería.

- Losing myself on an evening stroll through Santiago's medieval old town.

- Arriving at the parador in Baiona, knowing I have a room for the night.

- Eating fabada bean stew and drinking local cider, near the port in Ribadesella.

- Taking a deliberate wrong turn in the Picos de Europa, in search of forgotten mountain villages.

---

weekdays 10:30–2 and 4:30–8:30, Sat. 10:30–2 and 4:30–8, Sun. 11–2) has a large collection of clocks and sundials.

Where to Stay & Eat

$$–$$$$ ✕ **Mesón de Alberto.** This cozy venue has excellent Galician fare and professional service. The bar and adjoining bodega (winery) serve plenty of cheap *raciónes* (appetizers). The *surtido de quesos Gallegos* provides generous servings of four local cheeses; ask for some membrillo (quince jelly) to go with them and the brown, crusty corn bread. The dining room upstairs has an inexpensive set menu. ⊠ *Cruz 4* ☎ *982/228310* ▤ *AE, DC, MC, V* ☉ *Closed Sun.*

$$$ ▥ **Gran Hotel Lugo.** In a garden near the Praza Maior but outside the city walls, this modern, spacious hotel has comfortable rooms done in shades of yellow and brown. The rooms overlook the garden swimming pool or a broad street. ⊠ *Av. Ramón Ferreiro 21, 27002* ☎ *982/224152* 🖷 *982/241660* ⊕ *www.gh-hoteles.com* 📲 *156 rooms, 11 suites* ⚱ *Restaurant, pool, meeting rooms, parking (fee)* ▤ *AE, DC, MC, V.*

$$ ▥ **Casa Grande da Fervenza.** This graceful 17th-to-19th-century manor house, on the banks of the Miño river 14 km (8 mi) south of Lugo, is filled with heavy ceiling beams, wooden columns, exposed stone, chestnut floors, and hand-painted sinks and crockery. Rooms are rustic but comfortable. ⊠ *A Fervenza, O Corgo 27364* ☎ *982/150610* 🖷 *982/151610* ⊕ *www.fervenza.com* 📲 *8 rooms* ⚱ *Restaurant, pool, beach, bar; no a/c* ▤ *AE, DC, MC, V.*

Vilar de Donas

❸ *27 km (17 mi) southwest of Lugo.*

Southwest of Lugo, turn right in Ferradal onto the LU–4005, pass the picnic ground, and stop at the little **church** in Vilar de Donas to pay tribute to the knights of St. James, whose tombs line the inside walls. The afternoon sun spotlights carved-stone depictions, including the horizontal body of Christ. Portraits of the two medieval noblewomen who built the church are mixed with those of the apostles in the 15th-century frescoes on the apse. The church is open for visits April through

---

October, Tuesday through Sunday 11 to 2 and 3 to 6; to arrange a visit between November and March contact the **verger** (☎ 982/153833). Mass is held at 1 PM each Sunday.

Leboreiro

❹ *38 km (23 mi) west of Vilar de Donas.*

West of Vilar de Donas, the countryside flattens out. Just after the sign for Km 42 on the N547, turn left for Leboreiro, a farming hamlet with simple medieval stone houses surrounding a **Romanesque church.** On the west side of town, an old bridge and a stretch of the ancient pilgrims' road, paved with granite boulders, are surprisingly intact.

Santiago de Compostela

★ *277 km (172 mi) west of León, 650 km (403 mi) northwest of Madrid.*

A large, lively university makes Santiago one of the most exciting cities in Spain, but its cathedral makes it one of the most impressive. The building is opulent and awesome, yet its towers create a sense of harmony as a benign St. James, dressed in pilgrim's costume, looks down from his perch. Santiago de Compostela welcomes more than 4½ million visitors a year, with an extra 1 million during Holy Years (the next is in 2010), when St. James's Day, July 25, falls on a Sunday.

From the **Praza do Obradoiro,** climb the two flights of stairs to the main **❺** entrance to Santiago's **cathedral.** Although the facade is baroque, the interior holds one of the finest Romanesque sculptures in the world, the **Pórtico de la Gloria.** Completed in 1188 by Maestro Mateo (Master Mateo), this is the cathedral's original entrance, its three arches carved with biblical figures from the Apocalypse, the Last Judgment, and Purgatory. On the left are the prophets; in the center, Jesus is flanked by the four evangelists (Matthew, Mark, Luke, and John) and, above them, the 24 elders of the Apocalypse playing celestial instruments. Just below Jesus is a serene St. James, poised on a carved column. Look carefully and you can see five smooth grooves, formed by the millions of pilgrims who have placed their hands here over the centuries. On the back of the pillar, people, especially students preparing for exams, lean forward to touch foreheads with the likeness of Maestro Mateo in the hope that his genius can be shared. In his jeweled cloak, St. James presides over the **high altar.** The stairs behind itare the cathedral's focal point, surrounded by dazzling baroque decoration, sculpture, and drapery. Here, as the grand finale of their spiritual journey, pilgrims embrace St. James and kiss his cloak. In the crypt beneath the altar lie the remains of St. James and his disciples, St. Theodore and St. Athenasius.

A pilgrims' mass is celebrated every day at noon. On special, somewhat unpredictable occasions, the *botafumeiro* (huge incense burner) is attached to the thick ropes hanging from the ceiling and prepared for a ritual at the end of the pilgrims' mass: as small flames burn inside, eight strong laymen move the ropes to swing the vessel in a massive semicircle across the apse. In earlier centuries, this rite served as an air freshener—by the time pilgrims reached Santiago, they smelled, well, ripe.

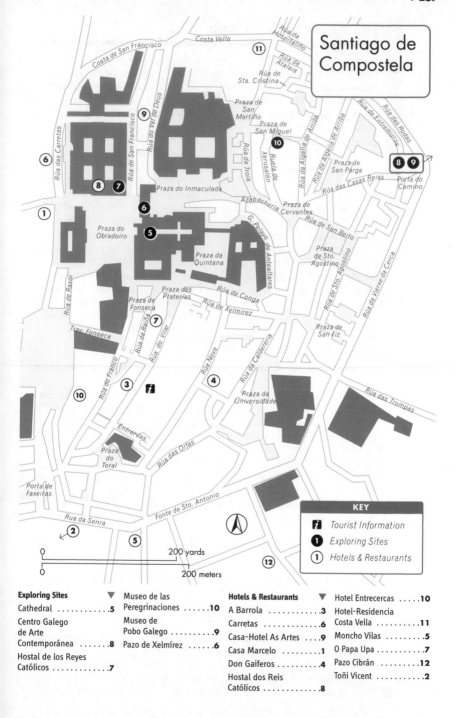

Santiago de Compostela

KEY

🛈 *Tourist Information*

➊ *Exploring Sites*

① *Hotels & Restaurants*

CLOSE UP

The Road to Santiago

NINTH-CENTURY SOURCES have the apostle James preaching in northwest Iberia, not far from Fisterra. Beheaded by Herod in AD 44 (Acts 12:2), Santiago's remains, according to legend, were placed in a stone boat and guided by God to the Galician river Iria Flavia, near Padrón. When, as the boat arrived, a horse on the shore bolted into deep water (only to emerge, with its rider, both covered in scallop shells), the scallop became the symbol of Saint James. Much later, in 813, religious leaders unearthed a sarcophagus said to contain the remains of the apostle James. ("Santiago" comes from *Sant Iago*, St. James; "Compostela" probably comes from the Latin *campus stellae*, field of stars.)

At the height of its fame in the 12th century, up to 2 million people made the trek to Santiago each year, nearly as many as those going to Rome and Jerusalem. Neither the Reformation nor 20th-century secularism managed to kill off the pilgrimage, now a mélange of believers, agnostics, and disaffected professionals taking to the hills to hear themselves think. As Nancy Louise Frey reports in *Pilgrim Stories: On and Off the Road to Santiago*, nearly 30,000 people made the pilgrimage in 1996, 16% declaring no belief in God and only about half of the rest practicing their faith. Although most medieval pilgrims were poor and infirm, today's average hiker is an educated, middle-class, thirtysomething western European. The main path is the *camino francés* (the French route), which enters Spain from France at Roncesvalles and hits Santiago 750 km (465 mi) later, a month's walk.

Spanish national television broadcasts this ceremony live on St. James's Day, July 25. A botafumeiro and other cathedral treasures are on display in the **museums** downstairs and next door. On the right (south) side of the nave is the **Porta das Praterías** (Silversmiths' Door), the only purely Romanesque part of the cathedral's facade. The statues on the portal were cobbled together from parts of the cathedral. The double doorway opens onto the **Praza das Praterías,** named for the silversmiths' shops that used to line it. The fountain here is a popular place to rest in nice weather. ⊠ *Praza do Obradoiro* ☎ *981/560527 (museum) or 981/583548 (cathedral)* ⌑ *Cathedral free, combined museum ticket €5* ☉ *Cathedral daily 7 AM–9 PM; museums June–Oct., Mon.–Sat. 10–2 and 4–8, Sun. 10–2; Nov.–May, Mon.–Sat. 10–1:30 and 4–6:30, Sun. 10–1:30.*

For excellent views of the city and the plazas surrounding the cathedral, join a tour across the granite steps of the **cathedral roofs.** Pilgrims made the same 100-foot climb in medieval times to burn their travel-worn clothes below the *Cruz dos Farrapos* (Cross of Rags). ⊠ *Pazo de Xelmírez, Praza do Obradoiro* ☎ *981/552985* ⌑ *€10* ☉ *Tues.–Sun. 10–2 and 4–8.*

The wide **Praza da Quintana** is the haunt of young travelers and folk musicians in summer. The **Porta Santa** (Holy Door) is open only during those years in which St. James's Day falls on a Sunday (such as 2010). The Praza is behind the Santiago cathedral. Stop into the rich 12th-century **⑥ Pazo de Xelmírez** (Palace of Archbishop Xelmírez), an unusual example of Romanesque civic architecture with a cool, clean, vaulted dining hall. The little figures carved on the corbels (supports) in this graceful, 100-foot-long space are lifelike, partaking of food, drink, and music with great medieval gusto. Each one is different; stroll around for a tableau of mealtime merriment. ⊠ *Praza do Obradoiro* 🎟 *Included in combined museum ticket* ☉ *Tues.–Sun. 10–2 and 4–8.*

❼ The **Hostal de los Reyes Católicos** (Hostel of the Catholic Monarchs), facing the cathedral from the left, was built in 1499 by Ferdinand and Isabella to house the pilgrims who slept on Santiago's streets every night. Having lodged and revived travelers for nearly 500 years, it's the oldest refuge in the world and was converted from a hospital to a luxury parador in 1953. The facade bears a Castilian coat of arms along with Adam, Eve, and various saints; inside, the four arcaded patios have gargoyle rainspouts said to be caricatures of 16th-century townsfolk. There's a small art gallery behind the lobby. Walk-in spectators without room keys risk being asked to leave, but for a negotiable cost, as part of a city tour, you can visit in the company of an official city guide from the tourist office. ⊠ *Praza do Obradoiro 1* 🕾 *981/582200 (hostel), 981/555129 (tourist office)* ☉ *Daily 10–1 and 4–6.*

Santiago's city hall and the president's offices of the regional government of Galicia, La Xunta de Galicia, are in the 18th-century **Pazo de Raxoi** (Rajoy Palace; ⊠ Praza do Obradoiro). It's directly opposite the cathedral. Take note of the 16th-century **Colexio de San Xerome** (⊠ Praza do Obradoiro), the offices of the rector of the University of Santiago. Its 15th-century entrance was brought from another city college and includes virgins and saints with the Virgin and Child above the door.

Santiago de Compostela's streets hold many old pazos (manor houses), convents, and churches that in most towns would receive headline attention. But the best way to spend your remaining time here is simply to walk around the **casco antiguo** (old town), losing yourself in its maze of stone-paved narrow streets and little plazas. The most beautiful pedestrian thoroughfares are Rúa do Vilar, Rúa do Franco, and Rúa Nova—portions of which are covered by arcaded walkways called *soportales,* designed to keep walkers out of the rain.

❽ On the north side of town off the Porta do Camino, the **Centro Galego de Arte Contemporánea** (Galician Center for Contemporary Art) is a stark but elegant modern building that offsets Santiago's ancient feel. Portuguese designer Álvaro Siza built the museum of smooth, angled granite, which mirrors the medieval convent of San Domingos de Bonaval next door. Inside, a gleaming lobby of white Italian marble gives way to white-wall, high-ceiling exhibition halls flooded with light from massive windows and skylights. The museum has a good permanent collection and even better changing exhibits. ⊠ *Rúa de Valle Inclán s/n* 🕾 *981/546619* ⊕ *www.cgac.org* 🎟 *Free* ☉ *Tues.–Sun. 11–8.*

❾ Next door to the Center for Contemporary Art is the **Museo do Pobo Galego** (Galician Folk Museum), in the medieval convent of Santo Domingo de Bonaval. Photos, farm implements, and other displays illustrate aspects of traditional Galician life. The star attraction is the 13th-century self-supporting spiral granite staircase that still connects three floors. ✉ *Rúa de Bonaval* ☎ *981/583620* ⊕ *www.museodopobo.es* 💵 *Free* ⊙ *Tues.–Sat. 10–2 and 4–8, Sun. 11–2.*

⑩ North of Azabachería (follow Ruela de Xerusalén) is the **Museo de las Peregrinaciones** (Pilgrimage Museum), with Camino de Santiago iconography from sculptures and carvings to *azabache* (compact black coal, or jet) items. For an overview of the history of the pilgrimage and the Camino's role in the development of the city itself, this is a key visit. ✉ *Rúa de San Miguel 4* ☎ *981/581558* 💵 *€2.50* ⊙ *Tues.–Fri. 10–8, Sat. 10:30–1:30 and 5–8, Sun. 10:30–1:30.*

Where to Stay & Eat

$$$$ ✗ **Casa Marcelo.** When it's actually open, this eruption into the culinary field of Santiago is a find. Leek-and-potato soup with clams and other refined cooking based on local favorites are the rule here. The €43 prix-fixe meal consists of a sample selection of six main dishes, and two desserts. ✉ *Rúa Hortas 1* ☎ *981/558580* 🖃 *AE, MC, V* ⊙ *Closed Sun.–Tues. and Feb.*

$$$–$$$$ ✗ **Toñi Vicent.** Galicia's most creative cuisine is concocted in this carefully furnished antiquary. *Marinada de lubina con ensalada amarga, aceite, limón, y eneldo* (marinade of sea bass with bitter salad, olive oil, lemon, and dill) is an example of the meeting of Galicia's finest produce with one of its most inventive chefs. ✉ *Rosalía de Castro 24* ☎ *981/594100* 🖃 *AE, MC, V* ⊙ *Closed Sun. and Dec. 23–Jan. 7.*

$$–$$$$ ✗ **A Barrola.** Polished wooden floors, a niche with wine and travel books, and a lively terrace make this tavern a favorite with university faculty. The house salads, mussels with *santiaguiños* (crabmeat), *arroz con bogavante* (rice with lobster), and seafood empanadas are superb. ✉ *Rúa do Franco 29* ☎ *981/577999* 🖃 *AE, MC, V* ⊙ *Closed Mon. and Jan.–Mar.*

$$–$$$$ ✗ **Don Gaiferos.** One of Santiago's most distinguished restaurants, this tavern serves jumbo prawns stuffed with smoked salmon and white Ribeiro and Albariño wines. The spicy fish stew is enough for two, and the *tarta de almendra* (almond tart) and the bilberry cheesecake are irresistible. ✉ *Rúa Nova 23* ☎ *981/583894* 🖃 *AE, DC, MC, V* ⊙ *Closed Jan. 1–15. No dinner Sun. and Mon.*

★ $$$ ✗ **Moncho Vilas.** The owner of the eponymous restaurant reached a zenith when he prepared a banquet for the late Pope John Paul II (the pontiff visited Santiago in 1989). Specialties include salmon with clams, *merluza a la gallega* (hake with paprika sauce) or *a la vasca* (in a green sauce), and steak with garlicky potatoes. ✉ *Av. Villagarcia 21* ☎ *981/598637* 🖃 *AE, DC, MC, V* ⊙ *No dinner Sun. Closed Mon.*

$$–$$$ ✗ **Carretas.** This casual spot for fresh Galician seafood is around the corner from the Hostal de los Reyes Católicos. Fish dishes abound, but the specialty here is shellfish. For the full experience, order the labor-intensive *variado de mariscos*, a comprehensive platter of langostinos, king prawns, crab, and goose barnacles that comes with a shell-cracker. *Salpicón de mariscos* presents the same creatures preshelled. ✉ *Rúa de Carretas 21* ☎ *981/563111* 🖃 *AE, DC, MC, V* ⊙ *Closed Sun.*

$$–$$$ ✗ **O Papa Upa.** A luscious assortment of shellfish and the entrecôte Papa Upa, a massive T-bone steak, are specialties. Chase your meal as the locals do—partake in the "rite of burning firewater" with queimada, flaming brandy served in a ceramic bowl. ⊠ *Rúa da Raiña 18* ☎ *981/ 566598* ⊟ *AE, DC, MC, V.*

★ **$$$$** ✕⊡ **Hostal dos Reis Católicos.** This 15th-century masterpiece was originally built as a royal hospital designed to take care of sick pilgrims as they arrived in the city. A mammoth baroque doorway gives way to austere courtyards of box hedge and simple fountains, and to rooms furnished with antiques, some with canopy beds. Also known as the Parador de Santiago de Compostela, this hotel is one of the most highly regarded in the state-run parador chain. Libredón, a restaurant ($$$–$$$$) in the grand, vaulted dining room, serves top-notch regional fare, including *lonchas de pulpo* (strips of octopus served with paprika and potato), foie gras, and *filloas de manzana y crema caramelizadas* (apple and caramel cream pancakes), and is well worth a visit. The tapas bar, Enxebre, is lively and informal. ⊠ *Praza do Obradoiro 1, 15705* ☎ *981/ 582200* 🖶 *981/563094* ⊕ *www.parador.es* 🖪 *137 rooms* 🛆 *2 restaurants, hair salon, bar, car rental, parking (fee)* ⊟ *AE, DC, MC, V.*

★ **$$** ⊡ **Casa-Hotel As Artes.** A stone's throw from the cathedral, this little inn offers sunny quarters at great rates. Each room has at least one stone wall, recessed windows with beveled wood shutters, polished hardwood floors, and a wrought-iron double bed; and each is named after a different artist and decorated accordingly. (The Vivaldi room, for instance, has music-manuscript curtains.) ⊠ *Travesía de Dos Puertas 2, off Rúa San Francisco, 15707* ☎ *981/572590 or 981/555254* 🖶 *981/ 577823* ⊕ *www.asartes.com* 🖪 *7 rooms* 🛆 *Sauna, bar* ⊟ *AE, DC, MC, V* ☾ *Closed Jan. 8–31.*

★ **$$** ⊡ **Hotel Entrecercas.** This house, just off the Rúa do Franco, was restored to highlight its exposed beams and stonework. There are five doubles and three single rooms, all with bath. The prices include tax and breakfast. Book early for this great location. ⊠ *Entrecercas 11 bajo, 15703* ☎ *981/571151* 🖶 *981/571112* 🖪 *8 rooms* 🛆 *Cafeteria, bar; no a/c* ⊟ *AE, DC, MC, V.*

★ **$$** ⊡ **Hotel-Residencia Costa Vella.** This inn snuggles up to Santiago's medieval wall at one of the highest points in the city. The house is classically Galician, but the interior is awash in smooth blond wood and natural light from floor-to-ceiling windows—the better to behold the perfect little garden, stone wall, red-tile rooftops, the baroque convent of San Francisco, and the green hills beyond. (Ask for a garden view.) There are also plenty of views from the airy breakfast room and reading area. ⊠ *Rúa Porta da Pena 17, 15704* ☎ *981/569530* 🖶 *981/569531* 🖪 *14 rooms* 🛆 *Bar, lounge* ⊟ *AE, DC, MC, V.*

★ **$$** ⊡ **Pazo Cibrán.** Charmingly restored, this 18th-century Galician farm mansion is 7 km (4 mi) from Santiago de Compostela. Owner Mayka Iglesias maintains six rooms in the main house and five large rooms in the old stable. The antiques-packed living room overlooks gardens with camellias, magnolias, palms, vines, and a bamboo walk. Breakfast is served in the pazo itself, with lunch and dinner available in the nearby Casa Roberto. To get here, take the N525 toward Ourense from Santiago and turn right at Km 11, after the gas station. ⊠ *San Xulián de Sales, 15885* ☎ *981/511515* 🖶 *981/814766* ⊕ *www.pazocibran.com* 🖪 *11 rooms* 🛆 *Library; no a/c* ⊟ *AE, DC, MC, V.*

Tapas Bars

Adega Abrigadoiro. A five-minute walk behind the Colegio San Jerónimo, this tapas emporium serves one of the best selections of Galician delicacies in town. ✉ *Carreira do Conde 5* ☏ *981/563163.*

La Bodeguilla de San Roque. One of Santiago's favorite spots for *tapeo* (tapas grazing) and *chiquiteo* (wine sampling), this tavern is just a five-minute walk from the cathedral. ✉ *San Roque 13* ☏ *981/564379.*

O Dezaseis. Specialists in small servings of great products, this traditional favorite near the town's center is a must on any tapas crawl. ✉ *Rúa de San Pedro 16* ☏ *981/577633.*

Prada a Tope. This rustic spot just behind the cathedral specializes in products from El Bierzo, either at the bar or in one of the dining rooms. ✉ *Troia 10* ☏ *981/581909.*

Cafés

Santiago is one of Spain's best cities for European-style coffee-nursing. Popular with students, **A Calderería** (✉ Calderería 26 ☏ 981/572045) juxtaposes contemporary and traditional aesthetics. Try Clip Nougat, ice cream with pistachios and toasted almonds. Once a gathering place for Galician poets, the **Cafe Bar Derby** (✉ Rúa das Orfas 29 ☏ 981/586417) remains a serene place for coffee and pastries. **Cafe Bar Literarios** (✉ Praza da Quintana 1 ☏ 981/565630) overlooks the plaza with generous windows and outdoor tables. Inside, a deliberately gaudy mural incorporates send-ups of famous paintings. Cozy **Iacobus** (✉ Azibechería 5 ☏ 981/582804 ✉ Calderería 42 ☏ 981/583415) blends stone walls with contemporary wood trim and light fixtures; look down to see a glass cache of coffee beans in the floor.

Nightlife & the Arts

Santiago's nightlife peaks on Thursday night, as many students spend weekends at home with their families. For up-to-date information on concerts, films, and clubs, pick up the student-run magazine *Compostelan* at any newsstand. Also check the monthly paper *Compostela*, available at the main tourist office on Rúa do Vilar, for current goings-on. Bars and seafood-theme tapas joints line the old streets south of the cathedral, particularly **Rúa do Franco, Rúa da Raiña,** and **Rúa do Vilar.** A great first stop, especially if you haven't eaten dinner, is **Rúa de San Clemente,** off the Praza do Obradoiro, where three bars in a row offer two or three plates of tapas free with each drink, an astonishing value.

O Beiro (✉ Rúa da Raiña 3 ☏ 981/581370) is a rustic wine bar with a laid-back professional crowd. Galicia's oldest pub is also one of its most unusual: **Modus Vivendi** (✉ Praza Feixóo 1) is in a former stable. The old stone feeding trough is now a low table, and instead of stairs you walk on ridged stone inclines designed for the former occupants—horses and cattle. A thirtysomething crowd packs the low-ceiling bar nightly, and on weekends the bar hosts live music (jazz, ethnic, Celtic) and sometimes storytelling. Drink to Galicia's Celtic roots with live music at **Casa das Crechas** (✉ Vía Sacra 3 ☏ 981/560751), where Celtic wood carvings hang from thick stone walls and dolls of playful Galician witches ride their brooms above the bar. **Retablo Concerto** (⊠ Rúa Nova 13 ☏ 981/564851) is cozy and has live music on weekends. **Blaster** (⊠ Av. República Argentina 6 ☏ 981/572809) is a hot musical bar.

The modern **Auditorio de Galicia** (⊠ Av. Burgo das Nacións ☏ 981/ 573855), north of town, has high-quality classical and jazz programs and a fine art gallery. In residence is the Royal Galician Philharmonic, which has hosted Il Giardino Armonico, the Academy of St. Martin-in-the-Fields, and the Leipzig Gewandhaus Orchestra. Players at Santiago's **Teatro Principal** (⊠ Rúa Nova 21 ☏ 981/528700) stage plays in Spanish, as well as dance performances and film festivals. The **Municipal tourist office** (⊠ Rua do Vilar 63 ☏ 981/555129) specializes in all things Santiago, including information about cultural events and venues.

Shopping
Galicia is known throughout Spain for its distinctive blue-and-white ceramics with bold modern designs, made in Sargadelos and O Castro. Peruse a wide selection at **Sargadelos** (⊠ Rúa Nova 16 ☏ 981/581905).

Look for beautifully crafted jewelry with the black stone azabache (jet, or compact black coal), at **Antonio Uzal Vázquez** (⊠ Abril Ares 8 ☏ 981/ 583483). A boutique founded in 1906 and run by **Augusto Otero** (⊠ Casa de Cabildo, Praza de Praterías 5 ☏ 981/581027) has fine handcrafted silver. On a tiny lane off Azabachería, **Noroeste** (⊠ Ruela de Xerusalén, 0 ☏ 981/577170) sells handmade jewelry.

In the fishing town of Camariñas, women fashion exquisite lace collars, scarves, and table linens. The best place to buy their work, and watch some of it being crafted, is **Bolillos** (⊠ Rúa Nova 40 ☏ 981/589776).

Pazo de Oca
⑪ *27 km (17 mi) southeast of Santiago.*

The barons who ruled over Galicia's peasants and the rest of its feudal society lived in pazos (country manor houses) like this one. Stroll the gardens to the lily pond and lake, where a stone boat stays miraculously afloat. ☏ *986/587435* ⊡ *€4, free Mon. 9–12:30* ☉ *Daily, 9–dusk.*

Padrón
⑫ *18 km (11 mi) south of Santiago.*

Having grown up beside the Roman port of Iría Flavia, Padrón is where the body of St. James is believed to have washed ashore after its miraculous maritime journey. The town is known for its *pimientos de Padrón,* tiny green peppers fried and sprinkled with sea salt. The fun in eating these is that one in five or so is spicy-hot. Galicia's biggest **food market** is held here every Sunday. Padrón was the birthplace of one of Galicia's heroines, the 19th-century poet Rosalía de Castro. The lovely **Casa-Museo Rosalía de Castro,** where she lived with her husband, a historian, now displays family memorabilia. ⊠ *Ctra. de Herbón* ☏ *981/811204* ⊡ *€1.50* ☉ *May–Sept., Tues.–Sat. 10–2 and 4–8, Sun. 10–1:30; Oct.–Apr., Tues.–Sat. 10–1:30 and 4–7, Sun. 10–1:30.*

Where to Stay & Eat

★ **$$** ✕▣ **A Casa Antiga do Monte.** This graceful manor house combines modern comfort and equipment with vintage furniture and Asturian architecture. The crackling fire in the dining room and the 18th-century horreo (granary) in the yard add up to perfect rustic comfort. Meals ($$) here include local culinary delights such as *fabada* (bean stew) and *chorizo a la sidra* (chorizo sausage with cider). ⊠ *Boca do Monte-Lestrove, 1½ km (1 mi) southwest of Padrón, 15916* ☎ *981/812400* 📠 *981/812401* ⊕ *www.susavilaocio.es* ↩ *16 rooms* ♢ *Restaurant, pool, gym, bar, parking (fee); no a/c* ▤ *AE, DC, MC, V.*

THE COSTA DA MORTE & RÍAS BAIXAS

West of Santiago, scenic C543 leads to the coast. Straight west, the shore is windy, rocky, and treacherous—hence its name, the "Coast of Death." The series of wide, quiet estuaries south of here is called the Rías Baixas (Low Estuaries). The hilly drive takes you through a green countryside dappled with vineyards, tiny farms, and Galicia's trademark horreos (granaries), most with a cross at one or both ends.

Fisterra

🔞 *50 km (31 mi) west of Santiago, 75 km (48 mi) southwest of A Coruña.*

There was a time when this lonely, windswept outcrop over raging waters was thought to be the end of the earth—the *"finis terrae"* (Cabo Finisterre in Castilian). The known western world sank into the ocean here with a flourish of rocky beaches. All that's left is a run-down stone *faro* (lighthouse) perched on a cliff; though it's not officially open to the public, you might find the door open. Aside from legends, the only draw in this tiny seaside town is its pleasant (barring storms) main plaza and the 12th-century church of **Santa Maria das Areas.** Romanesque, Gothic, and baroque elements combine in an impressive but rather gloomy facade. ⊠ *Manuel Lago País s/n* ☎ *Free* ⊙ *June–Sept., daily 9–2 and 3–6; Oct.–May, daily 10–2 and 4–6.*

Muros

🔞 *55 km (34 mi) southeast of Fisterra, 65 km (40 mi) southwest of Santiago.*

Muros is a popular summer resort with lovely, arcaded streets framed by Gothic arches. The quiet back alleys of the old town reveal some well-preserved characteristic Galician granite houses. The real action here takes place when fishing boats return to dock from the mussel-breeding platforms that dot the bay. Wander the port on a weekday afternoon during the unloading and mussel-sorting and rinsing. At around 6 PM a siren signals the start of the *lonja* (fish auction), and anyone is welcome, though you need a special license to buy. Trays upon trays—some spilling over with more than a dozen slimy octopi, or cod with heaving gills—line the floor, which in turn is covered in a sheen of saltwater, jet-black squid ink, and fish blood—the favored footwear is knee-high rubber boots. Good nearby beaches include Praia de San Francisco and Praia de Area.

Noia

⑮ *30 km (19 mi) east of Muros, 36 km (22 mi) west of Santiago.*

Deep within the Ría de Muros y Noia, the compact medieval town of Noia nuzzles up to the foot of the Barbanza mountain range. The Gothic church of **San Martín** rises over the old town's Praza do Tapal, facing resolutely out to sea. In the town center, **La Alameda** is a lovely sculpted park that gives way to a black-, white-, and red-tile pedestrian street lined with palm trees and stone and wrought-iron benches. You can catch glimpses of the ría through the trees; in the summer, the street fills with terrace cafés. Near Noia are the praias (beaches) Testal and Boa.

The 14th-century church of **Santa María a Nova** (⊠ Off Carreiriña do Ferreiro) has many well-preserved medieval tombstones, each carved with a family emblem and the tools or symbols of the buried artisan. One shipbuilder's stone depicts a compass, an anchor, and an ax.

Pontevedra

⑯ *55 km (34 mi) southeast of Noia, 59 km (37 mi) south of Santiago.*

At the head of its ría, Pontevedra is the largest city on Spain's northwest coast after A Coruña. You approach through prefab suburbs, but Pontevedra's old quarter is well preserved and largely undiscovered. Speckled with bars, it's lively-to-wild on weekends. The 16th-century seafarers' basilica of **Santa María Mayor,** with a 1541 facade, has lovely, sinuous vaulting and, at the back of the nave, a Romanesque portal. Above the door in the lower part of the basilica is a 16th-century image of Christ with the Virgin and St. John. At the end of the right nave is an 18th-century Christ by the Galician sculptor Ferreiro. ⊠ *Av. de Santa María s/n* ☎ *986/866185* 🎟 *Free* ☉ *Daily 11–1 and 6–8.*

★ Pontevedra's **Museo Provincial** is in two 18th-century mansions connected by a stone bridge. Displays include exquisite Celtic jewelry, silver from all over the world, and several large model ships. The original kitchen in this building is intact, complete with stone fireplace; nearby, take the tiny, steep wooden stairs down to the reconstructed captain's chamber on the battleship *Numancia,* which limped back to Spain after the Dos de Mayo battle with Peru in 1866. Completing the loop, upstairs in the first building, are Spanish and Italian paintings and some inlay work. ⊠ *Praza de Leña* ☎ *986/851455* 🎟 *Free* ☉ *Tues.–Sat. 10–2 and 4–7, Sun. 11–2.*

Where to Stay & Eat

★ **$$$–$$$$** ✕ **Casa Solla.** Pepe Solla brings Galicia's bounty to his terrace garden restaurant, 2 km (1 mi) outside of town toward O Grove. Try the *menu desgustacion* (tasting menu) to sample a selection of regional favorites, such as *lomo de caballa* (grilled mackerel) and *jarrete de cordero* (sliced lamb shank). ⊠ *Av. Sineiro 7, Crtra. de La Toja, Km 2, San Salvador de Poio* ☎ *986/872884* ☐ *AE, DC, MC, V* ☉ *Closed Mon. and late Dec.–early Jan. No dinner Thurs. or Sun.*

$$$ ✕🏠 **Casa del Barón.** A 16th-century manor house built on the foundations of an ancient Roman villa in the heart of the old quarter, the fairly dark Parador de Pontevedra has a baronial stone stairway winding up from the front lobby. Guest rooms have recessed windows with lace curtains and large wooden shutters; some face a small rose garden. The restaurant ($$–$$$$), which serves fine Galician food, is full of antique mirrors, candelabras, and portraits. ⊠ *Barón 19, 36002* ☎ *986/855800* 🖷 *986/852195* ⊕ *www.parador.es* ⇆ *47 rooms* ☖ *Restaurant, café, Wi-Fi, bar, library* ☰ *AE, DC, MC, V.*

$$$ 🍽 **Rectoral de Cobres.** This felicitous intersection of contemporary design and handsomely aging rustic charm was originally built as the village parsonage in 1729. With panoramic views over Vigo and the Strait of Rand where Francis Drake made a habit of sinking Spanish galleons, the Rectoral offers, along with impeccable comfort and taste, nearby golf, visits to the beautiful port of San Adrián de Cobres, scuba diving in search of sunken galleons, or visits to the prehistoric rock carvings at Campo Lameiro. ⊠ *San Adrián de Cobres, 36142* ☎ *986/673810* 🖷 *986/673803* ⊕ *www.rectoral.com* ⇆ *8 rooms* ☖ *Pool, bar, meeting rooms, parking* ☰ *AE, MC, V.*

Tapas Bars

La Navarra. Join the locals leaning on great oak wine barrels to watch soccer on the incongruous television and eat the spicy chorizo sausage that hangs from ceiling racks above the bar. ⊠ *Rúa Princessa 13* ☎ *986/ 851254.*

Jaqueyui. If you can cope with the lively, smoky atmosphere, then this cozy, central bar serves one of the most impressive slices of tortilla in Spain, ideally washed down with a glass of the fine house Rioja. ⊠ *Rúa de Doña Tareixa 1* ☎ *986/861820.*

┌ EN
└ ROUTE

While driving west on the C550, you'll pass **Albariño vineyards.** Wind your way through the small towns around here; it's still possible to come across the occasional donkey hauling wagons heaped with grapes.

O Grove

❶⓻ *31 km (19 mi) northwest of Pontevedra, 75 km (47 mi) south of Santiago.*

O Grove (El Grove in Castilian) throws an illustrious shellfish festival the second week of October, but you can enjoy the day's catch in taverns and restaurants year-round. From here you can cross a bridge to the island of **A Toxa** (La Toja), famous for its spas. Legend has it that a man abandoned an ailing donkey here and found it up on all fours, fully rejuvenated, upon his return; the waters are still said to have healing properties. The island's south side has a palm-filled garden anchored on one side by the **Capilla de San Sebastián,** a tiny church covered in cockleshells. Nearby Reboredo is the home of **Acquarium/galicia,** one of Spain's finest aquariums, devised to showcase marine life endemic to Galicia in an original and interactive manner. ⊠ *Punta Moreiras s/n* ☎ *986/731515* ⊕ *www.acquariumgalicia.com* ☒ *€9* ☉ *Mon. and Thurs. 10–5, Tues., Wed., and Fri.–Sun. 10–8.*

Where to Stay & Eat

$$–$$$$ ✕ **El Crisol.** Photos of famous diners greet you as you enter this secluded spot. The menu has lobster, shrimp, spider crabs, scallops, and freshly caught fish. If you can't make up your mind, a house stew, *sopa de pescados mixtos*, combines most of the above. Save room for the *torta de queso*, a rich cheesecake dessert. ✉ *Hospital 10* ☎ *986/730029* ▭ *AE, DC, MC, V* ⊙ *Closed Mon. Sept.–June. No lunch Mon. July and Aug.*

$$$$ ⊞ **Gran Hotel Hesperia La Toja.** Extravagant and exorbitant (for the region), this classic spa hotel is on the breezy island off O Grove, surrounded by pine trees. Guest rooms are simple, their charm slightly faded compared with the grandiose formality of the foyers and salons. Try to book a room with a sea view. The **Casino La Toja** (☎ *986/731000*) is steps from the hotel. ✉ *36991 Isla de la Toja* ☎ *986/730025* 📠 *986/730026* ⊕ *www.hesperia.com* ⤴ *197 rooms* ⚘ *Restaurant, Wi-Fi, 9-hole golf course, tennis court, 2 pools (1 indoors) health club, spa, beach, piano bar, casino, dance club* ▭ *AE, DC, MC, V.*

Cambados

⑱ *34 km (21 mi) north of Pontevedra, 61 km (37 mi) southwest of Santiago.*

This breezy seaside town has a charming, almost entirely residential old quarter. The impressive main square, **Praza de Fefiñanes,** is bordered on almost two sides by the imposing 17th-century Pazo de Fefiñanes, now an Albariño bodega.

Where to Stay & Eat

★ $$–$$$$ ✕ **María José.** From its privileged first-floor spot across from the parador, the Ribadomar family produces inventive dishes—salads of scallops or large prawns with bacon. Specialties are *arroz de marisco caldoso* (shellfish, stock, and rice), or *mariscada* (fresh seafood). ✉ *San Gregorio 2* ☎ *986/542281* ▭ *MC, V* ⊙ *Closed last wk in Dec. and 1st wk in Jan.; no dinner Sun. Oct.–June; closed Mon. Oct.–June.*

$$$ ✕⊞ **Parador de Cambados (El Albariño).** The bar of this airy mansion is large and inviting, with natural light and wooden booths. Rooms are warmly furnished with wrought-iron lamps, area rugs, and full-length wood shutters over small-pane windows. The kitchen's ($$–$$$$) *lenguado al vino albariño* (sole in Albariño wine sauce) is simply divine; be sure to order some local Albariño wine in its purest form. ✉ *Paseo de Cervantes s/n, 36630* ☎ *986/542250* 📠 *986/542068* ⊕ *www.parador.es* ⤴ *58 rooms* ⚘ *Restaurant, tennis court, pool, meeting rooms* ▭ *AE, DC, MC, V.*

Nightlife

Bar Laya (✉ Praza de Fefiñanes ☎ 986/542436) is easy to spot on the Praza de Fefiñanes, because it's filled with a youngish crowd day and night. Stone walls and close quarters keep this wine-tasting haven lively and inviting. A corner of the bar is given over to a substantial wine shop.

Shopping

Cambados is the hub for Albariño wines, one of Spain's best white wines—full bodied and fruity, yet fresh. **A Casa do Albariño** (✉ Rúa Principe 3

☎ 986/542236) is a tiny, tasteful emporium of Galician wines and cheeses. Head to **Cucadas** (✉ Praza de Fefiñanes ☎ 986/542511) for a particularly large selection of baskets, copper items, and Camariñas lace.

Vigo

⑲ *31 km (19 mi) south of Pontevedra, 90 km (56 mi) south of Santiago.*

Vigo's formidable port is choked with trawlers and fishing boats and lined with clanging shipbuilding yards. Its sights (or lack thereof) fall far short of its commercial swagger. The city's casual appeal lies a few blocks inland where the port commotion gives way to the narrow, dilapidated streets of the old town. On **Rúa Pescadería,** in the barrio called La Piedra, from 8:30 to 3:30 daily, Vigo's famed *ostreras*—a group of rubber-glove fisherwomen who have been peddling fresh oysters to passersby for more than 50 years—shuck their way through bushels of oysters hauled into port that morning. Healthy rivalry has made them expert hawkers who cheerfully badger all who walk by, occasionally talking up the oyster-as-aphrodisiac. You buy a dozen (for about €6), the women plate them and plunk a lemon on top, and you can then take your catch into any nearby restaurant and turn it into a meal. A short stroll southwest of the old town brings you to the fishermen's barrio of **El Berbés.** Here the day starts as early as 5 AM with the pungent and cacophonous *lonja* (fish market), where fishermen sell their morning catch to vendors and restaurants. **Ribera del Berbés,** facing the port, has several seafood restaurants, most with outdoor tables in summer. South of Vigo's old town is the hilltop **Parque del Castro** (✉ Between Praza de España and Praza do Rei, beside Av. Marqués de Alcedo), a quiet, stately park with sandy paths, palm trees, mossy embankments, and stone benches. Atop a series of steps are the remains of an old fort and a *mirador* (lookout) with fetching views of Vigo's coastline and the Islas Cíes.

Where to Eat

★ $$-$$$$　✕ **El Mosquito.** Signed photos from the likes of King Juan Carlos and Julio Iglesias cover the walls of this elegant rose- and stone-wall restaurant, open since 1928. The brother-and-sister team of Manolo and Carmiña have been at the helm for the last few decades; their specialties include *lenguado a la plancha* (grilled sole) and *navajas* (razor clams). Try the *tocinillos,* a sugary flan. The restaurant's name refers to an era when wine arrived in wooden barrels: If mosquitoes gathered at the barrel's mouth, it held good wine. (✉ *Praza da Pedra 4* ☎*986/224441* ☰ *AE, DC, MC, V* ۞ *Closed weekends and Aug.*

$-$$$　✕ **Bar Cocedero La Piedra.** This jovial tapas bar does a roaring lunch trade with Vigo locals. The chefs serve heaping plates of *mariscos* (shellfish) at market prices. Fresh and fruity Albariño wines are the beverage of choice; the chummy, elbow-to-elbow crowd sits at round tables covered with paper. (✉ *Rúa Pescadería 3* ☎ *986/223765* ☰ *AE, DC, MC, V.*

$　✕ **Tapas Areal.** This ample and lively bar flanked by ancient stone and exposed redbrick walls is a good spot for tapas and beer or Albariños and Ribeiros. (✉ *México 36* ☎ *986/418643* ☰ *MC, V.*

Shopping

Traditional musical instruments, such as the bagpipes, are studied, displayed, and sold at the **La Escuela de Artes y Oficios** (Universidade Popular de Vigo; ⊠ Av. García Barbón 5 ☎ 986/228087).

Islas Cíes

⑳ *35 km (21 mi) west of Vigo in Atlantic Ocean.*

The Cíes Islands are a nature reserve and one of the last unspoiled refuges on the Spanish coast. From July to September, about eight boats a day leave from Vigo's harbor, returning later in the day, for the round-trip fare of €12 for adults. The 45-minute ride brings you to fine white-sand beaches. Birds abound, and the only land transportation is your own two feet: It takes about an hour to cross the main island. For camping reservations (required), call **Camping Islas Cíes** (☎ 986/438358), open Easter week and June 15 through September 15.

Baiona

㉑ *12 km (8 mi) southwest of Vigo.*

At the southern end of the AP9 freeway and the Ría de Vigo, Baiona (Bayona in Castilian) is a summer haunt of affluent Gallegos. When Columbus's *Pinta* landed here in 1492, Baiona became the first town to receive the news of the discovery of the New World. Once a castle, **Monte Real** is one of Spain's most popular paradors; walk around the battlements for superb views. Inland from Baiona's waterfront, Paseo Marítima, a jumble of streets has seafood restaurants and lively cafés and bars. Calle Ventura Misa is one of the main drags. On your way into or out of town, check out Baiona's **Roman bridge.** The best nearby beach is Praia de América, north of town toward Vigo.

Where to Stay & Eat

★ **$$$$** ✕⌂ **Parador de Baiona.** This baronial parador was built inside the walls of a medieval castle on a hilltop fortified since 200 BC. The rooms are plush, and some even have balconies with ocean views toward the Islas Cíes. Try the *entremeses variados* (mixed appetizers) for a sampler of typical seafood ($$$–$$$$), or *parillada de pescados* (grilled swordfish, salmon, and cod). ⊠ *Ctra. de Baiona at Monterreal, 36300* ☎ *986/355000* ⎙ *986/355076* ⊕ *www.parador.es* ➭ *122 rooms* ⚫ *Restaurant, Wi-Fi, tennis court, pool, health club, beach, bar, playground* ⊟ *AE, DC, MC, V.*

Tui

㉒ *14 km (9 mi) southeast of Baiona, 26 km (16 mi) south of Vigo.*

Leave Vigo on the scenic coastal route PO552, which takes you up the banks of the Miño River along the Portuguese border. If time is short, jump on the inland A55: Both routes lead to Tui, where steep, narrow streets rich with emblazoned mansions suggest the town's past as one of the seven capitals of the Galician kingdom. Today it's an important border town, from which the mountains of Portugal are visible from the cathedral. Across the river in Portugal, the old fortress town of Vallença contains reasonable shops, bars, restaurants, and a hotel with splendid views of Tui. Crucial during the medieval wars between Castile and Portugal, Tui has a 13th-century **cathedral** that looks like a fortress. The cathedral's majestic cloister surrounds a lush formal garden. ⊠ *Pl. de San Fernando s/n* ☎ *986/600511* 🖼 *€2* ☉ *Daily 9:30–1:30 and 4–7.*

Where to Stay & Eat

$$$ ✕🖾 **Parador de Tui.** This granite-and-chestnut hotel on the bluffs overlooking the Miño has lobbies filled with rural antiques and paintings by local artists. Guest rooms are furnished with convincing reproductions. Views of the woods surround the dining room ($$–$$$$), where specialties from the river Miño include Atlantic salmon, lamprey eel, sea trout, and trout. For dessert, try the the *pececitos*, almond-flavor pastries made by local convent nuns. ⊠ *Av. del Portugal s/n, 36700* ☎ *986/600300* 🖼 *986/602163* ⊕ *www.parador.es* ⇆ *32 rooms* ⌂ *Restaurant, Wi-Fi, tennis court, pool, bar, playground, free parking* ⊟ *AE, DC, MC, V.*

A CORUÑA & RÍAS ALTAS

Galicia's gusty, rainy northern coast has inspired local poets to wax lyrical about raindrops falling continuously on one's head. Don't worry, the sun does shine here, and it suffuses town and country with a golden glow. North of A Coruña, the Rías Altas (Upper Estuaries) notch the coast as you head east toward the Cantabrian Sea.

A Coruña

㉓ *57 km (35 mi) north of Santiago.*

One of Spain's busiest ports, A Coruña (La Coruña in Castilian) prides itself on being the most progressive city in the region. The weather can be fierce, wet, and windy—hence the glass-enclosed, white-pane galleries on the houses lining the harbor. To see why sailors once nicknamed A Coruña *la ciudad de cristal* (the glass city), stroll **Dársena de la Marina,** said to be the longest seaside promenade in Europe. Although the congregation of boats is charming, the real sight is across the street: a long, gracefully curved row of houses. Built by fishermen in the 18th century, the houses actually face *away* from the sea—at the end of a long day, these men were tired of looking at the water. Nets were hung from the porches to dry, and fish was sold on the street below. When Galicia's first glass factory opened nearby, someone thought to enclose these porches in glass, like the latticed stern galleries of oceangoing galleons, to keep wind and rain at bay. The resulting **glass galleries** ultimately spread across the harbor and eventually throughout Galicia.

Plaza de María Pita is the focal point of the *ciudad vieja* (old town). Its north side is given over to the neoclassical **Palacio Municipal,** or city hall, built 1908–12 with three Italianate domes. The **monument** in the center, built in 1998, depicts the heroine herself, Maior (María) Pita, holding her lance. When England's notorious Sir Francis Drake arrived to sack A Coruña in 1589, the locals were only half finished building the defensive Castillo de San Antón, and a 13-day battle ensued. When

María Pita's husband died, she took up his lance, slew the Briton who tried to plant the Union Jack here, and revived the exhausted Coruñesos, inspiring women to join the battle as well.

The 12th-century church of **Santiago** (✉ Pl. de la Constitución s/n), the oldest church in A Coruña, was the first stop on the *camino inglés* (English route) toward Santiago de Compostela. Originally Romanesque, it's now a hodgepodge, with Gothic arches, a baroque altarpiece, and two 18th-century rose windows. The church smells of age and the sea. The **Colegiata de Santa María** (✉ Pl. de Santa María) is a Romanesque beauty from the mid-13th century, often called Santa María del Campo (St. Mary of the Field) because it was once outside the city walls. The facade depicts the Adoration of the Magi; the celestial figures include St. Peter, holding the keys to heaven. A quirk of this church is that, because of an architectural miscalculation, the roof is too heavy for its supports, so the columns inside lean outward, and the buttresses outside have been thickened. Couples who want to get married in the old town book this poetic church far in advance. At the northeastern tip of the old town is the **Castillo de San Antón** (St. Anthony's Castle), a 16th-century fort. Inside is A Coruña's **Museum of Archaeology**, with remnants of the prehistoric Celtic culture that once thrived in these parts. The collection includes silver artifacts as well as pieces of the Celtic stone forts called *castros*. ☎ *981/189850* 🔳 *€2* ⊙ *July and Aug., Tues.–Sat. 10–8:30, Sun. 10–2:30; Sept.–June, Tues.–Sat. 10–7, Sun. 10–2.*

The **Museo de Bellas Artes** (Museum of Fine Arts), housed in a converted convent on the edge of the old town, has French, Spanish, and Italian paintings, and a curious collection of etchings by Goya. ✉ *C. Zalaeta s/n* ☎ *981/223723* 🔳 *Free* ⊙ *Tues.–Fri. 10–8, Sat. 10–2 and 4:30–8, Sun. 10–2.* Across town, on a hill, is the **Casa de las Ciencias** (Science Museum), a hands-on museum where children can learn the principles of physics and technology. ✉ *Parque de Santa Margarita* ☎ *981/189844* ⊕ *www.casaciencias.org* 🔳 *Museum €2, planetarium €1* ⊙ *Sept.–June, daily 10–7; July and Aug., daily 11–9.*

Much of A Coruña sits on a peninsula, on the tip of which is the **Torre de Hercules**—the oldest still-functioning lighthouse in the world. Originally built during the reign of Trajan, the Roman emperor born in Spain in AD 98, the lighthouse was rebuilt in the 18th century and looks strikingly modern; all that remains from Roman times are inscribed foundation stones. Scale the 245 steps for superb views of the city and coastline—and if you're here on a summer weekend, return at night, when the tower opens for views of city lights along the Atlantic. Lining the approach to the lighthouse are sculptures depicting figures from Galician and Celtic legends. At the base of the structure, a museum displays items dug up during the restoration of the lighthouse and area. ✉ *Ctra. de la Torre s/n* ☎ *981/223730* 🔳 *€2* ⊙ *Sept.–June, daily 10–6; July and Aug., Sun.–Thurs. 10–6, Fri. and Sat. 10–11:45 PM.*

The slate-covered **Domus/Casa del Hombre** (Museum of Mankind) was designed by Japanese architect Arata Isozaki. In the shape of a ship's sail, this museum is dedicated to the study of the human being, and particularly the human body. A film showing a human birth and panels on

language are among the exhibits, many of which are interactive. ⊠ *C.
Santa Teresa 1* 🕾 *981/189840* 🖴 *Museum €2, IMAX €1* ⊙ *July and
Aug., daily 11–9; Sept.–June, daily 10–7.*

Where to Stay & Eat

$$$–$$$$ ✕ **Casa Pardo.** Near the port, this chic, double-decker dining room has
soft ocher tones, with perfectly matched wood furniture and cool light-
ing. Try the *rape a la cazuela* (bay leaf–scented monkfish and potatoes
drizzled with oil and sprinkled with paprika, baked in a clay casserole).
For dessert, there's flaky pastry with cream or chocolate soufflé. ⊠ *Novoa
Santos 15* 🕾 *981/280021* 🖃 *AE, DC, MC, V* ⊙ *Closed Sun.*

$$–$$$$ ✕ **El Coral.** The window is an altar of shellfish, with varieties of mol-
lusks and crustaceans you've probably never seen before. Inside, wood-
panel walls, crystal chandeliers, and 12 white-clad tables help create an
elegant yet casual experience. Specialties include *turbante de mariscos*
(a platter—literally, a "turban"—of steamed and boiled shellfish). ⊠ *Callejón de la Estacada 9, at Av. Marina* 🕾 *981/200569* 🖴 *Reservations essential* 🖃 *AE, DC, MC, V* ⊙ *Closed Sun.*

★ $$–$$$$ ✕ **Adega o Bebedeiro.** Steps from the ultramodern Domus, this tiny
restaurant is beloved by locals for its authentic food and low prices. It
feels like an old farmhouse, with stone walls, floors, and fireplace; pine
tables and stools; dusty wine bottles (*adega* means "wine cellar"); and
rustic implements. Appetizers, such as *setas rellenas de marisco y salsa
holandesa* (wild mushrooms with seafood and hollandaise sauce), are
followed by fresh fish at market prices. ⊠ *C. Ángel Rebollo 34* 🕾 *981/
210609* 🖃 *AE, DC, MC, V* ⊙ *Closed Mon., no dinner Sun.; closed last
2 wks in June and last 2 wks in Dec.*

★ $–$$$ ✕ **La Penela.** Try at least a few crabs or mussels with béchamel, for which
this restaurant is locally famous. If shellfish isn't your speed, make sure
you sample the equally popular roast veal. Enjoy the smart, contemporary, bottle-green dining room while feasting on fresh fish and sipping
some Albariño. The restaurant occupies a corner of the lively Praza María
Pita. ⊠ *Praza María Pita 12* 🕾 *981/209200* 🖃 *AE, DC, MC, V*
⊙ *Closed Sun. and Jan. 10–25.*

$$$$ 🏨 **Hesperia Finisterre.** This grande dame—where the old town joins the
bay—is the oldest of A Coruña's top hotels. A favorite with both busi-
nesspeople and families, it has large, carpeted rooms with modern wood
furnishings and bright upholstery. Ask for a room overlooking the bay.
⊠ *Paseo del Parrote 2, 15001* 🕾 *981/205400* 🖷 *981/208462* ⊕ *www.
hesperia-finisterre.com* 🛏 *92 rooms* ⅄ *Restaurant, in-room broadband, Wi-Fi, 2 tennis courts, 4 pools, health club, hair salon, bar, playground, meeting rooms* 🖃 *AE, DC, MC, V.*

$$ 🏨 **Tryp Coruña.** It's not charming, per se—fluorescent lighting abounds—
but soft blues and nautical prints offset its shortcomings while reinforc-
ing the maritime feel. Convenient to the El Corte Inglés department store
and the bus and train stations, this high-rise runs like a well-oiled ma-
chine. ⊠ *Ramón y Cajal 53, 15001* 🕾 *981/242711* 🖷 *981/236728*
⊕ *www.solmelia.com* 🛏 *181 rooms* ⅄ *Bar* 🖃 *AE, DC, MC, V.*

Nightlife

Begin your evening in the **Plaza de María Pita**—bars, cafés, and tapas
bars proliferate off the plaza's western corners and farther inland. **Calles**

Franja, Riego de Agua, Barrera, and **Galera** and the **Plaza del Humor** have many bars, some of which serve Ribeiro wine in bowls. Night owls head for the posh and pricey clubs around **Praia del Orzán** (Orzán Beach), particularly along Calle Juan Canalejo. For lower-key late-night entertainment, the old town has cozy taverns where you can grab a nightcap even as the new day dawns. Try **A Roda 2** (✉ Capitán Troncoso 8 ☎ 981/228671) for tapas—octopus in its own ink, garlic garbanzo beans—and a lively evening crowd.

Shopping

Calle Real has boutiques with contemporary fashions. A stroll down **Calle San Andres,** two blocks inland from Calle Real, or **Avenida Juan Flórez,** leading into the newer town, may yield some sartorial treasures. Galicia has spawned some of Spain's top designers, notably **Adolfo Dominguez** (✉ Avenida Finisterre 3 ☎ 981/252539). For hats and Galician folk clothing, stop into **Sastrería Iglesias** (✉ Rego do Auga 14 ☎ 981/221634)—founded 1864—where artisan José Luis Iglesias Rodrígues sells his textiles. Authentic Galician *zuecos* (hand-painted wooden clogs) are still worn in some villages to navigate mud; the cobbler **José López Rama** (✉ Rúa do Muiño 7 ☎ 981/701068) has a workshop 15 minutes south of A Coruña in the village of Carballo. **Alfares de Buño** (✉ Plazuela de los Angeles 6 ☎ No phone) sells glazed terra-cotta ceramics from Bunho, 40 km (25 mi) west of A Coruña on C552. These crafts are prized by aficionados—to see where they're made, drive out to Bunho itself, where potters work in private studios all over town. Stop into **Alfarería y Cerámica de Buño** (✉ C. Barreiros s/n, Bunho ☎ 981/721658) to see the results. A wide selection of classic blue-and-white pottery is sold at the factory and museum **Cerámicas del Castro** (✉ O Castro s/n, Sada ☎ 981/620200), north of Coruña in the nearby town of Sada.

Betanzos

★ **㉔** *25 km (15 mi) east of A Coruña, 65 km (40 mi) northeast of Santiago.*

The charming, slightly ramshackle medieval town of Betanzos is still surrounded by parts of its old city wall. It was an important Galician port in the 13th century but is now silted up. The 1292 monastery of **San Francisco** was converted into a church in 1387 by the nobleman Fernán Perez de Andrade, whose magnificent sepulchre, to the left of the west door, has him lying on the backs of a stone bear and boar, with hunting dogs at his feet and an angel receiving his soul by his head. The 15th-century church of **Santa María de Azougue** has 15th-century statues that were stolen in 1981 but subsequently recovered. It's a few steps uphill from the church of San Francisco. The tailors' guild put up the Gothic-style church of **Santiago,** which includes a Door of Glory inspired by the one in Santiago's cathedral. Above the door is a carving of St. James as the Slayer of the Moors.

Shopping

Visit a bagpipe workshop and buy the real thing at **Sellas y Gaitas** (✉ Cerca s/n ☎ No phone), open weekdays 10 to 1 and 5 to 8.

Vilalba

㉕ *87 km (52 mi) east of A Coruña.*

Known as *Terra Cha* (Flat Land) or the Galician Mesopotamia, Vilalba is the source of several rivers, most notably the Miño, which flows down into Portugal. Hills and knolls add texture to the plain.

Where to Stay & Eat

$$$ ✕🏨 **Parador Condes de Vilalba.** Part of the inn is in a massive 15th-century tower that was once a fortress. A drawbridge leads to the two-story lobby, hung with tapestries. The three large octagonal chambers in the tower have beam ceilings, wood floors, hand-carved Spanish furniture, and chandeliers. The restaurant ($$–$$$) offers empanada *de Rax,* made of beef loin, and empanada *de atún* (with tuna); for dessert, order the *San Simón,* a cone-shape, birch-smoked cheese served with apples or pears. ☒ *Valeriano Valdesuso s/n, 27800* ☎ *982/510011* 🖷 *982/ 510090* ⊕*www.parador.es* ➵*48 rooms* ⌂ *Restaurant, gym, sauna, Turkish bath, bar* ▱ *AE, DC, MC, V.*

Mondoñedo

㉖ *121 km (73 mi) northeast of A Coruña, 34 km (20 mi) northeast of Vilalba.*

Founded in 1156, this town was one of the seven capitals of the kingdom of Galicia from the 16th to early 19th century. The **cathedral,** consecrated in 1248, has a museum, a bishop's tomb with inlaid stone, and medieval murals showing the Slaying of the Innocents and St. Peter. The cathedral dominates the ancient **Plaza Mayor,** where a medieval pageant and market are held the first Sunday in August. The quiet streets and squares are filled with old buildings, monasteries, and churches, and include a medieval Jewish quarter. The shop **El Rey de las Tartas** (☒ Obispo Sarmiento 2 ☎ 982/521178) is known for its dessert pies, or *tartas,* made with pastry, sponge cake, *cabello de ángel* ("angel's hair," a filling of pumpkin and syrup, composed of fine strands), and almonds. The tartas are decorated with crystallized cherries and figs.

Where to Eat

$–$$$ ✕ **A Taberna do Valeco.** In a converted mill with exposed stone walls, this tavern on the outskirts of town has been family run since 1956. Pepe Bouso serves free crispy empanadas, sometimes made from wild boar, with each drink; the small restaurant upstairs serves game (in winter), fresh fish, and excellent meat. A good wine list rounds out the experience. ☒ *Rúa Os Muiños de Arriba 6* ☎ *982/521861* ▱ *AE, DC, MC, V* ☾ *No dinner Mon.*

Viveiro

★ ㉗ *119 km (71 mi) northeast of A Coruña, 81 km (50 mi) northeast of Vilalba.*

The once-turreted city walls of this popular summer resort are still partially intact. Two festivals are noteworthy: the Semana Santa processions, in which penitents follow religious processions on their knees, and the Rapa das Bestas, a colorful roundup of wild horses the first Sunday in July (on nearby Monte Buyo).

Where to Stay & Eat

$$ ✕▦ **Hotel Ego.** The view of the ría from this hilltop hotel outside Viveiro is unbeatable—tiny islets and all—and every room has it. Rooms are carpeted and have enormous mirrors and vanity tables. The glassed-in breakfast room faces the ría and a cascade of trees; on a rainy day, you'd much rather be cooped up here than in town. Adjoining the hotel is the elegant Nito restaurant ($$–$$$$), which serves excellent Galician cuisine, such as *percebes* (goose barnacles), spider crab, and lobster. ⊠ *Playa de Area, off N642, 27850* ☎ *982/560987* 🖷 *982/561762* 🛏 *29 rooms* ⟐ *Restaurant, bar* ▭ *AE, MC, V.*

OFF THE BEATEN PATH   Distinctive blue-and-white-glazed contemporary ceramics are made at **CERÁMICA DE SARGADELOS** (⊠ Ctra. Paraño s/n, Cervo ☎ 982/557841), 21 km (13 mi) east of Viveiro. Tour the factory and watch artisans work weekdays 8:30 to 12:30 and 2:30 to 5:30. Shop hours are 11 to 2 and 4 to 7 on weekends and holidays.

Ribadeo

㉘   *50 km (31 mi) southeast of Viveiro.*

Perched on the broad ría of the same name, Ribadeo is the last coastal town before Asturias. The views up and across the estuary are marvelous—depending on the wind, the waves appear to roll *across* the ría rather than straight inland. Salmon and trout fishermen congregate upriver. Take the scenic walk or drive north of town to the **Illa de la Pancha** lighthouse (a 5-km [3-mi] round-trip), connected to the coastal cliffs by a small bridge. If the bridge is closed, savor the briny air around the grassy cliff top.

Where to Stay & Eat

$$–$$$ ✕▦ **Parador de Ribadeo.** Most rooms here have glassed-in sitting areas with views (208 is best) across the ría to Asturias. Parquet floors and harvest-yellow walls are accented by watercolors and etchings of the area. In the dining room ($$–$$$$) a cornucopia of local shellfish is served, much of it swimming around in a holding tank. Try the *sopa de mariscos,* seafood soup with a light pastry top, and the ice cream that's been flavored with tetilla cheese and drizzled with honey. Fishing, horseback riding, and boating are easily arranged. ⊠ *Amador Fernández 7, 27700* ☎ *982/128825* 🖷 *982/128346* ⊕ *www.parador.es* 🛏 *46 rooms, 1 suite* ⟐ *Restaurant, bar* ▭ *AE, DC, MC, V.*

WESTERN ASTURIAS

As you cross into the Principality of Asturias, Galicia's intensely green countryside continues, belying the fact that this is a major mining region once exploited by the Romans for its iron- and gold-rich earth. More mountainous than Galicia, Asturias is bordered to the southeast by the imposing, snowcapped Picos de Europa.

Luarca

㉙ *75 km (47 mi) east of Ribadeo, 92 km (57 mi) northeast of Oviedo.*

The A8 autopista wanders along the entire Asturian coast through western Asturias toward Oviedo. The village of Luarca is tucked into a cove at the end of a final twist of the Río Negro, with a fishing port and, to the west, a sparkling bay. The town is a maze of cobblestone streets, stone stairways, and whitewashed houses, with a harborside decorated with painted flowerpots. The aromas wafting from the port's many bars and restaurants may tempt you to stop for some freshly caught seafood.

Where to Stay & Eat

★ **$$-$$$$** ✕ **Casa Consuelo.** Opened in 1935, Casa Consuelo, one of the most popular spots on Spain's northern coast, is famed for *merluza* (hake) with the northern Spanish delicacy *angulas* (baby eels) and blue cheese (at about €55 for two, depending on market prices). This dish and the busy restaurant itself are not to be missed. ⊠ *Ctra. N634, Km 511, 6 km (4 mi) west of Luarca, Otur* ☎ *985/641809* ⌕ *Reservations essential* ⊟ *AE, DC, MC, V* ⊘ *Closed Mon.*

$$-$$$ ✕ **Sport.** Large windows with river views lead into a kitchen adept at fabada (bean-and-sausage stew) as well as locally caught fish or *pulpo a la gallega* (octopus on boiled potatoes with olive oil, paprika, and garlic). ⊠ *Rivero 9* ☎ *985/641078* ⊟ *AE, DC, MC, V* ⊘ *Closed Jan. and Wed. Oct.–June.*

$-$$$ ✕ **El Barómetro.** This small, family-run seafood eatery in the middle of the harbor front has an inexpensive *menú del día* (daily menu) and a good choice of local fresh fish. For a bit more money, you can dig into *bogavante,* a large-claw lobster. ⊠ *Paseo del Muelle 4* ☎ *985/470662* ⊟ *MC, V* ⊘ *Closed late Sept.–late Oct. No dinner Wed.*

$$ 🏨 **Hotel Villa La Argentina.** Beautifully restored by the González family, this charming Asturian mansion on the hill above Luarca was built in 1899 by a wealthy *Indiano* (Spaniard who made his fortune in South America). There's a small antiques museum on-site. A restaurant is in the old coach house in the garden, surrounded by palm trees and imported shrubs. ⊠ *Villar de Luarca s/n, 33700* ☎ *985/640102* 🖷 *985/640973* ⊕ *www.villalaargentina.com* ⌕ *9 rooms, 3 suites* ⌕ *Restaurant (summer only), Wi-Fi, tennis court, pool, billiards, bar, library* ⊟ *DC, MC, V* ⊘ *Closed early Jan.–mid-Mar.*

$$ 🏨 **Torre de Villademoros.** An artistically restored 18th-century manor house with an elevated *panera* (grain-storage structure) and a medieval tower, this lovely retreat 14 km (8½ mi) east of Luarca is a find. Rooms and both sea and meadow views are superb, as is the cuisine. ⊠ *Villademoros, Valdés s/n, 33788* ☎ *985/645264* 🖷 *985/645265* ⌕ *10 rooms* ⌕ *Restaurant; no a/c* ⊟ *AE, DC, MC, V* ⊘ *Closed weekdays Nov.–Mar.*

EN ROUTE The coastal road leads to the little fishing village of **Cudillero** (35 km [22 mi] east of Luarca), clustered around its tiny port. The emerald green of the surrounding hills, the bright blue of the water, and the white of the houses make this village one of the prettiest in Asturias. Seafood and cider restaurants line the central street that turns into a boat ramp at the bottom of town. The town of **Pravia** and the river Narcea, one of

Spain's best salmon streams, are just inland. Pravia has several Art Nouveau *palacetes* (mansions) built by "Indianos," rich returnees from South America, famous for their trophy mansions and trophy wives—and for financing the local school.

Cornellana, a trout- and salmon-fishing town on the upper river Narcea, has a famous inn, La Fuente, where General Francisco Franco stayed while fishing for salmon, an event faithfully chronicled in the notorious No-Do's (*Noticias del Domingo*)—government newsreels shown before all movie screenings during the dictator's 40-year regime.

Oviedo

③⓪ *92 km (57 mi) southeast of Luarca, 50 km (31 mi) southeast of Cudillero, 30 km (19 mi) south of Gijón.*

Inland, the Asturian countryside starts to look a bit more prosperous. Wooden, thatch-roof horreos strung with golden bundles of drying corn replace the stark granite sheds of Galicia. A drive through the hills and valleys brings you to the capital city, Oviedo. Though primarily industrial, Oviedo has three of the most famous pre-Romanesque churches in Spain and a large university, giving it both ancient charm and youthful zest. Start your explorations with the two exquisite 9th-century chapels outside the city, on the slopes of Monte Naranco.

★ The church of **Santa María del Naranco,** with superb views, and its plainer sister, **San Miguel de Lillo** 300 yards uphill, are the jewels of an early architectural style called Asturian pre-Romanesque, a more primitive, hulking, defensive line that preceded Romanesque architecture by nearly three centuries. Commissioned as part of a summer palace by King Ramiro I when Oviedo was the capital of Christian Spain, these masterpieces have survived for more than 1,000 years. The **Reception Center** (☎ 985/114901 ☉ Wed.–Mon. 11–1:30 and 4–6) near the site provides videos in different languages explaining Asturian pre-Romanesque architecture. ✉ *Ctra. de los Monumentos, 2 km (1 mi) north of Oviedo* ☎ *676/032087* 💰 *€2.20 with guided tour, free Mon., without guide* ☉ *Apr.–Sept., Mon.–Sat. 9:30–1 and 3:30–7, Sun. 9:30–1; Oct.–Mar., Mon.–Sat. 10–12:30 and 3–4:30, Sun. 10–12:30.*

Western Asturias, a major mining region, was once a part of the Roman Gold Route. In Gijón you can view the Roman baths, Termas Romanos.

Oviedo's Gothic **cathedral** was built between the 14th and the 16th centuries around the city's most cherished monument, the **Cámara Santa** (Holy Chamber). King Ramiro's predecessor, Alfonso the Chaste (792–842), built this chamber to hide the treasures of Christian Spain during the long struggle with the Moors. Heavily damaged during the Spanish civil war, it has since been rebuilt. Inside is the gold-leaf **Cross of the Angels,** commissioned by Alfonso the Chaste in 808 and encrusted with pearls and jewels. On the left is the more elegant **Victory Cross,** actually a jeweled sheath crafted in 908 to cover the oak cross used by Pelayo in the battle of Covadonga. The crosses and other treasures were stolen from the cathedral in 1977 but were recovered relatively intact as thieves tried to spirit them out of Europe through Portugal. ⊠ *Pl. Alfonso II El Casto* ☎ *985/221033* 🎫 *Cathedral free, Cámara Santa €1.25, museum €3* ⊘ *Mon.–Sat. 10–1 and 4–7 (4–8 in July and Aug.), Sun. for mass only.*

From the cathedral, look directly across the Plaza Alfonso for the still-inhabited 15th-century **Palacio de la Rúa**, the oldest palace in town. Near the Palacio de la Rúa, on Calle San Francisco, is the beautifully clean 16th-century **Antigua Universidad de Oviedo**. Behind the cathedral, the **Museo Arqueológico**, housed in the splendid Monastery of San Vicente, contains fragments of pre-Romanesque buildings. ⊠ *San Vicente 3* ☎ *985/215405* 🎫 *Free* ⊘ *Tues.–Sat. 10–1:30 and 4–6, Sun. 11–1.*

To see Asturian paintings, visit the 9th-century church of **Santullano**. ⊠ *Pl. Santullano* 🎫 *Free* ⊘ *Tues.–Sat. 9:30–11:30 and Mon. 10–1:30.*

You might want to have a look at the exquisite **Hotel de la Reconquista**, a former 18th-century hospice. In the past, the Spanish crown prince (and prince of Asturias) has presented the annual International Achievement Awards at the hotel; judges for the award still stay there. ⊠ *Gil de Jaz 16* ☎ *985/241100.*

Where to Stay & Eat

★ **$$$–$$$$** ✕ **Casa Fermín.** Skylights, plants, and an air of modernity belie the age of this sophisticated pink-and-granite restaurant, which opened in 1924. Founder Luis Gil introduced traditional Asturian cuisine to seminars around the world. Specialties include fabada (bean-and-sausage stew) and wild game in season. The wine cellar is well stocked. ⊠ *San Francisco 8* ☎ *985/216452* ▤ *AE, DC, MC, V* ⊘ *Closed Sun.*

★ **$$$** ✕ **La Máquina.** For the best fabada in Asturias, head 6 km (4 mi) outside Oviedo toward Avilés and stop at the farmhouse with the miniature locomotive out front. This L-shape, whitewashed dining room has attracted diners from across Spain for decades, some of whom think nothing of making a weekend trip solely for the purpose of eating here. ⊠ *Av. Conde de Santa Bárbara 59, Lugones* ☎ *985/263636* ▤ *DC, MC, V* ⊘ *Closed Sun. and mid-June–mid-July. No dinner.*

$$–$$$ ✕ **El Raitán.** This place is styled like an old-fashioned kitchen, with an antique stove in the entrance. There are a selection of lunch menus, offering ample portions of Asturian specialties: seafood soup, crab bisque, vegetable-and-bean stew, fabada, potatoes stuffed with meat, onions filled with tomatoes, rice pudding, crepes, and nut pastries. ⊠ *Pl. Trascorrales 6* ☎ *985/214218* ▤ *AE, DC, MC, V* ⊘ *No dinner Sun.*

$$$$
Fodor'sChoice
★

🏨 **Hotel de la Reconquista.** In an 18th-century hospice emblazoned with a huge, stone coat of arms, the ultraluxurious Reconquista costs almost twice as much as any other hotel in Asturias. The wide lobby, encircled by a balcony, is decked out with velvet upholstery and 18th-century paintings. A pianist entertains nightly. Guest rooms are large and modern, with comfortable beds and large armchairs. ⊠ *Gil de Jaz 16, 33004* ☎ *985/241100* 🖨 *985/241166* ⊕ *www.hoteldelareconquista.com* ⤴ *132 rooms, 10 suites* ⚭ *Restaurant, coffee shop, Wi-Fi, hair salon, bar* ▤ *AE, DC, MC, V.*

$$$ 🏨 **NH Principado.** Try this hotel if you prize friendliness over flash. The NH chain is modern and functional, but this branch feels more distinguished than most. The hotel is conveniently located between the cathedral and the Plaza de la Escandalera. ☎ *San Francisco 6, 33003* ☏ *985/ 217792* 🖷 *985/213946* ⊕ *www.nh-hoteles.com* ↝ *97 rooms* ⚲ *Restaurant, Wi-Fi, bar* ☰ *AE, DC, MC, V.*

Nightlife & the Arts

The **Teatro Municipal** presents plays and concerts; check newspapers for schedules. The old town's main strip of dance clubs is on **Calle Canóniga.** A rather rowdy town after dark, Oviedo has plenty in the way of loud live music. **Calle Carta Puebla** is packed with pubs, many of which are Irish owing to the region's Celtic heritage. If you're still awake when the old town goes to sleep, try **Sir Lawrence** (✉ Eugenio Tamayo 3 ☎ No phone); you can dance out into daylight here.

Shopping

Some antiques shops are clustered together for a few blocks on **Calle de Mon.** On Thursday and Sunday mornings an outdoor market, **El Rastrillo,** which has all sorts of stuff, is held in El Fontan. Shops throughout the city carry **azabache jewelry** made of jet. For handcrafted leather bags and belts, check out **Artesania Escanda** (✉ Jovellanos 5 ☎ 985/210467). Vacuum-packed fabada is sold at **Casa Veneranda** (✉ Melquíades Álvarez 23 ☎ 985/212454).

Gijón

③ *30 km (19 mi) north of Oviedo, 95 km (59 mi) east of Luarca, 50 km (31 mi) east of Cudillero.*

Gijón can seem overwhelming at first, with its factories and warehouses. Full of hidden hot spots and friendly people, Gijón is part fishing port, part summer resort, and part university town, packed with inviting cafés and excellent restaurants. The promenade along **Praia San Lorenzo** extends from one end of town to the other. Across the narrow peninsula and the Plaza Mayor is the harbor, where the fishing fleet comes in with the day's catch. The steep peninsula is the old fishermen's quarter, **Cimadevilla,** now the hub of Gijón's nightlife. From the park at the highest point on the headland, beside Basque sculptor Eduardo Chillida's massive sculpture *Elogio del Horizonte* (In Praise of the Horizon), there's a panoramic view of the coast and city. Gijón's **Termas Romanas** (Roman baths), dating back to the time of Augustus, are under the plaza at the end of the beach. ✉ *Campo Valdés* ☎ *985/345147* 🎫 *€2.35* ⊙ *Tues.–Sat. 10–1 and 5–8, Sun. 11–2 and 5–7.*

The **Museo de la Gaita** (Bagpipe Museum) is across the river on the eastern edge of town, past Parque Isabel la Católica. A collection of bagpipes from all over the world is augmented by workshops where you can see the instruments crafted. ✉ *Paseo del Doctor Fleming 877, La Güelga s/n* ☎ *985/332244* 🎫 *€2.35* ⊙ *Sept.–June, Tues.–Sat. 10–1 and 5–8, Sun. 11–2 and 5–7; July and Aug., Tues.–Sat. 10–1:30 and 5–9, Sun. 11–2 and 5–8.*

Where to Stay & Eat

$$$–$$$$ ✕ **El Puerto.** This glass-enclosed dining room at the end of a quay overlooks the harbor and serves fine, imaginative shellfish, seafood, and meats. A specialty is *merluza con bogavante en salsa verde* (hake and lobster with a parsley sauce). Feast on a four-plate menu or a *parillada de mariscos* (mixed platter of grilled shellfish). Game is served in season, and the wine list is substantial. ⊠ *Claudio Alvargonzález* ☎ 985/ 349096 ⌃ *Reservations essential* ☰ *AE, DC, MC, V* ⊙ *No dinner Sun.*

$$–$$$$ ✗ **La Pondala.** This friendly, folksy, and romantic chalet was founded in 1891. When the weather cooperates, the terrace is a perfect spot for grilled meat with rice or one of many sweet and savory crepes, such as the crepe *de centolla* (crab). The restaurant is 3 km (2 mi) east of town. ⊠ *Av. Dioniso Cifuentes 58, Somió* ☎ 985/361160 ☰ *AE, DC, MC, V* ⊙ *Closed Thurs., last 2 wks in June, and last 2 wks in Nov.*

$$$ ✗▤ **Parador de Gijón.** In an old water mill in a park not far from the San Lorenzo beach, this parador is one of the simplest and friendliest in Spain. Rooms in the newer wing are small, with bleached-wood floors and thick pine shutters, but most have wonderful views over the adjacent lake or the park. In the restaurant ($–$$$), try the *tigres* (spicy stuffed mussels), *pimientos de piquillo rellenos* (green peppers stuffed with squid, mushrooms, and rice), or *oricios* (sea urchins), served raw or steamed with lemon juice or a spicy sauce. For dessert, try fresh figs (in season) with Cabrales cheese. ⊠ *Torcuato Fernández Miranda 15, 33203* ☎ 985/370511 ☒ 985/370233 ⊕ *www.parador.es* ☞ 40 rooms ⌃ *Restaurant, cafeteria, Wi-Fi* ☰ *AE, DC, MC, V.*

▌
▌EN
ROUTE

East of Gijón is apple-orchard country, the source of the famous hard cider of Asturias. Rolling green hills against a highland backdrop, grazing cows, and white chalets add up to a remarkably Alpine landscape.

Villaviciosa

㉜ *32 km (20 mi) east of Gijón, 45 km (28 mi) northeast of Oviedo.*

Cider-capital Villaviciosa has a big dairy and several bottling plants as well as an attractive old quarter. The Hapsburg Emperor Charles V first set foot in Spain just down the road from here. The town's annual five-day Fiesta de la Manzana (Apple Festival) begins the first Friday after September 8. To taste the regional hard cider, stop into **El Congreso** (⊠ Pl. Generalísimo 25 ☎ No phone), a popular *sidrería* (cider house) that also serves tasty tapas and shellfish straight from the tank. If time allows, check out Villaviciosa's restored 15th-century **castle** (⊠ 3 km [2 mi] west of town on N632). The beautiful sandstone walls, turrets, and archways now enclose a modern hotel and restaurant.

Where to Stay

$ ▤ **Carlos I.** From the common-area wood floors, antique furniture, potted plants, and oil paintings to the cozy bar-cafeteria, this late-17th-century mansion is loaded with character. Guest rooms are spotless and relatively large. ⊠ *Pl. Carlos I 4, 33300* ☎ 985/890121 ☒ 985/890051 ☞ 16 rooms ⌃ *Bar* ☰ *MC, V.*

Ribadesella

㉝ *67 km (40 mi) east of Gijón, 84 km (50 mi) northeast of Oviedo.*

The N632 twists around green hills dappled with eucalyptus groves and allows you glimpses of the sea and sandy beaches down plunging valleys. The snowcapped Picos de Europa loom inland. This fishing village and beach resort is famous for the international canoe races held on the Sella River the first Saturday of August; for copious fresh seafood; and for its cave. Discovered in 1968 by Señor Bustillo, the **Cueva Tito Bustillo** has 20,000-year-old paintings on par with those in Lascaux, France, and Altamira. Giant horses and deer prance about the walls. To protect the paintings, no more than 375 visitors are allowed inside each day. But for those turned away, there is a museum of Asturian cave finds open year-round. The guided tour is in Spanish. ☎ *985/861120* 🎫 €4 🕙 *Apr.–Sept., cave Wed.–Sun. 10–5; museum Wed.–Sun. 10–5.*

Where to Stay & Eat

$–$$ ✕ **El Repollu.** A block inland from the port and market, this small, homey grill specializes in fish. Try the fresh-grilled turbot; some sweet, grilled *gambas* (shrimp); and perhaps the house Cabrales cheese. ✉ *Santa Marina 2* ☎ *985/860734* 🚾 *AE, DC, MC, V* 🕙 *Closed Thurs. Oct.–June. No dinner Oct.–June.*

$$ 🏨 **Ribadesella Playa.** Passing a peaceful night in this quirky, restored turn-of-the-20th-century mansion on the beach is an unusually pleasant experience. It's family run, and has a timeless, stately charm that might remind you of black-and-white European art films. ✉ *Ricardo Cangas 3, 33560* ☎ *985/860715* 🖶 *985/860220* 🛏 *17 rooms* ⚲ *Bar; no a/c* 🚾 *AE, DC, MC, V.*

Llanes

34 *40 km (25 mi) east of Ribadesella.*

The sprightly beach town of Llanes is on a pristine stretch of the Costa Verde (Green Coast). Hug the shore in either direction outside town for vistas of vertical cliffs looming over white-sand beaches and isolated caves. The peaceful, well-conserved **Plaza Cristo Rey** marks the center of the old town, partially surrounded by the remains of its medieval walls. The 13th-century church of **Santa María** rises over the square. Nearby, off Calle Alfonso IX, a medieval tower houses the tourist office. A long canal, connected to a small harbor, cuts through the heart of Llanes, and along its banks rise yellow- and salmon-painted houses with glass galleries, against a backdrop of the Picos de Europa. At the daily portside fish market, usually held around 1 PM, vendors display heaping mounds of freshly caught seafood. Steps from the old town is **Playa del Sablón,** a little swath of sand that gets predictably crowded on summer weekends. On the eastern edge of town is the larger **Playa de Toró.** Just 1 km (½ mi) east of Llanes is one of the area's most secluded beaches, the immaculate **Playa Ballota,** with private coves for picnicking and one of the few stretches of nudist sand in Asturias. West of Llanes, the most pleasant beaches lie between the towns of Barro and Celorio. Farther west (8 km [5 mi] from Llanes) is partially nudist **Playa de Torimbia,** a wild, virgin beach yet untouched by development. You can reach it only via footpath, roughly a 15-minute walk.

Dotting the Asturian coast east and west of Llanes are *bufones* (blow-holes), which occur nowhere else in Spain. Active blowholes shoot streams of water as high as 100 feet into the air; unfortunately, it's hard to predict when this will happen, as it depends on the tide and the size of the surf. There's a blowhole east of Playa Ballota; try to watch it in action from the **Mirador Panorámico La Boriza,** near the entrance to the golf course. If you miss it, the view is still worth a stop—on a clear day you can see the coastline all the way east to Santander.

Where to Stay & Eat

$–$$$ ✕ **Mirentxu.** Minutes from the fish market, near the small harbor bobbing with colorful fishing boats, this friendly Basque-influenced restaurant serves heaping portions of grilled and fried fish. ⊠ *Marinero 14* ☎ *985/402236* ▤ *DC, MC, V* ⊗ *Closed Oct.–June.*

$$ ▥ **La Posada de Babel.** This exquisite family-run inn just outside Llanes has roaring fires in its public rooms. Expect plenty of personal attention here. One guest room is in a converted granary. ⊠ *La Pereda s/n, 33509* ☎ *985/402525* ▤ *985/402622* ⊕ *www.laposadadebabel.com* ⇰ *12 rooms* ⬧ *Restaurant, bicycles, horseback riding, bar, library* ▤ *DC, MC, V* ⊗ *Closed Nov.–Feb.*

Sports & the Outdoors

Three kilometers (2 mi) east of Llanes, near the village of Cué, is the 18-hole **Club de Golf La Cuesta** (☎ 985/403319 ⊕ www.golflacuesta.com). You could hardly ask for a more beautiful location: the course sprawls atop a plateau 300 feet above sea level, on the site of a former flying school (during the Spanish civil war, there was a Falangist airport here). Nine holes have views of the Asturian coastline, with all its misty coves and crashing waves; the other nine face the towering Picos de Europa.

THE PICOS DE EUROPA

With craggy peaks soaring up to the 8,688-foot Torre Cerredo, the northern skyline of the Picos de Europa has helped seafarers and fishermen navigate the Bay of Biscay for ages. To the south, pilgrims on their way to Santiago enjoy distant but inspiring views of the snowcapped range from the plains of Castile between Burgos and León. Some 300 million years ago, this area was a sea; over a period of 60 million years it collected a layer of calceous deposits more than a mile thick, and a massive shift of the earth's crust threw up the Picos (Peaks). Later, the fractured peaks acquired glaciers, which then left two lakes in their wake. Regular, very heavy rain and snow have created canyons plunging 3,000 feet, natural arches, caves, and sinkholes (one of which is 5,213 feet deep). The Picos de Europa National Park, covering 413½-square km (257 square mi), is perfect for climbers and trekkers. Explore the main trails, hang glide, ride horses, cycle, or canoe. There are two adventure-sports centers in Cangas de Onís, near the Roman Bridge.

Touring the Picos

The best-known road trip in the Picos connects Cangas de Onís and Riaño along the twisting Sella Gorge, the **Ruta de los Beyos** on the N625 road, a two-hour drive up to the pass at **Puerto del Pontón** (Pontón Pass; 4,232 feet). Just beyond the pass, turn left (northeast) for a drive up to the **Puerto** de **Panderruedas** (4,757 feet) for a panoramic view of the peaks, especially in the early evening sun. From here you can descend northeast to the town of Posada de Valdeón and continue on to Caín for a look at the upper end of the famous Ruta del Cares. Another drive, beginning from Cangas de Onis, takes you up past Covadonga to Lakes Enol and Ercina on the AS262.

For the **Ruta del Cares,** drive east on the AS114 from Cangas de Onís toward Panes, stopping just before Arenas de Cabrales: here the road descends a wide valley and reaches a mirador (lookout) onto the **Naranjo de Bulnes,** a huge tooth of rock way up in the peaks. The mountain was named for its occasional tendency to glow orange, *naranja,* at sunrise and sunset. Turn south in Arenas de Cabrales into the AS264 road to reach Poncebos, and leave the car near here for the four-hour Ruta de Cares walk to Caín through the **Garganta de Cares** gorge. The canyon presents itself fairly soon, so you can turn back without pangs if you don't want to make the full hike. This route is popular, so arrive in Poncebos early in the day to avoid parking problems. You can also enter the Ruta at the other end, as noted above—from **Puerto de Pontón,** a road leads to Puerto de Panderruedas, Posada de Valdeón, and Caín. Groups of friends with two cars sometimes leave them at Poncebos and Caín, then exchange keys when they meet to save the return walk.

If you have another day, leave Cangas and drive via Panes and Potes around the entire park. Consider relocating to the southern side and staying at the Parador de Fuente Dé. South of Panes, turn right at Urdón's hydroelectric power station to **Tresviso** for unforgettable views and a chance to buy some local cheese. South of La Hermida on the N621 the Garganta de La Hermida cuts through sheer 600-foot limestone cliffs up to Potes. West of Potes off the CA185 is the left turn for the **Monasterio de Santo Toribio de Liébana,** with a 13th-century Gothic church and 17th-century cloisters. The CA185 ends at Fuente Dé, where there's a Parador Nacional and a cable car that can whisk you to the top of the Picos. South of Potes the N621 continues south to Riaño, a two-hour drive. About halfway there, Puerta de San Glorio is the jumping-off point for the 2.2-km (1.3-mi) walk up to the **Monumento al Oso,** where a white stone bear marks another splendid view.

NEED A BREAK?

Nestled in the gorge, the simple **Hostal Poncebos** (☎ 985/846447), open from early March through October, serves solid mountain dishes such as fabada and *cabrito* (roast kid). Serious trekkers and mountaineers stay in the 18 rooms upstairs. A funicular provides 10-minute rides up and down the mountain.

Cangas de Onís

🟤 *25 km (16 mi) south of Ribadesella, 70 km (43 mi) east of Oviedo.*

Partly in the narrow valley carved by the Sella River, Cangas de Onís is the unofficial capital of the Picos de Europa National Park and has the feel of a mountain village. To help plan your rambles, consult the scale model of the park outside the **Picos de Europa visitor center** (✉ Casa Dago, Av. Covadonga 43 ☎ 985/848614). The store opposite (at No. 22), El

Llagar, sells maps and guidebooks, a few in English. Cangas was the first capital of Christian Spain. A high, humpback **medieval bridge** (also known as the Puente Romano, or Roman Bridge, because of its style) spans the Sella River gorge with a reproduction of Pelayo's Victory Cross, or the Cruz de la Victoria, dangling underneath.

Where to Stay & Eat

$–$$$ ✕ **Sidrería Los Arcos.** This busy tavern with lots of polished wood serves local cider, fine Spanish wines, and sizzling T-bone steaks. *Revuelto de morcilla* (scrambled eggs with blood sausage) is served on *torto de maiz* (a corn pastry base). ⊠ *Pl. del Ayuntamiento, enter on Av. Covadonga* ☎ 985/849277 ▤ *AE, MC, V.*

★ **$$$** ✕⌂ **Parador de Cangas de Onís.** On the banks of the Sella River Sella, just west of Cangas, this friendly parador is part 8th-century Benedictine monastery and part modern wing. The older building, connected to the newer one by a glass tunnel, has 11 period-style rooms, some with four-poster beds. Excellent local dishes ($$–$$$), such as *merluza del Cantabrica a la sidra* (hake cooked in cider) garnished with asparagus, are served in the bright dining room. ⊠ *Monasterio de San Pedro de Villanueva, Ctra. N624, from N634, take right turn for Villanueva, 33550* ☎ 985/849402 ☒ 985/849520 ⊕ *www.parador.es* ⇆ *64 rooms* ⚭ *Restaurant, bar, meeting room* ▤ *AE, DC, MC, V.*

$$ ⌂ **Aultre Naray.** This 19th-century mansion overlooking the Escapa mountain range is a rare find. It's perfectly placed for hiking, camping, canoeing, and swimming (all of which the staff can help organize). It's not rustic, though—guest rooms have modern furniture, plenty of light, and, in some cases, pleasant sitting rooms. The hotel is 15 km (9 mi) east of town. ⊠ *N634, Km 335, Los Campos, Peruyes, 33547* ☎ 985/840808 ☒ 985/840848 ⊕ *www.aultrenaray.com* ⇆ *10 rooms* ⚭ *Restaurant, bar* ▤ *DC, MC, V.*

$$ ⌂ **Hotel Los Lagos.** Each of the four floors of this bustling modern hotel has a different color scheme, ranging from cream to blue. Rooms have modern furniture and white-tile bathrooms. The hotel is in the center of town, near the tourist office. ⊠ *Jardines del Ayuntamiento 3, 33550* ☎ 985/849421 ☒ 985/848405 ⊕ *www.loslagos.as* ⇆ *45 rooms* ⚭ *Restaurant, Wi-Fi, bar, meeting room; no a/c* ▤ *AE, MC, V.*

$$ ⌂ **La Tiendona.** Conveniently situated halfway between the mountains of Cangas de Onís and the beaches of Ribadesella, this restored 19th-century roadhouse has country-style rooms. ⊠ *N634, Km 335, Margolles, 33547* ☎ 985/840474 ☒ 985/841316 ⇆ *26 rooms* ⚭ *Bar* ▤ *AE, DC, MC, V* ⊙ *Closed Jan.*

$ ⌂ **El Torrejón.** Built as a stone fortress in 1542, Torrejón has four charming but small doubles in the Torrejón proper and another nine in the *casa rural* (country house) annex next door. It's the only peach-color house around; it's at the back of town, a few blocks off the main road. Room prices include use of the kitchen. ⊠ *Calle Mayor s/n, Arenas de Cabrales 33554* ☎ 985/846428 ☒ 985/846411 ⊕ *www.eltorrejon. com* ⇆ *13 rooms* ▤ *AE, DC, MC, V.*

$ ⌂ **Hospedería del Peregrino.** This simple but adequate hotel looks out at a magnificent nearby church. Rooms are small but cozy and decorated with abundant fresh wood and checked curtains. ⊠ *Crtra. AS 262* *s/n, Covadonga 33589* ☎ *985/846047* 🖷 *985/846051* ⊕ *www. picosdeuropa.net/peregrino* ⇌ *7 rooms* ♨ *Restaurant, bar; no a/c* ▤ *AE, DC, MC, V* ⊗ *Closed Dec.–Feb.*

¢–$ 🏨 **Hotel La Plaza.** Expect clean, newly remodeled, and airy double rooms at bargain prices. Heading away from the Roman bridge, take the second right after the church on Avenida Covadonga. ⊠ *La Plaza 7, 33550* 🖷☎ *985/848308* ⊕ *www.orientedeasturias.com/hotelplaza* ⇌ *10 rooms* ♨ *No a/c* ▤ *AE, DC, MC, V.*

¢ 🏨 **La Naturaleza.** Poised at the foot of the Ruta del Cares, this place has views of Arenas de Cabrales and the Sella River. Four comfy rooms come with large, clean bathrooms. ⊠ *La Segada, 33554* ☎ *985/846487* 🖷 *985/846101* ⇌ *4 rooms* ♨ *Restaurant, bar; no a/c* ▤ *No credit cards* ⊗ *Closed Dec. and Jan.*

4

Covadonga

③⑥ *14 km (9 mi) southeast of Cangas de Onís.*

To see high alpine meadowland, some rare Spanish lakes, and views over the peaks and out to sea (if the mist ever disperses), take the narrow road up past Covadonga to **Lake Enol,** stopping for the view en route. Starting to the right of the lake, a three-hour walk takes in views from the **Mirador del Rey,** where you can find the grave of pioneering climber Pedro Pidal. Farther up the road from Lake Enol are a summer-only tourist office and **Lake Ercina,** where Pope John Paul II picnicked during his 1989 tour of Asturias and Galicia.

DISCOUNTS & DEALS

■ Visitors can get 20% off rural accommodation on selected Green Days and seniors and children get discounted or free tickets to museums and sights through the Galician tourist board, **Turgalicia.** ⊠ *Carretera Santiago–Noia Km 3, Santiago de Compostela* ☎ *981/542527 or 981/542511* ⊕ *www.turgalicia.es.*

■ **Compostela 48 Horas** is a €15 visitor's card that entitles you to discounts or free entry to all key Santiago sites. ⊠ *Rúa do Vilar 63, Santiago de Compostela* ☎ *981/555511* ⊕ *www. santiagoturismo.com.*

NEED A BREAK? Near Lake Enol is the **Restaurante el Casín,** with a small terrace bar overlooking the mountains and the lake. The set menu is a mere €9; à la carte options include roasts and restorative fabada bean stews. *Closed January and February.*

★ Covadonga's **shrine** is considered the birthplace of Spain. Here, in 718, a handful of sturdy Asturian Christians led by Don Pelayo took refuge in the Cave of St. Mary, about halfway up a cliff, where they prayed to the Virgin Mary to give them strength to turn back the Moors. Pelayo and his followers resisted the superior Moorish forces and set up a Christian kingdom that eventually led to the Reconquest. The cave has an 18th-century statue of the Virgin and Don Pelayo's grave. Covadonga itself has a **basilica,** and the **museum** has the treasures donated to the Virgin of the Cave, including a crown studded with more than 1,000 diamonds. ☎ *985/ 846096* ✆ €3 ☉ *Daily 10:30–2 and 4–7:30.*

Where to Stay & Eat

$$$ ✕⌂ **Parador de Fuente Dé.** You can find this modern parador in a valley beside a cable car that ascends a soaring rock face to 2,705 feet in about four minutes. Somewhat spartan, it's a fine no-frills base for serious climbers and walkers and has a good restaurant ($$–$$$) with *cocido lebaniego* (a sturdy local stew) and steaks topped with Cabrales, the local blue cheese. The parador is east of the Cantabrian border, 23 km (14 mi) west of Potes. ✉ *Fuente Dé, 39588* ☎ *942/736651* 🖷 *942/ 736654* ⊕ *www.parador.es* ✆ *78 rooms* ⚴ *Restaurant, bar, meeting room* ☰ *AE, DC, MC, V* ☉ *Closed Dec.–Feb.*

GALICIA & ASTURIAS ESSENTIALS

To research prices, get advice from other travelers, and book travel arrangements, visit www.fodors.com.

Transportation

BY AIR

Galicia's international airport is in Labacolla, 12 km (7 mi) east of Santiago de Compostela. Iberia flies daily from here to London, Paris, Zurich, Geneva, and Frankfurt, and domestic flights connect Santiago with the rest of Spain, including daily service to Madrid and Barcelona. Other Spanish airlines serving this area are Air Europa and Spanair. The region's other domestic airports are in A Coruña, Vigo, and near San Estéban de Pravia, 47 km (29 mi) north of Oviedo, Asturias. Airport shuttles usually take the form of ALSA buses from the city bus station. Occasionally, Iberia runs a private shuttle from its office out to the airport; inquire when you book your ticket.

🛈 Airport Information **A Coruña** ✉ Aeropuerto de Alvedro ☎ 981/187200. **Oviedo** ✉ Aeropuerto de Ranon ☎ 985/127500. **Santiago de Compostela** ✉ Aeropuerto de Labacolla ☎ 981/547500. **Vigo** ✉ Aeropuerto de Peinador ☎ 986/268200.

BY BIKE

The main Camino de Santiago (the St. James pilgrimage route) runs 800 km (525 mi) from St-Jean-Pied-de-Port on the Navarra-France border to Santiago. The official *El Camino de Santiago en Bicicleta* leaflet available from **Información Xacobeo** or from the Santiago tourist office warns that this is a very tough bike trip—bridle paths, dirt tracks, rough stones, and mountain passes. The best time of year is late spring or early autumn. Tourist offices in Asturias sell the booklet *Rutas de Montaña, Senderismo, Montañismo y Bicicleta de Montaña*, which outlines different routes, for about €1.20. Some hotels and campsites rent out bicycles, as do some adventure-sports organizations.

🛈 Bike Routes **Información Xacobeo** ✉ Pabellón de Galicia, San Lázaro s/n, Santiago de Compostela ⊕ www.xacobeo.es. **Santiago bike route information** ⊕ www. caminhodesantiago.com.

🛈 Bike Rentals **Bici Total** ✉ Av. de Lugo 221, Santiago de Compostela ☎ 981/564562.

BY BUS

ALSA runs daily buses from Madrid to Galicia and Asturias. Several other companies connect the region with other parts of Spain.

🚍 **Bus Company ALSA** ✉ Pl. Camilo Díaz Valiño s/n, Santiago de Compostela ☎ 981/586133, 981/586453, 902/422242 ⊕ www.alsa.es.

🚍 **Bus Stations A Coruña** ✉ Caballeros 21 ☎ 981/184335. **Lugo** ✉ Pl. de la Constitución s/n ☎ 982/223985. **Oviedo** ✉ Pl. Primo de Rivera 1 ☎ 902/422242. **Pontevedra** ✉ Calvo Sotelo s/n ☎ 986/852408. **Santiago** ✉ Rúa de San Caetano s/n ☎ 981/542416. **Vigo** ✉ Av. de Madrid 57 ☎ 986/373411.

BY CAR

The four-lane A6 expressway links northwestern Spain with Madrid in five hours (650 km [403 mi] to Santiago). Approaching by car is the best way to appreciate the arid Castilian steppe—which gives way to the northwest's stunning green countryside. The expressway north from León to Oviedo and Gijón is the fastest way to cross the Cantabrian Mountains. The AP9 north–south Galician ("Atlantic") expressway links A Coruña, Santiago, Pontevedra, and Vigo, and the A8 along the coast of Asturias links Santander to Ribadeo. Local roads along the coast or through the hills are more scenic but two or three times as slow.

If you're coming from the United States, remember that rental rates in Spain are as much as double as those you can arrange in advance back home. Plan ahead—reserve a car through Hertz, Budget, or National, all of which have offices in Santiago de Compostela, A Coruña, Vigo, Oviedo, and/or Gijón. Several airport branches are listed below.

🚗 **Rental Agencies Alamo** ✉ Aeropuerto de Coruña, A Coruña ☎ 981/662365 ✉ Aeropuerto de Labacolla, Santiago ☎ 981/599877 ⊕ www.alamo.com. **Avis** ✉ Aeropuerto de Ranon, Oviedo ☎ 985/562111 ✉ Aeropuerto de Labacolla, Santiago ☎ 981/547830 ✉ Aeropuerto de Peinador, Vigo ☎ 986/268276 ⊕ www.avis.com. **Europcar** ✉ Aeropuerto de Alvedro, A Coruña ☎ 981/650865 ✉ Aeropuerto de Labacolla, Santiago ☎ 981/547740 ⊕ www.europcar.es. **Hertz** ✉ Aeropuerto de Alvedro, A Coruña ☎ 981/663990 ✉ Aeropuerto de Labacolla, Santiago ☎ 981/598893 ⊕ www.hertz.com. **National/Atesa** ✉ Aeropuerto de Ranon, Oviedo ☎ 985/551217 ✉ Aeropuerto de Peinador, Vigo ☎ 986/486561 ⊕ www.atesa.com

BY TRAIN

RENFE runs several trains a day from Madrid to Oviedo (7 hours) and Gijón (8 hours), and a separate line serves Santiago (11 hours). Daytime first- and second-class cars are available. RENFE has ticket windows at the stations in Santiago, A Coruña, Oviedo, and Gijón. Local RENFE trains connect the major cities of Galicia and Asturias with most of the surrounding small towns, but be prepared for dozens of stops. Narrow-gauge FEVE trains clatter slowly across northern Spain, connecting Galicia and Asturias with Santander, Bilbao, and Irún, on the French border. Buy tickets at local travel agencies, any FEVE train station, or the FEVE office in Oviedo or Madrid. FEVE's Transcantábrico narrow-gauge train tour (⊕ www.transcantabrico.feve.es) is an eight-day, 1,000-km (600-mi) journey through the Basque country, Asturias, and Galicia. English-speaking guides narrate, and a private bus takes the group from train stations to artistic and natural attractions. Passengers sleep on the train in suites and dine on local specialties. Trains run from May through October, and the all-inclusive cost is €4,400 for two people in a suite.

⁊ Train Information FEVE ✉ C. Monte Gamonal s/n, near FEVE-Asturias train station, Oviedo ☎ 985/297656 or 985/981700 ✉ C. General Rodrígo 6, 2nd fl., Madrid ☎ 91/453-3828. **RENFE** ☎ 902/240202 ⊕ www.renfe.es.

⁊ Transcantábrico Information Marketing Ahead Inc. ✉ Suite 718, 381 Park Ave. S, New York, NY 10016 ☎ 212/686-9213 ⊕ www.marketingahead.com. **E. C. Tours** ✉ 12500 Riverside Dr., Valley Village, CA 91607 ☎ 818/755-9333 or 800/388-0877 ⊕ www. ectours.com. **PTG Tours** ✉ Gable House, Letcombe Hill, East Challow OX12 9RW, UK ☎ 01235/768855 ⊕ www.ptg.co.uk. **Transcantábrico** ✉ C. Monte Gamonal s/n, near FEVE-Asturias train station, Oviedo 33012 ☎ 91/453-3806.

Contacts & Resources

BANKS & EXCHANGING SERVICES

Although currency exchange offices are scarce, there are branches of all of Spain's major banks in city centers across Galicia and Asturias. They have 24-hour ATMs and offer currency exchange services during business hours.

⁊ Currency Exchange Cibernova ✉ Rúa Nova 50 Santiago de Compostela ☎ No phone. **El Corte Inglés** ✉ Ramón y Cajal 57 A Coruña ☎ 981/189400 ⊕ www. elcorteingles.es.

EMERGENCIES

⁊ Emergency Services Fire, Police or Ambulance ☎ 112. **Policía Local** ☎ 092. **Policía Nacional** ☎ 091. **Servicio Marítimo** (Air-sea rescue) ☎ 902/107981. **Guardia Civil** ☎ 062. **Cruz Roja** (Red Cross) ☎ 913/354545. **Insalud** (Public health service) ☎ 061. **Información Toxicológica** (Poison control) ☎ 915/620420.

INTERNET, MAIL & SHIPPING

Although Spain now has some of the best broadband Internet services in Europe, hotels are taking their time to catch up, with Wi-Fi access slowly finding its way into the smarter establishments. Internet cafés, however, are easy to locate in tourist areas.

Main post offices (*Correos,*) stay open until 8:30 during the week and will get your mail home eventually, but for urgent deliveries it is better to trust one of the main courier companies.

⁊ Internet Cafés Estrella Park Street ✉ Estrella 12 A Coruña ☎ 981/229070. **Cibercentro La Lila Street** ✉ La Lila 17 Oviedo ☎ 984/083400 ⊕ www.lalila.org. **Cibernova Street** ✉ Rúa Nova 50 Santiago de Compostela ☎ No phone **Ciber Station Street** ✉ Principe 22 Vigo ☎ No phone.

⁊ Post Offices ✉ Alcalde Manuel Casas s/n A Coruña ☎ 981/225175 ✉ Padre Ferrero 4 Oviedo ☎ 985/201306 ✉ Travesia Fonseca s/n Santiago de Compostela ☎ 981/581252 ✉ Plaza de Compostela 3 Vigo ☎ 986/438144.

⁊ Courier Services Seur ✉ Juan de Cierva 28-32 A Coruña ☎ 981/263600 ✉ Santa Susana 41 Oviedo ☎ 985/266005 ✉ Via Edison, Ciudad del Transporte, Poligono Industrial Tambre Santiago de Compostela ☎ 981/566160 ✉ Fragosiño s/n Vigo ☎ 986/411111.

MEDIA

Although no local English-language publications or broadcast outlets exist, English-language print media are on sale daily.

🚺 Bookstores Librería Abraxas ⊠ Montero Rios 50, Santiago de Compostela ☎ 981/580377. **Librería Follas Novas** ⊠ Montero Rios 37, Santiago de Compostela ☎ 981/594406. **Librería Ojanguren** ⊠ Pl. de Riego 1, Oviedo ☎ 985/218824.

TOUR OPTIONS

Call Santiago's association of well-informed **guides** (⊠ La Rosa 22, 3rd fl., Santiago de Compostela ☎ 981/569890) to arrange a private walking tour of the city and tailor-made tours to any place in Galicia.

VISITOR INFORMATION

The tourist office in Santiago de Compostela has information on all of Galicia; the office in Oviedo covers all of Asturias.

🚺 Regional Tourist Offices A Coruña ⊠ Dársena de la Marina s/n ☎ 981/221822 ⊕ www.turismocoruna.com. **Gijón** ⊠ Rodriguez San Pedro s/n ☎ 985/341771 ⊕ www.infogijon.com. **Pontevedra** ⊠ General Gutierrez Mellado 1 ☎ 986/850814 ⊕ www.turgalicia.com. **Santiago de Compostela** ⊠ Rúa do Vilar 63 ☎ 981/555129 ⊕ www.santiagoturismo.com. **Ourense** ⊠ Caseta do Legoeiro s/n, 32003 ☎ 988/372020 ⊕ www.turismourense.com. **Oviedo** ⊠ Cimadevilla 4 ☎ 902/300202 ⊕ www.ayto-oviedo.es.

🚺 Local Tourist Offices A Coruña ⊠ Edificio Sol, Sol s/n ☎ 981/184344. **Cangas de Onís** ⊠ Camila Beceña 1 ☎ 985/848005. **Covadonga** ⊠ Av. Covadonga s/n, Pl. del Ayuntamiento ☎ 985/846035. **Gijón** ⊠ Rodriguez San Pedro s/n ☎ 985/341771. **Lugo** ⊠ Praza Maior 27, Galerías ☎ 982/231361. **O Grove** ⊠ Pl. de Corgo 1 ☎ 986/731415 **Ourense** ⊠ Burgas 12 bajo ☎ 988/366064. **Oviedo** ⊠ Marqués de Santa Cruz 1 ☎ 985/227586. **Pontevedra** ⊠ Pl. de España ☎ 986/850814 ⊠ La Herreria ☉ July–Sept., outdoor kiosks. **Ribadeo** ⊠ Pl. de España ☎ 982/128689. **Ribadesella** ⊠ Paseo de Muelle ☎ 985/860038 ☉ Closed Mon. **Santiago de Compostela** ⊠ Rúa do Vilar 63 ☎ 981/555129. **Tui** ⊠ Colón s/n ☎ 986/601789. **Vigo** ⊠ Mercado, Pl. de la Piedra ☎ 986/810216. **Villaviciosa** ⊠ Parque Vallina ☎ 985/891759.

The Pyrenees

WORD OF MOUTH

"Zaragoza is a fantastic city! I lived there for two years and I think it would be a great place to stop. There are so many nice shops and restaurants as well as nice people."

—tropicalmango70

"I got to know a small part of the Pyrenees very well last summer, and simply for grandeur they cannot be beaten. Go to one of the national parks— the one I spent time at was Aigüestortes, but I think they are all wonderful."

—Sheila

By George
Semler

THE SNOWCAPPED PYRENEES, separating the Iberian Peninsula from the rest of the European continent, have always been a special realm, a source of legend and superstition. Along with the magic comes a surprising number of ancient cultures and languages, all Pyrenean and yet each profoundly different from the next. To explore the Pyrenees fully—appreciating the flora and fauna, the local gastronomy, the remote glacial lakes and streams, the Romanesque art in a thousand hermitages—could take a lifetime. Where to begin? Perhaps Hemingway's beloved Irati beech forest and river above Pamplona; the green hills of the Baztán Valley in Pyrenean Navarra; or the Romanesque churches of the Noguera de Tor valley and the lake country above at Sant Mauricio.Each Pyrenean mountain system is drained by one or more rivers, forming some three dozen valleys between the Mediterranean and the Atlantic; these valleys were all but completely isolated until around the 10th century. Local languages still abound, with Castilian Spanish and Euskera (Basque) in upper Navarra; Grausín, Belsetán, Chistavino, Ansotano, Cheso, and Patués (Benasqués), in Aragón; Aranés, a dialect of Gascon French, in the Vall d'Aran; and Catalan at the eastern end of the chain from Ribagorça to the Mediterranean.

The earliest inhabitants of the Pyrenees, originally cave dwellers, later shepherds and farmers, saw their first invaders when the Greeks landed at Empúries, in Northern Catalonia, in the 6th century BC. The seagoing Carthaginians colonized Spain in the 3rd century BC, and their great general Hannibal surprised Rome by crossing the eastern Pyrenees in 218 BC. After defeating the Carthaginians, the Romans built roads through the mountains. The Iberian Peninsula was the last of the Romanempire to be overtaken by the Visigoths in AD 409.

In the 8th century, the northern tribes then faced Moorish invaders from the south. Although Moorish influence was stronger in southern Spain, this region was nevertheless a meeting point for Arabic and European cultures at the end of the first millennium. The Moorish occupation sent Christianity fleeing to the hills, dotting the Pyrenees with Romanesque art and architecture. When Christian crusaders reconquered Spain, the Pyrenees were divided among three feudal kingdoms: Catalonia, Aragón, and Navarra, proud and independent entities with their respective spiritual "cradles" in the Romanesque mountain monasteries of Santa Maria de Ripoll, San Juan de la Peña, and San Salvador de Leyre.

Throughout the centuries, the Pyrenees have remained a strategic factor to be reckoned with. Charlemagne, moving south, lost Roland and his rear guard at Roncesvalles in 778, and his heirs lost all of Catalonia in 988. Napoléon never completed his conquest of the peninsula, largely because the Pyrenees presented insurmountable communication and supply problems. And Adolf Hitler was dissuaded by Francisco Franco from trying to use post–civil war Spain as a base camp for his African campaign, a decision that rendered the Pyrenees a path to freedom for Jews and others fleeing the Nazis.

Exploring the Pyrenees

For mountain worshippers, crossing the Pyrenees from the Mediterranean to the Atlantic (or vice versa) is a pilgrimage. It's a seven-week hike, but you can drive the route in anywhere from 2 to 14 days. As the crow flies, the Pyrenees stretch 435 km (270 mi) along Spain's border with France, though the sinuous borderline exceeds 600 km (370 mi). A drive across the N260 trans-Pyrenean axis connecting the destinations in this chapter would exceed 800 km (495 mi) in all. There are three main divisions: the Catalan Pyrenees from the Mediterranean to the Noguera Ribagorçana River south of Vielha, the central Pyrenees of Aragón extending west to the Roncal Valley, and the Basque Pyrenees falling gradually westward through the Basque Country to the Bay of Biscay and the Atlantic Ocean. The highest peaks are in Aragón—Aneto, in the Maladeta massif; Posets; and Monte Perdido, all of which are about 11,000 feet above sea level. Pica d'Estats (10,372 feet) is Catalonia's highest peak, and Pic d'Orhi (6,656 feet) is the highest in the Basque Pyrenees.

Numbers in the text correspond to numbers in the margin and on the Catalan Pyrenees and the Central & Western Pyrenees maps.

About the Restaurants

Pyrenean cuisine is characterized by thick soups, stews, roasts, and the use of local ingredients prepared differently in every valley, village, and kitchen from the Mediterranean to the Atlantic. The three main culinary schools correspond to the Pyrenees' three main regional and cultural identities—Catalan, Aragonese, and Basque—but within these are further subdivisions such as La Cerdanya, Vall d'Aran, Benasque, Roncal, and Baztán. Game is common throughout. Trout (now often raised in lakes and ponds fed by mountain streams), wild goat, deer, boar, partridge, rabbit, duck, and quail are roasted over coals or cooked in aromatic stews called *civets* in Catalonia and *estofadas* in Aragón and Navarra. Fish and meat are often seared on slabs of slate (*a la llosa* in Catalan, *a la piedra* in Castilian Spanish). Wild mushrooms are a local specialty in season, as are wild asparagus, leeks, and herbs such as marjoram, sage, thyme, and rosemary.

	WHAT IT COSTS In Euros				
	$$$$	**$$$**	**$$**	**$**	**¢**
AT DINNER	over €20	€15–€20	€10–€15	€6–€10	under €6

Prices are per person for a main course at dinner.

About the Hotels

Most hotels in the Pyrenees are informal and outdoorsy, with a large fireplace in one of the public rooms. They are usually built of wood and slate under a steep roof, blending with the surrounding mountains. Comfortable and protected, they reflect the tastes of the travelers, who are mostly skiers and hikers. Options include friendly family-owned establishments, rooms in Basque *caseríos* (farmhouses), and town houses.

GREAT ITINERARIES

IF YOU HAVE 3 DAYS
Starting from Barcelona, head north on the AP7 freeway. Take the C66 northwest (Exit 6) off AP7 north of Girona and then the trans-Pyrenean N260 at Besalú through Olot to the Capsacosta tunnel and 📷 **Camprodón ❶** for your first night. The next day, explore **Ripoll ❻, Puigcerdà ❼**, and 📷 **Llívia ❽**; then on your third day, drive west on N260 to 📷 **La Seu d'Urgell ⓬**. Head back to Barcelona through the Cadí Tunnel on the E9. Alternatively, if you're en route from Barcelona to the Basque Country, stay in **La Seu d'Urgell ⓬, Benasque ㉗**, and **Jaca ㉝** before driving out to Hondarribia (Fuenterrabía).

IF YOU HAVE 5 DAYS
Starting from Barcelona or the Costa Brava, devote your first afternoon and night to 📷 **Camprodón ❶**. Explore the Cerdanya Valley and 📷 **Llívia ❽** the next day; then head to 📷 **La Seu d'Urgell ⓬**–climbing to **Prat d'Aguiló ⓫** on the way–for your third day and night. From La Seu d'Urgell, drive two to three hours west on the N260 and then north up through the Noguera Pallaresa valley; spend your fourth day and night in the 📷 **Vall d'Aran ⓲**, and your fifth day absorbing **Taüll ㉓** and the Noguera de Tor Valley. If you have time, go through lake-dotted **Parc Nacional d'Aigüestortes i Estany de Sant Maurici ⓰**. Stop in **Huesca ㉕** and/or **Zaragoza ㉖** on your way out of the mountains.

IF YOU HAVE 10 DAYS
From Barcelona or the Costa Brava, the classic sea-to-sea crossing begins with a symbolic wade in the Mediterranean at Cap de Creus, peninsular Spain's easternmost point, just north of Cadaqués. From Cap de Creus cross westward to Hondarribia to do likewise at the Cabo Higuer lighthouse on the Bay of Biscay. On the westbound trip, a day's drive up through Figueres and Olot will bring you to 📷 **Camprodón ❶** and the surrounding unspoiled mountain towns. Stop next in 📷 **Llívia ❽**, moving on south to the sunny Cerdanya Valley. From there move westward through 📷 **La Seu d'Urgell ⓬** to **Parc Nacional d'Aigüestortes i Estany de Sant Maurici ⓰**, the **Vall d'Aran ⓲**, and the winter-sports center Baqueira-Beret. Stop at **Taüll ㉓** and the Noguera de Tor Valley's Romanesque churches. Farther west, spend the next few days in 📷 **Benasque ㉗**, 📷 **San Juan de Plan and the Gistaín Valley ㉙**, **Bielsa ㉚**, the remote valleys of Upper Aragón, **Parque Nacional de Ordesa y Monte Perdido ㉛**, and 📷 **Jaca ㉝**, the region's most important town. Finally, move west into the Basque Pyrenees to visit the Irati Forest. Explore the 📷 **Baztán Valley ㊵**, and then follow the Bidasoa River down to Hondarribia and the Bay of Biscay.

5

WHAT IT COSTS In Euros				
$$$$	$$$	$$	$	¢
FOR 2 PEOPLE over €180	€100–€180	€60–€100	€40–€60	under €40

Prices are for two people in a standard double room in high season, excluding tax.

Timing

If you're a hiker, stick to the summer (June through September, especially July), when the weather is better and there's less chance of a blizzard or lightning storm at high altitudes. October is ideal for the still-green Pyrenean valleys and a hunt for wild mushrooms. November brings colorful leaves, the last mushrooms, and the first frosts. The green springtime thaw, during which you can still ski on the snowcaps, is also spectacular. For skiing, come between December and April.

EASTERN CATALAN PYRENEES

Catalonia's easternmost Pyrenean valley, the Vall de Camprodón, is still hard enough to reach that it's retained much of its original character. It has several exquisite towns and churches and, above all, mountains, such as the Sierra de Catllar, thick with boar, mountain goat, wild trout, and snow partridge. Vallter 2000 and Núria are ski resorts at the eastern and western ends of the Pyrenees heights on the north side of the valley, but the middle reaches and main body of the valley have remained pasture for sheep, cattle, and horses, and de facto natural parks. To reach the Vall de Camprodón from Barcelona you can take the N152 through Vic and Ripoll; from the Costa Brava go by way of either Figueres or Girona, Besalú, and the Capsacosta tunnel. From France, drive southwest through the Col (Pass) d'Ares, which enters the head of the valley at an altitude of 5,280 feet from Prats de Molló.

Camprodón

❶ *127 km (80 mi) northwest of Barcelona.*

Camprodón, the capital of its *comarca* (county), lies at the junction of the Rivers Ter and Ritort—both excellent trout streams. The rivers flow by, through, and under much of the town, giving it a highland waterfront character (as well as a long history of flooding). The town owes much of its opulence to the summer folks from Barcelona who have built mansions along the leafy promenade, **Passeig Maristany,** at its northern edge. It's also known for its sausages of every imaginable size, shape, and consistency and for its two cookie factories, Birbas and Pujol, locked in eternal competition. (Birbas is better—look for the image of the bridge on the box.) Camprodón's best-known symbol is the elegant **12th-century stone bridge** that broadly spans the River Ter in the center of town.

Where to Stay

$$ ▦ **Edelweiss.** This friendly and comfortable Pyrenean inn is a good base camp for skiers, hikers, wild-mushroom seekers, equestrian enthusiasts,

IF YOU LIKE

FISHING

Well populated with trout, the Pyrenees' cold-water streams provide excellent angling from mid-March to the end of August. Notable places to cast a line are the Segre, Aragón, Gállego, Noguera Pallaresa, Arga, Esera, and Esca rivers. Pyrenean ponds and lakes also tend to be rich in trout.

NATIONAL PARKS

Nestled in the mountains between Espot, Caldes de Boí, and Taüll, lies Aigüestortes–Sant Maurici National Park. This Catalan Pyrenees gem has more than 200 glacial lakes, and forests rich with birch, beech, fir, and pine trees. In the neighboring Central Pyrenees, Spain's version of the Grand Canyon (albeit on a smaller scale), Ordesa and Monte Perdido National Park, is often overlooked. With its lovely falling waters, spectacular overlooks, and intriguing caves, the park, near Torla and Biescas, is the better of the two and worth a day's exploration. Its mountain trails are well marked and well maintained and lead to scenic vistas. Both national parks offer free admission.

ROMANESQUE ART & ARCHITECTURE

You could organize many a trip around the treasury of Romanesque chapels, monasteries, hermitages, and cathedrals in these mountains. Sites to seek out include the tiny chapel at Beget, above Camprodón; the superb rose window and 50 carved capitals of the cathedral of Santa Maria, in La Seu d'Urgell; the matched set of churches and bell towers in the Noguera de Tor Valley

south of Vall d'Aran; the San Juan de la Peña and Siresa monasteries, west of Jaca; and the village churches of Navarra's Baztán Valley.

WINTER SPORTS

Skiing is the main winter sport in the Pyrenees, and Baqueira-Beret, in the Vall d'Aran, is the leading resort. Thanks to artificial-snow machines, there is usually fine skiing from December through March at more than 20 resorts—from Vallter 2000 at Setcases, in the Camprodón Valley, west to Isaba and Burguete, in Navarra.

Although weekend skiing can be crowded in the eastern valleys, Catalonia's western Pyrenees tend to have more breathing room. Cerler-Benasque, Panticosa, Formigal, Astún, and Candanchú are the major ski areas in Huesca. Numerous resorts offer helicopter skiing and Nordic skiing. Leading Nordic areas include Lles, in the Cerdanya; Salardú and Beret, in the Vall d'Aran; and Panticosa, Benasque, and Candanchú, in Aragón. Jaca, Puigcerdà, and Vielha have public skating sessions, figure-skating classes, and ice-hockey programs.

The newspapers *El País*, *El Periódico de Catalunya*, and *La Vanguardia Española* print complete ski information every Friday in winter. Ski conditions are available at ⊕ www.pirineodigital. com/noticias-nieve.htm or ⊕ www. catski.net (for Catalonia), ⊕ www. aragob.es (for Aragón), and ⊕ www.aran.org and ⊕ www. baqueira.es (for Baqueira and environs).

5

GEORGE'S TOP 5

- Hike up to Prat d'Aguiló in the Cerdanya Valley for unforgettable views.

- Visit San Juan de Plan and the Gistaín Valley for a look at early-20th-century life in the Pyrenees.

- Walk through the Parque Nacional de Ordesa y Monte Perdido for stunning scenery.

- Stop at Taüll and see the Noguera de Tor Valley's exquisite Romanesque churches.

- Explore the lush Baztán Valley, and then follow the Bidasoa River down to Hondarribia and the Bay of Biscay.

and those interested in all manner of Camprodón Valley fauna. Rooms are simple but tasteful, with bright wood walls and a cheerful decor. The common rooms are low-key and informal, yet elegant and graceful spaces for socializing. ⊠ *Ctra. de Sant Joan 28, 17867* ☎ *972/740614* 🖷 *972/740605* ⊕ *www.edelweisshotel.net* ➷ *21 rooms* ♿ *Bar, lounge, meeting rooms, parking (fee)* ☲ *AE, DC, MC, V.*

Shopping

Cal Xec (⊠ C. Isaac Albèniz 1 ☎ 972/740084), the legendary sausage store at the end of the emblematic Camprodón Bridge, also sells the much-prized rectangular, shortbread-like, vanilla-flavored Birbas cookies.

EN ROUTE From Camprodón, take C151 north toward the French border at Col d'Ares and turn east toward **Rocabruna**, a village of crisp, clean Pyrenean stone at the source of the clear River Beget. The village is famous as a gastronomical pilgrimage to the excellent Can Po restaurant, *listed under* Beget, *below.*

Beget

★ ❷ *17 km (11 mi) east of Camprodón.*

The village of Beget, considered Catalonia's *més bufó* (cutest), was completely cut off from motorized vehicles until the mid-1960s, when a *pista forestal* (a jeep track) was laid down; in 1980 Beget was finally fully connected to the rest of the world by an asphalt roadway. Beget's 30 houses are eccentric stone structures with heavy wooden doors and a golden tone peculiar to the Camprodón Valley. Graceful stone bridges span the stream in which protected trout feast. The 11th-century Romanesque church of **Sant Cristófol** has a diminutive bell tower and a rare 6-foot Majestat, a polychrome wood carving of Christ in a head-to-foot tunic, dating from the 12th or 13th century. The church is usually closed, but townsfolk can direct you to the keeper of the key.

Where to Eat

$$–$$$ ✕**Can Po.** This ancient, ivy-covered, stone-and-mortar farmhouse perched over a deep gully in nearby Rocabruna serves carefully prepared local dishes from *entrecot amb crema de ceps* (veal in wild-mushroom sauce)

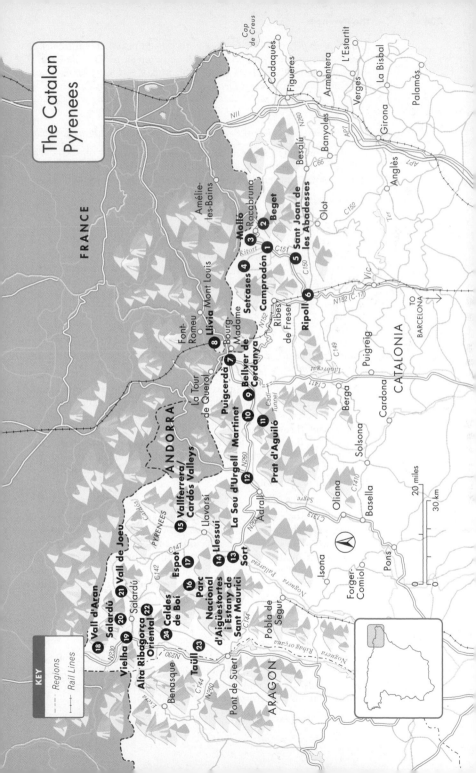

to *anec amb peras* (duck prepared with stewed pears). Try the *civet de porc senglar* (stewed wild boar) in season (winter). ✉ *Ctra. de Beget s/n, Rocabruna* ☎ *972/741045* ▭ *AE, DC, MC, V* ⊙ *Closed Mon.–Thurs. mid-Sept.–mid-July, except Dec. 26–Jan. 6 and Easter wk.*

Molló

❸ *25 km (16 mi) northwest of Beget, 24 km (15 mi) south of Prats de Molló.*

Molló lies on route C151 on the Ritort stream toward Col d'Ares. The 12th-century Romanesque church of **Santa Cecilia** is a work of exceptional balance and simplicity, with a delicate Romanesque bell tower.

Where to Stay

$$ 🏨 **Calitxó.** The rooms are small but comfortable at this friendly, family-run inn, and the views over the mountains in all directions are spectacular. After breakfast in the lush garden, this is an ideal base for hiking excursions to Beget and other points in the valley. A rustic chalet-type town house, the restaurant serves creative cuisine prepared with originality and fresh mountain ingredients. ✉ *Passatge el Serrat, 17868* ☎ *972/740386* 🖷 *972/740746* ⊕ *www.hotelcalitxo.com* 🛏 *23 rooms, 3 suites* ♨ *Restaurant; no a/c* ▭ *AE, DC, MC, V.*

Setcases

❹ *11 km (7 mi) north of Camprodón, 15 km (9 mi) west of Molló, 91 km (56 mi) northwest of Girona.*

Although Setcases ("seven houses") is somewhat larger than its name would imply, this tiny village nestled at the head of the valley has a distinct mountain spirit and a gravelly roughness, as if washed by the torrents flowing through and over its streets en route to the River Ter. On the road back down the valley from Setcases, **Llanars,** just short of Camprodón, has a 12th-century Romanesque church, **San Esteban,** of an exceptionally rich shade of ocher. The wood-and-iron portal depicts the martyrdom of St. Stephen.

Where to Stay

$$ 🏨 **La Coma.** Don't fear oversleeping here—*coma* is Catalan Pyrenean dialect for "high and fertile meadow." The proprietors are kind country folk who know the mountains and can help you plan excursions. Rooms in the modern stone house are done in bright wood trim. The restaurant, with garden seating in summer, specializes in mountain *civets* (stews) and *escudellas* (thick vegetable, bean, pasta, and pork soup). ✉ *Setcases 17869* ☎ *972/136074* 🖷 *972/136073* ⊕ *www.hotellacoma. com* 🛏 *20 rooms* ♨ *Restaurant, indoor/outdoor pool, gym; no a/c* ▭ *AE, DC, MC, V.*

Sports & the Outdoors

The **Vallter 2000 ski area** (☎ 972/136057 ⊕ www.vallter2000.com) above Setcases—built into a glacial cirque reaching a height of 8,216 feet—has a dozen lifts and, on very clear days at the top, views east all the way to the Bay of Roses on the Costa Brava.

Sant Joan de les Abadesses

❺ *21 km (13 mi) southeast of Setcases, 14 km (9 mi) south of Camprodón.*

Sant Joan de les Abadesses, site of an important church, is named for the 9th-century abbess Emma and her successors. Emma was the daughter of Guifré el Pilós (Wilfred the Hairy), the founder of the Catalonian nation and medieval hero of the Christian Reconquest of Ripoll. The town's arcaded Plaça Major looks and feels medieval, and the 12th-century bridge over the Ter is wide and graceful. The altarpiece in the 12th-century Romanesque church of **Sant Joan** (⊠ Plaça de la Abadía s/n ☎ 972/720013), a 13th-century polychrome wood sculpture of the Descent from the Cross, is one of the most expressive and human of that epoch.

Ripoll

❻ *10 km (6 mi) southwest of Sant Joan de les Abadesses, 105 km (62 mi) north of Barcelona, 65 km (40 mi) southeast of Puigcerdà.*

One of the first Christian strongholds of the Reconquest and a center of religious erudition during the Middle Ages, Ripoll is known as the *bressol* (cradle) of Catalonia's rescue from Moorish domination and modern nationhood. A dark, mysterious country town built around a **9th-century Benedictine monastery,** it was a focal point of culture throughout French Catalonia and the Pyrenees, from the monastery's AD 888 founding until the mid-1800s, when Barcelona began to eclipse it.

The 12th-century doorway to the church of **Santa Maria** is one of Catalonia's great works of Romanesque art, crafted as a triumphal arch by stone masons and sculptors of the Roussillon school (that is, the school centered around French Catalonia and the Pyrenees). The sculptures portray the glory of God and of all his creatures from the Creation onward. You can pick up a guide to the figures on the portal in the church or at the information kiosk nearby. ⊠ *Cloister €3, museum €6* ☉ *Tues.–Sun. 10–2 and 3–7.*

Fourteen kilometers (9 mi) north of Ripoll, the **cogwheel train** (☎ 972/732020) ride from Ribes de Freser up to Núria provides one of Catalonia's most unusual excursions. Known as the *cremallera* (zipper), the line was built in 1917 to connect Ribes with the Santuari de la Mare de Deu de Núria (Mother of God of Núria) and with mountain hiking and skiing. The ride takes 45 minutes and costs €16 round-trip. **Núria,** at an altitude of 6,562 feet at the foot of Puigmal, is a ski area, and in the 1950s it was the site of some of Spain's earliest ice-hockey activity.

The legend of the **Santuari de la Mare de Deu de Núria,** a Marian religious retreat, is based on the story of Sant Gil of Nîmes, who did penance in the Núria Valley during the 7th century. The saint left behind a wooden statue of the Virgin Mary, a bell he used to summon shepherds to prayer, and a cooking pot; 300 years later, a pilgrim found these treasures in this sanctuary. The bell and the pot came to have special importance to barren women, who were believed to be blessed with as many children as they wished by placing their heads in the pot and ringing the bell. ⊠ *Núria* 🎫 *Free* ☉ *Daily except during mass.*

LA CERDANYA

The Pyrenees' widest, sunniest valley is said to be in the shape of the handprint of God. High pastureland bordered north and south by snow-covered peaks, La Cerdanya starts in France, at Col de la Perche (near Mont Louis), and ends in the Spanish province of Lleida, at Martinet. Split into two countries and subdivided into two more provinces on each side, the valley has an identity all its own. Residents on both sides of the border speak Catalan, a Romance language derived from early Provençal French, and regard the valley's political border with undisguised hilarity. Unlike any other valley in the upper Pyrenees, this one runs east–west and thus has a record annual number of sunlight hours. If, as is nearly inevitable in La Cerdanya, you venture into France, Font Romeu offers sunny skiing; Porté-Puymorens is higher and colder. At the eastern end of the valley, the town of Mont Louis is a walled Vauban fortress, and Eyne offers excellent skiing and hiking. Remember that when you're north of the border, lunch is over by 2 PM.

Puigcerdà

❼ *170 km (105 mi) north of Barcelona, 65 km (40 mi) northwest of Ripoll.*

Puigcerdà (in Catalan, *puig* means "hill"; *cerdà* derives from "Cerdanya") is the largest town in the valley. From the promontory upon which it stands, the views down across the meadows of the valley floor and up into the craggy peaks of the surrounding Pyrenees give the town a schizophrenic sense of height and humility. The 12th-century Romanesque bell tower—all that remains of the town church destroyed in 1936 at the outset of the Spanish civil war—and the sunny sidewalk cafés facing it are among Puigcerdà's prettiest spots, as are the Gothic church of Santa Maria and its long square, the **Plaça del Cuartel.** On Sunday, markets sell clothes, cheeses, fruits, vegetables, and wild mushrooms to shoppers from both sides of the border.

From the balcony next to the **town hall** (⊠ Carrer Querol 1), you get an ample view of the Cerdanya Valley that stretches all the way past Bellver de Cerdanya down to the sheer granite walls of the Sierra del Cadí, at the end of the valley. A 300-yard walk west from the fountain near Carrer Font d'en Llanas around the edge of town will bring you to the stairs leading up from the train station to the balcony. The verse on the corner of the town hall to your left as you look out is by the Catalan poet Joan Maragall (1860–1910). In English, the fragment reads . . . *I love the balcony over the walls / When the townsfolk stroll there / and with nearly immobile eyes / follow the progress of the distant storm. . . .*

☺ **Le petit train jaune** (the little yellow train) leaves daily from Bourg-Madame and from La Tour de Querol, both simple walks into France from Puigcerdà. The border at La Tour, a longer but prettier walk, is marked only by a stone painted with the Spanish and French flags. This *carrilet* (narrow-gauge railway) is the last in the Pyrenees and is used for tours as well as transportation; it winds through the Cerdanya to the walled town of Villefranche de Conflent. The 63-km (39-mi) tour can take most of the day, especially if you stop to browse in Mont Louis or Villefranche. ⊠ *Boarding at SNCF stations at Bourg-Madame or La Tour de Querol, France* ☎ *33 (0)4–68–30–85–02* ⊕ *www.ter-sncf. com/languedoc* ⊠ *€33 La Tour de Querol–Villefranche-de-Conflent round-trip* ☉ *Schedule at Turismo office, Puigcerdà; or at RENFE station below Puigcerdà.*

Where to Stay & Eat

$$$–$$$$ ✕ **Josepmariamassó.** With sections of the medieval walls of Puigcerdà lining the downstairs dining rooms, and the postmodern creations of a young English-speaking chef with ideas and attitude, Josep Maria Massó, streaming out of the glass-walled kitchen, this is the town's top culinary showcase. The upstairs dining room is sleek and contemporary; the cellar is all ancient stone. ⊠ *Carrer d'Espanya 9* ☎ *972/884308* ▬ *AE, DC, MC, V* ☉ *Closed May 20–June 10, Nov. 15–30, and Mon. and Tues. except Aug.*

$$–$$$ ✕ **La Tieta.** A 500-year-old town house built into the remains of the ancient walls of Puigcerdà, this is one of the town's top restaurants. Its garden is ideal for a late-night drink in summer. The menu lists Cerdanya specialties such as *trinxat de Cerdanya* (a rib-sticking puree of cabbage and potatoes with bits of fried salt pork or bacon) as well as roasts cooked over coals. ⊠ *Carrer dels Ferrers 20* ☎ *972/880156* ▬ *AE, DC, MC, V* ☉ *Closed June 12–July 12 and Mon.–Wed. mid-Sept.–mid-June.*

$–$$$ ✕ **Madrigal.** The Pere Compte family has made this popular restaurant-bar near the town hall a Puigcerdà favorite for decades. The low-ceilinged, wood-trim dining room is filled with tables and benches. Selections include tapas and meals of assorted specialties, such as *codorniz* (quail), *caracoles* (snails), *calamares a la romana* (calamari dipped in batter), *albóndigas* (meatballs), *esqueixada* (raw codfish with peppers and onion), and wild mushrooms in season. ⊠ *Carrer Alfons I 3* ☎ *972/880860* ▬ *AE, DC, MC, V.*

$$$$ ✕▥ **La Torre del Remei.** About 3 km (2 mi) west of Puigcerdà is this splendid mansion, built in 1910 and brilliantly restored by José María and Loles Boix of the legendary restaurant Boix in Martinet, 26 km (16 mi) to the west. Everything is superb, from the Belle Epoque luxury of the manor house to the plush, tasteful suites, heated bathroom floors, huge bathtubs, and the bottle of Moët Chandon on your arrival. The restaurant ($$$$) serves fine international cuisine with an emphasis on local products such as lamb, trout, and game; reserve well in advance. ⊠ *Camí Reial s/n, Bolvir de Cerdanya 17539* ☎ *972/140182* ☎ *972/140449* ⊕ *www.torredelremei.com* ⇋ *5 rooms, 17 suites* ♨ *Restaurant, 18-hole golf course, putting green, pool* ▬ *AE, DC, MC, V.*

Fodor's Choice
★

$$$–$$$$ ▥ **Fontanals Golf.** This modern chalet-style ranch on the floor of the Cerdanya Valley places you within striking distance of ski slopes, trout streams, and a challenging golf course. Lavishly constructed with wood and glass, the resort has panoramic views into the Pyrenees on both sides of the valley. ⊠ *C. Fontanals 2, Soriguerola, 17538* ☎ *972/891818* ☎ *972/891740* ⊕ *www.hotelfontanals.com* ⇋ *60 rooms* ♨ *Restaurant, 18-hole golf course, tennis court, pool, bar* ▬ *AE, DC, MC, V.*

$$–$$$ ⊡ **Hotel del Prado.** Below town on the road to Llívia, a five-minute walk from France (Bourg-Madame), the relaxed and friendly "Hotel of the Meadow" is a good clubhouse and base for skiing, hiking, fishing, collecting wild mushrooms, and most outdoor activities in the Cerdanya Valley. The modernized rooms are chalet-style, with wood trimmings. ⊠ *Ctra. de Llívia, Km 1, 17520* ☎ *972/880400* 🖷 *972/141158* ⊕ *www. hotelprado.com* ⇌ *54 rooms* ⚹ *Restaurant, tennis court, pool, bar* ⊟ *AE, MC, V.*

$$ ⊡ **Hotel del Lago.** This comfortable old favorite near Puigcerdà's emblematic lake is a graceful, tastefully appointed series of buildings built around a central garden. A two-minute walk from the bell tower or the town market, it feels bucolic but is virtually in the center of town. ⊠ *Av. Doctor Piguillem 7, 17520* ☎ *972/881000* 🖷 *972/141511* ⊕ *www.hotellago.com* ⇌ *15 rooms* ⚹ *Indoor/outdoor pool, spa; no a/c* ⊟ *AE, DC, MC, V.*

Nightlife

Young Spanish and French night owls fill the town's many clubs until dawn. **No Ho Sé** (⊠ Ctra. 152, Km 170 ☎ 972/882248), 5 km (3 mi) south of town on the Barcelona road, is the favored disco on weekend and holiday nights. The **Le Clochard** (⊠ Carrer Major 54 ☎ 972/881615) rocks in midtown Puigcerdá.

Sports & the Outdoors

Pick up your **fishing license** after 7 PM, at the **Societat de Pesca de Puigcerdà** (⊠ Av. del Lago s/n ☎ 972/141172). With your Catalonia fishing license, you can buy a day pass (generally ranging from €4 to €9 though subject to change) for the Coto del Querol (reserved trout-fishing beat) on the Querol River (or the Segre) at **Tota Teca** (⊠ Ctra. N152, Km 169.5 ☎ 972/141027); there's also good take-out food here. The town's **ice rink** (☎ 972/880243) is worth checking out if you skate. The **Reial Club de Golf de la Cerdanya** (☎ 972/141408) near Puigcerdà has 18 holes. Near Puigcerdà, the challenging **Club de Golf de Fontanals** (☎ 972/144374), so called for its myriad water hazards, has 18 holes.

Shopping

Puigcerdà is one big shopping mall, and long a nexus for contraband clothes, cigarettes, and other items. **Carrer Major** is an uninterrupted row of stores selling everything—books, jewelry, sports equipment, and other items. The annual **equine fair,** in early November, is an unparalleled opportunity to study horses—and horse traders. The **Sunday market,** like those in most other Cerdanya towns, is a great place to look for local specialties such as herbs, goat cheese, wild mushrooms, honey, and basketry. It's as social as it is commercial; the Plaça del Cuartel fills with people and produce. In autumn, it's a great chance to learn about wild mushrooms of all kinds.

For the best *margaritas* (no, not those; these are crunchy-edged madeleines made with almonds) in town, look for **Pasteleria Cosp** (⊠ Carrer Major 20 ☎ 972/880103), founded in 1806 and the oldest pastry shop in the province of Girona.

Llívia

❽ *6 km (4 mi) northeast of Puigcerdà.*

A Spanish enclave in French territory, Llívia was marooned by the 1659 Peace of the Pyrenees treaty, which ceded 33 villages to France. Incorporated as a *vila* (town) by royal decree of Carlos V—who spent a night here in 1528 and was impressed by the town's beauty and hospitality—it managed to remain Spanish. At the upper edge of town, the fortified church **Mare de Deu dels Àngels** (⊠ Carrer dels Forns 13 ☎ 972/896301) is an acoustic gem; check to see if any choral events are scheduled, especially in August and December, when the Llívia music festival schedules top classical groups. Across from the church is the ancient pharmacy **Museu de la Farmacia** (⊠ Carrer dels Forns 12 ☎ 972/880103 ⊙ Daily Tues.–Fri. 10–4:20, weekends 10–1:50), founded in 1415 and thought to be the oldest in Europe.

Look for the **mosaic** in the middle of town commemorating Lampègia, *princesa de la pau i de l'amor* (princess of peace and of love), erected in memory of the red-haired daughter of the duke of Aquitania and lover of Munuza, a Moorish warlord who governed the Cerdanya during the Arab domination.

Where to Eat

★ $$$–$$$$ ✕ **Can Ventura.** Inside a quirky 17th-century town house, this attractive restaurant is one of the Cerdanya's best for cuisine and value. Trout and beef *a la llosa* (seared on slate) are house specialties, and the wide selection of *entretenimientos* (hors d'oeuvres) is delicious. ⊠ *Plaça Major 1* ☎ *972/896178* ⌲ *Reservations essential* ▭ *AE, DC, MC, V* ⊙ *Closed June 20–July 15, Mon. (except Nov.–May), and Tues.*

$$$–$$$$
Fodor'sChoice
★   ✕ **La Formatgeria de Llívia.** This conveniently situated restaurant on Llívia's eastern edge (en route to Saillagousse, France) is in a former cheese factory that still makes fresh mató cheese while you watch; there are tasting tables in the bar for trying the cheeses. Juanjo Meya and his wife, master chef Marta Pous, have had great success with fine local cuisine, panoramic views looking south toward Puigmal and across the valley, and creating general charm and good cheer. The innovative taster's menu adds a new and creative dimension to the restaurant. An ample garden with swings and slides allows children to let off steam while their parents sample wines, cheeses, and Havana tobacco. ⊠ *Pla de Rô, Gorguja* ☎ *972/146279* ⌲ *Reservations essential* ▭ *AE, DC, MC, V* ⊙ *Closed June 20–July 12, Tues., and Wed.*

Bellver de Cerdanya

★ **❾** *31 km (19 mi) southwest of Llívia, 25 km (16 mi) west of Puigcerdà.*

Bellver de Cerdanya has preserved its slate-roof and fieldstone Pyrenean architecture more successfully than many of the Cerdanya's larger towns. Perched on a promontory over the **River Segre,** which winds around much of the town, Bellver is a mountain version of a fishing village—trout fishing, of course. The river is the town's main event; whether the water is low or high, muddy or clear, warm or cold, it supplants the weather as the topic of conversation. Bellver's Gothic church of **Sant Jaume** and the arcaded **Plaça Major,** in the upper part of town, are lovely examples of traditional Pyrenean mountain-village design.

Where to Stay & Eat

$$ ✕▥ **Fonda Biayna.** This rustic retreat with woodsy furnishings seems happily stuck in an early Pyrenean time warp. Guest rooms are simple, old-fashioned, and cozy. The Catalan fare ($$–$$$) includes such dishes as roast rabbit *allioli* (a sauce of garlic and olive oil), *galtas de porc amb bolets* (pork cheeks with wild mushrooms), and *tiró amb naps i trumfes* (duck with turnips and potatoes). ⊠ *Carrer Sant Roc 11, 25720* ☎ *973/510475* 📠 *973/510853* ⊕ *www.fondabiayna.com* ⬐ *16 rooms* ⏶ *Restaurant; no a/c, no room phones, no room TVs* ▤ *AE, DC, MC, V.*

Sports & the Outdoors

The **Coto de Bellver,** a reserved section along the River Segre for trout fishing, was once one of Spain's best and is still a lovely place to spend time, fish or no fish. **Bar Blanch** (⊠ Carrer San Roc 13 ☎ 973/510208) is the town's de facto angling clubhouse, where, along with hearty mountain fare or a beer at the bar, you can buy licenses and day passes to the coto from mid-March through August.

Martinet

⑩ *10 km (6 mi) west of Bellver de Cerdanya.*

The town of Martinet hasn't much to offer except a few cozy watering spots that are hard to pass up in the heat of summer. For a course in trout economy and husbandry, have a close look over the railing along the River Segre just upstream from its junction with the Llosa River. Martinet's protected trout are famous in these parts: the fish dine from 1 to 4 in the afternoon, when the sun slants in and cooks off hatches of aquatic insects while illuminating every speckle and spot on the feeding trout.

For a spectacular excursion, drive or walk up the valley of the Llosa River into Andorra, or take the short but stunning walk from the village of **Aransa** to Lles: as you pull away from Aransa and onto an alpine meadow, the Cerdanya's palette changes with every twist of the trail. You'll even pass the ruins of a 10th-century hilltop hermitage. (The tourist office in La Seu d'Urgell has simple trail maps.) The village of **Lles** is a famous Nordic-skiing resort with 36 km (22 mi) of cross-country tracks.

Where to Stay & Eat

$$ ✕▥ **Cal Rei.** This graceful and rustic country inn built into former stables usually has a roaring fire in the common room and offers, when snow is abundant, direct access to one of the Pyrenees' finest cross-country ski areas. The cuisine is powerful mountain fare ($$–$$$$) designed to restore weary trekkers. Views of the Sierra del Cadí across the valley are spectacular. ⊠ *Cadí 4 Lles de Cerdanya 25726* ☎ *659–063–915 (mobile)* 📠 *973/515213* ✉ *www.cal.rei@lles.net* ⬐ *8 rooms* ⏶ *Restaurant; no a/c, no room phones, no room TVs* ▤ *AE, DC, MC, V.*

Prat d'Aguiló

⑪ *20 km (12 mi) south of Martinet.*

The spectacular Prat d'Aguiló, or Eagle's Meadow, is one of the highest points in the Cerdanya that you can access without either a four-wheel-drive vehicle or a hike. The winding, bumpy drive up the mountain takes about an hour and a half (start with a full tank) and opens onto some excellent vistas of its own. From the meadow, the roughly three-hour climb to the top of the sheer rock wall of the Sierra del Cadí, directly above, reaches an altitude of nearly 8,000 feet. On a clear day you can see Puigcerdà and beyond, with the Segre River seeming no more than a thin, silver ribbon on the valley floor. To get here from Martinet, take a dirt road that is rough but navigable by the average car. Follow signs for "Refugio Prat d'Aguiló."

La Seu d'Urgell

⑫ *24 km (15 mi) west of Martinet, 20 km (12 mi) south of Andorra la*
Fodor'sChoice *Vella (in Andorra), 50 km (31 mi) west of Puigcerdà.*
★

La Seu d'Urgell is an ancient town facing the snowy rock wall of the Sierra del Cadí. As the seat (*seu*) of the regional archbishopric since the 6th century, it has a rich legacy of art and architecture. The Pyrenean feel of the streets, with their dark balconies and porticoes, overhanging galleries, and colonnaded porches—particularly **Carrer dels Canonges**—makes Seu mysterious and memorable. Look for the medieval **grain measures** at the corner of Carrer Major and Carrer Capdevila. The tiny food shops on the arcaded Carrer Major are intriguing places to assemble lunch for a hike.

★ The 12th-century **Catedral de Santa Maria** is the finest cathedral in the Pyrenees. One of the most moving sights in northern Spain is the cathedral's show of sunlight casting the rich reds and blues of Santa Maria's southeastern rose window into the deep gloom of the transept. The 13th-century cloister is known for the individually carved, sometimes whimsical capitals on its 50 columns. (They were crafted by the same Roussillon school of masons who carved the doorway on the church of Santa Maria in Ripoll.) Don't miss either the haunting, 11th-century chapel of **Sant Miquel** or the **Diocesan Museum,** which has a striking collection of medieval murals from various Pyrenean churches and a colorfully illuminated 10th-century Mozarabic manuscript of the monk Beatus de Liébana's commentary on the Apocalypse, along with a short film explaining the manuscript. Ask for the attractive and well-organized book detailing every local church on the medieval Vía Románica (an itinerary covering the area's Romanesque churches)—it makes a great souvenir. ⊠ *Plaça dels Oms* ☎ *973/350981* ⊠ *Cathedral, cloister, and museum €3* ☉ *Daily 9–1 and 4–8.*

Where to Stay & Eat

$$–$$$ ✕ **Cal Pacho.** Sample traditional local specialties at very reasonable prices in this dark, rustic spot, built in the typical Pyrenean style with stone and wood beams. Count on the filling *escudella* (mountain soup

of vegetables, pork or veal, and noodles) in winter, and meat cooked over coals or on slate year-round. ⊠ *Carrer La Font 11* ☎ *973/352719* ⊟ *AE, DC, MC, V.*

★ $$$–$$$$ ╳▦ **El Castell de Ciutat.** Just outside Seu, this tall wood-and-slate structure is one of the finest places in the Pyrenees. Rooms on the second floor have balconies overlooking the river; those on the third have slanted ceilings and dormer windows. Suites include a salon. The restaurant ($$$–$$$$) specializes in mountain cuisine, such as *civet de jabalí* (wild-boar stew) and *llom de cordet amb trinxat* (lamb cooked over coals and served with puree of potatoes and cabbage). Reserve in advance during summer or Easter week. ⊠ *Ctra. de Lleida (N260), Km 229, 25700* ☎ *973/350000* 🖨 *973/351574* ⊕ *www.hotelelcastell.com* ⤷ *32 rooms, 6 suites* △ *Restaurant, 2 pools (1 indoor), gym, hair salon, sauna* ⊟ *AE, DC, MC, V.*

$$$ ▦ **Parador de la Seu d'Urgell.** These comfortable quarters right in town are built into the 12th-century church and convent of Sant Domènec. The interior patio—the cloister of the former convent—is a lush and tranquil hideaway. Rooms are simple but warm, and some face the mountains. ⊠ *Carrer Sant Domènec 6, 25700* ☎ *973/352000* 🖨 *973/352309* ⊕ *www.parador.es* ⤷ *77 rooms, 1 suite* △ *Restaurant, indoor pool, gym, meeting rooms* ⊟ *AE, DC, MC, V.*

┌─────
│ OFF THE
│ BEATEN
  PATH

CALBINYÀ – Ten minutes north of La Seu d'Urgell (off the road to Andorra), this Pyrenean village, with a Museu del Pagès (Farmer's Museum) and the 16th-century farmhouse and inn **Cal Serni,** is a place to find rustic charm, inexpensive meals, and a room for the night. ⊠ *Valls de Valira, 25798* ☎ *973/352809* ⤷ *6 rooms* ⊟ *AE, DC, MC, V.*

WESTERN CATALAN PYRENEES

"The farther from Barcelona, the wilder" is the rule of thumb, and this is true of the western part of Catalonia. Three of the greatest destinations in the Pyrenees are here: the Garonne-drained, Atlantic-oriented Vall d'Aran; the Noguera de Tor valley with its matching set of gemlike Romanesque churches; and Parc Nacional d'Aigüestortes i Estany de Sant Maurici, which has a network of pristine lakes and streams. The main geographical units in this section are the valley of the Noguera Pallaresa River, the Vall d'Aran headwaters of the Atlantic-bound Garonne, and the Noguera Ribagorçana River valley, Catalonia's western limit.

Sort

★ ⑬ *59 km (37 mi) west of La Seu d'Urgell.*

The capital of the Pallars Sobirà (Upper Pallars Valley) is a center for skiing, fishing, and white-water kayaking. Don't be content with the Sort you see from the main road: one block back, the town is honeycombed with tiny streets and protected corners built to stave off heavy winter weather. To get here from La Seu d'Urgell, take N260 toward Lleida, head west at Adrall, and drive 53 km (33 mi) over the Cantó Pass to Sort. Sort is the origin of the road into the unspoiled **Assua Valley,** a hidden pocket of untouched mountain villages, including Saurí and Olp.

Where to Eat

$$–$$$$ ✗**Fogony.** If you hit Sort at lunchtime, one of the finest dining establishments in the Pyrenees is a good reason to stop. Come here for local specialties such as *escudella* (a power stew with beans, pasta, pork, beef, fowl, and vegetables), roast lamb, or contemporary gems such as the *suquet de alcachofas* (stewed artichokes) before heading into the high country. ✉ *Av. Generalitat 45* ☎ *973/621225* 🖃 *AE, DC, MC, V* ⊘ *Closed 2 wks in Jan. Closed Mon. except Christmas wk, Easter wk, and Aug. No dinner Sun.*

Llessuí

⑭ *15 km (9 mi) north of Sort.*

Llessuí is at the head of the Upper Pallars Valley under the onetime ski slopes, now closed, of the Altars peak. The 12th-century Romanesque church of **Sant Pere** is topped with a typical conical bell tower resembling a pointed witch's hat. These are characteristic of the Vall d'Aran and its environs.

Where to Stay & Eat

$–$$ ✗**Cal Kiko.** This little restaurant, also known as "El Pigal," is famous throughout Catalonia for its simple but peerless Pyrenean cooking and for its "Filiberto," a dessert composed of whipped cream, yogurt, and red currants. ✉ *Ctra. de Llessuí s/n, Llessui 25567* ☎ *973/621715* 🖃 *No credit cards* ⊘ *Closed Oct., Wed. No dinner Tues.*

$ ✗🖾 **Vall d'Àssua.** A cozy refuge, this little family-run and family-oriented place is a sure bet for simple Pyrenean home cooking ($–$$) strong on thick stews and soups, and roasts cooked *a la brasa* (over coals). Guest rooms are small but comfortable. The family also rents out several apartments in country houses in the nearby village of Llagunes. ✉ *Ctra. de Llessuí, Altron 25567* ☎☎ *973/621738* ⇨ *11 rooms* ♻ *No room TVs* 🖃 *No credit cards* ⊘ *Closed Nov.*

Vallferrera & Cardós Valleys

⑮ *From Llavorsí—14 km (9 mi) from Sort on C14, at the junction of the Noguera Pallaresa and Cardós rivers—the road up to the Cardós and Vallferrera valleys branches off to the northeast.*

A trip up the Vallferrera Valley is a good way to penetrate some little-known countryside, explore icy trout streams, or browse through the Romanesque and Visigothic (pre-Romanesque) churches and chapels scattered in and around the village of **Alins** under Catalonia's highest mountain, the Pica d'Estats. In the neighboring Cardós Valley, the Romanesque bell tower of the church of **Santa Maria** rises amid green fields of alfalfa and early wheat and, in May, bright-red splashes of poppies.

Where to Stay & Eat

$–$$ ✗🖾 **Hotel Cardós.** As a base camp for summer hiking, climbing, or fishing excursions up the Cardós Valley, you can't do much better than this handy place in the village of Ribera de Cardós. The satisfying fare ($–$$$), featuring sturdy soups and civets, is welcome after you've spent some time at high altitude. The rooms are on the small side, but cozy and always spotless and comfortable. ✉ *Av. Hug Roger III 1, Ribera de Cardós 25570* ☎ *973/623100* 🖷 *973/623158* ⊕ *www.hotelcardos.com* 🛏 *47 rooms* △ *Restaurant, pool, bar; no a/c* 🖃 *AE, DC, MC, V* ◑ *Closed Oct.–Mar.*

Parc Nacional d'Aigüestortes i Estany de Sant Maurici

★ **16** *After Escaló, 12 km (7 mi) northwest of Llavorsí, the road to Espot and the park veers west.*

Running water and the abundance of high mountain terrain are the true protagonists in this wild domain in the shadow of the twin peaks of Els Encantats. More than 300 glacial lakes and lagoons (the beautiful Estany de Sant Maurici among them) drain through flower-filled meadows and woods to the two Noguera River watercourses, the Pallaresa to the east and the Ribagorçana to the west. The ubiquitous water is surrounded by bare rock walls carved out by the glacier that left these jagged peaks and moist pockets. The land ranges from soft lower meadows below 5,000 feet to the highest crags at nearly double that height: the twin Encantats measure more than 9,000 feet, and surrounding peaks Beciberri, Peguera, Montarto, and Amitges hover between 8,700 feet and just under 10,000 feet. Forested by pines, firs, beech, and silver birches, Aigüestortes (which means "twisted waters") also has ample pastureland inhabited by Pyrenean chamois (a kind of antelope), capercaillie (grouse), golden eagle, and snow partridge, also known as ptarmigan.

The dozen Aigüestortes mountain refuges are the stars of the Pyrenees, ranging from the 12-bunk Beciberri, the highest bivouac in the Pyrenees at 9,174 feet, to the 80-bunk, 7,326-foot Ventosa i Calvell at the foot of Punta Alta. Between June and September these mountain accommodations fill with tired and hungry hikers sharing trail tips and lore.

The park has strict rules: no camping, no fires, no vehicles beyond certain points, no unleashed pets. Access to the park is free. It is accessible from the Noguera Pallares and Ribagorçana valleys, and the Espot and Boí villages. For information and refuge reservations, contact the **park administration offices** (☎ 973/694000 Barruera, 973/696189 Boí, 973/624036 Espot ⊕ www.mma.es/parques/lared/).

Where to Stay

There are no hotels in the park, only refuges. The 66-bunk **Refugi d'Amitges** (☎ 973/250109) is near the Amitges lakes, at 7,920 feet. The 24-bunk **Refugi Ernest Mallafré** (☎ 973/250118) is at the foot of Els Encantats, near Lake Sant Maurici. **Refugi Josep Maria Blanc** (☎ 973/250108), at 7,755 feet, offers 40 bunks at the base of a peninsula reaching out into the Tort de Peguera lake.

Espot

17 *15 km (9 mi) northwest of Llavorsí, 166 km (100 mi) north of Lleida.*

Espot is at the heart of the valley, along a clear, aquamarine stream, and next to the eastern entrance of Aigüestortes–Sant Maurici National Park. **Super-Espot** is the local ski area. The **Pont de la Capella** (Chapel Bridge), a perfect, mossy arch over the flow, looks as though it might have grown directly from the Pyrenean slate.

Hiking in the Pyrenees

HIKING IS A SPECTACULARLY BEAUTIFUL Pyrenean activity year-round. Trails crisscross the region, most with truly unforgettable views. Walking the crest of the range, with one foot in France and the other in Spain, is an exhilarating experience and well within reach of the moderately fit.

In fall and winter the Alberes mountains between Cap de Creus, the Iberian Peninsula's easternmost point, and the border with France at Le Perthus is a sky-glide between the Côte Vermeille's curving strand to the north and the moist green patchwork of the Empordá to the south.

The eight-hour walk from Coll de Núria to Ulldeter over the Sierra Catllar, above Setcases, is a grassy corridor in good weather from April to October. The luminous Cerdanya Valley is a hiker's paradise year-round, while the summertime round-Andorra hike is a 360-degree tour of the principality.The Parque Nacional de Aigüestortes y Lago San Mauricio is superb for trekking from spring through fall. The ascent of the 11,168-foot Aneto peak above Benasque is a full day's round-trip best approached in summer and only by fit and experienced hikers. Much of the hike is over the Maladeta glacier, from the base camp at the Refugio de La Renclusa, where you can rent crampons and ice axes.

In Parque Nacional de Ordesa y Monte Perdido you can take day trips up to the Cola de Caballo waterfall and back around the southern rim of the canyon or, for true mountain goats, longer hikes via the Refugio de Góriz to La Brèche de Roland and Gavarnie or to Monte Perdido, the Parador at La Pineta, and the village of Bielsa.

Farther west, the Irati Forest and the Basque hills between the 6,617-foot Pic D'Orhi and the Bay of Biscay at Hondarribia are snow-free for nine months of the year. The Camino de Santiago walk from Saint-Jean-Pied-de-Port to Roncesvalles is a marvelous 8–10-hour trek and manageable any time of year, though weather reports should be checked carefully from October to June.

Local *excursionista* (outing) clubs can help you get started; local tourist offices may also have brochures and rudimentary trail maps. Keep in mind that the higher reaches are safely navigable only in summer

5

EN ROUTE From Esterri d'Aneu, C1412 reaches the sanctuary of Mare de Deu de Ares, a hermitage and shelter, at 4,600 feet, and the Bonaigua Pass, at 6,798 feet. The latter offers a dizzying look back at the Pallars Mountains and ahead to the Vall d'Aran and the Maladeta massif beyond.

Vall d'Aran & Environs

⑱ *From Esterri d'Aneu, the valley runs 46 km (27 mi) east to Vielha over the Bonaigua Pass.*

The Vall d'Aran is at the western edge of the Catalan Pyrenees and the northwestern corner of Catalonia. North of the main Pyrenean axis, it's the Catalan Pyrenees' only Atlantic valley, opening northward into the plains of Aquitania and drained by the Garonne, which flows into the Atlantic Ocean above Bordeaux. The 48-km (30-mi) drive from Bonaigua Pass to the Pont del Rei border with France follows the riverbed.

The valley's Atlantic personality is evidenced by its climate—wet and cold—and its language: the 6,000 inhabitants speak Aranés, a dialect of Gascon French derived from the Occitanian language group. With some difficulty, Aranés can be understood by speakers of Catalan and French. Originally part of the Aquitanian county of Comminges, the Vall d'Aran maintained feudal ties to the Pyrenees of Spanish Aragón and became part of Catalonia-Aragón in the 12th century. In 1389 the valley was assigned to Catalonia.

Neither as wide as the Cerdanya nor as oppressively narrow and vertical as Andorra, the Vall d'Aran has a sense of well-being and order, an architectural harmony unique in Catalonia. The clusters of iron-gray slate roofs, the lush vegetation, and dormer windows (a sign of French influence) all make the Vall d'Aran a distinct geographic and cultural pocket that happens to have washed up on the Spanish side of the border. Hiking and climbing are popular here; guides are available year-round and can be arranged through the **tourist office** (☎ 973/640110) in Vielha.

Vielha

 79 km (49 mi) northwest of Sort.

Vielha (Viella, in Spanish), capital of the Vall d'Aran, is a lively crossroads vitally involved in the Aranese movement to defend and reconstruct the valley's architectural, institutional, and linguistic heritage. The octagonal, 14th-century bell tower on the Romanesque parish church of **Sant Miquel** is one of the town's trademarks, as is the 15th-century Gothic altar. The partly damaged 12th-century polychrome wood carving *Cristo de Mig Aran,* displayed under glass, evokes a sense of mortality and humanity with a power unusual in medieval sculpture. The town also has an **ice rink** (☎ 973/642864).

North of Vielha, the tiny villages over the River Garonne hold intriguing little secrets, such as the sculpted Gallo-Roman heads (funeral stelae, or stone slabs, rehabilitated in the 12th century) carved into the village portal at **Gausac.** The bell tower in **Vilac** has an eccentric charm. The church in **Vilamós**, the oldest in the valley, is known for the three curious carved figures, thought to be Gallo-Roman funeral stelae, on its facade. The porticoed square in the border village of **Bossòst** has beautifully carved capitals on the supporting columns. East of Vielha is the village of **Escunhau,** with steep alley-stairways. **Arties** makes a good stop, with its famous Casa Irene restaurant and historic parador.

Where to Stay & Eat

★ **$$–$$$$** ✕ **Era Mola.** Also known as Restaurante Gustavo y María José, this former stable with whitewash walls serves French-inspired Aranese cuisine. The *confite de pato* (duck stewed with apple) and *magret de pato* (breast of duck served with *carradetas,* wild mushrooms from the valley) are favorites. ⊠ *Carrer Marrec 14* ☎ *973/642419* ⚄ *Reservations essential* ⊟ *AE, DC, MC, V* ⊗ *No lunch weekdays Dec.–Apr.*

★ **$$$–$$$$** ✕⊞ **Casa Irene.** A rustic haven, this inn 6 km (4 mi) east of Vielha is known for fine mountain cuisine with a French flair. Three tasting menus and dishes ($$$–$$$$) such as poached foie gras in black truffles and roast wood pigeon in nuts and mint have made Irene a national treasure. The personal style and spacious and elegant rooms make this a highly recommendable address for lodging as well as food. ⊠ *Carrer Major 3, 25599 Arties* ☎ *973/644364* 🖨 *973/642174* ⊕ *www. hotelcasairene.com* ↪ *22 rooms* ⚄ *Restaurant, parking (fee)* ⚄ *Reservations essential* ⊟ *AE, DC, MC, V* ⊗ *Closed Nov.*

$$$ ✕⊞ **Parador de Vielha.** This modern granite parador has a semicircular salon with huge windows and spectacular views over the Maladeta peaks of the Vall d'Aran. Rooms are furnished with traditional carved-wood furniture and floor-to-ceiling curtains. The restaurant ($$–$$$$) serves mainly Catalan cuisine, such as *espinacas a la catalana* (spinach cooked in olive oil with pine nuts, raisins, and garlic). ⊠ *Ctra. del Túnel s/n, 25530* ☎ *973/640100* 🖨 *973/641100* ⊕ *www.parador.es* ↪ *118 rooms* ⚄ *Restaurant, pool, meeting rooms* ⊟ *AE, MC, V.*

$$$ ⊞ **Parador de Arties.** Built around the Casa de Don Gaspar de Portolà, once home to the founder of the colony of California, this modern parador has panoramic views of the Pyrenees. Just 7 km (4 mi) from the Baqueira ski slopes and 2½ km (1½ mi) south of Vielha, it's big enough to seem festive, but small enough for intimacy. ⊠ *Ctra. Baqueira-Beret s/n, Arties 25599* ☎ *973/640801* 🖨 *973/641001* ⊕ *www.parador.es* ↪ *54 rooms, 3 suites* ⚄ *Restaurant, 2 pools (1 indoor), gym, meeting rooms, parking (fee)* ⊟ *AE, MC, V.*

$$ ⊞ **Hotel Pirene.** This modern hotel, with some of the best views in town, has rooms that are bright and simply furnished. The cozy sitting room and the charming family in charge make a stay here memorable. Book ahead during ski season: the place is 15 minutes from the slopes. It's on the left (or west) side side of the N230 into Vielha. ⊠ *Ctra. del Túnel s/n, 25530* ☎ *973/640075* 🖨 *973/642295* ⊕ *www.hotelpirene.com* ↪ *39 rooms* ⚄ *Restaurant, cable TV, bar; no a/c* ⊟ *AE, DC, MC, V.*

Nightlife

Glass (⊠ Centro Comercial Elurra, Betrén ☎ 973/640332) is in a commercial complex near Vielha filled with a dozen music bars, pubs, and discos. **Eth Clòt** (⊠ Plaça Sant Orenç, Arties ☎ 973/642060) is a hot *bar musicale*. **Bar Era Crin** (⊠ Carrer Sortaus 2, Escunhau ☎ 973/642061) has live performances and pop rock to dance to, as well as billiards and table football. **Bar la Lluna** (⊠ Carrer Major 10, Arties ☎ 973/641115), a local favorite, occupies a typical Aranese house and has live performances on Wednesday.

Salardú

⑳ *9 km (6 mi) east of Vielha.*

Convenient to Tredós, the Montarto peak, the lakes and Circ de Colomers, the Aigüestortes national park, and the villages of Unha and Mongarri, Salardú is a pivotal point in the Vall d'Aran. The town itself, with just over 700 inhabitants, is known for its steep streets and its octagonal fortified bell tower. The 12th-century **Sant Andreu** church's Romanesque wood sculpture of Christ is said to have miraculously floated up the Garonne River.

The tiny village of **Unha** perches on a promontory 3 km (2 mi) above Salardú, with the elegant Ço de Brastet (Brastet House) at its entrance. Unha's 12th-century church of Santa Eulàlia has a curiously bulging 17th-century bell tower. East of Salardú is the village of **Tredós,** home of the Romanesque church of Santa Maria de Cap d'Aran—symbol of the Aranese independence movement and meeting place of the valley's governing body, the Conseu Generau, until 1827.

Where to Stay & Eat

$–$$$ ✗ **Casa Rufus.** Pine and checkered tablecloths cozily furnish this restaurant nestled in the tiny, gray-stone village of Gessa, between Vielha and Salardú. Rufus himself, who also runs the ski school at Baqueira, specializes in local country cooking; try the *conejo relleno de ternera* (rabbit stuffed with veal). ✉ *Sant Jaume 8, Gessa* ☎ *973/645246 or 973/ 645872* ▤ *MC, V* ☉ *Closed May–mid-July, Nov., and weekdays in Oct. No dinner Sun. No lunch weekdays mid-Sept.–Apr.*

★ $$$$ ✗▥ **Meliá Royal Tanau.** This luxurious hotel 7 km (4 mi) east of Salardú is only a few steps from the lifts and offers services and amenities that include hydrotherapy massage and fine cuisine (with prices to match). Considered one of the top skiing hotels in the Pyrenees, it is a refuge where you can count on being well pampered between assaults on the snowy heights. Top-floor rooms can be snug, with duplex apartments and sleeping lofts with skylights opening directly out into the starry Pyrenean firmament. ✉ *Ctra. Baqueira-Beret, Km 7, 25598* ☎ *973/644446* ▤ *973/644344* ⊕ *www.meliaroyaltanau.solmelia.com* ☜ *30 rooms, 15 apartments* ⚒ *Restaurant, pool, hot tub; no a/c* ▤ *AE, MC, V.*

$$$–$$$$ ▥ **Val de Ruda.** For rustic surroundings light on luxury but long on comfort, and an outdoorsy, alpine feeling, this modern-traditional construction is a good choice. It was one of the first skiing hotels to go up here in the early '80s; it's just 660 feet from the slopes. This glass, wood, and stone refuge has a friendly staff and pine- and oak-beam warmth for après-ski wining and dining. ✉*Ctra. Baqueira-Beret Cota 1500, 25598* ☎ *973/645258* ▤ *973/645812* ⊕ *www.valderuda-bassibe.com* ☜ *34 rooms* ⚒ *Restaurant, bar; no a/c* ▤ *AE, DC, MC, V.*

Nightlife

Pachá (✉ Baqueira ☎ 973/646444) has successfully extended its disco tentacles from Ibiza to Barcelona to Baqueira.

Sports & the Outdoors

Skiing, white-water rafting, hiking, climbing, horseback riding, and fly-fishing are available throughout the Vall d'Aran. Consult the Vielha **tourist office** (☎ 973/640110) for information.

DOGSLEDDING **La Pirena** (☎ 974/360098 tourist office in Jaca), the Pyrenean version of the Iditarod, rages through the Vall d'Aran in early February. The race runs from Panticosa, above Jaca, to La Molina, near Puigcerdà, every winter in late January to early or mid-February.

SKIING The **Baqueira-Beret Estación de Esquí** (Baqueira-Beret Ski Station), visited annually by King Juan Carlos I and the royal family, offers Catalonia's most varied and reliable skiing. The station's 87 km (57 mi) of *pistas* (slopes), spread over 53 runs, range from the gentle Beret slopes to the vertical chutes of Baqueira. The Bonaigua area is a mixture of steep and gently undulating trails with some of the longest, most varied runs in the Pyrenees, from forest tracks to open hillsides to jagged drops through tight ravines. The internationally FIS-classified super-giant slalom run in Beret is Baqueira-Beret's star attraction, although the Hotel Pirene runs carefully guided helicopter outings to the surrounding peaks of Pincela, Areño, Parros, Mall de Boulard, Pedescals, and Bassibe, among others. A dozen restaurants and four children's areas are scattered about the facilities, and the thermal baths at Tredós are 4 km (2½ mi) away. ⊠ *Salardú* ☎ *973/639000* 🖷 *973/644488* ✉ *Barcelona office: Av. Diagonal 656, Barcelona* ☎ *93/205–8292* 🖷 *93/205–8290* ⊕ *www.baqueira.es.*

Vall de Joeu

㉑ *9 km (6 mi) northwest of Vielha.*

The Joeu Valley, above the town of Les Bordes, was for centuries the unsolved mystery of Vall d'Aran hydraulics. The Joeu River, one of the two main sources of the Garonne, appears to rise at Artiga de Lin, where it then cascades down in the Barrancs waterfalls. On July 19, 1931, speleologist Norbert Casteret proved, by dumping 132 pounds of colorant into a cavern in neighboring Aragón, that this "spring" was actually glacier runoff from the Maladeta massif in the next valley to the southwest. The glacier melt flows into a massive crater, Els Aïgualluts, and reappears 4 km (3 mi) northeast at the Uelhs deth Joeu (Eyes of Jupiter in Aranés, so named for the Roman deity's association with the heavens, weather, rainfall, and agriculture), where it flows north toward the Garonne and eventually the Atlantic.

Alta Ribagorça Oriental

㉒ *From Vall d'Aran take the 6-km (4-mi) Vielha tunnel to the Alta Ribagorça Oriental.*

This valley includes the east bank of the Noguera Ribagorçana River and the Llevata and Noguera de Tor valleys. The latter has the Pyrenees' richest concentration of medieval art and architecture. The quality and unity of design apparent in the Romanesque churches along the Noguera de Tor River, in towns such as Durro, Boí, Erill la Vall, and Taüll, are the result of the sponsorship—and wives—of the counts of

Erill. The Erill knights, away fighting Moors in distant battles of the Reconquest, left their spouses behind to supervise the creation of local houses of worship. The women then brought in Europe's leading masters of architecture, masonry, sculpture, and painting to build and decorate the churches. To what extent a single eye and sensibility was responsible for this extraordinarily harmonious and coherent set of churches may never be known, but it's clear that they all share certain distinguishing characteristics: a miniaturistic tightness combined with eccentric or irregular design, and slender rectangular bell towers that are light but forceful, perfectly balanced against the rocky background.

From Vielha, route N230 runs south 33 km (20 mi) to the intersection with N260 (sometimes marked C144), which goes west over the Fadas Pass to Castejón de Sos. Four kilometers (2½ mi) past this intersection, the road up the Noguera de Tor Valley turns to the northeast, 2 km (1 mi) short of Pont de Suert.

Taüll

㉓ *58 km (36 mi) south of Vielha.*

Taüll is a town of narrow streets and tight mountain design—wooden balconies and steep slate roofs. The churches of Sant Climent and Santa Maria are lovely, and important churches near Taüll include Sant Feliu, at Barruera; Sant Joan Baptista, at Boí; Santa Maria, at Cardet; Santa Maria, at Col; Santa Eulàlia, at Erill-la-vall; La Nativitat de la Mare de Deu and Sant Quirze, at Durro; Sant Llorenç, at Sarais; and Sant Nicolau, in the Sant Nicolau Valley, at the entrance to Aigüestortes–Sant Maurici National Park. Taüll has a ski resort, **Bohí Taüll**, at the head of the Sant Nicolau Valley.

★ The notable three-nave Romanesque church of **Sant Climent**, at the edge of town, was built in 1123 and has a six-story belfry. The proportions, the Pyrenean stone, the changing hues because of the light, and the general intimacy of the place create an exceptional balance and harmony. The church's murals, including the famous *Pantocrator,* the work of the "Master of Taüll," were moved to Barcelona's Museu Nacional d'Art de Catalunya in 1922; you can see reproductions here. ▨ €2 ☉ *Daily 10–2 and 4–8.*

Where to Eat

$–$$$ ✕ **La Cabana.** Lamb and goat cooked over coals are the specialties of this rustic place, which also serves a fine *escudella* (sausage, vegetable, and potato stew) and an excellent *crema de carredetes* (cream of meadow-mushroom) soup. ✉ *Ctra. de Tahüll* ☎ *973/696213* ▭ *AE, DC, MC, V* ☉ *Closed Apr. 15–June 23, Oct. 15–Nov. 9, and Mon. Oct.–June.*

Caldes de Boí

㉔ *6 km (4 mi) north of Taüll.*

The thermal baths in the town of Caldes de Boí include, between hot and cold sources, 40 springs. The caves inside the bath area are a singular natural phenomenon, with thermal steam seeping through the cracks in the rock. Take advantage of the baths' therapeutic qualities at either Hotel Caldes or Hotel Manantial—services range from a bath, at €6–€9, to an underwater body massage for €18. People with arthritis are frequent takers. ⊠ *Hotel Caldes* ☎ *973/696220* ⊠ *Hotel Manantial* ☎ *973/696210* ⊕ *www.caldesdeboi.com* ☉ *Hotels and baths closed Oct.–May.*

Where to Stay & Eat

$ ✕⚏ **Fondevila.** Wooden trim and simple country furnishings warm the interior of this stone structure 3 km (2 mi) north of Taüll. The rooms are generously proportioned and cozy. The country cuisine ($–$$$) includes game in season and various Catalan specialties. ⊠ *Carrer Única, 25528 Boí* ⚏⚏ *973/696011* ⚑ *46 rooms* ⚏ *No a/c, no TV in some rooms* ⊟ *AE, DC, MC, V* ☉ *Closed Nov. 10–Dec. 26 and Jan. 7–Feb. 1.*

ARAGÓN & CENTRAL PYRENEES

The highest, wildest, and most spectacular range of the Pyrenees is the middle section, farthest from sea level. From Benasque on Aragón's eastern side to Jaca at the western edge are the great heights and most dramatic landscapes of Alto Aragón (Upper Aragón), including the Maladeta (11,165 feet), Posets (11,070 feet), and Monte Perdido (11,004 feet) peaks, the three highest points in the Pyrenean chain.

Communications between the high valleys of the Pyrenees were all but nonexistent until the 19th century. Four-fifths of the region had never seen a motor vehicle of any kind until well into the 20th century, and the 150-km (93-mi) border with France between Portalet de Aneu and Vall d'Aran had never had an international crossing. This combination of high peaks, deep defiles, and isolation has produced some of the Iberian Peninsula's best-preserved towns and valleys. Today, numerous ethnological museums bear witness to a way of life that has nearly disappeared since the 1950s. Residents of Upper Aragón speak neither Basque nor Catalan, but local dialects, such as Grausín, Chistavino, Belsetá, and Benasqués (collectively known as *fabla*), and have more in common with each other and with Occitanian Langue d'Oc than with modern Spanish and French. Furthermore, each valley has its own variations on everything from the typical Aragonese folk dance, the *jota* (such as Bielsa's Chinchecle), to cuisine and traditional costume. Wildlife here includes several strains of mountain goat, deer, and, above Jaca between Somport and the French Vall d'Aspe, the Pyrenean brown bear.

The largely undiscovered cities of Huesca and Zaragoza are both useful Pyrenean gateways and destinations in themselves; Zaragoza is an unavoidable link between Barcelona and Bilbao. Both cities retain an authentic provincial character that is refreshing in today's cosmopolitan Spain. Huesca's lovely old quarter and Zaragoza's immense basilica, La Pilarica, are memorable places to explore.

Huesca

 75 km (46 mi) southwest of Aínsa, 72 km (45 mi) northeast of Zaragoza, 123 km (74 mi) northwest of Lleida.

Capital of Aragón until the royal court moved to Zaragoza in 1118, Huesca was founded by the Romans a millennium earlier. The city became an independent state with a senate and an excellent school system organized by the Roman general Sertorius in 77 BC. Much later, after centuries of Moorish rule, Pedro I of Aragón liberated Huesca in 1096. The town's university was founded in 1354 and now specializes in Aragonese studies. Huesca's fiestas for patron saint Lorenzo, held August 2 to 8, are nearly as riotous as Pamplona's San Fermín. *Albahaca* (basil) is Huesca's greatest crop and symbol; thus green neckerchiefs and sashes (as opposed to Pamplona's iconic red) are worn and sold everywhere in Huesca that week.

An intricately carved gallery tops the eroded facade of Huesca's 13th-century Gothic **cathedral**. Damián Forment, a disciple of the 15th-century Italian master sculptor Donatello, created the alabaster altarpiece with scenes from the Crucifixion. ⊠ *Pl. de la Catedral s/n* ☎ *974/ 292172* ☞ *Free* ☉ *Mon.–Sat. 8–1 and 4–6:30.*

Twice daily, the Huesca tourist office (in the former market at Plaza Luis Lopez Allué s/n) accompanies visitors into the Renaissance **ayuntamiento** (town hall) to see the 19th-century painting of the 12th-century beheading of a group of uncooperative nobles, ordered by Ramiro II. King Ramiro, having called a meeting for the purported pouring of a giant bell that would be audible throughout Aragón, proceeded to massacre the leading troublemakers; the expression *como la campana de Huesca* ("like the bell of Huesca") is still sometimes used to describe an event of surprising resonance. ⊠ *Pl. de la Catedral 1* ☎ *974/292170* ☞ *Free* ☉ *Mon.–Sat. at noon and 6.*

The **Museo Arqueológico Provincial** is an octagonal patio ringed by eight chambers, including the **Sala de la Campana** (Hall of the Bell), where the beheadings of 12th-century nobles took place. The museum is in parts of what was once the royal palace of the kings of Aragón and holds paintings by Aragonese primitives, including *La Virgen del Rosario* by Miguel Jiménez, and several works by the 16th-century Maestro de Sigena. ⊠ *Pl. de la Universidad* ☎ *974/220586* ☞ *Free* ☉ *Tues.–Sat. 10–2 and 5–8, Sun. 10–2.*

The church of **San Pedro el Viejo** has an 11th-century cloister with sculpted capitals. Ramiro II and his father, Alfonso I—the only Aragonese kings not entombed at San Juan de la Peña—rest in a side chapel. ⊠ *Pl. de San Pedro s/n* ☎ *974/292164* ☞ *Free* ☉ *Mon.–Sat. 10–2 and 6–8.*

OFF THE BEATEN PATH

CASTILLO DE LOARRE – This massively walled 11th-century monastery, 36 km (22 mi) west of Huesca off Route A132 on A1206, is nearly indistinguishable from the rock outcroppings that surround it. Inside the walls are a church, a tower, a dungeon, and even a medieval toilet with views of the almond and olive orchards in the Ebro basin.

Where to Stay & Eat

$$$–$$$$ ✕ **Las Torres.** Huesca's top dining establishment makes inventive use of first-rate local Pyrenean ingredients ranging from wild mushrooms to lamb. The glass-walled kitchen is as original as the cooking that emerges from it, and the wine list is strong in Somontanos, Huesca's own Denomination of Origin. Look for the *paticas de cordero deshuesados* (deboned lamb's trotters) for a taste of pure upper Aragón. ✉ *María Auxiliadora 3* ☎ *974/228213* ✉ *AE, DC, MC, V* ☉ *Closed 2 wks at Easter, Aug. 16–31, and Sun.*

$$–$$$ ⌸ **Pedro I de Aragón.** Huesca's best hotel by a wide margin, this modern structure over the leafy Parque Miguel Servet is lush with mirrors and marble in the lobby, and furnished with fresh and fragrant pine in the rooms. Comfort is guaranteed, and the service is excellent. ✉ *Parque 34, 22003* ☎ *974/220300* 🖨 *974/220094* ⊕ *www.gargallo-hotels. com* ➶ *125 rooms, 4 suites* ⚭ *Restaurant, minibars, pool, bar, meeting rooms; no a/c* ✉ *AE, DC, MC, V.*

$ ⌸ **San Marcos.** The building dates from 1890, and the rooms, though updated for comfort, remain tastefully decorated with traditional touches. Centrally located outside the 1st-century Roman walls, the hotel is a five-minute walk from Huesca's cathedral. ✉ *San Orencio 10, 22001* 🖨🖨 *974/222931* ➶ *29 rooms* ✉ *AE, DC, MC, V.*

Zaragoza

㉖ *72 km (43 mi) southwest of Huesca, 138 km (86 mi) west of Lleida, 307 km (184 mi) west of Barcelona, 164 km (98 mi) southeast of Pamplona, 322 km (193 mi) northeast of Madrid.*

In high spirits amid preparations for its 2008 Universal Exposition based on the theme of water and its own mighty river, Zaragoza is on the move. The AVE, Spain's high-speed railroad, now connects Zaragoza with Madrid in 2 hours and with Barcelona in 3¼: This provincial city is on the threshold of its greatest boom since the Romans established a thriving river port here in 25 BC. Rated one of Spain's most desirable places to live because of its air quality, cost of living, low population density, and other qualities, Zaragoza seems full of self-contained well-being. Despite its hefty size (pop. 610,976), this sprawling provincial capital midway between Barcelona, Madrid, Bilbao, and Valencia is nevertheless a detour from the well-beaten tourist track.

Straddling Spain's greatest river, the Ebro, 2,000-year-old Zaragoza was originally named Caesaraugusta for Roman emperor Augustus. Its legacy contains everthing from Roman ruins and Jewish baths to Arab, Romanesque, Gothic-Mudéjar, Renaissance, baroque, neoclassical, and Art Nouveau architecture. Parts of the city's landmark **Roman walls** are visible near the city's landmark Basílica de Nuestra Señora del Pilar. Nearby, the medieval **Puente de Piedra** (Stone Bridge) spans the Ebro. Checking out the **Lonja** (stock exchange), the Moorish **Aljafería** (jewel treasury), the **Mercado de Lanuza** (produce market), and the various **churches** in the old town—San Pablo, San Miguel, San Gil, Santa Engracia, San Carlos, San Ildefonso, San Felipe, Santa Cruz, and San Fernando—is a good way to navigate Zaragoza's jumble of backstreets.

Excursions from Zaragoza include Francisco José Goya y Lucientes' birthplace at **Fuendetodos,** 44 km (26 mi) to the southeast, and **Belchite,** another 20 km (12 mi) east of Fuendetodos, site of the ruins of a town destroyed in one of the fiercest battles of the Spanish civil war and left untouched since as a reminder of the tragedy of war.

Hulking on the banks of the Ebro, the **Basílica de Nuestra Señora del Pilar** (Basilica of Our Lady of the Pillar), affectionately known as "La Pilarica," is Zaragoza's symbol and pride. An immense baroque structure with no fewer than 11 tile cupolas, La Pilarica is the home of the Virgen del Pilar, the patron saint not only of peninsular Spain but of the entire Hispanic world. The fiestas honoring this most Spanish of saints, held the week of October 12, are events of extraordinary pride and Spanish fervor, with processions, street concerts, bullfights, and traditional *jota* dancing. The cathedral was built in the 18th century to commemorate the appearance of the Virgin on a pillar (*pilar*), or pedestal, to St. James, Spain's other patron saint, during his legendary incarnation as Santiago Matamoros (St. James the Moorslayer) in the 9th century. La Pilarica herself resides in a side chapel that dates from 1754. The frescoes in the cupolas, some of which are attributed to the young Goya, are among the basilica's treasures. The **Museo Pilarista** holds drawings and some of the Virgin's jewelry. The bombs displayed to the right of the altar of La Pilarica chapel fell through the roof of the church in 1936 and miraculously failed to explode. You can still see one of the holes overhead to the left. Behind La Pilarica's altar is the tiny opening where the devout line up to kiss the rough marble pillar where La Pilarica was allegedly discovered. ⊠ *Pl. del Pilar s/n* 🖀 *Basilica free, museum €1.50* ◔ *Basilica daily 5:45 AM–9:30 PM, museum daily 9–2 and 4–6.*

Zaragoza's cathedral, **La Seo** (Catedral de San Salvador), at the eastern end of the Plaza del Pilar, is the city's bishopric, or diocesan *seo* (seat). An amalgam of architectural styles, ranging from the Mudéjar brick-and-tile exterior to the Gothic altarpiece to exuberant, Churrigueresque doorways, the Seo nonetheless has an 18th-century baroque facade that seems to echo those of La Pilarica. The **Museo de Tapices** within contains medieval tapestries. The nearby medieval **Casa y Arco del Deán** form one of the city's favorite corners. ⊠ *Pl. del Pilar* 🖀 *Cathedral €2, museum €1.50* ◔ *Cathedral Mon.–Sat. 10–2 and 4–8, Sun. 5–8; museum Tues.–Sat. 10–2 and 4–6, Sun. 10–2.*

The **Iglesia de la Magdalena,** next to the remains of the Roman forum, has an ancient brick Mudéjar bell tower. The church is usually open in the mornings. ⊠ *Pl. de la Magdalena s/n* 🖀 *976/299598.* The **Museo del Foro** displays remains of the Roman forum and the Roman sewage system, though the presentation is in Spanish only. Two more Roman sites, the **thermal baths** at Calle de San Juan y San Pedro and the **river port** at Plaza San Bruno, are also open to the public. ⊠ *Pl. de la Seo s/n* 🖀 *976/399752* 🖀 *€2* ◔ *Tues.–Sat. 10–2 and 5–8.*

The **Museo Camón Aznar** has a fine collection of Goya's works, particularly his engravings. ⊠ *Carrer Espoz y Mina 23* 🖀 *976/397328* 🖀 *Free* ◔ *Tues.–Fri. 9–2 and 6–9, Sat. 10–2 and 6–9, Sun. 11–2.*

The **Museo del Centro de Historia** exhibits a wide range of memorabilia from Zaragoza's 2,000-year history, including audiovisual studies of different facets. The section on the River Ebro and the Roman exploitation of the port of Zaragoza are especially interesting. ⊠ *Pl. San Agustín 2* ☎ *976/205640* ⌨ *Free* ☉ *Tues.–Sat. 10–7:15, Sun. 10–1:15.* The **Museo Provincial de Bellas Artes** contains a rich treasury of Zaragoza's emblematic painter Francisco José Goya y Lucientes, including his portraits of Fernando VII, and his best graphic works: *Desastres de la guerra, Caprichos, and La tauromaquia.* ⊠ *Pl. de los Sitios 5* ☎ *976/222181* ⌨ *Free* ☉ *Tues.–Sat. 10–2 and 5–8, Sun. 10–2.* The **Museo Pablo Gargallo** is one of Zarargoza's most treasured and admired gems, both for the palace as well as for the collection—Gargallo, born near Zaragoza in 1881, was one of Spain's greatest modern sculptors. ⊠ *Pl. de San Felipe 3* ☎ *976/ 392058* ⌨ *Free* ☉ *Tues.–Sat. 9–2 and 5–9, Sun. 9–2.*

The **Museo del Teatro Romano** showcases a restored Roman amphitheater as well as the objects recovered during the excavation process, including theatrical masks, platters, and even Roman hairpins. ⊠ *C/San Jorge 12* ☎ *976/205088* ⌨ *€3.50* ☉ *Tues.–Sat. 10–9, Sun. 10–2.*

Palacio de La Aljafería is what remains of the Alhambra-esque original, which helps explain the importance of the nearly eight-century Moorish empire on the Iberian Peninsula. Originally an 11th-century fortress, the sprawling place underwent major restoration and redesign by Ferdinand and Isabella after 1492. Important as a seat of the Spanish Inquisition, it's now the home of the Cortes (Parliament) de Aragón. The 9th-century Torre del Trovador (Tower of the Troubadour) appears in Giuseppe Verdi's opera *Il Trovatore.* ⊠ *Diputados s/n* ☎ *976/289683* ⌨ *€3.50* ☉ *Mon.–Wed. and weekends 10–2 and 4–7, Fri. 4–7.*

Where to Stay & Eat

$$–$$$$
Fodor'sChoice
★ ✕ **El Fuelle.** Fine Aragonese fare distinguishes this rustic old-town favorite decorated with giant *fuelles* (bellows), farming tools, and random artifacts of every description. Specialties include *judias estofadas* (white beans stewed in sausage), *migas* (a traditional dish of chorizo, garlic, peppers, and bread crumbs soaked in olive oil and garlic), and a signature dish, *patatas asadas* (roast potatoes). ⊠ *Calle Mayor 59* ☎ *976/398033* ⊟ *AE, DC, MC, V.*

$$–$$$$ ✕ **La Venta del Cachirulo.** Outside Zaragoza, this roadhouse is worth a trip for authentic Aragonese cooking and folklore, including occasional *jota* dancing and singing. *Borrajas con almejas* (kale with clams) and *pato con cerezas* (duck with cherries) are among the local dishes served. ⊠ *Ctra. Logroño, N232, Km 1* ☎ *976/460146* ⊟ *AE, DC, MC, V* ☉ *Closed Sun. and Mon. and first 2 wks in Aug.*

$–$$ ✕ **Casa Emilio.** One of the city's most popular restaurants among artists, journalists, and writers, this haven of straightforward cooking and conversation near the Aljafería and the train station offers excellent value and a friendly environment. ⊠ *Av. Madrid 3–5* ☎ *976/435839* ⊟ *AE, DC, MC, V.*

★ $ ✕ **Los Victorinos.** Zaragoza's finest tapas emporium, which opens at 7:30, is a cozy tavern heavily adorned with bull-related paraphernalia. It's close behind La Seo. The items displayed on the bar are guaranteed to jump-start your appetite. ✉ *José de la Hera 6* ☎ *976/394213* 🖃 *AE, DC, MC, V* ⊗ *No lunch.*

$$$ 🏨 **Goya.** Smack in the city center, this hotel provides a balanced combination of comfort and proximity to the historic sights. It's a five-minute walk from the Basílica del Pilar and the Ebro River; here you can get the sense that you're part of the city's life. Rooms are modern, but not luxurious. ✉ *Cinco de Marzo 5, 50004* ☎ *976/229331* 🖷 *976/232154* ⊕ *www.palafoxhoteles.com* ↩ *148 rooms* ⚐ *Restaurant, café, minibars, cable TV, bar, meeting rooms, parking (fee)* 🖃 *AE, DC, MC, V.*

$–$$ 🏨 **Las Torres.** The rooms are small here, but the scenery is hard to beat. You may even be able to admire the domes of La Pilarica from your pillow (though if you're a light sleeper, you may need earplugs to muffle the bonging of the bells—they ring every 15 minutes all through the night; interior rooms are much quieter). ✉ *Pl. del Pilar 11, 50003* ☎ *976/394250* 🖷 *976/394254* ⊕ *www.hotellastorres.com* ↩ *54 rooms* ⚐ *Parking (fee)* 🖃 *AE, DC, MC, V.*

Shopping

El Tubo (✉ Cinegio 10 ☎ 976/391177), hidden away in the charming labyrinth of back streets between La Basílica del Pilar and Plaza de Espana, is the place to seek out for handmade leather boots from all over Spain.

Benasque

㉗
Fodor'sChoice
★

79 km (49 mi) southwest of Vielha.

Benasque, Aragón's easternmost town, has always been an important link between Catalonia and Aragón. This elegant mountain hub of a little more than 1,500 people packs a number of notable buildings, including the 13th-century Romanesque church of **Santa Maria Mayor** and the ancient, dignified manor houses of the town's old families, such as the **palace of the counts of Ribagorza**, on Calle Mayor, and the **Torre Juste.** Take a walk around and peer into the entryways and patios of these palatial facades, left open just for this purpose.

Anciles, 2 km (1 mi) south of Benasque, is one of Spain's best-preserved and best-restored medieval villages, a collection of farmhouses and *palacetes* (town houses). The summer classical-music series is a superb collision of music and architecture, and the village restaurant, Ansils, combines modern and medieval motifs in both cuisine and design.

▌ **OFF THE BEATEN PATH**

PICO DE ANETO – Benasque is the traditional base camp for excursions to Aneto, which, at 11,168 feet, is the highest peak in the Pyrenees. You can rent crampons and a *piolet* (ice ax) for the two- to three-hour crossing of the Aneto glacier at any sports store in town or at the Refugio de la Renclusa—a way station for mountaineers—an hour's walk above the parking area, which is 17 km (11 mi) north of Benasque, off A139. The trek to the summit and back is not difficult, just long—some 20 km (12 mi) round-trip, with a 1,500-yard vertical ascent. Allow a full 12 hours.

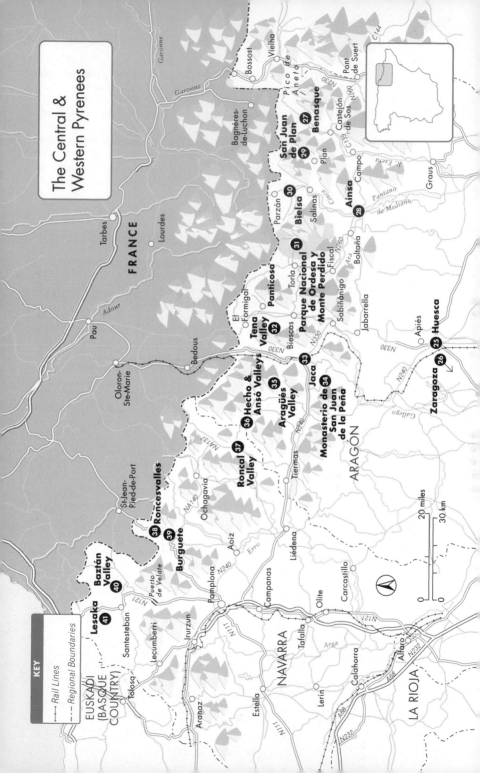

The Central & Western Pyrenees

FRANCE

ARAGÓN

NAVARRA

LA RIOJA

EUSKADI (BASQUE COUNTRY)

Garonne

Bossost
Vielha
Pico de Aneto
Pont de Suert
Bagnères-de-Luchon
San Juan de Plan **27**
Benasque **27**
Castejón de Sos
29
Plan
Campo
Graus
30 Bielsa
Parzán
Salinas
28 Ainsa
Pantano de Mediano
Boltaña
Fiscal
Ara
Tarbes
Lourdes
31 Parque Nacional de Ordesa y Monte Perdido
Torla
Bielsa
Sabiñánigo
Jabarrella
El Formigal
Panticosa
32 Tena Valley
Biescas
33 Jaca
Apiés
25 Huesca
26 Zaragoza
Adour
Pau
Bedous
Oloron-Ste-Marie
Hecho & Ansó Valleys **36**
35 Aragüés Valley
Monasterio de San Juan de la Peña **34**
Tiermas
Roncal Valley **37**
St-Jean-Pied-de-Port
Roncesvalles **38**
39 Burguete
Ochagavia
Liédena
Carcastillo
Aoiz
Erro
Campanas
Olite
Baztán Valley **40**
Puerto de Velate
Pamplona
Tafalla
Alfaro
Lesaka **41**
Santesteban
Irurzun
Lecumberri
Aranaz
Tolosa
Estella
Lerín
Calahorra
Garonne
R. Esera
Cinca
Gállego
Arga

20 miles
30 km

Where to Stay & Eat

$$–$$$$ ✕ **Asador Ixarso.** Roast goat or lamb cooked over a raised fireplace in the corner of the dining room is why this place is a fine refuge in chilly weather. The *revuelto de setas* (eggs scrambled with wild mushrooms) is superb, as are the salads. ⊠ *Calle San Pedro 9* ☎ *974/552057* ☰ *AE, DC, MC, V* ☉ *Closed weekdays mid-Sept.–1st wk in Dec. and Easter–June.*

$$–$$$$ ✕ **Restaurante Ansils.** This rustic place, ingeniously designed in glass, wood, and stone, specializes in local Benasqués dishes, such as *civet de jabalí* (wild-boar stew) and *recau* (a thick vegetable broth). Holiday meals are served on Christmas and Easter. ⊠ *Anciles* ☎ *974/551150* ☰ *AE, DC, MC, V* ☉ *Closed weekdays Oct.–June.*

$$–$$$ ✕▣ **Hospital de Benasque.** Some 13 km (8 mi) north of Benasque off the A139 road, this mountain retreat is an ideal base camp for hiking and cross-country skiing. Constructed and furnished in stone and fresh wood, rooms are simple and clean lined. The restaurant ($$–$$$) serves classical Pyrenean fare in a glassed-in dining room flooded with natural light. ⊠ *Camino Real de Francia s/n, 22440* ☎ *974/552012* ☒ *974/551052* ⊕ *www.llanosdelhospital.com* ⏎ *57 rooms* ⟁ *Restaurant, meeting rooms, free parking; no a/c* ☰ *AE, DC, MC, V.*

$$ ✕▣ **Gran Hotel Benasque.** This spacious, modern hotel within walking distance from Benasque is bracketed by the highest crests in the Pyrenees (Aneto and Posets) and serves as an impeccably comfortable base for exploring them. The restaurant's mountain fare ($$–$$$$) includes *sopa Benasquesa* (a thick highland stew) and *crepas Aneto* (crepes with ham, wild mushroom, and béchamel sauce). ⊠ *Ctra. de Anciles s/n, 22440* ☎ *974/551011* ☒ *974/552821* ⊕ *www.hoteles-valero.com* ⏎ *69 rooms* ⟁ *Restaurant, 2 pools, gym, sauna, bar, meeting rooms* ☰ *AE, MC, V* ☉ *Closed Nov.*

$$ ✕▣ **La Casa del Río.** Just south of Benasque, this ramshackle Pyrenean house offers comfortable lodging and fly-fishing (guided excursions can be arranged) within casting distance of your pillow. The cuisine ($–$$$) includes mountain specialties and roasts cooked over coals. ⊠ *Crtra. Benasque Km 49.9 22467 Vilanova* ☎☎ *974/553493* ⊕ *www.lacasadelrio.com* ⏎ *8 rooms* ⟁ *Restaurant, free parking; no a/c* ☰ *AE, DC, MC, V.*

Sports & the Outdoors

The **Cerler ski area** (☎ 974/551012 ⊕ www.cerler.com), 6 km (4 mi) east of Benasque on the Cerler road, covers the slopes of the Cogulla peak. Built on a shelf over the valley at an altitude of 5,051 feet, Cerler has 26 ski runs, 3 lifts, and a guided helicopter service to drop you at the highest peaks. The outfitter **Danica Guías de Pesca** (☎ 974/553493 or 659/735376 ⊕ www.danicaguias.com) can show you the top spots and techniques for Pyrenean fly-fishing.

EN ROUTE South of Castejón de Sos, down the Esera Valley and through the Congosto de Ventamillo—a sheer slice through the rock made by the Esera River—a turn west on N260 cuts over to Aínsa, at the junction of the Rivers Cinca and Ara.

Aínsa

28 *66 km (41 mi) southwest of Benasque.*

Aínsa's arcaded Plaza Mayor and old town are classic examples of medieval village design, with heavy stone archways and tiny windows. The 12th-century Romanesque church of **Santa María** has a quadruplevaulted door. ⊠ *Old Quarter* 🏛 *Free* ⊗ *Daily 9–2 and 4–8.*

Where to Stay & Eat

$$–$$$$ ✕ **Bodegas del Sobrarbe.** Superb lamb roasted in a wood oven is the specialty of this fine restaurant built into an 11th-century wine cellar. The setting is medieval: Expect vaulted ceilings of heavy wood and stone. ⊠ *Pl. Mayor 2* 🕾 *974/500237* ▤ *AE, DC, MC, V* ⊗ *Closed Jan. and Feb.*

$$ ✕🏠 **Bodegón de Mallacán y Posada Real.** If you want to sit at a table under the massive medieval porticoes of Aínsa's Plaza Mayor, consider this breezy spot, which is wonderfully cool in summer. Inside, the ceramic-tile murals (and the views south) are lovely. The cuisine is classic mountain fare ($$–$$$): roasts and stews of lamb, venison, and wild boar. The fresh, wood-trim rooms in the hotel annex, La Casa del Marqués, are simple and elegant, with beams overhead and a lovely combination of modern restoration techniques and vintage materials. ⊠ *Pl. Mayor 6* 🕾 *974/500977* 🖨 *974/500953* ⊕ *www.posadareal.com* 📮 *6 rooms* ▤ *AE, DC, MC, V* ⊗ *Closed Jan. and Feb.*

$ 🏠 **Casa Cambra.** A once-abandoned village between Barbastro and Aínsa lodges this little inn, a perfect base for mountain sports of all kinds. The restored 18th-century house of stone and timber has rooms for two to four people and is part of a tourist complex that includes a restaurant. ⊠ *Ctra. Barbastro–Aínsa, A138, Km 41.8, Morillo de Tou 22395* 🖨🖨 *974/500793* ⊕ *www.morillodetou.com* 📮 *17 rooms* � *No a/c, no room TVs* ▤ *MC, V.*

| OFF THE BEATEN PATH | **AÑISCLO GORGES –** On the road north from Aínsa, the Añisclo Canyon is 5 km (3 mi) north of the town of Escalona. A road to the west runs 14 km (9 mi) along the edge of the sheer rock divide to Urbez. As you drive into Urbez, you can see the ancient stone bridge. On the far bank of the river is the cave chapel named for St. Urbez, a hermit monk from Bordeaux who lived there in the 8th century. |

San Juan de Plan & the Gistaín Valley

29 *14 km (8½ mi) east of Salinas.*

This detour begins with a well-marked road heading east of Salinas, 25 km (15 mi) north of Aínsa. The Cinqueta River drains the Gistaín Valley, flowing by or through the mountain villages of Sin, Señes, Saravillo, Serveta, and Salinas. The town of San Juan de Plan presides at the head of the valley, where an ethnographic museum, a water-powered sawmill, and an early music and dance ensemble are the pride of the region. The mid-February carnival is among the most distinct and traditional celebrations in the Pyrenees. The **Museo Etnográfico** is a fascinating glimpse into a traditional way of life (dress, kitchen utensils, bedclothes, field

tools) that endured largely intact until about 1975. ⊠ *Pl. Mayor s/n*
☎ *974/506052* ▣ *€2* ۞ *Daily 9–2 and 4–8.*

Where to Stay & Eat

$$ ✕⊞ **Hotel Anita.** This modern stone building has become San Juan de Plan's hub and nerve center. Rooms are bright and well equipped, and the restaurant ($–$$$) is known as the best in town—its Pyrenean fare includes seasonal game, from partridge to wild boar. For a taste of pure lunacy, try to be here when the Pirene, a 200-husky dogsled race, comes through in late January. ⊠ *Calle Alta s/n, 22367* ☎ *974/506211* 🖨 *974/ 506196* ⊕ *www.hotelcasaanita.com* ⤴ *18 rooms* ♲ *Restaurant, cable TV, bar; no a/c* ▭ *AE, DC, MC, V* ۞ *Closed Nov.*

★ $–$$ ✕⊞ **Casa la Plaza.** Josefina Loste's pleasant inn has cozy rooms with antique furniture. Each room tucked into the eaves is different. The restaurant ($–$$$) serves excellent local dishes using the freshest ingredients in inventive yet traditional ways. ⊠ *Pl. Mayor s/n, 22367* ☎ *974/ 506052* ⤴ *13 rooms* ♲ *No a/c* ▭ *AE, DC, MC, V* ۞ *Closed sporadically Oct.–May; call to confirm.*

Bielsa

③⓪ *34 km (21 mi) northeast of Aínsa.*

Bielsa, at the confluence of the Cinca and Barrosa rivers, is a busy summer resort with some lovely mountain architecture and an ancient, porticoed town hall. Northwest of Bielsa the **Monte Perdido glacier** and the icy **Marboré Lake** drain into the **Pineta Valley** and the Pineta Reservoir. You can take three- or four-hour walks from the parador up to Larri, Munia, or Marboré Lake among remote peaks.

Where to Stay & Eat

$$$ ✕⊞ **Parador de Bielsa.** Glass, steel, and stone define this modern structure overlooking the national park, the peak of Monte Perdido, and the source of the Cinca River. Rooms are done in bright wood, but the best part is your proximity to the park and the views. The restaurant ($$–$$$) specializes in Aragonese mountain dishes, such as *pucherete de Parzán* (a stew with beans, sausage, and vegetables). ⊠ *Valle de Pineta s/n, 22350* ☎ *974/501011* 🖨 *974/501188* ⊕ *www.parador.es* ⤴ *39 rooms* ♲ *Restaurant, cable TV, bar; no a/c* ▭ *AE, DC, MC, V.*

★ $–$$ ✕⊞ **Hotel Valle de Pineta.** This corner castle overlooking the river junction is the most spectacular refuge in town. The restaurant ($$–$$$) is excellent, the views without compare. Try for the top corner room, which looks across both valleys. ⊠ *Baja s/n, 22350* ☎ *974/501010* 🖨 *974/ 501191* ⊕ *www.hotelvalledepineta.com* ⤴ *26 rooms* ♲ *Restaurant, cable TV, pool, bar; no a/c* ▭ *AE, DC, MC, V* ۞ *Closed Nov., Jan., and Feb.*

Parque Nacional de Ordesa y Monte Perdido

③① *108 km (67 mi) west of Bielsa; from Aínsa, turn west on N260 for the* **Fodor'sChoice** *53-km (33-mi) drive to Torla.*
★

Ordesa and Monte Perdido National Park is one of Spain's great but often overlooked wonders, a domain many consider comparable, if on a somewhat smaller scale, to North America's Grand Canyon. The entrance lies under the vertical walls of Monte Mondarruego, source of the Ara River and its tributary, the Arazas, which forms the famous Ordesa Valley. The park was founded by royal decree in 1918 to protect the natural integrity of the Central Pyrenees, and it has expanded from 4,940 to 56,810 acres as provincial and national authorities have added the Monte Perdido massif, the head of the Pineta Valley, and the Escuain and Añisclo canyons. Defined by the Ara and Arazas rivers, the Ordesa Valley is endowed with pine, fir, larch, beech, and poplar forests; lakes, waterfalls, and high mountain meadows; and protected wildlife, including trout, boar, chamois, and the *Capra Pyrenaica* mountain goat.

Well-marked and well-maintained mountain trails lead to waterfalls, caves, and spectacular observation points. The standard tour, a full day's hike (eight hours), runs from the parking area in the Pradera de Ordesa, 8 km (5 mi) northeast of Torla, up the Arazas River, past the *gradas de Soaso* (Soaso risers; a natural stairway of waterfalls) to the *cola de caballo* (horse's tail), a lovely fan of falling water at the head of the Cirque de Cotatuero, a sort of natural amphitheater. A return walk on the south side of the valley, past the Refugio de los Cazadores (hunters' hut), offers a breathtaking view followed by a two-hour descent back to the parking area. A few spots, although not technically difficult, may seem precarious. Information and guidebooks are available at the booth on your way into the park at Pradera de Ordesa. The best time to come is from May to mid-November, but check conditions with regional tourist offices before driving into a blizzard in May or missing out on *el veranillo de San Martín* (Indian summer) in fall. ☎ *974/243361 Pradera de Ordesa information office* ⊕ *www.mma.es* ⧆ *Free.*

EN ROUTE | **Broto** is a prototypical Aragonese mountain town with an excellent 16th-century Gothic church. Nearby villages, such as **Oto,** have stately manor houses with classic local features: baronial entryways, conical chimneys, and wooden galleries. **Torla** is the park's entry point and a popular base camp for hikers.

Where to to Stay & Eat

$–$$ ✕ **El Rebeco.** In this graceful and rustic building in the upper part of town, the dining rooms are lined with historic photographs of Torla. The black marble and stone floor and the *cadiera*—a traditional open fireplace room with an overhead smoke vent—are extraordinary. In late fall, *civets* (stews) of deer, boar, and mountain goat are the order of the day. ⊠ *Calle Lafuente 55, Torla 22376* ☎ *974/486068* ▭ *AE, DC, MC, V* ⊘ *Closed Dec.–Easter.*

$–$$ ▥ **Villa de Torla.** This rustic gem has rooms in various shapes and sizes, all sharing typical Pyrenean decor and a great deal of comfort. Sundecks and terraces and a private dining room make it easy to forget that Spain's Grand Canyon is just up the valley. ⊠ *Pl. Aragón 1, 22376* ☎ *974/486156* 🖷 *974/486365* ⊕ *www.hotelvilladetorla.com* ⤺ *38 rooms* ⚏ *Restaurant, cable TV, pool, bar, parking* ▭ *AE, DC, MC, V.*

EN ROUTE | Follow N260 (sometimes marked C140) west over the Cotefablo Pass from Torla to Biescas. This route winds interminably through the pine forest leading up to and down from the pass; expect it to take five times longer than it looks like it should.

Panticosa & the Tena Valley

㉜ *40 km (25 mi) west of Ordesa.*

The Valle de Tena, a north–south hexagon of 400 square km (154 square mi), is formed by the Gállego River and its tributaries, principally the Aguaslimpias and the Caldares. A glacial valley surrounded by peaks rising to more than 10,000 feet (such as the 10,900-foot Vignemale), Tena is a busy hiking and winter-sports center. **Sallent de Gállego,** at the head of the valley, has long been a jumping-off point for excursions to **Aguaslimpias, Piedrafita,** and the meadows of the Gállego headwaters at **El Formigal** (a major ski area) and **Portalet.** The lovely Pyrenean *ibon* (glacial lake) of **Respumoso** is accessible by a 2½-hour walk above the old road from Sallent to Formigal. The villages lining the valley are each unique, with Tramacastilla, Escarrilla, and Piedrafita especially representative of ancient Pyrenean village architecture. **Lanuza,** a ghost town since the reservoir built in 1975 flooded half the village, comes alive every summer when a floating stage hosts performers in the Pirineos Sur music festival.

Where to Stay & Eat

$–$$ ✕ **Mesón Sampietro.** This cozy spot not far from Panticosa's lovely church blossoms after the skiing or hiking day ends. The house specialty, potatoes in olive oil, garlic, parsley, and vinegar is not to be missed. Take a seat at a traditional *susulia* bench—they have little fold-down tables between the two seats, making them good for dinner for two in front of a roaring fire. ⊠ *C. La Parra 5* ☎ *974/487244* ☐ *AE, DC, MC, V.*

$–$$ ▦ **Hotel Vicente.** Rooms here are simple but impeccable and look south over the town to Panticosa's ski area and the jagged peaks of the Sierra de Tendeñera mountains beyond. The lower access spills directly down into town, a five-minute walk from the gondola station. ⊠ *Ctra. del Balneario 12, Panticosa 22661* ☎ *974/487022* 🖷 *974/487529* ⊕ *www. hotelvicente.com* ↵ *16 rooms* ⚭ *Restaurant; no a/c, no room TVs* ☐ *AE, DC, MC, V.*

Jaca

㉝ *24 km (15 mi) southwest of Biescas; down the Tena Valley through Biescas, a westward turn at Sabiñánigo onto N330 leaves a 14-km (9-mi) drive to Jaca.*

Jaca, the most important municipal center in Alto Aragón (with a population of more than 15,000), is anything but sleepy. Bursting with ambition, and blessed with the natural resources and first-rate facilities to express their relentless drive, Jacetanos are determined to be the site of a Winter Olympics someday. The town is already Spain's winter-sports capital, playing frequent host to major competitions, such as the World Figure Skating Championships and the national King's Cup in ice hockey.

Founded in 1035 as the kingdom of Jacetania, Jaca was an important stronghold during the Christian Reconquest of the Iberian Peninsula and proudly claims never to have bowed to the Moorish invaders. Indeed, the town still commemorates, on the first Friday of May, the decisive battle in which the appearance of a battalion of women, their hair and jewelry flashing in the sun, so intimidated the Moorish cavalry that they beat a headlong retreat.

NEED A BREAK? One of Jaca's most emblematic restaurants is **La Campanilla** (Escuelas Pías 8), behind the ayuntamiento, or town hall. The baked potatoes with garlic and olive oil are an institution, unchanged for as long as anyone can remember.

An important stop on the pilgrimage to Santiago de Compostela, Jaca has the 11th-century **Catedral de Santa María,** one of the oldest in Spain. The **Museo Diocesano,** near the cloisters, is filled with excellent Romanesque and Gothic murals and artifacts. ☎*974/356378 Museo* 🎟*€4* ☉*June–Sept., Tues.–Sun. 10–2 and 4–8; Oct.–May, Tues.–Sun. 11–1:30 and 4–7.*

The door to Jaca's **ayuntamiento** (town hall) has a notable Renaissance design. The massive **Ciudadella** (Citadel) is a good example of 17th-century military architecture. It has a display of thousands of military miniatures. ✉ *Av. Primer Viernes de Mayo s/n* ☎ *974/363018* 🎟 *€4* ☉ *Daily 11–noon and 4–6.*

In summer a free guided **tour** departs from the local RENFE station, covering the valley and the mammoth, semiderelict Belle Epoque railroad station at Canfranc, surely the largest and most ornate building in the Pyrenees. The train ticket costs €3; ask the tourist office for schedules.

Where to Stay & Eat

$$–$$$$ ✕ **La Cocina Aragonesa.** This Jaca mainstay in the Hotel Conde Aznar is known far and wide for fresh and innovative cuisine, especially game in season: venison, wild boar, partridge, duck. Try the partridge stuffed with foie gras. ✉ *Cervantes 5* ☎ *974/361050* ▭ *AE, DC, MC, V* ☉ *Closed Nov. 15–30, Wed. June–Sept.*

$–$$$ ✕ **La Tasca de Ana.** Ana's *tasca* (tavern) is one of Jaca's simplest and best. Nearly anyone in town will send you here for superb tapas of every kind. Invent your own meal by starting with a round of olives and working through, say, cured *jamó ibérico* (Iberian ham), *sepia* (cuttlefish), *albóndigas* (meatballs), and *civet de jabalí* (wild-boar stew), concluding with cheese from the neighboring Roncal Valley. ✉ *Pl. Ramiro I 3* ☎ *974/363621* ▭ *AE, DC, MC, V* ☉ *Closed Mon.*

★ $–$$ ✕ **El Fau.** Tucked next to the cathedral, El Fau overlooks Jaca's finest carved capitals and serves excellent *cazuelitas,* small earthenware casseroles containing anything from piping-hot garlic shrimp to wild mushrooms. In summer the cold beer here is legendary. ✉ *Pl. de la Catedral* ☎ *974/361719* ▭ *AE, DC, MC, V* ☉ *Closed Mon.*

$$–$$$ 🏨 **Gran Hotel.** This rambling hotel, which serves as Jaca's official clubhouse, is central to both life and tourism in Jaca. Done up in wood, stone, and glass, it has a garden and dining wing. The comfortable rooms have rich colors and practical wood furniture. ✉ *Paseo de la Constitución 1, 22700* ☎ *974/360900* 🖨 *974/364061* ⊕ *www.inturmark.es* ⬦ *165 rooms* ⬧ *Restaurant, pool, meeting rooms* ▭ *AE, DC, MC, V.*

$–$$ 🏨 **Hostal Somport.** A good budget option, this tidy little spot in the center of Jaca is halfway between the cathedral and the town hall. The rooms, beds, and baths are all well kept, and the location is an ideal crawling distance from the nearby taverns and music bars on Calle Gil Bergés. ⊠ *Calle Echegaray 11, 22700* 🏨 *974/363410* 📞 *17 rooms* ♿ *Restaurant; no a/c* 🞕 *AE, DC, MC, V.*

$–$$ 🏨 **Hotel Mur.** This simple but sound lodging option in the middle of Jaca offers traditional highland town-house decor, a helpful staff, and a central location for cruising the après-ski scene in this booming winter party center. ⊠ *Santa Orosia 1, 22700* 🏨 *974/360100* 🏨 *974/356162* ⊕ *www. hotelmur.com* 📞 *78 rooms* ♿ *Restaurant; no a/c* 🞕 *AE, DC, MC, V.*

Nightlife

Discos such as **Dimensión** and **Oroel** are thronged with skiers and hockey players in season (October–April), but the main nocturnal attractions are Jaca's so-called *bares musicales* (music bars), usually less loud and smoky than the discos. Most of these are in the old town, around Plaza Ramiro I and along Calle Gil Bergés and Calle Bellido.

Sports & the Outdoors

The **ski areas** of Candanchú and Astún are 32 km (20 mi) north of Jaca, on the road to Somport and the French border. If you like to skate, check out the town's **ice rink** (🏨 974/361032).

THE WESTERN & BASQUE PYRENEES

The Aragüés, Hecho, and Ansó valleys, drained by the Estarrún, Osia, Veral, and Aragón Subordán rivers, are the westernmost valleys in Aragón and rank among the most pristine parts of the Pyrenees. Today these sleepy hollows are struggling to generate an economy that will save this endangered species of Pyrenean life. Less frequented by tourists, with cross-country (Nordic) skiing only, the mountain towns here retain ways and means of life more firmly entrenched than in, say, Jaca and the Tena Valley. As you move west into the Roncal Valley and the Basque Country, you will note smoother hills and softer meadows as the rocky central Pyrenees of Aragón fade into the past. These wet and fertile uplands and verdant beech forests seem reflected in the wide lines and flat profiles of the Basque *caseríos* (farmhouses) hulking firmly into the landscape. The Basque highlands of Navarra, from Roncal through the Irati Forest to Roncesvalles, and along the Bidasoa River leading down to the Bay of Biscay, all seem like some Arcadian paradise with progressively less stone and more vegetation as the Pyrenean heights give way to sheep-filled pasturelands.

Monasterio de San Juan de la Peña

★ ➌➍ *22 km (14 mi) southwest of Jaca.*

South of the Aragonese valleys of Hecho and Ansó is the Monastery of San Juan de la Peña, a site connected to the legend of the Holy Grail and another "cradle" of Christian resistance during the 700-year Moorish occupation of Spain. Its origins can be traced to the 9th century, when a hermit monk named Juan settled here on the *peña* (cliff). A monastery was founded on the spot in 920, and in 1071 Sancho Ramirez, son of King Ramiro I, made use of this structure, which was built into the mountain's rock wall, to found the Benedictine Monasterio de San Juan de la Peña. The **cloister,** tucked under the cliff, dates from the 12th century and contains intricately carved capitals depicting biblical scenes. From Jaca, drive 11 km (7 mi) west on N240 toward Pamplona to a left turn clearly signposted for San Juan de la Peña. From there it's another 11 km (7 mi) to the monastery. ✉ *Off N240* ☎ *974/355119* 🎫 *€6* ⊙ *Oct.–mid-Mar., Tues.–Sun. 11–1:30 and 4–5:30; mid-Mar.–May, Tues.–Sun. 10–1:30 and 4–7; June–Sept., daily 10–noon and 4–8.*

⌐ EN ROUTE To get to the westernmost Pyrenean valleys in Aragón from Jaca, head west on N240 for 20 km (12 mi), take a hard right at Puente de la Reina (after turning right to cross the bridge), and continue north along the Aragón-Subordán River. The first right after 15 km (9 mi) leads into the Aragüés Valley along the Osia River to Aisa and then Jasa.

Aragüés Valley

5

㉟ *Aragüés del Puerto is 2 km (1 mi) from Jasa.*

Aragüés del Puerto is a tidy mountain village with stone houses and lovely little corners, doorways, and porticoes. The distinctive folk dance in Aragüés is the *palotiau,* a variation of the *jota* performed only in this village. The **Museo Etnográfico** (Ethnographic Museum), in an ancient chapel in Aragüés del Puerto (ask for the caretaker at the town hall), offers a look into the past, from the document witnessing the 878 election of Iñigo Arista as king of Pamplona to the quirky manual wheat grinder. At the source of the River Osia, the Lizara **cross-country ski area** is in a flat expanse between the Aragüés and Jasa valleys. Look for 3,000-year-old megalithic dolmens sprinkled across the flat.

Hecho & Ansó Valleys

㊱ *Hecho Valley is 49 km (30 mi) northwest of Jaca; Ansó Valley is 25 km (15 mi) west of Hecho.*

You can reach the Valle de Hecho from the Aragüés Valley by returning to the valley of the Aragón-Subordan and turning north again on the A176. The **Monasterio de San Pedro de Siresa,** above the town of Hecho, is the area's most important monument, a 9th-century retreat of which only the 11th-century church remains. *Cheso,* a medieval Aragonese dialect descended from the Latin spoken by the Siresa monks, is thought to be the closest to Latin of all Romance languages and dialects. Cheso has been kept alive in the Hecho Valley, especially in the works of the poet Veremundo Mendez Coarasa. ✉ *Calle San Pedro, Siresa* 🎫 *Free* ⊙ *July and Aug., daily 11–1 and 5–8; other months, call the Ayuntamiento de Siresa (☎ 974/375002) for key.*

The **Selva de Oza** (Oza Forest), at the head of the Hecho Valley, is above the **Boca del Infierno** (Mouth of Hell), a tight draw where road and river barely squeeze through. Beyond the Oza Forest is a **Roman road** used before the 4th century to reach France through the Puerto del Palo—one of the oldest routes across the border on the pilgrimage to Santiago de Compostela.

The **Valle de Ansó** is Aragón's western limit. Rich in fauna (mountain goats, wild boar, and even a bear or two), the Ansó Valley follows the Veral River up to Zuriza. The three **cross-country ski areas** above Zuriza are known as the Pistas de Linza. Near Fago is the sanctuary of the **Virgen de Puyeta,** patron saint of the valley. Towering over the head of the valley is Navarra's highest point, the 7,989-foot **Mesa de los Tres Reyes** (Plateau of the Three Kings), named not for the Magi but for the kings of Aragón, Navarra, and Castile, whose 11th-century kingdoms all came to a corner here—allowing them to meet without leaving their respective realms. Try to be in the town of **Ansó** on the last Sunday in August, when residents dress in their traditional medieval costumes and perform ancestral dances of great grace and dignity.

Where to Stay & Eat

$ ✕⛉ **Gaby-Casa Blasquico.** This cozy inn, famed as Hecho's top restaurant ($–$$$), is known for its Aragonese mountain cuisine. Especially strong on game recipes from wild boar to venison to partridge or migratory pigeon, the menu also lists lamb and vegetable dishes. Make sure you call ahead: Gaby often opens for anyone who reserves in advance, even if the place is theoretically closed. ⊠ *Pl. Palacio 1, Hecho* ☎ *974/375007* ⌕ *Reservations essential* 🛏 *6 rooms* ♻ *Restaurant; no a/c* ▤ *MC, V* ☉ *Closed 1st 2 wks in Sept.; restaurant closed weekdays Sept.–Holy Week.*

$–$$ ⛉ **Usón.** For a base to explore the upper Hecho Valley or the Oza Forest, look no further. The staff at this friendly little Pyrenean inn will tell you where to rent a bike, get you a trout-fishing permit, or send you off in the right direction for a climb or hike. ⊠ *Ctra. Selva de Oza, HU2131, Km 7, Usón 22720* 🕿 *974/375358* 🛏 *14 rooms* ♻ *Restaurant; no a/c* ▤ *MC, V* ☉ *Closed Nov. 2–Mar. 15.*

▐ EN
 ROUTE

From Ansó, head west to Roncal on the narrow and winding but panoramic 17½-km (11-mi) road through the Sierra de San Miguel. To enjoy this route fully, count on taking a good 45 minutes to reach the river Esca and the Valle de Roncal.

Roncal Valley

㊲ *17½ km (11 mi) west of Ansó Valley.*

The Roncal Valley, the eastern edge of the Basque Pyrenees, is famous for its sheep's-milk cheese, Roncal, and as the birthplace of Julián Gayarre (1844–90), the leading tenor of his time. The 34-km (21-mi) drive through the towns of **Burgui** and **Roncal** to **Isaba** winds through green hillsides and Basque *caseríos*, which house both farming families and their livestock. Burgui's red-tile roofs backed by rolling pastures contrast with the vertical rock and steep slate roofs of the Aragonese and Catalan Pyrenees; Isaba's wide-arched bridge across the Esca is a graceful reminder of Roman aesthetics and engineering techniques. To get to the valley from Jaca, take N240 west along the Aragón River; a right turn north on NA137 follows the Esca River from the head of the Yesa Reservoir up the Roncal Valley.

Try to be in the Roncal Valley for **El Tributo de las Tres Vacas** (the Tribute of the Three Cows), which has been celebrated every July 13 since

1375. The mayors of the valley's villages, dressed in traditional gowns, gather near the summit of San Martín to receive the symbolic payment of three cows from their French counterparts, in memory of the settlement of ancient border disputes. Feasting and celebrating follow.

The road west (NA140) to **Ochagavia** through the Puerto de Lazar (Lazar Pass) has views of the Anie and Orhi peaks, towering over the French border. Two kilometers (1 mi) south of Ochagavia, at Escároz, a small secondary roadway winds 22 km (14 mi) over the Abaurrea heights to **Aribe,** known for its triple-arched medieval bridge and ancient *horreo* (granary). A 15-km (9-mi) detour north through the town of Orbaiceta up to the headwaters of the Irati River, at the Irabia Reservoir, gets you a good look at the **Selva de Irati** (Irati Forest), one of Europe's major beech forests and the source of much of the timber for the fleet Spain commanded during her 15th-century golden age.

Roncesvalles

★ ③⑧ *2½ km (1½ mi) north of Burguete, 48 km (30 mi) north of Pamplona, 64 km (40 mi) northwest of Isaba in the Roncal Valley.*

Roncesvalles (Orreaga, in Euskera) is the site of the Colegiata, cloister, hospital, and 12th-century **chapel of Santiago,** the first Navarran church on the Santiago pilgrimage route. The **Colegiata** (Collegiate Church), built at the orders of King Sancho VII el Fuerte (the Strong), houses the king's tomb, which measures more than 7 feet long. The 3,468-foot **Ibañeta Pass,** above Roncesvalles, is a gorgeous route into France. A **menhir** (monolith) marks the traditional site of the legendary battle in *The Song of Roland* in which Roland fell after calling for help on his ivory battle horn. The well-marked eight-hour walk to or from St-Jean-Pied-de-Port is one of the most beautiful and dramatic sections of the pilgrimage.

Where to Stay

$ 🏨 **La Posada.** This 17th-century building with a heavy stone entry is an ancient way station for pilgrims bound for Santiago de Compostela. The accommodattons are simple but far more comfortable than the pilgrims' quarters in the neighboring Colegiata. ✉ *Ctra. Pamplona–Francia, C135, Km 48, 31650* 📞 *948/760225* 🖷 *948/760266* 🛏 *18 rooms* 🍴 *Restaurant; no a/c* 🖃 *AE, DC, MC, V* 🌣 *Closed Nov.*

Burguete

③⑨ *2½ km (1½ mi) south of Roncesvalles, 120 km (75 mi) northwest of Jaca.*

Burguete (Auritz in Euskera) lies between two mountain streams forming the headwaters of the Urobi River. The town was immortalized in Ernest Hemingway's *The Sun Also Rises,* with its evocative description of trout fishing in an ice-cold stream above a Navarran village.

Where to Stay & Eat

$–$$ ✕🏨 **Hostal Burguete.** Hemingway's character Jake Barnes spends a few days here clearing his head before plunging back into the psychodrama of the San Fermín festival and his impossible passion for Lady Brett Ashley. The inn still works for this sort of thing, though there don't seem to be as many trout around these days. Good value and simple Navarran cooking ($–$$$) make this stalwart Basque town house a good stop for a meal or a night. With a little luck you can even sleep in Hemingway's bed; his room is kept exactly as it was when the novelist bunked here in the summer of 1924. ⊠ *Calle Única 51, 31640* ☎ *948/760005* 🖷 *948/790488* ⥀ *22 rooms* ⚇ *Restaurant; no a/c* ☰ *AE, DC, MC, V* ⊘ *Closed Feb. and Mar.*

EN ROUTE

To skip Pamplona and stay on the trans-Pyrenean route, continue 21 km (13 mi) southwest of Burguete on NA135 until you reach NA138, just before Zubiri. A right turn takes you to Urtasun, where the small NA252 leads left to the town of Iragui and over the pass at Col d'Egozkue (from which there are superb views over the Arga and Ultzana River valleys) to Olagüe, where it connects with NA121 some 20 km (12 mi) north of Pamplona. Turn right onto N121A and climb over the Puerto de Velate (Velate Pass)—or, in bad weather or a hurry, through the tunnel—to the turn for Elizondo and the Baztán Valley, N121B.

Baztán Valley

④⓪ *80 km (50 mi) north of Pamplona.*

Tucked neatly over the headwaters of the Bidasoa River and under the peak of the 3,545-foot Garramendi mountain, which looms over the border with France, the rounded green hills of the Valle de Baztán make an ideal halfway stop between the central Pyrenees and the Atlantic. Each village in this enchanted Basque valley seems smaller and simpler than the next: tiny clusters of whitewashed, stone-and-mortar houses with red-tile roofs group around a central *frontón* (handball court).

Where to Stay & Eat

★ $–$$$ ✕ **Galarza.** The kitchen in this stone town house overlooking the Baztán River turns out excellent Basque fare, with a Navarran emphasis on vegetables. Try the *txuritabel* (roast lamb with a special stuffing of egg and vegetables), which is best in the spring (though available year-round), or *txuleta de ternera* (veal raised in the valley), good anytime of year. ⊠ *Calle Santiago 1, Elizondo* ☎ *948/580101* ☰ *MC, V* ⊘ *Closed late Sept.–early Oct.*

★ ¢–$ ✕🖸 **Fonda Etxeberria.** This tiny inn, set in an old farmhouse with creaky floorboards and oak doors, has small, handsome rooms. The palatial bathrooms are shared by guests (usually one bathroom per two to three rooms). The restaurant ($–$$) prepares simple country dishes such as *alubias de Navarra estofadas* (Navarran white beans stewed with chorizo) and roast lamb. ⊠ *Antxitonea Trinketea (next to frontón court) s/n, 31700 Arizkun* ☎ *948/453013* 🖷 *948/453433* ⥀ *16 rooms without bath* ⚇ *Restaurant; no a/c, no room TVs* ☰ *MC, V.*

Lesaka

④① *21 km (13 mi) west of Elizondo in the Baztán Valley, 71 km (43 mi) northwest of Pamplona.*

If you're around for Pamplona's festival of San Fermín (July 6–14), stop at Lesaka, just 2 km (1 mi) off the N121. Lesaka's patron saint is also

San Fermín, and its *sanfermines txikos* (miniature San Fermín fests) may more closely resemble the one described in *The Sun Also Rises* than Pamplona's modern-day international beer brawl does.

OFF THE BEATEN PATH

CABO HIGUER – Follow the Bidasoa River down through Vera de Bidasoa to Irún, Hondarribia (Fuenterrabía), and, for its symbolic value as well as the view out into the Atlantic, Cabo Higuer. This is the end of the road, one of two geographical bookends—Cap Creus, on the Mediterranean, is the other—of a complete trans-Pyrenean trek.

PYRENEES ESSENTIALS

To research prices, get advice from other travelers, and book travel arrangements, visit www.fodors.com.

Transportation

5

BY AIR

Barcelona's international airport, El Prat de Llobregat, is the largest gateway to the Catalan Pyrenees. Farther west, the airports at Zaragoza, Pamplona, and Hondarribia (Fuenterrabía) serve the Pyrenees of Aragón, Navarra, and the Basque Country. From Madrid, fly to Barcelona on Iberia's shuttle, or fly any of several airlines to Hondarribia or Pamplona.

BY BIKE

Because most roads do not include extra pavement for bicyclists, travel across the Pyrenees is challenging and somewhat dangerous. Experienced cyclists recommend "taking the road," that is, fully occupying a lane, as the safest way to travel. The best cycling options are local day trips and mountain-bike circuits on off-road tracks, trails, former railroad lines, and livestock paths. (Check with local tourist offices for details.) The Cerdanya's nearly flat 50-km (30-mi) east–west valley is one of the prettiest and gentlest portions to cycle; the Baztán Valley between Pamplona and the French border, though steeper, is a lush, generally cool run to bike. Benasque at Aragón's eastern edge is another valley made for biking, from the town itself out to Ansils and up to the flatland around Hospice de France and the French border. In addition, Benasque has many miles of off-road and back-road trails. Generally, trans-Pyrenean biking is a series of long, grueling ascents and vertiginous, perilous descents that ought to be tackled only by experienced cyclists.

🚲**Bike Rentals Esports Iris** ✉Av. de Francia, Duana, near French border at Bourg Madame, Puigcerdà ☎972/882398. **Top Bike** ✉Pla d'Arenes, Ctra. Nacional 152, Puigcerdà ☎972/882042. **Deportes Aïgualluts** ✉Av. de los Tilos s/n, Benasque ☎974/551215. **El Baúl** ✉Av. de Francia, Benasque ☎974/551039. **Vit's** ✉Pl. Mayor s/n, Benasque ☎974/552088. **Deportes Azus** ✉Villanúa, Jaca ☎974/378217. **Ciclos Larequi** ✉Av. de Zaragoza 56, Pamplona ☎948/150645.

BY BUS

Bus travel in the Pyrenees is the only way, other than hiking or driv-

---

TIP

If you're planning a long-distance hiking trip, the bus will get you to your starting point and retrieve you from the finish line.

ing, to cross from east to west, though this will often mean zigzagging down to the major lowland hubs (Barcelona, Lleida, Zaragoza, Huesca, and Pamplona) and busing back up the valleys. Communications from the lowland cities and the main highland distributors (Puigcerdà, La Seu d'Urgell, Vielha, Benasque, and Jaca) generally include four buses daily, two early in the morning and two in the afternoon. Buses will get you anywhere you want to go in the Pyrenees, eventually, but the time lost waiting for them and planning your trip around departures makes this option a last resort. On the other hand, if you're planning a long-distance hiking trip, the bus will get you to your starting point and retrieve you from the finish line.

Serving Catalunya, Barcelona's bus line, Alsina Graells, connects Barcelona with the Pyrenees; in La Seu d'Urgell, it also links Puigcerdà with Lleida, connects directly with Barcelona via Cervera and Igualada, and, in Lleida, dispatches two buses daily (9 AM and 4 PM) to Vielha and to La Seu d'Urgell. From Zaragoza, Ágreda La Oscense sends frequent buses to Huesca and Jaca; in Huesca, the company connects with Jaca, Panticosa, Ordesa National Park, Bielsa, and Benasque. Pamplona's La Baztanesa has three buses a day to Elizondo and through to Irún. La Roncalesa dispatches three buses daily east to Jaca.

◪ Bus Lines Ágreda La Oscense ⊠ Paseo María Agustín 7, Zaragoza ☎ 976/229343 ⊠ Estación Intermodal, Ronda de la Estación s/n, Huesca ☎ 974/210700. **Alsina Graells** ⊠ Calle Ali Bei 80, Barcelona ☎ 93/265-6508 ⊠ Av. Garriga i Masó s/n, La Seu d'Urgell ☎ 972/350020 ⊠ Calle Saracibar s/n, Lleida ☎ 973/271470. **La Baztanesa** ⊠ Calle Conde Oliveta 6, Pamplona ☎ 948/226712. **La Roncalesa** ⊠ Estación de Autobuses, Calle Conde Oliveta 6, Pamplona ☎ 948/222079.

◪ Bus Depots Estació d'autobusos de Barcelona Nord ⊠ Alí Bei 80, Barcelona ☎ 902/260606. **Estació d'autobusos** ⊠ Av. Garriga i Masó s/n, La Seu d'Urgell ☎ 973/350020. **Estació d'autobusos** ⊠ Saracibar s/n, Lleida ☎ 973/271470. **Estación de autobuses** ⊠ Paseo María Agustín 7, Zaragoza ☎ 976/229343. **Estación Intermodal** ⊠ Ronda de la Estación s/n, Huesca ☎ 974/210700. **Estación de Autobuses** ⊠ Calle Conde Oliveta 6, Pamplona ☎ 948/226712.

BY CAR

Short of hiking, the only practical way to tour the Pyrenees is by car. The Collada de Toses (Tosses Pass) to Puigcerdà is the most difficult route into the Catalan Pyrenees, but it's free and the scenery is spectacular. Safer and faster, if more expensive (tolls total more than €20 from Barcelona to La Cerdanya) and somewhat less scenic, is the E9 through the Tuñel del Cadí (Cadí Tunnel). Once you're there, most of the Cerdanya Valley's two-lane roads are wide and well paved. As you move west, roads can be more difficult to navigate, but the Eje Pirenaico (Pyrenean Axis), or N260, is a carefully engineered, safe cross-Pyrenean route. Many Pyrenean roads wind dramatically through mountain passes, so allow extra driving time no matter how well the road is paved. You can rent cars at airports at both ends of the Pyrenees.

BY TRAIN

There are three small train stations deep in the Pyrenees: Puigcerdà, in the Cerdanya Valley; Pobla de Segur, in the Noguera Pallaresa Valley; and Canfranc, north of Jaca, below the Candanchú and Astún ski resorts. The larger gateways are Huesca and Lleida. From Madrid, connect through Barcelona for the eastern Pyrenees, Zaragoza and Huesca for the central Pyrenees, and Pamplona or San Sebastián for the western Pyrenees.

🚆 **RENFE** ☎ 902/240202 ⊕ www.renfe.es/ingles.

Sports & the Outdoors

FISHING

Ramón Cosiallf and Danica can take you fly-fishing anywhere in the world by horse or helicopter, but the Pyrenees are their home turf. For about €145 a day (depending on equipment), you'll be whisked to high Pyrenean lakes and ponds, streams, and rivers and armed with equipment and expertise. You can buy a fishing license for each autonomous region (Catalonia, Aragón, Navarra) at local rod-and-gun clubs, known as Asociaciones de Pesca and/or Caza. In Puigcerdà, licenses are available weekdays 9–2 at the office of Agricultura, Ramadería i Pesca.

🚆 **Agricultura, Ramadería i Pesca** ✉ Calle de la Percha 17, Puigcerdà ☎ 972/880515. **Agricultura, Ramadería i Pesca** ✉ Av. Meridiana 38, Barcelona ☎ 93/409-2090. **Danica** ☎ 659/735376 or 974/553493 ⊕ www.danicaguias.com. **Departamento de Medio Ambiente** ✉ Travessera de Gràcia 56, Barcelona ☎ 93/567-0815.

SKIING

Spain's daily newspaper, *El País,* prints complete ski information every Friday in season (December through mid-April). For an up-to-the-minute ski report in Spanish or Catalan, call the ski-report hotline in Barcelona. For general information, contact the Catalan Winter Sports Federation. Jaca, Puigcerdà, and Vielha have excellent ice rinks with public skating sessions.

🚆 **Federació Catalana Esports d'Hivern** (Catalan Winter Sports Federation) ✉ Carrer Casp 38, Barcelona ☎ 93/415-5544. **Ski report** ☎ 93/416-0194.

Contacts & Resources

EMERGENCIES

🚆 **Emergency Services General emergency** ☎ 091. **Red Cross** ☎ 972/216400 in Girona, 974/221186 in Huesca, 973/267011 in Lleida, 948/203540 in Navarra. **Police** ☎ 972/201381 in Girona, 974/244711 in Huesca, 973/245012 in Lleida, 948/237000 in Navarra.

INTERNET, MAIL & SHIPPING

Most hotels, especially in the larger cities and towns of Puigcerdà, La Seu d'Urgell, Vielha, Benasque, Vielha, Zaragoza, and Jaca, provide free Internet access—getting online is now more the rule than the exception. If you prefer a cybercafé, you'll find them everywhere. Just ask at your hotel's front desk, and they should be able to point you in the right direction.

Federal Express and DHL Offices (local transporters are MRW and SEUR) are available only in larger Pyrenean destinations.

🚆 **Cybercafé & Internet Centers Online** ✉ Carrer d'Espanya 23, Puigcerdà ☎ 972/140820. **Oficina de Turismo del Consell Comarcal** ✉ Pg. Joan Brudieu, La Seu d'Urgell ☎ 973/353112. **Cybercafé** ✉ Pl. Coto Marzo 1, Vielha ☎ 973/641156. **La Biblioteca de** la Casa de la Cultura ✉ San Sebastián 5, Benasque ☎ 974/551289. Osc@.com ✉ C. San José de Calasanz 13, Huesca ☎ 974/292166. **Change** ✉ C. Jardiel s/n, Zaragoza ☎ 976/297625. **Ciberciva** ✉ Av. Regimiento Galicia 2, Jaca ☎ 974/356775.

🖪 **Overnight Services MRW** ✉ Av. de Francia Edificio Balbenas (bajos), Benasque ☎ 974/551722 ✉ Calle Huesca 2, Jaca ☎ 974/356031 ✉ Valles de Andorra s/n, La Seu d'Urgell ☎ 973/354499 ✉ Calle Breton 48, Zaragoza ☎ 976/357600. **SEUR** ✉ C/ Agricultura, Polígono Industrial Lucas Mayadas, Huesca ☎ 974/229970 ✉ Carrer Escoles Pies 9, Puigcerdà ☎ 972/880602 ✉ Poligono Industrial de Mig Aran, Vielha ☎ 973/640588.

MEDIA

The national newspaper *El País* is available throughout the Pyrenees. *El Punt Diari* (in Catalan) is available throughout Girona province. In the Vall d'Aran, the monthly *Tot Aran* is the local sheet, along with *Aran,* published in Barbastro, both in Catalan. The *Diario de Alto Aragón,* in Spanish, informs Huesca, Jaca, and all of upper Aragón. Zaragoza's *Heraldo de Aragón* is the city's main paper, and Pamplona's *Diario de Navarra* is found throughout Navarra. The *International Herald Tribune* is easily found in major towns such as Puigcerdà, Huesca, Zaragoza, and Jaca. Librería General in Zaragoza (✉ Paseo de la Independencia 22, Zaragoza ☎ 976/22448) has the city's largest offering of books and periodicals in English.

The Pyrenees receives all of the six Spanish television stations, as well as many French stations. Most four- and five-star hotels also receive CNN and European stations such as SKY TV. In Catalunya, TV3 is the Catalan language station and, in the Basque Country, Euskal Telebista transmits in Euskera, the Basque language.

TOUR OPTIONS

The Puigcerdà travel agency Touring Cerdanya can arrange guides, horses, or jeeps for treks to upper lakes, peaks, and meadows.

🖪 **Touring Cerdanya** ✉ Escuelas Pías 19, Puigcerdà ☎ 972/880602 or 972/881450.

VISITOR INFORMATION

🖪 **Regional Tourist Offices Barcelona** ✉ Palau Robert, Passeig de Gràcia 107, at Av. Diagonal ☎ 93/238–4000. **Girona** ✉ Rambla de la Llibertat 1 ☎ 972/202679. **Huesca** ✉ Coso Alto 23 ☎ 974/225778. **Lleida** ✉ Plaça de la Paeria 11 ☎ 973/248120. **Navarra** ✉ Duque de Ahumada 3, Pamplona ☎ 948/211287. **Zaragoza (Aragón)** ✉ Torreon de la Zuda, Glorieta de Pío XII ☎ 976/393537.

🖪 **Local Tourist Offices Aínsa** ✉ Av. Pirenaica 1 ☎ 974/500767. **Benasque** ✉ Plaça Mayor 5 ☎ 974/551289. **Bielsa** ✉ Pl. del Ayuntamiento ☎ 974/501000. **Camprodón** ✉ Plaça Espanya 1 ☎ 972/740010. **Jaca** ✉ Av. Rgto. Galicia ☎ 974/360098. **La Seu d'Urgell** ✉ Av. Valira s/n ☎ 973/351511. **Panticosa** ✉ C. San Miguel s/n ☎ 974/487318. **Puigcerdà** ✉ Carrer Querol 1 ☎ 972/880542. **Sant Joan de les Abadesses** ✉ Plaça de la Abadía 9 ☎ 972/720599. **Taüll** ✉ Av. Valira s/n ☎ 973/694000. **Vielha** ✉ Av. Castiero 15 ☎ 973/641196.

Barcelona & Northern Catalonia

WORD OF MOUTH

"What I like about Barcelona is the buzz, the areas that are so different from one another: narrow Gothic Quarter streets, wide Eixample lanes, trendy Born shops and bars, alternative Raval streets, the Parc de la Ciutadella on a Sunday afternoon, the beach for bonfires on a hot summer night, the new architecture in the Port Olímpic en Diagonal del Mar, the fresh air of Montjuïc, the mountain feel of Tibidabo, the cozy atmosphere of Gràcia."

—stardust

"Our winner—attending a concert at Palau de la Música Catalana. If you like classical music at all, buy tickets to a concert here."

—julies

By George
Semler

CAPITAL OF CATALONIA, 2,000-year-old Barcelona commanded a vast Mediterranean empire when Madrid was still a dusty Moorish outpost on the Spanish steppe. Relegated to second-city status only after Madrid became the seat of the royal court in 1561, Barcelona has long rivaled and often surpassed Madrid's supremacy. One of Europe's most visually stunning cities, Barcelona balances the medieval intimacy of its Gothic Quarter with the grace and distinction of the wide boulevards in the Modernista Eixample—just as the Mediterranean Gothic elegance of the church of Santa Maria del Mar provides a perfect counterpoint to Gaudí's riotous Sagrada Família. Mies van der Rohe's pavilion seems even more minimalist after a look at the Art Nouveau Palau de la Música Catalana, and such exciting contemporary creations as Bofill's neoclassical, Parthenon-under-glass Teatre Nacional de Catalunya, Frank Gehry's waterfront goldfish, Norman Foster's Torre de Collserola, and Jean Nouvel's Torre Agbar all add new spice to Barcelona's visual soup.

Barcelona has long had a frenetically active cultural life. It was the home of architect Antoni Gaudí, whose buildings are the most startling statements of Modernisme. Other leading Moderniste architects include Lluís Domènech i Montaner and Josep Puig i Cadafalch. The painters Joan Miró, Salvador Dalí, and Antoni Tàpies are also strongly identified with Catalonia. Pablo Picasso spent his formative years in Barcelona, and one of the city's treasures is a museum devoted to his works. Barcelona's opera house, the Liceu, is the finest in Spain; and the city claims such native Catalan musicians as cellist Pablo (Pau, in Catalan) Casals, opera singers Montserrat Caballé and José (Josep) Carreras, and early music master Jordi Savall. Barcelona's fashion industry is hard on the heels of those of Paris and Milan, and FC (Futbol Club) Barcelona is arguably the world's most glamorous soccer club.

In 133 BC the Roman Empire annexed the city. The Visigoths roared down from the north in the 5th century; the Moors invaded in the 8th; and in 801 the Franks under Charlemagne captured the city and made it their buffer zone at the edge of the Moors' Iberian empire. By 988, the autonomous Catalonian counties had gained independence from the Franks. Not until 1137 was Catalonia united through marriage with the House of Aragón, and yet another marriage, that of Ferdinand II of Aragón and Isabella of Castile (and queen of León) in 1474, brought Aragón and Catalonia into a united Spain. As the capital of Aragón's Mediterranean empire, Barcelona grew powerful between the 12th and the 14th centuries and began to falter only when maritime emphasis shifted to the Atlantic after 1492. Despite Madrid being the seat of Spain's Royal Court, Catalonia enjoyed autonomous rights and privileges until 1714, when, in reprisal for having backed the Austrian Hapsburg pretender to the Spanish throne, all institutions and expressions of Catalan identity were suppressed by Felipe V of the French Bourbon dynasty. Not until the mid-19th century would Barcelona's industrial growth bring about a renaissance of nationalism and a cultural flowering that recalled Catalonia's former opulence.

Catalan nationalism continued to strengthen in the 20th century. After the abdication of Alfonso XIII and the establishment of the Second Span-

GREAT ITINERARIES

IF YOU HAVE 3 DAYS
Begin with the **Rambla neighborhood and Boqueria market** ⑲ to get the feel of Barcelona before plunging into **the Gothic Quarter** to see the **Catedral de la Seu** ①, **Plaça del Rei** ③, and the Catalan and Barcelona government palaces in **Plaça Sant Jaume** ⑨. Next, cross Via Laietana to the **Barri de la Ribera** (waterfront neighborhood), which contains the paradigmatic Catalan Gothic **Santa Maria del Mar** ⑦ and **Museu Picasso** ⑤. For dinner, head to Cal Pep in **Plaça de les Olles**. An evening concert at the **Palau de la Música Catalana** ㊷ ends the day.

Make Day 2, especially if it's sunny, a Gaudí day. Visit the **Temple Expiatori de la Sagrada Família** ㉛ first thing, followed by **Parc Güell** ㊳; in the afternoon tour **Casa Vicens,** ㊶ and then, on Passeig de Gràcia **Casa Milà,** ㉘ and **Casa Batlló,** part of the **Manzana de la Discòrdia** ㉕. **Palau Güell,** ⑭ off the lower Rambla, is probably too much Gaudí for one day, but don't miss it.

On Day 3, climb Montjuïc for the **Museu Nacional d'Art de Catalunya** ㊾, in the hulking Palau Nacional. Investigate the **Fundació Miró,** ㊻ **Estadi Olímpic,** ㊽ the **Mies van de Rohe Pavilion** ㊱ and **Casaramona** (aka Caixaforum) ㊽. At lunchtime, take the cable car across the port for seafood in **Barceloneta** ㊴.

IF YOU HAVE 5 DAYS
On Day 1, after exploring the **Rambla and Boqueria market** ⑲, head into **the Gothic Quarter** (Barri Gòtic) at Plaça del Pi or through sunny **Plaça Reial** ⑩. The **Catedral**

de la Seu ① and its surroundings offer hours of exploring before visiting the Roman columns at **Carrer Paradis** and government seats at **Plaça Sant Jaume** ⑨. The next day, explore the **Barri de la Ribera** and **Barceloneta,** ㊴ including the **Museu Picasso** ⑤ and the church of **Santa Maria del Mar** ⑦. **Barceloneta,** ㊴ the **Port Olímpic** ㊵ or the *rompeolas* (breakwater) are a good hike along the Mediterranean.

On the third morning explore the **Raval** to the west of the Rambla, and visit the **Museu d'Art Contemporani de Barcelona (MACBA)** ㉒ and the **Centre de Cultura Contemporànea de Barcelona (CCCB)** ㉓ as well as the medieval **Antic Hospital de La Santa Creu** ㉑ and Barcelona's oldest church, **Sant Pau del Camp** ㉕. Don't miss the splendid Gothic shipyards and the **Museu Marítim** ⑬ and its Drassanes Reials shipyards. Next take a guided tour of the **Palau de la Música Catalana** ㊷ and pick up tickets to a concert. Devote your fourth day to Gaudí by following the Day 2 schedule in the three-day suggested itinerary—again, the **Palau Güell,** ⑭ off the lower Rambla is a de rigueur Gaudí visit.

On Day 5, explore **Montjuïc,** visiting the **Museu Nacional d'Art de Catalunya** ㊾ in the Palau Nacional, the **Fundació Miró** ㊻, the **Mies van der Rohe Pavilion** ㊱, and the **Casaramona (Caixaforum)** ㊽. Take the cable car across the port and have lunch in **Barceloneta** ㊴ before a tour of the **Port Olímpic** ㊵ and, farther up the coast, the **Diagonal Mar.**

6

ish Republic in 1931, Catalonia enjoyed autonomy and cultural freedom. Once again backing a losing cause, Barcelona was a Republican stronghold and hotbed of anti-fascist sentiment during the 1936–39 civil war, with the result that Catalan language and identity were suppressed under the 1939–75 Francisco Franco regime by such means as book burning, the renaming of towns, and the banning of the Catalan language in schools and the media. This repression had little lasting effect; Catalans jealously guard their language and culture and generally think of themselves as Catalans first, Spaniards second.

Catalonian home rule was granted after Franco's death in 1975, and Catalonia's governing body, the ancient Generalitat, was reinstated in 1980. Catalan is now Barcelona's co-official language, along with Castilian Spanish, and is eagerly promoted through free classes funded by the Generalitat. Street names are signposted in Catalan, and newspapers, radio stations, and a TV channel publish and broadcast in Catalan. The triumphant culmination of this rebirth was the staging of the Olympics in 1992—ring roads and freeways were installed, stadiums and pools were renovated, new harborside promenades were created, and an entire set of train tracks was moved to make way for the Olympic Village. In the 21st century, innovative structures, such as the Ricardo Bofill *Vela* (sail) hotel, demonstrate Barcelona's insatiable appetite for novelty and progress.

EXPLORING BARCELONA

Barcelona is made up of four distinct areas. Between Plaça Catalunya and the port lies the Old City, or Ciutat Vella, including El Barri Gòtic (the Gothic Quarter), La Ribera (the waterfront, also known as Born-Ribera), and El Raval, the former slums or outskirts southwest of the Rambla. Above Plaça Catalunya is the grid-pattern expansion built after the city's third series of defensive walls were torn down in 1860. Known as the Eixample ("Widening"), this area contains most of Barcelona's Moderniste architecture. Farther north and west are the former outlying towns of Gràcia and Sarrià, the Pedralbes area, and, rising up behind the city to the northwest, the green hills of the Collserola nature reserve. Diagonal Mar, from Torre Agbar and Plaça de les Glòries east, is the new Barcelona built for the 2004 Forum de les Cultures.

Numbers in the margin correspond to points of interest on the neighborhood maps.

El Barri Gòtic & La Ribera

This walk explores Barcelona's Gothic Quarter and spills across Via Laietana into the Barri de la Ribera, where the Picasso Museum, Santa Maria del Mar, and El Born are the main visits. Parts of the Barri Gòtic and the Barri Xinès (or Barrio Chino), Barcelona's notorious red-light district, have been much improved since the early 1990s; you'll happen on squares freshly begotten by the demolition of whole blocks and the planting of palm trees. Nonetheless, bag snatching is common in this part of town, so keep your wits about you, and if at all possible, carry nothing in your hands, while keeping any belongings on your personhood se-

GEORGE'S TOP 5

La Boqueria—Barcelona's in-town produce market is the most beautiful and exciting metropolitan cornucopia in the world. A browse through the hundred-odd stalls and a taste of local morsels is Barcelona at its best. Try Pinotxo or Quim de la Boqueria for top tastes.

Santa Maria del Mar—Peerless Mediterranean Gothic; the breathtaking purity and symmetry here is unrivaled in Barcelona. It is a top site for concerts, and hearing Renaissance polyphony sung by The Sixteen in this architectural gem is the ultimate musical moment.

La Sagrada Família—Gaudí's midcity assemblage of stalagmites, stalactites, and cylindrical towers is the city's most surprising and eye-

cure. The Barri de la Ribera, once the waterfront district, surrounds the basilica of Santa Maria del Mar and includes Carrer Montcada, Barcelona's poshest street in the 14th and 15th centuries. Much of the Barri de la Ribera was torn down in 1714 by the victorious Spanish and French army of Felipe V to create a glacis, an open no-man's land outside the walls of the occupying stronghold, La Ciutadella fortress.

rattling architectural marvel. A thorough exploration of this work in progress will leave you ravenous for a paella on the Barceloneta beach.

El Palau de la Música Catalana—A concert in this Art Nouveau wonder is unforgettable no matter what happens on stage. Cavalry erupts from the wings, a stained-glass chandelier plummets from above, and floral mayhem is everywhere.

Castellers and Sardanas—If you get lucky enough to see human castles constructed on a Sunday morning, or the *sardana*, Catalonia's national dance, performed in front of the cathedral, you will have seen two of this nation-within-a-nation's most beloved symbols of identity.

A GOOD
WALK

A good walk through the Barri Gòtic could begin at **Catedral de la Seu ❶ ▶** and move through and around the cathedral to the **Museu Frederic Marès ❷** (and its little terrace café, surrounded by Roman walls). Next, pass the patio of the Arxiu de la Corona d'Aragó (Archives of the House of Aragón); then turn left again and down into **Plaça del Rei ❸**. As you leave Plaça del Rei, the **Museu d'Història de la Ciutat ❹** is on your left. Crossing Via Laietana, pass through the Plaça del Angel and walk down Carrer Princesa; this will take you to Carrer Montcada followed by a right turn to the **Museu Picasso ❺**. Walk along Carrer Montcada and see some of Barcelona's most elegant medieval palaces, before emerging into the Passeig del Born, with the giant steel hangar of the city's onetime main produce market, **El Born ❻**, looming at the far end. To your right is the back entrance of the church widely considered Barcelona's best, the Catalan Gothic **Santa Maria del Mar ❼**. After spending some time inside (note that the basilica closes each afternoon between 1:30 and 4:30), stop into La Vinya del Senyor, the excellent wine bar opposite the main door. Walk around the church's eastern side through the **Fossar de les Moreres ❽**. On the west side of Santa Maria

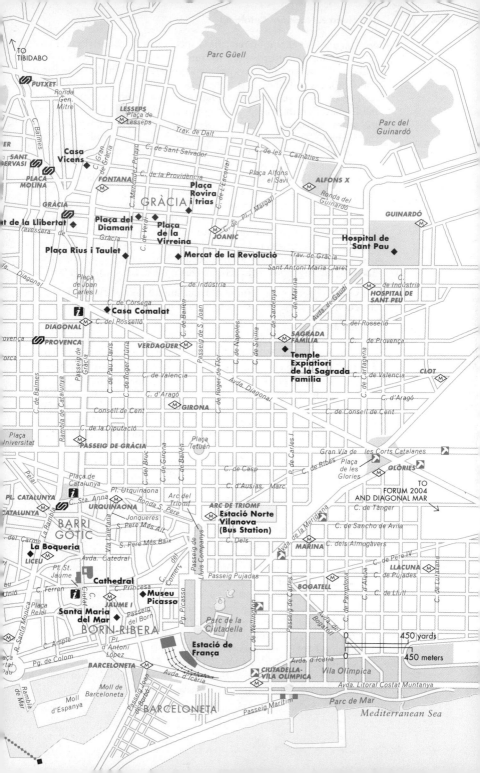

del Mar are Carrer Sombrerers, the Gispert spice shop, and the entrance to Carrer Banys Vells, lined with interesting shops and restaurants. Walk to the far end of Banys Vells and go left through Barra de Ferro and Cotoners to Princesa. A walk back across Via Laietana into Carrer Ferran will take you to **Plaça Sant Jaume ❾**. From this square, once the Roman Forum, walk up Carrer Paradís (facing La Generalitat it's the second street to your right), take a sharp right, and have a look at the **Roman Columns** inside the entryway at Carrer Paradís 10. For a tour of Barcelona's *call* (from the Hebrew *qahal*, "meeting"), the medieval Jewish quarter, leave Plaça Sant Jaume on Carrer del Call, turn right on Sant Domènech del Call, and proceed to the next corner. Early Barcelona's **Sinagoga Major** (Main Synagogue) opens into Carrer Marlet across the intersection to your left. On the next corner—on the right is a stone with Hebrew inscriptions, and a Spanish translation on a plaque—Arc de Sant Ramón del Call is another reminder of the Jewish community that prospered here until a 1391 pogrom decimated it a century before the 1492 expulsion. Take a left here, onto Carrer del Call, and then turn right on Carrer Ferran to reach the neoclassical **Plaça Reial ❿**.

TIMING   This walk covers some 3 km (2 mi) and should take about three hours, depending on stops. Allow another hour for the Picasso Museum.

What to See

▶ ❶ **Catedral de la Seu.** On Saturday afternoons, Sunday mornings, and occasional evenings, Barcelona folk gather in the Plaça de la Seu to dance the *sardana,* a somewhat demure circular dance and a great symbol of Catalan identity. The Gothic cathedral was built between 1298 and 1450, with the spire and neo-Gothic facade added in 1892. Architects of Catalan Gothic churches strove to make the high altar visible to the entire congregation, hence the unusually wide central nave and slender side columns. The first thing you see upon entering are the high relief sculptures on the choir stalls, telling the story of **Santa Eulàlia** (Barcelona's co-patron along with La Mercé, Our Lady of Mercy). The first scene, on the left, shows St. Eulàlia in front of Roman Consul Decius with her left hand on her heart and her right hand pointing at a cross in the distance. In the next scene, Eulàlia is tied to a column and flagellated by Decius's thugs. To the right of the choir entrance, the senseless Eulàlia is hauled away, and in the final scene she is lashed to the X-shape cross upon which she was crucified in the year 303. To the right of this high relief is a sculpture of St. Eulàlia, standing with her emblematic cross, resurrected as a living saint. Other highlights are the beautifully carved choir stalls; St. Eulàlia's tomb in the crypt; and the battle-scarred crucifix in the Lepanto Chapel to the right of the main entrance. The tall cloisters surround a tropical garden, and outside, at the building's front right corner, is the intimate Santa Llúcia chapel. The cathedral is floodlighted in striking yellows at night, and the stained-glass windows are backlighted. ⊠ *Pl. de la Seu* ☎ *93/342–8260* ⊕ *www.catedralbcn.org* 🎫 *€4 for special visit* ☉ *Daily 7:45 AM–7:45 PM; during a special visit time, between 1 and 5, visitors can see entire cathedral, museum, bell tower, and rooftop* Ⓜ *Catalunya, Liceu, Jaume I.*

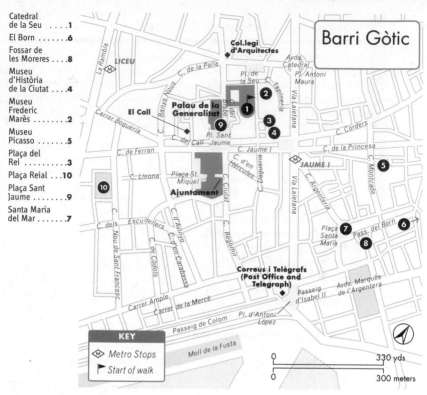

Barri Gòtic

KEY

◈ *Metro Stops*

┏ *Start of walk*

0 _____ 330 yds

0 _____ 300 meters

6

**NEED A
BREAK?**

Mercat de Santa Caterina. Across Via Laietana is the restored Santa Caterina market where the late Enric Miralles, architect of the Scottish Parliament building, devised a revolutionary marketplace executed by his widow, architect Benedetta Tagliabue. Undulating wood and ceramic mosaic roofing with colors recalling both Gaudí and Miró covers a glass floor through which sections of the original convent are visible. The spacious, clean-lined Santa Caterine Cuines restaurant offers an original menu with vegetable, rice, pasta, meat, fish, and eggs from left to right across the top with vegetarian, Mediterranean, Asian, cooked over coals (*carbo*), and desserts down the side. The numbered dishes appear at the intersections while daily specials flash on an electronic message board overhead. Meat and vegetable stands remain the prime attraction, though a supermarket with home delivery and an Internet ordering system have created an ultramodern facility between the neoclassical walls and the medieval and Visigothic remains beneath. ⊠ *Av. Francesc Cambo 16, Born-Ribera* ☎ *93/ 268–9918* ⊕ *www.mercatsbcn.com* Ⓜ *Catalunya.*

⑥ El Born. Once the site of medieval jousts, the Passeig del Born is at the end of Carrer Montcada behind the church of Santa Maria del Mar. The numbered cannonballs under the benches are by the late Joan Brossa

Catalonia's National Dance

THE *SARDANA*, CATALONIA'S NATIONAL DANCE, is often perceived as anything but exuberant, a solemn and dainty affair usually danced by senior citizens in front of the Barcelona Cathedral at midday on weekends. Look for an athletic young *colla* (troupe), though, and you will see the grace and fluidity the sardana can create. The long faces and intense concentration are the result of the mathematical precision of a dance consisting of 76 steps in sets of four, each dancer needing to know exactly where he or she is at all times. The Basque fandango or the Aragonese jota are athletic explosions of joy, whereas the sardana is melancholic, reflective, and subtle.

Said to be a representation of the passing of time, a choreography of the orbits and revolutions of the moon and stars, the circular sardana is recorded in Greek chronicles dating back 2,000 years. The name of the dance may have come from the 14th-century Catalan colony on the Mediterranean island of Sardinia, though the alternate spelling *cerdana* suggests it may have originated in the Pyrenean Cerdanya valley.

Pep Ventura, famous *tenora* (oboe) master and sardana composer, made his debut in 1837; the sardana's popularity skyrocketed with Ventura's own. Performed in circles of all sizes and of dancers of all ages, the sardana is accompanied by the *cobla* (sardana combo), five wind instruments, five brass, and the director, who plays a three-holed flute called the *flabiol* and a small drum, the *tabal*, which he wears attached to his flute arm, normally the right. The sardana, for all its delicate primness and numerical rigor, never fails to communicate a strong emotion, a combination of nostalgia and *enyorança*, a sense of longing for old traditions and glories past and future.

"poet of space" in memory of the 1714 siege of Barcelona that concluded the 14-year War of the Spanish Succession. The Bourbon forces obliged local residents to tear down more than 900 of their own houses, about a fifth of the city, to create an open no-man's land, for the fortress built for the occupying army of the great villain of Barcelona history, Felipe V, grandson of Louis XIV. Walk down to the Born itself—a great iron hangar designed by Josep Fontseré in 1876. Once the city's main produce market, it was modeled after Les Halles in Paris. Renovation of El Born uncovered the perfectly preserved lost city of 1714, complete with blackened fireplaces, taverns, wells, and the canal that brought water into the city. Sand dunes visible in the cellars attest to La Ribera's early position on the Barcelona waterfront before landfill created Barceloneta and the present harbor. The Museu de Història de la Ciutat offers free visits overlooking the ruins of the 14th-to-18th-century Barri de la Ribera weekends 10 to 3. ⊠ *Born-Ribera* Ⓜ *Jaume I.*

❽ **Fossar de les Moreres** (Cemetery of the Mulberry Trees). This low marble monument is on the eastern side of the church of Santa Maria del Mar, honoring the defenders of Barcelona who gave their lives in the 1714 siege that ended the War of the Spanish Succession and established

Felipe V on the Spanish throne. The inscription (EN EL FOSSAR DE LES MOR-ERES NO S'HI ENTERRA CAP TRAIDOR, or IN THE CEMETERY OF THE MULBERRY TREES NO TRAITOR LIES) refers to the story of the graveyard keeper who refused to bury those who had fought on the invading side, even when one of them turned out to be his son. The torch-sculpture over the marble monument, often referred to as a *pebetero* (Bunson burner), was erected in 2002. ⊠ *Fossar de les Moreres, La Ribera.*

4 **Museu d'Història de la Ciutat** (City History Museum). Just off the Plaça del Rei, this fascinating museum traces the evolution of Barcelona from its first Iberian settlement to its alleged founding by the Carthaginian Hamilcar Barca in about 230 BC to Roman and Visigothic times and beyond. Antiquity is the focus here: Romans took the city during the Punic Wars, and the striking underground remains of their Colonia Favencia Julia Augusta Paterna Barcino, through which you can roam on metal walkways, are the museum's main treasure. Archaeological finds include parts of walls, fluted columns, and recovered busts and vases. Above ground, off the Plaça del Rei, the **Palau Reial Major,** the splendid **Saló del Tinell,** the chapel of **Santa Àgata,** and the **Torre del Rei Martí,** a lookout tower with views over the Barri Gòtic, complete the self-guided tour. ⊠ *Palau Padellàs, Carrer del Veguer 2, Barri Gòtic* ☎ *93/315–1111* ⊕ *www.museuhistoria.bcn.es* ⊠ *€4 (also covers admission to Monestir de Pedralbes, Park Güell Centre d'Interpretation, and Museu-Casa Verdaguer)* ☉ *Oct.–May, Tues.–Sat. 10–2 and 4–8; June–Sept., Tues.–Sat. 10–8; Sun. 10–3* Ⓜ *Catalunya, Liceu, Jaume I.*

OFF THE BEATEN PATH

MUSEU DEL CALÇAT – Hunt down the tiny Shoe Museum, between the cathedral and Carrer Banys Nous. The collection includes a pair of clown's shoes and a pair worn by Pablo Casals. The tiny square, originally a graveyard, is just as interesting as the museum, with its shrapnel-pocked walls and quiet fountain. ⊠ *Pl. Sant Felip Neri, Barri Gòtic* ☎ *93/301–4533* ⊠ *€2.50* ☉ *Tues.–Sun. 11–2* Ⓜ *Catalunya, Liceu, Jaume I.*

2 **Museu Frederic Marès** (Frederic Marès Museum). Off the left (north) side of the Catedral de la Seu, you can browse for hours among the miscellany assembled by the early-20th-century sculptor-collector Frederic Marès. Everything from paintings and polychrome wood carvings, such as Juan de Juní's 1537 masterpiece *Pietà* and the Master of Cabestany's late-12th-century *Apparition of Christ to His Disciples at Sea,* to Marès's collection of pipes and walking sticks is stuffed into this rich potpourri. ⊠ *Pl. Sant Iu 5, Barri Gòtic* ☎ *93/310–5800* ⊕ *www.museumares.bcn.es* ⊠ *€3 (free 1st Sun. of month and Wed. afternoon)* ☉ *Tues., Wed., Fri., and Sat. 10–7, Thurs. 10–5, Sun. 10–3* Ⓜ *Catalunya, Liceu, Jaume I.*

5 **Museu Picasso.** Carrer Montcada is known for Barcelona's most elegant medieval and Renaissance palaces, five of which are occupied by the Picasso Museum. Picasso spent his key formative years in Barcelona (1895–1904), and though the 3,600-work permanent collection is strong on his early production, don't expect to find any of the artist's most famous works. Picasso's longtime crony and personal secretary Jaume Sabartés donated his private collection in 1960, and Picasso himself donated another 1,700 works in 1970. Displays include childhood and ado-

Fodor'sChoice ★

6

Picasso's Barcelona

BARCELONA'S CLAIM TO PABLO PICASSO (1881–1973) has been contested by Málaga, the painter's birthplace, as well as by Madrid, where *Guernica* hangs, and even by the town of Gernika itself, victim of the 1937 Luftwaffe saturation bombing that inspired the famous canvas. Picasso, a staunch anti-Franco opponent after the war, refused to return to Franco's Spain. In turn, the Franco regime allowed no public display of Picasso's work until 1961, when the artist's Sardana frieze at Barcelona's Architects' Guild was unveiled. Picasso never set foot on Spanish soil for the last 39 years of his life.

Picasso spent a sporadic but formative period of his youth in Barcelona between 1895 and 1904, after which he moved to Paris to join the fertile art scene in the French capital. Picasso's father had been appointed art professor at the Reial Acadèmia de les Belles Arts in La Llotja. Picasso, a precocious draftsman, began advanced classes in the academy at the age of 15. Working in different studios between academic stints in Madrid, the 19-year-old Picasso first exhibited at Els Quatre Gats, a tavern still thriving on Carrer Montsió. Much intrigued with the Bohemian life of Barcelona's popular neighborhoods, Picasso's early cubist painting, *Les Demoiselles d'Avignon*, was inspired not by the French town but by the Barcelona street Carrer d'Avinyó, then known for its brothel. After his move to Paris, Picasso returned occasionally to Barcelona until his last visit in summer of 1934.

Considering Picasso's off-and-on tenure in Barcelona, followed by a 36-year residence in Paris and a 39-year self-imposed exile, it's remarkable that Barcelona and Picasso should be so intertwined in the world's perception of the city. The Picasso Museum, although an excellent visit, is only the fourth-most important art venue on any art connoisseur's list of Barcelona galleries. The museum was the brainchild of the artist's longtime friend Jaume Sabartés, who believed that his vast private collection of Picasso works should be made public. After much wrangling with the Franco regime, who were loath to publicly recognize such a prominent anti-Franco figure and author of a work titled *The Dream and the Lie of Franco* (1937), the Picasso Museum finally opened in 1963. Spread through three Renaissance palaces, the collection's best works are Picasso's childhood drawings made in La Coruña between the ages of 10 and 14; his early portraits, such as the 1897 *Science and Charity;* his 1901–04 Blue Period paintings, including *Terrats de Barcelona* (1902); and his 44 cubist Las Meninas studies.

Iconoserveis Culturals (✉ C. Muntaner 185 Eixample ☎ 93/410–1405 ⊕ www.iconoserveis.com) gives walking tours through the key spots in Picasso's Barcelona life, covering studios, galleries, taverns, Picasso family apartments, and the painter's favorite haunts and hangouts.

lescent sketches, works from Picasso's Blue and Rose periods, and the famous 44 cubist studies based on Velázquez's *Las Meninas*. The sketches, oils, schoolboy caricatures and drawings from Picasso's early years in La Coruña and, later, in Barcelona are perhaps the most fascinating part of the museum, showing the facility the artist possessed from an early age. His *La Primera Communión (First Communion)*, painted at the age of 15, for which he was given a short review in the local press, was an important achievement for the young Picasso, and the Las Meninas studies and the bright *Pichones (Pigeons)* series provide a final explosion of color and light. *Suite 156*, a series of erotic and playful drawings on display when temporary exhibits allow space, may be the best of all. ✉ *Carrer Montcada 15–23, Born-Ribera* ☎ *93/319–6310* ⊕ *www.museupicasso.bcn.es* ✉ *Permanent collection €6, temporary exhibits €5, combined ticket €8.50; free 1st Sun. of month* ☉ *Tues.–Sat. 10–8, Sun. 10–3* Ⓜ *Catalunya, Liceu, Jaume I.*

❸ Plaça del Rei. The plaza is long held to be the scene of Columbus's triumphal return from his first voyage to the New World—Ferdinand and Isabella, as chronicled in legend, song, and painting, received him on the stairs fanning out from the corner. (However, it turns out they were actually at a summer palace outside of town). The **Palau Reial Major** was the Catholic Monarchs' official residence in Barcelona. Its main room is the **Saló del Tinell,** a banquet hall built in 1362. Also around the square: the dark 15th-century **Torre Mirador del Rei Martí** (King Martin's Watchtower), above the Saló del Tinell; to the left, the **Palau del Lloctinent** (Lieutenant's Palace); the 14th-century **Capilla Reial de Santa Àgueda** (Royal Chapel of Saint Agatha), to the right of the stairway; and the **Palau Clariana-Padellàs** (Clariana-Padellàs Palace), moved here stone by stone from Carrer Mercaders in the early 20th century and now the entrance to the Museu d'Història de la Ciutat. The hulking bronze sculpture, *Topos* (Greek for "Place") by Basque sculptor Eduardo Chillida (1924–2002), the tiny shrine to St. Agatha behind glass above a 1638 Barcelona coat of arms, and, if you're lucky, the resonating notes of classical-guitar music on a quiet afternoon can all add up to a memorable Barcelona moment. Ⓜ *Catalunya, Liceu, Jaume I.*

❿ Plaça Reial. A symmetrical mid-19th-century arcaded square, Plaça Reial is bordered by elegant ocher facades with balconies overlooking the **Fountain of the Three Graces** and lampposts designed by Gaudí in 1879. Restaurants and cafés, identifiable as tourist traps by the photo-menus (the only good one is Taxidermista), line the square. On Sunday morning, crowds gather to sell and trade stamps and coins. After dark the square is a nightlife hot spot starring Jamboree for jazz and boogy, Los Tarantos for flamenco, and Glaciar for young beer-drinking internationals. Ⓜ *Catalunya, Liceu.*

❾ Plaça Sant Jaume. This central square behind the Catedral de la Seu is the site of both Catalonia's and Barcelona's governments and was the center of the Roman forum 2,000 years ago. The Plaça was cleared in the 1840s, but the two imposing buildings facing each other across it are much older. The 15th-century *Ajuntament* (city hall) contains impressive black-and-burnished-gold murals (1928) by Josep Maria Sert and the famous

Saló de Cent, from which the Council of One Hundred, Europe's earliest proto-democratic body founded in 1372, governed until Felipe V abolished Catalonia's autonomous institutions in 1715. Filled with art, the ajuntament is open to the public on Sunday morning (10 to 1) and on special holidays. During the week, check listings for free concerts or events here. The **Palau de la Generalitat**, seat of the Catalan government, is a majestic 15th-century palace—through the front windows you can see the gilded ceiling of the Saló de Sant Jordi (Hall of St. George), named for Catalonia's dragon-slaying patron saint. Normally you can visit the Generalitat only on certain holidays, such as the Día de Sant Jordi (St. George's Day), April 23; check with the *protocolo* (protocol office). The Generalitat hosts carillon concerts, open to the public, on occasional Sundays at noon. ✉ *Pl. Sant Jaume 1, Barri Gòtic* ☎ *93/402-7000* ⊕ *www. bcn.es* ☉ *Sun. 10–1* Ⓜ *Catalunya, Liceu, Jaume I.*

★ ➐ **Santa Maria del Mar.** The most elegant of all Barcelona's churches is on the Carrer Montcada end of Passeig del Born. Simple and spacious, this pure and classical space enclosed by soaring columns is something of an oddity in ornate and complex Moderniste Barcelona. Santa Maria del Mar (Saint Mary of the Sea) was built from 1329 to 1383, an extraordinarily prompt construction time in that era, in fulfillment of a vow made a century earlier by Jaume I to build a church to watch over all Catalan seafarers. The cry of "Santa Maria" was the war cry of the Catalan sailors and soldiers who conquered the Balearic Islands from the Moors in 1229 and went on to extend their empire as far as Athens by 1311. The architect in charge of the construction, a mere stonemason named Montagut de Berenguer, designed a bare-bones basilica (an oblong Roman royal hall used for public meetings and later adapted for early Christian or medieval churches) that is now considered the finest existing example of Catalan (or Mediterranean) Gothic architecture. Early Gothic with Romanesque echoes and overtones, the number eight (or multiples thereof)—the medieval numerological symbol for the Virgin Mary—runs through every element of the basilica's construction: 16 octagonal pillars rising 16 meters before arching out another 16 meters to the painted keystones at the apex of the arches 32 meters overhead. The sum of the lateral aisles, 8 meters each, equals the width of the center aisle, and the difference in height between the central and lateral naves, 8 meters, equals their width. The result of all this proportional balance is a tonic sense of peace and uplift, a sweeping and symmetrical grace enhanced by a lovely rose window whose circular mass in blues and crimsons perfectly offsets the golden sandstone verticality of the columns. Any excuse to spend time in Santa Maria del Mar, from eavesdropping on a wedding, to hearing a concert, to using it merely as a shortcut through to the Passeig de Born, is valid. The haunting "Cant de la Sibil.la" ("Song of the Sibyl") performed on Christmas Eve before the midnight Mass, is a concert not to miss, and Handel's *Messiah* at Christmas and Haydn's *Creation* at Easter are also annual events. Any chance to hear Renaissance choral music here—performing the works of such composers as Tomás Luís de Victoria, Guerrero, Tallis, and Byrd—especially if performed by The Sixteen or the Tallis Scholars, is an unmissable treat. ✉ *Pl. de Santa Maria, Born-Ribera* ☎ *93/310-2390* ☉ *Daily 9–1:30 and 4:30–8* Ⓜ *Catalunya, Jaume I.*

The Rambla & the Raval

Barcelona's best-known promenade is a constant and colorful flood of humanity past flower stalls, bird vendors, mimes, musicians, newspaper kiosks, and outdoor cafés. Federico García Lorca called this street the only one in the world that he wished would never end; traffic plays second fiddle to the endless *paseo* (stroll) of locals and travelers alike. The whole avenue is referred to as Las Ramblas (Les Rambles, in Catalan) or La Rambla, but each section has its own name: Rambla Santa Monica is at the southeastern, or port, end; Rambla de les Flors in the middle; and Rambla dels Estudis at the top, near Plaça de Catalunya. El Raval is the area to the west of the Rambla, originally a slum outside Barcelona's second set of walls, which ran down the left side of the Rambla. Alas, Rambla-happy tourists are tempting prey for thieves and scam artists. Do *not* play the shell game, dress conservatively, keep maps and guidebooks hidden, conceal cameras, and leave wallets and passports in your hotel safe. A credit card and a little cash are all you need.

A GOOD WALK

Start on the Rambla opposite the Plaça Reial and wander down toward the sea, to the **Monument a Colom** ⓫ ▶ and the Rambla de Mar. From here you might make a brief probe into the unprepossessing modern **Port** ⓬. As you move back to the Columbus Monument, investigate the **Museu Marítim** ⓭ and its medieval Drassanes Reials shipyards. Gaudí's **Palau Güell** ⓮ on Carrer Nou de la Rambla is the next stop before the **Gran Teatre del Liceu** ⓯, and along the way take a peek at Barcelona's red-light district, the **Barri Xinès** ⓰. At the Miró mosaic at Pla de la Boqueria, cut right to the Plaça del Pi and the church of **Santa Maria del Pi** ⓱. Back on the Rambla, take in the facade and perhaps some savories at **Antigua Casa Figueres** ⓲, stroll through the **Boqueria** ⓳ food market and the **Palau de la Virreina** ⓴ exhibition center next door, and then cut around to the courtyards of the medieval **Antic Hospital de la Santa Creu** ㉑. Next, visit the **Museu d'Art Contemporani de Barcelona** (MACBA) ㉒ and the **Centre de Cultura Contemporània de Barcelona** (CCCB) ㉓, on Carrer Montalegre, before returning to the Rambla. Finish your walk along Carrer Tallers, ending up in **Plaça de Catalunya** ㉔.

6

TIMING

This walk covers 3 km (2 mi). With stops, allow three hours.

What to See

㉑ **Antic Hospital de la Santa Creu.** The 15th-century medieval hospital now houses libraries, cultural and educational institutions, and the Escola Massana art school. Approach it from the back door of the Boqueria starting at the Carrer del Carme end, where, across from the Reial Acadèmia de Cirurgia i Medecina, the courtyard of the Casa de Convalescència leads in past scenes from the life of St. Paul portrayed in lovely blue-and-white ceramic tiles hand-painted by master craftsman Llorenç Passolas in 1680–81. The green-and-white-tiled patio inside houses the Institut d'Estudis Catalans. The second-floor garden behind the clock is dedicated to Catalan novelist Mercé Rodoreda. Turn right as you leave the entryway, take a look into the beautifully vaulted reading rooms on either side down the stairs, and continue through the orange grove in the hospital patio to the stairs leading up to the right for a look at the

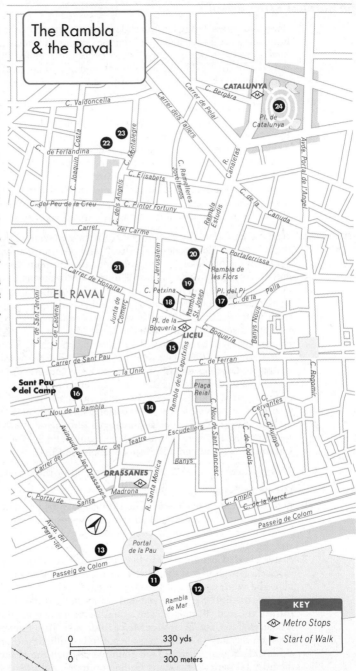

The Rambla
& the Raval

CATALUNYA
Pl. de
Catalunya

C. Valdoncella

C. Bergàra

Carrer de Pelai

C. dels Tallers

Costa

de Ferlandina

C. Joaquin

Montaleqre

C. del Peu de la Creu

C. Elisabets

C. dels Angels

C. Pintor Fortuny

Carrer   del Carme

Ramelleres

Jovellamos

Rambla

Estudis

C. de la

Canuda

Avda. Portal de l'Angel

R.

Canaletas

Carrer de Hospital

C. Jerusalem

C. Portaferrissa

Rambla
les Flors

C. de Sant Jeróni

C. de Cadena

Junta de
Comerç

C. Petxina

Rambla

St. Josep

Pl. del Pi

C. de la

Palla

Palau

EL RAVAL

Pl. de la
Boqueria

LICEU

C. Boqueria

Banys Nous

Carrer de Sant Pau

C. la Unió

Rambla dels Caputxins

C. de Ferran

C. Reganit

Sant Pau
del Camp

C. Nou de la Rambla

Plaça
Reial

C. Nou de Sant Francesc

Cervantes

C. d'Avoyo

C. de Codols

Arc   del   Teatre

Escudellers

Banys

Avinguda de les Drassanes

Carrer del

DRASSANES

Madrona

R. Santa Mònica

C. Ample

C. de la Mercé

C. Portal de   Santa

Avda. del   Paral·lel

Passeig de Colom

Portal
de la Pau

Passeig de Colom

Rambla
de Mar

0   330 yds

0   300 meters

KEY

Ⓜ Metro Stops

▶ Start of Walk

wide Gothic arches inside the Biblioteca de Catalunya. Out on Carrer Hospital to the left is **La Capella**, once the hospital chapel and now a gallery with contemporary art. ✉ *Carrer del Carme 45, or Carrer Hospital 56, Raval* ⊕ *www.gencat.es/bc* Ⓜ *Catalunya, Liceu.*

⓲ **Antigua Casa Figueres.** This Moderniste café, grocery, and pastry store on the corner of Carrer Petxina has a splendid mosaic facade and exquisite Art Nouveau fittings. ✉ *La Rambla 83, Rambla* ☎ *93/301–6027* ⊕ *www.escriba.es* Ⓜ *Catalunya, Liceu* ⊙ *Daily 8:30 AM–9 PM.*

⓰ **Barri Xinès.** As you walk from Plaça Reial toward the sea, Barcelona's red-light district, the Barri Xinès (traditionally called the Barrio Chino in Castilian Spanish) is on your right. Though literally translatable as Chinatown, China had nothing to do with this; the name is a generic reference to foreigners of all kinds. The area is ill-famed for prostitutes, drug pushers, and street thieves, but it's not as dangerous as it looks; the reinforced police presence here may make it safer than other parts of the Gothic Quarter.

★ ⓳ **Boqueria.** Barcelona's most spectacular food market, also known as the Mercat de Sant Josep, is an explosion of life and color sprinkled with delicious little bar-restaurants. **Pinotxo** has long been a sanctuary for food lovers; **El Kiosco Universal** and **Quim de la Boqueria** are hot on its heels. Don't miss mushroom expert, and author Petràs and his mad display of wild mushrooms, herbs, nuts, and berries (*Fruits del Bosc—* Fruits of the Forest) at the very back. ✉ *La Rambla 91, Rambla* ⊕ *www. boqueria.info* ⊙ *Mon.–Sat. 8–8* Ⓜ *Liceu.*

㉓ **Centre de Cultura Contemporànea de Barcelona** (CCCB). In the renovated Casa de la Caritat, a former medieval convent and hospital, the CCCB, a combination museum, lecture hall, and concert hall, now has a reflecting wall, in which you can see over the rooftops to Montjuïc and beyond. ✉ *Montalegre 5, Raval* ☎ *93/306–4100* ⊕ *www.cccb.org* ✉ *€6; entry to patio and bookstore free* ⊙ *Tues., Thurs., and Fri. 11–2 and 4–8, Wed. and Sat. 11–8, Sun. 11–7* Ⓜ *Catalunya.*

⓯ **Gran Teatre del Liceu.** Along with Milan's La Scala, Barcelona's opera house has long been considered one of the most beautiful in Europe. First built in 1848, this cherished landmark was torched in 1861, bombed in 1893, and once again gutted by a blaze of mysterious origins in early 1994. Barcelona's soprano Montserrat Caballé stood on the Rambla in tears as her beloved venue was consumed. Five years later, a restored and renewed Liceu, equipped for modern productions, opened anew. Even if you don't see an opera, don't miss a tour of the building; some of the Liceu's oldest and most spectacular rooms were untouched by the fire. The downstairs Espai Liceu features a cafeteria; a shop specializing in opera-related gifts, books, and recordings; an intimate 50-person-capacity circular concert hall; and a Mediateca with recordings and films of past opera productions. ✉ *La Rambla 51–59, Rambla* ☎ *93/ 485–9900* ⊕ *www.liceubarcelona.com* ✉ *Guided tours €6* ⊙ *Tours daily at 10 AM in English. For an extra €3, the 75-min visit includes Círculo del Liceu, with the extraordinary Ramon Casas collection of* *paintings. Express tours at 11 AM, noon, and 1 PM are shorter (20 mins) and less comprehensive; cost is €4* Ⓜ *Liceu.*

➤ **⓫ Monument a Colom** (Columbus Monument). At the foot of the Rambla, take an elevator to the top of this monument for a bird's-eye view over the city. (The entrance is on the harbor side.) ✉ *Portal de la Pau s/n, Rambla* ☎ *93/302–5224* ☜ *€2.25* ☉ *Daily 9–8:30* Ⓜ *Drassanes.*

㉒ Museu d'Art Contemporani de Barcelona (Barcelona Museum of Contemporary Art; MACBA). Designed by American architect Richard Meier, this 1992 building's 20th-century masters include Calder, Rauschenberg, Oteiza, Chillida, and Tàpies. The optional guided tour is excellent. ✉ *Pl. dels Àngels 1, Raval* ☎ *93/412–0810* ⊕ *www.macba.es* ☜ *€7.50* ☉ *Mon. and Wed.–Fri. 11–7:30, Sat. 10–8, Sun. 10–3; reduced admission Wed. €3; free guided tours daily at 6, Sun. at noon.* Ⓜ *Catalunya.*

⓭ Museu Marítim. The superb Maritime Museum is in the 13th-century **Drassanes Reials** (Royal Shipyards), to the right at the foot of the Rambla. This vast medieval space, one of Barcelona's finest Gothic structures, seems more like a cathedral than a boatyard and is filled with ships, including a life-size reconstructed galley, figureheads, and early navigational charts. Take the self-guided tour. ✉ *Av. de les Drassanes s/n, Rambla* ☎ *93/342–9920* ⊕ *www.museumaritimbarcelona.org* ☜ *€6; free 1st Sat. of month after 3* ☉ *Daily 10–7* Ⓜ *Drassanes.*

⓴ Palau de la Virreina. The neoclassical Virreina Palace, built by a viceroy to Peru in 1778, is now an exhibition center for paintings, photography, and historical items. The building also has a bookstore and a municipal tourist office. ✉ *La Rambla 99, Rambla* ☎ *93/316–1000* ⊕ *www.bcn.es/virreinaexposicions* ☜ *Free; €3 charge for some exhibits* ☉ *Mon.–Sat. 11–8, Sun. 11–3* Ⓜ *Liceu.*

⓮ Palau Güell. Antoni Gaudí built this mansion during the years 1886–89 for his patron, a textile baron named Count Eusebi de Güell, and soon found himself in the international limelight. The dark facade is a dramatic foil for the treasure house inside, where spear-shape Art Nouveau columns frame the windows and prop up a series of minutely detailed wood ceilings. Gaudí is most himself on the roof, where his playful, polychrome ceramic chimneys fit right in with later works such as Parc Güell and La Pedrera. Tours are guided. ✉ *Nou de la Rambla 3–5, Rambla* ☎ *93/317–3974* ☉ *Closed until Jan. 2007; call for update* Ⓜ *Drassanes, Liceu.*

㉔ Plaça de Catalunya. Barcelona's main transport hub, the Plaça de Catalunya is the frontier between the old city and the post-1860 Eixample. Café Zurich, at the head of the Rambla and the mouth of the metro, is a classic rendezvous point.

⓬ Port. Beyond the Columbus Monument—behind the Duana, or former customs building, now site of the Barcelona Port Authority—is the **Rambla de Mar,** a boardwalk with a drawbridge. The Rambla de Mar extends out to the **Moll d'Espanya,** with its Maremagnum shopping center, IMAX theater, and aquarium. Next to the Duana, you can board a Golondrina boat for a tour of the port or take a boat to the end of the *rompeolas,* 3 km (2 mi) out to sea, and walk back into the old fishing village of Barceloneta, now Barcelona's beachfront section. From the Moll de Barcelona's Torre de Jaume I, farther to the right, you can catch a cable car to Montjuïc or Barceloneta.

⑰ Santa Maria del Pi (St. Mary of the Pine). Like Santa Maria del Mar, the church of Santa Maria del Pi is another example of Mediterranean Gothic architecture, though its bulky, somber interior makes its soaring and elegant sister ship seem even more astounding by comparison. The gigantic rose window is best seen from inside in the late afternoon. The adjoining squares, **Plaça del Pi** and **Plaça de Sant Josep Oriol**, are two of the liveliest, most appealing spaces in the Gothic Quarter. ⊠ *Pl. del Pi s/n, Rambla* ☎ *93/318–4743* ⊗ *Daily 9–1:30 and 4:30–8* Ⓜ *Liceu.*

OFF THE
BEATEN
PATH

Fodor'sChoice
★

SANT PAU DEL CAMP. Barcelona's oldest church was originally outside the city walls (*del camp* means "in the fields") and was a Roman cemetery as far back as the 2nd century, according to archaeological evidence. A Visigothic belt buckle found in the 20th century confirmed that Visigoths used the site as a cemetery between the 2nd and 7th centuries. What you see now was built in 1127 and is the earliest Romanesque structure in Barcelona, redolent of the pre-Romanesque Asturian churches or of the pre-Romanesque Sant Michel de Cuxà in Prades, Catalunya Nord (Catalonia North, aka southern France). Elements of the church (the classical marble capitals atop the columns in the main entry) are thought to be from the 6th and 7th centuries. The hulking mastodonic shape of the church is a reminder of the fortress or refuge it must have served as through Moorish invasions and sackings. Check carefully for musical performances here, because the church is an acoustical gem. Note the tiny stained-glass window high on the facade facing Carrer Sant Pau. If Santa Maria del Pi's rose window is Europe's largest, this is quite probably the smallest. The tiny cloister, the only way in during afternoon opening hours, is Sant Pau del Camp's best feature, one of Barcelona's semisecret treasures. From inside the church, the right side of the altar leads out into this patio surrounded by porches or arcades. Sculpted Corinthian capitals portraying biblical scenes support triple Mudéjar arches. ⊠ *Sant Pau 101, Raval* ☎ *93/441–0001* ⊗ *Cloister weekdays 4:30–7:30. Sun. mass at 10:30, 12:30, and 8 PM* Ⓜ *Catalunya, Liceu, Paral.lel.*

The Moderniste Eixample

North of Plaça de Catalunya is the checkerboard known as the Eixample. With the dismantling of the city walls in 1860, Barcelona embarked upon an expansion scheme fueled by the return of rich colonials, by an influx of provincial aristocrats who had sold their country estates after the debilitating second Carlist War (1847–49), and by the city's growing industrial power. The street grid was the work of urban planner Ildefons Cerdà; much of the building here was done at the height of Modernisme. The Eixample's principal thoroughfares are Rambla de Catalunya and Passeig de Gràcia, where the city's most elegant shops vie for space among its best Art Nouveau buildings.

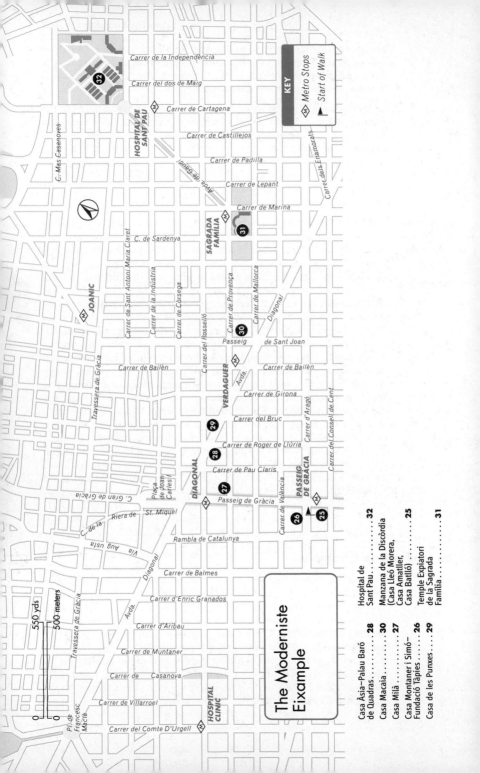

The Moderniste Eixample

KEY

◈ Metro Stops

▲ Start of Walk

Carrer de la Independència

Carrer del dos de Maig

Carrer de Cartagena

HOSPITAL DE SANT PAU

Carrer de Castillejos

Carrer de Padilla

Carrer de Lepant

Carrer de Marina

Avda. de Gaudí

C.-Mas Casanoves

SAGRADA FAMÍLIA

C. de Sardenya

JOANIC

Carrer de Sant Antoni Maria Claret

Carrer de la Indústria

Carrer de Còrsega

Carrer del Rosselló

Carrer de Provença

Carrer de Mallorca

Diagonal

Passeig de Sant Joan

VERDAGUER

Carrer de Bailèn

Carrer de Bailèn

Carrer de Girona

Carrer del Bruc

Carrer de Roger de Llúria

Carrer de Pau Claris

Passeig de Gràcia

PASSEIG DE GRÀCIA

Carrer de València

Carrer d'Aragó

Carrer del Consell de Cent

DIAGONAL

Plaça de Joan Carles I

St. Miquel

Riera de

C. Gran de Gràcia

Travessera de Gràcia

Rambla de Catalunya

Carrer de Balmes

Carrer d'Enric Granados

Carrer d'Aribau

Carrer de Muntaner

Carrer de Casanova

Carrer de Villarroel

Carrer del Comte D'Urgell

HOSPITAL CLÍNIC

Travessera de Gràcia

Pl. de Francesc Macià

Via Augusta

Diagonal

Avda.

550 yds
500 meters
0
0

A GOOD TOUR

Starting in the Plaça de Catalunya, walk up Passeig de Gràcia until you reach the corner of Consell de Cent. Enter the Bermuda Triangle of Moderniste architecture, the **Manzana de la Discòrdia** ㉕ ▶. The **Casa Montaner i Simó–Fundació Tàpies** ㉖ is around the corner on Carrer Aragó. Gaudí's **Casa Milà** ㉗, known as La Pedrera, is three blocks farther up Passeig de Gràcia; after touring the interior and rooftop, walk up Passeig de Gràcia to Vinçon for a look through one of Barcelona's top design stores, with views into the back of Casa Milà. Just around the corner, at Diagonal 373, is Puig i Cadafalch's intricately sculpted **Palau Baró de Quadras** ㉘, now housing the Casa Asia cultural center. Two minutes farther is his Nordic castlelike **Casa de les Punxes** ㉙ at No. 416–420. From here it's a 10-minute hike to yet another Puig i Cadafalch masterpiece, **Casa Macaia** ㉚. Finally, take a taxi to Gaudí's emblematic **Temple Expiatori de la Sagrada Família** ㉛. If you've still got energy and curiosity to burn, stroll over to Domènech i Montaner's **Hospital de Sant Pau** ㉜.

TIMING   Depending on how many taxis you take, this is a four- to five-hour tour.

What to See

㉘ **Casa Àsia–Palau Baró de Quadras.** The neo-Gothic and plateresque (intricately carved in silversmithlike detail) house built by Puig i Cadafalch in 1904 for Baron Quadras displays, on its facade, some of the most spectacular Eusebi Arnau sculptures in town (Palau de la Música Catalana, Casa Martí–Quatre Gats, Casa Amatller, Casa Lleó Morera, and Hotel Espanya are other Arnau sites). Look for St. George slaying the dragon, and don't miss the alpine chalet–like windows across the top floor. Casa Àsia, with an excellent library for cultural and business (Asia-related) research, offers free visits to its main floors and art gallery. ✉ *Av. Diagonal 373, Eixample* ☎ *93/238–7337* ⊕ *www.casaasia.es* 🎟 *Free* ☉ *Tues.–Sat. 10–8, Sun. 10–2* Ⓜ *Diagonal.*

★ ㉗ **Casa Milà.** Gaudí's Casa Milà, usually referred to as **La Pedrera** (The Stone Quarry), has a curving stone facade that undulates around the corner of the block. When the building was unveiled, in 1905, residents weren't enthusiastic about these cavelike balconies. Don't miss Gaudí's rooftop chimney park, especially in late afternoon, when the sunlight slants over the city into the Mediterranean. The handsome **Espai Gaudí** (Gaudí Space) in the attic has excellent critical displays of Gaudí's works, theories, and techniques, including an upside-down model of the Sagrada Família made of hanging beads. The **Pis de la Pedrera,** a restored apartment, gives an interesting glimpse into the life of its resident family in the early 20th century. Guided tours are offered weekdays at 6 PM and weekends at 11 AM. ✉ *Provença 261–265, Eixample* ☎ *902/ 400973* 🎟 *Espai Gaudí €5, Pis de la Pedrera €4, combined ticket €8* ☉ *Daily 10–8; guided tours weekdays at 6. Espai Gaudí roof terrace open for drinks evenings June–Sept.* Ⓜ *Diagonal, Provença.*

㉖ **Casa Montaner i Simó–Fundació Tàpies.** This former publishing house was converted to a modern, airy, split-level showcase for the work of contemporary Catalan painter Antoni Tàpies, as well as temporary exhibits. The bookstore is strong on Tàpies and Asian art. ✉ *Carrer d'Aragó 255, Eixample* ☎ *93/487–0315* 🎟 *€4.50* ☉ *Tues.–Sun. 10–8.*

㉙ Casa de les Punxes (House of the Spikes). Also known as Casa Terrades for the family that commissioned it, this cluster of six conical towers ending in impossibly sharp needles is one of several Puig i Cadafalch inspirations rooted in the Gothic architecture of northern Europe, an ur-Bavarian or Danish castle in downtown Barcelona. It is one of the few freestanding Eixample buildings visible from 360 degrees. ⊠ *Av. Diagonal 416–420, Eixample* Ⓜ *Diagonal.*

㉜ Hospital de Sant Pau. Certainly one of the most beautiful hospital complexes in the world, visible down Avinguda Gaudí from the Sagrada Família's Nativity facade, the Hospital de Sant Pau is notable for its Mudejar motifs and sylvan plantings. The hospital wards are set among gardens under exposed brick facades intensely decorated with mosaics and polychrome ceramic tile. Begun in 1900, this monumental production won Lluís Domènech i Montaner his third Barcelona "Best Building" award, in 1912. (His previous two prizes were for the Palau de la Música Catalana and Casa Lleó Morera.) The Moderniste enthusiasm for nature is apparent here; the architect believed patients are more apt to recover if they are surrounded by trees and flowers than in sterile hospital wards. Domènech i Montaner also believed in the therapeutic properties of form and color and decorated the hospital with Pau Gargallo sculptures and colorful mosaics. ⊠ *Carrer Sant Antoni Maria Claret 167, Eixample* ☎ *93/291–9000* ⊕ *www.santpau. es* 🖱 *Free; tour €5* ⊙ *Daily 9–8; tours weekends 10–2, weekdays by advance arrangement* Ⓜ *Hospital de Sant Pau.*

㉕ Manzana de la Discòrdia. A pun on the Spanish word *manzana*, meaning both city block and apple, the reference is to the classical myth of the Apple of Discord, in which Eris, goddess of strife, angered by not being invited to the marriage of Peleus and Thetis, tosses a golden apple with the inscription "to the fairest" among the guests. Hera, Athena, and Aphrodite all claim the apple; Paris is chosen to settle the dispute and awards the apple to Aphrodite, who promises him Helen, the most beautiful of women. Paris abducts Helen from Sparta and unleashes the Trojan War. The architectural counterpoint on this block, where the three main Moderniste architects go hand to hand, draws steady crowds of architecture buffs. Of the three, Casa Batlló is clearly the star.

Fodor'sChoice
★

Casa Lleó Morera (No. 35) was extensively rebuilt (1902–06) by Palau de la Música Catalana architect Domènech i Montaner and is a treasure chest of Modernisme. The facade is covered with ornamentation and sculptures of female figures using the modern inventions of the age: the telephone, the telegraph, the photographic camera, and the Victrola. The inside is currently closed to the public, but a quick glimpse into the entryway on the corner will give an idea of what's upstairs.

The pseudo-Flemish **Casa Amatller** (No. 41) was built by Josep Puig i Cadafalch in 1900 when the architect was 33 years old. Puig i Cadafalch's architectural historicism sought to recover Catalonia's proud past, in combination with eclectic elements from Flemish or Netherlandish architectural motifs. The Eusebi Arnau sculptures range from St. George and the dragon to the figures of a handless drummer with his dancing bear. The flowing-haired "Princesa" is thought to be Amatller's daugh-

CLOSE UP

Gaudí: Evangelist in Stone

PERHAPS NO SINGLE ARCHITECT HAS EVER marked a major city as comprehensively and spectacularly as Antoni Gaudí (1852–1926) imprinted Barcelona. The great Moderniste (or Art Nouveau) master's still unfinished Temple Expiatori de la Sagrada Família (Expiatory Temple of the Holy Family) has become Barcelona's most emblematic structure, and another dozen-odd mansions, parks, schools, gateways, lampposts, and other works in and around Barcelona provide a constant Gaudí presence throughout the Catalonian capital.

Cátedra Gaudí–Pabellones Güell (✉ Av. Pedralbes 7, Pedralbes ☎ 93/204–5250), a Gaudí library and study center, is directed by Joan Bassegoda i Nonell, Barcelona's top Gaudí expert. In one of his many articles, Bassegoda described Gaudí's approach with his legendary "originality is a return to origins." Bassegoda explains the master's conviction that, throughout the history of architecture, architects had become prisoners of the forms they were able to create with the tools of their trade: the compass and the T-square. Buildings had been composed of shapes these instruments could draw: circles, triangles, squares, and rectangles that in three dimensions became prisms, pyramids, cylinders, and spheres used for the construction of pillars, planes, columns, and cupolas.

Gaudí observed that in nature these shapes are unknown. Admiring the structural efficiency of trees, mammals, and the human form, he noted that ". . . neither are trees prismatic, nor are bones cylindrical, nor are leaves triangular." A closer study of natural forms revealed that bones, branches, muscles, and tendons are all composed of and supported by fibers. Thus, though a surface curves, it is supported from within by a fibrous network that Gaudí translated into what he called "ruled geometry," a system of inner reinforcement he designed to construct hyperboloids, conoids, helicoids, or parabolic hyperboloids, all complicated terms for simple forms and familiar shapes.

Gaudí, then, was more than a sculptor playing with form—he was an engineer experimenting with construction. His parabolic (naturally looping) arches were functional techniques first and formal exercises on a second level. His catenary (from *cadena*, for "chain") arches were inverted from chains hanging from stress points over mirrors. Gaudí's evolution away from the T-square and the compass can be traced from his first project onward. Casa Vicens (1883–85) was colorful and daring though angular and rectilinear; in the Palau Güell (1885–89), only his rooftop chimneys hint at what's to come; then in Casa Calvet (1898–1900) the vestibule, elevator, and stairwell are beginning to warp and heave into organic suggestions. Just a few years later arrives the undulating stone face of Casa Milà (La Pedrera, 1905). Casa Batlló (1907), done shortly after, incorporates a scaly dragon back of a roof and its tibias, femurs, and skulls. Finally, the project that consumed the last 20 years of his life, the phantasmagorical Sagrada Família, was a virtual midtown massif and forest.

6

ter, and the animals up above are pouring chocolate, a reference to the source of the Amatller family fortune. Casa Amatller is closed to the public (call or ask about any change in this), but an office on-site dispenses tickets for the Ruta del Modernisme tour.

At No. 43, the colorful and bizarre **Casa Batlló**—Gaudí at his most spectacular—with its mottled facade resembling anything from an abstract pointillist painting to a rainbow of sprinkles on an ice-cream cone, is usually easily identifiable by the crowd of tourists snapping photographs on the sidewalk. Nationalist symbolism is at work here: the scaly roofline represents the Dragon of Evil impaled on St. George's cross, and the skulls and bones on the balconies are the dragon's victims. These motifs are allusions to Catalonia's Middle Ages, with its codes of chivalry and religious fervor. The interior design follows a gently swirling maritime motif in stark contrast to the terrestrial strife represented on the facade. ☏ *93/216–0306* ⊕ *www.casabatllo.es* ✉ *€16* ⏱ *Daily 9–8* ✉ *Passeig de Gràcia 43, between Consell de Cent and Aragó, Eixample* ⏱ *Daily 9–8* Ⓜ *Passeig de Gràcia.*

③① **Temple Expiatori de la Sagrada Família.** Barcelona's most unforgettable
FodorsChoice landmark, Antoni Gaudí's Sagrada Família was conceived as nothing
★ short of a Bible in stone. This landmark is one of the most important architectural creations of the 19th to 21st centuries. No building in Barcelona, and few in the world, is more deserving of half a day's scrutiny. Consider bringing binoculars.

Start at the **Nativity facade,** where Gaudí addresses the fundamental mystery of Christianity: why does God the Creator become, through Jesus Christ, a creature? Gaudí's answer-in-stone is that God wanted to free man from the slavery of selfishness, symbolized here by the iron fence around the serpent at the base of the central column. The column depicts the genealogy of Christ. Overhead are the constellations in the Christmas sky at Bethlehem. Higher up is the Crowning of the Virgin under an overhang, atop which is a pelican feeding its young with its blood, a symbol of the eucharistic sacrifice. Below, two angels adore the initials of Christ (JHS) under the symbols of the cross, the Alpha and Omega. The cypress at the top is the evergreen symbol of eternity pointing to heaven; the white doves, souls seeking eternity.

To the right, the Portal of Faith, above Palestinian flora and fauna, shows scenes from the youth of Jesus, including his preaching at the age of 13. Higher up are grapes and wheat, symbols of the eucharist, and a sculpture of a hand and eye, symbols of divine providence. The left-hand Portal of Hope begins at the bottom with flora and fauna from the Nile; the Slaughter of the Innocents; the flight of the Holy Family into Egypt; Joseph, surrounded by his carpenter's tools, contemplating his son; and the marriage of Joseph and Mary. Above this is a sculpted boat with anchor (representing the church), piloted by St. Joseph assisted by the Holy Spirit. Overhead is a typical spire from the Montserrat massif. Gaudí intended these towers to house a system of tubular bells capable of playing more complex music than standard bell systems. The towers' peaks represent the apostles' successors in the form of miters, the official headdress of bishops of the Western church.

The **Passion facade** on the southwestern side, at the entrance to the grounds, is a dramatic contrast to the Nativity facade. Josep Maria Subirachs, the sculptor chosen in 1986 to execute Gaudí's plans—initially an atheist, and author of statements such as "God is one of man's greatest creations"—now confesses to a respectful agnosticism. Known for his distinctly angular, geometrical interpretations of the human form, Subirachs boasted that his work "has nothing to do with Gaudí." When in 1990 artists, architects, and religious leaders called for his resignation after he sculpted an anatomically complete naked Christ on the cross, Subirachs defended the piece as part of the stark realism of the scene he intended to portray. Subirachs pays double homage to Gaudí in the Passion facade: over the left side of the main entry is the blocky figure of Gaudí making notes or drawings, and the Roman soldiers are modeled on Gaudí's helmeted chimneys on the roof of La Pedrera.

Framed by leaning tibialike columns, the bones of the dead, the scenes begin at the left with the Last Supper. The faces of the disciples are contorted in confusion and dismay, especially that of Judas, who clutches a bag of money behind his back over the figure of a reclining hound (symbol of fidelity and foil to the perfidy of Judas). The next sculptural group represents the prayer in the Garden of Gethsemane and Peter awakening, followed by the kiss of Judas. The numerical cryptogram behind this contains 16 numbers that can be added 310 different ways for a total of 33, the age of Christ at his death.

In the center, Jesus is lashed to a pillar during his flagellation, a tear track carved into his expressive countenance. The column's top stone is off kilter, a reminder of the stone to be removed from Christ's sepulchre. The knot and broken reed at the base of the pillar symbolize Jesus' physical and psychological suffering. To the right of the door is a rooster, with Peter lamenting his third denial "before the cock crows" of Christ. Farther to the right are Pilate and Jesus with a crown of thorns, and just above, back on the left, is Simon of Cyrene helping Jesus with the cross after his first fall. Over the center, where Jesus consoles the women of Jerusalem ("Don't cry for me; cry for your children"), is a faceless Veronica—faceless because her story is considered apocryphal, holding the veil with which she wiped Christ's face, only to find his likeness miraculously imprinted upon it. To the left is a sculpture of Gaudí making notes, the evangelist in stone, and farther left the equestrian figure of a centurion piercing the side of the church with his spear, the church representing the body of Christ. Above are the soldiers rolling dice for Christ's clothing and the naked, crucified Christ. The moon to the right of the cross refers to the darkness at the moment of Christ's death and to the full moon of Easter; to the right are Peter and Mary at the sepulchre, the egg above Mary symbolizing the Resurrection. At Christ's feet is a figure with a furrowed brow, perhaps suggesting the agnostic's anguished search for certainty, thought to be a self-portrait of Subirachs characterized by the sculptor's giant hand and an "S" on his right arm. High above is a gold figure of the resurrected Christ.

Future of the project. Architect Jordi Bonet, director of the work on the Sagrada Família, predicts that the apse will be covered by 2007, in time to celebrate mass inside on March 19, the 125th anniversary of the laying of the first stone of a project initially instigated by a society dedicated to Saint Joseph. This covered apse will have space for 15,000 people and a choir loft for 1,500, and occupy an area large enough to encompass the entire Santa Maria del Mar basilica. ✉ *Mallorca 401, Eixample* ☎ *93/207–3031* ⊕ *www.sagradafamilia.org* 🎫 *€8, bell tower elevator €2.* ⏱ *Oct.–Mar., daily 9–6; Apr.–Sept., daily 9–8* Ⓜ *Sagrada Família.*

Upper Barcelona: Gràcia, Parc Güell, Pedralbes & Sarrià

Barcelona's upper reaches begin with Pedralbes, a neighborhood of graceful mansions grouped around a stunning Gothic monastery. Parc Güell is Gaudí's Art Nouveau urban garden. Sarrià and Gràcia were outlying villages swallowed up by the expanding metropolis. The Monestir de Pedralbes closes at 2, so start with Pedralbes and Sarrià, then visit Parc Güell and Gràcia. Tibidabo, with its amusement park and Norman Foster's Torre de Collserola should be considered only on an (increasingly unusual) unsmoggy day.

A GOOD TOUR

From the **Monestir de Pedralbes** ㉝ ➤, a 15-minute walk gets you to the main square of **Sarrià** ㉞. After exploring Sarrià, another 20-minute walk downhill through the Jardins de la Villa Amèlia leads past Gaudí's Finca Güell gate and gatehouse (now the Cátedra Gaudí research center) to the **Palau Reial de Pedralbes** ㉟, which, in turn, is a 10-minute walk downhill to the FC Barcelona soccer stadium. **Tibidabo** ㊱ has wonderful vistas on clear days, and the restaurant La Venta is a fine place for lunch in the sun. A truly fantastic photo op awaits at **Torre de Collserola** ㊲. Free transportation is provided to the tower from Plaza Tibidabo. Gaudí's **Parc Güell** ㊳ is most easily reached by taxi. While there, don't miss the **Casa-Museu Gaudí** ㊴. After the park, walk down through **Gràcia** ㊵ to **Casa Vicens** ㊶. Parc Güell and Tibidabo are best seen in mid- to late afternoon, when the sun backs around to the west and illuminates the Mediterranean.

TIMING If you do it all at once, this is a five- to six-hour outing. Add another two hours if you want to go up to the Collserola Tower.

What to See

㊶ **Casa Vicens.** Gaudí's first important commission as a young architect was built between 1883 and 1885, at which time he had not yet thrown away his architect's tools, particularly the T-square. The historical eclecticism of the early–Art Nouveau movement is evident in the Orientalist themes and Mudejar details lavished on the facade. The house was commissioned by a ceramics merchant, which may explain the eye-catching color ceramic tiles that render most of the facade a striking checkerboard—Barcelona's first example of this now-omnipresent technique. The palm leaves on the gate and surrounding fence have been attributed to Gaudí assistant, Francesc Berenguer, and the comic iron lizards and bats oozing off the facade are Gaudí's playful nod to the Gothic gargoyle. ✉ *Carrer de les Carolines 24–26, Gràcia.*

㊴ The **Casa-Museu Gaudí,** within Parc Güell, is in a pink, Alice-in-Wonderland house designed by Gaudí's assistant and right hand, Francesc

KEY

⬨ Metro Stops

▲ Start of Walk

Parc Güell

VALLCARCA

LESSEPS

FONTANA

MARIA
CRISTINA

PALAU REIAL

550 yds

500 meters

Upper Barcelona: Gràcia & Parc Güell, Pedralbes & Sarrià

Berenguer (1866–1914); this is where Gaudí lived with his niece from 1906 to 1926. Exhibits include Gaudí-designed furniture, decorations, drawings, portraits, and a bust of the architect. ✉ *Parc Güell, up hill to right of main entrance, Gràcia* ☎ *93/219–3811* 🎫 *€4* 🕐 *May–Sept., daily 10–8; Oct.–Feb., daily 10–6; Mar. and Apr., daily 10–7.*

⑩ Gràcia. Gràcia, as well as a neighborhood, is a state of mind, a virtual village republic that has periodically risen in rebellion against city, state, and country. The street names (Llibertat, Fraternitat, Progrès, Venus) reveal the ideological history of this nucleus of working-class sentiment. Barcelona's first collectivized manufacturing operations (i.e., factories) were clustered here—a dangerous precedent, as workers organized into radical groups ranging from anarchists to feminists to esperantists. Once an outlying town, Gràcia joined Barcelona only under duress and attempted to secede from the Spanish state in 1856, 1870, 1873, and 1909. Lying above the Diagonal from Carrer de Córsega up to Parc Güell, this jumble of streets is filled with appealing bars and restaurants, movie theaters, and outdoor cafés, usually thronged by hip couples. The August Festa Major fills the streets with the rank-and-file residents of this lively yet intimate little pocket of resistance to Organized Life.

From Parc Güell, dig out your city map and follow Carrer Larrard across Travessera de Dalt and down Carrer Torrent de les Flors through upper Gràcia to **Plaça Rovira i Trias,** where a bronze effigy of architect Antoni Rovira i Trias sits on a bench. Continue downhill and west to **Plaça de la Virreina** to see the work of Francesc Berenguer at Carrer del Or 44. (If Barcelona was Gaudí's sandbox, Gràcia was Berenguer's—nearly every major building in this neighborhood is his creation.) Cut over to **Plaça del Diamant** to see in bronze the heroine of Mercé Rodoreda's famous 1962 novel *La Plaça del Diamant.* Moving through Plaça Trilla, cross Gran de Gràcia to Carrer de les Carolines to see Gaudí's very first house, **Casa Vicens.**

Your next stop is the produce market **Mercat de la Llibertat,** an uptown Boqueria. Cut east along Cisne, cross Gran de Gràcia, and pass another Berenguer creation on Ros de Olano, the Mudejar-style **Centre Moral Instructiu de Gràcia. Plaça del Sol,** one of Gràcia's most popular squares, is downhill. From here, continue east to Gràcia's other market, the **Mercat de la Revolució.** Walk three blocks back over to Gràcia's main square, **Plaça Rius i Taulet,** with its emblematic clock tower. From Plaça Rius i Taulet, cut out to **Gran de Gràcia** for a look at some more Art Nouveau buildings by Berenguer (Nos. 15, 23, 35, 49, 51, 61, and 77). For lunch, consider Galician seafood at Botafumeiro, Basque fare at Ipar Txoko just below Plaça Rius i Taulet, or, near the bottom of Gràcia above Carrer Còrsega, the exquisite Jean Luc Figueras—a few steps from the Art Nouveau gem, **Casa Comalat.**

▶ **㉝ Monestir de Pedralbes.** One of Barcelona's hidden treasures, this monastery (in fact, a convent) was founded by Reina Elisenda, widow of Catalonia's Sovereign Count Jaume II, for Clarist nuns in 1326. The unusual, three-story Gothic cloister is the finest in Barcelona. The abess's day cell, the Capella de Sant Miquel, has famous murals painted in 1346 by Ferrer Bassa, a Catalan master much influenced by the Italian Renaissance.

Scratched into the painting, on the right side between Saints Francis and Clare, you can make out what is widely considered Barcelona's earliest graffito: *Joan no m'oblides* (John, don't forget me), proof that not all of the novotiates were there by their own choice. You can also visit the medieval living quarters and kitchen. Look for the ruts broken into the arcaded walkways by Napoléonic cannon during the 1809 French occupation. The museum shows religious paintings and artifacts collected over the centuries. ⊠ *Baixada Monestir 9, Pedralbes* ☎ *93/203–9282* ⊕ *www.museuhistoria.bcn.es* ▩ *€4; free 1st Sun. of month* ۞ *Oct.–May, Tues.–Sun. 10–2, June–Sept., Tues.–Sun. 10–5.* Ⓜ *Reina Elisenda.*

OFF THE
BEATEN
PATH

Ⓢ **COSMOCAIXA–MUSEU DE LA CIÈNCIA FUNDACIÓ "LA CAIXA"** – Young scientific minds work overtime in this ever-more-interactive science museum, just below Tibidabo. Among the many displays designed for children seven and up are the Geological Wall, a history of rocks and rock formations studied through a transversal cutaway section; and the Underwater Forest, showcasing the climate and species of an Amazonian rain forest in a large greenhouse. Expositions of sustainable exploitation techniques such as "The Red Line: How to Make Wood Without Damaging the Forest" are accompanied by explanations of environmental problems and how to correct them. ⊠ *Teodor Roviralta 55, Sant Gervasi* ☎ *93/212–6050* ⊕ *www.cosmocaixa.com* ▩ *€3 (€2 per interactive activity inside)* ۞ *Tues.–Sun. 10–8* Ⓜ *Avinguda de Tibidabo and Tramvía Blau halfway.*

6

❸❺ **Palau Reial de Pedralbes** (Royal Palace of Pedralbes). Built in the 1920s for King Alfonso XII, the palace houses the **Museu de Ceràmica,** covering Spanish ceramic art from its Moorish beginnings up through medieval work from Manises and Paterna to Talavera de la Reina and Puente del Arzobispo. Catalan tile work, porcelain from Alcora, and Picasso and Miró creations complete the exhibit. The **Museu de les Arts Decoratives** exhibits household and design objects from medieval times through the Industrial Revolution and Spanish civil war up to contemporary design. ⊠ *Av. Diagonal 686, Pedralbes* ☎ *93/280–5024 decorative arts museum, 93/280–1621 ceramic museum* ⊕ *www.museuceramica.bcn.es* ⊕ *www. museuartsdecoratives.bcn.es* ▩ *€4 includes both museums; free 1st Sun. of month* ۞ *Tues.–Sat. 10–6, Sun. 10–3* Ⓜ *Palau Reial.*

❸❽ **Parc Güell.** Güell Park is one of Gaudí's, and Barcelona's, most pleasant and stimulating places to spend a few hours; it's light and playful, alternately shady, green, floral, and sunny. Named for and commissioned by Gaudí's main patron, Count Eusebio Güell, the park was intended as a hillside garden suburb on the English model. Barcelona's bourgeoisie seemed happier living closer to "town," however, so only two of the houses were ever built. The Güell family eventually turned the land over to the city as a public park. Gaudí highlights include an Art Nouveau extravaganza with gingerbread gatehouses topped with a hallucinogenic red-and-white fly ammanite wild mushroom (rumored to have been a Gaudí favorite) on the right and a *phallus impudicus* mushroom (no translation necessary) on the left. The gatehouse on the right holds the **Center for the Interpretation and Welcome to Parc Güell,** with plans, scale models, photos, and suggested routes analyzing the park in detail. Other highlights include the ⇨ **Gaudí Casa–Museu** (the house where Gaudí lived with his niece for 20 years), the Room of a Hundred Columns—a covered market supported by tilted Doric-style columns and mosaic-encrusted buttresses, and guarded by a patchwork lizard—and the fabulous serpentine, polychrome bench that snakes along the main square. ✉ *Carrer d'Olot s/n; take Metro to Lesseps; then walk 10 mins uphill or catch Bus 24 to park entrance, Gràcia* ☉ *Oct.–Mar., daily 10–6; Apr.–June, daily 10–7; July–Sept., daily 10–9* Ⓜ *Lesseps.*

㉞ Sarrià. This 1,000-year-old village was once a cluster of farms and country houses overlooking Barcelona from the hills. Start at the main square, Plaça Sarrià, which holds an antiques market on Tuesday morning, a book market on Friday, occasional *sardana* dances on Sunday morning, and Christmas fairs in season. The Romanesque church tower, lighted a warm ocher at night, looms overhead. Across Passeig Reina Elisenda from the church, wander through the brick-and-steel **produce market** and the tiny **Plaça Sant Gaietà** behind it. Back in front of the church, cut through the Placeta del Roser to the left of the main door and you'll come to the elegant **town hall** in the Plaça de la Vila; note the buxom bronze sculpture of Pomona, goddess of fruit and the harvest, by famed Sarrià sculptor Josep Clarà (1878–1958). After a peek at the massive ceiling beams (and tempting set lunch menu) in the restaurant Vell Sarrià, at the corner of Major de Sarrià, go back to the Pomona bronze and turn left toward Carrer dels Paletes (with its tiny Sant Antoni, patron saint of workers, or *paletes,* overhead to the right). Back on Major de Sarrià, continue down this pedestrian-only street and turn left onto **Carrer Canet,** with its cottagelike artisans' quarters, formerly factory workers' housing provided by a nearby 19th-century textile mill. The house at No. 15 is an original two-story village house. No. 21 has unusual floral ornamentation on the facade, and No. 23 is a rustic village dwelling painted a characteristic earthy Mediterranean orange.

Turn right on Carrer Cornet i Mas and walk two blocks down to Carrer Jaume Piquet. A quick probe to the left will take you to No. 30, Barcelona's most perfect small-format **Moderniste house,** complete with faux-medieval upper windows, wrought-iron grillwork, floral and fruit ornamentation, and organically curved and carved wooden doors. Don't miss the restored wooden door at No. 9, or the Falangist eagle over the entrance of what was until 1976 the local telegraph office. Farther down at No. 15 is a fascist symbol left over from the 1951 Instituto Nacional de Vivienda (National Housing Institute). The tiny pink house down at No. 36 is another typical Sarrià village house. The next stop down Cornet i Mas is Sarrià's most picturesque square, **Plaça Sant Vicens,** a leafy space ringed by early village houses and centered on a statue of Sarrià's patron saint. Note the other renditions of the saint over the square's upper right corner. The café Can Pau is the local hangout, once a haven for such authors as Gabriel García Marquez and Mario Vargas Llosa, who lived in Sarrià in the early 1970s, on the cusp of their fame. Check out the Gouthier oyster-, salmon-, foie-, caviar-, and wine-tasting bar on the lower corner of the square. To get to the Monestir de Pedralbes from Plaça Sant Vicens, walk back up Mayor de Sarrià and through the market to the corner of Sagrat Cor and Ramon Miquel Planas; then turn left and walk straight west for 15 minutes, past the splendid upper-city mansions of Pedralbes. Other Sarrià landmarks include the two **Foix** pastry stores, one at Plaça Sarrià 9–10 and the other on Major de Sarrià 57, above Bar Tomás. Both have excellent pastries, artisanal breads, and cold *cava* sparkling white wine). The late J. V. Foix, son of the store's founders, was one of the great Catalan poets of the 20th century, a key player in keeping the Catalan language alive during the 40-year Franco regime. The store in Plaça Sarrià, a good place for homemade ice cream, has a bronze bust of the poet, and the Major de Sarrià shop has a plaque identifying the house with one of the poet's most memorable verses: *Tota amor és latent en l'altra amor / tot llenguatge és saó d'una parla comuna / tota terra batega a la pàtria de tots / tota fe serà suc d'una mes alta fe.* (Every love is latent in the other love / every language is part of a common tongue / every country touches the fatherland of all / every faith will be the lifeblood of a higher faith.) ⊠ *Pl. Sarrià; take Bus 22 from bottom of Av. de Tibidabo, or U-6 train on FFCC subway to Reina Elisenda Sarrià.*

NEED A BREAK? **Bar Tomás** (⊠ Major de Sarrià 49, Sarrià ☎ 93/203–1077 Ⓜ Sarrià), on the corner of Jaume Piquet, is a Barcelona institution, home of the finest potatoes in town. Order the *doble mixta* of potatoes with *allioli* (garlic and olive oil) and a splash of fiery hot sauce. Draft beer (ask for a *caña*) is the de rigueur drink.

6

🟤**36** **Tibidabo.** When the wind blows the smog out to sea, the views from this hill are legendary, particularly from the 850-foot communications tower, Torre de Collserola. There's not much to see here except the vista, particularly from the tower. Clear days are few and far between in 21st-century Barcelona, but if (and only if) you hit one, this excursion is worth considering. The restaurant **La Venta,** at the base of the funicular, is excellent, a fine place to sit in the sun in cool weather (the establishment provides straw sun hats). The bar **Mirablau** is a popular hangout for evening drinks. ⊠ *Take Tibidabo train (U-7) from Pl. de Catalunya or buses 24 and 22 to Pl. Kennedy. At Av. Tibidabo, catch Tramvía Blau (Blue Trolley), which connects with funicular to summit* Ⓜ *Tibidabo.*

🟤**37** **Torre de Collserola.** The creation of Norman Foster, the Collserola Tower was erected for the 1992 Olympics amid controversy over defacement of the traditional mountain skyline. It's now considered the best piece of architecture in the city's upper reaches. ⊠ *Av. de Vallvidrera. Take the funicular up to Tibidabo; from Pl. Tibidabo there is free transport to the tower.* ☎ *93/406–9354* ⊕ *www.torredecollserola.com* 🎫 *€5.50* 🕐 *Wed.–Fri. 11–2:30 and 3:30–6, weekends 11–6* Ⓜ *Tibidabo.*

Sant Pere, La Ribera, La Ciutadella & Barceloneta

Barcelona's old textile neighborhood, around the church of Sant Pere, includes the flagship of the city's Moderniste architecture, the Palau de la Música Catalana. Barceloneta, once the open sea, silted in and became a salt marsh until 1753, when French military engineer Prosper de Verboom designed a housing project for families who had lost their homes in *La Ribera.* Together, these areas form a good walk within and around what were once Barcelona's 13th-century walls.

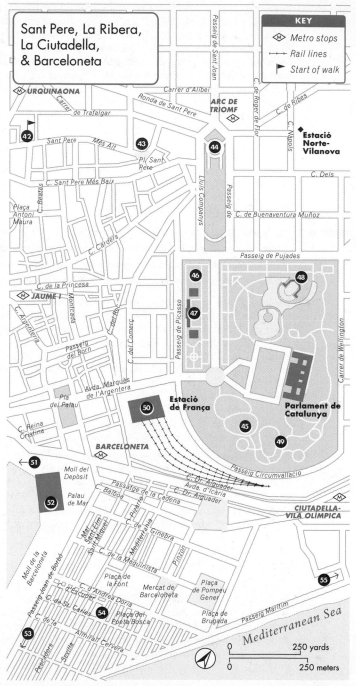

Sant Pere, La Ribera,
La Ciutadella,
& Barceloneta

KEY

Ⓜ *Metro stops*

⊢⊣⊢⊣ *Rail lines*

▶ *Start of walk*

A GOOD WALK

These neighborhoods northeast of the Gothic Quarter begin with the **Palau de la Música Catalana** ㊷ ⚑, a 10-minute walk from Plaça Catalunya. After the Palau, continue along Carrer Sant Pere Més Alt past the church of **Sant Pere de les Puelles** ㊸ and out to the **Arc del Triomf** ㊹, on Passeig de Sant Joan. From there, walk through the **Parc de la Ciutadella** ㊺, past the **Castell dels Tres Dragons** ㊻, the **Museu de la Geologia** ㊼, and the **La Cascada** ㊽ (a waterfall with rocks, by a young architecture student named Antoni Gaudí). The Barcelona **Zoo** ㊾ has dolphins, rhinos, and an albino gorilla. Leaving the zoo, pass the **Estació de França** ㊿, and continue on to the edge of **Port Vell** (51) next to the Palau de Mar. For a look at Catalonia's version (for once) of its own history, check out the interactive **Museu d'Història de Catalunya** (52). Then walk around the port to the **El Transbordador Aeri del Port** (53) for a ride over the harbor, or walk through **Barceloneta** (54) and along the beach to the **Port Olímpic** (55).

TIMING Depending on the number of stops, this walk can take a full day. Count on at least four hours of actual walking time.

What to See

㊹ **Arc del Triomf.** This imposing, exposed-redbrick arch on Passeig de Sant Joan was built by Josep Vilaseca as the grand entrance for the Universal Exposition of 1888. Similar in size and sense to the triumphal arches of ancient Rome, this one refers to Jaume I El Conqueridor's 1229 conquest of the Moors in Mallorca—as suggested by the bats, always part of Jaume I's coat of arms, on either side of the arch.

(54) **Barceloneta.** Once Barcelona's pungent fishing port, Barceloneta retains much of its maritime flavor. It's an exciting and colorful walk through narrow streets with lines of laundry snapping in the breeze. Stop in Plaça de la Barceloneta to see the baroque church of **Sant Miquel del Port,** with its oversize sculpture of the winged archangel himself. Look for the Barceloneta market and the restaurant Can Ramonet on Carrer de la Maquinista, and for the original two-story houses and the restaurant Can Solé on Carrer Sant Carles. Barceloneta's **beach,** though overcrowded in midsummer, offers swimming, surfing, and a lively social scene from late May through September.

NEED A BREAK?

Friendly Can Manel la Puda (☎ 93/221-5013), at Passeig de Joan de Borbó 60-61 in Barceloneta, is always good for an inexpensive feast in the sun. Serving lunch until 4 and starting dinner at 7, it's a popular place for *suquets* (fish stew), paella, and *arròs a banda* (rice with de-shelled seafood). It's closed Monday, and they accept all major plastic. On Monday or if Can Manel is booked solid, La Mar Salada next door is just as good.

㊻ **Castell dels Tres Dragons** (Castle of the Three Dragons). Built by Domènech i Montaner as a restaurant for the Universal Exposition of 1888, this arresting structure was named in honor of a popular mid-19th-century comedy by the father of the Catalan theater, Serafí Pitarra. Greeting you on the right as you enter the Ciutadella from Passeig Lluí Companys, the building has exposed brickwork and visible iron supports, both radical innovations of their time. Moderniste architects later met here to exchange ideas and experiment with traditional crafts; the castle now holds Barcelona's **Museum of Zoology.** ✉ *Passeig Picasso 5, La Ciu-tadella* ☎ *93/319–6912* ⊕ *www.bcn.es/medciencies* 💳 *€3.75* ⊙ *Tues., Wed., Fri., Sat., and Sun. 10–2:30, Thurs. 10–6:30* Ⓜ *Arc de Triomf.*

❸ El Transbordador Aeri del Port (cable car). The cable car leaving from the tower at the end of Passeig Joan de Borbócan connects the Torre de San Sebastián on the Moll de Barceloneta, the tower of Jaime I in the boat terminal, and the Torre de Miramar on Montjuïc. The Torre de Altamar restaurant in the tower at the Barceloneta end serves excellent food and wine along with nonpareil views. ✉ *Passeig Joan de Borbó s/n, Barceloneta* ☎ *93/225–2718* 💳 *€9 round-trip, €7.50 one-way* ⊙ *Daily 10:45–7* Ⓜ *Barceloneta.*

❺⓪ Estació de França. Once Barcelona's main train station, the gracefully re-stored Estació de França is outside the west gate of the Ciutadella. Wander in for a rush of European railroad nostalgia. ✉ *Marquès de l'Argentera s/n, Born-Ribera* Ⓜ *Barceloneta.*

❹❽ La Cascada. Take a break by this lake, and, behind it, the monumental *Cascada,* by Josep Fontseré, designed for the Universal Exposition of 1888. The waterfall's rocks were the work of a young architecture stu-dent named Antoni Gaudí—his first public works, appropriately natu-ral and organic, a hint of things to come. ✉ *La Ciutadella* Ⓜ *Arc de Triomf, Ciutadella.*

❹❼ Museu de la Geologia. The Museum of Geology is next to the Castell dels Tres Dragons and the Umbracle, the black slats of which help create jun-gle lighting for a valuable collection of tropical plants. Barcelona's first public museum, it has rocks, minerals, and fossils from Catalonia and the rest of Spain. ✉ *Off Passeig de Picasso, La Ciutadella* ☎ *93/319–6895* ⊕ *www.bcn.es/museuciencies* 💳 *€3.50; free 1st Sun. of month* ⊙ *Tues., Wed., Fri., Sat., and Sun. 10–2, Thurs. 10–6:30* Ⓜ *Arc de Tri-omf, Ciutadella.*

❺❷ Museu d'Història de Catalunya. Built into what used to be a port ware-house, this state-of-the-art interactive museum makes you part of Cat-alonian history from prehistoric times through more than 3,000 years and into the contemporary democratic era. Explanations of the exhibits appear in Catalan, Castilian, and English. Guided tours are available on Sunday at noon and 1 PM. The rooftop cafeteria, open to the general pub-lic, has excellent views over the harbor. ✉ *Pl. Pau Vila 3, Barceloneta* ☎ *93/225–4700* ⊕ *www.mhcat.net* 💳 *€3.50; free 1st Sun. of month* ⊙ *Tues. and Thurs.–Sat. 10–7, Wed. 10–8, Sun. 10–2:30* Ⓜ *Barceloneta.*

▶ ❹❷ Palau de la Música Catalana. A riot of color and form, Barcelona's Music Palace is the flagship of the city's Moderniste architecture. Designed by Lluís Domènech i Montaner in 1908, it was originally conceived by the Orfeó Català musical society as a vindication of the importance of music at a popular level—as opposed to the Liceu opera house's iden-tification with the Catalan (often Castilian-speaking monarchist) aris-tocracy. The Palau's exterior is remarkable in itself, albeit hard to see because there's no room to back up and behold it. Above the main en-trance are busts of Palestrina, Bach, Beethoven, and (around the corner on Carrer Amadeu Vives) Wagner. Look for the colorful mosaic pillars

CLOSE UP

Moderniste Barcelona

CHARACTERIZED BY INTENSE ORNAMENTATION and the use of natural or organic lines and forms, Modernisme (Art Nouveau) swept Europe between 1880 and 1914, though nowhere did it proliferate as it did in Barcelona, beginning with the Universal Exposition of 1888. Here it tapped into the playful Catalan artistic impulse (as evidenced in the works of Gaudí) because it coincided with Barcelona's late-19th-century industrial prosperity and the resulting surge in regional ebulliance, and because the post-1860 Eixample neighborhood was in the process of being built by a rich bourgeoisie eager to outshine each other with opulent mansions.

A cultural movement that went beyond architecture, Barcelona's Modernisme affected the design of everything from clothes to hairstyles to tombstones. Painters such as Ramón Casas and Santiago Russinyol, sculptors such as Miquel Blay and Eusebi Arnau, stained-glass artisans, ceramicists, acid engravers, and wood-carvers all played a part in the explosion of artistic exuberance.

The curved line replaced the straight; natural elements such as flowers and fruits were sculpted into facades; and the classical and pragmatic gave way to decorative excess. Barcelona's Palau de la Música Catalana by Lluís Domènech i Montaner, the flagship of the movement, is a stunning compendium of Art Nouveau decorative techniques, including acid-etched glass and stained glass, polychrome ceramic ornamentation, carved wooden arches, and sculptures. Antoni Gaudí is the most famous of the Moderniste architects.

Josep Puig i Cadafalch's Casa Amatller and Casa de les Punxes are examples of Modernisme's eclectic, historical tendencies. Josep Graner i Prat's Casa de la Papallona, Joan Rubió Bellver's Casa Golferichs, Gaudí's Casa Batlló, and Salvador Valeri i Pupurull's Casa Comalat are Moderniste mansions that make Barcelona's Eixample a living architecture museum.

The Ruta del Modernisme is an itinerary through the Barcelona of Gaudí, Domènech i Montaner, and Puig i Cadafalch, the architects who, along with others, made Barcelona the world capital of Modernisme in the late 19th and early 20th centuries: palaces, private houses, the temple that has become a symbol of the city, and a huge hospital join pharmacies, lampposts, and benches—115 works in all—tracing Art Nouveau's explosion in Barcelona.

There are three Modernisme Centers (☎ 902/076621), which sell items related to the route, including a route pack with discount vouchers, a map showing all 115 works, a guide to Moderniste bars and restaurants, a pencil, a notebook, and a bag in which to carry it all. The *Modernisme Route* guidebook—the most comprehensive Modernisme study in Barcelona—is available for €12 in most local bookstores and at all three Modernisme Centers. It offers discount vouchers good for up to 50% on all Moderniste monuments in the city and in another 13 towns.

6

RECOMMENDED MODERNISTE MONUMENTS

- Casa Amatller
- Casa Batlló
- Casa Calvet
- Casa Comalat
- Casa de les Punxes
- Casa Lleó Morera
- Casa Milà, la Pedrera
- Casa Fuster
- Casa Macaya
- Casa Planells
- Casa Terrades
- Casa Thomas
- Casa Vicens
- Conservatori Municipal de Música

- CosmoCaixa, Museu de la Ciència
- Hidroelèctrica
- Hospital de la Santa Creu i Sant Pau
- MNAC
- Museu de Zoologia
- Observatori Fabra
- Palau Güell
- Palau de la Música Catalana
- Palau del Baró de Quadras
- Palau Montaner
- Pavellons Güell
- Temple Expiatori de la Sagrada Família
- Torre Bellesguard

on the second upper level, a preview of what's inside. The Miquel Blay sculptural group over the corner of Sant Pere Més Alt and Amadeu Vives depicts everyone from St. George the dragon slayer (at the top) to fishermen with oars over their shoulders.

The interior is an uproar. Wagnerian cavalry erupts from the right side of the stage over a heavy-browed bust of Beethoven, and Catalonia's popular music is represented by the flowing maidens of Lluís Millet's song *Flors de Maig* (*Flowers of May*) on the left. Overhead, an inverted stained-glass cupola seems to offer the divine manna of music; painted rosettes and giant peacock feathers explode from the tops of the walls. Even the stage is populated with muselike Art Nouveau musicians, each half bust, half mosaic. The visuals alone make music sound different in here, and at any important concert the excitement is palpably thick. If you can't attend one, take a tour of the hall. *Ticket office ⊠ Sant Francesc de Paula 2, just off Via Laietana, around corner from hall, Sant Pere* ☎ *902–442–882* ⊕ *www.palaumusica.org* ⊠ *Tour €8* ☉ *Tours daily 10–3:30, 10–7 July and Aug.* Ⓜ *Catalunya.*

Ⓒ ㊺ **Parc de la Ciutadella** (Citadel Park). Once a fortress designed to consolidate Madrid's military occupation of Barcelona, the Ciutadella is now the city's main downtown park. The clearing dates from shortly after the War of the Spanish Succession, when Felipe V demolished some 2,000 houses in what was then the Barri de la Ribera (waterfront neighborhood) to build a fortress and barracks for his soldiers and fields of fire for his artillery. The fortress walls were pulled down in 1868 and replaced by gardens laid out by Josep Fontserè. Within the park are a cluster of museums, the Catalan parliament, and the city zoo.

⑤ Port Olímpic. Choked with yachts, restaurants, and tapas bars of all kinds, the Olympic Port is 2 km (1 mi) up the beach, marked by the mammoth Frank Gehry goldfish sculpture in front of Barcelona's first real skyscraper, the Hotel Arts. The port rages on Friday and Saturday night, especially in summer, with hundreds of young people circling and grazing until daybreak. Ⓜ *Ciutadella, Vila Olimpica.*

⑤ Port Vell (Old Port). From Pla del Palau, cross to the edge of the port, where the Moll d'Espanya, the Moll de la Fusta, and the Moll de Barceloneta meet. Just beyond the Lichtenstein sculpture *Barcelona Head,* in front of the post office, the modern Port Vell complex stretches up the grassy hill to the wood-panel *Ictineo II* reproduction of the submarine created by Narcis Monturiol (1819–85)—the world's first, launched in the Barcelona port in 1862. Beyond are the IMAX theater, the aquarium, and the Maremagnum shopping mall along the Moll d'Espanya. The Moll de Barceloneta, with its five (somewhat pricey and impersonal) quayside terrace restaurants, stretches along the sport marina across the way. Ⓜ *Barceloneta.*

④③ Sant Pere de les Puelles (St. Peter of the Novices). One of the oldest medieval churches in Barcelona, this one has been destroyed and restored so many times that there's little left to see except the beautiful stained-glass window, which illuminates the stark interior. *Puelles* comes from the Latin *puella* (girl)—the convent here was known for the beauty and nobility of its young women. ✉ *Lluís El Piadós 1, Sant Pere* ☎ *93/268–0742* ⊙ *Open for mass only* Ⓜ *Catalunya, Jaume I.*

④⑨ Zoo. Barcelona's zoo (said to be moving out of town, at least partially) occupies the bottom part of the Parc de la Ciutadella. Reptiles, and a full complement of African animals reside in this colony squeezed in between the Catalan Parliament and the Universidad Pompeu Fabra. Look for the statue of *La Senyoreta del Paraigua* (Lady with Umbrella) near the dolphins. ✉ *La Ciutadella* ☎ *93/225–6780* ⊕ *www.zoobarcelona. com* 🎟 *€14* ⊙ *Daily 10–7* Ⓜ *Arc de Triomf, Ciutadella.*

Montjuïc

This hill to the south of town may have been named for the Jewish cemetery once on its slopes, though an alternate explanation has it named for the Roman deity Jove, or Jupiter. The most dramatic approach is by way of the cross-harbor cable car from Barceloneta or from the mid-station in the port; but Montjuïc is normally accessed by taxi or Bus 61 (or on foot) from Plaça Espanya, or by the funicular that operates from the Paral.lel. Ⓜ *Paral.lel.*

◼ A GOOD WALK
Walking from sight to sight on Montjuïc is possible but not recommended. You'll want fresh feet to see the sights here, especially the Romanesque art in the Palau Nacional and the Miró Foundation.

The *El Transbordador Aeri del Port* cable car drops you at the Jardins de Miramar, a 10-minute walk from the Plaça de Dante. From here, another small cable car takes you up to the **Castell de Montjuïc ⑤⑥** ▶. From

6

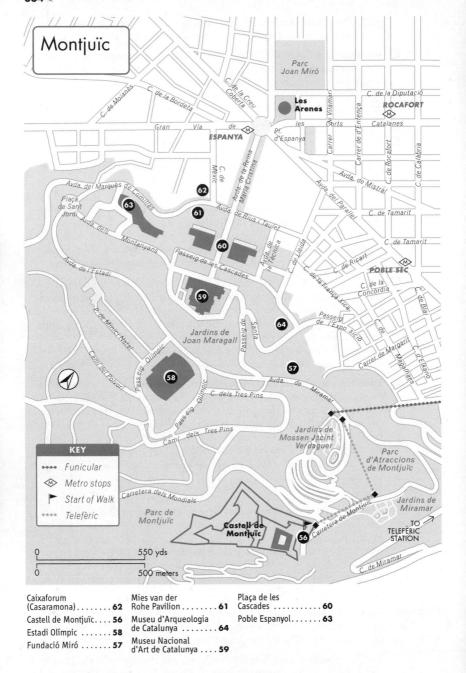

Montjuïc

Parc
Joan Miró

Les
Arenes

ROCAFORT

ESPANYA

Pr.
d'Espanya

POBLE SEC

62

63

61

60

59

64

57

Jardins de
Joan Maragall

58

Jardins de
Mossen Jacint
Verdaguer

Parc
d'Atraccions
de Montjuïc

Jardins de
Miramar

KEY

◆◆◆◆ Funicular
Ⓜ Metro stops
▶ Start of Walk
◆◆◆◆ Telefèric

Parc de
Montjuïc

Castell de
Montjuïc

56

TO
TELEFÈRIC
STATION

0 _____ 550 yds
0 _____ 500 meters

the bottom station, the **Fundació Miró** ⑤⑦ is a few minutes' walk, and beyond it is the **Estadi Olímpic** ⑤⑧. From the stadium, walk straight down to the Palau Nacional and its **Museu Nacional d'Art de Catalunya** ⑤⑨. From here, a wide stairway leads down toward Barcelona's convention fairgrounds; the Plaça de Espanya, behind the so-called Venetian Towers, was built as the grand entrance to Barcelona's 1929 World's Fair. As you descend this stairway past the **Plaça de les Cascades** ⑥⓪, the **Mies van der Rohe Pavilion** ⑥① is on your left, and across the street is Casaramona (1913), now the **CaixaForum** ⑥②. Uphill to the left is **Poble Espanyol** ⑥③, a miniature-scale sampling of architecture from all over Spain, and the **Museu d'Arqueologia de Catalunya** ⑥④ is around to the right of the stairs.

TIMING   With unhurried visits to the Miró Foundation and the Romanesque exhibit in the Palau Nacional, this is a four- to five-hour excursion. Have lunch afterward in the Poble Espanyol.

What to See

⑥② **Caixaforum** (Casaramona). Built by architect Josep Puig i Cadafalchto in 1911 to house a textile factory, this redbrick Art Nouveau fortress opened in early 2002 as a center for art exhibits, concerts, lectures, and other cultural events. Casaramona has come back to life as one of Barcelona's hottest new art venues. The contemporary entryway was designed by Arata Isozaki, architect of the nearby Palau Sant Jordi. ⊠ *Av. Marquès de Comillas 6–8, Montjuïc* ☏ *93/476–8600* ⊕ *www.fundacio. lacaixa.es* ⊠ *Free; charge for evening concerts* ⊙ *Tues.–Sun. 10–8; later for concerts.*

▶ ⑤⑥ **Castell de Montjuïc.** Built in 1640 by rebels against Felipe IV, the castle has been stormed several times, most famously in 1705 by Lord Peterborough for Archduke Carlos of Austria. In 1808, during the Peninsular War, it was seized by the French under General Dufresne. During an 1842 civil disturbance, Barcelona was bombed from its heights by a Spanish artillery battery. The moat has lush green gardens, with one side given over to an archery range, and the terraces have views of the city and the sea. ⊠ *Ctra. de Montjuïc 66, Montjuïc* ☏ *93/329–8613* ⊡ *€3* ⊙ *Tues.–Sun. 9:30–8.*

⑤⑧ **Estadi Olímpic.** The Olympic Stadium was originally built for the International Exposition of 1929, with the idea that Barcelona would then be the site of the 1936 Olympics (ultimately staged in Hitler's Berlin). After failing twice, Barcelona celebrated the attainment of its long-cherished goal by renovating the semi-derelict stadium in time for 1992, providing seating for 70,000. The **Galeria Olímpica,** a museum about the Olympic movement in Barcelona, displays objects and shows audiovisual replays from the 1992 games. An information center traces the history of the modern Olympics from Athens in 1896 to the present. Next door and just downhill stands the futuristic **Palau Sant Jordi Sports Palace,** designed by the noted Japanese architect Arata Isozaki. The Isozaki structure has no pillars or beams to obstruct the view. The roof was built first, then hydraulically lifted into place. ⊠ *Passeig Olímpic 17–19, Montjuïc* ☏ *93/426–0660* ⊕ *www.fundaciobarcelonaolimpica.es* ⊡ *€3 gallery* ⊙ *Tues.–Sat. 10–2 and 4–7.*

6

★ ⑤ **Fundació Miró.** The Miró Foundation was a gift from the artist Joan Miró to his native city and is one of Barcelona's most exciting showcases of contemporary art. The airy, white building was designed by Josep Lluís Sert and opened in 1975; an extension was added by Sert's pupil Jaume Freixa in 1988. Miró's unmistakably playful and colorful style, filled with Mediterranean light and humor, seems a perfect match for its surroundings, and the exhibits and retrospectives that open here tend to be progressive and provocative, from Moore to Mapplethorpe. Look for Alexander Calder's mercury fountain. Miró himself rests in the cemetery on Montjuïc's southern slopes. During the Franco regime, which he strongly opposed, Miró first lived in self-imposed exile in Paris, then moved to Majorca in 1956. When he died in 1983, the Catalans gave him a send-off amounting to a state funeral. ⊠ *Av. Miramar 71, Montjuïc* ☎ *93/443–9470* ⊕ *www.bcn.fjmiro.es* ☒ *€7.50* ⊙ *Tues., Wed., Fri., and Sat. 10–7, Thurs. 10–9:30, Sun. 10–2:30.*

⑥ **Mies van der Rohe Pavilion.** The reconstructed Mies van der Rohe Pavilion—the German contribution to the International Exposition of 1929, reassembled between 1983 and 1986—is a "less is more" study in interlocking planes of white marble, green onyx, and glass: the aesthetic opposite of the Moderniste Palau de la Música. ⊠ *Av. Marquès de Comillas s/n, Montjuïc* ☎ *93/423–4016* ⊕ *www.miesbcn.com* ☒ *€3.50* ⊙ *Daily 10–8.*

⑥ **Museu d'Arqueologia de Catalunya.** Just downhill to the right of the Palau Nacional, the Museum of Archaeology holds important finds from the Greek ruins at Empúries, on the Costa Brava. These are shown alongside fascinating objects from, and explanations of, Megalithic Spain. ⊠ *Passeig Santa Madrona 39–41, Montjuïc* ☎ *93/424–6577* ⊕ *www.mac.es* ☒ *€2.50* ⊙ *Tues.–Sat. 9:30–7, Sun. 10–2:30.*

⑤ **Museu Nacional d'Art de Catalunya** (MNAC; Catalonian National Museum
Fodor'sChoice of Art). Housed in the imposingly domed, towered, frescoed, and columned
★ **Palau Nacional,** built in 1929 as the centerpiece of the World's Fair, this superb museum was renovated in 1995 by Gae Aulenti, architect of the Musée d'Orsay in Paris. In 2004 the museum's three collections—Romanesque, Gothic, and the Cambó Collection, an eclectic trove, were joined by the 19th- and 20th-century collection of Catalan impressionist and Moderniste painters. Also now on display is the Thyssen-Bornemisza collection of early masters, with works by Zurbarán, Rubens, Tintoretto, Velázquez, and others. With this influx of artistic treasure, the MNAC becomes Catalonia's grand central museum. Pride of place goes to the Romanesque exhibition, the world's finest collection of Romanesque frescoes, altarpieces, and wood carvings, most of them rescued from chapels in the Pyrenees during the 1920s to save them from deterioration, theft, and art dealers. Many, such as the famous *Cristo de Taüll* fresco (from the church of Sant Climent de Taüll in Taüll), have been reproduced and replaced in their original settings. ⊠ *Mirador del Palau 6, Montjuïc* ☎ *93/622–0375* ⊕ *www.mnac.es* ☒ *€9* ⊙ *Tues.–Sat. 10–7, Sun. 10–2:30.*

⑥ **Plaça de les Cascades.** At night near the Mies van der Rohe Pavilion is a multicolor fountain in the Plaça de les Cascades. For a scenic stroll, meander down the esplanade past the exhibition halls, to the large and frenetic **Plaça d'Espanya.** Across the square is Les Arenes bullring, no longer used for bullfights, its neo-Mudéjar facade of exposed brick horseshoe arches containing an ultramodern shopping, leisure, and performance complex. From here, you can take the metro or Bus 38 back to the Plaça de Catalunya.

🖐 ㉓ **Poble Espanyol.** The Spanish Village was created for the International Exposition of 1929. A sort of artificial Spain-in-a-bottle, with reproductions of Spain's architectural styles, it takes you from the walls of Ávila to the wine cellars of Jerez de la Frontera amid shops, houses, and crafts workshops en route. The liveliest time to come is at night, and a reservation at one of the half-dozen restaurants gets you in free, as does the purchase of a ticket for the two discos or the Tablao del Carmen flamenco club. ✉ *Av. Marquès de Comillas s/n* ☎ *93/508–6300* ⊕ *www.poble-espanyol. com* ✉ *€7.50* ⊙ *Mon. 9–8, Tues.–Thurs. 9–2, Sat. 9–4, Sun. 9–noon.*

BEACHES

Ever since Barcelona revamped its beaches for the 1992 Olympics, the summer beach scene has been multitudinous. Five kilometers (3 mi) of beaches now run from the Platja (beach) de Sant Sebastià, a nudist enclave, northward through the Barceloneta, Port Olímpic, Nova Icària, Bogatell, Mar Bella, Nova Mar Bella, and Novíssima Mar Bella beaches to the Fòrum complex and the rocky Illa Pangea swimming area. Next to the mouth of the Besòs River is Platja Nova. Topless bathing is common. The beaches immediately north of Barcelona include Montgat, Ocata, Vilasar de Mar, Arenys de Mar, Canet, and Sant Pol de Mar, all accessible by train from the RENFE station in Plaça de Catalunya. Especially worthy is **Sant Pol,** with clean sand and a handsome old part of town and Carme Ruscalleda's famous **Sant Pau,** one of the top three restaurants in Catalonia. The farther north you go, toward the Costa Brava, the better the beaches. Ten kilometers (6 mi) south is **Castelldefels,** with a long, sandy beach and a series of bars and restaurants. A 15-minute train ride from Passeig de Gràcia's (or Plaça de Catalunya's) RENFE station to Gavà or Castelldefels deposits you on a 10-km-long (6-mi-long) beach for a (usually) windy walk in the sand. From October to March the sun sets into the Mediterranean here, thanks to the westward slant of the coastline. There are several good places for lamb chops, *calçots* (spring onions), and paella; the best, **Can Patricio,** (✉ Passeig Maritim 59 ☎ 93/665–1347) serves lunch until 4:30. **Sitges,** another 25 minutes south, has better sand and clearer water.

BARS & CAFÉS

Barcelona may have more bars and cafés per capita than any other place in the world. Here you can find a wide selection of colorful tapas places, sunny outdoor cafés, tearooms, chocolaterias, and, of course, *coctelerías* (cocktail bars), *whiskerias* (often singles bars filled with professional escorts), *xampanyerias* (serving champagne and cava, Catalan sparkling wine), and beer halls. Most stay open until about 2:30 AM.

6

Cafés

Café de l'Opera. Opposite the opera house, this high-ceiling Art Nouveau space has welcomed operagoers and performers for more than 100 years. For locals, it's a central point on the Rambla traffic pattern. ⊠ *La Rambla 74, Rambla* ☎ *93/317–7585* ☉ *Daily 9:30 AM–2:15 AM* Ⓜ *Liceu.*

Café Paris. This café is a lively place to kill time. Everyone from Prince Felipe, heir to the Spanish throne, to poet and pundit James Townsend Pi Sunyer can be spotted here in season. The tapas are excellent, the beer is cold, and the place is open 365 days a year. ⊠ *C. Aribau 184, at Carrer Paris, Eixample* ☎ *93/209–8530* ☉ *Daily 8 AM–2:30 AM* Ⓜ *Provença.*

Café Viena. The rectangular perimeter of this inside bar is always packed with travelers in a party mood. The pianist upstairs lends a cabaret touch. ⊠ *La Rambla dels Estudis 115, Rambla* ☎ *93/349–9800* ☉ *Daily 8 AM–2:30 AM* Ⓜ *Catalunya.*

Café Zurich. Ever of key importance to Barcelona society, this classic spot at the top of the Rambla is the city's prime meeting place. The outdoor tables offer peerless people-watching; the elegant interior has a high ceiling. ⊠ *Pl. de Catalunya 1, Rambla* ☎ *93/317–9153* ☉ *Daily 8 AM–2:30 AM* Ⓜ *Catalunya.*

Els Quatre Gats. Picasso staged his first exhibition here, in 1899, and Gaudí and the Catalan impressionist painters Ramón Casas and Santiago Russinyol held meetings of their Centre Artistic de Sant Lluc in the early 20th century. The restaurant is undistinguished, but the café is a good place to read and people-watch. ⊠ *Montsió 3, Barri Gòtic* ☎ *93/302–4140* ☉ *Daily 8 AM–2:30 AM* Ⓜ *Catalunya.*

Espai Barroc. Filled with baroque embellishments and music, this unusual "space" *(espai)* is on Carrer Montcada's most beautiful patio, the 15th-century Palau Dalmases. The stairway, with a bas-relief of the rape of Europa, leads up to the Omnium Cultural, a center for the study and diffusion of Catalan history and culture. The patio merits a look even if you find the café too lugubrious. ⊠ *Carrer Montcada 20, La Ribera* ☎ *93/310–0673* ☉ *Tues.–Sat. 8 PM–midnight* Ⓜ *Jaume I.*

La Bodegueta. If you can find this dive, you can also find a cluttered space with a dozen small tables, a few places at the marble counter, and happy couples having coffee or beer—and maybe some ham or *tortilla española de patatas* (a typically Spanish, omeletlike potato-and-onion delicacy). ⊠ *La Rambla de Catalunya 100, Eixample* ☎ *93/215–4894* ☉ *Daily 8 AM–1 AM* Ⓜ *Provença.*

Schilling. Near Plaça Reial, Schilling is always packed. Have coffee by day, drinks and tapas by night. ⊠ *Ferran 23, Barri Gòtic* ☎ *93/317–6787* ☉ *Daily 10 AM–2:30 AM* Ⓜ *Catalunya, Liceu.*

Travel Bar. With entrances on Carrer de la Boqueria and Placeta del Pi, and tables in the shady square behind Sant Maria del Pi, this hot spot for young travelers offers everything from Internet access to walking tours. ⊠ *Boqueria 27, Barri Gòtic* ☎ *93/342–5252* ☉ *Daily 8 AM–2:30 AM* Ⓜ *Catalunya, Liceu.*

Coctelerías

Almirall. This Moderniste bar in the Raval is quiet, dimly lighted, and dominated by an Art Nouveau mirror and frame behind the marble bar. It's an evocative spot, romantic and mischievous. ✉ *Joaquín Costa 33, Raval* ☎ *93/302–4126* ◷ *Daily 11* AM*–2:30* AM Ⓜ *Catalunya, Liceu, Sant Antoni.*

Boadas. A small, rather formal saloon near the top of the Rambla, Boadas is emblematic of the Barcelona *coctelería* concept, which usually entails a mixture of decorum and expensive mixed drinks amid wood and leather. ✉ *Tallers 1, Rambla* ☎ *93/318–9592* ◷ *Daily 11* AM*–2:30* AM Ⓜ *Catalunya.*

Dry Martini Bar. The eponymous specialty is the best bet at this spot, which exudes a kind of genteel wickedness. This seems to be a popular hangout for mature romantics, husbands, and wives, though not necessarily each other's. The speakeasy restaurant through the kitchen is excellent, too. ✉ *Aribau 162, Eixample* ☎ *93/217–5072* ◷ *Daily 11* AM*–2:30* AM Ⓜ *Provença.*

El Born. This former codfish emporium is now a charming and intimate haven for drinks, raclettes, and fondues. The marble cod basins in the entry and the spiral staircase to the second floor are the quirkiest details. ✉ *Passeig del Born 26, La Ribera* ☎ *93/319–5333* ◷ *Daily 7* PM*–2:30* AM Ⓜ *Jaume I.*

El Copetín. Right on Barcelona's best-known cocktail avenue, this bar has good cocktails and Irish coffee. Dimly lighted, it has a romantic South Seas motif. ✉ *Passeig del Born 19, La Ribera* ☎ *93/317–7585* ◷ *Daily 7* PM*–2:30* AM Ⓜ *Jaume I.*

El Paraigua. Behind the *ajuntament* (city hall), this pricey but stylish bar serves cocktails and classical-music recordings. ✉ *Pl. Sant Miquel, Barri Gòtic* ☎ *93/217–3028* ◷ *Daily 11* AM*–2:30* AM Ⓜ *Jaume I, Liceu.*

Miramelindo. The bar has a range of herbal liquors, fruit cocktails, pâtés, and cheeses; recorded music is usually jazz. ✉ *Passeig del Born 15, La Ribera* ☎ *93/319–5376* ◷ *Daily 7* PM*–2:30* AM Ⓜ *Jaume I.*

6

Tapas Bars

As a result of Catalonia's distinct social mores, tapas have historically never been an important part of Barcelona life. But stand by: astute Catalans and Basque chefs are busy transforming Barcelona into an emerging tapas capital (until now, San Sebastian, Sevilla, Cadiz, or perhaps Madrid led the tapas charge). Especially around Santa Maria del Mar and the Passeig del Born area, nomadic wine tippling and tapa tasting are proliferating. Beware of the tapas places along Passeig de Gràcia: although they're minimally acceptable, the tapas here are over-large, microwaved, and far from Barcelona's best.

FodorśChoice ★ **Cal Pep.** A two-minute walk east from Santa Maria del Mar toward the Estació de França, Pep's has Barcelona's best and freshest selection of tapas, cooked and served piping hot in this boisterous space. ✉ *Pl. de les Olles 8, Born-Ribera* ☎*93/319–6183* ◷ *Tues.–Sat. 1–4* PM *and 8–midnight, Mon. 8* PM*–midnight* Ⓜ *Jaume I.*

Fodor'sChoice **Casa Lucio.** With preserved and fresh ingredients and original dishes flow-
★ ing from the kitchen, this handsome (though expensive) little gem just
two blocks south of the Mercat de Sant Antoni is well worth tracking
down. Lucio's wife, Maribel, is relentlessly inventive. Try the *tastum al-
barole* (cured sheep cheese from Umbria) or the *pochas negras con morcilla* (black beans with black sausage). ☒ *Viladomat 59, Eixample*
☎ *93/424–4401* ◷ *Mon.–Sat. 1–4 PM and 8–11 PM* Ⓜ *Sant Antoni.*

Fodor'sChoice **Cata 1.81.** Small delicacies such as truffle omelets and foie gras make this
★ a taste treat as well as a wine-tasting *(cata)* sanctuary. The wine selections
are thoughtfully and carefully worked out, and the contemporary design
is refreshing and exciting. ☒ *Valencia 181, Eixample* ☎ *93/323–6818*
◷ *Tues.–Sat. 1–4 PM and 8–midnight, Mon. 8 PM–midnight* Ⓜ *Provença.*

Cerveseria La Catalana. This booming bar is filled for a reason: excellent food at fair prices. Try the small *solomillos* (filet mignons)—mini-
morsels that will take the edge off your carnivorous instincts without
undue damage. ☒ *Mallorca 236, Eixample* ☎ *93/216–0368* ◷ *Daily
8 AM–1:30 AM* Ⓜ *Provença.*

Ciudad Condal. A Barcelona hot spot, this restaurant and grazing ground
serves fine tapas to a well-heeled crowd. ☒ *La Rambla de Catalunya
18, Eixample* ☎ *93/318–1997* ◷ *Daily 7:30 AM–1:30 AM* Ⓜ *Passeig de
Gràcia.*

El Irati. Between Plaça del Pi and the Rambla, this boisterous Basque bar
has only one drawback: it's hard to squeeze into. Try coming around 1
PM or 7:30 PM. The standard beverage here is *txakolí,* a white Basque
wine. The restaurant in back is excellent. ☒ *Cardenal Casañas 17,
Barri Gòtic* ☎ *93/302–3084* ◷ *Tues.–Sun. 12:30 PM–midnight.*

El Vaso de Oro. At the uptown edge of Barceloneta, this bar has become
more and more popular over the last few years. If you can catch it when
it's not crammed with customers, you're in for some of the best beer
and tapas in town. ☒ *Balboa 6, Barceloneta* ☎ *93/319–3098* ◷ *Daily
9 AM–midnight* Ⓜ *Barceloneta.*

Euskal Etxea. The tapas and canapés speak for themselves here at this
gastronomical oasis just down from the Picasso Museum. ☒ *Pl. de
Montcada 13, Born-Ribera* ☎ *93/310–2185* ◷ *Mon.–Sat. 9 AM–1 AM,
Sun. 9 AM–4:30 PM* Ⓜ *Jaume I.*

Inòpia Clàssic Bar. Albert Adrià, younger brother and chief culinary re-
searcher for his hyper-famous brother Ferran of tapas bar El Bulli fame
has opened his own tapas bar just a few blocks west of the Mercat de
Sant Antoni. Products and preparations are uniformly interesting and
excellent here, from the fragrant Torta del Casar cheese, to the olive sampler served in a ceramic flute, or the ham croquettes. ☒ *Tamarit 104,
Eixample* ☎ *93/424–5231* ◷ *Tues.–Sat. 7:30 PM–11 PM, Sun. 1–4 PM*
Ⓜ *Rocafort, Poble Sec.*

Jaizkibel. One of Barcelona's off-the-beaten-track secrets, this proto-Basque
enclave is six blocks from the Sagrada Família, five from the Casa
Macaia Fundació La Caixa art gallery and concert hall, three from the
Monumental bullring, and just three from the Auditori, all contributing to this being a handy place to add in after an afternoon or evening
at any of these locales. ☒ *Sicília 180, Eixample* ☎ *93/245–6569*
◷ *Sept.–July, Tues.–Sun. 8 AM–2 AM* Ⓜ *Arc de Triomf.*

Mantequeria Can Ravell. For lovers of exquisite wines, hams, cheeses, oils, whiskies, cigars, caviars, baby eels, and any other delicacy you can think of, this is your spot. The backroom table, where strangers share tastes, is open from about 10 AM to 8 PM; it's first-come, first-served. ✉ *Aragó 313, Eixample* ☎ *93/457–5114* ☉ *Tues.–Sat. 8 AM–9 PM.*

Sagardi. This attractive, wood-and-stone cider house comes close to re-creating its Basque prototype, with cider shooting from mammoth (fake) barrels and piping-hot tapas out front, and *txuletas de buey* (beefsteaks) prepared over coals in the restaurant out back. ✉ *Carrer Argenteria 62, La Ribera* ☎ *93/319–9993* ☉ *Daily 10 AM–1 AM.*

Taller de Tapas. Next to Plaça del Pi, facing the eastern lateral facade of Santa Maria del Pi, this fine tapas specialist has it all: cheery young staff, traditional Catalan dishes in bite-size format, and service from midday to midnight. The other Taller de Tapas at Argenteria 51 near Santa Maria del Mar is equally excellent. ✉ *Pl. de Sant Josep Oriol 9, Barri Gòtic* ☎ *93/302–6243* ☉ *Daily 10 AM–2 AM.*

Xampanyerias & Wine Bars

El Xampanyet. Just down Carrer Montcada from the Picasso Museum, hanging *botas* (wineskins) mark one of Barcelona's liveliest saloons, usually stuffed to the gills. Caveat: The sparkling wine served here is not cava but a sweet brew of indeterminate origin. Stick with beer or one of their excellent wines. ✉ *Montcada 22, La Ribera* ☎ *93/319–7003* ☉ *Closed Mon.*

La Vinya del Senyor. Ambitiously named "The Lord's Vineyard," this excellent wine bar across from the entrance to Santa Maria del Mar changes its savvy by-the-glass wine selections every fortnight. ✉ *Pl. de Santa Maria 5, La Ribera* ☎ *93/310–3379* ☉ *Closed Mon.*

El Bitxo. An original wine list and ever-changing choices of interesting cava selections accompany creative tapas and small dishes from foie (duck or goose liver) to iberico hams and cheeses, all 50 yards from the Palau de la Música. ✉ *Verdaguer i Callis 9, Sant Pere* ☎ *93/268–1708.*

La Taverna del Palau. This little tavern is perfect for a hit of cava during intermission or a beer and a *flauta* (thin, flute-like sandwich) of cured ham directly under the Palau de Música's colorful facade. ✉ *Sant Pere més Alt 8, Sant Pere* ☎ *93/268–8481.*

WHERE TO EAT

Barcelona's restaurant scene is an ongoing surprise. Between the cutting-edge of avant-garde culinary experimentation and the cosmopolitan and rustic dishes of traditional Catalan fare is a fleet of inventive chefs producing some of Europe's finest Mediterranean cuisine.

Catalans are legendary lovers of fish, vegetables, rabbit, duck, lamb, game, and natural ingredients from the Pyrenees or the Mediterranean. The *mar i muntanya* (sea and mountain—that is, surf and turf), a recipe combining seafood with upland products, is a standard. Rabbit and prawns, cuttlefish and meatballs, chickpeas and clams are just a few examples. Combining salty and sweet tastes—a Moorish legacy—is another common theme, as in duck with pears, rabbit with figs, or lamb with olives.

The Mediterranean diet, which is based on olive oil, seafood, fibrous vegetables, onions, garlic, and red wine, is at home in Barcelona, and food tends to be seasoned with Catalonia's four basic sauces—*allioli* (pure garlic and olive oil), *romescu* (almonds, hazelnuts, tomato, garlic and olive oil), *sofregit* (fried onion, tomato, and herbs), and *samfaina* (a ratatouillelike vegetable mixture).

Typical entrées include *habas a la catalana* (a spicy broad-bean stew), *bullabesa* (fish soup-stew similar to the French bouillabaisse), and *espinacas a la catalana* (spinach cooked with oil, garlic, pine nuts, raisins, and bits of bacon). Bread is often doused with olive oil and spread with tomato to make *pa amb tomaquet,* delicious on its own or as a side order.

Menús del día (menus of the day), served only at lunchtime, are good values. Lunch is served from 1 to 4, dinner 9 to 11. Certain restaurants serve continuously from 1 PM to 1 AM. Beware of the *advice* of hotel concierges and taxi drivers, who have been known to warn that the place you are going is either closed or no good anymore and to recommend places where they get kickbacks.

Catalan wines from the nearby Penedès region, especially the local *méthode champenoise* (sparkling white wine known in Catalonia as *cava*), adequately accompany regional cuisine. Meanwhile, winemakers from the Priorat, Ampurdan, and Costers del Segre regions are producing some of Spain's most exciting new wines.

WHAT IT COSTS In Euros				
$$$$	$$$	$$	$	¢
BARCELONA				
AT DINNER	over €25	€18–€25	€12–€18	€8–€12	under €8
SIDE TRIPS FROM BARCELONA				
AT DINNER	over €20	€15–€20	€10–€15	€6–€10	under €6

Restaurant prices are per person for a main course at dinner.

Ciutat Vella (Old City)

Ciutat Vella comprises the Rambla, Barri Gòtic, Ribera, and Raval districts between Plaça de Catalunya and the port. Chic new restaurants and cafés seem to open daily in Barcelona's Old City.

$$$$ ✗ **Àbac.** In the tradition of Catalonia's finest restaurants, Xavier Pellicer leaves no detail to chance here, preparing carefully selected ingredients in innovative recipes based on sound culinary canons. As of January 2007, Àbac will have

> **DINING TIP**
>
> If you make a reservation and change your mind, be polite and call to cancel. Also, beware of the *advice* of hotel concierges and taxi drivers who warn that the place you are going is either closed or no good anymore and recommend places where they get kickbacks.

moved to upper Barcelona (Av. Tibidabo 3–7) and will offer a spa and 17 luxury suites for snoozing off lunch. ☒ *Rec 79–89 Born-Ribera* ☎ *93/319–6600* ⌂ *Reservations essential* ☰ *AE, DC, MC, V* ⊘ *Closed Sun. and Aug. No lunch Mon.* Ⓜ *Jaume I.*

$$$–$$$$ ✕ **Ca l'Isidre.** Just inside the Raval from Avinguda del Paral.lel, this is a favorite with Barcelona's art crowd. Pictures and engravings, some original, by Dalí and other stars line the walls. The traditional Catalan cooking draws on fresh produce from the nearby Boqueria and has a slight French accent. Isidre's wines are invariably novelties from all over the Iberian Peninsula; ask for his advice and you will get a great wine as well as an oenology, geography, and history course delivered with charm, brevity, and wit. The homemade foie gras is superb. Come and go by cab at night; the area can be shady. ☒ *Les Flors 12, Raval* ☎ *93/441–1139* ⌂ *Reservations essential* ☰ *AE, MC, V* ⊘ *Closed Sun., Easter wk, and mid-July–mid-Aug.* Ⓜ *Paral.lel.*

$$$–$$$$
Fodor'sChoice
★
✕ **Casa Leopoldo.** Hidden in the dark Raval west of the Rambla, this restaurant owned by the Gil family serves fine seafood and Catalan fare. To get here, approach along Carrer Hospital, take a left through the Passatge Bernardí Martorell, and go 50 feet right on Sant Rafael to the Gil front door. Try the *revuelto de ajos tiernos y gambas* (eggs scrambled with young garlic and shrimp) or the famous *cap-i-pota* (stewed head and hoof of pork). Albariños and Priorats are Rosa Gil's favorites. ☒ *Sant Rafael 24, Raval* ☎ *93/441–3014* ☰ *AE, DC, MC, V* ⊘ *Closed Mon. No dinner Sun.* Ⓜ *Liceu.*

$$$–$$$$ ✕ **Comerç 24.** Artist, aesthete, and chef Carles Abellan playfully reinterprets traditional Catalan favorites at this sleek, designer dining spot. Try the deconstructed *tortilla de patatas* (potato omelet), or the *huevo kinder* (an egg with surprises inside, based on a popular children's toy). For dessert, prepare for a postmodern version of the traditional afterschool snack of chocolate, olive oil, salt, and bread. Abellán's cuisine is always original and, though sometimes flirting with the border between fine dining and playing with your food, unfailingly delicious. ☒ *Carrer Comerç 24, Born-Ribera* ☎ *93/319–2102* ⌂ *Reservations essential* ☰ *AE, DC, MC, V* ⊘ *Closed Sun.* Ⓜ *Jaume I.*

$$$–$$$$ ✕ **Mey Hofmann.** Just up Argenteria from Santa Maria del Mar is glamorous Mey Hofman's cooking academy and first-rate restaurant specializing in Mediterranean cuisine. The young waiters and waitresses are chefs-in-training and are usually encyclopedic about ingredients and preparations, from aperitif wines to cheeses and desserts. ☒ *Argenteria 74–78, Born-Ribera* ☎ *93/319–5889* ☰ *AE, DC, MC, V* ⊘ *Closed weekends* Ⓜ *Jaume I.*

$$–$$$$ ✕ **Nonell.** This excellent new addition to the city's gastronomic scene serves a cuisine that chef Oliver Balteo unabashedly calls eclectic, drawn from his experiences as a culinary professor in Venezuela and his Lebanese roots. Dishes range from classical Mediterranean to Castilian roast suckling pig to eastern creams and sauces. The wine list is entirely

6

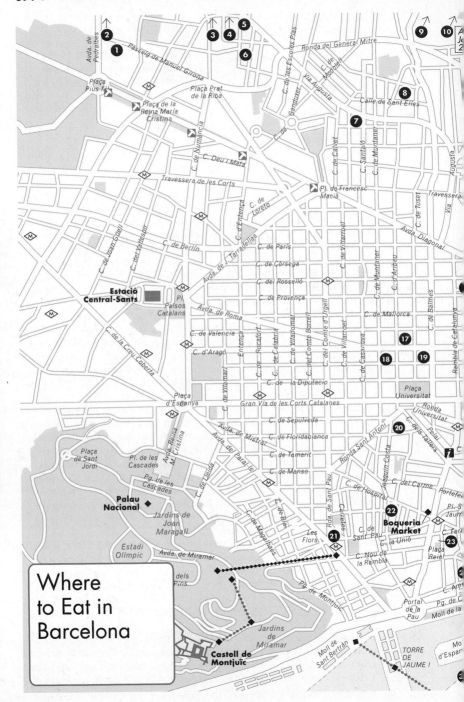

Where to Eat in Barcelona

original, featuring labels you have never heard of but are glad to get to know; the service is impeccable and delivered with panche and a twinkle in the eye—and in perfect English. ⊠ *Pl. Isidre Nonell, Barri Gòtic* ☎ 93/301–1378 ▤ *AE, DC, MC, V* Ⓜ *Catalunya, Liceu.*

$$–$$$$ ✗ **Shunka.** Widely regarded as Barcelona's finest Japanese restaurant, this cozy hideaway behind the Hotel Colón serves straight across the counter from the burners to the diners. Mediterranean and Japanese cuisines have much in common (such as raw fish dishes, for starters). ⊠ *Sagristans 5, Barri Gòtic* ☎ 93/412–4991 ▤ *AE, DC, MC, V* Ⓜ *Liceu.*

$$–$$$ ✗ **Café de l'Acadèmia.** With wicker chairs, stone walls, and background classical music, this place is sophisticated-rustic, and the excellent Catalan cuisine makes it much more than a mere café. It's frequented by politicians and functionaries from the nearby Generalitat and is always boiling with life. Be sure to reserve at lunchtime. ⊠ *Lledó 1, Barri Gòtic* ☎ 93/319–8253 ▤ *AE, DC, MC, V* Ⓜ *Jaume I.*

$$–$$$ ✗ **Cometacinc.** This stylish place in the Barri Gòtic, an increasingly chic neighborhood of artisans and antiquers, is a fine example of Barcelona's new-over-old architecture and interior design panache. Although the 30-foot floor-to-ceiling wooden shutters are already a visual feast, the carefully prepared interpretations of old standards, such as the *carpaccio de toro de lidia* (carpaccio of fighting bull) with basil sauce and pine nuts, are also brilliant. ⊠ *Carrer Cometa 5, Barri Gòtic* ☎ 93/310–1558 ▤ *AE, DC, MC, V* ⊘ *Closed Tues.* Ⓜ *Jaume I.*

$$–$$$ ✗ **La Taxidermista.** Don't worry: No road kill is served here. Once a natural-science museum and taxidermy shop (from which Dalí once purchased 200,000 ants and a stuffed rhinoceros), this is the only recommendable restaurant in the sunny Plaça Reial. Interior decorator Beth Gali designed the interior around original beams and steel columns. Delicacies such as *bonito con escalivada y queso de cabra* (white tuna with braised eggplants, peppers, and goat cheese) are served at outside tables best enjoyed in the winter sun. ⊠ *Pl. Reial 8, Rambla* ☎ 93/412–4536 ▤ *AE, DC, MC, V* ⊘ *Closed Mon.* Ⓜ *Liceu.*

★ $–$$ ✗ **Agut.** Wainscoting and 1950s canvases are the background for the mostly Catalan crowd in this homey restaurant in the lower reaches of the Gothic Quarter. Agut was founded in 1924, and its popularity has never waned—not least because the hearty Catalan fare is a fantastic value. In season (September through May), try the *pato silvestre agridulce* (sweet-and-sour wild duck). There's a good selection of wine, but no frills such as coffee or liqueur. ⊠ *Gignàs 16, Barri Gòtic* ☎ 93/315–1709 ▤ *AE, MC, V* ⊘ *Closed Mon. and July. No dinner Sun.* Ⓜ *Jaume I.*

$–$$ ✗ **Ca l'Estevet.** Facing the journalism school and around the block from Barcelona's *La Vanguardia* daily, this romantic little spot near the MACBA (contemporary art museum) is popular with journalists, students, and artists. Estevet and family are charming, and the carefully elaborated Catalan cuisine sparkles, especially at these prices. Try the asparagus cooked over coals, the *chopitos gaditanos* (deep-fried baby octopus), or the *magret de pato* (duck breast). The house wine is inexpensive and perfectly drinkable. ⊠ *Valdoncella 46, Raval* ☎ 93/302–4186 ▤ *AE, DC, MC, V* ⊘ *Closed Sun.* Ⓜ *Catalunya.*

$-$$ ✕ **El Foro.** This hot spot near the Born is always full to the rafters with lively young and not-so-young people. Painting and photographic exhibits line the walls, and the menu is dominated by pizzas, salads, and meat cooked over coals. Flamenco and jazz performances downstairs are a good post-dinner option. ⊠ *Princesa 53, Born-Ribera* 🕾 *93/310–1020* 🖃 *AE, DC, MC, V* ⊙ *Closed Mon.* Ⓜ *Jaume I.*

Barceloneta & the Port Olímpic

Barceloneta and the Port Olímpic (Olympic Port) have little in common beyond their seaside location, the former a traditional fishermen's quarter and the latter a crazed disco strip with thousand-seat restaurants.

$$$$ ✕ **Torre d'Altamar.** Seafood of every stripe, spot, fin, and carapace emanates from the kitchen here, but the filet mignon, under a colossal slab of foie (duck or goose liver), is a tour de force, too. The restaurant is in the cable-car tower over the far side of the port and has spectacular views of Barcelona as well as far out into the Mediterranean. ⊠ *Passeig Joan de Borbó 88–Torre de San Sebastián, Barceloneta* 🕾 *93/221–0007* 🖃 *AE, DC, MC, V* ⊙ *Closed Sun. No lunch Mon.* Ⓜ *Barceloneta.*

$$$-$$$$ ✕ **Antiga Casa Solé.** Two blocks from the sea side of Plaça de Sant Miquel, Barceloneta's prettiest square, you can find this traditional midday-Sunday pilgrimage site, which occupies a characteristic waterfront house and serves fresh, well-prepared, piping-hot seafood. Whether it's *lenguado a la plancha* (grilled sole) or the exquisite *arroç negre amb sepia en su tinta* (black rice with squid in its ink), everything here comes loaded with flavor. In winter try to sit near the open kitchen for the aromas, sights, sounds, and warmth. ⊠ *Sant Carles 4, Barceloneta* 🕾 *93/221–5012* 🖃 *AE, DC, MC, V* ⊙ *Closed Mon. and last 2 wks of Aug. No dinner Sun.* Ⓜ *Barceloneta.*

$$$-$$$$ ✕ **Barceloneta.** This enormous riverboatlike building at the end of the yacht marina in Barceloneta is not an intimate space where you feel your dinner has been lovingly prepared just for you. On the other hand, the food is delicious, the service impeccable, the hundreds of fellow diners make the place feel like a cheerful New Year's Eve celebration, and, all in all, a bad time is rarely had here. Rice and fish dishes are the specialty, and the salads are excellent. ⊠ *L'Escar 22, Barceloneta* 🕾 *93/221–2111* 🖃 *AE, MC, V* Ⓜ *Barceloneta.*

★ **$$$-$$$$** ✕ **Can Majó.** On the beach in Barceloneta stands one of Barcelona's premier seafood restaurants. House specialties include *caldero de bogavante* (a cross between paella and lobster bouillabaisse) and *suquet* (fish stewed in its own juices), but whatever you choose will be excellent. In summer the terrace overlooking the Mediterranean is the closest you can come to beachside dining. ⊠ *Almirall Aixada 23, Barceloneta* 🕾 *93/221–5455* 🖃 *AE, DC, MC, V* ⊙ *Closed Mon. No dinner Sun.* Ⓜ *Barceloneta.*

$$$-$$$$ ✕ **Reial Club Marítim.** For sunset or harbor views, excellent maritime fare, and a sense of remove from the city, try Barcelona's yacht club, just around the harbor through Barceloneta. Highlights are paella *marinera* (seafood paella), *rodaballo* (turbot), *lubina* (sea bass), and *dorado* (sea bream). Ask for the freshest fish they have and you won't be disappointed.

✉ *Moll d'Espanya, Barceloneta* ☎ *93/221–7143* 🖃 *AE, DC, MC, V* ⊘ *No dinner Sun.* Ⓜ *Barceloneta.*

$$–$$$$ ✕ **Andaira.** This creative young couple fresh in from the Balearic Islands has brought new flavors and innovative, contemporary cooking to a Barceloneta dining scene all too familiar with rice and traditional fish concoctions. Its not that Andaira doesn't do them, but they do them with a sleek, modern flair, and they do a variety of other things as well, all within sight of the Mediterrenean. ✉ *Vila Joiosa 52–54, Barceloneta* ☎ *93/221–1616* 🖃 *AE, DC, MC, V* Ⓜ *Barceloneta.*

$$–$$$ ✕ **Suquet de l'Almirall.** With an intimate terrace for alfresco dining in summer, "The Admiral's Fish Stew" indeed serves fare fit for the admiralty. Specialists in rice dishes and *caldoso de bogavante,* an abundantly brothy rice dish with lobster, this is one of Barceloneta's best seafood havens. ✉ *Passeig Joan de Borbó 65, Barceloneta* ☎ *93/221–6233* 🖃 *AE, DC, MC, V* ⊘ *No dinner Sun. Closed Mon.* Ⓜ *Barceloneta.*

$–$$ ✕ **Can Manel la Puda.** The first choice for paella in the sun, year-round, Can Manel is near the end of the main road out to the Barceloneta beach. Any time before 4 PM will do; it then reopens at 7. *Arròs a banda* (rice with peeled shellfish) and paella marinera (seafood and rice) or *fideuà* (with noodles instead of rice) are all delicious. ✉ *Passeig Joan de Borbó 60, Barceloneta* ☎ *93/221–5013* 🖃 *AE, DC, MC, V* ⊘ *Closed Mon.* Ⓜ *Barceloneta.*

Eixample

Eixample dining, invariably upscale and elegant, ranges from traditional cuisine in Moderniste houses to designer fare in sleek minimalist-experimental spaces.

★ $$$$ ✕ **Can Gaig.** This Barcelona favorite is famous for combining superb design and carefully prepared cuisine. Market-fresh ingredients and original combinations are solidly rooted in traditional recipes from Catalan home cooking, and the menu balances seafood and upland specialties, game, and homegrown products of all kinds. Try the *perdiz asada con jamón ibérico* (roast partridge with Iberian ham), or, if it's available, *becada* (woodcock), one of Carles Gaig's signature dishes. ✉ *Carrer d'Aragó 214, Eixample* ☎ *93/429–1017* 🖨 *93/429–7002* ⌱ *Reservations essential* 🖃 *AE, DC, MC, V* ⊘ *Closed Mon., Easter wk, and Aug.* Ⓜ *Passeig de Gràcia.*

★ $$$$ ✕ **Drolma.** Named (in Sanskrit) for Buddha's female side, Fermin Puig's intimate refuge was an instant success. The *menú de degustació* (taster's menu) might have pheasant cannelloni in foie-gras sauce with fresh black truffles or giant prawn tails with *trompettes de la mort* (black wild mushrooms) with *sôt-l'y-laisse* (literally "fool leaves it there"; in fact, chicken nuggets). Fermin's foie gras *a la ceniza con ceps* (cooked over wood coals with wild mushrooms) is typical of Drolma's blend of tradition and inspiration. ✉ *Majestic Hotel, Passeig de Gràcia 70, Eixample* ☎ *93/496–7710* ⌱ *Reservations essential* 🖃 *AE, DC, MC, V* ⊘ *Closed Sun. and Aug.* Ⓜ *Provença, Passeig de Gràcia.*

$$$–$$$$ ✕ **Casa Calvet.** This Art Nouveau space in Antoni Gaudí's 1898–1900 Casa Calvet just a block down from the Ritz is an opportunity to break bread in one of the great Moderniste's creations. The dining room is a graceful and spectacular design display featuring signature Gaudí ornamentation from looping parabolic door handles to polychrome stained glass, acid engravings, and wood carved in floral and organic motifs. The menu is Mediterranean, with an emphasis on light, contemporary fare. ⊠ *Casp 48, Eixample* ☎ *93/412–4012* ☰ *AE, DC, MC, V* ⊘ *Closed Sun. and last 2 wks of Aug.* Ⓜ *Urquinaona.*

$$$–$$$$ ✗ **Cinc Sentits.** The engaging Artal family—maître d' and owner Rosa, server and eloquent food narrator Amy, and chef Jordi—a Catalan family with a couple of decades in Canada and the United States, offers a unique Barcelona experience: cutting-edge, one-of-a-kind cuisine in a minimalist setting explained in detail in native English. Three tasting menus—light, tasting, and *omakase* (a "trust the chef" menu, including wine pairings of the chef's choice)—provide a wide range of tastes and textures. At the end of the meal, a printout reprises the nine mini-courses and seven wines that have just crossed your palate. ⊠ *Aribau 58, Eixample* ☎ *93/323–9490* ☰ *AE, DC, MC, V* ⊘ *Closed Sun. No dinner Mon.* Ⓜ *Provença.*

$$$–$$$$ ✗ **El Tragaluz.** *Tragaluz* means skylight—literally, "light-swallower"—and this is an excellent choice if you're still on a design high from Gaudí's Pedrera. The sliding roof opens to the stars in good weather, and the chairs, lamps, and fittings by Javier Mariscal (creator of 1992 Olympic mascot Cobi) reflect Barcelona's passion for whimsy and playful design. The Mediterranean cuisine is light and innovative. ⊠ *Passatge de la Concepció 5, Eixample* ☎ *93/487–0196* ☰ *AE, DC, MC, V* ⊘ *Closed Jan. 5. No lunch Mon.* Ⓜ *Diagonal.*

$$$–$$$$ ✗ **Gorría.** One of the two best Basque restaurants in Barcelona (the other is Taktika Berri, which is very hard to get into), this establishment serves everything from the stewed *pochas* (white beans) to the heroic *chuletón* (steak) is as pure as the Navarran Pyrenees. The Castillo de Sajazarra reserva '95, a brick-red Rioja, provides perfect accompaniment at this delicious pocket of Navarra in the Catalan capital. ⊠ *Diputació 421, Eixample* ☎ *93/245–1164* ☰ *AE, DC, MC, V* ⊘ *Closed Sun.* Ⓜ *Monumental.*

$$$–$$$$ ✗ **Lasarte.** Martin Berasategui's landing in the Catalan capital comes at a moment when the great chefs are in general expansion around the peninsula. Alex Garés, chief cook in Berasategui's absence, trained with the best (Pellicer of Àbac and Manolo de la Osa in Las Rejas) and serves an eclectic selection of Basque, Mediterranean, market, and personal interpretations and creations. Expect whimsical and playful aperitifs to deepen to surprising and serious combinations such as foie and smoked eel or simple wood pigeon cooked to perfection. ⊠ *Mallorca 259, Eixample* ☎ *93/445–0000* ☰ *AE, DC, MC, V* ⊘ *Closed weekends* Ⓜ *Provença.*

$$$–$$$$ ✗ **L'Olivé.** Specializing in Catalan home cooking, this busy, attractive Eixample spot is always filled with trendy diners having a great time. You soon see why: excellent hearty food, smart service, and some of the best *pa amb tomaquet* (toasted bread with olive oil and squeezed tomato) in town. ⊠ *Balmes 47, Eixample* ☎ *93/452–1990* ☰ *AE, DC, MC, V* ⊘ *No dinner Sun.* Ⓜ *Provença.*

★ $$$–$$$$ ✗ **Manairó.** A *manairó* is a mysterious Pyrenean (obviously culinary) elf who helps make things happen, and Jordi Herrera may be one. A demon for everything from blow torch–fried eggs to meat cooked *al clavo ardiente* (à la burning nail), filets warmed from within by red-hot spikes producing meat both rare and warm and never undercooked, Jordi also

6

cooks cod under a lightbulb at 220 degrees (*bacalao iluminado*—illuminated codfish) and serves a palate-cleansing gin and tonic with liquid nitrogen, gin, and lime. ✉ *Diputació 424, Eixample* ☎ *93/231–0057* ⚭ *Reservations essential* 🖃 *AE, DC, MC, V* ⊘ *Closed Sun., Mon., and last 3 wks of Aug.* Ⓜ *Monumental.*

$$–$$$ ✕ **Mantequeria Ya Ya Amelia.** Delicatessen and wine emporium, this *mantequeria* (literally, "buttery") two blocks uphill from Gaudí's Sagrada Família church serves lovingly prepared and clued-in dishes ranging from warm goat-cheese salad to foie (duck or goose liver) to beef. The wine list, of course, is exquisite and the service is cheerful. Ask for the chef's table by the kitchen. The original Ya Ya Amelia (*Ya Ya* is Spanish for "grandmother") around the corner at Sardenya 364 (93/456–4573) is closed on Sunday, but open on Monday (so one or the other is always available). Both restaurants serve continuously from 1 PM to midnight. The Mantequeria is usually fresher, less smoky, and less frequented. ✉ *Còrsega 537, Eixample* ☎ *93/435–8048* 🖃 *AE, DC, MC, V* ⊘ *Closed Mon.* Ⓜ *Sagrada Família.*

Gràcia

This exciting yet intimate neighborhood has everything from the most sophisticated cuisine in town to Basque taverns in a lively context.

$$$$ ✕ **Botafumeiro.** Fleets of waiters in white outfits move at the speed of light in Barcelona's best Galician restaurant, a seafood medley from shellfish to finfish to cuttlefish to caviar. An assortment of *media ración* (half-ration) selections is available at the bar, where *pulpo a feira* (squid on potato) and *jamón bellota de Guijuelo* (acorn-fed ham) make peerless late-night fare. People-watching is tops, and the waiters are stand-up comics. ✉ *Gran de Gràcia 81, Gràcia* ☎ *93/218–4230* 🖃 *AE, DC, MC, V* Ⓜ *Gràcia.*

$$$$ ✕ **Jean-Luc Figueras.** A Gràcia town house contains this perennial favorite on everyone's short list of Barcelona restaurants. The berry-pink walls, polished dark-wood floors, and brass sconces make a rich backdrop for unforgettable Catalan cuisine with a French accent. The menú de degustació is, for value and variety, the best choice for innovative interpretations such as the fried prawn with ginger pasta and mustard-and-mango sauce. ✉ *Carrer Santa Teresa 10, Gràcia* ☎ *93/ 415–2877* ⚭ *Reservations essential* 🖃 *AE, DC, MC, V* ⊘ *Closed Sun. No lunch Sat.* Ⓜ *Diagonal.*

$–$$ ✕ **Folquer.** This little hideaway in the bottom of Gràcia is a good way to end a tour of this village within a city. With one of the best-value taster's menus in Barcelona, Folquer serves creatively prepared traditional Catalan specialties that use first-rate ingredients. ✉ *Torrent de l'Olla 3, Gràcia* ☎ *93/217–4395* 🖃 *AE, DC, MC, V* ⊘ *Closed Sun. and last 2 wks of Aug. No lunch Sat.* Ⓜ *Diagonal.*

Sarrià-Pedralbes & Sant Gervasi

Take an excursion to the upper reaches of town for an excellent selection of restaurants, along with cool summer evening breezes and a sense of village life in Sarrià.

$$$$ ✕ **El Racò d'en Freixa.** Chef Ramó Freixa, one of Barcelona's established culinary lights, is taking founding father José María's work to another level. His clever reinterpretations of traditional recipes, all made with high-quality raw ingredients, have qualified the younger Freixa's work as *cuina d'autor* (designer cuisine). One specialty is *peus de porc en escabetx de guatlle* (pig's feet with quail in a garlic-and-parsley gratin). ⬚ *Sant Elíes 22, Sant Gervasi* ☎ *93/209–7559* ▭ *AE, DC, MC, V* ⊗ *Closed Mon., Easter wk, and Aug. No dinner Sun.* Ⓜ *Sant Gervasi.*

★ **$$$$** ✕ **Neichel.** Chef Jean-Louis Neichel skillfully manages a wide variety of exquisite ingredients such as foie, truffles, wild mushrooms, herbs, and the best seasonal vegetables. His flawless Mediterranean delicacies include *ensalada de gambas de Palamós al sésamo con puerros* (shrimp from Palamós with sesame-seed and leeks) and *espardenyes amb salicornia* (sea slugs and sea asparagus) on sun-dried-tomato paste. ⬚ *Carrer Bertran i Rózpide 1, off Av. Pedralbes, Pedralbes* ☎ *93/203–8408* ⌾ *Reservations essential* ▭ *AE, DC, MC, V* ⊗ *Closed Sun., Mon., and Aug.* Ⓜ *Maria Cristina.*

$$$–$$$$ ✕ **Le Quattro Stagioni.** For excellent, streamlined Italian cuisine that will remind you more of postmodern Catalan cooking than of *The Godfather*, this chic spot just down from the Bonanova metro stop on the Sarrià line is a winner. It's always filled with intriguing-looking *bons vivants* (evenly balanced between hip locals and clued-in tourists), and the garden is cool and fragrant on summer nights. ⬚ *Dr. Roux 37, Sant Gervasi* ☎ *93/205–2279* ▭ *AE, DC, MC, V* Ⓜ *Tres Torres.*

★ **$$$–$$$$** ✕ **Tram-Tram.** At the end of the old tram line above the village of Sarrià, Isidre Soler and his stunning wife, Reyes, have put together one of Barcelona's finest culinary offerings. Try the *menú de degustaciò* and you might score marinated tuna salad, cod medallions, and venison filet mignons. Perfect portions and a streamlined reinterpretation of space within this traditional Sarrià house—especially in or near the garden out back—make this a memorable dining experience. ⬚ *Major de Sarrià 121, Sarrià* ☎ *93/204–8518* ▭ *AE, DC, MC, V* ⊗ *Closed Sun. and late Dec.–early Jan. No lunch Sat.* Ⓜ *Reina Elisenda.*

$$–$$$$ ✕ **Vivanda.** Just above the Plaça de Sarrià, this leafy garden is especially wonderful between May and mid-October, when outside dining is a delight. The menu has Catalan specialties such as *espinacas a la catalana* (spinach with raisins, pine nuts, and garlic) and inventive combinations of seafood and inland products. ⬚ *Major de Sarrià 134, Sarrià* ☎ *93/203–1918* ▭ *AE, DC, MC, V* ⊗ *Closed Sun.* Ⓜ *Reina Elisenda.*

$$–$$$ ✕ **Acontraluz.** This stylish covered terrace in the leafy upper-Barcelona neighborhood of Tres Torres has a strenuously varied menu ranging from game in season, such as *rable de liebre* (stewed hare) with chutney, to the more northern *pochas con almejas* (beans with clams). Dishes are prepared with care and flair; the lunch menu is a bargain. ⬚ *Milanesat 19, Tres Torres* ☎ *93/203–0658* ▭ *AE, DC, MC, V* Ⓜ *Tres Torres.*

$$ ✕ **El Mató de Pedralbes.** Named for the *mató* (cottage cheese) traditionally prepared by the Clarist nuns across the street in the Monestir de Pedralbes, this is a fine stop after touring the monastery, which closes at 2. The restaurant has one of the most typically Catalan, best-value menus in town. Look for *sopa de ceba gratinée* (onion soup), *trinxat*

6

(chopped cabbage with bacon bits), and *truite de patata i ceba* (potato-and-onion omelet). ⊠ *Obispo Català, Pedralbes* ☎ *93/204–7962* ⊟ *AE, DC, MC, V* ⊙ *Closed Sun.* Ⓜ *Reina Elisenda.*

$$ ✗ **Silvestre.** This sleek youngster in Barcelona's culinary firmament serves modern cuisine to some of Barcelona's most distinguished diners. Just below Via Augusta in upper Barcelona, a series of intimate dining rooms and cozy corners are carefully tended by chef Guillermo Casañé and Marta Cabot, his charming (and perfect-English-speaking) partner and maître d'. Look for fresh market produce lovingly prepared and dishes such as tuna tartare or noodles and shrimp. ⊠ *Santaló 101, Sant Gervasi* ☎ *93/241–4031* ⊟ *AE, DC, MC, V* ⊙ *Closed Sun., 2 wks in Aug., and Easter wk. No lunch Sat.* Ⓜ *Muntaner.*

Tibidabo

$$$–$$$$ ✗ **El Asador de Aranda.** Designed by Art Nouveau architect Rubió i Bellver, this immense palace rising 1,600 feet above the Avenida Tibidabo metro station is a hike—but worth remembering if you're in upper Barcelona. The kitchen specializes in *cordero lechal* (roast lamb); try *pimientos de piquillo* (hot, spicy peppers) on the side. The dining room has a terracotta floor and a full complement of Art Nouveau ornamentation ranging from intricately carved wood trimmings to stained-glass partitions, acid-engraved glass, and Moorish archways. ⊠ *Av. del Tibidabo 31, Tibidabo* ☎ *93/417–0115* ⊟ *AE, DC, MC, V* ⊙ *Closed Easter wk and Sun. in Aug. No dinner Sun.* Ⓜ *Av. Tibidabo.*

Outskirts of Barcelona

With the many fine in-town dining options available in Barcelona, any out-of-town recommendations should rank somewhere in the uppermost stratosphere of excellence. These two, both among the top five or six establishments below the Pyrenees, undoubtedly do.

★ $$$$ ✗ **Sant Pau.** Carme Ruscalleda's Sant Pol de Mar treasure is a scenic 40-minute train ride along the beach from Plaça Catalunya's RENFE station: The Calella train stops at the door. (The last evening train is too early for dinner, so attempt this only for lunch.) Star dishes include *vieiras* (scallops) with crisped artichoke flakes on roast potato, and *lubina* (sea bass) on baby leeks and chard in *garnatxa* (sweet Catalan wine) sauce. If you're there for Saint Valentine's Day, the *misiva de amor* (love letter) is a pastry envelope with slivers of raspberries, wild strawberries, blueberries, and julienned peaches. ⊠ *Nou 10, Sant Pol de Mar* ☎ *93/760–0662* ⊟ *AE, DC, MC, V* ⊙ *Closed Mon., 2 wks in Mar., and 2 wks in Nov. No dinner Sun.*

$$$–$$$$
Fodor'sChoice
★ ✗⛊ **El Racó de Can Fabes.** Santi Santamaria's master class in Mediterranean cuisine merits the 45-minute train ride (or 30-minute drive) north of Barcelona to Sant Celoni. One of the top three restaurants ($$$$) in Spain, this is a must for anyone interested in fine dining. Every detail, from the six flavors of freshly baked bread to the cheese selection, is superb. The taster's menu is the wisest solution. The RENFE stations are at Passeig de Gràcia or Sants—the last train back is at 10:24 PM, so this is a lunchtime-only transport solution. However, El Racó has five

sleek rooms so you can always reach a bed just a short crawl from the dinner table. ⊠ *Sant Joan 6, Sant Celoni* ☎ *93/867–2851* 🖷 *93/867–3861* ⊕ *www.canfabes.com* ⇔ *5 rooms,* ♿ *Restaurant, cable TV, parking (fee)* ▤ *AE, DC, MC, V* ☺ *Closed Mon., 1st 2 wks of Feb., and late June–early July. No dinner Sun.*

WHERE TO STAY

Barcelona's hotels offer clear distinctions. Hotels in the Ciutat Vella (Old City)—the Gothic Quarter and along the Rambla—are charming and convenient for sightseeing, though sometimes short on peace and quiet. Relative newcomers such as the Neri, the Duquesa de Cardona, the Banys Orientals, and the Casa Camper Barcelona are contemporary design standouts inhabiting medieval architecture, a combination at which Barcelona architects and decorators are peerless. Eixample hotels (including most of the city's best) are late-19th- or early-20th-century town houses restored and converted into exciting modern environments. Downtown hotels, including the Ritz, the Claris, the Majestic, the Condes de Barcelona, and the Hotel Omm best combine style and luxury with a sense of place, and the peripheral palaces (the Hotel Arts, the Eurostar Grand Marina, and the Rey Juan Carlos I) are less about Barcelona and more about generic luxury. Sarrià and Sant Gervasi upper-city hotels get you up out of the urban crush, and Olympic Port and Diagonal Mar hotels are in high-rise towers (requiring transport to and from the real Barcelona). Smaller budget hotels are less than half as expensive as some of the luxury addresses and more a part of city life.

> **LODGING TIP**
>
> Hotels will negotiate room rates if they're not full. Ask about weekend rates, which are often half; faxing for reservations may also get you a good deal. Business travelers may get a 40% break.

6

WHAT IT COSTS In Euros				
$$$$	$$$	$$	$	¢
BARCELONA				
FOR 2 PEOPLE over €225	€150–€225	€80–€150	€50–€80	under €50
SIDE TRIPS FROM BARCELONA				
FOR 2 PEOPLE over €180	€100–€180	€60–€100	€40–€60	under €40

Hotel prices are for two people in a standard double room in high season, excluding tax.

Ciutat Vella (Old City)

$$$$ 🏨 **Eurostars Grand Marina Hotel.** A tower built around a central patio, this ultracontemporary monolith offers maximum luxury two minutes from the Rambla over Barcelona's port. With stunning views of the city or Mediterranean, the Grand Marina is in the middle of, though well above, Barcelona's best sights. Rooms are bright and comfortable, albeit somewhat generic, and the public spaces are geometrical expanses of sleek glass and steel. Guests tend to be conventioneers and business travelers. ⊠ *Moll de Barcelona s/n, World Trade Center, Port Olímpic, 08039* ☎ *93/603–9000* 🖷 *93/603–9090* ⊕ *www.grandmarinahotel. com* 🖙 *291* ⚴ *3 restaurants, minibars, cable TV, pool, health club, hair salon, bar, parking (fee)* ☰ *AE, DC, MC, V* Ⓜ *Drassanes.*

$$$$ 🏨 **Hotel Neri.** Owner Bruno Figueras and designer Cristina Gabà have created a unique oasis of taste in the heart of the Gothic Quarter. Built into a 17th-century palace over one of the Gothic Quarter's smallest and most charming squares, Plaça Sant Felip Neri, the Neri is a singular counterpoint of ancient and avant-garde design. The rooms are medievalesque yet clean lined, hard edged, and equipped with great facilities. ⊠ *St. Sever 5, Barri Gòtic, 08002* ☎ *93/304–0655* 🖷 *93/304–0337* ⊕ *www. hotelneri.com* 🖙 *22 rooms* ⚴ *Restaurant, minibars, cable TV, in-room data ports, bar, meeting room* ☰ *AE, DC, MC, V* Ⓜ *Liceu, Catalunya.*

$$$$ 🏨 **Le Meridien.** The top Rambla hotel, this supremely luxurious giant offers a variety of rooms and suites, many of which overlook Barcelona's most emblematic promenade. Painted in pastel hues with brightly colored bedding and curtains, rooms include complete laptop and fax hookups. Rooms over the Rambla are completely soundproofed. Ask to have a look at the presidential suite for a peek at one of Barcelona's greatest hideaways (for clients with an extra two grand per night on their hands). ⊠ *La Rambla 111, Rambla, 08002* ☎ *93/318–6200, 800/543–4300 reservations in U.S. and Canada* 🖷 *93/301–7776* ⊕ *www.lemeridien-barcelona. com* 🖙 *390 rooms* ⚴ *Restaurant, in-room safes, bar, babysitting, business services, car rental, parking (fee)* ☰ *AE, DC, MC, V* Ⓜ *Catalunya.*

$$$–$$$$
Fodor'sChoice
★
🏨 **Colón.** Surprisingly charming and intimate for such a sizable hotel, this Barcelona standby is directly across the plaza from the cathedral, overlooking weekend *sardana* dancing, Thursday antiques markets, and, of course, the floodlighted cathedral by night. Rooms are comfortable and tasteful; try to get one with a view of the cathedral. The Colón was a favorite of Joan Miró. Considering its combination of comfort, style, and location, it may be the best hotel in Barcelona. ⊠ *Av. Catedral 7, Barri Gòtic, 08002* ☎ *93/301–1404* 🖷 *93/317–2915* ⊕ *www. hotelcolon.es* 🖙 *140 rooms, 5 suites* ⚴ *Restaurant, minibars, cable TV, in-room data ports, bar, babysitting, meeting room, car rental, travel services* ☰ *AE, DC, MC, V* Ⓜ *Catalunya.*

$$$–$$$$
Fodor'sChoice
★
🏨 **Duquesa de Cardona.** This refurbished 16th-century town house overlooking the port has ultracontemporary facilities with designer touches, all in an early-Renaissance structure. The exterior rooms have views of the harbor, the World Trade Center, and the passenger-boat terminals. The hotel is a 10-minute walk from everything in the Gothic Quarter or Barceloneta, and no more than a 30-minute walk from the main Eixample attractions. The miniature rooftop pool, more a plunge than a swimming venue, is cooling in summer. ⊠ *Passeig de Colom 12, Rambla, 08002* ☎ *93/268–9090* 🖷 *93/268–2931* ⊕ *www. hduquesadecardona.com* 🖙 *44 rooms* ⚴ *Restaurant, cafeteria, minibars, cable TV, in-room data ports, pool, meeting rooms* ☰ *AE, DC, MC, V* Ⓜ *Drassanes.*

$$$–$$$$ 🏨 **Grand Hotel Central.** Recently opened in the famous Cambó house on the edge of the Gothic Quarter very near the Barcelona cathedral, this hot new midtown hideaway is becoming a nomenclature magnet for the hip and swashbuckling from around Europe and beyond. Rooms are impeccably furnished and equipped with high-tech design features, from flat-screen TVs to DSL hookups. The restaurant, supervised by internationally acclaimed chef Ramón Freixa, is bound for glory, and the top-floor pool offers a unique perch over the city's 2000-year-old Roman and Gothic central nucleus. ☒ *Via Laietana 30, Barri Gòtic, 08003* 🕾 *93/295-7900* 🖷 *93/268-1215* ⊕ *www.grandhotelcentral.com* ↘ *147 rooms* ♧ *Restaurant, health club, pool, sauna, bar, meeting rooms, DSL connections, parking (fee)* ▭ *AE, DC, MC, V* Ⓜ *Catalunya.*

$$$–$$$$ 🏨 **H1898.** This elegant hotel overlooking the Rambla occupies a building with an illustrious history as the headquarters of the Compañia de Tabacos de Filipinas, a prestigious Barcelona business concern for nearly 100 years. Named for the fateful year when Spain was stripped of its final colonial possesions, the Philippines among them, the hotel's elegance is an homage to bygone glories as well as a sign of the city's present opulence. Rooms are superbly equipped with state-of-the-art appliances (such as flat-screen plasma TVs), and the location is unbeatable. ☒ *La Rambla 109, Rambla, 08002* 🕾 *93/552-9552* 🖷 *93/552-9550* ⊕ *www.nnhotels.es* ↘ *166 rooms, 3 suites* ♧ *Restaurant, health club, pool, sauna, bar, meeting rooms, DSL connections, parking (fee)* ▭ *AE, DC, MC, V* Ⓜ *Catalunya.*

$$$–$$$$ 🏨 **Montecarlo.** The ornate, illuminated entrance takes you from the Rambla through an enticing marble hall; upstairs, you enter a sumptuous reception room with a dark-wood Art Nouveau ceiling. Guest rooms are modern, bright, and functional, and many overlook the Rambla. ☒ *La Rambla 124, Rambla, 08002* 🕾 *93/412-0404* 🖷 *93/318-7323* ⊕ *www.montecarlobcn.com* ↘ *55 rooms, 1 suite* ♧ *Cafeteria, bar, meeting room, parking (fee)* ▭ *AE, DC, MC, V* Ⓜ *Catalunya.*

$$–$$$$ 🏨 **Rivoli Ramblas.** Behind this upper-Rambla facade lies an imaginative interior with marble floors. The rooms are pastel in hue and contemporary in design. The roof-terrace bar has panoramic views. ☒ *La Rambla 128, Rambla, 08002* 🕾 *93/481-7676* 🖷 *93/317-5053* ⊕ *www.rivolihotels.com* ↘ *81 rooms, 9 suites* ♧ *Restaurant, health club, sauna, bar, meeting rooms, parking (fee)* ▭ *AE, DC, MC, V* Ⓜ *Catalunya.*

$$$ 🏨 **Casa Camper Barcelona.** This revolutionary new hotel halfway between the Rambla and the MACBA (Museum of Contemporary Art) is the mutual brainchild of the Camper footwear empire and Barcelona's nonpareil Vinçon design store. No smoking, no tips, a free 24-hour snack facility to which you can invite your friends, ecologically recycled residual waters, children up to 12 staying free of charge, and the Foodball restaurant next door serving spheroids of natural ingredients such as garbanzo beans and spinach all add up to a unique address in the formerly grim Raval. ☒ *C. Elisabets 11, Raval, 08001* 🕾 *93/342-6280* 🖷 *93/342-7563* ⊕ *www.casacamper.com* ↘ *20 rooms, 5 suites* ♧ *Restaurant, meeting rooms, parking (fee); no smoking* ▭ *AE, DC, MC, V* ⦿❙ *BP* Ⓜ *Catalunya.*

$$$ 🏨 **Nouvel.** Centrally located below Plaça de Catalunya, this hotel blends white marble, etched glass, elaborate plasterwork, and carved, dark wood-

6

work in its handsome Art Nouveau interior. The rooms have marble floors, firm beds, and smart bathrooms. The narrow street is pedestrian-only and therefore quiet, but views are nonexistent. ⊠ *Santa Anna 18–20, Rambla, 08002* ☎ *93/301–8274* 🖶 *93/301–8370* ⊕ *www.hotelnouvel. com* ⇱ *71 rooms* ⚫ *Restaurant, coffee shop, in-room safes, cable TV, bar* ⊟ *AE, DC, MC, V* Ⓜ *Catalunya.*

$$$ 🏨 **Racó del Pi.** This sleek, modern space on a bustling Gothic Quarter street offers first-rate service and flawless if somewhat characterless accommodations. Equidistant from the cathedral, the Boqueria market, Plaça Catalunya, and the Palau de la Musica, this cozy *racó* (corner) is as practical as it is spotless. ⊠ *Carrer del Pi 7, Rambla, 08002* ☎ *93/ 342–6190* 🖶 *93/342–6191* ⊕ *www.h10.es* ⇱ *37 rooms* ⚫ *Minibars, cable TV, bar* ⊟ *AE, DC, MC, V* Ⓜ *Catalunya, Liceu.*

$$–$$$ 🏨 **Citadines.** This Rambla *aparthotel* (a hotel that rents apartments with kitchens) is impeccably bright and modern, soundproof, and generally well equipped. All rooms have kitchenettes and small dining areas. The rooftop solarium has views of Montjuïc and the Mediterranean. ⊠ *La Rambla 122, Rambla, 08002* ☎ *93/270–1111* 🖶 *93/412–7421* ⊕ *www.citadines.com* ⇱ *115 studios, 16 apartments* ⚫ *Kitchenettes, minibars, bar, meeting rooms* ⊟ *AE, DC, MC, V* Ⓜ *Catalunya.*

$$ 🏨 **Continental.** This modest hotel stands at the top of the Rambla, below Plaça de Catalunya. Space is tight, but rooms manage to accommodate large, firm beds. It's high enough over the Rambla to escape street noise, so ask for a room overlooking Barcelona's most emblematic street. George Orwell stayed here with his wife in 1937 after recovering from a bullet wound. ⊠ *La Rambla 138, Rambla, 08002* ☎ *93/ 301–2570* 🖶 *93/302–7360* ⊕ *www.hotelcontinental.com* ⇱ *35 rooms* ⚫ *In-room safes, cable TV* ⊟ *AE, DC, MC, V* Ⓜ *Catalunya.*

$$ 🏨 **Jardí.** Perched over the traffic-free and charming Plaça del Pi and Plaça Sant Josep Oriol, this budget hotel has rooms with views of the Gothic church of Santa Maria del Pi. All rooms have pine furniture and small bathrooms. The in-house breakfast is excellent, and the alfresco tables at the Bar del Pi, downstairs, are ideal in summer. With five floors and an elevator, this is not the Ritz: beds and furniture are flimsy, and the square can be noisy in summer, but it's still a great value. ⊠ *Pl. Sant Josep Oriol 1, Barri Gòtic, 08002* ☎ *93/301–5900* 🖶 *93/342–5733* ⊕ *www.hoteljardi-barcelona.com* ⇱ *40 rooms* ⊟ *AE, DC, MC, V* Ⓜ *Liceu, Catalunya.*

$$ 🏨 **Suizo.** The public rooms have elegant, modern seating and good views over the noisy square east of Plaça del Rei. The guest rooms have bright walls and wood or tile floors. ⊠ *Pl. del Àngel 12, Barri Gòtic, 08002* ☎ *93/310–6108* 🖶 *93/315–0461* ⊕ *www.gargallo-hotels.com* ⇱ *59 rooms* ⚫ *Snack bar, in-room safes, minibars, bar, laundry service* ⊟ *AE, DC, MC, V* Ⓜ *Jaume I.*

$–$$ 🏨 **Hostal Gat Xino.** A cheery space in what was once the darkest Raval, Gat Raval's sister ship places the adventurous traveler in the middle of what may seem more like a North African souk than a modern textile and design metropolis. Near the intersection of Carrers Carmen and Hospital, the Gat Xino gives you an up-close look at one of Barcelona's most cosmopolitan and traditionally tumultuous neighborhoods. Rooms are decorated in bright colors, and the value is unbeatable. In the bargain, you may discover that the Raval and its raucous street life are inhabited by Barcelona's friendliest citizens. ⊠ *Hospital 155, Raval, 08001* ☎ *93/324–8833* 🖷 *93/324–8834* ⊕ *www.gataccommodation.com* 🛏 *35 rooms* ⚐ *Dining room* ☰ *AE, DC, MC, V* Ⓜ *Sant Antoni.*

\$ **▣ Hostal Gat Raval.** This hip little hole-in-the-wall opens into a surprisingly bright and sleekly designed modern space with rooms that come in different shapes, styles, and number of beds, all cheerily appointed and impeccably maintained. Just around the corner from the MACBA, the Gat Raval seems to have been influenced by Richard Meier's shining contemporary structure, though you'd never guess it from the street. ⊠ *Joaquín Costa 44, Raval, 08001* ☎ *93/481–6670* 🖷 *93/342–6697* ⊕ *www.gataccommodation.com* 🛏 *22 rooms* ☰ *AE, DC, MC, V* Ⓜ *Universitat.*

FodorśChoice ★

Barceloneta & the Port Olímpic

★ \$\$\$\$ **▣ Hotel Arts.** This luxurious Ritz-Carlton monolith overlooks Barcelona from the Olympic Port, providing unique views of the Mediterranean, the city, and the mountains behind. The hotel's main drawback is that it's somewhat in a world of its own, a short taxi ride from the center of the city. That said, its world is an exciting one. True to its name, fine art—from Chillida drawings to Susana Solano sculptures—hangs everywhere. Sergi Arola's restaurant is a chic, postmodern culinary playground. ⊠ *Calle de la Marina 19, Port Olímpic, 08005* ☎ *93/221–1000* 🖷 *93/ 221–1070* ⊕ *www.harts.es* 🛏 *397 rooms, 59 suites, 27 apartments* ⚐ *3 restaurants, room service, minibars, cable TV, pool, hair salon, beach, bar, parking (fee)* ☰ *AE, DC, MC, V* Ⓜ *Ciutadella–Vila Olímpica.*

\$ **▣ Marina Folch.** This little Barceloneta hideaway is crisp, clean, and contemporary. Five minutes from the beach, with views over the port, an excellent restaurant (the Peru) downstairs, and a generous and caring family at the helm, it's a winner. ⊠ *Carrer Mar 16 pral., Barceloneta, 08003* ☎ *93/310–3709* 🖷 *93/310–5327* 🛏 *11 rooms* ⚐ *Restaurant* ☰ *AE, DC, MC, V* Ⓜ *Barceloneta.*

Eixample

\$\$\$\$ **▣ Claris.** Widely considered Barcelona's best hotel, this midtown refuge is a fascinating mélange of design and tradition. The rooms come in 60 modern layouts, some with restored 18th-century English furniture and some with contemporary furnishings from Barcelona's endlessly playful legion of lamp and chair designers. Lavishly endowed with wood and marble, the hotel also has a Japanese water garden. The restaurant East 47 is stellar. ⊠ *Carrer Pau Claris 150, Eixample, 08009* ☎ *93/487– 6262* 🖷 *93/215–7970* ⊕ *www.derbyhotels.es* 🛏 *80 rooms, 40 suites* ⚐ *2 restaurants, cable TV, pool, gym, sauna, bar, laundry service, meeting rooms, parking (fee)* ☰ *AE, DC, MC, V* Ⓜ *Passeig de Gràcia.*

FodorśChoice ★

\$\$\$\$ **▣ Fira Palace.** Built in the early '90s, this hotel has established itself as one of Barcelona's finest business and convention havens. Close to the Convention Palace, it offers easy access to Montjuïc and its attractions. Impeccably modern, it's also a solid choice for generic creature comfort rather than local color. ⊠ *Av. Rius i Taulet 1, Eixample, 08004* ☎ *93/ 426–2223* 🖷 *93/424–8679* ⊕ *www.fira-palace.com* 🛏 *258 rooms, 18*

6

suites ⌂ *Restaurant, minibars, cable TV, in-room data ports, pool, gym, hair salon, massage, squash, bar, meeting room, car rental, parking (fee)* ⊟ *AE, DC, MC, V* Ⓜ *Poble Sec.*

$$$$ 🖭 **Gallery.** In the upper part of the Eixample, just below the Diagonal, this modern hotel offers impeccable comfort and service and a central location for middle and upper Barcelona. (In the other direction, you're only a half-hour walk from the waterfront.) It's named for its proximity to the city's prime art-gallery district, a few blocks away on Rambla de Catalunya and Consell de Cent. ⊠ *Rosselló 249, Eixample, 08008* ☎ *93/415–9911* 🖷 *93/415–9184* ⊕ *www.galleryhotel.com* ↝ *108 rooms, 5 suites* ⌂ *Restaurant, cafeteria, minibars, cable TV, in-room data ports, health club, bar, meeting rooms, parking (fee)* ⊟ *AE, DC, MC, V* Ⓜ *Provença.*

$$$$ 🖭 **Hotel Omm.** Another member of Barcelona's lengthening list of design hotels, this postmodern architectural tour de force created by a team of designers seeks to create, in a playful way, a mystic sense of peace consonant with its eponymous mantra. The rooms, reception area, pool, and upper rooms overlooking the roof terrace of Gaudí's Casa Milá all contribute to this aura. The restaurant, Moo, is an oasis of modern cuisine orchestrated by the Roca brothers—Joan, Josep, and Jordi—who have achieved international prestige with their Celler de Can Roca near Girona. Roca offerings range from the bizarre to the classical, but one word to the wise: unless the taste of swallowing a cigar appeals to you, avoid the chocolate stogie. ⊠ *Rosselló 265, Eixample, 08008* ☎ *93/445–4000* 🖷 *93/445–4004* ⊕ *www.hotelomm.es* ↝ *58 rooms, 1 suite* ⌂ *Restaurant, minibars, cable TV, pool, hair salon, bar, wine bar, parking (fee)* ⊟ *AE, DC, MC, V* Ⓜ *Diagonal, Provença.*

★ $$$$ 🖭 **Hotel Palace.** Founded in 1919 by Caesar Ritz, this grande dame of Barcelona hotels has been restored to the splendor of its earlier years. The imperial lobby is at once loose and elegant; guest rooms contain Regency furniture, and some have Roman baths and mosaics. The restaurant, Diana, serves superb French and Catalan cuisine. ⊠ *Gran Via 668, Eixample, 08010* ☎ *93/510–1130* 🖷 *93/318–0148* ⊕ *www. hotelpalacebarcelona.com* ↝ *122 rooms* ⌂ *Restaurant, coffee shop, gym, sauna, bar, babysitting, business services, meeting rooms* ⊟ *AE, DC, MC, V* Ⓜ *Passeig de Gràcia.*

$$$$
Fodor'sChoice
★
✕🖭 **Majestic.** On Barcelona's most stylish boulevard, surrounded by fashion emporiums, you can find this near-perfect place to stay. The building is part Eixample town house and part modern extension, but pastels and Mediterranean hues warm each room. The superb restaurant, Fermin Puig's internationally acclaimed Drolma, is a destination in itself. ⊠ *Passeig de Gràcia 68, Eixample, 08008* ☎ *93/488–1717* 🖷 *93/488–1880* ⊕ *www.hotelmajestic.es* ↝ *273 rooms, 30 suites* ⌂ *2 restaurants, minibars, cable TV, in-room data ports, pool, health club, bar, parking (fee)* ⊟ *AE, DC, MC, V* Ⓜ *Passeig de Gràcia.*

$$$–$$$$ 🖭 **AC Diplomatic.** Well placed in the middle of the Eixample, within walking distance of nearly everything in town, this newly outfitted, high-tech hotel offers much more value than many of its more expensive neighbors. From flat-screen TVs to the free minibar, everything in the building, even the service, seems a little better than it has any right to be, especially if you can negotiate a weekend, low-season bargain. Spare, wood-paneled rooms, the outside pool, and the Mediterranean market-driven cuisine at Nichte, the hotel restaurant, can make this refuge a hard place to leave. ⊠ *Carrer Pau Claris 122, Eixample, 08009* ☎ *93/272–3810* 🖹 *93/272–3811* ⊕ *www.ac-hotels.com* 🛏 *211 rooms* ♿ *Restaurant, health club, pool, sauna, bar, meeting rooms, in-room data ports, free minibar, parking (fee)* ⊟ *AE, DC, MC, V* Ⓜ *Diagonal.*

$$$–$$$$
Fodor'sChoice
★
🏨 **Condes de Barcelona.** Reserve well in advance—this is one of Barcelona's most popular hotels. The pentagonal lobby has a marble floor and the original columns and courtyard from the 1891 building. The newest rooms have hot tubs and terraces overlooking interior gardens. An affiliated fitness club nearby has golf, squash, and swimming. The restaurant, Lasarte, where Martin Berasategui–trained chef Alex Garès serves fine Basque-influenced cuisine, is one of Barcelona's hot new stars. ⊠ *Passeig de Gràcia 75, Eixample, 08008* ☎ *93/445–0000* 🖹 *93/445–3232* ⊕ *www.condesdebarcelona.com* 🛏 *181 rooms, 2 suites* ♿ *Restaurant, in-room safes, minibars, cable TV, 2 pools (1 indoor), gym, hot tub, piano bar, business services, meeting room, parking (fee)* ⊟ *AE, DC, MC, V* Ⓜ *Passeig de Gràcia.*

$$$–$$$$
🏨 **Regente.** Moderniste furnishings and copious stained glass lend style and charm to this smallish hotel. The public rooms are carpeted in a mix of patterns; guest rooms, fortunately, are restrained. The verdant roof terrace and the prime position on the Rambla de Catalunya seal the positive verdict. ⊠ *La Rambla de Catalunya 76, Eixample, 08008* ☎ *93/487–5989* 🖹 *93/487–3227* ⊕ *www.hcchotels.com* 🛏 *79 rooms* ♿ *Restaurant, in-room safes, minibars, cable TV, pool, bar, meeting room* ⊟ *AE, DC, MC, V* Ⓜ *Passeig de Gràcia.*

$$–$$$
🏨 **Calderón.** On leafy Rambla de Catalunya, this modern high-rise has facilities normally found in hotels farther out of town. Public rooms are huge, with cool, white-marble floors, and the bedrooms follow suit. For stunning views, ask for one of the higher rooms. ⊠ *La Rambla Catalunya 26, Eixample, 08007* ☎ *93/301–0000* 🖹 *93/412–0120* ⊕ *www.nh-hoteles.com* 🛏 *224 rooms, 29 suites* ♿ *Restaurant, minibars, cable TV, 2 pools (1 indoor), health club, bar, piano bar, parking (fee)* ⊟ *AE, DC, MC, V* Ⓜ *Passeig de Gràcia.*

★ **$$**
🏨 **Continental Palacete.** This former in-town mansion, or *palacete*, provides a splendid drawing room, two elegant suites, a location nearly dead center between all of Barcelona's main attractions, views over the leafy tree-lined tunnel of Rambla Catalunya and a 24-hour free buffet. Ask specifically for one of the exterior rooms; the interior rooms on the elevator shaft can be noisy. ⊠ *La Rambla de Catalunya 30, Eixample, 08007* ☎ *93/445–7657* 🖹 *93/445–0050* ⊕ *www.hotelcontinental.com* 🛏 *17 rooms, 2 suites* ♿ *Minibars, cable TV* ⊟ *AE, DC, MC, V* Ⓜ *Passeig de Gràcia.*

$$
🏨 **Gran Via.** This 19th-century town house is a Moderniste enclave, with an original chapel, hall-of-mirrors breakfast room, ornate Moderniste staircase, and Belle Epoque phone booths. Guest rooms have plain alcoved walls, bottle-green carpets, and Regency-style furniture; those overlooking Gran Vía itself have better views but are quite noisy. ⊠ *Gran Vía 642, Eixample, 08007* ☎ *93/318–1900* 🖹 *93/318–9997* ⊕ *www.nnhotels.es* 🛏 *53 rooms* ♿ *Minibars, parking (fee)* ⊟ *AE, DC, MC, V* Ⓜ *Passeig de Gràcia.*

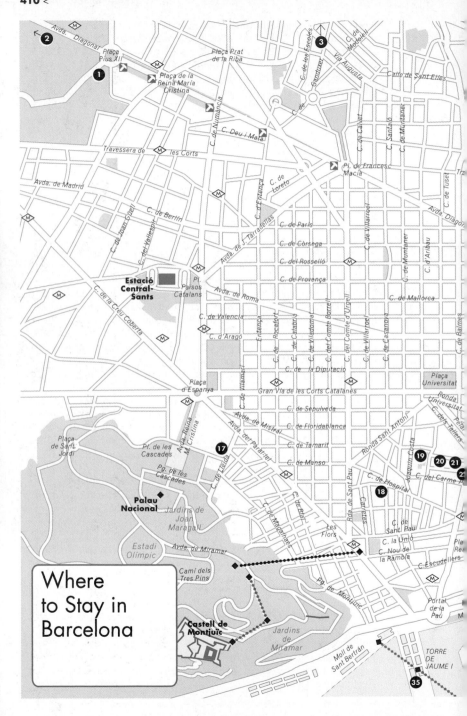

Where
to Stay in
Barcelona

KEY

- •••• Funicular
- ◈ Metro Stations
- 🄵 FGC Stations
- ┼─┼ Railway Lines
- •••• Telefèric
- 🅸 Tourist Information
- ↗ Tram stops

$–$$ ⌸ **Paseo de Gràcia.** Formerly a hostel, the Paseo has soft-color bedrooms with plain, good-quality carpets and sturdy wooden furniture. Add the location, on a handsome Eixample boulevard, and you have a good budget option. Some rooms, though not necessarily the newest, have balconies with views west over the city and the Collserola hills beyond. ⊠ *Passeig de Gràcia 102, Eixample, 08008* ☎ *93/215–5828* 🖷 *93/215–3724* ⌖ *33 rooms* ⊟ *AE, DC, MC, V* Ⓜ *Passeig de Gràcia.*

Sarrià-Pedralbes & Sant Gervasi

$$$$ ⌸ **Princesa Sofía.** This modern high-rise has numerous facilities and everything from shops to three different restaurants. The rooms, decorated in soft colors, are ultracomfortable. ⊠ *Pl. Pius XII 4, Diagonal, 08028* ☎ *93/508–1000* 🖷 *93/508–1001* ⊕ *www.expogrupo.com* ⌖ *475 rooms, 25 suites* ⚬ *3 restaurants, cable TV, 2 pools (1 indoor), health club, hair salon, sauna, bar, parking (fee)* ⊟ *AE, DC, MC, V* Ⓜ *Maria Cristina.*

★ **$$$$** ⌸ **Rey Juan Carlos I.** Towering over the western end of Barcelona's Avinguda Diagonal, this luxury hotel is also an exciting commercial complex where you can even buy or rent a fur or limousine. The lush garden, which includes a pond with swans, has an Olympic-size swimming pool, and the green expanses of Barcelona's finest in-town country club, El Polo, are beyond. The restaurant Chez Vous serves French cuisine, and Café Polo has a sumptuous buffet. ⊠ *Av. Diagonal 661–671, Diagonal, 08028* ☎ *93/364–4040* 🖷 *93/364–4264* ⊕ *www.hrjuancarlos. com* ⌖ *375 rooms, 37 suites* ⚬ *2 restaurants (3 in summer), minibars, cable TV, in-room data ports, tennis court, pool, health club, hair salon, spa, paddle tennis, 2 bars, meeting rooms, parking (fee)* ⊟ *AE, DC, MC, V* Ⓜ *Zona Universitària.*

$$–$$$ ⌸ **Turó de Vilana.** Surrounded by bougainvillea-festooned villas and
FodorśChoice mansions above Barcelona's Passeig de la Bonanova, this shiny entry
★ has a hot tub in every room; immaculate and gleaming halls and public areas of stone, steel, and glass; and a pleasant staff. Rooms are luminous. In summer, upper Barcelona is noticeably cooler, not to mention quieter at night. The Turó de Vilana is a 10-minute walk from the Sarrià train that connects you with the city center in 15 minutes. ⊠ *Vilana 7, Sant Gervasi, 08017* ☎ *93/434–0363* 🖷 *93/418–8903* ⊕ *www. turodevilana.com* ⌖ *20 rooms* ⚬ *Restaurant, room service, minibars, cable TV, meeting rooms* ⊟ *AE, DC, MC, V* Ⓜ *Sarrià.*

Tibidabo

$$$$ ⌸ **Gran Hotel la Florida.** This David Stein Group gem provides unaparalleled views over Barcelona, water sculptures everywhere but in your bed, a superb restaurant (L'Orangerie), and designer suites that are difficult to leave behind. Twenty minutes (and euros) from the port, this design hotel first opened in 1925 has roared back to the forefront of Barcelona's most stylish lodgings. ⊠ *Carretera Vallvidrera al Tibidabo 83–93, Tibidabo, 08035* ☎ *93/259–3000* 🖷 *93/259–3001* ⊕ *www.hotellaflorida. com* ⌖ *74 rooms, 22 suites* ⚬ *Restaurant, in-room safes, minibars, cable TV, indoor-outdoor pool, health club, hair salon, spa, Turkish bath, bar, nightclub, parking (fee)* ⊟ *AE, DC, MC, V* Ⓜ *Tibidabo.*

NIGHTLIFE & THE ARTS

Barcelona's art and nightlife scenes start early and never quite stop. To find out what's on, look in newspapers or the weekly *Guía Del Ocio*, which has a section in English, available at newsstands all over town. *Activitats*, available at the Palau de la Virreina (La Rambla 99) or the Centre Santa Monica (La Rambla 7) lists cultural events.

The Arts

Classical Music

The basilica of Santa Maria del Mar, the church of Santa Maria del Pi, the Monestir de Pedralbes, Drassanes Reials, and the Saló del Tinell, among other ancient and intimate spaces, hold concerts. Barcelona's music festival brings a long series of concerts in June and July. In late September, the **International Music Festival** is part of the feast of Nostra Senyora de la Mercè (Our Lady of Mercy), Barcelona's patron saint. Pop concerts are held in the Palau Sant Jordi on Montjuïc.

Barcelona's most famous concert hall is the Moderniste **Palau de la Música Catalana** (⊠ Sant Francesc de Paula 2, Sant Pere ☎93/295–7200), with performances September through June. Tickets go from €6 to €100 and are best purchased well in advance, though a last-minute *palco sin vistas* (box seat with no sight of the stage) is a good way to get into the building for a concert. The contemporary **Auditori de Barcelona** (⊠ Lepant 150, near Plaça de les Glòries, Eixample ☎ 93/247–9300) has classical music, with occasional jazz and pop thrown in. Barcelona's **Gran Teatre del Liceu** (Box office ⊠ La Rambla de Capuchinos 63, Rambla ☎ 93/485–9900) stages operas and recitals.

Dance

L'Espai de Dansa i Música de la Generalitat de Catalunya (⊠ Travessera de Gràcia 63, Eixample ☎ 93/414–3133)—generally listed as L'Espai, or "The Space"—is the prime venue for ballet and modern dance, as well as some musical offerings. **El Mercat de les Flors** (⊠ Lleida 59, Eixample ☎ 93/426–1875), near Plaça de Espanya, is a traditional venue for seeing modern dance and theater.

Film

Though many foreign films are dubbed, Barcelona has a full complement of original-language cinema; look for listings marked "v.o." (*versión original*). **Verdi** (⊠ Carrer Verdi 32, Gràcia) screens current releases with original-version sound tracks in a fun neighborhood for pre- and post-movie eating and drinking. The **Icaria Yelmo** (⊠ Salvador Espriu 61, Port Olímpic Ⓜ Carles I) complex in the Olympic Port has the city's largest selection of English-language films. **Renoir Les Corts** (⊠ Eugeni d'Ors 12, behind Diagonal's El Corte Inglés, Diagonal) is a good choice for recently released English-language features of all kinds. **Casablanca** (⊠ Passeig de Gràcia 115, Eixample) plays (generally art-flick) original-language movies.

Flamenco

Barcelona is not richly endowed with flamenco haunts, because Catalans consider flamenco—like bullfighting—a foreign import from An-

6

dalusia. On the Plaça Reial, **Los Tarantos** (✉ Pl. Reial 17, Barri Gòtic ☎ 93/318–3067) spotlights Andalusia's best flamenco. **El Patio Andaluz** (✉ Aribau 242, Eixample ☎ 93/209–3378) has rather touristy flamenco shows twice nightly (10 and midnight) and a karaoke section upstairs. Tour groups in search of flamenco gravitate to **El Cordobés** (✉ La Rambla 35, Rambla ☎ 93/317–6653). **El Tablao de Carmen** (✉ Poble Espanyol, Montjuïc ☎ 93/325–6895) hosts touring flamenco troupes up on Montjuïc. **La Taberna Flamenca** (✉ Art 12, Horta-Guinardó ☎ 93/351–8757) is a *sala rociera*, meaning they sing a salve to La Virgen del Rocío every night and welcome amateur flamencos.

Theater

Most plays are performed in Catalan, though some are in Spanish. Barcelona is known for avant-garde theater and troupes that specialize in mime, large-scale performance art, and special effects (La Fura dels Baus, Els Joglars, Els Comediants). **Teatre Lliure** has English subtitles on Wednesday, to make theater accessible for visitors. Other theaters are beginning to follow this lead. Call ahead for details. Several theaters along Avinguda Parallel specialize in musicals. The **Teatre Nacional de Catalunya** (✉ Pl. de les Arts 1 ☎ 93/306–5700), near Plaça de les Glories at the eastern end of the Diagonal, is a glass-enclosed classical temple designed by Ricardo Bofill, architect of Barcelona's airport. Programs cover everything from Shakespeare to ballet to avant-garde theater. The **Teatre Poliorama** (✉ La Rambla Estudios 115, Rambla ☎ 93/317–7599) is below Plaça de Catalunya. The **Teatre Romea** (✉ Hospital 51, Raval ☎ 93/301–5504) is behind the Boqueria. The **Teatre Tívoli** (✉ Casp 8, Eixample ☎ 93/412–2063), above Plaça de Catalunya, has theater and dance performances. Gràcia's **Teatre Lliure** (✉ Montseny 47, Gràcia ☎ 93/218–9251) stages theater, dance, and musical events. The **Mercat de les Flors** (✉ Lleida 59, Montjuïc ☎ 93/426–1875), near Plaça de Espanya, is the city's most traditional dance and theater venue.

Nightlife

Cabaret

Near the bottom of the Rambla, the minuscule **Bar Pastis** (✉ Santa Mònica 4, Rambla ☎ 93/318–7980) has both live performances and LPs of every Edith Piaf song ever recorded. **Arnau** (✉ Paral.lel 60, Eixample ☎ 93/242–2804) is an old-time music hall that's still going strong. **Starlets** (✉ Av. Sarrià 44, Eixample ☎ 93/430–9156) has a combination cabaret and disco program. **Joy's** (✉ Rocafort 231, Eixample ☎ 93/430–9156) hosts a floor show, cabaret, and dancing.

Casino

The **Gran Casino de Barcelona** (✉ Carrer de la Marina, Port Olímpic ☎ 93/225–7878), under the Hotel Arts, is open daily from 1 PM to 5 AM.

Jazz & Blues

The Palau de la Música Catalana holds an **international jazz festival** in November. The Gothic Quarter's **Harlem Jazz Club** (✉ Comtessa Sobradiel 8, Barri Gòtic ☎ 93/310–0755) is small but atmospheric, with good jazz and country bands. **Jamboree-Jazz & Dance-Club** (✉ Pl. Reial 17, Rambla ☎ 93/301–7564) is a center for jazz, rock, and flamenco. **Luz de Gas**

(✉ Muntaner 246, Eixample ☎ 93/209–7711) hosts every genre from Irish fusion to Cuban sounds. **Luna Mora** (✉ Port Olímpic, next to Hotel Arts, Port Olímpic ☎ 93/221–6161) stages the gamut, from country blues to salsa and soul. **Nao Colón/Club Bamboo** (✉ Av. Marques de l'Argentera 19, Born-Ribera ☎ 93/268–7633) combines the sounds and the cuisine of the Mediterranean followed by jazz, blues, flamenco, fusion, hard rock, and house after midnight. The bustling **Zacarías** (✉ Av. Diagonal 477 Eixample ☎ 93/207–5643) stages live music from a variety of musical genres, including jazz, rock, folk, and blues.

Late-Night Bars

Bar musical is Spanish for any bar with music loud enough to drown out conversation. Wildly active but, on balance, better to *avoid,* are the **Port Olímpic** and the Port Vell's **Maremagnum**. Especially in summer and on weekends, these are far from Barcelona's best nightlife options.

Universal (✉ Marià Cubí 182–184, Eixample ☎ 93/200–7470) has been the hottest bar in town for 30 years. **Mas i Mas** (✉ Marià Cubí 199, Eixample ☎ 93/209–4502), across the street from Universal, is so crowded that social intimacy is guaranteed. **Nick Havanna** (✉ Rosselló 208, Eixample ☎ 93/215–6591) has, along with a consistently hot program of live music, Barcelona's most entertaining urinals. **L'Ovella Negra** (✉ Sitjàs 5, Raval ☎ 93/317–1087) is the top student tavern. **Glaciar** (✉ Pl. Reial 13, Rambla ☎ 93/302–1163) is *the* spot for young out-of-towners. For a more laid-back scene, with high ceilings, billiards, tapas, and hundreds of students, visit the popular **Velodrom** (✉ Muntaner 211–213, Eixample ☎ 93/230–6022), below the Diagonal. Two blocks from Velodrom is the intriguing *barmuseo* (bar-cum-museum) **La Fira** (✉ Provença 171, Eixample ☎ 93/323–7271). Downtown, deep in the Barrio Chino, try the **London Bar** (✉ Nou de la Rambla 34, Raval ☎ 93/302–3102), an Art Nouveau circus haunt with a trapeze suspended above the bar. **Bar Almirall** (✉ Joaquin Costa 33, Raval ☎ 93/412–1535) has an Art Nouveau chicness. **Bar Muy Buenas** (✉ Carme 63, Raval ☎ 93/442–5053) is an Art Nouveau gem. Over by the Sagrada Família, the **Michael Collins Irish Pub** (✉ Pl. Sagrada Família 4, Eixample ☎ 93/459–1964) has a strong Anglo following. Above Via Augusta in upper Barcelona, the **Sherlock Holmes** (✉ Copernic 42–44, Eixample ☎ 93/414–2184) is an ongoing Brit-fest with live musical performances and darkly intimate corners. Above Via Augusta, **Opiniao** (✉ Ciutat de Balaguer 67, below Bonanova, La Bonanova ☎ 93/418–3399) is another upper-Barcelona dive, a hot local club. **George & Dragon** (✉ Diputació 269, Eixample ☎ 93/488–1765), named for Barcelona's ubiquitous symbols of good and evil, is a rollicking English pub just off Passeig de Gràcia. Café-restaurant-bar **Salero** (✉ Carrer del Rec 60, Eixample ☎ 93/488–1765) is always packed with young miscreants.

Nightclubs & Discos

Most clubs have a discretionary cover charge and like to inflict it on foreigners, so dress up and be prepared to talk your way past the bouncer. Any story can work; for example, you own a chain of nightclubs and are on a world tour. Don't expect much to happen until 1:30 or 2. Tops for some time now is the prisonesque nightclub **Otto Zutz** (✉ Lincoln 15, Eixample ☎ 93/238–0722), off Via Augusta. The nearly classic **Up and Down** (✉ Numancia 179, Eixample ☎ 93/280–2922), pronounced "Pen-*dow*," is a good choice for elegant carousers. A line forms at **Bikini** (✉ Deu i Mata 105, at Entença, Eixample ☎ 93/322–0005) on festive Saturday nights. **Torres de Avila** (✉ Marquès de Comillas 25, Montjuïc ☎ 93/424–9309), in Pueblo Espanyol, is wild and woolly until broad daylight on weekends. **Danzatoria** (✉ Av. Tibidabo 61, Tibidabo ☎ 93/211–6261), a fusion of Salsitas and Partycular, is a "multispace" with five venues (disco, hall, dance, chill-out, garden) and fills with models and hopeful guys. **Sala Razzmatazz** (✉ Almogavers 122, Poble Nou ☎ 93/320–8200) offers Friday and Saturday disco madness until dawn. Weeknight concerts have international stars such as Ani DiFranco and Enya. **Bucaro** (✉ Aribau 195, Eixample ☎ 93/209–6562) rocks until dawn, albeit largely for the extremely young. **Buda Barcelona** (✉ Pau Claris 92, Eixample ☎ 93/318–4252) is the hottest nightspot in the Eixample, with celebrities and glamour galore. The beachfront **CDLC** (✉ Passeig Maritim 32, Port Olímpic ☎ 93/224–0470) has compartmentalized *sofa-camas* (sofa beds of a sort) for horizontal time. **DosTrece** (✉ Carme 40, Raval ☎ 93/443–0341) packs in young internationals for dancing and carousing and general hooking up. **It Café** (✉ Joaquin Costa 4, Raval ☎ 93/443–0341) is a design oasis not far from the MACBA in the Raval. The **Loft** (✉ Pamplona 88, Poble Nou ☎ 93/272–0910), an offshoot of Sala Razzmatazz, is dedicated to electronic music. **Row Club** (✉ Rosselló 208, Eixample ☎ 93/237–5405) is big on techno. **Sala Cibeles** (✉ Córsega 363, Eixample ☎ 93/272–0910) has big sound and singing DJs. Salsa sizzles at the exuberantly Caribbean **Antilla BCN Latin Club** (✉ C. Aragó 141, Eixample ☎ 93/451–4564). **Luz de Luna** (✉ C. Comerç 21, La Ribera ☎ 93/310–7542) lays down wall-to-wall salsa; oxygen masks are advised. **Agua de Luna** (✉ Viladomat 211, Eixample ☎ 93/410–0440) is a torrid salsa scene in the western Eixample. **Pachá** (✉ Dr. Maranon 17, Pedralbes-Les Corts ☎ 93/204–0412) offers two raging discos and a restaurant.

Costa Breve (✉ Aribau 230, Eixample ☎ 93/200–7346) accepts postgraduates with open arms. **El Otro** (✉ Valencia 166, Eixample ☎ 93/323–6759) is kind to aging (over-thirty) miscreants. For big-band tango in an old-fashioned *sala de baile* (dance hall), head to **La Paloma** (✉ Tigre 27, Raval ☎ 93/301–6897), with kitschy 1950s furnishings.

SPORTS & THE OUTDOORS

Golf

Call ahead to reserve tee times. Weekday greens fees range from about €36 at most courses to €72 on weekends and holidays. San Cugat's **Club de Golf de San Cugat** (✉ Calle Villa s/n ☎ 93/674–3908) has 18 hilly holes. Greens fees are €65 on weekdays and €130 on weekends. Sitges' **Club de Golf Terramar** (✉ Passeig Maritim s/n ☎ 93/894–0580) offers 18 along the beach. Greens fees are €75 during the week and €90 on weekends.

Health Clubs

For specifics, look in the *Páginas Amarillas/Pàgines Grogues* (*Yellow Pages*) under "Gimnasios/Gimnasis." The **DiR** (☎ 901/304030 general information ✉ Main branch ✉ DiR Diagonal, Ganduxer 25–27, Eixample ☎ 93/202–2202) network of fitness centers is worthy, with addresses all over Barcelona. A day membership, €11, includes aerobics classes and the use of a sauna, a steam room, a swimming pool, squash courts, and MTV.

Hiking

The **Collserola** hills behind the city offer well-marked trails, fresh air, and lovely views. Take the San Cugat, Sabadell, or Terrassa FFCC train from Plaça de Catalunya and get off at Baixador de Vallvidrera; the information center, 10 minutes uphill next to **Vil.la Joana** (now the Jacint Verdaguer Museum), has maps of this mountain woodland 20 minutes from downtown. The walk back into town can take from two to five hours, depending on your speed and the trails you pick. **Club Excursionista de Catalunya** (✉ Paradis 10, Barri Gòtic ☎ 93/315–2311) has information on hiking in Barcelona's outskirts. Ask the **Asociació Excursionista, Etnográfica i Folklorica** (✉ Avinyó 19, Barri Gòtic ☎ 93/302–2730) about hikes, including treks in the Pyrenees.

Soccer

If you're in Barcelona between September and June, go see the celebrated FC Barcelona play soccer (preferably against Real Madrid, if you can get in) at Barcelona's gigantic stadium, **Camp Nou** (✉ Arístides Maillol, Les Corts ☎ 93/496–3608 ⊕ www.fcbarcelona.com ✉ Museum €5.30, combined ticket including tour of museum, field, and sports complex €9.50 ☉ Museum Mon.–Sat. 10–6:30, Sun. 10–2 Ⓜ Collblanc, Palau Reial). Games are played Saturday night at 9 or Sunday afternoon at 5, though there may be international Champion's League games on Tuesday or Wednesday evening as well. Ask your hotel concierge how to get tickets, or call the club in advance. The stadium seats 98,000 and fills to capacity for big games. A worthwhile alternative to seeing a game is the guided tour of the FC Barcelona museum and facilities. The museum has a five-screen video showing the club's most memorable goals, along with player biographies and displays chronicling the history of one of Europe's most colorful soccer clubs.

Swimming

Piscines Bernat Picornell (✉ Av. del Estadi 30–40, Montjuïc ☎ 93/423–4041) comprises indoor and outdoor pools plus a sauna, gymnasium, and fitness equipment. Overlooking the beach from Barceloneta, the **Club Natació de Barceloneta** (✉ Passeig Joan de Borbó, Barceloneta ☎ 93/221–0010), also known as Complex Esportiu Municipal Banys Sant Sebastiá, has an indoor pool.

Tennis

Vall d'Hebron (✉ Passeig Vall d'Hebron 178–196, Vall d'Hebron ☏ 93/427–6500 ✍ Clay courts €15 per hour, hard courts €17 ⊗ 8 AM until 11 PM) has Olympic tennis facilities. **Complejo Deportivo Can Caralleu** (Can Caralleu Sports Complex; ✉ Calle Esports 2–8 ☏ 93/203–7874 ✍ €8 per hour by day, €10 by night ⊗ daily 8 AM–11 PM), above Pedralbes, a 30-minute walk uphill from the Reina Elisenda subway stop (FFCC de la Generalitat), has hard courts and clean air. **Club Vall Parc** (✉ Ctra. de la Rabassada 79, Tibidabo ☏ 93/212–6789 ✍ €15 per hour by day, €19 by night ⊗ Daily 8 AM–midnight) is upscale.

SHOPPING

Between fashions, designer home furnishings, foodstuffs, and art and antiques, Barcelona is the best place in Spain to unload extra ballast from your wallet. True, bargains are few outside saffron and rope-sole shoes, but quality and selection are excellent. Most stores are open Monday through Saturday 9 to 1:30 and 5 to 8, but some close in the afternoon. Virtually all close on Sunday.

Shopping Districts

For high fashion, browse along Passeig de Gràcia and the Diagonal between Plaça Joan Carles I and Plaça Francesc Macià. There are two-dozen antiques shops in the Gothic Quarter, another 70 shops off Passeig de Gràcia on Bulevard dels Antiquaris, and still more in Gràcia and Sarrià. Barcelona's prime shopping districts are the Passeig de Gràcia, Rambla de Catalunya, Plaça de Catalunya, Porta de l'Àngel, and Avinguda Diagonal up to Carrer Ganduxer. For old-fashioned Spanish shops, prowl the Gothic Quarter, especially **Carrer Ferran.** The area surrounding **Plaça del Pi,** from the Boqueria to Carrer Portaferrissa and Carrer de la Canuda, is thick with boutiques, jewelry, and design shops. The **Barri de la Ribera,** around Santa Maria del Mar, has design and food shops. Design, jewelry, and knick-knack shops cluster on Carrer Banys Vells and Carrer Flassaders, near Carrer Montcada. The shopping colossus **L'Illa,** on the Diagonal beyond Carrer Ganduxer, includes the department store FNAC and other temptations. **Carrer Tuset,** north of the Diagonal, has lots of small boutiques. The **Maremagnum** mall, in Port Vell, is convenient to downtown. **Diagonal Mar,** at the eastern end of the diagonal, along with the **Fòrum 2004** complex offer many shopping options in a mega-shopping-mall environment.

SHOPPING HOT SPOTS

Antiques Center: Carrer de la Palla
Ceramics Studio: Art Escudellers
Bookstore: La Central
Cobbler: La Manual Alpargartera
Gourmet Food Market: Mantequeria Can Ravell
Music Store: Discos Castelló
Spice Shop: Casa Gispert
Stationery Boutique: Papirum

Specialty Stores

Antiques

Antiques shopping is headquartered in the Gothic Quarter, where **Carrer de la Palla** and **Carrer Banys Nous** are lined with shops full of prints, maps, books, paintings, and furniture. An antiques market is held in front of the **cathedral** every Thursday from 10 to 8. In upper Barcelona, the entire village of **Sarrià** is becoming an antiquer's destination, with shops along Cornet i Mas, Pedró de la Creu, and Major de Sarrià. The Eixample's **Centre d'Antiquaris** (⊠ Passeig de Gràcia 55, Eixample) contains 75 antiques stores. Moderniste aficionados should check out **Gothsland** (⊠ Consell de Cent 331, Eixample). **La Maison Coloniale** (⊠ Sant Antoni Abat 61, Raval) has 15th-century stone vaulting and colonial treasures. **Novecento** (⊠ Passeig de Gràcia 75, Eixample) has antique art and jewelry. **Alcanto** (⊠ Passeig de Gràcia 55–57, Eixample) is a clearinghouse for buying and selling. **Antiguedades J. Pla** (⊠ C. Aragó 517, Eixample) buys and sells antiques.

Art

There's a cluster of art galleries on Carrer Consell de Cent between Passeig de Gràcia and Carrer Balmes, and around the corner on Rambla de Catalunya. The Born–Santa Maria del Mar quarter is another art destination, along Carrer Montcada and the parallel Carrer Bany Vells. **Galeria Joan Prats** (⊠ La Rambla de Catalunya 54, Eixample) is a veteran, known for the quality of its artists' works. **Eude** (⊠ Consell de Cent 278, Eixample) showcases young artists. **Sala Dalmau** (⊠ Consell de Cent 347, Eixample) is an established art outlet. **Sala Rovira** (⊠ La Rambla de Catalunya 62, Eixample) has shown top artists Tom Carr and Blanca Vernis. The **Joan Gaspar** (⊠ Pl. Letamendi 1, Eixample) started with Picasso and Miró. Carrer Petritxol, which leads down into Plaça del Pi, is lined with galleries, notably **Sala Parès** (⊠ Petritxol 5, Barri Gòtic).

Books

La Central (⊠ C. Mallorca 237, Eixample) is Barcelona's best bookstore. **La Central del Raval** (⊠ C. Elisabets 6, Eixample), in the former chapel of the Casa de la Misericòrdia, sells books on architectureas well. **Altair** (⊠ Gran Vía 616, Eixample) is Barcelona's premier travel and adventure bookstore, with many titles in English. **BCN Books** (⊠ Roger de Llúria 118, Eixample) is a top store for books in English. **Casa del Llibre** (⊠ Passeig de Gràcia 62, Eixample) is a book feast with English titles. **Laie** (⊠ Pau Claris 85, Eixample) is a book lover's sanctuary, with cultural events as well as stacks. The bookstore in the **Palau de la Virreina** (⊠ La Rambla 99, Rambla) has books on art, design, and Barcelona in general. **El Corte Inglés,** especially the branch in Porta del Àngel, sells English guidebooks and novels.

Boutiques & Jewelry

Chanel, Armani, Loewe, and the other big names have stores on Passeig de Gràcia. **El Bulevard Rosa** (⊠ Passeig de Gràcia 53–55, Eixample) is a collection of boutiques with the latest outfits. The stretch of Avinguda Diagonal between Passeig de Gràcia and Carrer Ganduxer is lined with high-end shops. **Adolfo Domínguez** (⊠ Passeig de Gràcia 35, Av. Diagonal 570, Eixample) is one of Spain's leading designers. **Groc** (✉ C. Muntaner 382, Eixample ✉ La Rambla de Catalunya 100, Eixample), Toni Miró's two shops, have the latest looks for men, women, and children. **David Valls** (✉ C. Valencia 235, Eixample) represents new, young Barcelona fashion design. **May Day** (✉ C. Portaferrissa 16, Barri Gòtic) carries cutting-edge clothing, footwear, and accessories. **Joaquim Berao** (✉ C. Rosselló 277, Eixample) is a top jewelry designer. Beatriz Würsch displays her unusual jewelry designs in **Forum Ferlandina** (✉ Ferlandina 31, Raval), next to the MACBA. Young designers show their work in New Yorker Annie George's **Candela** (✉ Santa Maria 6, La Ribera) next to Santa Maria del Mar in a superb 17th-century house.

Ceramics
Art Escudellers (✉ C. Escudellers 23–25, Barri Gòtic) has ceramics from all over Spain, with more than 200 different artisans represented and maps showing where the work is from. In addition, the art gallery and the wine-, Iberian ham–, and cheese-tasting bar downstairs makes this the best studio in town. **Itaca** (✉ C. Ferrán 26, Barri Gòtic) has ceramic plates, bowls, and pottery from Talavera de la Reina and La Bisbal. For Lladró, try **Pla de l'Os** (✉ Boqueria 3, Barri Gòtic), off the Rambla. In Sarrià, behind the market on your way into bougainvillea-choked Plaça Sant Gaietà, check out the ceramics store **Nica & Bet** (✉ Pare Miquel de Sarrià 10, Sarrià); don't miss the beautifully restored wooden doors. Although perusing smaller establishments is always worthwhile, one of Barcelona's big department stores, **El Corte Inglés**, at Plaça Catalunya or Diagonal, is a good bet for ceramics shoppers.

Department Stores
Among other emporiums, Plaça de Catalunya includes **FNAC** and **Habitat**, which also has stores on Tuset at the Diagonal. The ubiquitous **El Corte Inglés** has four locations: Plaça de Catalunya 14, Porta de l'Angel 19–21, Avinguda Francesc Macià 58, and Avinguda Diagonal 617.

Design & Interiors
The area around the church of Santa Maria del Mar, an artisans' quarter since medieval times, is full of cheerful design stores and art galleries.

Vinçon (✉ Passeig de Gràcia 96, Eixample) occupies a rambling Moderniste house and carries everything from Filofaxes to handsome kitchenware. You can also find one of Barcelona's most spectacular Art Nouveau fireplaces, complete with a stylized face for a hearth. Upscale **Gimeno** (✉ Passeig de Gràcia 102, Eixample) has everything from clever suitcases to the latest in furniture design. **bd** (Barcelona design; ✉ Carrer Mallorca 291–293, Eixample) is a spare, cutting-edge home-furnishing store in another Moderniste gem, Domènech i Montaner's Casa Thomas. **Vientos del Sur** (✉ C. Argenteria 78, La Ribera), part of the Natura chain, has a good selection of crafts. **Ici et Là** (✉ Pl. Santa Maria del Mar 2, La Ribera) is across the square and has an eclectic selection of clothing, gifts, and knickknacks. **Fem** (✉ Palau 6, behind ajuntament, Barri Gòtic) has interesting artifacts and artisanship. **Papers Coma** (✉ Montcada 20, La Ribera) has inventive knickknacks. **Estudi Pam2** (✉ Sabateret 1–3, La Ribera), behind Carrer Montcada, sells ingenious design items. **Suspect** (✉ Comerç 29, La Ribera), north of the Born, specializes in clothes and furniture made by Spastor, a group of Barcelona designers. **Gotham** (✉ Cervantes 7, Barri Gòtic), behind Town Hall, restores furniture from the '50s and '60s. It's a perennial set for Almodóvar movies. Amid mouthwatering interior design, **La Comercial** (✉ Rec 52 and 73, La Ribera) off Passeig del Born has clothes by Paul & Joe, Paul Smith, and Isabel Marant. **Sita Murt** (✉ Avinyó 18, Barri Gòtic) is a stunning subterranean space with a clever play of mirrors and collections from Antik Batik, Save the Queen, and Esteve Sita Murt.

Fine Foods

Casa Gispert (✉ Sombrerers 23, La Ribera), on the inland side of Santa Maria del Mar, is one of the most aromatic and esthetically perfect shops in Barcelona, bursting with spices, saffron, chocolates, and nuts. **Jobal** (✉ C. Princesa 38, La Ribera) is a charming and fragrant saffron and spice shop. **La Barcelonesa** (✉ C. Comerç 27, La Ribera) specializes in dry goods, spices, tea, and saffron. **Tot Formatge** (✉ Passeig del Born 13, La Ribera) has cheeses from all over Spain and the world. **Vila Viniteca** (✉ C. Agullers 7, La Ribera), near Santa Maria del Mar, is one of the best wine shops in Barcelona, and the produce store across the way sells some of the best cheeses around. **La Botifarreria de Santa Maria** (✉ Carrer Santa Maria 4, La Ribera), next to the church of Santa Maria, has excellent cheeses, hams, pâtés, and homemade *sobrassadas* (pork pâté with paprika). **El Magnífico** (✉ C. Argenteria 64, La Ribera) is famous for its coffees. Behind the Picasso Museum, **Born Cooking** (✉ Corretger 9, La Ribera) is a work of art in itself, serving delicious cakes, quiches, and all manner of sweets and savories.

La Casa del Bacalao (✉ Condal 8, off Portal del Angel, Barri Gòtic) specializes in salt cod and books of codfish recipes. **La Palmera** (✉ C. Enric Granados 57, Eixample) has a superb collection of wines, hams, cheeses, and olive oils. **Caelum** (✉ C. de la Palla 8, Barri Gòtic) sells crafts and such foods as honey and preserves, made in convents and monasteries all over Spain. **Mantequeria Can Ravell** (✉ Aragó 313, Eixample) restaurant and delicatessen, is Barcelona's number one all-around wine, cheese, ham, and fine foods specialist. **La Cave** (✉ Av. J. V. Foix 80, Sarrià) is a wine cellar with a flair. Polyglot Claude Cohen and company not only sell wine, but teach it. **Vilaplana** (✉ C. Francesc Perez Cabrero, Eixample) is famous for its pastries, cheeses, hams, pâtés, caviars, and fine deli items. **Tutusaus** (✉ C. Francesc Perez Cabrero 5, Sant Gervasi) specializes in fine Iberian hams and superb cheeses from all over Europe. **OroLíquido** (✉ C. de la Palla 8, Barri Gòtic) sells the finest olive oils from Spain and the world at large.

Food & Flea Markets

Spectacular food markets include the Mercat de la Llibertat, near Plaça Gal.la Placidia, and Mercat de la Revolució, on Travessera de Gràcia, both in Gràcia. On Thursday, a natural-produce market (honeys, cheeses) fills Plaça del Pi with interesting tastes and aromas. On Sunday morning, a stamp and coin market fills Plaça Reial; also on Sunday, the Plaça Sant Josep Oriol holds a painter's market, along with another general crafts and flea market near the Columbus Monument at the port end of the Rambla. The **Boqueria** (✉ La Rambla 91, Rambla) is Barcelona's most colorful food market and the oldest of its kind in Europe. Open Monday through Saturday 8 to 8, it's most active before 3 PM. Barcelona's biggest flea market, **Els Encants** (⊠ Dos de Maig, on Plaça de les Glòries, Eixample Ⓜ Glòries) is held Monday, Wednesday, Friday, and Saturday 8 to 7. The **Mercat Gòtic** (⊠ Pl. de la Seu, Barri Gòtic) fills the area in front of the Catedral de la Seu on Thursday. The **Mercat de Sant Antoni** (⊠ Ronda Sant Antoni, Eixample) is an old-fashioned food, clothing, and used-book (many in English) market that's best on Sunday.

Gifts & Miscellany

Stationery lovers will want to linger in the Gothic Quarter's **Papirum** (⊠ Baixada de la Llibreteria 2, Barri Gòtic), a tiny, medieval-tone shop with exquisite hand-printed papers and writing implements. **La Manual Alpargartera** (⊠ Avinyó 7, Barri Gòtic), off Carrer Ferran, specializes in handmade rope-sole sandals and espadrilles. **Solé** (⊠ C. Ample 7, Barri Gòtic) makes shoes by hand and sells others from all over the world. **La Lionesa** (⊠ C. Ample 21, Barri Gòtic) is an old-time grocery store. Barcelona's best music store is **Discos Castelló** (⊠ C. Tallers 3, Raval). For textiles, try **Teranyina** (⊠ C. Notariat 10, Raval). **Baclava** (⊠ C. Notariat 10, Raval) shares an address with Teranyina and sells artisanal products. **Otman** (⊠ Carrer Cirera 4, La Ribera) has light and racy frocks, belts, blouses, and skirts. Cutlery flourishes at the stately **Ganiveteria Roca** (⊠ Pl. del Pi 3, Barri Gòtic), opposite the giant rose window of the Santa Maria del Pi church.

SIDE TRIPS

Numbers in the margin correspond to points of interest on the Side Trips from Barcelona map.

Montserrat

❶ *50 km (30 mi) northwest of Barcelona.*

A nearly obligatory side trip from Barcelona is the shrine of La Moreneta, the Black Virgin of Montserrat, high in the mountains of the Serra de Montserrat. These weird, sawtooth peaks have given rise to countless legends: here St. Peter left a statue of the Virgin Mary carved by St. Luke, Parsifal found the Holy Grail, and Wagner sought inspiration for his opera. Montserrat is as memorable for its strange, pink hills as it is for its religious treasures, so be sure to explore the area. The vast monastic complex is dwarfed by the grandeur of the jagged peaks, and the crests are bristling with chapels and hermitages. The hermitage of **Sant Joan** can be reached by funicular. The views over the mountains to the Mediterranean and, on a clear day, to the Pyrenees are breathtaking; the rugged, boulder-strewn terrain makes for dramatic walks and hikes.

Although a monastery has stood on the same site in Montserrat since the early Middle Ages, the present 19th-century building replaced the rubble left by Napoléon's troops in 1812. The shrine is world-famous, and one of Catalonia's spiritual sanctuaries—honeymooning couples flock here by the thousands seeking La Moreneta's blessing on their marriages, and twice a year, on April 27 and September 8, the diminutive statue of

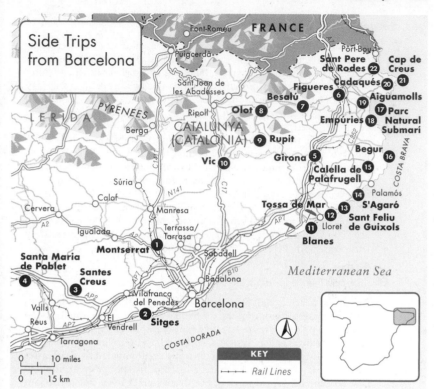

Side Trips
from Barcelona

Montserrat's Black Virgin becomes the object of one of Spain's greatest pilgrimages. To get here, follow the A2/A7 *autopista* on the upper ring road (Ronda de Dalt), or from the western end of the Diagonal as far as Salida (Exit) 25 to Martorell. Bypass this industrial center and follow signs to Montserrat. Alternatively, you can take a train from the Plaça Espanya metro station (hourly from 8:36 to 6:36, connecting with the funicular leaving every 15 minutes) or go on a guided tour with Pullmantur or Julià.

Only the basilica and museum are regularly open to the public. The **basilica** is dark and ornate, its blackness pierced by the glow of hundreds of votive lamps. Above the high altar stands the famous polychrome statue of the Virgin and Child, to which the faithful can pay their respects by way of a separate door. ☎ 93/877–7777 ⏰ *Daily 6 AM–10:30 AM and noon–6:30 PM.*

The monastery's **museum** has two sections: the Secció Antiga has old masters, among them works by El Greco, Correggio, and Caravaggio, and the amassed gifts to the Virgin; the Secció Moderna concentrates on recent modern Catalan painters. ☎ 93/877–7766 *abbey and museum* ⏰ *Secció Antiga Tues.–Sat. 10:30–2, Secció Moderna Tues.–Sat. 3–6.*

Sitges, Santes Creus & Poblet

This trio of attractions south and west of Barcelona can be seen comfortably in a day. Sitges is the prettiest and most popular resort in Barcelona's immediate environs, flaunting an excellent beach, a whitewashed and flowery old quarter. It's also one of Europe's premier gay resorts. The Cistercian monasteries west of here, at Santes Creus and Poblet, are characterized by monolithic Romanesque architecture and beautiful cloisters. By car, head southwest along Gran Vía or Passeig Colom to the freeway that passes the airport on its way to Castelldefels. From here, the freeway and tunnels will get you to Sitges in 20 to 30 minutes. From Sitges, drive inland toward Vilafranca del Penedès and the A7 freeway. The A2 (Lleida) leads to the monasteries. Regular trains leave Sants and Passeig de Gràcia for Sitges; the ride takes a half hour. To get to Santes Creus or Poblet from Sitges, take a Lleida-line train to L'Espluga de Francolí, 4 km (2½ mi) from Poblet. For Poblet, you can also stay with the train to Tarragona and catch a bus to the monastery (Autotransports Perelada ☎ 973/202058).

Sitges

❷ *43 km (27 mi) southwest of Barcelona.*

The Sitges beach is well provided with fine sand that is carefully maintained in pristine condition, and the human flora and fauna usually found sun-worshipping on it are dazzling specimens for every taste and preference, lending the display of sea, sand, and celebrants a nearly catwalk-like intensity. The eastern end of the strand is dominated by an albaster statue of the 16th-century painter El Greco, usually more at home in Toledo, where he spent most of his professional career. The artist Santiago Rusinol is to blame for this surprise, as he was such an El Greco fan that he not only installed two El Greco paintings in his Museu Cau Ferrat but had this sculpture planted on the beach.

The most interesting museum here is the **Cau Ferrat**, founded by Santiago Rusinol (1861–1931) and containing some of his own paintings together with two El Grecos. Connoisseurs of wrought iron will love the beautiful collection of *cruces terminales,* crosses that once marked town boundaries. Next door is the **Museu Maricel de Mar**, with more artistic treasures, and **Casa Llopis**, a romantic villa offering a tour of the house and local wine tasting is a short walk across town. ⊠ *Fonollar s/n* ☎ *93/894–0364* ⊕ *www.diba.es* ✉ *€3.75, valid for all three museums; free 1st Wed. of month* ☽ *June 14–Sept. 30., Tues.–Sat. 9:30–2 and 4–7; Oct. 1–June 13, Tues.–Sat. 9:30–2 and 3:30–6:30; Sun. 10–2.*

NEED A BREAK? Linger over excellent Mediterranean products and cooking with a nonpareil sea view at **Vivero** (⊠ Passeig Balmins ☎ 93/894–2149). The clean-lined contemporary style enhances both the seascapes and the seafood. The restaurant is closed Tuesday from February through April.

EN ROUTE After leaving Sitges, make straight for the A2 *autopista* by way of Vilafranca del Penedès. Wine buffs may want to stop here to taste some excellent Penedès wines; you can tour and sip at the **Bodega Miguel Tor-**

res (✉ C. Comerç 22 ☎ 93/890–0100). There's an interesting **Museu del Vi** (Wine Museum) in the Royal Palace, with descriptions of wine-making history. ⊞ €4 ⊙ *Tues.–Sun. 10–2 and 4–7.*

Santes Creus

❸ *95 km (59 mi) west of Barcelona.*

Founded in 1157, Santes Creus is the first of the monasteries you'll come upon as A2 branches west toward Lleida. Three austere aisles and an unusual 14th-century apse combine with the newly restored cloisters and the courtyard of the royal palace. ✉ *Off A2* ☎ *977/638329* ⊞ *€4* ⊙ *Mid-Mar.–mid-Sept., Tues.–Sun. 10–1:30 and 3–7; mid-Sept.–mid-Jan., Tues.–Sun. 10–1:30 and 3–5:30; mid-Jan.–mid-Mar., Tues.–Sun. 10–1:30 and 3–6.*

Montblanc is off A2 at Salida (Exit) 9, its ancient gates too narrow for cars. A walk through its tiny streets reveals Gothic churches with stained-glass windows, a 16th-century hospital, and medieval mansions.

Santa Maria de Poblet

❹ *8 km (5 mi) west of Santes Creus.*

This splendid Cistercian foundation at the foot of the Prades Mountains is one of the great masterpieces of Spanish monastic architecture. The cloister is a stunning combination of lightness and size; on sunny days the shadows on the yellow sandstone are extraordinary. Founded in 1150 by Ramón Berenguer IV in gratitude for the Christian Reconquest, the monastery first housed a dozen Cistercians from Narbonne. Later, the Crown of Aragón used Santa Maria de Poblet for religious retreats and burials. The building was damaged in an 1836 anticlerical revolt, and monks of the reformed Cistercian Order have managed the difficult task of restoration since 1940. Today, monks and novices again pray before the splendid retable over the tombs of Aragonese rulers, restored to their former glory by sculptor Frederic Marès; they also sleep in the cold, barren dormitory and eat frugal meals in the stark refectory. You can join them if you'd like—18 very comfortable rooms are available (for men only). Call **Padre Benito** (☎ 977/870089) to arrange a stay of up to 15 days within the stones and silence of one of Catalonia's gems. ✉ *Off A2* ☎ *977/870254* ⊞ *€4* ⊙ *Guided tours by reservation Apr.–Sept., daily 10–12:30 and 3–6; Oct.–Mar., daily 10–12:30 and 3–5:30.*

OFF THE BEATEN PATH

VALLS – The town of Valls, famous for its early spring *calçotada* (long-stem onion roast) held on the last Sunday of January, is 10 km (6 mi) from Santes Creus and 15 km (9 mi) from Poblet. Even if you miss the big day, *calçots* are served from November to April at rustic and rambling farmhouses such as **Cal Ganxo** (☎ 977/605960) in nearby Masmolets, and the Xiquets de Valls, Catalonia's most famous *castellers* (human castlers), might be putting up a human skyscraper.

Girona & Northern Catalonia

Often ignored by travelers who bolt from its airport to the resorts of the Costa Brava, Girona is an easy and worthy day trip from Barcelona. Much of the city's charm comes from its narrow medieval streets—with frequent stairways, as required by the steep terrain. Historic sites include the cathedral, which dominates the city; Arab baths; and a charming Jewish quarter. Northern Catalonia is memorable for the soft, green hills of the Ampurdan farm country, the Alberes mountain range at the eastern end of the Pyrenees, and the rugged Costa Brava. Sprinkled across the landscape are *masías* (farmhouses) with austere, grayish or pinkish staggered-stone rooftops and ubiquitous square towers that make them look like fortresses. Even the tiniest village has its church, arcaded square, and *rambla,* where villagers take their evening *paseo.*

Girona
⑤ *97 km (60 mi) northeast of Barcelona.*

If you drive here, park in the free lot next to the River Onyar, under the train trestle. Walk along the river to Plaça de la Independencia, admiring Girona's best-known view as you go: the town's pastel yellow, pink, and orange waterfront facades, their windows draped with a colorful mix of drying laundry reflected in the shimmering Onyar. Cross the bridge from under the arcades in the corner of the Plaça and find your way to the tourist office, to the right at La Rambla Llibertat 1. Then work your way up through the labyrinth of steep streets, using the cathedral's huge baroque facade as a guide.

At the base of the Girona cathedral's 90 steps and left through the Sobreportes gate are the **Banys Arabs,** or Arab Baths. Built by Morisco craftsmen in the late 12th century, long after Girona's Islamic occupation (795–1015) had ended, the baths are both Romanesque and Moorish in design. 🖼 *€2.50 ☉ May–Sept., Tues.–Sat. 10–2 and 4–7, Sun. 10–2; Oct.–Apr., Tues.–Sun. 10–1.*

Across the Galligants River is the church of **Sant Pere** (Holy Father), finished in 1131 and notable for its octagonal belfry and the detailed capitals atop the cloister columns. Next door is the **Museu Arqueològic,** which documents the region's archaeological history since Paleolithic times. 🖼 *€3 ☉ Church and museum daily 10–1 and 4:30–7.*

A five-minute walk from the cathedral leads to the **Torre de Gironella,** the highest point in the Jewish quarter. It was here that Girona's Jewish community took refuge in August 1391, emerging 17 weeks later to find their houses in ruins. Even though Spain's expulsion decree didn't take effect until 1492, this attack ended the Girona Jewish community. On December 20, 1998, the first Hanukkah celebration in 607 years was held in the gardens, with representatives of the Jewish communities of Spain, France, Portugal, Germany, and the United States present and Jerusalem's chief Sephardic rabbi, Rishon Letzion, presiding.

To see the inside of Girona's **cathedral,** designed by Guillem Bofill in 1416, complete the loop around it. The cathedral is known for its immense, uncluttered Gothic nave, which at 75 feet is the widest in the world and the epitome of the spatial ideal of Catalan Gothic architects. The **museum** contains the famous *Tapis de la Creació* (*Tapestry of the Creation*) and a 10th-century copy of Beatus's manuscript *Commentary on the Apocalypse.* The stepped Passeig Arqueològic runs below the walls of the Old City; climb through the Jardins de la Francesa to the highest ramparts for a view of the 11th-century Romanesque **Torre de Carlemany** (Charlemagne Tower), the oldest part of the cathedral. ☒ €3 ⊘ *Oct.–June, daily 9:30–1:15 and 3:30–7; July–Sept., daily 9:30–7.*

Next door to Girona's cathedral is **Palau Episcopal** (Bishop's Palace), which houses the **Museu d'Art,** a good mix of Romanesque, Catalan Gothic, and modern art. ☒ €3 ⊘ *Tues.–Sat. 10–7, Sun. 10–1.*

What was once the cramped and squalid center of the 13th-century *Call,* or Jewish quarter, is the sight of the **Centre Bonastruc ça Porta,** the lifeblood of the activities that refer to the recuperation of the Jewish heritage of Girona. Its **Museu de Història dels Jueus** (Museum of Jewish History) has 21 stone tablets, one of the finest collections in the world of medieval Jewish funerary slabs. ⊠ *Carrer de la Força 8* ☎ *972/ 216761* ☒ €3 ⊘ *Tues.–Sat. 10–2 and 4–7, Sun. 10–2.*

The **Museu d'Història de la Ciutat,** on Carrer de la Força, is filled with memorabilia from Girona's long and embattled past, from pre-Roman objects to paintings and drawings from the notorious siege at the hands of Napoléonic troops to the early municipal lighting system and the medieval printing press. ⊠ *Carrer de la Força 27* ☎ *972/222229* ⊕ *www. ajuntament.gi/museu_ciutat* ☒ €3 ⊘ *May–Sept., Mon.–Sat. 10–8, Sun. 10–3; Oct.–Apr., Mon.–Sat. 10–6, Sun. 10–3.*

The interactive **Museu del Cinema** has artifacts and movie-related paraphernalia going all the way back to Chinese shadows, the first rudimentary moving pictures. Look for the Cine Nic toy filmmaking machines, originally developed in 1931 by the Nicolau brothers of Barcelona and now being relaunched commercially. ⊠ *Carrer Sèquia 1* ☎ *972/412777* ⊕ *www.museudelcinema.org* ☒ €4 ⊘ *May–Sept., Mon.–Sat. 10–8, Sun. 10–3; Oct.–Apr., Mon.–Sat. 10–6, Sun. 10–3.*

WHERE TO
STAY & EAT
$$$–$$$$

✕ **Albereda.** Excellent Ampurdan cuisine is served in a bright yet soothing dining room. Try the *galleta con langostinos glaceada,* a zucchini bisque with prawns. ⊠ *C. Albereda 7 bis* ☎ *972/226002* ⊟ *AE, DC, MC, V* ⊘ *Closed Sun.*

$$$–$$$$
Fodor'sChoice
★

✕ **El Celler de Can Roca.** Girona's best restaurant and one of Catalonia's top six, this unusual spot west of town might serve anything from steak tartare with mustard ice cream to simple *vieiras* (scallops) with peas or a surf and turf of *pies de porc amb espardenyes* (trotters with sea slugs). ⊠ *Ctra. Taialà 40, 2 km (1½ mi) west of Girona, Sant Gregori first roundabout to Taialà* ☎ *972/222157* ⊟ *AE, DC, MC, V* ⊘ *Closed Dec. 23–Jan. 15, 1st 2 wks in July, and Sun. and Mon.*

★ $$–$$$

✕ **Cal Ros.** Tucked under the arcades just behind the north end of Plaça de la Llibertat, this perennial favorite combines ancient stone arches with a crisp, contemporary interior and cheerful lighting. The cuisine is gamey and delicious: hot goat-cheese salad with pine nuts and *garum* (black-olive-and-anchovy paste dating back to Roman times), *oca amb naps* (goose with turnips), and a blackberry sorbet not to miss. ⊠ *C. Cort Reial 9* ☎ *972/217379* ⊟ *AE, DC, MC, V* ⊘ *Closed Mon. No dinner Sun.*

★ $$$

▥ **Hotel Històric y Apartaments Històric Girona.** This boutique hotel has one room (the suite) with views of the cathedral and Gothic vaulting overhead. The apartments, in a 9th-century house, include parts of a

3rd-century Roman wall and a Roman aqueduct on the ground floor and in one of the apartments. One dining room even contains a wall made in the pre-Romanesque *opus spicatum* herringbone pattern. Casilda Cruz rents these good-value apartments in the old quarter for as many days as you'd like, from one day to one month. ⊠ *Carrer Bellmirall 4A, 17004* ☏ *972/223583* 🖷 *972/200932* ⊕ *www.hotelhistoric.com* ⤶ *8 rooms, 7 apartments, 1 suite* ♢ *Dining room, kitchens, minibars, microwaves* 🖃 *AE, DC, MC, V.*

$$ 🖫 **Bellmirall.** This gorgeous little inn across the Onyar in the Jewish quarter offers top value in the heart of Girona's most historic section. ⊠ *Carrer Bellmirall 3, 17001* ☏ *972/204009* ⤶ *7 rooms* ♢ *No a/c, no room phones, no room TVs* 🖃 *AE, DC, MC, V* ☉ *Closed Jan. and Feb.*

Figueres

❻ *37 km (23 mi) north of Girona on the A7.*

This bustling country town is the capital of the Alt Empordà (Upper Ampurdan). Take a walk along the Figueres Rambla, scene of the *passeig* (*paseo* in Castilian; the constitutional midday or evening stroll), and have a coffee in one of several traditional cafés. The **Teatre-Museu Dalí** pays spectacular homage to a unique artist. The museum is installed in a former theater next to the bizarre, ocher-color Torre Galatea, where Dalí lived until his death in 1989. The remarkable Dalí collection includes a vintage Cadillac with ivy-cloaked passengers whom you can water for less than a euro. Dalí himself is entombed beneath the museum. ⊠ *Pl. Gala-Salvador Dalí 5* ☏ *972/677500* ⊕ *www.salvador-dali.org* 🖼 *€10* ☉ *Oct.–June, Tues.–Sun. 10:30–5:15; July–Sept., daily 9–7:15.*

> ### SALVADOR DALÍ SITES
>
> Artist Salvador Dalí is entombed beneath the Teatre-Museu Dalí in Figueres. His former home, a castle in Pubol, is where his lover is buried. His summer home in Portlligat bay, to the north of Cadaqués, is now a museum focused on the surrealist's life and work.

WHERE TO STAY & EAT

$$ ✕🖫 **Hotel Duràn.** Once a stagecoach relay station, the Duràn is now a hotel and restaurant ($–$$) open every day of the year. Salvador Dalí had his own private dining room here, and you can take a meal amid pictures of the great surrealist. Try the *mandonguilles amb sepia al estil Anna* (meatballs and cuttlefish), a *mar i muntanya* (surf-and-turf) specialty of the house. ⊠ *C. Lasauca 5, 17600* ☏ *972/501250* 🖷 *972/502609* ⊕ *www.hotelduran.com* ⤶ *65 rooms* ♢ *Restaurant, bar, meeting rooms, parking (fee)* 🖃 *AE, MC, V.*

$$
Fodor's Choice
★ ✕🖫 **Hotel Empordà.** A mile north of town, this hotel and elegant restaurant run by Jaume Subirós is hailed as the birthplace of modern Catalan cuisine and has become a pilgrimage destination for foodies seeking superb French, Catalan, and Spanish cooking ($$$–$$$$). Try the *terrina calenta de lluerna a l'oli de cacauet* (hot pot of gurnard fish in peanut oil) or, if it's winter, *llebre a la Royal* (boned hare cooked in red wine). Guest rooms have parquet floors and sparkling bathrooms, and you can sit in the sun and have a drink on the terrace. The hotel is 1½ km (1 mi)

north of town. ✉ *Antiga Carretera de França s/n, 17600* ☎ *972/500562* 🖷 *972/509358* ⊕ *www.hotelemporda.com* 🛏 *42 rooms* ⚎ *Restaurant, cable TV, bar, meeting rooms, some pets allowed* ☰ *AE, DC, MC, V.*

┌ **OFF THE**
BEATEN
PATH

AMPURDAN UPLANDS – To explore the Alt Empordà (Upper Ampurdan), take N2 10 km (6 mi) north of Figueres and turn west on GI502. Work your way 13 km (8 mi) west to the village of Maçanet de Cabrenys. Continue to the Santuari de les Salines, where you can find a chapel and a tiny restaurant open in summer. Above Salines is one of the greatest beech forests in the Pyrenees. Follow signs from Le Perthus to Puig Neulós, at 4,148 feet the highest point in the Alberes range and the easternmost major Pyrenean peak. One of the greatest walks in the Pyrenees is the six-hour hike from Puig Neulós to Banyuls-sur-Mer, on the Mediterranean: The grassy border crest has views south over the Ampurdan and north over the curving yellow strand of the Côte Vermeille.

Besalú

❼ *34 km (21 mi) north of Girona.*

Once the capital of a feudal county as part of Charlemagne's 8th- and 9th-century Spanish March, Besalú is 25 km (15 mi) west of Figueres on C260. This ancient town's most emblematic sight is its **fortified bridge,** complete with crenellated battlements. **Sant Vicenç** (✉ Carrer de Sant Vicenç s/n) is Besalú's best Romanesque church. The church of **Sant Pere** (✉ Pl. de Sant Pere s/n) is all that remains of the 10th-century Benedictine monastery torn down in 1835. The ruins of the convent of **Santa Maria** on the hill above town are a panoramic vantage point over Besalú. The **tourist office** (☎ 972/591240) in the arcaded Plaça de la Llibertat can provide opening hours for Sant Pere as well as keys to the *miqwe,* the rare Jewish baths discovered in the 1960s. A **Tren Turístic** leaves from the bridge every 45 minutes and visits the baths and the two churches for a cost of €3. The extraordinary town of **Castellfollit de la Roca** perches on its prowlike basalt cliff over the Fluvià River 16 km (10 mi) west of Besalú.

WHERE TO EAT
★ **$$–$$$$**

✗ **Els Fogons de Can Llaudes.** A faithfully restored 11th-century Romanesque chapel holds proprietor Jaume Soler's outstanding restaurant, one of Catalonia's best. A typical main dish is *confitat de bou amb patates al morter i raïm glacejat* (beef confit with glacé grapes, served with mashed potatoes with nutmeg). The *menú de degustació* (taster's menu) is recommended; call at least one day in advance to reserve this menu. ✉ *Prat de Sant Pere 6* ☎ *972/590858* ⚎ *Reservations essential* ☰ *AE, MC, V* ☉ *Closed Tues. and Nov.*

Olot

❽ *21 km (13 mi) west of Besalú, 55 km (34 mi) northwest of Girona, 130 km (78 mi).*

Capital of the Garrotxa area, Olot is famous for its 19th-century school of landscape painters and has several excellent Art Nouveau buildings, including one with a facade by Moderniste master Lluís Domènech i Montaner. The **Museu Comarcal de la Garrotxa** (County Museum of La Garrotxa) has an assemblage of Moderniste art as well as sculptures by Miquel Blai, creator of the long-tressed maidens who support the balconies along

Olot's main boulevard. ⊠ *Carrer Hospici 8* ☏ *972/279130* ⌨ €3 ☉ *Mon. and Wed.–Sat. 10–1 and 4–7, Sun. 10–1:30.*

The villages of **Vall d'En Bas** lie south of Olot off A153. The twisting old road goes past farmhouses whose dark wooden balconies are bedecked with bright flowers. Turn off for **Sant Privat d'En Bas** for a step back in time. The village of **Els Hostalets d'En Bas** eloquently defines rustic. A modern freeway cuts across this countryside to Vic, but you'll miss a lot by taking it.

WHERE TO
STAY & EAT
$$–$$$$

✕ **Restaurante Ramón.** Ramon's eponymous restaurant is the opposite of rustic: sleek, modern, refined, and international. Samples of the *cuina de la terra* (home cooking of regional specialties) include *patata de Olot* (potato stuffed with veal) and *cassoleta de judias amb xoriç* (white haricot with sausage). ⊠ *Carrer Bolós 22* ☏ *972/261001* ⌨ *Reservations essential* ☰ *AE, DC, MC, V* ☉ *Closed Thurs.*

$–$$

⌂ **La Perla d'Olot.** Known for its friendly family ambience, this hotel is always the first in Olot to fill up. On the edge of town toward the Vic road, it's within walking distance of two parks. ⊠ *Av. Santa Coloma 97/La Deu 9, 17800* ☏*972/262326* ⌨*972/270774* ⊕*www.laperlahotels. com* ⌨*30 rooms, 37 apartments* ⌂ *Restaurant, bar, Internet room, some pets allowed; no a/c in some rooms* ☰ *AE, DC, MC, V.*

Rupit

9 *33 km (20 mi) south of Olot, 97 km (60 mi) north of Barcelona.*

Rupit is a spectacular stop for its medieval houses and its food, the highlight of which is beef-stuffed potatoes. Built into a rocky promontory over a stream in the rugged Collsacabra region (about halfway from Olot to Vic), the town has some of the most aesthetically perfect **stone houses** in Catalonia, some of which were reproduced for Barcelona's "Spain-in-a-bottle" architectural sampler, Poble Espanyol.

WHERE TO
STAY & EAT
$
Fodor'sChoice
★

✕⌂ **El Repòs.** Hanging over the river that runs through Rupit, this restaurant ($–$$$) serves the best meat-stuffed potatoes around. Ordering a meal is easy: just learn the word *patata*. Other specialties include duck and lamb. Rooms are rustic but cozy. ⊠ *C. Barbacana 1* ☏ *93/ 852–2100* ⌨ *11 rooms* ☰ *AE, DC, MC, V* ☉ *Closed weekdays Oct.–Easter. Will open by arrangement.*

Vic

10 *66 km (41 mi) north of Barcelona.*

Known for its conservatism and Catalan nationalism, Vic rests on a 1,600-foot plateau at the confluence of two rivers and serves as the area's commercial, industrial, and agricultural hub. The wide **Plaça Major,** surrounded by Gothic arcades and well supplied with bars and cafés, perfectly expresses the city's personality. Vic's religiosity is demonstrated by its 35 churches, of which the largely neoclassical **cathedral** (⊠ Pl. de la Catedral s/n ☏ 93/886–4449 ⌨ €1 ☉ Mon.–Sat. 10–1 and 4–7, Sun. 10–1:30) is the foremost. The 11th-century Romanesque tower, El Cloquer, built by the Abbot Oliva, and the powerful modern murals painted twice by Josep Maria Sert (first in 1930 and again after fire damage in 1945) are the cathedral's high points. The **Museu Episcopal** (Bishop's Museum; ⊠ Pl. de la Catedral s/n ☏ 93/886–4449 ⊡ €4 ☉ Mon.–Sat. 10–1 and 4–7, Sun. 10–1:30) has a fine collection of religious elics.

WHERE TO EAT ✕ **Art de Coch.** Named for Catalonia's first medieval cookbook, this cen-
$$–$$$$ tral location a few steps from Vic's Plaça Major serves modern versions of antique recipes, as the early Catalan would suggest. The interior patio is intimate and quiet, and the cuisine is carefully elaborated with fresh market products. ⊠ *Sant Miquel dels Sants 1* ☏ *93/886–4033* ☲ *AE, DC, MC, V* ☉ *Closed Mon. and 1st 2 wks in Sept. No dinner Sun.*

$$ ✕ **Ca l'U.** Translated as "The One," Ca l'U is in fact *the* place in Vic for hearty local cuisine with a minimum of pretense and expense. Try the *llangostinos i llenguado* (prawns and sole) or the regional standard, *botifarra i mongetas* (sausage and beans). ⊠ *Pl. Santa Teresa 4–5* ☏ *93/ 886–3504* ☲ *MC, V* ☉ *Closed Mon. No dinner Sun.*

Girona & Northern Catalonia Essentials

ARRIVING & 🚃 By Bus **Sarfa** ⊠ Estació Norte–Vilanova C. Alí Bei 80 ☏ 93/265–1158
DEPARTING has buses every 1½ hours to Girona, Figueres, and Cadaqués. If you want to go to Vic, contact **Segalés** ☏ 93/889–2577. For Ripoll, call **Teisa** ⊠ Pau Claris 118 ☏ 93/488–2837.

🚗 By Car Barcelona is surrounded by a network of *rondas*, or ring roads, with quick access from every corner of the city. Look for signs for these *rondas*; then follow signs to France (Francia), Girona, and the A7 *autopista*, which goes all the way to France. For Girona, roughly a one-hour drive from Barcelona, leave the autopista at Salida (Exit) 7.

🚆 By Train RENFE ☏ 902/240202 operates trains, which leave Sants and Passeig de Gràcia every 1½ hours for Girona, Figueres, and Port Bou (France). Some trains for northern Catalonia and France also leave from the França Station. For Vic and Ripoll, catch a Puigcerdà train (every hour or two) from Sants or Plaça de Catalunya.

The Costa Brava

The Costa Brava (Wild Coast) is a rocky stretch of shoreline that begins at Blanes and continues north through 135 km (84 mi) of coves and beaches to the French border at Port Bou. This tour concentrates on selected pockets—Tossa, Cap de Begur, Cadaqués—where the rocky terrain has discouraged the worst excesses of real-estate speculation. Here, on a good day, the luminous blue of the sea still contrasts with red-brown headlands and cliffs; the distant lights of fishing boats reflect on wine-color waters at dusk; and umbrella pines escort you to the fringes of secluded *calas* (coves) and sandy white beaches.

Exploring the Costa Brava

⑪ The beaches closest to Barcelona are at **Blanes,** where small boats can take you to Cala de Sant Francesc or the double beach at Santa Cristina between May and October. (⊠ Crucetours ☏ 972/314969)

⑫ The next stop north from Blanes on the coast road is **Tossa de Mar,** christened "Blue Paradise" by painter Marc Chagall, who summered here in 1934. The only Chagall painting in Spain is in Tossa's **Museu Municipal** (Municipal Museum; ☏ 972/340709), open Tuesday through Sunday 10 to 1 and 5 to 8. Admission is €3.50. Tossa's walled **medieval town** and pristine beaches are among Catalonia's best.

⑬ Sant Feliu de Guixols follows Tossa de Mar, after 23 km (15 mi) of hairpin curves over hidden inlets. Tiny turnouts or parking spots on this route nearly always lead to intimate coves with stone stairways winding down from the road. Visit Sant Feliu's two fine beaches, church and monastery, Sunday market, and lovely **Passeig del Mar.**

⑭ S'Agaró, one of the Costa Brava's best clusters of seaside mansions, is 3 km (2 mi) north of Sant Feliu. The 30-minute walk along the **sea wall** from Hostal de La Gavina to Sa Conca beach is a delight. Likewise, the one-hour hike from Sant Pol beach over to Sant Feliu de Guixols for lunch and back is a superb look at the Costa Brava at its best.

Up the coast from S'Agaró, a road leads east to **Llafranc,** a small port ⑮ with quiet waterfront hotels and restaurants, and forks right to **Calella de Palafrugell,** a pretty fishing village known for its July Habaneras (Catalan-Cuban sea chanties inspired by the Spanish-American War) festival. Just south is the panoramic promontory **Cap Roig,** with views of the barren Formigues (Ants) Isles and a fine botanical garden that you can tour with a guide March–December, daily 9–9, for €4. The left fork drops down to **Tamariu,** one of the Costa's prettiest inlet towns. A climb over the bluff leads down to the parador at **Aiguablava,** a modern eyesore overlooking magnificent cliffs and crags.

⑯ From **Begur,** north of Aiguablava, you can go east through the *calas* or take the inland route past the rose-color stone houses and ramparts of the restored medieval town of **Pals.** Nearby **Peratallada** is another medieval town with fortress, castle, tower, palace, and well-preserved walls. North of Pals there are signs for **Ullastret,** an Iberian village dating from the 5th century BC.

⑰ L'Estartit is the jumping-off point for the spectacular **Parc Natural Submarí** (Underwater Natural Park) by the Medes Isles, famous for diving and for underwater photography.

⑱ The Greco-Roman ruins at **Empúries** are Catalonia's most important archaeological site. This port, complete with breakwater, is one of the most monumental ancient engineering feats on the Iberian Peninsula. As the Greeks' original point of arrival in Spain, Empúries was also where the Olympic Flame entered Spain for Barcelona's 1992 Olympic Games.

⑲ The **Aiguamolls** (Marshlands), a nature reserve with migratory waterfowl from all over Europe, lies mainly around **Castelló d'Empúries,** but the main information center is at El Cortalet, on the road in from Sant Pere Pescador. Follow the road from Empúries, crossing the Fluvià River at Sant Pere Pescador, and proceed north through the wetlands to Castelló. From Castelló d'Empúries, a series of roadways and footpaths traverses the marshes, the latter well marked on the information center's maps.

⑳ Cadaqués, Spain's easternmost town, still has the whitewashed charm that made this fishing village into an international artists' haunt in the early 20th century. The Marítim is the central hangout both day and night; after dark, you might also enjoy the Jardí, across the square. Salvador Dalí's house, now a museum, still stands at Portlligat, a 30-minute walk north of town.

The **Casa Museu Salvador Dalí** was Dalí's summerhouse and a site long associated with the artist's notorious frolics with everyone from poets such as Federico García Lorca and Paul Eluard (whose wife, Gala, became Dalí's muse and spouse) to filmmaker Luis Buñuel. Filled with bits and pieces of the surrealist's daily life, it's an important point in the "Dalí triangle," completed by the castle at Pubol and the Museu Dalí, in Figueres. ⊠ *Port Lligat, 3-km (2-mi) walk from Cadaqués town center, along beach* ☎ *972/251015* ⊕ *www.salvador-dali.org* ⊠ *€10* ◷ *By appointment, Mar. 15–Jan. 7, Tues.–Sun.*

The **Castillo Pubol,** Dalí's former castle-home, is now the resting place of Gala, his perennial model and mate. It's a chance to wander through yet more Dalíesque landscape: lush gardens, fountains decorated with masks of Wagner (the couple's favorite composer), and distinctive elephants with giraffe's legs and claw feet. Two lions and a giraffe stand guard near Gala's tomb. ⊠ *Rte. 255 toward La Bisbal, 15 km (9 mi) east of A7* ☎ *972/488655* ⊠ *€10* ◷ *Mar. 15–June 14 and Sept. 16–Jan. 6, Tues.–Sun. 10:30–5:15; June 15–Sept. 15, daily 10:30–8.*

㉑ **Cap de Creus,** north of Cadaqués, Spain's easternmost point, is a fundamental pilgrimage, if only for the symbolic geographical rush. The hike out to the lighthouse—through rosemary, thyme, and the salt air of the Mediterranean—is unforgettable. The Pyrenees officially end (or rise) here. New Year's Day finds mobs of revelers awaiting the first emergence of the "new" sun from the Mediterranean.

㉒ The monastery of **Sant Pere de Rodes,** 7 km (4½ mi) by car (plus a 20-minute walk) above the pretty fishing village El Port de la Selva, is the last site, and one of the most spectacular, on the Costa Brava. Built in the 10th and early 11th centuries by Benedictine monks—and sacked and plundered repeatedly since—this Romanesque monolith, now being restored, commands a breathtaking panorama of the Pyrenees, the Empordà plain, the sweeping curve of the Bay of Roses, and Cap de Creus. (Topping off the grand trek across the Pyrenees, Cap de Creus is a spectacular six-hour walk from here on the well-marked GR-11 trail.)

Where to Stay & Eat

$$$$ ✕ **El Bulli.** This seaside hideaway has become such a global phenomenon that getting a table involves reserving months, possibly years, in advance. Only dinner is served here, so getting back to Barcelona at midnight after five hours, a table is a challenge. Chef Ferran Adrià will make your palate his playground with a 35-course taster's menu that began with concepts such as *espuma de humo* (foam of smoke), progressed through rosewater bubbles and *aire de zanahoria con coco amargo* (air of carrot with bitter coconut), and has moved on past Ferran's recent passion in culinary chemistry: "freeze-frying" eggs in liquid nitrogen. Cala Montjoi is 7 km (4½ mi) southeast of Roses, the same distance from Cadaqués by boat or footpath and 22 km (14 mi) by car. ⊠ *Cala Montjoi, Roses, Girona* ☎ *972/150457* 🖷 *972/150717* ⊕ *www.elbulli.com* ⌦ *Reservations essential* ▤ *AE, DC, MC, V* ◷ *Closed Oct.–Mar. No lunch.*

$$–$$$ ✕ **Can Pelayo.** This tiny, family-run restaurant serves the best fish in Cadaqués. It's hidden behind Plaça Port Alguer, a few minutes' walk

south of the town center. ✉ *Carrer Nou 11, Cadaqués* ☎ *972/258356* 🖃 *AE, DC, MC, V* ⊘ *Closed weekdays Oct.–May.*

\$\$–\$\$\$ ✕ **La Xicra.** The local fare here includes, in winter, *es niu*, a powerful combination of game fowl, fish tripe, pork meatballs, and cuttlefish, stewed in a rich sauce. ✉ *C. Estret 17, Palafrugell* ☎ *972/305630* 🖃 *AE, DC, MC, V* ⊘ *Closed Wed. and Nov. No dinner Tues.*

\$–\$\$\$ ✕ **Royal.** This sunny, beachside spot serves fisherman-style creations of impressive freshness and quality. The *suquet* (fish cooked slowly to create its own juice, or *suc*) is especially commendable. ✉ *Passeig de Mar 9, Tamariu* ☎ *972/620041* 🖃 *MC, V.*

\$\$\$–\$\$\$\$ ✕🖫 **El Hostal de la Gavina.** At the eastern corner of Sant Pol beach in S'Agaró, La Gavina is a superb display of design and food founded in 1932 by Josep Ensesa, who invented S'Agaró itself. Fine comforts and dining (\$\$\$–\$\$\$\$) are augmented by nearby tennis, golf, and horseback riding. ✉ *Pl. de la Rosaleda s/n, S'Agaró 17248* ☎ *972/321100* 🖷 *972/321573* ⊕ *www.lagavina.com* ⟿ *58 rooms, 16 suites* ⚫ *Restaurant, café, minibars, cable TV, 2 tennis courts, pool, health club, bar, meeting rooms* 🖃 *AE, DC, MC, V* ⊘ *Closed Nov.–Easter except Dec. 30–Jan. 2.*

\$–\$\$ ✕🖫 **Bar Cap de Creus.** Right next to the Cap de Creus lighthouse, this restaurant (\$–\$\$\$) has spectacular views. The food is simple and good, and the proprietor rents three apartments (four beds each) upstairs. ✉ *Cap de Creus, Cadaqués 17488* ☎ *972/199005* 🖃 *MC, V* ⊘ *Closed Mon.–Thurs. Oct.–June.*

\$ ✕🖫 **La Riera.** Built into a medieval house, this rustic hotel-restaurant (\$–\$\$) is a quiet hideaway in lovely Peratallada, near Begur. The dining room is in the former wine cellar, and the rooms have ceiling beams over painted ceramic tiles. Food includes such local specialties as *anec amb naps* (duck with turnips) and *peu de porc amb cargols* (pig's feet with snails). ✉ *Pl. de les Voltes 3, Peratallada 17113* ☎ *972/634142* 🖷 *972/635040* ⟿ *8 rooms* ⚫ *Restaurant, bar* 🖃 *AE, DC, MC, V.*

\$\$\$ 🖫 **Parador de Aiguablava.** The service is impeccable at this modern parador on a promontory overlooking sheer cliffs and surging seas. ✉ *Platja D'Aiguablava Begur 17255* ☎ *972/622162* 🖷 *972/622166* ⊕ *www.parador.es* ⟿ *78 rooms* ⚫ *Restaurant, minibars, cable TV, pool, gym, sauna, bar* 🖃 *AE, DC, MC, V.*

\$\$\$ 🖫 **Playa Sol.** Open for more than 40 years, this hotel has the experience that comes with age. The rooms are done tastefully in red and ocher; some overlook the sea. The Playa Sol is in the cove of Es Pianc on the left side of the bay of Cadaqués as you face the sea, a five-minute walk from the village center. Boaters will love this place—all types of craft tie up here, as Catalan writer Josep Pla spread its fame as the best place to drop anchor in Cadaqués. ✉ *Platja Pianc 3, Cadaqués, Girona 17488* ☎ *972/258100* 🖷 *972/258054* ⊕ *www.playasol.com* ⟿ *49 rooms* ⚫ *Restaurant, cable TV, pool, bar, library* 🖃 *AE, DC, MC, V* ⊘ *Closed mid-Dec.–mid-Feb.* ▯◯▮ *BP.*

\$\$–\$\$\$ 🖫 **Mar Menuda.** This modern Costa Brava hideaway offers as much peace and quiet—*and* as many varieties of water sports—as you can possibly handle. Equipment and instruction are available for windsurfing, sailing, swimming, and scuba diving. The hotel terrace overlooks the coast and the town of Tossa de Mar, with a medieval castle and an old quarter full of cobble streets. ✉ *Platja Mar Menuda s/n, Tossa de Mar*

17320 ☎ *972/341000* 📠 *972/340087* ⊕ *www.marmenuda.com* ⇔ *50 rooms* ⚒ *Restaurant, minibars, tennis court, pool, bar, meeting rooms* ▭ *AE, DC, MC, V* ⊙ *Closed Nov.–Dec. 26.*

Costa Brava Essentials

ARRIVING & **⊓** By Bus **Sarfa** ⊠ Estació Norte–Vilanova C. Alí Bei 80 ☎ 93/265–1158 Ⓜ Arc de
DEPARTING Triomf operates buses to Blanes, Lloret, Sant Feliu de Guixols, Platja d'Aro, Palamos, Begur, Roses, and Cadaqués.

⊓ By Car For the fastest trip from Barcelona, start up A7 *autopista* as if to Girona and take Salida (Exit) 10 for Blanes. Coastal traffic can be slow and frustrating, and the roads tortuous.

⊓ By Train The local train to the Costa Brava pokes along the coast to Blanes every 30 minutes, departing Sants at 13 and 43 minutes after every hour and Plaça de Catalunya 5 minutes later.

GUIDED TOURS Bus and boat tours from Barcelona to the Costa Brava, Girona, and Figueres are run by **Julià Travel** (⊠ Ronda Universitat 5 ☎ 93/317–6454 ⊕ www.juliatravel.com). Buses leave Barcelona at 9 and return at 6. The prices range from €80 per person with lunch for the Costa Brava to €90 for Girona and Figueres. **Pullmantur** (⊠ Gran Vía 635 ☎ 93/318–5195) runs tours to several main points on the Costa Brava.

6

BARCELONA & N. CATALONIA ESSENTIALS

To research prices, get advice from other travelers, and book travel arrangements, visit www.fodors.com.

Transportation

Modern Barcelona, above the Plaça de Catalunya, is built on a grid system. The old town, however, from the Plaça de Catalunya to the port, is a labyrinth of narrow streets, so you'll need a good street map. Most sightseeing can be done on foot—you won't have any choice in the Barri Gòtic—but you'll have to use the metro, buses, or taxis to link sightseeing areas. The Dia T1 pass is valid for one day of unlimited travel on all subway, bus, and FFCC lines. Maps showing bus and metro routes are available free from booths in the Plaça de Catalunya; for general information on public transport, call 93/412–0000. Turisme de Barcelona sells two-, three-, four-, and five-day versions of the very worthwhile Barcelona Card. For €23, €28, €31, and €34, you get unlimited travel on all public transport as well as discounts at 27 museums, 10 restaurants, 14 leisure sites, and 20 stores. Travel cards, covering transport only, cost €9.20, €13.20, €16.20, and €20 for two-, three-, four-, and five-day passes. Other services include walking tours of the Gothic Quarter, an airport shuttle, a bus to Tibidabo, and the Tombbus, which connects key shopping areas.

Barcelona's new tramway system is divided into two subsectors: **Trambaix** serves the western end of the Diagonal between Plaça Francesc Macià and destinations in the Baix Llobregat, L'Hospitalet de Llobregat, Cornellà, Sant Joan Despí, Esplugues de Llobregat, Sand Just Desvern, and Sand Feliu de Llobregat; **Trambesòs** serves the eastern end of the Diagonal between Plaça de les Glòries, Diagonal Mar, and the Fòrum 2004 area in the delta of the river Besòs.

🛈 **Turisme de Barcelona** ✉ Pl. de Catalunya 17 bis, Eixample ☎ 93/285-3834.

BY AIR

All international and domestic flights arrive at the spectacular glass, steel, and marble El Prat de Llobregat airport, 14 km (9 mi) south of Barcelona.

Most flights from the United States connect in Madrid or at other European points such as London, Amsterdam, Paris, or Frankfurt; only Continental, Delta, and Iberia fly nonstop to Barcelona.

The Aerobus leaves the airport for Plaça de Catalunya every 15 minutes (6 AM–11 PM) on weekdays and every 30 minutes (6:30 AM–10:30 PM) on weekends. From Plaça de Catalunya, it leaves for the airport every 15 minutes (5:30 AM–10 PM) on weekdays and every 30 minutes (6:30 AM–10:30 PM) on weekends. The fare is €3.50.

Cab fare from the airport into town is about €20. If you're driving your own car, follow signs to the Centre Ciutat and you'll enter the city along Gran Vía. For the port area, follow signs for the Ronda Litoral. The journey to the center of town can take anywhere from 15 to 45 minutes, depending on traffic (*see* Traffic, *below*).

At present, the airport train to Barcelona is either a great bargain or an unmitigated disaster as a result of ongoing construction scheduled to last until early 2008. If you're traveling light (always recommended, especially in the light of recent frequent baggage-loss or delay problems), a 10-minute walk to the train, much of it on a moving walkway, is no problem. A 10-ride Metro ticket (€6.65) will get you into town for the price of a single ride during the construction project. However, there is a train change in the village of El Prat de Llobregat that can be nearly instantaneous or much delayed. The train goes to Estació de Sants, Plaça de Catalunya, Arc de Triomf, and Clot. Trains run to and from the airport from 6 in the morning until 10 at night. With little at stake (meeting a plane or arriving without a rush, for example) the train makes sense. But for outgoing flights train transport will be uncertain until 2008.

🛈 **Aeroport del Prat** ☎ 902/404704. **Airport Lost and Found** ☎ 93/298-3349.

BY BIKE

Bicitram is a bike-rental outfit that stays open on weekends and holidays. Los Filicletos rents bikes, skates, and scooters. Un Menys—"One Less," in Catalan, meaning one less car on the streets of Barcelona—organizes increasingly popular outings that tack drinks, dinner, and dancing on to a gentle, guided bike ride for a total price of about €30 (which includes bike rental).

🛈 **Bike Rentals Bicitram** ✉ Marquès de l'Argentera 15 ☎ 636/401997. **Los Filicletos** ✉ Passeig de Picasso 38 ☎ 93/319-7811. **Un Menys** ✉ Esparteria 3 ☎ 93/268-2105 🖷 93/319-4298.

BY BUS

Barcelona's main bus station is Estació del Nord, east of the Arc de Triomf. Buses also depart from the Estació de Sants as well as from the depots of Barcelona's various private bus companies. Rather than pound the pavement (or the telephone, usually futile because of overloaded lines) trying to sort out Barcelona's complex and confusing bus system, go through a travel agent, who can quickly book you the best bus passage to your destination, or reserve online.

City buses run daily from 5:30 AM to 11:30 PM. The fare is €1.20. For multiple journeys purchase a Targeta T10 (valid for bus or metro), which buys you 10 rides for €6.65. Route maps are displayed at bus stops. Note that those with a red band always stop at a central square— Catalunya, Universitat, or Urquinaona—and blue indicates a night bus. Barcelona's 30 night buses generally run until about 4:30 AM, though some stop as early as 3:30 AM and others continue until as late as 5:20 AM (the morning buses start up at 5 AM). Schedules are available at bus and metro stations or at ⊕ www.bcn.es/guia/welcomea.htm

BY CABLE CAR

The Montjuïc Funicular is a cog railroad that runs from the junction of Avinguda Paral.lel and Nou de la Rambla to the Miramar station on Montjuïc (Paral.lel). It operates daily 11 AM to 9:30 PM in summer, and weekends and holidays 11 AM to 8 PM in winter; the fare is €1.20. A *telefèric* then takes you up to Montjuïc Castle. In winter the telefèric runs weekends and holidays 11 to 2:45 and 4 to 7:30; in summer, daily 11:30 to 9. The fare is €3.75. A Transbordador Aeri Harbor Cable Car runs between Miramar and Montjuïc across the harbor to Torre de Jaume I, on Barcelona's *moll* (quay), and on to Torre de Sant Sebastià, at the end of Passeig Joan de Borbó in Barceloneta. You can board at either stage. The fare is €9 round-trip (€7 one-way), and the car runs October through June, weekdays noon to 5:45, weekends noon to 6:15, and July through September, daily 11 to 9. To reach the summit of Tibidabo, take the metro to Avinguda de Tibidabo, then the Tramvía Blau (€2.30 one-way, €3 round-trip) to Peu del Funicular, and finally the Tibidabo Funicular (€2 one-way, €3 round-trip) from there to the Tibidabo fairground. It runs every 30 minutes, 7:05 AM to 9:35 PM ascending, 7:25 AM to 9:55 PM descending.

BY CAR

Getting around Barcelona by car is generally more trouble than it's worth. The *rondas* (ring roads) make entering and exiting the city easy, unless it's rush hour, in which case traffic comes to a halt. Between parking, navigating, *alcoholemia* (alcohol blood-level) patrols, and the general wear and tear of driving in the city, the subway, taxis, buses, and walking are your best bets in Barcelona.

For travel outside of Barcelona, the freeways to Girona, Figueres, Sitges, Tarragona, and Lleida are surprisingly fast. Routine cruising speed on Spanish freeways is 140 km/h (84 mph) or more. If you drive at the official speed limit of 120 km/h (72 mph), you seriously risk high-speed rear-ending. The distance to Girona, 97 km (58 mi), is a 45-minute shot. The French border is an hour away. Perpignan is, at 188 km (113 mi), an hour and 20 minutes.

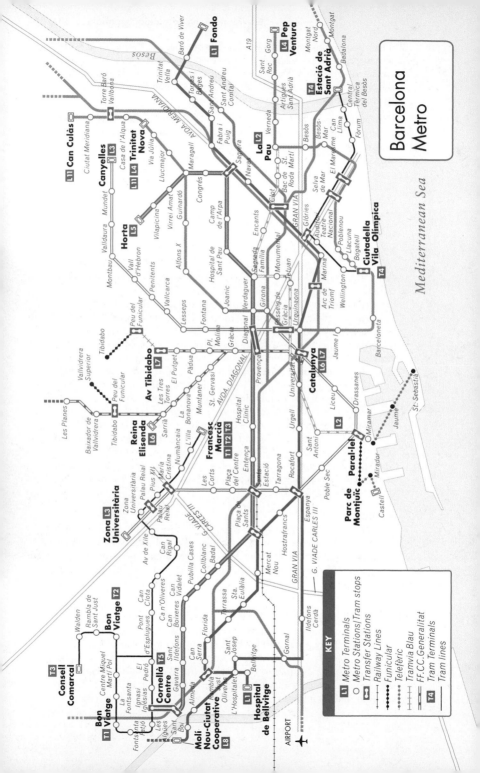

Barcelona Metro

On freeways (possibly because official driving-school manuals date before the invention of Spain's excellent network of freeways), do not expect motorists coming down the inside lane to move left and give way. The "merging" concept does not exist in Spain. Expect to come to a full stop at the red yield triangle at the end of the on-ramp and wait for a break in traffic.

Spanish highway engineers have discovered the British roundabout. Remember that the motorist *in the roundabout* has the right of way, even if you're the vehicle to the right (which is the normal rule of thumb elsewhere: vehicles coming from your right have right of way).

Note that National Car Rental is affiliated with the Spanish agency Atesa, or Avis. Europcar has good weekend deals. Vanguard rents motorcycles as well as cars.

PARKING You can often find a legal and safe parking place on the street, and underground public parking is plentiful, easy, and cheap.

TRAFFIC Barcelona's rush hours take place from 8:30 to 9:30 AM, from 2 to 3 PM, and, intermittently, from 5 to 9 PM.

Major Agencies Avis ⊠ Casanova 209, Eixample ☎ 93/209-9533 ⊠ Aragó 235, Eixample ☎ 93/487-8754 ⊕ www.avis.com. **Europcar** ⊠ Viladomat 214, Eixample ☎ 93/439-8403 ⊠ Estació de Sants ☎ 93/491-4822 ⊕ www.europcar.com. **Hertz** ⊠ Còrsega 293 Eixample ☎ 93/237-5680 ⊠ Tuset 10, Eixample ☎ 93/217-3248 ⊕ www.hertz.com.

Local Agencies Atesa ⊠ El Prat Airport, El Prat ☎ 93/298-3433 ⊠ Muntaner 45, Eixample ☎ 93/323-0266. **Vanguard** ⊠ Londres 31, Eixample ☎ 93/439-3880.

BY SUBWAY

The subway is the fastest, cheapest, and easiest way to get around Barcelona. You pay a flat fare of €1.20 no matter how far you travel (with free transfers for up to an hour and 15 minutes), but it's more economical to buy a 10-ride Targeta T10 for €6.65 valid for Metro and FGC Generalitat trains, the Tramvía Blau blue tram, and the Montjuïc Funicular. This card can be shared by up to ten people. Fares are scheduled to increase by up to 15 centimes after January 1, 2007. Metro lines are color coded, and the FGC trains are marked with a reclining S-like blue and white icon. Lines 2, 3, and 5 run weekdays 5 AM to midnight. Lines 1 and 4 close at 1 AM. On Friday, Saturday, and holiday evenings all trains run until 2 AM. The FGC Generalitat trains run until 12:30 on weekdays and 2:15 AM on weekends and eves of holidays. Sunday trains run on weekday schedules.

BY TAXI

Taxis (☎ 93/387-1000, 93/490-2222, 93/357-7755 24 hours a day) are black and yellow and show a green rooftop light when available for hire. The meter starts at €1.45 (€1.55 at night and on weekends and holidays). There are supplements for luggage, night travel, Sunday and holidays, rides from a station or to the airport, and for trips to or from the bullring or a soccer *(fútbol)* match. There are cab stands all over town, and you can also hail cabs on the street. One of the prime taxi stands is at the head of the Rambla on Plaça Catalunya, though lines often form there. Another handy one is at Plaça Sant Jaume, dead center in the Gothic Quarter. Within 200 yards of a taxi stand, cabdrivers generally refuse to respond to a hail, referring you to the line at the stand.

BY TRAIN
Almost all long-distance trains arrive and depart from Estació de Sants. En route to or from Sants, some trains stop at another station on Passeig de Gràcia at Carrer Aragó; this can be a good way to avoid the long lines that form at Sants during holidays. The Estació de França, near the port, now handles only a few long-distance trains within Spain. For schedules and fares, call RENFE. Although overnight train travel is convenient, time efficient, and easy if you like to sleep on trains, beware: Unless you have a fairly pricey compartment for two (or four), you will be packed in with strangers in a four-person compartment with often suffocating heat and windows that do not open. The air shuttle (or a scheduled flight) between Madrid and Barcelona can, if all goes well, get you door to door in less than three hours for only about €40 more.

⑦ Train Information & Stations Estació de França ✉ Av. Marquès de l'Argentera s/n, La Ribera. **Estació de Sants** ✉ Pl. dels Països Catalans s/n, Eixample. **RENFE** ☎ 902/ 240202.

Contacts & Resources

CHILDREN IN BARCELONA
Check listings in daily newspapers for children's activities on Saturday and Sunday morning. The Fundació Miró is one of Barcelona's most child-friendly venues, with clowns, storytellers, and events of all kinds 10 to 2 on weekends. The Barcelona zoo—especially the dolphin show—are great favorites with small *barcelonins*. The Museu de la Ciència offers excellent interactive scientific games and virtual experiences. Drassanes Reials and the Museu Marítimo have superb displays designed for children. Last of all is the amusement park up on Tibidabo, a once-popular children's event that has simply been eclipsed by superior activities.

EMERGENCIES
Tourist Attention, a service provided by the local police department, can help if you're the victim of a crime or need medical or psychological assistance. English interpreters are on hand. To find out which pharmacies are open late at night or 24 hours on a given day, look on the door of any pharmacy or in any local newspaper under "Farmacias de Guardia." Alternatively, dial 010.

⑦ Emergency Services Ambulance ☎ 93/300-2020 Creu Roja. **Hospital Clinic** ✉ Villarroel 170, Eixample ☎ 93/454-6000 or 93/454-7000 Ⓜ Blue line to Hospital Clinic. **Medical assistance** ☎ 061. **Police** ☎ 091 or 092 ◪ Main police station ✉ Via Laietana 43, Barri Gòtic ☎ 93/301-6666. **Tourist Attention** ✉ Guardia Urbana, La Rambla 43, Rambla ☎ 93/290-3440. **24-Hour Pharmacies** ☎ 010.

INTERNET, MAIL & SHIPPING
Surrounded by medieval stone, the art gallery–cum–Internet café bcnet offers everything from e-mail checking to video conferences until 1 AM. Another venue, Idea, which also has a bookstore, is perfect for e-mail.

◢ Internet Cafés **Bar Travel** ✉ Boqueria 27, Barri Gòtic ☎ 93/410-8592. **bcnet** ✉ Barra de Ferro 3, La Ribera ☎ 93/268-1507. **Cafe Internet Navego** ✉ Provença 546, Eixample ☎ 93/436-8459. **Idea** ✉ Pl. Comercial 2, El Born ☎ 93/268-8787.

TOUR OPTIONS

BOAT TOURS **Golondrina** (☎ 93/442–3106 ⊕ www.lasgolondrinas.com) harbor boats make short trips around the harbor from the Portal de la Pau, near the Columbus Monument. The fare is €4 for a 40-minute tour. The 90-minute ride in a glass-bottom catamaran that parallels the coast up past Barcelona's Olympic Port to the Fòrum complex at the northeastern end of the Diagonal costs €10. For an interesting amphibean loop, get off at the Fòrum and take the grassy tramway line back for a look at the new Diagonal Mar neighborhood and Barcelona's new architecture from the low triangular Fòrum building itself, past the Oscar Tusquets–designed Hotel Princess, Jean Nouvel's Torre Agbar, Ricardo Bofill's Teatre Nacional de Catalunya, the Diposit de les Aigues, to the Ciutadella-Vila Olímpica tram and metro stop behind the zoo.

Depending on the weather, the catamarans leave every hour on the half hour from 11:30 to 5:30 (6:30 from Holy Week through September). Regular Golondrina departures are spring and summer (Holy Week through September), daily 11 to 7; fall and winter, weekends and holidays only, 11 to 5. It's closed mid-December through early January.

BUS TOURS From mid-June to mid-October, the Bus Turistic (9:30–7:30 every 30 minutes) runs on a circuit that passes all the important sights. A day's ticket, which you can buy on the bus, costs €9 (€6 half day) and also covers the fare for the Tramvía Blau, funicular, and Montjuïc cable car across the port. The ride starts at the Plaça de Catalunya. Julià Tours and Pullmantur run day and half-day excursions outside the city. The most popular trips are those to Montserrat and the Costa Brava resorts, the latter including a cruise to the Medes Isles.
◢ Julià Tours ✉ Ronda Universitat 5, Eixample ☎ 93/317-6454. **Pullmantur** ✉ Gran Vía 635, Eixample ☎ 93/318-5195.

WALKING TOURS The **Barcelona Tourist Office** (⊕ www.barcelonaturisme.com) offers weekend walking tours of the Gothic Quarter (at 10 AM) for €9. **Ruta Gourmet** walking tours through emblematic points of the city's gastronomic life are also available, with tastings, for €11. The **Mercat de la Boqueria** offers tours of the market with breakfast, cooking classes, and tastings. **Urbancultours** has English-language walking tours covering Gaudí's Sagrada Família, the medieval Jewish quarter, and other sights. For Thursday afternoon boat tours of the harbor and the fishermen's quarter (€10), and visits to the daily fish auction (€7), reserve ahead with **Consorci El Far de Barcelona.**
◢ Aula Gastronómica del Mercat de la Boqueria ✉ La Rambla 91, Rambla ☎ 93/304-0272. **Consorci El Far de Barcelona** ✉ L'Escar s/n, Barceloneta ☎ 93/221-7457. **Palau de la Virreina** ✉ La Rambla 99, Rambla. **Turisme de Barcelona** ✉ Pl. de Catalunya 17 bis, Eixample ☎ 93/285-3832. **Urbancultours** ☎ 93/417-1191.

6

DISCOUNTS & DEALS

Obtainable in Turisme de Barcelona offices in Plaça de Catalunya and Plaça Sant Jaume (both open Monday–Saturday 9–9 and Sunday 10–2), as well as in the Sants train station (open daily 8–8) and the El Prat airport, the Barcelona Card offers discounts in nearly all of Barcelona's major museums and stores, access to public transport gratis, and discounts on theater and music events.

Turisme de Barcelona sells the multi-attraction Barcelona Card in single-day through five-day versions. For €17 up to €30, you get unlimited travel on all public transport as well as discounts at 27 museums, 10 restaurants, 14 recreational sites, and 20 stores, as well as additional services. You can buy the card at all tourist offices, the El Corte Inglés department store, and the Barcelona Aquarium, among other sites.

🛈 **Estació de Sants** ✉ Pl. dels Països Catalans s/n, Eixample. **Pl. de Catalunya** ✉ Pl. de Catalunya 17 bis, Eixample ☎ 906/301282. **Pl. Sant Jaume** ✉ Pl. Sant Jaume 1, Barri Gòtic ☎ 906/301282.

VISITOR INFORMATION

Turisme de Barcelona has two main locations, both open Monday through Saturday 9 to 9 and Sunday 10 to 2: Plaça de Catalunya, in the center of town, and Plaça Sant Jaume, in the Gothic Quarter. There are smaller facilities at the Sants train station, open daily 8 to 8; the Institut de Cultura (at La Rambla 99 and La Rambla 7) open Monday through Saturday 9 to 9 and Sunday 10 to 2, has cultural information only. The Palau de Congressos is open daily 10 to 8 during trade fairs and conventions only. For general information in English, dial 010 between 8 AM and 10 PM any day but Sunday. El Prat Airport has two offices (in terminals A and B) with tourist information, open Monday through Saturday 9:30 to 8 and Sunday 9:30 to 3. The tourist office in Palau Robert, open Monday–Saturday 10 to 7, specializes in provincial Catalonia. From June to mid-September, tourist information aides patrol the Gothic Quarter and La Rambla area 9 AM to 9 PM. They travel in pairs and are recognizable by their uniforms of red shirts, white trousers or skirts, and badges.

🛈 **City Tourist Offices Palau de Congressos** ✉ Av. María Cristina s/n, Eixample ☎ 902/233200. **Pl. de Catalunya** ✉ Pl. de Catalunya 17 bis, Eixample ☎ 807/117222 ⊕ www.barcelonaturisme.com. **Pl. Sant Jaume** ✉ Pl. Sant Jaume 1, Barri Gòtic ☎ 906/301282. **Institut de Cultura** ✉ La Rambla 99, Rambla ☎ 93/316-1000. **Institut de Cultura Centro de Arte Santa Mónica** La Rambla 7, Rambla ☎ 93/316-2811.
🛈 **Regional Tourist Offices El Prat Airport** ☎ 93/478-4704. **Palau Robert** ✉ Passeig de Gràcia 107, at Diagonal, Eixample ☎ 93/238-4000.

Southern Catalonia & the Levante

WORD OF MOUTH

"Tarragona has a large beach . . .. There is an impressive Roman amphitheater right beside the main beach and other Roman ruins sprinkled around, [including] a double-decker aqueduct. A nice small old quarter, too . . .. We stayed one night and wished we had more time."

–Ian

Updated by
Michael
Kessler

THIS REGION STRADDLES CATALONIA (Catalunya) and Valencia, allowing you to sample the differences and similarities between these two feuding Mediterranean cousins. Valencia was part of the House of Aragón, Catalonia's medieval Mediterranean empire, after Jaume I conquered it in the 13th century. Valencia was incorporated, along with Catalonia, into a united Spanish state in the 15th century, but the most energetic cultivators of its separate cultural and linguistic identity still resent their centuries of Catalan domination. The Catalan language prevails in Tarragona, a city and province of Catalonia, but Valenciano, widely considered a dialect of Catalan (many valencianos consider it a language proper), is spoken and written on street signs in the Valencian provinces. You may notice the subtle difference in dialect as you move south.

The *huerta* (a fertile, irrigated coastal plain) is devoted mainly to citrus and vegetable farming, which lends color to the landscape and fragrance to the air. Grayish, arid mountains form a stark backdrop to the lush coast. Over the years these shores have entertained Phoenician, Greek, Carthaginian, and Roman visitors—the Romans stayed several centuries and left archaeological reminders all the way down the coast, particularly in Tarragona, the capital of Rome's Spanish empire by 218 BC. Rome's dominion did not go uncontested, however; the most serious challenge came from the Carthaginians of North Africa. The three Punic Wars, fought over this territory between 264 BC and 146 BC, led to the immortalization of the Carthaginian general Hannibal.

The same coastal farmland and beaches that attracted the ancients call to modern-day tourists, though a chain of ugly developments has marred much of this shore. Inland, however, local culture has survived intact. This rugged and often beautiful territory is dotted with small fortified towns, several of which bear the name of Spain's 11th-century national hero, El Cid, as proof of the battles he fought here against the Moors 900 years ago. Each town has a porticoed Plaza Mayor, a warren of whitewashed houses, and countless coats of arms. Founded by the Greeks, the city of Valencia was in Moorish hands from 712 to 1238, apart from a brief interlude from 1094 to 1102, when El Cid reconquered it. Colorful *azulejos* (glazed, patterned tiles) and bright-blue church cupolas reflect Moorish traditions here. Spain's golden age left striking souvenirs of the 15th century as well: the Gothic Lonja (Silk Exchange) and mansions, and the primitive paintings of Jacomart and Juan Reixach in the Museum of Fine Arts. The flamboyant Palacio de las Dos Aguas embodies the vitality of Churrigueresque, the early Spanish baroque.

Exploring Tarragona to Valencia

The ancient city of Tarragona—with a Roman amphitheater and aqueduct—infuses the northern wedge of Southern Catalonia with a medieval flavor. Southwest of Tarragona are the wetlands of the Ebro Delta, rich in birdlife. Inland lie the rugged Sierra de Beceite mountains and the walled town of Morella. The Ebro River snakes its way through the interior, passing through the historical town of Tortosa. Southern Catalonia's interior is best accessed by car, as the bus and trains have limited routes.

GREAT ITINERARIES

Numbers in the text correspond to numbers in the margin and on the Southern Catalonia & the Levante and the Valencia maps.

IF YOU HAVE 3 DAYS

Spend one day exploring the Roman, Visigothic, medieval, and modern wonders of ▦ **Tarragona ❶**, stopping occasionally to savor its sweeping sea views. Have lunch in the Serallo fishing quarter, dine within the Roman walls, and spend the night in the heart of town. Set out the next morning for the **Delta de l'Ebre ❻** and explore its world-famous nature preserve before having lunch at the restaurant-museum Estany, near Villafranca del Delta. Head south to ▦ **Peñíscola ❼** for your second night, and devote your third day to **Valencia ㉑– ㉝**.

IF YOU HAVE 5 DAYS

Begin with ▦ **Tarragona ❶**. After a night there, move on to explore the **Delta de l'Ebre ❻**, taking a late lunch at the restaurant-museum Estany. Drive up to ▦ **Tortosa ❼** for a night in the Castillo de la Zuda parador. Devote Day 3 to the **Sierra de Beceite ❾**, **Gandesa ❽**, Calaceite, Valderrobres, Beceite, and Fredes before an overnight in ▦ **Morella ⓫**. On Day 4, drive through the Maestrazgo mountains to see some of the least visited valleys and villages on the entire Iberian Peninsula. Take the slow but scenic CS802 around the small town of Villafranca del Cid before driving through **Ares del Maestre ⓬** and **San Mateu ⓯** on your way to ▦ **Peñíscola ⓱**, where you can spend the night. Finally, travel down the Costa del Azahar to ▦ **Valencia ㉑– ㉝**.

South of Tortosa, lively resort towns—including Benicarló, Peñíscola, and Benicàssim—dot the Costa del Azahar. The region's crown jewel is artistic Valencia, perched on the southern end of the Costa del Azahar.

About the Beaches

Beaches here are endless swaths of fine-grain sand. At the northern end of the region, Salou has the best beaches, along with a lively, palm-lined promenade. More tranquil are the beaches of the Ebro Delta, the best of which is Playa de los Eucaliptos, reached by a scenic road from Amposta via Montells. There are views of the wetlands and, as you approach the beach, of the sea. Peñíscola's beach seems to go on forever—the sand is soft, and the old city rises out of the sea at one end. Alcocéber has a series of small uncrowded sandy crescents, and just to its north is the sophisticated marina at Las Fuentes. Benicàssim's long, crescent-shape beach is the most dramatic, with mountains rising steeply in the background. Valencia itself has a long beach that's wonderful for sunning and has numerous restaurants, but it's not the best place to swim; for cleaner water, head south to El Saler.

About the Restaurants

In and around Valencia, indeed all along the Mediterranean coast, you're in the homeland of *paella valenciana*—a hearty rice dish flavored with saffron and embellished with seafood, poultry, meat, peas, and peppers. Prepared to order in a *caldero* (shallow pan), paella takes a full 20 minutes to cook, so it's not for when you're in a hurry. Good paella is fabulous, but it's often overpriced because of tourist demand, and it's usually best not to choose paella from a *menú del día*—it'll probably be bland and disappointing. For the optimum experience, find a restaurant that specializes in paella, one where you can be sure of the freshest ingredients. A variant is *arroz a la banda,* in which the fish and rice are cooked separately; the fish is fried in garlic, onion, and tomato, and the rice is boiled in the resulting stock. *Romesco,* a spicy blend of almonds, peppers, and olive oil, is used as a fish and seafood sauce in Tarragona, especially during the *calçotada* (spring onion) feasts of February. If you're here for September's Santa Tecla festival, look for *espineta amb cargolins* (tuna with snails), perhaps accompanied by some excellent wine from the nearby Penedés or Priorato vineyard. The Ebro Delta is renowned for its fresh fish and eels, as well as specialties such as *rossejat* (fried rice in a fish broth, dressed with garlic sauce). *Jamones* (hams), *cecinas* (smoked meats), and *carnes a la brasa* (meats cooked over coals) are all staples of cooking in the Maestrazgan mountain range, along with good *trucha* (trout), *conejo* (rabbit), and local *trufas* (truffles).

WHAT IT COSTS In Euros				
	$$$$	$$$	$$	$	¢
AT DINNER	over €20	€15–€20	€10–€15	€6–€10	under €6

Prices are per person for a main course at dinner.

About the Hotels

Antique, one-of-a-kind lodgings are in gratifying abundance on the Ebro Delta and in the Maestrazgo mountains. On the shore, hotels are more mundane, with modern high-rises predominating. Tarragona has several standard hotels. Just north and south of Valencia, the towns of Puzol and El Saler have some famous luxury properties; the city itself offers a reasonable mix of hotels. Book your room months in advance if you plan to be in Valencia during Las Fallas or America's Cup.

WHAT IT COSTS In Euros				
	$$$$	$$$	$$	$	¢
FOR 2 PEOPLE	over €180	€100–€180	€60–€100	€40–€60	under €40

Prices are for two people in a standard double room in high season, excluding tax.

Timing

In general, avoid this region in summer. The weather is hot and dry, and the beaches are crowded. Fall and spring are probably the best times to come, though anyone who has seen slanting December light in the delta

IF YOU LIKE

FIESTAS
In Valencia, **Las Fallas** fill an entire week in March, reaching their climax on March 19, El Día de San José (St. Joseph's Day), when families throughout Spain celebrate Father's Day. The time-honored feast of Las Fallas grew from the fact that St. Joseph is the patron saint of carpenters; in medieval times, carpenters' guilds celebrated his feast day by making huge bonfires with their wood shavings. Today Valencia explodes into a weeklong celebration of fireworks, flower-strewn floats, carnival processions, bullfights, and uncontrolled merrymaking. On March 19, huge and often grotesque effigies of popular and not-so-popular figures are ceremoniously burned, inspiring a surprising sense of nostalgia and the ephemerality of life itself. If you're allergic to firecrackers or large crowds, stay away from this one. Tarragona's most important fiestas are those of **St. Magí** (August 19) and **St. Tecla** (September 23), both marked by colorful processions.

or the dramatic shadows that winter sun casts on medieval stone facades might recommend a winter visit just as heartily.

TARRAGONA

❶ *98 km (60 mi) southwest of Barcelona, 251 km (155 mi) northeast of Valencia.*

Just over an hour from Barcelona, Tarragona gives you a mix of activities in a fresh provincial capital. An ancient outpost of the Roman Empire, it remains a fishing port, busy shipping harbor, and vibrant cultural center. As capital of the Roman province of Tarraconensis (from 218 BC), Tarraco, as it was then called, formed the empire's principal stronghold in Spain, and by the 1st century BC the city was regarded as one of the empire's finest urban creations. Its wine was already famous, and its people were the first in Spain to become Roman citizens. The apostle Paul preached here in AD 58, and Tarragona became the seat of the Christian church in Spain until it was superseded by Toledo in the 11th century. Tarragona was selected by UNESCO in 2000 as a World Heritage Site for its extensive Roman remains and exceptional and ongoing excavations. Check out the €8 combination ticket, which includes admission to the amphitheater, Circus Maximus, Praetorium, and Casa Castellarnau. Valid for one year, the pass is a good deal if you plan to explore several of the major sites.

Approaching the city from Barcelona, 19 km (12 mi) north of Tarragona, you pass the **triumphal arch of Berà,** dating from the 3rd century BC. From the Lleida (Lérida) road, or *autopista,* you can see the 1st-century **Roman aqueduct** that helped carry fresh water 32 km (19 mi) from the River Gayo. Tarragona is divided clearly into old and new by the Rambla Vella—the old town and most of the Roman remains are to the north, and modern Tarragona spreads toward the south.

Start your tour at the acacia-lined Rambla Nova, at the end of which is a balcony overlooking the sea, the Balcó del Mediterràni. Walking up-hill along Passeig de les Palmeres, you arrive at the remains of Tarrag-

★ ona's **amphitheater,** sitting in the shadow of the modern, semicircular Hotel Imperial Tarraco, artfully echoing the amphitheater's curve. Walk down the steps to the amphitheater to see just how well preserved it is— you're free to wander through the access tunnels and along the seating rows. In the center of the theater are the remains of two superimposed churches, the earlier of which was a Visigothic basilica built to mark the martyrdom of St. Fructuosus and his deacons in AD 259 (they were burned alive). ⊠ *Parc de Miracle* ☎ *977/242579* ⊡ *€2 or €8 combination ticket* ☯ *Wk after Easter–Sept., Tues.–Sat. 9–9, Sun. 9–3; Oct.–Holy wk, Tues.–Sat. 9–5, Sun. 9–3.*

Explore the excavated vaults from the 1st-century Roman **Circus Maximus.** The plans just inside the gate show that these formed only a small corner of a vast arena (350 yards long), where 23,000 spectators gathered to watch chariot races. As medieval Tarragona grew, the city gradually swamped the Circus. The Circus is across the Rambla Vella from the Tarragona amphitheater. ☎ *977/241952* ⊡ *€2, joint entry with Praetorium, or €8 combination ticket* ☯ *Wk after Easter–Sept., Tues.–Sat. 9–9, Sun. 9–3; Oct.–Easter wk, Tues.–Sat. 9–7, Sun. 9–3.*

The former **Praetorium** served as Augustus's town house and is said to be the birthplace of Pontius Pilate. In the Middle Ages, it housed the kings of Catalonia and Aragón during their visits to Tarragona. The Praetorium now has a **Museu d'Història** (History Museum), with plans showing the evolution of the city; the highlight is the **Hippolytus sarcophagus,** which has a bas-relief depicting the legend of Hippolytus and Fraeda. The Praetorium is around the corner from the Circus Maximus. ⊠ *Passeig Sant Antoni* ☎ *977/221736* ⊡ *€2, joint entry with Circus Maximus, or €8 combination ticket* ☯ *Wk after Easter–Sept., Tues.–Sat. 9–9, Sun. 9–3; Oct.–Easter wk, Tues.–Sat. 9–7, Sun. 9–3.*

★ Next door to the Praetorium, in a 1960s neoclassical building, is **Museu Nacional Arqueològic.** It includes Roman statuary, keys, bells, and belt buckles, and the Head of Medusa, with its piercing stare. There's an excellent video on Tarragona's history. ⊠ *Pl. del Rei 5* ☎ *977/221736* ⊕ *www.mnat.es* ⊡ *€2.40, free Tues.* ☯ *June–Sept., Tues.–Sat. 10–8, Sun. 10–2; Oct.–May, Tues.–Sat. 10–1:30 and 4:30–7, Sun. 10–2.*

Under the arcade on the Carrer de la Merceria is a stairway leading to Tarragona's **cathedral.** If no mass is in progress, enter through the cloister. The main attraction is the **altarpiece** of St. Tecla, a detailed depiction of the life of Tarragona's patron saint. ⊠ *Pla de la Seu* ☎ *977/238685* ⊡ *€2.40* ☯ *June–mid-Oct., Mon.–Sat. 10–7; mid-Oct.–mid-Nov., Mon.–Sat. 10–5; mid-Nov.–mid-Mar., Mon.–Sat. 10–2; mid-Mar.–May, Mon.–Sat. 10–1 and 4–7.*

Built by Tarragona nobility in the 18th century, **Casa Castellarnau,** a Gothic *palacete,* or town house, is now a museum with furnishings from the 18th and 19th centuries. The last member of the Castellarnau family vacated the house in 1954. ⊠ *Carrer Cavallers* ☎ *977/242220* ⊡ *€2* *or €8 combination ticket ☉ June–Sept., Tues.–Sat. 9–9, Sun. 9–3; Oct.–May, Tues.–Sat. 9–7, Sun. 9–3.*

Les Voltes (✉ End of Carrer Cavallers at Plaça Pallol), is a Roman forum with a Gothic upper story and also one of the prettiest corners in Tarragona. The **Passeig Arqueològic** (✉ Through Portal del Rose) is a path that skirts the 3rd-century BC Ibero-Roman ramparts and is built on even earlier walls of giant rocks. The glacis was added by English military engineers in 1707, during the War of the Spanish Succession. Look for the rusted bronze of Romulus and Remus. At the **Serallo** fishing quarter, boats unload their catch at the quayside. Peek inside the market, where fish are swiftly auctioned off to fishmongers and restaurateurs. The market is accessible by Bus 2 if you happen to be traveling from the Portal del Rose. Near the fish market is the **Necròpolis i Museu Paleocristià** (Tomb and Paleochristian Museum). ✉ *Av. Ramón y Cajal 80* ☎ *977/211175* 💳 *Combined ticket with Museu Arqueològic €2.40, free Tues.* ☉ *June–Sept., Tues.–Sat. 10–1 and 4:30–8, Sun. 10–2; Oct.–May, Tues.–Sat. 10–1:30 and 3–5:30, Sun. 10–2.*

Where to Stay & Eat

$$$$ ✕ **La Puda.** The prime quayside location guarantees fresh seafood, including a mixed platter of hake, sole, and monkfish with spicy *salsa Romesco.* Locals love this place, even though the menu is written in several languages. The restaurant is simply decorated: a tile floor, salmon-color walls, and white tablecloths. ✉ *Muelle Pescadores 25* ☎ *977/211511* 💳 *AE, DC, MC, V* ☉ *No dinner Sun. Oct.–May.*

★ **$$$–$$$$** ✕ **Les Coques.** If you have time for only one meal in Tarragona, take it at this elegant little restaurant in the heart of the old town. Both mountain and Mediterranean food are served, from hearty *cordero* (lamb) to *calamarsets* (baby calamari sautéed in olive oil, garlic, and secret seasonings) and *lubina* (sea bass). ✉ *Carrer San Lorenzo 15* ☎ *977/228300* 🍴 *Reservations essential* 💳 *AE, DC, MC, V* ☉ *Closed Sun. Closed 1st 2 wks in Feb. and late July–mid-Aug.*

★ **$$$** ✕ **Les Voltes.** Built into the vaults of the Roman Circus Maximus, this out-of-the-way spot is a combination of 2,000-year-old chiseled stone, contemporary polished steel, and thick plate glass. The hearty menu of fish dishes and international fare includes oven-baked sea bass with vegetables and the specialty of the house, *rap al all cremat* (monkfish in fried garlic). In winter, *calçotadas* (spring onions) are available; it's best to order them a day in advance. The bar is a popular late-night spot. ✉ *Carrer Trinquet Vell 12* ☎ *977/230651* 💳 *MC, V* ☉ *Closed Mon. No dinner Sun.*

$ ✕ **El Tiberi.** Just steps off the Rambla Nova sits this bustling, rustic restaurant with wood tables. Here you can graze on a buffet of Catalan dishes, from *butifarra* (Catalan sausage) to *pa amb tomaquet* (toasted bread smeared with tomato and drizzled in olive oil). Finish off with *crema catalana,* Catalonia's answer to crème brûlée. ✉ *Carrer Martí d'Ardenya 5* ☎ *977/235403* 💳 *MC, V* ☉ *Closed Mon.*

$$$ 🏨 **Imperial Tarraco.** Overlooking the Mediterranean, this large, white, half-moon-shape hotel has plain but comfortable guest rooms, and each has a private balcony. Ask for a sea view. The large public rooms have cool marble floors and black leather furniture. The hotel caters to business travelers and conferences during the week, so off-season weekend rates (Fri.–Sun., Sept.–May) are a steal at half the regular price. ✉ *Passeig Palmeres s/n 43003* ☎ *977/233040* 📠 *977/216566* ⊕ *www.husa. es* ⌨ *170 rooms* ♨ *Restaurant, tennis court, pool, hair salon, bar, meeting room* ☰ *AE, DC, MC, V* ⏐◯⏐ *BP.*

$–$$ ⊞ **Hotel Lauria.** Guest rooms are spacious and comfortable, and their terraces overlook the serene pool and patio area, the Rambla Nova, or the sea. This is the most pleasant place to stay downtown. ✉ *Rambla Nova 20, 43004* ☎ *977/236712* 📠 *977/236700* ⊕ *www.hlauria.es* ⌨ *72 rooms* ♨ *Bar* ☰ *AE, DC, MC, V* ⏐◯⏐ *CP.*

¢–$ ⊞ **Pensión La Noria.** Rising above the spirited Plaça de la Font, this small place sports a cheery yellow facade with wrought-iron balconies. The interior is drab and institutional, but the basic, functional rooms (linoleum floors, simple furnishings) are clean and fresh smelling, and some have small balconies, making this one of Tarragona's better budget digs. The entrance is through the bar-cafeteria. ✉ *Pl. de la Font 53, 43003* ☎ *977/238717* ⌨ *24 rooms* ♨ *Bar* ☰ *MC, V.*

Nightlife & the Arts

The **Teatro Metropol** (✉ Rambla Nova 46 ☎ 977/244795) is Tarragona's center for music, dance, theater, and cultural events ranging from *castellers* (human-castle formations), usually performed in August and September, to folk dances. Castellers is a centuries-old Catalan tradition. Dressed in typical Catalan dress, participants climb atop one another to create a towering human castle. On Rambla Nova, near Plaça Imperial Tarraco, is a life-size paean to Tarragona's gravity-defying castellers. At the very top of this bronze sculpture is a child with his hand in the air, the official gesture that signals the dismantling of the tower.

Nightlife in Tarragona takes two forms: older and quieter in and around the Casco Viejo, and younger and more raucous in the southern, newer part of town, south of Rambla Nova. There's a row of restaurants and dance spots in the Puerto Deportivo, a pleasure-boat harbor separate from the working port; young folks flock here on weekends and summer nights. For a dose of culture to go with your cocktail, try **Antiquari** (✉ Santa Anna 3 ☎ 977/241843), a bar with film screenings (usually Wednesday at 10 PM), and live music on Thursday, Friday, and Saturday nights. It's closed Sunday and Monday. For quiet talking, tippling, and tapas tasting, **El Cándil** (✉ Pl. del Forum ☎ 977/230916) is a serene spot. In the shadow (literally) of Tarragona's cathedral is the casual café-bar **Pla La Seu** (✉ Pl. de la Seu 5 ☎ 977/230407). You can sample ice-cream concoctions on the Plaça while admiring the cathedral's impressive facade;on summer weekends there's live jazz.

Shopping

Expect to haggle for bargains; **Carrer Major** has some exciting antiques stores. Rummage thoroughly, as the gems are often hidden away. You might also try the shops in front of the cathedral. **Poblet** (✉ Carrer Major 27–29 ☎ 977/23492) has antique furniture, lamps, fans, watches, porcelain, and bronze busts. **Mercat d'Antiguitats** (antiques market) fills the Pla de la Seu on Sunday 9 to 3. For Tarragona crafts, browse the ceramics and Roman-style candleholders and plates at **Mosaic** (✉ Carrer Major 19 ☎ 977/234246).

MICHAEL'S TOP 5

- Viewing Valencia from atop the Miguelete Tower.
- Relaxing at the beach in El Saler.
- Dining on seafood at Joan Gatell's in Cambrils.

- Bird-watching at Delta de l'Ebre.
- Celebrating into the wee hours with the crowd at Las Fallas in mid-March.

Lleida

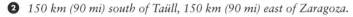 *150 km (90 mi) south of Taüll, 150 km (90 mi) east of Zaragoza.*

The pleasant provincial capital of Lleida (Lérida in Castilian) borders the banks of the River Segre in the heart of Catalonia's agricultural and farm country. The Romans settled here around 200 BC, and the Arabs took control of the city in the 8th century.

The landmark **La Seu Vella,** the old cathedral, was built between the 13th and 15th centuries in a transitional Romanesque-Gothic style and was converted to a military barracks after the 1707 siege of Felipe V. That explains its appearance—its Vauban-style walls and esplanades make it seem like a fortress. It's especially panoramic in late afternoon, when the low light spotlights the city, the Segre river, and the countryside beyond. Open daily from 10 to 1:30 and 4 to 7:30, it can be reached by escalator and elevator from Plaça Sant Joan or on foot via Carrer Cavallers. The medieval chapel of **Sant Jaume Peu de Rome** is on the Catalan route of the Camino de Santiago pilgrimage. Lleida's sculptor Jaume Gort fashioned the Sculpture of Saint James, and local artist Miquel Roig Nadal painted a work hung in the altar.

One block inside the old town, the most vital pedestrian artery, **Carrer Major,** runs parallel to the river. After 8 PM the newer area around Plaça Ricard Vinas is the hub of café, terrace, and restaurant life. Two key architectural sights here are **La Paeria,** a 13th-century Gothic mansion distinguished by massive stone archways, and the immense arched entrance to the **Antic Hospital de Santa Maria,** now the city's Cultural Center. Worth checking out while you're here is the **Arc del Pont,** opposite the Pont Vell (Old Bridge), the bridge leading across the Segre just upstream from La Paeria. This arch was the ancient gateway into the walled city; the bronze figures depict the two fallen heroes of the local Ilergetes tribe, Indíbil and Mandoni. The 14th-century church of **Sant Llorenç,** has a slender bell tower and porticoed doorway.

SOUTH TO THE MAESTRAZGO

This segment goes from the purely recreational, such as the Port Aventura theme park, to the sublime, encompassing the extraordinary natural resources from the Ebro Delta to the Sierra de Beceite. The wildly varied route takes you from below sea level (in parts of the delta) to high stone villages in the hills; from wetlands to the arid hinterlands of Tarragona.

Reus

❸ *13 km (8 mi) northwest of Tarragona.*

Reus is an industrial town with the distinction of having been the birthplace of Antoni Gaudí, as well as the longtime home of his fellow Moderniste architect Lluís Domènech i Montaner. If you're into Moderniste buildings, Lluís Domènech's **Casa Navàs** is well worth the short detour. Follow the signs to the center of Reus and you arrive at the Plaça del Mercadal; the Casa Navàs is beside the *ajuntament* (town hall). The rich interior decoration includes mosaics, stained glass, tiles with characteristic Moderniste floral motifs, and oddly shaped leather chairs. There are no formal visiting hours, but the house is usually open Thursday through Saturday 10 to 1. (It's generally closed December through February. Stop by the **tourist office** (⊠ Pl. de la Llibertad s/n ☎ 977/778149) to arrange a visit; they only allow groups with a minimum of six people to tour the house. Admission is €5. **Teatre Fortuny** (⊠ Pl. Prim 4 ☎ 902/332211) is the Reus's primary theater and opera showcase.

Salou

❹ *11 km (7 mi) south of Reus.*

If you're starting to crave a sunny afternoon on the beach, stop in Salou, a modern resort with a long esplanade of young palms. The town itself is long on glitz but short on charm. History buffs might appreciate that the conquerors of Mallorca set out from the old port here in 1229. On the edge of Salou, the **Universal Port Aventura** (⊠ Autovéia Salou/Vila-Seca, Km 2, Apartat 90/43480 Vila-Seca, Tarragona ☎ 902/202220 or 977/779000 ⊕ www.portaventura.es) boldly offers "the adventure of your life" to anyone brave enough to shell out €35 or €28 per child under 11 for rides, waterslides, and steam engines. Prices rise €2 during the peak summer months of July and August; the park is closed from early January to late March. Port Aventura's hotel offers reasonably budgeted lodging aimed at families.

Cambrils

❺ *7 km (4½ mi) west of Salou, 18 km (11 mi) southwest of Tarragona.*

Food lovers come to coastal Cambrils to dine in the Joan Gatell restaurant. Refreshingly less developed than Salou, Cambrils has a marina and a bustling fishing port, where each day's catch is hauled in. The fine-sand beaches draw Spanish families, who stroll the town's cobbled streets after sunset and ease into the evening over excellent seafood.

Where to Eat

$$$$
Fodor'sChoice
★

✕ **Joan Gatell.** Since 1970, Joan Pedrell Font—assisted by wife Fanni and now also by son Jordi—has been preparing exquisite local meals starring the freshest seafood from the Costa Daurada. Try the baby eels, *fideos negros amb sepionets* (paella in baby-squid ink), or the superb *suquet,* a traditional Catalan fish stew. Bring your wallet! ⊠ *Miramar 26* ☎ *977/360057* ▭ *AE, DC, MC, V* ⊘ *Closed Mon., mid-Dec.–mid-Jan., 1st 2 wks of May. No dinner Sun.*

Delta de l'Ebre

❻ *77 km (48 mi) southwest of Tarragona, 60 km (37 mi) south of Cambrils.*

The Ebro Delta, a flat piece of wetland à la the Netherlands, juts into the Mediterranean on land deposited over the years by the Ebro River. The largest wetland park in Catalonia, the 20,000-acre **Parc Natural del Delta de l'Ebre** has endless salt marshes, sand dunes, reed beds, and rice paddies. The delta's waters teem with fish (largemouth bass, pike, black bullheads), and frogs, toads, and spiny-footed lizards populate the marshlands and beaches. The park is a major stopping and breeding place for more than 200,000 birds of more than 300 species—an impressive 60% of Europe's bird species can be seen here during the year. A vast variety of waterbirds (shoveler ducks, mallards, coots) descend by the thousands in October and November, when the rice has been harvested but the fields are still full of water. Morning and early evening in autumn and winter yield the best bird-watching. Unfortunately, the delta's most widespread critter is the mosquito, so you'll need a strong repellent to explore the wetlands. To get to the park, take N230 and follow signs to Sant Jaume d'Enveja; at Sant Jaume, take a ferry to the town of Deltebre. Staff at the **Park Information Office** (⊠ Carrer Doctor Martí Buera 22 ☎ 977/489679 ⊕ www.parcsdecatalunya.net) can tell you how to visit the reserve proper—which occupies the delta's northern, eastern, and southern tips—and give you the required permit. The information office is open Monday through Saturday 10 to 2 and 3 to 6 and Sunday 10 to 1.

Where to Stay & Eat

\$\$–\$\$\$ ✗ **L' Estany.** At this restaurant (also known as Casa de la Fusta) smack in the middle of wetlands and rice paddies, chef-owner Luis Garcia is committed to serving the best fish and game, caught just off the doorstep—and to the cultural heritage of the area. During Sunday's lunch hour (2:30–4:30) musicians perform Ebro Delta folk music for diners. In a separate building, groups of 20 or more can arrange for a meal of regional fare served by a waitstaff in traditional dress. ⊠ *Partida La Encanyissada s/n, en route from Amposta to Sant Jaume* ☎ *977/261026* ▭ *MC, V* ⊘ *Closed Mon. Nov.–Feb. No dinner Mon.–Thurs. Oct.–June.*

\$ ⬚ **Lo Molí de Rosquilles.** Once an olive-oil mill, this old stone building with original furnishings functions as a charming and cozy hotel. A library stocked with regional books invites you to delve into the history, geography, and ecology of the Ebro Delta. Food is served for guests only; don't miss the excellent bread, cooked in a wood-burning oven. The hotel is in Masdenverge, 20 km (12 mi) west of Deltebre and 5 km (3 mi) north of Amposta (en route to Santa Barbara). ⊠ *C. Catalunya 6, Masdenverge 43878* ☎ *977/718052 or 629/358929* ⊅ *8 rooms* ⚭ *Dining room, massage, sauna, library; no TV in some rooms* ▭ *MC, V.*

Tortosa

❼ *80 km (50 mi) southwest of Tarragona.*

Tortosa, straddling the Ebro River 10 km (6 mi) inland, was successively Roman, Visigothic, Moorish, and Christian. The town was the scene of one of the Spanish civil war's bloodiest battles. The Republicans, loyal to the democratically elected government and already in control of Catalonia, crossed the Ebro in July 1936 to attack the rebel Nationalists' rear guard. They got no farther than Tortosa, and were pinned down in trenches until they were forced to retreat, having lost 150,000 lives. You can cover the city's sights in a few hours.

Tortosa's local parador, in the ruined hilltop **Castillo de la Zuda,** is worth visiting even if you don't stay the night. Originally a Templar fortress, the castle (and town) passed into the hands of the Moors around the year 713, where it remained until its reconquest in 1153 by Ramón Berenguer IV, count of Barcelona. From the castle walls are views across the fertile Ebro Valley to the Sierra de Beceite. ⊠ *Parador Castillo de la Zuda* ☎ *977/444450.*

The Renaissance **Colegio Sant Lluís** has an arcaded patio, embellished with a frieze depicting the kings of Aragón. It houses an impressive archival collection, including a population map of Tortosa dated 1149 and signed by Ramón Berenguer IV. The 13th-century *El Llibre de les Costums de Tortosa* is the first judicial text written in Catalan. ⊠ *Sant Domènec s/n.*

Tortosa's **cathedral** looks baroque, but if you enter through the cloister you can see that the building itself is purely Gothic. It was common in 18th-century Spain to tack these exuberant stuccos on to Gothic structures; the style is called Churrigueresque, after its first practitioner, José Churriguera. ⊠ *Croera s/n* ☉ *Cloister daily, cathedral for mass only.*

Where to Stay & Eat

$$–$$$ ✕ **Rosa Pinyol.** Following in his mother's illustrious footsteps, chef and owner Joan Pinyol concocts regional dishes based on the Ebro Delta's teeming underwater population, from sea bass to sole, and fresh seasonal vegetables, including asparagus. His careful preparation of each dish can sometimes delay your food—but it's worth the wait. Try the *rape asado con calçots* (grilled monkfish with calçots, a springtime green onion native to this region). The small restaurant is just west of the old town, across the Pont de l'Estat (Estat Bridge). ⊠ *Hernan Cortés 17* ☎ *977/502001* ▤ *AE, DC, MC, V* ☉ *Closed Sun. No dinner Mon.*

$$–$$$ ✕ **Sant Carles.** Joan Ros, chef-owner of this long-running restaurant on the northern edge of old town, excels in seafood and freshwater fish from the Ebro Delta, including *almejas a la marinera* (marinated clams), *lubina a la plancha* (grilled sea bass), *rodaballo* (turbot), and sole. ⊠ *Rambla Felip Pedrell 13* ☎ *977/441048* ▤ *AE, DC, MC, V* ☉ *Closed Sun.*

★ $$$ ▥ **Parador de Tortosa.** Few sights around Tortosa can equal the superb view from the old Arab Castillo de la Zuda across the Ebro Valley to the Sierra de Beceite. Dark shades of mahogany and copious tapestries evoke the past. Guest rooms have heavy wood furniture, terra-cotta floors, rugs, and plain walls. The restaurant serves Catalan fare, including *bacalao con espinacas y allioli* (cod with spinach and garlic mayonnaise) and *pato del Delta con mandarinas* (Delta duck with mandarins). ⊠ *Castillo de la Zuda s/n, Tortosa 43500* ☎ *977/444450* 🖶 *977/444458* ⊕ *www.parador.es* ◻ *72 rooms* ♨ *Restaurant, pool, bar, playground, meeting room, free parking* ⊟ *AE, DC, MC, V.*

Nightlife & the Arts

October marks the **Felip Pedrell Musical Festival,** when classical and chamber music concerts are showcased at the **Teatre Auditori Felip Pedrell** (⊠ Pl. Salvador Videllet ☎ 977/510144).

Gandesa

❽ *87 km (54 mi) west of Tarragona.*

The terrain surrounding Gandesa is rugged, and some of the mountainsides are covered in pine trees. There are views of the fields and orchards in the valleys below. Renowned for its strong wine (up to 16% alcohol), Gandesa also has two architectural landmarks. The extraordinary **Cooperativa Agrícola** (Wine Cooperative) was designed by the Moderniste architect Cèsar Martinell in 1919. The white, Islamic-looking facade does little to prepare you for the remarkable vaulting inside, constructed entirely of small bricks ingeniously arranged to allow for expansion and contraction. This is a working building (open weekdays 9 to 1 and 3 to 7, Saturday 9 to 1, Sunday 10 to 2), and you can buy some local wine here for a sleepy picnic on the way to Alcañiz or Beceite. ⊠ *Av. Catalunya 28, Gandesa* ☎ *977/420017.*

Where to Stay & Eat

¢ ✕▦ **Hostal Piqué.** Though uninviting from the outside, this modern roadhouse has a large, smart dining room with white tablecloths and professional service. The menu mixes everyday local options with rarer, pricier delicacies. The *menú del día* (menu of the day) is an excellent bargain ($), and may include *ensalada de queso de cabra* (salad with goat cheese), *sopa de cebolla* (onion soup), peppers stuffed with seafood, and steak. Rooms are comfortable and economical. ⊠ *Via Catalunya 68, 43780* ☎ *977/420068* 🖶 *977/420329* ◻ *48 rooms* ♨ *Restaurant; no a/c, no TV in some rooms* ⊟ *AE, MC, V.*

Sierra de Beceite

❾ *15 km (9 mi) southwest of Gandesa on N420.*

The mountains of the Sierra de Beceite offer a beautiful excursion near Gandesa, as long as you and your car can handle some bumpy roads. Just after the entrance to the Aragonese province of Teruel is **Calaceite** on your right: explore its ancient, labyrinthine streets, which converge at the arcaded Plaza Porticada. For a closer inspection of the Beceite massif, turn left at the Calaceite crossroads and drive along TE301. Turn right after 18 km (11 mi) at a T junction to reach **Valderrobres,** with a fortified palace and a Renaissance town hall that served as the model for Barcelona's Poble Espanyol. Continue to **Beceite** and follow signs to a *panorama* for a bumpy drive culminating in an impressive vista. Depending on the condition of these forest roads, you can drive all the way to **Fredes,** due south of Beceite: the kings of Catalonia, Aragón, and Valencia are said to have met near here, on the Tossal dels Tres Reis (4,450 feet), to iron out disputes. The best way to explore these hills is on foot (or on horseback); a sign on the way into Beceite points you toward the tourist office, which has trail maps and can arrange horseback rides. From Valderrobres, you can cut back to the Alcañiz road via TE300, which follows the River Matarraña.

Alcañiz

⑩ *62 km (38 mi) west of Gandesa, 74 km (46 mi) north of Morella.*

Alcañiz lies on a plain, encircled by the River Guadaloupe and surrounded by ugly, modern apartment blocks, the result of a population explosion following the success of the nearby olive and almond orchards. The highway (N420) enters the town along a street that bustles with ongoing construction. For the old town, turn left at the end of this street to the Plaza Mayor. The **Lonja** (✉ Exchange, Pl. Mayor) has pointed arches defining its Gothic origin. The galleries and overhanging eaves on both buildings of the Renaissance *ayuntamiento* (✉ Town hall, Pl. Mayor, adjoining the Lonja) mark them as Aragonese. The **Colegiata** (✉ Pl. Mayor) church has a baroque facade and an impressively ornate portal; by comparison, the painted interior is simple and rather dull. Alcañiz's hilltop **castle** (✉ Castillo de Calatrava ☎ 978/830400) was the seat of the Calatrava Knights in the 14th century and is now a parador.

Where to Stay & Eat

★ **$$$** ✕⌂ **Parador de Alcañiz.** Installed in the sturdy castle of the Calatrava Knights, this hotel grandly surveys the olive-growing plain and the foothills of the Maestrazgo. Guest rooms have terra-cotta tile floors, patterned rugs, dark furniture, generous beds, and good views. The traditional restaurant ($–$$$) is spacious and warm, and serves Aragonese fare, such as *ternasco asado* (grilled lamb) and sweet *almendrados* (small almond cakes). ✉ *Castillo de Calatrava, 44600* ☎ *978/830400* 📠 *978/830366* ⊕ *www.parador.es* 🛏 *37 rooms* ⌂ *Restaurant, sauna, bar, meeting room* ▤ *AE, DC, MC, V.*

Morella

★ **⑪** *74 km (46 mi) south of Alcañiz, 64 km (40 mi) northwest of Benicarló.*

The walled town of Morella stands on a towering crag in Castellón, the northernmost Valencian province. It's not immediately evident if you approach from the north, but from the south and east the land drops away sharply, creating a natural fortress—the scene of several bloody battles. Morella's main thoroughfare is the arcaded **Calle Don Blasco de Alagón.** The numerous bars here are packed on weekends. Morella's **castle** is accessible through the gate on the Plaza de San Francisco, on the uppermost of the town's contoured streets. Just inside the gate is the ruined cloister and small church of an old Franciscan monastery; inside the church vault are several polychrome reliefs of Saint Francis. In 1088 El Cid scaled these walls and wreaked havoc on the occupying Moors. During the Carlist Wars of the 16th century, the castle became a stronghold for General Cabrera, who captured Morella in 1838 for Don Carlos, pretender to the Spanish throne. The walk up to the castle takes a good 15 minutes. ☎ *964/173128* ☒ *€1.50* ۞ *Oct.–Mar., daily 10:30–6:30; Apr.–Sept., daily 9–9.*

The blue-tile dome on the beautiful church of **Santa María la Mayor** lends an exotic note to this otherwise Gothic structure. The larger of the church's two doorways, depicting the Apostles, dates from the 14th century. A spiral marble staircase leads to the raised, flat-vaulted choir. The sanctuary got the full baroque treatment, as did the high altar. The **museum** has a painting by Francisco Ribalta and some 15th-century Gothic panels. The church is near Morella's castle on Calle Hospital. ☒ *€1.50* ۞ *June–Sept., daily 11–2 and 4–7; Oct.–May, daily noon–2 and 4–6.*

Where to Stay & Eat

★ $$$ ✕ **Restaurante El Mesón del Pastor.** In a restored 14th-century stone mansion on a side street off Calle Don Blasco de Alagón, chef José Ferrer specializes in Maestrazgan fare such as *conejo relleno trufado* (rabbit stuffed with truffles) and dishes with wild and farmed mushrooms. Desserts include *buñuelos con miel* (fried dumplings with honey), *tarta de almendras* (almond tart), and homemade *cuajada*, a firm curd yogurt. In November the restaurant hosts a mushroom specialty week. Next door is a simple 12-room inn ($$). ☒ *Cuesta Jovaní 5–7* ☎ *964/160249* ⊕ *www.hoteldelpastor.com* ☰ *AE, DC, MC, V* ۞ *Closed Wed. Sept.–July. No dinner weekdays. No lunch Sat. Sept.–July.*

$$ ✕⊞ **Cardenal Ram.** In what was originally the 14th-century ancestral
FodorsChoice home of the famous Spanish prelate Cardinal Ram, this hotel reveals
★ its history with its bare, stone walls and ubiquitous coats of arms. The lobby has a huge tapestry depicting the 1414 visit of Antipope Papa Luna, named Pope Benedict XIII during the Great Schism of 1378–1417—Cardinal Ram was named by the antipope, whom he then served. Rooms have pine floors, bare white walls, high-beamed ceilings, and magnificent heavy furniture. The fine restaurant ($$–$$$) serves a succulent *solomillo* (sirloin) and fragrant *perdiz* (partridge). ☒ *Cuesta Suñer 1, 12300* ☎ *964/173085* ⊕ *www.cardenalram.com* ☒ *964/173218* ☞ *19 rooms* ዻ *Restaurant; no a/c* ☰ *MC, V.*

$ ⊞ **Hostal La Muralla.** Right on the street that delineates Morella's city walls, this hostelry is comfortable and clean. Several of the exterior rooms offer romantic *vistas al muralla* (views of the wall). ☒ *Muralla 12, 12300* ☎ *964/160243* ☞ *19 rooms* ዻ *Cafeteria; no a/c* ☰ *MC, V* ⊠ *CP.*

Shopping

The Maestrazgo region produces brightly colored handwoven woolens. The best buys are striped *mantas morellanas* (Morellan bedspreads), available along Calle Blasco de Alagón and around Plaza Arciprestal.

Ares del Maestre

⑫ *50 km (31 mi) southwest of Morella on N232, the main road to Villafranca del Cid, and CS802 toward Albocácer.*

Ares del Maestre is on the most dramatic site of any village in this area—like Morella, it rests on a crag, but here the drop is more severe and the vistas are more rewarding. Lush valleys dotted with well-tended fields unfold far below, in marked contrast to the surrounding terrain of stark mountains and craggy cliffs. A very steep climb, windy in winter and scorching in summer, takes you to a ruined **castle.**

Teruel

⑬ *110 km (68 mi) southwest of Ares del Maestre, backtrack on CS802 toward Morella, then get on TE811 at Villafranca del Cid, 148 km (92 mi) northwest of Valencia.*

This provincial Aragonese capital is famous for its Mudejar architecture, its medieval lovers of lore, and its cured ham—displayed proudly in grocery stores throughout town. Once part of the city walls, Teruel's **Mudejar towers** were built between the 12th and 16th centuries in a style more reminiscent of Muslim minarets than Christian belfries. The highlight of the **cathedral** is its coffered ceiling with 13th-century court and hunting scenes, visible from the upper gallery.

The church of **San Pedro** has a Mudejar tower but is best known for its adjoining **Mausoleo de los Amantes** (Lovers' Mausoleum). Here lie the tombs of Diego and Isabel, two 13th-century Teruel lovers who died, it's said, of broken hearts. A wealthy merchant's daughter named Isabel de Segura fell in love with a young man named Diego de Marcilla, who had no means to marry a woman of Isabel's status. Her father naturally forbade the match. Determined to marry his true love and prove himself worthy in her father's eyes, Diego set out to seek his fortune. He returned five years later in triumph to ask for Isabel's hand—only to find that she was being married that very day to the son of a wealthy merchant from the nearby town of Albarracín. Overcome with grief, Diego died on the spot; the next day, at his funeral, Isabel, devastated, also died. Their story—Spain's version of Romeo and Juliet—captured the imagination of 16th-century European artists, including Tirso de Molina and Hartzenbusch. ⊠ *North of Pl. Bretón.*

Where to Stay & Eat

$$–$$$ ✕🏨 **Parador de Teruel.** Teruel's parador was built in 1956 to match the town's famous Mudejar-style architecture. The spacious rooms have parquet floors and floral wallpaper befitting an Aragonese palacete. The flower and herb gardens are beautifully maintained, as are the pool and tennis courts. The restaurant ($$–$$$) serves both regional and national cuisine—everything from paella valenciana to *caldereta de cordero* (lamb stew). ⊠ *Ctra. Sagunto–Burgos, N234, Km 124, 44080* ☎ *978/601800* 🖨 *978/608612* ⊕ *www.parador.es* ⇥ *58 rooms, 2 suites* ♿ *Restaurant, 2 tennis courts, pool* ☰ *AE, DC, MC, V.*

7

Albarracín

⑭ *37 km (23 mi) west of Teruel, 185 km (116 mi) northwest of Valencia.*

West of Teruel are the grand Sierras de Albarracín, a vast massif carved into spectacular ravines by the powerful Guadalaviar and Curvo rivers. Rocky mountain plateaus loom above fertile valleys rich with wild vegetation, hulking pine and fir trees, and a population of deer and wild boar—which often end up as succulent dishes on the menus of mountain restaurants. Trekking trails cross the region, much of which remains refreshingly untamed, and there are 30-odd delightful villages, with ancient stone-and-wood houses and cobblestone streets. The area's natural and cultural riches all seem to come together in the small town of Albarracín. Perched at 3,840 feet above a luxuriant gorge with the Guadalaviar rushing below, the village makes an eye-catching picture of ancient stone houses and crenellated walls, against a gorgeous backdrop of evergreen hills and craggy cliffs. Climb the steep cobblestone streets past tiny old-fashioned *carnicerías* (butcher shops) and groups of old men leaning on their canes, and you really start feeling like you're deep in Spain. Rising above the Plaza Mayor is the **cathedral,** with a beautiful 16th-century *retablo* (altarpiece) featuring St. Peter.

Where to Stay & Eat

★ **$$** ✕⊞ **Casa de Santiago.** At the top of an ancient staircase near the Plaza Mayor is this family-run hotel in a beautifully restored country house. The fresh-smelling rooms are all individually decorated, and there are ample sitting rooms on every floor. A cozy common room is outfitted with oversize brown-leather sofas that you can sink into, a rope-woven rocking chair, and big baskets of magazines. One flight up is a sunlighted attic suite with a wrought-iron writing desk and splendid views of the valley and the red-tile roofs of town. The small restaurant ($$–$$$) serves excellent Aragonese fare, including roast veal and *migas*, fried spiced-bread crumbs with chopped pork and onions. ✉ *Subida a las Torres 11, 44100* ☎ *978/700316* ⊕ *www.casadesantiago.net* ⌂ *8 rooms, 1 suite* ⌂ *Restaurant; no a/c, no room TVs* ▤ *MC, V* ⊘ *Closed Feb.*

San Mateu

⑮ *26 km (16 mi) west of Benicarló, take CS802 southeast from Ares del Maestre to Albocácer, and then turn left.*

The small town of San Mateu proudly bears the subtitle Capital del Maestrazgo because it was from here that King Jaume I set out on his decisive reconquering raids in the 13th century, freeing the region finally from Moorish control. Sturdy Gothic mansions near the Plaza Mayor attest to San Mateu's regal past. Visit the Iglesia Arciprestal (Archpriest's Church) on the corner of the plaza—its nave is a fine example of the Catalan Gothic style, and the vault covers a wide expanse, dispensing with the need for columns.

THE COSTA DEL AZAHAR

Named for the orange blossom and its all-pervading fragrance along this sweet coastal plain, the Costa del Azahar was transformed by the tourist-inspired building boom of the 1960s and '70s. Benicarló and Peñíscola are, with Vinaròs, the northernmost towns on the Costa del Azahar (province: Castellón de la Plana), and Sagunto marks the start of the Costa de Valencia.

Benicarló

16 *55 km (34 mi) south of Tortosa.*

Benicarló has become a major tourist center. The harbor is a lively confusion of fishing and pleasure craft, and the beaches are jammed with locals and northern European sunseekers most of the year.

Where to Stay & Eat

$$$–$$$$ ✕ **Casa Pocho.** This restaurant is named after its owner, Paco Puchal—also known as El Pocho, or "the Tubby One." Wood paneling and maritime motifs set the scene for the restaurant's famously good seafood. *Langostinos* (prawns) are a good choice, as are the *almejas* (clams), *lubina* (sea bass), and fillet of sole. ✉ *San Gregorio 49, Vinaròs* 🕾 *964/451095* ▤ *MC, V* ⊘ *Closed Mon. No dinner Sun.*

$$$ ▥ **Parador de Benicarló.** The main attraction here is the large, semiformal garden, which runs down to the sea—a perfect place to rest, away from the crowded beaches. Public rooms are huge and bright, with white-wicker furniture and white walls. Guest rooms have tile floors and functional furniture; ask for a seaside view. Travelers with disabilities are well accommodated. ✉ *Av. Papa Luna 5, 12580* 🕾 *964/470100* 🖷 *964/470934* ⊕ *www.parador.es* ➷ *108 rooms* ⚐ *Restaurant, tennis court, pool, bar, meeting rooms* ▤ *AE, DC, MC, V.*

Peñíscola

17 *7 km (4½ mi) south of Benicarló, 60 km (37 mi) northeast of Benicàssim.*

Peñíscola owes its foundation to the Phoenicians. It later became the bridgehead by which the Carthaginian Hamilcar (father of Hannibal) imported his elephants and munitions to wage the first of the three Punic Wars. Carthaginian influence in Iberia reached its zenith some 20 years later, in 230 BC, but was eventually eroded by that of Rome. Peñíscola's **old town** is a cluster of white houses and tiny narrow streets leading up to the castle on a promontory, which gave people perfect surveillance of the coast. The beach here is one of the best in the area. You can drive up to the **castle,** but in summer the traffic makes it smarter to leave your car by the town walls and walk. Of chief interest are the chapel and study of the antipope Papa Luna, to whom the 14th-century castle passed in the 15th century. Hardly any of Papa Luna's effects remain, but while you're in his drafty quarters, try to imagine this 90-year-old Frenchman (formerly Pope Benedict XIII) passing the last six years of his life attend-

FodorśChoice
★

7

ing mass and composing schismatic bulls while surrounded by hostile Moorish townsfolk. ☎ *964/480021* ⌚ *€2* ⊙ *Apr.–mid-June and mid-Sept.–mid-Oct., daily 9–8:30; mid-June–mid-Sept. 9:30–2 and 4:30–9:30; mid-Oct.–Mar., daily 9:30–1 and 3:15–6.*

Where to Stay & Eat

$$$ ✕⌂ **Hostería del Mar.** Officially a "semiparador," this modern, white hotel next to Peñíscola's long beach meets the paradores' high standards. Most guest rooms have balconies; some overlook the old town and others the beach. Inside, they have white walls, tile floors, and Castilian-style dark-wood and leather furniture. The rustic, beamed public rooms surround a leafy pool terrace. The Los Ficus restaurant—named after a regional tree—serves fish in season, including *rape, merluza* (hake) and tasty *chuletas* (pork chops). ⊠ *Av. Papa Luna 18, 12598* ☎ *902/ 480600* ⊕ *www.hosteriadelmar.net* 🖨 *964/481363* 🛏 *86 rooms* ⚭ *Restaurant, tennis court, pool, bar, some pets allowed (fee)* ▭ *AE, DC, MC, V.*

▊ EN
ROUTE

A trip down the Costa del Azahar south of Peñíscola takes you through carob and orange plantations. The autopista is the fastest road south, but the N340 shares the same scenery and grants easier access to places en route. The town of **Alcalá de Chivert** can claim the tallest belfry in the Valencian provinces. This stretch of the road is separated from the sea by the Sierra de Hirta, whose rugged outlines contain some ruined castles easily visible from the road. **Alcocéber** is an expanding but still quiet vacation town with two good beaches.

Benicàssim

⑱ *60 km (37 mi) southwest of Peñíscola, 13 km (8 mi) northeast of Castellón de la Plana.*

Geographically blessed, the coastal town of Benicàssim is backed by the dramatic shapes of the Desierto de las Palmas mountain range, and the Mediterranean laps the town's long, sandy swimming beaches. Early vacationers—mostly wealthy Valencians—were suitably charmed, and the first vacation villa was built here in 1887. By 1900, Benicàssim was a genteel getaway, prompting its nickname: the Biarritz of the Costa de Azahar. This all changed during Spain's tourist boom in the early 1960s, when package tours arrived en masse along the coast; resorts replaced rusticity, and the local flavor of many coastal towns faded in the face of high-rise concrete jungles and quadrilingual menus. Although Benicàssim has its share of characterless apartment blocks, it was spared the worst resort-style excesses. Pleasant pedestrian promenades run alongside its clean, sandy beaches, and today most summer visitors are vacationing Spanish families. The well-preserved 16th-century **Torre de San Vicente,** a watchtower (not open to the public), once guarded against marauding pirates and looms over a popular beach of the same name.

Seven kilometers (4 mi) inland from Benicàssim and set against the soothing backdrop of silent mountain peaks is the **Monasterio del Desierto de las Palmas,** a Carmelite monastery founded in 1694. The small museum houses Carmelite religious figurines and clothing from centuries past. ⊠ *Carretera Desierto de las Palmas s/n* ☎ *964/300950* 🖃 €2 ⊙ *Monastery daily 10:30–1, museum Sun. noon–2.*

Where to Stay & Eat

$$$ ✕ **Villa del Mar.** This secludedold country manor house has a dining terrace ringed by palms and pines. The food international and regional; try the *arroces valencianos* (Valencian rice dishes). On summer evenings a barbecue is held in the garden. ⊠ *Paseo Marítimo Pilar Coloma 24* ☎ *964/302852* 🖃 *AE, MC, V* ⊙ *Closed Nov.*

$$$ 🏨 **Orange.** If it's facilities you're after, look no farther: this huge, modern, chalet-style hotel has them. It's central—only 150 yards from the beach—and surrounded by trees and a garden. Loud patterns in brown and orange set the tone in the public rooms, and the plain guest rooms are no more than functional. Ask for a sea view: rooms over the pool can be noisy. ⊠ *Av. Gimeno Tomás 9, 12560* ☎ *964/394400* 🖃 *964/ 301541* ⊕ *www.intur.com* ⤳ *415 rooms* ♨ *Restaurant, cafeteria, miniature golf, tennis court, 3 pools, bar, meeting rooms* 🖃 *AE, DC, MC, V* ⊙ *Closed early Nov.–mid-Feb.* ⟨◯⟩ *CP.*

$$–$$$ 🏨 **Voramar.** On the beach at the north end of town, this small neoclassical hotel is encircled by ample balconies. Ask for a room overlooking the sea, and you'll have a large balcony to yourself, with the sand directly below and gorgeous vistas of the Mediterranean. Prices dip considerably if you opt for a mountain-facing room, and even more so for a room with no balcony, just a window with a view (if you can call it that) of the parking lot. Rooms are plain and functional, with tile floors, white walls, and 1970s furniture. ⊠ *Paseo Pilar Coloma 1, 12560* ☎ *964/300150* 🖃 *964/300526* ⊕ *www.voramar.net* ⤳ *58 rooms* ♨ *Restaurant, tennis court, bar, some pets allowed* 🖃 *AE, DC, MC, V* ⟨◯⟩ *CP.*

Nightlife & the Arts

Since 1995 Benicàssim has made a name for itself on the indie-music circuit. Thousands descend for the annual **Festival Internacional de Benicàssim** (FIB; ⊕ www.fiberfib.com) held in August, which has headlined such bands as Nick Cave, Mouse on Mars, and Björk. On a more traditional note, late July brings the **Festival de Habaneras,** featuring sorrowful sailor songs on the guitar, often with a Cuban rhythm.

In summer, Benicàssim pulsates with the liveliest *marcha* (night "scene") on the Costa de Azahar. The city center is the nocturnal hot spot; **Plaza de los Dolores** and **Calle Santo Tomás** are packed with pubs and clubs. Enjoy the Mediterranean's balmy nights on Benicàssim's seaside promenade, **Paseo del Pilar Coloma,** where graceful 19th-century villas have been converted into classy terrace bars and restaurants. A classic drinking spot is the elegant **Villa María** (⊠ Bernat Artola 36 ☎ 964/300662). The outdoor terrace, surrounded by well-tended gardens, draws couples and groups of coworkers out for an evening cocktail. Dinner is also a popular option: Mediterranean cuisine—the fresh sea bass is excellent—is served in the spacious dining room. At the north end of the promenade is the **Voramar Hotel** (⊠ Paseo Pilar Coloma 1 ☎ 964/300150) with a lovely beachfront terrace bar. A lively mix of tourists and locals enjoy the breezes off the sea in the early evening; the summer beverage of choice is a *clara* (beer mixed with lemon soda). Groove to rock and pop at **K'asim** (✉ Av. Gimeno Tomás), a happening nightclub that swarms with locals and foreigners in the summer.

Sagunto

 65 km (40 mi) southwest of Benicàssim, 23 km (14 mi) northeast of Valencia.

Sagunto will ring a bell if you've read Caesar's history: Saguntum, as the Romans called it, was the sparking point for the Second Punic War. When Hannibal laid siege to the town (at that time a port, from which the sea has since receded), the people heroically held out, faithfully expecting a Roman relief force, and eventually burned the town rather than surrender to the Carthaginians. Rambling Moorish fortifications dominate Sagunto from the hilltops, and within this citadel earlier **Roman remains** are now being excavated. In the citadel (on Plaza de San Fernando) is the **Antiquarium Epigráfico,** a collection of inscriptions on marble and epigraphs dedicated to various Roman emperors, and Roman funeral stones. Visit the well-restored **amphitheater.** More complete than Tarragona's, it went up during the Roman rebuilding five years after Hannibal's siege. ⬛ *Free* ☉ *Amphitheater and citadel: May–Sept., Tues.–Sat. 10–8, Sun. 10–2; Oct.–Apr., Tues.–Sat. 10–6, Sun. 10–2. Epigraph collection: May–Sept., Tues.–Sat. 10–2 and 5–8, Sun. 10–2; Oct.–Apr., Tues.–Sat. 10–2 and 4–6, Sun. 10–2.*

Nightlife & the Arts

The month of August brings **Sagunto a Escena** (✉ Pl. Cronista Chabret ☎ 962/662213), a festival of classical Mediterranean drama for which theater groups perform ancient plays in Sagunto's Roman amphitheater.

VALENCIA & ENVIRONS

Spain's third-largest city and the capital of the Levante, Valencia is nearly equidistant from Barcelona and Madrid. If you have time for a day trip (or you decide to stay in the coastal town of El Saler), make your way to the Albufera, a scenic coastal wetland teeming with native wildlife, especially migratory birds. Tourist buses leave from Plaza de la Reina daily (☎ 963/414400).

Valencia

 362 km (224 mi) south of Barcelona, 351 km (218 mi) southeast of Madrid.

Despite its proximity to the Mediterranean, Valencia's history and geography have been defined most significantly by the River Turia and the fertile floodplain (*huerta*) that surrounds it. The city has been fiercely contested ever since it was founded by the Greeks. El Cid captured Valencia from the Moors in 1094 and won his strangest victory here in 1099: he died in the battle, but his corpse was strapped to his saddle and so frightened the waiting Moors that it caused their complete defeat. In 1102, his widow, Jimena, was forced to return the city to Moor-

America's Cup in Valencia: June 2007

IN 2007, from June 23 through July 7, the 32nd America's Cup comes to Valencia. The last time the America's Cup was held on European waters, the year was 1851 and Queen Victoria watched as the yacht *America,* representing the New York Yacht Club, beat 15 British vessels racing around the Isle of Wight.

Reliable wind conditions and the promise of a new sailing village that will bring the race closer to spectators helped Valencia take the honor of hosting the world's oldest sporting trophy event.

Spain's third-largest city will be the first non-English-speaking nation to hold the sailing competition—since the mid-19th century, the races have been held only in Britain, the United States, Australia, and New Zealand. This year's event also will be the first Cup not to be staged in the home waters of the holders.

The Cup will deliver major infrastructure improvements to the city—including an airport expansion, a subway line from the airport to the transformed port (with a new 700-berth marina), a competitor's village, and vantage points that not only will be inclusive of the city's residents but attract a foreign tourism euro splash not seen in the city before.

Spanish King Juan Carlos will be over the moon—he's a yachting freak and devoted competitor in Mallorca's sailing season. His son Felipe was a competitor for Spain in the 1992 Barcelona Olympics. (⊕ www. americascup.com).

---

ish rule; Jaume I finally drove them out in 1238. Modern Valencia was best known for its flooding disasters until the River Turia was diverted to the south in the late 1950s. Since then the city has been on a steady course of urban beautification. The lovely *puentes* (bridges) that once spanned the Turia look equally graceful spanning a wandering municipal park, and the spectacular futuristic Ciudad de las Artes y de las Sciencias (City of Arts and Sciences) designed by Valencian-born architect Santaigo Clalatrava has at long last created an exciting architectural link between this river town and the Mediterranean. Valencia's port, and parts of the city itself, are undergoing major structural refurbishment in anticipation of the 2007 America's Cup sailing classic to be held here.

A GOOD WALK

Begin your stroll through Valencia's historic center at the **cathedral** ⑳ ➤ in the Plaza de la Reina (climb the Miguelete Tower for good city views). Cross the **Plaza de la Virgen** and before you to the left stands the Gothic **Palau de la Generalitat** ㉑. Continuing down Calle Caballeros, you pass Valencia's oldest church, **San Nicolás** ㉒. After spending time inside, walk to the Plaza del Mercado and the 15th-century **Lonja de la Seda** ㉓. Travel down Avenida María Cristina to the **Plaza del Ayuntamiento** ㉔, one of the city's liveliest areas. After a five-minute walk down Avenida Marqués de Sotelo, you'll find the Moderniste **Estación del Tren (train station)** ㉕. Next to it is the **Plaza de Toros** ㉖. Head back to the city center via the bustling Plaza del Ayuntamiento and then walk along Calle

Poeta Querol to the wedding-cake facade of the **Palacio del Marqués de Dos Aguas** ㉗. Cross the Calle Poeta Querol to Plaza Patriarca and enter the **Real Colegio del Patriarca** ㉘. Wander old town's streets on your way north toward the Turia River—cross by Puente de la Trinidad to see the **Museo de Bellas Artes** ㉙, adjoined by the **Jardines del Real** (Royal Gardens). Walk up Calle San Pio V to the Puente de Serranos and cross back to the 14th-century **Torre de Serranos**, which once guarded the city's entrance. Turn right for the **Casa Museo José Benlliure** ㉚, and continue west to the **Institut Valencià d'Art Modern (IVAM)** ㉛. On a separate outing, cross the Turia and stroll south to the **Palau de la Música** ㉜ and **Ciutat de les Arts i les Ciències** ㉝.

TIMING   Allow a full day for a tour of the old quarter, the Museo de Bellas Artes, and the IVAM. Tack on a few hours the next day for the Palau de la Música and Ciutat de les Arts i les Ciències.

What to See

㉚ **Casa Museo José Benlliure.** Cross the Puente de Serranos, turn right down Calle Blanquerías, and stop at No. 23. The modern Valencian painter-sculptor Jose Benlliure is known for his portraits and large-scale historical and religious paintings, many of which hang in Valencia's Museo de Bellas Artes (Museum of Fine Arts). Here in his elegant house and studio are 50 of his works, including paintings, ceramics, sculptures, and drawings. On display are also works by his son, Pepino, who painted in the small, flower-filled garden in the back of the house, and iconographic sculptures by Benlliure's brother, the well-known sculptor Mariano Benlliure. ☎ 963/919103 ⊠ Free ⊘ Tues.–Sat. 9:30–2 and 4:30–8, Sun. 9:30–2.

▶ ⑳ **Cathedral.** Valencia's 13th- to 15th-century cathedral is the heart of the city. The building has three portals—Romanesque, Gothic, and rococo respectively. Inside, Renaissance and baroque marble were removed in a successful restoration of the original Gothic style, as is now the trend in Spanish churches. The Capilla del Santo Cáliz (Chapel of the Holy Chalice) displays a purple agate vessel once said to be the Holy Grail (Christ's cup at the Last Supper) and thought to have been brought to Spain in the 4th century. Behind the altar you can see the left arm of **St. Vincent,** who was martyred in Valencia in 304. Stars of the cathedral **museum** are Goya's two famous paintings of St. Francis de Borja, Duke of Gandia. To the left of the cathedral entrance is the octagonal tower **El Miguelete,** which you can climb: the roofs of the old town create a kaleidoscope of orange and brown terra-cotta, and the sea appears in the background. It's said that you can see 300 belfries from here, including bright-blue cupolas made of ceramic tiles from nearby Manises. The tower was built in 1381, and the final spire added in 1736. ⊠ Pl. de la Reina ☎ 963/918127 ⊠ Cathedral free, museum €1.20, tower €1.20 ⊘ Cathedral Mon.–Sat. 7:30–1 and 4:30–8:30, Sun. 7:30–1 and 5–8:30; museum and chapel Dec.–Feb., Mon.–Sat. 10–1; Mar.–May, Oct., and Nov., Mon.–Sat. 10–1 and 4:30–6; June–Sept., Mon.–Sat. 10–1 and 4:30–7; tower weekdays 10–12:30 and 4:30–6:30, weekends 10–1:30 and 5–6:30.

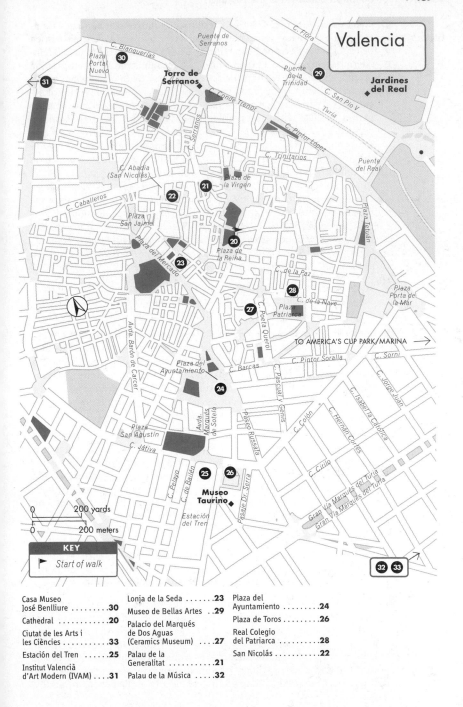

Valencia

ⓒ ⑬ **Ciutat de les Arts i les Ciències.** Designed by native son Santiago Cala-
Fodor's Choice trava, this sprawling futuristic complex is the home of Valencia's **Museu**
★ **de les Ciències Príncipe Felipe** (Prince Philip Science Museum), **L'Hemisfèric** (Hemispheric Planetarium), **L'Oceanogràfic** (Oceanographic
Park), and **Palau de les Arts** (Palace of the Arts). With resplendent buildings resembling combs and crustaceans, the Ciutat is a favorite of architecture buffs and curious kids. The Science Museum has soaring
platforms filled with lasers, holograms, simulators, and hands-on lab
experiments. The eye-shape planetarium projects 3-D virtual voyages
on its huge IMAX screen. At the Oceanographic Park you can take a
submarine ride through a coastal marine habitat. New additions include
an amphitheater, an indoor theater, and a chamber-music hall. ⊠ *Av.
Autovía del Saler 7* ☎ *902/100031* 🖷 *961/974505* ⊕ *www.cac.es*
🎟 *Museu de les Ciències €7.50, L'Hemisfèric €7.50, €11.20 for admission to both, L'Oceanogràfic €22, €29.90 for admission to all 3*
⊙ *Museum Sun.–Fri. 10–8, Sat. 10–9 (July–mid-Sept., daily 10–9),
L'Oceanogràfic Sun.–Fri. 10–6, Sat. 10–8 (July–mid-Sept. 10–mid-
night), L'Hemisfèric daily shows generally every hr on the hr 11–8 (on
Fri. and Sat., additional show at 9 PM).*

㉕ **Estación del Tren.** Designed by Demetrio Ribes Mano in 1917, the train
station is a splendid Moderniste pile replete with citrus motifs. ⊠ *Down
Av. Marqués de Sotelo from ayuntamiento.*

㉛ **Institut Valencià d'Art Modern (IVAM).** Dedicated to modern and contemporary pieces, the art institute has a permanent collection of 20th-cen-
tury avant-garde works, European Informalism (including the Spanish
artists Saura, Tàpies, and Chillida), pop art, and photography. The museum is out near the Turia riverbed's elbow. ⊠ *Guillem de Castro 118*
☎ *963/863000* ⊕ *www.ivam.es* 🎟 *€2, free Sun.* ⊙ *June–Aug.,
Tues.–Sun. 10–10; Sept.–May, Tues.–Sun. 10–8.*

㉓ **Lonja de la Seda** (Silk Exchange). Downhill from San Nicolás, on the Plaza
del Mercado, is the 15th-century Lonja. It is a product of Valencia's golden
age, when the arts came under the patronage of Ferdinand I. Widely regarded as one of Spain's finest Gothic buildings, it has a perfect Gothic
facade decorated with ghoulish gargoyles, complemented inside by high
vaulting and twisted columns. Opposite the Lonja stands the **Iglesia de
los Santos Juanes** (Church of the St. John), whose interior was destroyed during the civil war, and, next door, the Moderniste **Mercado
Central** (Central Market), built entirely of iron and glass. The bustling
food market is open Monday to Saturday, 8 AM to 2 PM, with stall after
stall of fresh fruits and vegetables, meat, fish, and dried fruits and nuts.
🎟 *Free* ⊙ *Tues.–Fri. 9:30–2 and 4:30–8, weekends 9:30–1:30.*

★ ⓒ ㉙ **Museo de Bellas Artes** (Museum of Fine Arts). Valencia was a thriving center of artistic activity in the 15th century, and the city's Museum of Fine
Arts is one of the best in Spain. To get here, walk behind the cathedral
and cross the Puente de la Trinidad (Trinity Bridge) to the river's north
bank; the museum is at the edge of the **Jardines del Real** (Royal Gardens),
with fountains, rose gardens, tree-lined avenues, and a small zoo. The
Royal Gardens are open daily 8 to dusk. Many of the best paintings by

Jacomart and Juan Reixach, two of several artists known as the Valencian Primitives, are here, as is work by Hieronymus Bosch—or El Bosco, as they call him here. The ground floor has the murky, 17th-century Tenebrist masterpieces of Francisco Ribalta and his pupil José Ribera, together with a Velázquez self-portrait and a room devoted to Goya. Upstairs, look for Joaquín Sorolla (Gallery 66), the luminous Valencian painter of everyday Spanish life in the 19th century. ⊠ *C. San Pío V s/n* ☎ *963/ 932046* ⊕ *www.cult.gva.es/mbav* ⊠ *Free* ⊙ *Tues.–Sun. 10–8.*

★ ㉗ **Palacio del Marqués de Dos Aguas.** This building, near the Plaza Patriarca and across Calle Poeta Querol, has a fascinating baroque alabaster facade. Embellished with fruits and vegetables, it centers on the figures of the *Dos Aguas* (*Two Waters*), carved by Ignacio Vergara in the 18th century. The palace contains the **Museo Nacional de Cerámica**, with a magnificent collection of mostly local ceramics. Look for the Valencian kitchen on the second floor. ⊠ *C. Poeta Querol 2* ☎ *963/516392* ⊠ *Palace and museum €2.40, free Sat. afternoon and Sun. morning* ⊙ *Tues.–Sat. 10–2 and 4–8, Sun. 10–2.*

㉑ **Palau de la Generalitat.** On the left side of the Plaza de la Virgen, fronted by orange trees and box hedges, is the elegant eastern facade of what was once the Gothic home of the Valencia Cortés (Parliament), until it was suppressed by Felipe V for supporting the wrong (losing) side during the War of the Spanish Succession in the 18th century. The two *salones* (reception rooms) in the older of the two towers have superb woodwork on the ceilings. Call in advance for permission to enter. ☎ *963/863461* ⊙ *Weekdays 9–2.*

㉜ **Palau de la Música** (Concert Hall). On one of the nicest stretches of the Turia riverbed, a pond is backed by a huge glass vault: Valencia's Palace of Music. Supported by 10 porticoed pillars, the dome gives the illusion of a greenhouse, both from the street and from within its sun-filled, tree-landscaped interior. Home of the Orquesta de Valencia, the main hall also hosts performers on tour from around the world, including chamber and youth orchestras, opera, and an excellent concert series featuring early, baroque, and classical music. For concert schedules, pick up a *Turia* guide or one of the local *periodicos* (newspapers) at any newsstand. To see the building without concert tickets, pop into the **art gallery,** which is host to free changing exhibits. ⊠ *Paseo de la Alameda 30* ☎ *963/375020* ⊕ *www.palauvalencia.com* ⊙ *Gallery daily 10:30–1:30 and 5:30–9.*

㉔ **Plaza del Ayuntamiento.** Down Avenida María Cristina from the market, this plaza is the hub of city life, a fact well conveyed by the massiveness of its baroque facades. The **ayuntamiento** itself contains the city tourist office and a museum on the history of Valencia. ⊙ *Ayuntamiento weekdays 8:30–2:30.*

Plaza de la Virgen. From the cathedral's Gothic Puerta de los Apóstoles (Apostle Door), emerge on this pedestrian plaza, a lovely place for a refreshing *horchata* (tiger-nut milk) in the late afternoon. Next to its portal, market gardeners from the huerta bring their irrigation disputes before the Water Tribunal, which has met every Thursday at noon since 1350. It is said that it is the oldest surviving legal system in the world. Verdicts are given on the spot, and sentences have ranged from fines to deprivation of water.

26 Plaza de Toros. Adjacent to the train station is the bullring, one of the oldest in Spain. The best bullfighters are featured during the Fallas in March, particularly March 18 and 19. Just beyond, down Pasaje Dr. Serra, the **Museo Taurino** (Bullfighting Museum) has bullfighting memorabilia, including bulls' heads and matadors' swords. ▣ *Free* ⊙ *Bullring and museum Mon. 10–2, Tues.–Sun. 10–8.*

28 Real Colegio del Patriarca (Royal College of the Patriarch). The colegio stands on the far side of Plaza Patriarca, toward the center of town. Founded by San Juan de Ribera in the 16th century, it has a lovely Renaissance patio and an ornate church, and its museum holds works by Juan de Juanes, Francisco Ribalta, and El Greco. ⊠ *Entrance off C. de la Nave* ▣ *€1.20* ⊙ *Daily 11–1:30.*

22 San Nicolás. A small plaza contains Valencia's oldest church, once the parish of the Borgia Pope Calixtus III. The first portal you come to, with a tacked-on, rococo bas-relief of the Virgin Mary with cherubs, hints well at what's inside: every inch of the originally Gothic church is covered with Churrigueresque embellishments. ⊠ *C. Abadía San Nicolás* ▣ *Free* ⊙ *Open for mass daily 8–9 AM and 7–8 PM; Sat. 6:30–8:30 PM; Sun. various masses 8–1:15.*

Where to Eat

$$$$ ✗ Civera. This restaurant (and its sister establishment, Civera Centro), is run by the well-known Civera seafood merchants family. It enjoys local renown for its fresh fish and seafood, especially the *langosta* (lobster) cooked *a la plancha* (grilled), *hervidos* (boiled), or *a la sal* (baked in salt). The marine theme is underscored by white walls, beams, and sumptuous displays of fish, fruit, and vegetables. The restaurant is three blocks northwest of the Museo de Bellas Artes. ⊠ *C. Lérida 11* ☎ *963/475917* ▤ *AE, DC, MC, V* ⊙ *Closed Mon., Easter wk, and Aug. No dinner Sun.*

$$$$ ✗ Eladio. West of the city center is this welcoming restaurant decorated with oak and marble. The many Galician fish dishes here are prepared with a mixture of tradition and invention—and some Swiss influences by chef Eladio Rodríguez, who spent some formative years in Switzerland. Try the *rape* (monkfish) or *lubina* (sea bass) *a la brasa* (grilled), or *rodaballo a la Gallega* (turbot with sweet paprika oil), and finish up with a mouthwatering *tarta* (cake) of *almendras* (almonds) or chocolate. ⊠ *Chiva 40* ☎ *963/842244* ▤ *AE, DC, MC, V* ⊙ *Closed Sun. and Aug.*

$$$$
Fodor'sChoice
★
✗ La Sucursal. La Sucursal is solid proof that Valencia can match the cutting-edge contemporary cuisine of its big brother Barcelona. A thoroughly modern but also very cozy spot within the IVAM (Institut Valencía d'Modern Art), it is simply a taste sensation. You won't leave with a full wallet, but then again it's unlikely you'll sample deer carpaccio anywhere else or partake of an *arroz caldoso de bogavante* (rice soup with lobster) as good. At times the food veers toward the indescribable, but there's barely a weakness. Best to let the attentive staff make sug-

gestions and go with it. ✉ *Guillén de Castro 188* ☎ *963/746655* ⚭ *Reservations essential* 🗖 *AE, DC, MC, V* ☯ *Closed Sun.*

$$$–$$$$ ✕ **Gargantua.** Intimate and chic, this 1910 town house has apricot-color rooms crowded with pictures. The cooking is nouvelle and imaginative; *Esgarrat* (grilled cod with green peppers) is a good regional dish. Just east of the city center, Gargantua's a 15-minute walk from Plaza de la Reina. ✉ *Navarro Reverter 18* ☎ *963/346849* 🗖 *AE, DC, MC, V* ☯ *Closed Sun., Easter wk, and last 2 wks of Aug. No lunch Sat.*

$$–$$$$ ✕ **La Riuà.** This local secret, which serves Valencian food, is decorated with beautiful ceramic tiles. House specialties include *anguilas* (eels) prepared with *all i pebre* (garlic and pepper), *pulpitos guisados* (stewed baby octopus), and traditional rice dishes. Wash it down with a cold bottle of *Llanos de Titaguas,* a dry yet snappy white Valencian table wine. The restaurant is just off Plaza de la Reina. ✉ *C. del Mar 27* ☎ *963/914571* 🗖 *AE, DC, MC, V* ☯ *Closed Sun., Easter wk, and Aug. No dinner Mon.*

$$$ ✕ **El Timonel.** Decorated like the inside of a yacht, this central restaurant (two blocks east of the bullring) serves outstanding shellfish. The cooking is simple yet benefits from the freshest ingredients; try the *pescado de roca* (rockfish), grilled *lenguado* (sole), or *lubina* (sea bass). Also top-notch are the eight different kinds of *arrozes* ("rice dishes," the term commonly used by Spaniards for paella), including paella with lobster and peeled *mariscos* (shellfish). For a sweet finale, delve into the house special *naranjas a la reina,* oranges spiced with rum and topped with *salsa de fresa* (strawberry sauce). Lunch attracts businesspeople, and dinner brings in a crowd of locals and foreigners. ✉ *Félix Pizcueta 13* ☎ *963/526300* 🗖 *AE, DC, MC, V* ☯ *Closed Mon.*

$$$ ✕ **La Pepica.** For the best in Valencia's seafood paella, head to the waterfront. At this bustling longtime family restaurant, dig into *arroz marinero* (seafood paella) topped with shrimp and mussels or hearty platters of *calamare* (squid) and *langostinos* (prawns). Save room for the delectable tarts made with fruit in season. ✉ *Paseo Neptuno 6* ☎ *963/710366* 🗖 *AE, DC, MC, V* ☯ *Closed last 2 wks of Nov. No dinner Mon.–Thurs. Sept.–May.*

$$ ✕ **Patos.** Small, cozy, and very popular with locals, this restored 18th-century town house has an earthy look, thanks to the terra-cotta tiles, wood-panel walls, and overhead beams. On weekdays, the set lunch menu is a real bargain at €10 and usually includes *ternera* (veal) and *lomo* (pork loin). The set dinner (and weekend) menu is €18 and sometimes includes *cordero* (lamb) and *solomillo* (pork sirloin). Get here by 9:30 PM to snag a table; you can also dine outside in summer. The restaurant is just north of Calle de la Paz, in the old quarter. ✉ *C. del Mar 28* ☎ *963/921522* 🗖 *MC, V* ☯ *No dinner Sun. and Mon.*

Where to Stay

$$–$$$ ✕🖭 **Ad Hoc.** Small and beautifully designed, this 19th-century town house offers immediate access to the old quarter and the Turia gardens. Owner Luis García Alarcón is an antiquarian, and the hotel reflects his eye for ancient design and architectural elegance. Weekend rates (a third less than weekday prices) are a great value. A buffet breakfast is included on weekends only. The excellent restaurant ($$$–$$$$) draws a pleasant mix of Valencian locals and hotel guests; tuck into paellas or one of the creative meat dishes, including duck with pine nuts, lentils and shrimp, cod with spinach, and a divine passion-fruit sorbet. ⊠ *Boix 4, 46003* ☎ *963/919140* 📠 *963/913667* ⊕ *www.adhochoteles.com* 🗗 *28 rooms* ♿ *Restaurant, some pets allowed* 🖃 *AE, DC, MC, V.*

$$$–$$$$ 🏨 **Monte Picayo.** If you want a casino nearby and don't mind looking at the sea from a distance, consider this place. Set into a hill and draped in greenery, its modern, tiered structure overlooks the huerta north of Valencia. The public areas and guest rooms are spacious and cheerful, and service is impeccable. Each room has a terrace, and six junior suites have private pools. ⊠ *Urbanización Monte Picayo, Autopista Valencia–Barcelona, Puzol, 46530* ☎ *961/420100* 📠 *961/422168* ⊕ *www.hot-hlghotels.com* 🗗 *83 rooms* ♿ *Restaurant, tennis court, pool, hair salon, bar, casino* 🖃 *AE, DC, MC, V.*

★ **$$$–$$$$** 🏨 **Reina Victoria.** Valencia's grande dame is an excellent choice if you want timeworn charm and a good location, next to the Plaza del Ayuntamiento. The spacious reception rooms have cool marble floors (with rugs to take the chill off), as does the smart, classy restaurant. The smallish guest rooms are clothed in green or burgundy chintz and deep-pile carpets with a subdued pattern. A buffet breakfast is included on the weekends only. ⊠ *Barcas 4, 46002* ☎ *963/520487* 📠 *963/522721* ⊕ *www.husa.es* 🗗 *97 rooms* ♿ *Restaurant, bar* 🖃 *AE, DC, MC, V.*

$$$–$$$$ 🏨 **Sidi Saler.** The stretch of coastline just south of Valencia suffers from ongoing construction, but this hotel, surrounded by the Saler Nature Park, is an oasis of luxury. Many of the modern and bright guest rooms have views of the sea. Breakfast is included in the price—fill up on a buffet of *revueltos* (scrambled eggs), a variety of breads, and fresh fruit. Ask about weekend rates, which are often considerably less than on weekdays. ⊠ *Playa del Saler, 46012* ☎ *961/610411* 📠 *961/610838* ⊕ *www. hotelessidi.es* 🗗 *276 rooms* ♿ *Restaurant, cable TV with movies, 2 tennis courts, 2 pools (1 indoor), hair salon, sauna, spa, squash, 2 bars, meeting rooms, some pets allowed (fee)* 🖃 *AE, DC, MC, V* 🍽 *BP.*

★ 🕐 **$$–$$$** 🏨 **Holiday Inn Valencia.** The Holiday Inn is great value compared with may other similar establishments. Close to the city center, its rooms are light and spacious, and have high-speed Internet access. The staff is attentive, and the Mezzo & Mezzo restaurant serves good Italian and international fare—a real bonus is that kids under 12 can eat for free. The bar at the rooftop pool is a bonus. ⊠ *Paseo de La Alameda 38, 46023* ☎ *963/032100* ⊕ *www.valencia.holiday-inn.com* 🗗 *200 rooms* ♿ *Two restaurants, pool, bar, gym* 🖃 *AE, DC, MC, V.*

$$–$$$ 🏨 **Meliá Confort Inglés.** Once the palace of the dukes of Cardona, this hotel is convenient to the old town. Rooms are plush and ultramodern; ask for one overlooking the alabaster doorway of the neighboring Palacio del Marqués de Dos Aguas, with the brawny twin atlantes pouring water from two amphorae in illustration of the marqués's name. Ask about weekend rates—prices dip considerably. ⊠ *Marqués de Dos Aguas 6, 46002* ☎ *963/516426* 📠 *963/940251* ⊕ *www.solmelia.com* 🗗 *63 rooms* ♿ *Restaurant, cable TV with movies, bar* 🖃 *AE, DC, MC, V.*

$–$$ 🏨 **Villarreal.** Rustic on the outside, modern on the inside, this little family-friendly hotel is between the Mercado Central and Plaza del

Ayuntamiento. In a neighborhood where a moderately priced room is a scarce commodity, this is your very best bet. The neutral-hue rooms are spotless. Breakfast is included on the weekends. ✉ *Ángel Guimerá 58, 46008* ☎ *963/824633* 🖷 *963/840247* 🛏 *25 rooms* ⚭ *Cafeteria* ▤ *AE, DC, MC, V.*

Nightlife & the Arts

Sleep seems to be anathema here. You can experience Valencia's nocturnal way of life at any time except summer, when locals disappear on vacation and the international set moves to the beach. Nightlife in the old town centers around Barrio del Carmen, a lively web of streets that unfolds north of Plaza del Mercado. A string of bars and pubs dot Calle Caballeros, leading off Plaza de la Virgen—these establishments are very popular, if not a little tired; the Plaza del Tossal also has some popular cafés, as does Calle Alta, leading off Plaza San Jaime. Some of the funkier and newer places are to be found in and around Plaza del Carmen. Across the river in the new town, look for appealing hangouts along Avenida Blasco Ibáñez and on Plaza de Cánovas del Castillo and Plaza Zuquer. Out by the sea, Paseo Neptuno and Calle de Eugenia Viñes are lined with loud clubs and bars. Castellón and Valencia jointly publish *Que y Donde*, the major listings magazine; *Turia* focuses on Valencia.

Fodor'sChoice
★ If you want nonstop nightlife at its frenzied best, come during **Las Fallas** in March, when revelers throng the streets and last call at many of the bars and clubs isn't until the wee hours of morning, if at all. The **Feria de Julio** is July's monthlong festival of theater, film, dance, and music (☎ 963/520694).

The **Filmoteca** (✉ Pl. del Ayuntamiento 17 ☎ 963/539300) has changing monthly programs of films in their original language (look for *v.o.— versión original*) and an artsy haunt of a café. An 11th-century Arab wall is incorporated into the 18th-century palace that is **Carmen** (✉ C. Caballeros 38 ☎ 963/925273), a sleek bar-club whose many floors are connected by ramps. There are several art installations, and the music is always sharp. The airy, perennially popular, bar-club-performance-space **Radio City** (✉ Santa Teresa 19 ☎ 963/914151) offers an eclectic nightly showcase from flamenco (on Tuesday at 11 PM) and Afro-jazz fusion to theater. For quiet after-dinner drinks, try the jazzy, light-hearted bar **Café de la Seu** (✉ Santo Cáliz 7 ☎ 963/915715), with contemporary art and animal-print chairs. For a taste of *el ambiente andaluz* (Andalusian atmosphere) tuck into tapas and cocktails at **El Albero** (✉ Ciscar 12 ☎ 963/337428). At 11 PM Thursday through Saturday, there's Andalusian singing. Locals out for a cocktail before hitting the clubs start their evening at **Xuquer Palace** (✉ Pl. Xuquer 8 ☎ 963/615811), with Barcelona-style Moderniste furnishings. **Casablanca** (✉ Eugenia Viñes 152 ☎ 963/713366) has an elegant postwar look; it's open Thursday through Sunday and has everything from waltz to swing music. Valencia has a lively gay nightlife, with a string of bars and clubs on Calle Quart and around the Plaza del Mercado. Follow the trendsters to the hopping **Venial** (✉ Quart 26 ☎ 963/917356), where you can enjoy a tipple or two, groove on the packed dance floor, or just take in the *gran espectaculos* of sequinned and/or muscled performers strutting their stuff on stage.

Shopping

A flea market is held every Sunday morning by the cathedral. Another crafts and flea market takes place on Sunday morning in Plaza Luis Casanova, near the *campo de fútbol* (soccer stadium).

Albufera Nature Park

③④ *11 km (7 mi) south of Valencia.*

This beautiful freshwater lagoon was named by Moorish poets—*albufera* means "the sun's mirror." Dappled with rice paddies, the Parque Natural de la Albufera is a nesting site for more than 250 bird species, including herons, terns, egrets, ducks, and gulls. Admission is free, and there are miles of lovely walking trails. (☎ 961/627345)

From Valencia, buses depart from the corner of Sueca and Gran Vía de Germanías on the hour (every half hour in summer) daily 7 AM to 9 PM.

Where to Eat

★ $$$–$$$$ ✕ **La Matandeta.** With its white garden walls, this engaging restaurant appears from a distance to be a shining island in a sea of rice paddies. Thanks to the local birdlife—snowy egrets, gray herons—a lunchtime drive to La Matandeta can be almost as eye-opening as the culinary creations of its proprietors, Maria Dolores Baixauli and Rafael Galvez. A traditional main dish is the *paella de pato, pollo, y conejo* (paella with duck, chicken, and rabbit). Don't forget to specify which of the 50 types of olive oil you'd like on your whole-wheat bread or salad. (⊠ *Ctra. Alfafar, Km 4* ☎ *962/112184* ⊟ *MC, V* ☉ *Closed Mon.*

S. CATALONIA & THE LEVANTE ESSENTIALS

To research prices, get advice from other travelers, and book travel arrangements, visit www.fodors.com.

Transportation

BY AIR

El Prat de Llobregat in Barcelona, 100 km (62 mi) north of Tarragona, is the international airport closest to the northern end of this terrain. Valencia has an international airport with direct flights to London, Paris, Brussels, Lisbon, Zurich, and Milan.

🛪 Airports **Aeropuerto de Valencia** ☎ 961/598500. **Aeropuerto del Prat** ☎ 93/298-3838. **Iberia** ☎ 902/400500.

🛪 Carriers **Iberia** ☎ 902/400500.

BY BUS

The trip from Barcelona to Tarragona is easy; 8–10 buses leave Barcelona's Estación Vilanova-Norte every day. Connections between Tarragona and Valencia are frequent, and from Valencia buses continue down the coast and on to Madrid. Valencia's bus station is across the river from the old town; take Bus 8 from the Plaza del Ayuntamiento. Transport inland to

Morella and Alcañiz can be arranged from Vinaròs, and Castellón and Sagunto have bus lines west to Teruel. Within Valencia, buses are the main mode of public transport; central lines begin at the Plaza del Ayuntamiento. Buses to the beaches and suburbs leave from the Plaza Puerta del Mar. The tourist office has details.

🚩 Bus Information Bacoma SA bus line ✉ Pl. Imperial Tarraco s/n, Tarragona ☎ 977/222072. **Valencia bus station** ✉ Av. Menendez Pidal 13 ☎ 963/497222.

BY CAR

The A7 autopista leads into this region at both ends. The coastal N340 can get clogged, so you're often better off paying to use the autopista. A car is extremely valuable, even necessary, if you want to explore the inland Maestrazgo mountains, where much of the driving is smooth, uncrowded, and scenic.

In Tarragona, Avis works out of the travel agency Viajes Vibus. In Valencia you have a choice of Avis, Hertz, or Europcar.

🚩 National Agencies Avis ✉ Pin Soler 10, Tarragona ☎ 977/219156 ⊕ www.avis.com ✉ Gran Vía Ramón y Cajal, 2, Valencia ☎ 963/168019. **Europcar** ✉ Antiguo Reino de Valencia 7, Valencia ☎ 963/741512 ⊕ www.europcar.es ✉ Airport, Valencia ☎ 961/521872 ✉ Estación RENFE, Játiva 24, Valencia ☎ 963/3519055. **Hertz** ✉ Segorbe 7, Valencia ☎ 963/415036 ⊕ www.hertz.es ✉ Airport, Valencia ☎ 961/523791.

BY TRAIN

The AVE train travels from Madrid to Lleida (with a stop in Zaragoza). The trip to Zaragoza is just under two hours and starts at €45 each way; to Lleida, the trip is just under three hours and starts at €55 each way. Sometime in 2007 it is expected that the AVE will be expanded to continue to Barcelona. From Lleida, there are numerous train connections to the rest of Catalonia, especially north to the Pyrenees.

Trains bound for Tarragona (via Zaragoza) leave Barcelona's Passeig de Gràcia and Sants stations every half hour or so. Tarragona's RENFE station is downhill from the Mediterranean Balcony, south toward the port. Leaving Valencia, you have a choice of train connections to Madrid (via Cuenca) or Alicante (via Játiva). The main station, Estación del Norte, is on Calle Játiva next to the bullring, a short walk or cab ride from most hotels. Within the region, trains run more or less down the coast: Tarragona to Salou, Cambrils to Tortosa, Vinaròs to Peñíscola, Benicàssim to Castellón, and Sagunto to Valencia. A line also goes from Valencia to Zaragoza by way of Sagunto and Teruel; local lines go around Valencia from the Cronista Rivelles station.

🚩 Train Information RENFE ☎ 902/240202 ⊕ www.renfe.es. **Valencia–Cronista Rivelles** ☎ 902/240202. **Valencia–Estación del Norte** ☎ 902/240202.

Sports & the Outdoors

GOLF

All golf courses are near or on the coast. They are listed from north to south; call in advance to reserve tee times.

🚩 Campo de Golf de Manises 🖉 Apdo. 22029 Valencia ☎ 961/523804, 9 holes. **Campo de Golf El Saler** 🖉 Apdo. 9034 Valencia ☎ 961/611186, 18 holes. **Club de Campo del**

Mediterráneo ✉ Urbanización La Coma, Borriol ☎ 964/321227, 18 holes. **Club de Campo El Bosque** ✉ Chiva, 31 km (19 mi) west of Valencia ☎ 963/263800, 18 holes. **Club de Golf Costa de Azahar** ✉ Ctra. Grao–Benicàssim, Grao de Castellón ☎ 964/280979, 9 holes. **Club de Golf Costa Dorada** ✆ Apdo. 43, Calafells Tarragona ☎ 977/168032, 9 holes. **Club de Golf Escorpión** ✆ Apdo. 1, Betera Valencia ☎ 961/601211, 18 holes.

SAILING

The safe waters off Spain's eastern coast make for good sailing conditions. Ask the local tourist office about procuring a boat, contact one of the clubs below, or just chance upon rental outfits.

🖪 **Club Náutico Castellón** ✉ Escollera de Poniente ☎ 964/280354. **Club Náutico Salou** ✉ Port Salou ☎ 977/382166. **Club Náutico Valencia** ✉ Camino del Canal 91 ☎ 963/679011. **Real Club Náutico Tarragona** ✉ Puerto Deportivo ☎ 977/240360.

Contacts & Resources

BANKS & EXCHANGING SERVICES

All of Spain's major banks and accompanying ATMs can be found in Tarragona and Valencia. In smaller towns and villages it's better to check ahead—most will have one or two branches. Valencia and Tarragona also have their own local banks and building societies, which are just as functional for ATM exchanges. Currency-exchange centers are easily found in Valencia's old town, in hotels, and at the airport. They're more scarce in Tarragona—a good tip is to ask at your hotel (or any hotel, for that matter). Most currency-exchange centers are open daily until 10 PM.

🖪 **La Caixa** ⊕ www.lacaixa.es. Tarragona **American Express (in Worldjet Viatjes)** ✉ Fortuny 10 ☎ 977/250099. Valencia **American Express (in Viajes Duna)** ✉ Cirilo Amoros 88 ☎ 963/741562.

EMERGENCIES

Generally, emergency services in Spain are run by local *Ayuntamientos* (councils). The smaller the town, the less likely you are to receive help in English. The good news is that many hospital-based doctors speak fluent English. The attitude of local police can vary widely in Spain, but in the last 10 years or so there has been a considerable focus on tourists. The Tarragona and Valencia regions are popular tourist destinations, so it is in the interests of both the police and the local government to ensure that the tourist is well attended to by their emergency services. Few operators speak English, so if you need to contact the police or a hospital, if possible, do so with the help of English-speaking staff at a hotel or tourist office.

🖪 **Emergency Services Ambulance** ☎ 964/211253 in Castellón, 977/244728 in Gandesa, 964/160962 in Morella, 977/252525 in Tarragona, 963/677375 in Valen-

---

HELP IN SPANISH

A few universal phrases if you're in trouble:
¡Ayudame!–Help me!
¡Me han robado!–I've been robbed!
¡Me he hecho dano.–I'm hurt.

cia. **Hospital Clínico** ✉ Valencia ☎ 963/862600. **Hospital Joan XXIII** ✉ Tarragona ☎ 977/295800. **Hospital Provincial** ✉ Castellón ☎ 964/210522. **Police** ☎ 091 national toll-free.

INTERNET, MAIL & SHIPPING

Numerous cybercafés can be found in the center of Tarragona and Valencia and in outlying suburbs—Valencia's barrio Carmen has the best. Internet access also is available in most of the three- and higher-star hotels, though, curiously, the vast majority tend to be dial-up, whereas the broadband boom has extended to most homes, offices, and cybercafés. A number of hotels in both Tarragona and Valencia, however, have Wi-Fi zones. Access to them for guests and visitors varies from hotel to hotel. Ask at reception. Another option are the fledgling Starbucks café stores. Access is limited to certain hours, and it isn't cheap.

Most post offices are open Monday to Friday from 8:30 AM to 8:30 PM, and 8:30 AM to 2 PM on Saturday. This may vary in very small towns. The Web site for Spain's *Correos* department lets you search for every outlet in the country.

🔲 Wi-Fi **Hotel Husa Imperial** ✉ Passeig Palmares, Rambla Vella, Tarragona ☎ 977/233040. **Ra Beach Thalasso Hotel** ✉ Av. Santori 1, Tarragona ☎ 977/694200. **Holiday Inn Valencia Bonnaire** ✉ Parque Comercial y de Ocio Aldaia, Valencia ☎ 963/063000. **Hotel Abba Acteon** ✉ Vicente Beltrán Grimal 2, Valencia ☎ 963/310707. **Hotel Astoria Palace** ✉ Pl. Rodrigo Botet 5, Valencia ☎ 963/981000. **Hotel Husa Reina Victoria** ✉ Barcas 4, Valencia ☎ 963/520487.

🔲 Cybercafés **Cantonet** ✉ Av. Vicente Blasco Ibáñez, Valencia. **Netcraft** ✉ Guardia Civil 18, Valencia ⊕ www.netcraftvalencia.net ☎ 963/621503. **Ono** ✉ San Vicente 22, Valencia ☎ 963/281901.

🔲 Correos (Post Offices) **Tarragona** ✉ Pl. Corsini s/n ☎ 977/240149 ✉ Av. San Salavador 48 ☎ 977/522961. **Valencia** ✉ Pl. Ayuntamineto 24 ☎ 963/512370 ✉ Av. Menendez Pidal 15 (El Cote Ingles) ☎ 963/470308 ⊕ www.correos.es.

LODGING

APARTMENT & VILLA RENTALS Throughout Catalonia are farmhouses (called a *casa rural* in Spanish and a *casa de pagès* in Catalan and Valenciano). Accommodations vary widely, from small rustic homes with a few rooms to spacious farmhouses with wood-beam ceilings, fireplaces, and outdoor pools. The high-end farmhouses are called Gîtes. Most tourist offices have a pamphlet, called *Gîtes de Catalunya*, with color photos, and also sell a book on the *Cases de Pagès de Catalunya*. You can also peruse listings of farmhouses on the Catalunya Tourist Office Web site (⊕ www.gencat.es/probert).

🔲 Local Agents **Torrecorinto Apartamentos Turisticos** ✉ Av. de Corinto 1, Playa de Canet, Sagunto ☎ 962/608911. **Federació d'Agroturisme i Turisme Rural Comarques de Tarragona** ✉ Sant Francesc 1, 43360 Cornudella de Montsant ☎ 977/821082 ⊕ www. agroturisme.org.

TOUR OPTIONS

In Tarragona, the city tourist office (just below the cathedral) leads a tour of the cathedral and archaeological sites. The Tarraco Guide Bureau runs guided tours through the Roman sights of Tarragona (€10 per person). They also conduct day tours to the Ebro Delta and Peñíscola. Throughout the year, the double-decker Valencia Bus Turistic (daily 10:30–7:30, until 9 in summer; departing every hour) travels on a circuit throughout the city that passes all the main sights. A 24-hour ticket (€10) allows you to get on and off when you wish at four main boarding points: Plaza de la Reina, Institut Valencià d'Art Modern (IVAM), Museo de Bellas Artes, and Ciutat de les Arts i les Ciències. The Valencia Bus Turistic company also offers a two-hour guided trip (€12) to and around the Albufera Nature Park. The bus departs from the Plaza de la Reina in the center of Valencia. In the summer (and during the rest of the year, depending on demand) Valencia's regional tourist office also organizes tours of the Albufera Nature Park. You tour the port area before continuing south to the lagoon itself, where you can visit a traditional *barraca* (thatch farmhouse). You'll end up in the Devesa Gardens, where you can hire a boat to explore the rice paddies.

🚩 **Tour Operators Tarraco Guide Bureau** ⊠ Rambla Nova 21 ☎ 977/248866. **Valencia Bus Turistic** ⊕ www.valenciabusturistic.com.

VISITOR INFORMATION

Regional tourist offices—in Castellón, Tarragona, and Valencia—have area-wide information. There are local tourist offices in Albarracín, Benicàssim, Morella, Peñíscola, Reus, Sagunto, Tarragona, Teruel, Tortosa, and Valencia. Castellón and Valencia also have information phone lines.

🚩 **Regional Tourist Offices Castellón** ⊠ Pl. María Agustina 5 ☎ 964/358688 ⊕ www.castellon-costaazahar.com. **Tarragona** ⊠ Rambla Nova 118 ☎ 977/238033. **Valencia** ⊠ Paz 48 ☎ 963/986422 ⊕ www.comunidad-valenciana.com.

🚩 **Local Tourist Offices Albarracín** ⊠ Diputación 4 ☎ 978/710251. **Benicàssim** ⊠ Médico Segarra 4 ☎ 964/300962 ⊕ www.benicassim.org. **Morella** ⊠ Pl. San Miguel ☎ 964/173032 ⊕ www.morella.net. **Peñíscola** ⊠ Paseo Marítimo ☎ 964/480208. **Reus** ⊠ San Juan s/n ☎ 977/778149 ⊕ www.reus.net. **Sagunto** ⊠ Pl. Cronista Chabret ☎ 962/662213 ⊕ www.sagunt.com/turismo. **Tarragona** ⊠ Carrer Major 39 ☎ 977/245203. **Teruel** ⊠ Tomás Nogués 1 ☎ 978/602279 ⊕ www.teruel.net. **Tortosa** ⊠ Pl. España ☎ 977/442567. **Valencia** ⊠ Pl. Ayuntamiento 1 ☎ 963/510417 ⊠ Estación RENFE, Játiva 24 ☎ 963/528573.

The Southeast

WORD OF MOUTH

"I really loved Cabo de Gata . . .. My favorite beaches, . . . still unspoiled by tourists, are Monsul beach (smaller and maybe better) and Los Genoveses beach, close to San Jose."
–Pedro

Updated by
Norman
Renouf

SPAIN'S SOUTHEASTERN CORNER is a land of natural contrasts. To the north, the *huerta* (fertile, irrigated coastal plain) generates an orange harvest from late November through April; in spring, fragrant flowers adorn the same trees. The rice paddies stretching south from the Albufera lagoon to Gandía give rise to Valencia's culinary specialty, paella. The farther south you go, the drier and more mountainous the land, until you reach the desert-lunar landscape of Almería—backdrop for spaghetti-western films in the 1960s. The inland province of Albacete, historically part of Murcia, was the scene of Don Quijote's exploits in the Castilian expanse of La Mancha. The striking architecture in most southeastern towns attests to the area's long Moorish occupation. Alicante was in Moorish hands from 718 to 1249; Murcia, from 825 to 1243; and Almería, from 712 to 1489, when it was finally reconquered by Ferdinand and Isabella.

During the civil war, many towns were bombarded and churches looted throughout these provinces. The ensuing reconstruction was painfully slow—a situation that continued until the 1960s, when tourism on the Spanish coasts was boosted by the first package-tour vacationers. Agriculture and industry have also continued to grow, and Alicante is now the fourth-wealthiest province in Spain.

Despite the large number of foreign residents and the annual swell of summer visitors, locals have remained fiercely protective of their regional culture. The traditional fiestas here are wonderfully colorful and exuberant, as are the distinctive local cuisine and craftsmanship.

Exploring the Southeast

From Valencia's Albufera to the beginning of the Costa Blanca and down the coast through Alicante then on through the Murcia coastline, this part of Spain is rich in beaches, salt lagoons, steppes, mountain villages, and Mediterranean port cities. The Costa Blanca coastline of coves and white-sand beaches stretches from just north of Denia all the way south to the border with the Murcia coastline. It's peppered with resorts— Benidorm being far and away the splashiest and most crowded—and the resulting onslaught of summer tourists. Just tucked inland from the coast is a splattering of interesting villages, attractions, and larger towns, including Elche, Murcia, and Lorca.

About the Restaurants

Rice grows better in the Valencian provinces than anywhere else in Spain, which explains why paella was born here. Remember that paella should be eaten immediately after it's cooked—don't order it from a *menú del día* (menu of the day) unless you can be sure it's fresh. Another rice dish to try is *arroz a la banda* (rice and vegetables with meat or fish, cooked over a wood fire). Alicante and Jijona are known for their *turrón*, nougat made with almonds and flavored with honey. In Elche you can savor fresh dates. Murcian cooking uses products of the huerta and the sea, with a marked Arab influence in preparation. *Caldero de Mar Menor,* a traditional fisherman's rice dish, is cooked in huge iron pots, has a distinctly oily consistency, and is flavored by fish cooked in its own

GREAT ITINERARIES

Wanderers can choose from three different coastal experiences (the lagoon, the populous beaches of the Costa Blanca, and the deserted strands south of Mojácar), two distinct inland programs (the steppe around Albacete and the mountains near Murcia), and four major cities (Alicante, Albacete, Murcia, and Almería).

IF YOU HAVE 3 DAYS
Start with the lakeside village of **El Palmar** and **La Albufera** ❶, and continue south through **Cullera** ❷ and the elegant coastal town of **Denia** ❹ to the beautiful curved bay at **Cabo de la Nao** ❻. Treat yourself to an overnight stay at the El Rodat in 🖼 **Jávea** ❺. Begin the next day in the stylish small village of **Altea** ❾, then head to **Alicante** ⓫ for a leisurely lunch before moving inland through **Elche** ⓱ and stay at the Huerto del Cura hotel. Next morning, on the third day, head to 🖼 **Murcia** ㉓, with its superb cathedral, and then continue on to **Cartagena** ⓳ to explore that fascinating city and stop there for the night.

IF YOU HAVE 5 DAYS
Explore **El Palmar** and the watery patchwork of **La Albufera** ❶ before moving through **Cullera** ❷ and the pretty coastal town of **Denia** ❹ to the dramatic **Cabo de la Nao** ❻. Stay at the El Rodat, in **Jávea** ❺, for a treat. The next day visit the stylish small village of **Altea** ❾; then hook inland and enjoy a wander around the unspoiled villages of **Polop** ⓯ and **Guadalest** ⓮ before swinging back to the coast and taking a quick look at **Benidorm** ❿. Stay overnight in 🖼 **Alicante** ⓫. On Day 3, make the first stop **Santa Pola** ⓬. In summer take the boat trip to **Tabarca Island** ⓭ and stay there for the night; if it's not summer, head east to the lush palm groves of 🖼 **Elche** ⓱ and stay overnight there. On Day 4 head south to check out the cathedral in **Murcia** ㉓, then explore the ancient town of **Cartagena** ⓳. Continue on to the playground of **La Manga del Mar Menor** ⓲. On your last day, explore the coast from **Cartagena** ⓳ to **Águilas** ⓴, a very pleasant town surrounded by beautiful beaches.

8

juices. Delicious as tapas or a first course are *muchirones* (broad beans in a spicy sauce, similar to the Catalan *habas a la catalana*) and *cocas* (meat pies akin to empanadas).

	WHAT IT COSTS In Euros				
	$$$$	**$$$**	**$$**	**$**	**¢**
AT DINNER	over €20	€15–€20	€10–€15	€6–€10	under €6

Prices are per person for a main course at dinner.

About the Hotels
Many hotels on this coast are modern high-rises. There are also some very tasteful independent hotels. Some coastal hotels close for the winter.

WHAT IT COSTS In Euros				
	$$$$	$$$	$$	$	¢
FOR 2 PEOPLE	over €180	€100–€180	€60–€100	€40–€60	under €40

Prices are for two people in a standard double room in high season, excluding tax.

Timing

Try to visit this region between mid-October and April; summer gets oppressively hot. Mild temperatures in spring and fall allow you to vacation before and after the thickest crowds. Easter is interesting for its often-bizarre pageants and processions, especially in remote towns.

Numbers in the text correspond to numbers in the margin and on the Southeast map.

VALENCIA TO THE COSTA BLANCA

This short drive takes you through the Albufera wetlands and into the northern end of the Costa Blanca, known as La Marina Alta (the High Shore). Compared with the sunbathers' strip south of Denia, these lonely marshlands and deserted beaches are wonderfully undiscovered.

La Albufera

❶ *16 km (10 mi) south of Valencia.*

One of the largest bodies of freshwater in Spain, the **Parque Natural L'Albufera de Valencia** supports four main environments: a sandbar, a marsh, the Albufera lagoon, and (to a lesser extent) hills and woodlands. More than 250 species of birds have been identified here—90 species breed here regularly. ✉ *Centre d'Informació Raco del'Olla, El Palmar* ☎ *96/162–7345* ⊙ *Mon., Wed., and Fri. 9–2, Tues., Thurs., and weekends 9–2 and 3:30–5:30.*

El Palmar, the major village in the area, is home to numerous restaurants specializing in paella Valenciana, made with game birds and seafood. Throughout the area there are numerous outlooks to stop and observe the birds—in some places local fishermen offer boat rides to get an even closer look.

Where to Stay

$$$$ ⌂ **Hotel Sidi Saler.** On the edge of La Albufera, and just south of the city of Valencia, this modern hotel is next to miles of unspoiled beaches. With a free shuttle bus to and from Valencia, it makes a good base from which to explore the city as well as the natural park and El Palmar. ✉ *Playa el Saler, Valencia, 46012* ☎ *96/161–0411* 🖷 *96/161–0838* ⊕ *www.sidi-saler.com* ⇖ *256*

> **NORMAN'S TOP 5**
>
> ■ Castillo de Santa Barbara, Alicante
>
> ■ Cartagena, Murcia
>
> ■ Guadalest, Alicante
>
> ■ Cabo de Gato Nature Reserve, Almería
>
> ■ La Manga, Murcia

IF YOU LIKE

BEACHES

The southeastern coastline varies from the long stretches of sand dunes north of Denia and south of Alicante to the coves and crescents of the Costa Blanca. The benign climate permits lounging on the beach almost year-round. Major beaches have Cruz Roja (Red Cross) stations with helicopters and flags to warn swimmers of conditions: green for safety, red for danger.

Altea, popular with families, is busy and pebbly, but the old town is pretty. Benidorm's two white, crescent-shape beaches, packed in summer, extend for more than 5 km (3 mi) and are widely considered the best in Spain. Benidorm takes all prizes for après-beach entertainment. Calblanque is on the road between Los Belones and Cabo de Palos, which takes you down a longish, rough track to a succession of nearly deserted sands frequented mainly by young Murcians. Calpe's beaches have the scenic advantage of the sheer outcrop Peñón de Ifach (Cliff of Ifach), which stands guard over stretches of sand to either side. Denia and Jávea both have family beaches where children paddle in relatively safe waters. Gandía's sandy beach is well kept, its promenade lined with bars and restaurants.

If you have a car, try some of the deserted beaches to the south. There are no facilities except for the odd water tap for campers; nudity, though illegal, seems generally accepted here, at Calblanque, and just north of Cullera. In Moraira, the best beach is Playa Castillo, just outside the center. Santa Pola and Guardamar del Segura are other good options, with fine, clean sand and pine trees behind the dunes.

FIESTAS

Almería's lively **Festival Internacional de Títeres** (Puppet Theater Festival) is held in January. Denia throws a **mini Fallas** March 16 to 19. Alcoy's spectacular **Moros y Cristianos** (Moors and Christians) festival, held April 21 to 24, includes a reenactment of clashes from the Christian Reconquest, the battle to dislodge the Moors at the end of the 15th century. Murcia's **Semana Santa** (Holy Week) processions are among the most illustrious in Spain; those in Lorca are known for the opulent costumes of both Christian and Roman participants and for the penitents' solemn robes. Altea's **Moros y Cristianos** spectacle, staged the third Sunday in May, is a combination of battle reenactment and pageantry, complete with elaborate costumes and local kids dressed up as knights in shining armor. Alicante's main festival is **Hogueras de San Juan** (St. John's Day Bonfires), June 21 to 24. **El Misteri** (the Mystery Play) is performed in Elche in two parts, August 14 to 15, preceded by a public dress rehearsal.

8

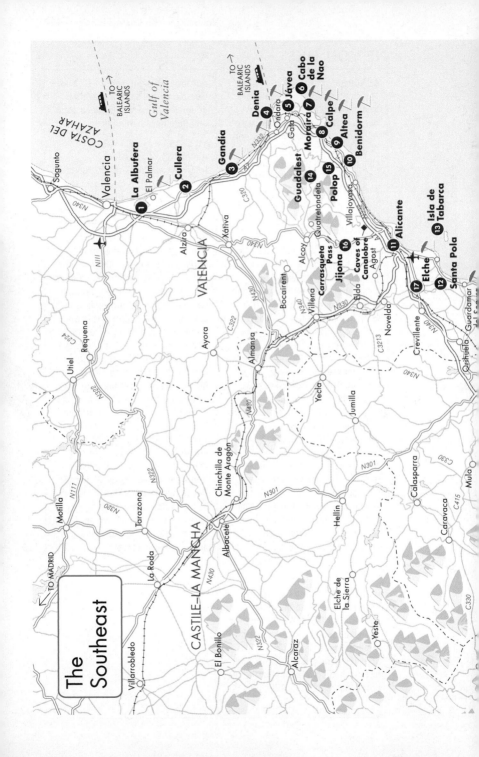

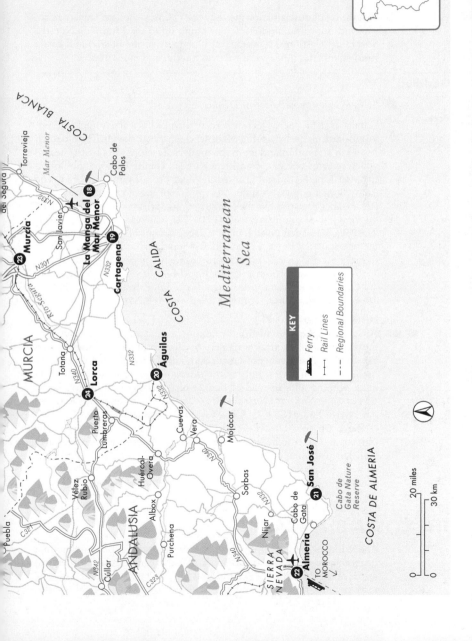

rooms, 16 suites ᐩ 2 restaurants, putting green, 2 tennis courts, 2 pools (1 indoor), health club, hair salon, beach, piano bar, shop, business services, free parking ▤ AE, DC, MC, V.

Cullera

❷ *39 km (24 mi) south of Valencia, 27 km (17 mi) north of Gandía.*

Past the lighthouse and around the rocky point is modern Cullera, a resort with futuristic high-rises. The climb up to the **Ermita de Nuestra Señora del Castillo** (Hermitage of Our Lady of the Castle) and **castle ruins** culminates in views of the sea, huerta, and mountains.

Gandía

❸ *30 km (19 mi) northwest of Denia.*

Fodor'sChoice
★

Gandía is a prosperous commercial town with a lively nightlife enjoyed, particularly, by visiting Madrileños on the weekends. The old town lies 4 km (2½ mi) inland from the modern developments by the beach, which remains one of Costa Blanca's best. Gandía became the Borgia fief after King Ferdinand granted the duchy to the family in 1485. The canny Borgia pope Alexander VI was one of the most notorious of all Renaissance prelates, but the family's reputation was later redeemed by the local Jesuit St. Francis Borgia (1510–72), who was canonized in 1671. The **Palau Ducal dels Borja** (Ducal Palace), signposted from the city center, was founded by St. Francis in 1546 and serves as a Jesuit college. Elaborate ceilings and bright-color *azulejos* (glazed tiles) adorn the 17th-century state rooms. ☎ 96/287–1465 ⊕ *www.palauducal.com* ▨ €3 ⊗ *Guided tours June–Aug., Tues.–Sat. hrly 10–2 and 5–9, Sun. 10–2; Sept.–May, Tues.–Sat. hrly 10–2 and 4–8, Sun. 10–2.*

Where to Eat

$$–$$$ ✕ **Gamba Marisqueria.** Justifiably famous around these parts, this restaurant is a family-run affair—namely by three brothers and their wives. The food is attractively presented, and only the freshest ingredients are used. The menu varies, but try the *fideua de mariscos* (seafood paella made with noodles instead of rice), which feeds two, if it's available. ⊠ *Carretera Nazaret-Oliva s/n* ☎ *96/284–1310* ⚫ *Reservations essential* ▤ *AE, DC, MC, V* ⊗ *Closed Mon. No dinner.*

$–$$ ✕ **Mesón Gallego.** This Galician restaurant is a lucky discovery in the port area. The rough, simple surroundings complement such hearty Galician dishes as *pulpo* (octopus) or the fish and meat specialties cooked over coals. Ask for Galician *culcas,* shallow ceramic bowls for drinking the young Ribeiro wines. ⊠ *Levante 37, Grao de Gandía* ☎ *96/284–1892* ▤ *AE, MC, V* ⊗ *Closed Wed. No dinner Tues.*

THE COSTA BLANCA

The White Coast is the popular name for the stretch of coastline that begins between Gandía and Denia and ends near Murcia's border, just north of the Mar Menor. The largest city, by far, is Alicante, and the most popular resort is Benidorm. A drive down this shore allows for some quiet and picturesque stops, especially off-season. One especially scenic segment is the coastal road that branches off N332 at Els Poblets, heading to the towns of Denia and Jávea.

Denia

④ *100 km (62 mi) south of Valencia, 8 km (5 mi) north of Jávea and east of Ondara.*

The northernmost beach resort on the Costa Blanca, Denia is a busy tourist town known for its fishing boats and fiestas, which culminate in the midsummer St. John's Day bonfires (June 23). Backed by the Montgó massif, rising to more than 2,100 feet to the west, Denia's beaches to the north—Les Marines, Les Bovetes, and Les Deveses—are smooth and sandy, whereas the coast to the south is rocky, forming *calas* (tiny secluded inlets that recall the Costa Brava, north of Barcelona).

Known as the gastronomic capital of the Costa Blanca, Denia is a good place to sample fresh Mediterranean seafood—try *picaetes de sepia y calamar* (squid and cuttlefish) or *suquet de rape* (stewed monkfish).

Denia's most interesting architectural attraction is the **Palau del Governador,** the Governor's Palace, within a Moorish-era castle. Overlooking the town, the castle has an interesting archaeological museum as well as a Renaissance bastion and a Moorish portal with a lovely horseshoe arch. One notable church is **Iglesia de la Asunción** (Church of the Assumption).

Denia has the closest ferry connections to the Balearic Islands. **Balearia** (☎ 902/160180 ⊕ www.balearia.com) and **Iscomar** (☎ 902/119128 ⊕ www.iscomar.com) make sailings to Ibiza, and then onward to Palma de Mallorca.

★ Inland from Denia, the **Cueva de las Calaveras** (Caves of Canalobre) (☎ 96/640–4235 🎫 €3 ☉ Daily 9–8), near Benidoleig, was inhabited by prehistoric humans some 50,000 years ago. The Cave of Skulls has numerous bones from that period. The cave of stalactites and stalagmites is more than 300 yards long, with domes rising to more than 60 feet. **Safari Park Vergel** (✉ Carretera CV-700, Vergel-Pego, El Verger ☎ 96/643–9808 🎫 €13.50 ☉ Spring, daily 10–6; summer, daily 10–7; fall and winter, daily 10–5) has 145 species of animals, including lions, Bengal tigers, yaks, elephants, and exotic birds.

Where to Eat

$ ✕ **Drassanes.** Built into Denia's original medieval shipyards (for which **Fodor'sChoice** it's named), Drassanes is a well-known place for fresh local seafood. The ★ food is authentic and good. *Arroz a la banda* (rice with seafood) is the house specialty. ✉ *C. Puerto 15* ☎ *96/578–1118* 🖃 *AE, MC, V* ☉ *Closed Mon. and Nov.*

$ ✕ **El Port.** Found in the old seamen's quarter, just across from the port, **Fodor'sChoice** this is one of those very popular restaurants that features all kinds of ★ fish and shellfish dishes, as well as rice specialties, tapas, and mouthwatering desserts. ✉ *Esplanada Bellavista 12* ☎ *96/578–4973* 🖃 *AE, MC, V* ☉ *Closed Mon.*

Where to Stay

♨ **$$$** ⊞ **Denia Marriott La Sella Golf Resort & Spa.** This large hotel, about 15 minutes west of Denia and 1½ km (1 mi) past the small town of La Xara, is ideal if you want to combine sporting facilities and a fine spa with sightseeing and the beaches of the coast. The rooms are larger than in most other places, and it's a child-friendly hotel, with on-site babysitting and a seasonal Kids Club. ⊠ *Alqueria Ferrando, Jesus Pobre, 03749* ☎ *96/645–4054* 🖷 *96/575–7880* ⊕ *www.marriott.com* ⟿ *178 rooms, 8 suites ♨ 2 restaurants, minibars, cable TV, 18-hole golf course, tennis court, pool, health club, bar, shops, babysitting, dry cleaning, laundry facilities, business services, free parking, some pets allowed, no-smoking rooms* ⊟ *AE, DC, MC, V.*

$$$ ⊞ **La Posada del Mar.** Directly under Denia castle, and a few steps across from the harbor, this hotel has a light, modern decor. Many of the rooms have balconies and views over the harbor and sea. The rooftop terrace is particularly inviting. ⊠ *Plaça de les Drassanes s/n, 03700* ☎ *96/643–2966* 🖷 *96/642–0155* ⊕ *www.laposadadelmar.com* ⟿ *20 rooms, 5 suites ♨ In-room safes, in-room broadband, wine bar, laundry facilities, free parking* ⊟ *AE, DC, MC, V.*

$$ ⊞ **Hotel Chamarel.** Inside a 19th-century mansion in the town center, this eclectic hotel is also charming. Expect art deco–style furniture, bright pastel colors, modern art, high-tech facilities, the soothing sound of water, and four-poster beds. ⊠ *Calle Cavallers 13, 03700* ☎ *96/643–5007* 🖷 *96/643–5600* ⊕ *www.hotelchamarel.com* ⟿ *10 rooms, 3 suites ♨ Cafeteria, massage, parking (fee)* ⊟ *AE, DC, MC, V.*

Jávea

❺ *108 km (67 mi) southeast of Valencia, 92 km (57 mi) northeast of Alicante, 8 km (5 mi) south of Denia.*

A labyrinth of tiny streets and houses with arched portals and Gothic windows, Jávea has an antique aspect contrasted only (ironically) by its modern church, **Santa María de Loreto.** The church-fortress of **San Bartolomé** is the town's architectural gem. Restaurants around the port's **Aduanas del Mar** area serve *arroz a la marinera* (seafood paella).

The **Soler Blasco,** an ethnological and archaeological museum, has a superb set of Iberian gold jewelry discovered in 1904 during building excavation works. ⊠ *Calle Primicies s/n* ☎ *96/579–1098* 🎟 *Free* ⊙ *Mar.–Oct., Tues.–Fri. 10–1 and 6–8, weekends 10–1; Nov.–Feb., Tues.–Sun. 10–1.*

Where to Stay & Eat

$$$–$$$$ ✕ **Restaurante Puerto.** On the first floor of a delightful building and with a nifty terrace, right between the beach and the harbor, this has the best location in Jvea. The cuisine is Valenciana, and the specialties here are paellas, *zarzuela con mariscos,* (shellfish) and rice dishes. There are special lunchtime menú del días for €10 and €16. ⊠ *Aduanas del Mar* ☎ *96/579–1064* ⊟ *AE, DC, MC, V* ⊙ *No lunch Mon.*

$$$ ⊞ **El Rodat.** This distinguished hotel has an inviting location off the bay. The rooms are spacious, and have character. ⊠ *Ctra. al Cabo de la Nao s/n, 03730* ☎ *96/647–0710* 🖷 *96/647–1550* ⊕ *www.elrodat.com* ⟿ *34* *suites, 8 villas* ⚐ *Restaurant, pool, spa, bar, free parking, Internet room* 🖃 *AE, DC, MC, V.*

$$$ 🏨 **Parador de Jávea.** Ensconced in a lush palm grove, with terrific views of the bay and white-sand beach below, this modern parador is four stories tall and far more tasteful than the high-rise hotels elsewhere on the Costa Blanca. The oak-trim, ceramic-tile guest rooms are airy and pleasant. ⊠ *Av. del Mediterráneo 7, 03730* ☎ *96/579–0200* 🖷 *96/579–0308* ⊕ *www.parador.es* ⚐ *70 rooms* ⚐ *Restaurant, cable TV, in-room data ports, pool, gym, sauna, bar* 🖃 *AE, DC, MC, V.*

$$ 🏨 **Hotel Miramar.** This small, unpretentious hotel is a little basic when it comes to facilities but makes up for that with its location right on the promenade by the bay. ⊠ *Plaza Almirante Bastarreche 12, 03730* ☎ *96/ 579–0100* 🖷 *96/579–0102* ⚐ *26 rooms* ⚐ *Restaurant* 🖃 *MC, V.*

Cabo de la Nao

❻ *10 km (6 mi) southeast of Jávea.*

Cabo de la Nao (Cape Nao) is a great spur of land jutting into the Mediterranean toward Ibiza, barely 100 km (62 mi) away. As you round the point, you turn from a coast that looks toward Italy to one that faces Africa. In the same few miles, you pass from an agriculture of oranges and rice to one of olives and palms, and from a benign (if variable) climate to one of tawny aridity.

Moraira

❼ *12 km (7 mi) northeast of Calpe, 20 km (12 mi) southeast of Jávea.*

The narrow streets leading down to Moraira's harbor preserve an air of seclusion. The *casco viejo* (old town) has a good selection of bars and restaurants, and the outskirts give way to chalets and private homes. The **castle** and watchtower overlooking the port were built in the Middle Ages to ward off Mediterranean pirates.

Where to Stay

$$$ 🏨 **Swiss Moraira.** Reopened in April 2006 and secluded in a pine forest above Moraira (off the road to Calpe), this low-rise luxury hotel is ideal if you're looking for peace and comfort. Smart, modern rooms—three of the superior ones have hot tubs—are arranged around a creatively shaped swimming pool. The beach and marina are 3 km (2 mi) away. ⊠ *C. Haya 175, Urb. Club Moraira, 03724* ☎ *965/747104* 🖷 *965/ 747074* ⚐ *33 rooms* ⚐ *Restaurant, tennis court, pool, bar, free parking, some in-room hot tubs* 🖃 *AE, DC, MC, V.*

EN ROUTE The **Cabo de Sant Antoni** promontory, just north of Jávea, rises to 525 feet and is much steeper on its northern side than the southern. After the reconquest in the early 13th century, religious hermits lived at the very end. Later fortifications were built there to protect against the Barbary Pirates. The fortifications were replaced by the lighthouse that now stands there near the end of the 19th century. The views to the south are best, encompassing the bay all across to the Cap de Sant Marti.

Calpe

★ ⑧ *15 km (9 mi) southwest of Jávea, 8 km (5 mi) north of Altea.*

The road from Moraira to Calpe is very scenic, winding through the cliffs and hills covered in villas and passing small, rocky, and pebbly bays. Calpe has an ancient history, and its strategic location has attracted Phoenicians, Greeks, Romans, and Moors, with the latter dedicated to agriculture and fishing. After the reconquest by Jaume I, the Christians and Moors lived together peacefully, but between the 14th and 17th century they were under almost constant threat from the Barbary Pirates. This led to the construction of numerous fortifications such as the Torreó de la Peça, a defense tower named after an artillery piece used to defend the city. (Two of these cannons can be seen next to the Torreó.) Today the Old Town, full of striking small streets and squares, is a charming place to wander.

Calpe has always been dominated by the **Peñón d'Ifach,** a huge calcareous rock more than 1,100 yards long, 1,090 feet high, and joined to the mainland by a narrow isthmus. The area is rich in flora and fauna, with more than 300 species of plantlife and 80 species of land and marine birds identified here. Marine plant and wildlife also thrive on its shelves, with Mediterranean coral in the submerged walls and seaweed spreading across the sandy bottom. A visit to the top is not for the fainthearted; wear shoes with traction for the hike, which includes a trip through a tunnel to the summit. The views are spectacular, reaching to the island of Ibiza on a clear day.

The fishing industry is still very important in Calpe, and every evening the fishing boats return to port with their catch. The subsequent auction at the **Fish Market** can be watched from the walkway of La Lonja de Calpe. Many fish restaurants are near the port, and those displaying the round *Peix de Calp* symbol are using fish unloaded and sold in the harbor and fish market here. ⊠ *Port* ⊙ *Weekdays 5–7.*

Close to the port is another connection to the fish industry in Calpe. The **Baños de la Reina,** a group of six rooms, was built into the sea in the late-Roman period, around the 5th century. Legend says that it was reminiscent of a spa of a Moorish queen; in fact, though, the rooms were hatcheries, used by the Romans to dry and salt fish. ⊠ *South of port.*

The **Mundo Marino** company offers a complete range of sailing trips, including cruises between the towns up and down the coast. Some of the vessels have glass bottoms, so you can keep an eye on the abundant marine life here. ⊠ *Port* ⊕ *www.mundomarino.es.*

Where to Stay & Eat

$$–$$$$ ✕**Playa.** Quite simply, this and its sister restaurant La Lonja, is a seafood and shellfish lovers' paradise. Just opposite the fishing port, it has an array of sample dishes that is staggering, from a few oysters for a handful of euros up to family-style combination plates at €100. You may even get treated to a free sample and glass of sangria just for looking. ⊠ *Explanada del Puerto* ☏ *96/583–0032* ⊙ *MC, V.*

$$$ 🏨 **Roca Esmeralda & Spa.** This neat hotel on the Levante beach is 2½ km (1½ mi) north of the town center and is linked to it by a half-hourly shuttle bus. More than half of the rooms include a lounge. ✉ *Ponent 1, Playa de Levante, 03710* ☎ *96/583–6101* 🖷 *96/583–6004* ⊕ *www. rocaesmeralda.com* ⚲ *212 rooms* ☼ *2 restaurants, snack bar, 4 pools (1 indoor), gym, massage, sauna, spa, dance club, shop, free parking* ⊟ *AE, DC, MC, V.*

$$ 🏨 **SH Ifach.** Architecturally unusual, this 15-story hotel that's 150 yards from the beach is impossible to miss in Calpe. Most rooms offer spectacular views from their terraces. ✉ *Calle Juan Carlos I s/n, 03710* ☎ *96/ 587–4500* 🖷 *96/587–4530* ⊕ *www.sh-hoteles.com* ⚲ *192 rooms, 1 suite* ☼ *Restaurant, cafeteria, minibars, 2 pools (1 indoor), gym, sauna, 2 bars, free parking* ⊟ *AE, DC, MC, V.*

$ 🏨 **Venta la Chata.** This pretty hotel was an 18th-century horse-changing post on the Valencia–Alicante road. The lower floor is rustic, as are the wood furnishings and *azulejo* (tiled) floors in the rooms. Ask for a room with a balcony or terrace. The terrace gardens have sea views. ✉ *Ctra. de Valencia, N332, Km 172, 03710* ☎🖷 *96/583–0308* ⚲ *17 rooms* ☼ *Tennis court, Ping-Pong, bar* ⊟ *AE, DC, MC, V.*

Altea

❾ *10 km (6 mi) south of Calpe, 11 km (7 mi) north of Benidorm.*

Altea is an old fishing village with white houses and a striking church with a blue ceramic-tile dome. One of the best-conserved towns on the Costa Blanca, it serves as a foil to the skyscraping tourist towers of Benidorm. The beach here is pebbly. North of town, the Altea Hills area is more built up, with pretty villas lining the hills and cliffs.

Where to Eat

$$$–$$$$ ✕ **La Costera.** This extremely popular restaurant mixes excellent Swiss cooking with bizarre furnishings and a nightly show. Specialties include the delicious, typically Swiss dish *rostit con carne troceada y champiñon* (chopped meat with mushrooms and potatoes). ✉ *Costera del Mestre la Música 8* ☎ *96/584–0230* ⚱ *Reservations essential* ⊟ *MC, V* ☾ *Closed Nov.–Feb. No lunch.*

Benidorm

❿ *11 km (7 mi) south of Altea, 42 km (26 mi) northeast of Alicante.*

Benidorm is an overdeveloped resort with tens of thousands of hotel beds and a seemingly bottomless capacity for tourists. Its twin, white crescent-shape beaches were its claim to fame when Benidorm first became popular with mass tourism from northern Europe in the 1960s, and they're still a great attraction today. The city hasn't looked back since those early tourism days, and hundreds of thousands still flock here annually. As a consequence, the numerous karaoke clubs and British-run pubs offering all-day breakfasts and satellite soccer games give it a decidedly un-Spanish feel—and it's certainly not the place for those seeking a quiet vacation by the Mediterranean. Those with children, though, may appreciate the nearby famous Terra Mítica theme park and animal and

8

water parks as well as the available boat trips. For a fantastic view, follow signs to Club Sierra Dorada at the eastern edge of town and climb up to the **Rincón de Loix** (Loix Corner).

ⓒ **Mundomar.** This park's variety of marine and exotic animals includes colorful parrots. In addition to a children's playground there are dolphin, sea lion, and parrot shows. ⊠ *Sierra Helada s/n, Rincón de Loix* ☎ *96/586–9101* ⊕ *www.mundomar.es* ⊠ *€18.*

ⓒ **Excursiones Marítimas Benidorm.** Of the many boat trips offered by this company, the excursion to the Isla de Benidorm is one of the best. Here you can swim and look at the local birdlife. Boats depart every hour 10–5. The fare is €10 for adults. If you want to see more of the beautiful coastline here, opt for the one-hour cruise up to Calpe; this allows a little time for sightseeing there. These trips depart every day but Sunday at 11, with a return sail to Calpe at 3:30. ☎ *96/585–0052* ⊕ *www. excursionesmaritimasbenidorm.com.*

ⓒ **Terra Mítica.** Owned by Paramount, this is one of Europe's largest theme parks. The theme is the cultural development of the Mediterranean, with nods to the ancient civilizations of the Iberians, Romans, Greeks, and Egyptians. In addition to many rides, there are shows that include pirate battles, chariot races, and fighting gladiators. ⊠ *Just outside Benidorm* ☎ *902/020220* ⊕ *www.terramiticapark.com* ⊠ *1-day ticket €32* ⊙ *Apr., May, and Sept., daily 10–8; June–Aug., daily 10–midnight; Oct.–Dec. and mid- to late Mar., weekends 10–8.*

ⓒ **Limon Expres.** Starting at Benidorm train station, this train from the 1920s makes an 80-minute trip north past Altea, Calpe, Benissa, and Teulada to the Gata de Gorgo, where you have time to shop at the area's wicker shops and visit a guitar factory. On the outbound journey there's a guided commentary and the train stops for photo opportunities. The return trip is far more lighthearted, with a party atmosphere helped along by Limon Expres champagne and music. ⊠ *Benidorm* ☎ *902/020220* ⊠ *€22* ⊙ *Tues.–Fri., departure at 9:40, return at 1:40.*

Where to Stay & Eat

$$–$$$ ✕ **Tiffany's.** At this relaxed restaurant, you can eat such dishes as *salmón con langostinos* (salmon with shrimp), *entrecôte al roquefort* (steak with Roquefort cheese), and *lubina a la sal* (sea bass cooked in its own juices), accompanied by piano music. ⊠ *Av. Mediterráneo, Edifício Coblanca 3* ☎ *96/585–1680* ⊟ *AE, DC, MC, V* ⊙ *Closed Jan. No lunch.*

$ ✕ **I Fratelli.** The cooking here is Italian, with contemporary French and international accents. Neapolitan music complements the stylish Moderniste touches: sleek black chairs, white tablecloths, and exotic potted plants. Best bets are pasta and *pescados a la sal* (fish baked in salt). ⊠ *Dr. Orts Llorca* ☎ *96/585–3979* ⊟ *AE, DC, MC, V* ⊙ *Closed Nov.*

$$$$ ⊞ **Montiboli.** A few miles south of Benidorm, this hotel on various levels and in an Arabic–eastern coast style sits on a cliff, overlooking a beautiful bay. Surrounded by luxuriant vegetation and the blue Mediterranean waters, it is, undoubtedly, the hotel of choice for many miles around. The rooms are totally luxurious and peaceful—as are the public rooms and the gourmet restaurant. ⊠ *Partida Montiboli s/n, Villajoysa, 03570*

☎ 96/589–0250 🖷 96/589–3857 ⊕ *www.servigroup.es* ⇘ *89 rooms* ⚶ *Restaurant, pool, bar, free parking* ⊟ *MC, V.*

$$$ ⊡ **Gran Hotel Delfín.** This hotel's quiet, calm location isan impressive feat, especially in summer. The salon downstairs has '70s-style furniture. The bedrooms are Castilian-style, with bric-a-brac on the walls. Ask for a room at the front, overlooking the beach. ⊠ *Av. Mont Benidorm 13, 03500* ☎ *96/585–3400* 🖷 *96/585–7154* ⊕ *www.granhoteldelfin.com* ⇘ *92 rooms, 1 suite* ⚶ *Restaurant, cable TV, tennis court, pool, bar* ⊟ *AE, DC, MC, V* ⊙ *Closed early Jan.–early Apr.*

$$ ⊡ **Gran Hotel Bali.** Housed in two futuristic buildings, one with 19 floors and the other with 43, this hotel would not look out of place in Manhattan; it says much about Benidorm that it does not look out of place here either. There are marvelous views from the upper floors and the terrace. The hotel is 400 yards from the beach and a little more than a mile from both the center of town and the Terra Mítica theme park. ⊠ *Calle Luis Prendes s/n, 03502* ☎ *96/681–5200* 🖷 *96/681–5208* ⊕ *www.granhotelbali.com* ⇘ *688 rooms, 84 suites* ⚶ *2 restaurants, cafeteria, 3 pools, health club, hair salon, 4 bars, cabaret, laundry facilities, Internet room* ⊟ *AE, DC, MC, V.*

$$ ⊡ **Poseidon Playa.** This hotel, 17 stories high, has a privileged position across from Poniente beach and a short walk from old-town Benidorm. Expect modern rooms with terraces that have sea views. The hotel has a full program of entertainment in the summer. ⊠ *Av. Armada Española s/n, 03502* ☎ *96/585–4850* 🖷 *96/680–4247* ⊕ *www. hotelesposeidon.com* ⇘ *306 rooms* ⚶ *Restaurant, pool, billiards, Ping-Pong, bar, cabaret, Internet room, free parking* ⊟ *AE, DC, MC, V.*

Nightlife

Countless bars and discos with names such as Jockey's and Harrods (reflecting Benidorm's popularity with Brits and Germans) line Avenida de Europa and the Ensanche de la Playa de Levante. The **Benidorm Palace** (⊠ Av. Severo Ochoa ☎ 96/585–1661 ⊕ www.benidorm-palace.com) offers a cabaret Tuesday through Saturday, with Spanish dance and an international musical show. Dinner starts at 8:30; the show at 10. Since its opening in 1977 this has been one of the major tourist attractions for the region, with capacity for 1,500. Admission for dinner and show is €39; for the show only, €24. Don a crown at the **Nuevo Gran Castillo Conde de Alfaz** (⊠ Camino Viejo del Albir ☎ 96/686–5265) and dine in front of jousting medieval knights. Dinner, drinks, and the show (Friday and Saturday only) cost €37 per person.

Alicante

⓫ *82 km (51 mi) northeast of Murcia, 183 km (113 mi) south of Valencia by coast road, 42 km (26 mi) south of Benidorm.*

A crossroads for inland and coastal routes, Alicante has always been known for its luminous skies. The Greeks called it Akra Leuka (White Summit)and the Romans named it Lucentum (City of Light). The city is dominated by the Castillo de Santa Bárbara, but also memorable is its grand **Explanada,** lined with date palms. Directly under the castle is

8

the city beach, the Playa del Postiguet. The city's pride is the long, curved Playa de San Juan, which runs north from the Cap de l'Horta to El Campello. The small TRAM train (⊕ www.tram-alicante.com) runs from the city center on the beach to El Campello. From the same open-air station in Alicante the FGV train departs to Denia, with stops in El Campello, Benidorm, Altea, Calpe, and elsewhere.

Old Town

Concatedral of San Nicolás de Bari. Built between 1616 and 1662 on the site of a former mosque, this church has an austere facade that was designed by Agustín Bernardino, an admirer of Herrera (of Escorial fame). Inside, it's dominated by a dome nearly 150 feet high, a pretty cloister, and a lavish baroque side chapel. It was named because of the day that Alicante was reconquered, December 6, 1248—the feast day of St. Nicolás. ⊠ *Pl. del Abad Penalva 1* ☏ *96/521–2662* ◷ *Daily 7:30–12:30 and 5:30–8:30.*

Iglesia de Santa María. Constructed in a Gothic style over the city's main mosque between the 14th and 16th centuries, this is Alicante's oldest church. The main door is flanked by beautiful baroque stonework by Juan Bautista Borja. ⊠ *Place de Santa María* ☏ *96/521–6026.*

Museo de Bellas Artes Gravina. Inside a beautiful palace and opened in 2001, MUBAG, as it's known, has art collections from the 16th to early 20th centuries. ⊠ *Gravina 13–15* ☏ *96/514–6780* ▦ *Free* ◷ *May–Oct., Tues.–Sat. 10–2 and 5–9; Nov.–Apr., Tues.–Sat. 10–2 and 4–8.*

Ayuntamiento. Constructed between 1701 and 1780, the town hall is a beautiful example of baroque civic architecture. Take a look inside and ask gate officials for permission to explore the ornate halls and rococo chapel on the first floor. ⊠ *Plaza de Ayuntamiento* ☏ *96/514–9100.*

Outside Old Town

Santa Bárbara Castle (Castillo de Santa Bárbara). The Benacantil mountain, rising to a height of 545 feet, forms a strategic position overlooking not just the city but the sea and the whole Alicante plain for many miles. Remains from civilizations dating from the Bronze Age onward have been found here, and the oldest parts, at the highest level, are from the 9th to 13th centuries. Most of the work was undertaken between 1562 and 1580 during the reign of Felipe II. This is one of the largest existing medieval fortresses in Europe. The castle is named after a virgin martyr whose day coincided with the date that the castle was reconquered, December 4, 1248. ⊠ *Castle is most easily reached by first walking through a 200-yard tunnel entered from Av. Jovellanos 1, along Postiguet beach by pedestrian bridge, and then taking elevator up 472 feet to castle* ☏ *96/516–2128* ▦ *Free, elevator €2.40* ◷ *Elevator and castle daily 10–7; last elevator up at 6:30.*

Capa Collection. Professor Eduardo Capa donated this collection of contemporary Spanish sculpture, the largest such collection in the world. Some 250 of the total of 700 works are permanently displayed here, including pieces by Benlliure, Pérez Comendador, and Alberto Sánchez. ⊠ *Castillo de Santa Bárbara* ☏ *96/515–2969* ▦ *Free* ◷ *Tues.–Sat. 10:30–2:30 and 4–6:30, Sun. and holidays 10:30–2:30.*

Museo Arqueológico Provincial (MARQ). Inside the old hospital of San Juan de Dios, this museum has exhibits dating from the Palaeolithic era to modern times, with a particular emphasis on Iberian art. ✉ *Plaza Dr. Gómez Ulla s/n* ☎ *96/514–9000* ⊕ *www.marqalicante.com* ☑ *€6* ◷ *Tues.–Sat. 10–7, Sun. and holidays 10–2.*

Museo Taurino. In the Plaza de Toros, the Bullfighting Museum is a must for aficionados of the sport. There are fine examples of costumes (the "suits of lights"), bulls' heads, posters, capes, and sculptures. ✉ *Plaza de España s/n* ☎ *96/521–9930* ☑ *Free* ◷ *Tues.–Fri. 10:30–1:30 and 5–8, Sat. 10:30–1:30.*

Museo de Fogueres. Bonfire festivities are popular in this part of Spain, and the effigies can be elaborate and funny. Every year the best *ninots* (effigies) are saved from the flames and placed in the Bonfire Festivities Museum, which also has a video of the festivities, scale models, photos, and costumes. ✉ *Av. Rambla de Méndez Núñez 29* ☎ *96/514–6828* ☑ *Free* ◷ *May–Oct. Tues.–Sat. 10–2 and 6–9, Sun. and holidays 10–2.*

Where to Stay & Eat

$$–$$$ ✕ **Dársena.** The Marina Deportiva, a stretch of harbor front lined with restaurants and cafés, is the location of this old Alicante standard. Mediterranean rice dishes (more than 140 options) are the house specialty, but pay close attention to the outstanding fish specials, which vary depending on the season and the luck of the local fishermen. Highlights include paella *con bogavante* (with lobster) and *arroz de caracoles y calamares* (short-grain rice with escargots and calamari). ✉ *Marina Deportiva–Muelle de levante 6* ☎ *96/520–7399* ⊕ *www.darsena.com* ☰ *AE, DC, MC, V.*

$–$$ ✕ **Casa Dimas.** This may be a small and easily missed restaurant, but for those who love Galician cuisine such as *Pulpo Gallego* washed down with inexpensive, but tasty, white Albariño wine served in typical Galician bowls called Riveiros, this Old Town eatery, near the Amérigo hotel, is the place to head for. ✉ *Pórico de Ansaldo 2* ☎ *96/520–8086* ☰ *MC, V* ◷ *Closed Tues.*

$–$$ ✕ **El Buen Comer.** On the edge of the Old Town, this unostentatious restaurant serves its enticing dishes in plentiful portions. Specialties include roast suckling pig, lamb chops, and baby lamb in garlic sauce. The rice dishes, made for a minimum of two people, include rice with monkfish and clams and rice with vegetables. Another option is pork and snails in *fidugá* (noodles). ✉ *Calle Mayor 8* ☎ *96/521–3103* ☰ *MC, V.*

$$$$ 🛏 **Amérigo.** This used to be the Dominican convent right in the historic center of Alicante, but it has been tastefully refurbished to blend its historic tendencies with the best of modern features and technology to become the newest, and best, luxury hotel in the city center. It also incorporates a cool tapas bar, a roof-top terrace and pool, and on-site private parking—a real luxury in Alicante. From here it is a short walk to nearby places of interest, including the Postiguet beach. ✉ *Rafael Altamira 7, 03002* ☎ *96/514–6570* 🖨 *96/514–6571* ⊕ *www.hospes.es* ⤵ *59 rooms* ⚐ *Restaurant, pool (covered in winter), gym, sauna, 2 bars, parking (fee)* ☰ *MC, V.*

8

$$$$ ⊞ **Sidi San Juan.** Overlooking the Playa de San Juan, this luxury hotel has many sporting facilities plus arrangements at a nearby golf course, compensating for the couple miles' distance from Alicante's center (which can be reached via a free shuttle bus). ⊠ *Playa de San Juan, 03540* ☎ *96/516–1300* 🖨 *96/516–3346* ⊕ *www.sidisanjuan.com* ☞ *163 rooms, 13 suites* ⚘ *2 restaurants, driving range, putting green, 5 tennis courts, 2 pools (1 indoor), health club* ▭ *AE, DC, MC, V.*

$$ ⊞ **Tryp Gran Sol.** This 24-story hotel towers over the center of Alicante, and the upper floors and restaurant have spectacular views over the marina and beach. Some rooms have small sitting areas. ⊠ *Rambla Méndez Núñez 3* ☎ *96/520–3000* 🖨 *96/521–1439* ⊕ *www.solmelia.com* ☞ *123 rooms* ⚘ *Restaurant, bar, parking (fee)* ▭ *AE, DC, MC, V.*

¢–$ ⊞ **Hostal Les Monges Palace.** In a restored 18th-century building, this family-run pension is behind the *ayuntamiento* (town hall) in Alicante's central old quarter. Rooms are furnished with a quirky charm. The Japanese Suite (*suite japonés*) is equipped with hot tub and sauna. ⊠ *C. San Agustín 4, 03002* ☎ *96/521–5046* 🖨 *96/514–7189* ⊕ *www.lesmonges.net* ☞ *16 rooms, 2 suites* ⚘ *Some in-room hot tubs, cable TV, in-room data ports, parking (fee)* ▭ *MC, V.*

Fodor'sChoice ★

Nightlife

Run-down bars populate the streets behind the *ayuntamiento*. In summer the liveliest places are along the water, on the Ruta del Puerto and Ruta de la Madera. Among the slicker pubs and discos is **Z-Club** (⊠ Calle San Fernando s/n ☎ 96/521–0646), where Alicante twentysomethings groove to house and techno. Thirtysomething couples gather at **Byblos** (⊠ C. San Francisco s/n ☎ 647/654298).

Shopping

Local **crafts** include basketwork, embroidery, leatherwork, and weaving, each specific to a single town or village. You can find these in the major resorts, though their prices may be inflated. The most satisfying places to shop are often neighborhood markets, so inquire about market days. For **ceramics** travel to the town of Agost, 20 km (12 mi) inland from Alicante. Potters here make jugs and pitchers from the local white clay, with porosity that is ideal for keeping liquids cool. You're bound to see a few potters at work in Agost, and you can learn more about their craft, and, more to the point, shop for ceramics at the **Museo de Alfarería** (Pottery Museum). ⊠ *Teuleria 11* ☎ *96/569–1199* 🎫 €1.50 ☉ *Tues.–Sat. 11–2 (Oct.–Mar.), and 11–2 and 5–8 (Apr.–Sept.); Sun. 11–2 (Sept.–May) and 5–9 (June–Aug.).*

Santa Pola

☾ ⑫ *19 km (11.8 mi) south of Alicante.*

This fishing town, which has nearly 15 km (10 mi) of mainly fine-sand and safe beaches with shallow, clear water, is an ideal location for families with children. The closest mainland city to Tabarca Island, Santa Pola has the port for several boats that make regular trips here.

There are records showing that people have lived in this area since the third millennium BC. A fortified city was built in the 4th century BC to protect the settlers, who fished and traded with other Mediterranean societies. The population increased with the coming of the Romans in the 1st century BC, who made it one of their main ports. Many of the fortifications seen today, including the town's castle, date from the 16th century and were built to defend the town from raids by the Barbary Pirates, who had taken over nearby Tabarca Island.

Exhibits at **Museo del Mar** detail Santa Pola's history and its close relationship with the sea, from prehistoric times through the fortification of the coast. ⊠ *Santa Pola Castle* ☎ *96/669–1532* ⌨ *€0.60* ☉ *Summer, Tues.–Sat. 11–1 and 6–10, Sun. 11–1:30; winter, Tues.–Sat. 11–1 and 4–7, Sun. 11–1:30.* The eight rooms of **Museo de la Pesca** detail the life of fishermen in Santa Pola. ⊠ *Santa Pola Castle* ☎ *96/541–3351* ⌨ *€1.50* ☉ *Tues.–Sat. 11–1 and 6–10 (4–7 in off-season), Sun. 11–1:30.*

Inside an old salt mill within the natural park, **Museo de la Sal** details all aspects of salt extraction, as well as its uses and characteristics. There are also bird-watching observatories. ⊠ *Av. Zaragoza 45* ☎ *96/669–3546* ⌨ *Free* ☉ *Fri.–Mon. and Wed., 9–2:30; Tues. and Thurs. 9–2:30 and 4–6.*

Acuario. This aquarium has nine large tanks with creatures native to the local Mediterranean environment—including *musolas* (a type of shark), crossbow fish, conger eels, octopi, and morays. ⊠ *Plaza Fernández Ordóñez s/n* ☎ *96/541–6916* ⌨ *€2.40* ☉ *Summer, daily 11–1 and 6–10; winter, Tues.–Sat. 10–1 and 5–7, Sun. 10–1.*

Parque Natural de Les Salines de Santa Pola. This natural park of 6,103 acres overlaps with an old early 18th-century hunting and fishing reserve. It wasn't until a salt factory was opened in 1890 that the area was transformed. By making the seawater flow through a circuit of ponds to precipitate out the salt, the area has developed its own ecosystem. The park supports about 8,000 flamingos, one of the few places on the Iberian Peninsula with a permanent flock, as well as many other species, including sandpipers, osprey, and herons. The old Tamarit Tower, dating from the 16th century, stands in an isolated position by the side of N332. ⊠ *South of Santa Pola, on either side of N332 Rd.*

8

☺ **Rio Safari Elche.** Surrounded by more than 4,000 palm trees, you can take a small train to view large animals; visit smaller ones, such as crocodiles, reptiles, and birds; take in the animal shows; and even take a dip in the pool. ⊠ *Ctra. Santa Pola-Elche* ☎ *96/663–8288* ⊕ *www.riosafari. com* ⌨ *€14* ☉ *Summer, daily 10:30–8 with shows at 1, 5, and 8; winter, daily 10:30–6 with shows at 1 and 6.*

La Lonja. Every evening the fishing boats come back home, and their catch is auctioned off at the fish market here. It's a fascinating sight. ⊠ *Puerto Pesquero.*

Where to Stay

$$ ⊞ **Polamar.** This hotel has a good location, with one side facing the town and the other the beach. The interior has classic Spanish decor, a summer terrace, and a bar and restaurant overlooking the sea. ⊠ *Astilleros, 12 (Playa de Levante), 03130* ☎ *96/541–3200* ☐ *96/541–3183* ⊕ *www.*

polamar.com ⤳*71 rooms, 4 suites* ⅋ *Restaurant, laundry facilities, parking (free)* ▤ *AE, DC, MC, V.*

Isla de Tabarca

⑬ *4½ km (3 mi) east of Santa Pola.*

The only inhabited island off the Valenciano coast became a base for the Barbary Pirates in the Middle Ages. In 1760 Carlos III fortified it and populated it with about 600 Genoan fishermen after an agreement with the king from the Tabarka peninsula (between Tunisia and Algeria). These ancestors account for the Italian surnames of many of today's island dwellers. A little more than a mile long and 437 yards wide, and car-free, the small fortified enclosure was listed as a National Historic Artistic Complex in 1964. The few restaurants specialize in seafood; the secluded beaches are great for snorkeling or simply sunbathing.

Cruceros Baeza-Parodi (☏ 608/330422 or 639/893920) and **Cruceros La Gola de Guadarmar** (☏ 689/123623) operate glass-bottom catamarans between Santa Pola and Tabarca. Crossings, which run four times a day, take around 25 minutes and costs €11 each way.

INLAND FROM THE COASTA BLANCA

Guadalest

⑭ *24 km (15 mi) north of Benidorm.*

The old town of Guadalest, originally Moorish, perches atop a crag within the walls of a castle ruined in a 1644 earthquake. Because of the steep terrain here, the tiny streets are stepped. To the north are splendid views over a large reservoir. The population is only 200, but this tiny village is the second-most-visited place in Spain, after the Prado Museum. People are drawn here for the seven museums in town and the one just outside it. The most interesting are detailed below.

Built after the earthquake of 1644 by a family of nobility, the **Museo Municipal Casa Orduña** was plundered during the War of Succession in 1708. All the furnishings on display here belong to the family and demonstrate how the affluent lived in the 19th century. The museum also serves as the entrance to the castle itself. ▨*Iglesia 2* ☏*96/588–5393* ▨€3 ⊙*May–Oct., daily 10:15–1:45 and 3:15–8; Nov.–Apr., daily 10:15–1:45 and 3:15–6.*

Attached to a natural rock, the **Antonio Marco Museum** contains miniature models of churches and homes made by Antonio Marco. On the top floor is a huge nativity scene, weighing 12 tons. ▨ *Calle de la Virgen 2* ☏ *96/588–5323* ▨ €3 ⊙ *May–Oct., daily 10–9; Nov.–Apr., daily 10–6.*

The name says it all at the **Museo de Tortura Medieval** you can see torture methods used from the Spanish Inquisition through the 20th century. ▨ *Honda 2* ☏ *61/005–1001* ▨ €3 ⊙ *May–Oct., daily 10:30–9; Nov.–Apr., 10:30–6.* The **Museo Ribera Girona,** the first of its kind in the province, exhibits contemporary art from numerous artists, including those of the founder, Ribera Girona. Many of the works here have been displayed in famous museums around the world. ⊠ *Peña 1* ☎ *96/588–5062* 🖃 *€4* ⊘ *May–Oct., daily 10–8; Nov.–Apr., daily 10–6.*

Where to Eat

★ $ ✕ **El Tossal.** Just outside the pedestrian-only area of the old town, El Tossal, has a wood-beam dining room and outside terraces. On weekdays there's a set meal with a selection of tapas, main course, dessert, wine, and bread—all for less than €9. ⊠ *Aitana* ☎ *96/588–5352* 🖃 *MC, V.*

Polop

⑮ *10 km (6 mi) northwest of Altea.*

This hilltop town has two interesting features: a castle and the Plaza Fuente de la Provincia, which holds a collection of 221 taps for water, each donated by a different town in the province. Villagers armed with jugs can obtain free, constant mountain water from this square.

Jijona

⑯ *24 km (15 mi) north of Alicante.*

Jijona is the home of *turró,* an almond-and-honey-based nougat of Moorish origin, still produced by more than 25 family-run businesses.

Museo del Turrón. This museum is in the old Turrones El Lobo carpentry works, in a business park on the outskirts of Jijona on the road to Busot. Guided tours (in Spanish, along with brochures in English) of this three-floored museum explain the production of *turrón,* marzipan, and other confections that have been the economic foundation of this town since the early 20th century. ⊠ *Poligon industrial "Ciutat del Turró," sector 10, 2, Ctra. Xixona-Busot, Km 1* ☎ *96/561–0225* ⊕ *www. museodelturron.com* ⊘ *Weekdays guided tours hourly 10–7, weekend tours hourly 10–1.*

▌ EN
ROUTE

Caves of Candelabra, one of the most spacious caves in Spain, has a length of 50 feet and a high ceiling. The stalagtites have created weird shapes, and the acoustic properties are put to use with musical shows. At an elevation of 2,300 feet on the slopes of the Cabezón de Oro (Golden Head) mountain, the location offers impressive views across the Mediterranean and the plain of Alicante. ⊠ *3 km (2 mi) north of Busot* ☎ *96/569–9250* 🖃 *€4* ⊘ *July–Sept., daily 10:30–7:50; Oct.–June daily 11–5:50.*

Elche

⑰ *24 km (15 mi) southwest of Alicante, 34 km (21 mi) northeast of Orihuela, 58 km (36 mi) northeast of Murcia.*

If Alicante is torrid in summer, Elche is even hotter. The largest palm forest in Europe surrounds Elche, however, granting some escape from the worst of the heat. The Moors first planted the palms for dates, Europe's most reliable crop, and the trees still produce these as well as yellow fronds. (Throughout Spain the fronds are blessed on Palm Sunday and hung on balconies to ward off evil during the coming year.) Colo-

8

nized by ancient Rome, Elche was later ruled by the Moors for 500 years. The remarkable stone bust known as *La Dama de Elche,* one of the earliest examples of Iberian sculpture (now in Madrid's Museum of Archaeology), was discovered here in 1897.

Elche's history dates back to the Neolithic period, when it was a mile south of the present town—it was at this site, L'Alcudia, that La Dama de Elche was discovered. Museum exhibits are from the Copper and Bronze ages as well as pieces from the Iberian and Roman eras. ⊠ *Ctra. Dolores, Km 2* ☎ *96/661–1506* ⊠ *€2.50* ⊘ *Tues.–Sat. 10–2 and 4–8 (10–5 only in off-season), Sun. 10–2.*

Fodor'sChoice
★ **Elche Palm Grove.** The Moors originally irrigated the land and started planting palm trees here, and these days there are more than 200,000 palm trees growing within the city. Many of the plantations have been turned into public parks, and efforts are being made to bring back traditional crafts. The blanched palm leaves are used in Elche's two most important cultural events—the Palm Sunday procession and the Mystery Play of Elche. ⊠ *Porta de la Morera* ☎ *96/545–1936* ⊠ *€4* ⊘ *Apr.–Sept., daily 9–8:30; Oct.–Mar., daily 9–6.*

In the cellar of the 16th-century **Arab Baths Convent of Our Lady of Mercy** is an intriguing complex of Arab baths, with tiled walls and ceilings. ⊠ *Passeig de les Eres de Santa Llúcia 13* ☎ *96/545–2887* ⊠ *Free.*

Where to Stay & Eat

$$–$$$ ✕ **Els Capellans.** This restaurant within the Huerto del Cura hotel is exceptional. Cold appetizers might include spider crab and avocado cake with green apples, and creamed asparagus with salmon croquettes. Main dishes might include lamb kebab on a bed of eggplant and grilled fillets of sole with razor clams in an artichoke cream sauce. ⊠ *Porta de la Morera 14* ☎ *96/661–0011* ▭ *AE, DC, MC, V.*

★ **$$$** ▤ **Huerto del Cura.** A subtropical location and a large, private garden in Elche's palm grove make this modern hotel perfect for relaxation. The bedrooms, in bungalow huts, are gloomy because of the shady location but are tastefully decorated. ⊠ *Porta de la Morera 14, 03203* ☎ *96/661–0011* 🖷 *96/542–1910* ⊕ *www.huertodelcura.com* ↩ *81 rooms, 10 suites* 🔥 *Restaurant, cafeteria, cable TV with movies, putting green, tennis court, pool, gym, sauna, bar* ▭ *AE, DC, MC, V.*

THE MURCIA COAST

The Murcia Coast is markedly different from the coastline to the north. Here you are met by the curious Mar Menor, an inland sea hemmed in by La Mangor, the narrow strip of land that has beaches on either side. These days, La Manga is famous for its numerous hotels, particularly the huge La Manga complex on the mainland, just before the Cabo de Palos. The main town along the coast is Cartagena, which has a long and glorious history and is well worth a visit. Águilas, almost at the border with Andalusia, is a pleasant surprise, with a mild climate and fine beaches with clear water in town and for many miles north and south.

La Manga del Mar Menor

⓲ *45 km (28 mi) southeast of Murcia.*

The advance of rocks and sand from two headlands into the Mediterranean Sea transformed what was once a bay into the Mar Menor (Smaller Sea), a famously calm expanse of water about 20 feet deep. The Mar Menor is Europe's largest saltwater lake (170 square km [105 square mi]), and, because of its high salt and iodine content, it's used as a therapeutic health resort for rheumatism patients. The Manga ("sleeve") is the 21-km (13-mi) spit of sand averaging some 990 feet wide that separates it from the Mediterranean. Four canals, called *golas,* connect the Mar Menor with the Mediterranean. The Manga has 42 km (26 mi) of immense, sandy beaches on both the Mediterranean and the Mar Menor sides, allowing swimmers to choose more or less exposed locations and warmer or colder water according to season and weather.

Museo de Carruajes y Motocicletas Zamar (Museo de Carruajes y Motocicletas Zamar). Just before the exit to the Hyatt Regency La Manga, this museum has an interesting collection of carriages from the 17th century to the present, as well as one of the largest collections of motorcycles in Spain. ⊠ *Ctra. La Unión, Km 2, El Algar* ☎ *96/813–6656* ⊕ *www.museodecarruajeszamar.com* ☉ *Tues.–Sun. 10–2 and 4–9.*

Where to Stay & Eat

$ **✕ D'Bistro.** This is where the locals go—nothing fancy, but great food in good quantities. The prix-fixe lunch, at €8, is a great value, especially with a bottle of wine thrown in. ⊠ *C. Zoco D'Levante, 1st fl.* ☎ *96/814–0370* ▤ *MC, V.*

$$$$ **▥ Hyatt Regency La Manga.** Golf pervades this superbly situated luxury clubhouse-hotel, just above the Mar Menor. For nongolfers, the resort has no fewer than 22 tennis courts and a regulation cricket pitch, the latter of which may account for the surfeit of British-registered Range Rovers in the parking lot. You can also rent apartments or villas. ⊠ *Los Belones, Murcia 30385* ☎ *96/833–1234* 🖷 *96/833–1235* ⊕ *www. lamanga.hyatt.com* 🖙 *192 rooms ⚭ Restaurant, cable TV with movies, 3 18-hole golf courses, 22 tennis courts, pool, hot tub, sauna, horseback riding, squash, 2 bars* ▤ *AE, DC, MC, V.*

Sports & the Outdoors

Notable for its absence of waves of any kind, the Mar Menor is a serious sailing destination. Various schools offer windsurfing, waterskiing, catamaran sailing, and other marine diversions.

Socaire Watersports School. In Santiago de la Ribera, to the north on the mainland side of the Mar Menor, this school offers sailing and windsurfing courses using a variety of vessels, and rents out equipment to qualified adults who wish to sail around the lake. ⊠ *Playa del Castillico* ☎ *606/111813* ⊕ *www.socaire.com.*

8

Cartagena

 48 km (29 mi) south of Murcia.

Founded in the 3rd century BC by the Carthaginians, this is Spain's principal naval base. From Cartagena you have easy access to the resort La Manga del Mar Menor and the twisty, scenic 100-km (62-mi) drive along N332 to the start of the Costa de Almería.

General Asdrúbal founded Cartagena in 227 BC. Even then its natural harbor surrounded by five hills made it a busy port. It was from here that Hannibal set out in 218 BC with a mighty army and his elephants crossing the Pyrenees and the Alps before narrowly failing to destroy the Roman Republic. The Romans had their revenge in 209 BC, when they conquered Cartagena during the Second Punic War. This began a period of splendor under Roman rule that lasted until the beginning of the 2nd century AD.

In 44 BC Cartagena was honored with the title of Colony—Colonia Urbs Iulia Nova Carthago—and it prospered because of its mines and its easily defended natural harbor and the inland sea, Mar Menor then known as El Almarjal, directly to the north. As elsewhere, when the Romans left there was a long period of decadence and troubles, with the Visigoths controlling for long periods before being replaced by the Moors in 734 AD. The reconquest came early here, in 1245 led by a prince who later became Alfonso X "The Wise." The Catholic monarchs began fortifications around the hills of the harbor to defend the city against the Moors, who retained power in nearby Granada until 1492, and after that the Spanish Armada was stationed here for defensive purposes and to support military attacks on North Africa and the Mediterranean. At this time, in the early 16th century, castles and the huge city walls were constructed—many can be seen

> **WORD OF MOUTH**
>
> "Cartagena is a very cute old Roman/Carthaginain seaport.
> —WishIwasthere.

today—but they couldn't stop Sir Francis Drake from sacking Cartagena in 1585. The city was named as capital of the Mediterranean Maritime Department in 1728, resulting in a large population growth to support the construction of arsenals, barracks, and castles. Mining remained economically important at this time, and remained so until the end of the 1920s. After the Cantonal Revolution in 1873 many of the buildings seen today were constructed. During the Spanish civil war Cartagena remained steadfastly loyal to the Republican government, and was one of the last cities in Spain to surrender to Generalissimo Francisco Franco's troops. These days, it's been largely replaced as an important port by the larger ones of Barcelona, Málaga, and Valencia, and therefore, Cartagena is looking to its illustrious historical past for its economic future by carefully, and cleverly, developing its touristic potential.

A **tour bus** departs from outside the tourist office, directly across from the Punic Wall. With commentary about the city's attractions, the tour is a good introduction to Cartagena. ⊠ *Tourist Office* ☎ €3.50.

Most of what can be seen of the **Castillo de la Concepción** today was built by Enrique III in the 14th century, using the remains of nearby Roman ruins. The views from here are astounding, reaching out over the town, harbor, and the Mediterranean. A **panoramic lift** (elevator) on Calle Gisbert rises nearly 150 feet to a gangway that leads to the Concepción Castle. Besides saving a strenuous walk, the gangway also offers great views on the way up. The lift costs €1. ⊠ *Concepción Hill* ☎ *96/852–5326* ⌨ *€3.50* ☉ *Mid-June–mid-Sept., daily 10:30–8:30.*

Cartagena suffered through much aerial bombardment during the Spanish civil war, since it was the base for most the Republican fleet. For the safety of its citizens, shelters with a capacity of 5,500 were built into the sides of the Concepción hill. At the **Refugio Museo de la Guerra Civil,** visitors today can see the conditions people had to endure during those harrowing days. ⊠ *Gisbert 10* ⌨ *€3.50.*

The **Pabellón de Autopsias,** near the panoramic lift, was a part of the naval hospital when it was built in 1768. Autopsies and anatomy lessons were held here as part of the research into the constant epidemics that swept Cartagena in the late 18th century. Exhibits cover the anatomy sessions of those days. Across the road, and under Plaza de Toros, are some remains of the Roman Amphitheatre. Dating from the 1st century BC, it's one of the oldest of its kind on the Iberian Peninsula. ⊠ *Calle Gisbert* ⌨ *€1.50.*

Across from the tourist office on the San José hill, the **Muralla Púnica** (Punic Wall) dates from 227 BC. The walls enclosed and helped defend the Punic city that became the capital of the Carthaginians on the Iberian Peninsula. ⊠ *San Diego 25* ☎ *96/852–5477* ⌨ *€3.50.* At the remains of the **Casa de la Fortune,** which belonged to a wealthy family of the 1st century BC, the most attractive feature is the fresco painted on the dining-room walls. It's to the south of the tourist office, down the main road. ⊠ *Plaza del Risueño* ⌨ *€2.50* ☉ *Tues.–Sun. 10:30–2:30.*

On display at the **Decumano Calzada Romana** is a section of the Roman road known as the Decumano Maximo, which joined the harbor to the Forum. ⊠ *Plaza de los Tres Reyes s/n* ⌨ *€2.* Discovered in 1987, the **Teatro Romano** dates from the late 1st century BC. It was built into the northern slopes of the Cocepción hill. ⊠ *Plaza Condesa Peralta s/n.*

A little distance outside the old town, and built over the 4th-century Roman necropolis of San Antón, the **Museo Arqueológico** is the headquarters for all archaeological study in this area. ⊠ *Ramón y Cajal 45* ☎ *96/853–9027.*

With all of Cartagena's maritime influences, it's appropriate to take to the water and find out more about this natural harbor. Guides on the **Barco Turístico** (Tourist Catamaran) talk about the harbor's system of fortifications, as well as intriguing legends and stories about the town's trading and military role of Cartagena. ⊠ *Muelle Alfonso XII* ⌨ *€5.*

Where to Eat

$$$–$$$$ ✕ **Mare Nostrum.** On the ground floor is a bar for snacks and tapas, and upstairs is a dining room offering seafood, shellfish, and meat entrées,

accompanied by such rice dishes as *arroz caldero* (fish and rice stew) and *arroz con Bogavante* (rice with lobster). ⊠ *Paseo Alfonso XII s/n, at the Puerto Deportivo* ☎ *968/522131* ▭ *AE, DC, MC, V.*

Águilas

⑳ *96 km (60 mi) southwest of Cartagena.*

Águilas, the last town of any size in Murcia, sits in a privileged position between two fine beaches and under the 16th-century Castillo de San Juan, which dominates a 280-foot-tall promontory in the center of town. The crystal-clear waters along the coastline hold fascinating, colorful underwater life. **Centro de Buceo–Águilas** leads dives between Águilas and Cabo Cope, rents all necessary equipment, and runs diving courses. ⊠ *Isaac Peral 13* ☎ *617/910973.*

Where to Stay & Eat

$$–$$$ ✗ **Delicias del Mar.** This large restaurant has an equally large terrace, with both having delightful views across the bay over the marina to the commanding castle. The menu offers a wide range of typical dishes with an emphasis on seafood and shellfish. ⊠ *Aire 145* ☎ *968/449496* ▭ *MC, V* ☺ *No dinner Mon.–Wed.*

$$ ▣ **Calypso.** This hotel is in the first small community over the border, into the province of Almería a few miles south of Águilas. On the corner of a charming beach, Calypso has bright, simply furnished rooms with balconies overlooking the Mediterranean. ⊠ *Playa de San Juan de los Terreros, 04648* ☎ *950/466032* ♨ *950/466160* ⊕ *www.calypsoalmeria.com* ⇥ *28 rooms* ♿ *Restaurant, cafeteria, health club, snorkeling, laundry facilities, free parking.*

$$ ▣ **Don Juan Spa & Resort.** This new hotel is directly on the Playa Poniente in the southern part of Águilas and considered the best place to stay in town. The rooms are large and modern, with unparalleled views of the Mediterranean. Facilities include the Mondariz Spa & Beauty center. ⊠ *Av. del Puerto Deportivo 1, Playa Poniente, 30880* ☎ *968/493493* ♨ *968/414949* ⊕ *www.hoteldonjuan.es* ⇥ *128 rooms* ♿ *Restaurant, 2 pools (1 indoor), gym, massage, sauna, spa, bar, piano bar, concierge, Internet room* ▭ *AE, DC, MC, V.*

San José & the Cabo de Gata Nature Reserve

㉑ *40 km (25 mi) east of Almería, 86 km (53 mi) south of Mojácar.*

San José is the largest village in the southern part of the park and has a very nice bay, but these days it has rather outgrown itself and can get busy in the summer months. Those preferring smaller, quieter places should look a little farther north at places such as La Isleta and Agua Amarga and the often-deserted beaches between them. Just south of San José is the **Parque Natural Marítimo y Terrestre Cabo de Gata–Níjar** (nature reserve; ⊠ Road from Almería to Cabo de Gata, Km 6 ☎ 950/160435). Birds are the main attraction; the park is home to several species native to Africa, including the *camachuelo trompetero* (large beaked bullfinch), which is not found anywhere else outside Africa. The **Centro Las Amuladeras visitor center,** at the park entrance, has an exhibit and information on the region. For beach time, follow signs south to the **Playa Los Genoveses** and **Playa Monsul.** A dirt track follows the coast around the spectacular cape, eventually linking up with the N332 to Almería.

Where to Stay

$$$-$$$$ ⊞ **Mikasa.** Specifically designed for rest and relaxation, this stylish hotel has some rooms with king-size beds and whirlpools as well as sea views; a gourmet breakfast is served on the terrace or in the delightful garden, and the restaurant, exclusively for guests, serves an intriguing mix of local and international cuisine. If you don't fancy the beach, relax at one of the two pools (one is heated) or luxuriate in the spa. ⊠ *Ctra. de Carboneras s/n, Agua Amarga, 04149* ☎ *950/138073* ⊕ *www.mikasasuites. com* ⤳ *20 rooms* ♿ *Restaurant, 2 pools, spa, bar* ⊟ *AE, DC, MC, V.*

Almería

❷❷ *219 km (136 mi) southwest of Murcia, 183 km (114 mi) east of Málaga.*

Warmed by the sunniest climate in Andalusia, Almería is a youthful Mediterranean city, basking in sweeping views of the sea from its coastal perch. Almería is also a capital of the grape industry, thanks to its wonderfully mild climate in spring and fall. Rimmed by tree-lined boulevards and some landscaped squares, the city's core is still a maze of narrow, winding alleys formed by flat-roof, distinctly Mudéjar houses. Though now surrounded by modern apartment blocks, these dazzling-white older homes give Almería an Andalusian flavor. Dominating the city is its **Alcazaba** (fortress) built by Caliph Abd ar-Rahman I and provided with a bell tower by Carlos III. From here you have sweeping views of the port and city. Among the ruins of the fortress, damaged by earthquakes in 1522 and 1560, are landscaped gardens of rock flowers and cacti. ⊠ *C. Almanzor* ☎ *950/271617* ⊠ *€1.50; free for EU citizens* ⌚ *Apr.–Oct., Tues.–Sun. 10–8; Nov.–Mar., Tues.–Sun. 9–6:30.*

Below the Alcazaba stands the **cathedral,** whose buttressed towers make it look like a castle. It is Gothic in design, but with some classical touches around the doors. ⊠ *€3* ⌚ *Weekdays 10:30–4:30, Sat. 10–1.*

Where to Stay & Eat

$$ ✗ **Veracruz.** In Almería's beach barrio, El Zapillo, this justly popular seafood restaurant has its own storage tank for oysters, clams, prawns, and lobsters. The specialty is *parillada de pescado,* a mixed grill of everything that swims in the Mediterranean. ⊠ *Av. Cabo de Gata 119* ☎ *950/251220* ⊟ *AE, MC, V.*

$–$$ ✗ **Valentin.** This popular, central spot serves fine regional specialties, such as *cazuela de rape* (monkfish baked in a sauce of almonds and pine nuts). The surroundings are Andalusian: white walls, wood, and glass. Come on the early side (around 9) to get a table. ⊠ *Tenor Iribarne 7* ☎ *950/264475* ⊟ *AE, MC, V* ⌚ *Closed Mon. No dinner Sun.*

$$ ✗⊞ **Torreluz III.** Value is the overriding attraction of this comfortable yet elegant modern hotel. Guest rooms are slick and bright, with the kind of installations for which you'd expect to pay more. Its restaurant, Torreluz Mediterráneo, is famous among locals for robust portions and

8

brisk lunchtime service. It serves an excellent cross section of southeastern fare—try the *zarzuela de marisco a la marinera* (mixed seafood in a zesty red marinade). The cheaper Torreluz Hotel, with just 24 rooms ($) next door (with the same phone number) is also good value, as are the nearby apartments, which offer more space for the same price as the main hotel. ⊠ *Plaza Flores 3, 04001* ☎ *950/234399* 🖷 *950/281428* ⊕ *www.torreluz.com* 📞 *94 rooms* ♿ *2 restaurants, cafeteria, cable TV, bar* ▤ *AE, DC, MC, V.*

$$ 🏨 **NH Ciudad de Almería.** One of the newest hotels in Almería, this has the appealing mix of traditional and modern style—including avant-garde art pieces—often found in NH hotels, and offers larger rooms than is usually expected in the region. It also has a fine strategic location, just to the east of the town center and directly across from the train and bus station. ⊠ *Jardín de Medina s/n, 04006* ☎ *950/182500* 🖷 *950/273010* ⊕ *www.nh-hotels.com* 📞 *139 rooms* ♿ *Restaurant, bar, laundry facilities, Internet room* ▤ *AE, DC, MC, V.*

$ 🏨 **Hostal Sevilla.** If you want inexpensive comfort, look no further. In the labyrinth of the old town, you'll find healthy doses of Andalusian style and charm. The rooms vary; those on the street side have small terraces, whereas those on the quiet interior look over the courtyards and rooftops of the old town. All have ceramic-tile floors. ⊠ *Granada 25, 04001* ☎🖷 *950/230009* 📞 *37 rooms* ▤ *MC, V.*

Nightlife

Nocturnal action centers on **Plaza Flores,** moving down to the beach in summer. In town, try the small **Cajón de Sastre** (⊠ Plaza Marques de Heredia 8) for typical *copas* (libations) and a mainly Spanish crowd. For an ancient Greek experience minus the toga, look into **Pub Minerva** (⊠ C. Marchales 44). **El Café del Irlandés** (⊠ C. General Segura 15) offers darts and hearty beers in an Irish environment. **Alabama** (⊠ C. Pablo Picasso 22) plays a blend of country and classic rock.

INLAND FROM THE MURCIA COAST

There are only two towns inland that are worth venturing away from the coast to explore: the capital, Murcia, these days a busy, modern city, and Lorca, a considerably smaller community to the southwest.

Murcia

㉓ *82 km (51 mi) southwest of Alicante, 146 km (91 mi) southeast of Albacete, 219 km (136 mi) northeast of Almería.*

A provincial capital and university town of more than 300,000, Murcia was first settled by Romans; later, in the 8th century, the conquering Moors used Roman bricks to build the city proper. The result was reconquered and annexed to the crown of Castile in 1243. The Murcian dialect contains many Arabic words, and many Murcians clearly reveal Moorish ancestry.

★ Murcia's **cathedral** is a masterpiece of eclectic architecture. Begun in the 14th century, the cathedral received its magnificent facade—considered one of Spain's fullest expressions of the Churrigueresque style—as late as 1737; the 19th-century English traveler Richard Ford described it as "rising in compartments, like a drawn out telescope." The 15th century brought the Gothic **Door of the Apostles** and, inside, the splendid chapel of **Los Vélez,** with a beautiful, star-shape stone vault. Carvings by the 18th-century Murcian sculptor Francisco Salzillo were added later. The **museum** has been undergoing restoration; call ahead before planning to visit. The **bell tower,** built between 1521 and 1792, is also undergoing repairs and is sometimes closed to the public. ☎ *96/821–6344* 🖂 *€1.20* ⊙ *Daily 10–1 and 5–8, (4–7 in off-season).*

Wander north on the pedestrian shopping street Calle Trapería and you soon reach the 19th-century **Casino,** which retains the aura of a British gentleman's club. Despite the name, this has never been a gambling center—Murcians (that is, Murcian men) come to read the newspaper and play billiards. ⊠ *C. Trapería.*

The **Museo Salzillo,** out by the bus station, has the main collection of Francisco Salzillo's disturbingly realistic polychrome *pasos* (carvings), carried in Easter processions. ⊠ *Plaza San Agustín 1* ☎ *96/829–1893* ⊕ *www. museosalzillo.es* 🖂 *€3* ⊙ *Tues.–Sat. 9:30–2 and 5–8, Sun. 11–2.*

Where to Stay & Eat

★ **$$–$$$** ✗ **Hispano.** For a typically Spanish brand of rusticity, look no further than this establishment run by a well-known Murcian family of restaurateurs-hoteliers named Abellán, who opened the Hispano in 1979. It is popular for Murcian and nouvelle cuisine, and traditional fare such as paella and *solomillo* (veal). ⊠ *Arquitecto Cerdá 3* ☎ *96/821–6152* ▭ *AE, DC, MC, V* ⊙ *Closed Sun. in July and Aug.*

★ **$$** ✗▦ **Rincón de Pepe.** In the center of the old town, this comfortable hotel is 50 yards from the cathedral's apse. Guest rooms are bright and modern, and the lobby and reception rooms have cool marble floors. The fine restaurant ($$–$$$)serves a good selection of *tapeo murciano,* samples of favorite Murcian dishes. Chef Francisco Gonzáles uses produce from the hotel's own organic farm, plus fish from the nearby Mar Menor and lamb from Segura. Highlights on the extensive menu include *cordero segureño asado a la murciana* (local lamb roasted Murcian-style). ⊠ *Apóstoles 34, 30002* ☎ *96/821–2239* 🖨 *96/822–1744* ⊕ *www.nh-hoteles.com* 🛏 *148 rooms* ⚙ *Restaurant, cable TV with movies, parking (fee)* ▭ *AE, DC, MC, V* ⊙ *No dinner Sun.*

$$ ▦ **Hispano 1.** Rooms at this central budget hotel are bright and airy, and the public sitting area is large and tasteful. Ask for an exterior room, with a view of the pedestrian street below. ⊠ *Trapería 8–10, 30001* ☎ *96/821–6152* 🖨 *96/821–6859* 🛏 *45 rooms, 35 with bath* ⚙ *Restaurant, cable TV, bar, parking (fee)* ▭ *AE, DC, MC, V.*

Nightlife

Murcia is a university town, which in Spain generally guarantees a good time, but this place has some additional creative energy that many other cities lack. Bars come and go, but you can always find action on both edges of the university, especially **Calle Doctor Fleming.** West of campus, a well-dressed young set gathers on the streets in front of the Teatro

Romea; **Los Claveles** (✉ C. Alfaro 10 ☎ No phone) is the center of action in this zone. It's closed Sunday through Tuesday. When the university bars close, there's always the main disco in the city center, **Dance Club** (✉ Centrofama, C. Puerta Nueva s/n ☎ No phone).

Lorca

★ ㉔ *62 km (39 mi) southwest of Murcia, 158 km (98 mi) northeast of Almería, 37 km (23 mi) inland from Mediterranean at Águilas.*

Leave the highway for a glimpse of Lorca, an old market town and the scene of some of Spain's most colorful Holy Week celebrations. The Casa de los Guevara, on Lope Gisbert, houses the tourist office; from here head down Alamo to the elegant **Plaza de España**, ringed by rich baroque buildings, including the *ayuntamiento* (town hall), law courts, and Colegiata (collegiate church). Follow signs from the plaza up to the **castle**.

Where to Eat

★ $ ✕ **Cándido.** Just outside the town center, this rustic, relaxed, old-fashioned restaurant has been going strong on home cooking for more than half a century. A happy mix of Lorcans and travelers partake of the food, which is locally inspired; try the classic *trigo con conejo y caracoles* (bulgar wheat with rabbit and snails). ✉ *Santo Domingo 13* ☎ *96/846–6907* ▤ *MC, V* ☉ *No dinner Sun.*

THE SOUTHEAST ESSENTIALS

To research prices, get advice from other travelers, and book travel arrangements, visit www.fodors.com.

Transportation

BY AIR

Iberia (www.iberia.com) has the most flights to this part of Spain. There are three airports serving the region: Valencia, Alicante, and San Javier (for Mar Menor and Murcia).

🛈 **Airports Aeropuerto de Valencia** ☎ 96/159–8500. **Alicante** ✉ El Altet, 12 km (7 mi) south of town ☎ 96/691–9000. **San Javier** ✉ Mar Menor north shore, off N332 ☎ 96/857–0073.

🛈 **Carriers Iberia** ☎ 902/400500 ⊕ www.iberia.com.

BY BOAT & FERRY

Balearia (⊕ www.balearia.net) and **Iscomar** (⊕ www.iscomarferrys.com) offer ferry services from Denia to Ibiza and Palma de Mallorca. In summer you can cross from Santa Pola to the tiny island of Tabarca. Boat excursions leave from most resorts along the coast, including some with underwater viewing areas.

BY BUS

Private companies run buses down the coast and from Madrid to Valencia, Benidorm, and Alicante. Bus travel is generally inexpensive and comfortable, although few tourists use the service, preferring trips organized by local travel agencies and hotels.

BY CAR

The *autopista* (toll highway) A7 from Barcelona runs through Valencia and Alicante as far as Murcia, and the A37 branches off just south of Elche on to Cartagena. Tolls, though quite high, are often worth it for the time saved, as well as the safe driving conditions. The other main links with the region are the A3 from Madrid to Valencia and the N111/A31 from Madrid to Murcia via Albacete.

The N332 offers a nontoll (but slower) alternative down the coast from Valencia to Águilas, but between Denia and Calpe it's necessary to take smaller (and even slower) roads if you want to be near the sea.

There are numerous car-rental companies, from all the major firms to local operations. Always shop around for the best price. Autoeurope usually has the best rates. Reservations are generally essential only during the Christmas and Easter holidays.

🔒 Rental Agencies **Autoeurope** ☎ 888/223-5555 ⊕ www.autoeurope.com. **Europa Rent-a-Car** ✉ Av. de la Comunidad Valenciana 10, Benidorm ☎ 96/680-2902 ⊕ www. europa-rentacar.es ✉ Aeropuerto de Alicante ☎ 96/568-3362. **Hertz** ✉ Av. de la Estacíon 22, Alicante ☎ 96/513-1123 ⊕ www.hertz.com.

BY TAXI

In the main towns, taxis can be hailed on the street. Alternatively, ask for the nearest taxi stand (*parada de taxi*). Taxis use meters to calculate the fare. Drivers may charge separate fees for luggage.

🔒 Taxi Companies **Cooperativa de Taxis** ☎ 96/578-6565 in Denia. **Radio Taxi** ☎ 96/525-2511 in Benidorm.

BY TRAIN

RENFE trains serve the region's chief cities. Alicante has a RENFE station at which you can book train trips to anywhere in Spain.

The local FGV line (not affiliated with RENFE) runs along the Costa Blanca from Denia to Alicante. The FGV station is at the far end of Playa Postiguet and can be reached by buses C1 and C2 from downtown. The Limon Expres tourist train provides a regular excursion along the Costa Blanca from Benidorm with stops including Gata de Gorgos, where passengers visit a guitar factory.

🔒 Rail Lines **FGV Station, Alicante** ☎ 96/526-2731. **Limon Expres** ☎ 96/680-3103. **RENFE** ☎ 902/240202 ⊕ www.renfe.es.

🔒 Train Stations **Alicante-FGV** ☎ 96/585-1895 ⊕ www.fgv.es. **Alicante-RENFE** ✉ Av. Salamanca ☎ 902/240202. **Murcia** ✉ Industria ☎ 902/240202.

Contacts & Resources

EMERGENCIES

In case of an emergency, dial 091 or 092 for the police.

🔒 Emergency Services **Fire, Police or Ambulance** ☎ 112. **Guardia Civil** ☎ 062. **Insalud** (Public health service) ☎ 061. **Policía Local** (Local police) ☎ 092. **Policía Nacional** (National police) ☎ 091. **Información Toxicológica** (Poisoning) ☎ 915/620420.

TOUR OPTIONS

Numerous companies up and down the coast offer all kinds of tours; information on them can often be found in hotel lobbies and local tourist offices (*see* Visitor Information, *below*).

Alicante's *ayuntamiento* (town hall) and travel agencies arrange tours of the city and bus and train tours to Guadalest, the Algar waterfalls, Benidorm, the Peñón de Ifach (Calpe), and Elche. In Benidorm, large hotels arrange similar excursions. Elche's town hall organizes tours of the city and environs. Alicante's town hall runs tours to Jijona, where you can visit one of the famous turrón factories before seeing the amazing stalactites and stalagmites at the Cuevas de Canalobre.

🚩 **Tour Operators Alicante ayuntamiento** ⊠ Plaza del Ayuntamiento ☎ 96/514-9100 ⊕ www.comunitat-valenciana.com. **Elche ayuntamiento** ⊠ Plaça de Baix ☎ 96/665-8000 ⊕ www.ayto-elche.es.

VISITOR INFORMATION

🚩 **Regional Tourist Offices Alicante** ⊠ Rambla de Mendez Nuñez 23 ☎ 96/520-0000 ⊕ www.comunidad-valenciana.com. **Murcia** ⊠ Plaza Julian Romea 4 ☎ 902/101070 ⊕ www.murciaturistica.com.

🚩 **Local Tourist Offices Aguilas** ⊠ Plaza Antonio Cortijo s/n ☎ 96/849-3173 ⊕ www. aguilas.org. **Albacete** ⊠ Posada del Rosario/del Tinte 2 ☎ 96/758-0522 ⊕ www.albacity. org. **Alicante** ⊠ Rambla Mendez Nuñez 23 ☎ 96/520-0000 ⊕ www.costablanca. org. **Benidorm** ⊠ Av. Martínez Alejos 16 ☎ 96/585-3224 ⊕ www.benidorm.org. **Calpe** ⊠ Av. Ejércitos Españoles s/n ☎ 96/583-6920. **Cartagena** ⊠ Plaza Almirante Bastarreche ☎ 968/506483 ⊕ www.cartagena.es. **Denia** ⊠ Plaza Oculista Builges 9 ☎ 96/642-2367. **Elche** ⊠ Parque Municipal ☎ 96/665-8140 ⊕ www.turismedelx. com. **Gandía** ⊠ Marqués de Campo s/n ☎ 96/287-7788 ⊕ www.gandia.org. **Jávea** ⊠ Plaza Almirante Bastarreche 11 ☎ 96/579-0736 ⊕ www.xabia.org. **Lorca** ⊠ López Gisbert ☎ 96/846-6157 or 968/479700 ⊕ www.ayuntlorca.es. **Murcia** ⊠ Plaza Cardenal Belluga ☎ 96/835-8749 ⊕ www.murciaciudad.com. **Santa Pola** ⊠ Plaza Diputación ☎ 96/669-2276 ⊕ www.santapola.com.

The Balearic Islands

9

Updated by
Jared Lubarsky

PART OF THE PHOENICIAN, Roman, and Byzantine empires before the Moors invaded them in 902, the Balearic Islands—Majorca (Mallorca), Minorca (Menorca), Ibiza, and Formentera—have long been important maritime trading and staging posts. Lying between 80 and 242 km (50 and 150 mi) from Spain's Mediterranean coast, they are halfway between France and Africa. Beaches, of course, are a major attraction here.

Between 1229 and 1235, the Moors were ousted by Jaume I of the House of Aragón. The islands were part of the independent kingdom of Majorca (which included Roussillon and the Cerdanya Valley on the mainland) from 1276 until 1343, when they returned to the Crown of Aragón under Pedro IV. Upon the marriage of Isabella of Castile to Ferdinand of Aragón in 1469, the Balearics became part of a united Spain. During the War of the Spanish Succession, Great Britain occupied Minorca in 1704 to secure the superb natural harbor of Mahón as a naval base. The British stayed for almost a century, interrupted only by an invasion in 1756, which gave the French control for 12 years, and a shorter reoccupation by the Spanish 20 years later. Under the Treaty of Amiens, Britain finally returned Minorca to Spain in 1802.

Minorca diverged once more during the Spanish civil war, remaining loyal to Spain's democratically elected Republican government while Majorca and Ibiza sided with Franco's insurgents. Majorca became a home base for the Italian fleet supporting the fascist cause. This topic is still broached delicately on the islands; they remain fiercely independent of one another in many ways. Even Mahón and Ciutadella, at opposite ends of Minorca—all of 44 km (27 mi) apart—remain locked in bitter opposition over differences dating from the war with Britain.

The tourist boom, which began during Francisco Franco's regime (1939–75), turned great stretches of Majorca's and Ibiza's coastlines into strips of high-rise hotels, fast-food restaurants, and discos.

In 1983 the Balearics became an Autonomous Community. One result has been the replacement of Castilian Spanish by the Catalan language (banned for official use by Franco) in its Mallorquín, Menorquín, and Ibizencan dialects. This can be confusing, because outside the islands you can still hear island locations named in Spanish. Within the islands, the problem is compounded by road signs that have not been officially altered and are often obliterated by spray paint. This guide uses Catalan or Spanish according to whichever is used locally. *Avinguda* (avenue), *carrer* (street), and *plaça* (square) are Catalan; *avenida, calle,* and *plaza* are Spanish. Note that *cala* is the local word for "cove" or "inlet."

Exploring the Balearic Islands

Of the four main islands, Majorca and Ibiza are the most heavily developed. Formentera has relatively little tourism outside the summer months; much of Minorca, the favorite destination of mainland Catalan visitors, is still farm- and pastureland, but with more and more vacation homes rising every year. The north coast of Majorca and parts of Ibiza have spectacular rocky coastlines, protected areas, and wonderfully clear waters. In general, go to Formentera for solitude and in-

GREAT ITINERARIES

IF YOU HAVE 3 DAYS

Fly to 🚉 **Palma de Mallorca ❶** and spend that day and the next morning exploring the historic city center. The next day, head for the hills—specifically the Sierra de Tramuntana, on the island's north coast—and see the Raixa palace on your way to the **Jardins d'Alfàbia ❷**, **Sóller ❸**, **Deià ❹** (where the English writer and poet Robert Graves lived during much of the 20th century), the **Son Marroig ❺** estate, and the spectacular Sa Foradada rock peninsula. Spend the night in 🚉 **Valldemossa ❻**, and visit the church, pharmacy, and museum at the Royal Carthusian Monastery the next morning. Then, for the remainder of your third day, finish exploring the Tramuntana mountains: see the open-air Majorcan countryside museum at **Sa Granja** and hike down into the **Torrent de Pareis ⓭** ravine and beach. Visit the monastery at

Lluc ⓬ before exploring the town and the port of **Pollença ⓫**. Make the Roman and Moorish ruins at **Alcúdia ❿** your last stop before the 40-minute drive back to Palma for your last night.

IF YOU HAVE 5 DAYS

You can either do the Majorca loop from Palma (along the north coast and back through the center), with more time to settle in and explore, *or* devote your trip to Minorca, a good fit for a five-day visit. Spend your first day exploring 🚉 **Mahón ⓳**. On Day 2, visit the megalithic ruins at **Torre d'en Gaumés** and **Torralba,** on your way to Es Mercadal and Minorca's highest point, **Monte Toro ㉑**. Have dinner in Fornells or Mercadal. On Day 3, take in the beaches at Fornells and Cap de Cavalleria before heading to 🚉 **Ciutadella ⓴**. Dedicate your last two days to explorations of the city and its environs.

9

timacy; Ibiza for wilderness with heavy concentrations of humanity; Majorca for Palma's history and culture, and wild north coast; and Minorca for what may be the best blend of all of the above.

About the Beaches

MAJORCA The closer a beach is to Palma, the more crowded it's likely to be. West of the city, the lovely, narrow beach of Palma Nova/Magalluf is backed by one of the noisiest resorts on the Mediterranean. Paguera, with several small beaches, is the only sizable local resort not overshadowed by high-rises. Camp de Mar, with a good beach of fine white sand, is small and relatively undeveloped but is sometimes overrun with day-trippers from other resorts. Sant Telm, at the end of this coast, has a pretty little bay and a tree-shaded parking lot. East of Palma, a 5-km (3-mi) stretch of sand runs along the main coastal road from C'an Pastilla to Arenal, forming a package-tour nexus also known collectively as Playa de Palma. The crowded beach is long with fine white sand.

On the northwest coast, there's a popular beach at Port de Sóller. Farther north, the lovely Sa Calobra beach, with its fine white sand and quiet cove, draws lots of day-visitors in the summer. Moderately developed Cala St. Vicenç has fine, soft sand in two narrow bays. At Port de Pollença, on the north coast, the sand is imported, but the resort is attractive and has good water sports. There's frequent water-taxi service from Port de Pollença to Formentor, one of the finest beaches on Majorca. The north coast also has the island's longest sand beach; it stretches 8 km (5 mi) from Port de Alcúdia to beyond C'an Picafort. Ses Casetes, near Port des Pins, is the best stretch.

Majorca's Levante, or southeast coast, is peppered with beaches and coves, though few are easily reachable by car. Canyamel, near the Caves of Artà, is a large, undeveloped strand. Farther south, Costa d'es Pins is an extensive, expensive urbanization, but it has a good sandy stretch backed by a thin line of pines. Tourist buses, which look like train engines, run from here to Cala Millor, where the beach is accessible only on foot. Farther south, Cala d'Or is a pleasant resort, and Cala Gran, a short walk away, is even more attractive. Cala Mondrajó is a tiny, sandy bay with little development; it's most easily reached by boat from Portopetre or Cala Figuera. On the south coast, the dune-backed beach at Es Trenc, near Colònia de Sant Jordi, is a quiet seaside patch. The 10-km (6-mi) walk along the beach from Colònia de Sant Jordi to the Cap Salines lighthouse is one of Majorca's treasures.

MINORCA   Cala Mesquida, north of Mahón, is popular with the Mahonese; you'll see few tourists here. Another small beach, also development-free, lies on a headland beyond one of Minorca's many watchtowers. Farther west, Es Grau, a sandy stretch with dunes behind it, is a bit littered. Behind Es Grau is the S'Albufera nature reserve. Before the lighthouse at the end of Cap Faváritx are the nudist beaches Cala Presili and Playa Tortuga. Arenal d'en Castell, a sheltered circular bay, and Arenal de Son Saura (Son Parc) are the north's biggest sandy beaches. At the junction of the Mahón–Fornells and Mercadal–Fornells roads, take the small lane leading west and follow signs to Binimellà, an excellent sandy beach. It's often deserted, and the caves in the tiny coves to the west provide welcome shade in the summer.

The only reasonable and generally accessible beach north of Ciutadella is Cala Morell. Minorcans claim that the inlets and beaches at Cala Algaiarens are the nicest on the island. Son Saura, Cala en Turqueta, Macarella, and Cala Galdana at the west end of the south coast are all

---

JARED'S TOP 5

- Driving along the rugged coast of Majorca's Tramuntana from Valldemossa to Soller, by way of Deià and Son Marroig.
- Taking tea on the terrace at the Gran Hotel Son Net, in Puigpunyent, with its lovely view of the Mallorcan countryside.
- Getting really pampered, with a full-course, no-holds-barred wellness session in the spa at Agroturismo Atzaró in Ibiza.
- Enjoying a meal of *caldereta de langosta* (spiny lobster stew) at a waterfront restaurant on Minorca.
- Walking through the woods to the (still relatively) isolated little crescent of beach at Cala'n Turqueda, on Minorca's south coast, for a morning swim.

IF YOU LIKE

MAJORCA FIESTAS

Sant Joan Pelós is celebrated June 23–24 in Felanitx; a man dressed in sheepskins represents John the Baptist. The **Romería de Sant Marçal** (Pilgrimage of St. Mark), held June 30 in Sa Cabaneta, involves primitive ceramic whistles.

MINORCA FIESTAS

Ciutadella's feast of **Sant Joan** (June 23–24) has townspeople dancing on horseback, trying to keep the horses up on their hind legs while the crowd gathers beneath. **Sant Lluís**, at the end of August, spotlights equestrian activities; Mahón's **Fiestas de Gràcia** (September 7–8) are the season's final celebrations.

IBIZA FIESTAS

Ibiza's patron saint, **Mare de Déu dels Neus** (Our Lady of the Snows), is honored on August 8 in memory of the conquest of Ibiza. **Sant Antoni d'Abat** (January 17) has processions of pets, cavalry, and livestock. On February 12 the **Festes de Santa Eulalia** is a boisterous winter carnival with folk dancing and live music. **Sant Josep** (March 19) is known for folk dancing, which you can also see in Sant Joan every Thursday evening. On June 23–24, witness the islandwide **Festa Major de Sant Joan** (Feast of St. John the Baptist). The **Festa del Mar**, honoring the Mare de Déu del Carme (Our Lady of Carmen), is held July 15–16 in Eivissa, Santa Eulalia, Sant Antoni, and Sant Josep, and on Formentera.

FORMENTERA FIESTAS

On July 15–16 islanders honor the **Virgen del Carmen**, patron saint of sailors, with processions of boats and anything else that floats. On July 25, Sant Francesc dances in honor of **Sant Jaume** (St. James), Spain's male patron saint.

reached by driving southeast from Ciutadella toward Son Saura. All three are classic Minorcan beaches with trees down to the water's edge, horseshoe coves, and white sand. To the east, Cala Mitjana, Cala Trebaluger, Cala Fustam, and Cala Escorxada are accessible on land only by foot, but you can rent boats with outboard engines to reach them or Son Saura. You can get to the long, straight, sandy stretches of Binigaus, Sant Adeodato, and Santo Tomas from Mercadal, and to Son Bou, the island's longest beach (with a nudist section), from Alaior. Cala'n Porter is a British enclave sheltered by cliffs. On the southeastern tip of the island is the windswept, white-sand beach at Punta Prima.

IBIZA Immediately south of Ibiza Town is a long, sandy beach, the nearly 3-km (2-mi) Playa d'en Bossa, almost entirely developed. Farther on, a left turn at Sant Jordi on the way to the airport leads across the salt pans to Cavallet and Ses Salines, two of the most natural beaches on the island. Topless bathing is accepted all over Ibiza, but Es Cavallet is the official nudist beach. The remaining beaches on this part of the island are accessible from the Ibiza–Sant Josep–Sant Antoni highway, down side roads that often end in rough tracks. North of Sant Antoni, there are no easily accessible beaches until you reach Puerto San Miguel, an almost rectangular cove with relatively restrained development. Next along the north coast, accessible via San Juan, is Portinatx, a series of small coves with sandy beaches, of which the first and last, Cala Xarraca and Caló d'Es Porcs, are the best. East of San Juan is the long, curved cove beach of Cala San Vicente. Popular with families, it has a more leisurely pace than Ibiza's other resorts. The beaches on the east coast have been developed, but Santa Eulalia remains attractive. The resort has a narrow, sloping beach in front of a pedestrian promenade that is much less frenetic than Sant Antoni.

FORMENTERA Wild and lonely beaches are the rule on Formentera. The undeveloped Playa de Mitjorn stretches for 7 km (4 mi) along the south of the island. Trucadors, a long, thin spit at the north, has 2 km (1 mi) of sand on each side, and in summer you can wade to Es Palmador, where you can find more sandy beaches and a preponderance of nude bathers.

About the Restaurants

MAJORCA Seafood forms the basis of many local specialties, such as *espinigada* (a pie topped with tiny eels and spinach) and *panades de peix* (fish pies). Lamb, chicken, pork, and their derivatives are also traditional. *Sobrasada*, the bright-red Majorcan sausage paste, is basically pork and red pepper, and even the fluffy, super-sweet *ensaimada*—a powdery spiral pastry that ranges in size from a breakfast snack to a gift-box party special a foot in diameter—is based on *saim* (pork fat). Other specialties are *butifarra* and *llonganissa* sausages, *coques amb verdura* and *trampó* (pizzalike pastries covered with vegetables or finely chopped salad), and *cocarrois* (pastries filled with meat or a mixture of vegetables). *Sopa mallorquina* is a meal of fried vegetables in meat stock, usually served over pieces of thinly sliced bread. *Escaldum* is a stew of chicken legs with potatoes and ground almonds; *tumbet* is a stew of meat or fish with peppers, tomatoes, potatoes, and eggplant.

Artà, Benissalem, Felanitx, and Inca are all wine-making areas. Majorca also makes sweet or dry herb liquors.

MINORCA Minorcan restaurant fare used to consist almost entirely of seafood and was served mainly along the harbors in Mahón, Ciutadella, and the fishing village of Fornells, famous for its very expensive *llagosta* (lobster), sold by weight and grilled or served as *caldereta* (soup). A country influence has also developed, based on inland and upland products such as rabbit, pork, and other meats often made into stews and roasts. Mayonnaise—which was invented in Minorca during the French occupation and named after Mahón—is usually freshly prepared. Local tapas include *tornellas*—sheep's intestines stuffed with bread crumbs, garlic, and meat, then braided and cooked. Mahón cows' cheese on Minorca has been made since 3000 BC, and the best handcrafted Mahón cheeses have a *Denominación de Origen* label. The *curado*, fully cured, is the best. The British occupation left a tradition for making excellent, aromatic *ginebra* (gin).

IBIZA & Because much produce comes to Ibiza and Formentera from mainland
FORMENTERA Spain via Palma, the cost of dining is high, especially in such simple surroundings. Many local products, however, such as potatoes and the na-

tive sea bass and bream, are prized for their distinctive taste. You can find authentic Balearic specialties inland, off the tourist track; look for *sofrit pagès* (potatoes and red peppers stewed in olive oil and garlic) and *ratjada eivissenca* (grilled, semipoached ray).

WHAT IT COSTS In Euros					
	$$$$	**$$$**	**$$**	**$**	**¢**
AT DINNER	over €20	€15–€20	€10–€15	€6–€10	under €6

Prices are per person for a main course at dinner.

About the Hotels

Many hotels on the islands include a continental or full buffet breakfast in the price of a room.

MAJORCA Majorca's newer resorts—more than 1,500 of them—are concentrated mainly on the southern coast, and mainly serve the package-tour industry. Perhaps the best accommodations on the island are the number of grand old country estates and town houses that have been converted into boutique hotels, ranging from simple and relatively inexpensive *agroturismos* to stunning outposts of luxury.

MINORCA Apart from a few hotels and hostels in Mahón and Ciutadella, almost all of Minorca's tourist lodgings are in beach resorts. As on the other islands, many of these are fully reserved by travel operators in the high season and often require a week's minimum stay, so it's generally most economical to book a package that combines airfare and accommodations. Alternatively, inquire at the tourist office about boutique and country hotels, especially in and around Sant Lluis.

IBIZA Ibiza's hotels are mainly in coastal Sant Antoni and Playa d'en Bossa. Many of these are excellent, but unless you're eager to be part of a mob, Sant Antoni has little to recommend it. Playa d'en Bossa, close to the town of Ibiza, is less brash, but it lies under the flight path to the airport. To get off the track and into the island's largely pristine interior, look for *agroturismo* lodgings in Els Amunts (The Uplands) and in villages such as Santa Gertrudis or Sant Miquel de Balanzat.

FORMENTERA If July and August are the only months you can visit, reserve well in advance. To get the true feel of this smallest major member of the archipelago, look for the most out-of-the-way calas and fishing villages.

WHAT IT COSTS In Euros					
	$$$$	**$$$**	**$$**	**$**	**¢**
FOR 2 PEOPLE	over €180	€100–€180	€60–€100	€40–€60	under €40

Prices are for two people in a standard double room in high season, excluding tax.

Timing

Summer is hot and crowded. May and October are ideal, with June and September just behind. Winter (November–March) is quiet, sometimes too cold for the beach, but fine for hiking, golfing, and exploring. Be aware that between November and February many hotels, restaurants, and other facilities—especially on Minorca and Formentera—are closed for their own holidays or for seasonal repairs.

MAJORCA

More than five times the size of either Minorca or Ibiza, Majorca is shaped roughly like a saddle. The Sierra de Tramuntana, a dramatic mountain range soaring to nearly 5,000 feet, runs the length of its northwest coast, and a ridge of hills borders the southeast shores; between the two lies a great, flat plain that in early spring becomes a sea of almond blossoms, "the snow of Majorca." The island draws more than 10 million visitors a year—Palma's international airport is bigger than Barcelona's—the largest numbers of them bound for summer vacation packages in the coastal resorts. Elsewhere, Majorca has relatively undiscovered charms, particularly in the mountains of the northwest and in the interior: caves, bird sanctuaries, abandoned monasteries, tiny museums, outdoor cafés, and village markets form a good mixture of sights.

Numbers in the text correspond to numbers in the margin and on the Majorca, the Minorca, and the Ibiza & Formentera maps.

Palma de Mallorca

❶ *40-min flight from Barcelona.*

If you look north of the cathedral (La Seu, or the "seat" of the Bishopric, to Majorcans) on a map of the city of Palma, you can see around the Plaça Santa Eulalia the jumble of tiny streets that made up the early town. Farther out, a ring of wide boulevards, known as the Avenues, zigzags around—these follow the path of the walls built by the Moors to defend the larger city that had grown up by the 12th century. The zigzags mark the bastions that jutted out at regular intervals. By the end of the 19th century the walls were largely torn down; the only place where you can still see the massive defenses is Ses Voltes, along the seafront west of the cathedral.

A streambed (*torrent*) used to run through the middle of the old city, dry for most of the year but often a raging flood in the rainy season, causing destruction and drowning. In the 17th century it was diverted to the east, along the moat that ran outside the city walls. The stream's natural course is now followed by La Rambla and the Passeig d'es Born, two of Palma's main arteries. The traditional evening *paseo* (promenade) takes place on the Born.

If you come to Palma by car, park in the garage beneath the Parc de la Mar and stroll along the park. Beside it run the huge bastions guarding the Almudaina Palace; the cathedral, golden and massive, rises beyond. The park has several **ceramic murals** by the late Catalan artist and Majorca resident Joan Miró, as well as various modern **sculptures.**

If you begin early enough, a walk along the ramparts at Ses Voltes from the **mirador** (lookout) beside the Palma cathedral is spectacular. The first rays of the sun turn the upper pinnacles of La Seu bright gold and begin

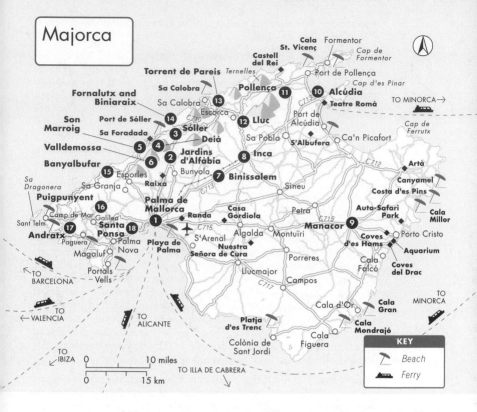

Majorca

Cala St. Vicenç · Formentor
Cap de Formentor
Castell del Rei
Torrent de Pareis · Ternelles
Port de Pollença
Sa Calobra · Pollença · 11 · 10 · Alcúdia
Fornalutx and Biniaraix · Sa Calobra · 13 · C713 · Teatre Romà · TO MINORCA →
Escorca · Cap d'es Pinar
Son Marroig · Port de Sóller · 14 · C710 · 12 · Lluc · Port de Alcúdia
Sa Foradada · 3 · Sóller · Sa Pobla · Cap de Ferrutx
Valldemossa · 5 · 4 · Deià · S'Albufera · Ca'n Picafort
Banyalbufar · 6 · 2 · Jardins d'Alfàbia · 8 · Inca · Artà
Sa Dragonera · 15 · Esporles · Bunyola · Canyamel
Puigpunyent · Sa Granja · Raixa · 7 · Binissalem · Sineu · Costa d'es Pins
Camp de Mar · Galilea · 16 · Palma de Mallorca · Petra · Auto-Safari Park · Cala Millor
Sant Telm · Santa Ponsa · 1 · Randa · Casa Gordiola · Manacor · 9 · Porto Cristo
Andratx · 17 · 18 · S'Arenal · Algalda · Montuïri · Coves d'es Hams · Aquarium
Paguera · Palma Nova · Playa de Palma · Nuestra Señora de Cura · Porreres · Cala Falcó · Coves del Drac
Magaluf · Llucmajor · Campos
Portals Vells
TO BARCELONA
TO VALENCIA
TO ALICANTE
Cala d'Or · Cala Gran · TO MINORCA
Platja d'es Trenc · Cala Mondrajó
Colònia de Sant Jordi · Cala Figuera
TO IBIZA · 0 · 10 miles · 0 · 15 km · TO ILLA DE CABRERA

KEY
Beach
Ferry

to work their way down the sandstone walls. From the Parc de la Mar, follow Avinguda Antoni Maura past the steps to the palace. Just below the Plaça de la Reina, where the **Passeig d'es Born** begins, turn left on Carrer de la Boteria into the Plaça de la Llotja (don't miss a chance to visit the Llotja itself, the Mediterranean's finest civic Gothic building, if it's open), and stroll from there through the Plaça Drassana to the **Museu d'Es Baluard,** at the end of Carrer Sant Pere.

Retrace your steps to Avinguda Antoni Maura. Walk up the Passeig d'es Born to Plaça Joan Carles I, then left on Avenida de La Unió and up Carrer de Sant Joan. About 110 yards west of the Plaça Joan Carles I, on the Plaça del Mercat, is **San Nicolau** (⊠ Plaça del Mercat), a 14th-century church with a hexagonal bell tower. The ornate facades of the **Casas Casasayas** (⊠ Plaça del Mercat, 13, 14), on opposite corners of Carrer Santa Cilia, were designed by Moderniste architect Francesc Roca Simó in 1908; the ground floors are occupied by a bank and a boutique. Brilliant examples of the Moderniste style as they are, the Casas Casasayas are outshone by the **Gran Hotel,** across the square (⊠ Plaça Weyler 3), built between 1901 and 1903 by Luis Domènech i Montaner, author of Barcelona's Palau de la Música Catalana. The alabaster facade of the building is sculpted like a wedding cake, with floral motifs, angelic heads, and coats of arms; the original interiors, alas, have been "refurbished." Don't miss the permanent exhibit of Majorcan impressionist Anglada Camarassa.

Take time to appreciate the neoclassical symmetry of the **Teatre Principal** (✉ Top of the Plaça Weyler), under renovation until 2007. Near the steps leading up to the right of the Teatre Principal is the **Forn des Teatre** (✉ Plaça Weyler 12), a unique bakery known for its *ensaimadas* (a typically Spanish fluffy pastry) and *cocas* (meat pies). From the Forn des Teatre, climb the steps to the **Plaça Major**. A crafts market fills this elegant neoclassical square on Monday, Friday, and Saturday between 10 and 2. A flight of steps on the east side of the Plaça Major leads down to the **Rambla**, a pleasant promenade lined with flower stalls.

Walk south from the Plaça Major on Carrer Colom, and above the Cacao Sampaka chocolate shop on the right, at the next small square, contemplate another Art Nouveau delight: the **Can Forteza Rei** (✉ Plaça Marqués Palmer 1), designed by the original owner, Luis Forteza Rei, in 1909. The building has twisted wrought-iron railings and surfaces inlaid with bits of polychrome tile, signature touches of Gaudí and his contemporaries. A wonderful carved stone face, in a painful grimace, flanked by dragons, ironically frames the stained-glass windows of a third-floor dental clinic. Carrer Colom brings you to the 17th-century **Ajuntament** (Town hall; ✉ Plaça Cort); stop in to see the collection of *gigantes*—the huge painted and costumed mannequins paraded through the streets at festivals—on display in the lobby. The olive tree on the right side of the square is one of Majorca's so-called *olivos milenarios*—thousand-year-old olives—and may be even older.

West from the Ajuntament, a few steps along the Carrer de la Cadena bring you to the imposing Gothic church of **Santa Eulalia**. During his wild youth, the eminent 13th-century scholar Ramón Llull allegedly rode his horse into this church, in pursuit of a married noblewoman with whom he'd fallen in love. In 1435, 200 Jews were converted to Christianity in this church after their rabbis were threatened with being burned at the stake. ✉ *Plaça Santa Eulalia, Barrio Antiguo.*

From the Plaça de Sant Eulalia, take the Carrer del Convent de Sant Francesc to the beautiful 13th-century monastery church of **Sant Francesc,** established by Jaume II when his eldest son took monastic orders and gave up rights to the throne. Fra Junípero Serra, the missionary who founded San Francisco, California, was later educated here; his statue stands to the left of the main entrance. The basilica houses the tomb of Ramón Llull. Enter the church and cloisters through the collegiate buildings on the east side. ✉ *Plaça Sant Francesc, Barrio Antiguo* ☉ *Mon.–Sat. 9:30–1 and 3:30–6* ✉ *€1.*

NEED A BREAK?

When you're ready to sink your teeth into an ensaimada, head for the soothing Ca'n Joan de S'aigo, on a hard-to-find side street behind the church of Sant Francesc (✉ C. de C'an Sanç 10, Barrio Antiguo ☎ 971/710759 ☉ open Mon. and Wed.–Fri. 8–9, Sat. 8–9:15). Founded in 1700, this café-confectionery has been serving sweets longer than anyone on the island.

From the Plaça Sant Francesc, take Carrer Pere Nadal south toward the bay; the street changes names as it descends, crossing Carrer del Call (in many Spanish cities and towns, the term *call* indicates the site of the medieval Jewish quarter) to become Carrer Santa Clara, then Carrer de Can Pont i Vic. On the left as it turns to Carrer de la Portella is the **Museu de Mallorca.** Housed in the 18th-century ducal palace of the Condes de Ayamans, the museum displays Moorish art and some prehistoric bronze objects culled from local archaeological digs. ✉ *Portella 5, Barrio Antiguo* ☎ *971/717540* 🖃 *Weekdays €2.40, weekends free* ⊙ *Tues.–Sat. 10–7, Sun. 10–2; under renovations at time of this writing.*

From the Museu de Mallorca, walk down Carrer de la Portella and turn left before the archway at the bottom of the street; follow the signs to one of Palma's oldest monuments, the 10th-century **Banys Arabs** (Arab Baths), in a wonderful walled garden of tall palms, palmettos, and lemon trees. In its day, it was not merely a public bathhouse but a social institution, an oasis where you could soak your cares away at the end of the day and gossip with your neighbors. ✉ *Serra 7, Barrio Antiguo* ☎ *971/721549* 🖃 *€1.50* ⊙ *Dec.–Mar., daily 9–6; Apr.–Nov., daily 9–7:30.*

Fodor's Choice ★ Palma's **cathedral** is an architectural wonder that took almost 400 years to build (1230–1601). It can be approached by turning left from the top of Carrer de Can Serra and following the meandering streets west to the Plaça Almoina, where there's a cluster of antiques shops and re-

> **WORD OF MOUTH**
>
> "Palma is great, and (the) villages in Sierra Tramuntana are charming." -elina.

storers. The extraordinarily wide (63-foot) expanse of the nave is supported on 14 extraordinarily slender 70-foot-tall columns, which fan out at the top like palm trees. The nave is dominated by an immense rose window, 40 feet in diameter, from 1370. Look up into the nave: suspended above the Royal Chapel is the curious **asymmetrical canopy** built by Antoni Gaudí, who remodeled the chapel in the early 1900s. Lights within the canopy come on at regular intervals. The **bell tower** above the cathedral's Plaça Almoina door holds nine bells, the largest of which is known as N'Eloi, meaning "praise." N'Eloi was cast in 1389, weighs 5½ tons, needs six men to ring it, and has shattered stained-glass windows with its sound. Continue around the cathedral to see the **west facade,** whose blocked windows are the result of alterations after earthquake damage in 1851. ✉*Pl. Almoina s/n, Barrio Antiguo* ☎*971/723130* 🖃 *€3.50* ⊙ *Apr., May, and Oct., weekdays 10–5, Sat. 10–2; June–Sept., weekdays 10–6, Sat. 10–2; Nov.–Mar., weekdays 10–3, Sat. 10–2.*

Opposite Palma's cathedral is the **Palau de l'Almudaina** (Almudaina Palace), residence of the royal house of Majorca during the Middle Ages and originally an Arab citadel. It's now a military headquarters. Guided tours generally depart hourly during open hours. ✉ *Carrer Palau Reial s/n, Barrio Antiguo* ☎ *971/214134* 🖃 *€3.20; €4 with a guided tour; European Union citizens free Wed.* ⊙ *Weekdays 10–2 and 4–6, Sat. 10–2.*

The **Llotja** (Exchange), on the seafront west of the Plaça de la Reina, was built in the 15th century and is connected by an interior courtyard to the **Consolat de Mar** (Maritime Consulate). With its decorative turrets, battlements, fluted pillars, and Gothic stained-glass windows—part fortress, part church—it attests to the veneration of wealth Majorca achieved in its heyday as a Mediterranean trading power. It can be visited inside only when there are special exhibitions in the Merchants Chamber. ✉ *Pl. de la Llotja, La Llotja* ☎ *971/711705* ◷ *During exhibits, Tues.–Sat. 11–2 and 5–9, Sun. 11–2.*

★ Inaugurated in January 2004, the **Museu d'Es Baluard** (Museum of Modern and Contemporary Art of Palma) rises on a long-neglected archaeological site at the western end of the city, parts of which date back to the 12th century. The building itself is an outstanding convergence of old and new: the exhibition space uses and merges into the surviving 16th-century perimeter walls of the fortified city, with a stone courtyard facing the sea and a promenade along the ramparts. There are three floors of galleries; the collection includes work by Miró, Picasso, Magritte, Tapiès, Calder, and other major artists The café-terrace Restaurant del Museu (Tues.–Sat. 1–4, 8–11), in the courtyard, affords a fine view of the marina. ✉ *Plaça Porta de Santa Catalina 10 Puig Sant Pere* ☎ *971/ 908200* ⊕ *www.esbaluard.org* ▣ *€6* ◷ *Oct.–May, Tues.–Sun. 10–8; June–Sept., Tues.–Sun. 10 AM–11 PM.*

The **Castell de Bellver** (Bellver Castle) overlooks the city and the bay from a hillside above the Terreno nightlife area. Built in the 14th century on a circular design, it's a sturdy fortress complete with dry moat and drawbridge. Within the walls is a fascinating **museum** that chronicles the history of Mallorca and of the castle. Archaeological finds from around the island include Roman and Moorish pottery, coins, and jewelry. ✉ *Camilo José Cela s/n* ☎ *971/730657* ▣ *€2* ◷ *Oct.–Mar., Mon.–Sat. 8–7:15; Apr.–Sept., Mon.–Sat. 8–8:30.*

The **Museu Fundació Pilar y Joan Miró** (Pilar and Joan Miró Foundation Museum) has many works by the Catalan artist, who spent his last years on Majorca (1979–83). The museum is 3 km (2 mi) west of the city center, off the Passeig Marítim. ✉ *Carrer Joan de Saridakis 29, Cala Major, Marivent* ☎ *971/701420* ⊕ *www.a-palma.es/fpjmiro* ▣ *€5* ◷ *Mid-Sept.–mid-May., Tues.–Sat. 10–6, Sun. 10–3; mid-May–mid-Sept., Tues.–Sat. 10–7, Sun. 10–3.*

The **Poble Espanyol** (Spanish Village), in Palma's western suburbs, is a reproduction of Spanish buildings, complete with shops and studios. It's based on the much larger and perennially popular Poble Espanyol in Barcelona. ✉ *Carrer Poble Espanyol s/n, Poble Espanyol* ☎ *971/ 737075* ▣ *€5* ◷ *Apr.–Sept., village daily 9–7, crafts shops daily 9–6, some closed Sun.; Oct.–May, village daily 9–6, some crafts shops close at 5 or earlier, closed on Sun.*

OFF THE BEATEN PATH

ILLA DE CABRERA – Off the south coast of Majorca lies one of the last unspoiled verdant slivers in the Mediterranean—the Illa de Cabrera, largest of the 19 islands and islets that make up the Cabrera archipelago. Determined to protect it, local environmental activists succeeded in 1991 in having the archipelago, with its dramatic landscape, wildlife, and lush vegetation, declared a national park.

Throughout its history, Cabrera has had its share of visitors, from the Romans to the Arabs. Today, the only intact historical remains are those of a 14th-century castle overlooking the harbor. You can hike trails that meander through the island: a steep trek leads to the castle, where you're rewarded with views of the Mediterranean. Several tour boats make day trips to the island (usually only between April and October), including **Excursiones a Cabrera** (☎ 971/649034 ⊕ www. excursionsacabrera.com). Boats generally depart from Colònia de Sant Jordi, 47 km (29 mi) southeast of Palma, around 9:30 AM, returning at 6 PM; tickets are €29, with lunch provided for an additional cost. Boat companies and departure times vary from year to year, so inquire at any of the Palma tourist offices for current information. If you have your own boat, you are required to get written permission to visit the island from the **Oficina de Parque Nacional** (National Park Office; ⊠ Plaza de España 8, Palma ☎ 971/725010 ⊙ Weekdays 9–2)

Where to Stay & Eat

$$–$$$$ ✕ **Koldo Royo.** Crowded with modern art, this chic yellow dining room overlooks the marina through glass walls. Chef-owner Koldo Royo conjures up Basque specialties such as lamprey eel, salt cod, tripe, and stuffed quail; try the *cochinillo confitado con salsa de miel* (roast suckling pig with honey sauce) or the *merluza con risotto del calamar* (grilled hake with risotto in black squid ink). ⊠ *Av. Gabriel Roca 3, Paseo Marítimo* ☎ *971/732435* ⊟ *AE, MC, V* ⊙ *Closed Sun. and Mon.*

$–$$ ✕ **La Bóveda.** Within hailing distance of the Llotja, with a huge front window, this bustling, popular eatery serves tapas and inexpensive platters such as chicken or ham croquettes, grilled cod topped with tomato sauce, garlic shrimp, and *revuelto con setas y jamón* (scrambled eggs with mushrooms and ham). Tables are at a premium; there's additional seating at the counter, or on stools around upended wine barrels. Nothing fancy here: just ample portions of good food. ⊠ *Carrer de la Botería 3, La Llotja* ☎ *971/714863* ⊟ *AE, MC, V* ⊙ *Closed Sun.*

$$$$ ✕🏠 **Castillo Hotel Son Vida.** Emerging in March 2006 after a year of renovations and a €30 million investment, the Castillo still reigns as Majorca's only grand hotel, with room rates to match. The original building—a turreted 13th-century *possession* (country estate)—now has a five-story atrium lobby with a stained-glass cupola inspired by the cosmology of Ramón Llull; a vast terrace looks out over the whole of Palma and the bay. Public spaces are hung with tapestries and antique portraits from the owner's private collection; even the most basic double rooms have love seats upholstered in pale gold brocade, marble bathtubs, and huge flat-screen TVs that disappear silently into mahogany sideboards at the touch of a button. The hotel's ultra-elegant Es Vi features French and Mediterranean dishes, and a wine list with bottles that will set you back more than the price of a small car. ⊠ *Carrer Raixa 2, Son Vida, 07013* ☎ *971/493493* 🖶 *971/493494* ⊕ *www.hotelsonvida. com* ⇆ *152 rooms, 12 suites* ⚫ *2 restaurants, in-room safes, minibars, cable TV, in-room DVD, in-room data ports, 3 18-hole golf courses, 4*

9

tennis courts, 3 pools (1 indoor), health club, hair salon, 3 bars, library, playground, some pets allowed ☰ AE, DC, MC, V ❁ BP.

$$$$ ✕☒ **Convent de la Missió.** Acquiring part of a 17th-century convent and converting it to a modern hotel posed a major design challenge—but it was solved brilliantly. With so many rules of historical preservation to observe, the owners opted for a Zen-like simplicity of decor that respects and even enhances the character of the building. The lobby, accented by a fireplace, leads back to an art gallery with a vaulted stone ceiling, originally the refectory of the convent, and from there to the elegant Refectori restaurant. Rooms have bed canopies and deep-pile white shag rugs on hardwood floors; the sundeck has a white-stone Japanese garden. ⊠ Carrer de la Missió 7A Barrio Antiguo, 07003 ☎ 971/227347 ☐ 971/227348 ⊕ www.conventdelamissio.com ⇶ 11 rooms, 3 suites ⚖ Restaurant, in-room safes, minibars, cable TV, in-room data ports, sauna, bar, meeting room ☰ AE, DC, MC, V ❁ BP.

★ $$$$ ✕☒ **Read's Hotel.** A 15-minute drive from Palma, this peaceful retreat occupies part of an 18th-century country house, on a 10-acre finca (farm). It has spacious rooms, large gardens, and a superb restaurant with 17th-century-style murals. Chef Marc Fosh, considered one of the best in Spain, presents a menu of light French–Mediterranean cuisine with vegetable- and herb-infused sauces and broths. Try the sea bass drizzled in a parsley-and-anise sauce. ⊠ Ctra. Santa María–Alaró s/n, 07320 ☎ 971/140261 ☐ 971/140762 ⊕ www.readshotel.com ⇶ 8 rooms, 15 suites ⚖ Restaurant, in-room safes, cable TV, in-room DVD, Wi-Fi, tennis court, 2 pools (1 indoor), spa, bicycles, horseback riding, bar, library, meeting rooms ☰ AE, DC, MC, V ❁ BP.

$$$$ ☒ **Maricel.** A colonnade of marble arches runs the full length of the lobby, offering a stunning view out over the terrace to the sea. Stone staircases descend to the pool and cabanas, then to a private jetty. Rooms are a bit small, but sumptuously furnished with leather armchairs, mahogany side tables, and big claw-foot tubs in the bathrooms. Room service is round the clock. There are jazz concerts in the bar on Thursday, with a deli service of champagne, caviar, and oysters. Chef Juan Partillo serves a seven-course "tasting menu" breakfast (€30) to die for. During high season, there is a four-night minimum stay. It's about a 10-minute drive from Palma. ⊠ Carretera d'Andratx 11 C'As Català Calvìa, 07181 ☎ 971/707744 ☐ 971/707745 ⊕ www.hospes.es ⇶ 24 rooms, 5 suites ⚖ Restaurant, in-room safes, minibars, cable TV, in-room DVD, in-room data ports, pool, massage, 2 bars, meeting room; no children under 12 June–Sept. ☰ AE, DC, MC, V.

★ $$$–$$$$ ☒ **Palau Sa Font.** Warm Mediterranean tones and crisp, clean lines give this boutique hotel an atmosphere very different from anything else in Palma. A 16th-century Episcopal palace (the bishop's residence), restored as a hotel in 2000, it has ample rooms with linen curtains and plump comforters. The light, airy breakfast room has chairs in pastel yellow, lime green, and orange. From the terrace in the tower, you have 360-degree views of Palma's old quarter. ⊠ Carrer Apuntadores 38, Barrio Antiguo, 07012 ☎ 971/712277 ☐ 971/712618 ⊕ www.palausafont.com ⇶ 19 rooms ⚖ Dining room, minibars, cable TV, bar, some pets allowed ☰ AE, MC, V ❁ BP.

$$$ 🏨 **Dalt Murada.** Dating back to the 15th century, this town house in the old part of Palma was the Sancha Moragues family home until 2001, when, with no real experience in the business, the family opened it as a hotel. Most of the furniture, paintings, and furnishings were the family's own, handed down for generations, but with modernization came enormous hot tubs in the tile bathrooms. Weather permitting, a basic breakfast is served in the lovely interior garden, overgrown with bougainvillea, orange, and lemon trees. The location, a minutes' walk or so to the cathedral, is ideal. ✉ *Carrer Almudaina 6A Barrio Antiguo, 07001* ☎ *971/425300* 🖷 *971/719708* ⊕ *www.daltmurada.org* ⤳ *8 rooms* ⚇ *In-room safes, minibars, in-room DVD* ▭ *AE, MC, V* ⌾❘ *BP.*

$$–$$$ 🏨 **Born.** Romanesque arches and a giant palm tree spectacularly cover the central courtyard and reception area of this hotel, which occupies the former mansion of a noble Majorcan family. Guest rooms are modest, though some have the original coffered and painted ceilings, but the rates are more than reasonable. A buffet breakfast is included in the price. The Born is on a quiet street off the busy Plaça Rei Juan Carlos. ✉ *Carrer Sant Jaume 3, Centro, 07012* ☎ *971/712942* 🖷 *971/718618* ⊕ *www.hotelborn.com* ⤳ *29 rooms* ⚇ *Cable TV* ▭ *AE, DC, MC, V.*

$ 🏨 **Hostal Apuntadores.** It's easy to see why this is Palma's hostal of choice among budget travelers. It's cheap; the rooftop terrace has arguably the city's best view—overlooking the cathedral and the sea; and it's in the heart of the old town, within strolling distance of the bustling Passeig d'es Born. Rooms are basic (and some are cramped) but clean; ask for a room with a balcony. There is one dormitory-style room that sleeps six. The owners also run the Hostal Terramar near the port, where they often have rooms available if Hostal Apuntadores is full. ✉ *Carrer Apuntadores 8, Barrio Antiguo, 07012* ☎ *971/713491* ⊕ *www.palma-hostales.com* ⤳ *29 rooms, 15 with bath* ⚇ *Cafeteria, Wi-Fi, bar; no room TVs* ▭ *MC, V.*

Nightlife & the Arts

THE ARTS Outside in summer, the City of Palma Symphony Orchestra performs about twice a month at the **Auditorium** (✉ Passeig Marítim 18, Paseo Marítimo ☎ 971/734735 ⊕ www.auditorium-pm.com), which also hosts performances by guest soloists and chamber orchestras, rock concerts, musicals, and plays throughout the year. The neoclassical **Teatre Principal** (✉ Plaça del Hospital 4, Centro ☎ 971/713346 ⊕ www.teatreprincipal.com) is the city's venue for opera, choral music, and drama.

NIGHTLIFE With some 200 discos and music bars scattered throughout the city and across the island, Majorca's nightlife is never hard to find. The most incandescent hot spots are concentrated 6 km (4 mi) west of Palma at **Punta Portals,** in Portals Nous, where King Juan Carlos I often moors his yacht along with many of Europe's most beautiful people. Try the pubs **Flannigan's** (☎ 971/679191) or **Tristan** (the best and most expensive). (☎ 971/675547) **Wellies Pub** (✉ Portals Nous ☎ 971/676444) has great views of the marina and serves upscale pub grub, including juicy burgers, chicken kebabs, and on Friday, fish-and-chips.

In Palma, the section of the Passeig Marítim known as **Avinguda Gabriel Roca** is a nucleus of taverns, pubs, and clubs. The ever-popular night-

9

club **Pacha** (☎ 971/455908) thumps to house music until the wee hours. Once a week (usually Sunday) they host gay night, "Pacha Loca," with an infectious anything-goes vibe; the cover charge can be pricey (€10–20). You could pick a different cocktail every night for a month and still not run out of options at the lively waterfront bar **Tonic** (✉ Passeig Marítim 21 ☎ 971/454468). Outdoor elevators transport you from Avinguda Gabriel Roca to a large, packed-with-foreigners dance floor at the sleek and futuristic **Tito's** (☎ 971/730017).

★ The **Plaça de la Llotja** and surrounding streets are the place to go for *copas* (drinking, tapas sampling, and general carousing). Elegant **Abaco** (✉ Carrer de Sant Joan 1, La Llotja ☎ 971/714939) offers baroque music amid fragrant flowers and fruit.

Carrer Apuntadores (✉ Carrer Apuntadores 3, La Llotja ☎ 971/720817), on the Born's west side in the old town, has casual bars popular with those in their twenties and thirties. On the weekends, you can often come across impromptu live rock and pop acts performed on small back stages. Some of Palma's best jazz acts play the small, smoky jazz club **Barcelona** (✉ Carrer Apuntadores s/n, La Llotja ☎ No phone) on weekends. Relax over cocktails at the low-lighted, genteel **Golden Door**.

The cobblestone streets of the old town are jammed with restaurants and bars. Join the after-work crowd basking in the Palma of yesteryear at **Grand Café Capuccino** (✉ Carrer Sant Miquel 53, Barrio Antiguo ☎ 971/719764), an elegant bar-restaurant in a traditional Mallorcan town house. **Bluesville** (✉ Carrer Ma de Morro 3, Barrio Antiguo ☎ No phone) is a laid-back bar popular with both locals and foreigners. You can listen to rock and blues on Saturday nights. In summer (June–September), head to the nearby suburb of Magalluf and dance the night away at the gargantuan disco **BCM Planet Dance** (✉ Av. S'Olivera s/n, Magalluf ☎ No phone), popular with a pan-European crowd.

Palma's **Gran Casino de Mallorca** is a short distance from the harbor. There's an admission charge of €4, and you'll need your passport to enter; dress is informal, but T-shirts, shorts, and sandals are considered inappropriate. ✉ *Urb. Sol de Mallorca s/n Calvìa* ☎ *971/130000* ⊕ *www.casinodemallorca.com* ☻ *Daily, 5 PM to 5 AM.*

Sports & the Outdoors

Turisme Actiu, a leaflet that details all sports clubs, describes everything from sea diving to skydiving, and is available at tourist offices.

BALLOONING For spectacular views of the island, head up, up, and away with **Mallorca Balloons** (✉ Ca'n Melis 22, Cala Rajada ☎ 971/818182, 639/818109 in winter).

BICYCLING The Majorca tourist board has an excellent series of leaflets on bike routes with maps, details about the terrain, sights, and distances. The tourist office of Cala Ratjada, in northeast Majorca, has a 12-page brochure that includes maps and photographs.

BIRD-WATCHING Majorca has two notable nature reserves, ideal for bird-watchers. **S'Albufera de Mallorca** (✉ Ctra. Port d'Alcúdia–Ca'n Picafort, Hotel Parc Natural ☎ 971/892250 ⊕ www.mallorcaweb.net/salbufera ☻ Apr.–Sept., daily 9–7; Oct.–Mar., daily 9–5) is the largest wetlands zone in Majorca, with binoculars for rent. **Sa Dragonera** (☎ 971/180632 ⊘ Apr.–Sept., daily 9–5; Oct.–Mar., daily 9–4) has a large colony of sea falcons and is accessible by boats from Sant Elm, the western tip of Majorca.

Cruceros Margarita excursion boats to **Sa Dragonera** leave Sant Elm Monday through Saturday (except in January) at 10:15, 11:15, and 12:15. The fare is €10. ☎ *639/617545.*

GOLF   Majorca has more than a score of 18-hole golf courses, among them PGA championship venues of fiendish difficulty. For more information, contact the **Federación Balear de Golf** (Balearic Golf Federation; ✉ Av. Jaime III 17, Palma ☎ 971/722753 ⊕ www.fbgolf.com).

Son Vida Golf (✉ Next to Castillo Son Vida hotel, 5 km [3 mi] from Palma, Son Vida ☎ 971/791210) offers 18 holes. **Golf Alcanada** (✉ Carretera del Faro s/n Alcúdia ☎ 971/220966) is an 18-hole course designed by Robert Trent Jones Jr. and Sr.

HANG GLIDING   For memorable views of the island, glide above it on an ultralight. Arrange a trip at **Escuela de Ultraligeros "El Cruce"** (✉ Ctra. Palma–Manacor, Km 42, Petra ☎ 629/392776). For hang gliding, contact **Parapente Alfàbia** (✉ Camino d'es Puig, Finca Es Puxet, Alcúdia ☎ 971/891366 ⊕ www.alfabia.galeon.com). **Club Vol Lliure Mallorca** (✉ Baluard del Princep 10C, 3rd fl. B, Palma ☎ 971/754316 ⊕ www.cvlmallorca. com) conducts weekend and intensive hang-gliding courses.

HIKING-WALKING   Majorca is an excellent destination for hiking. In the Sierra de Tramuntana, you can easily arrange to trek one way and take a boat, bus, or train back. Ask the tourist office for the free booklet *20 Hiking Excursions on the Island of Majorca,* with detailed maps and itineraries. For excellent drawings and maps, track down *12 Classic Hikes Through Majorca,* by the German author Herbert Heinrich, available in the bookstores at key sights. For more hiking information contact the **Grup Excursionista de Mallorca** (Majorcan Hiking Association; ✉ Carrer Andreu Feliu 20, Palma ☎ 871/947900 ⊕ www.gemweb.org). A useful outfit for foreign trekkers is **Explorador** (✉ Pueblo Espanyol, Despacho 7, 07014 Palma ☎ 600/557770 ⊕ www.exploradors.com).

SAILING   For information on sailing, call the **Federación Balear de Vela** (Balearic Sailing Federation; ✉ Av. Joan Miró 327, Palma ☎ 971/402412). The **Escuela Nacional de Vela de Calanova** (National Sailing School; ✉ Av. Joan Miró 327, Palma ☎ 971/402512) can clue you in about sailing in the Balearics. The **Club de Mar** (✉ Muelle de Pelaires, south end of Passeig Marítim, La Llotja, Palma ☎ 971/403611 ⊕ www.clubdemar-mallorca. com) is famous among yachties. It has its own hotel, bar, disco, and restaurant. Charter a yacht at **Cruesa Mallorca Yacht Charter** (✉ Passeig Marítim 16, Edificio Tròpic, Palma ☎ 971/282821).

SCUBA DIVING   Ask about scuba diving at **Escuba Palma** (✉ Via Rey Jaume l, 84, Santa Ponsa ☎ 971/694968). **Big Blue** (✉ Marti Ros García 6, Edificio Ski Club, Palma Nova, Calvià ☎ 971/681686) is a resource for scuba divers.

TENNIS   Tennis is very popular here; there are courts at many hotels and private clubs, and tennis schools as well. For information about playing in the area, call the **Federació de Tennis de les Illes Balears** (Balearic Tennis Federation; ⊠ Via Aleman 11 Palma ☎ 971/720956 ⊕ www.ftib.net).

WATER SPORTS   You can rent windsurfers and dinghies at most beach resorts; both skin- and scuba diving are excellent; and the island has some 30 yacht marinas. On the northwest coast at Port de Sóller, canoes, windsurfers, dinghies, motor launches, and waterskiing gear are available for rent from Easter to October at **Escola d'Esports Nàutics** (⊠ Paseo Playa d'en Repic s/n, Port de Sóller ☎ 971/633001 ⊕ www.nauticsoller.com).

Shopping

Majorca's specialties are leather shoes and clothing, porcelain, souvenirs carved from olive wood, handblown glass, artificial pearls, and espadrilles. Top-name fashion boutiques line **Avinguda Jaume III** and the nearby Plaça Joan Carles I. You can find several antiques shops on Plaça Almoina. Less-expensive shopping strips are **Carrer Sindicat** and **Carrer Sant Miquel**—both pedestrian streets running north from the Plaça Major—and the small streets south of the Plaça Major. The **Plaça Major** itself has a modest crafts market Monday, Thursday, Friday, and Saturday 10 to 2. In summer the market is open daily 10 to 2; January and February, it's open weekends only. Another crafts market is held May 15 through October 15, 8 PM to midnight in **Plaça de les Meravelles**.

Leather is best in the high-end **Loewe** (⊠ Av. Jaime III 1, Centro ☎ 971/715275), a branch of the famed Spanish firm founded in 1846. Bags, jackets, and the like are artfully displayed in classy, perfumed surroundings; the expert staff provides personal attention. **Rampel** (⊠ Av. Jaime III 21, Centro ☎ 971/715139) sells high-quality leather coats and bags. **Barrats** (⊠ Av. Jaime III 5, Centro ☎ 971/213024) specializes in leather coats and shoes for women. Mallorca's most popular footwear export—in summer, it seems like every Spaniard sports a pair—are its simple, comfortable slip-on espadrilles (usually with a leather front over the first half of the foot and a strap across the back of the ankle). They come in every color of the rainbow. Look for a pair at **Alpargatería La Concepción** (⊠ Concepción 17, Barrio Antiguo ☎ 971/710709).

Mediterráneo (⊠ Av. Jaume III 11, Centro ☎ 971/712159) sells high-quality artificial pearls in its elegant sit-down showroom. **Persépolis** (⊠ Av. Jaume III 23, Centro ☎ 971/724539) carries high-quality antiques. **Las Columnas** (⊠ C. Sant Domingo 24, Barrio Antiguo) has ceramics from all over the Balearic Islands. Visit **Gordiola** (⊠ Carrer de la Victoria 8–12, Centro ☎ 971/711541), glassmakers since 1719, for a variety of original bowls, bottles, plates, and decorative objects. The company's workshop is in Alguida, on the Palma-Manacor road, where you can watch the glass being blown and even try your hand at making a piece. Stop by **La Casa del Olivo** (⊠ Carrer Pescateria Vella, Centro ☎ 971/727025), just off Carrer Jaume II, for olive-wood crafts, from bowls to cutting boards.

For gift-wrapped ensaimadas, pop into **Forn des Teatro** (⊠ Pl. Weyler 9, at the foot of the steps leading to Pl. Major, Barrio Antiguo ☎ 971/715254). The much-photographed shop front of **Colmado Sto. Domingo** (⊠ Santo Domingo 1, Barrio Antiguo ☎ 971/714887) explains why this is the place for *sobrasada* (sausage paste) plus liqueurs and other local produce. Local, national, and foreign wines are on sale at **La Vinoteca** (⊠ Plaza Virgen de la Salud 3, Plaza de España ☎ 971/728829).

Side Trip to Randa
Southeast 26 km (16 mi) southeast from Palma is the tiny village of Randa, with its three separate hermitages. Take C715 east from Palma to PM501, turn right, and follow signs to Llucmajor until, after about 3 km (2 mi), a left turn leads to Randa. At the center of town, turn right and follow a twisting road up the Puig de Randa. Long a pilgrimage destination for the sick, the Franciscan monastery of **Nuestra Señora de Cura** (El Santuari de Cura) was founded in the 13th century by philosopher Ramón Llull; its library has valuable books that you may be able to see. The monastery also houses a simple hotel with clean, basically furnished rooms; doubles cost €46 a night. ⊠ *Puig de Randa* ☎ *971/ 120260 hotel, 971/660994 library* ⊕ *www.santuariodecura.com* ✉ *Donation suggested* ◔ *Library daily 11–1:30 and 4–6.*

Jardins d'Alfàbia

❷ *17 km (10½ mi) north of Palma.*

You don't often hear in the Majorcan interior what you hear in the Alfàbia Gardens: the sound of falling water. The Moorish viceroy of the island developed the springs and hidden irrigation systems here sometime in the 12th century, to create this remarkable oasis with its 40-odd varieties of trees, climbers, and flowering shrubs. The 17th-century manor house, furnished with antiques and painted panels, has a collection of original documents that chronicle the history of the estate. ⊠ *Ctra. Palma–Sóller, Km 17* ☎ *971/613123* ✉ *€4.50* ◔ *Nov.–Mar., weekdays 9–5:30, Sat. 9–1; Apr.–Oct., Mon.–Sat. 9–6:30.*

Where to Eat
$$$–$$$$ ✕ **Ses Porxeres.** Former stables at the gardens' edge have been converted into a rustic restaurant. Catalan and Majorcan specialties include pheasant stuffed with tiny plums, rabbit prepared with snails, and cod in garlic sauce. For dessert, try the *crema catalana* (Catalonia's answer to crème brûlée topped with a crackly layer of burned sugar) or the *tarta de chocolate* (chocolate tart). ⊠ *Ctra. Palma–Sóller, Km 17* ☎ *971/ 613762* ▭ *AE, MC, V* ◔ *Closed Aug. and Mon. No dinner Sun.*

Sóller

❸ *13 km (8 ½ mi) north of Jardins d'Alfàbia, 30 km (19 mi) north of Palma.*

You can reach Sóller on the railway from Palma, which still uses carriages dating from 1912; trains depart four to five times a day from Plaça d'Espanya. If you're driving, take the tunnel (€4) at Alfàbia. (The road over the mountains is spectacular—lemon and olive trees on stone-walled terraces, farmhouses perched on the edges of forested cliffs—but demanding.) Sóller is a delightful little town, with many stately houses dating from the 16th through 18th century, ideally placed for walks through the hills to Deià or for excursions to the beach at nearby Port de Sóller. Find your way to the Plaça Constitució, dominated by the cathedral, and arm yourself with a map at the tourist office, in the city hall.

Where to Stay & Eat

$$ ✕⌨ **El Guía.** Typical of the houses built by Sóller's merchants on the rich rewards of the citrus trade, this hotel is furnished in that fin-de-siècle style. The excellent restaurant serves Majorcan specialties. ⊠ *Carrer Castanyer 2, 07100* ☎ *971/630227* ☒ *971/632634* ⊸ *18 rooms* ♦ *Restaurant; no a/c in some rooms, no room TVs* ☰ *MC, V* ⊗ *Closed Nov.–Mar.* ⍗ *BP.*

Deià

❹ *9 km (5½ mi) southwest of Sóller.*

★ Deià was made famous by the English poet and writer Robert Graves, who lived here off and on from 1929 until his death in 1985. The village is still a favorite haunt of writers and artists, including Graves's son Tomás, author of *Pa amb oli (Bread and Olive Oil)*, a guide to Majorcan cooking, and British painter David Templeton. The setting is unbeatable; all around Deià rise the steep cliffs of the Sierra de Tramuntana. There's live jazz on summer evenings. On warm afternoons, literati gather at the beach bar in the rocky cove at Cala de Deià, 2 km (1 mi) downhill from the village. Walk up the narrow street to the village church; the small **cemetery** behind it affords views of mountains terraced with olive trees and of the coves below. It's a fitting spot for Graves's final resting place, in a quiet corner beneath a simple slab.

Where to Stay & Eat

$$$$ ✕⌨ **La Residencia.** Two 16th–17th-century manor houses have been artfully combined to make this exceptional hotel on a hill above the village of Deià. Reopened in March 2006 after a major face-lift, it is superbly furnished with Majorcan antiques, modern canvases, and canopied four-poster beds. Britain's late Princess Diana was a regular guest here, in one of the four suites with private pool. Herbs, olives, fruit, and flowers come straight to the kitchen and guest rooms from the hotel's lush landscaped gardens. El Olivo, the restaurant ($$$–$$$$), offers an inventive Spanish and continental menu. The hotel has its own shuttle to the sea at Lluc al Cari. ⊠ *Son Canals s/n, 07179* ☎ *971/639011* ☒ *971/639370* ⊕ *www.hotel-laresidencia. com* ⊸ *67 rooms* ♦ *3 restaurants, cable TV, in-room data ports, Wi-Fi, 2 tennis courts, 3 pools (1 indoor), spa, bar, business services, no-smoking rooms; no kids under 10 July–Aug. 18, Oct. 20–31, or the wk between Christmas and New Year's days* ☰ *AE, DC, MC, V* ⍗ *BP.*

Fodor's Choice
★

Son Marroig

❺ *4 km (2½ mi) west of Deià.*

West of Deià is Son Marroig, one of the estates of Austrian archduke Luis Salvador (1847–1915), who arrived in Majorca as a young man and fell in love with the place. Speaker of 14 languages and a prolific writer, the archduke acquired estates and built great houses, mostly along the northwest coast, which he then furnished with miradors at each spectacular viewpoint. Now a museum, Son Marroig contains the archduke's collections of Mediterranean pottery and ceramics, old Majorcan furniture, and paintings. From April through early October, the Deià International Festival holds classical concerts here.

From the mirador you can see, nearly 1,000 feet below, **Sa Foradada,** a spectacular rock peninsula pierced by a huge archway, beneath which the archduke moored his yacht. A pathway, beginning near the café in the parking area, leads down to Sa Foradada (1 hour down, 1½ hours up). Four kilometers (2½ mi) farther, behind the restaurant C'an Costa, on the right, is another of the archduke's miradors, **Ses Pites,** named for the spiky cactus plants that surround it. ✉ *Ctra. Deià–Valldemossa s/n* ☎ *971/639158* ⬛ *€3* ⏱ *May–Sept., Mon.–Sat. 10–8; Oct.–Apr., Mon.–Sat. 10–5:30.*

On the road south from Deià to Valldemossa is the **Monestir de Miramar,** founded in 1276 by Ramón Llull, who established a school of Asian languages here. It fell into disuse, and was bought in 1872 by the Archduke Luis Salvador—the first coastal property he bought—and restored as a mirador. Explore the garden and the tiny cloister, then walk below through the olive groves to a spectacular lookout. ✉ *Ctra. Deià–Valldemossa s/n* ☎ *971/616073* ⬛ *€3* ⏱ *Mon.–Sat. 10–5.*

Valldemossa

⑥ *18 km (11 mi) north of Palma.*

The **Reial Cartuja** (Royal Carthusian Monastery) was founded in 1339, but when the monks were expelled in 1835, it was privatized, and the cells became lodgings for travelers. Later they were leased as summer apartments, which they largely remain today. The most famous lodgers were Frédéric Chopin and the (female) French novelist George Sand, who spent three difficult months here in the winter of 1838–39 (the weather and their affair are always described as tempestuous). The tourist office, in the plaza next to the church, sells a ticket good for all of the monastery's attractions.

In the **church,** note the frescoes above the nave—the monk who painted them was Goya's brother-in-law. The next stop, in the cloisters, is perhaps the most interesting: it's a **pharmacy,** equipped by the monks in 1723 and almost completely preserved. Up a long, wide corridor are the apartments occupied by Chopin and Sand, furnished in period style. The piano is original. Nearby, another set of apartments houses the local **museum,** with mementos of Archduke Luis Salvador and a collection of old printing blocks. From here you return to the ornately furnished **King Sancho's palace,** a group of rooms originally built by King Jaume II for his son Sancho. ✉ *Pl. de la Cartuja* ☎ *971/612106* ⬛ *€7.50* ⏱ *Oct. and Nov., Mon.–Sat. 9:30–4, Sun. 10–1; Dec. and Jan., Mon.–Sat. 9:30–4; Feb.–May, Mon.–Sat. 9:30–5:30, Sun. 10–1; June–Sept., Mon.–Sat. 9:30–6:30, Sun. 10–1.*

Where to Stay

★ **$$$$** 🏨 **Valldemossa Hotel.** The breathtaking vistas alone are worth the visit. Once part of the Valldemossa Carthusian monastery, this beautifully restored Mallorcan stone house–turned–luxury hotel sits on a hill amid acres of olive trees and has sweeping views of the Bay of Palma and the Tramuntana mountains. Modern rooms have snowy white curtains and comforters, and antique bedsteads. You can relax on rattan chairs shaded by palms in the sunny patio and then ease into the evening at the elegant restaurant, which serves Mediterranean and international dishes. Between June 15 and August 20, a minimum stay of three nights is required. ✉ *Ctra. Valldemossa s/n, 07170* ☎ *971/612626* 🖶 *971/612625* ⊕ *www.valldemossahotel.com* ↩ *3 rooms, 9 suites* ⚃ *Restaurant, in-room safes, minibars, cable TV, in-room DVD, in-room broadband, 2 pools, sauna, bar* ▤ *AE, MC, V* ¶❶ *BP.*

$$$ 🏨 **Ca's Garriguer.** Search out this lovely, small *agroturismo* hotel amid 250 acres of olive groves overlooking the sea. The original country manor home has been faithfully restored, and the sitting rooms and bedrooms have exposed beams, solid furnishings, and comfortable beds. ✉ *Ctra. Valldemossa–Andratx, Km 2.5, 07170* ☎ *971/612300* 🖶 *971/612583* ⊕ *www.vistamarhotel.es* ↩ *10 rooms* ⚃ *Cable TV, Wi-Fi, pool, sauna* ▤ *AE, MC, V* ☾ *Closed mid-Nov.–mid-Feb.* ¶❶ *BP.*

Binissalem

❼ *18 km (11 mi) northeast of Palma.*

Binissalem is the center of one of Majorca's two D.O.O. (Denominación de Orígen) registered wine-producing regions—the other being Pla i Llevant. The town is an ideal base, not just for visits to the local **bodegas** (wineries), but for forays around the island: neither Palma, the north coast beaches, nor the rugged Serra de Tramuntana are much more than half an hour by car; trains run frequently through the day to Palma.

Where to Stay

$$$–$$$$ 🏨 **Scott's.** American George Scott and Brit Judy Brabner converted this 18th-century Majorcan town house into a graceful, tranquil hideaway. A lovely interior garden leads back to rooms and suites facing the courtyard, done in a range of decors from traditional—with canopied beds—to modern. A memorable breakfast is included in the room price. The couple also run a sister hotel, similarly lovely and soothing, set in a former artists' colony above the village of Galilea, northwest of Palma; ask about a package combining stays at both hotels for a discount. ✉ *Pl. Iglesia 12, 07350* ☎ *971/870100* 🖶 *971/870267* ⊕ *www.scottshotel.com* ↩ *13 rooms, 4 suites* ⚃ *Pool, no-smoking rooms; no room TVs, no kids under 12* ▤ *MC, V* ¶❶ *BP.*

⌐ EN ROUTE In and around Binissalem are some of Majorca's best wineries, most of them open for tastings and tours. One of the largest is **Bodegas José Ferrer** (✉ Conquistador 103 ☎ 971/511050). A hard winery to find, but worth a detour, since it exports none of its production, is Antonio Nadal's **Finca Son Roig** (✉ Camino de Son Roig s/n ☎ 971/451146).

Inca

❽ *28 km (17 mi) northeast of Palma.*

Inca is known for its leather factories and its Thursday open-air market, the largest on Majorca—closing all the streets in the heart of town and making parking a nightmare. If you don't find what you want among the stalls, hunt for crafts, leather, and pottery at the emporium outside town, on the left side of the road to Alcúdia. Be sure to try some *galletas* (a local kind of cookies).

Where to Eat

$$–$$$ ✕ **Celler C'an Amer.** A *celler* is a uniquely Majorcan combination of wine cellar and restaurant, and Inca has no fewer than six. C'an Amer is the best, with heavy oak beams and huge wine vats lining the walls behind the tables and banquettes. Antonia, the dynamic chef-owner, serves some of the best *lechona* (suckling pig) and *tumbet* (vegetables baked in layers) on the island. Portions here are heroic. Winter specialties include a superb oxtail soup prepared with red wine and seasonal mushrooms; year-round, C'an Amer makes its own terrific bread. ⊠ *Carrer Pau 39* ☎ *971/501261* ▤ *AE, MC, V* ☉ *Closed weekends, Mar. to Sept. No dinner Sun.*

Manacor

❾ *50 km (30 mi) east of Palma.*

Majorca's second-largest town, Manacor is known primarily for its Majórica artificial-pearl industry; it's an ideal center from which to storm the island's southeastern vacation coast. Prehistoric settlement sites abound in this area; later, the Romans moved in, followed by the Moors, who built a mosque where the Gothic parish church of **Nostra Senyora de les Dolores** (Our Lady of Sorrows) now stands.

Where to Stay & Eat

$$$$ ✕🖭 **La Reserva Rotana.** This luxury hotel is in a beautifully restored manor house 3 km (2 mi) north of Manacor. Most of the original coffered ceilings, ancient woodwork, and Venetian stucco are still in place. The 500-acre Rotana estate has its own 9-hole golf course, orchards, and kitchen gardens, which supply the excellent restaurant ($$–$$$$) with fresh produce for its excellent Mediterranean cuisine. Hotel rates include breakfast and greens fee. ⊠ *Camí de S'Avall Km 3, Manacor 07500* ☎ *971/ 845685* 🖷 *971/555258* ⊕ *www.reservarotana.com* ➴ *22 rooms* ⅋ *Restaurant, minibars, cable TV, in-room DVD, Wi-Fi, 9-hole golf course, putting green, tennis court, pool, gym, sauna* ▤ *AE, DC, MC, V* ☉ *Closed Dec. and Jan.* †◎�b *BP.*

Shopping

The weekly market in Manacor is held on Monday morning. To see Majorca's famous artificial pearls being made, go to **Fábrica de Perlas Majórica** (⊠ Vía Majórica ☎ 971/550200).

Alcúdia

❿ *54 km (34 mi) northeast of Palma.*

The first city on the site of Alcúdia was a Roman settlement, in 123 BC. The Moors reestablished a town here, and after the Reconquest it became a feudal possession of the Knights Templars; the first ring of city walls dates to the early 14th century. Begin your visit at the **Church of**

Sant Jaume, and walk through the maze of narrow streets inside to the **Porta de Xara,** with its twin crenelated towers—the most impressive feature of the surviving fortifications.

The **Museu Monogràfic de Pollentia** has an excellent collection of Roman items. ⊠ *Carrer Sant Jaume 30* ☎ *971/547004* 🗹 *Joint ticket for museum and Roman ruins* €2 ۞ *Tues.–Fri. 10–3:30, weekends 10:30–1.*

Just outside Alcúdia, off the port road, a signposted lane leads to the small, 1st-century BC **Teatre Romà** (Roman Amphitheater), excavated in the 1950s. From the Teatre Romà, turn back toward Alcúdia, but at the Inca junction keep right for **Port de Pollença,** less hectic than many of Majorca's coastal resorts.

Sports & the Outdoors

BICYCLING   You can find excellent bicycling in the flatlands around Port de Pollença, and Alcúdia and C'an Picafort—on the north coast—are ideal. The roads have bike lanes, and there are rental outlets on every block.

Pollença

❶   *5 km (3 mi) inland of the port.*

This cozy port town has lovely views of the water, plus a weekly market on Sunday morning. Climb the **Calvari,** a stone staircase with 365 steps. At the top is a tiny **chapel** with a Gothic wooden crucifix and a view of the bays Alcúdia and Pollença, and Capes Formentor and Pinar. Almost opposite the turnoff to Ternelles is Pollença's **Roman bridge.**

OFF THE BEATEN PATH   **CAP DE FORMENTOR –** If you enjoy twisty, scenic roads to nowhere, pack a picnic and drive to Cap de Formentor, north of Puerto de Pollença. The road threads its way among huge teeth of rock before reaching a lighthouse at the extreme tip, where the view is spectacular.

Where to Stay

$$$$ 🏨 **Formentor.** This famous hotel, founded in 1929, is perched on a cliff at Majorca's northern tip; it reopened after renovations in spring 2006. Terrace gardens descend to an attractive private beach, where a barbecue is fired up at lunchtime. The building is long and white, and the rooms are comfortable. The furniture is modern, and decors are in soothing white, yellow, pale gray, and blue. Former guests include the Duke of Windsor, Winston Churchill, Charlie Chaplin, Aristotle Onassis, and the Spanish royal family. ⊠ *Playa de Formentor s/n, Port de Pollença 07470* ☎ *971/899101* 🖷 *971/865155* ⊕ *www.hotelformentor.net* ➷ *125 rooms* ৬ *Restaurant, cable TV, Wi-Fi, 2 pools, massage, sauna, bar, Internet room* ➡ *AE, DC, MC, V* ۞ *Closed end of Oct.–Easter* ⍥ *BP.*

The Arts

Pollença hosts an acclaimed international **music festival** in July and August. Founded in 1961, it has drawn the likes of Mstislav Rostropovic, Jessye Norman, and the Alban Berg Quartet. Concerts are performed in the cloisters of the former monastery of Santo Domingo. For information, contact Pollença's **Ajuntament** (⊠ Calvari 2 ☎ 971/534012 or 971/534016 ⊕ www.festivalpollenca.org).

Lluc

⑫ *20 km (12 mi) southwest of Port de Pollença.*

The **monastery** in the remote mountain village of Lluc is widely considered Majorca's spiritual sanctuary. La Moreneta, also known as La Virgen Negra de Lluc (the Black Virgin of Lluc), is here in the 17th-century church. The **museum** has an eclectic collection of ceramics, paintings, clothing, folk costumes, and religious items. A boys' choir sings psalms in the chapel weekdays at 11:15 AM and around 4:45 PM, and at 11 AM for Sunday mass; hours change during holidays and the summer. The Christmas Eve performance of the pre-Christian Cant de la Sibila (Song of the Sybil) is an annual choral highlight. ☎ *971/871525* ☜ *Museum €2.60; admission to the monastery free* ☉ *Daily 10–1:15 and 2:30–5:15.*

Where to Stay & Eat

¢ ✕☷ **Santuari de Lluc.** The Lluc monastery offers simple, clean, and cheap accommodation, mostly in cells once occupied by priests. Although the vast building has one bar and three Majorcan restaurants, nightlife is restricted, and guests are asked to be silent after 11 PM. ⊠ *Santuari de Lluc, Plaça Pelegrins s/n 07315* ☎ *971/871525* ☷ *971/517096* ⤺ *110 rooms* ⚲ *3 restaurants, cafeteria, bar, shop; no a/c, no room TVs* ▤ *V.*

Torrent de Pareis

⑬ *2 km (1 mi) east of Sa Calobra.*

From Escorca's church of Sant Pere, you can hike down the Torrent de Pareis, a ravine that drops dramatically to the sea. Use proper footwear, don't go alone, and don't go at all if rain is forecast. The "torrent" becomes just that after a downpour and can cause drownings.

Fornalutx & Biniaraix

⑭ *3 km (2 mi) northeast of Sóller.*

Both Fornalutx and Biniaraix have been spruced up by tourist cash, but their cobbled, honey-color plazas and stepped streets remain undeniably charming. Each village has a resident artists' colony.

Banyalbufar

⑮ *23 km (14 mi) northwest of Palma.*

Originally terraced by the Romans, this tiny town overlooks its tiny harbor from high on a cliff. A 1½-km (1-mi) walk southwest leads to the **Mirador Ses Animes** observation point.

Where to Stay

★ $$–$$$ ☷ **Mar i Vent.** This small, friendly, family-run hotel is at the north end of Banyalbufar. Paths lead down to two small, rocky coves for sea swimming. All guest rooms have balconies with sea or mountain views, and are furnished in traditional style with simple blond-wood furniture and tile floors. Ask at the desk for an English-language guide to local

9

walking tours, especially through the mountains toward Son Marroig; find out why luminaries from the Archduke Lluis Salvador to Chopin to Michael Douglas have described this wild, breathtaking stretch of coast as the most beautiful on earth. ⊠ *Carrer Major 49, Banyalbufar 07191* ☎ *971/618000* 🖶 *971/618201* ⊕ *www.hotelmarivent.com* ⇝ *29 rooms* ⚐ *Restaurant, in-room data ports, Wi-Fi (in main building), tennis court, pool, hiking, bar, no-smoking rooms; no TV in some rooms* ▤ *MC, V* ⊘ *Closed Dec. and Jan.* ⦿l *BP.*

Puigpunyent

🔟 *25 km (15 mi) northwest of Palma.*

This village and the little roadways leading to and from it in all directions are a welcome relief from some of Majorca's more heavily traveled routes and routines. Visit the parish church, look through the Son Bru historical center, and hike up the nearby Puig de Galatzó (3,368 feet).

Where to Stay & Eat

★ $$$$ ✕🖼 **Gran Hotel Son Net.** This restored estate house—parts of which date back to 1672—is one of Majorca's most luxurious hotels. Poplars and palms shade the terrace above the 30-meter pool, with the village of Puigpunyent and the surrounding countryside spread out below. Room decors can be a bit over the top—a lot of red and rose pink—but the bathrooms are truly palatial. The restaurant, L'orangerie, set in an ancient olive press, is an ideal showcase for the creations of chef Christian Rullan, trained at Le Nôtre in Paris but fiercely proud of his Majorcan roots; try his lamb in rosemary sauce with sauteed artichokes and wild mushrooms. (A sister hotel, Son Julia, opened in 2006 near Llucmajor, to the southeast.) ⊠ *Carrer Castillo de Son Net, Puigpunyent 07194* ☎ *971/147000* 🖶 *971/147001* ⊕ *www.sonnet.es* ⇝ *16 rooms, 9 suites* ⚐ *2 restaurants, minibars, cable TV, Wi-Fi, tennis court, pool, gym, massage, bar* ▤ *AE, DC, MC, V.*

Andratx

🔢 *23 km (14 mi) southwest of Banyalbufar.*

Andratx is a charming cluster of white and ocher hillside houses, rather like cliff dwellings, with the 3,363-foot Mt. Galatzó behind it. Many of the towns on Majorca are at some distance from their seafronts; from Andratx you can take a 4-km (1½-mi) drive through S'Arracó to Sant Elm and on to the rocky shore opposite Sa Dragonera—an island shaped indeed like the long-armored back of a dragon. Local history has it that the tiny island of Pantaleu, just to the west of it, was where Jaume I chose to disembark in September 1200, on his campaign to retake Majorca from the Moors.

Where to Stay & Eat

$$$–$$$$ ✕🖼 **Villa Italia.** This ornate, rose-color hideaway, once a 1920s *palacito*, was built in a Florentine style, with marble floors and faux-classical columns. It has fine views over the port from the main building. The rococo suites in pink and salmon are truly palatial; doubles, with an-

tique oak beams and rough plaster walls, are a bit small for the price, but all have comfortable private terraces. The elegant restaurant, Club Royal, serves Mediterranean cuisine. ⊠ *Camino San Carlos 13, Port D'Andratx 07157* 🕾 *971/674011* 🖷 *971/673350* ⊕ *www.hotelvillaitalia. com* ↪ *10 rooms, 6 suites* ♨ *Restaurant, minibars, cable TV, pool, gym, massage, bar, some pets allowed* ⊟ *AE, MC, V* ⦿ *BP.*

Santa Ponsa

⑱ *15 km (9 mi) west of Palma.*

Santa Ponsa has a sandy beach on its north side and a small fishing port to the south. Some time on the beach and lunch in the port may be a great idea before you return to Palma by way of the C719 and the *autopista* (divided highway).

MINORCA

Minorca, the northernmost Balearic island, is a knobby, cliff-bound plateau with a single central hill—Monte Toro—from whose 1,100-foot summit you can see the whole island. Prehistoric monuments—*taulas* (huge stone T-shapes), *talayots* (spiral stone cones), and *navetes* (stone structures shaped like overturned boats)—left by the first Neolithic settlers are everywhere on the island, rising up out of a landscape of small, tidy fields bounded by hedgerows and drystone walls, where sheep and Holstein cattle graze. Tourism came late to Minorca, as it was traditionally more prosperous than its neighbors, and Franco punished the Republican island by restricting development here. Having sat out the early Balearic boom, Minorca has avoided many of the other islands' industrialization troubles: there are no high-rise hotels, and the herringbone road system, with a single central highway, means that each resort is small and separate.

9

Mahón (Maó)

⑲ *Overnight ferry, fast hydrofoil (about 3 hours), or 40-min flight from Barcelona; 6-hr ferry from Palma.*

Established as the island's capital in 1722, when the British began their nearly 80-year occupation, Mahón stills bears the stamp of its former rulers. The streets nearest the port are lined with four-story Georgian town houses in various states of repair; the Mahónese still nurse a craving for Chippendale furniture; English is widely spoken. Mahón is quiet for much of the year, but between June and September the waterfront pubs and restaurants swell with foreigners.

Begin your tour at the northwest corner of the Plaça de S'Esplanada and turn right onto Carrer de Sa Rovellada de Dalt. Stop in at No. 25, the **Ateneo,** a cultural and literary society with wildlife, seashells, seaweed, minerals, and stuffed birds. Side rooms include paintings and mementos of Minorcan writers, poets, and musicians. ⊠ *Rovellada de Dalt 25* 🕾 *971/360553* 🖾 *Free* ⊙ *Weekdays 10–2 and 4–10, Sat. 10–2 and 5–9.*

From Sa Rovellada de Dalt, turn left on Carrer de ses Moreres, then right on Carrer Bastió to where it becomes Carrer Costa d'en Deià, and—if it's open—have a look at the **Teatre Principal** (✉ C. Costa d'en Deia s/n ☎ 971/355776). The theater was built in 1824 as an opera house, with five tiers of boxes, red plush seats, and gilded woodwork—a La Scala in miniature. Opera companies from Italy would make this their first port of call, en route to their mainland tours; anything that went down poorly with the critical audience in Mahón would get cut from the repertoire. Fully restored in 2005, the Principal is now mainly a movie house, but if you're visiting in the first week of December or June, when it hosts its own brief opera season, get tickets at all costs.

Carrer Costa d'en Deaià descends to the Plaça Reial (a bit grandiosely named, for an unimposing little rectangle dominated by a café called the American Bar), where it becomes the Carrer sa Ravaleta. Ahead is the church of **La Verge del Carme** (✉ Plaça del Carme ☎ 971/362402), which has a fine painted and gilded altarpiece. Adjoining the church are the cloisters, now used as a **public market,** the intervals between the massive stone arches filled with stalls selling fresh produce and a variety of local specialties such as cheeses and sausages.

> Opera companies from Italy made the Teatre Principal in Mahón their first port of call; if something went down poorly in Mahón, it would get cut from the repertoire.

A few steps north from the Cloister del Carme bring you to the church of **Santa María** (✉ Pl. de la Constitució ☎ 971/363949), which dates from the 13th century but was rebuilt during the British occupation and restored after being sacked during the civil war. The church's pride is its 3,200-pipe baroque organ, imported from Austria in 1810. There are concerts (€3) here weekdays 11:30–12:30. Behind the church of Santa María is the **Plaça de la Conquesta,** with a statue of Alfons III of Aragón, who wrested the island from the Moors in 1287.

From the Plaça de la Conquesta, walk up Carrer Alfons III and turn right at the The **Ajuntament** (✉ Pl. de la Constitució 1 ☎ 971/369800) to Carrer Isabel II, a street lined with many of the more imposing Georgian homes. Turn west from Carrer Isabel II on Carrer Rector Mort, and at the far end of the street is the massive gate of **Puerta de San Roque,** the only surviving portion of the 14th-century city walls, rebuilt in 1587 to protect Mahón from the pirate Barbarossa (Redbeard).

Where to Stay & Eat

★ $$$$ ✕ **Marivent.** This restaurant changed ownership in 2002, and is now generally conceded by knowledgeable Mahónese to be the best in town. Chef Lydia Barben trained locally and does wonders with a menu that changes with the season but always features fresh fish and Minorcan free-range beef. The sea bream with black rice risotto and Mahón cheese is wonderful. Marivent has a second-floor patio for dining alfresco; the third-floor main room, with a harbor view, is done in understated elegance with white walls and uprights, and narrow black beams. The staff is attentive, and the wine list has some 200 Spanish and French labels. ✉ Moll de Llevant 314 ☎ 971/369801 or 699/062117 ⚐ Reservations essential ▭ AE, MC, V ☉ Closed Tues. and Christmas–3rd wk of Jan.; Feb.–May, Mon., Wed., and Sun., lunch only.

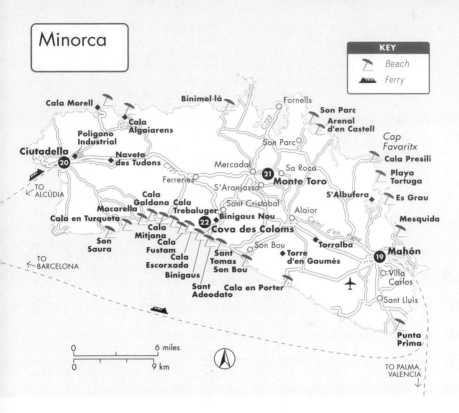

Minorca

KEY

🏖 Beach

⛴ Ferry

Cala Morell

Cala Algaiarens

Binimel·là

Fornells

Son Parc

Arenal d'en Castell

Polígono Industrial

Ciutadella **20**

TO ALCÚDIA

Naveta des Tudons

Son Parc

Cap Favaritx

Cala Presili

Mercadal **21** Sa Roca **Monte Toro**

Playa Tortuga

Ferreries

S'Aranjassa

S'Albufera

Es Grau

Cala Galdana Cala Trebaluger

Macarella

Sant Cristobal

Binigaus Nou

Alaior

22 **Cova des Coloms**

Mesquida

Cala en Turqueta

Cala Mitjana

Son Saura

Cala Fustam

Son Bou

Torralba

Mahón **19**

TO BARCELONA

Cala Escorxada

Binigaus

Sant Tomas Son Bou

Torre d'en Gaumés

Villa Carlos

Sant Adeodato

Cala en Porter

Sant Lluís

0   6 miles
0   9 km

Punta Prima

TO PALMA, VALENCIA

$$$–$$$$ ✕ **El Jàaro.** The daily catch of fish is whisked from the boat into the kitchen at this simple waterfront restaurant with a terrace. The lunchtime crowd comes for the inexpensive platter of lightly fried mixed fish with potatoes; in the evening, enjoy grilled *pescado de roca* (rockfish), *sepia* (cuttlefish), or *bacalao* (salt cod). The menu takes a quantum leap in price for the €72 spiny lobster, a local delicacy, in its various forms: grilled, thermidor, and in the savory stew called *caldereta*. ⊠ *Moll de Llevant 334* ☎ *971/362390* 🖃 *AE, MC, V* ☺ *No dinner Sun. Closed Mon.*

$$–$$$ ✕ **Es Moli de Foc.** Enjoy fresh Mediterranean cooking in a charming old house 3 km (2 mi) outside Mahón. Book a table in summer on the interior patio. ⊠ *Sant Llorenç 65, Sant Climent* ☎ *971/153222* 🖃 *MC, V* ☺ *Closed Mon. and Jan. No dinner Sun. Oct.–June.*

$$–$$$ ✕ **Pilar.** On a side street a few steps from the Plaça de l'Esplinada, in the center of Mahón, this pleasant little restaurant (eight tables) has a simple decor of white walls and beams, and antique sideboards. Under owners Jesus Saavedra and Fanny Mateu it offers a range of traditional Spanish dishes—including a hearty *sopa de ajo* (garlic soup) with cured ham, chorizo (spicy sausage), and whole cooked cloves of garlic. ⊠ *Carrer des Forn 61* ☎ *971/366817* 🖃 *DC, MC, V* ☺ *Closed Jan. 1–15, Sept. 6–8; Oct.–June, no dinner Mon.–Thurs., closed Sun.*

$–$$ ✕ **Itake.** On the port since 1994, Itake is an amiable clutter of 12 tables, specials of the day on a chalkboard, ceiling fans, paper place mats, and frosted-glass lamps. This is arguably the best place in Mahón for an inexpensive, informal meal with a different touch. Where neighboring eateries pride themselves on fresh fish, Itake serves goat cheese and burgers, kangaroo steaks in mushroom sauce, and ostrich breast with strawberry coulis. That said, nothing here is made with any real elaboration: orders come out of the kitchen at nearly the rate of fast food. ⊠ *Moll de Llevant 317* ☏ *971/354570* ▤ *AE, DC, MC, V* ◷ *No dinner Sun. Closed Mon.*

$$$–$$$$ 🏠 **Hotel Biniarroca.** An English artist and a fashion designer have charmingly restored the 15th-century farmhouse near Mahón. The rooms are all different, with tile floors, pastel shades, and exposed wooden beams. One ground-floor room has wheelchair access. The garden is colorful, and the fine restaurant has a summer terrace. ⊠ *Ctra. Villacarlos s/n, San Luis 07780* ☏ *971/150059, 619/460942* 🖷 *971/151250* ⊕ *www.biniarroca. com* ◞ *18 rooms, 2 suites* ♿ *Restaurant, cable TV, 2 pools, bar, lounge, library, free parking, some pets allowed* ▤ *MC, V* ◷ *Closed Jan. and Feb.*

$$$–$$$$ 🏠 **Port Mahón.** This hotel overlooks the harbor from terrace gardens in a quiet residential district; the suites on the second floor, with private terraces, have the best sea views. The piano bar has banquettes and red plush stools, but room decors are undistinguished. Service can be a bit quirky. Steps across from the hotel lead directly down to the fashionable bars and restaurants on the Moll de Llevant. The price includes breakfast. ⊠ *Av. Fort de l'Eau 13, 07701* ☏ *971/362600* 🖷 *971/351050* ⊕ *www.sethotels.com* ◞ *73 rooms, 9 suites* ♿ *Restaurant, minibars, cable TV, pool, hair salon, bar, piano bar* ▤ *AE, DC, MC, V* ⋈ *BP.*

★ $$$ 🏠 **Sant Joan de Binissaida.** Approach this lovely restored farmhouse, some 15 km (9 mi) from Mahón, on an avenue lined with chinaberry and fig trees. The terrace, where meals are served in season, offers a spectacular view of La Mola at the mouth of the port; a row of adjoining stables has been converted to additional guest rooms, facing the 20-meter pool. All the rooms at Sant Joan are named for composers (owner Josep Maria Quintana is a serious opera fan); the first-floor "Rossini" is fully wheelchair-accessible. The decors are antique, including a wonderful common room with deep leather chairs, a baize-topped card table—and an oratory. ⊠ *Camí de Binissaida 108 Es Castell 07720* ☏ *971/355598, 618/874381* 🖷 *971/355001* ⊕ *www.binissaida.com* ◞ *9 rooms, 2 suites* ♿ *Restaurant, in-room safes, cable TV, Wi-Fi, pool, massage, bicycles, library* ▤ *AE, MC, V* ◷ *Closed Jan.–Mar.*

$$–$$$ 🏠 **Casa Alberti.** The most centrally located of the Mahón hotels, the Casa Alberti was built in 1740 as a private home, during the British occupation, and is registered as a *patrimonio historico-cultural*. The house had been empty some 15 years when Dani Crespo and his partners bought it and turned it into a friendly, comfortable boutique hotel in 2004. The house has 15-foot ceilings, the original marble staircases, and tile floors; the rooms are furnished in rustic style from local and Barcelona antiques shops. Rates include breakfast in the big communal kitchen and adjoining interior patio. ⊠ *Carrer Isabel II, 9, 07701* ☏ *971/354210, 686/393569* 🖷 *971/354210* ⊕ *www.casalberti.com* ◞ *4 rooms, 2 suites* ♿ *No room phones, no room TVs* ▤ *AE, MC, V.*

$$–$$$ ▣ **Sol Mirador des Port.** Just a five-minutes walk from the docks, this is a convenient base for exploring the eastern end of Minorca. The rooms, which have modern wooden furnishings, range from basic to excellent, depending on the location; the best doubles, above the terrace, have a spectacular view by night of the Romanesque Church of Sant Francesc and the whole extent of the harbor. The restaurant serves breakfast and dinner only; the simple, filling fare includes vegetable stew and grilled hake. ⊠ *Dalt Vilanova 1, 07701* ☎ *971/360016* 🖷 *971/367346* ⊷ *73 rooms* ⅄ *Restaurant, cafeteria, minibars, cable TV, pool, bar, meeting rooms* ▤ *AE, DC, MC, V.*

Nightlife

The bars opposite the ferry terminal in Mahón's harbor fill with locals late at night. **Cova d'en Xoroi** (⊠ C. Cova s/n ☎ 971/377236) hides in a series of cliff-side caves high above the sea and is reached by a path. By day it's a tourist attraction and by night a wild disco. The longtime favorite **Mambo** (⊠ Moll de Llevant 209 ☎ 971/351852) has rustic stone walls and tasty cocktails. **Latitude 40** (⊠ Moll de Llevant 265 ☎ 971/364176) is where yachtsmen and their chic companions enjoy evening cocktails and tapas; it's closed on Sunday. **Akelarre** (⊠ Anden de Poniente 41 ☎ 971/368520) is a smart drinking venue near the port, often with loud music; on Friday night, groove to live jazz and blues. Catch live jazz Tuesday (May–September) at the **Casino** (⊠ Sant Jaume 4, Sant Climent ☎ 971/153418) bar and restaurant. Sant Climent is 4 km (2½ mi) southwest of Mahón.

Sports & the Outdoors

DIVING The clear Mediterranean waters here are ideal for diving. Equipment and lessons are available at Cala En Bosc, Son Parc, Fornells, and Cala Tirant. For scuba diving, compressed air is available at **Club Marítimo** (⊠ Moll de Llevant, 287, Mahón ☎ 971/365022). For exploring the waters off the western end of the island, equipment and services are available at **Club Náutico** (⊠ Camí del Baix s/n, Ciutadella ☎ 971/383918).

GOLF Minorca's sole golf course is the 18-hole **Golf Son Parc** (⊠ Urb. Son Parc ☎ 971/188875 ⊕ www.golfsonparc.com), 9 km (6 mi) east of Mercadal.

WALKING In the south, each cove is approached by a *barranca* (ravine or gully), often from several miles inland. The head of **Barranca Algendar** is down a small, unmarked road immediately on the right of the Ferreries–Cala Galdana Road; the barranca ends at the local beach resort, and from there you have a lovely walk north along the sea to an unspoiled half-moon of sand at **Cala Macarella**. Extend your walk north, if time allows, through the forest along the riding trail to **Cala Turqueta**, where you find some of the island's most impressive sea grottoes.

WINDSURFING & Knowledgeable windsurfers and sailors head for Fornells Bay. Several
SAILING miles long and a mile wide, but with a narrow entrance to the sea and virtually no waves, it gives the beginner a feeling of security and the expert plenty of excitement. **Wind Fornells** (⊠ Nou 33, Es Mercadal ☎ 971/188150 or 659/577760) rents boards, dinghies, and catamarans, and gives lessons in English or Spanish; they're open from May to October.

9

A little south of Fornells, at Ses Salines in Bahia Fornells, Tim Morris of **Minorca Sailing Holidays** (☏ 971/376589 ✉ 58 Kew Rd., Richmond, Surrey, England TW9 2PQ ☏ 0181/948–2100) sells a package that includes airfare and accommodations along with various activities. Charter a yacht from **Nautica Matias** (✉ Pl. Quintana de Mar 2, Ciutadella ☏ 971/380538 ⊕ www.nauticamatias.com). For charters and trips around the island, contact **Blue Mediterraneum–Rago** (✉ Moll de Llevant s/n, Mahón ☏ 971/154677 or 609/305314 ⊕ www.chartermenorca.com).

Shopping

Minorca is known for shoes and leather wear, cheese, gin—and recently, wine. In Mahón, buy leather goods at **Marks** (✉ S'Arravaleta 18 ☏ 971/322660). **Musupta** (✉ S'Arravaleta 26 ☏ 971/364131) is another source in the capital for leather wear. Inland, the showroom of **Pons Quintana** (✉ Calle San Antonio 120, Alaior ☏ 971/371050) has a full-length window overlooking the factory where they make their ultrachic women's shoes. The company also has a shop in Mahón, at Sa Ravaleta 21. The showroom of **Jaime Mascaro,** on the main highway from Alaior to Cuitadella (✉ Poligon Industrial s/n Ferreries ☏ 971/374072), features not only shoes and bags but fine leather coats and belts for men and women. Mascaro also has a shop in Mahón, at Carrer ses Moreres.

Mahón is one of the 12 *denominacion de origin* cheese-producing regions in Spain. A good place to buy the tangy, Parmesan-like Mahón cheese is **Hort de Sant Patrici** (✉ Camino Ruma-Sant Patrici s/n, Ferreries ☏ 971/373702 ⊕ www.santpatrici.com). You can't visit the dairy itself, but Sant Patrici has a shop, beautiful grounds with a small vineyard and botanical garden, and a display of traditional cheese-making techniques and tools.

In the 18th century, wine was an important part of the Minorcan economy: the British, who knew a good place to grow wine when they saw one, planted the island thick with vines. Viticulture was simply abandoned when Minorca returned to the embrace of Spain, and it has emerged again only in the past few years. The most promising of the small handful of new Minorcan wineries is **Bodegas Binifadet** (✉ Ses Barraques s/n, Sant Lluis ☏ 971/150715 ⊕ www.binifadet.com), which began as a hobby for founder Carlos Angles and his son Lluis, a labor of love that evolved into a determination to produce high-quality local wines in market volume. They did a creditable job of it, now making 5,000 bottles a year of white (Chardonnay, Muscat) and 20,000 of red (Merlo-Cabernet, Syrah). The robust young Binifada wines are on the shelves all over Minorca; the winery is open for tastings May through October, Monday to Saturday 10 to 1 and 4 to 8, and well worth a visit.

The other gastronomic legacy of the British occupation was, of course, gin. Visit the **Xoriguer distillery** (✉ Anden de Poniente 91 ☏ 971/362197), on Mahón's quayside, near the ferry terminal, and take a guided tour, sample various types of gin, and buy some to take home.

Side Trip to Torralba

Puzzle over Minorca's prehistoric past at **Torralba.** Driving west from Mahón, you turn south at Alaior on the road to Cala en Porter. Torralba, a megalithic site with a number of stone constructions, is 2 km (1 mi) ahead at a bend in the road, marked by an information kiosk on the left. The massive, T-shape stone **taula** is through an opening to the right. Behind it, from the top of a stone wall, you can see, in a nearby field, the monolith **Fus de Sa Geganta.**

Ciutadella

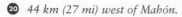 *44 km (27 mi) west of Mahón.*

Ciutadella was Minorca's capital before the British settled in Mahón, and its history is richer than Mahón's. As you arrive via the C721 across the island, turn left at the traffic light and circle the old part of the city to the north end of the coniferous **Plaça de s'Esplanada.** Turn left here, down Camí de Sant Nicolau. At the end, near the **Castell de Sant Nicolau** watchtower (visits daily, June–October 10–1 and 5–10) and three rusty cannons, is a **monument to David Glasgow Farragut,** the first admiral of the U.S. Navy, whose father emigrated from Ciutadella to the United States. From the Farragut monument, return up Sant Nicolau and park near the Plaça d'es Born. From a passage on the left side of Ciutadella's columned and crenelated **Ajuntament** (⊠ Pl. d'es Born), on the west side of the Born, steps lead up to the **Mirador d'es Port,** a lookout from which you can survey the harbor. The local **Museu Municipal** museum houses artifacts of Minorca's prehistoric, Roman, and medieval past, including records of land grants made by Alfons III to the local nobility after defeating the Moors. It's in an ancient defense tower at the east end of the harbor, the Bastió de Sa Font (Bastion of the Fountain). ☎ 971/380297 ⊕ *www.ciutadella.org/museu* ⊠ €2.13, free Wed. ⊙ *June–Sept., Tues.–Sat. 10–2 and 6–9.*

The monument in the middle of the Plaça d'es Born commemorates the citizens' resistance of a Turkish invasion in 1588. South from the plaza along the east side of the Born is the block-long 19th-century **Palau Torresaura** (⊠ Carrer Major del 8orn 8), built by the Baron of Torresaura, one of the many noble families from Aragón and Catalonia that repopulated Minorca after it was captured from the Moors in the 13th century. The interesting facade faces the plaza, though the entrance is on the side street (it is not open to the public). The **Palau Salort,** on the opposite side of the Carrer Major, is the only noble home regularly open to the public. The coats of arms on the ceiling are those of the families Salort (a salt pit and a garden: *sal* and *ort,* or *huerta*) and Martorell (a marten). ⊠ *Carrer Major des Born* ⊠ €2.50 ⊙ *May–Oct., Mon.–Sat. 10–2.*

The Carrer Major leads to the Gothic **Cathedral** (⊠ Pl. de la Catedral at Plaça Píus XII), which has some beautifully carved, intricate choir stalls. The side chapel has round Moorish arches, remnants of the mosque that once stood on this site.

Follow the arcade of Carrer de Quadrado north from the cathedral and turn right on Carrer del Seminari, lined on the west side with some of the city's most impressive historical buildings. Among them is the **Seminari** of the 17th-century Convent and Església del Socors (⊠ Carrer del

9

Seminari at Carrer Obispo Vila), which hosts Ciutadella's summer festival of classical music.

Ciutadella's **port** is accessible from steps that lead down from Carrer Sant Sebastià. The waterfront here is lined with seafood restaurants, some of which burrow into caverns far under the Born.

Where to Stay & Eat

$$–$$$$ ✕ **Cafe Balear.** Seafood doesn't get much fresher than this. The owners' boat docks nearby with its catch each day—except Sunday—and the restaurant fish tank is seldom empty. The house special, *arroz caldoso de langosta* (lobster and rice stew), is a masterpiece (€45), as are *pulpo a la gallega* (octopus in paprika and olive oil), *cigalas* (crayfish), lobster with onion, and grilled *navajas* (razor clams). *Merluza* (hake) and *bacalao* (cod) are also winners. ⊠ *Paseo San Juan 15* ☎ *971/380005* ☰ *AE, DC, MC, V* ☺ *Closed Nov., Sun. July–Sept., and Mon. Oct.–June. No dinner Sun.*

$$–$$$ ⊡ **Hesperia Patricia.** This hotel on a quiet boulevard south of the main plaza is close to Ciutadella Creek. The marble hall is light and modern, and the bedrooms have pale carpets and pastel wallpaper. ⊠ *Camí Sant Nicolau 90–92, 07760* ☎ *971/385511* ☐ *971/481120* ⊕ *www.hoteles-hesperia.com* ⬦ *40 rooms, 4 suites* ⟁ *Cafeteria, pool, bar, meeting rooms* ☰ *AE, DC, MC, V* ☑ *BP.*

$ ⊡ **Hostal-Residencia Ciutadella.** A block southwest of the Plaça Alfonso III, this pleasant bar-restaurant has guest rooms upstairs, which are clean and comfortable but purely functional—white walls, tile floors, laminated furniture, no wasted space. ⊠ *Carrer Sant Eloi 10, 07760* ☎☎ *971/383462* ⬦ *20* ⟁ *Restaurant, bar* ☰ *AE, MC, V* ☑ *CP.*

Shopping

Gin, shoes, leather, costume jewelry, and cheese are the items to shop for here; try the Ses Voltes area, the Es Rodol zone near Plaça Artrutx and Ses Voltes, and along the Camí de Maó between Plaça Palmeras and Plaça d'es Born. The industrial complex *(polígono industrial)* on the right as you enter Ciutadella has shoe factories, each with shops. Prices may be the same as in stores, but the selections are greater. In Plaça d'es Born, a market is held on Friday and Saturday. For Mahón cheeses and sausages, go to **Ca Na Riera** (⊠ Hospital de Santa Magdalena 7 ☎ 971/380748). Visit ARTEME (Artesanos de Menorca;; ⊠ Carrer Curniola 17 ☎ 971/353907) for the town's only **alfarería** (pottery maker).

Monte Toro

❷¹ *24 km (15 mi) northwest of Mahón.*

Follow signs in Es Mercadal (the crossroads at the island's center) to the peak of Monte Toro, Minorca's highest point, at all of 1,555 feet. From the monastery on top you can see the whole island and across the sea to Majorca.

Where to Eat

$$$–$$$$ ✕ **Es Pla.** The modest wooden exterior of this waterside restaurant in Fornells' harbor, on the north coast, is misleading. King Juan Carlos is

said to make regular detours here during Balearic jaunts to indulge in the *Es Pla caldereta de langosta* (a rich lobster stew)—which at €65.50 skews an otherwise reasonably priced menu. Excellent fish dishes include scallops "Gallega" style, anglerfish with *maresco* (seafood) sauce, and grilled scorpion fish—a local specialty. ⊠ *Pasaje Es Pla, Puerto de Fornells* ☎ *971/376655* ▤ *AE, DC, MC, V.*

$$–$$$ ✕ **Ca N' Olga.** It's hard to find, but the inventive country cuisine served here—local snails, quail in sherry—is worth it. Off the Camino de Tramuntana, in central Mercadal, Olga's is under an archway to the left (ask for directions if you don't see it). Make for the small patio. ⊠ *Pont Na Macarrana s/n, Mercadal* ☎ *971/375459* ▤ *AE, DC, MC, V* ⊗ *Closed mid-Dec.–Mar., and Tues. Nov.–Dec. and Mar.–May. No lunch June–Oct., or Mon. and Wed. Nov., Dec., and Mar.–May.*

$$–$$$ ✕ **Molí d'es Reco.** The hotel is an old mill just off the Mahón–Ciutadella highway, on the north end of Mercadal. In winter or on cold evenings, the ground floor offers snug dining, and the rustic, airy terrace is ideal on warm summer days. Minorcan specialties here include rabbit dishes, snails with aioli, and chicken with *centollo* (spider crab). ⊠ *Carrer Major 53, Mercadal* ☎ *971/375392* ▤ *AE, DC, MC, V.*

Cova des Coloms

㉒ *40 km (24 mi) west of Mahón.*

The massive Cova Des Coloms (Cave of Pigeons), also known as the Cathedral, is the most spectacular cave on Minorca. Eerie rock formations rise up to a 77-foot-tall ceiling. To reach the cave, take the Ferreries road at San Cristobal and turn up to the primary school; beyond the school the paved road continues for about 3 km (2 mi) toward Binigaus Nou. You'll see wheel marks and possibly cars at the designated parking area; leave the car. Climb a stile and take the path that follows the right-hand side of the barranca (ravine or gully) toward the sea—you'll come to a well-trodden path bearing down into the bottom of the barranca and up the other side. The entrance to the cave is around an elbow, camouflaged by a tree. A flashlight helps.

9

IBIZA

Settled by the Carthaginians in the 5th century BC, Ibiza managed to maintain its unique character through successive waves of invasion and occupation until the 1960s, when it emerged as a wild, anything-goes gathering place for hippies and the international jet set. With a full-time population of only some 260,000, it gets some 5 million visitors a year. Blessed with beaches—50 of them, by one count—it also has the world's largest disco, with a capacity of 12,000. About 25% of the people who live on Ibiza year-round are foreigners.

Agroturismo is a new notion here; there are some 30 of these small rural accommodations, with more on the way, but most visitors put up in heavily developed beach resorts such as Santa Eulària and Sant Antoni, the latter a Balearic version of Torremolinos on the Costa del Sol.

Ibiza & Formentera

Cala Xarraca
Caló d'Es Porcs
Portinatx
Puerto Sant Miguel
Sant
Vicent
Cala Sant Vicent
Sant Miguel
Sant Joan
Sant Mateo
Balafi
Sant Carles
Santa Agnes
Sant Llorenç
Bahía de Sant Antoni
Santa Gertrudis
Santa Eulária des Riu 24
Santa Eulalia
Sant Antoni
Santa
Sant Rafael
Ibiza Town (Eivissa)
Sant Josep
23
Sant Jordi
Es Vedrà
Playa d'En Bossa
Mitjorn
Cavallet
Ses Salines
Es Palmador
Trucadors
Estany Pudent
Puerto de La Sabina
Es Pujols
Estany d'es Peix
Sant Ferran
Sant Francesc Xavier
Cala Sahona
25
El Pilar
Formentera
Playa de Mitjorn
Cabo de Berbería

↑ TO BARCELONA
TO PALMA
←TO VALENCIA

KEY
⊿ *Beach*
⛴ *Ferry*

0   10 miles
0   15 km

Ibiza Town (Eivissa)

㉓ *40-min flight from Barcelona.*

Hedonistic and historical, Ibiza Town (Eivissa, in Majorcan and Catalan) is a city of jam-packed nightspots and trendy boutiques presided over by sturdy medieval walls and a Gothic cathedral. Explore the web of ancient streets in Dalt Vila, the walled old town, and then dance the night away to music spun by Europe's top DJs at the clubs.

Running along the quay is the area known as **Sa Penya** (the Crag, or the Cliff). Once a quiet fisherman's quarter, this neighborhood is a tourist haunt, springing into life each evening with lively bars, restaurants, and flea markets.

Enter Sa Penya via Carrer Rimbau, which you can find at the end of Passeig Vara de Rey opposite Hotel Montesol, whose fashionable pavement café is a favorite place for people-watching. **Carrer Rimbau** has some of the exotic boutiques that Ibiza is renowned for, and the alleys off it are crammed with stalls, more boutiques, and restaurants. Continue on Carrer Major to the **Plaça de la Constitució**, north of the church of San Telmo, where a little building that looks something like a miniature Parthenon houses the local market. Beyond it, a ramp leads up to the Portal de ses Taules, the main gate of **Dalt Vila,** the walled upper town. On each side stands a statue, Roman in origin and now headless: Juno on the right, an armless male on the left.

Inside Dalt Vila, the ramp continues to the right between the outer and inner walls and opens into a long, narrow plaza lined with stalls and sidewalk cafés. Don't worry about losing your way: aim uphill for the cathedral, downhill for the gate. A little way up Sa Carroza, a sign on the left points back toward the **Museu d'Art Contemporani,** housed in the gateway arch. ⊠ *Ronda Pintor Narcis Putget s/n* ☎ *971/302723* ☞ *€1.20* ☉ *Oct.–Apr., Tues.–Fri. 10–1:30 and 4–6, weekends 10–1:30; May–Sept., Tues.–Fri. 10–1:30 and 5–8, weekends 10–1:30.*

Uphill from the museum is a sculpture of a priest sitting on one of the stone seats in the gardens. On the left, the wide **Bastió de Santa Llúcia** (Bastion of St. Lucia) has a panoramic view.

Wind your way up past the 16th-century church of **Sant Domingo** (⊠ Carrer de Balanzat), its roof an irregular landscape of tile domes, and turn right in front of the ajuntament housed in the church's former monastery. From the church of San Domingo, follow any of the streets or steps leading uphill to Carrer Obispo Torres (Carrer Major). The **cathedral** is on the site of religious structures from each of the cultures that have ruled Ibiza since the Phoenicians. Built in the 13th and 14th centuries and renovated in the 18th century, the cathedral has a Gothic tower and a baroque nave. ⊠ *Carrer Major* ☎ *971/312774* ☉ *Weekdays 10–1, Sun. 10:30–noon.*

The **Museu Arqueològic** has Phoenician, Punic (Carthaginian), and Roman artifacts. It's across the plaza from the cathedral. ⊠ *Plaça Catedral 3* ☎ *971/301231* ☞ *€2.40* ☉ *Mid-Oct.–mid-Mar., Tues.–Sat. 9–3, Sun. 10–2; mid-Mar.–mid-Oct., Tues.–Sat. 10–2 and 6–8, Sun. 10–2.*

Behind the cathedral, from the **Bastió de Sant Bernat** (Bastion of St. Bernard), a promenade with sea views runs west to the bastions of Sant Jordi and Sant Jaume, past the **Castell**—a fortress formerly used as an army barracks, turned over to the city of Ibiza in 1973, and left to fall apart until 2006, when work began to transform it into a 70-room luxury parador. The promenade ends at the steps to the **Portal Nou** (New Gate). From the Portal Nou, cross the Carrer Joan Xico and walk up the Vía Romana to reach, on the left, the Puig des Molins (Hill of Windmills). A major Punic necropolis, with more than 3,000 tombs, has been excavated here and can be visited; many of the finds will be on display in the **Museu Puig des Molins** (Punic Archaeological Museum) adjacent to it. At this writing, the museum was closed for major restoration; it is scheduled to open in late 2007. ⊠ *Vía Romana 31* ☎ *971/ 301771* ☞ *Museum €1.80, necropolis free* ☉ *Mon.–Sat. 10–1.*

Where to Stay & Eat

$$$–$$$$ ✕ **S'Oficina.** Some of the best Basque cuisine on Ibiza is served at this restaurant just 2 km (1 mi) outside town. Marine prints hang on the white walls and ships' lanterns from the ceiling; the bar is adorned with

ships' wheels. *Lomo de merluza con almejas* (hake with clams) and *kokotxas* (cod cheeks) are among the specialties. ✉ *C. Begonias 17. From Ibiza Town, take Carretera toward airport and turn off for Playa d'en Bossa* ☎ *971/390081* ⊟ *AE, DC, MC, V* ☯ *Closed Mon. No dinner Sun.*

★ **$$–$$$$** ✕ **Ca Na Joana.** Joana Biarnés, a well-known journalist in a former life, has put together one of the finest restaurants in the Balearics in this small, 200-year-old country house on a hillside in Sant Josep (10 km [6 mi] from Ibiza). It feels like a private house, and there's an acclimatized wine cellar below. House specialties include rack of roast lamb and potato slices layered with truffles. ✉ *Ctra. Eivissa–Sant Josep, Km 10* ☎ *971/ 800158* ⊟ *AE, MC, V* ☯ *Closed Mon. and Nov.–mid-Jan. No dinner Sun. Jan.–May. No lunch June–Oct.*

★ **$$$$** ▦ **Atzaró.** The idea of *agroturismo*—country inns—has developed only recently on Ibiza; opened just this century, Atzaró is one of the newest entries in that category, and arguably one of the best. The original building was a 300-year-old family farmhouse; as the hotel grew, it added separate suite cottages, a pool, and a luxurious spa. Rooms are huge, with natural wood beams, stone walls, tile floors, and rustic furniture. The spacious grounds are laid out like a Balinese retreat, with accent pools and fountains, stone lanterns and wood sculptures, and small private pavilions with hand-carved ceilings and deep, inviting divans. ✉ *Ctra. Sant Joan, Km 15, Santa Eulària, 07840* ☎ *971/338838* 🖷 *971/ 331650* ⊕ *www.atzaro.com* ➳ *7 rooms, 9 suites* ☐ *Restaurant, room service, in-room safes, minibars, cable TV, in-room DVD, in-room broadband, Wi-Fi, 3 pools, gym, spa, Turkish bath, bicycles, bar, business services* ⊟ *AE, MC, V* ⫴ *BP.*

$$$$ ▦ **Cas Gasí.** With splendid views of Ibiza's one and only mountain, the 1,567-foot Sa Talaiassa, this lovely late-19th-century manor house is surrounded by hills of olive trees, redolent of Tuscany. Airy, rustic rooms with wood-beam ceilings are sparsely and gracefully furnished with brass beds and contemporary designer chairs. Dinner is served on request; breakfast daily on a terrace. ✉ *Cami Vell a Sant Mateu s/n, Santa Gertrudis 07814* ☎ *971/197700* 🖷 *971/197899* ⊕ *www.casgasi. com* ➳ *12 rooms, 2 suites* ☐ *Dining room, in-room safes, minibars, cable TV, in-room DVD, in-room data ports, 2 pools, massage, sauna, spa, bar, business services, airport shuttle, some pets allowed* ⊟ *AE, DC, MC, V* ⫴ *BP.*

★ **$$$$** ▦ **Hacienda Na Xamena.** Ibiza's most exclusive hotel is also its most isolated: it's on a rocky headland in Sant Miquel, toward the north end of the island. Access to the sea is difficult, involving a long hike down steep steps. The rooms, arranged around a little patio with a fountain and trees, are spare—classical Ibizan with clean lines—and all the bathrooms have whirlpools. Reserve well in advance. ✆ *Apdo. 423, San Miguel 07815* ☎ *971/334500* 🖷 *971/334514* ⊕ *www.hotelhacienda-ibiza. com* ➳ *56 rooms, 9 suites* ☐ *4 restaurants, café, in-room safes, minibars, cable TV, Wi-Fi, tennis court, 3 pools (1 indoor), spa, boating, bicycles, bar, shop, some pets allowed* ⊟ *AE, MC, V* ☯ *Closed Nov.–Apr.*

$$$–$$$$ ▦ **Torre del Canónigo.** Built into a 16th-century tower at the top of the Dalt Vila, 55 yards from the cathedral, the modern rooms have open fireplaces. Three have a view of the port and sea. Vehicle access is limited. ⊠ *Carrer Major 8, Dalt Vila, 07800* ☏ *971/303884* 🖷 *971/307843* ⊕ *www.elcanonigo.com* 🖙 *8 rooms* △ *Snack bar, minibars, cable TV, in-room DVD, no pets* ⊟ *AE, DC, MC, V* ⊗ *Closed mid-Jan.–mid-Mar.*

★ $$$ ⌂ **Cas Pla.** Surrounded by thousand-year-old olive trees and blessed with views over the sea and the fortified church in the village of Sant Miquel, this rural hotel is tastefully decorated and well managed. A cozy retreat from the Ibiza scene, it's still a short hop to the beach. ⊠ *Apdo. 777, Cam Putel, San Miguel de Balanzat, San Juan, 07800* ☏ *971/334587* 🖷 *971/334604* 🖙 *16 rooms* △ *Dining room, pool, sauna, bar, cable TV, Wi-Fi, some pets allowed* ⊟ *MC, V* ⊗ *Closed Nov.–Mar.*

$$$ ⌂ **Los Molinos.** A brisk 10-minute walk from Ibiza brings you to this beachfront hotel, over the hill that separates the city from neighboring Figueretas. Guest rooms are modern, with blue bedspreads and blue-beige curtains and upholstery; the more expensive ones have balconies facing the bay. Breakfast is billed separately at €9.50. ⊠ *Carrer Ramón Muntaner 60, Figueretas 07800* ☏ *971/302250* 🖷 *971/302504* ⊕ *www.thbhotels.com* 🖙 *165 rooms, 3 suites* △ *2 restaurants, cafeteria, room service, in-room safes, minibars, cable TV, Wi-Fi, 2 pools, gym, hair salon, spa, 2 bars, car rental* ⊟ *AE, DC, MC, V* �[○⟨ *BP.*

$$–$$$ ⌂ **La Ventana.** From the dainty, green-shuttered *ventanas* (windows) to the lushly painted rooms with handsome beds draped in romantic white canopies, this intimate hillside hotel is a breath of fresh air in the heart of Dalt Vila. Tucked behind the medieval walls, it's surrounded by the cobbled streets of history but within a 10-minute stroll of the port. The roof terrace has Morrocan-style sofas to sink into and gorgeous vistas of the old town and the Mediterranean. ⊠ *Sa Carrossa 13, 07800* ☏ *971/390857* 🖷 *971/390145* ⊕ *www.laventanaibiza.com* 🖙 *14 rooms* △ *Restaurant, cable TV* ⊟ *AE, MC, V.*

Nightlife

If the arts are relatively neglected on Ibiza, nightlife certainly is not. **Ibiza's discos** are famous throughout Europe. Keep your eyes open during the day for free invitations to discos, handed out on the street. This will save you a sometimes expensive (€10 to €40) entry fee. Also note that a handy, all-night "Discobus" service (☏ 971/192456) runs between Ibiza, Sant Antoni, Santa Eulalia, and the major discos. Some discos—such as Amnesia, Privilege, and Space—are open only from June to September, plus New Year's Eve.

Down in the town, the trendy place to start the evening is **Keeper** (⊠ Paseo Marítimo Ibiza Nueva ☏ 971/310509), where you can sip your drink sitting on a carousel horse. A lively, very young scene rocks **El Divino Café** (⊠ C. Vara De Ray ☏ 971/119-0177). In summer, boats depart between 1 AM and 4 AM from in front of El Divino Café for the marina and **El Divino Disco** (⊠ Puerto de Ibiza Nueva ☏ 971/190176 ⊕ www.eldivino-ibiza.com), which is a typical Ibiza disco with throbbing dance music (and spectacular views of Ibiza Town). The "in" place for older nighthawks is the stylish bar in the foyer of the former **Teatre Pereira** (⊠ Carrer Comte Roselló 3 ☏ 971/191468). A young, international crowd dances to techno at **Pacha** (⊠ Av. 8 de Agosto s/n ☎ 971/ 313612 ⊕ www.pacha.com). The popular **Amnesia San Rafael** (⊠ Sant Antoni road, opposite Km 5 marker ☎ 971/198041) has several ample dance floors that throb to house and funk. **Privilege** (⊠ Ctra. Ibiza–Sant Antoni, Km 7, San Rafael ☎ 971/198477) is the grande dame of Ibiza's nightlife, with a giant dance floor, a swimming pool, and more than a dozen bars. **Space** (⊠ Playa d'en Bossa ☎ 971/396793 ⊕ www.space-ibiza.es), which doesn't even open until other discos have closed, is where the serious clubbers come to dance "after hours." Ibiza's **casino,** under reconstruction at this writing, is in temporary quarters until a scheduled reopening sometime in 2007. ⊠ *Carrer del Metge Domingo Nicolau Balansat s/n* ☎ *971/313312* ⊕ *www.casinoibiza.com* ☽ *Weekdays 10 AM–4 AM, weekends 10 AM–5 AM.*

Gay nightlife converges on **Carrer de la Verge** in Sa Penya, where a multinational crowd bar-hops until the wee hours. The ever-popular gay bar **Dome** (⊠ Carrer Alfonso XII ☎ No phone) has a leafy terrace that overflows with revelers in summer. In Dalt Vila, join the rest of gay Ibiza at the fashionable, electronica-blasting **Disco Anfora** (⊠ Carrer San Carlos 7 ☎ 971/302893), one of the few discos open year-round.

Sports & the Outdoors
For information on sports on Ibiza and Formentera, obtain a free copy of the magazine **Touribisport** (⊕ www.touribisport.com), available locally.

BICYCLING **Mr. Bike** (⊠ Av. Isidoro Nacabich 63A bajo, Ibiza Town ☎ 971/392300) rents bicycles in Ibiza Town.

BOATING Explore Ibiza by sea with **Coral Yachting** (⊠ Marina Botafoc, Ibiza Town ☎ 971/313524). **Cruiser Ibiza** (⊠ Marina Botafoc s/n, Ibiza Town ☎ 971/316170 ⊕ www.cruiser-ibiza.com) runs charters.

GOLF Ibiza's only 18-hole course is **Golf de Ibiza** (⊠ Ctra. Jesús–Cala Llonga, Km 6, Santa Eulalia ☎ 971/196118 ⊕ www.golfibiza.com). **Club Roca Lisa** (⊠ Ctra. Jesús–Cala Llonga, Km 8, Santa Eulalia ☎ 971/313718) has 9 holes.

HORSEBACK RIDING **Centro Ecuestre Easy Rider** (Easy Rider Equestrian Center; ⊠ Camí del Sol d'en Serra, Cala Llonga, Santa Eulalia des Riu ☎ 971/339192) offers a two-hour ride along the coast and inland.

SCUBA DIVING Year-round a team with a decompression chamber is on standby at the **Policlinica de Nuestra Señora del Rosario** (⊠ Via Romana s/n, Ibiza Town ☎ 971/301916). Scuba in Sant Antoni with **Centro de Buceo Sirena** (⊠ Balanzat 21 bajo, Sant Antoni ☎ 971/342966). Dive in Sant Joan with **Centro Subfari** (⊠ Portinatx, San Joan ☎ 971/333067). **Diving Center San Miguel** (⊠ Puerto de San Miguel ☎ 971/334539 ⊕ www.divingcenter-sanmiguel.com) also offers diving. **Active Dive** (⊠ Cantabra 2, Bahíia de San Antoni ☎ 971/804125) is a scuba source in Sant Antoni. Dive in Santa Josep with **Orca Sub** (⊠ Club Hotel Tarida Beach, Santa Josep ☎ 971/806307). Rent scuba gear in Ibiza Town at **Vellmari** (⊠ Marina Botafoc, Ibiza Town ☎ 971/192884 ⊕ www.vellmari.com).

TENNIS **Ibiza Club de Campo** (⊠Ctra. Sant Josep, Km 2, Ibiza Town ☎971/391458 ⊕ www.ibiza-spotlight.com/clubdecampo), with six clay and two composition courts, is the largest tennis club on the island. Nonmembers can play here for €6 per hour during the day and €9.60 per hour at night. There are public tennis courts at **Port Sant Miquel**, available on a first-come, first-served basis.

WALKING **Ecoibiza** (✉ C. Abad y Lasierra 35, Ibiza Ciutat 07800 ☎ 971/302347 ⊕ www.ecoibiza.com) has lots of ecologically friendly countryside hikes, and can also arrange horseback riding, sailing, and sea fishing.

Shopping

In the late 1960s and '70s, Ibiza built a reputation for extremes of fashion. Little of this phenomenon survives, though the softer designs of Smilja Mihailovich (under the Ad Lib label) still prosper. Along Carrer d'Enmig is an eclectic collection of shops and stalls selling fashion and crafts. Although the Sa Penya area of Ibiza Town still has a few designer boutiques, much of the area is now called the Mercat dels Hippies ("hippie market"), with more than 80 stalls of overpriced tourist ephemera. For trendy casual gear, sandals, belts, and bags, try **Ibiza Republic** (✉ Antoni Mar 15, Ibiza Town ☎ 971/314175). For wines and spirits, visit **Enotecum** (✉ Av. d'Isidoro Macabich 43, Ibiza Town ☎ 971/399167).

Santa Eulària des Riu

㉔ *15 km (9 mi) northeast of Ibiza.*

At the edge of this town (at Santa Eulària des Riu), to the right below the road, a Roman bridge crosses what is claimed to be the only permanent river in the Balearics (hence "des Riu," or "of the river"). Ahead, on the hilltop, are the cubes and domes of the church—to reach it, look for a narrow lane to the left, signed PUIG DE MISSA, itself so named for the hill where regular mass was once held. A stoutly arched, crypt-like covered area guards the entrance; inside are a fine gold reredos and blue-tile stations of the cross.

Where to Eat

$–$$$ ✕ **Mezzanotte.** Opened in March 2006, this charming little portside restaurant is a branch of the popular Mezzanotte in Ibiza Town. There are just 12 tables inside, softly lighted with candles and track lights; in summer, seating expands to an interior patio and tables on the sidewalk. The kitchen prides itself on hard-to-find fresh ingredients flown in from Italy. The linguini with jumbo shrimp, saffron, and zucchini—or with *bottarga* (dried and salted mullet roe from Sicily)—is wonderful. Value for price here is excellent; the €15 prix-fixe lunch menu is an absolute bargain. ✉ *Paseo de s'Alamera 22 Santa Eulària* ☎ *971/319498* ▤ *MC, V* ⊘ *Closed Jan. and Mon.*

★ $$ ✕ **C'as Pagès.** Meat eaters will love this restaurant in an old farmhouse with bare stone walls, wood beams, and columns made of giant olive-press screws. Try the leg of *cordero asado* (roast lamb with baked potato) or *sofrit pagès* (lamb and chicken stew), and finish with *graixonera*, a mixture of sugar, milk, eggs, and cinnamon. ✉ *Ctra. de San Carlos, Km 10, Pont de S'Argentara* ☎ *971/319029* ▤ *No credit cards* ⊘ *Closed Tues. and Feb.–mid-Mar.* ⌖ *Reservations are not accepted.*

9

Sports & the Outdoors

Charter yachts from **Tagomago Yachting** (✉ Puerto Deportivo, Santa Eulalia ☎ 971/338101).

Club Terra Nova (✉ Ctra. Cala Llonga, Km 10, Santa Eulalia ☎ 971/319116) has six tennis courts plus archery, badminton, Ping-Pong, bowling, a swimming pool, and a hot tub. (The property was sold in 2006, so there may be changes under way; call ahead.)

FORMENTERA

For a calm respite from Ibiza's dance-until-you-drop madness, sleepy little Formentera is the answer. Just south of Ibiza, Formentera has managed to sidestep rampant overdevelopment. Though it can still get crowded in the summer, many of the island's long white-sand beaches are generally unspoiled, and you can pedal along quiet country roads in relative solitude.

Formentera

㉕ *90 mins by ferry from Ibiza, 30–40 mins by fast boat.*

You can begin this tour from Ibiza Town, Sant Antoni, or Santa Eulalia, as all have ferries to La Sabina—though the fast boats all connect from Ibiza Town. Because Formentera is mostly beach and countryside, you may be inspired to picnic; if so, buy supplies in Ibiza. It's worth standing on deck during the short passage for the excellent views of Ibiza's Dalt Vila and the smaller islands en route. Look for Trucadors, the stretch of sand that almost links Formentera with Es Palmador.

La Sabina has several car-, bicycle-, and moped-rental agencies, and most people rent bikes to explore this flat little island. From La Sabina, it's only 3 km (2 mi) to Formentera's tiny capital, **Sant Francesc Xavier,** a few yards off the main road. There's an active hippie market in the small plaza before the church. The interior of the whitewashed church, with its weathered wooden door, encased in iron and studded with nails, has a simple sturdiness inside as well. Down a short street directly opposite the church, on the left, an antiques and junk shop has a small art gallery with paintings and olive-wood carvings. At the main road, turn right toward Sant Ferran, 2 km (1 mi) away. Beyond Sant Ferran the road travels for 7 km (4 mi) along a narrow isthmus, keeping slightly closer to the rougher, northern side, where waves come crashing over the rocks when a wind is blowing.

The plateau on the island's east side ends at the lighthouse **Faro de la Mola.** Nearby is a **monument to Jules Verne,** who set part of his novel *Journey Through the Solar System* in Formentera. Despite being trampled by tourists, the bare rock around the lighthouse is carpeted with flowers, purple thyme, and sea holly in spring and fall.

Back on the main road, turn right at Sant Ferran toward Es Pujols. The few hotels here are the closest Formentera comes to beach resorts, even if the beach is not the best. Beyond Es Pujols the road skirts **Estany Pu-**

dent, one of two lagoons that almost enclose La Sabina. Salt was once extracted from Pudent, hence its name, which means "stinking pond," although the pond now smells fine. At the northern tip of Pudent, a road to the right leads to a footpath that runs the length of **Trucadors,** a narrow sand spit. The long, windswept beaches here are excellent.

Where to Stay & Eat

$–$$$ ✕ **Sa Palmera.** On the beachfront in Es Pujols, Sa Palmera is known for paella and extremely fresh fish, such as the grilled *dorada* (sea bream) and *lubino* (sea bass). The locals' favorite is the *parrillada*, a platter of three types of grilled fish (depending on the catch of the day) served with potatoes and a salad. ⊠ *Playa Es Pujols, Es Pujols* ☎ *971/328356* ▤ *MC, V* ⊙ *Closed Nov.–Feb.*

★ **$–$$** ✕▦ **Fonda C'an Rafalet.** This simple inn is just a few steps from the water at the tiny fishing cove of Es Caló; stay here, and one of the fishing boats drawn up on the rocky strand is likely to have come in that morning with your lunch. Paellas are the specialities here; don't miss the rice with *bogavante* (lobster). The lack of a sandy beach has saved Es Caló from rampant development, but the setting is lovely: the brilliant blue-green of the water is bounded on the east by a long, dramatic line of cliffs. The hotel is 12 km (7 mi) from La Sabina. ⊠ *Ctra. La Mola, Km 12, Apdo. de Correos 225, Es Caló de Sant Agustí, Sant Francesc Xavier 07860* ☎▨ *971/327016* ⌂ *15 rooms* ⌂ *Restaurant, bar; no a/c, no room TVs* ▤ *MC, V* ⊙ *Closed Nov.–Mar.*

$$–$$$ ▦ **Sa Volta.** Near the beach in Es Pujols, one of the island's busiest villages, this is a cozy and, if you choose one of the more modest rooms, economical lodging choice. ⊠ *Miramar 94, Es Pujols 07860* ☎ *971/328125* ▨ *971/328228* ⊕ *www.guiaformentera.com/savolta* ⌂ *22 rooms, 3 suites* ⌂ *Cafeteria, pool, cable TV, Internet room* ▤ *MC, V* ⊙ *Closed Jan.–Mar.*

$$ ▦ **Roca Bella.** Balanced atop craggy rocks overlooking the Mediterranean Sea, this simple, pleasant hotel offers the best of both worlds: head in one direction, and you have the beach, waves, and wilderness all to yourself; saunter in the opposite direction and you hit crowds, shops, and the nightlife of Es Pujols. The price is more than reasonable, so this hotel often gets booked up by agencies; call ahead to make reservations. ⊠ *Playa Es Pujols, Es Pujols 07870* ☎ *971/328130* ▨ *971/328002* ⌂ *60 rooms* ⌂ *Restaurant, bar, cafeteria, cable TV in some rooms, Wi-Fi* ▤ *MC, V* ⊙ *Closed Dec.–Apr.*

Shopping

El Pilar is the chief crafts village of Formentera. Stores and workshops sell handmade items, including bags, ceramics, jewelry, and leather goods. El Pilar's crafts market draws shoppers on Sunday afternoon, May to September; from June to August, the market is also on Wednesday afternoon. From May to September, crafts are sold in the morning at the San Francesc Xavier market and in the evening in Es Pujols.

Sports & the Outdoors

BICYCLING You can rent bikes and motorcycles in La Sabina at **Moto Rent Mitjorn** (⊠ Playa de Migjorn ☎ 971/328611 ⊕ www.guiaformentera.com/mitjorn).

BOATING   The graceful sloop **Princesa de Mar** (☎ 971/390068) travels around and between Ibiza and Formentera daily. The young crew provides plenty of laughs, and lovely views await aboard the sunset cruise. The boat departs from Ibiza's port or La Sabina in Formentera and costs €35 per person. Boats are for hire at **Náutica Pins** (⊠ Av. Mediterráneo 15–19, La Sabina ☎ 971/322651 ⊕ www.formenteraonline.com/comercial/nauticapins).

DIVING   You can take diving courses at **Vell Marí** (⊠ Puerto Deportivo Marina de Formentera s/n, La Sabina ☎ 971/322105).

BALEARIC ISLANDS ESSENTIALS

To research prices, get advice from other travelers, and book travel arrangements, visit www.fodors.com.

Transportation

BY AIR

Iberia, Spanair, and Air Europa have daily direct flights between Palma and Barcelona, Madrid, Alicante, Valencia, Minorca, and Ibiza, as well as direct flights two or three times a week to Bilbao and Vitoria. Interisland flights should be booked well in advance for summer travel. Iberia and a large number of charter operators also serve other European cities. Iberia flies direct to Mahón from Barcelona and Palma three or four times daily, and most of these flights start and end in Madrid. Air Europa and Spanair also fly to Mahón, and in summer several European cities send charter flights to Minorca. Iberia has direct daily flights to Ibiza from Barcelona, Madrid, Valencia, and Palma.

TRANSFERS   Bus 1 runs between Palma's airport and the bus station on Plaça d'Espanya, next to the Inca train station. The last bus from town is around 2:30 AM; the last bus from the airport leaves at 2:15 AM. The fare is €1.80, and the trip takes 30 minutes. A taxi is about €20. A meter taxi to Mahón from the airport costs about €12. An hourly bus service runs between Ibiza's airport and Ibiza Town from 7 AM to 10:30 PM (on the hour from town, on the half hour from the airport; fare €2.70, journey time is about 20 minutes). By taxi, the same trip costs about €16.

🛫 **Airports Aeropuerto de Ibiza (IBZ)** ☎ 971/809000. **Aeropuerto de Menorca (MAH)** ☎ 971/157000. **Aeropuerto de Palma de Mallorca (PMI)** ☎ 971/789099.
🛫 **Carriers Air Europa** ☎ 902/401501 ⊕ www.air-europa.com. **British Airways** ☎ 971/787737 ⊕ www.britishairways.com. **British Midland** ☎ 971/789269 ⊕ www.flybmi.com. **Easyjet** ☎ 902/299992 ⊕ www.easyjet.com. **Iberia** ☎ 902/400500 ⊕ www.iberia.com. **Spanair** ☎ 902/131415 ⊕ www.spanair.com.

BY BIKE

The Balearic Islands—especially Formentera and Ibiza—are ideal for exploration by bicycle. Parts of Majorca are quite mountainous, with challenging climbs through spectacular scenery; along some country roads, there are designated bicycle lanes Bicycles are easy to rent, and tourist offices have details on recommended routes. Minorca is relatively flat, with lots of roads that wander through pastureland and olive groves to small coves and inlets. Ibiza, too, is relatively flat and easy to negotiate, though side roads can be in poor repair. Formentera is level, with bicycle lanes on all connecting roads.

BY BOAT AND FERRY

BARCELONA For die-hard romantics with time to spare, the best way to get to the Balearic Islands is by overnight ferry from Barcelona on one of the three lines departing from the Terminal Drassanes, at the foot of the Ramblas. Depending on the line and the season, the Transmediterránea, Balearia, and Iscomar car ferries to Palma, Majorca, sail between 11 and 11:30 PM; on a clear night, you can watch the lights of Barcelona sinking into the horizon for three hours or more—and when you arrive in Palma, around 6 AM, the spires of the cathedral should just be bathed in the light of the morning sun. All three lines serve Minorca and Ibiza as well. Fast ferries and 43-knot catamarans, for passengers only, speed from Barcelona to Palma and Alcúdia (Majorca), to Ciutadella (Minorca), and to Eivissa (Ibiza); depending on the destination, the trip takes between three and five hours.

Overnight ferries have both lounges and private cabins; the fast ferries and catamarans have only lounge seating. Depending on the line, the season, and the points of departure and destination, round-trip fares are around €140 for lounges and range from about €280 to €360 for a double cabin. In the high summer season, it's wise to reserve a cabin well in advance. Major credit cards are accepted for all mainland–Balearic and most interisland fares.

DENIA Balearia runs a daily two-hour "Super Fast Ferry" service for passengers and cars between Denia (Alicante) and Ibiza Town, and a similar three-hour service between Denia and Palma on weekends. Iscomar runs a slower car-and-truck ferry service between Denia and Sant Antoni, Ibiza.

VALENCIA Trasmediterránea ferries leave Valencia in midmorning for Palma, arriving early evening. There are also ferries from Valencia to Ibiza and Minorca: departure days and times vary with the season; service is more frequent in summer.

MAJORCA Trasmediterránea sails daily (and twice on Sunday) from Palma to Barcelona, daily from Palma to Valencia, and weekly (Sunday) from Palma to Mahón and Ibiza. Balearia has a daily "Super Fast Ferry" car ferry service between Palma and Denia, direct on weekends but via Ibiza on weekdays. From June to September, a twice-weekly Euromer service connects Palma with Sète, France.

MINORCA Trasmediterránea sails between Mahón and Barcelona six days a week in summer (mid-June to mid-September) and to Palma and Valencia every Sunday.

IBIZA Trasmediterránea sails to Barcelona and Valencia from Ibiza, and once a week (Sunday) to Palma. From May to October there's also a daily hydrofoil service from Palma and Denia, as well as less frequent serv-

9

ice from Valencia and Barcelona. Balearia runs a "Super Fast Ferry" to Denia daily, which takes two hours. In summer, Flebasa runs a daily 2½-hour hovercraft between Sant Antoni (Ibiza) and mainland Benidorm; contact Coral Travel. Flebasa also runs a car ferry and a fast hydrofoil between Sant Antoni (Ibiza) and mainland Denia, with bus connections from Denia to Madrid and Valencia. A Euromer service operates between Sète (France) and Ibiza twice a week, June to September, calling at Palma on the way.

INTERISLAND   Boats from Palma, Majorca, to neighboring beach resorts leave from the jetty opposite the Auditorium, on the Passeig Marítim. The tourist office has a schedule. In summer, excursions to Minorca's remotest beaches leave daily from the jetty next to the Nuevo Muelle Comercial, in Mahón's harbor. Daily ferries connect Alcúdia (Majorca) and Ciutadella (Minorca) in three to four hours, depending on the weather; a hydrofoil makes the same journey in about an hour. From May to October, a daily hydrofoil service connects Palma and Ibiza; call Naviera Mallorquina. There are frequent car and fast ferry services between Ibiza and Formentera operated by Balearia, Mediterránea Pitiusa, and other local lines.

▉ **Boat & Ferry Information Balearia** ✉ Estación Marítima, Barcelona ☎ 902/160180 ⊕ www.balearia.com. **Coral Travel** ✉ Carrer Mar 11, Sant Antoni, Ibiza ☎ 971/343711 or 971/343752 ✉ Carrer Isadoro Macabich 14, Santa Eulalia, Ibiza ☎ 971/330512 or 971/330561. **Euromer** ☎ 33/467-65-9513 ⊕ www.euromer.net. **Flebasa** ✉ Estación Marítim, Ibiza ☎ 971/310711 ✉ Edificio Faro, Sant Antoni, Ibiza ☎ 971/342871 ✉ Madrid ☎ 91/473-2055 ✉ Denia ☎ 96/784011. **Formentera port information** ☎ 971/320157. **Inserco** ☎ 971/322210. **Iscomar** ✉ Estación Marítima, Barcelona ☎ 902/119128 ⊕ www.iscomar.com. **Mediterránea Pitiusa** ☎ 971/32244. **Naviera Mallorquina** ☎ 971/710153. **Pitra** ☎ 971/191068. **Transmapi Ibiza** ☎ 971/322930, 971/322703 on Formentera. **Trasmediterránea** ✉ Estación Marítima, Barcelona ☎ 902/454645 ⊕ www.trasmediterranea.es ✉ Estación Marítima, Valencia ☎ 963/676512 ✉ Estación Marítima 2, Muelle de Paraires, Palma de Mallorca ☎ 971/707377 ✉ Nuevo Muelle Comercial, Mahón, Minorca ☎ 971/366050 ✉ Ibiza, Estación Marítima ☎ 971/315050. **Umafisa Lines** ☎ 902/191068.

BY BUS

A good network of bus service fans out from Palma to towns throughout Majorca. Most buses leave from the city station, next to the Inca railway terminus on the Plaça d'Espanya; a few terminate at other points in Palma. The tourist office on the Plaça d'Espanya has schedules. Several buses a day run the length of Minorca between Mahón and Ciutadella, stopping at Alaior, Mercadal, and Ferreries en route. From smaller towns there are daily buses to Mahón and connections, though often indirect, to Ciutadella. A regular bus service from the west end of Ciutadella's Plaça Explanada shuttles beachgoers between town and the resorts to the south and west. On Ibiza, buses run every half hour from Ibiza Town (Avinguda Isidoro Macabich) to Sant Antoni and Playa d'en Bossa, roughly hourly to Santa Eulalia. Buses from Ibiza to other parts of the island are less frequent, as is the cross-island bus between Sant Antoni and Santa Eulalia. The schedule is published in newspapers. A very limited bus service connects Formentera's villages, shrinking to one bus each way between San Francisco and Pilar on Saturday and disappearing altogether on Sunday and holidays.

7 Bus Stations Ciutadella ✉ Plaça de S'Esplanada, across from tourist office. **Ibiza Town** ✉ At Av. Isidoro Macabich and Extremadura ⊕ www.ibizabus.com. **Palma de Mallorca** ✉ Estación Central ☎ 971/752224.

BY CAR

Majorca's main highways are well surfaced, and a fast, 25-km (15-mi) motorway penetrates deep into the island between Palma and Inca. Palma is ringed by an efficient beltway, the Vía Cintura. For destinations in the north and west, follow the ANDRATX and OESTE signs on the beltway; for the south and east, follow the ESTE signs. Driving in the mountains that parallel the northwest coast and descend to a cliff-side corniche is a different matter; you'll be slowed not only by winding roads but by tremendous views and tourist traffic. The tunnel through the mountains to Sóller makes the island's northwest coast a safe, simple, 20-minute drive from downtown Palma—the twisting route through the mountains is spectacular but tiring.

A car is essential if you want to beach-hop on Minorca, as few of the beaches and calas are served by public transport. However, most historic sights are in Mahón or Ciutadella, both of which have reasonable bus service from other parts of the island, and once you're in town, everything is within walking distance. You can see the island's archaeological remains in a day's drive, so you may want to rent a car for just part of your visit. Ibiza is best explored by car or motor scooter: many of the beaches lie at the end of rough, unpaved roads.

In 2005, work began on Ibiza on a six-lane divided highway connecting the capital with the airport and Sant Antoni. It's still a bit confusing to get in and out of Ibiza Town, but once you're past the construction sites, driving is easy—and remains the only feasible way of getting to some of the island's smaller coves and beaches. Tiny Formentera can almost be covered on foot, but renting a car at La Sabina is an obvious time-saver.

If you use a car on any of the Balearics, eventually you will have to park it somewhere. Finding a legal space on the street—indicated by painted blue lines—can be a nightmare; if and when you do, you then have to find a parking ticket dispenser on the sidewalk nearby, feed it coins for the time you want (dispensers won't take paper money), then take the ticket back to the car and lock it inside, on the dashboard. The meter maids are super-vigilant; the fine for parking overtime is usually €6, payable—also in the dispensers—on the spot.

RENTALS Although reserving a car from home through a major agency can often lead to savings, don't count out the local companies, whose rates are often inexpensive. Many of these local vendors also rent out *motos* (motor scooters) and bicycles.

7 National Agencies Avis ☎ 902/135531 ⊕ www.avis.com. **Europcar** ☎ 902/105030 ⊕ www.europcar.es. **Hertz** ☎ 902/402405 ⊕ www.hertz.es. **National/Atesa** ☎ 902/100101 ⊕ www.atesa.com.

9

BY TAXI
Taxis in Palma are metered. For trips beyond the city, charges are posted at the taxi stands. On Minorca, you can pick up a taxi at the airport or in Mahón and Ciutadella; on Ibiza, taxis are available at the airport and in Ibiza Town, Figueretas, Santa Eulalia, and Sant Antoni. On Formentera, there are taxis in La Sabina and Es Pujols. Most taxis in Minorca, Ibiza, and Formentera are not metered.

⌘ Taxi Companies Majorca ✉ Palma ☎ 971/728081 ✉ Palma ☎ 971/755440 ✉ Palma ☎ 971/401414. **Minorca** ✉ Explanada, Mahón ☎ 971/367111 ✉ Carrer Josep Antoni, Ciutadella ☎ 971/381896. **Ibiza** ✉ Aeropuerto de Ibiza ☎ 971/305230 ✉ Passeig Vara de Rey, Ibiza Town ☎ 971/307000, or 971/306602 ✉ Figueretas ☎ 971/301676 ✉ Santa Eulalia ☎ 971/333033 ✉ Sant Antoni ☎ 971/340074 or 971/341721. **Formentera** ✉ La Sabina ☎ 971/322002 ✉ Sant Francesc ☎ 971/322016 ✉ Es Pujols ☎ 971/322080.

BY TRAIN
The Palma–Inca line travels to Inca, with stops at about half a dozen villages en route, from the Palma terminus. A journey on the privately owned Palma–Sóller railway is a must: built by the citrus-fruit magnates of Sóller in 1912, it still uses the carriages of that era. The line trundles across the plain to Bunyola, then winds through tremendous mountain scenery to emerge high above Sóller. An ancient tram connects the Sóller terminus to Port de Sóller, leaving every hour on the hour, 9–6; the Palma terminal is near the corner of the Plaça d'Espanya, on Calle Eusebio Estada next to the Inca rail station.

⌘ Train Information Palma train station ✉ Ferrocarriles de Majorca, Plaça d'Espanya ☎ 971/752245. **Sóller tram** ✉ Eusebi Estada 1 ☎ 971/752051.

Contacts & Resources

BANKS & EXCHANGING SERVICES
You can change currency virtually anywhere in the Balearics, from the ports and airports to the shopping districts in all of the major cities, towns, and beach resorts. The local banks—**Banco de Credito Balear, sa Nostra** and **la Caixa**—are the most prominent; all are authorized to make currency exchanges.

EMERGENCIES
⌘ Emergency Services Fire, Police or Ambulance ☎ 112. **Guardia Civil** ☎ 062. **Insalud** (Public health service) ☎ 061. **Policía Local** (Local police) ☎ 092. **Policía Nacional** (National police) ☎ 091. **Información Toxicológica** (Poisoning) ☎ 915/620420. **⌘ 24-Hour Pharmacies 24-Hour Pharmacy Emergency Line** ☎ 112.

LANGUAGE
The regional language is a version of Catalan, but everyone speaks Castilian Spanish. Road signs are in Catalan or Castilian. English and German are widely understood at most tourist venues.

LODGING
Villas, apartments, and rural houses are rented out to tourists throughout the Balearic Islands. There are hundreds of real estate agents offer-

ing properties for short-term rentals. Contact the tourist offices or check the local papers for listings, but also consider booking through a travel agent, who can usually put together an attractive lodging package that includes transportation. **Kuhn and Partner** (✉ Plaça de la Lonja 1, Palma 07001 ☎ 971/228880 ⊕ www.kuhn-partner.com) is a major Majorca real estate agency with numerous branches. For information on more than 75 small country hotels away from the crowds, contact **Associació Agroturisme Balear** (✉ Av. Gabriel Alomar i Villalonga 8A, 2A, Palma de Mallorca 07006 ☎ 971/721508 ☎ 971/717317).

MEDIA

Majorca's daily English-language newspaper, the *Majorca Daily Bulletin* (☎ 971/788400 ⊕ www.majorcadailybulletin.es); its useful Web site has information on all the islands; the city's weekly English-language paper is the *Reader.* Ibiza's sole English-language publication is the *Ibiza Sun* (☎ 971/342815 ⊕ www.theibizasun.com); the **Ibiza Spotlight** Web page (⊕ www.ibiza-spotlight.com) is also worth a look.

Kiosks in Palma, Mahón, Cuitadella, Ibiza Town—indeed, everywhere in the islands tourists are likely to spend time—stock a wide variety of foreign-language newspapers.

TOUR OPTIONS

In Palma, take in the sights from an open-top **City Sightseeing** (☎ 902/101081) bus that departs from various stops throughout the town, including Plaça de la Reina, and travels along the Passeig Marítim and up to the Castell de Bellver. Tickets (€13) are valid for 24 hours, and you can get on and off as many times as you wish along the way. All of Palma's tourist offices have information and details. Also in Palma, groups of up to four or five can hire a horse-drawn carriage with driver at the bottom of the Born; on Avinguda Antonio Maura; in the nearby cathedral square; and on the Plaça d'Espanya, at the side farthest from the railway station. A tour of the city costs about €25.

Most Majorca hotels offer guided tours. Typical itineraries are the Caves of Artà or Drac, on the east coast, including the nearby Auto Safari Park and an artificial-pearl factory in Manacor; the Chopin museum in the old monastery at Valldemossa, returning through the writers' and artists' village of Deià; the port of Sóller and the Arab gardens at Alfàbia; the Thursday market and leather factories in Inca; Port de Pollença; Cape Formentor; and northern beaches. Nearly every Majorcan resort runs excursions to neighboring beaches and coves—many inaccessible by road—and to the islands of Cabrera and Dragonera. You can also take a morning shopping trip by boat from Magalluf or Palma Nova to Palma; the tourist office has details. Sightseeing trips leave Mahón's harbor from the quayside near the Xoriguer gin factory; several boats have glass bottoms. Fares average around €10. Every Ibiza resort runs trips to neighboring beaches and to smaller islands off the coast. Trips from Ibiza to Formentera include an escorted bus tour. In Sant Antoni, which has little to offer in the way of beaches, a whole flotilla advertises trips.

9

VISITOR INFORMATION
The regional tourist office for the Balearic Islands is the**Consellaria de Turismo de Balear** (✉ Plaça de la Reina 2, Palma de Mallorca 07012 ☎ 971/712216 ⊕ www.visitbalears.com). Several tourist offices in Palma's airport have information on Majorca and towns nearby. The offices in Mahón and Ciutadella have local information.

⑦ Local Tourist Offices–Majorca Oficina de Turismo de Mallorca ✉ Aeropuerto de Palma ☎ 971/789556. **Alcúdia** ✉ Passeig Marítim s/n ☎ 971/547257. **Manacor** ✉ Plaça Ramon Llull s/n ☎ 971/847241. **Palma** ✉ Plaça de la Reina 2 ☎ 971/712216 ✉ Passeig d'es Born 27 ☎ 971/729634 ✉ Parc de ses Estacions, across from train station and near Plaça España ☎ 971/292758. **Pollença** ✉ Sant Domingo 2 ☎ 971/535077. **Sóller** ✉ Plaça de Sa Constitució 1 ☎ 971/630200 ✉ Carrer Canónigo Oliver ☎ 971/630101. **Valldemossa** ✉ Av. de Palma 7 ☎ 971/612019.

⑦ Local Tourist Offices–Minorca Ciutadella ✉ Plaça de la Catedral 5 ☎ 971/382693. **Mahón** ✉ Plaça Esplanada s/n ☎ 971/363790. **Minorca** ✉ Aeropuerto de Menorca ☎ 971/157115.

⑦ Local Tourist Offices–Ibiza (Eivissa) & Formentera Aeropuerto de Ibiza ☎ 971/809118. **Formentera** ✉ Port de La Sabina ☎ 971/322057 ⊕ www.formentera.es/en/turismo. **Ibiza Town** ✉ Carrer Antonio Riquer 2 ☎ 971/301900. **Santa Eulalia** ✉ Carrer Mariano Riquer Wallis 4 ☎ 971/330728. **Sant Antoni** ✉ Passeig de Ses Fonts s/n ☎ 971/343363. **Sant Joan** ✉ Ajuntament ☎ 971/333003.

The Costa del Sol

10

By Hilary
Bunce

Updated by
Mary McLean

THE STRETCH OF ANDALUSIAN SHORE known as the Costa del Sol runs
west from the Costa Tropical, near Granada, to the tip of Tarifa, the
southernmost tip of Europe, just beyond Gibraltar. For most of the Europeans who have flocked here over the past 40 years, though, the Sunshine Coast has been largely restricted to the 70-km (43-mi) sprawl of
hotels, vacation villas, golf courses, marinas, and nightclubs between
Torremolinos, just west of Málaga, and Estepona, down toward Gibraltar. Since the late 1950s this area has mushroomed from a group of impoverished fishing villages into an overdeveloped seaside playground and
retirement haven.

Construction continued unabated along the coast until the early '90s,
which saw a brief economic slump caused, in part, by a drop in international airfares. Travelers became more adventurous, and Spain's favorite coast was now competing with seemingly more sophisticated
locations. Local municipalities poured money into elaborate landscaping, and better roads and infrastructure. It paid off. In 1997 the prestigious Ryder Cup was held in Sotogrande, seeming to mark the Costa
del Sol's return to the world stage. The result was more golf courses,
luxury marinas, villa developments, and upscale hotels. The Costa averages some 320 days of sunshine a year, and balmy days are not unknown even in January or February. Despite the hubbub, you *can*
unwind here, basking or strolling on mile after mile of sandy beach.

Choose your base carefully. Málaga is a vibrant Spanish city, virtually
untainted by tourism. Despite the tour bus trade, Ronda is also intrinsically Andalusian, with the added perk of a stunning inland setting. Back
on the coast, Torremolinos is a budget destination catering almost exclusively to the mass market; it appeals to young families, the gay community, and to those who come purely for the sunbronzing and late-night
scene. Fuengirola is quieter, with a large, and notably middle-aged, foreign resident population; farther west, the Marbella–San Pedro de Alcántara area is more exclusive—and expensive.

Exploring the Costa del Sol

The towns and resorts along the Costa del Sol vary considerably according to whether they lie to the east or to the west of Málaga. To the east
lies the Costa Tropical, a rugged and less developed stretch of coastline.
Towns such as Nerja also act as a gateway to the dramatic mountainous region of La Axarquía. Heading west from Málaga along the Costa
del Sol proper, the strip between Torremolinos and Marbella is the most
densely populated. Seamless though it may appear, as one resort merges
into the next, each town has a distinctive character, with its own sights,
charm, and activities.

About the Beaches

Lobster-pink sun worshippers from northern Europe pack these beaches
in summer so that there's little towel space on the sand. Beach chairs
can be rented for around €4 a day. Beaches range from shingle and pebbles (Almuñecar, Nerja, Málaga) to fine, gritty sand (from Torremolinos westward). The best—and most crowded—beaches are El Bajondillo
and La Carihuela, in Torremolinos; the stretch between Carvajal, Los

GREAT ITINERARIES

IF YOU HAVE 3 DAYS

Start with a gentle initiation to Andalusia by exploring the relatively unspoiled villages of the Costa Tropical. Wander around quaint **Salobreña** ❶ before hitting the larger coastal resort of **Nerja** ❸ for lunch at a sea-view restaurant. Visit **Frigiliana** ❹, before proceeding to 🖼 **Málaga** ❻ for an evening of touring the tapas bars. The next morning, check out the Museo Picasso or one of Málaga's many other sights before heading into the hills for lunch in **Antequera** ❼. Make the 100-km (62-mi) drive to the stunning mountain-top town of 🖼 **Ronda** ⓰ for your second night. Explore Ronda in the morning before hitting the coast at **Marbella** ⓮, the Costa del Sol's swankiest resort, followed by lunch at Puerto Banús. Head west to **Gibraltar** ㉕-㊲ for an afternoon of shopping and sightseeing before returning to the coast and 🖼 **Torremolinos** ❿ for a night on the town.

IF YOU HAVE 5 DAYS

Follow the itinerary above for your first day, settling down in 🖼 **Málaga** ❻ for the night. On Day 2 explore Málaga's many sights, followed by a seafood lunch by the beach. Head into the hills for sunset and a night in the parador in 🖼 **Antequera** ❼. On Day 3, drive to the village of Alora, follow a small road north to the impressive **Garganta del Chorro** ❽, and lunch on the terrace at one of the restaurants overlooking the lake. Continue on to 🖼 **Torremolinos** ❿ for a night out on the town. On Day 4, explore the village of **Mijas** ⓭ before continuing to **Marbella** ⓮ to check out the glitterati. Alternately, escape into the hills and the village of **Ojén** ⓯. In early evening, enjoy a sunset drive to 🖼 **Ronda** ⓰ via stunning countryside. On Day 5 check out Ronda, then explore its environs, including the dramatically situated village of **Setenil de las Bodegas** ⓱ and **Olvera's** ⓲ castle and church, followed by a stroll and picnic in the gorgeous **Sierra de Grazalema** ⓴ countryside. For a complete change of mood, head to the luxurious port at Sotogrande near **San Roque** ㉓ for an early evening cocktail overlooking the yachts before carrying on to 🖼 **Gibraltar** ㉕-㊲ for an English dinner and overnight stay.

10

Boliches, and Fuengirola; and those around Marbella. You may find a secluded beach west of Estepona. For wide beaches of fine golden sand, head west past Gibraltar, to Tarifa and the Cádiz coast, though winds are quite strong, hence all the sails.

All beaches are free, and are packed July through August and on Sunday May through October. It's acceptable for women to go topless; if you want to take it *all* off, go to beaches designated *playa naturista*. The most popular nude beaches are in Maro (near Nerja) and near Tarifa.

About the Restaurants

Spain's southern coast is known for fresh seafood, breaded with fine flour and fried quickly in sizzling olive oil. Sardines barbecued on skewers at beachside restaurants are another popular and unforgettable treat. Gazpacho and *ajo blanco* (a cold soup based on almonds, grapes, and garlic) are typical cold soups that are refreshing in hot weather. Málaga is best for traditional Spanish cooking, with a wealth of bars and seafood restaurants serving *fritura malagueña,* the city's famous fried fish. Torremolinos' Carihuela district is also a locus for lovers of Spanish seafood. The resorts serve every conceivable foreign cuisine as well, from Thai to the Scandinavian smorgasbord. Expect to pay more at the internationally renowned restaurants in Marbella.

At the other end of the scale, and often even more enjoyable, are the *chiringuitos.* Strung out along the beaches, these rough-and-ready, summer-only restaurants serve seafood fresh off the boats. Because there are so many foreigners, meals on the coast are served earlier than elsewhere in Andalusia, with restaurants opening at 1 or 1:30 for lunch and 7 or 8 for dinner. Reservations are advisable for the pricier restaurants in Marbella and Málaga; elsewhere, they're rarely necessary. Expect beach restaurants, such as Málaga's Adolfo and all those on the Carihuela seafront in Torremolinos, to be packed after 3 PM on Sunday.

WHAT IT COSTS In Euros				
$$$$	**$$$**	**$$**	**$**	**¢**
AT DINNER	over €20	€15–€20	€10–€15	€6–€10	under €6

Prices are for per person for a main course at dinner.

About the Hotels
Most hotels on the developed stretch, between Torremolinos and Fuengirola, offer large, functional rooms near the sea at competitive rates. The area's popularity as a budget destination means that most such hotels are booked in high season by package-tour operators. Finding a room at Easter, in July and August, or over holiday weekends can be difficult if you haven't reserved in advance. Málaga has several new lodging establishments but is still poorly endowed with high-quality hotels for a city of its size, aside from an excellent but small parador that can be hard to book. Marbella, conversely, has more than its fair share of grand hotels, including some of Spain's most expensive accommodations. Rooms in Gibraltar's handful of hotels tend to be more expensive than most comparable lodgings in Spain.

WHAT IT COSTS In Euros				
$$$$	**$$$**	**$$**	**$**	**¢**
FOR 2 PEOPLE	over €180	€100–€180	€60–€100	€40–€60	under €40

Prices are for two people in a standard double room in high season, excluding tax.

Timing
Fall and spring are the best times to visit the coast. There's plenty of sunshine but fewer tourists. Winter can have bright sunny days, but it also feels chilly, especially if you're used to central heating; many ho-

IF YOU LIKE

FERIAS & FIESTAS

Throughout Spain but particularly in Andalusia, the year revolves around annual ferias and fiestas (a feria is a more general and usually lengthier celebration, but a fiesta celebrates a specific event or day). Málaga has a parade on January 5, the eve of the **Día de los Tres Reyes** (Feast of the Three Kings); the city's **Semana Santa** (Holy Week) processions are dramatic. Nerja and Estepona celebrate **San Isidro** (May 15) with typically Andalusian ferias with plenty of flamenco and fino (sherry). Midsummer, or the feast of **San Juan** (June 23–24), is marked by midnight bonfires on beaches along the coast. The **Virgen del Carmen** is the patron saint of fishermen, so coastal communities honor her feast day (July 16) with processions. The annual **ferias** in Málaga (early August) and Fuengirola (early October) are among the best on the coast for sheer exuberance and party spirit.

GOLF

Nicknamed the Costa del Golf, the Sun Coast has the unbeatable combination of year-round sunshine and a choice of some 40 golf courses within putting distance of the Mediterranean, making it one of the prime destinations for golfers in Europe. Most of the courses are between Rincón de la Victoria (east of Málaga) and Gibraltar. The best season is October to June; greens fees are lower in summer. Pick up *Sun Golf*, a free magazine, at hotels and golf clubs. Additionally, the *Andalucía Golf Guide*, published by Andalusia's tourist office, details all the courses on the Costa del Sol.

tels in the lower price bracket have heating for only a few hours a day. You can also expect several days of rain. Avoid July and August; it's too hot and crowded. May, June, and the fall are better, with longer days and more space on the beach. Holy Week offers memorable ceremonies and processions, and most of the tourists will be Spanish.

Numbers in the text correspond to numbers in the margin and on the Costa del Sol and Gibraltar maps.

10

THE COSTA TROPICAL

East of Málaga and west of Almería lies the Costa Tropical. It has escaped the worst excesses of the property developers, and its tourist onslaught has been mild. A flourishing farming center, this area earns its keep from tropical fruit, including avocados, mangoes, and papaws (also known as custard apples). Housing developments are generally inspired by Andalusian village architecture rather than bland high-rise design. You may find packed beaches and traffic-choked roads at the height of the season, but for most of the year the Costa Tropical is relatively free of tourists, if not devoid of expatriates.

Salobreña

❶ *102 km (63 mi) east of Málaga.*

You can reach Salobreña by descending through the mountains from Granada or by continuing west from Almería on N340. A detour to the left from the highway brings you to this unspoiled village of near-perpendicular streets and old white houses, slapped onto a steep hill beneath a Moorish fortress. It's a true Andalusian pueblo, separated from the beachfront restaurants and bars in the newer part of town.

Almuñecar

❷ *85 km (53 mi) east of Málaga.*

Almuñecar has been a fishing village since Phoenician times, 3,000 years ago, when it was called Sexi. Later, the Moors built a castle here for the treasures of Granada's kings. Today Almuñecar is a small-time resort with a shingle beach, popular with Spanish and northern-European vacationers. The road west from Motril and Salobreña passes through the former empire of the sugar barons who brought prosperity to Málaga's province in the 19th century. The cane fields are now giving way to litchis, limes, mangoes, papaws, and olives; avocado groves line your route as you descend into Almuñecar. The village is actually two, separated by the dramatic rocky headland of Punta de la Mona. To the east is Almuñecar proper, and to the west is **La Herradura**, a quiet fishing community. Between the two is the Marina del Este yacht harbor, a popular diving center along with La Herradura.

> Shingle beaches are popular with European vacationers. For wide beaches of fine golden sand, head west past Gibraltar, to Tarifa and the Cádiz coast.

Crowning Almuñecar is the **Castillo de San Miguel** (St. Michael's Castle). A Roman fortress once stood here, later enlarged by the Moors, but the castle's present aspect owes more to 16th-century additions. The building was bombarded during the Peninsular War at the beginning of the 19th century, and what was left became initially a cemetery until the 1990s, when excavation and restoration began. You can wander the ramparts and peer into the dungeon; the skeleton at the bottom is a reproduction of human remains discovered on the spot. ☑ €2, *includes admission to Cueva de Siete Palacios* ⊘ *July and Aug., Tues.–Sat. 10:30–1:30 and 6–9, Sun. 10–2; Sept.–June, Tues.–Sat. 10:30–1:30 and 4–6:30, Sun. 10:30–2.*

Beneath the Castillo de San Miguel is a large, vaulted stone cellar of Roman origin, the **Cueva de Siete Palacios** (Cave of Seven Palaces), now Almuñecar's archaeological museum. The collection is small but interesting, with Phoenician, Roman, and Moorish artifacts. ☑ €2, *includes admission to Castillo de San Miguel* ⊘ *July and Aug., Tues.–Sat. 10:30–1:30 and 6–9, Sun. 10–2; Sept.–June, Tues.–Sat. 10:30–1:30 and 4–6:30, Sun. 10:30–2.*

Where to Stay & Eat

$$ ✗ **Jacquy-Cotobro.** One of the finest French restaurants on Spain's southern coast is at the foot of the Punta de la Mona. The dining area is cozy,

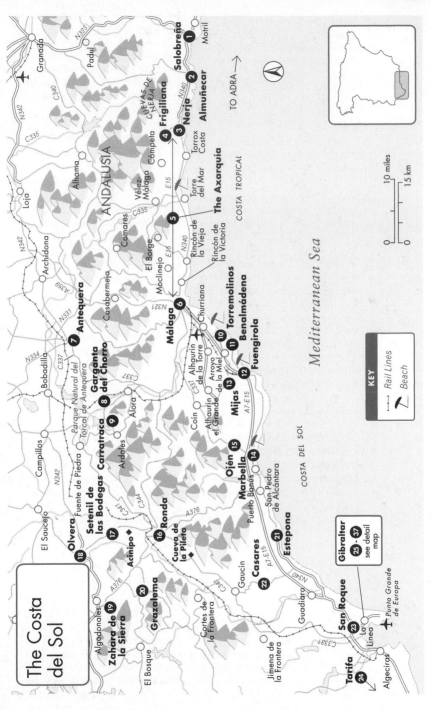

with bare brick walls and green wicker chairs; a beachfront terrace is open in summer. Try the *menú de degustación*, with three courses plus dessert; it might include fresh pasta topped with oyster mushrooms and prawns, lobster salad with truffle oil, or duck in orange sauce. Crown your meal with the calorific delight of strawberry mousse drizzled with Kirsch. ⊠ *Edificio Río, Playa Cotobro* ☎ *958/631802* ▭ *MC, V* ⊘ *Closed Mon.*

$$$ 🏨 **Sol Los Fenicios.** Near the beach in La Herradura, this modern, Andalusian-style hotel has views of the bay and the cliffs of Punta de Mona to the east and the rocky headland of Cerro Gordo to the west. The rooms are set around a traditional interior patio and are spacious with terraces and sitting areas; ask for a room with a sea view. ⊠ *Paseo de Andrés Segovia s/n, La Herradura 18697* ☎ *958/827900* 🖷 *958/827910* ⊕ *www.sollosfenicios.solmelia.com* 🛏 *43 rooms* ⚸ *Restaurant, cafeteria, minibars, cable TV, in-room data ports, pool, meeting room, parking (fee)* ▭ *AE, DC, MC, V* ❙◯❙ *BP* ⊘ *Closed late Nov.–early Mar.*

$–$$ 🏨 **Casablanca.** There's something quaint about this family-run hotel with a neo-Moorish facade. Rooms are spacious and have modern fittings juxtaposed with antiques. The building is next to the beach near the botanical park; rooms have either balconies or picture windows. Try the specialty—paella (rice with seafood, saffron, peppers, and spices)—in the restaurant. ⊠ *Pl. San Cristóbal 4, 18690* ☎ *958/635575* ⊕ *www.almunecar.info/casablanca* 🛏 *35 rooms* ⚸ *Restaurant, bar, parking (fee)* ▭ *D, MC, V.*

MARY'S TOP 5

- Spending a morning strolling around Marbella's old town, stopping for a drink at Plaza de los Naranjos (Orange Square).

- Heading for Málaga's Cathedral and the surrounding tangle of pedestrian streets, including Calle Agustín, home to the Picasso Museum.

- Checking out the weekly market in one of the Costa resorts—the best place to pick up cut-price souvenirs, such as ceramics or Spanish music CDs.

- Basking in the five-star splendor of Puerto Banús, where everything is more exclusive, extravagant, and expensive, but I can sit and pose or watch for free.

- Tucking into a dish of *fritura malagueño* (fried fish, anchovies, and squid) at one of La Carihuela's seafood restaurants in Torremolinos.

Nerja

★ ❸ *52 km (32 mi) east of Málaga, 22 km (14 mi) west of Almuñecar.*

Nerja—the name comes from the Moorish word *narixa*, meaning "abundant springs"—has a large foreign resident community living mainly outside town in *urbanizaciones* ("village" developments). The old village is on a headland above small beaches and rocky coves, which offer reasonable swimming despite the gray, gritty sand. In high season, Nerja is packed with tourists, but the rest of the year it's a pleasure to wander the old town's narrow streets. Nerja's highlight is the **Balcón de Europa,** a tree-lined promenade with magnificent views, on a promontory just off the central square. The **Cuevas de Nerja** (Nerja Caves) lie between Almuñecar and Nerja on a road surrounded by giant cliffs and dramatic seascapes. Signs point to the cave entrance above the village of Maro, 4 km (2½ mi) east of Nerja. The caves were discovered in 1959 by children who were supposedly chasing a pig; the caves are now floodlighted for better views of the spires and turrets created by millennia of dripping water. One suspended pinnacle, 200 feet long, is in fact the world's largest known stalactite. The awesome subterranean chambers create an evocative setting for concerts and ballets during the Nerja Caves Festival, held annually during the second and third weeks of July. ☎ 952/529520 ⊕ *www.cuevanerja.com* ☒ €6 ☼ *Oct.–Apr., daily 10–2 and 4–6:30; May–Sept., daily 10–2 and 4–8.*

Where to Stay & Eat

$$–$$$ ✕ **Udo Heimer.** Your eponymous host, a genial German, welcomes you warmly to this stylish art-deco villa in a development to the east of Nerja. The visual flair extends to the food, which mixes German and Spanish flavors. Try the rack of lamb with rosemary and thyme or prawns wrapped in bacon with cayenne rice and a sweet curry sauce. The excellent wine list has rarities from all over Spain. ☒ *Pueblo Andaluz 27* ☎ *952/520032* ▤ *MC, V* ☼ *Closed Wed. No lunch.*

$$ ✕ **Casa Luque.** One of Nerja's most authentic Spanish restaurants, Casa Luque is an old Andalusian house in a lovely square just off the Balcón de Europa. The menu has dishes from northern Spain, often of Basque or Navarrese origin, with an emphasis on meat and game; tapas and seafood are also on offer. Ask to sit on the patio during the summer. ☒ *Pl. Cavana 2* ☎ *952/521004* ▤ *AE, DC, MC, V* ☼ *Closed Wed. and Sun.*

$$$ ✕▥ **Parador de Nerja.** On a cliff's edge is this modern parador with its disarmingly bland exterior. The rooms are far more agreeable, with balconies overlooking a garden and the sea. Rooms in the newer, single-story wing open onto their own patios; some have whirlpool baths. An elevator descends to the rocky beach. The restaurant ($$–$$$) is known for its fish offerings, which might include *pez espada a la naranja* (swordfish in orange sauce) or giant *langostino* (shrimp). ☒ *Almuñecar 8, 29780* ☎ *952/520050* ▤ *952/521997* ⊕ *www.parador.es* ➷ *98 rooms* ☆ *Restaurant, cable TV, in-room data ports, tennis court, pool, piano bar, Internet room, free parking* ▤ *AE, DC, MC, V* ⦿| *BP.*

★ $$–$$$ ▥ **Hotel Carabeo.** Tucked away down a side street near the center of town and the sea, this British-owned boutique hotel has bookshelves, antiques, and cozy overstuffed sofas in the downstairs sitting room. The walls throughout are hung with colorful oil paintings by local artist David Broadhead. In the main building there are seven rooms, five with sea views, and a private terrace overlooking the sea. In the newer annex there are six more rooms, plus a small gym and games room. ☒ *C. Hernando de Carabeo 34, 29780* ☎ *952/525444* ▤ *952/522677* ⊕ *www. hotelcarabeo.com* ➷ *13 rooms* ☆ *Restaurant, cable TV, pool, gym, bar, public Internet* ▤ *MC, V* ☼ *Closed mid-Nov.–mid–Dec. and early Jan.–mid-Mar.*

10

Nightlife & the Arts

El Colono (✉ Granada 6, Nerja ☎ 952/521826) is a flamenco club in the town center. Dinner shows begin at 9 PM on Wednesday and Friday from February until the end of October. You can choose from five prix-fixe menus.

Frigiliana

④ *58 km (36 mi) east of Málaga.*

The village of Frigiliana sits on a mountain ridge overlooking the sea. One of the last battles between the Christians and the Moors was waged here in 1567. The short drive off the highway rewards you with spectacular views and an old quarter of narrow, cobbled streets and dazzling white houses decorated with pots of geraniums. (If you don't have a car, take a bus here from Nerja.)

The Axarquía

⑤ *Vélez-Málaga: 36 km (22 mi) east of Málaga.*

The Axarquía region is in the eastern third of Málaga's province, stretching from Nerja to Málaga. Its coast consists of narrow, pebbly beaches and drab fishing villages on either side of the high-rise resort town of Torre del Mar. The region's charm lies in its mountainous interior, peppered with pueblos, vineyards, and tiny farms. The four-lane E15 highway speeds across the region a few miles in from the coast; traffic on the old coastal road (N340) is slower. **Vélez-Málaga** is the capital of the Axarquía. A pleasant agricultural town of white houses, Vélez-Málaga is a center for strawberry fields and vineyards. Worth quick visits are the **Thursday market,** the ruins of a **Moorish castle,** and the church of **Santa María la Mayor,** built in Mudejar style on the site of a mosque that was destroyed when the town fell to the Christians in 1487.

If you have a car and an up-to-date road map, explore the Axarquía's inland villages. You can follow the **Ruta del Vino** (Wine Route) 22 km (14 mi) from the coast, stopping at villages that produce the sweet, earthy local wine, particularly Cómpeta. Alternatively you can take the **Ruta de la Pasa** (Raisin Route) through Moclinejo, El Borge, and Comares. Comares perches like an eagle's nest atop one of La Serrazuela's highest mountains and dates back to Moorish times. This area is especially spectacular during the late-summer grape-harvest season or in late autumn, when the leaves of the vines turn gold. A short detour to Macharaviaya (7 km [4 mi] north of Rincón de la Victoria) might lead you to ponder the past glory of this now sleepy village: In 1776 one of its sons, Bernardo de Gálvez, became Spanish governor of Louisiana and later fought in the American Revolution (Galveston, Texas, takes its name from the governor). Macharaviaya prospered under his heirs and for many years enjoyed a lucrative monopoly on the manufacture of playing cards for South America. Both the Ruta del Vino and the Ruta de la Pasa are signposted locally.

Where to Stay & Eat

$ ✕ **Museo del Vino.** There's no museum here—instead it's a rambling arts-and-crafts shop as well as a bodega lined with barrels and bottles of muscatel wine. An attached restaurant is suitably rustic, with brick walls and a wood-beam ceiling. Start out the evening sampling wines and tasty tapas, including pungent Manchego cheese, cured hams, and olives. If you're still hungry, settle in for a full meal featuring grilled meats, the house specialty. ⊠ *Av. Constitución s/n, Cómpeta* ☏ *952/553314* ☐ *MC, V* ☉ *Closed Mon. and last 2 wks in Jan.*

$$–$$$ ✕▦ **Molino de Santillán.** This small country hotel and restaurant is typically Andalusian, with arches, terra-cotta floors, and dark oak furniture throughout. There are superb countryside views from the rooms as well as from the timbered restaurant, where the cooks use organic ingredients (much of the produce is grown in the hotel's greenhouse and garden). At the end of a signposted dirt road north of the main highway, the hotel is a short drive away from the Añoreta golf club and course and 5 km (2½ mi) from the nearest beach. ⊠ *Ctra. de Macharaviaya, Km 3, Rincón de la Victoria 29730* ☏ *952/400949* ☐ *952/115782* ⊕ *www.molinodesantillan.es* ⬎ *22 rooms* ☖ *Restaurant, cable TV, Wi-Fi, pool, hot tub* ☐ *AE, DC, MC, V.*

★ ¢–$ ▦ **El Molino de los Abuelos.** Under a canopy of jasmine and bougainvillea, this former olive mill has a cobbled courtyard where you can enjoy a glass of fino at sundowner time. The rooms are all different, varying from small and simple with shared bath to a sumptuous suite with hot tub. The restaurant serves solidly traditional fare, with an emphasis on fish—despite the fact that this pueblo blanco sits some 3,000 feet above sea level. ⊠ *Plaza 2, Comares 29195* ☏ *952/509309* ☐ *952/214220* ⬎ *6 rooms* ☖ *Restaurant; no TV in some rooms* ☐ *AE, MC, V.*

MÁLAGA & INLAND

The city of Málaga and the towns of the upland hills and valleys to the north create the kind of contrast that makes travel in Spain so tantalizing. The region's Moorish legacy is a unifying visual theme, connecting the tiny streets honeycombing the steamy depths of Málaga, the rocky cliffs and gorges between Alora and Archidona, the layout of the farms, and the crops themselves, including olives, grapes, oranges, and lemons.

10

Málaga

❻ *175 km (109 mi) southeast of Córdoba.*

With about 550,000 residents, the city of Málaga is technically the capital of the Costa del Sol, though most travelers head straight for the beaches west of the city. Approaching Málaga from the airport, you'll be greeted by huge 1970s high-rises that march determinedly toward Torremolinos. But don't despair: In its center and its eastern suburbs, Málaga is a pleasant port city, with ancient streets and lovely villas amid exotic foliage. Blessed with a subtropical climate, it's covered in lush vegetation and averages some 324 days of sunshine a year.

Málaga has been spruced up with tastefully restored historic buildings and the gradual emergence of more sophisticated shops, bars, and restaurants. The opening of the prestigious Picasso Museum has similarly boosted tourism to this Costa capital, although there are still far fewer visitors here than in the other grand-slam Andalusian cities of Seville, Córdoba, and Granada. Most hotels organize sightseeing tours, and there's an inexpensive open-top tourist bus that travels to the major sights. Tickets (€13) allow you to hop on and off as many times as you like within a 24-hour period. Note that more tourists usually means more pickpockets, so stay alert, particularly around the historic city center.

Arriving from Nerja, you'll enter Málaga through the suburbs of El Palo and Pedregalejo, once traditional fishing villages in their own right. Here you can eat fresh fish in the numerous *chiringuitos* (beachside bars) and stroll Pedregalejos' seafront promenade or the tree-lined streets of El Limonar. At sunset, walk along the **Paseo Marítimo** and watch the lighthouse start its nightly vigil. A few blocks inland from here is Málaga's bullring, **La Malagueta,** built in 1874.

Continuing west you soon reach the city center and inviting **Plaza de la Marina;** with cafés and an illuminated fountain overlooking the port, it's a pleasant place for a drink. From here, stroll through the shady, palm-lined gardens of the **Paseo del Parque** or browse on **Calle Marqués de Larios,** the elegant pedestrian-only main shopping street.

The narrow streets and alleys on each side of Calle Marqués de Larios have charms of their own. Wander the warren of passageways around **Pasaje Chinitas,** off Plaza de la Constitución, and peep into the dark, vaulted bodegas, where old men down glasses of *seco añejo* or *Málaga Virgen,* local wines made from Málaga's muscatel grapes. Silversmiths and vendors of religious books and statues ply their trades in shops that have changed little since the early 1900s. Backtrack across Larios, and, in the streets leading to Calle Nueva, you can see shoeshine boys, lottery-ticket vendors, Gypsy guitarists, and tapas bars with wine served from huge barrels.

From the Plaza Felix Saenz, at the southern end of Calle Nueva, turn onto Sagasta to reach the **Mercado de Atarazanas,** the most colorful market in all of Andalusia. Stalls sell fresh fish, spices, and vegetables. The typical 19th-century iron structure incorporates the original **Puerta de Atarazanas,** the exquisitely crafted 14th-century Moorish gate that once connected the city with the port.

NEED A BREAK? The **Antigua Casa de Guardia** (⊠ Alameda 18 ☎ 952/214680), around the corner from the Mercado de Atarazanas, is Málaga's oldest bar, founded in 1840. Andalusian wines flow straight from the barrel, and the floor is ankle-deep in discarded shrimp shells.

Málaga's **cathedral,** built between 1528 and 1782, is a triumph, although a generally unappreciated one, having been left unfinished when funds ran out. Because it lacks one of its two towers, the building is nicknamed *La Manquita* (The One-Armed Lady). The enclosed choir, which miraculously survived the burnings of the civil war, is the work of 17th-century artist Pedro de Mena, who carved the wood wafer-thin in some places to express the fold of a robe or shape of a finger. The choir also has a pair of massive 18th-century pipe organs, one of which is still used for the occasional concert. Adjoining the cathedral is a small museum of religious art and artifacts, and a walk around the cathedral on Calle Cister will take you to the magnificent Gothic Puerta del Sagrario. ⊠ *C. de Molina Larios* ☎ *952/215917* 🎫 *€3.50* ⊙ *Mon.–Sat. 10–6:45.*

Palacio Episcopa (Bishop's Palace), which faces the cathedral's main entrance, has one of the most stunning facades in the city. It's now a venue for temporary art exhibitions. ⊠ *Pl. Obispo 6* ☎ *952/602722* 🎫 *Free* ⊙ *Tues.–Sun. 10–2 and 6–9.*

Fodor'sChoice The charm of the **Museo Picasso,** the city's latest and most prestigious mu-
★ seum, is that it's such a family affair. These are the works that Pablo Picasso kept for himself or gave to his family and include the heartfelt *Paulo con gorro blanco* (Paulo with a white cap), a portrait of his first-born son painted in the early 1920s, and *Olga Kokhlova con mantilla* (Olga Kokhlova with mantilla), a 1917 portrait of his certifiably insane first wife. The holdings were largely donated by two family members—Christine and Bernard Ruiz-Picasso, the artist's daughter-in-law and grandson. The works are displayed in chronological order according to the periods that marked his development as an artist, from Blue and Rose to Cubism, and beyond. The museum is housed in a former palace where, during restoration work, Roman and Moorish remains were discovered. These are now on display, together with the permanent collection of Picassos and temporary exhibitions. ⊠ *C. de San Agustín* ☎ *952/602731* 🎫 *Permanent exhibition €6, combined permanent and temporary exhibition €8, last Sun. of every month free* ⊙ *Tues.–Thurs. 10–8, Fri. and Sat. 10–9.*

On the Plaza de la Merced, No. 15 was the childhood home of Málaga's most famous native son, Pablo Picasso, born here in 1881. Now the **Fundación Picasso,** the building has been painted and furnished in the style of the era and houses a permanent exhibition of Picasso's early sketches and sculptures, as well as memorabilia, including the artist's christening robe and family photographs. ⊠ *Pl. de la Merced 15* ☎ *952/600215* 🎫 *€1* ⊙ *Mon.–Sat. 10–8, Sun. 10–2.*

Just beyond the ruins of a Roman theater on Calle Alcazabilla, the Moorish **Alcazaba** is Málaga's greatest monument. This fortress was begun in the 8th century, when Málaga was the principal port of the Moorish kingdom, though most of the present structure dates from the 11th century. The inner palace was built between 1057 and 1063, when the Moorish emirs took up residence; and Ferdinand and Isabella lived here for a while after conquering Málaga in 1487. The ruins are dappled with orange trees and bougainvillea and include a small museum; from the highest point you can see over the park and port. ⊠ *Entrance on Alcazabilla* 🎫 *€1.90, €3.15 combined entry with Gibralfaro* ⊙ *Nov.–Mar., Tues.–Sun. 8.30–7; Apr.–Oct., Tues.–Sun. 9:30–8.*

Magnificent vistas beckon at **Gibralfaro,** which is floodlighted at night. The fortifications were built for Yusuf I in the 14th century; the Moors called them Jebelfaro, from the Arab word for "mount" and the Greek word for "lighthouse," after a beacon that stood here to guide ships into

10

the harbor and warn of pirates. The beacon has been succeeded by a small parador. You can drive here by way of Calle Victoria or take a minibus that leaves 10 times a day between 11 and 7, or roughly every hour, from the bus stop in the park near the Plaza de la Marina. ⊠ *Gibralfaro Mountain* ☎ *952/220043* 🕾 *€1.90 €3.15 combined entry with Alcazaba* ☉ *Nov.–Mar., daily 9–5:45; Apr.–Oct., daily 9–7:45.*

🌀 In the old Mesón de la Victoria, a 17th-century inn, is the **Museo de Artes Populares** (Arts and Crafts Museum). On display are horse-drawn carriages and carts, old agricultural implements, folk costumes, a forge, a bakery, an ancient grape press, and Malagueño painted clay figures and ceramics. ⊠ *Pasillo de Santa Isabel 10* ☎ *952/217137* 🕾 *€2* ☉ *Oct.–May, weekdays 10–1:30 and 4–7, Sat. 10–1:30; June–Sept., weekdays 10–1:30 and 5–8, Sat., 10–1:30.*

A 150-year-old botanical garden, **La Concepción** was created by the daughter of the British consul, who married a Spanish shipping magnate—the captains of the Spaniard's fleet had standing orders to bring back seedlings and cuttings from every "exotic" port of call. The garden is just off the exit road to Granada—too far to walk, but well worth the cab fare from the city center. ⊠ *Ctra. de las Pedrizas, Km 166* ☎ *952/252148* 🕾 *€3.10* ☉ *Tues.–Sun. 10 AM–dusk.*

Where to Stay & Eat

$$–$$$ ✕ **Adolfo.** On Málaga's Paseo Marítimo, this small restaurant has a solid reputation for Spanish food with a contemporary touch. The dining room has a wood floor and exposed-brick walls; service is smooth and professional; and there's a good wine list. Entrées include *rape con almejas* (halibut with clams) and *cabrito lechal a la miel de romero* (roast kid in rosemary-honey sauce). ⊠ *Paseo Marítimo Pablo Ruíz Picasso 12* ☎ *952/601914* ☐ *AE, D, MC, V* ☉ *Closed Sun.*

$$–$$$ ✕ **El Chinitas.** Decorated with traditional mosaic tiles and original paintings by Malagueño artists, this place sits at one end of Pasaje Chinitas, Málaga's most *típico* (typical) street. The tapas bar is popular, especially for its cured ham. The second floor has three private dining rooms—groups of 12 to 20 can reserve the Sala Antequera, with a Camelot-style round table—and a banquet hall. Try the *sopa castellana,* garlic soup made with fresh garlic, bread, paprika, and egg, followed by *solomillo al vino de Málaga,* fillet steak in Málaga wine sauce. ⊠ *Moreno Monroy 4* ☎ *952/210972* ⊕ *www.chinitas.arrakis.es* ☐ *AE, DC, MC, V.*

$–$$ ✕ **La Posada de Antonio.** Local *Malagueño* actor Antonio Banderas owns this restaurant, one of a chain of four. Decked out in traditional bodega style, the brick-and-beam interior has barrel tables and a long bar displaying available tapas, including such local specialties as *berenjenos con miel* (fried eggplant slices drizzled with honey) and *porra Antequerana* (a gazpacho mix of tomato, garlic, egg, and salami). Main dishes include grilled meats, seafood dishes, and oxtail stew. The restaurant is in Plaza Mayor, 6 km (4 mi) west of the airport, a commercial complex with some 58 restaurants loosely designed after an Andalusian village. ⊠ *Plaza del Azahar, Plaza Mayor* ☎ *952/172629* ☐ *MC, V.*

$ ✕ **El Vegetariano de la Alcazabilla.** This restaurant is arguably the best of the handful of vegetarian restaurants on this carnivorous Costa. The position is pleasantly atmospheric, tucked up a side street just around the corner from the Roman amphitheater. Dishes include vegan options and more mainstream vegetarian choices, including spinach cannelloni, Roquefort-and-celery turnovers, and plenty of salads. The daily set menu prices fluctuate from a reasonable €6.50 to €8.50 and, refreshingly, this restaurant is not too pious to include a healthy wine list and some delicious calorie-laden desserts. ⊠ *Pozo del Rey 5* ☎ *952/214858* ▤ *MC, V* ⊘ *Closed Sun.*

$　✕ **Tintero.** Come to this sprawling and noisy restaurant for the entertainment rather than the food. There's no menu—the waiters circle the restaurant carrying various dishes and you choose whatever looks good to you. The bill is totaled up according to the number and size of the plates on the table at the end of the meal. On the El Palo seafront, Tintero specializes in catch-of-the-day seafood, such as *boquerones* (fresh anchovies), *sepia* (cuttlefish), and the all-time familiar classic, *gambas* (prawns). ⊠ *Playa del Dedo, El Palo* ☎ *952/204464* ▤ *No credit cards* ⊘ *No dinner.*

¢–$　✕ **Logueno.** Shoehorned into a deceptively small space, the original well-
Fodor'sChoice　loved traditional tapas bar is on a side street near Calle Larios. More
★　recently Logueno has expanded to encompass a second bar space across the street. Check out the original with its L-shape wooden bar crammed with a choice of more than 75 tantalizing tapas, including many Logueno originals, such as grilled oyster mushrooms with garlic, parsley, and goat cheese. There's an excellent selection of Rioja wines, and the service is fast and good, despite the lack of elbow room. ⊠ *Marin Garcia s/n* ☎ *No phone* ▤ *No credit cards* ⊘ *Closed Sun.*

¢–$　✕ **Pitta Bar.** Tables spill out onto the attractive street fronting this bright pine-clad Middle Eastern restaurant. Falafel, kebabs, hummus, and tabbouleh salad are on the menu, along with a choice of 14 stuffed pita breads, spicy sausage, and french fries. The location is ideal if you're sightseeing—it's between the cathedral and Picasso Museum, in the old part of town. ⊠ *Echegaray 8* ☎ *952/608675* ▤ *No credit cards* ⊘ *Closed Sun.*

$$$　✕▦ **Parador de Málaga–Gibralfaro.** Surrounded by pine trees on top of
Fodor'sChoice　Gibralfaro, 3 km (2 mi) above the city, this cozy, gray-stone parador
★　has spectacular views of Málaga and the bay. Rooms are attractive—with blue curtains and bedspreads, and woven rugs on bare tile floors—and are some of the best in Málaga. Reserve well in advance. The restaurant ($–$$$) excels at such classic Mediterranean dishes as calamari and fried green peppers. ⊠ *Monte de Gibralfaro s/n, 29016* ☎ *952/221902* 🖷 *952/221904* ⊕ *www.parador.es* ⤳ *38 rooms* ⚭ *Restaurant, cafeteria, minibars, cable TV, in-room broadband, pool, bar, meeting room, free parking* ▤ *AE, DC, MC, V.*

$$$　▦ **Don Curro.** Just around the corner from the cathedral, this family classic is going through continual renovations, but an old-fashioned air permeates the wood-panel common rooms and fireplace lounge. The revamped rooms have parquet floors, spot lighting, and classy cream and white fabrics. The ground floor bingo parlor is a quirky surprise. Prices drop considerably on weekends. ⊠ *Sancha de Lara 9, 29015* ☎ *952/227200* 🖷 *952/215946* ⊕ *www.hoteldoncurro.com* ⤳ *112*

10

rooms, 6 suites ☼ Restaurant, cafeteria, minibars, cable TV, in-room data ports, parking (fee) ☰ *AE, DC, MC, V.*

$$$ ▦ **Larios.** On the central Plaza de la Constitución, Larios is inside a 19th-century building that's been elegantly restored. Black-and-white tile floors lend subdued elegance to the second-floor lobby; the rooms are furnished in art-deco style with photographs and jazzy bedspreads. The roof terrace, which has views of the cathedral, is just the place to unwind with a glass of fino after a day of sightseeing. There are special discount weekend rates. ✉ *Marqués de Larios 2, 29005* ☎ *952/222200* 🖷 *952/222407* 🌐 *www.hotel-larios.com* ⌨ *35 rooms, 6 suites ☼ Restaurant, minibars, cable TV with movies, Wi-Fi, meeting room* ☰ *AE, DC, MC, V* ◯| *BP.*

$$ ▦ **Humaina.** In this small hotel 16 km (10 mi) north of the city, the rooms
Fodor'sChoice are painted a sunny yellow and are furnished with terra-cotta tiles. Bal-
★ conies overlook a thickly forested park of olive, pine, and oak trees. Solar energy, an organic garden, and serious recycling are part of the ecofriendly package; horse riding, bird-watching, and rambling excursions can be arranged. The restaurant dishes up healthful, tasty dishes, and vegetarians are happily accommodated—a rarity in these parts. ✉ *Parque Natural Montes de Málaga, Carretera del Colmenar s/n, 29013* ☎ *952/641025* 🖷*952/640115* 🌐*www.hotelhumaina.es* ⌨*12 rooms ☼ Restaurant, pool, library* ☰ *MC, V* ◯| *BP.*

$$ ▦ **Los Naranjos.** This is a solid no-surprises hotel, on an elegant stretch of street, east of the city center. Although the lobby and downstairs salon are fairly bland, the rooms have benefited from a recent lick of paint. Head for one of the upper-floor rooms for the best sea and coastline views. There are private balconies, and the decor is cream-and-salmon Regency style with good-size bathrooms, most with a bathtub as well as shower. Agreeable extras include super-fluffy towels and tasteful original paintings throughout. ✉ *Paseo de Sancha 35, 29016* ☎ *952/224316* 🖷 *952/225975* 🌐 *www.hotel-losnaranjos.com* ⌨ *41 rooms ☼ Restaurant, Wi-Fi, bar, meeting room, parking (fee)* ☰ *AE, DC, MC, V.*

$ ▦ **Castilla.** You can't beat the location of this great little hostel: It's between the city's main artery, the Alameda, and the port. Rooms are done in burgundy and cream; some have balconies. There's an underground garage, and plenty of cafés and restaurants are nearby. ✉ *Córdoba 7, 29001* ☎ *952/218635* ⌨ *37 rooms ☼ Parking (fee)* ☰ *MC, V.*

Nightlife & the Arts

The region's main theater is the **Teatro Cervantes** (✉ Ramos Marín ☎952/224109 or 952/220237 🌐 www.teatrocervantes.com), whose programs include Spanish-language plays, concerts, and flamenco. The **Málaga Symphony Orchestra** has a winter season of orchestral concerts and chamber music, with most performances held at the Teatro Cervantes. In summer, larger concerts are staged in the bullring or the **Palacio Municipal de Deportes** (☎ 952/176392); past big-name billings have included Bryan Ferry and Bob Dylan. Málaga's main nightlife districts are Maestranza, between the bullring and the Paseo Marítimo, and the beachfront in the suburb of Pedregalejos. Central Málaga also has a lively bar scene.

Shopping

The **Corte Inglés** department store offers one-stop shopping over its six vast floors, plus an excellent basement supermarket selling many kinds of imported goodies. Head to the fifth floor for year-round sale items. ⊠ *Av. de Andalucía 4–6* ☎ *952/300000* ☉ *Mon.–Sat. 10–10.*

Antequera

❼ *64 km (40 mi) northwest of Málaga, 43 km (27 mi) northeast of Pizarra, 108 km (67 mi) northeast of Ronda, via Pizarra.*

Antequera became a stronghold of the Moors after their defeat at Córdoba and Seville in the 13th century. Its fall to the Christians in 1410 paved the way for the reconquest of Granada—the Moors retreated, leaving a **fortress** on the town heights. Next door is the former church of **Santa María la Mayor,** one of 27 churches, convents, and monasteries in Antequera. Built of sandstone in the 16th century, it has a fine ribbed vault and is now a concert hall. The church of **San Sebastián** has a brick baroque Mudejar tower topped by a winged figure called the Angelote ("big angel"), the symbol of Antequera. The church of **Nuestra Señora del Carmen** (Our Lady of Carmen) has an extraordinary baroque altarpiece that towers to the ceiling.

Antequera's pride and joy is Efebo, a beautiful bronze statue of a boy that dates back to Roman times. Standing almost 5 feet high, it's on display in the **Museo Municipal.** ⊠ *Pl. Coso Vieja* ☎ *952/704051* 🖭 *€3* ☉ *Tues.–Fri. 10–1:30 and 4:30–6:30, Sat. 10–1:30, Sun. 11–1:30.*

The mysterious prehistoric **dolmens** are megalithic burial chambers, built some 4,000 years ago out of massive slabs of stone weighing more than 100 tons each. The best-preserved dolmen is La Menga. They're just outside Antequera. ⊠ *Signposted off the Málaga exit Rd.* 🖭 *Free* ☉ *Tues. 9–3:30, Wed.–Sat. 9–6, Sun. 9:30–2:30.*

Europe's major nesting area for the greater flamingo is **Fuente de Piedra,** a shallow saltwater lagoon. In February and March, these birds arrive from Africa by the thousands to breed, returning to Africa in August when the water dries up. The visitor center has information on wildlife. Don't forget your binoculars. ⊠ *10 km (6 mi) northwest of Antequera, off A92 to Seville* ☎ *952/111715* 🖭 *Free* ☉ *May–Sept., Wed.–Sun. 10–2 and 4–6, Oct.–Apr., Wed.–Sun. 10–2 and 6–8.*

East of Antequera, along N342, is the dramatic silhouette of the **Peña de los Enamorados** (Lovers' Rock), an Andalusian landmark. Legend has it that a Moorish princess and a Christian shepherd boy eloped here one night and cast themselves to their deaths from the peak the next morning. The rock's outline is often likened to the profile of the Córdoban bullfighter Manolete.

About 8 km (5 mi) from Antequera's Lovers' Rock, the village of **Archidona** winds its way up a steep mountain slope beneath the ruins of a Moorish castle. This unspoiled village is worth a detour for its **Plaza Ochavada,** a magnificent 17th-century square resplendent with contrast-

10

ing red and ocher stone. ⊠ *8 km (5 mi) beyond Peña de los Enamorados, along N342, Antequera.*

Fodor'sChoice Well-marked walking trails guide you at the **Parque Natural del Torcal de**
★ **Antequera** (El Torcal Nature Park). You can walk among eerie pillars of pink limestone sculpted by aeons of wind and rain. Wear sturdy shoes and keep to the well-marked paths. A guide can be arranged for longer hikes. The visitor center includes a small museum. ⊠ *Centro de Visitantes, Ctra. C3310, 10 km (6 mi) south of Antequera* ☎ *649/472688* ▨ *Free* ☉ *Daily 10–5.*

Where to Stay & Eat

$$ ✕ **El Angelote.** Across the square from the Museo Municipal, these two
Fodor'sChoice wood-beam dining rooms are usually packed. Try the *porrilla de setas*
★ (wild mushrooms in an almond-and-wine sauce) or *perdiz hortelana* (stewed partridge). Antequera's typical dessert is *bienmesabe* (literally, "tastes good to me"), a delicious concoction made of almonds, chocolate, and apple custard. ⊠ *Pl. Coso Viejo* ☎ *952/703465* ▤ *DC, MC, V* ☉ *Closed Mon. No dinner Sun.*

$ ✕ **Caserío San Benito.** If it weren't for the cell-phone transmission tower looming next to this country restaurant 11 km (7 mi) north of Antequera, you might think you've stumbled into an 18th-century scene. Many of the items found during the renovation of this former farmhouse fronted by a cobbled courtyard are displayed in a small adjacent museum. Popular dishes include *porra antequerana* (a thick version of gazpacho) and *migas* (fried bread crumbs with sausage). ⊠ *Ctra. Málaga–Córdoba, Km 108* ☎ *952/111103* ▤ *AE, MC, V* ☉ *Closed Mon. and 1st 2 wks in July. No dinner Tues.–Thurs.*

$$ ✕▥ **Parador de Antequera.** Overlooking the *vega*, Antequera's fertile valley, this modern white parador stands on a hill. Common rooms are simple but tasteful, with antique carpets on tile floors and bull prints on the walls. The comfortable guest rooms have twin beds, covered with woven rugs, and spacious tile bathrooms. The large dining room ($–$$$), with a lofty wood ceiling, serves good local dishes, such as *pío antequerano* (a salad of orange, cod, and olives) and the delicious dessert, *bienmesabe* (almond cream). ⊠ *García del Olmo s/n, 29200* ☎ *952/840261* 🖷 *952/841312* ⊕ *www.parador.es* ⇶ *55 rooms* ⚐ *Restaurant, cable TV with movies, in-room broadband, pool, bar* ▤ *AE, DC, MC, V.*

$$$–$$$$ ▥ **La Posada del Torcal.** Surrounded by the lunar landscape of El Torcal, this small hotel is just the place to chill out and relax after a long day on the trail. There are king-size and four-poster beds and a fireplace in each room. You can find skillful copies of Spanish paintings throughout. The Posada's restaurant specializes in local Spanish food, including several vegetarian options. ⊠ *Partido de Jeva, Villanueva de la Concepción, 29230* ☎ *952/031177* 🖷 *952/031006* ⊕ *www.eltorcal.com/PosadaTorcal* ⇶ *10 rooms* ⚐ *Restaurant, cable TV, tennis court, pool, gym, sauna, horseback riding, bar* ▤ *AE, MC, V* ☉ *Closed Dec. and Jan.* ⑩ *BP.*

The Guadalhorce Valley

Leave Antequera via the El Torcal exit and turn right onto A343. From
8 the village of Alora, follow a small road north to the awe-inspiring **Gar-**

ganta del Chorro (Gorge of the Stream) , a deep limestone chasm where the Guadalhorce River churns and snakes its way some 600 feet below the road. The railroad track that worms in and out of tunnels in the cleft is, amazingly, the main line heading north from Málaga for Bobadilla junction and, eventually, Madrid. Clinging to the cliff side is the **Caminito del Rey** (King's Walk), a suspended catwalk built for a visit by King Alfonso XIII at the beginning of the 19th century. At this writing, the catwalk was closed for major construction and renovations; it is not expected to reopen until early 2007.

North of the gorge, the Guadalhorce has been dammed to form a series of scenic reservoirs surrounded by piney hills, which constitute the **Parque de Ardales** nature area. Informal, open-air restaurants overlook the lakes and a number of picnic spots. Driving along the southern shore of the lake, you reach Ardales and, turning onto A357, the old spa town **⑨** of **Carratraca**. Once a favorite watering hole for both Spanish and foreign aristocracy, it has a Moorish-style *ayuntamiento* (town hall) and an unusual **polygonal bullring.** Carratraca's old hotel, the **Hostal del Príncipe,** once sheltered Empress Eugénie, wife of Napoléon III; Lord Byron also came seeking the cure. The splendid Roman-style marble-and-tile **bathhouse** has benefited from extensive restoration.

THE COSTA DEL SOL

After you rejoin N340 11 km (7 mi) west of Málaga, the sprawling outskirts of Torremolinos signal that you're leaving the "real" Spain and entering, well, the "real" Costa del Sol, with its beaches, high-rise hotels, and serious tourist activity.

Torremolinos

⑩ *11 km (7 mi) west of Málaga, 16 km (10 mi) northeast of Fuengirola, 43 km (27 mi) east of Marbella.*

Torremolinos is all about fun in the sun. It may be more subdued than it was in the action-packed '60s and '70s, but scantily attired northern Europeans of all ages still jam its streets in season, shopping for bargains on Calle San Miguel, downing sangría in the bars of La Nogalera, and congregating in the karaoke bars and English pubs. By day, the sunseekers flock to the beaches El Bajondillo and La Carihuela, where, in high summer, it's hard to find a patch to call your own.

Torremolinos has two sections. The first, **Central Torremolinos,** is built around the Plaza Costa del Sol; Calle San Miguel, the main shopping street; and the brash Nogalera Plaza, which is full of overpriced bars and restaurants. The Pueblo Blanco area, off Calle Casablanca, is more pleasant; and the Cuesta del Tajo, at the far end of San Miguel, winds down a steep slope to the Bajondillo beach. Here, crumbling walls, bougainvillea-clad patios, and old cottages hint at the quiet fishing village of bygone years. The second, much nicer, section is **La Carihuela.** (To find it, head west out of town on Avenida Carlota Alessandri and turn left following the signs.) Far more authentically Spanish, the Car-

10

ihuela still has a few fishermen's cottages and excellent seafood restaurants. The traffic-free esplanade makes for a pleasurable stroll, especially on a summer evening or Sunday at lunchtime, when it's packed with Spanish families.

Ⓒ Just inland on the Churriana road, **Senda** bird park, botanical garden and mini-zoo opened in 2005 in former historical gardens. Exhibits include an aquarium, reptile enclosure, and plenty of exotic birds, all viewed in a lush tropical setting. ⊠ *Ctra. Coín, Km 88, Churriana* ☎ *952/623540* ⊠ *€20* ⊙ *May–Sept., daily 10–10, Oct.–Apr., daily 10–6.*

Where to Stay & Eat

★ $$$ ✕ **Med.** Med is tucked away around the corner from the car-free San Miguel. An elevator whisks you up to an elegant restaurant with wooden beams, a blue-and-white nautical theme, seamless Mediterranean views, and impeccable service. The beautifully presented food is from a menu that changes every six months, with dishes such as *solomillo de ternero con setas, patata machacona y tempura de verduras* (braised veal with oyster mushrooms, creamed potatoes, and vegetable tempura) followed by *sorbete de limón o mandarina con cava* (lemon or orange sorbet with champagne). There's also an excellent wine selection. ⊠ *Las Mercedes 12* ☎ *952/058830* ⪦ *Reservations essential* ☐ *AE, DC, MC, V.*

$$ ✕ **Casa Juan.** The restaurant, an institution among Malagueño families who flock here on weekends to sample the legendary fresh seafood, has recently broadened its girth with still more tables—try for one on the square overlooking the mermaid fountain. This is a good place to indulge in *fritura malagueña* (fried seafood) or *arroz marinera* (seafood with rice), another specialty. As usual in seafood restaurants here, the desserts are disappointing: frozen, commercially made, and overpriced. Buy an ice-cream cone on the beach instead. ⊠ *Plaza San Gines, La Carihuela* ☎ *952/373512* ☐ *MC, V.*

$ ✕ **Matahambre.** Opened in mid-2005, the interior has a stylish yet rustic feel with its brick-barrel vault ceiling, terra-cotta tiles, and walls washed in dark ocher and sky blue. There are outside tables on the Plaza del Panorama—aptly named, as the views of the coast from here are stunning. The affordable restaurant takes its wines seriously, with more than 80 reds to choose from. To accompany your tipple choose from dishes such as *morcilla de Burgos y morrones y cebollas salteada* (black pudding from Burgos with roasted sweet peppers and onion), or, for lightweights, goat-cheese salad with bacon and walnuts. ⊠ *Las Mercedes 14* ☎ *952/381242* ☐ *MC, V.*

$$$ ⊞ **Don Pedro.** Extremely comfortable and well maintained, this three-story hotel was built in traditional low-rise Andalusian-style with ocher-painted walls. The rooms are spacious and have balconies, although sea views get snapped up fast. The bodega-style bar gets popular at happy hour; nightly entertainment there includes flamenco shows. The hearty breakfast buffet should set you up for the day. ⊠ *Av. del Lido, 29620* ☎ *952/386844* ⊟ *952/386935* ⊕ *www.solmelia.com* ⪧ *524 rooms* ⚘ *Restaurant, cable TV, 2 pools, beach* ☐ *AE, DC, MC, V* ⦿❘ *BP.*

$$$ ⊞ **Meliá Costa del Sol.** In the Bajondillo (eastern beach) section of town, the Meliá looks somewhat boxy from the outside. Inside, however, it's

modern and well run. Every room has a sea-view balcony and gets lots of sun; before you book a room, decide whether you prefer morning or evening sunlight. ⊠ *Paseo Marítimo 11, Playa del Bajondillo, 29620* ☎ *952/386677* 🖷 *952/386417* ⊕ *www.solmelia.es* ⇔ *535 rooms, 18 suites* ⚐ *Restaurant, cable TV, in-room broadband, pool, health club, spa, Internet room, meeting rooms, free parking.* ⊟*AE, DC, MC, V* ⊚❘*BP.*

$$$ 🏨 **Tropicana.** On the beach at the far end of the Carihuela, in one of the most pleasant parts of Torremolinos, you'll find this low-rise resort hotel, which has its own beach club. A tropical theme runs throughout, from the purple passion-flower climbers covering the brickwork to the common areas, with exotic plants, raffia floor mats, and bamboo furniture, to the rooms, with their warm color schemes complemented by lashings of white linen. The hotel has a friendly, homey feel that keeps many guests returning year after year. ⊠ *Trópico 6, La Carihuela, 29620* ☎*952/386600* 🖷*952/380568* ⊕*www.hoteltropicana.es* ⇔*84 rooms* ⚐*Restaurant, cable TV, pool, beach, piano bar* ⊟ *AE, DC, MC, V* ⊚❘ *BP.*

$$ 🏨 **Miami.** Something of a find, this small hotel dates from 1950, when it was designed by Manolo Blascos, Picasso's cousin, for the well-known flamenco Gypsy dancer Lola Medina. Rooms are individually furnished, if a little dated, and there's a sitting area with a cozy fireplace. The inn is surrounded by a shady garden west of the Carihuela, making a stay here like visiting a private Spanish home. Reserve ahead. ⊠ *Aladino 14, at C. Miami, 29620* ☎ *952/385255* ⊕ *www.residencia-miami.com* ⇔*26 rooms* ⚐ *Pool, bar, some pets allowed; no room TVs* ⊟ *No credit cards* ⊚❘ *CP.*

$ 🏨 **Cabello.** The rooms at this small hotel have few frills, but most have impressive sea views—it's just a block from the beach, in La Carihuela. Near the ground-floor bar is a comfortable sitting area, with overstuffed chairs, a piano, and a pool table. The owners are friendly and helpful, though they speak only Spanish. ⊠ *Calle Chiriva 28, 29620* ☎ *952/384505* ⇔ *19 rooms* ⚐ *Bar* ⊟ *No credit cards.*

Nightlife & the Arts

Most nocturnal action is in the center of town. Some bars have live music, but Torremolinos is best known for its discos. Many of the better hotels stage flamenco shows, but you may also want to check out the **Taberna Flamenca Pepe López** (⊠ Pl. de la Gamba Alegre ☎ 952/381284). There are nightly shows at 10 PM from April to October. The rest of the year shows are on weekends only.

As the gay capital of the Costa del Sol, Torremolinos has numerous bars and clubs catering to a gay clientele. Most are in or around La Nogalera—this includes the **Parthenon** (⊠ La Nogalera Local 712 ☎ No phone), a small bar that gets packed on weekends. A popular disco for gay patrons is **Disco Séfora** (⊠ Av. Montemar 21 ☎ 658/031235).

Benalmádena

⓫ *9 km (5½ mi) west of Torremolinos, 9 km (5½ mi) east of Mijas.*

★ **Benalmádena-Pueblo,** the village proper, is on the mountainside 7 km (4 mi) from the coast and is surprisingly unspoiled, with a glimpse of the old Andalusia. **Benalmádena-Costa,** the beach resort, is practically an extension of Torremolinos, and run almost exclusively by package-tour operators. It has little for the independent traveler, although the marina has shops, restaurants, and bars aimed at a sophisticated clientele.

In Benalmádena-Costa's marina, **Sea Life Benalmádena** is a better-than-average aquarium with fish from local waters, including rays, sharks, and sunfish. ⊠ *Puerto Marina Benalmádena* ☎ *952/560150* ⊕ *www. sealife.es* ▨ *€10.50* ⊙ *May–Sept., daily 10* AM*–midnight; Oct.–Apr., daily 10–6.*

The Costa del Sol's leading amusement park is **Tivoli World,** with rides, Wild West shows, and 40-odd restaurants and snack bars. A 4,000-seat, open-air auditorium showcases international stars alongside cancan, flamenco, and Spanish ballet performances. On Sunday mornings there's a flea market. Take a cable car to the top of Calamorro Mountain for hiking trails. ⊠ *Av. Tivoli s/n, Arroyo de la Miel* ☎ *952/7577016* ⊕ *www.tivoli.es* ▨ *€4.50, €1 Sun. 11–2* ⊙ *May–Sept., daily 1* PM*–1* AM; *Oct.–Apr., weekends noon–8.*

Where to Stay & Eat

$$$–$$$$ ✕ **Mar de Alborán.** Next to the yacht harbor, this restaurant has a touch more class than most of its peers, including a decent wine list. Fish dishes, such as the Basque-inspired *lomo de merluza con kokotxas y almejas* (hake stew with clams) or *bacalao al pil-pil* (salted cod in a spicy sauce) can be a welcome switch from standard Costa fare. ⊠ *Av. de Alay 5* ☎ *952/446427* ▤ *AE, MC, V* ⊙ *No dinner Sun. Closed Mon. mid-Dec.–mid-Jan.*

$–$$ ✕ **Casa Fidel.** This Benalmádena-Pueblo restaurant is in a typical Andalusian house complete with arches, terra-cotta tiles, a large fireplace, and a small leafy patio. For a starter, try *crema fría de aguacate con salmón marinado* (cold avocado soup with marinated salmon) or *ensalada templada de setas y gambas* (warm salad with shrimp and wild mushrooms). Main courses include *langostinos con chalotas y puré de garbanzos* (king prawns with shallots and garbanzos) and T-bone steak for two. ⊠ *Maestra Ayala 1* ☎ *952/449165* ▤ *AE, DC, MC, V* ⊙ *Closed Tues. and Aug. 1–15. No lunch Wed.*

★ $–$$ ✕ **Ventorillo de la Perra.** If you've been scouring the coast for something typically Spanish, you may find it at this old inn, which dates from 1785. Outside, there's a leafy patio; inside is a cozy dining room and bar with hams hanging from the ceiling. Choose between local Malagueño cooking, including *gazpacuelo malagueño* (a warm gazpacho of potatoes, rice, and shrimp), and typical Spanish food, such as *conejo en salsa de almendras* (rabbit in almond sauce). The *ajo blanco* (a cold, garlicky almond-based soup) is particularly good. ⊠ *Av. Constitución 115, Km 13, Arroyo de la Miel* ☎ *952/441966* ▤ *AE, DC, MC, V* ⊙ *Closed Mon. and Nov.*

$$ ▤ **La Fonda.** You'll find a true taste of Andalusia at this small hotel on one of the prettiest streets in the pueblo. Rooms have white walls, marble floors, and brightly floral fabrics. Some rooms have peerless views of the coast and the Mediterranean; others look onto the cool interior patio. In the same building, under different management, is an excellent restaurant run by Málaga's official hotel school; it's open for lunch on weekdays. ⊠ *Santo Domingo 7, 29639* ☎ *952/568324* 🖷 *952/ 568273* ⊕ *www.fondahotel.com* ⇥ *26 rooms* ⚘ *Minibars, cable TV, pool, bar* ▤ *AE, DC, MC, V* ᵀ⊙ᴵ *BP.*

Nightlife
For discos, piano bars, and karaoke, head for the port. The **Fortuna Night-club** in the **Casino Torrequebrada** (⊠ Av. del Sol s/n, Benalmádena Costa ☎ 952/446000 ⊕ www.torrequebrada.com) has flamenco and an international dance show with a live orchestra, starting at 10:30 PM. A passport, jacket, and tie are required in the casino, open daily 9 PM–4 AM.

Fuengirola

⑫ *16 km (10 mi) west of Torremolinos, 27 km (17 mi) east of Marbella.*

Fuengirola is less frenetic than Torremolinos. Many of its waterfront high-rises are vacation apartments that cater to budget-minded sunseekers from northern Europe and, in summer, a large contingent from Córdoba and other parts of Spain. The town is also a haven for British retirees (with plenty of English and Irish pubs to serve them) and a shopping and business center for the rest of the Costa del Sol. Its Tuesday market is the largest on the coast, and a major tourist attraction.

The most prominent landmark in Fuengirola is **Castillo de Sohail.** The original structure dates from the 12th century, but the castle served as a military fortress until the early 19th century. Just west of town, the castle makes a dramatic performance venue for the annual summer season of music and dance. 🖾 €*1.30* ⊙ *Tues.–Sun. 10–3.*

ᶜᴮ The American company Rain Forest operate the **Fuengirola Zoo.** This cageless zoo with four different habitats create a natural environment for the animals, which include chimpanzees, big cats, and dolphins. The company is also heavily involved with worldwide conservation programs. ⊠ *Av. José Cela 6* ☎ *952/666301* 🖾 €*9.50* ⊙ *Daily 10 AM–dusk.*

Where to Stay & Eat

$$–$$$ ✕ **Patrick Bausier.** Patrick was a student of Paul Bocuse, the grandfather
FodorŚChoice of nouvelle cuisine in Paris. And it shows. Don't worry: the food *is* a
★ work of art, but you won't go hungry. Dishes include exquisitely prepared fowl and fish, such as pot-au-feu of crayfish and Norwegian smoked salmon blinis and vodka. The desserts are fabulous and the service is impeccable. There's complimentary champagne and hors d'oeuvres. ⊠ *Rotondade la Luna 1, Pueblo López* ☎ *952/585120* ⚘ *Reservations essential* ▤ *AE, MC, V* ⊙ *Closed Sun. No lunch.*

$–$$ ✕ **Bistro.** This part of Fuengirola is the most charming, with its low-rise buildings punctuated by the occasional fisherman's cottage. The Bistro has a loyal following from foreign residents, here for the reliably good menu and reasonable prices. Spread over several pine-clad rooms, the cuisine caters to international palates with dishes such as chicken salad with Philadelphia cheese sauce, crepes stuffed with spinach, and fillet steak with a choice of sauces. The bow-tied waiters are charming and efficient. No smoking. ⊠ *Calle Palangreros 30* ☎ *952/477701* ▤ *MC, V* ⊙ *Closed Sun.*

10

$–$$ ✕ **Bodega La Solera.** On a quiet pedestrian street near the main square, this bodega-style bar and restaurant has a sophisticated *madrileño* (Madrid) feel, with a main bar lined with dusty bottles from the selection of more than 500 vintages. The wine is served in giant goblets; as you sip, you can snack on classy canapes such as Roquefort and dates, or go for a palate-blowing main course such as *pulpo a la Gallega con cachelos* (Galician-style braised octopus with new potatoes). ✉ *Calle San Antonio 17* ☎ *952/467708* ☰ *MC, V* ◷ *Closed Tues.*

$$ ⊡ **Villa de Laredo.** This is the place to stay if you want to be near Fuengirola's nightlife and restaurants, although you may need earplugs on a Saturday night. One block east of the port, it has a prime location on the seaside promenade. Recently expanded over two blocks, the rooms are warmly decorated in forest green; all have terraces and most have sea views. ✉ *Paseo Marítimo 42, Rey de España, 29640* ☎ *952/477689* 🖨 *952/477950* ⊕ *www.hotelvilladelaredo.com* ⇱ *74 rooms* ᴥ *Restaurant, minibars, cable TV, in-room data ports, pool* ☰ *AE, DC, MC, V.*

$ ⊡ **Hostal Italia.** Right off the main plaza and near the beach, this small, family-run hotel is deservedly popular. People come here year after year, particularly during the October feria. The rooms are small yet comfy, and nearly all have balconies. There's a larger sun terrace for catching the rays. ✉ *C. de la Cruz 1, 29640* ☎ *952/474193* 🖨 *952/461909* ⊕ *www.hostal-italia.com* ⇱ *40 rooms* ☰ *MC, V.*

Nightlife & the Arts

Amateur local troupes regularly stage plays and musicals in English at the **Salón de Variétés Theater** (✉ Emancipación 30 ☎ 952/474542). For concerts—from classical to rock to jazz—check out the modern **Palacio de la Paz** (✉ Recinto Ferial, Av. Jesús Santo Rein ☎ 952/589349) between Los Boliches and the town center.

Mijas

★ ⓭   *8 km (5 mi) north of Fuengirola, 18 km (11 mi) west of Torremolinos.*

Mijas is in the foothills of the sierra just north of the coast. Buses leave Fuengirola every half hour for the 20-minute drive through hills peppered with villas. If you have a car and don't mind a mildly hair-raising drive, take the more dramatic approach from Benalmádena-Pueblo, a winding mountain road with splendid views. Mijas was discovered long ago by foreign retirees, and though the large, touristy square may look like an extension of the Costa, beyond this are hilly residential streets with time-worn homes. Try to arrive late in the afternoon, after the tour buses have left. Park in the underground parking garage signposted on the approach to the village. The **Museo Mijas** occupies the former town hall. Themed rooms, including an old-fashioned bakery and bodega, surround a patio. Regular art exhibitions are mounted in the upstairs gallery. ✉ *Plaza de la Libertad* ☎ *952/590380* 🎫 *Free* ◷ *Daily 10–2 and 5–8.*

Bullfights take place throughout the year, usually on Sunday at 4:30 PM, at Mijas's tiny **bullring**. One of the few square bullrings in Spain, it's off the Plaza Constitución—Mijas's old village square—and up the slope beside the Mirlo Blanco restaurant. Entrance is via an uninspired small museum of bullfighting memorabilia. ⊠ *Pl. Constitución* ☎ *952/485248* 🖾 *€3* ☉ *June–Sept., daily 10–10; Oct.–Feb., daily 9:30–7; Mar., daily 10–7:30; Apr. and May, daily 10–8:30.*

Worth a visit is the delightful village church **Iglesia Parroquial de la Inmaculada Concepción** (The Immaculate Conception). It's impeccably decorated, especially at Easter, and the terrace and spacious gardens have a splendid panoramic view. The church is up the hill from the Mijas bullring. ⊠ *Pl. Constitución.*

NEED A BREAK?

The **Bar Porras** on Plaza de la Libertad (at the base of Calle San Sebastián–the most photographed street in the village) attracts a regular crowd of crusty locals with its good-value tasty tapas.

Mijas extends down to the coast, and the coastal strip between Fuengirola and Marbella is officially called **Mijas-Costa**. This area has several hotels, restaurants, and golf courses.

Where to Stay & Eat

$$$–$$$$ ✕ **El Padrastro.** Perched on a cliff above the Plaza Virgen de la Peña, "The Stepfather" is accessible by an elevator from the square or, if you're energetic, by stairs. A view over Fuengirola and the coast is the restaurant's main draw. Dishes might include *lubina cocida con ragout de alcachofa y mantequilla al limón* (sea bass cooked with ragout of artichokes and lemon butter). When the weather's right, you can dine alfresco on the large terrace. ⊠ *Paseo del Compás 22* ☎ *952/485000* ☰ *AE, DC, MC, V.*

$$$ ✕ **Mirlo Blanco.** In an old house on the pleasant Plaza de la Constitución, with a terrace for outdoor dining, this place is run by a Basque family that has been in the Costa del Sol restaurant business for decades. Good choices here are such Basque specialties as *txangurro* (spider crab) and *kokotxas de bacalau* (cod cheeks). ⊠ *Pl. de la Constitución 2* ☎ *952/485700* ☰ *AE, MC, V* ☉ *Closed Jan.*

$$–$$$ ✕ **Valparaíso.** Halfway up the road from Fuengirola to Mijas, this sprawling villa stands in its own garden, complete with swimming pool. There's live music nightly ranging from flamenco to opera and jazz. Valparaíso is a favorite among local (mainly British) expatriates, some of whom come in full evening dress to celebrate their birthdays. In winter, logs burn in a cozy fireplace. Try the *pato a la naranja* (duck in orange sauce). ⊠ *Ctra. de Mijas–Fuengirola, Km 4* ☎ *952/485996* ☰ *AE, DC, MC, V* ☉ *No dinner Sun. No lunch Oct.–June.*

★ $$$$ ✕🖾 **Byblos Andaluz.** On the edge of Mijas's golf course (closer to Fuengirola than to Mijas) and in a huge garden of palms, cypresses, and fountains, this is the most expensive hotel on the entire Costa del Sol. It's primarily a spa known for its thalassotherapy, a skin treatment using seawater and seaweed, which is applied in a Roman-like temple of cool, white-and-blue marble tiles. Three outstanding restaurants serve savory regional and international dishes. The menu changes according to season but may include such gourmet delights as roast duck breast flambéed with Jerez brandy. ⊠ *Urbanización Mijas-Golf, Mijas-Costa 29640* ☎ *952/473050* 🖾 *952/476783* ⊕ *www.byblos-andaluz.com* 🖅 *109 rooms, 35 suites* ⚴ *3 restaurants, minibars, cable TV with movies, in-*

10

room broadband, Wi-Fi, 2 18-hole golf courses, 4 tennis courts, 3 pools (1 indoor), health club, hair salon, spa, 2 bars, Internet room, some pets allowed ▭ AE, DC, MC, V ⦿I BP.

$$$$ 🏨 **La Cala Resort.** Set within its own two golf courses a few miles inland, this stylish modern resort is a world unto itself. The rooms, decorated in earth tones, have large balconies with views over the fairways, greens, and countryside, as well as the inevitable but more recent development of vacation apartments, which are tastefully designed. ✉ *La Cala de Mijas, Mijas-Costa 29649* 🖀 *952/669000* 🖷 *952/669039* ⊕ *www.lacala.com* ⇝ *98 rooms, 5 suites* ⚴ *2 restaurants, cafeteria, minibars, cable TV, Wi-Fi, 2 18-hole golf courses, 2 tennis courts, 2 pools (1 indoor), sauna, squash, bar, Internet room, meeting rooms* ▭ *AE, DC, MC, V* ⦿I *BP.*

$$$ 🏨 **Mijas.** It's easy to unwind here, thanks to the poolside restaurant and bar, and the gardens with views of the hillsides stretching down to Fuengirola and the sea. The hotel has new management as of 2006 but retains its tasteful decor with marble floors throughout, wrought-iron window grilles, and wooden shutters. The lobby is large and airy, and there's an attractive glass-roof terrace. All rooms are well furnished, with wood fittings and marble floors. The hotel is at the entrance to Mijas village and has recently completed a 100-room extension. ✉ *Urbanización Tamisa, 29650* 🖀 *952/485800* 🖷 *952/485825* ⇝ *204 rooms, 2 suites* ⚴ *Restaurant, coffee shop, cable TV, in-room data ports, tennis court, pool, health club, hair salon* ▭ *AE, DC, MC, V.*

Marbella

⑭ *27 km (17 mi) west of Fuengirola, 28 km (17 mi) east of Estepona, 50 km (31 mi) southeast of Ronda.*

Playground of the rich and home of movie stars, rock musicians, and dispossessed royal families, Marbella has attained the top rung on Europe's social ladder. Dip into any Spanish gossip magazine and chances are the glittering parties that fill its pages are set in Marbella. Much of this action takes place on the fringes—grand hotels and luxury restaurants line the waterfront for 20 km (12 mi) on each side of the town center. In the town itself, you may well wonder how Marbella became so famous. The main thoroughfare, Avenida Ricardo Soriano, is distinctly charmless, and the Paseo Marítimo, though pleasant enough, with a mix of seafood restaurants and pizzerias overlooking an ordinary beach, is far from spectacular.

Marbella's appeal lies in the heart of the **old village**, which remains miraculously intact. Here, a block or two back from the main highway, narrow alleys of whitewashed houses cluster around the central **Plaza de los Naranjos** (Orange Square), where colorful, albeit pricey, restaurants vie for space under the orange trees. Climb onto what remains of the old fortifications and stroll along the Calle Virgen de los Dolores to the Plaza de Santo Cristo. Wander the maze of lanes and enjoy the geranium-speckled windows and splashing fountains.

The **Museo del Grabado Español Contemporáneo,** in a restored 16th-century palace in the heart of the old town, has contemporary Spanish prints and temporary exhibitions. ⊠ *Hospital Bazán* 🖷 *952/765741* ⊕ *www.museodelgrabado.com* 🖾 *€2.50* ⊙ *Tues.–Sat. 10–2 and 5:30–8:30.*

In a modern building just east of Marbella's old quarter, the **Museo de Bonsai** has a collection of miniature trees, including a 300-year-old olive tree from China. ⊠ *Parque Arroyo de la Repesa, Av. Dr. Maiz Viñal* 🖷 *952/862926* 🖾 *€3* ⊙ *June–Sept., daily 10:30–1:30 and 5–8:30; Oct.–May., daily 10:30–1:30 and 4–7.*

⊓ **NEED A BREAK?** | Enjoy a glass of wine and a transplanted Basque delight at **La Taberna del Pintxo** (⊠ *Av. Miguel Cano 7* 🖷 *952/829321*). A *pintxo* is a little morsel served on a slice of bread or with a toothpick. There's platter after platter of creative examples, from shellfish to slices of omelet to mushrooms baked in garlic to vegetables in vinaigrette.

Marbella's wealth glitters most brightly along the Golden Mile, a tiara of star-studded clubs, restaurants, and hotels west of town stretching from Marbella to **Puerto Banús**. Here, a mosque, Arab banks, and the onetime residence of Saudi Arabia's King Fahd betray the influence of oil money in this wealthy enclave. About 7 km (4½ mi) west of central Marbella (between Km 175 and Km 174), a sign indicates the turnoff leading down to Puerto Banús. Though now hemmed in by a belt of high-rises, Marbella's plush marina, with 915 berths, is a gem of ostentatious wealth, a Spanish answer to St. Tropez. Huge and flashy yachts, beautiful people, and countless expensive stores and restaurants make up the glittering parade that marches long into the night. The backdrop is an Andalusian pueblo—built in the 1960s to resemble the fishing villages that once lined this coast.

Where to Stay & Eat

$$$–$$$$ ╳ **La Hacienda.** In a large, pleasant villa 12 km (7 mi) east of Marbella, the Hacienda was founded in the early '70s by the late Belgian chef Paul Schiff, who helped transform the Costa del Sol culinary scene with his modern approach and judicious use of local ingredients. His legacy lives on here through his family. Schiff's signature dish, *pintada con pasas al vino de Málaga* (guinea fowl with raisins in Málaga wine sauce), is often available. ⊠ *Urbanización Las Chapas, N340, Km 193* 🖷 *952/831267* 🖓 *Reservations essential* ⊟ *AE, MC, V* ⊙ *Closed Mon. and Tues. mid-Nov.–mid-Dec. No lunch July and Aug.*

$$–$$$$ ╳ **Santiago.** Facing the seafront promenade, this busy place, recently slickly redecorated, has long been considered the best fish restaurant in Marbella. Try the *ensalada de langosta* (lobster salad), followed by *besugo al horno* (baked red bream). The menu also has roasts, such as *cochinillo* (pig) and *cordero* (lamb) of the owner's native Castile. Around the corner from the original restaurant (and sharing the same phone number) is Santiago's popular tapas bar. ⊠ *Paseo Marítimo 5* 🖷 *952/770078* ⊟ *AE, DC, MC, V* ⊙ *Closed Nov.*

$$–$$$ ╳ **Aquavit.** Cream-and-yellow paintwork, titanium cutlery, and hand-crafted illuminated tables provide a sunny, snazzy look. Fusion starters include sushi nori rolls, Thai fish cakes, and fresh arugula salad; the signature dish just has to be the potato-and-anchovy gratin with a shot of

10

(what else?) chilled aquavit liquor. More than 35 different vodkas are available, as well as some unusual wines and liqueurs. ⊠ *Plaza del Puerto, Puerto Banús* ☎ *952/819127* ⊟ *AE, MC, V* ⊗ *No lunch.*

$$–$$$ ✕ **La Comedia.** This Swedish-run restaurant is on one of the old town's most traditional Andalusian plazas and has one of the most imaginative menus among Marbella's 600-plus restaurants. Starters include such delights as blue mussel carpaccio topped with grilled scallops and truffles. Entrées include avocado-and-salmon spring rolls with mango and marie rose sauce (a thousand island-style dressing) and tandoori sweet curried chicken. Desserts might include the unusual deep-fried apple-cinnamon wonton with vanilla and white chocolate mousse. ⊠ *Plaza de la Victoria* ☎ *952/776478* ⚄ *Reservations essential* ⊟ *AE, DC, MC, V* ⊗ *Closed Mon. No lunch.*

$$–$$$ ✕ **Zozoi.** Tucked into the corner of one of the town's squares, upbeat, art
Fodor'sChoice deco Zozoi receives rave reviews from the local press. The fashionably
★ Mediterranean menu makes little distinction between starters and main courses; all the portions are generous. Imaginative use of ingredients is shown in such dishes as fish kebabs with curry and roasted duck breast with black cherries and pepper. For dessert, try the red forest fruits with *mille feuilles* (puff pastry) or lemon sorbet spiked with vodka. ⊠ *Plaza Altamirano 1* ☎ *952/858868* ⚄ *Reservations essential* ⊟ *MC, V.*

$$$$ ✕⌂ **Marbella Club.** The grande dame of Marbella hotels was a creation
Fodor'sChoice of the late Alfonso von Hohenlohe, a Mexican-Austrian aristocrat who
★ turned Marbella into a playground for the rich and famous. The exquisite grounds have lofty palm trees, dazzling flower beds, and a beachside tropical pool area. The bungalow-style rooms vary in size; some have private pools. The main restaurant has a classy eclectic menu of modern Mediterranean cuisine. If you can't afford to stay, at least stop by for afternoon tea, served between 4 and 6:30 daily with a selection of finger sandwiches, pastries, and strawberries and cream (in summer.) ⊠ *Blvd. Principe Alfonso von Hohenlohe at Ctra. de Cádiz, Km 178, 3 km (2 mi) west of Marbella, 29600* ☎ *952/822211* 🖷 *952/829884* ⊕ *www.marbellaclub.com* ⏎ *84 rooms, 37 suites, 16 bungalows* ⚄ *3 restaurants, minibars, cable TV with movies, in-room broadband, in-room data ports, Wi-Fi, 2 pools, gym, sauna, Internet room, free parking* ⊟ *AE, DC, MC, V* ⧈ *BP.*

★ $$$$ ✕⌂ **Puente Romano.** West of Marbella, between the Marbella Club and Puerto Banús, is this palatial hotel designed like an Andalusian pueblo, complete with gardens and trickling fountains. As the name suggests, there's a genuine Roman bridge on the landscaped grounds, which run right down to the beach. There are four restaurants, including El Puente, and Roberto; the latter serves Italian food in the hotel's beach club, a popular summer nightlife venue. In summer there's a beachfront chiringuito (seafood restaurant), where you can sample fresh fish. ⊠ *Ctra. Cádiz, Km 177, 29600* ☎ *952/820900* 🖷 *952/775766* ⊕ *www. puenteromano.com* ⏎ *149 rooms, 77 suites* ⚄ *4 restaurants, minibars, cable TV with movies, in-room data ports, 10 tennis courts, 2 pools, nightclub, meeting room* ⊟ *AE, DC, MC, V* ⧈ *BP.*

$$$ ⌂ **Artola.** Painted with yellow trim and green shutters, this traditional hotel has expansive gardens and direct access to the beach. The rooms are pleasant, if a little on the small side; some have balconies. Golfers can perfect their game within putting distance of the Med. Artola is between Fuengirola and Marbella. ✉ *Ctra. de Cádiz, Km 194, 29600* ☎ *952/831390* 🖶 *952/830450* ⊕ *www.hotelartola.com* 🛏 *35 rooms* ⚴ *Restaurant, cable TV, 9-hole golf course, pool, bar, some pets allowed* ▭ *AE, DC, MC, V* ⦷ *BP.*

$$$ ⌂ **Fuerte Miramar Spa.** This slick new hotel with marble floors is a sister to the somewhat stuffier El Fuerte Hotel a couple of blocks away. The rooms are elegant, with a gold and pale-blue color scheme, choice of pillows, balconies, and sea views. Agreeable extras include the hydrotherapy treatments, such as the anti-stress program, and massages on the beach out front. The historic center of town is a five-minute stroll away. ✉ *Plaza José Luque Manzano s/n, 29600* ☎ *952/768400* 🖶 *952/768414* ⊕ *www.hotelfuertemiramar.com* 🛏 *226 rooms* ⚴ *Restaurant, cafeteria, in-room data ports, Wi-Fi, pool, hair salon, sauna, spa, Turkish bath, piano bar, Internet room, parking (fee)* ⦷ *BP.*

$$ ⌂ **Lima.** Here's a good midrange option in downtown Marbella, two blocks from the beach. The recently redecorated rooms have dark-wood furniture, bright floral bedspreads, and balconies; the corner rooms are the largest. Underground parking is available at an extra cost. ✉ *Av. Antonio Belón 2, 29600* ☎ *952/770500* 🖶 *952/863091* ⊕ *www.hotellimamarbella.com* 🛏 *64 rooms* ⚴ *Cable TV, parking (fee)* ▭ *AE, DC, MC, V.*

¢   ⌂ **Juan.** On a quiet pedestrian street, this no-frills cheapie with a small courtyard is a short stroll from the beach and Marbella's historic center. Because the rooms have refrigerators, this is a good place if you're economizing on eating out. ✉ *Calle Luna 18, 29600* ☎ *952/779475* 🛏 *4 rooms* ⚴ *Fans, refrigerators; no a/c* ▭ *No credit cards* ⦷ *EP.*

Nightlife & the Arts

Art exhibits are held in private galleries and in several of Marbella's leading hotels, notably the Puente Romano. The **tourist office** (✉ Glorieta de la Fontanilla ☎ 952/822818 ⊕ www.pgb.es/marbella) can provide a map of town and monthly calendar of exhibits and events.

Much of the nighttime action revolves around the **Puerto Banús,** in such bars as Sinatra's and Joy's Bar. Marbella's most famous nightspot is the **Olivia Valére disco** (✉ Ctra. de Istán, Km 0.8 ☎ 952/828861), decorated to resemble a Moorish palace; head inland from the town's mosque (an easy-to-spot landmark).

Fodor'sChoice
★

The trendy **Dreamers** (✉ CN 340 km, Puerto Banús ☎ 952/812080) attracts a young, streetwise crowd with its live bands, go-go girls, and a massive dance space. The **Casino Nueva Andalucía** (✉ Bajos Hotel Andalucía Pl., N340 ☎ 952/814000), open 8 PM to 6 AM May through October (until 5 AM November through April), is a chic gambling spot in the Hotel Andalucía Plaza, just west of Puerto Banús. Jacket and tie are required for men, and passports for all. In the center of Marbella, **Ana María** (✉ Pl. de Santo Cristo 5 ☎ 952/775646) is a popular flamenco venue but open only from May to September.

10

Ojén

⑮ *10 km (6 mi) north of Marbella.*

For a contrast to the glamour of the coast, drive up to Ojén, in the hills above Marbella. Take note of the beautiful **pottery** and, if you're here the first week in August, don't miss the *Fiesta de Flamenco,* which attracts some of Spain's most respected flamenco names, including the Juan Peña El Lebrijano, Chiquetete, and El Cabrero. Four kilometers (2½ mi) from Ojén is the **Refugio del Juanar,** a former hunting lodge in the heart of the Sierra Blanca, at the southern edge of the Serranía de Ronda, a mountainous wilderness. Not far from the Refugio, you might spot the **wild ibex** that dwell among the rocky crags; the best times to watch are dawn and dusk, when they descend from their hiding places. A bumpy trail takes you a mile from the Refugio to the **Mirador** (lookout), with a sweeping view of the Costa del Sol and the coast of northern Africa.

Where to Stay & Eat

$$$ ✕🖼 **Castillo de Monda.** Designed to resemble a castle, this hotel incorporates the ruins of Monda's Moorish fortress, some of which date back to the 8th century. The interior is decorated with ceramic tiles, elaborate arches, and extensive use of Moorish-style stucco bas-relief. The guest rooms are sumptuous and fun, with four-poster beds, marble heated bathroom floors, and colorful fabrics. The main restaurant, which resembles a medieval banquet hall, has terrific views of the surrounding countryside. ✉ *Monda 29110* ☎ *952/457142* 🖷 *952/457336* ⊕ *www.mondacastle.com* ➱ *17 rooms, 6 suites* ⏚ *Restaurant, cable TV, in-room data ports, Wi-Fi, pool, bar* ⊟ *AE, MC, V.*

$$–$$$ ✕🖼 **Refugio del Juanar.** Once an aristocratic hunting lodge (King Alfonso XIII came here), this secluded hotel and restaurant was sold to its staff in 1984 for the symbolic sum of 1 peseta. The hunting theme prevails, both in the common areas—where a log fire roars in winter—and on the restaurant menu, where game is emphasized. The rooms are simply decorated in a rustic style, and six (including the three suites) have their own fireplace. ✉ *Sierra Blanca s/n, 29610* ☎🖷 *952/881000* ⊕ *www.juanar.com* ➱ *23 rooms, 3 suites* ⏚ *Restaurant, cafeteria, cable TV, tennis court, pool, meeting room* ⊟ *AE, DC, MC, V.*

RONDA & THE PUEBLOS BLANCOS

Ronda and the whitewashed villages of the mountains behind the Costa del Sol form one of Spain's most scenic and emblematic driving routes. The contrast with Torremolinos is dramatic.

Ronda

⑯
Fodor'sChoice
★
61 km (38 mi) northwest of Marbella, 108 km (67 mi) southwest of Antequera (via Pizarra).

Ronda, one of the oldest towns in Spain, is known for its spectacular position and views. Secure in its mountain fastness on a rock high over the River Guadalevín, the town was a stronghold for the legendary Andalusian bandits who held court here from the 18th to early 20th century. Ronda's most dramatic element is its ravine (360 feet deep and 210 feet across)—known as El Tajo—which divides La Ciudad, the old Moorish town, from El Mercadillo, the "new town," which sprang up after the Christian Reconquest of 1485. Tour buses roll in daily with sightseers from the coast 49 km (30 mi) away, and on weekends affluent Sevillanos flock to their second homes here. Stay overnight midweek to see this noble town's true colors.

The most attractive approach is from the south. The winding but well-maintained A376 from San Pedro de Alcántara travels north up through the mountains of the Serranía de Ronda. Take the first turnoff to Ronda from A376. Entering the lowest part of town, known as El Barrio, you can see parts of the old walls, including the 13th-century **Puerta de Almocobar** and the 16th-century **Puerta de Carlos V** gates. The road climbs past the Iglesia del Espíritu Santo (Church of the Holy Spirit) and up into the heart of town.

Begin in El Mercadillo, where the **tourist office** (✉ Paseo de Bas Infante s/n ☎ 952/187119 ⊕ www.andalucia.org ⊘ Weekdays 9:30–6:30, weekends 10–2) in the Plaza de España can supply you with a map. Immediately south of the Plaza de España is Ronda's most famous bridge, the **Puente Nuevo** (New Bridge), an architectural marvel built between 1755 and 1793. The bridge's lantern-lighted parapet offers dizzying views of the awesome gorge. Just how many people have met their ends here nobody knows, but the architect of the Puente Nuevo fell to his death while inspecting work on the bridge. During the civil war, hundreds of victims were hurled from it. Cross the Puente Nuevo into **La Ciudad,** the old Moorish town, and wander the twisting streets of white houses with birdcage balconies.

The so-called House of the Moorish King, **Casa del Rey Moro,** was actually built in 1709 on the site of an earlier Moorish residence. Despite the name and the *azulejo* (painted tile) plaque depicting a Moor on the facade, it's unlikely that Moorish rulers ever lived here. The garden has a great view of the gorge, and from here a stairway of some 365 steps, known as **La Mina,** descends to the river. However, the steps are steep and poorly lighted and should be tackled only by the agile. The house, across the Puente Nuevo on Calle Santo Domingo, is being converted into a luxury hotel due for completion in late 2006, although you can visit the gardens and La Mina. ✉ *Calle Santo Domingo 17* ☎ *952/187200* ▣ €4 ⊘ *May–Sept., daily 10–8; Oct.–Apr., daily 10–7.*

10

The excavated remains of the **Baños Arabes** (Arab Baths) date from Ronda's tenure as capital of a Moorish *taifa* (kingdom). The star-shape vents in the roof are an inferior imitation of the ceiling of the beautiful bathhouse in Granada's Alhambra. The baths are beneath the Puente Arabe (Arab Bridge) in a ravine below the Palacio del Marqués de Salvatierra. ▣ €2 ⊘ *Weekdays 10–6, weekends 10–3.*

The collegiate church of **Santa María la Mayor,** which serves as Ronda's cathedral, has roots in Moorish times: originally the Great Mosque of Ronda, the tower and adjacent galleries, built for viewing festivities in the square, retain their Islamic design. Overall, however, the church was rebuilt by the Christians and dedicated to the Virgen de la Encarnacion after the Reconquest. The naves are late Gothic, and the main altar is heavy with baroque gold leaf. The church is around the corner from the remains of a mosque, Minarete Árabe (Moorish Minaret) at the end of the Marqués de Salvatierra. ⊠ *Pl. Duquesa de Parcent* ▨ *€2* ⊙ *May–Sept., daily 10–8; Oct.–Apr., daily 10–6.*

A stone palace with twin Mudejar towers, the **Palacio de Mondragón** (Palace of Mondragón) was probably the residence of Ronda's Moorish kings. Ferdinand and Isabella appropriated it after their victory in 1485. Today you can wander through the patios, with their brick arches and delicate, Mudejar stucco tracery, and admire the mosaics and *artesonado* (coffered) ceiling. The second floor holds a small museum with archaeological items found near Ronda, plus the reproduction of a dolmen. ⊠ *Plaza Mondragón* ☎ *952/878450* ▨ *€2* ⊙ *Apr.–Oct., weekdays 10–6, weekends 10–3; May–Sept., weekdays 10–8, weekends 10–3.*

The main sight in Ronda's commercial center, El Mercadillo, is the **Plaza de Toros.** Pedro Romero (1754–1839), the father of modern bullfighting and Ronda's most famous native son, is said to have killed 5,600 bulls here during his long career. In the museum beneath the plaza you can see posters for Ronda's very first fights, held here in 1785. The plaza was once owned by the late bullfighter Antonio Ordóñez, on whose nearby ranch Orson Welles's ashes were scattered (as directed in his will)—indeed, the ring has become a favorite of filmmakers. Every September, the bullring is the scene of Ronda's *corridas goyescas,* named after Francisco Goya, whose bullfight sketches (*tauromaquias*) were inspired by the skill and art of Pedro Romero. Both participants and the dignitaries in the audience don the costumes of Goya's time for the occasion. Seats for these fights cost a small fortune and are booked far in advance. Other than that, the plaza is rarely used for fights except during Ronda's May festival and sometimes in September. ☎ *952/874132* ▨ *€5* ⊙ *Daily 10–6, 10–8 in summer.*

▌ NEED A BREAK? Beyond the bullring in El Mercadillo, you can relax in the shady **Alameda del Tajo** gardens, one of the loveliest spots in Ronda. At the end of the garden, a balcony protrudes from the face of the cliff, offering a vertigo-inducing view of the valley below. Stroll along the cliff-top walk to the Reina Victoria hotel, built by British settlers from Gibraltar at the turn of the 20th century as a fashionable rest stop on their Algeciras–Bobadilla railroad line.

Where to Stay & Eat

★ **$$$$** ✗ **Tragabuches.** Málagueño chef Benito Goméz has taken over the culinary helm here, but the menu remains daringly innovative. The menú de degustación, a taster's menu of five courses and two desserts, includes imaginative choices such as *tocino con jugo de almejas, morcilla y lemongrass* (pork with blood sausage in a clam-and-lemongrass sauce) and white-garlic ice cream with pine nuts. Traditional and modern furnishings blend in the two dining rooms (one with a picture window). The restaurant is around the corner from Ronda's parador and the tourist office, and you can purchase a cookbook containing some of the its best-loved dishes. ⊠ *José Aparicio 1* ☎ *952/190291* ▭ *AE, DC, MC, V* ☉ *Closed Mon. No dinner Sun.*

\$\$–\$\$\$ ✕ **Restaurante del Escudero.** Sergio Lopéz, winner of the Best Young Chef in Spain award, moved here from Tragabuches and has predictably raised the culinary stakes. Dishes are simple (a surprise from Lopéz) but exquisitely prepared. They include *berenjenas rellenas y gratinadas con carne* (baked eggplant with a meat-and-cheese sauce) and the down-to-earth *chorizo y morcilla* (black pudding and sausage). Three elegant dining rooms, separated by graceful arches, are in a colonial-style house with sweeping Tajo views. An outside terrace for dining alfresco and an ample wine list complete the picture. ⊠ *Paseo de Blas Infante 1* ☎ *952/ 871367* ▭ *AE, DC, MC, V.*

\$\$ ✕ **Pedro Romero.** Named after the father of modern bullfighting, this restaurant opposite the bullring is packed with colorful bullfight paraphernalia. Mounted bull heads peer down at you as you tuck into the *sopa de la casa* (the house soup, made with ham and eggs), *rabo de toro,* (oxtail) or *perdiz estofada con salsa de vino blanco y hierbas* (stewed partridge with white-wine-and-herb sauce), and, for dessert, *helado de higos con chocolate* (fig ice cream topped with house-made chocolate sauce). ⊠ *Virgen de la Paz 18* ☎ *952/871110* ▭ *AE, DC, MC, V.*

\$\$\$ ✕▥ **Parador de Ronda.** The exterior of this parador is the old town hall, perched at the very edge of the Tajo gorge. Aside from the downstairs seating area and corridors, which are old-fashioned and starting to look a little shabby, the decor is modern, with a glass-enclosed courtyard. The large, comfortable rooms are done in cream tones and have enormous bathrooms with double sinks and full-size baths. If you want a view of the gorge, it will cost an extra €20. The restaurant (\$–\$\$\$) is famous in its own right: try the gazpacho based on green peppers, a regional specialty. ⊠ *Pl. de España, 29400* ☎ *952/877500* 🖶 *952/878188* ⊕ *www.parador.es* ☞ *70 rooms, 8 suites* ⚐ *Restaurant, minibars, cable TV, pool, meeting room* ▭ *AE, DC, MC, V.*

\$\$–\$\$\$ ✕▥ **Ancinipo.** The artistic legacy of its former owners, Ronda artist Téllez Loriguillo and acclaimed Japanese watercolor painter Miki Haruta, is evidenced throughout this boutique hotel. The interior has exposed stone panels, steel-and-glass fittings, and mosaic-tile bathrooms—and many murals and paintings. There are dramatic mountain views from most of the rooms, and the Atrium restaurant dishes up such traditional favorites as *migas* (fried bread crumbs) and oxtail stew, followed by chestnuts with brandy and cream. ⊠ *José Aparicio 7, 29400* ☎ *952/161002* ⊕ *www.hotelacinipo.com* ☞ *14 rooms* ⚐ *Restaurant, minibars, cable TV, in-room data ports, bar* ▭ *AE, DC, MC, V.*

\$\$ ✕▥ **Alavera de los Baños.** This small, German-run hotel was used as a backdrop for the film classic *Carmen.* Fittingly, given its location next to the Moorish baths, there's an Arab-influenced theme throughout, with terra-cotta tiles, graceful arches, and pastel-color washes. The two rooms on the first floor have their own terraces, opening up onto the split-level garden. The restaurant is open for dinner and uses predominantly organic foods. ⊠ *Hoya San Miguel s/n, 29400* ☎☎ *952/879143* ⊕ *www.andalucia.com/alavera* ☞ *9 rooms* ⚐ *Restaurant, pool, lounge, library; no a/c* ▭ *MC, V* ⦿ *BP.*

10

$$ ✕⊡ **El Molino del Santo.** In the now-converted "Saint's Mill" next to a rushing stream near Benaoján, 10 km (7 mi) from Ronda, this British-run establishment was one of Andalusia's first country hotels. Guest rooms are arranged around a pleasant patio and come in different sizes, some with a terrace. This is a good base for walks in the mountains, and the hotel rents mountain bikes as well. There's also a small station nearby with trains to Ronda and other villages. The restaurant has an excellent reputation with vegetarian options. The hotel also adopts such ecological practices as using solar panels for hot water and the pool. ✉ *Estación de Benaoján s/n, Benaoján 29370* ☎ *952/167151* 🖷 *952/167327* ⊕ *www.andalucia.com/molino* ⤢ *18 rooms* ⚲ *Restaurant, pool, bicycles* ▭ *AE, DC, MC, V* ☯ *Closed mid-Nov.–mid-Feb.* ⍟ *BP.*

$$$ ⊡ **Reina Victoria.** Built in 1906 by the Gibraltar British as a weekend stop for passengers on the rail line between Algeciras and Bobadilla, this classic Spanish hotel rose to fame in 1912, when the ailing German poet Rainer Maria Rilke came here to convalesce. (His room has been preserved as a museum.) Although the Queen Victoria has had more than a lick of paint, it still exudes old-fashioned charm with large Edwardian-style windows, hunting prints, and gracious lounges. The views from the cliff-top gardens, hanging over a roughly 500-foot precipice, are particularly dramatic. ✉ *Jerez 25, 29400* ☎ *952/871240* 🖷 *952/871075* ⊕ *www.hotelreinavictoriaronda.com* ⤢ *90 rooms* ⚲ *Restaurant, minibars, cable TV, pool, parking (fee), some pets allowed* ▭ *AE, DC, MC, V.*

$$ ⊡ **Finca la Guzmana.** This traditional Andalusian *corijo* (cottage) 4 km (2½ mi) east of Ronda has been lovingly restored with bright, fresh decor to complement the original beams, the wood-burning stoves, and a sublime setting surrounded by olive trees and grapevines. Walkers, birdwatchers, and painters are frequent guests. The owners also organize trips (guided or unguided) through the white villages in a classic sports car. The breakfast is more generous than most, with homemade bread, preserves, and local cheeses. ✉ *Aptdo de Correos 408, 29400* ☎ *600/006305* ⊕ *www.laguzmana.com* ⤢ *5 rooms* ⚲ *Pool, library* ▭ *No credit cards* ⍟ *CP.*

★ $$ ⊡ **San Gabriel.** In the oldest part of Ronda, this hotel is run by a family who converted their 18th-century home into an elegant, informal hotel (the family still lives in part of the building). The common areas, furnished with antiques, are warm and cozy, and include a DVD screening room with autographed photos of actors. (John Lithgow, Isabella Rossellini, and Bob Hoskins, in town to film the 2000 television movie version of *Don Quixote,* were among the first to stay at the hotel.) Some guest rooms have small sitting areas; all are stylishly furnished with antiques. ✉ *Marqués de Moctezuma 19, 29400* ☎ *952/190392* 🖷 *952/190117* ⊕ *www.hotelsangabriel.com* ⤢ *15 rooms, 1 suite* ⚲ *Cafeteria, minibars, cable TV, free parking* ▭ *AE, MC, V.*

Around Ronda: Caves, Romans & Pueblos Blancos

This area of spectacular gorges, remote mountain villages, and ancient caves is fascinating to explore and a dramatic contrast with the clamor and crowds of the coast. About 20 km (12 mi) west of Ronda toward Seville is the prehistoric **Cueva de la Pileta** (Pileta Cave). Exit left for the village of Benaoján—from here the caves are well signposted. A Spanish-speaking guide will hand you a paraffin lamp and lead you on a roughly 90-minute walk that reveals prehistoric wall paintings of bison, deer, and horses outlined in black, red, and ocher. One highlight is the Cámara del Pescado (Chamber of the Fish), whose drawing of a huge fish is thought to be 15,000 years old. ☎ 952/167343 ⊠ €6 ⊗ *Daily 10–1 and 4–5, 4–6 in summer.*

Ronda la Vieja (Old Ronda), 20 km (12 mi) west of Ronda, is the site of the old Roman settlement of **Acinipo.** A thriving town in the 1st century AD, Acinipo was abandoned for reasons that still baffle historians. Today it's a windswept hillside with piles of stones, the foundations of a few Roman houses, and what remains of a theater. Excavations are often under way at the site, in which case it will be closed to the public. Call the tourist office in Setenil before visiting to get an update. ⊠ *Take A376 toward Algodonales; turnoff for ruins is 9 km (5 mi) from Ronda on MA449* ☎ *956/134261* ⊕ *www.setenil.com* ⊠ *Free* ⊗ *Weekdays 10–2:30 and 5–8, weekends noon–2 and 5–8.*

⑰ **Setenil de las Bodegas,** 8 km (5 mi) north of Acinipo, is in a cleft in the rock cut by the Guadalporcín River. The streets resemble long, narrow caves, and on many houses the roof is formed by a projecting ledge of heavy rock.

⑱ In **Olvera,** 13 km (8 mi) north of Setenil, two imposing silhouettes dominate the crest of its hill: the 11th-century castle Vallehermoso, a legacy of the Moors, and the neoclassical church of La Encarnación, reconstructed in the 19th century on the foundations of the old Moorish mosque.

⑲ A solitary watchtower dominates a crag above the village of **Zahara de la Sierra,** its outline visible for miles around. The tower is all that remains of a Moorish castle where King Alfonso X once fought the emir of Morocco; the building remained a Moorish stronghold until it fell to the Christians in 1470. Along the streets you can see door knockers fashioned like the hand of Fatima: the fingers represent the five laws of the Koran and serve to ward off evil. ⊠ *From Olvera, drive 21 km (13 mi) southwest to the village of Algodonales.*

10

Sierra de Grazalema

Village of Grazalema: 28 km (17 mi) northwest of Ronda, 23 km (14 mi) northeast of Ubrique.

The 323-square-km (125-square-mi) Sierra de Grazalema straddles the provinces of Málaga and Cádiz. These mountains trap the rain clouds that roll in from the Atlantic and thus have the distinction of being the wettest place in Spain, with an average annual rainfall of 88 inches. Thanks to the park's altitude and prevailing humidity, it's one of the last habitats for the rare fir tree *Abies pinsapo*; it's also home to ibex, vultures, and birds of prey. Parts of the park are restricted, accessible only on foot and accompanied by an official guide. Standing dramatically at the entrance to the park, the village of **Grazalema** is the prettiest of the pueblos blancos. Its cobblestone streets of houses with pink-and-ocher roofs

⑳

wind up the hillside, red geraniums splash white walls, and black wrought-iron lanterns and grilles cling to the house fronts.

From Grazalema, A374 takes you to **Ubrique,** on the slopes of the Saltadero Mountains, and known for its leather tanning and embossing industry. Look for the **Convento de los Capuchinos** (Capuchin Convent), the church of **San Pedro,** and 4 km (2½ mi) away the ruins of the Moorish castle **El Castillo de Fátima.** Another excursion from Grazalema takes you through the heart of the nature park: follow the A344 west through dramatic mountain scenery, past Benamahoma, to **El Bosque,** home to a trout stream and information center.

Where to Stay

☾ $ 🏠 **Villa Turística de Grazalema.** Across the valley from the village of Grazalema, this complex consists of a hotel proper and 38 semidetached apartments sleeping two to six. Most have splendid views of the village and the mountains beyond. It's popular with families, so the noise level can rise during school vacations. ⊠ *El Olivar, exit just before village, Grazalema 11610* 🕾 *956/132136* 🖷 *956/132213* ⊕ *www.tugasa. com* 🛌 *24 rooms, 38 apartments* ⌂ *Restaurant, pool, meeting room* 🖃 *MC, V* ⍧⊙ *BP.*

ESTEPONA TO TARIFA

You can still see Estepona's fishing village and Moorish old quarter amid its booming coastal development. Just inland, Casares piles whitewashed houses over the bright-blue Mediterranean below. Sotogrande, with its golf courses and long beach, and old San Roque are the last stops before the windy town of Tarifa marks the southernmost tip of mainland Europe.

Estepona

㉑ *17 km (11 mi) west of San Pedro de Alcántara.*

Estepona is a pleasant and relatively tranquil seaside resort, despite being surrounded by an ever-increasing number of urban developments. The beach, more than 1 km (½ mi) long, also has better-quality sand than the Costa norm, and the promenade is lined with well-kept, aromatic flower gardens. The gleaming white **Puerto Deportivo** is lively and packed with restaurants, serving everything from fresh fish to pizza and Chinese food. Back from the main Avenida de España, the old quarter of narrow streets and bars is surprisingly unspoiled.

Where to Stay & Eat

$$–$$$ ✕ **Alcaría de Ramos.** José Ramos, a winner of Spain's National Gastronomy Prize, opened this restaurant in the El Paraíso complex, between Estepona and San Pedro de Alcántara, and has watched it garner a large and enthusiastic following. Try the ensalada *de lentejas con salmón ahumado* (with lentils and smoked salmon), followed by *zarzuela de pescados y mariscos* (seafood casserole), leaving room for Ramos's exemplary crepes suzette with raspberry sauce. ⊠ *Urbanización El Paraíso, Ctra. N340, Km 167* 🕾 *952/886178* 🖃 *MC, V* ⊙ *Closed Sun. No lunch.*

$$-$$$ ✕ **La Rada.** Locals flock to this bright, busy establishment for freshly caught fish and shellfish. Service is brisk—waiters dash among the tables in the two dining rooms. Ask about the daily specials or dig into the house specialty, *arroz a la marinera* (seafood rice). ⊠ *Av. España 16* ☎ *952/791036* ☱ *AE, MC, V.*

$$$$ 🏨 **Kempinski.** From the outside, this luxury resort between the coastal highway and the beach looks like a cross between a Moroccan casbah and the Hanging Gardens of Babylon. Tropical gardens, with a succession of large swimming pools, meander down to the beach. The rooms are spacious, modern, and luxurious, with faux–North African furnishings and balconies overlooking the Mediterranean. The Sunday-afternoon jazz brunch, with a live band and lavish buffet, is something of a social occasion for locals. ⊠ *Playa El Padrón, Ctra. N340, Km 159, 29680* ☎ *952/809500* 🖨 *952/809550* ⊕ *www.kempinski-spain.com* ⟿ *133 rooms, 16 suites* ⚴ *Restaurant, minibars, cable TV with movies, in-room broadband, in-room data ports, Wi-Fi, 4 pools (1 indoor), gym, hair salon, shop, some pets allowed* ☱ *AE, DC, MC, V* ⟦⊙⟧ *BP.*

★ **$$$$** 🏨 **Las Dunas.** Rising like a multicolor apparition next to the beach, this spectacular hotel is halfway between Estepona and Marbella. Trickling fountains and copious exotic plants help create a sense of the palatial, and the large guest rooms are suitably sumptuous. Sea views command a premium. The restaurant serves first-class international food, and the health center offers several alternative therapies. Families will appreciate the well-organized kids' club. ⊠ *La Boladilla Baja, Ctra. de Cádiz, Km 163.5, 29689* ☎ *952/794345* 🖨 *952/794825* ⊕ *www.las-dunas.com* ⟿ *33 rooms, 39 suites, 33 apartments* ⚴ *2 restaurants, children's programs, minibars, cable TV with movies, in-room broadband, Wi-Fi, pool, health club, spa, meeting rooms, free parking* ☱ *AE, DC, MC, V* ⟦⊙⟧ *BP.*

★ **$$$** 🏨 **Albero Lodge.** Owner Myriam Perez Torres' love for travel infuses this boutique hotel, where each room is named after a city, with decor to match. Exotic Fez has rich fabrics and colors; European rooms, such as Florence and Berlin, are elegantly decorated with antiques. In playful contrast, the New York room is dramatically avant-garde with a black-and-white theme. There are private terraces, and a sandy path leads to the beach. Myriam can arrange hiking, bicycling, and boat trips, as well as therapeutic massages. ⊠ *Urb. Finca La Cancelada, Calle Támesis 16, 29689* ☎ *952/880700* 🖨 *952/885238* ⊕ *www.alberolodge.com* ⟿ *8 rooms* ⚴ *Minibars, cable TV, pool* ☱ *AE, DC, MC, V.*

Casares

㉒ *20 km (12 mi) northwest of Estepona.*

The mountain village of Casares lies high above Estepona in the Sierra Bermeja. Streets of ancient white houses piled one on top of the other perch on the slopes beneath a ruined but impressive Moorish castle. The heights afford stunning views over orchards, olive groves, and cork woods to the Mediterranean, sparkling in the distance.

San Roque

㉓ *92 km (57 mi) southwest of Ronda, 64 km (40 mi) west of Marbella.*

The town of San Roque was founded within sight of Gibraltar by Spaniards who fled the Rock when the British captured it in 1704. Almost 300 years of British occupation have done little to diminish the ideals of San Roque's inhabitants, who still see themselves as the only genuine Gibraltarians. Fourteen kilometers (10 mi) east of San Roque is the luxury **Sotogrande** complex, a gated community with sprawling millionaires' villas, a yacht marina, and four golf courses, including the legendary Valderrama, which once hosted the Ryder Cup.

Where to Stay & Eat

$$–$$$ ✕ **Los Remos.** The dining room in this gracious colonial villa has peach-color walls with quasi-baroque adornments: gilt rococo mirrors, swirling cherubs, friezes of grapes, and crystal lamps. It overlooks a formal, leafy garden full of palms, cedars, and trailing ivy. Entrées include *potaje de sepia con garbanzos.* (cuttlefish stew with chickpeas). All the seafood comes from the Bay of Algeciras area—the restaurant's name means "The Oars"—and the wine cellar contains some 20,000 bottles. ⊠ *Villa Victoria, Campomento de San Roque* 🕾 *956/698412* ▤ *AE, DC, MC, V* ☻ *Closed Mon. No dinner Sun.*

$$$$ 🏨 **San Roque Club.** In this Moorish-Andalusian-style pueblo, the main building houses the reception area, golf clubhouse, and two restaurants, one specializing in Japanese food. The rooms and suites are in white houses scattered around a garden with fountains and exotic plants; each room has a little garden patio, and each suite has an enclosed courtyard as well. The houses are connected by paved paths, on which the cleaning staff tool around on golf carts. The hotel is next to the San Roque golf course, halfway between the village and Sotogrande. ⊠ *San Roque Club, Ctra. N340, Km 127, 11360* 🕾 *956/613030* 🖷 *956/613013* ⊕ *www. sanroqueclub.com* ⋑ *50 rooms, 50 suites* ⅃ *2 restaurants, minibars, cable TV with movies, in-room data ports, 18-hole golf course, 4 tennis courts, pool, horseback riding, some pets allowed* ▤ *AE, DC, MC, V* ¶⋑ *BP.*

$$$ 🏨 **NH Almenara Golf Hotel & Spa.** This deluxe Sotogrande resort is a complex of semidetached Andalusian-style houses clustered around a main building on the edge of an 18-hole golf course, 6 km (4 mi) from the coast. Gardens surround each house, accessible via golf cart. Each house also has a private terrace or patio. Facilities at the marble-clad spa include a Finnish sauna, Turkish bath, and hydromassage pool. ⊠ *Av. Almenara s/n, Sotogrande 11310* 🕾 *956/582000* 🖷 *956/582001* ⊕ *www. sotogrande.com* ⋑ *136 rooms, 12 suites* ⅃ *Restaurant, snack bar, minibars, cable TV with movies, in-room data ports, Wi-Fi, 18-hole golf courses, pool, spa, bar* ▤ *AE, DC, MC, V.*

Nightlife

The **Casino de San Roque** (⊠ Ctra. N340, Km 124 🕾 956/780100 ☻ Mar.–Sept., daily 8 PM–5 AM; Oct.–Feb., daily 9 PM–5 AM) has a gaming room with roulette and blackjack tables and a less formal slot-machine area. Passports, and a jacket and tie for men, are required in the casino.

Tarifa

㉔ FodorsChoice ★ *35 km (21 mi) west of San Roque.*

On the Straits of Gibraltar at the southernmost tip of mainland Europe—where the Mediterranean and the Atlantic meet—Tarifa was one of the earliest Moorish settlements in Spain. Strong winds kept Tarifa off the tourist maps for years, but they have ultimately proven a source of wealth; the vast wind farm on the surrounding hills creates electricity, and the wide, white-sand beaches stretching north of the town have become Europe's biggest wind- and kite-surfing center. As a result, the town has continued to grow and prosper. Downtown cafés which, a couple of years ago, were filled with men in flat caps playing dominoes and drinking *anís,* now serve croissants with their *café con leche* and make fancier tapas for a more cosmopolitan crowd.

Tarifa's 10th-century **castle** is famous for its siege of 1292, when the defender Guzmán el Bueno refused to surrender even though the attacking Moors threatened to kill his captive son. In defiance, he flung his own dagger down to them, shouting, "Here, use this"—or something to that effect. (And they did indeed kill his son afterward.) The Spanish military turned the castle over to the town in the mid-1990s, and it now has a **museum** on Guzmán and the sacrifice of his son. 🖼 €1.50 ☉ *Tues.–Sun. 10–2 and 4–6.*

Ten kilometers (6 mi) north of Tarifa on the Atlantic coast are the Roman ruins of **Baelo Claudia.** This settlement was a thriving production center of *garum,* a salty fish paste appreciated in Rome. ☎ 956/688530 🖼 *Free* ☉ *July–mid-Sept., Tues.–Sat. 10–6, Sun. 10–2; mid-Sept.–June, Tues.–Sat. 10–5, Sun. 10–2.*

Where to Stay

$$$ 🏨 Hurricane Hotel. A laid-back, palm-kissed hotel next to the beach, this is a favorite hangout of the wind- and kite-surfing set. It's fun and informal, and the rooms are simple but adequate. The staff can organize horseback-riding trips along the beach or inland, as well as courses on surfing (wind and kite) ⊠ *Ctra. Cádiz–Málaga, Km 77.5, 11380* ☎ *956/684919* 🖨 *956/680329* ⊕ *www.hurricanehotel.com* 🛏 *28 rooms, 5 suites* ♿ *Restaurant, cable TV, pool, horseback riding, some pets allowed* 🍽 *AE, MC, V* 🍴 *BP.*

$$ 🏨 Convento de San Francisco. Rooms are comfortable and basic, but the main draw here is the setting: an aesthetically restored 17th-century convent in the spectacular village of Vejer, just west of Tarifa, overlooking the coast. Breakfast is served in the former refectory. ⊠ *La Plazuela, 11150* ☎ *956/451001* 🖨 *956/451004* ⊕ *www.tugasa.com* 🛏 *25 rooms* ♿ *Restaurant, cafeteria* 🍽 *MC, V.*

GIBRALTAR

The tiny British colony of Gibraltar—nicknamed Gib, or simply "the Rock"—whose impressive silhouette dominates the strait between Spain and Morocco, was one of the two Pillars of Hercules in ancient times, marking the western limits of the known world. Gibraltar today is a bizarre anomaly of Moorish, Spanish, and British influences in an ace position commanding the narrow pathway between the Mediterranean Sea and the Atlantic Ocean.

The Moors, headed by Tariq ibn Ziyad, seized the peninsula in 711 as a preliminary to the conquest of Spain. After the Moors had ruled for 750 years, the Spaniards recaptured Tariq's Rock in 1462. The English, heading an Anglo-Dutch fleet in the War of the Spanish Succession, gained control in 1704, and, after several years of local skirmishes, Gibraltar was finally ceded to Great Britain in 1713 by the Treaty of Utrecht. Spain has been trying to get it back ever since. In 1779 a combined French and Spanish force laid siege to the Rock for three years to no avail. During the Napoléonic Wars, Gibraltar served as Admiral Horatio Nelson's base for the decisive naval Battle of Trafalgar, and during the two World Wars, it served the Allies well as a naval and air base. In 1967 Franco closed the land border with Spain to strengthen his claims over the colony, and it remained closed until 1985.

Dominating the strait between Spain and Morocco, Gibraltar is an anomaly of cultures, but essentially, the Rock is like Britain with a suntan.

The Rock is like Britain with a suntan. There are double-decker buses, policemen in helmets, and bright red mailboxes. Millions of dollars have been spent in developing the Rock's tourist potential, while a steady flow of expatriate Britons come here from Spain to shop at Safeway and High Street shops. Gibraltar's economy is further boosted by its important status as an offshore financial center. Britain and Spain have been talking about joint Anglo-Spanish sovereignty, much to the ire of the majority of Gibraltarians, who remain fiercely patriotic to the crown.

Exploring the Rock

25–**37** *20 km (12 mi) east of Algeciras, 77 km (48 mi) southwest of Marbella.*

There must be few places in the world that you enter by walking or driving across an airport runway, but that's what happens in Gibraltar. First, show your passport; then make your way out onto the narrow strip of land linking Spain's La Linea with Britain's Rock. Unless you have a good reason to take your car—such as loading up on cheap gas or duty-free goodies—you're best off leaving it in a guarded parking area in La Linea, the Spanish border town—and don't bother hanging around here; it's a seedy place. In Gibraltar you can hop on buses and taxis that expertly maneuver the narrow, congested streets. The Official Rock Tour—conducted either by minibus or, at a greater cost, taxi—takes about 90 minutes and includes all the major sights, allowing you to choose which places to come back to and linger at later. When you call Gibraltar from Spain, the area code is 9567; when you call from another country, the code is 350. Prices in this section are given in British pounds; Gibraltar permits the use of U.K. currency and its own sterling government notes and coins. Euros can also be used in most of the shops, but the exchange rate may be high.

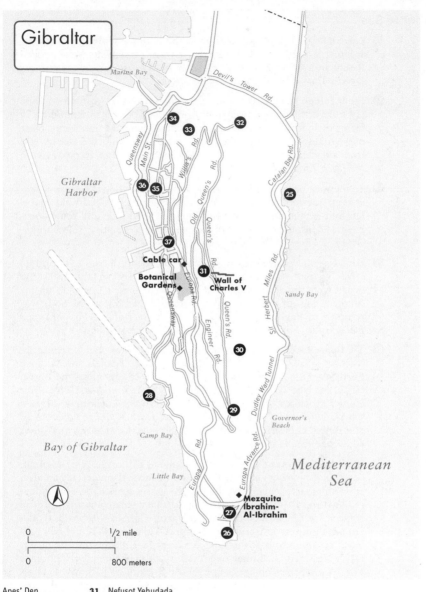

Gibraltar

Marina Bay

Devil's Tower Rd.

Queensway

Main St.

Willis's Rd.

Old Queen's Rd.

Queen's Rd.

Catalan Bay Rd.

Gibraltar Harbor

Gibraltar Harbor

Cable car

Botanical Gardens

Wall of Charles V

Sandy Bay

Europa Rd.

Queensway

Engineer Rd.

Queen's Rd.

Sir Herbert Miles Rd.

Dudley Ward Tunnel

Governor's Beach

Camp Bay

Europa Rd.

Europa Advance Rd.

Bay of Gibraltar

Little Bay

Mediterranean Sea

Mezquita Ibrahim-Al-Ibrahim

0   1/2 mile

0   800 meters

What to See

㉕ **Catalan Bay,** a fishing village founded by Genoese settlers, is now a resort on the eastern shores. The massive water catchments once supplied the colony's drinking water. ⊠ *From the Rock's eastern side, go left down Devil's Tower Rd. as you enter Gibraltar.*

㉖ From **Europa Point,** have a look across the straits to Morocco, 23 km (14 mi) away. You're now standing on one of the two ancient Pillars of Hercules. In front of you, the lighthouse has dominated the meeting place of the Atlantic and the Mediterranean since 1841; sailors can see its light from a distance of 27 km (17 mi). ⊠ *Continue along the coast road to the Rock's southern tip.*

㉗ To the west of the lighthouse is the **Shrine of Our Lady of Europe,** venerated by seafarers since 1462. Once a mosque, the small Catholic chapel has a little museum with a 1462 statue of the Virgin and some documents. ⊠ *Just west of Europa Point and lighthouse, along Rock's southern tip* ⋑ *Free* ⊙ *Weekdays 10–7.*

㉘ For a fine view, drive high above **Rosia Bay,** to which Nelson's flagship, HMS *Victory,* was towed after the Battle of Trafalgar in 1805. On board were the dead, who were buried in Trafalgar Cemetery on the southern edge of town—except for Admiral Nelson, whose body was returned to England preserved in a barrel of rum. ⊠ *From Europa Flats, follow Europa Rd. back along Rock's western slopes.*

㉙ The **Upper Rock Nature Preserve,** accessible from Jews' Gate, includes St. Michael's Cave, the Apes' Den, the Great Siege Tunnels, the Moorish Castle, and the Military Heritage Center, which chronicles the British regiments who have served on the Rock. ⊠ *From Rosia Bay, drive along Europa Rd. as far as Casino, above Alameda Gardens. Make a sharp right here up Engineer Rd. to Jews' Gate, a lookout over docks and Bay of Gibraltar to Algeciras* ⋑ *£8, includes all attractions, plus £1.50 per vehicle* ⊙ *Daily 9:30–6:30.*

㉚ **St. Michael's Cave** is the largest of Gibraltar's 150 caves. A series of underground chambers hung with stalactites and stalagmites, it's an ideal performing-arts venue. Sound-and-light shows are held here most days at 11 AM and 4 PM. The skull of a Neanderthal woman (now in the British Museum) was found at nearby Forbes Quarry eight years *before* the world-famous discovery in Germany's Neander Valley in 1856; nobody paid much attention to it at the time, which is why this prehistoric race is called Neanderthals rather than *Homo calpensis* (literally, "Gibraltar Man"—after the Romans' name for the Rock, *Calpe*). St. Michael's is on Queens Road. You can reach St. Michael's Cave—or ride all the way

★ to the top of Gibraltar—on a **cable car.** The car doesn't go high off the ground, but the views of Spain and Africa from the Rock's pinnacle are superb. It leaves from a station at the southern end of Main Street. ⋑ *Cable car £8 round-trip* ⊙ *Daily 9:30–5:45.*

The famous Barbary Apes are a breed of cinnamon-color, tailless monkeys native to Morocco's Atlas Mountains. Legend holds that as long as the apes remain in Gibraltar, the British will keep the Rock; Winston Churchill went so far as to issue an order for their preservation when the apes' numbers began to dwindle during World War II. They are pub-

③ licly fed twice daily, at 8 and 4, at **Apes' Den,** a rocky area down Old Queens Road and near the Wall of Charles V. Among the apes' mischievous talents are grabbing food, purses, and cameras.

㉜ The **Great Siege Tunnels,** formerly known as the Upper Galleries, were carved out during the Great Siege of 1779–82. You can plainly see the openings from whence the guns were pointed at the Spanish invaders. These tunnels form part of what is arguably the most impressive defense system anywhere in the world.

㉝ The **Moorish Castle** was built by the descendants of Tariq, who conquered the Rock in 711. The present Tower of Homage dates from 1333, and its besieged walls bear the scars of stones from medieval catapults (and, later, cannonballs). Admiral George Rooke hoisted the British flag from its summit when he captured the Rock in 1704, and it has flown here ever since. The castle is on Willis's Road.

㉞ **Casemates Square,** in the northern part of town, is Gibraltar's social hub, and pedestrianized. There are now plenty of places to sit out with a drink and watch the world go by. There's a small **branch tourist office** (☎ 9567/50762 ⊙ Weekdays 9 AM–5:30 PM, weekends 10 AM–4 PM) here.

> "The skull of a Neanderthal woman was found at Forbes Quarry eight years *before* the world-famous discovery in Germany's Neander Valley in 1856."

㉟ The colorful, congested **town of Gibraltar** is where the dignified Regency architecture of Great Britain blends well with the shutters, balconies, and patios of southern Spain. Shops, restaurants, and pubs beckon on busy Main Street; at the Governor's Residence, the ceremonial Changing of the Guard takes place six times a year and the Ceremony of the Keys takes place twice a year. Also make sure you see the Law Courts, where the famous case of the sailing ship *Mary Celeste* was heard in 1872; the Anglican Cathedral of the Holy Trinity; and the Catholic Cathedral of St. Mary the Crowned. The **main tourist office** (⊠ Duke of Kent House, Cathedral Sq. ☎ 9567/45000 ⊙ Weekdays 9 AM–5:30 PM) is on Cathedral Square.

10

㊱ The **Gibraltar Museum** houses a beautiful 14th-century Moorish bathhouse, an 1865 model of the Rock, and has displays that evoke the Great Siege and the Battle of Trafalgar. There's also a reproduction of the "Gibraltar Woman," the Neanderthal skull discovered here in 1848. ⊠ *Bomb House La.* ☎ *9567/74289* ⊙ *£2* ⊙ *Weekdays 10–6, Sat. 10–2.*

㊲ The 18th-century **Nefusot Yehudada Synagogue,** on Line Wall Road, is one of the oldest synagogues on the Iberian Peninsula, dating back to 1724. There are guided tours twice a day at 12:30 PM and 2:30 PM, accompanied by a short history of the Gibraltar Jewish community.

WHAT IT COSTS In £				
$$$$	$$$	$$	$	¢
RESTAURANTS over £25	£18–£25	£12–£18	£5–£12	under £5
HOTELS over £165	£120–£165	£80–£120	£30–£80	under £30

Restaurant prices are per person for a main course at dinner. Hotel prices are for two people in a standard double room in high season, excluding tax.

Where to Stay & Eat

$$–$$$ ✕ **Terrace Restaurant.** Upstairs from the casino, this is one of the best restaurants for sea views. Tarifa's colorful kite-surfers and Africa's Atlas mountains are visible on a clear day. The menu here is comfortably traditional and as good as the black bow-tie service. Dishes include beef Wellington, chicken Roquefort, and lobster thermidor. Afterward, choose from the diet-defying dessert trolley with classic English desserts, such as trifle, and fresh fruit tarts. ⊠ *7 Europa Rd.* ☎ *9567/76666* ⚓ *Reservations essential* ▭ *AE, DC, MC, V* ◎ *Closed Sun. No lunch.*

$ ✕ **Sacarello's.** Right off Main Street, this place is as well known for its excellent coffee and cakes as its adjacent restaurant. There's a daily lavish salad buffet, as well as filled baked potatoes, panfried noodles with broccoli, mussels, and chicken, and rack of lamb with wine and fine herbs. Top your meal off with a specialty coffee with cream and vanilla. There are several rooms warmly decorated in English-pub style featuring cozy corners, dark-wood furnishings, and low ceilings. ⊠ *57 Irish Town* ☎ *9567/70625* ▭ *MC, V* ◎ *No dinner Sun.*

$$$$ ▥ **The Eliott.** If you want to stay at the most slick and modern of the Rock's hotels, try this place right in the center of the town, in what used to be the Gibraltar Holiday Inn. Rooms have been revamped, so you can expect all the extras. Ask for a room at the top of the hotel, with a view over the Bay of Gibraltar. ⊠ *2 Governor's Parade* ☎ *9567/70500* 🖨 *9567/70243* ⇥ *106 rooms, 8 suites* ⚏ *2 restaurants, cable TV with movies, in-room data ports, Wi-Fi, pool, sauna, 2 bars, meeting room; no smoking* ▭ *AE, DC, MC, V* ◎| *BP.*

$$$$ ▥ **The Rock.** Overlooking Gibraltar, this hotel first opened in 1932. Furnishings in the rooms and restaurants are modern and colorful, yet they manage to preserve something of the English colonial style—bamboo, ceiling fans, and a fine terrace bar with a wisteria-covered terrace. There's a 20% discount if you book online. ⊠ *3 Europa Rd.* ☎ *9567/73000* 🖨 *9567/73513* ⊕ *www.rockhotelgibraltar.com* ⇥ *101 rooms, 2 suites* ⚏ *Restaurant, cable TV, in-room data ports, Wi-Fi, pool, hair salon, bar, meeting room* ▭ *AE, DC, MC, V* ◎| *BP.*

$ ▥ **Bristol.** This colonial-style hotel in the heart of town has splendid views of the bay and the cathedral. Rooms are spacious and comfortable, and the downstairs lounge exudes a faded elegance with sink-into sofas and chandeliers. The tropical garden is a haven. ⊠ *10 Cathedral Sq.* ☎ *9567/76800* 🖨 *9567/77613* ⊕ *www.bristolhotel.gi* ⇥ *60 rooms* ⚏ *Cable TV, pool, bar, free parking* ▭ *AE, DC, MC, V.*

Nightlife

At the **Ladbrokes Casino** (✉ 7 Europa Rd. ☎ 9567/76666) the gaming room is open 9 PM–4 AM, the cocktail bar 7:30 PM–4 AM. Dress is smart casual.

Sports & Outdoors

Bird- and dolphin-watching, diving, and fishing are popular activities on the Rock. For details on tours and outfitters, visit the Gibraltar government Web site's "On Holiday" page (⊕ www.gibraltar.gov.uk/hol) or call the local tourist office (☎ 9567/74950).

THE COSTA DEL SOL ESSENTIALS

To research prices, get advice from other travelers, and book travel arrangements, visit www.fodors.com.

Transportation

BY AIR

ARRIVING & DEPARTING
Air Plus Comet operates a direct flight from New York to Málaga every Thursday. All other flights from the United States connect in Madrid. Iberia and British Airways fly once daily from London, and numerous British budget airlines, such as easyJet and Monarch, link London with Málaga. This can be an inexpensive route if you are flying from the West Coast of the United States with inexpensive flights from major cities such as Los Angeles, provided by airlines such as Virgin Airways. Aside from London, most major European cities have direct flights to Málaga on Iberia or their own national airlines. Iberia has up to eight flights daily from Madrid (flying time is 1 hour), three flights a day from Barcelona (1½ hours), and regular flights from other Spanish cities. The only flights into and out of Gibraltar airport are from the United Kingdom.

GETTING AROUND
By far the region's busiest point of entry, Málaga's Pablo Picasso airport is 10 km (6 mi) west of town. Trains connect the airport with Málaga every half hour (airport to Málaga 7 AM–10:40 PM, journey time 12 minutes, €1.20 single) and southwest to Fuengirola every half hour (airport to Fuengirola 6:45 AM–10:40 PM, journey time 25 minutes, €1.65 single), stopping at several resorts en route, including Torremolinos and Benalmádena. There's a bus service to Málaga every half hour from 6:30 AM to 11:30 PM at a fare of €1. Ten daily buses (more July–September) run between the airport and Marbella, with a journey time of one hour and fare of €4 single. Taxis are plentiful, and official fares to Málaga, Torremolinos, and other resorts are posted inside the terminal. The trip from the airport to Marbella costs about €45, to Torremolinos €10, to Fuengirola €24. Many of the better hotels and all tour companies will arrange for pickup at the airport.

If you're coming from Britain and heading for the coast west of Marbella, fly into Gibraltar instead: The runway at Gibraltar airport cuts across the main road to the town center, so that the road has to be closed whenever any plane arrive or departs. Once you've crossed into Spain you can get buses in La Linea for all coastal resorts.

10

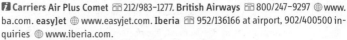

Carriers Air Plus Comet ☏ 212/983–1277. **British Airways** ☏ 800/247–9297 ⊕ www. ba.com. **easyJet** ⊕ www.easyjet.com. **Iberia** ☏ 952/136166 at airport, 902/400500 inquiries ⊕ www.iberia.com.
Airports Aeropuerto de Málaga (AGP) ☏ 952/048804 ⊕ www.ccoo-agp.com. **Gibraltar Airport (GIB)** ☏ 9567/73026.

BY BIKE

The Costa del Sol is famous for its sun and sand, but many people supplement their beach time with mountain-bike forays into the hilly interior, particularly around Ojén, near Marbella, and also along the mountain roads around Ronda. A popular route, which affords sweeping vistas, is via the mountain road from Ojén west to Istán. The Costa del Sol's temperate climate is ideal for biking, though it's best not to exert yourself on the trails in July and August, when temperatures soar. There are numerous bike-rental shops around the Costa del Sol, particularly in Marbella, Ronda, and Ojén; many shops can also arrange bike excursions. The cost to rent a mountain bike for the day ranges between €15 and €20. Guided bike excursions, which include the bikes and support staff and cars, generally start at about €62 a day.

Bike Rentals Monte Aventura ✉ Pl. de Andalucía 1, Ojén ☏ 952/881519. **Sierra Cycling** ✉ Urbanization Pueblo Castillo No. 7, Fuengirola ☏ 952/471720 ⊕ www.sierracycling. com. **Spanish Cycling Federation** ✉ Ferraz 16, 28008 Madrid ☏ 91/542–0421.

BY BOAT & FERRY

ARRIVING & DEPARTING   There are no direct ferries to Andalusia; the only possible option is to go to the northern Spanish coast from the United Kingdom via the Portsmouth-to-Bilboa route or the Plymouth-to-Santander route and then catch a train south.

GETTING AROUND   If you opt for the ferry from the United Kingdom to northern Spain, you can take the train from Bilboa to Málaga (journey time 14 hours, one daily).

P & O Ferries ☏ 944/234477 ⊕ www.poferries.com. **Brittany Ferries** ☏ 942/360611. **RENFE Trains** ☏ 902/240202 ⊕ www.renfe.es.

BY CAR

Málaga is 580 km (360 mi) from Madrid, taking the N–IV to Córdoba, then N331 to Antequera and the N321; 182 km (114 mi) from Córdoba via Antequera; 214 km (134 mi) from Seville; and 129 km (81 mi) from Granada by the shortest route of N342 to Loja, then N321 to Málaga. A car allows you to explore some of Andalusia's famous mountain villages. Mountain driving can be an adventure—hair-raising curves, precipices, and mediocre road services are common—but it's getting more manageable as highways are resurfaced, widened, and in some cases completely rebuilt. Gas stations are also plentiful, with a fair percentage open 24 hours.

There are some beautiful scenic drives here about which the respective tourist offices can advise you. The A369 heading southwest from Ronda to Guacín passes through stunning whitewashed villages (*pueblo blancos*). Another camera-clicking route is the N334 from Churriana to Coín, via

Alhaurín de la Torre and Alhaurín el Grande. From here, continue on to Coín, then take the 337 toward Marbella, which travels via the villages of Monda and Ojen, finally ending at the coast just north of Marbella.

On major roads and motorways the speed limit is 120 km/h (75 mph); in urban areas it is 50 km/h (31 mph), and on other roads it is either 90 km/h (55 mph) or 100 km/h (62½ mph).

Parking in the smaller villages can be fraught with danger (such as getting your vehicle sideswiped on winding, narrow streets), so it is advisable to park on the edge of the center and walk. In larger towns head for the nearest parking garage. The major resorts have improved their parking, and you should have no problem. You can expect to pay around €1.20 an hour. Blue lines on the street mean you must pay at the nearest meter to park during working hours, around €0.50 an hour. Yellow lines mean no parking. If your car is towed, you will be fined approximately €65 to claim it.

To take a car into Gibraltar you need, in theory, an insurance certificate and a logbook (a certificate of vehicle ownership). In practice, all you need is your passport. Prepare for parking problems on the Rock, as space is scarce.

Severe fines are enforced throughout Spain for driving under the influence of alcohol. Spot breath checks are often carried out, and you will be cited if the level of alcohol in your bloodstream is found to be 0.05 percent or above.

Local car-rental agencies can be less expensive than the large chains. **🚗 Car-Rental Agencies Autopro** ✉ Carril de Montañez 49, Málaga ☎ 952/176030 🌐 www.autopro.es. **Crown Car Hire** ☎ 952/176486 🌐 www.crowncarhire.com. **Niza Cars** ☎ 952/236179 🌐 www.nizacars.com.

BY TAXI

Taxis are plentiful throughout the Costa del Sol and may be hailed on the street or from specified taxi ranks marked TAXI. Restaurants are usually obliging and will call you a taxi, if requested. Fares are reasonable and meters are strictly used. There are extra charges for luggage. You are not required to tip taxi drivers, although rounding off the amount will be appreciated. **🚗 Taxi Companies Radio Taxi Torremolinos** ☎ 952/380600. **Radio Taxi Fuengirola** ☎ 952/471000. **Morales Rodriguez–Málaga** ☎ 952/430077.

BY BUS

Buses are the best way to reach the Costa del Sol from Seville or Granada, and the best way to get around once you're here. The buses are modern, inexpensive, and comfortable. Larger towns usually have a bus station where all out-of-town buses stop. During holidays it is wise to reserve your seat in advance for long-distance bus travel. On the Costa del Sol, the bus service connects Málaga with Cádiz (4 daily), with Córdoba (5 daily), with Granada (18 daily), and with Seville (12 daily). Also in Fuengirola you can catch buses for Mijas, Marbella, Estepona, and Algeciras. The Portillo bus company serves most of the Costa del Sol; Alsina

Gräells serves Granada, Córdoba, Seville, and Nerja. Los Amarillos serves Cádiz, Jerez, Ronda, and Seville. Málaga's tourist office has details on other bus lines.

🚌 **Bus Depots Algeciras** ✉ Av. Virgen del Carmen 15 ☎ 956/51055. **Estepona** ✉ Av. de España ☎ 952/800249. **Fuengirola** ✉ Av. Alfonso XIII ☎ 952/475066. **Málaga** ✉ Paseo de los Tilos ☎ 952/350061. **Marbella** ✉ Av. Trapiche ☎ 952/764400. **Torremolinos** ✉ Calle Hoyo ☎ 952/382419.

🚌 **Bus Lines Alsina Gräells** ☎ 952/318295. **Los Amarillos** ✉ Málaga bus station ☎ 902/210317. **Portillo** ✉ Málaga bus station ☎ 952/360191.

BY TRAIN

Málaga is the main rail terminus on the Costa del Sol, with eight trains a day from Madrid and one from Barcelona and Valencia. Most Madrid–Málaga trains leave Madrid from Atocha station, though some leave from Chamartín. Travel time varies between 4½ and 10 hours; the best and fastest train is the daytime *Talgo 200* from Atocha. All Madrid–Málaga trains stop at Córdoba. A new AVE high-speed service is under construction that will connect Málaga to Madrid in around 2½ hours. The current date for completion is late 2007. From both Seville (4 hours, five daily) and Granada (3–3½ hours, three daily) to Málaga, you have to change at Bobadilla, making buses a more efficient mode of travel from those cities. In fact, aside from the direct Madrid–Córdoba–Málaga line, trains in Andalusia can be slow because of the hilly terrain. Málaga's train station is a 15-minute walk from the city center, across the river. Check the RENFE Web site for schedules and fares. You can book tickets online for most services.

A useful suburban train service connects Málaga, Torremolinos, and Fuengirola, stopping at the airport and all resorts along the way. The train leaves Málaga every half hour between 6 AM and 10:30 PM and Fuengirola every half hour from 6:35 AM to 11:35 PM. For the city center get off at the last stop—Centro-Alameda—not the previous stop, which will land you at Málaga's RENFE station. A daily train connects Málaga and Ronda via the dramatic Chorro gorge, with a change at Bobadilla. Travel time is about three hours. Three trains a day make the direct two-hour trip between Ronda and Algeciras on a spectacular mountain track. All routes are operated by RENFE.

EURAIL PASS   North Americans can purchase a Eurail Spain Pass, available in both first- and second-class sections, which allows three days' unlimited travel within a two-month period for around $200 ($225 for first-class and $175 for second-class).

🚆 **Eurail Pass** ⊕ www.raileurope.com/us. **Málaga train station** ✉ Explanada de la Estación ☎ 952/360202. **RENFE** ☎ 902/240202 ⊕ www.renfe.es.

Contacts & Resources

EMERGENCIES

In an emergency, call one of the Spain-wide emergency numbers for police, ambulance, or fire services. The local Red Cross (Cruz Roja) can also dispatch an ambulance in case of an emergency. Also, there are numerous private ambulance services, which are listed under *ambulancias* (ambulances) in the *Paginas Amarillas* (Yellow Pages). The Hospital Carlos Haya in Málaga has a 24-hour emergency department. For nonemergencies, there are private medical clinics throughout the Costa del Sol, which often have staff members who can speak some English. Every town has at least one pharmacy open 24 hours; the address of the on-duty pharmacy is posted on the front door of all pharmacies. You can also dial Spain's general information number for the location of a doctor's office or pharmacy that's open nearest you.

7 Emergency Services Directory Enquiries ☎ 11818. **Emergencies** ☎ 112. **Fire department** ☎ 080. **Hospital Carlos Haya** ☎ 952/390400. **Local police** ☎ 092. **Medical service** ☎ 061. **National police** ☎ 091. **Red Cross** ☎ 952/443545.

INTERNET, MAIL & SHIPPING

There are plenty of places to get connected to the Internet in Málaga and throughout the Costa del Sol resorts. These are typically in the main shopping and commercial centers; the respective tourist office can provide you with a list. Many of the better hotels now provide Wi-Fi and broadband connection for guests. For shipping, most of the international couriers have representatives on the Costa del Sol, including MRW and Mail Boxes Etc.

7 Internet Cafés Cristanet ✉ Cristamar Commercial Centre, Puerto Bánus, Marbella 29600 ☎ 952/799591. **Microfun** ✉ Av. de Los Boliches, Fuengirola 29640 ☎ 952/661424. **Navegaweb** ✉ Calle Molina Lario 11, Málaga 29005 ☎ 952/352300. **7 Couriers Mail Boxes Etc.** ✉ C. Medellin 1, Málaga 29006 ☎ 952/311482. **MRW** ✉ C. Paris 45, Málaga 29006 ☎ 952/171760.

LODGING

APARTMENTS & VILLAS
The Costa del Sol caters to those in search of some uninterrupted R&R and, accordingly, there's no shortage of apartments and villas for both short- and long-term stays. The coast and rural interior are peppered with accommodations from traditional Andalusian farmhouses to self-catering rustic cottages to luxury villas. An excellent source for apartment and villa rentals is ⊕ www.andalucia.com.

7 Local Agents Gilmar ✉ Av. Ricardo Soriano 56, Marbella 29600 ☎ 952/861341 ⊕ www.gilmarinmobiliaria.com. **Viajes Rural Andalus** ✉ Calle Montes de Oca 18, Málaga 29007 ☎ 952/276229.

MEDIA

Many newspaper stands sell international periodicals and paperbacks in English. The glossy, monthly magazines *Essential* and *Absolute Marbella* have chatty articles on entertainment, culture, travel, and restaurants around the Costa del Sol. The weekly newspaper *Costa del Sol News* reports local and international news and has TV and entertainment listings. On Friday an English version of the Spanish daily *Sur* is published with local news and a large classifieds section.

There are a number of English-language radio stations on the dial in the Costa del Sol, all of which offer a mix of tunes and talk. Many also broadcast the BBC news throughout the day, usually in the evening and

10

on weekends. REM (104.8 FM) and Onda Cero (101.6 FM) are the two main English-language stations. They both air international news on an hourly basis and include interviews and chat on topics of interest to English-speaking foreign residents on the Costa del Sol.

TOUR OPTIONS

Many one- and two-day excursions from Costa del Sol resorts are run by the national company Pullmantur and by smaller firms. All local travel agents and most hotels can book you a tour; excursions leave from Málaga, Torremolinos, Fuengirola, Marbella, and Estepona, with prices varying by departure point. Most tours last half a day, and in most cases you can be picked up at your hotel. Popular tours include Málaga, Gibraltar, the Cuevas de Nerja, Mijas, Marbella, and Puerto Banús; a burro safari in Coín; and a countryside tour of Alhaurín de la Torre, Alhaurín el Grande, Coín, Ojén, and Ronda. Night tours include a barbecue evening, a bullfighting evening with dinner, and a night at the Casino Torrequebrada. The varied landscape here is also wonderful for hiking and walking, and several companies offer walking tours. All provide comprehensive information on their Web sites.

If you plan to visit Málaga independently, but are on a tight schedule, the colorful, open-topped Málaga Tour City Sightseeing Bus is a good way to view the city's attractions within a day. The bus stops at all the major sights in town, including the Gibralfaro and the cathedral.

🔁 Tour Operators **Málaga Tour City Sightseeing Bus** ✉ Málaga ☎ 952/363133 ⊕ www.citysightseeing-spain.com. **Pullmantur** ✉ Av. Imperial, Torremolinos ☎ 952/384400. **Walking Holidays** ⊕ www.walksinspain.com or www.realadventures.com.

VISITOR INFORMATION

The official Web site of the Andalucian government is www.andalucia.org; it has further information on sightseeing and events as well as contact details for the following regional and local tourist offices. Tourist offices are generally open 10 to 2 and 5 to 8 Monday through Saturday.

🔁 Regional Tourist Office **Málaga** ✉ Pasaje de Chinitas 4 ☎ 952/213445.

🔁 Local Tourist Offices **Almuñecar** ✉ Palacete de La Najarra, Av. Europa ☎ 958/631125. **Antequera** ✉ Palacio de Najera, Coso Viejo ☎ 952/702505. **Benalmádena Costa** ✉ Av. Antonio Machado 14 ☎ 952/442494. **Estepona** ✉ Av. San Lorenzo 1 ☎ 952/802002. **Fuengirola** ✉ Av. Jesús Santos Rein 6 ☎ 952/467625. **Gibraltar** ✉ 6 Kent House, Cathedral Sq. ☎ 9567/74950. **Málaga** ✉ Av. Cervantes 1, Paseo del Parque ☎ 952/604410. **Marbella** ✉ Glorieta de la Fontanilla ☎ 952/822818. **Nerja** ✉ Puerta del Mar 2 ☎ 952/521531. **Ronda** ✉ Pl. de España 1 ☎ 952/871272. **Torremolinos** ✉ Pl. Blas Infante 1 ☎ 952/379512.

Granada, Córdoba & Eastern Andalusia

WORD OF MOUTH

"We visited the Alhambra in late September 2004. Hot! The good news is that the Moors knew this, and there are fountains and water features everywhere to cool the air. You'll have no problem finding places to sit down and rest."

—Craigellachie

"We spent some time hiking outside of Ronda, which is very scenic, as are the white villages in that area."

—Zootsi

Updated by
Norman
Renouf

ANDALUSIA RINGS with echoes of the Moors from the dark mountains of the Sierra Morena down to the mighty, snowcapped peaks of the Sierra Nevada. These North African Muslims dwelled in southern Spain for almost 800 years, from their first conquest of Spanish soil (Gibraltar) by the Visigoths in AD 711 to their final expulsion from Granada in 1492. The name Andalusia (Andalucía) comes from the Moors' own name for their new acquisition: Al-Andalus. Two of Spain's most famous monuments, Córdoba's mosque and Granada's Alhambra palace, were the inspired creations of Moorish architects and craftsmen. Typical Andalusian architecture—brilliant-white villages with narrow, shady streets; thick-walled houses clustered around cool, private patios; whitewashed facades with modest grilled windows—comes from centuries of Moorish occupation. The Guadalquivir, the Moors' "Great River," runs through the entire region; town names such as Úbeda and Jaén are derivations of old Arabic names; ruined *alcázares* (fortresses) dot the landscape; and *azahar* (orange blossom) perfumes the patios.

The Moors left their mark here, but so did the Christian conquerors and their descendants: Andalusia today has Gothic chapels, Renaissance cathedrals, and baroque monasteries and churches. The sturdy sandstone mansions of Úbeda and Baeza contrast intriguingly with the humble, basic villages elsewhere in the province.

The landscape, too, is varied and powerful. Granada's plain (known as *la vega*), covered with lush orchards and tobacco and poplar groves, stretches up to the mountains of the majestic Sierra Nevada. Covered in snow half the year, this range has the highest peaks on mainland Spain, Mulhacén (11,407 feet) and Veleta (11,125 feet). Farther north the Guadalquivir flows west toward Córdoba from the heights of the Sierra de Cazorla, bounded by the rugged, shrub-covered Sierra Morena to the north and by the olive groves of Jaén to the south. Fruit and almond trees line the river's banks in Córdoba's orchards. Vineyards cover the Córdoban *campiña* (fertile plain south of the Guadalquivir), and villages cling to hillsides beneath ruined castles.

Exploring Eastern Andalusia

Eastern Andalusia includes fabled Granada, in a province that spans the Sierra Nevada mountains and the beautifully rugged Alpujarras. This is where you can find some of the prettiest, most ancient villages; it has become one of the foremost destinations for Andalusia's increasingly popular rural tourism. To the west is the magnificent city of Córdoba, surrounded by countryside in the fertile valley of the Guadalquivir River. The coastline of Eastern Andalusia is similarly stunning, with towering cliffs, coves, and unspoiled seaside resorts.

Numbers in the text correspond to numbers in the margin and on the Andalusia, Granada to Córdoba, Granada, and Córdoba maps.

About the Restaurants

Lunch is the main meal in this part of the country. Córdoba has numerous high-quality restaurants; in Granada the selection is more limited. Restaurants start serving around 2, but they don't fill up until at least

GREAT ITINERARIES

IF YOU HAVE 3 DAYS
Begin in 🏙 **Granada ❶-⓱**. On Day 1, visit the Alhambra, and wander the Albaicín, Granada's ancient Moorish quarter. Have lunch along the Calderería. Spend the afternoon in the alleyways of the Alcaicería, visiting the cathedral and the Capilla Real; then take an evening tour of the Alhambra (only the Palacios Nazaríes). The morning of the second day, leave Granada for Alcalá la Real to discover the Fortaleza de la Mota and then head north to the historic twin towns of Úbeda and Baeza before heading to 🏙 **Córdoba ㉙-㊼** for the night. Spend the morning of the third day touring Córdoba's Mezquita and wandering the Judería. Walk out to the Guadalquivir River and cross the Puente Romano to the Torre de la Calahorra.

IF YOU HAVE 5 DAYS
Explore 🏙 **Córdoba ㉙-㊼** on Day 1, lingering in the Mezquita and Judería. Stay the night; then head the next morning toward Granada, stopping at Alcalá la Real to discover the Fortaleza de la Mota. Explore the Alhambra in the afternoon and spend the night in 🏙 **Granada ❶-⓱**. The next morning, discover the Capilla Real and Cathedral in Granada, before taking the short drive to the **Alpujarras ㉒** and the high mountain village of Trévelez—famous for its dry-cured hams—and spend the night in one of the rustic places in this fascinating region. On Day 4 take a change of scenery by heading south to Motril, with its subtropical climate, and then head along the Costa Tropical to **Almería** (*see* Chapter 8) and its magnificent castle. On the last day, head inland to the desert of Tabernas and the mini-Hollywood studios before spending the last night in a cave at **Guadix ㉓**.

3, and most people are still at the table at 5. After such a long, late lunch, few Andalusians dine out in the evening; instead, they make the rounds of the bars, dipping into tapas and plates of ham or cheese. You shouldn't have trouble getting a table if you show up early—around 2 for lunch, 9 or 10 for dinner.

Habas con jamón de Trevélez (broad beans with ham from the Alpujarran village of Trevélez) is Granada's most famous regional dish, with *tortilla al Sacromonte* (an omelet made of calf's brains, sweetbreads, diced ham, potatoes, and peas) just behind. *Sopa sevillana* (tasty fish and seafood soup made with mayonnaise), surprisingly named for Granada's most direct rival city, is another staple, and *choto albaicinero* (braised kid with garlic, also known as *choto al ajillo*) is also a specialty. Moorish dishes such as *bstella* (from the Moorish *bastilla*, a salty-sweet puff pastry with pigeon or other meat, pine nuts, and almonds) and spicy *crema de almendras* (almond cream soup) are not uncommon on Granada menus. Local taverns serve the earthy *vino de la costa*, from the Alpujarras region. And thanks to its Moorish heritage, Granada serves some of the best mint tea in Spain. Córdoba's specialties are *salmorejo* (a thick version of gazpacho topped with hard-boiled egg) and *rabo de toro* (bull's-tail or oxtail stew), and many Córdoban restaurants are inventing new dishes based on old Arab recipes. Here, *fino de Montilla*, a dry, sherry-like wine from the Montilla-Moriles district, makes a good aperitif.

WHAT IT COSTS In Euros					
	$$$$	**$$$**	**$$**	**$**	**¢**
AT DINNER	over €20	€15–€20	€10–€15	€6–€10	under €6

Prices are per person for a main course at dinner.

About the Hotels

Andalusia has lodging for all budgets, from simple inns to historic paradors and luxury, private hotels. At the high end, the Parador de Granada, beside Granada's Alhambra, is a magnificent way to enjoy Granada and the storied past of southern Spain. Bed-and-breakfast and rural lodgings, close to, or in, many villages, give you better access to the countryside and its rich folk traditions. In Córdoba, several pleasant hotels occupy houses in the old quarter, close to the mosque. It's easy to find a room in Córdoba, even if you haven't reserved one—just watch out for Holy Week and the May Patio Festival. Granada can be very difficult, as the Alhambra is the second-most popular tourist attraction in Spain (after the Prado in Madrid). The city has plenty of hotels, but peak season runs long—from Easter to late October. Hotels on the Alhambra hill, especially the Parador, must be reserved long in advance, and those in the city center, around the Puerta Real and Acera del Darro, are unbelievably noisy—ask for rooms toward the back. Beware of Holy Week and the International Festival of Music and Dance (mid-June–mid-July). Also, if you're driving, inquire with hotels in both cities about parking, especially in Córdoba.

WHAT IT COSTS In Euros					
	$$$$	**$$$**	**$$**	**$**	**¢**
FOR 2 PEOPLE	over €180	€100–€180	€60–€100	€40–€60	under €40

Prices are for per two people in a standard double room in high season, excluding tax.

Timing

Spring and autumn are the best seasons to visit. Summer can be stifling, especially in Córdoba; in winter, temperatures can drop to the 30s, and the wind off the Guadalquivir in Córdoba can be as stiff as any in New England. Granada can be extremely hot in summer, but with its proximity to the towering Sierra Nevada peaks, expect cold and even snow in winter. Note that most

---

NORMAN'S TOP 5

- Alhambra & Generalife, Granada
- Mezquita, Córdoba
- Capilla Real, Granada
- Alcalá la Real, Jaén
- Sierra de Cazorla

IF YOU LIKE

SOUTHERN COOKING

Southern Andalusia is an arid region, with a terrain best suited to grapevines and olive trees; its people love life with a cheerful disposition and simplicity of attitude—and the cuisine follows suit. Although neither Granada nor Córdoba is a coastal city, fish reigns supreme at many of the finer restaurants. Wonderfully colorful produce markets inspire chefs with their purple figs, glossy red peppers, curly green chard, or brilliant orange pumpkin.

In Granada and Córdoba, the cuisine's Moorish influence is reflected in the use of almonds, bitter oranges, dates and figs, and the combinations of savory and sweet. Sugar mills were one of the chief sources of Granada's wealth until well into the 19th century, and as a result pastries made of syrups, almonds, and flour became specialties, particularly in convents. In Córdoba province, hams from the Pedroches valley and the Alpujarran village of Trevélez are famous throughout Spain.

HIKING & WALKING

Thanks to outdoor clubs and an interest in preserving the wilderness, Andalusia has many parks for recreation and camping. The village of Cazorla, in the province of Jaén, leads to the pine-clad slopes of the Cazorla Nature Park. South of Granada, the Sierra Nevada and the Alpujarras have some of the most impressive vistas in all of Spain, plus terrific skiing in winter and many outdoor sports in summer.

FIESTAS

Granada observes **La Toma** (the Capture), the 1492 surrender to the Catholic Monarchs, on January 2. On January 5, the eve of the **Día de los Reyes Magos** (Feast of the Three Magic Kings), every city and village holds processions of the three Wise Men. On February 1, Granada organizes a *romería* (pilgrimage) to the Monastery of San Cecilio, on Sacromonte. Both Granada and Córdoba party hard during **Carnival,** on the days leading up to Ash Wednesday; and both celebrate **Semana Santa** (Holy Week) with dramatic religious processions. The shrine of the **Virgen de la Cabeza,** near Andújar in the province of Jaén, is the scene of one of Spain's biggest romerías on the last weekend in April. May brings to Córdoba **Las Cruces de Mayo** (May Days of the Cross), the **Fiesta de los Patios** (Patio Festival), and the **Feria de Nuestra Señora de la Salud** (Feast of Our Lady of Health). In Granada **Día de la Cruz** (Day of the Cross) is observed the first Sunday in May, **San Isidro** on May 15, and **Mariana Pineda** (a 19th-century political heroine) on May 26. In mid-June, Granada celebrates **Corpus Christi** and **San Pedro** (June 29); the **Festival Internacional de Música y Danza** (International Festival of Music and Dance), with some events in the Alhambra, begins in late June and runs into July. The **International Guitar Festival** brings major artists to Córdoba in early July.

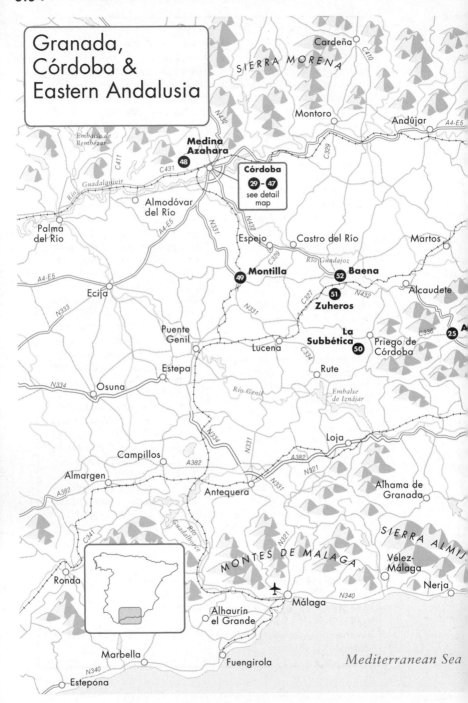

Granada, Córdoba & Eastern Andalusia

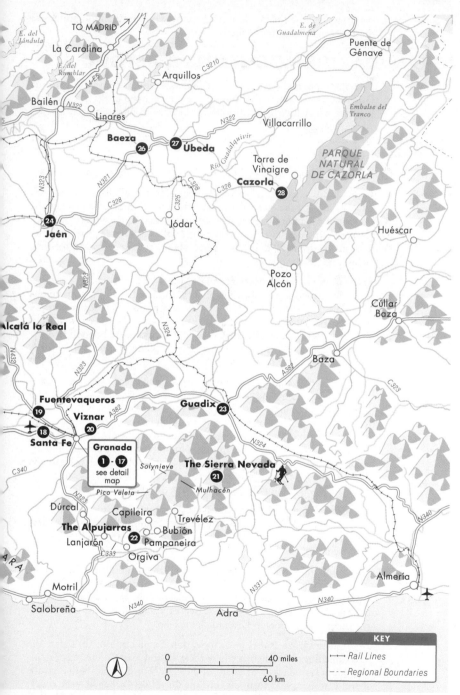

TO MADRID

E. del
Lindula

La Carolina

E. del
Rumblar

Arquillos   C3210

Bailén   N322

Linares

A4-E5

Baeza ㉖   ㉗ **Úbeda**

Villacarrillo

N322

Río Guadalquivir

Torre de
Vinaigre

E. de
Guadalmeña

Puente de
Génave

*Embalse del
Tranco*

*PARQUE
NATURAL
DE CAZORLA*

N321

C328

N323

C328   C328   **Cazorla**
                        ㉘

Jaén
㉔

C325

Jódar

Huéscar

N323

Pozo
Alcón

Cúllar
Baza

lcalá la Real

N4324

N323

Baza

A-382

C-323

Fuentevaqueros
⑲   A-382   **Guadix** ㉓

⑱   Viznar
Santa Fe   ⑳

N324

C340

Granada
❶ · ⑰
see detail
map

Solynieve

Pico Veleta

The Sierra Nevada
㉑

Mulhacén

N340

Dúrcal

N323

Capileira   Trevélez

The Alpujarras   ㉒   ○ Bubión
Lanjarón   Pampaneira
         C333   Orgiva

N331

Almería

Motril

N340

Salobreña   Adra   N340

0   40 miles
0   60 km

KEY
⊢—⊣ *Rail Lines*
- - - *Regional Boundaries*

monuments close for lunch, anywhere between 1:30 and 4, and most museums are closed on Monday.

GRANADA, THE MOUNTAINS & BEYOND

The Alhambra and the tomb of the Catholic Monarchs are the pride of Granada. Overlooking the city are the snowcapped peaks of the Sierra Nevada, which hide the traditional whitewashed villages and crafts-rich Alpujarra region.

Granada

❶–⓱ *430 km (265 mi) south of Madrid, 261 km (162 mi) east of Seville.*

Granada rises majestically from a plain onto three hills, dwarfed—on a clear day—by the Sierra Nevada. Atop one of these hills perches the pink-gold Alhambra palace. The stunning view from its mount takes in the sprawling medieval Moorish quarter, the caves of the Sacromonte, and, in the distance, the fertile *vega* (plain), rich in orchards, tobacco fields, and poplar groves.

Split by internal squabbles, Granada's Moorish Nasrid dynasty gave Ferdinand of Aragón an opportunity in 1491; spurred by Isabella's religious fanaticism, he laid siege to the city for seven months, and on January 2, 1492, Boabdil, the "Rey Chico" (Boy King), was forced to surrender the keys of the city to the Catholic Monarchs. As Boabdil fled the Alhambra by the Puerta de los Siete Suelos (Gate of the Seven Floors), he asked that the gate be sealed forever.

Granada can be characterized by its major neighborhoods. East of the Darro River and up the hill is La Alhambra. South of it and around a square and a popular hangout area, Campo del Príncipe, is Realejo. To the west of the Darro and going from north to south are the two popular neighborhoods, Sacromonte and Albaicín. The latter is the young and trendy part of Granada, full of color, flavor, and charming old architecture and narrow streets going uphill. On either side of Gran Vía de Colón and the streets that border the cathedral (Reyes Católicos and Recogidas—the major shopping areas) is the city center.

These days much of the Alhambra and Albaicín areas are closed to cars, because of the difficult access, but starting from the Plaza Nueva there are now minibuses—numbers 30, 31, 32, and 34—that run frequently to these areas.

A GOOD WALK

Save a full day for the **Alhambra ❶** ▶ and the neighboring sites on the Alhambra hill: the Alcazaba, Generalife, Alhambra Museum, Fundación Rodríguez Acosta, **Casa-Museo de Manuel de Falla ❷**, and **Carmen de los Mártires ❸**. The following walk deserves a day of its own and covers the other major spots in Granada's nucleus.

Begin at the Plaza Isabel la Católica (at the junction of the Gran Vía and Calle Reyes Católicos), where there's a statue of Columbus presenting Queen Isabella with his maps of the New World. Walk south on Calle Reyes Católicos and turn left into the **Corral del Carbón ❹**—the oldest

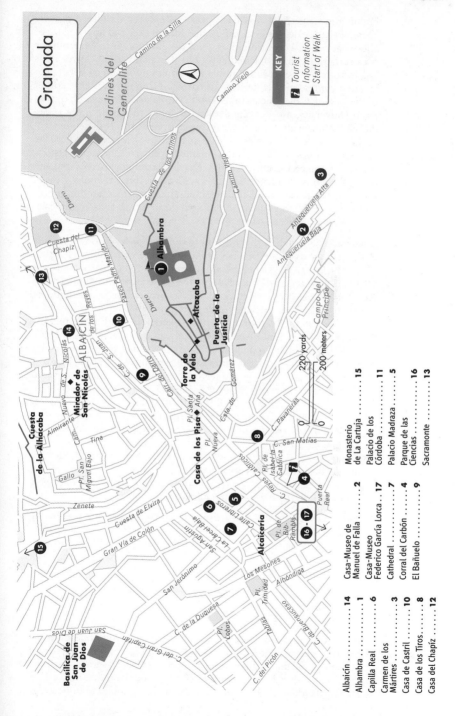

Granada

KEY

🛈 Tourist
ℹ Information
▲ Start of Walk

Jardines del Generalife

Camino de la Silla
Camino Viejo
Camino Viejo

Cuesta de los Chinos

Antequeruela Alta
Antequeruela Baja

Campo del Príncipe

Alhambra
▲ 1

Atcazaba
Puerta de la Justicia
Torre de la Vela
Pl. Santa Ana
Casa de los Pisa

Cuesta del Chapiz
ALBAICÍN
Mirador de San Nicolás
Cuesta de la Alhacaba

Paseo Padre Manjón
Carr. del Darro
Duero
Duero

Almirante
Camino Nuevo de S.
Tina
Gallo
Pl. San Miguel Bajo
Zenete
Cuesta de Elvira
Gran Vía de Colón

Basílica de San Juan de Dios

San Juan de Dios
C. del Gran Capitán
San Jerónimo
C. de la Duquesa
Pl. Lobos
Pl. Trinidad
Tablas
C. del Picón
Los Mesones
Alhóndiga

Cuesta del Chapiz
Carr. de los reyes
Carr. S. Juan de los
C. de los
Pl. Nueva
Csta. de Gómerez
C. Pavaneras
C. San Matías
Pl. de Isabel la Católica
C. Reyes Católicos
Puerta Real
Alcaicería
Calle Libreros
La Cárcel Baja
San Agustín
Pl. de Bib-Rambla

220 yards
200 meters

building in Granada. Cross back over Calle Reyes Católicos: directly ahead is the Alcaicería, once the Arabs' silk market and now a maze of alleys packed with souvenir shops and restaurants. Turn left from the Alcaicería to reach the relaxed Plaza Bib-Rambla, with its flower stalls and historic Gran Café Bib-Rambla, the latter famous for its hot chocolate and *churros* (a deep-fried flour fritter). From the northeast corner of the square, Calle Oficios takes you to the **Palacio Madraza ❺**, the old Arab University, and the **Capilla Real ❻**, next to which is the **cathedral ❼**. Just outside the cathedral's west front is the 16th-century Escuela de las Niñas Nobles, with a plateresque facade. Next to the cathedral, just off Calle Libreros, are the impressive Curia Eclesiástica, used as an Imperial College until 1769; the Palacio del Arzobispo; and the 18th-century Iglesia de Sagrario, with Corinthian columns. Behind the cathedral is the Gran Vía de Colón, named after Columbus, one of Granada's main thoroughfares. Cross the Gran Vía and head right, back to Plaza de Isabel la Católica.

If it's after 2:30, make a short detour to the **Casa de los Tiros ❽** (on Calle Pavaneras, across Calles Reyes Católicos). Make your way back a couple of blocks to Plaza Isabel la Católica and turn right and follow Reyes Católico to reach the Plaza Nueva, overlooked by the 16th-century Real Cancillería (Royal Chancery) with its ornate facade. The building now houses the Tribunal Superior de Justicia (High Court). Artisans have set up shops in the surrounding area. At the north end of the plaza is the adjacent Plaza Santa Ana, where you can find the church of Santa Ana, designed by Diego de Siloé. Nearby is the interesting **Casa de los Pisa.** Walk north through the Plaza Santa Ana onto Carrera del Darro—recently renovated, with new hotels and restaurants—and you come to the 11th-century Arab bathhouse, **El Bañuelo ❾**. Just up Carrera del Darro is the 16th-century **Casa de Castril ❿**, site of Granada's Archaeological Museum. Follow the river along the Paseo del Padre Manjón—also known as the Paseo de los Tristes—to the end, to see the attractive **Palacio de los Córdoba ⓫**. Head north up the Cuesta del Chapíz to the Morisco **Casa del Chapíz ⓬**. East of here are the caves of the **Sacromonte ⓭**, and the **Centro de Interpretación del Sacromonte (Cuevas).** (Both sights are a long walk away; there's a minibus to help you get here.) For now, turn west and plunge into the streets of the **Albaicín ⓮**.

Granada's other major sights are just outside town and best reached by car or taxi: 2 km (1 mi) north of the city center, off Calle Real de Cartuja, is the 16th-century baroque **Monasterio de La Cartuja ⓯**. To the south are the **Parque de las Ciencias ⓰**, an interactive science museum, and **Casa-Museo Federico García Lorca ⓱**.

TIMING   This walk takes the better part of a day; remember that it does not include the Alhambra hill.

What to See

⓮ **Albaicín.** Covering a hill of its own, across the Darro ravine from the Alhambra, this ancient Moorish neighborhood is a mix of dilapidated white houses and immaculate *carmenes* (private villas in gardens enclosed by high walls). It was founded in 1228 by Moors who fled Baeza after Saint King Ferdinand III captured the city. Full of cobblestone alleyways

FodorśChoice
★

and secret corners, the Albaicín guards its old Moorish roots jealously, though its 30 mosques were converted to baroque churches long ago. A stretch of the Moors' original city wall runs beside the Cuesta de la Alhacaba. If you're walking—the best way to explore—you can enter the Albaicín from either the Cuesta de Elvira or the Plaza Nueva. Alternatively, on foot or by taxi (parking is impossible), begin in the Plaza Santa Ana and follow the Carrera del Darro, Paseo Padre Manjón, and Cuesta del Chapíz. One of the highest points in the quarter, the plaza in front of the church of San Nicolás—called the **Mirador de San Nicolás**—has one of the finest views in all of Granada: on the hill opposite, the turrets and towers of the Alhambra form a dramatic silhouette against the snowy peaks of the Sierra Nevada. The sight is most magical at dawn, dusk, and on nights when the Alhambra is floodlighted. Interestingly, given the area's Moorish history, the two sloping, narrow streets of Calderería Nueva and Caldería Vieja that meet at the top by the Iglesia San Gregorio have developed into something of a North African bazaar. They are full of shops and stalls selling clothes, bags, crafts, and trinkets. The numerous little teahouses and restaurants here have a decidedly Moroccan flavor. Be warned that there have been some thefts in the Albaicín area, so keep your money and valuables out of sight.

► **1** **Alhambra.** With around 2 million visitors a year, the Alhambra is Spain's
Fodor'sChoice most popular attraction. Walking *to* the Alhambra can be as inspiring
★ as walking *around* it. If you're up to a long, and rather steep, scenic approach, start in the Plaza Nueva and climb the Cuesta de Gomérez—through the slopes of green elms planted by the Duke of Wellington—to reach the Puerta de las Granadas (Pomegranate Gate), a Renaissance gateway built by Charles V and topped by three pomegranates, symbols of Granada. More easily, simply take one of the minibuses, numbers 30 and 32, up from the Plaza Nueva. They run every few minutes; pay the fare of €0.90 on board. Just past the gate, take the path branching off to the left to the Puerta de la Justicia (Gate of Justice), one of the Alhambra's entrances. Yusuf I built the gate in 1348; its two arches have carvings depicting a key and a hand. The five fingers of the hand represent the five laws of the Koran. If you're driving, you approach the Alhambra from the opposite direction. There's a large parking lot. Don't be tempted to park on the surrounding streets, which may leave your car vulnerable to a break-in. Alternatively, you can park in the underground lot on Calle San Agustín, just north of the cathedral, and take a taxi or the minibus from the Plaza Nueva. The complex has three main parts: the Alcazaba, the Palacios Nazaríes (Nasrid Royal Palace), and the Generalife.

The Alhambra was begun in the 1240s by Ibn el-Ahmar, or Alhamar, the first king of the Nasrids. The great citadel once comprised a complex of houses, schools, baths, barracks, and gardens surrounded by defense towers and seemingly impregnable walls. Today, only the Alcazaba and the Palacios Nazaríes, built chiefly by Yusuf I (1334–54) and his son Mohammed V (1354–91), remain. The palace is an endless, intricate conglomeration of patios, arches, and cupolas made from wood, plaster, and tile; lavishly colored and adorned with marquetry and ceramics in geometric patterns; and topped by delicate, frothy profusions

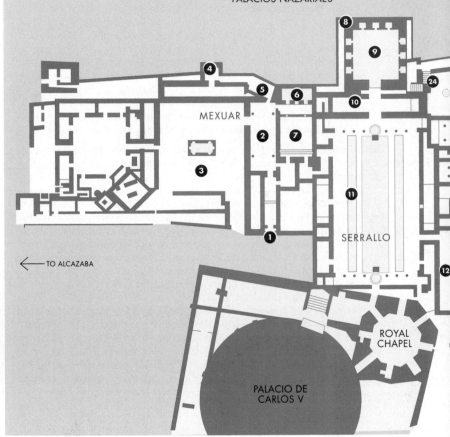

The Alhambra

PALACIOS NAZARIÁES

MEXUAR

← TO ALCAZABA

SERRALLO

ROYAL CHAPEL

PALACIO DE CARLOS V

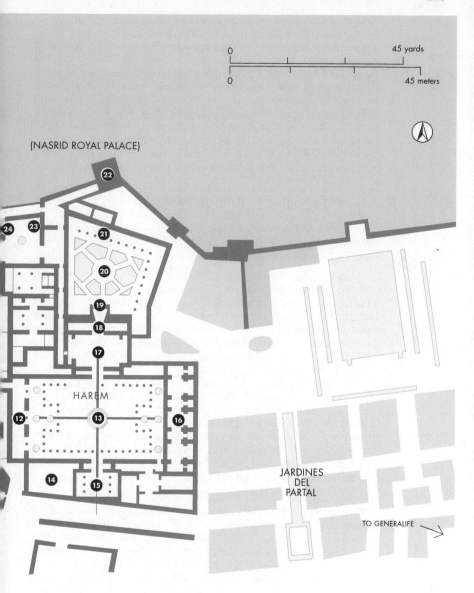

(NASRID ROYAL PALACE)

HAREM

JARDINES
DEL
PARTAL

TO GENERALIFE

0   45 yards

0   45 meters

Sala de las Dos Hermanas
(Hall of the
Two Sisters) **17**

Sala de los
Mocárabes **12**

Sala de los Reyes
(Kings Gallery) **16**

Salón de Embajadores
(Hall of the
Ambassadors) **9**

Torre de Comares
(Comares Tower) **8**

Torre de los Punales
(Tower of the Punales) . . **4**

of lacelike stucco and *mocárabes* (ornamental stalactites). Built of perishable materials, it was never intended to last but to be forever replenished and replaced by succeeding generations. By the early 17th century, ruin and decay had set in, and the Alhambra was abandoned by all but tramps and stray dogs. Napoléon's troops commandeered it in 1812, but their attempts to destroy it were, happily, foiled. In 1814, the Alhambra's fortunes rose with the arrival of the Duke of Wellington, who came here to escape the pressures of the Peninsular War. Soon afterward, in 1829, Washington Irving arrived to live on the premises and helped revive interest in the crumbling palace, in part through his 1832 book *Tales of the Alhambra*. In 1862, Granada finally launched a complete restoration program that has been carried on ever since.

Across from the main entrance is the original fortress, the **Alcazaba.** Its ruins are dominated by the Torre de la Vela (Watchtower); from its summit you can see, to the north, the Albaicín; to the northeast, the Sacromonte; and to the west, the cathedral. The tower's great bell was once used, by both the Moors and the Christians, to announce the opening and closing of the irrigation system on Granada's great plain.

A wisteria-covered walkway leads to the heart of the Alhambra, the **Palacios Nazaríes,** sometimes also called the Casa Real (Royal Palace). Here, delicate apartments, lazy fountains, and tranquil pools contrast vividly with the hulking fortifications outside, and the interior walls are decorated with elaborately carved inscriptions from the Koran. The Palacios Nazaríes is divided into three sections. The first is the *mexuar,* where business, government, and palace administration were headquartered. These chambers include the Oratorio (Oratory) and the Cuarto Dorado (Golden Room); gaze at the Albaicín and Sacromonte from their windows. The second section of the Palacios Nazaríes is the *serrallo,* a series of state rooms where the sultans held court and entertained their ambassadors. In the heart of the *serrallo* is the Patio de los Arrayanes (Court of the Myrtles), with a long goldfish pool. At its northern end, in the Salón de Embajadores (Hall of the Ambassadors)—which has a magnificent cedar door—King Boabdil signed the terms of surrender and Queen Isabella received Christopher Columbus.

The third and final section of the Palacios Nazaríes is the harem, which in its time was entered only by the sultan, his wives and the rest of his family, and their most trusted servants, most of them eunuchs. To reach it, pass through the Sala de los Mocárabes (Hall of the Ornamental Stalactites): note the splendid, though damaged, ceiling, and the elaborate stalactite-style stonework in the arches above. The postcard-perfect Patio de los Leones (Court of the Lions) is the heart of the harem. From the fountain in the center, 12 lions, thought to represent the months or signs of the zodiac, leer out at you (these will be removed in January during renovations). Four streams flow symbolically to the four corners of the cosmos and more literally to the surrounding state apartments.

The **Sala de los Abencerrajes** (Hall of the Moors), on the south side of the palace, may be the Alhambra's most beautiful gallery, with its fabulous, ornate ceiling and a star-shape cupola reflected in the pool below. Here Boabdil's father is alleged to have massacred 16 members of the

Alhambra Tickets

11

ENTRANCE TO THE ALHAMBRA COMPLEX of the Alcazaba, Nasrid Palaces, Mosque Baths, and Generalife is strictly controlled by quotas. There are three types of timed tickets: morning, afternoon, and evening, but the evening ticket is valid only for the Nasrid Palaces.

November through February, morning visits are daily from 8:30 to 2 with a maximum capacity of 3,300; afternoon visits are daily from 2 to 6 with a maximum capacity of 2,100; and evening visits are Friday and Saturday from 8 to 9:30 with a maximum capacity of 400.

March to October, morning visits are daily from 8:30 to 2 with a maximum capacity of 3,300; afternoon visits are daily from 2 to 8 with a maximum capacity of 3,300; and evening visits are Tuesday through Saturday from 10 to 11:30 with a maximum capacity of 400.

Visits to the monument's main gardens are allowed daily from 8:30 to 2 year-round and from 2 to 6 November through February and from 2 to 8 March through October.

Tickets for the Alhambra complex and the Nasrid Palaces cost €10. Because the number of tickets is limited and subject to availability, try to book your tickets in advance. You can do this in several ways: via the Web, www.alhambratickets.com; via phone (902/224460 in Spain, 34 91/5379178 outside Spain); and at any BBVA branch in Spain.

If you wait and take your chances at the ticket office, its hours are March to October, daily from 8 to 7 and 9:30 to 10:30, and November to February, daily from 8 to 5 and 7:30 to 8:30.

Wheelchairs are available on request, and information for those with physical disabilities is available at the Entrance Pavilion.

The Alhambra open every day except December 25 and January 1.

Abencerrajes family—whose chief was the lover of his favorite daughter, Zoraya—and piled their bloodstained heads in this font. The Sala de los Reyes (Hall of the Kings) lies on the patio's east side, decorated with ceiling frescoes thought to be the work of a visiting Christian Spaniard and painted during the last days of the Moors' tenure. To the north, the Sala de las Dos Hermanas (Hall of the Two Sisters) was Zoraya's abode. Its stuccoed ceiling is done in an intricate honeycomb pattern. Note the symmetrically placed patterned pomegranates on the walls.

The **Baños Reales** (Arab Baths), the Alhambra's semi-subterranean bathhouse, is where the sultans' favorites luxuriated in brightly tiled pools beneath star-shape pinpoints of light from the ceiling above. The baths are open to visitors only on specific days, which change throughout the year. An up-to-date timetable can be obtained from the tourist office.

The Renaissance **Palacio de Carlos V** (Palace of Charles V), with a perfectly square exterior but a circular interior courtyard, is where the sultans' private apartments once stood. Designed by Pedro Machuca—a pupil of Michelangelo—and begun in 1526, the palace once was the site of bullfights and mock tournaments. Today its acoustics are perfect for the summer symphony concerts held during Granada's International Festival of Music and Dance. Part of the building houses the **Museo de la Alhambra** (Museum of the Alhambra; ✑ Free ☉ Tues.–Sat. 9–2:30), devoted to Islamic art. Upstairs is the more modest **Museo de Bellas Artes** (Museum of Fine Arts). (At this writing, the museum was closed for major repairs. Check with the tourist office for updates.) You can visit the Palace of Charles V and the museums independently of the Alhambra.

Over on the Cerro del Sol (Hill of the Sun) is the **Generalife,** ancient summer palace of the Nasrid kings. Its name comes from the Arabic *gennat alarif* (garden of the architect) and its terraces and promenades grant incomparable views of the city that stretch to the distant vega. During the summer's International Festival of Music and Dance, stately cypresses are the backdrop for evening ballets in the Generalife amphitheater. Between the Alhambra and Generalife is the 16th-century convent of San Francisco, one of Spain's most luxurious paradors. ⊠ *Cuesta de Gomérez, Alhambra* ⊕ *www.alhambra-patronato.es.*

Baños Árabes. Baths played a very important part in Muslim life, and as a measure of that status were often situated near a mosque or in the *souk* (market). At the re-created baths, you can relax with friends in this series of baths, get a massage, and even take tea and be entertained by a belly dancer. ⊠ *Santa Ana 16* ☏ *958/229978* ⊕ *www.hammamspain. com* ✑ *Baths €15; baths, aromatherapy, and Tea Hammam €24* ☉ *Daily by appt. at 10, noon, 2, 4, 6, 8, 10, midnight.*

❻ Capilla Real (Royal Chapel). Catholic Monarchs Isabella of Castile and Ferdinand of Aragón are buried at this shrine. The couple originally planned to be buried in Toledo's San Juan de los Reyes, but Isabella changed her mind when the pair conquered Granada in 1492. When she died in 1504, her body was first laid to rest in the Convent of San Francisco (now a parador), on the Alhambra hill. The architect Enrique Egas began work on the Royal Chapel in 1506 and completed it 15 years later, creating a masterpiece of the ornate Gothic style now known in Spain as Isabelline. In 1521 Isabella's body was transferred to a simple lead coffin in the Royal Chapel crypt, where it was joined by that of her husband, Ferdinand, and later her unfortunate daughter, Juana la Loca (Joanna the Mad), and son-in-law, Felipe el Hermoso (Philip the Handsome). Felipe died young, and Juana had his casket borne about the peninsula with her for years, opening the lid each night to kiss her embalmed spouse good night. A small coffin to the right contains the remains of Prince Felipe of Asturias, a grandson of the Catholic Monarchs and nephew of Juana la Loca who died in his infancy. The underground **crypt** containing the five lead coffins is quite simple, but it's topped by elaborate marble **tombs** showing Ferdinand and Isabella lying side by side (commissioned by their grandson Charles V and sculpted by Domenico Fancelli). The **altarpiece,** by Felipe Vigarini (1522), comprises 34 carved panels depicting religious and historical scenes; the bottom row shows Boabdil surrendering the keys of the city to its conquerors and the forced baptism of the defeated Moors. The **sacristy** holds Ferdinand's sword, Isabella's crown and scepter, and a fine collection of

Flemish paintings once owned by Isabella. ✉ *Oficios, Centro* ☎ *958/ 229239* ⊕ *www.capillarealgranada.com* 🖼 *€3* ⊙ *Apr.–Oct., Mon.–Sat. 10:30–1 and 4–7, Sun. 11–1 and 4–7; Nov.–Mar., Mon.–Sat. 10:30–1 and 3:30–5:30, Sun. 11–1 and 3:30–6:30.*

❸ Carmen de los Mártires. Up the hill from the Hotel Alhambra Palace, this turn-of-the-20th-century Granada carmen, or private villa, and its gardens—the only area open to tourists—are like a Generalife in miniature. ✉ *Paseo de los Mártires, Alhambra* ☎ *958/227953* 🖼 *Free* ⊙ *Apr.–Oct., weekdays 10–2 and 5–7, weekends 10–7; Nov.–Mar., weekdays 10–2 and 4–6, weekends 10–6.*

❿ Casa de Castril. Bernardo Zafra, secretary to Queen Isabella, once owned this richly decorated 16th-century palace. Before you enter, notice the exquisite portal, and the facade carvings depicting scallop shells and a phoenix. Inside is the **Museo Arqueológico** (Archaeological Museum), where you can find artifacts from provincial caves and from Moorish times, Phoenician burial urns from the coastal town of Almuñécar, and a copy of the *Dama de Baza* (Lady of Baza) a large Iberian sculpture discovered in northern Granada province in 1971 (the original is in Madrid). ✉ *Carrera del Darro 41, Albaicín* ☎ *958/225640* 🖼 *€1.50, EU citizens free* ⊙ *Tues. 2:30–8, Wed.–Sat. 9–8:30, Sun. 9–2:30.*

NEED A BREAK?

The park at **Paseo Padre Manjón,** along the Darro River—also known as the Paseo de los Tristes (Promenade of the Sad) because funeral processions once passed this way—is a terrific place for a coffee break at one of the cafés or bars along the paseo. Dappled with fountains and stone walkways, the park has a stunning view of the Alhambra's northern side.

Casa de los Pisa. Originally built in 1494 for the Pisa family, this house's claim to fame is its relationship to St. John of God (San Juan de Dios), who came to Granada in 1538 and founded a charity hospital to take care of the poor and abandoned. Befriended by the Pisa family, he was taken into the Pisa home when he fell ill in February 1550. A month later, he died there, at the age of 55. Since that time, devotees of the saint have traveled from around the world to this house with a stone Gothic facade, now run by the Hospital Order of St. John. Inside are numerous pieces of priceless religious works of art, an extensive collection of paintings and sculptures depicting St. John, jewelry, and furniture. ✉ *Convalencia 1* ☎ *958/222144* 🖼 *€2.50* ⊙ *Mon.–Sat. 10–1.*

❽ Casa de los Tiros. This 16th-century palace, adorned by the coat-of-arms of the Grana Venegas family who owned it, was named House of the Shots for the musket barrels that protrude from its facade. The stairs to the upper-floor displays are flanked by portraits of miserable-looking Spanish royals, from Ferdinand and Isabella to Philip IV. The highlight is the carved wooden ceiling in the Cuadra Dorada (Hall of Gold), adorned with gilded lettering and portraits of royals and knights. Old lithographs, engravings, and photographs show life in Granada in the 19th and early 20th centuries. ✉ *Pl. Padres Suarez, Realejo* ☎ *958/221072* 🖼 *€1.50* ⊙ *Tues. 2:30–8:30, Wed.–Sat. 9–8:30, Sun. 9–2:30.*

⑫ Casa del Chapíz. There's a delightful garden in this fine 16th-century Morisco house (built by Moorish craftsmen under Christian rule). It houses the School of Arabic Studies and is not generally open to the public, but if you knock, the caretaker might show you around. ☒ *Cuesta del Chapíz at Camino del Sacromonte, Albaicín.*

② Casa-Museo de Manuel de Falla. The composer Manuel de Falla (1876–1946) lived and worked for many years in this rustic house, tucked into a charming little hillside lane with lovely views of the Alpujarra mountains. In 1986 Granada paid homage to Spain's classical-music composer by naming its new concert hall (down the street from the Carmen de los Mártires) the Auditorio Manuel de Falla—and from this institution, fittingly, you have a view of his little white house. Note the bust in the small garden: it stands where the composer once sat to enjoy the sweeping view. ☒ *C. Antequeruela Alta 11, Alhambra* ☎ *958/ 228318* 🖳 *€2* ⊙ *Tues.–Sat. 10–1:30. Guided 30-min tours.*

⑰ Casa-Museo Federico García Lorca. Granada's most famous native son, the poet Federico García Lorca, gets his due here, in the middle of a park devoted to him on the southern fringe of the city. Lorca's onetime summer home, **La Huerta de San Vicente,** is now a museum—run by his-niece Laura García Lorca—with such artifacts as his beloved piano and changing exhibits on specific aspects of his life. ☒ *Parque García Lorca, Virgen Blanca s/n, Arabial* ☎ *958/258466* ⊕ *www.huertadesanvicente. com* 🖳 *€1.80, free Wed.* ⊙ *July and Aug., Tues.–Sun. 10–3; Apr., May, June, and Sept., Tues.–Sun. 10–1 and 5–8; Oct.–Mar. 10–1 and 4–7. Guided tours every 45 mins until 30 mins before closing.*

⑦ Cathedral. Granada's cathedral was commissioned in 1521 by Charles V, who considered the Royal Chapel "too small for so much glory" and wanted to house his illustrious late grandparents someplace more worthy. Charles undoubtedly had great designs, as the cathedral was created by some of the finest architects of its time: Enrique Egas, Diego de Siloé, Alonso Cano, and sculptor Juan de Mena. Alas, his ambitions came to little, for the cathedral is a grand and gloomy monument, not completed until 1714 and never used as the crypt for his grandparents (or parents). You enter through a small door at the back, off the Gran Vía. Old hymnals are displayed throughout, and there's a museum, which includes a 14th-century gold-and-silver monstrance (used for communion) given to the city by Queen Isabella. Audio guides are available for €3. ☒ *Gran Vía s/n, Centro* ☎ *958/222959* 🖳 *€3* ⊙ *Apr.–Oct., Mon.–Sat. 10:30–1:30 and 4–8, Sun. 4–8; Nov.–Mar., Mon.–Sat. 10:45–1:30 and 4–7, Sun. 4–7.*

Centro de Interpretación del Sacromonte. A word of warning: Even if you take the 30 or 32 minibus or the city sightseeing bus to get here, you will still be left with a steep, arduous walk to reach the center. The Museo Etnográfico shows how people lived here, and other areas show the flora and fauna of the area as well as cultural activities. ☒ *Barranco de los Negros s/n* ☎ *958/215120* ⊕ *www.sacromontegranada.com* 🖳 *€4 museum, €1 for other areas* ⊙ *Apr.–Oct., Tues.–Fri. 10–2 and 5–9; Nov.–Mar., Tues.–Fri. 10–2 and 4–7, weekends 11–7.*

❹ Corral del Carbón (Coal House). This building was used to store coal in the 19th century, but its history goes further back. Dating from the 14th century, it was used by Moorish merchants as a lodging house, and then later by Christians as a theater. It's one of the oldest Moorish buildings in the city, and is the only Arab structure of its kind in Spain.

❾ El Bañuelo (Little Bath House). These 11th-century Arab steam baths might now be a little dark and dank, but try to imagine them filled, some 900 years ago, with Moorish beauties. The dull brick walls were then backed by bright ceramic tiles, tapestries, and rugs. Light comes in through star-shape vents in the ceiling, à la the bathhouse in the Alhambra. ⊠ *Carrera del Darro 31, Albaicín* ☎ *958/027800* ⊠ *Free* ☉ *Tues.–Sat. 10–2.*

Fundación Rodríguez-Acosta/Instituto Gómez Moreno. A few yards from the impressive Alhambra Hotel, this nonprofit organization was founded at the bequeath of the painter José Marí Rodríguez-Acosta. Inside a typical Granadino carmen (private villa), it houses works of art, archaeological findings, and a library collected by the Granada-born scholar Manuel Gómez-Moreno Martínez. Other exhibits include valuable and unique objects from Asian cultures and the prehistoric and classical eras. ⊠ *Callejón Niños del Rollo 8* ☎ *958/227497* ⊕ *www.fundacionrodriguezacosta.com* ⊠ *€4* ☉ *Wed.–Sun. 10–2; last entrance 30 mins before closing.*

❶❺ Monasterio de La Cartuja. This Carthusian monastery in northern Granada (2 km [1 mi] from the center and reached on a number 8 bus) was begun in 1506 and moved to its present site in 1516, though construction continued for the next 300 years. The exterior is sober and monolithic, but inside are twisted, multicolor marble columns; a profusion of gold, silver, tortoiseshell, and ivory; intricate stucco; and the extravagant sacristy—it's easy to see why Cartuja has been called the Christian answer to the Alhambra. ⊠ *Camino de Alfacar, Cartuja* ☎ *958/161932* ⊠ *€3* ☉ *Apr.–Oct., Mon.–Sat. 10–1 and 4–8, Sun. 10–noon and 4–8; Nov.–Mar., Mon.–Sun. 10–1 and 3:30–6.*

❶❶ Palacio de los Córdoba. At the end of the Paseo Padre Manjón, this palace was a noble house in the 17th century. Today it keeps Granada's municipal archives and is used for municipal functions and art exhibits. You're free to wander around the large garden.

❺ Palacio Madraza. This building conceals the old Islamic seminary built in 1349 by Yusuf I. The intriguing baroque facade is elaborate; inside, across from the entrance, an octagonal room is crowned by a Moorish dome. There are occasional free art and cultural exhibitions. ⊠ *C. Zacatín s/n, Centro* ☎ *958/223447.*

❶❻ Parque de las Ciencias (Science Park). Across from Granada's convention center, and easily reached on either a number 1 or 5 bus, this museum has a planetarium and interactive demonstrations of scientific experiments. The 165-foot observation tower has views to the south and west. This is the most-visited museum in Andalusia. ⊠ *Av. del Mediterráneo, Zaidín* ☎ *958/131900* ⊕ *www.parqueciencias.com* ⊠ *Park €4.50, planetarium €2* ☉ *Tues.–Sat. 10–7, Sun. and holidays 10–3. Closed Sept. 15–30.*

⓭ Sacromonte. The third of Granada's three hills, the Sacromonte rises behind the Albaicín. The hill is covered with prickly pear cacti and riddled with caverns. These caves may have sheltered early Christians; 15th-century treasure hunters found bones inside and assumed they belonged to San Cecilio, the city's patron saint. Thus the hill was sanctified—*sacro monte* (holy mountain)—and an abbey built on its summit, the **Abadía de Sacromonte** (✉ Camino del Sacromonte, Sacromonte 🕾 958/221445 ✉ €3 ⊙ Tues.–Sat. 11–1 and 4–6, Sun. 4–6; guided tours every ½ hr). The Sacromonte has long been notorious as a domain of Granada's gypsies and a den of pickpocketing, but its reputation is largely undeserved. The quarter is more like a quiet Andalusian *pueblo* (village) than a rough neighborhood. Many of the quarter's colorful *cuevas* (caves) have been restored as middle-class homes, and some of the old spirit lives on in a handful of *zambras*—flamenco performances in caves garishly decorated with brass plates and cooking utensils. These shows differ from formal flamenco shows in that the performers mingle with you, usually dragging one or two onlookers onto the floor for an improvised dance lesson. Ask your hotel to book you a spot on a cueva tour, which usually includes a walk through the neighboring Albaicín and a drink at a tapas bar in addition to the zambra.

Where to Eat

$$–$$$$ ✗ **Azafrán.** It is rather a charming surprise when entering this restaurant, nestled at the foot of the Albaicín by the side of the Darro river and in the shadow of the Alhambra, to find such a bright and modern decor. It is newly opened, and you can expect an interesting and varied menu with fish and meat dishes as well as pasta, couscous, and an enticing rice-and-fish casserole. ✉ *Paseo de los Tristes 1* 🕾 *958/226882* 🖃 *MC, V.*

★ **$$$** ✗ **Ruta del Veleta.** It's worth the short drive 5 km (3 mi) out of town to this Spanish restaurant, which serves some of the best food in Granada. House specialties include *carnes a la brasa* (succulent grilled meats) and fish dishes cooked in rock salt, as well as seasonal dishes such as *Solomillo de jabalí con frutos de otoño y salsa de vinagre* (wild boar fillet with autumn fruits in a vinegar-and-honey sauce). Dessert might be *morito de chocolate templado con helado de gachas* (warm chocolate sponge cake with ice cream). ✉ *Ctra. del Sierra 136, on road to Sierra Nevada, Cenes de la Vega* 🕾 *958/486134* ⊕ *www.rutadelveleta.com* 🖃 *AE, DC, MC, V* ⊙ *No dinner Sun. in summer.*

$$–$$$ ✗ **Cunini.** Around the corner from the cathedral is Granada's best fish house, where seafood, often fresh from the boats at Motril, is displayed in the window at the front of the tapas bar. Both the *pescaditos fritos* (fried) and the *parrillada* (grilled) fish are good choices, and if it's chilly, you can warm up with *caldereta de arroz, pescado y marisco* (rice, fish, and seafood stew). There are tables outdoors in warm weather. ✉ *Pescadería 14, Centro* 🕾 *958/250777* 🖃 *AE, DC, MC, V* ⊙ *Closed Mon. No dinner Sun.*

$$–$$$ ✗ **La Ermita en la Plaza de Toros.** As the name implies, this classy restaurant is under the seats of the Plaza de Toros; the decor, with *carteles* (bullfighting posters), bulls' heads, and bullfighter suits, reflects that fact. Meat selections such as *rabo de toro estofado al vino tinto* (bull's tail cooked in red wine) and *lomo de buey Gallego a la parrilla* (grilled beef tenderloin) dominate, but there are also seafood dishes and daily specials. ⊠ *Dr. Olóriz 25* ☎ *958/290257* ▭ *MC, V.*

$$–$$$ ✗ **Luna Verde.** This strangely named restaurant, the Green Moon, has a terrace with marvelous views across to the Alhambra and Sierra Nevada. Regional dishes here might include toasted and stuffed eggplants with pâté, stuffed sea bass and vegetables, and hake with prawns. ⊠ *Nuevo de San Nicolás 16* ☎ *958/291794* ▭ *MC, V.*

★ **$$–$$$** ✗ **Mirador de Morayma.** Buried in the Albaicín, this place is hard to find and might appear to be closed (ring the doorbell). Once inside, you'll have unbeatable views across the gorge to the Alhambra, particularly from the wisteria-laden outdoor terrace. The adequate menu has some surprises, such as smoked *esturión* (sturgeon) from Riofrío, served cold with cured ham and a vegetable dip, and the *ensalada de remojón granadino,* a salad of cod, orange, and olives. ⊠ *Pianista García Carrillo 2, Albaicín* ☎ *958/228290* ▭ *AE, MC, V* ☾ *No dinner Sun.*

★ **$$–$$$** ✗ **Sevilla.** Since 1930 this colorful, central two-story restaurant has fed the likes of the composer de Falla and the poet García Lorca. There are four dining rooms and an outdoor terrace overlooking the Royal Chapel and Cathedral. There's a small but superb tapas bar; the dinner menu includes Granadian favorites such as *sopa sevillana* (soup with fish and shellfish) and *tortilla al Sacromonte* (with bull's brains and testicles) as well as more elaborate dishes. ⊠ *Oficios 12, Centro* ☎ *958/221223* ▭ *AE, DC, MC, V* ☾ *No dinner Sun.*

¢–$$$ ✗ **Taberna Tendido 1.** Also found under the Plaza de Toros, this is next to the La Ermita but more informal. The menu of salads, cheeses, smoked fish, and popular tapas is served in three sizes—tapa, half-ración, and ración (€2–€18)—and fits neatly onto the barrel tops. Fixed-price menus are also available. ⊠ *Dr. Olóriz 25* ☎ *958/203136* ⊕ *www.tendido1.com* ▭ *MC, V.*

$$ ✗ **Jardines Alberto.** Spacious and well located near the Alhambra, this restaurant has two outside patios with stunning views of the Generalife, plus a summer bar and barbecue. The interior is cozy and rustic, and the food, classically Granadian with a choice of five-course menu (€30–€41) includes dishes such as *lobo de cerdo iberico confitado al ajo y hierbas serranas con pure de castañas* (honeyed pork with garlic, wild herbs, and chestnut sauce) followed by the diet-defying *mousse de turron y crema de cafe* (nougat mousse with coffee cream). ⊠ *Av. Alixares del Generalife s/n, Alhambra* ☎ *958/224818* ▭ *AE, MC, V* ☾ *Closed Sun. No dinner Mon.*

$$ ✗ **La Yedra Real.** This is a very modern-style restaurant with a terrace that has a large selection of good, typical Spanish dishes at reasonable prices. Because it is very close to the main entrance of the Alhambra, it is an ideal stop for those visiting this amazing monument. ⊠ *Paseo de la Sabika 15* ☎ *958/229145* ▭ *MC, V* ☾ *Closed Mon.*

$$ ✗ **Velázquez.** Tucked into a side street one block west of the Puerta de Elvira and Plaza del Triunfo, this cozy, very Spanish restaurant has long been popular with locals. At street level, the brick-wall bar is hung with hams; the intimate, wood-beam dining room is upstairs. House specialties include *zancarrón cordero a la miel* (lamb with honey) and *lomitos* *de rape* (braised monkfish medallions). ⊠ *Emilio Orozco 1, Triunfo* ☎ *958/280109* ▭ *MC, V* ☉ *Closed Sun.*

¢–$$ ✗ **Bodegas Castañeda.** A block from the Cathedral across Gran Vía, this is a delightfully typical Granadino bodega. In addition to its wines, the specialties here are *jamón Ibérico* and *embutidos* (cold meats). The extensive list of tapas includes the likes of *queso viejo en aceite* (cured cheese in olive oil), bacon with Roquefort cheese, and *jamón de Trevélez* (ham from the Alpujarran village of Trevélez—the the highest point in Spain). Combination plates and *raciónes* (family-style platters) both come in two sizes. ⊠ *Almireceros 1–3* ☎ *958/223222* ▭ *MC, V.*

$ ✗ **Kasbah Tetería.** On a sloping street that feels very North African, Kasbah Tetería has a menu that's fairly short. Dishes here include couscous with chicken, lamb, and vegetables, as well as tasty *pasteles árabes* (cakes). ⊠ *Calderería Nueva 4* ☎ *958/227936* ▭ *MC, V.*

$ ✗ **Mesón Blas Casa.** In the choicest square in the Albaicín, this restaurant serves solidly traditional cuisine that includes *rabo de toro* (oxtail) and habas con jamón. There's a cheap and filling *menú del día* (daily menu) and a fireplace for warming the toes when there's snow on the Sierras. ⊠ *Plaza San Miguel Bajo 15, Albaicín* ☎ *958/273111* ▭ *MC, V* ☉ *Closed Mon.*

¢–$ ✗ **Antigua Bodega Castañeda.** This typical and traditional-style bodega, close to Plaza Nueva, is the idea place to pop into for a snack and a quick drink. It features salads, sandwiches—made with toasted chapatta bread—smoked fish, cheeses, pates, stews, tapas, stuffed baked potatoes, and desserts, and a range of wines to wash it down with. ⊠ *Elvira 5* ☎ *958/226362* ▭ *MC, V.*

¢–$ ✗ **Meknes Rahma.** This Moroccan restaurant has an unusual location—on the edge of Albaicín at the junction of the road to Sacromonte—but can be easily reached on the minibus numbers 31 or 32 from Plaza Nueva. In addition to dishes such as Moroccan soup and shish kebab, there's a selection of Eastern teas, and, for entertainment, belly dancing. ⊠ *Peso de la Harina 1* ☎ *958/227430* ▭ *MC, V.*

Where to Stay

$$$$ 🖫 **Alhambra Palace.** Built by a local duke in 1910, this neo-Moorish hotel

Fodor'sChoice is on leafy grounds at the back of the Alhambra hill. The interior is very

★ Arabian Nights, with orange-and-brown overtones, multicolor tiles, and Moorish arches and pillars. Even the bar is decorated as a mosque. Rooms overlooking the city have incredible views, as does the terrace, a perfect place to watch the sun set on Granada and its fertile plain. ⊠ *Peña Partida 2, Alhambra, 18009* ☎ *958/221468* 🖶 *958/226404* ⊕ *www.h-alhambrapalace.es* ⇆ *124 rooms, 11 suites* ⚭ *Restaurant, minibars, cable TV with movies, in-room data ports, 2 bars, free parking* ▭ *AE, DC, MC, V.*

$$$$ 🖫 **Casa de los Migueletes.** This very attractive 17th-century mansion with patios and galleries is found close to the popular Plaza Nueva. Expect to find antique or handmade furnishings in the individually decorated rooms—some with Alhambra views. It comes by its name from the fact that it was once the headquarters of the Migueletes, a 19th-century rural police force. It is 100% nonsmoking. Parking arrangements are at the Plaza Puerta Real garage some distance away. ⊠ *Benalua 11, 18010*

☎ *958/210700* 🖷 *958/210702* ⊕ *www.casamigueletes.com* 🖃 *25 rooms* ▭ *AE, DC, MC, V.*

★ **$$$$** ⊞ **Palacio de los Patos.** This beautiful palace is unmissable, as it sits proudly on its own in the middle of one of Granada's busiest shopping streets. While retaining its 19th-century classical architecture, it also, thanks to remodeling and renovation, incorporates absolutely everything—including a gastronomic restaurant and spa—that even the most discriminating 21st-century traveler could desire. Some consider this Granada's finest hotel. ✉ *Solarillo de Gracia 1, 18002* ☎ *958/536516* 🖷 *958/ 536517* ⊕ *www.hospes.es* 🖃 *42 rooms* ⚬ *Restaurant, in-room broadband, indoor pool, massage, sauna, spa, bar, parking (fee)* ▭ *AE, DC, MC, V.*

$$$$ ⊞ **Parador de Granada.** This is Spain's most expensive and popular
Fodor's Choice parador, and it's right in the Alhambra precinct. The building, a former
★ Franciscan monastery built by the Catholic Monarchs after they captured Granada, is soul-stirringly gorgeous. If possible, go for a room in the old section where there are beautiful antiques, woven curtains, and bedspreads. The rooms in the newer wing are also charming but simple. Reserve four to six months in advance. ✉ *Real de la Alhambra s/ n, Alhambra, 18009* ☎ *958/221440* 🖷 *958/222264* ⊕ *www.parador. es* 🖃 *36 rooms, 2 suites* ⚬ *Restaurant, minibars, in-room data ports, bar, free parking* ▭ *AE, DC, MC, V.*

★ **$$$-$$$$** ⊞ **Casa Morisca Hotel.** The architect-owner of this 15th-century building transformed it into a hotel and received the 2001 National Restoration Award for the project. The brick building has many original architectural elements, three floors, and a central courtyard with a small pond and well. The rooms aren't large, but they get a heady Moorish feel through wonderful antiques and views of the Alhambra and Albaicín. ✉ *Cuesta de la Victoria 9, Albaicín, 18010* ☎ *958/221100* 🖷 *958/215796* ⊕ *www.hotelcasamorisca.com* 🖃 *12 rooms, 2 suites* ⚬ *Dining room, minibars, cable TV, in-room data ports* ▭ *AE, DC, MC, V.*

$$-$$$$ ⊞ **Palacio de Santa Inés.** It's not often you stay in a 16th-century palace, and this one in particular has a stunning location in the heart of the Albaicín. Rooms on the two upper floors are centered on a courtyard with frescoes painted by a disciple of Raphael. Each room is magnificently decorated with antiques and modern art; some have balconies with Alhambra views. ✉ *Cuesta de Santa Inés 9, Albaicín, 18010* ☎ *958/ 222362* 🖷 *958/222465* ⊕ *www.palaciosantaines.com* 🖃 *15 rooms, 20 suites* ⚬ *Dining room, minibars, cable TV, parking (fee)* ▭ *AE, DC, MC, V.*

$$$ ⊞ **Carmen.** This hotel has a prized city-center location on a busy shopping street, and is directly across from the El Corte Inglés department store. The rooms are spacious and have a mix of modern and classic decor. The rooftop terrace and pool offer stunning views of the city. ✉ *Acera del Daro 62, 18005* ☎ *958/258300* 🖷 *958/256462* ⊕ *www. hotelcarmen.com* 🖃 *270 rooms, 13 suites* ⚬ *Restaurant, cafeteria, pool, bar, business services, parking (fee)* ▭ *AE, D, MC, V.*

$$$ ⊞ **Carmen de la Alcubilla del Caracol.** In a traditional Granadino carmen–style house, on the slopes of the Alhambra, this is one of Granada's most stylish hotels. The rooms are bright, airy, and furnished with antiques; they also have views over the city and the Sierra Nevada. The traditional terraced garden, with water troughs fed by an irrigation system from the Alhambra itself, is a peaceful oasis. ⊠ *Aire Alta 12, 18009* ☎ *958/215551* ⊕ *www.alcubilladelcaracol.com* ⇆ *7 rooms* ⚹ *Cafeteria, Wi-Fi, bar, library, free parking* ▭ *MC, V* ⊗ *Closed Aug.*

$$$ ⊞ **El Ladrón de Agua.** Situated by the side of the Darro river, in an interesting area directly under the imposing shadow of the Alhambra itself, this 16th-century mansion is called The Water Thief—a name inspired from a Juan Ramón Jiménez (winner of the Nobel Prize for Literature in 1956) poem. The rooms, traditionally decorated, are all named after poems by Federico García Lorca and Manuel deFalla, and are found around the galleries of the two floors, with the best found in the tower; eight of the rooms overlook the Alhambra, There is no nearby parking. ⊠ *Carrera del Darro 13, 18010* ☎ *958/215040* 🖶 *958/ 224345* ⊕ *www.elladrondeagua.com* ⇆ *15 rooms* ⚹ *Restaurant, café, Wi-Fi, bar* ▭ *AE, DC, MC, V.*

$$$ ⊞ **Palacio de los Navas.** In the center of the city, this was built by aristocrat Francisco Navas in the 16th century and later became the Casa de Moneda (Mint). It retains original architectural features while also blending in new features with the old to become a particularly charming hotel. ⊠ *Navas 1, 18009* ☎ *958/215760* 🖶 *958/215760* ⊕ *www. palaciodelosnavas.com* ⇆ *19 rooms* ⚹ *Parking (fee)* ▭ *AE, DC, MC, V.*

★ $$$ ⊞ **Reina Cristina.** In the former Rosales family residence, where the poet Lorca was arrested after taking refuge when the Spanish civil war broke out, the Reina Cristina is near the lively and central Plaza de la Trinidad. Plants trail from the windowsills of the reception area; a covered patio with a small marble fountain and a marble stairway leads to the guest rooms, which are simply but cheerfully furnished with red fabrics on a white background. ⊠ *Tablas 4, Centro, 18002* ☎ *958/253211* 🖶 *958/ 255728* ⊕ *www.hotelreinacristina.com* ⇆ *43 rooms* ⚹ *Restaurant, cafeteria, cable TV, bar, parking (fee)* ▭ *AE, DC, MC, V* ⑩ *BP.*

$$–$$$ ⊞ **Alojamientos con Encanto.** A bargain for groups and families, these elegant, comfortable, and large apartments are on the hills of the Albaicín. Tiles, wrought-iron headboards, and other local crafts accent the apartments; quarters at the top of the neighborhood share a pebble patio crowded with plants and a terrace with magnificent views of the Alhambra. ⊠ *C. Cuesta del Chapíz 54, Albaicín, 18010* ☎ *958/222428* 🖶 *958/222810* ⊕ *www.granada-in.com* ⚹ *In-room broadband, free parking* ▭ *AE, DC, MC, V.*

$$–$$$ ⊞ **Casa del Capitel Nazarí.** This hotel's Nazarí capital (the top structure of a column) is carved in alabaster and original to the former palace, built in 1503. Rooms are sober but elegant, with dark wooden beams and furniture. The two-story hotel is east of the River Darro. ⊠ *Cuesta Aceituneros 6, Albaicín, 18010* ☎ *958/215260* 🖶 *958/215260* ⇆ *17 rooms* ⚹ *Dining room, cable TV, in-room data ports, lounge* ▭ *AE, DC, MC, V.*

$$–$$$ ⊞ **Inglaterra.** The interior of this 19th-century house is comfortable and modern. Guest rooms are painted in pastel tones and have functional furniture and polished-wood floors. The hotel is in the heart of town, two blocks east of the Gran Vía de Colón. ⊠ *Cetti Meriem 4, Centro, 18010* ☎ *958/221558* 🖶 *958/227100* ⊕ *www.nh-hoteles.com* ⤳ *36 rooms* ♿ *Restaurant, meeting room, parking (fee)* ☰ *AE, DC, MC, V.*

$$ 🖵 **Guadalupe.** This charming hotel is another option for those who want to be close to the Alhambra. The rooms, in single, double, and triple sizes, are traditionally styled and of a generous size. ⊠ *Av. de los Alixares s/n, 18009* ☎ *958/223423* 🖶 *958/223798* ⊕ *www.hotel-guadalupe. com* ⤳ *58 rooms* ♿ *Restaurant, snack bar* ☰ *AE, DC, MC, V.*

$$ 🖵 **Hotel Los Tilos.** With a comfortable modern interior and a central location overlooking a pleasant square with a daily flower market, this good-value no-frills hotel is worth a try. Best of all is the fourth-floor terrace where you can sip a drink, read a book, or just enjoy the panoramic view of the skyline. ⊠ *Plaza Bib-Rambla 4, Centro, 18001* ☎ *958/266712* 🖶 *958/266801* ⊕ *www.hotellostilos.com* ⤳ *30 rooms* ♿ *Parking (fee)* ☰ *MC, V.*

¢ 🖵 **Britz.** If you plan on spending considerable time at the Alhambra and don't have wads of cash, consider this hostel, which is within walking distance. Rooms are more than adequate, and some have terraces and brightly tiled bathrooms. Its location on the bustling Plaza Nueva means noise can be a problem, but on the other hand there is also a wide choice of sidewalk cafés a short stroll away. ⊠ *Cuesta de Gomérez 1, Centro, 18010* ☎ *958/223652* ⊕ *www.lisboaweb.com* ⤳ *22 rooms, some with bath* ♿ *No room TVs* ☰ *MC, V.*

Nightlife & the Arts

THE ARTS Get the latest on arts events at the **Diputacíon de Cultura** (Department of Culture), in the **Palacio de los Condes de Gabia** (⊠ Pl. de los Girones 1, Centro ☎ 958/247383); the palace holds art and photography exhibitions as well. Free magazines at the tourist offices also have schedules of cultural events. Granada's orchestra performs in the **Auditorio Manuel de Falla** (⊠ Paseo de los Mártires, Realejo ☎ 958/222188). Plays are staged at the **Teatro Alhambra** (⊠ Molinos 56, Realejo ☎ 958/220447). Granada's **Festival Internacional de Teatro** fills 10 days with drama each May. Contact the **tourist office** (⊠ Pl. Mariana Pineda 10, Centro ☎ 958/247128) for details. The **Festival Internacional de Música y Danza de Granada** (☎ 958/220691, 958/221844 tickets ⊕ www.granadafestival. org) is held annually from mid-June to mid-July, with some events in the Alhambra itself. Contact the tourist office or visit the Web site for information on November's **Festival Internacional de Jazz de Granada** (⊕ www.jazzgranada.net).

FLAMENCO Flamenco is played throughout the city, especially in the *cuevas* (caves) of the Albaicín and Sacromonte, where *zambra* shows—informal performances by gypsies—take place almost daily. The most popular cuevas are along the Camino de Sacromonte, the major street in the neighborhood of the same name. For any Sacromonte show, prepare to part with lots of money (€18–€20 is average). In August free shows are held at the delightful El Corral del Carbón square—home of the tourist office. The annual *Encuentro Flamenco* festival held during the first days of December typically attracts some of the country's best performers. If you do not want to show up randomly at the flamenco clubs, join a tour through a travel agent or your hotel, or contact **Los Tarantos** (⊠ Camino del Sacromonte 9, Sacromonte ☎ 958/224525), which has lively nightly shows with midnight performances on Friday and Saturday. **Sala Alhambra** (⊠ Parque Empresarial Olinda, Edif. 12 ☎ 958/412269 or 958/412287) runs well-organized, scheduled performances. **La Rocío** (⊠ Sacromonte 70, Albaicín ☎ 958/227129) is a good spot for authentic flamenco shows. **María La Canastera** (⊠ Camino de Sacromonte 89, Sacromonte ☎ 958/121183) is another one of the several cuevas on Camino de Sacromonte with unscheduled zambra shows.

TAPAS BARS   Poke around the streets between the Carrera del Darro and the Mirador de San Nicolás, particularly around the bustling Plaza San Miguel Bajo, for Granada's most colorful twilight hangouts. Also try the bars and restaurants in the arches underneath the Plaza de Toros (Bullfighting Ring), on the west of the city and a bit farther from the city center. For a change, check out some Moroccan-style tea shops, known as *Teterías*—these first emerged in Granada and are now equally popular in Seville and Málaga, particularly among students. Tea at such places can be expensive, so be sure to check the price of your brew before you order. The highest concentration is in the Albaicín, particularly around Calle Calderería Nueva where, within a few doors from each other, you find Tetería Kasbah, Tetería Oriental, and El Jardín de los Sueños, which also sells delicious milk shakes—try the almond and pistachio.

La Trastienda (⊠ Cuchilleros 11, Centro ☎ 958/226985) is named "The Backroom" because of where you eat the tapas, which are served on wooden plates. After you get the tapas and your drink, take them to the dining area in back. **Le Gran Taberna** (⊠ Plaza Nueva 12, Centro ☎ 958/228846) serves unusual tapas, such as trout with cottage cheese and Roquefort with beets, and goat's-cheese canapés, as well as the more standard selections. **Taberna Salínas** (⊠ Elvira 13, Centro ☎ 958/221411) has a brick-and-beam decor and great wine to accompany its delicious tapas. More filling fare is also available. Off Calle Navas in Plaza Campillo is **Chikito** (⊠ Plaza del Campillo 9, Puerta Real ☎ 958/223364), best known for its tasty sit-down meals, but the bar is an excellent place for tapas. The place is usually packed, so additional tables are set up on the square in summer. **La Taberna de Baco** (⊠ Campo del Príncipe 22, Realejo ☎ 958/226732) fuses Ecuadoran and Andalusian flavors. **El Pilar del Toro** (⊠ C. Hospital de Santa Ana 12, Albaicín ☎ 958/225470) is a bar and restaurant with a beautiful patio. The popular **Bodegas Castañeda** (⊠ Elvira 6, Centro ☎ 958/226362) serves classic tapas, as well as baked potatoes with a choice of fillings. **Bodega Peso La Harina** (⊠ Placeta del Peso de la Harina, Sacromonte), on a square right at the entrance of Camino de Sacromonte, prepares reliably good tapas. Southeast of Granada's cathedral, **Café Botánico** (⊠ Málaga 3, Centro ☎ 958/271598) is a modern hot spot with a diverse menu that serves twists on traditional cuisine for a young, trendy crowd.

NIGHTLIFE   Granada's ample student population makes for a lively bar scene. Some of the trendiest bars are in converted houses in the Albaicín and Sacromonte and in the area between Plaza Nueva and Paseo de los Tristes.

Calle Elvira and Caldería Vieja and Nueva are crowded with laid-back coffee and pastry shops. In the modern part of town, Pedro Antonio de Alarcón and Martinez de la Rosa have larger but less glamorous offerings. Another nighttime gathering place is the Campo del Príncipe, a large plaza surrounded by typical Andalusian taverns.

El Eshavira (✉ Postigo de la Cuna 2, Albaicín ☎ 958/290829) is a smoky, dimly lighted club where you can hear sultry jazz and occasional flamenco. **Planta Baja** (✉ C. Horno de Abad 11, Centro ☎ 958/207607) is a funky late-night club that hosts bands playing everything from exotic pop to garage and soul. **Fondo Reservado** (✉ Santa Inés 4, Albaicín ☎ 958/222375) is a hip hangout for mainly students, and has late-night dance music. **Granada 10** (✉ Carcel Baja 10, Centro ☎ 958/224001), with an upscale crowd, is a discotheque in a former theater. **La Industrial Copera** (✉ Paz 7, Ctra. de la Armilla ☎ 958/258449) is a popular disco, especially on Friday night. **Zoo** (✉ C. Mora 2, Puerta Real) is one of the longest-established and largest discos in town.

Shopping

A Moorish aesthetic pervades Granada's silver-, brass- and copperware, ceramics, marquetry (especially the *taraceas,* wooden boxes with inlaid tiles on their lids), and woven textiles. The main shopping streets, centering on the Puerta Real, are the Gran Vía de Colón, Reyes Católicos, Zacatín, Ángel Ganivet, and Recogidas. Most antiques stores are on Cuesta de Elvira, and Alcaicería—off Reyes Católicos—and Cuesta de Gómerez, on the way up to the Alhambra, also has many handicraft shops. **Cerámica Fabre** (✉ Pl. Pescadería 10, Centro), near the cathedral, has typical Granada ceramics: blue-and-green patterns on white, with a pomegranate in the center. For wicker baskets and esparto-grass mats and rugs, head off the Plaza Pescadería to **Espartería San José** (✉ C. Jaudenes 22, Centro).

EN ROUTE Eight miles (12 km) south of Granada on N323, the road reaches a spot known as the **Suspiro del Moro** (Moor's Sigh). Pause here a moment and look back at the city, just as Granada's departing "Boy King," Boabdil, did 500 years ago. As he wept over the city he'd surrendered to the Catholic Monarchs, his scornful mother pronounced her now legendary rebuke: "You weep like a boy for the city you could not defend as a man."

Santa Fe

⑱ *8 km (5 mi) west of Granada just south of N342.*

Santa Fe was founded in winter 1491 as a campground for Ferdinand and Isabella's 150,000 troops as they prepared for the siege of Granada. It was here, in April 1492, that Isabella and Columbus signed the agreements that financed his historic voyage, and thus the town has been called the Cradle of America. Santa Fe was originally laid out in the shape of a cross, with a gate at each of its four ends, inscribed with Ferdinand and Isabella's initials. The town has long since transcended those boundaries, but the gates remain—to see them all at once, stand in the square next to the church at the center of the old town.

Fuentevaqueros

⑲ *10 km (6 mi) northwest of Santa Fe.*

Federico García Lorca was born in this village on June 5, 1898, and lived here until the age of six. The **Museo Casa Natal Federico García Lorca,** the poet's childhood home, opened as a museum in 1986, when Spain commemorated the 50th anniversary of Lorca's assassination and celebrated his reinstatement as a national figure after 40 years of nonrecognition during the Francisco Franco regime. The house has been restored with original furnishings, and the former granary, barn, and stables have been converted into exhibition spaces, with temporary art shows and a permanent display of photographs, clippings, and other memorabilia. A two-minute video shows the only existing footage of Lorca. ⊠ *Poeta García Lorca 4* ☎ *958/516453* ⊕ *www.museogarcialorca.org* ⊠ *€1.80* ⊙ *Closed on Mon.*

Viznar

⑳ *9 km (5½ mi) northeast of Granada; head northeast on N342, then turn left, then left again when you see signs for Viznar.*

If you're a Lorca devotee, make the short trip to Viznar. The **Federico García Lorca Memorial Park,** 3 km (2 mi) from Viznar up a narrow winding road, marks the spot where Lorca was shot without trial by Nationalists at the start of the civil war in August 1936 and where he's probably buried. Lorca, who's now venerated by most Spaniards, was hated by fascists for his liberal ideas and his homosexuality.

The Sierra Nevada

㉑ The drive southeast from Granada to Pradollano along the N420/A395—Europe's highest road, by way of Cenes de la Vega—takes about 45 minutes. It's wise to carry snow chains even as late as April or May. The mountains here make for an easy and worthwhile excursion, especially for those keen on trekking. The **Pico de Veleta,** Spain's third-highest mountain, is 11,125 feet, and the view from its summit across the Alpujarra range to the sea, at distant Motril, is stunning; on a very clear day you can see the coast of North Africa. In July and August you can drive or take a minibus to within hundreds of yards of the summit—a trail takes you to the top. It's cold up here, so bring a warm jacket and scarf, even if Granada is sizzling hot. Away to your left, the mighty **Mulhacén,** the highest peak in mainland Spain, soars to 11,427 feet. Legend has it that it came by its name when Boabdil, the last Moorish king of Granada, deposed his father, Muly Abdul Hassan, and had the body buried at the summit of the mountain so that it couldn't be desecrated. For more information on trails to the two summits, call the **Natural Park's Service office** (☎ 958/763127) at Pampaneira. The Sierra Nevada ski resort's two stations—Pradollano and the higher Borreguiles—draw crowds from December to May. In winter, **buses to Pradollano** (⊠ Autocares Bonal ☎ 958/465022) leave Granada three times a day weekdays, and four times on weekends and holidays. They depart from

Granada's bus station, where can you also buy tickets for €6 round-trip. As for Borreguiles, you can get there only on skis.

Skiing

The **Estación de Esquí Sierra Nevada** is Europe's southernmost ski resort and one of its best equipped. At the Pradollano and Borreguiles stations there's good skiing from December through May. Both stations have a special snowboarding circuit, floodlighted night slopes, a children's ski school, and après-ski sun and swimming in the Mediterranean less than an hour (33 km [20 mi]) away. There's an **information center** (☎ 958/249100) at Plaza de Andalucía 4 ⊕ *www.cetursa.es.*

Where to Stay

$$$$ ⊞ **El Lodge.** A fantastic slope-side location and friendly, professional service adds up to the best hotel in the Sierra Nevada. It's built of Finnish wood—unusual for southern Spain, but perfectly appropriate in this alpine area—and has a warm, cozy quality. Know, however, that accommodations are not particularly large. Rooms are entirely wood—ceiling, walls, and floors. ⊠ *C. Maribel 8, 18196* ☎ *958/480600* 🖨 *958/481314* 📨 *16 rooms, 4 suites* ⌂ *Restaurant, cable TV, health club, bar, meeting rooms* 🚭 *AE, DC, MC, V* ⊗ *Closed May–Oct.* ⎮⊙⎮ *BP.*

The Alpujarras

㉒ *Village of Lanjarón: 46 km (29 mi) south of Granada.*

A trip to the Alpujarras, on the southern slopes of the Sierra Nevada, takes you to one of Andalusia's highest, most remote, and most scenic areas, home for decades to painters, writers, and a considerable foreign population. The Alpujarras region was originally populated by Moors fleeing the Christian Reconquest (from Seville after its fall in 1248, then from Granada after 1492). It was also the final fiefdom of the unfortunate Boabdil, conceded to him by the Catholic Monarchs after he surrendered Granada. In 1568 rebellious Moors made their last stand against the Christian overlords, a revolt ruthlessly suppressed by Philip II and followed by the forced conversion of all Moors to Christianity and their resettlement farther inland and up Spain's eastern coast. The villages were then repopulated with Christian soldiers from Galicia, who were granted land in return for their service against the Moors. To this day the Galicians' descendants continue the Moorish custom of weaving rugs and blankets in the traditional Alpujarran colors of red, green, black, and white, and they sell their crafts in many of the villages. Be on the lookout for handmade basketry and pottery as well. Houses here are squat and square; they spill down the southern slopes of the Sierra Nevada, bearing a strong resemblance to the Berber homes in the Rif Mountains, just across the sea in Morocco. If you're driving, the road as far as Lanjarón and Orgiva is smooth sailing; after that come steep, twisting mountain roads with few gas stations. Beyond sightseeing, the area is a haven for outdoor activities such as hiking and horseback riding. Inquire at the **Information Point** at Plaza de la Libertad s/n, at Pampaneira.

EN
ROUTE
Lanjarón, the western entrance to the Alpujarras some 46 km (29 mi) from Granada, is a spa town famous for its mineral water, collected from the melting snows of the Sierra Nevada and drunk throughout Spain. **Orgiva,** the next and largest town in the Alpujarras, has a 17th-century castle. Here you can leave C348 and follow signs for the villages of the Alpujarra Alta (High Alpujarra), including **Pampaneira, Capileira,** and especially **Trevélez,** which lies on the slopes of the Mulhacén at 4,840 feet above sea level. Reward yourself with a plate of the locally produced *jamón serrano* (cured ham). Trevélez has three levels, the Barrio Alto, Barrio Medio, and Barrio Bajo; the butchers are concentrated in the lowest section (Bajo). Also explore the higher levels, which have narrow cobblestone streets, whitewashed houses, and shops.

Where to Stay & Eat

If you're looking for the unusual—or a slightly longer stay—rural houses scattered throughout the region are an affordable alternative. For information, contact the tourist office of Granada or **Rustic Blue** (✉ Barrio de la Ermita, Bubión ☎ 958/763381 ⊕ www.rusticblue.com), which also organizes walking and riding excursions.

$ ✕⊡ **Taray.** This hotel has its own farm and makes a perfect base for exploring the Alpujarras. Public areas and guest rooms are in a low, typical Alpujarran building. The sunny quarters are decorated with Alpujarran handwoven bedspreads and curtains; three rooms have rooftop terraces, and there's a pleasant common terrace. Most of the restaurant's food comes from the estate, including trout and lamb; in season, you can even pick your own raspberries or oranges for breakfast. ✉ *Ctra. Tablate–Albuñol, Km 18, Órgiva 18400* ☎ *958/784525* 📠 *958/784531* ⊕ *www.turgranada.com/hoteltaray* ⤴ *15 rooms* ⚘ *Restaurant, cafeteria, cable TV, pool* ▤ *AE, DC, MC, V.*

¢–$ ✕⊡ **La Fragua.** Spotless rooms with baths (and some with balconies), fresh air, and views over the rooftops of Trevélez to the valley beyond are the perks at this small, friendly hotel in a typical village house behind the town hall. The restaurant is in a separate house up the street, serving regional dishes such as *arroz liberal* (hunter's rice with sausage and salami), *lomo a los aromas de la sierra* (pork loin with herbs), and *choto al ajillo* (piglet meat in garlic sauce). ✉ *San Antonio 4, Barrio Medio, Trevélez 18417* ☎ *958/858626* 📠 *958/858614* ⤴ *14 rooms* ⚘ *Restaurant* ▤ *MC, V* ⊙ *Closed Mid-Jan.–mid-Feb.*

$–$$ ⊡ **Alquería de Morayma.** Close to the banks of the Guadalfeo River and on many different levels, all of the buildings in this complex have been remodeled in the old Alpujarreño style, including some rooms that are in an old chapel. Look, also, for an old bodega, an oversize gameboard on the terrace, and the nearby home farm. This is really a charming hotel. ✉ *Cádiar, 18440* 📠📠 *958/343221* ⤴ *13 rooms, 5 apartments* ⚘ *Restaurant, pool, library, free parking* ▤ *MC, V.*

Guadix

㉓ *47 km (30 mi) east of Granada on A92.*

Guadix was an important mining town as far back as 2,000 years ago and has its fair share of monuments, including a cathedral (built

1594–1706) and a 9th-century Moorish *alcazaba* (citadel). But Guadix and the neighboring village of Purullena are best known for their cave communities. Around 2,000 caves were carved out of the soft, sandstone mountains, and most are still inhabited. Far from being troglodytic holes in the wall, they are well furnished and comfortable, with a pleasant year-round temperature; a few serve as hotels. Follow signs to the **Cueva Museo,** a small cave museum in Guadix's cave district. Toward the town center, the **Cueva la Alcazaba** has a ceramics workshop. A number of private caves have signs welcoming you to inspect the premises, though a tip is expected if you do. Purullena, 6 km (4 mi) from Guadix, is also known for ceramics.

Where to Stay & Eat

$–$$ ✗▥ **Comercio.** In the historic center of Guadix is this enchanting little family-run hotel. Rooms in the 1905 building have dark-wood classic furniture, modern bathrooms, and, except for the few that are carpeted, marble floors. The public areas include an art gallery, a jazz concert room, and the best restaurant in Guadix, with such local specialties as roast lamb with raisins and pine nuts. ⊠ *C. Mira de Amezcua 3, 18500* ☎ *958/660500* 📠 *958/665072* ⊕ *www.hotelcomercio.com* ⬐ *23 rooms* ₰ *Restaurant, cafeteria, free parking* ▤ *AE, DC, MC, V.*

$$ ▥ **Cuevas Pedro Antonio de Alarcón.** If you're looking for a so-called authentic experience, consider staying in a cave. In a "suburb" outside Guadix, this unique lodging comprises 19 adjoining caves and one suite. Each cave sleeps two to five and has a kitchenette; the honeymoon cave has a whirlpool bath. The whitewashed walls and polished clay-tile floors are decorated with charming Granadian crafts and colorful rugs; handwoven Alpujarran tapestries serve as doors between the rooms. The restaurant, also subterranean, serves regional dishes. ⊠ *Barriada San Torcuato, 18500* ☎ *958/664986* 📠 *958/661721* ⬐ *19 rooms, 1 suite* ₰ *Restaurant, some in-room hot tubs, kitchenettes, cable TV, pool; no a/c* ▤ *AE, MC, V.*

JAÉN & EASTERN JAÉN PROVINCE

Jaén is dominated by its alcázar. To the northeast are the historic, olive-producing twin towns of Baeza and Úbeda. Cazorla, the gateway to the Parque Natural Sierra de Cazorla Segura y Las Villas, lies beyond.

Jaén

㉔ *93 km (58 mi) north of Granada.*

Nestled in the foothills of the Sierra de Jabalcuz, Jaén is surrounded by towering peaks and olive-clad hills. The Arabs called it Geen (Route of the Caravans) because it formed a crossroad between Castile and Andalusia. Captured from the Moors by Saint King Ferdinand III in 1246, Jaén became a frontier province, the site of many a skirmish and battle over the next 200 years between the Moors of Granada and Christians from the north and west. Today the province earns a living from its lead and silver mines and endless olive groves.

★ The **Castillo de Santa Catalina,** perched on a rocky crag 400 yards above the center of town, is Jaén's star monument. The castle may have originated as a tower built by Hannibal; the site was fortified continuously over the centuries. The Nasrid king Alhamar, builder of Granada's Alhambra, constructed an alcázar here, but King Ferdinand III captured it from him in 1246 on the feast day of Santa Catalina (St. Catherine). Catalina consequently became Jaén's patron saint, so when the Christians built a castle and chapel here, they dedicated both to her. ⊠ *Castillo de Santa Catalina* ☎ *953/120733* ⊠ *€3* ⊙ *Thurs.–Tues. 10–2 and 4:30–7 in summer, Thurs.–Tues. 10–2 and 3:30–6 in winter.*

Jaén's **cathedral** is a hulk that looms above the modest buildings around it. Begun in 1492 on the site of a former mosque, it took almost 300 years to build; its chief architect was Andrés de Vandelvira (1509–75), many more of whose buildings can be seen in Úbeda and Baeza. The ornate facade was sculpted by Pedro Roldán, and the figures on top of the columns include San Fernando (King Ferdinand III) surrounded by the four evangelists. The cathedral's most treasured relic is the **Santo Rostro** (Holy Face), the cloth with which, according to tradition, St. Veronica cleansed Christ's face on the way to Calvary, leaving his image imprinted on the fabric. The rostro is displayed every Friday. In the underground **museum,** look for the *Immaculate Conception,* by Alonso Cano; *San Lorenzo,* by Martínez Montañés; and a Calvary scene by Jácobo Florentino. ⊠ *Pl. Santa María* ⊠ *Cathedral free, museum €3* ⊙ *Cathedral Mon.–Sat. 8:30–1 and 5–8, Sun. 9–1 and 6–8; museum Tues.–Sat. 10–1 and 5–8.*

Explore the narrow alleys of old Jaén as you walk from the cathedral to the **Baños Árabes** (Arab Baths), which once belonged to Ali, a Moorish king of Jaén, and probably date from the 11th century. Four hundred years later, in 1592, Fernando de Torres y Portugal, a viceroy of Peru, built himself a mansion, the **Palacio de Villardompardo,** right over the baths, so it took years of painstaking excavation to restore them to their original form. The palace contains a small museum of folk crafts and a larger museum devoted to native art. There are guided tours of the baths, one of the largest and best conserved in Spain, every 30 minutes. ⊠ *Palacio de Villardompardo, Pl. Luisa de Marillac* ☎ *953/ 248068* ⊠ *Free (bring ID or passport)* ⊙ *Tues.–Fri. 9–8, weekends 9:30–2:30.*

Jaén's **Museo Provincial** has one of the best collections of Iberian (pre-Roman) artifacts in Spain. The newest wing has 20 life-size Iberian sculptures discovered by chance near the village of Porcuna in 1975. The museum proper is in a 1547 mansion, on a patio with the facade of the erstwhile Church of San Miguel. The fine-arts section has a roomful of Goya lithographs. ⊠ *Paseo de la Estación 29* ☎ *953/250600* ⊠ *€1.50, EU citizens free* ⊙ *Sun. 9–2:30; Wed.–Sat. 9–8:30, except Tues. 3–8 and 2:30–8:30.*

Where to Stay & Eat

$$$ ✕ **Casa Antonio.** Exquisite Andalusian food is served at this somber and elegant restaurant with three small dining rooms—all with cherrywood-

11

panel walls, dark plywood floors, and a few modern-art paintings on display. Try the *foie y queso en milhojas de manzana verde caramelizada en aceite de pistacho* (liver and cheese with green apples caramelized in pistachio oil in a pastry puff) or *salmonetes de roca en caldo tibio de molusco y aceite de vainilla* (red mullet in a warm mollusk broth and vanilla oil). ⊠ *Fermín Palma 3* ☎ *953/270262* ⊟ *AE, MC, V* ⊘ *Closed Aug. and Mon. No dinner Sun.*

$$ ✕ **Casa Vicente.** Locals typically pack this popular family-run restaurant around the corner from the cathedral square. You can have drinks and tapas in the colorful tavern, then move on to the cozy courtyard dining room. The traditional Jaén dishes—game casseroles, Jaén-style spinach, and *cordero Mozárabe* (Mozarab-style roast lamb with a sweet-and-sour sauce)—are especially good. ⊠ *Francisco Martín Mora 1* ☎ *953/232222 or 953/232816* ⊟ *AE, MC, V* ⊘ *No dinner Sun.*

$$$ ▦ **Parador de Jaén.** Built amid the mountaintop towers of the Castillo
Fodor'sChoice de Santa Catalina, this is one of the showpieces of the parador chain
★ and a reason in itself to visit Jaén. The parador's grandiose exterior echoes the castle next door, as do the lofty ceilings, tapestries, baronial shields, and suits of armor inside. Comfortable bedrooms, with canopy beds, have balconies overlooking fields stretching toward a dramatic mountain backdrop. ⊠ *Castillo de Santa Catalina, 23001* ☎ *953/230000* ⊞ *953/230930* ⊕ *www.parador.es* ⇘ *45 rooms* ⏃ *Restaurant, minibars, cable TV, in-room data ports, pool* ⊟ *AE, DC, MC, V.*

Alcalá la Real

㉕ *75 km (46.5 mi) south of Jaén on N432 and A316.*

This ancient city, known to the Iberians and Romans, grew to prominence under the Moors who ruled here for more than 600 years. And it was they who gave it the first part of its name, Alcalá, which originated from a word meaning "fortified settlement." The **Fortaleza de la Mota.** as it's known today, was started by the Moors in 727 and sits imperiously at an elevation of 3,389 feet, dominating not only the town but the whole area for miles around. From here, you can see spectacular views of the towering peaks of the Sierra Nevada on the southern horizon.

During the 12th century the city changed hands frequently as the Moors fought to keep their control of the area. Finally, in 1341 Alfonso XI reconquered the town for good, adding Real (Royal) to its name. It remained of strategic importance until the Catholic Monarchs finally reconquered Granada—indeed, it was from here that they rode out to accept the keys of the city and the surrender. Hundreds of years later, the French forces left the town in ruins after their retreat in the early 19th century.

The town itself was gradually rebuilt, but the fortress, consisting of the alcazaba (citadel) and the Abbey church that Alfonso XI built, were more or less ignored. Up until the late 1990s, it was possible just to drive up and look around—exposed skeletons were visible in some open tombs on the floor of the church. These days, things are more organized. After you buy a ticket, you face a long, uphill climb to the complex, which also has a small archaeology museum. ☎ *639/647796* 🖼 *€1.50* 🕐 *July–Sept. 10:30–1:30 and 5–8; Oct.–June 10:30–1:30 and 3:30–6:30.*

Where to Stay

$ 🖼 **Don Pedro.** There are few hotels in Alcalá la Real, and the parking situation is atrocious, so it's probably a good idea to travel about 15 mi south to Granada to this very pleasant roadside hotel. The rooms, with terraces and views of olive groves and mountains, are pleasantly furnished; the restaurant's specialty is Mediterranean cuisine. ☒ *Av. de Andalucía s/n, Puerto Lope, 18249* ☎ *958/418137* 🖼 *958/418192* 🛏 *16 rooms ⌂ Restaurant, cafeteria, bar, free parking* ☰ *MC, V.*

Baeza

26 *48 km (30 mi) northeast of Jaén on N321.*

Fodor'sChoice
★

The historic town of Baeza is nestled between hills and olive groves. Founded by the Romans, it later housed the Visigoths and became the capital of a *taifa* (kingdom) under the Moors. The Saint King Ferdinand III captured Baeza in 1227, and for the next 200 years it stood on the frontier of the Moorish kingdom of Granada. In the 16th and 17th centuries, local nobles gave the city a wealth of Renaissance palaces. The **Casa del Pópulo,** in the central paseo—where the Plaza del Pópulo (or Plaza de los Leones) and Plaza de la Constitución (or Plaza del Mercado Viejo) merge to form a delightful cobblestone square—is a beautiful structure from around 1530. The first Mass of the Reconquest was supposedly celebrated on its curved balcony, and it now houses Baeza's tourist office. In the center of the town square is an ancient Iberian-Roman statue thought to depict Imilce, wife of Hannibal; at the foot of her column is the **Fuente de los Leones** (Fountain of the Lions).

To find Baeza's **university,** follow the steps on the south side of the Plaza del Pópulo. The college opened in 1542, closed in 1824, and later became a high school in which the poet Antonio Machado taught French from 1912 to 1919. The building now functions as a cultural center (a new school has been built next door). You can visit Machado's classroom—request the key—and the patio. ☒ *Beato Juan de Ávila s/n* ☎ *953/740154* 🕐 *Thurs.–Tues. 10–2 and 4–6.*

Baeza's **cathedral** was originally begun by Ferdinand III on the site of a former mosque. The structure was largely rebuilt by Andrés de Vandelvira, architect of Jaén's cathedral, between 1570 and 1593, though the west front has architectural influences from an earlier period. A fine 14th-century rose window crowns the 13th-century Puerta de la Luna (Moon Door). Don't miss the baroque silver monstrance (a vessel in which the consecrated Host is exposed for the adoration of the faithful), which is carried in Baeza's Corpus Christi processions—the piece is kept in a concealed niche behind a painting, but you can see it in all its splendor by putting a coin in a slot to reveal the hiding place (money well spent). Next to the monstrance is the entrance to the clock tower, where a small donation and a narrow spiral staircase take you to one of the best views of Baeza. The remains of the original mosque are in the cathedral's Gothic cloisters. Entrance to the cloister and small museum is €2. ☒ *Pl. de Santa*

María ☎ *953/744157* ☼ *Summer, daily 10–1 and 5–7; winter, 10:30–1 and 4–6.*

Plaza de Santa María. The main square of the medieval city is surrounded by not just the cathedral but also other palaces. The highlight is the fountain of the same name, built in 1564 and resembling a triumphal arch.

Iglesia de Santa Cruz. This rather small and quite plain church dates from the early 13th century. Not only was it one of the first built here after the Reconquest, but it's also one of the earliest Christian churches in all of Andalusia. It has two Romanesque portals and a curved stone altar. ⊠ *Plaza de Santa Cruz* ☼ *Mon.–Sat. 11–1 and 4–5:30, Sun. noon–2.*

Casa Museo de Vera Cruz. Found immediately behind the Santa Cruz church, and housed in a building dating from 1540, this museum has religious artifacts from the 16th, 17th, 18th, and 19th centuries. There's also a small shop selling local products. ⊠ *Plaza de Santa Cruz* 🎫 €1 ☼ *Daily 11–1 and 4–6.*

Palacio de Jabalquinto. Built between the 15th and 16th centuries by Juan Alfonso de Benavides as a palatial home, this palace has a flamboyant Gothic facade and a charming marble colonnaded Renaissance patio. It's a perfect example of how the old can be retained and incorporated into the new. ⊠ *Plaza de Santa Cruz* ☼ *Weekdays 9–2.*

The ancient student custom of inscribing names and graduation dates in bull's blood (as in Salamanca) is still evident on the walls of the seminary of **San Felipe Neri** (⊠ Cuesta de San Felipe), built in 1660. It's opposite Baeza's cathedral. Baeza's **ayuntamiento** (Town hall; ⊠ Pl. Cardenal Benavides, just north of Pl. del Pópulo) was designed by cathedral master Andrés de Vandelvira. The facade is ornately plateresque; look between the balconies for the coats of arms of Felipe II, the city of Baeza, and the magistrate Juan de Borja. Arrange for a visit to the *salón de plenos,* a major hall with painted, carved woodwork. The 16th-century **Convento de San Francisco** (⊠ C. de San Francisco) is one of Vandelvira's architectural religious masterpieces. You can see its restored remains—the building was spoiled by the French army and partially destroyed by a light earthquake in the beginning of the 19th century. It's a few blocks west of the ayuntamiento.

Where to Stay & Eat

$$–$$$ ✕ **Vandelvira.** Seldom do you have the chance to eat in a 16th-century convent. The restaurant, within two galleries on the first floor of the Convento de San Francisco, has lots of character and magnificent antiques. Specialties include the *paté de perdiz con aceite de oliva virgen* (partridge paté with olive oil) and the *manitas de cerdo rellenas de perdiz y espinacas* (pig's knuckles filled with partridge and spinach). It has a summer terrace that doubles as a tavern and night bar. ⊠ C. *de San Francisco 14* ☎ *953/748172* 🖃 *MC, V* ☼ *Closed Mon. No dinner Sun.*

$–$$ ✕🖫 **Juanito.** Rooms in this small, unpretentious hotel are simple and comfortable. The restaurant's proprietor is a champion of Andalusian food, and the chef has revived such regional specialties as *alcachofas*

Luisa (braised artichokes), *ensalada de perdiz* (partridge salad), and *cordero con habas* (lamb and broad beans); desserts are based on old Moorish recipes. The hotel is next to a gas station on the edge of town, toward Úbeda. ✉ *Paseo Arca del Agua, 23440* ☎ *953/740040* ⊜ *953/ 742324* ⊕ *www.juanitobaeza.com* ⇨ *36 rooms, 1 suite* ⚭ *Restaurant, tennis court, pool, soccer* ☰ *MC, V* ☉ *No dinner Sun. and Mon.*

$$ 🏨 **Hospedería Fuentenueva.** It's hard to believe, but this small, charming hotel was once a women's prison. The interior has undergone a sophisticated overhaul: colors are harmonious and warm, and there's stenciling on salmon-color walls. Floors are marble, furnishings modern, and there's a bubbling fountain in the interior patio. The result is an upbeat, contemporary look. There are also regular art exhibitions here. ✉ *Carmen, 15 23440* ☎ *953/743100* ⊜ *953/743200* ⊕ *www. fuentenueva.com* ⇨ *12 rooms* ⚭ *Restaurant, cafeteria, cable TV, in-room data ports, pool* ☰ *AE, MC, V.*

¢ 🏨 **El Patio.** Considering the setting—the former 16th-century palace of the Marqués Cuentacilla—you're getting a rather good deal here. The place is comfortable and homey, and several generations of the owner's family are often around. Basic rooms are set around a vast central patio interspersed with original columns and filled with overstuffed, heavily brocaded furniture. The location—on a cobblestone side street leading to an old church—is wonderfully quiet and reasonably central to shops and restaurants. ✉ *C. Conde Romanones 13, 23440* ☎ *953/740200* ⇨ *12 rooms* ☰ *MC, V.*

Úbeda

㉗ *9 km (5½ mi) northeast of Baeza on N321.*

Fodor'sChoice
★

Úbeda is in the heart of Jaén's olive groves, and olive oil is indeed the main concern here. Although this modern town of 30,000 is relatively dull (it has a reputation as being a serious, religious place), the *casco antiguo* (old town) is one of the most outstanding enclaves of 16th-century architecture in Spain. Follow signs to the *Zona Monumental* (Monumental Zone), where there are countless Renaissance palaces and stately mansions, most closed to the public. The Plaza del Ayuntamiento is crowned by the privately owned **Palacio de Vela de los Cobos.** It was designed by Andrés de Vandelvira (1505–75), a key figure in the Spanish Renaissance era for Úbeda's magistrate, Francisco de Vela de los Cobos. The corner balcony has a central white-marble column that's echoed in the gallery above.

Vandelvira's 16th-century Palacio Juan Vázquez de Molina is better known by its nickname, the **Palacio de las Cadenas** (House of Chains), because decorative iron chains were once affixed to the columns of its main doorway. It's now the town hall and has entrances on both Plaza Vázquez de Molina and Plaza Ayuntamiento. Molina was a nephew of Francisco de los Cobos, and both served as secretary to the emperors Carlos V and Felipe II.

The Plaza Vázquez de Molina, in the heart of the old town, is the site of the **Sacra Capilla del Salvador.** This building is photographed so often that it has become the city's unofficial symbol. Sacra Capilla was built by Vandelvira, but he based his design on some 1536 plans by Diego de Siloé, architect of Granada's cathedral. Considered one of the masterpieces of Spanish Renaissance religious art, the chapel was sacked in the frenzy of church burnings at the outbreak of the civil war. However, it retains its ornate west front and altarpiece, which has a rare Berruguete sculpture. ⊠ *Pl. Vázquez de Molina* ☎ *953/758150* 🖾 *€2.25* ⊘ *Mon.–Sat. 10–2 and 4:30–7, Sun. 10:45–2 and 4:30–7.*

The **Ayuntamiento Antiguo** (Old Town Hall), begun in the early 16th century but restored as a beautiful arcaded baroque palace in 1680, is now a conservatory of music. From the hall's upper balcony, the town council watched celebrations and autos-da-fé ("acts of faith"—executions of heretics sentenced by the Inquisition) in the square below. On the north side is the 13th-century church of San Pablo, with an Isabelline south portal. ⊠ *Pl. Primero de Mayo, off C. María de Molina* ⊘ *1-hr tour 7–8 PM.*

The **Hospital de Santiago,** sometimes jokingly called the Escorial of Andalusia, is a huge, angular building in the modern section, and yet another one of Andrés de Vandelvira's masterpieces in Úbeda. The plain facade is adorned with ceramic medallions, and over the main entrance is a carving of Santiago Matamoros (St. James the Moorslayer) in his traditional horseback pose. Inside are an arcaded patio and a grand staircase. Now a cultural center, it holds some of the events at the annual International Spring Dance and Music Festival that takes place in May and June. ⊠ *Av. Cristo Rey* ☎ *953/750842* ⊘ *Daily 8–3 and 4–10.*

Museo Agrícola. Found within the Barbacoa restaurant, this curious museum exhibits more than 4,000 agricultural items from the area. ⊠ *San Cristóbal 17* ☎ *953/790473* 🖾 *Free* ⊘ *Tues.–Thurs. 5–10 PM, Fri.–Sat. 5–11 PM.*

Where to Stay & Eat

¢–$ ✕ **Libra.** A very pleasant and comfortable combination of cafeteria, pub, and bar, Libra is on a busy plaza on the edge of the older part of town. Combination plates consist of *huevos fritos, calamares, y patatas fritas* (fried eggs, squid, and french fries) and *bacon, huevos fritos, patatas fritas, y asadillo* (bacon, fried eggs, french fries, and red peppers) as well as a tempting selection of sandwiches. ⊠ *Plaza Andalucía 3–5* ☎ *953/757480* ▭ *MC, V.*

$$–$$$ ✕▥ **Parador de Úbeda.** This splendid parador is in a 16th-century ducal
Fodor'sChoice   palace on the Plaza Vázquez de Molina, next to the Capilla del Salvador.
★   A grand stairway, decked with tapestries and suits of armor, leads up to the guest rooms, which have tile floors, lofty wood ceilings, dark Castilian-style furniture, and large bathtubs. The dining room, specializing in regional dishes, serves perhaps the best food in Úbeda; try one of the *perdiz* (partridge) entrées. There's a bar in the vaulted basement. ⊠ *Pl. Vázquez de Molina s/n, 23400* ☎ *953/750345* 🖾 *953/751259* ⊕ *www. parador.es* ⇆ *35 rooms, 1 suite* ᏸ *Restaurant, minibars, cable TV, bar* ▭ *AE, DC, MC, V.*

$$$ ▥ **Palacio de la Rambla.** In old Úbeda, the wonderfully beautiful 16th-century mansion has been in the same family since it was built, and part

of it still hosts the regal Marquesa de la Rambla when she's in town. Eight of the rooms are open to overnighters; each is unique, but all are large and furnished with original antiques, tapestries, and works of art; some have chandeliers. The palace is arranged on two levels, around a cool, ivy-covered patio. ✉ *Pl. del Marqués 1, 23400* ☎ *953/750196* 🖷 *953/750267* ✑ *palaciorambla@terra.es* ➷ *7 rooms, 1 suite* ₰ *Minibars, cable TV, parking (fee)* ▤ *AE, MC, V.*

$$ 🏨 **María de Molina.** In the heart of the Monumental Zone (Zona Monumental), this hotel is in a large town house formerly known as La Casa de los Curas (The Priests' House), because it once housed two priests who were twins. Each room is different, but all are done in warm pastels and elegant Andalusian furnishings; some have balconies. Rooms 204–207 have the best views over the town's rooftops. The rates go up on weekends and holidays. ✉ *Pl. del Ayuntamiento s/n, 23400* ☎ *953/795356* 🖷 *953/793694* ⊕ *www.hotel-maria-de-molina.com* ➷ *27 rooms* ₰ *Cafeteria, cable TV, bar, meeting room* ▤ *AE, DC, MC, V.*

$$ 🏨 **Rosaleda de Don Pedro.** This beautiful 16th-century mansion, in the city's Monumental Zone (Zona Monumental), blends the best of the old with all the comforts a modern traveler would expect. The rooms and public areas are spacious, and the pool offers relief from the summer heat. A unique feature is its parking facility—you drive your car into an elevator to be taken down to the car park. ✉ *Obispo Toral 2, 23400* ☎ *953/795147* 🖷 *953/795149* ⊕ *www.rosaledadedonpedro.com* ➷ *30* ₰ *Restaurant, cafeteria, pool, bar, Internet room, free parking* ▤ *AE, DC, MC, V.*

$–$$ 🏨 **Hospedería El Blanquillo.** This hotel is in a small palace from the 16th century, and it's close to the walls and the Hospital Salvador. The simply furnished rooms surround a central patio. The restaurant's specialty is Mediterranean cuisine. ✉ *Plaza del Carmen 1, 23400* ☎ *953/795405* 🖷 *953/795406* ➷ *16 rooms, 1 suite* ₰ *Restaurant, bar, laundry facilities* ▤ *MC, V.*

Shopping

Little Úbeda is the crafts capital of Andalusia, with workshops devoted to carpentry, basket weaving, stone carving, wrought iron, stained glass, and, above all, the city's distinctive green-glaze pottery. Calle Valencia is the traditional potters' row, running from the bottom of town to Úbeda's general crafts center, northwest of the old quarter (follow signs to Calle Valencia or Barrio de Alfareros). Úbeda's most famous potter was Pablo Tito, whose craft is carried on at three different workshops run by two of Tito's sons (Paco and Juan) and a son-in-law, Melchor, each of whom claims to be the sole true heir to the art. The extrovert **Juan Tito** (✉ Pl. del Ayuntamiento 12 ☎ 953/751302) can often be found at the potter's wheel in his rambling shop, which is packed with ceramics of every size and shape. **Paco Tito** (✉ C. Valencia 22 ☎ 953/751496) devotes himself to clay sculptures of characters from *Don Quixote*, which he fires in an old Moorish-style kiln. His shop has a small museum as well as a studio. **Melchor Tito** (✉ C. Valencia 44 ☎ 953/753365) focuses on classic green-glaze items. **Antonio Almazara** (✉ Valencia 34 ☎ 953/753692 ✉ Fuenteseca 17

☎ 953/753365) is one of several shops specializing in Úbeda's green-glaze pottery. All kinds of ceramics are sold at **Alfarería Góngora** (✉ Cuesta de la Merced 32 ☎ 953/754605). For handmade esparto-grass ware, such as rugs, mats, and baskets, go to **Artesanía Blanco** (✉ Real 47 ☎ 953/750456), supplied by its own local factory.

Cazorla

28 *48 km (35 mi) southeast of Úbeda.*

Unspoiled and remote, the Andalusian village of Cazorla is at the east end of the province of Jaén. The pine-clad slopes and towering peaks of the Cazorla and Segura sierras rise above the village, and below it stretch endless miles of olive groves. In spring, purple jacaranda trees blossom in the plazas. For a break from human-made sights, drink in the scenery or watch for wildlife in the ☾ **Parque Natural Sierra de Cazorla, Segura y Las Villas** (Cazorla, Segura and Las Villas Nature Park). Try to avoid the summer and late spring months, when the park teems with tourists and locals. It's almost impossible to get accommodations in fall, particularly when it's deer rutting season (September and October). For information on hiking, camping, canoeing, horseback riding, or going on guided excursions, contact **Agencia de Medio Ambiente** (✉ Tejares Altos ☎ 953/720125) in Cazorla or in **Jaén** (✉ Fuente de Serbo 3 ☎ 953/012400), or the park visitor center. For hunting or fishing permits, apply to the Jaén office well in advance. Deer, wild boar, and mountain goats roam the slopes of this carefully protected patch of mountain wilderness 80 km (50 mi) long and 30 km (19 mi) wide, and hawks, eagles, and vultures soar over the 6,000-foot peaks. Within the park, at **Cañada de las Fuentes** (Fountains' Ravine), is the source of Andalusia's great river, the Guadalquivir. The road through the park follows the river to the shores of **Lago Tranco de Beas.** Alpine meadows, pine forests, springs, waterfalls, and gorges make Cazorla a perfect place to hike. A short film shown in the **Centro de Interpretación Torre del Vinagre** (✉ Ctra. del Tranco, Km 37.8 ☎ 953/713040 ☉ Daily 11–2 and 4–6), in Torre de Vinagre, introduces the park's main sights; displays explain the park's plants and geology; and the staff can advise you on camping, fishing, and hiking trails. There's also a **hunting museum,** with such cheerful attractions as the interlocked antlers of bucks who clashed in autumn rutting season, became helplessly trapped, and died of starvation. Nearby are a **botanical garden** and a **game reserve.** Between June and October the park maintains seven well-equipped **campsites.** Past Lago Tranco and the village of Hornos, a road goes to the **Sierra de Segura** mountain range, the park's least crowded area. At 3,600 feet, the spectacular village of **Segura de la Sierra,** on top of the mountain, is crowned by an almost perfect castle with impressive defense walls, a Moorish bath, and an almost rectangular bullring.

Déjate Guiar-Excursiones organizes four-wheel-drive trips into restricted areas of the park to observe the flora and fauna and photograph the larger animals. ✉ *Paseo del Santo Cristo 17, Bajo, Edificio Parque, Cazorla* ☎ *953/721351* ⊕ *www.turisnat.org.*

**EN
ROUTE**

Leave Cazorla Nature Park by an alternative route—the spectacular **gorge** carved by the Guadalquivir River, a rushing torrent beloved by kayak enthusiasts. At the El Tranco dam, follow signs to Villanueva del Arzobispo, where N322 takes you back to Úbeda, Baeza, and Jaén.

Where to Stay & Eat

$$–$$$ ✕☷ **Parador de Cazorla.** Isolated in a valley at the edge of the nature reserve, 26 km (16 mi) above Cazorla village, lies this white, modern parador with red-tile roof. It's a quiet place, popular with hunters and anglers. The restaurant serves regional dishes such as *pipirrana* (a salad of finely diced peppers, onions, and tomatoes) and, in season, game. ⊠ *Sierra de Cazorla, 23470* ☎ *953/727075* 🖷 *953/727077* ⊕ *www. parador.es* 🖃*33 rooms* ⌕ *Restaurant, cable TV, pool, free parking* ▭ *AE, DC, MC, V* ☉ *Closed Dec. and Jan.*

$$ ✕☷ **Villa Turística de Cazorla.** On a hill with superb views of the village of Cazorla, this leisure complex rents semidetached apartments sleeping one to six. Each has a balcony or terrace as well as a kitchenette—some have a full kitchen—and fireplace. The restaurant, done in welcoming warm ocher tones, specializes in trout, lamb, and game. ⊠ *Ladera de San Isicio s/n, Cazorla 23470* ☎*953/710100* 🖷*953/710152* ⊕*www.villacazorla.com* 🖃*32 units* ⌕ *Restaurant, cafeteria, kitchenettes, pool, bar, meeting rooms* ▭ *MC, V.*

$ ✕☷ **La Hortizuela.** Deep in the heart of Cazorla Nature Park, in what was once a game warden's house, is a small hotel that's the perfect base for exploring the wilderness. Guest rooms are in the back, beyond the central courtyard, and most have unhindered views of the forest-clad mountainside (a few look onto the patio). Wild boar, game, deer, and fresh trout are usually available in the restaurant. ⊠ *Ctra. del Tranco, Km 50.5, 2 km (1 mi) east of visitor center up dirt track, Coto Ríos 23478* ☎🖷 *953/713150* ⊕ *www.lahortizuela.com* 🖃 *23 rooms* ⌕ *Restaurant, cafeteria, pool, free parking* ▭ *MC, V* ⑩ *CP.*

$$ ☷ **Coto del Valle.** This delightful new hotel in Cazorla's foothills is easily recognized by the huge fountain outside. The hotel, with traditional stone-style architecture, offers rooms with a mountain decor and a restaurant with a huge fireplace and stuffed animals. ⊠ *Ctra. del Tranco, Km 34.3, 23470* ☎ *953/124067* ⊕ *www.hotelcotodelvalle.com* 🖃 *59 rooms* ⌕ *Restaurant, cafeteria, pool, bar, shop, free parking* ▭ *AE, DC, MC, V.*

$–$$ ☷ **Casa Rural La Calerilla.** Tucked into the mountainside, on the road leading down to Cazorla away from the valley and almost hidden from the road itself, is this rather charming and new stone-designed casa rural. The rooms are bright with a traditional decor, and the garden and pool area is a great place to wind down. ⊠ *Ctra. de la Sierra, Km 24.5, Burunchel, 23479* ☎*953/727326* 🖷*953/727034* ⊕*www.casaruralcalerilla. com* 🖃 *11 rooms* ⌕ *Restaurant, cafeteria, pool, bar, free parking* ▭ *MC, V.*

CÓRDOBA & ENVIRONS

Córdoba has one of Spain's most spectacular monuments, the Moorish Mezquita (mosque), which dates from the 8th through the 10th century.

11

The city's old quarters, particularly the old Jewish Quarter, invite quiet exploration: you wander through narrow, ancient alleys past plant-filled tiled patios, and visit the only synagogue in Andalusia to survive the expulsion of the Jews in 1492. If you have time to go beyond Córdoba, head west to the ruins of Medina Azahara, site of a once-magnificent palace complex, or south to the wine country around Montilla and the Subbética region, a cluster of small towns virtually unknown to travelers.

Córdoba

29–**47** *166 km (103 mi) northwest of Granada, 407 km (250 mi) southwest of Madrid.*

On the north bank of the Guadalquivir, Córdoba is integral to the cultural history of the Iberian Peninsula. It was both the Roman and Moorish capital of Spain, and its old quarter, clustered around its famous mosque (Mezquita), remains one of the country's grandest and yet most intimate examples of its Moorish heritage. The Romans invaded in 206 BC, later making it the capital of its section of Spain. Nearly 800 years later, the Visigoth king Leovigildus took control. The tribe was soon supplanted by the Moors, whose emirs and caliphs of the West held court here from the 8th century to the early 11th century. At that point Córdoba was one of the greatest centers of art, culture, and learning in the Western world; one of its libraries had more than 400,000 volumes, a staggering number at the time. Moors, Christians, and Jews lived together in harmony within its walls. Chroniclers of the day put the city's population at around a million, making it the largest city in Europe, though historians believe the real figure was closer to half a million (there are fewer than 300,000 today). In that era, it was considered second in importance behind only Constantinople. However, in 1009 Prince Muhammad II and Omeyan led a rebellion that broke up the Caliphate, leading to power flowing to separate Moorish kingdoms.

Córdoba remained in Moorish hands until it was conquered by King Ferdinand in 1236 and repopulated with people from the north of Spain. Later the Catholic Monarchs used the city as a base from which to plan the conquest of Granada. In Columbus's time, the Guadalquivir was navigable as far upstream as Córdoba, and great galleons sailed its waters. Today, the river's muddy water and marshy banks evoke little of Córdoba's glorious past, but the city's bridge—of Roman origin, though much restored by the Arabs and successive generations—and an old Arab waterwheel recall a far grander era.

Córdoba is a very manageable city to explore. It spans out from the mosque and the Judería. North of this pair, and emerging from Plaza de las Tendillas, is the commercial center of the city. To the east of the Judería, following the river, is the San Basilio neighborhood. Its farthest edge is encircled by Avenida del Corregidor, which flows into the Jardínes de la Victoria, the large park that borders the city to the east. The park ends on Avenida de América, which cuts diagonally through the city. Avenida de América leads into Avenida del Brillante, which heads north and gives its name to the neighborhood on the hills overlooking the city.

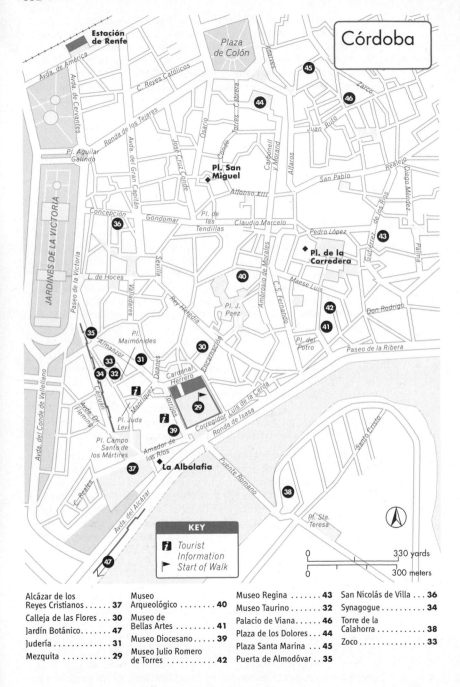

Córdoba

KEY

🛈 Tourist Information

▶ Start of Walk

0 _____ 330 yards
0 _____ 300 meters

Across the river and opposite the mosque is the neighborhood Campo de la Verdad. Out of the old part of the city, locals (and taxi drivers) unofficially name neighborhoods based on a major or representative church of the area.

┌─
**A GOOD
WALK**

Begin on Cardenal Herrero, at the **Mezquita** ㉙ ☞. Facing the western side of the mosque, in the sacristy of a former hospital on Calle Torrijos, is the regional tourist office. Walk up Calle Velázquez Bosco to a tiny alleyway known as **Calleja de las Flores** ㉚. Come back to Cardenal Herrero and enter the **Judería** ㉛. Go up Calle Judería and continue along Calle Albucasis past the Plaza Juda Levi. Just around the corner, in the Plaza Maimónides, is Córdoba's **Museo Taurino** ㉜. Leading northwest from here, Calle Judíos goes past the tiny Plaza Tiberiades and the statue of Maimónides, the 12th-century Jewish doctor and philosopher. Continue along Calle Judíos to the **Zoco** ㉝ on the right, and go through the arch to the courtyard, where a former Arab souk (market) houses working artisans by day and flamenco on summer evenings. A bit farther up Calle Judíos, on the left, is Córdoba's **synagogue** ㉞. The **Puerta de Almodóvar** ㉟ marks the western limit of the Judería.

From the Puerta de Almodóvar, you can go north to **San Nicolás de Villa** ㊱, a church with Islamic decoration, or instead, travel down Cairuán along a restored section of Córdoba's Moorish walls past the statue of 12th-century Moorish philosopher Averröes (another prominent Córdoban) to the Plaza Campo Santo de los Mártires. On the far side of the square is the **Alcázar de los Reyes Cristianos** ㊲. From Plaza Campo Santo, you can hire a *coche caballo* (horse and buggy) for a city tour (€30 for a 45-minute ride) and head back to the shops on Deanes and Cardenal Herrero by way of Manríquez and Plaza Juda Levi; or walk back along Amador de los Ríos to the bottom of Torrijos, turn down past the Puerta del Puente (Gate of the Bridge), and cross the Puente Romano (Roman Bridge), whose 16 arches span the Guadalquivir. From the bridge you have a good view of **La Albolafia**, the huge wheel once used to carry water to the gardens of the Alcázar. On the far side of the bridge is the **Torre de la Calahorra** ㊳, now a history museum.

Next, backtrack to the Mezquita. Facing the south side of the mosque is the **Museo Diocesano** ㊴ (currently closed). Walk around the Mezquita and head up Encarnación to Plaza Jerónimo Paez; at the plaza's northeast corner is the **Museo Arqueológico** ㊵. Off to the east is the Plaza del Potro (Colt Square)—named after its Fuente del Potro (Colt Fountain). The cafés around the square are good rest stops; here, too, are the **Museo de Bellas Artes** ㊶ and the adjacent **Museo Julio Romero de Torres** ㊷. Go northwest to the **Plaza de la Corredera** (some maps call it Plaza Constitución), an arcaded square built around 1690. After a couple of blocks east on Calle Lineros, take Carlos Rubio north. Just after it merges with Gutierrez de los Rios, you can see the **Museo Regina** ㊸ on your right. Head west on Pedro López, past the Plaza de la Corredera, and you pass the town hall and the towering columns of what was once a **Roman temple** on your way to the Plaza de las Tendillas.

If you've had enough walking, head down Jesús María and back to the Mezquita, saving the remaining sights for another time. If you have the strength, follow Calle Diego León from the north side of the Plaza de las Tendillas to the small **Plaza San Miguel,** whose 13th-century Gothic-Mudejar church dates from the time of Córdoba's conquest by King Ferdinand. North of the Plaza San Miguel is the small, charming **Plaza de los Dolores** ㊹, and around the corner from Dolores is the Casa de los Fernández de Córdoba, with a plateresque facade. At the nearby **Plaza Santa Marina** ㊺, on the edge of the Barrio de los Toreros, is a statue of the bullfighter Manolete. On the way you pass the fascinating Gothic churches of San Pablo and San Lorenzo. Southeast of here stands the **Palacio de Viana** ㊻. Córdoba's **Jardín Botánico** ㊼, across from the zoo by the river south of the city center, is best visited by car (there's plenty of parking) or taxi.

TIMING Allow a full day for this walk. Córdoba's council authorities and private institutions frequently change the hours of the city's sights; confirm hours with the tourist office or the sight itself.

What to See

㊲ **Alcázar de los Reyes Cristianos** (Fortress of the Christian Monarchs). Built by Alfonso XI in 1328, the Alcázar is a Mudejar-style palace with splendid gardens. (The original Moorish Alcázar stood beside the Mezquita, on the site of the present Bishop's Palace.) This is where, in the 15th century, the Catholic Monarchs held court and launched their conquest of Granada. Boabdil was imprisoned here in 1483, and for nearly 300 years the Alcázar served as the Inquisition's base. The most important sights here are the Hall of the Mosaics and a Roman stone sacrophagus from the 2nd or 3rd century. ⊠ *Pl. Campo Santo de los Mártires, San Basilio* ☎ *957/420151* ⊡ *€4, free Fri.* ☉ *May–Sept., Tues.–Sat. 10–2 and 6–8, Sun. 9:30–3; Oct.–Apr., Tues.–Sat. 10–2 and 4:30–6:30, Sun. 9:30–2:30.*

㊿ **Calleja de las Flores.** You'd be hard pressed to find prettier patios than those along this tiny street, a few yards off the northeastern corner of the Mezquita. Patios, many with ceramics, foliage, and iron grilles, are key to Córdoba's architecture, at least in the old quarter, where life is lived behind sturdy white walls—a legacy of the Moors, who honored both the sanctity of the home and the need to shut out the fierce summer sun. Between the second and the third week of May, right after the **Crosses Competition,** Córdoba throws a **Patio Festival,** during which private patios are filled with flowers, opened to the public, and judged in a municipal competition. Córdoba's council publishes a map with an itinerary of the best patios in town. Note that most of the patios are open only in the late afternoon during the week and all day on weekends.

㊼ **Jardín Botánico** (Botanical Garden). Across from Córdoba's modest zoo is its modern botanical garden, with outdoor spaces—including a section devoted to aromatic herbs—as well as greenhouses full of plants from South America and the Canary Islands. The **Museo de Etnobotánica** explores the way in which humans interact with the plant world. ⊠ *Av. del Zoológico, Parque Zoológico* ☎ *957/200018* ⊡ *€2* ☉ *Apr.–Oct., Tues.–Sun. 10–2:30 and 5:30–7:30; Nov.–Mar., Tues.–Sat. 10:30–2:30 and 4:30–6:30, Sun. 10:30–6:30.*

③ Judería. Córdoba's medieval Jewish Quarter is its most photogenic war-
Fodor'sChoice ren, a fascinating labyrinth of narrow streets and alleyways lined with
★ ancient white houses. Alas, the streets around the Mezquita leading up
to the Judería have a few too many tourist shops selling the same souvenirs.

**NEED A
BREAK?**

The lively **Plaza Juda Levi,** surrounded by a maze of narrow streets and squares,
lies at the heart of the Judería and makes a great spot for indulging in a little
people-watching. Sit outside here with a drink or, better still, an ice cream from
Helados Juda Levi.

▶ ㉙ Mezquita (Mosque). Built between the 8th and 10th centuries, Cór-
Fodor'sChoice doba's mosque is one of the earliest and most transportingly beautiful
★ examples of Spanish Muslim architecture. The plain, crenellated walls
of the outside do little to prepare you for the sublime beauty of the interior. As you enter through the **Puerta de las Palmas** (Door of the
Palms), some 850 columns rise be-
fore you in a forest of jasper, marble, granite, and onyx. The pillars
are topped by ornate capitals taken
from the Visigothic church that was
razed to make way for the mosque.
Crowning these, red-and-white-
stripe arches curve away into the
dimness. The ceiling is carved of
delicately tinted cedar. The

> **WORD OF MOUTH**
>
> "If you want to have a good lunch
> before or after seeing the
> Mezquita, El Caballo Rojo is just
> off the Mezquita square. -Eloise.

Mezquita has served as a cathedral since 1236, but its origins as a
mosque are clear. Built in four stages, it was founded in 785 by Abd ar-
Rahman I (756–88) on a site he bought from the Visigoth Christians.
He pulled down their church and replaced it with a mosque, one-third
the size of the present one, into which he incorporated marble pillars
from earlier Roman and Visigothic shrines. Under Abd ar-Rahman II
(822–52), the Mezquita held an original copy of the Koran and a bone
from the arm of the prophet Mohammed and became a Muslim pilgrimage site second only to Mecca in importance.

Al Hakam II (961–76) built the beautiful **Mihrab,** the Mezquita's greatest jewel. Make your way over to the **Qiblah,** the south-facing wall in
which this sacred prayer niche was hollowed out. (Muslim law decrees
that a Mihrab face east, toward Mecca, and that worshippers do likewise when they pray. Here, because of an error in calculation, the
Mihrab faces more south than east. Al Hakam II spent hours agoniz-
ing over a means of correcting such a serious mistake, but he was per-
suaded by wise architects to let it be.) In front of the Mihrab is the
Maksoureh, a kind of anteroom for the caliph and his court; its mosaics and plasterwork make it a masterpiece of Islamic art. The last addition to the mosque as such, the Maksoureh was completed around
987 by Al Mansur, who more than doubled its size.

After the Reconquest, the Christians left the Mezquita largely undisturbed,
dedicating it to the Virgin Mary and using it as a place of Christian worship. The clerics did erect a wall closing off the mosque from its court-

yard, which helped dim the interior and thus separate the house of worship from the world outside. In the 13th century, Christians had the **Capilla de Villaviciosa** built by Moorish craftsmen, its Mudejar architecture blending with the lines of the mosque. Not so the heavy, incongruous baroque structure of the **cathedral,** sanctioned in the very heart of the mosque by Charles V in the 1520s. To the emperor's credit, he was supposedly horrified when he came to inspect the new construction, exclaiming to the architects, "To build something ordinary, you have destroyed something that was unique in the world" (not that this sentiment stopped him from tampering with the Alhambra, to build the Palacio Carlos V, or with Seville's Alcázar). Rest up and reflect in the **Patio de los Naranjos** (Orange Court), perfumed in springtime by orange blossoms. The **Puerta del Perdón** (Gate of Forgiveness), so named because debtors were forgiven here on feast days, is on the north wall of the Orange Court. It's the formal entrance to the mosque.

The **Virgen de los Faroles** (Virgin of the Lanterns), a small statue in a niche on the outside wall of the mosque along the north side on Cardenal Herrero, is behind a lantern-hung grille, rather like a lady awaiting a serenade. The painting of the Virgin is by Julio Romero de Torres, an early-20th-century Córdoban artist. The **Torre del Alminar,** the minaret once used to summon the faithful to prayer, has a baroque belfry. Wheelchairs are available, and audio guides can be rented for €3 Monday through Saturday. ☒ *Torrijos and Cardenal Herrero, Judería* ☏ *957/ 470512* ▦ *€8* ☉ *Jan. and Dec. 10–5:30, Feb. and Nov. 10–6, Mar. and July–Oct. 10–7, Apr.–June 10–7:30.*

⓵ **Museo Arqueológico.** In the heart of the old quarter, the Museum of Archaeology has finds from Córdoba's varied cultural past. The ground floor has ancient Iberian statues, and Roman statues, mosaics, and artifacts; the upper floor is devoted to Moorish art. By chance, the ruins of a Roman theater were discovered right next to the museum in 2000—have a look from the window just inside the entrance. It is currently undergoing a major extension. Avoid exploring this area in the deserted siesta hours, when it's prime territory for muggers. At busier times of day and evening, the alleys and steps along Altos de Santa Ana make for great wandering. ☒ *Pl. Jerónimo Paez, Judería* ☏ *957/ 474011* ▦ *€1.50, EU citizens free* ☉ *Tues. 2:30–8:30, Wed.–Sat. 9–8:30, Sun. 9–2:30.*

⌐ NEED A BREAK? **Wander over to the Plaza de las Tendillas, which is halfway between the Mezquita and Plaza Colón. The terraces of the Café Boston and Café Siena are both enjoyable places to relax with a coffee when the weather is warm.**

⓶ **Museo de Bellas Artes.** Hard to miss because of its deep-pink facade, Córdoba's Museum of Fine Arts, in a courtyard just off the Plaza del Potro, belongs to a former Hospital de la Caridad (Charity Hospice). It was founded by Ferdinand and Isabella, who twice received Columbus here. The collection includes paintings by Murillo, Valdés Leal, Zurbarán, Goya, and Sorolla. ☒ *Off Pl. del Potro, San Francisco* ☏ *957/ 473345* ▦ *€1.50, EU citizens free* ☉ *Tues. 2:30–8:30, Wed.–Sat. 9–8:30, Sun. 9–2:30.*

㊷ **Museo Julio Romero de Torres.** Across the courtyard from the Museum of Fine Arts, this museum is devoted to the early-20th-century Córdoban artist Julio Romero de Torres, who specialized in portraits of demure, partially dressed Andalusian temptresses and is regarded locally as something of a hero. ⊠ *Pl. del Potro 1, San Francisco* ☎ *957/491909* 🎫 *€4, free Fri.* ☉ *Tues.–Sat. 10–2 and 4:30–6:30, Sun. 9:30–2:30.*

★ ㊸ **Museo Regina.** You can watch craftsmen at work here creating the delicate silver filigree pieces for which Córdoba is famous. Construction unearthed the Roman and Moorish archaeological remains that are on display on the ground floor. ⊠ *Plaza Luís Venegas 1, Centro* ☎ *957/ 496889* ⊕ *www.museoregina.com* 🎫 *€3* ☉ *June–mid-Sept., daily 9–2 and 5:30–9; mid-Sept.–Apr., daily 10–3 and 5–8.*

㉜ **Museo Taurino** (Museum of Bullfighting). Two adjoining mansions on the Plaza Maimónides (or Plaza de las Bulas) house this museum. It's worth a visit, as much for the chance to see a restored mansion as for the posters, Art Nouveau paintings, bull's heads, suits of lights (bullfighter outfits), and memorabilia of famous Córdoban bullfighters including the most famous of all, Manolete. To the surprise of the nation, Manolete, who was considered immortal, was killed by a bull in the ring at Linares in 1947. ⊠ *Pl. Maimónides, Judería* ☎ *957/ 201056* 🎫 *€3, free Fri.* ☉ *Tues.–Sat. 10–2 and 6–8, 4:30–6:30 in winter, Sun. 9:30–3.*

㊻ **Palacio de Viana.** This 17th-century palace is one of Córdoba's most splendid aristocratic homes. Also known as the **Museo de los Patios,** it contains 12 interior patios, each one different; the patios and gardens are planted with cypresses, orange trees, and myrtles. Inside the building are a carriage museum, a library, embossed leather wall hangings, filigree silver, and grand galleries and staircases. As you enter, note that the corner column of the first patio has been removed to allow the entrance of horse-drawn carriages. ⊠ *Pl. Don Gomé, Barrio de los Toreros* ☎ *957/496741* 🎫 *Patios only €3, patios and interior €6* ☉ *Mid-June–Sept., Mon.–Sat. 9–2; Oct.–Apr., Mon.–Sat. 10–1 and 4–6.*

㊹ **Plaza de los Dolores.** The 17th-century Convento de Capuchinos surrounds this small square north of Plaza San Miguel. The square is where you feel most deeply the city's languid pace. In its center, a statue of **Cristo de los Faroles** (Christ of the Lanterns) stands amid eight lanterns hanging from twisted wrought-iron brackets. ⊠ *Centro.*

㊺ **Plaza Santa Marina.** At the edge of the **Barrio de los Toreros,** a quarter where many of Córdoba's famous bullfighters were born and raised, stands a statue of the famous bullfighter Manolete (1917–47). Not far from here, on the Plaza de la Lagunilla, is a Manolete bust. ⊠ *Barrio de los Toreros.*

㉟ **Puerta de Almodóvar.** Outside this old Moorish gate at the northern entrance of the Judería is a statue of **Seneca,** the Córdoban-born philosopher who rose to prominence in Nero's court in Rome and was forced to commit suicide at his emperor's command. The gate stands at the top of the narrow and colorful Calle San Felipe. ⊠ *Judería.*

㊱ San Nicolás de Villa. This classically dark Spanish church displays the Mudejar style of Islamic decoration and art forms. Córdoba's well-kept city park, the **Jardínes de la Victoria**, with tile benches and manicured bushes, is a block west of here. ⊠ *C. San Felipe, Centro.*

㉞ Synagogue. The only Jewish temple in Andalusia to survive the expulsion and inquisition of the Jews in 1492, Córdoba's synagogue is also one of only three ancient synagogues left in all of Spain (the other two are in Toledo). Though it no longer functions as a place of worship, it's a treasured symbol for Spain's modern Jewish communities. The outside is plain, but the inside, measuring 23 feet by 21 feet, contains some exquisite Mudejar stucco tracery. Look for the fine plant motifs and the Hebrew inscription saying that the synagogue was built in 1315. The women's gallery, not open for visits, still stands, and in the east wall is the ark where the sacred scrolls of the Torah were kept. ⊠ *C. Judíos, Judería* ☎ *957/202928* 💶 *€0.30, EU citizens free* ☉ *Tues.–Sat. 9:30–2 and 3:30–5:30, Sun. 9:30–1:30.*

㊳ Torre de la Calahorra. The tower on the far side of the Puente Romano (Roman Bridge) was built in 1369 to guard the entrance to Córdoba. It now houses the **Museo Vivo de Al-Andalus** (Museum of Al-Andalus), with films and audiovisual guides (in English) on Córdoba's history. Climb the narrow staircase to the top of the tower for the view of the Roman bridge and city on the other side of the Guadalquivir. ⊠ *Av. de la Confederación, Sector Sur* ☎ *957/293929* 💶 *€4.50, €5.20 with audiovisual show* ☉ *May–Sept., daily 10–2 and 5:30–8:30 with audiovisual shows at 10:30, 11:30, midday, 5, 6, and 7; Oct.–Apr., daily 10–6 with audiovisual shows at 11, midday, 1, 3, and 4.*

㉝ Zoco. Zoco is the Spanish word for the Arab souk, the onetime function of this courtyard near the synagogue. It now is the site of a daily crafts market, where you can see artisans at work, and evening flamenco in summer. ⊠ *Judíos 5, Judería* ☎ *957/204033* 💶 *Free.*

Where to Eat

$$$–$$$$
Fodor'sChoice
★
✕ **El Caballo Rojo.** This is one of the most famous traditional restaurants in Andalusia, frequented by royalty and society folk. The interior resembles a cool, leafy Andalusian patio, and the dining room is furnished with stained glass, dark wood, and gleaming marble. The menu mixes traditional specialties, such as *rabo de toro* (oxtail stew) and *salmorejo* (a thick version of gazpacho), with dishes inspired by Córdoba's Moorish and Jewish heritage, such as *alboronia* (a cold salad of stewed vegetables flavored with honey, saffron, and aniseed), *cordero a la miel* (lamb roasted with honey), and *rape mozárabe* (grilled monkfish with Arab spices). ⊠ *Cardenal Herrero 28, Judería* ☎ *957/475375* ⊕ *www.elcaballorojo.com* 🖃 *AE, DC, MC, V.*

$$–$$$$
✕ **Los Marqueses.** Los Marqueses is in the heart of the Judería area, inside a delightful 17th-century palace. It specializes in Mediterranean cuisine; dishes may include fried eggplant with honey, mushrooms risotto with prawns, and turbot fillets with potato and mascarpone sauce. The lunch menu, served Monday through Saturday, is €21.90. ⊠ *Tomás Conde 8* ☎ *957/202094* 🖃 *AE, DC, MC, V* ☉ *Closed Mon. and 15 days in Sept.*

★ $$$ ✗ **Bodegas Campos.** A block east of the Plaza del Potro, this restaurant in a traditional old wine cellar is the epitome of all that is great about Andalusian cuisine and service. The dining rooms are in a warren of barrel-heavy and leafy courtyards. Regional dishes include *ensalada de bacalao y naranja* (salad of salt cod and orange with olive oil) and *solomillo con salsa de setas* (sirloin with an oyster-mushroom sauce). The *menu degustacíon* (taster's menu) is a good value at €35. ✉ *Los Lineros 32, San Pedro* ☎ *957/497643* 🖃 *AE, MC, V* ☺ *No dinner Sun.*

★ $$$ ✗ **El Churrasco.** The name suggests grilled meat, but this restaurant in the heart of the Judería serves much more than that. Try tapas such as the *berenjenas crujientes con salmorejo* (crispy fried eggplant slices with thick gazpacho) in the colorful bar. The grilled fish is also supremely fresh, *and* the steak is the best in town. On the inner patio, there's alfresco dining when it's warm outside (covered in winter). ✉ *Romero 16, Judería* ☎ *957/290819* ⊕ *www.elchurrasco.com* 🖃 *AE, DC, MC, V* ☺ *Closed Aug.*

$–$$$ ✗ **Los Alarifes.** This delightful restaurant serves a fine selection of typical Spanish dishes, including leek salad with Iberian ham, smoked salmon and carrot vinaigrette, cod with red peppers, and partridge. The daily set menu is less than €18. ✉ *Hotel Alfaros, Alfaros 18* ☎ *957/491920* 🖃 *AE, DC, MC, V.*

$$ ✗ **Tabernas Salinas.** This has been an established favorite in Córdoba since 1879: the tiles, paintings, wooden furniture, glassed-in patio, bodega with barrels, and small bar all reflect this era. The cuisine, typical of the Córdobese mountains, might include goat's cheese, meatballs, blood sausage, and lamb chops. ✉ *Tundidores 3* ☎ *957/480135* ⊕ *www.tabernasalinas.com* 🖃 *AE, DC, MC, V* ☺ *Closed Sun.*

$–$$ ✗ **El Burlaero.** A block from the front of the Mezquita, El Burlaero has wooden beams in its bar and one dining room: the space is furnished with much bullfighting memorabilia as well as deer heads and other hunting artifacts. There's also a terrace for outdoor dining. Typical dishes include grilled swordfish, meat-and-vegetable brochette, Iberian pork, and partridge with onions. ✉ *Calleja de la Hoguera 5* ☎ *957/472719* 🖃 *MC, V.*

$ ✗ **El Tablón.** Opened in 1890 as a bodega, El Tablón became a restaurant with simple decor in 1985. From inside or on the pleasing columned patio, you can select from a typical Córdoba-style menu that includes a good choice of two plates plus drink and dessert for just €9. Pizzas, tapas, and sandwiches are also available. The small bar, with no seats and a marble counter, retains a 19th-century feel. ✉ *Cardenal González 69* ☎ *957/476061* 🖃 *MC, V.*

¢–$ ✗ **La Abacería.** La Abacería is by the west side of the Mezquita, close to the tourist office, and has a large bar, pleasing open central patio, and full restaurant. It has homemade tapas: *patatas allioli* (potatoes in oil), *berenjenas fritas* (fried eggplant), *calamares fritos* or *plancha* (squid fried or grilled), and a Spanish omelet, all sold in half or full portions. ✉ *Corregidor Luis de la Carda 73* ☎ *957/487050* 🖃 *MC, V.*

¢ ✗ **Bar Santos.** This very small, typically Spanish bar, with no seats and numerous photos of matadors and flamenco dancers, seems out of place surrounded by the tourist shops and overshadowed by the Mezquita.

Its appearance—and its prices—are part of its charm. Tapas, such as *morcillo Iberico* (Iberian blood sausage), start at €1.20, and €3.30 for a ración. *Bocadillos* (sandwiches) range from €1.65 to €2.40. A large glass of sangria will set you back just €2. ⊠ *Magistral Gonzalez Francés 3.*

¢ ✕ **Hostal El Pilar del Potro.** A part of the budget hotel of the same name, this restaurant serves an interesting selection of tapas that include *rabo de toro* (bull's tail), tortillas, and fried squid rings in either half or full ració sizes; combination plates with veal, chicken breast, and pork chops at €5, sandwiches between €2 and €3.50, and pizzas at €4. An Internet café is in the next room. ⊠ *Lucano, 12* 🕾 *957/492966* ⊟ *MC, V.*

Where to Stay

$$$$ 🏨 **Palacio del Bailío.** Set to open in summer of 2006 at this writing, the beautiful 17th-century mansion is built over the ruins of a Roman house in the heart of the historical center of Córdoba. No doubt, once opened, it will immediately jump to the top of Córdoba's hotel league. The company specializes in carefully and tastefully renovating impressive and historic buildings to the highest of expected modern standards, and this is another exemplary example of its work. Archaeological remains, mixed with high-tech features (such as Internet access), and a relaxing spa complete the enticing cocktail. ⊠ *Ramirez de las Casas Deza 10–12, 14001* 🕾 *957/498993* 🖷 *957/498994* ⊕ *www.hospes.es* 🛏 *53 rooms* ⚘ *Restaurant, tapas bar, in-room broadband, Wi-Fi, 2 pools, (1 indoor), spa, bicycles, bar, laundry facilities, Internet room* ⊟ *MC, V.*

$$$ 🏨 **Amistad Córdoba.** Two 18th-century mansions that look out on the
Fodor'sChoice Plaza de Maimónides in the heart of the Judería are now a stylish hotel.
★ (You can also enter through the old Moorish walls on Calle Cairuán.) There's a cobblestone Mudejar courtyard, carved-wood ceilings, and a plush lounge area; the newer wing across the street is done in blues and grays and Norwegian wood. Guest rooms are large and comfortable. ⊠ *Pl. de Maimónides 3, Judería, 14004* 🕾 *957/420335* 🖷 *957/420365* ⊕ *www.nh-hoteles.com* 🛏 *84 rooms* ⚘ *Restaurant, room service, minibars, cable TV, in-room data ports, bar, laundry service, parking (fee)* ⊟ *AE, DC, MC, V.*

$$$ 🏨 **Casa de los Azulejos.** Although renovated in 1934, this 17th-century house still has its underground rooms with vaulted ceilings. Decorated with colorful tiles, it mixes Andalusian and Latin American influences. All rooms, painted in warm, pastel colors and filled with antique furnishings, open onto the central patio. There's an Andalusian–Latin American restaurant and a Mexican cantina on the premises. ⊠ *Fernando Colón 5, 14002* 🕾 *957/470000* 🖷 *957/475496* ⊕ *www.casadelosazulejos.com* 🛏 *7 rooms, 1 suite* ⚘ *2 restaurants, Internet room* ⊟ *MC, V.*

$$$ 🏨 **Conquistador.** Ceramic tiles and inlaid marquetry adorn the bar and public rooms at this contemporary, Andalusian-Moorish-style hotel next to the Mezquita. The reception area overlooks a colonnaded patio, fountain, and small enclosed garden. Rooms are comfortable and classically Andalusian; those at the front have small balconies overlooking the mosque, which is floodlighted at night. ⊠ *Magistral González Francés 17, Judería, 14003* 🕾 *957/481102 or 957/481411* 🖷 *957/474677* ⊕ *www.hotelconquistadorcordoba.com* 🛏 *99 rooms, 3 suites* ⚘ *Room*

service, minibars, cable TV with movies, in-room data ports, bar, laundry service, business services, parking (fee) ▭ *AE, DC, MC, V.*

$$$ **La Hospedería de El Churrasco.** As should be expected from a place associated with the nearby restaurant of the same name, this small hotel is one of the most beautiful and tasteful places to stay in Córdoba. Each room is individually furnished with fine antiques, but also comes with such modern facilities as plasma TVs. The terrace-solarium here has fine views of the Mezquita. ✉ *Romero 38, 14003* ☎ *957/294808* 📠 *957/421661* 🌐 *www.elchurrasco.com* *9 rooms* *Minibars, in-room data ports, free parking* ▭ *AE, DC, MC, V* 🍽 *BP.*

$$$ **Lola.** Lola, the owner, has decorated the rooms in this former 19th-century palace with decorative flair and attention to detail. There are original beams, woven rugs, antique wardrobes, and art-deco decorative pieces. The bathrooms are airy, modern, and marbled. Tucked down a side street, Lola is away from the tour groups, but a short stroll away from all the big-city sights. The roof terrace has Mezquita tower views. There's parking on nearby Plaza Vallinas. ✉ *Romero 3, Judería, 14003* ☎ *957/200305* 📠 *957/422063* 🌐 *www.hotelconencantolola.com* *8 rooms* *Cable TV* ▭ *AE, MC, V* 🍽 *CP.*

$$$ **Maciá Alfaros.** One of the advantages of this elegant hotel is that it's in a quieter part of the city but just a 15-minute walk from the Mezquita. The rooms are large, with modern furnishings and a terrace or balcony. The rooms opening onto the inner patio overlook the pool. ✉ *Alfaros 18, 14001* ☎ *957/491920* 📠 *957/492210* *133 rooms* *Restaurant, cafeteria, minibars, in-room data ports, pool, bar, dry cleaning, laundry service, business services, free parking* ▭ *AE, D, MC, V.*

$$$ **Maimónides.** The lobby here has a colonnaded sand-color hall with tile floors and a remarkable *mocárabe* (ornamental wood) ceiling. Outside there's a small patio with wrought-iron tables and chairs. Rooms and bathrooms have marble floors and are decorated in light tones. Some of the rooms make you feel like you're so close to the Mezquita you can touch it. ✉ *Torrijos 4, Judería, 14003* ☎📠 *957/471500* 🌐 *www.hotusa.es* *82 rooms* *Restaurant, minibars, cable TV, in-room data ports, Internet room, parking (fee)* ▭ *MC, V.*

$$$ **Parador de Córdoba.** A peaceful, leafy garden surrounds this modern parador on the slopes of the Sierra de Córdoba, 5 km (3 mi) north of town. Rooms are sunny, with wood or wicker furnishings, and the pricier ones have balconies overlooking the garden or facing Córdoba. ✉ *Av. de la Arruzafa, El Brillante, 14012* ☎ *957/275900* 📠 *957/280409* 🌐 *www.parador.es* *89 rooms, 5 suites* *Restaurant, room service, minibars, cable TV, in-room data ports, tennis court, pool, free parking* ▭ *AE, DC, MC, V.*

$$ **Gonzalez.** A few minutes from the Mezquita, Gonzalez was originally built as a 16th-century palace and has been converted into a small hotel with an elegant marble entrance and a typical Córdobese central patio. Many of the single, double, twin, and triple rooms here overlook the patio. ✉ *Marnique 3, 14003* ☎ *957/479819* 📠 *957/486187* *17 rooms* ▭ *MC, V.*

$$ **Mezquita.** Across from the mosque, this hotel in a restored 16th-century home is filled with bronze sculptures depicting Andalusian themes, and the public areas are filled with antiques collected by the owner. The best rooms face the interior patio, and one of them is what used to be the house's old chapel. All have elegant dark wooden headboards and matching pink curtains and bedspreads. The only real drawback is the lack of parking; your best bet is nearby Plaza Vallinas. ⊠ *Pl. Santa Catalina 1, Judería, 41003* ☎ *957/475585* 🖥 *957/476219* 🛏 *21 rooms* ⚇ *Cable TV, in-room data ports, bar* ☰ *AE, MC, V.*

$ 🖥 **El Tablón.** Close to the Mezquita, this comfortable hostal has pleasantly decorated rooms in a traditional old-fashioned Spanish style. There's a restaurant and bar across the street. ⊠ *Cardenal González 69, 14003* ☎ *957/476061* ⊕ *www.hostaleltablon.com* 🖥 *957/486240* 🛏 *8 rooms, 1 suite* ⚇ *Restaurant, bar* ☰ *MC, V.*

¢–$ 🖥 **Hotel Maestre.** Rooms here overlook a gracious inner courtyard framed by arches. The Castilian-style furniture, gleaming marble, and high-quality oil paintings add elegance to excellent value. The hotel is around the corner from the Plaza del Potro. The management also runs an even cheaper lodging, the Hostal Maestre, and two types of apartments down the street; the top of the lot are large and clean and offer one of the best deals in town. ⊠ *Romero Barros 4–6, San Pedro, 14003* ☎ *957/472410* 🖥 *957/475395* ⊕ *www.hotelmaestre.com* 🛏 *26 rooms* ⚇ *Parking (fee)* ☰ *AE, MC, V.*

Nightlife & the Arts

During the **Patio Festival,** on the second and third weeks of May, the city is invaded by flamenco dancers and singers. The **Festival de Córdoba-Guitarra** attracts Spanish and international guitarists for more than two weeks of great music in July, and orchestras perform in the Alcázar's garden on Sunday throughout summer. The **Feria de Mayo** (the last week of May) draws popular performers to the city. See concerts, ballets, and plays year-round in the **Gran Teatro** (⊠ Gran Capitán 3, Centro ☎ 957/ 480644 ⊕ www.teatrocordoba.com).

FLAMENCO   Córdoba's most popular flamenco club, the year-round **Tablao Cardenal** (⊠ Torrijos 10, Judería ☎ 957/483320 ⊕ www.tablaocardenal.com), facing the Mezquita, is worth the trip just to see the courtyard of the 16th-century building, which was Córdoba's first hospital. Admission is €20. **Mesón la Bulería** (⊠ Pedro López 3, Judería ☎ 957/483839) stages flamenco shows between Easter and September. Flamenco is performed in the **Zoco** (⊠ Off C. Judíos, Judería ☎ 957/483839) on summer evenings.

NIGHTLIFE   Córdoba locals hang out mostly in the areas of Ciudad Jardín (the old university area), Plaza de las Tendillas, and the top section of the Avenida Gran Capitán. **Café Málaga** (⊠ Málaga 3, Centro), a block away from Plaza de las Tendillas, is a laid-back hangout. **Salón de Té** (⊠ Buen Pastor 13, Judería), a few blocks away from the Mezquita, is a beautiful place for tea, with a courtyard, side rooms filled with cushions, and a shop selling Moroccan clothing. It closes at midnight. **Sojo** (⊠ Benito Pérez Galdós 3, off Av. del Gran Capitán, Centro ☎ 957/487211 ⊠ José Martorell 12, Judería) has a trendy crowd. The branch in the Judería has DJs on weekends. **O'Donoghue's** (⊠ Gran Capitán 38, Centro ☎ 957/ 481678) is an Irish pub favored by locals. For some of the best views of Córdoba, drop by **Hotel Hesperia** (⊠ Av. de la Confederación 1, Sector Sur ☎ 957/421042 ⊕ www.hesperia-cordoba.com), across the Guadalquivir River, almost facing the Mezquita. The hotel has a rooftop bar, open only in summer.

Shopping

Córdoba's main shopping district is around Avenida Gran Capitán, Ronda de los Tejares, and the streets leading away from Plaza Tendillas. **Artesanía Andaluza** (⊠ Tomás Conde 3, Judería), near the Museo Taurino, sells Córdoban crafts, including fine embossed leather (a legacy of the Moors) and jewelry made of filigree silver from the mines of the Sierra Morena. Córdoba's artisans sell their crafts in the **Zoco** (⊠ C. Judíos, opposite synagogue, Judería ☎ 957/204033); note that many stalls are open May to September only. **Meryan** (⊠ Calleja de las Flores 2 and Encarnación, 12 ☎ 957/475902 ⊕ www.meryancor.com) is one of Córdoba's best workshops for embossed leather.

Medina Azahara

48 *8 km (5 mi) west of Córdoba on C431.*

The ruins and partial reconstruction of the Muslim palace Medina Azahara (sometimes spelled Madinat Al-Zahra) are well worth a detour. Begun in 936, Medina Azahara was built in the foothills of the Sierra Morena by Abd ar-Rahman III for his favorite concubine, az-Zahra (the Flower). Historians say it took 10,000 men, 2,600 mules, and 400 camels 25 years to erect this fantasy of 4,300 columns in dazzling pink, green, and white marble and jasper brought from Carthage. Here, on three terraces, stood a palace, a mosque, luxurious baths, fragrant gardens, fishponds, an aviary, and a zoo. In 1013 the place was sacked and destroyed by Berber mercenaries. In 1944 the Royal Apartments were rediscovered, and the Throne Room was carefully reconstructed. The outline of the mosque has also been excavated. The only covered part of the site is the Salon de Abd Al Rahman III; the rest is a sprawl of foundations, defense walls, and arches that hint at the splendor of the original city-palace. There is no public transport out to here, but the authorities run a daily tourist bus, so check with the tourist offices for hours and place of departure. ⊠ *Off C431; follow signs en route to Almodóvar del Río* ☎ *957/329130* ⊠ *€1.50, EU citizens free* ☉ *Mid–late Sept. and May–mid-June, Tues.–Sat. 10–2; mid-June–mid-Sept., Tues.–Sat. 10–1:30; Oct.–Apr., Tues.–Sat. 10–6:30, Sun. 10–2.*

Montilla

49 *46 km (28 mi) south of Córdoba.*

Heading south from Córdoba to Málaga through hills ablaze with sunflowers in early summer, you reach the Montilla-Moriles vineyards of the Córdoban campiña. Every fall, 47,000 acres' worth of Pedro Ximénez grapes are crushed here to produce the region's rich Montilla wines. Producing a wine that's similar to sherry, the local grapes contain so much sugar (transformed into alcohol during fermentation) that they are not fortified with the addition of extra alcohol. For this reason, the locals claim that Montilla wines do not give you a hangover. Recently, Montilla has started developing a young white wine similar to Portugal's Vinho Verde.

On the outskirts of town, coopers' shops produce barrels of various sizes, some small enough to serve as creative souvenirs. On the main road, **Tonelería J. L. Rodríguez** is well worth a stop not just to see the barrels and other things for sale, but also to pop in the back and see them being made. Local wines are also for sale here. ⌂ *Ctra. Córdoba-Málaga, Km 43.3* ☎ *957/650563* ⊕ *www.toneleriajlrodriguez.com.*

Bodegas Alvear. Founded in 1729, this bodega in the center of town is Montilla's oldest. Besides being informative, the fun tour and wine tasting gives you the chance to buy a bottle or two of Alvear's tasty version of the sweet Pedro Ximenez aged sherry. ⌂ *María Auxiliadora 1* ☎ *957/ 664014* ⊕ *www.alvear.es* ⌂ *€1.50 for tour; €2.95–3.95 with wine tasting* ☉ *Guided tour and wine tasting Mon.–Sat. 12:30; shop Mon. 4:30–6:30, Tues.–Fri. 10–2 and 4:30–6:30, Sat. 11–1:30.*

Where to Stay & Eat

★ $–$$ ✕**Las Camachas.** The best-known restaurant in southern Córdoba province is in an Andalusian-style hacienda outside Montilla—near the main road toward Málaga. Start with tapas in the attractive tiled bar, and then move to one of six dining rooms. Regional specialties include *alcachofas al Montilla* (artichokes braised in Montilla wine), *salmorejo* (a thick version of gazpacho), *perdiz campiña* (country-style partridge), and *cordero a la miel* (lamb with honey). You can also buy local wines here. ⌂ *Antigua Carretera Córdoba–Málaga* ☎ *957/650004* ▭ *AE, DC, MC, V.*

$$ 🏨 **Don Gonzalo.** Just 2 km (1 mi) south of Montilla is one of Andalusia's better roadside hotels. The wood-beam common areas have a mixture of decorative elements; note the elephant tusks flanking the TV in the lounge. The clay-tile rooms are large and comfortable; some look onto the road, others onto the garden and pool. Ask to see the wine cellar. ⌂ *Ctra. Córdoba–Málaga, Km 47, 14550* ☎ *957/650658* ⌂ *957/ 650666* ⊕ *www.hoteldongonzalo.com* ➥ *35 rooms, 1 suite △ Restaurant, cable TV, in-room data ports, tennis court, pool, bar, dance club, meeting rooms* ▭ *AE, MC, V.*

La Subbética

🔟 *Priego de Córdoba: 103 km (64 mi) southeast of Córdoba.*

In the southeastern corner of Córdoba's province lies a largely undiscovered cluster of villages, small towns, and countryside known to locals as the Subbética. The entire region is protected as a natural park. The mountains, canyons, and wooded valleys are stunning. You'll need a car to explore the area, and in some parts of the park, the roads are rather rough. For general information or hiking advice, contact the **Mancomunidad de la Subbética** (⌂ Ctra. Carcabuey–Zagrilla, Km 5.75, Carcabuey ☎ 957/704106 ⊕ www.subbetica.org). You can also pick up handy information, including a pack of maps titled *Rutas Senderistas de la Subbética,* from any local tourist office. The packet details 10 walks on handy cards with sketched maps.

This is Córdoba province's main olive-producing region, with the town of Lucena at its center. By following the Ruta del Aceite (oil route) you pass by some of the province's most picturesque villages. In **Lucena,** often called the city of the three cultures (Christian, Arab, and Jewish), is the Torre del Moral, where Boabdil was imprisoned in 1483 after launching an unsuccessful attack on the Christians, and the Parroquia de San Mateo, a small but remarkable Renaissance–Gothic cathedral. Today the town makes furniture and brass and copper pots. At the southern tip of the province, southeast of Lucena, C334 crosses the **Embalse de Iznájar** (Iznájar Reservoir) amid spectacular scenery. On C334 halfway between Lucena and the reservoir, in **Rute,** you can sample the potent *anís* (anise) liqueur for which this small, whitewashed town is famous.

The jewel of this area is **Priego de Córdoba,** a town of 14,000 at the foot of Mt. Tinosa. (From Lucena, head north 5 km [3 mi] on C334 to Cabra, and turn right, or east, on C340; after 32 km [20 mi], you'll reach Priego.) Wander down Calle del Río opposite the town hall to see 18th-century mansions, once the homes of silk merchants. At the end of the street is the Fuente del Rey (King's Fountain), with some 130 water jets, built in 1803. Don't miss the lavish baroque churches of La Asunción and La Aurora or the Barrio de la Villa, an old Moorish quarter with a maze of narrow streets of white-wall buildings.

Zuheros
51 *80 km (50 mi) southeast of Córdoba.*

At the northern edge of the Subbética and at an altitude of 2,040 feet, Zuheros one of the most attractive villages in the province of Córdoba. From the road up, it's hidden behind a dominating rock face topped off by the dramatic ruins of a castle built by the Moors over a Roman castle. The view from here back over the valley is immense. Next to the castle is the Santa María church, built over a mosque. The base of the minaret is the foundation for the bell tower.

The **Museo Histórico-Arqueológico Municipal** displays archaeological remains found in local caves and elsewhere; some date back to the Middle Palaeolithic period some 35,000 years ago. You can also visit the remains of the Renaissance rooms in the castle, across the road. Call ahead for tour times. ✉ *Plaza de la Paz 2* ☎ *957/694545* 💶 *€1.80* ☉ *Apr.–Sept., Tues.–Fri. 10–2 and 5–7; weekends 10–7; Oct.–Mar., Tues.–Fri. 10–2 and 4–6; weekends 10–6.*

Opened in 2002, and housed in an impressive square mansion from 1912, the **Museo de Costumbres y Artes Populares Juan Fernandez Cruz** is at the edge of the village. Exhibits here detail the way of life and local customs and traditions. ✉ *Santo s/n* ☎ *957/694690* 💶 *€2* ☉ *Tues.–Sun. 11–2 and 4–7.*

Found some 4 km (2½ mi) above Zuheros along a windy, twisty road, the **Cueva de los Murciélagos** (Cave of the Bats) runs for about 2 km (1¼ mi), although only about half of that expanse is open to the public. The main attractions are the wall paintings dating from the Neolithic Age (6,000–3,000 BC) and Chalcolithic Age (3,000–2,000 BC), but excavations have identified that the cave was already inhabited 35,000 years ago. Items from the Copper and Bronze ages as well as from the Roman period and the Middle Ages have also been found here. ✉ *Information and reservations: Nueva 1, Zuheros* ☎ *957/694545 weekdays 10–2:30 and 5–7* ◫ *€4.60* ◷ *By appointment only: Apr.–Sept., weekdays noon–5:30; weekends 11–6:30; Oct.–Mar., weekdays 12:30–4:30; weekends 11–5:30.*

Baena

52 *68 km (42 mi) southeast of Zuheros.*

Outside the boundaries of Subbética and surrounded by chalk fields producing top-quality olives, Baena is an old town of narrow streets, whitewashed houses, ancient mansions, and churches clustered beneath Moorish battlements.

The **Museo del Olivar y el Aceite** is housed in the old olive mill owned and operated by Don José Alcalá Santaella until 1959. The machinery on display dates from the middle of the 19th century, when the mill was capable of processing up to 3 tons a day. The museum aims to demonstrate the most important aspects of olive cultivation, olive-oil production, and the way of life of workers in this most important industry in this region. ✉ *Cañada 7* ☎ *957/691641* ⊕ *www.museoaceite.com* ◫ *€2* ◷ *Summer, Tues.–Sat. 11–2 and 6–8, Sun. 11–2; winter, Tues.–Fri. 11–2 and 4–6, Sun. 11–2.*

Where to Stay & Eat

$–$$$ ✗ **Los Palancos.** Literally built into the cliff face of the towering mountain that Zuheros is built upon, this is a small restaurant/bar of some charm. Expect local mountain-style cuisine featuring roast young goat, rabbit, partridge, and suckling pig, and choose from many items of local produce to take home with you. ✉ *Llana 43* ☎ *957/694538* ▭ *MC, V.*

★ $$$$ ✗▦ **Barceló La Bobadilla.** Standing on its own 1,000-acre estate amid olive and holm-oak trees, this complex 14 km (9 mi) west of Loja resembles a Moorish village, or a rambling *cortijo* (ranch). It has white walls, tile roofs, patios, fountains, and an artificial lake. Guest buildings center around a 16th-century-style chapel that houses a 1,595-pipe organ. Each room has either a balcony, a terrace, or a garden. One restaurant serves highly creative international cuisine, and the other serves more down-to-earth regional items. The hotel is just south of the La Subbética region, but it's by far the best one in the general area. ✉ *Finca La Bobadilla, Apdo 144 E, 18300* ☎ *958/321861* ☒ *958/321810* ⊕ *www. la-bobadilla.com* ↝ *62 rooms, 8 suites* ♧ *2 restaurants, minibars, cable TV with movies, 2 tennis courts, 2 pools (1 indoor), gym, hot tub, sauna, mountain bikes, horseback riding, convention center* ▭ *AE, DC, MC, V.*

$$ ▦ **Fuente las Piedras.** This stylish hotel opened in 2004, on the edge of the Parque Natural Sierra Subbéticas. Its rooms are modern and generous in size. A large pool is surrounded by verdant gardens. ✉ *Av. Fuente de las Piedras s/n, 14940* ☎ *957/529740* ☒ *957/521407* ↝ *61 Rooms* ♧ *Restaurant, café, pool, bar, dry cleaning, laundry facilities, business services, free parking* ▭ *MC, V.*

$$ ⌂ **Villa Turística de Priego.** Clustered to form an Andalusian pueblo, the semidetached units of this gleaming-white complex sleep between two and six people each. Some have a terrace or balcony. It's in the heart of the Subbética nature park—near Zagrilla, 6 km (4 mi) from Priego de Córdoba. ⊠ *Aldea de Zagrilla, 14816* ☎ *957/703503* 🖷 *957/703573* ⊕ *www.villadepriego.com* ⌻ *14 rooms, 38 villas* ⚸ *Restaurant, some kitchenettes, pool, bar* ☰ *AE, DC, MC, V* ⊙ *Closed Jan.*

$–$$ ⌂ **Señorios de Zuheros.** In a central location, Señorios de Zuheros offers 10 apartments with three or four beds as well as six studios with sleeping accommodations for two people. All rooms are modern and well equipped. ⊠ *Horno 3, 14870* ☎ *957/694527* ⊕ *www.zuherosapartamentos.com* ⌻ *10 apartments, 6 rooms* ⚸ *Restaurant, cafeteria, bar, laundry facilities* ☰ *MC, V.*

$ ⌂ **Zuhayra.** On a narrow street in Zuheros, this small hotel has comfortable large rooms with views over the village rooftops to the valley below. There's a cozy bar and dining room with original beams and an open fireplace. Groups of artists on organized trips often stay here. ⊠ *C. Mirador 10, Zuheros 14870* ☎ *957/694693* 🖷 *957/694702* ⌻ *18 rooms* ⚸ *Restaurant, bar* ☰ *AE, DC, MC, V.*

EASTERN ANDALUSIA ESSENTIALS

To research prices, get advice from other travelers, and book travel arrangements, visit *www.fodors.com.*

BY AIR

There are only very limited direct services from North America to this region, and then only to Málaga International airport (the most important point of arrival for visitors from other European countries). Iberia has daily flights to Málaga from within Spain.

Málaga airport (AGP) on the Costa del Sol is one of Spain's major hubs and therefore a possible access point for Granada, Córdoba, and Almería. These cities are approximately two hours away by car. Granada's airport, Aeropuerto de Granada (GRX), is 18 km (11 mi) west of the city; Almería's airport (LEI) is 9 km (just over 5 mi) east of the city. Seville's San Pablo airport (SVQ) is 10 km (6 mi) east of the city on the main road to Córdoba.

By taxi, which is more convenient as well as more expensive, expect to pay around €17 to the city center and €25 to the Alhambra.

J. González (☎ 958/490164) buses (€3) run between the center of Granada and the airport, leaving from the Palacio de Congresos, and making a few other stops along the way to the airport. Times are listed at the bus stop; service is reduced in winter.

Line 14 (☎ 950/221422), €0.70, municipal bus service operates between the airport and the city center.

🖪 **Airports Aeropuerto de Málaga** ☎ 95/204-8838. **Aeropuerto de Granada** ☎ 958/245223. **Aeropuerto de Almería** ☎ 950/213700. **Aeropuerto de Sevilla** ☎ 95/444-9000.

🖪 **Airlines Iberia** ☎ 800/772-4642 ⊕ www.iberia.com.

BY BUS

If you're not driving, buses are the best way to get around this region. They serve most small towns and villages, and they're generally faster and more frequent than trains. From Granada, Alsina Gräells serves Alcalá la Real, Almería, Almuñecar, Cazorla, Córdoba, Guadix, Jaén, Lanjarón, Motril, Órgiva, Salobreña, Seville, and Úbeda.

Autocares Bonal operates between Granada and the Sierra Nevada.

Granada's bus station is on the highway to Jaén.

Buses serve Córdoba as well, but the various routes are covered by myriad companies. For schedules and details, go to Córdoba's bus station—next to the AVE (high-speed train) station—and inquire with the appropriate company. Alsina Gräells connects Córdoba with Granada, Seville, Cádiz, Badajoz, and Málaga.

🚌 Granada Bus Information Bus station ✉ Ctra. Jaén ☎ 958/185010.
🚌 Córdoba Bus Information Bus station ✉ Glorieta de las Tres Culturas ☎ 957/404040.
🚌 Bus Lines Alsina Gräells ⊕ www.alsinagraells.es ✉ Almería ☎ 950/238197
✉ Córdoba ☎ 957/278100 ✉ Granada ☎ 958/185480 ✉ Jaén ☎ 953/255014
✉ Málaga ☎ 95/2341738 ✉ Seville ☎ 95/4418811. Autocares Bonal ☎ 958/273100.

BY BUS WITHIN GRANADA & CÓRDOBA

Granada and Córdoba have extensive public bus networks. The average waiting time usually does not exceed 15 minutes.

Normally, buses in both cities start running around 6:30 to 7 AM and stop around 11 PM in Granada and midnight in Córdoba. However, schedules can be slightly reduced for some lines. In Granada, you can buy 6- and 21-trip discount passes on the buses and 10-trip passes at newsstands. In Córdoba, newsstands and the bus office at Plaza de Colón sell 10-trip discount tickets. The single-trip fares are €0.85 in Granada and Córdoba. Rober and Aucorsa manage the bus networks in Granada and Córdoba, respectively.

🚌 Aucorsa ☎ 957/764676 ⊕ www.aucorsa.net. Rober ☎ 958/813750 or 900/710900 ⊕ www.transportesrober.com.

BY CAR

With the exception of parts of La Alpujarra, most roads in this region are smooth. Driving is one of the most enjoyable ways to see the countryside.

Be prepared for serious parking problems. In both Granada and Córdoba (particularly the former), parking problems are exacerbated by the substantial threat of break-ins. It's best to park in an underground lot. There are a couple of good-size lots in the center of Granada. Follow the large blue "P" signs, which will guide you through the baffling one-way system of streets to the city center. You can take a cab or shuttle bus from the center to the Alhambra or Albaicín. Most of Córdoba's hotels are ensconced in a labyrinth of narrow streets that can be a nightmare to negotiate, even with a small car.

A good bet for Córdoba parking is in the underground lot near the Campo Santo de los Mártires, west of the Judería; or try to park in that general area or across the river, on Avenida de la Confederación and its nearby streets. In Córdoba, all the sights are within walking distance of one another. Other towns, too, date from Moorish times and are ill suited to present-day traffic, so look out for underground parking lots that are usually found in the city-town centers.

BY TAXI

Taxis can be hailed on the street in both Granada and Córdoba. In Granada there's a taxi station, or *paradas de taxis,* in almost every major area. In Córdoba there are taxi stations at Avenida de América near the Hotel Gran Capitán, at the corner of El Corte Inglés, and near the hotel Meliá, among other locations. You can also phone Tele Radio Taxi or Asociación de Radio Taxi in Granada. Call Radio Taxi in Córdoba.

In both cities, taxis are metered; the minimum fare is about €3. Fares are based on the time of the day, and are higher at night and on public holidays. In Córdoba taxis charge an additional amount for picking up passengers at the train station, as well as for each piece of luggage (the latter is true in Granada also). At this writing, those extra fares didn't exceed €0.50. When in doubt, check the sticker of official fares found in taxi back windows. If you're dissatisfied with either the fare or the driver, remember to record the taxi's license number.

🚖 **Taxi Companies Asociació de Radio Taxi** ☎ 958/132323. **Radio Taxi** ☎ 957/764444. **Tele Radio Taxi** ☎ 958/280654.

BY TRAIN

The wonderful, high-speed AVE connects Madrid with Córdoba in less than two hours. Trains also link Madrid with Almería, Granada, and Jaén, via Linares-Baeza for all and also Guadix for Almería. Train service from Córdoba to Granada routes goes through the important junction of Bobadilla, and then runs via Andújar to Jaén. Almería, Granada, and Jaén are all terminals, and although the latter two are geographically close, the rail route is roundabout.

🚆 **Train Information RENFE** ☎ 902/240202 ⊕ www.renfe.es.

Contacts & Resources

EMERGENCIES

The **national emergency number** is ☎ 112; it does not yet directly cover all of Spain, but operators can redirect you if you provide them with additional information.

🚑 **Emergency Services Ambulance** ☎ 061. **Police: Local** (Policía Local) ☎ 092. **Police: National** (Policía Nacional) ☎ 091.

INTERNET, MAIL & SHIPPING

Granada's main post office is in the Plaza Real, whereas the main office in Córdoba—the only one open in the afternoon—is north of the mosque near the Plaza de las Tendillas. Internet cafés with competitive prices are plentiful in both cities, especially Granada, which has a large student population.

MEDIA

You can get English books from Granada's Librería Metro and also from the Kioscos by the Puerta Real and Acera de Darro in Granada, and the Plaza Tendillas in Córdoba. Tourist shops around the Mezquita and the Judería area also carry English-language materials. In other cities and towns they can usually be found at Kioscos in the city center or the train station, but not usually at the bus station.

Librería Metro ⊠ C. Gracia 31, Granada 🕾 958/261565

TOUR OPTIONS

GENERAL TOURS   Pullmantur and Julià Tours run numerous excursions to this region; you can book them through most travel agents, many hotels, or through the companies' Madrid and Costa del Sol offices. GranaVisión and Córdoba Visión offer both day- and nighttime tours, including an excursion to Medina Azahara. In Granada and Jaén, contact an English-speaking guide through the Asociación Provincial de Guías. Pópulo is also a good company for touring Baeza. Artificis also leads tours of Úbeda as well as Baeza. In Córdoba, you can hire an English-speaking guide for the mosque and synagogue through the Asociación Profesional de Informadores Turísticos.

CitySightseeing Granada bus tours include informative commentary on major sights. Tickets, which cost €10 and are valid for 24 hours, allow you to hop on and off both the large open-topped bus that takes in the sights in the lower city and the minibus that winds up to the Alhambra and through the narrow streets of Albaicín.

Tour Operators Pullmantur ⊠ Av. Imperial, Torremolinos 🕾 952/384400 ⊕ www.pullmantur.es. **Julià Tours** ⊠ Gran Vía 68, Centro, Madrid 🕾 91/559-9605 ⊕ www.juliatours.es. **Artificis** ⊠ Juan Ruíz González 19, next to parador, Úbeda 🕾 953/758150 ⊕ www.artificis.com. **Asociación Profesional de Informadores Turísticos** ⊠ Museo Diocesano, Torrijos 12, Judería, Córdoba 🕾 957/486997. **Asociación Provincial de Guías** ⊠ Pl. Nueva 2, Albaicín, Granada 🕾 958/229936 ⊠ Jaén 🕾 957/254442. **CitySightseeing Granada** ⊠ Outside the Cathedral, Granada 🕾 902/101081. **Córdoba Visión** ⊠ Av. de Doctor Fleming, Centro, Córdoba 🕾 957/760241. **GranaVisión** ⊠ Reyes Católicos 47-49, Centro, Córdoba 🕾 958/535875 ⊕ www.granavision.com. **Pópulo** ⊠ Pl. de los Leones 1, Baeza 🕾 953/744370 ⊕ www.baezamonumental.com.

SPORTS-RELATED TOURS   Based in the Alpujarras, Nevadensis leads guided tours of the region on foot, horseback, and mountain bike. In Granada, Sólo Aventura offers one- to seven-day outdoor sports—trekking, mountaineering, climbing, mountain biking, and other activities—around the Alpujarras, Sierra Nevada, and the rest of the province. Kayak Sur organizes kayaking and canoeing trips to the River Guadalfeo. Granada Romántica takes up to five people in balloon trips above the city and its surroundings. Quercus arranges jeep and horseback trips and special-interest nature tours. Excursiones Bujarkay leads guided hikes as well as horseback and four-wheel-drive tours.

The Alúa in Zuheros can help you with planning and getting the equipment for hiking, rock climbing, mountain biking, caving, and other active sports.

Horseback-riding tours, some with English-speaking guides, are offered in the villages of the Alpujarras, Sierra Nevada, and in the Sierra de Cazorla; Cabalgar Rutas Alternativas is one established Alpujarras agency. Dallas Love offers trail rides for up to 10 days in the Alpujarras. The price includes overnight stays and most meals.

🚩 **Tour Operators Alúa** ⊠ Horno 3, Zuheros ☎ 957/694527 ⊕ www.aluactiva.com. **Cabalgar Rutas Alternativas** ⊠ Bubión, Alpujarras ☎ 958/763135 ⊕ www.ridingandalucia. com. **Dallas Love** ⊠ Ctra. de la Sierra, Bubión, Alpujarras ☎☎ 958/763038 ⊕ www. spain-horse-riding.com. **Excursiones Bujarkay** ☎ 953/721111 ⊕ www.guiasnativos. com. **Kayak Sur** ⊠ Arabial, Urbanizació Parque del Genil, Edificio Topacio, Sur, Granada ☎ 958/523118 ⊕ www.kayaksur.com. **Nevadensis** ⊠ Pl. de la Libertad, Pampaneira ☎ 958/ 763127 ⊕ www.nevadensis.com. **Quercus** ☎ 953/720115. **Sólo Aventura** ⊠ Pl. de la Romanilla 1, Centro, Granada ☎ 958/804937 ⊕ www.soloaventura.com.

VISITOR INFORMATION

The regional tourist offices in Granada and Córdoba will supply you with information, including free periodicals and city guides, some for a nominal fee. The *where 2* bimonthly magazine offers an alternative guide to Granada, Sierra Nevada, La Alpujarra, Guadix, and Costa Tropical.

One of the most informative Web sites for the region is www.andalucia. org, the official tourism site of the Junta de Andalusia. The site includes a tourist atlas with detailed information on a wide range of subjects relating to the province.

🚩 **Regional Tourist Offices Córdoba** ⊠ Palacio de Exposiciones, Torrijos 10, opposite mosque, Judería ☎ 957/471235. **Granada** ⊠ Mariana Pineda, 10 Centro ☎ 958/247146 ⊕ www.turismodegranada.org. **Junta de Andalusia** ⊕ www.andalucia.org

🚩 **Local Tourist Offices Baeza** ⊠ Pl. del Pópulo ☎ 953/740444. **Córdoba** ⊠ Pl. Juda Levi, Judería ☎ 957/200522 ☎ 957/200277. **Granada** ⊠ Pl. Mariana Pineda 10, Centro ☎ 958/247128. **Jaén** ⊠ C. Maestra, 13-Bajo ☎ 953/242624. **Montilla** ⊠ Capitán Alonso de Vargas 3 ☎ 957/652462 ⊕ www.turismomontilla.com. **Úbeda** ⊠ Palacio Marqués del Contadero, C. Baja del Marqués 4 ☎ 953/750897.

Seville & Western Andalusia

WORD OF MOUTH

"We attended the Royal Equestrian School Dancing Horses show in Jerez de la Frontera. We did not reserve tickets in advance and there were empty seats during the performance (first week in July). Although they offer a range of prices for seating, frankly every seat is the same for viewing. No need to pay more for any seating category . . .. Show lasts about 90 minutes with a 10-minute intermission. It is lovely and sedate. Do not expect to see circus tricks, a Fantasia, or much drama. This is a subtle and elegant presentation."

–winnie

By Mary
McLean

ALL THE ROMANTIC IMAGES of Andalusia—and Spain in general—spring vividly to life in Seville. Spain's fourth-largest city is an olé cliché of matadors, flamenco, tapas bars, gypsies, geraniums, and strolling guitarists. So tantalizing is this city that many travelers spend their entire Andalusian time here—but don't; Western Andalusia holds many surprises, from the aristocratic towns and Roman ruins of Seville's *campiña* (fertile plains) to the farmlands, sandy coastline, and tree-clad sierras of the neighboring provinces of Cádiz and Huelva.

Predating Seville by a millennium, the ancient city of Cádiz sits like a worn but still-shining jewel at the tip of a sandy isthmus in an Atlantic bay. Stretching north from here is the gently sloping Marco de Jerez area, bordered by the towns of Jerez de la Frontera, Sanlúcar de Barrameda, and Puerto de Santa María—a land of bull ranches, prancing Andalusian horses, and one of the world's best-known wines, sherry, aged in cobweb-filled cellars that have barely changed in centuries. In the province of Huelva, across the Guadalquivir River from the sherry region, stretches Doñana National Park, where marshy wetlands alternate with pine forests and shifting sand dunes. Beyond the park are coastal towns that played key roles in modern Western history: Christopher Columbus set sail from these shores in 1492. To the north is the Sierra de Aracena, where free-range Iberian pigs fatten in one of Andalusia's prettiest highland oak forests.

Today's Andalusian scenery is of fairly recent vintage. Flowing west at a sluggish pace from Jaén's Sierra Morena to the Atlantic Ocean, the mighty Guadalquivir River has shaped the landscape and history of southwestern Spain. Two thousand years ago, as the capricious river shifted course, it left the thriving Roman city of Itálica high and dry. As Itálica slid gradually into oblivion, nearby Hispalis—today's Seville—rose on the river's banks 11 km (7 mi) away. Seville's fortunes would continue to climb under the Moors, and again after its conquest by the Castilian Christians under King Ferdinand "the Saint" in the 13th century. During their reign the city acquired its cathedral—the largest Gothic building in the world—and its Moorish-inspired palace, the Alcázar.

With the discovery of the New World, Seville reached even dizzier heights of splendor, outshining Madrid in riches and culture as Spanish ships loaded with booty from the Americas sailed upriver past the Torre de Oro (Tower of Gold) and into Seville's port. Much of this treasure was siphoned off to pay for the Spanish throne's increasingly expensive foreign entanglements and bankers' debts, but enough was left over to fuel a cultural flowering and building bonanza that can still be seen today in Seville's lovely houses, courtyards, palaces, and monuments.

Exploring Seville & Western Andalusia

Although exploring the city of Seville is the main event here, there's also nearby Itálica, with its Roman ruins, as well as the farmland south of the Guadalquivir River known as La Campiña, along the *vega* (fertile river basin) of the Upper Guadalquivir. Huelva's Sierra de Aracena is an hour to the southwest, and the Doñana wetlands at the mouth of the

Guadalquivir River offer a chance to explore some of the Iberian Peninsula's wildest country. Cádiz and the triangle formed by Jerez de la Frontera, El Puerto de Santa María, and Sanlúcar de Barrameda offer culinary delights, beaches, Andalusian equestrian art, and flamenco dance and music, and Arcos de la Frontera is the gateway to the Sierra de Grazalema and the highlands.

About the Beaches

Overall this is not an area renowned for its beaches. The closest beach to Seville, Mataslascañas, is in Huelva province. It gets predictably crowded, especially on weekends in summer. For whiter sand and fewer people, head west to Mazagón or the Costa de la Luz east of Cádiz.

About the Restaurants

Spaniards drive for miles to sample the succulent seafood of Puerto de Santa María and Sanlúcar de Barrameda and to enjoy *fino* (a dry and light sherry from Jerez) and *manzanilla* (a dry and delicate Sanlúcar sherry with a hint of saltiness). Others come just to feast on tapas in Seville or Cádiz. The village of Jabugo, in Huelva, is famous for its cured ham from the free-ranging Iberian pig. Look for *jamon serrano,* a delicacy throughout Andalusia, on the menu at better restaurants. Note that many restaurants are closed on Sunday evenings, and several close for a month's vacation in August. Most restaurants and bars in this region offer a *menú del día,* mainly at lunchtime, which will include a starter, main course, sweet or coffee, bread, and wine or beer for between €8 and €12.

WHAT IT COSTS In Euros				
	$$$$	**$$$**	**$$**	**$**	**¢**
AT DINNER	over €20	€15–€20	€10–€15	€6–€10	under €6

Prices are per person for a main course at dinner.

About the Hotels

Western Andalusia has four paradores, including converted palaces at Carmona and Arcos de la Frontera, both worth a special visit. The parador at Mazagón and the parador Hotel Atlántico, in Cádiz, are comfortable modern hotels. You can also stay at a converted monastery, in Puerto de Santa María, or on a private luxury ranch, near Arcos de la Frontera. Seville has grand old hotels, such as the Alfonso XIII, and a number of former palaces converted into sumptuous hostelries. For top hotels during Seville's Holy Week or April Fair, Jerez's Horse Fair or Harvest Festival, or the Carnival of Cádiz, book early—six to eight months in advance. Prices in hotels can rise by at least 50% during fiesta time.

WHAT IT COSTS In Euros				
	$$$$	**$$$**	**$$**	**$**	**¢**
FOR 2 PEOPLE	over €180	€100–€180	€60–€100	€40–€60	under €40

Prices are for two people in a standard double room in high season, excluding tax.

GREAT ITINERARIES

If time is short, two days will cover Seville. From there, you can wander Doñana National Park and visit coastal villages, or head south to sip sherry in Jerez de la Frontera, relax in the village of Arcos de la Frontera, and feast on seafood in Cádiz.

IF YOU HAVE 3 DAYS

Base yourself in **Seville ❶ – ㉜**. On Day 1, visit the cathedral, the Giralda, and the nearby Alcázar, and walk through the Barrio de Santa Cruz. On Day 2, explore the Barrio de Macarena in the morning, starting at the Mercado de Feria and ending at the Museo de Bellas Artes. In the afternoon stroll in the Parque de María Luisa, the Plaza de América, and the Plaza de España. In the evening cross the Guadalquivir and visit the Barrio de Triana and the tapas bars of Calle Betis. Devote the next day to the ancient town of **Carmona ㉝**, with its Roman necropolis, and then the Roman ruins at **Itálica ㉞** before returning to Seville.

IF YOU HAVE 5 DAYS

Follow the itinerary above for the first day and a half. On the afternoon of the second day, walk the Paseo de Colón by the river–to see the Maestranza Bullring and visit the Torre de Oro. On Day 3, wander the Parque de María Luisa, stopping at the Plaza de América and Plaza de España. When returning to the city center, look for the University of Seville, the former tobacco factory of *Carmen* fame. In the afternoon cross the Guadalquivir to explore the Barrio de Triana. On Day 4, head south to ▦ **Jerez de la Frontera ㊸**. If it's a Thursday, catch the spectacular horse show at the Royal Andalusian School of Equestrian Art. Spend your last night in ▦ **Puerto de Santa María ㊻**, and on your final day visit **Cádiz ㊼** before heading back.

Timing

Aside from timing your visit with a fiesta, spring and late fall are particularly pleasant, when the weather is warm but not too hot. Avoid July and August, when the heat can be stifling. Winters are mild and uncrowded. Bear in mind that many museums and monuments are closed on Monday and that many restaurants close in January.

Numbers in the text correspond to numbers in the margin and on the Andalusia: Seville & Western Andalusia and Seville maps.

SEVILLE & ENVIRONS

Seville's whitewashed houses, bright with bougainvillea, its ocher-color palaces, and its baroque facades have long enchanted both Sevillanos and travelers. Lord Byron's well-known line, "Seville is a pleasant city famous for oranges and women," may be true, but is far too tame. Yes, the orange trees are pretty enough, but the fruit is too bitter to eat except as Scottish-made marmalade. As for the women, stroll down the swankier pedestrian shopping streets and you can't fail to notice just how good-looking *everyone* is. Aside from being blessed with even features and flashing dark eyes, there's a cool sophistication of style about the Sevillanos that seems more Catalan than Andalusian.

This bustling city of almost 800,000 does have a darker side, however: traffic-choked streets, high unemployment, a notorious petty-crime rate, and at times the kind of impersonal treatment you won't find in smaller cities such as Granada and Córdoba. If you want to venture out of Seville on a day trip, head to Carmona—the parador is perfect for a leisurely lunch—or Itálica, with its fascinating Roman ruins.

Seville

①–㉜   *550 km (340 mi) southwest of Madrid, 220 km (140 mi) northwest of Málaga.*

Seville has a long and noble history. Conquered by the Romans in 205 BC, it gave the world two great emperors, Trajan and Hadrian. The Moors held Seville for more than 500 years and left it one of their greatest works of architecture, the much-loved Giralda tower. Saint King Ferdinand (Ferdinand III) lies enshrined in the glorious cathedral; and his rather less saintly descendant, Pedro the Cruel, builder of the Alcázar, is buried here as well. Seville is justly proud of its literary and artistic associations. The painters Diego Rodríguez de Silva Velázquez (1599–1660) and Bartolomé Estéban Murillo (1617–82) were sons of Seville, as were the poets Gustavo Adolfo Bécquer (1836–70), Antonio Machado (1875–1939), and Nobel Prize winner Vicente Aleixandre (1898–1984). The tale of the ingenious knight of La Mancha was begun in a Seville jail—Don Quijote's creator, Miguel de Cervantes, twice languished in a debtors' prison. Tirso de Molina's Don Juan seduced in Seville's mansions, and Rossini's barber, Figaro, was married in the Barrio de Santa Cruz. It was at the old tobacco factory where Bizet's sultry Carmen first met Don José.

Seville's color and vivacity are most intense during Semana Santa (Holy Week), when lacerated Christs and bejeweled, weeping statues of Mary from the city's 24 parishes are paraded through the streets on floats borne by penitents, who often walk barefoot. A week later, and this time in flamenco costume, Sevillanos throw their April Fair. This celebration began as a horse-trading fair in 1847 and still honors its equine origins: midday horse parades include men in broad-brim hats and Andalusian riding gear astride prancing steeds, with their women in ruffled dresses riding sidesaddle behind them. Bullfights, fireworks, and all-night singing and dancing in the fairground's *casetas* (tents) complete the spectacle.

**▌ ◀
A GOOD
WALK**

Start with the **cathedral ① ▶**, in the Plaza Virgen de los Reyes. Then climb the Giralda, the minaret of the former Moorish mosque. Walk down Avenida de la Constitución until you reach the **Archivo de las Indias ②**. Behind the archives is the **Alcázar ③**, surrounded by high walls. Allow at least a couple of hours to explore this superb Moorish fortress and palace, surrounded by lush tropical gardens.

Backtrack to the Giralda and the Plaza Virgen de los Reyes and plunge into the **Barrio de Santa Cruz ④**, a tangle of narrow streets and squares lined with orange trees that was the home of Seville's Jews in the Mid-

IF YOU LIKE

BULLFIGHTING

In Seville is one of Spain's most celebrated bullrings: the Maestranza. Few *toreros* (bullfighters) gain nationwide recognition until they have fought in this "cathedral of bullfighting." The season runs from Easter until late October, but it peaks early on, when Seville's April Fair draws Spain's leading toreros for a string of daily fights.

FIESTAS

The weeklong **Carnival** in Cádiz, celebrated in February, is one of the best in the land. Seville's dramatic **Semana Santa** (Holy Week) processions and April Fair draw visitors worldwide. Many Seville attractions are closed during this time, especially on Holy Thursday and Good Friday. Jerez and Cádiz also have Semana Santa processions. The **Feria de Abril** (two weeks from the day after Holy Week) Seville's annual city fair, is celebrated with top bullfights, horse parades, flamenco costumes, and singing, dancing, and fireworks nightly in the fairground across the river. In May, Jerez de la Frontera shows off its Andalusian horses in the **Feria del Caballo** (Horse Fair). **Corpus Christi** (the second Thursday after Pentecost; June 7 in 2007) is celebrated with processions in Cádiz, Jerez, and Seville. In early June, worshippers make a Whitsuntide pilgrimage to the shrine of the **Virgen del Rocío** (Virgin of the Dew) in the village of El Rocío (Huelva). The **Asunción** (Assumption) is celebrated throughout Spain on August 15, but especially in Seville, where it's the day of the city's patron, **Nuestra Señora de los Reyes** (Our Lady of the Kings). In September, all wine-producing towns in the province of Cádiz celebrate the **Fiesta de la Vendimia** (Grape Harvest Festival). Jerez's **Fiesta de Otoño** (Autumn Festival) is spectacular. Cádiz commemorates its patron, the **Virgen del Rosario** (Virgin of the Rosary), in October.

FLAMENCO

Seville and Jerez de la Frontera are headquarters for this quintessentially Andalusian art form combining dance, song, guitar, and percussion. Seville offers flamenco opportunities ranging from professional clubs to the grassroots amateur *cante jondo* (literally, "deep song") heard in little taverns, *tablaos* (clubs), and *peñas* (societies) all over town. What the commercial clubs lack in spontaneity they make up for in skill and polish, but authentic flamenco, with its true emotion, its *duende* (power or magnetism), is best found in performances that break out off the beaten tourist track. Head to the *tascas* (bars) of popular barrios, such as Triana and La Macarena, or in the great flamenco factory of Las Tres Mil Viviendas, Seville's outlying, largely Gypsy, community. Ask around—at the tourism office, your hotel, or just about any bar—for the peñas (societies), semiprivate clubs. In such places, improvised flamenco, the real thing, may materialize.

12

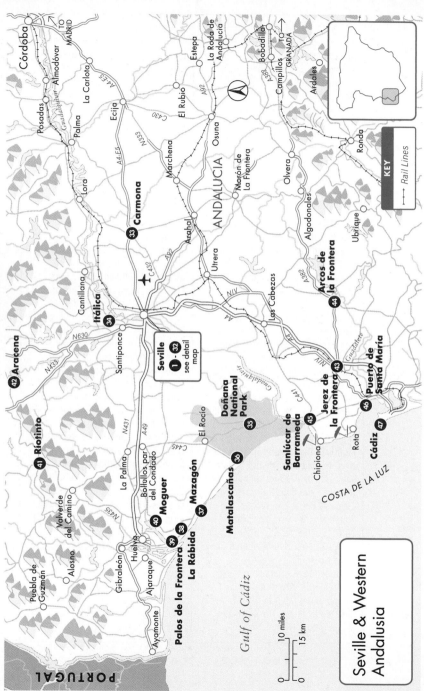

PORTUGAL

TO MADRID →

Córdoba

Posadas
Almodóvar
Guadalquivir
Palma
La Carlota
Lora
Cantillana
Ecija
El Rubio
La Roda de Andalucía
Estepa
Bobadilla
TO GRANADA →
Campillos
Ardales

33 Carmona

Marchena
Arahal
Osuna
Marón de La Frontera
Olvera
Ronda
Ubrique
Algodonales
Ardales

ANDALUCIA

34 Itálica

Santiponce

Seville **1** - **32** see detail map

Utrera
Las Cabezas

42 Aracena

Riotinto **41**

Valverde del Camino
Alosno
Puebla de Guzmán

La Palma

Bollullos par del Condado

El Rocio

Doñana National Park **35**

Guadalquivir

36

45 Sanlúcar de Barrameda
Chipiona

Arcos de la Frontera **44**

Jerez de la Frontera **43**

Puerto de Santa María **46**

Rota

Cádiz **47**

Moguer **40**
38 La Rábida
39

Mazagón **37**

Matalascañas

Palos de la Frontera

Huelva
Gibraleón
Ajaraque
Ayamonte

Gulf of Cádiz

COSTA DE LA LUZ

KEY

Rail Lines

Seville & Western Andalusia

0 ⊢—⊢—⊢ 10 miles
0 ⊢—⊢—⊢ 15 km

dle Ages. While you're in the neighborhood, don't miss the baroque **Hospital de los Venerables** ❺, a hospice for the elderly with a plant-filled patio and several notable paintings. On Calle Santa Teresa is the **Museo Casa de Murillo** ❻; from there you can stroll through the **Jardines de Murillo** ❼. At the far end of the gardens is the **University of Seville** ❽, once the tobacco factory where the mythical Carmen worked as a cigar roller. Across the Glorieta de San Diego is the **Parque de María Luisa** ❾, which encompasses the **Plaza de España** ❿ at its east end as well as the **Plaza de América** ⓫ at its south end. In the Plaza de América you can find the **Museo Arqueológico** ⓬, with marble statues and mosaics from the Roman era. Opposite is the **Museo de Artes y Costumbres Populares** ⓭. Head back north along the Paseo de las Delicias toward the city center. Near downtown Seville, on Avenida de Roma, is the baroque **Palacio de San Telmo** ⓮, home of the Andalusian regional government. Behind the Palacio is the Mudejar-style **Hotel Alfonso XIII** ⓯. On the north side of Puerta de Jerez is **Palacio de Yanduri** ⓰, birthplace of the Nobel Prize winner Vicente Aleixandre.

Walking toward the Guadalquivir River along Calle Almirante Lobo, you come to the riverside **Torre de Oro** ⓱, which stands opposite the **Teatro de la Maestranza** ⓲. Behind the theater is the **Hospital de la Caridad** ⓳, with a collection of works by Seville's leading painters. Continuing north along the river, you reach the **Plaza de Toros Real Maestranza** ⓴. Finally, head away from the river toward the Plaza Nueva, in the heart of Seville, and have a look at the **ayuntamiento** ㉑.

If you have energy and two more hours, walk north from the town hall along the pedestrian **Calle Sierpes** ㉒, Seville's most famous shopping street. Backtrack down Calle Cuna, parallel to Sierpes, stopping at No. 8 to see the **Palacio de la Condesa de Lebrija** ㉓. Continue down Calle Cuna to Plaza del Salvador and the **Iglesia del Salvador** ㉔, a former mosque. Walk up Alcaicería to Plaza de la Alfalfa and along Sales Ferre toward Plaza Cristo del Burgos—in a small alley off the square is the **Casa Natal de Velázquez** ㉕, where the painter was born in 1599. From Plaza Cristo de Burgos follow the narrow streets Descalzos and Caballerizas to the **Casa de Pilatos** ㉖, believed to be modeled on Pilate's house in Jerusalem.

A number of other sights are scattered throughout northern Seville and require separate trips. If you're an art lover, set aside half a day for the **Museo de Bellas Artes** ㉗. From here, head down to the river and across the Pasarela de la Cartuja bridge to the island of **La Cartuja** ㉘. Take a look at the Carthusian monastery, now home to the Andalucian Center of Contemporary Art. Another half day should be set aside to explore the **Triana** ㉙ neighborhood, on the river's western bank. To visit the **Basílica de la Macarena** ㉚, site of the Virgen de la Macarena, it's best to take a taxi from the city center. Other religious sites in the Macarena area are the Gothic **Convento de Santa Paula** ㉛ and the church of **San Lorenzo y Jesús del Gran Poder** ㉜, where colorful floats used in Seville's Holy Week processions are on display. If you just feel like a leisurely trip, hire a horse-drawn carriage; alternatively, you can hop on a city tour bus.

680 <

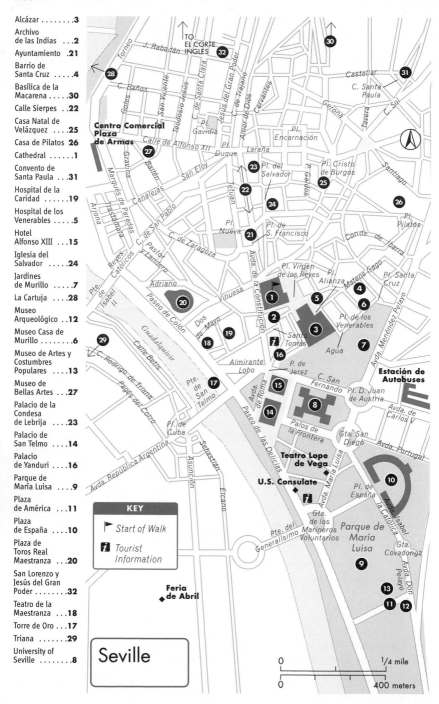

TIMING Allow a full day for the grand Seville tour. A trip to the Museo de Bellas Artes and the monastery at La Cartuja takes half a day (allow more time if you're visiting the island's theme park), and Triana and La Macarena each take two to three hours. Note that hours for the city's monuments and other sights change seasonally.

12

What to See

★ ❸ **Alcázar.** The Plaza Triunfo forms the entrance to the Mudejar palace built by Pedro I (1350–69) on the site of Seville's former Moorish *alcázar* (fortress). Don't mistake the Alcázar for a genuine Moorish palace, like Granada's Alhambra—it may look like one, and it was indeed designed and built by Moorish workers brought in from Granada, but it was commissioned and paid for by a Christian king more than 100 years after the reconquest of Seville. In its construction, Pedro the Cruel incorporated stones and capitals he pillaged from Valencia, from Córdoba's Medina Azahara, and from Seville itself. The palace serves as the official Seville residence of the king and queen.

You enter the Alcázar through the Puerta del León (Lion's Gate) and the high, fortified walls. You'll first find yourself in a garden courtyard, the **Patio del León** (Courtyard of the Lion). Off to the left are the oldest parts of the building, the 14th-century **Sala de Justicia** (Hall of Justice) and, next to it, the intimate **Patio del Yeso** (Courtyard of Plaster), the only part of the original 12th-century Almohad Alcázar. Cross the **Patio de la Montería** (Courtyard of the Hunt) to Pedro's Mudejar palace, arranged around the beautiful **Patio de las Doncellas** (Court of the Damsels), resplendent with delicately carved stucco. Its name refers to the annual gift of 100 maidens to the Moorish sultans. Opening off this patio, the **Salón de Embajadores** (Hall of the Ambassadors), with its cedar cupola of green, red, and gold, is the most sumptuous hall in the palace. It was here that Carlos V married Isabel of Portugal in 1526. The balconies were added by Felipe II.

Other royal rooms include Felipe II's dining hall and the three baths of Pedro's wily mistress, María de Padilla. María's hold over her royal lover—and apparently over his courtiers, too—was so great that legend goes that they all lined up to drink her bathwater. The **Patio de las Muñecas** (Court of the Dolls) takes its name from two tiny faces carved on the inside of one of its arches, no doubt as a joke on the part of its Moorish creators. Here Pedro reputedly had his half brother, Don Fadrique, slain in 1358; and here, too, he murdered guest Abu Said of Granada for his jewels—one of which is now among England's crown jewels. (The huge, uncut ruby came to England by way of the Black Prince—Edward, Prince of Wales [1330–76], eldest son of Edward III. Pedro gave the ruby to him as payment for help in fighting the revolt of his illegitimate brother in 1367.)

You come next to the Renaissance **Palacio de Carlos V** (Palace of Charles V), built by the emperor at the time of his marriage and endowed with a rich collection of Flemish tapestries depicting Carlos's victories at Tunis. Look for the map of Spain: it shows the Iberian Peninsula upside down, as was the custom in Arab mapmaking. There are more goodies—rare clocks, antique furniture, paintings, and more tapestries—on the Alcázar's upper floor, in the **Estancias Reales** (Royal Chambers). These are the apartments used by King Juan Carlos I and his family when in town. The required guided tour (a separate ticket from the Alcázar) leads you through the dining room, other protocol rooms, and the king's office. Tours depart in the morning only, every half hour in summer and every hour in winter.

At the end of your visit, pause in the **gardens** to inhale jasmine and myrtle, wander among terraces and ornamental baths, and peer into the well-stocked goldfish pond. In the midst of this green oasis is an orange tree said to have been planted in the time of Pedro the Cruel. From the gardens, a passageway leads to the **Patio de las Banderas** (Court of the Flags), which has a classic view of the Giralda. ☒ *Pl. del Triunfo, Santa Cruz* ☏ *95/450–2323* ⊕ *www.patronato-alcazarsevilla.es* ☒ *€5, tour of Royal Chambers €3* ⊘ *Apr.–Sept., Tues.–Sat. 9:30–8, Sun. 9:30–6; Oct.–Mar., Tues.–Sat. 9:30–5, Sun. 9:30–1:30.*

② **Archivo de las Indias** (Archives of the Indies). Opened in 1785 in the former Lonja (Merchants' Exchange), this dignified Renaissance building was designed by Juan de Herrera, architect of El Escorial, in 1572. The archives include more than 40,000 documents, including drawings, trade documents, plans of South American towns, even the autographs of Columbus, Magellan, and Cortés. ☒ *Av. de la Constitución, Santa Cruz* ☏ *95/421–1234* ☒ *Free* ⊘ *Mon.–Sat. 10–6.*

㉑ **Ayuntamiento** (City Hall). This Diego de Riaño original, built between 1527 and 1564, is in the heart of Seville's commercial center. A 19th-century, plateresque facade overlooks the Plaza Nueva. Walk around to the other side, on the Plaza de San Francisco, to see Riaño's work. ☒ *Pl. Nueva 1, Centro* ☏ *95/459–0101* ☒ *Free* ⊘ *Tours Tues.–Thurs. at 5:30.*

★ **④** **Barrio de Santa Cruz.** The twisting alleyways and traditional ocher houses add to the tourist charm of this barrio. On some streets, bars alternate with antiques stores and souvenir shops, but most of the quarter is quiet and residential. The Callejón del Agua, beside the wall of the Alcázar's gardens, has some of the quarter's finest mansions and patios. Pause to enjoy the antiques shops and outdoor cafés on the **Plaza Alianza.** Take a look at the simple crucifix hanging on one of the dazzling-white walls shrouded in bougainvillea. In the **Plaza de Doña Elvira,** with its fountain and *azulejo* (painted tile) benches, young Sevillanos gather to play guitars. Here you can see one side of the **Hospital de los Venerables.** Just around the corner from the hospital, at Callejón del Agua and Jope de Rueda, Rossini's Figaro serenaded Rosina on her **Plaza Alfaro** balcony. Adjoining the Plaza Alfaro, in the **Plaza Santa Cruz,** flowers and orange trees surround a 17th-century filigree iron cross, which marks the site of the erstwhile church of Santa Cruz, destroyed by Napoléon's General Soult. The painter Murillo was buried here in 1682, though his current resting place is unknown.

㉚ **Basílica de la Macarena.** This church holds Seville's most revered image, the Virgin of Hope—better known as La Macarena. Bedecked with candles and carnations, her cheeks streaming with glass tears, the Macarena steals the show at the procession on Holy Thursday, the highlight of Seville's Holy Week pageant. She's the patron of gypsies and the protector of the matador. So great are her charms that the Sevillian bullfighter Joselito spent half his personal fortune buying her four emeralds. When he was killed in the ring at the tender age of 25, in 1920, the Macarena was dressed in widow's weeds for a month. There's a small adjacent museum devoted to her costumes and jewels. ⊠ *C. Bécquer 1, La Macarena* ☎ *95/490–1800* ⊠ *Basilica free, museum €3* ⊙ *Basilica daily 9–2 and 5–9, museum daily 9:30–2 and 5–8.*

12

㉒ **Calle Sierpes.** This is Seville's classy main shopping street. Near the southern end, at No. 85, a plaque marks the spot where the Cárcel Real (Royal Prison) once stood (now a bank). Miguel de Cervantes began writing *Don Quijote* in one of its cells.

❻ **Museo Casa de Murillo.** Bartolomé Estéban Murillo (1617–82) lived here for a time; there's a small museum here dedicated to the painter's life, but it's open only for special exhibitions. Call or contact the tourist office for more information. ⊠ *C. Santa Teresa 8, Alfalfa* ☎☎ *95/422–9415* ⊠ *Free* ⊙ *Weekdays 10–2 and 4–7.*

㉕ **Casa Natal de Velázquez.** One of Spain's greatest painters, Diego de Velázquez was born in this *casa de vecinos* (town house shared by several families) in 1599. The house fell into ruin, but was bought in the 1970s by the well-known fashion designers Victorio y Lucchino, who restored it for use as their studio. It's not open to the public. ⊠ *Padre Luis María Llop 4, Centro.*

㉖ **Casa de Pilatos.** This palace was built in the first half of the 16th century by the dukes of Tarifa, ancestors of the present owner, the Duke of Medinaceli. It's known as Pilate's House because Don Fadrique, first marquis of Tarifa, allegedly modeled it on Pontius Pilate's house in Jerusalem, where he had gone on a pilgrimage in 1518. With its fine patio and superb azulejo decorations, the palace is a beautiful blend of Spanish Mudejar and Renaissance architecture. The upstairs apartments, which you can see on a guided tour, have frescoes, paintings, and antique furniture. ⊠ *Pl. Pilatos 1, Santa Cruz* ☎ *95/422–5298* ⊠ *€8; lower floor only, €5* ⊙ *Daily 9–6:30.*

▶ ❶ **Cathedral.** After Ferdinand III captured Seville from the Moors in 1248, the great mosque begun by Yusuf II in 1171 was reconsecrated to the Virgin Mary and used as a Christian cathedral. But in 1401 the people of Seville decided to erect a new cathedral, one that would equal the glory of their great city. They promptly pulled down the old mosque, leaving only its minaret and outer court, and set about constructing the existing building in just over a century—a remarkable feat for the time. The clergy renounced their incomes for the cause, and a member of the chapter is said to have proclaimed, "Let us build a church so large that we shall be held to be insane." This they proceeded to do, for the cathedral can be described only in superlatives: it's the largest and highest cathedral in Spain, the largest Gothic building in the world, and the world's third-largest church, after St. Peter's in Rome and St. Paul's in London.

Head first for the **Patio de los Naranjos** (Courtyard of Orange Trees), on the northern side and part of the original mosque. The fountain in the center was used for ablutions before people entered the mosque. Near the Puerta del Lagarto (Lizard's Gate), in the corner near the Giralda, try to find the wooden crocodile—thought to have been a gift from the emir of Egypt in 1260 as he sought the hand of the daughter of Alfonso the Wise—and the elephant tusk, found in the ruins of Itálica. The cathedral's exterior, with its rose windows and flying buttresses, is a monument to pure Gothic beauty. Aside from the well-lighted high altar, the dimly illuminated interior can be disappointing, its five naves and numerous side chapels shrouded in gloom; Gothic purity has been largely submerged in ornate baroque decoration. Enter the cathedral through the Puerta de la Granada or the Puerta Colorada. In the central nave rises the **Capilla Mayor** (Main Chapel) and its intricately carved altarpiece, begun by a Flemish carver in 1482. This magnificent *retablo* (altarpiece) is the largest in Christendom (65 feet by 43 feet). It depicts some 36 scenes from the life of Christ, with pillars carved with more than 200 figures. The whole work is lavishly adorned with gold leaf.

Make your way to the opposite (southern) side of the cathedral to see the **monument to Christopher Columbus**. The great explorer knew both triumph and disgrace but found no repose—he died, bitterly disillusioned, in Valladolid in 1506. No one knows for certain where he is buried: he was reportedly laid to rest for the first time in the Dominican Republic and then moved over the years to other locations. Still, his remains are thought to be here. Columbus's coffin is borne aloft by the four kings representing the medieval kingdoms of Spain: Castile, León, Aragón, and Navarra. Columbus's son Hernando Colón (1488–1539), is also interred here; his tombstone, inscribed with the words A CASTILLA Y A LEÓN, MUNDO NUEVO DIO COLÓN (to Castile and León, Columbus gave a new world), lies between the great west door, the Puerta Mayor, and the central choir.

Between the elder Columbus's tomb and the Capilla Real, at the eastern end of the central nave, the cathedral's treasures include gold and silver (much of it from the New World), relics, and other works of art. In the **Sacristía de los Cálices** (Sacristy of the Chalices) look for Martínez Montañés's wood carving *Crucifixion, Merciful Christ*; Valdés Leal's *St. Peter Freed by an Angel*; Zurbarán's *Virgin and Child*; and Goya's *St. Justa and St. Rufina*. The **Sacristía Mayor** (Main Sacristy) holds the keys to the city, which Seville's Moors and Jews presented to their conqueror, Ferdinand III. Finally, in the dome of the **Sala Capitular** (Chapter House), in the cathedral's southeastern corner, is Murillo's *Immaculate Conception*, painted in 1668.

One of the cathedral's highlights, the **Capilla Real** (Royal Chapel), is reserved for prayer and concealed behind a ponderous curtain, but you can duck in if you're quick, quiet, and properly dressed (no shorts or sleeveless tops). To do so, explore the rest of the cathedral and the Giralda and enter again from a separate door, the Puerta de los Palos, on Plaza Virgen de los Reyes (signposted ENTRADA PARA CULTO—entrance for worship). Along the sides of the chapel are the tombs of the wife of 13th century's Ferdinand III, Beatrix of Swabia, and his son Alfonso X, called The Wise); in a silver urn before the high altar rest the precious relics of Ferdinand III himself, Seville's liberator. Canonized in 1671, he was said to have died from excessive fasting. In the (rarely open) vault below lie the tombs of Ferdinand's descendant Pedro the Cruel and Ferdinand's mistress, María de Padilla. Above the entrance, a Jerónino Roldán sculpture of Ferdinand III receives the keys to Seville.

12

Before you duck into the Capilla Real, climb to the top of the **Giralda,** which dominates Seville's skyline. Once the minaret of Seville's great mosque, from which the faithful were summoned to prayer, it was built between 1184 and 1196, just 50 years before the reconquest of Seville. The Christians could not bring themselves to destroy this tower when they tore down the mosque, so they incorporated it into their new cathedral. In 1565–68 they added a lantern and belfry to the old minaret and installed 24 bells, one for each of Seville's 24 parishes and the 24 Christian knights who fought with Ferdinand III in the Reconquest. They also added the bronze statue of Faith, which turned as a weather vane— *el giraldillo,* or "something that turns," thus the name Giralda. To give it a rest after 400 years of wear and tear, the original statue was replaced with a copy in 1997. With its baroque additions, the slender Giralda rises 322 feet. Inside, instead of steps, 35 sloping ramps—wide enough for two horsemen to pass abreast—climb to a viewing platform 230 feet up. It is said that Ferdinand III rode his horse to the top to admire the city he had conquered. If you follow in his (horse's) footsteps, you'll be rewarded with a view of tile roofs and the Guadalquivir shimmering beneath palm-lined banks. ⊠ *Pl. Virgen de los Reyes, Santa Cruz* ☎ *95/ 421–4971* 🖃 *Cathedral and Giralda €6, Sun. free* ☉ *Cathedral Mon.–Sat. 11–5, Sun. 2:30–6, and for Mass.*

③① **Convento de Santa Paula.** This 15th-century Gothic convent has a fine
Fodor'sChoice facade and portico, with ceramic decoration by Nicolaso Pisano. The
★ chapel has some beautiful azulejos and sculptures by Martínez Montañés. There's a small museum and shop selling delicious cakes and jams made by the nuns. ⊠ *C. Santa Paula 11, La Macarena* ☎ *95/453– 6330* 🖃 *€2* ☉ *Tues.–Sun. 10–1.*

⑲ **Hospital de la Caridad.** Behind the Maestranza Theater is this almshouse for the sick and elderly, where six paintings by Murillo (1617–82) and two gruesome works by Valdés Leal (1622–90) depicting the Triumph of Death are displayed. The baroque hospital was founded in 1674 by Seville's original Don Juan, Miguel de Mañara (1626–79). A nobleman of licentious character, Mañara was returning one night from a riotous orgy when he had a vision of a funeral procession in which the partly decomposed corpse in the coffin was his own. Accepting the apparition as a sign from God, Mañara renounced his worldly goods and joined the Brotherhood of Charity, whose unsavory task it was to collect the bodies of executed criminals and bury them. He devoted his fortune to building this hospital and is buried before the high altar in the chapel. There's a series of paintings by the artist Murillo, a friend of Mañara's. ⊠ *C. Temprado 3, Arenal* ☎ *95/422–3232* 🖃 *€4* ☉ *Mon.–Sat. 9–1:30 and 3:30–6:30, Sun. 9–1.*

⑤ Hospital de los Venerables. Once a retirement home for priests, this baroque building now has a cultural foundation that organizes art exhibitions here. The required 20-minute guided tour takes in a splendid azulejo patio with an interesting sunken fountain (designed to cope with low water pressure) and upstairs gallery, but the hospital's highlight is its chapel, with frescoes by Juan Valdés Leal. ⊠ *Pl. de los Venerables 8, Santa Cruz* ☎ *95/456–2696* ⊡ *€4.75 with guide* ☉ *Daily 10–2 and 4–8.*

⑮ Hotel Alfonso XIII. Seville's most emblematic hotel, this grand, Mudejar-style building next to the university was built—and named—for the king's visit to the 1929 fair. Nonguests are welcome to admire the gracious Moorish-style courtyard, best appreciated while sipping an ice-cold *fino* from the adjacent bar. ⊠ *San Fernando 2, El Arenal* ☎ *95/491–7000.*

Fodor'sChoice
★

㉔ Iglesia del Salvador. Built between 1671 and 1712, the Church of the Savior stands on the site of Seville's first great mosque, and remains can be seen in the Courtyard of the Orange Trees. Also of note are the sculptures of *Jesus de la Pasión* and St. Christopher by Martínez Montañés. In 2003 archaeologists discovered an 18th-century burial site here; digs are still being carried out with walkways installed to facilitate visits. ⊠ *Pl. del Salvador, Centro* ☎ *95/459–5405* ⊡ *€2 with guide* ☉ *Weekends only 10–2 and 4–8.*

⑦ Jardines de Murillo (Murillo Gardens). From the Plaza Santa Cruz you can embark on a stroll through these shady gardens, where you'll find a statue of Christopher Columbus.

㉘ La Cartuja. Named after its 14th-century Carthusian monastery, the island of La Cartuja, across the river from northern Seville, was the site of the decennial Universal Exposition (Expo) in 1992. Four bridges were built across the river for this event. The island has the Teatro Central, used for concerts and plays; Parque del Alamillo, Seville's largest and least-known park; and the Estadio Olímpico, a 60,000-seat covered stadium. The eastern shore holds the ۞ **Isla Mágica**, with 14 different attractions around a lake, including the hair-raising Jaguar roller coaster. ☎ *902/161716* ⊕ *www.islamagica.es* ⊡ *Apr. and May €21, June–Oct. €23.50* ☉ *Apr. and May, weekends 11 AM–midnight; June–Oct., daily 11 AM–midnight.*

The 14th century **Monasterio de Santa María de las Cuevas,** or the Monasterio de La Cartuja, was regularly visited by Christopher Columbus, who was buried here for a few years. Part of the building houses the Centro Andaluz de Arte Contemporáneo, which has an absorbing collection of contemporary art, plus regular temporary exhibitions. ⊠ *Isla de la Cartuja* ☎ *95/503–7070* ⊡ *€3, free Tues. for EU citizens* ☉ *Tues.–Fri. 10–7:30, Sat. 11–8, Sun. 10–2:30.*

⑫ Museo Arqueológico (Museum of Archaeology). A fine Renaissance-style building has artifacts from Phoenician, Tartessian, Greek, Carthaginian, Iberian, Roman, and medieval times. Displays include marble statues and mosaics from the Roman excavations at Itálica and a faithful replica of the fabulous Carambolo treasure found on a hillside outside Seville in 1958: 21 pieces of jewelry, all of them 24-karat gold, dating

CLOSE UP

Easter Week in Seville

HOLY WEEK IN SEVILLE combines religious emotion, Gypsy passion, and pagan joy. From Palm Sunday to Good Friday some 65 *cofradías* (brotherhoods) parade more than 120 *pasos* (floats) with vivid representations of Christ on the cross followed by the grieving Virgin Mary. More than 50,000 pointy-hooded penitents, known as *Nazarenos* (20,000 of them lugging wooden crosses), accompany processions through the streets, while central Seville becomes a vast wine-and-tapas fest. Throughout Holy Week,

and the Feria de Abril a week later, Seville is officially *"de fiesta,"* partying, with the whole community decked out as if headed to weddings, possibly their own.

The week builds to a crescendo with *La Madrugá* (dawn), from midnight Thursday into the early hours of Good Friday. *El Llamador*, the official program, has timetables and information about the cofradías, the icons, the music, and the number of Nazarenos.

12

---

from the 7th and 6th centuries BC. ⊠ *Pl. de América, El Porvenir* ☎ 95/ 423–2401 ☒ €1.50, free for EU citizens ☉ Tues. 3–8, Wed.–Sat. 9–8, Sun. 9–2.

⑬ Museo de Artes y Costumbres Populares (Museum of Folklore). The Mudejar pavilion opposite the Museum of Archaeology is the site of this museum of mainly 19th- and 20th-century Spanish folklore. The first floor has re-creations of a forge, a bakery, a wine press, a tanner's shop, and a pottery studio. Upstairs, exhibits include 18th- and 19th-century court dress, stunning regional folk costumes, carriages, and musical instruments. ⊠ *Pl. de América 3, El Porvenir* ☎ 95/423–2576 ☒ €1.50, free for EU citizens ☉ Tues. 3–8, Wed.–Sat. 9–8, Sun. 9–2.

Fodor's Choice
★

㉗ Museo de Bellas Artes (Museum of Fine Arts). Along with Bilbao's Guggenheim, this museum is second only to Madrid's Prado in Spanish art. It's in the former convent of La Merced Calzada, most of which dates from the 17th century. The collection includes Murillo, Zurbarán, Valdés Leal, and El Greco; outstanding examples of Seville Gothic art; and baroque religious sculptures in wood (a quintessentially Andalusian art form). In the rooms dedicated to Sevillian art of the 19th and 20th centuries, look for Gonzalo Bilbao's *Las Cigarreras*, a group portrait of Seville's famous cigar makers. ⊠ *Pl. del Museo 9, El Porvenir* ☎ 95/422–0790 ☒ €1.50, free for EU citizens ☉ Tues. 2:30–8:15, Wed.–Sat. 9–8:15, Sun. 9–2:15.

㉓ Palacio de la Condesa de Lebrija. This lovely palace has three ornate patios, including a spectacular courtyard graced by a Roman mosaic taken from the ruins in Itálica, surrounded by Moorish arches and fine azulejos. The side rooms house a collection of archaeological goodies. ⊠ *Cuna 8, Centro* ☎ 95/422–7802 ☒ €7, €4 for ground floor only ☉ Weekdays 10:30–1:30 and 4:30–7:30, Sat. 10–2.

⓮ **Palacio de San Telmo.** This splendid baroque palace is largely the work of architect Leonardo de Figueroa. Built between 1682 and 1796, it was first a naval academy and then the residence of the Bourbon dukes of Montpensier, during which time it outshone Madrid's royal court for sheer brilliance. The palace gardens are now the Parque de María Luisa, and the building itself is the seat of the Andalusian government. The main portal, vintage 1734, is a superb example of the fanciful Churrigueresque style. Call in advance if you want to arrange a visit. ☒ *Av. de Roma, El Arenal* ☎ *95/503–5500.*

⓰ **Palacio de Yanduri.** Nobel Prize–winning poet Vicente Aleixandre was born here. ☒ *North side of Puerta de Jerez, Santa Cruz.*

➒ **Parque de María Luisa.** Formerly the garden of the Palacio de San Telmo, the park is a blend of formal design and wild vegetation. In the burst of development that gripped Seville in the 1920s, it was redesigned for the 1929 Exhibition, and the impressive villas you see now are the fair's remaining pavilions, many of them consulates or schools. Note the **statue of El Cid** by Rodrigo Díaz de Vivar (1043–99), who fought both for and against the Muslim rulers during the Reconquest, and the old **Casino** from the 1929 Hispanic-American Exhibition, now the Teatro Lope de Vega. ☒ *Main entrance: Glorieta San Diego, El Arenal.*

⓫ **Plaza de América.** Walk to the south end of the Parque de María Luisa, past the Isla de los Patos (Island of Ducks), to find this plaza, typically carpeted in white doves and designed by Aníbal González. It's a blaze of color, with flowers, shrubs, ornamental stairways, and fountains tiled in yellow, blue, and ocher. The three impressive buildings surrounding the square—in neo-Mudejar, Gothic, and Renaissance styles— were built by González for the 1929 fair. Two of them now house Seville's museums of archaeology and folklore.

🅒 ➓ **Plaza de España.** This grandiose half-moon of buildings on the eastern edge of the Parque de María Luisa was Spain's centerpiece pavilion at the 1929 Exhibition. The brightly colored azulejo pictures represent the 50 provinces of Spain, while the four bridges symbolize the medieval kingdoms of the Iberian Peninsula. You can rent small boats for rowing along the arc-shape canal.

⓴ **Plaza de Toros Real Maestranza** (Royal Maestranza Bullring). Sevillanos have spent many a thrilling Sunday afternoon in this bullring, built between 1760 and 1763. Painted a deep ocher, the stadium is the one of the oldest and loveliest *plazas de toros* in Spain. An adjoining museum has prints and photos. ☒ *Paseo de Colón 12, El Arenal* ☎ *95/422–4577* ⌨ *Plaza and bullfighting museum €4 with English-speaking guide* ☉ *Daily 9:30–7, 9:30–3 only on bullfight days.*

㉜ **San Lorenzo y Jesús del Gran Poder.** This 17th-century church has many fine works by such artists as Montañés and Pacheco, but its outstanding piece is Juan de Mesa's *Jesús del Gran Poder* (*Christ Omnipotent*). ☒ *C. Jesús del Gran Poder, Alameda* ☎ *95/438–4558* ⌨ *Free* ☉ *Daily 8–1:30 and 6–9.*

⑱ **Teatro de la Maestranza** (Maestranza Theater). Opposite the Torre de Oro is Seville's opera house. One of Europe's leading halls, the Maestranza presents opera, classical music, *zarzuela* (Spanish light opera), and jazz. ✉ *Paseo de Colón 22, El Arenal* ☎ *95/422–6573 or 95/422–3344* ⊕ *www.teatromaestranza.com.*

12

⑰ **Torre de Oro.** The Tower of Gold stands on the banks of the Guadalquivir near the Puerta de Jerez. A 12-sided tower built by the Moors in 1220 to complete the city's ramparts, it served to close off the harbor when a chain was stretched across the river from its base to another tower on the opposite bank. In 1248 Admiral Ramón de Bonifaz broke through this barrier, and thus did Ferdinand III capture Seville. The tower now houses a small naval museum. ☎ *95/422–2419* ☞ €1 ⊙ *Tues.–Sat. 10–2.*

㉙ **Triana.** Across the Guadalquivir from central Seville, Triana used to be the city's gypsy quarter. Today it has a tranquil, neighborly feel by day, and its atmospheric clubs and flamenco bars throb at night. Enter Triana by the **Puente Isabel II** (better known as the Puente de Triana), built in 1852, the first bridge to connect the city's two sections. Walk across Plaza Altozano up Calle Jacinto and turn right at **Calle Alfarería** (Pottery Street) to see a slew of pottery stores and workshops. Return to Plaza Altozano and walk down Calle Pureza as far as the small **Capilla de los Marineros** (Seamen's Chapel), home to a venerated statue of Mary called the Esperanza de Triana, which native-born Trianeros claim is prettier than the rival Virgen de la Macarena across the river. Head back toward the river and **Calle Betis** for some of the city's most colorful bars, clubs, and restaurants.

⑧ **University of Seville.** At the far end of the Jardines de Murillo, opposite Calle San Fernando, stands what used to be the **Real Fábrica de Tabacos** (Royal Tobacco Factory). Built between 1750 and 1766, the factory employed some 3,000 *cigarreras* (female cigar makers) less than a century later, including, of course, the heroine of Bizet's opera *Carmen,* who reputedly rolled her cigars on her thigh. You're free to wander around the lower floors and courtyards, usually teeming with students. The enormous building has been the university's home only since the 1950s; today's factory is across the river. ✉ *C. San Fernando, Santa Cruz* ☎ *95/455–1000* ☞ *Free* ⊙ *Weekdays 9–8:30.*

Where to Eat

★ $$$$ ✗ **Egaña-Oriza.** Owner José Mari Egaña is Basque, but he is considered one of the fathers of modern Andalusian cooking. The restaurant, on the edge of the Murillo Gardens opposite the university, has spare contemporary decor with high ceilings and wall-to-wall windows. The menu might include *lomos de lubina con salsa de erizos de mar* (sea bass with sea urchin sauce) or *solomillo con foie natural y salsa de ciruelas* (fillet steak with foie gras and plum sauce). On the downside, the service can be slow; you can always drop into the adjoining Bar España for an hors d'oeuvre tapa such as stuffed mussels with béchamel sauce. ✉ *San Fernando 41, Jardines de Murillo* ☎ *95/422–7211* ⊟ *AE, DC, MC, V* ⊙ *Closed Sun. and Aug. No lunch Sat.*

★ $$$–$$$$ ✗ **La Albahaca.** Overlooking one of Seville's prettiest small plazas in the Barrio de Santa Cruz, this wonderful old family manor house was built by the celebrated architect Juan Talavera as a home for his own family; inside, four dining rooms are decorated with tiles, antique oil paintings, and leafy plants. There's a Basque twist to many of the dishes—consider the *lubina al horno con berenjenas y yogur al cardamomo* (baked sea bass with eggplant in a yogurt-and-cardamom sauce) or *foie de oca salteado* (lightly sautéed goose liver perfumed with honey vinegar) followed by the delicious fig mousse. There's an excellent €27 daily menu. Readers have complained of being turned away without a reservation here, so do book your table ahead. ⊠ *Pl. Santa Cruz 12, Santa Cruz* ☎ *95/422–0714* ⚸ *Reservations essential* ⊟ *AE, DC, MC, V* ⊘ *Closed Sun.*

$$$ ✗ **Poncio.** In the three small, comfortable dining rooms, diners enjoy dishes
Fodor's Choice based on Andalusian tradition with a French flair. Chef Willy Moya trained
★ in Paris and blends local and cosmopolitan cuisine flawlessly. Try the *salmorejo encapotado* (thick, garlic-laden gazpacho topped with diced egg and ham), or the *besugo con gambitas* (sea bream with shrimp). Desserts include a delectable version of French toast, showered with slivered almonds and garnished with rich cinnamon ice cream. The restaurant is around the corner from the Iglesia de Santa Ana, Seville's oldest church. ⊠ *C. Victoria 8, Triana* ☎ *95/434–0010* ⊟ *AE, DC, MC, V* ⊘ *Closed Sun.*

$$$ ✗ **Taberna del Alabardero.** Installed in a 19th-century mansion near the Plaza Nueva, this highly regarded restaurant is also a hotel with seven guest rooms. Preceded by a courtyard and a bar, the dining area is decorated in Sevillian tiles. Modern dishes include *bacalao a la parrilla trija de hongos sobre pil-pil y aceite de jamón* (grilled cod with mushrooms in a spicy chili-and-ham sauce). There's a training school for chefs here—always a good sign. ⊠ *Zaragoza 20, Arenal* ☎ *95/456–0637* ⊟ *AE, DC, MC, V* ⊘ *Closed Aug.*

$$–$$$ ✗ **Becerrita.** The affable Jesus Becerra runs this cozy—verging on cramped—establishment. Diligent service and tasty modern treatments of such classic Spanish dishes as *lomo de cordero a la miel* (loin of lamb in a honey sauce) and *rape con salsa de manzana* (angler fish with applesauce) have won the favor of Sevillanos. ⊠ *Recaredo 9, Santa Catalina* ☎ *95/441–2057* ⊕ *www.becerrita.com* ⚸ *Reservations essential* ⊟ *AE, MC, V* ⊘ *No dinner Sun. and Aug.*

★ $$ ✗ **Enrique Becerra.** Excellent tapas await at this restaurant run by the fifth generation of this family of celebrated restaurateurs. Enrique's brother Jesus helms nearby Becerrita. The tiled bar is a lively meeting place for locals. The menu focuses on traditional, home-cooked Andalusian dishes, such as *pez espada al amontillado* (swordfish cooked in dark sherry) and *cordero a la miel con espinacas* (honey-glazed lamb stuffed with spinach and pine nuts). Don't miss the cumin seed–laced *espinacas con garbanzos* (spinach with chickpeas). ⊠ *Gamazo 2, Arenal* ☎ *95/421–3049* ⊟ *AE, DC, MC, V* ⊘ *Closed Sun. and last 2 wks of July.*

$$ ✗ **La Isla.** Using fresh fish from Cádiz and Huelva, La Isla serves wonderful *parrillada de mariscos y pescados*, a fish and seafood grill for two people. *Zarzuela*, the Catalan seafood stew, is another favorite, and simple meat dishes are also served. The dining room and tapas bar are adorned

with traditional Sevillano tiles. ⊠ *Arfe 25, Arenal* ☎ *95/421–5376* ▭ *AE, DC, MC, V* ☺ *Closed Aug.*

$$ ✕ **San Marco.** In a 17th-century palace in the shopping district, this Italian restaurant has original frescoes, a gracious patio, and a menu that combines Italian, French, and Andalusian cuisine. Pasta dishes, such as ravioli stuffed with shrimp and pesto sauce, are notable. The restaurant now has four satellites, but this one, the original, is the most charming. ⊠ *Cuna 6, Centro* ☎ *95/421–2440* ⚠ *Reservations essential* ▭ *AE, DC, MC, V.*

$–$$ ✕ **El Corral del Agua.** Abutting the outer walls of the Alcázar on a narrow pedestrian street in the Santa Cruz neighborhood is a restored 18th-century palace, with a patio filled with geraniums and a central fountain. Andalusian specialties, such as *cola de toro al estilo de Sevilla* (Seville-style bull's tail), are prepared with contemporary flair. ⊠ *Callejón del Agua 6, Santa Cruz* ☎ *95/422–4841* ▭ *AE, DC, MC, V* ☺ *Closed Sun. and Jan. and Feb.*

$–$$ ✕ **Hostería del Laurel.** This restaurant—also a small hotel—has a large tapas selection and is geared toward tourists, capitalizing on its location in the Barrio de Santa Cruz. In summer you can dine outdoors on the plaza, surrounded by beautiful white and ocher houses. Inside, the dining room ceilings are festooned with hanging hams, garlic, dried herbs, peppers, squash, and corn cobs. Dishes include squid in garlic and hearty tortillas. ⊠ *Pl. de los Venerables 5, Santa Cruz* ☎ *95/422–0295* ⊕ *www.hosteriadellaurel.net* ▭ *AE, DC, MC, V.*

$ ✕ **Modesto.** The downstairs is a lively, crowded tapas bar; upstairs is the dining room, which has stucco walls decorated with blue-and-white tiles. The house specialty is a crisp *fritura Modesto* (a selection of small fish fried in top-quality olive oil); another excellent choice is the *cazuela al Tío Diego* ("Uncle Jim's Casserole"—ham, mushrooms, and shrimp). You can dine cheaply here, but beware: *mariscos* (shellfish) take the bill to another level. ⊠ *Cano y Cueto 5, Santa Cruz* ☎ *95/441–6811* ▭ *AE, DC, MC, V.*

¢–$ ✕ **Habanita.** A vegetarian restaurant in the buzzing Alfalfa barrio is a rarity. The menu is vast, with an emphasis on Cuban and Mediterranean fare. Dishes might include yucca with garlic, black beans with rice, tamales, and strict vegan fare. There's a healthy choice of girth-expanding desserts and a good wine list. Some meat dishes are available. ⊠ *Golfo 3, Alfalfa* ☎ *606/716456* ▭ *MC, V* ☺ *No dinner Sun.*

¢–$ ✕ **Mesón Don Raimundo.** Tucked into an alleyway off Calle Argote de Molina near the cathedral, this former 17th-century convent with its eclectic decor of religious artifacts tends to attract the tour buses. Still, it's worth the trip for its generous portions of traditional fare, including Mozarab-style wild duck (braised in sherry) and solomillo *a la castellana* (Castilian-style steak). Start with the crisp *tortillitas de camarones* (batter-fried shrimp pancakes) or stuffed peppers. ⊠ *Argote de Molina 26, Santa Cruz* ☎ *95/422–3355* ▭ *AE, DC, MC, V.*

Where to Stay

★ **$$$$** ✕▣ **El Bulli Hotel Hacienda Benazuza.** This five-star luxury hotel is in a rambling country palace near Sanlúcar la Mayor, 15 km (9 mi) outside

Seville off the main road to Huelva. Surrounded by olive and orange trees and in a courtyard with towering palms, the building incorporates an 18th-century church. The interior has clay-tile floors and ocher walls. The acclaimed restaurant, La Alquería, serves Spanish and international dishes, creative variations on the recipes of superstar Catalan chef (and hotel owner) Ferran Adrià. ⊠ *C. Virgen de las Nieves, Sanlúcar la Mayor 41800* ☎ *95/570–3344* 🖷 *95/570–3410* ⊕ *www.hbenazuza.com* ⤵ *41 rooms, 3 suites ⚖ 2 restaurants, cable TV, in-room broadband, tennis court, pool, paddle tennis, Internet room, meeting room, free parking, some pets allowed* ⊟ *AE, DC, MC, V* ⊘ *Closed Jan.*

$$$$
Fodor'sChoice
★
🏨 **Alfonso XIII.** Inaugurated by King Alfonso XIII on April 28, 1929, this grand hotel is a splendid, historical Mudejar-style palace, built around a huge central patio and surrounded by ornate brick arches. The public rooms have marble floors, wood-panel ceilings, heavy Moorish lamps, stained glass, and ceramic tiles in the typical Seville colors. There is a Spanish and Japanese restaurant, as well as an elegant bar. ⊠ *San Fernando 2, El Arenal, 41004* ☎ *95/491–7000* 🖷 *95/491–7099* ⊕ *www.westin.com/hotelalfonso* ⤵ *127 rooms, 19 suites ⚖ 2 restaurants, cable TV, in-room data ports, Wi-Fi, pool, hair salon, bar, Internet room, meeting room, parking (fee)* ⊟ *AE, DC, MC, V.*

$$$$
🏨 **Casa Imperial.** Adjoining the Casa de Pilatos, and once connected to it via underground tunnel, this restored 16th-century palace is the former residence of the marquis of Tarifa. Public areas surround four plant-filled patios. The 24 suites are approached by a stairway adorned with trompe l'oeil tiles. Each suite is different—one has a private courtyard with a trickling fountain—but all have kitchenettes. There's a roof terrace with gorgeous views. ⊠ *Imperial 29, Santa Catalina, 41003* ☎ *95/450–0300* 🖷 *95/450–0330* ⊕ *www.casaimperial.com* ⤵ *24 suites ⚖ Restaurant, kitchenettes, cable TV, in-room broadband, Wi-Fi, bar, meeting room, free parking* ⊟ *AE, DC, MC, V* ⦿ *BP.*

★ $$$$
🏨 **Los Seises.** This hotel is in a section of Seville's 16th-century Palacio Episcopal (Bishop's Palace), and the combination of modern and Renaissance architecture is striking: Room 219, for instance, is divided by a 16th-century brick archway, and breakfast (for an extra €16) is served in the old chapel. A pit in the center of the basement restaurant reveals the building's foundations and some archaeological finds, including a Roman mosaic. The rooftop pool and summer restaurant are in full view of the Giralda. ⊠ *Segovias 6, Santa Cruz, 41004* ☎ *95/422–9495* 🖷 *95/422–4334* ⊕ *www.hotellosseises.com* ⤵ *42 rooms, 2 suites ⚖ Restaurant, cable TV, Wi-Fi, pool, parking (fee), meeting rooms* ⊟ *AE, DC, MC, V* ⦿ *BP.*

$$$$
🏨 **Meliá Colón.** Built for the 1929 Exhibition, the grand old Colón has a white-marble staircase that leads up to the central lobby—which has a magnificent stained-glass dome and crystal candelabra. Downstairs is the El Burladero restaurant, with a bullfight theme, and La Tasca tavern, packed midday with slick local businessmen. The old-fashioned rooms are elegantly furnished with silk drapes and bedspreads, and wood fittings. ⊠ *Canalejas 1, San Vicente, 41001* ☎ *95/450–5599* 🖷 *95/422–0938* ⊕ *www.solmelia.com* ⤵ *204 rooms, 14 suites ⚖ Restaurant, cable TV, Wi-Fi, bar, Internet room, meeting room* ⊟ *AE, DC, MC, V* ⦿ *BP.*

$$$ ☒ **Casa Numero 7.** Voted by Tatler Magazine as Best Small Hotel in Europe, this exquisite hotel is owned by a director of González Byass, the famous sherry producer, who has lovingly restored this private mansion. Dating from 1847, the interior retains a homey, lived-in feel with family-owned antiques, original oil paintings, and plush furnishings throughout. Each room is individually designed, and there is an elegant salon with fireplace and comfy chairs. The roof terrace has Giralda views, and in the dining room, the breakfast is better than most, with fluffy scrambled eggs an agreeable option. ☒ *C. Virgenes 7, 41003* ☎ *95/422–1581* 🖨 *95/421–4527* ⊕ *www.casanumero7.com* ↵ *6 rooms* ⚴ *Bar* ⊟ *AE, V* ⫶⊙⫶ *BP.*

$$$ ☒ **Doña María.** In a 14th-century former mansion, one of Seville's most charmingly old-fashioned hotels is near the cathedral. Some rooms are comparatively modern, but most are more ornate and furnished with antiques. Room 310 has a four-poster double bed, and 305 has two single four-posters; bathrooms throughout are spacious. There's also a rooftop pool with a view of the Giralda. ☒ *Don Remondo 19, Santa Cruz, 41004* ☎ *95/422–4990* 🖨 *95/421–9546* ⊕ *www.hdmaria.com* ↵ *64 rooms* ⚴ *Minibars, cable TV, Wi-Fi, pool* ⊟ *AE, DC, MC, V.*

$$$ ☒ **Las Casas de la Judería.** This labyrinthine hotel occupies three of the barrio's old palaces, each arranged around inner courtyards. Ocher predominates in the palatial common areas; the spacious guest rooms are painted in subdued pastel colors and decorated with prints of Seville. The hotel is tucked into a passageway off the Plaza Santa María. ☒ *Callejón de Dos Hermanas 7, Santa Cruz, 41004* ☎ *95/441–5150* 🖨 *95/442–2170* ⊕ *www.casasypalacios.com* ↵ *103 rooms, 3 suites* ⚴ *Restaurant, minibars, cable TV, in-room data ports, bar, parking (fee)* ⊟ *AE, DC, MC, V.*

$$$ ☒ **Vincci La Rábida.** The Barrio de Santa Cruz is steps from this 18th-century palace. Rooms are elegant yet traditional, with terra-cotta tiling and wrought-iron bed frames with en suite marble bathrooms. The lounge areas and stunning central patio are sumptuous, and the large sun terrace—complete with outdoor hot tub—has superb city and cathedral views. ☒ *Castelar 24, 41001* ☎ *95/450–1280* 🖨 *95/421–6600* ⊕ *www.vinccihoteles.com* ↵ *79 rooms, 2 suites* ⚴ *Restaurant, cable TV, in-room data ports, Wi-Fi, hot tub, sauna, Internet room, parking (fee)* ⊟ *AE, MC, V.*

★ **$$–$$$** ☒ **Hotel Amadeus.** With pianos in the soundproof rooms and a music room off the central patio and lobby, this acoustical oasis is ideal for touring professional musicians and music fans in general. Classical concerts are regularly held in the patio. The 18th-century manor house has been equipped with such modern amenities as in-room data ports for Internet access and a small glass-wall elevator that whips quietly up and down a corner of the central patio. You can enjoy breakfast (an extra €7) on the roof terrace overlooking the Judería and Giralda. ☒ *Calle Farnesio 6, Barrio de Santa Cruz, 41004* ☎ *95/450–1443* 🖨 *95/450–0019* ⊕ *www. hotelamadeussevilla.com* ↵ *14 rooms* ⚴ *Dining room, minibars, cable TV, high-speed Internet access, parking (fee)* ⊟ *AE, DC, MC, V.*

$$ ☒ **Adriano.** Opened in 2004 in an 18th-century mansion, this small hotel has good-size rooms centered around three patios. A short stroll from the cathedral, the river, and the sophisticated shops on Calle Sierpes, Adriano has rooms decorated in a straightforward style with striped burgundy-and-cream fabrics and shiny marble on the floors and in the bathroom. There's a bar downstairs, just one of many on the street. ✉ C. *Adriano 12, 41001* ☎ *95/4293800* ⊕ *www.hoteladriano.net* ↩ *34 rooms* ⚹ *Cable TV, hot tub, bar, meeting room, parking (fee).*

$$ 🖼 **Hostal Picasso.** You can't beat this situation for the price, within confessional distance of the Cathedral and a short stroll away from both the shops and the Barrio de Santa Cruz. In this traditional building festooned with potted plants, the rooms vary in size, so check first, but they are all as neat as a pin, with sunny yellow paintwork. Several have small balconies. The same management owns the nearby Van Gogh, which is equally good value if the Picasso is full. ✉ *C. San Gregorio 1, 41001* ☎ *95/4210864* ⊕ *www.grupo-piramide.com* ↩ *17 rooms* ▭ *AE, V.*

$$ 🖼 **Hostería del Laurel.** A small, tree-lined square in the heart of the Barrio de Santa Cruz is an unbeatable position for this hotel. Hostería del Laurel is known for its bodega, which is mentioned in Zorilla's popular 19th-century play *Don Juan Tenorio*, as well as for the adjoining restaurant, which specializes in traditional local cuisine, such as *pollo a la Sevillana* (chicken in a rich gravy sauce) and *espinacas* (spinach) and squid in garlic. The rooms are a relatively recent addition, spread between two floors. They are spotlessly clean and simply furnished. ✉ *Plaza de los Venerables 5, 41004* ☎ *95/422–0295* 🖨 *95/421–0450* ⊕ *www.hosteriadellaurel.com* ↩ *21 rooms* ⚹ *Restaurant, cable TV, bar* ▭ *MC, V* ⧓ *BP.*

$$ 🖼 **San Francisco.** An 18th-century town house near the cathedral and the main shopping area houses this modest hotel. A central patio enlivens the entrance, and the simple rooms have en suite marble bathrooms. The upstairs terrace has five-star cathedral views. The friendly owner speaks some English. ✉ *Álvarez Quintero 38, Santa Cruz, 41004* ☎ *95/450–1541* ↩ *17 rooms* ▭ *MC, V.*

$$ 🖼 **Simón.** In a rambling turn-of-the-19th-century town house, this hotel is a good choice for inexpensive, comfortable accommodations near the cathedral. The spacious, fern-filled, azulejo-tile patio makes a fine initial impression; the elegant marble stairway and high-ceiling and pillared dining room are cool and stately spaces. The rooms are less grand, but the mansion's style permeates throughout the house. ✉ *García de Vinuesa 19, El Arenal, 41001* ☎ *95/422–6660* 🖨 *95/456–2241* ⊕ *www.hotelsimonsevilla.com* ↩ *29 rooms* ⚹ *Dining room, some pets allowed* ▭ *AE, DC, MC, V.*

$ 🖼 **Hostal Londres.** What with the nearby art treasures, the lively nightlife around the Barrio de San Lorenzo, and the good vibrations emanating from the plaque to Manuel Machado (fellow poet and brother of the more famous Antonio) across from the door of the hotel, Hostal Londres is a find. This simple but comfortable place near the Museo de Bellas Artes is a good value. Rooms are plain but clean, and some have balconies. ✉ *San Pedro Mártir 1, El Arenal, 41001* ☎ *95/421–2896* 🖨 *95/450–3830* ↩ *22 rooms* ▭ *MC, V.*

Nightlife & the Arts

Seville has lively nightlife and plenty of cultural activity. The monthly magazine *El Giraldillo* (⊕ www.elgiraldillo.es) lists classical and jazz concerts, plays, dance performances, art exhibits, and films in Seville and all major Andalusian cities. (For American films in English, look for the designation *v.o.,* for *versión original.*) The magazine is free and available at tourist offices and other venues in the city.

THE ARTS Concerts are performed at various venues, including the cathedral; check *El Giraldillo* for details. Long prominent in the opera world, Seville is particularly proud of its opera house, the **Teatro de la Maestranza** (⊠ Paseo de Colón 22, Arenal ☎ 95/422–3344 ⊕ www.teatromaestranza.com). Classical music and ballet are performed at the **Teatro Lope de Vega** (⊠ Av. María Luisa s/n, Parque de María Luisa ☎ 95/459–0853). The modern **Teatro Central** (⊠ José de Gálvez s/n, Isla de la Cartuja ☎ 95/503–7200 ⊕ www.teatrocentral.com) stages theater, dance, and classical and contemporary music. Seville's music college, the **Conservatorio Superior de Música** (⊠ Baños 48, San Vicente ☎ 95/491–5630), offers its own performances. Built for outdoor shows at Expo '92, the **Auditorio de Sevilla** (⊠ Camino de los Descubrimientos s/n, Isla de la Cartuja ☎ 915/186229 ⊕ www.auditoriodesevilla.com) stages concerts. The **Teatro Alameda** (⊠ Crédito 13, Alameda ☎ 95/438–8312) stages plays in Spanish, including some for children.

FLAMENCO Seville has a handful of regular flamenco clubs, patronized more by tourists than locals. Tickets are sold in most hotels; otherwise, make your own reservations (essential for groups, advisable for everyone in high season) by calling the club in the evening.

La Carbonería is a former coal yard and is spread over two dark, atmospheric bars. The flamenco is spontaneous when this place gets packed, which is most Thursdays. ⊠ *C. Levíes 18 Santa Cruz* ☎ *95/421–4460.*

El Arenal is in the back room of the traditionally tiled Mesón Dos de Mayo. Here you get your own table, rather than having to sit in rows. ⊠ *Rodo 7, Arenal* ☎ *95/421–6492* ▤ *Dinner and show €64, show only €33* ☉ *Shows nightly at 9:30 and 11:30.*

El Tamboril is a late-night bar in the heart of the Barrio de Santa Cruz noted for its great glass case in which the Virgin of Rocío sits in splendor. At 11 each night, locals pack in to sing the *Salve Rociera,* an emotive prayer to her. Afterward everything from flamenco to salsa continues until the early hours. ⊠ *Pl. Santa Cruz, Santa Cruz* ▤ *Free.*

Los Gallos is an intimate club in the heart of the Barrio de Santa Cruz. Performances are good and reasonably authentic. ⊠ *Pl. Santa Cruz 11, Santa Cruz* ☎ *95/421–6981* ⊕ *www.tablaolosgallos.com* ▤ *€27 with 1 drink* ☉ *Shows nightly at 8 and 10:30* ☉ *Closed Jan.*

TAPAS BARS **Bar Giralda.** This old Moorish bathhouse across from the Giralda has been a tapas bar since 1934. The outdoor seating area has lofty cathedral views. Specialties here include *patatas a la importancia* (fried potatoes stuffed with ham and cheese). ⊠ *Mateos Gago 1, Barrio de Santa Cruz* ☎ *95/422–7435.*

Bar Gran Tino. Named for the giant wooden wine cask that once dominated the bar (but no longer does so), this busy spot on the funky Plaza Alfalfa is always alive and serves an array of Andalusian tapas, including *calamares fritos* (fried squid) and wedges of crumbly Manchego cheese. ⊠ *Plaza Alfalfa 2, Centro* ☎ *95/421–0883.*

Bar Rincón San Eloy. This place is always heaving with a happy mix of shoppers and students. You can buy stacked mini-sandwiches, as well as traditional tapas and sherry from the barrel. If there are no tables left, grab a pew on the tiled steps, along with everyone else. ⊠ *San Eloy 2, Centro* ☎ *95/421–8079.*

Bodega Santa Cruz. A young college crowd frequents this spot in Seville's famous former Jewish quarter. There's an excellent selection of traditional tapas, including a mini-tortilla. Your bill is chalked up at your place at the bar. ⊠ *Mateo Gago 8, Barrio de Santa Cruz* ☎ *95/421–3246.*

Bodega San Jose. At this funky old 1893 bar decorated with faded Semana Santa posters and shelves of dusty bottles, the wine and sherry is served straight from the barrel and accompanied by *gambas* (prawns), the house specialty, prepared in several delicious ways. ⊠ *Adriano 10, Arenal* ☎ *95/422–4105.*

El Rinconcillo. Founded in 1670, this lovely spot continues to serve a classic selection of dishes such as the *caldereta de venado* (venison stew), a superb *salmorejo* (thick gazpacho-style soup), and *espinacas con garbanzos* (creamed spinach with chickpeas). The views of the Iglesia de Santa Catalina out the front window are unbeatable. Your bill is chalked up on the wooden counters. ⊠ *C. Gerona 40, Barrio de la Macarena* ☎ *95/422–3183* ⊗ *Closed Wed.*

Sports & the Outdoors

BOATING　Paddleboats, canoes, and river cruises on the Guadalquivir are great ways to see Seville from the water. Inquire about rentals at the tourist office or on the riverbank near the Torre del Oro. **Cruceros Torre del Oro** (⊠ Paseo Alcalde Marqués de Contadero, beside Torre del Oro, Arenal ☎ 95/561–692 ⊕ www.crucerostorredeloro.com) runs river cruises daily from 10 AM every half hour (April to October 11 AM to midnight, November to March 11 to 7 and at 8 PM and 9 PM), for €12 per person.

BULLFIGHTING　Bullfighting season is from Easter through Columbus Day, with most *corridas* (bullfights) held on Sunday. The season highlight is the April Fair, with Spain's leading toreros; other key dates are Corpus Christi (date varies; about seven weeks after Easter), Assumption (August 15), and the last weekend in September. Fights take place at the **Maestranza Bullring** (☎ 95/422–4577), on the Paseo de Colón 12. Bullfighting tickets are expensive; buy them in advance from the official *despacho de entradas* (Ticket office; ☎ 95/450–1382) on Calle Adriano 37, alongside the bullring. Other despachos sell tickets on Calle Sierpes, but these are unofficial and charge a 20% commission.

Shopping

Seville is the region's main shopping area and the place for archetypal Andalusian souvenirs, most of which are sold in the Barrio de Santa Cruz and around the cathedral and Giralda, especially on Calle Alemanes.

The main shopping street for Sevillanos themselves is Calle Sierpes, along with its neighboring streets Cuna, Tetuan, Velázquez, Plaza Magdalena, and Plaza Duque—boutiques abound here. Near the Puente del Cachorro bridge, the old Estación de Córdoba train station has been converted into a stylish shopping center, the **Centro Comercial Plaza de Armas** (⊠ Enter on Pl. de la Legión, Almas), with boutiques, bars, fast-food joints, a microbrewery, and a cinema complex. The pan-Spanish department store **El Corte Inglés** stays open all day; check out Seville's **main branch** (⊠ Pl. Duque 8, Centro ☎ 95/422–0931).

12

ANTIQUES For antiques, look along Mateos Gago, opposite the Giralda, and in the Barrio de Santa Cruz on Jamerdana and on Rodrigo Caro, just off Plaza Alianza.

BOOKS A large assortment of books in English, Spanish, French, and Italian is sold at the American-owned **Librería Vértice** (⊠ San Fernando 33–35, Santa Cruz ☎ 95/421–1654), near the cathedral.

CERAMICS In the Barrio de Santa Cruz, browse along Mateos Gago; Romero Murube, between Plaza Triunfo and Plaza Alianza, on the edge of the barrio; and between Plaza Doña Elvira and Plaza de los Venerables. Look for traditional azulejo tiles and other ceramics in the Triana **potters' district**, on Calle Alfarería and Calle Antillano Campos. **Cerámica Santa Isabel** (⊠ Alfarería 12, El Zurraque ☎ 95/434–4608) is one of a string of Triana ceramics shops. In central Seville, **Martian Ceramics** (⊠ Sierpes 74, Centro ☎ 95/421–3413) has high-quality dishes, especially the flowers-on-white patterns native to Seville. It's a bit touristy but fairly priced. A permanent arts-and-crafts market near the cathedral is **El Postigo** (⊠ Arfe s/n, Arenal ☎ 95/456–0013).

FANS **Casa Rubio** (⊠ Sierpes 56, Centro ☎ 95/422–6872) is Seville's premier fan store, no mean distinction, with both traditional and contemporary designs.

FLAMENCO WEAR Flamenco wear can be expensive; local women will gladly spend a month's grocery money, or more, on their frills, with dresses ranging from €100 to €400 or more. Recommended shops: **María Rosa** (⊠ Cuna 13, Centro ☎ 95/422–2143) and **Molina** (⊠ Sierpes 11, Centro ☎ 95/422–9254), which also sells the traditional foot-tapping shoes. For privately fitted and custom-made flamenco dresses, try **Juan Foronda** (⊠ Virgen de los Reyes 3, Centro ☎ 95/421–1856).

GUITARS **Cayuela** (⊠ Zaragoza 4, Arenal ☎ 95/422–4557) is run by the second generation of a family of guitar makers from Andújar, near Jaén. They carry unique, handcrafted guitars and high-quality factory-made instruments.

PASTRIES Seville's most celebrated pastry outlet is **La Campana** (⊠ Sierpes 1, Centro ☎ 95/422–3570), founded in 1885. Andalusia's convents are known for their homemade pastries—sample sweets from several convents at **El Torno** (⊠ Pl. del Cabildo s/n, Santa Cruz ☎ 95/421–9190).

PORCELAIN La Cartuja china, originally crafted at La Cartuja Monastery but now made outside Seville, is sold at **La Alacena** (⊠ Alfonso XII 25, San Vicente ☎ 95/422–8021). **El Corte Inglés** department stores are a good second choice.

STREET MARKETS   The **Plaza del Duque** has a crafts market on Friday and Saturday. The flea market **El Jueves** is held on Calle Feria on Thursday morning. A Sunday morning crafts market is a weekly happening at the **Alameda de Hercules**. The **Plaza del Cabildo** is for the coin and stamp aficionados. There's a Sunday pet market in **Plaza Alfalfa**.

TEXTILES   You can find all kinds of blankets, shawls, and embroidered tablecloths woven by local artisans at the three shops of **Artesanía Textil** (✉ García de Vinuesa 33, Arenal ☎ 95/456–2840 ✉ Sierpes 70, Centro ☎ 95/422–0125 ✉ Pl. de Doña Elvira 4, Santa Cruz ☎ 95/421–4748).

Carmona

㉝ *32 km (20 mi) east of Seville off NIV.*

Claiming to be one of the oldest inhabited places in Spain (the Phoenicians and Carthaginians had settlements here), Carmona, on a steep, fortified hill, became an important town under both the Romans and the Moors. Its Roman necropolis contains about 900 tombs dating from the 2nd century BC. As you wander its ancient, narrow streets, you can see many Mudejar and Renaissance churches, medieval gateways, and simple whitewashed houses of clear Moorish influence, punctuated here and there by a baroque palace. Local fiestas are held September 8 to 16 each year.

Park your car near the Puerta de Sevilla in the imposing **Alcázar de Abajo** (Lower Fortress), a Moorish fortification built on Roman foundations at the edge of the old town. In the tower beside the gate is the tourist office, where you can grab a map. On the edge of the "new town," across the road from the Alcázar de Abajo, is the church of **San Pedro** (✉ Calle San Pedro), begun in 1466. Its interior is an unbroken mass of sculptures and gilded surfaces, and its baroque tower, erected in 1704, is an unabashed imitation of Seville's Giralda.

Up Calle Prim is the **Plaza San Fernando,** in the heart of the old town, whose 17th-century houses have Moorish overtones. The Gothic church of **Santa María** (✉ Calle Martín) was built between 1424 and 1518 on the site of Carmona's former Great Mosque. Santa María is a contemporary of Seville's cathedral, and it, too, retains its beautiful Moorish courtyard, studded with orange trees. Behind Santa María is the **Museo de la Ciudad,** in a former 18th-century palace, with exhibits centered on the history of

MARY'S TOP 5
■ Spending an evening on a tapas crawl in the historic center.
■ Soaking up the history and beauty of the Alcázar and cathedral, topped off by climbing the Giralda for the best view of the city.
■ Enjoying a foot-tapping flamenco show at one of the clubs in the Barrio de Santa Cruz.
■ Basking in the golden age of Spanish art at the superb Museo de Belles Artes.
■ Enjoying a glass of fino (dry sherry) in the palatial surrounds of the Hotel Alfonso XIII's bar, with its traditional courtyard setting.

Carmona. There's plenty for children, with interactive exhibits clearly labeled in English and Spanish. ☎ 95/414–0128 ✆ €2 ⊙ Oct.–May, Wed.–Mon. 11–7, Tues. 11–2; June–Sept., Wed.–Mon. 10–2 and 6:30–9:30, Tues. 10–2.

Stroll down to the **Puerta de Córdoba** (Córdoba Gate) on the eastern edge of town. This old gateway was first built by the Romans around AD 175, then altered by Moorish and Renaissance additions. The Moorish **Alcázar de Arriba** (Upper Fortress) was built on Roman foundations and later converted by King Pedro the Cruel into a fine Mudejar palace. Pedro's summer residence was destroyed by a 1504 earthquake, but the parador amid its ruins has a breathtaking view.

At the western end of town lies the splendid **Roman necropolis.** Here, in huge underground chambers, some 900 family tombs were chiseled out of the rock between the 2nd and 4th centuries BC. The walls, decorated with leaf and bird motifs, have niches for burial urns. The most spectacular tombs are the **Elephant Vault** and the **Servilia Tomb,** which resembles a complete Roman villa with its colonnaded arches and vaulted side galleries. ⊠ C. Enmedio ☎ 95/414–0811 ✆ €2 ⊙ Mid-Sept.–mid-June, Tues.–Fri. 9–4:45, weekends 10–1:45; mid-June–mid-Sept., Tues.–Fri. 8:30–1:45, Sat. 10–2.

Where to Stay & Eat

$–$$$ ✕ **San Fernando.** You enter from a side street, but this second-floor restaurant looks out onto the Plaza de San Fernando. Set in an 18th-century palace, the beige dining room is pleasant in its simplicity, with nothing to distract from the view of daily life below. The kitchen serves Spanish dishes with flair—as in cream of apple soup or light fried potato slivers shaped like a bird's nest. Game, including partridge, are perennial favorites, and there's a fine dessert selection. ⊠ Sacramento 3 ☎ 95/414–3556 ☐ AE, DC, MC, V ⊙ Closed Mon. and Aug. No dinner Sun.

$$$$ ✕🏨 **Alcázar de la Reina.** Stylish and contemporary, this hotel has public areas that incorporate three bright and airy courtyards, with marble floors and pastel walls. Guest rooms are spacious and comfortable. The elegant Ferrara ($–$$$) serves a tasty combination of Italian and Spanish dishes, served à la carte or on a menú de degustación (gourmet menu) with four courses and dessert. ⊠ Pl. de Lasso 2, 41410 ☎ 95/419–6200 🖷 95/414–0113 ⊕ www.alcazar-reina.es ↵ 66 rooms, 2 suites ⚲ Restaurant, café, cable TV, some in-room broadband, pool, bar, meeting rooms, parking (fee), some pets allowed ☐ AE, DC, MC, V ⊺⊙⏐ BP.

$$$ 🏨 **Casa de Carmona.** Every guest room has a different tone in this former 16th-century palace, some with Moorish accents, but all are luxuriously furnished. Rooms vary in size from the homey, intimate Room 21 to the enormous Suite Azul (Blue Suite). Public rooms are decorated with antiques, rich fabrics, and museum-quality rugs. Relax in the Arabian-style garden, with orange trees and a fountain. ⊠ Pl. de Lasso 1, 41410 ☎ 95/419–1000 🖷 95/419–0189 ⊕ www.casadecarmona.com ↵ 32 rooms, 1 suite, 1 apartment ⚲ Restaurant, cable TV, in-room DVD/VCR, in-room broadband, pool, bar, library, laundry service, concierge, meeting rooms, free parking, some pets allowed ☐ AE, DC, MC, V ⊺⊙⏐ BP.

★ $$$ ⊞ **Parador Alcázar del Rey Don Pedro.** The Parador de Carmona has superb views from its hilltop position among the ruins of Pedro the Cruel's summer palace. The public rooms surround a central, Moorish-style patio, and the vaulted dining hall and adjacent bar open onto an outdoor terrace overlooking the sloping garden. Spacious rooms have rugs and dark furniture. All but six, which face onto the front courtyard, look south over the valley; the best rooms are on the top floor. ⊠ *Alcázar s/n, 41410* ☎ *95/414–1010* 🖨 *95/414–1712* ⊕ *www.parador.es* ⇖ *63 rooms* ♿ *Restaurant, cable TV, in-room data ports, Wi-Fi, pool, bar* ▭ *AE, DC, MC, V.*

Itálica

34 *12 km (7 mi) north of Seville, 1 km (½ mi) beyond Santiponce.*

Fodor'sChoice
★ Founded by Scipio Africanus in 205 BC as a home for veteran soldiers, Itálica had grown into one of Roman Iberia's most important cities by the 2nd century AD and had given the Roman world two great emperors, Trajan (52–117) and Hadrian (76–138). Ten thousand people once lived here, in 1,000 dwellings. About 25% of the site has been excavated, and work is still in progress. You can find traces of city streets, cisterns, and the floor plans of several villas, some with mosaic floors, though all the best mosaics and statues have been removed to Seville's Museum of Archaeology. Itálica was abandoned and plundered as a quarry by the Visigoths, who preferred Seville. It fell into decay around AD 700. The huge, elliptical **amphitheater** held 40,000 spectators. Other remains, including a **Roman theater** and **Roman baths,** are visible in the small town that has grown up next door, Santiponce. ☎ *95/599–7376 or 95/599–6583* 🖾 *€1.50, free for EU citizens* ⊙ *Oct.–Mar., Tues.–Sat. 9–5:30, Sun. 10–4; Apr.–Sept., Tues.–Sat. 8:30–8:30, Sun. 9–3.*

PROVINCE OF HUELVA

When you've had enough of Seville's urban bustle, nature awaits in Huelva. From the Parque Nacional de Doñana to the oak forests of the Sierra de Aracena, nothing is much more than an hour's drive from Seville. Then glean a sense of history by hopping on the miners' train at Riotinto, or visit Aracena's spectacular caves. Columbus's voyage to the New World was also sparked near here, at the monastery of La Rábida and in Palos de la Frontera. From Seville, turn off the Seville–Huelva highway and drive through Almonte and El Rocío—scene of the Whitsuntide pilgrimage to the Virgin of the Dew. Stop off at the visitor center at La Rocina for more information about Doñana.

Doñana National Park

35 *100 km (62 mi) southwest of Seville.*

Fodor'sChoice
★ One of Europe's last swaths of wilderness, these wetlands are beside the Guadalquivir estuary. The site was named for Doña Ana, wife of a 16th-century duke: prone to bouts of depression, she crossed the river and wandered into the wetlands one day, never to be seen alive again. The 188,000-acre park sits on the migratory route from Africa to Europe

and is the winter home and breeding ground for as many as 150 species of rare birds. Habitats range from beaches and shifting sand dunes to marshes, dense brushwood, and sandy hillsides of pine and cork oak. Two of Europe's most endangered species, the imperial eagle and the lynx, make their homes here, and kestrels, kites, buzzards, egrets, storks, and spoonbills breed among the cork oaks. A good base of exploration is the hamlet of **El Rocío,** on the park's northern fringe. In spring, during the Romería del Rocío pilgrimage (40 days after Easter Sunday), up to a million people converge on the local *santuario* (shrine) to worship the Virgen del Rocío. The rest of the year, many of El Rocío's pilgrim-brotherhood houses are empty. Most of the streets are unpaved to make them more comfortable for horses, as many of the yearly pilgrimage events are on horseback or involve horse-drawn carts.

At the Doñana visitor center at **La Rocina** (☎ 959/442340), less than 2 km (1 mi) from El Rocío, you can peer at the park's many bird species from a 3½-km (2-mi) footpath. It's open daily 9 to 2 and 3 to sunset. Five kilometers (3 mi) away, an exhibit at the **Palacio de Acebrón** (☎ No phone) explains the park's ecosystems. It's open daily 9 to 3 and 4 to dusk; last entrance is one hour before closing. Two kilometers (1 mi) before Matalascañas, you can find **Acebuche** (☎ 959/430432 jeep tours ⊕ www.parquenacionaldonana.com), the park's main interpretation center and the departure point for jeep tours, which must be reserved in advance. The center is open June–September, daily 8 AM to 9 PM and October to May, daily 9 to 7. Tours leave daily June to September at 8:30 and 5 and October to May at 8:30 and 3 and last four hours; they cover a 70-km (43-mi) route across beaches, sand dunes, marshes, and scrub. Cost is €21. Off-season (November to February) you can usually book a tour with just a day's notice; at other times, book as far in advance as possible.

Where to Stay

$$$ ☒ **El Cortijo de Los Mimbrales.** On the Rocío–Matalascañas road, this convivial, one-story Andalusian farm-hacienda is perched on the park's edge, a mere 1 km (½ mi) from the visitor center at La Rocina. Spend a relaxed evening with fellow nature lovers in comfy chairs by the fireplace in the large common lounge. Pick a colorfully decorated room, or a bungalow that sleeps two to four, with a kitchenette and small private garden. Some rooms and bungalows have fireplaces. There are stables on the premises, and the hotel can arrange horseback rides on the fringes of the park. ☒ *Ctra. del Rocío a Matalascañas (A483), Km 30, 21750* ☎ *959/442237* 🖷 *959/442443* ⊕ *www.cortijomimbrales.com* ⇄ *24 rooms, 2 suites, 5 bungalows* ⚐ *Restaurant, pool, horseback riding, bar, some pets allowed; no a/c* ▤ *AE, DC, MC, V* ⍟ *BP.*

$$ ☒ **Toruño.** Despite its location behind the famous Rocío shrine, the theme at this simple, friendly hotel is nature: it's run by the same cooperative that leads official park tours and has become a favorite of bird-watchers. Each room is named after a local bird species. Those on the first floor have balconies and priceless views over the marshes. ☒ *Pl. del Acebuchal 22, 21750* ☎ *959/442323* 🖷 *959/442338* ⇄ *30 rooms* ⚐ *Restaurant* ▤ *MC, V* ⍟ *BP.*

Matalascañas

36 *3 km (2 mi) south of Acebuche, 85 km (53 mi) southwest of Seville.*

Its proximity to Acebuche, the main reception center at Doñana, makes Matalascañas a convenient lodging base for park visitors. Otherwise, it's a rather incongruous and ugly sprawl of hotels and vacation homes, very crowded at Easter and in summer and eerily deserted the rest of the year (most hotels are closed from November to March). There are some nice beaches for those who just want to relax, and the local ocean waters attract windsurfers.

Where to Stay

$$$ 🖼 **Tierra Mar.** Try this large beachfront hotel if you want to combine Doñana with the seashore. The nearby 18-hole Dunes golf course (€30 greens fee) is windy and challenging year-round; the more gentle prospect of lawn bowling is available within the hotel's grounds. The rooms are modern, spacious, and have balconies. ⊠ *Matalascañas Parcela 120, Sector M, 21760* 🖼 *959/440300* 🖼 *959/440720* ⊕ *www.atlanticclub-hoteles.com* ⤴ *250 rooms* ⚸ *Restaurant, café, in-room data ports, tennis court, pool, gym, sauna, meeting room* ▤ *AE, DC, MC, V.*

Mazagón

37 *22 km (14 mi) northwest of Matalascañas.*

There isn't much to see or do in this coastal town, but its parador makes a good base for touring La Rábida, Palos de la Frontera, and Moguer. Mazagón's beautiful beach is among the region's nicest, because of its sweeping sandy beach sheltered by steep cliffs.

Where to Stay & Eat

$$$ ✕🖼 **Parador de Mazagón.** This peaceful modern parador stands on a cliff surrounded by pine groves, overlooking a sandy beach 3 km (2 mi) southeast of Mazagón. Most rooms have balconies overlooking the garden. The restaurant serves Andalusian dishes and local seafood specialties, such as stuffed baby squid, and hake medallions. ⊠ *Playa de Mazagón, 21130* 🖼 *959/536300* 🖼 *959/536228* ⊕ *www.parador.es* ⤴ *63 rooms* ⚸ *Restaurant, cable TV, in-room data ports, Wi-Fi, 2 tennis courts, pool, hot tub, sauna, fishing, bicycles, horseback riding, bar, meeting room, free parking* ▤ *AE, DC, MC, V.*

La Rábida

38 *30 km (19 mi) northwest of Doñana, 8 km (5 mi) northwest of Mazagón.*

You may want to extend your Doñana tour to see the monastery of **Santa María de La Rábida,** "the birthplace of America." In 1485 Columbus came from Portugal with his son Diego to stay in this Mudejar-style Franciscan monastery. Here he discussed his theories with friars Antonio de Marchena and Juan Pérez, who interceded on his behalf with Queen Isabella. The early 15th-century church holds a much-venerated 14th-century statue of the **Virgen de los Milagros** (Virgin of Miracles). The frescoes in the gatehouse were painted by Daniel Vázquez Díaz in 1930. ☏ 959/350411 ⊡ €3 *with audio guide,* €2.50 *without* ☺ *Mar.–July, Sept., and Oct., Tues.–Sun.* 10–1 *and* 3–7; *Aug., Tues.–Sun.* 10–1 *and* 4:45–8; *Nov.–Feb., Tues.–Sun.* 10–1 *and* 4–6:15.

Two kilometers (1 mi) from the monastery, on the seashore, is the **Muelle de las Carabelas** (Caravels' Wharf), a reproduction of a 15th-century port. The star exhibits here are the full-size models of Columbus's flotilla, the *Niña, Pinta,* and *Santa María,* built using the same techniques as in Columbus's day. Board each one and learn more about the discovery of the New World in the adjoining museum. ✉ *Paraje de la Rábida* ☏ 959/ 530597 *or* 959/530312 ⊡ €3 ☺ *Oct.–Mar., Tues.–Sun.* 10–7; *Apr.–Sept., Tues.–Fri.* 10–2 *and* 5–9, *weekends* 11–8 ☺ *Closed Jan.*

Palos de la Frontera

③⑨ *4 km (2½ mi) northwest of La Rábida, 12 km (7 mi) northeast of Mazagón.*

> **SHIPS ASAIL**
>
> Most of the crew of the *Niña*, the *Pinta*, and the *Santa María* were men from Palos and Moguer.

On August 2, 1492, the *Niña,* the *Pinta,* and the *Santa María* set sail from Palos de la Frontera. Most of the crew were men from Palos and neighboring Moguer. At the door of the church of **San Jorge** (1473), the royal letter ordering the levy of the ships' crew and equipment was read aloud, and the voyagers took their water supplies from the Fontanilla (fountain) at the town's entrance.

Moguer

④⓪ *12 km (7 mi) northeast of Palos de la Frontera.*

The inhabitants of this old port town now spend more time growing strawberries than they do seafaring, as you can see from the surrounding fields. The **Convento de Santa Clara** dates from 1337. ✉ *Pl. de los Monjes s/n* ☏ 959/370107 ⊡ €1.80 ☺ *Tues.–Sat. guided tours in Spanish only at* 11, *noon,* 1, 5, 6, *and* 7.

While in Moguer, see the **Casa-Museo Juan Ramón Jiménez**, former home of the Nobel Prize–winning poet who penned the much-loved *Platero y Yo.* At this writing, the Casa-Museo building was at the final phase of renovations and the exhibition (same price and hours) had been moved to the **Casa Natal** (✉ Ribera 2), the house where Ramón Jiménez was born. Check at the tourist office for an update. ✉ *C. Juan Ramón Jiménez* ☏ 959/372148 ⊡ €1.80 ☺ *Tues.–Sat. guided tours hrly* 10:15–1:15 *and* 5:15–7:15; *Sun. hrly* 10:15–1:15.

Riotinto

④① *74 km (46 mi) northeast of Huelva.*

Heading north from Palos and Huelva on the N435, you can reach the turnoff to Minas de Riotinto, the mining town near the source of the

Riotinto (literally, "Red River"). The waters are the color of blood because of the minerals leached from the surrounding mountains: this area has some of the richest copper deposits in the world, as well as gold and silver. In 1873 the mines were taken over by the British Rio Tinto Company Ltd., which started to dig an open-pit mine and build a 64-km (40-mi) railway to the port of Huelva to transport mineral ore. The British left in 1954, but mining activity continues today, albeit on a smaller scale.

Riotinto's landscape, scarred by centuries of intensive mining, can be viewed as part of a **tour** conducted by the Fundación Riotinto. The tour's first stop, the **Museo Minero** (Museum of Mining), has archaeological finds and a collection of historical steam engines and rail coaches. Next comes the **Corta Atalaya**, one of the largest open-pit mines in the world (4,000 feet across and 1,100 feet deep), and **Bellavista,** the elegant English quarter where the British mine managers lived. The tour ends with an optional ride on the **Tren Minero** (Miners' Train), which follows the course of the Riotinto along more than 24 restored km (15 mi) of the old mining railway. You can opt for the full tour as described (offered the first Sunday of each month, October–May), or just visit the individual sights. ☎ 959/590025 *Fundación Riotinto* 🖃 *Full tour €15* ◷ *Museum daily 10:30–3 and 4–7; miners' train mid-July–mid-Sept., daily at 1:30 PM; mid-June–mid-July, weekends at 4 PM; mid-Apr.–mid-May and mid-Sept.–mid-Oct., weekends at 5 PM; mid-Oct.–mid-Apr., weekends at 4 PM.*

Aracena

㊷ *105 km (65 mi) northeast of Huelva, 100 km (62 mi) northwest of Seville.*

Stretching north of the Riotinto mines is the 460,000-acre Sierra de Aracena nature park, an expanse of hills cloaked in cork and holm oak. This region is known for its cured hams, which come from the prized free-ranging Iberian pigs that gorge on acorns in the autumn months before slaughter; the hams are buried in salt and then hung in cellars to dry-cure for at least two years. The best hams come from the village of **Jabugo.** The capital of the region is Aracena, whose main attraction is the spectacular cave known as the **Gruta de las Maravillas** (Cave of Marvels). The 12 caverns hide long corridors, stalactites and stalagmites arranged in wonderful patterns, and stunning underground lakes. ✉ *Pl. Pozo de Nieves, Pozo de Nieves* ☎ *959/128355* 🖃 *€7.70* ◷ *Guided tours, if sufficient numbers, daily hrly 10:30–1:30 and 3–6.*

Where to Stay & Eat

$–$$ ✕ **Casas.** There's not much wall space left in the intimate beamed dining room of this typical Sierra Morena restaurant: plates, pots, pans, mirrors, and religious pictures cover every inch. Specializing in the region's famous ham and pork, the honest, home-style cooking is at its best with dishes prepared according to what is in season. ✉ *Colmenetas 41* ☎ *959/128044* 🖃 *MC, V* ◷ *No dinner.*

$$$ 🏠 **Finca Buenvino.** This lovely country house inn, nestled in 150 acres of woods, is run by a charming British couple, Sam and Jeannie Chesterton. The room price includes a big breakfast; dinner with tapas is

available for a moderate extra sum. Jeannie also conducts Spanish cookery and tapas courses for groups of up to six people. Three woodland self-catering cottages are available, each with its own pool. The house is 6 km (4 mi) from Aracena. ✉ *Crtra. N433, Km 95, 21293 Los Marines* ☎ *959/124034* 🖷 *959/501029* ⊕ *www.fincabuenvino. com* 🖙 *5 rooms, 3 cottages* ⚭ *Restaurant, some kitchens, 4 pools, bar; no a/c, no room phones, no room TVs* ▤ *MC, V* ☉ *Closed mid-July–mid-Sept.* ⦿| *MAP.*

★ **$$** ⬚ **Finca de la Silladilla.** In a wild Iberian pig–infested oak forest, this ranch offers a chance to see Spain's most prized products priming themselves for your palate. The rooms and small stone houses are impeccably decorated in heavy slabs of beautifully finished wood, and the bathrooms have unusual ceramic-and-copper washbasins. Communal areas combine warm tones with whites, ochers, and terra-cottas. The staff can organize tours of the Sierra de Aracena, and equestrian outings, or visits to nearby Jabugo, *bellota* (acorn-fed) ham capital of Spain. ✉ *Ctra. Los Romeros, Los Romeros, Jabugo 21290* ☎ *959/501350* 🖷 *959/501184* 🖙 *2 rooms, 2 suites, 3 houses for 4, 1 house for 6* ⚭ *Kitchens, pool, horseback riding, some pets allowed* ▤ *AE, DC, MC, V* ⦿| *BP.*

$–$$ ⬚ **Galaroza Sierra.** The common areas in this stone-clad hotel are done in light wood with rustic furnishings and woven textiles. Rooms have small balconies and views of the mountains, and the four bungalows face the swimming pool. Pork dishes are the restaurant's specialty. Galaroza Sierra is on the outskirts of the village of Galaroza, 3 km (2 mi) from Jabugo; the surrounding countryside is ideal for walking, and there's a pretty stream nearby. ✉ *Ctra. Sevilla–Lisboa, Km 69.5, Galaroza 21291* ☎ *959/123237* 🖷 *959/123236* ⊕ *www.hotelgalaroza. com* 🖙 *22 rooms, 7 bungalows* ⚭ *Restaurant, pool* ▤ *DC, MC, V.*

$ ⬚ **Los Castaños.** A few minutes' walk from the caves, rooms here are modern and spacious with balconies. The best view is from the dining room, which looks out to the surrounding Sierra de Aracena. ✉ *Av. de Huelva 5, Aracena 21200* ☎ *959/126300* 🖷 *959/126287* 🖙 *33 rooms* ⚭ *Restaurant, café, parking (fee); no a/c in some rooms* ▤ *AE, DC, MC, V.*

PROVINCE OF CÁDIZ

A trip through Cádiz is a trip back in time. Winding roads take you through scenes ranging from flat and barren plains to seemingly endless vineyards, and the rolling countryside is carpeted with blindingly white soil known as *albariza*—unique to this area, and the secret to the grapes used in sherry. Throughout the province, *los pueblos blancos* (the white villages) provide striking contrasts with the terrain, especially at Arcos de la Frontera, where the village sits dramatically on a crag overlooking the gorge of the Guadalete River. In Jerez, you can savor the town's internationally known sherry or delight in the skills and forms of purebred Carthusian horses. Finally, in the city of Cádiz, absorb about 3,000 years of history: this may be the oldest continuously inhabited city in the Western world.

Jerez de la Frontera

★ 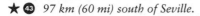   *97 km (60 mi) south of Seville.*

Jerez, world headquarters for sherry, is surrounded by vineyards of chalky soil, whose Palomino grapes have funded a host of churches and noble mansions. Names such as González Byass, Domecq, Harvey, and Sandeman are inextricably linked with Jerez. The word *sherry,* first used in Great Britain in 1608, is an English corruption of the town's old Moorish name, Xeres. Both sherry and horses are very much the domain of Jerez's Anglo-Spanish aristocracy, whose Catholic ancestors came here from England centuries ago.

At any given time, more than half a million barrels of sherry are maturing in Jerez's vast aboveground wine cellars. If you visit a **bodega** (winery), your guide will explain the *solera* method of blending old wine with new, and the importance of the *flor* (a sort of yeast that forms on the surface of the wine as it ages) in determining the kind of sherry. Most bodegas welcome visitors, but it's advisable to phone ahead for an appointment, if only to make sure you join a group that speaks your language. Cellars usually charge an admission fee of €3 to €6, and some close in August. Tours, about an hour, go through the aging cellars, with their endless rows of casks. (You won't see the actual fermenting and bottling, which take place in more modern, less romantic plants outside town.) Finally, you'll be invited to sample generous amounts of pale, dry fino; nutty *amontillado*; or rich, deep *oloroso,* and, of course, to purchase a few robustly priced bottles in the winery shop. For the other attractions, an hour's stroll around the city center is all you'll need. May and September are the most exciting times to visit Jerez, as their spectacular fiestas transform the town. For the Feria del Caballo (Horse Fair), in early May, carriages and riders fill the streets, and purebreds from the School of Equestrian Art compete in races and dressage displays. September brings the Fiesta de Otoño (Autumn Festival), when the first of the grape harvest is blessed on the steps of the cathedral.

If you have time for only one bodega, tour the **González Byass** (☎ 956/357000 ⊕ www.gonzalezbyass.com), home of the famous Tío Pepe. This tour is well organized and includes La Concha, an open-air aging cellar designed by Gustave Eiffel. Jerez's oldest bodega is **Domecq** (☎ 956/151500), founded in 1730. Aside from sherry, Domecq makes the world's best-selling brandy, Fundador. **Harveys** (☎ 956/319650) is the source of Harvey's Bristol Cream. **Sandeman** (☎ 956/301100 ⊕ www.sandeman.com) is known for its man-in-a-cape logo.

Museo de Vino (⊠ Cervantes 3, La Atalaya, Jerez de la Frontera ☎ 956/182100 ⊠ €5 ☉ Tues.–Sun. 10–2), a sherry museum, offers a multimedia show twice daily at 10 and noon, plus an exhibition, a bar, a restaurant, and a shop.

The 12th-century **Alcázar** was once the residence of the caliph of Seville. Its small, octagonal **mosque** and **baths** were built for the Moorish governor's private use. The baths have three sections: the *sala fria* (cold room), the larger *sala templada* (warm room), and the *sala caliente* (hot room), for steam baths. In the midst of it all is the 17th-century **Palacio de Villav-icencio,** built on the site of the original Moorish palace. A camera obscura, a lens-and-mirrors device that projects the outdoors onto a large indoor screen, offers a 360-degree view of Jerez and its principal monuments from the palace's highest tower. ⊠ *Alameda Vieja* ≊ *€1.35, €3.35 including camera obscura* ☉ *Mid-Sept.–Apr., daily 10–6; May–mid-Sept., daily 10–8.*

NEED A
BREAK?

Bar Juanito (Pescadería Vieja 8 and 10, ☎ 956/334838) has a flowery patio and is a past winner of the national Best Tapas Bar in Spain award. Jolly Faustino Rodríguez and his family serve 50 different tapas and larger-portion raciones. It's closed Monday and during El Rocó pilgrimage.

Across from the Alcázar and around the corner from the González Byass winery, the **cathedral** (⊠ Pl. del Arroyo ☉ Open for mass only) has an octagonal cupola and a separate bell tower. On the **Plaza de la Asunción,** one of Jerez's most intimate squares, you can find the Mudejar church of **San Dionisio** and the ornate **cabildo municipal** (city hall), whose lovely plateresque facade dates from 1575. The unusual **Museo de los Relojes,** within the grand Centro Temático La Atalaya, is a museum devoted entirely to clocks, with 300 timepieces. ⊠ *C. Cervantes 3* ☎ *956/182100* ≊ *€6* ☉ *Feb.–mid-Jan., Tues.–Sat. 10–2 and 5–7, Sun. 10–2.*

The **Centro Andaluz de Flamenco** is a modern flamenco museum, complete with an audio-and-visual library, and a multimedia show. ⊠ *Palacio Pemartín, Pl. San Juan 1* ☎ *956/322711* ⊕ *http://caf.cica.es* ≊ *Free* ☉ *Weekdays 9–2.*

Diving into the maze of streets that form the scruffy San Mateo neighborhood east of the town center, you come to the **Museo Arqueológico,** one of Andalusia's best archaeological museums. The collection is strongest on the pre-Roman period. The star item, found near Jerez, is a Greek helmet dating from the 7th century BC. ⊠ *Pl. del Mercado s/n* ☎ *956/341350* ≊ *€1.75* ☉ *Sept.–mid-June, Tues.–Fri. 10–2 and 4–7, weekends 10–2:30; mid-June–Aug., Tues.–Sun. 10–2:30.*

Just west of the town center the **Parque Zoológico** is set within lush botanical gardens where you can usually spy up to 33 storks' nests. Primarily a place for the rehabilitation of injured or endangered animals native to Spain, the zoo also houses white tigers, elephants, and a giant red panda. ⊠ *C. Taxdirt* ☎ *956/153164* ⊕ *www.zoobotanicojerez.com* ≊ *€5.30* ☉ *June–Sept, Tues.–Sun. 10–8, Oct.–May, Tues.–Sun. 10–6.*

The **Real Escuela Andaluza del Arte Ecuestre** (Royal Andalusian School of Equestrian Art) operates on the grounds of the Recreo de las Cadenas, a 19th-century palace. This prestigious school was masterminded by Alvaro Domecq in the 1970s. Every Thursday the Cartujana horses— a cross between the native Andalusian workhorse and the Arabian— and skilled riders in 18th-century riding costume demonstrate intricate dressage techniques and jumping in the spectacular show "Cómo Bailan los Caballos Andaluces" (roughly, "The Dancing Horses of Andalusia"). Reservations are essential. Admission price depends on how close to the arena you sit; the first two rows are the priciest. The rest of the week,

Fodor's Choice
★

you can visit the stables and tack room, watch the horses being schooled, and see **rehearsals** for the show. ⌨ €8 ⊙ *Mon.–Wed. and Thurs. 10–1.* ⊠ *Av. Duque de Abrantes s/n* ☎ *956/319635* ⊕ *www.realescuela.org* ⌨ *€15–€23* ⊙ *Nov.–Feb., Thurs. at noon; Mar.–July 14, Tues. and Thurs. at noon; July 15–Oct., Fri. at midday; in Mar. fair nightly at 10:30.*

Just outside Jerez de la Frontera is **Yeguada de la Cartuja,** the largest state-run stud farm in Spain for Carthusian horses. In the 15th century, a Carthusian monastery on this site started the breed for which Jerez and the rest of Spain are now famous. Every Saturday at 11 AM a full tour and show begin. Book ahead. ⊠ *Finca Fuente El Suero, Ctra. Medina–El Portal, Km 6.5* ☎ *956/162809* ⊕ *www.yeguadacartuja.com* ⌨ *€10.50* ⊙ *Sat. 11 AM.*

Bullfighting

Jerez's bullring is on Calle Circo, northeast of the city center. Tickets are sold at the official ticket office on Calle Porvera, though only about five bullfights are held each year, in May and October. Six blocks from the bullring is the **Museo Taurino,** a bullfighting museum where admission includes a drink. ⊠ *Pozo del Olivar 6* ☎ *956/319000* ⌨ *€3* ⊙ *Weekdays 9–2.*

Where to Stay & Eat

$$–$$$ ✕ **La Carboná.** This cavernous restaurant in a former bodega has a suitably rustic atmosphere with arches, original beams, and a central fireplace for winter nights. During the summer you can often enjoy live music, including flamenco, while you dine. The current chef has worked at several top-grade restaurants; his menu provides an innovative twist to classic dishes, such as *pechuguitas de cordorniz rellenas de pétalos de rosa y foié* (quail stuffed with rose petals and liver pâté). There's an excellent wine list as well. ⊠ *C. San Francisco de Paula 2* ☎ *956/347475* ⊟ *MC, V* ⊙ *Closed Tues.*

$–$$ ✕ **El Bosque.** Housed in a modern villa with contemporary paintings of bullfighting themes, this is one of the most stylish dining spots in town. Most tables are round and seat four; the smaller of the two dining rooms has picture windows overlooking a park. The food is contemporary Spanish. *Sopa de galeras* (soup of mantis shrimp) makes a rich appetizer; follow up with *confit de pato de laguna* (leg of wild duck) or *perdiz estofado con castañas* (stewed partridge with chestnuts). ⊠ *Av. Alcalde Alvaro Domecq 26* ☎ *956/307030* ⊟ *AE, DC, MC, V* ⊙ *Closed Mon. No dinner Aug.*

$–$$ ✕ **Gaitán.** Within walking distance of the riding school, this restaurant has brick arches and white walls decorated with colorful ceramic plates and photos of famous guests. It's crowded with businesspeople at lunchtime. The menu is Andalusian, with a few Basque dishes thrown in. *Setas* (wild mushrooms) make a delicious starter in season; follow them with *cordero asado* (roast lamb) in a sauce of honey and Jerez brandy. ⊠ *Gaitán 3* ☎ *956/345859* ⊟ *AE, DC, MC, V* ⊙ *No dinner Sun.*

$–$$ ✕ **Venta Antonio.** Crowds come to this roadside inn for superb, fresh seafood cooked in top-quality olive oil. You enter through the busy bar, where lobsters await their fate in a tank. Try the specialties of the Bay of Cádiz, such as *sopa de mariscos* (shellfish soup) followed by succulent *bogavantes de Sanlúcar* (local lobster). ✉ *Ctra. de Jerez–Sanlúcar, Km 5* ☎ *956/140535* ▭ *AE, DC, MC, V* ⊘ *No dinner Sun.*

★ $ ✗ **La Mesa Redonda.** Owner José Antonio Valdespino spent years research-ing the classic recipes once served in aristocratic Jerez homes, and now his son, José, presents them in this small, friendly restaurant off Avenida Alcalde Alvaro Domecq, around the corner from the Hotel Avenida Jerez. Don't be put off by the bland exterior—within, the eight tables are sur-rounded by watercolors and shelves are lined with cookbooks. (The round table at one end of the room gives the restaurant its name.) Ask the chef's mother, Margarita—who has an encyclopedic knowledge of Spanish wines—what to eat. ✉ *Manuel de la Quintana 3* ☎ *956/340069* ▭ *AE, DC, MC, V* ⊘ *Closed Sun. and mid-July–mid-Aug.*

★ $$$ ▥ **Hotel Sherry Park.** Set back from the road in an unusually large, tree-filled garden, this modern hotel is designed around several patios filled with exotic foliage. The sunny hallways are hung with contemporary paintings. Rooms are bright and airy and decorated in sunny peach and blue; most have balconies overlooking the garden and pool. There are good deals out of season, as well as special weekend packages. ✉ *Av. Alvaro Domecq 11, 11407* ☎ *956/317614* 🖷 *956/311300* ⊕ *www. hipotels.com* ⟿ *172 rooms* ⌂ *Restaurant, coffee shop, minibars, cable TV, 2 pools (1 indoor), gym, hair salon, sauna, bar, meeting room* ▭ *AE, DC, MC, V* ⫯⊙⫯ *BP.*

$$$ ▥ **Hotel Villa Jerez.** This hacienda-style, tastefully furnished hotel has luxury to offer in the historic part of town. The mature gardens sur-round a traditional courtyard and are lushly landscaped with palm trees and a dazzle of colorful plants and flowers. Facilities include an elegant restaurant with terrace, a saltwater swimming pool, and a gym. Bedrooms are plush and well equipped, and the staff is friendly and ef-ficient. ✉ *Av. de la Cruz Roja 7, 11407* ☎ *956/153100* 🖷 *956/304300* ⊕ *www.villajerez.com* ⟿ *14 rooms, 4 suites* ⌂ *Restaurant, minibars, cable TV, in-room broadband, pool, bar* ▭ *AE, DC, MC, V.*

$$$ ▥ **Montecastillo Hotel and Golf Resort.** Outside Jerez near the racetrack, the sprawling, modern Montecastillo adjoins a golf course designed by Jack Nicklaus—ask for a room with a terrace overlooking the course. The spacious common areas have marble floors. Rooms are cheerfully decorated, with bright floral bedspreads and rustic clay tiles. ✉ *Ctra. de Arcos, Km 9.6, 11406* ☎ *956/151200* 🖷 *956/151209* ⊕ *www. montecastillo.com* ⟿ *119 rooms, 2 suites, 20 villas* ⌂ *Restaurant, in-room data ports, Wi-Fi, 18-hole golf course, tennis court, 3 pools (1 in-door), health club, spa, soccer* ▭ *AE, DC, MC, V* ⫯⊙⫯ *BP.*

$ ▥ **Ávila.** This friendly, inexpensive hotel on a side street off Calle Arcos offers affordable central lodgings. The rooms have basic furnishings and tile floors; beds are European twin-size. A TV lounge and a small bar/breakfast room adjoin the lobby. ✉ *Ávila 3, 11401* ☎ *956/334808* 🖷 *956/336807* ⟿ *32 rooms* ⌂ *Bar, parking (fee)* ▭ *AE, DC, MC, V.*

$ ▥ **El Ancla.** El Ancla's architecture is classic Jerez, with yellow-and-white paintwork, wrought-iron balconies, and wooden shutters. The hotel dou-bles as a popular local bar, which is good for atmosphere but means it can be noisy at night. Rooms are plainly furnished but comfortable. The underground parking lot across the street is a bonus. ✉ *Plaza del*

Mamelón, 11405 ☎ *956/321297* 🖨 *956/325005* ⏋ *20 rooms* ⟡ *Parking (fee).*

Sports
Formula One Grand Prix races—including the Spanish motorcycle Gran Prix on the first weekend in May—are held at Jerez's racetrack, the **Circuito Permanente de Velocidad** (✉ Ctra. Arcos, Km 10 ☎ 956/151100 ⊕ www.circuitodejerez.com).

Shopping
Browse for wicker and ceramics along **Calle Corredera** and **Calle Bodegas. Duarte** (✉ Lancería 15 ☎ 956/342751) is the best-known saddle shop in town, sending its beautifully wrought leather all over the world (it even sells to the British royal family).

Arcos de la Frontera

★ ④④ *31 km (19 mi) east of Jerez.*

Its narrow and steep cobblestone streets, whitewashed houses, and finely crafted wrought-iron window grilles make Arcos the quintessential Andalusian pueblo blanco. Make your way to the main square, the Plaza de España, the highest point in the village: one side of the square is open, and a balcony at the edge of the cliff offers views of the Guadalete valley. On the opposite end is the church of **Santa María de la Asunción,** a fascinating blend of architectural styles: Romanesque, Gothic, and Mudejar, with a plateresque doorway, a Renaissance retablo, and a 17th-century baroque choir. The *ayuntamiento* (town hall) stands at the foot of the old castle walls on the northern side of the square; across from here is the Casa del Corregidor, one-time residence of the governor and now a parador. Arcos is the most western of the 19 pueblos blancos, whitewashed towns dotted around the Sierra de Cádiz.

Where to Stay & Eat

$$ ✕ **El Convento.** With tables set around a graceful Andalusian patio, this rustic-style restaurant (owned by but separate from the hotel) is known for its fine regional cooking. The *sopa de tagarninas* (wild asparagus soup) is one of the town treasures, as are the *garbanzos con tomillo* (chickpeas with thyme) and the *abajado* (wild rabbit or lamb stew). ✉ *Marqués de Torresoto 7* ☎ *956/703222* ▭ *AE, DC, MC, V* ⊘ *Closed Jan.*

★ **$$–$$$** ✕▨ **Parador Casa del Corregidor.** Expect a spectacular view from the terrace—the Parador de Arcos de la Frontera clings to the cliff side, overlooking the rolling valley of the Guadalete River. Public rooms include a popular bar and restaurant that opens onto the terrace, and an enclosed patio. Spacious rooms are furnished with dark Castilian furniture, *esparto* (reed) rugs, and abundant tiles. The best rooms are Nos. 15–18, which overlook the valley. At the restaurant, try a local dish such as *berenjenas arcenses* (spicy eggplant with ham and chorizo) or sample 10 different regional specialties with the *menú degustacíon* (gourmet menu €25). ✉ *Pl. del Cabildo, 11630* ☎ *956/700500* 🖨 *956/701116* ⊕ *www.parador.es* ⏋ *24 rooms* ⟡ *Restaurant, café, minibars, cable TV, in-room data ports, Wi-Fi, bar* ▭ *AE, DC, MC, V.*

$$ ☐ **El Convento.** Perched on top of the cliff behind Parador Casa del Corregidor, this tiny hotel shares the same amazing view, though the rooms are much smaller—and cheaper. Some rooms have balconies, and there's a large rooftop terrace on the edge of the cliff. The building is a former convent. ✉ *Maldonado 2, 11630* ☎ *956/702333* 📠 *957/704128* ⊕ *www.webdearcos.com/elconvento* 🛏 *11 rooms* ♨ *Restaurant* ⊟ *AE, DC, MC, V* ☺ *Closed Jan.*

12

$$ ☐ **La Casa Grande.** Built in 1729, this extraordinary 18th-century mansion encircles a lushly vegetated central patio and is perched on the edge of the 400-foot cliff to which Arcos de la Frontera clings. Each room has been restored by Catalan owners Elena Posa and Ferran Grau. The artwork, the casually elegant design of the living quarters, and inventive bathrooms are all a delight. The breakfast terrace allows you to look down on falcons circling hundreds of feet above the riverbed below. The rooftop rooms "El Palomar" (the pigeon roost) and "El Soberao" (the attic) are the best. ✉ *C. Maldonado 10, 11630* ☎ *956/703930* 📠 *956/703930* ⊕ *www.lacasagrande.net* 🛏 *5 rooms, 2 suites* ♨ *Library* ⊟ *AE, DC, MC, V* ❢ *BP.*

FodorsChoice
★

$ ☐ **Real de Veas.** This tastefully converted 19th-century town house is home to this gem of a hotel. Rooms are set around a central glass-covered patio and are decorated in neutral tones agreeably coupled with rustic furniture. The marble-clad bathrooms have all the extras, including whirlpool baths and hair dryers. The congenial Spanish owners also dish up a more-generous-than-most breakfast, which includes cheese and cold cuts. ✉ *C. Corredera 12, 11630* ☎ *956/717370* 🛏 *13 rooms* ♨ *Restaurant, cafeteria, minibars, in-room data ports* ⊟ *MC, V* ❢ *BP.*

Sanlúcar de Barrameda

45 *24 km (15 mi) northwest of Jerez.*

Columbus sailed from this harbor on his third voyage to the Americas, in 1498. Twenty years later, Magellan began his circumnavigation of the globe from here. Today this fishing town has a crumbling charm and is best known for its *langostinos* (giant shrimp) and manzanilla, an exceptionally dry sherry. The most popular restaurants are in the **Bajo de Guía** neighborhood, on the banks of the Guadalquivir. Here, too, is the Fábrica de Hielo, which serves as a visitor center for Doñana National Park. Boat trips can take you up the river, stopping at various points in the park; the **Real Fernando** makes a four-hour cruise, with bar and café, up the Guadalquivir to the Coto de Doñana. ✉ *Bajo de Guía, Sanlúcar de Barrameda* ☎ *956/363813* ⊕ *www.visitasdonana.com* 💶 *€15.50* ☺ *Cruises Apr., May, and Oct., daily at 10 AM and 4 PM; Nov.–Mar., daily at 10 AM; June–Sept., daily at 10 AM and 5 PM.*

From the *puerto pesquero* (fishing port) of **Bonanza**, 4 km (2½ mi) upriver from Sanlúcar, there's a fine view of fishing boats and the pine trees of Doñana on the opposite bank. Sandy beaches extend along Sanlúcar's southern promontory to Chipiona, where the Roman general Scipio Africanus built a beacon tower.

Where to Stay & Eat

$$ ✗ **Mirador de Doñana.** This Bajo de Guía landmark overlooking the water serves delicious *chocos* (crayfish), shrimp, and the signature dish *mi barca mirador* (white fish in a tomato sauce). The dining area overlooks the large, busy tapas bar. ☒ *Bajo de Guía* ☎ *956/364205* ▭ *MC, V* ⊘ *Closed Jan.*

$–$$ ✗ **Casa Balbino.** After the sunset at Bajo de Guía beach, the serious tapas and tippling begins in the Plaza del Cabildo, Sanlúcar's party nerve center. Balbino is the best of these taverns—though the *patatas aliñá* (potatoes dressed in an olive oil vinaigrette) at nearby Bar Barbiana are noteworthy as well. ☒ *Plaza del Cabildo 14* ☎ *956/362647* ▭ *AE, DC, MC, V* ⊘ *Closed Jan.*

$–$$ ✗ **Casa Bigote.** Colorful and informal, this spot on the beach is known for its fried *acedias* (a type of small sole) and langostinos, which come from these very waters. The seafood paella is also catch-of-the-day fresh. Reservations are essential in summer. ☒ *Bajo de Guía* ☎ *956/ 362696* ▭ *AE, DC, MC, V* ⊘ *Closed Sun. and Nov.*

$$ ▥ **Los Helechos.** Named for the ferns *(los helechos)* that dominate the patio and entryway, this breezy place with a lovely rooftop terrace has the distinct advantage of being out of earshot but within stumbling distance of the Plaza del Cabildo. ☒ *Plaza Madre de Dios 9, 11540* ☎ *956/ 361349* ⊟ *956/369650* ⇆ *56 rooms* ♨ *Restaurant, cable TV, bar, parking (fee)* ▭ *AE, DC, MC, V.*

Puerto de Santa María

❹❻ *12 km (7 mi) southwest of Jerez, 17 km (11 mi) north of Cádiz.*

This attractive, if somewhat dilapidated, little fishing port on the northern shores of the Bay of Cádiz, with lovely beaches nearby, has white houses with peeling facades and vast green grilles covering the doors and windows. The town is dominated by the Terry and Osborne sherry and brandy bodegas. Columbus once lived in a house on the square that bears his name (Cristóbal Colón), and Washington Irving spent the autumn of 1828 at Calle Palacios 57. The marisco bars along the Ribera del Marisco (Seafood Way) are Puerto de Santa María's current claim to fame. Casa Luis, Romerijo, La Guachi, and Paco Ceballos are among the most popular, along with Er Beti, at Misericordia 7. The tourist office has a list of six tapas routes taking in 39 tapas bars, listing their specialties.

The **Castillo de San Marcos** was built in the 13th century on the site of a mosque. Created by Alfonso X, it was later home to the Duke of Medinaceli. Among the guests were Christopher Columbus—who tried unsuccessfully to persuade the duke to finance his voyage west—and Juan de la Cosa, who, within these walls, drew up the first map ever to include the New World. The red lettering on the walls is a 19th-century addition.

> **NOTABLE RESIDENTS**
>
> Christopher Columbus and Washington Irving once lived in the little fishing village of Puerto de Santa María.

⊠ *Pl. del Castillo* ☎ *965/851751* ⊡ *€5, free Tues.* ☉ *Tues., Thurs., and Sat. 10–2.*

This stunning neo-Mudejar **Plaza de Toros** was built in 1880 thanks to a donation from the winemaker Thomas Osborne. It originally had seating for exactly 12,816 people, the population of Puerto at that time. ⊠ *Los Moros* ⊡ *Free* ☉ *Apr.–Oct., Thurs.–Tues. 11–1:30 and 6–7:30; Nov.–Mar., Thurs.–Tues. 11–1:30 and 5:30–7. Closed bullfight days plus 1 day before and after each bullfight.*

Where to Stay & Eat

$$–$$$ ✕ **El Faro de El Puerto.** In a villa outside town, the "Lighthouse in the Port" is run by the same family that established the classic El Faro in Cádiz. Like its predecessor, it serves excellent fish; also available are such delicacies as veal rolls filled with foie gras in a sweet sherry sauce and several vegetarian options. ⊠ *Ctra. Fuenterabia–Rota, Km 0.5* ☎ *956/ 858003 or 956/870952* ⊕ *www.elfarodelpuerto.com* ▤ *AE, DC, MC, V* ☉ *No dinner Sun. except Aug.*

$–$$ ✕ **Casa Flores.** Across from the water, this place serves the same fresh seafood as the neighboring Ribera del Marisco haunts, but is a bit more upmarket. Specialties include *filete de urta al camarón* (fillet of bream in shrimp sauce) and *fritos de la bahía* (assorted fried fish caught locally). You approach the delightful dining rooms, decorated with tiles and wood paneling, through a long bar hung with hams. ⊠ *Ribera del Río 9* ☎ *956/543512* ⊕ *www.casaflores.com* ▤ *AE, DC, MC, V.*

★ $$$ ▦ **Monasterio San Miguel.** Dating from 1733, this monastery is a few blocks from the harbor. There's nothing spartan about the former cells; they're now air-conditioned rooms with all the trappings. The restaurant is in a large, vaulted hall (formerly the nuns' laundry); the baroque church is now a concert hall; and the cloister's gardens provide a peaceful refuge. Beam ceilings, polished marble floors, and huge brass lamps enhance the 18th-century feel. If you're traveling out of season, check the Web site for discounts. ⊠ *C. Virgen de los Milagros 27, 11500* ☎ *956/ 540440* ⊟ *956/542604* ⊕ *www.jale.com* ⇄ *139 rooms, 11 suites* ⟁ *Restaurant, cable TV, in-room data ports, Wi-Fi, pool, paddle tennis, squash, bar, parking (fee)* ▤ *AE, DC, MC, V.*

Nightlife

The **Casino Bahía de Cádiz,** on the road between Jerez and Puerto de Santa María, is the only casino in this part of Andalusia. You can play the usual games, and there's a restaurant. You must present your passport to enter. On weekends there's a disco and, in summer, live shows. ⊠ *NIV, Km 649, Puerta de Santa María* ☎ *956/871042* ⊡ *€3; free for second visit; also free entry vouchers at tourist office* ☉ *Sun.–Wed. 5 PM–3 AM, Thurs. 5 PM–4 AM, weekends and daily in Aug. 5 PM–6 AM.*

Cádiz

★ ㊼ *32 km (20 mi) southwest of Jerez, 149 km (93 mi) southwest of Seville.*

Surrounded by the Atlantic Ocean on three sides, Cádiz was founded as Gadir by Phoenician traders in 1100 BC and claims to be the oldest continuously inhabited city in the Western world. Hannibal lived in Cádiz for a time, Julius Caesar first held public office here, and Columbus set out from here on his second voyage, after which the city became the home base of the Spanish fleet. When the Guadalquivir silted up in the 18th century, Cádiz monopolized New World trade and became the wealthiest port in Western Europe. Most of its buildings—including the cathedral, built in part with gold and silver from the New World—date from this period.

The old city is African in appearance and immensely intriguing—a cluster of narrow streets opening onto charming small squares. The golden cupola of the cathedral looms above low white houses, and the whole place has a slightly dilapidated air. Spaniards flock here in February to revel in the famous Carnival celebrations, but few foreigners have yet to discover the city's real charm.

Begin your explorations in the Plaza de Mina, a large, leafy square with palm trees and plenty of benches. On the square's western flank, the ornamental facade of the **Colegio de Arquitectos** (College of Architects) is especially beautiful. In the northwestern corner of the square is the tourist office. On the east side of the Plaza de Mina, is the **Museo de Cádiz** (Provincial Museum). Notable pieces include works by Murillo and Alonso Cano as well as the *Four Evangelists* and set of saints by Zurbarán, which have much in common with his masterpieces at Guadalupe, in Extremadura. The archaeological section contains Phoenician sarcophagi from the time of this ancient city's birth. ⊠ *Pl. de Mina* ☎ *956/212281* 🖼 *€1.50, free for EU citizens* ☉ *Tues. 2:30–8, Wed.–Sat. 9–8, Sun. 9–2.*

A few blocks east of the Plaza de Mina, next door to the Iglesia del Rosario, is the **Oratorio de la Santa Cueva,** an oval 18th-century chapel with three frescoes by Goya. ⊠ *C. Rosario 10* ☎ *956/222262* 🖼 *€2* ☉ *Tues.–Fri. 10–1 and 4:30–7:30, weekends 10–1.*

Heading up Calle San José from the Plaza de la Mina, you see the **Oratorio de San Felipe Neri.** Spain's first liberal constitution was declared at this church in 1812, and here the Cortes (Parliament) of Cádiz met when the rest of Spain was subjected to the rule of Napoléon's brother, Joseph Bonaparte (more popularly known as Pepe Botella, for his love of the bottle). On the main altar is an *Immaculate Conception* by Murillo, the great Sevillian artist who in 1682 fell to his death from a scaffold while working on his *Mystic Marriage of St. Catherine* in Cádiz's Chapel of Santa Catalina. ⊠ *Santa Inés 38* ☎ *956/211612* 🖼 *€2* ☉ *Mon.–Sat. 10–1.*

Next door to the Oratorio de San Felipe Neri, the small but pleasant **Museo de las Cortes** has a 19th-century mural depicting the establishment of the Constitution of 1812. Its real showpiece, however, is a 1779 ivory-and-mahogany model of Cádiz, with all of the city's streets and buildings in minute detail, looking much as they do now. ⊠ *Santa Inés 9* ☎ *956/221788* 🖼 *Free* ☉ *Oct.–May, Tues.–Fri. 9–1 and 4–7, weekends 9–1; June–Sept., Tues.–Fri. 9–1 and 5–8, weekends 9–1.*

Four blocks west of Santa Inés is the Plaza Manuel de Falla, overlooked by an amazing neo-Mudejar redbrick building, the **Gran Teatro Manuel**

de Falla. The classic interior is impressive as well; try to attend a performance. ✉ *Pl. Manuel de Falla* ☎ *956/220828.*

Backtrack along Calle Sacramento toward the city center to **Torre Tavira.** At 150 feet, this tower, attached to an 18th-century palace that's now a conservatory of music, is the highest point in the old city. More than a hundred such watchtowers were used by Cádiz ship owners to spot their arriving fleets. A camera obscura gives a good overview of the city and its monuments; the last show is a half hour before closing time. ✉ *Marqués del Real Tesoro 10* ☎ *956/212910* ✉ *€3.50* ⊙ *Mid-June–mid-Sept., daily 10–8; mid-Sept.–mid-June, daily 10–6.*

Five blocks southeast of the Torre Tavira are the gold dome and baroque facade of Cádiz's **cathedral,** begun in 1722, when the city was at the height of its power. The Cádiz-born composer Manuel de Falla, who died in 1946 at the age of 70, is buried in the **crypt.** The cathedral **museum,** on Calle Acero, displays gold, silver, and jewels from the New World, as well as Enrique de Arfe's processional cross, which is carried in the annual Corpus Christi parades. The cathedral is known as the New Cathedral because it supplanted the original 13th-century structure next door, which was destroyed by the British in 1592, rebuilt, and renamed the church of **Santa Cruz** when the New Cathedral came along. The entrance price includes the crypt, museum, and church of Santa Cruz. ✉ *Pl. Catedral* ☎ *956/259812* ✉ *€4* ⊙ *Mass Sun. at noon; museum Tues.–Fri. 10–2 and 4:30–7:30, Sat. 10–1.*

Next door to the church of Santa Cruz are the remains of a 1st-century BC **Roman theater** (✉ Free ⊙ Daily 10–2) discovered by chance in 1982; the theater is still under excavation.

The impressive **ayuntamiento** overlooks the Plaza San Juan de Diós, one of Cádiz's liveliest hubs. Built in two parts, in 1799 and 1861, the building is attractively illuminated at night. The **Plaza San Francisco,** near the ayuntamiento, is a pretty square surrounded by white-and-yellow houses and filled with orange trees and elegant street lamps. It's especially lively during the evening *paseo* (promenade).

Where to Stay & Eat

$$–$$$
Fodor's Choice
★

✕ **El Faro.** Gonzalo Córdoba's fishing-quarter restaurant is deservedly known as the best restaurant in the province. Outside, it's one of many low-rise, white houses with bright-blue flowerpots; inside it's warm and inviting, with half-tile walls, glass lanterns, oil paintings, and photos of old Cádiz. Fish dominates the menu, but alternatives include *cebón al queso de cabrales* (venison in blue-cheese sauce). If you don't want to go for the full splurge, there's an excellent tapas bar as well. ✉ *San Felix 15* ☎ *956/211068* ⊟ *AE, DC, MC, V.*

★ **$$**
✕ **El Ventorrillo del Chato.** Standing on its own on the sandy isthmus connecting Cádiz to the mainland, this former inn was founded in 1780 by a man ironically nicknamed "El Chato" (pug-nosed) for his prominent proboscis. Run by a scion of El Faro's Gonzalo Córdoba, the restaurant serves tasty regional specialties in charming Andalusian surroundings. Seafood is a favorite, but meat, stews, and rice dishes are also well

represented on the menu, and the wine list is very good. ⊠ *Vía Augusta Julia s/n* ☎ *956/250025* 🍴 *AE, DC, MC, V* ☺ *Closed Sun.*

$–$$ ✕ **Casa Manteca.** Cádiz's most quintessentially Andalusian tavern is just down the street from El Faro restaurant and a little deeper into the La Viña barrio (named for the vineyard that once grew here). *Chacina* (Iberian ham or sausage) served on waxed paper and manzanilla (sherry from Sanlúcar de Barrameda) are standard fare at this low wooden counter that has served bullfighters and flamenco singers, as well as dignitaries from around the world since 1953. ⊠ *Corralón de los Carros 66* ☎ *956/213603* 🍴 *AE, DC, MC, V* ☺ *Closed Mon. No lunch Sun.*

$$$ ▣ **Parador de Cádiz.** Cádiz's modern Parador Atlántico has a privileged position on the headland overlooking the bay and is the only hotel in its class in the old part of Cádiz. The spacious indoor public rooms have gleaming marble floors, and tables and chairs surround a fountain on the small patio. The cheerful, bright-green bar, decorated with ceramic tiles and bullfighting posters, is a popular meeting place for Cádiz society. Most rooms have small balconies facing the sea. ⊠ *Av. Duque de Nájera 9, 11002* ☎ *956/226905* 🖷 *956/214582* ⊕ *www.parador.es* 🛏 *143 rooms, 6 suites* ⚒ *Restaurant, cable TV, in-room data ports, Wi-Fi, pool, gym, sauna, bar, free parking, some pets allowed* 🍴 *AE, DC, MC, V* ⓇⓁ *BP.*

$–$$ ▣ **Bahía.** Just off the bustling Plaza de San Juan de Dios, on a tree-lined pedestrian street, this is a budget winner. The beds are firm, and most rooms have small balconies. The lack of dining room is compensated for by the choice and proximity of bars and restaurants. ⊠ *Plocia 5, 11002* ☎ *956/259061* 🖷 *956/254208* 🛏 *21 rooms* 🍴 *MC, V.*

Nightlife & the Arts

The cultural hub in Cádiz is the **Gran Teatro Manuel de Falla** (⊠ Pl. Manuel de Falla ☎ 956/220828). The tourist office has performance schedules.

Shopping

Traditional Andalusian handicrafts, especially ceramics and wicker, are plentiful in Cádiz. Just off the Plaza de la Mina, **Belle Epoque** (⊠ Antonio Lopez 2 ☎ 956/226810) is one of the city's better—and more reasonably priced—antiques stores, specializing in furniture.

SEVILLE & W. ANDALUSIA ESSENTIALS

To research prices, get advice, and book travel arrangements, visit www. fodors.com.

Transportation

BY AIR

Seville is a relatively easy destination to reach via air, although from the United States you will need to connect, ideally in Madrid or London. Ryan Air operates an inexpensive no-frills flight from London Stansted airport to Seville on a daily basis for as little as €30 return. Iberia and British Airways also have a daily nonstop flight between London and Seville. You can alternatively connect in other major European cities, including Amsterdam, Brussels, Frankfurt, and Paris.

Domestic flights connect the Andalusian capital with Madrid, Barcelona, Valencia, and other major cities. Iberia flies from Jerez de la Frontera to numerous Spanish cities, including Almería, Madrid, Barcelona, Bilbao, Valencia, Ibiza, and Zaragoza, and Spanair and Air Europa have daily nonstop flights to and from Barcelona to Seville. Ryan Air operates a daily flight to and from London Stansted and Jerez. Iberia has at least two direct daily flights to and from Madrid and Barcelona and Jerez.

The region's main airport belongs to Seville, 7 km (3 mi) east of the city on the NIV to Córdoba. There's a bus from the airport to the center of Seville every half hour on weekdays (between 6:30 AM and 8 PM), and every hour on weekends and holidays. It costs €2.30 one way. The smaller Aeropuerto de Jerez is 7 km (4 mi) northeast of Jerez on the road to Seville. There's no public transport into Jerez, you will need to take a taxi (approximately €12).

🚹 Airports **Aeropuerto de Jerez** ☎ 956/150000 Jerez. **Aeropuerto de Sevilla** ☎ 95/444-9000.

🚹 Airlines **Air Europa** ✉ Aeropuerto de Sevilla, Seville ☎ 95/444-9179 ⊕ www.aireuropa.com. **British Airways** ✉ Aeropuerto de Sevilla ☎ 902/111333 ⊕ www.ba.com. **Iberia** ✉ Avenida Buhaira 8, Seville ☎ 95/498-7357, 902/400500 at Aeropuerto de Sevilla, 956/150010 at Jerez de la Frontera airport ⊕ www.iberia.es. **Ryan Air** ☎ 0818/303030 (from the U.K.) ⊕ www.ryanair.com. **Spanair** ✉ Aeropuerto de Sevilla, Seville ☎ 902/131415 ⊕ www.spanair.com.

BY BIKE

If you're thinking of bringing a bicycle with you, Spain has severe restrictions on taking bikes on trains (⇨ Bike Travel *in* Smart Travel Tips). Seville city is perfect for bike travel since it's flat, but make sure you have a good lock or two handy. For rentals, contact Alkimoto. The route from Seville to Puerto de Santa María, Jerez, and Cádiz is also flat, but it's hillier toward Portugal and northward. Many local tourist offices have details of mountain-bike routes.

In Seville or Cádiz, if you want to rent a four-wheel bike (these modern-day rickshaws are good with children or bags) or a bike with an audio guide, call Cyclotour/Telebike. In Puerto de Santa María, Bigote will rent you a bike.

🚹 **Alkimoto** ✉ Fernando Tirado 5, Seville ☎ 954/584927 ⊕ www.alkimoto.com. **Bigote** ✉ Rodrigo de Bastidas 6, Puerto de Santa María ☎ 956/875418. **Cyclotour/ Telebike** ✉ Residencial Virgen de Rocío 3, 4th fl., A, Mairena del Aljarafe, Seville ☎ 605/252-8312 ⊕ www.cyclotouristic.com.

BY BOAT & FERRY

Boats cruise along the Guadalquivir River, which links both places. From Cádiz, Trasmediterránea operates truck, car, and passenger ferry services to the Canary Islands. For foot passengers, boats leave every Tuesday at 6 PM, stopping at Gran Canaria, Tenerife, and La Palma. Fares range from €200 to €429 for this trip, which takes 36 to 48 hours.

There are no direct ferries to Sevilla; the only possible option is to go to the northern Spanish coast from the United Kingdom via the

Portsmouth-to-Bilboa route or the Plymouth-to-Santander route and then catch a train south.

7 Trasmediterránea ⊠ Estación Marítima ☎ 956/227421 or 902/454645 ⊕ www. trasmediterranea.es.

BY BUS

Alsa long-distance buses connect Seville with Madrid; with Cáceres, Mérida, and Badajoz in Extremadura; and with Córdoba, Granada, Málaga, Ronda, and Huelva in Andalusia. Regional buses connect all of the towns and villages in this region—indeed, buses within Andalusia (and between Seville and Extremadura) tend to be more frequent and convenient than trains. The coastal route links Granada, Málaga, and Marbella to Cádiz. From Ronda, buses run to Arcos, Jerez, and Cádiz. Seville has two bus stations: Estación del Prado de San Sebastián, serving the west and northwest, and the Estación Plaza de Armas, which serves central and eastern Spain. Cádiz also has two bus stations: Comes, which serves most destinations in Andalusia, and Los Amarillos, which serves Jerez, Seville, Córdoba, Puerto de Santa María, Sanlúcar de Barrameda, and Chipiona. The bus station in Jerez, on Plaza Madre de Dios, is served by two companies: La Valenciana and Los Amarillos.

Seville's urban bus service is efficient and covers the greater city area. Bus Nos. C1, C2, C3, and C4 run circular routes linking the main transportation terminals with the city center. The No. C1 goes east in a clockwise direction, from the Santa Justa train station via Avenida de Carlos V, Avenida de María Luisa, Triana, the Isla de la Cartuja, and Calle de Resolana. The No. C2 follows the same route in reverse. The C3 runs from the Avenida Menéndez Pelayo to the Puerta de Jerez, Triana, Plaza de Armas, and Calle de Recaredo. The C4 does the same route counterclockwise.

Buses do not run within the popular tourist area Moorish Santa Cruz because the streets are too narrow.

Seville's city buses operate limited night service between midnight and 2 AM, with no service between 2 and 4 AM. Single rides cost €1, but it is more economical to buy a ticket for 10 rides, which costs €5 for use on any bus and €4 for use on only the city's urban bus service. There's also a ticket valid for any ride during 30 days, which costs €28 and is transferrable. Tickets are on sale at newspaper kiosks and at the main bus station, Prado de San Sebastián.

7 Bus Companies Alsa ☎ 902/422242 Spain ⊕ www.alsa.es. **Comes** ⊠ Pl. Hispanidad, Cádiz ☎ 956/224271. **La Valenciana** ⊠ Bus station, Pl. Madre de Dios, Jerez de la Frontera ☎ 956/341063. **Los Amarillos** ⊠ Diego Fernández Herreras 34, Cádiz ☎ 956/285852, 956/329347 Jerez.

7 Bus Stations Cádiz–Estación de Autobuses Comes ⊠ Pl. de la Hispanidad 1 ☎ 956/342174. **Huelva–Estación de Autobuses** ⊠ Av. Doctor Rubio s/n ☎ 959/ 256900. **Jerez de la Frontera–Estación de Autobuses** ⊠ Cartuja ☎ 956/345207.

Seville–Estación del Prado de San Sebastián ⊠ Prado de San Sebastián s/n ☎ 95/441-7111. **Seville–Estación Plaza de Armas** ⊠ Cristo de la Expiración ☎ 95/490-7737. ⚑ **Local Bus Information Prado de San Sebastián** ⊠ Pl. San Sebastián ☎ 95/441-7111, open weekdays 8–3.

12

BY CAR

The main road from Madrid is the NIV through Córdoba, a four-lane *autovía* (highway), but it's one of Spain's busiest roads, and trucks can cause delays. From Granada or Málaga, head for Antequera; then take A39 *autovía* by way of Osuna to Seville. Road trips from Seville to Córdoba, Granada, and the Costa del Sol (by way of Ronda) are reasonably quick and pleasant. From the Costa del Sol, the coastal N340 highway is rarely very busy west of Algeciras. Driving within Western Andalusia is easy—the terrain is mostly flat land or slightly hilly, and the roads are straight. From Seville to Jerez and Cádiz, you can choose between NIV and the faster A4 toll road. The only way to access Doñana National Park by road is to take the A49 Seville–Huelva highway, exit for Almonte/Bollullos par del Condado, then follow the signs for El Rocío and Matalascañas. The A49 west of Seville will also lead you to the freeway to Portugal and the Algarve.

There are some pretty scenic drives here about which the respective tourist offices can advise you. One good route is heading northwest from Seville on the N433. This passes through some stunning scenery; turn east on the 435 to Santa Olalla de Cala and after a few miles you come to the village of Zufre, with its dramatic setting on the ridge of a gorge. Backtrack and continue on to Aracena. Return via the Minas de Riotinto (signposted from Aracena), which will bring you back to the N433 heading east to Seville.

Getting in and out of Seville is not difficult thanks to the SE30 ring road, but getting around the city by car is still trying. In Seville and Cádiz, avoid the lunchtime rush hour (around 2–3 PM) and the 7:15 to 8:30 PM rush hour. Don't try to bring a car to Cádiz at Carnival time (pre-Lent) or to Seville during Holy Week or the April Fair—processions close most of the streets to traffic.

Seville and the larger cities in this area have increased their parking. Just follow the blue "P" sign when you enter town, which will lead you to the nearest underground parking lot. You can expect to pay around €1.20 an hour. Blue lines on the street mean you must pay at the nearest meter to park during working hours, around €0.50 an hour. Yellow lines mean no parking. If your car is towed, you will be fined approximately €65 to claim it.

On major roads and motorways the speed limit is 120 km/h (75 mph); in urban areas it is 50 km/h (31 mph), and on other roads it is either 90 km/h (55 mph) or 100 km/h (62.5 mph). Severe fines are enforced throughout Spain for driving under the influence of alcohol. Spot breath checks are often carried out, and you will be cited if the level of alcohol in your bloodstream is found to be 0.05 percent or above.

Local car-rental agencies can be less expensive than the international chains.

⚠ Rental Agencies Crown Car Hire ☎ 952/176486 ⊕ www.crowncarhire.com. **Niza Cars** ☎ 952/236179 ⊕ www.nizacars.com. **Autopro** ✉ Carril de Montañez 49, Málaga ☎ 952/176030 ⊕ www.autopro.es.

BY SUBWAY

The first line of a three-line metro is due to open in Seville by late 2006. This will cover a distance of 19 km (13 mi) and run from Aljarafe to Montequinto with 23 stations, including Puerta de Jerez and Plaza de Cuba. (⊕ www.metrodesevilla.net).

BY TAXI

Taxis are plentiful throughout Western Andalusia and may be hailed on the street or from specified taxi ranks marked TAXI. Restaurants are usually obliging and will also call you a taxi, if required. Fares are reasonable, and meters are strictly used. There are extra charges for luggage. You are not required to tip taxi drivers, although rounding off the amount is appreciated.

⚠ Taxi Companies Radio Teléfono Giralda ✉ Seville ☎ 95/467-5555. **Tele Taxi** ✉ Jerez de la Frontera ☎ 956/344860. **Tele Taxi** ✉ Huelva ☎ 959/250022. **Unitaxi** ✉ Cádiz ☎ 956/212121.

BY TRAIN

Seville, Jerez, and Cádiz all lie on the main rail line from Madrid to southwestern Spain. Trains leave from Madrid for Seville (via Córdoba) almost hourly, most of them high-speed AVE trains that reach Seville in 2½ hours. Two of the non-AVE trains continue on to Jerez and Cádiz; travel time from Seville to Cádiz is 1½ to 2 hours. Trains also depart regularly for Barcelona (3 daily, 11 hours), Cáceres (1 daily, 6 hours), and Huelva (4 daily, 1½ hours). From Granada, Málaga, Ronda, and Algeciras, trains go to Seville by way of Bobadilla, where, more often than not, you have to change. A dozen or more local trains each day connect Cádiz with Seville, Puerto de Santa María, and Jerez. There are no trains to Doñana National Park, Sanlúcar de Barrameda, or Arcos de la Frontera or between Cádiz and the Costa del Sol. In Seville, the sprawling Santa Justa station is on Avenida Kansas City. Cádiz's station is on Plaza de Sevilla near the docks. Jerez's station is on Plaza de la Estación, off Diego Fernández Herrera, in the eastern part of town. *Al Andalus* is a vintage 1920s luxury train that makes a weekly six-day trip in season from Seville to Córdoba, Granada, and Antequera, with side trips to Carmona and Jerez.

North Americans can purchase a Eurorail Spain Pass, available in both first- and second-class sections, which allows three days of unlimited travel within a two-month period for $225/$113 (adult/child) for first class and $175/$88 (adult/child) for second class.

⚠ Train Information RENFE ☎ 902/240202 ⊕ www.renfe.es. **Eurorail** ⊕ www.raileurope.com/us

⚠ Train Stations Seville-Estación Santa Justa ☎ 95/454-0202. **Huelva-Estación** ✉ Av. de Italia ☎ 959/246666. **Cádiz-Estación** ✉ Av. de Gibraltar (Cortadura) ☎ 956/251010. **Jerez de la Frontera-Estación** ✉ Pl. de la Estación s/n ☎ 956/342319.

Contacts & Resources

BANKS & EXCHANGING SERVICES

Banks are generally in town and city centers; the majority will have an ATM, enabling you to withdraw euros with your credit or debit card (you must have a PIN). Your card issuer is likely to charge you a fee for using an ATM abroad. Banks are open from 8:30 AM to 2 PM, Monday to Friday, plus on Saturday from October to April. Currency-exchange offices are also common—however, they generally charge a higher commission than the banks. You can also change money in your hotel, although this again will cost you more than the banks. One of the main banks in Spain is BBVA (⊕ www.bbva.es).

EMERGENCIES

In an emergency, call one of the Spain-wide emergency numbers, for police, ambulance, or fire services. The local Red Cross (Cruz Roja) can also dispatch an ambulance in case of an emergency. Also, there are numerous private ambulance services, which are listed under *ambulancias* (ambulances) in the *Paginas Amarillas* (Yellow Pages). The Centro de Salud El Porvenir is a public clinic with a 24-hour emergency department. For nonemergencies, there are private medical clinics throughout the region, which often have staff members who can speak some English. Every town has at least one pharmacy open 24 hours; the address of the on-duty pharmacy is posted on the front door of all pharmacies. You can also dial Spain's general information number for the location of a doctor's office or pharmacy that's open nearest you.

🔁 Emergency Services **Fire, Police or Ambulance** ☎ 112. **Guardia Civil** ☎ 062. **Insalud** (Public health service) ☎ 061. **Centro de Salud El Porvenir** (Health Clinic) ☎ 955/0377817. **Policía Local** (Local police) ☎ 092. **Policía Nacional** (National police) ☎ 091. **Servicio Marítimo** (Air-Sea Rescue) ☎ 902/202202. **Información Toxicológica** (Poisoning) ☎ 915/620420.

HOLIDAYS

In Seville city, local public holidays are as follows: San Fernando, May 30; Virgen de los Reyes, August 15; plus *Semana Santa* (the week between Palm Sunday and Easter), and the Feria de Abril (two weeks after Easter). In Cádiz, holidays are La Festividad del Rosario, October 7; and Carnival week in February. Celebrated in Huelva are San Sebastian, January 20; Virgen de la Cinta, September 8; and Colombinas Fiestas, first week in August. In Jerez, holidays are La Merced September 24; and San Dionisio, October 9 (with the Fiesta de Otoño in between).

INTERNET, MAIL & SHIPPING

There are several work stations with free Internet access for one hour at Seville's new provincial tourist office between Plaza Nueva and Calle Sierpes. Internet cafés are also widespread; the tourist office can provide you with a comprehensive list. Some online cafés also offer courier drop-off service.

The main post office in Seville is opposite the cathedral. It's open weekdays 8:30 to 8:30 and Saturday 9:30 to 2.

Several international courier companies have branches at Seville airport, including DHL. National courier companies include Seur and MRW; both have branches and drop-off locations throughout the country.
🔒 **Cybercafés Amazonas Cyber** ⊠ Conde de Barajas 6 Alameda ☎ 95/437-2491. **First Centre** ⊠ Av. de la Constitucíon 34, Centro ☎ 95/421-5622. **Seville Internet Centre** ⊠ C. Almirantazgo 2, Centro ☎ 95/450-0275. **Turismo de la Provincia** ⊠ Plaza del Triunfo 1, Centro ☎ 95/450-1001. **WORKCenter** ⊠ San Fernando, 1, Centro ☎ 95/423-8292.
🔒 **Couriers DHL** ⊠ Aeropuerto de Seville ☎ 902/122-424. **MRW** ⊠ Aeropuerto de Seville ☎ 900/300-400. **SEUR** ⊠ Aeropuerto de Seville ☎ 902/101-010.

LODGING

APARTMENT & VILLA RENTALS

Rural accommodations are available throughout Western Andalusia.
🔒 **Local Agents Asociación de Hoteles Rurales de Andalusia** ⊠ Edif. Congreso, C. Ramal Hoyo, Cristo Rey 2, Torremolinos 23400 Málaga ☎ 952/378775 ⊕ www.ahra. es. **Viajes Rural Andalus** ⊠ Montes de Oca 18, Málaga 29007 ☎ 952/276229 ⊕ www. ruralandalus.es.

MEDIA

There are no local English-language newspapers in Seville and Western Andalusia. U.K. papers and the *International Herald Tribune* are available at main news outlets. English-language books and guides are sold at several outlets, including International House, Librería Beta, and Casa del Libro.
🔒 **English-Language Bookstores Casa del Libro** ⊠ Calle Velázquez 8, Centro, Seville ☎ 95/450-2950. **International House** ⊠ Mendez Nuñez 13, Centro, Seville ☎ 95/450-2792. **Librería Beta** ⊠ Constitución 27, Centro, Seville ☎ 95/456-0703.

SAFETY

Seville has long been notorious for petty crime. Tourists continue to be thieves' favored victims, so take common sense precautions at the very least. In the car, drive with your doors locked, lock all your luggage out of sight in the trunk, and keep a wary eye on scooter riders, who have been known to snatch purses or even smash the windows of moving cars—and *never* leave *anything* in a parked car. When walking around, take only a small amount of cash and one credit card with you. Leave your passport, traveler's checks, and other credit cards in the hotel safe, if possible, and avoid carrying purses and expensive cameras or wearing valuable jewelry.

TOUR OPTIONS

In Seville, A.P.I.T., Guidetur, and I.T.A. can hook you up with a qualified English-speaking guide. Sevilla Walking Tours offers a two-hour walking tour in English, leaving Plaza Nueva (Statue of San Fernando) at 10:30 AM Monday through Saturday. The fee is €10. The tourist office has information on open-bus city tours run by Servirama, Hispalense de Tranvias, and others; buses leave every half hour from the Torre del Oro, with stops at Parque María Luisa and the Isla Mágica theme park. You can hop on and off at any stop; the complete tour lasts about 90 minutes. For an English-speaking guide in Cádiz or Jerez, contact the local tourist office.
🔒 **Tour Operators Asociación Provincial de Informadores Turísticos** ⊠ Glorieta de Palacio de Congresos, Seville ☎ 95/425-5957. **Guidetour** ⊠ Mateos Gago 29-Bajo ☎ 95/

422-2374 or 95/422-2375 ⊕ www.guidetur.com. **Hispalense de Tranvias** ✉ Teniente Coronel Segui 2, Centro ☎ 95/421-4169 or 95/422-9006. **ITA** ✉ Santa Teresa 1 ☎ 95/422-4641. **SevillaTour** ✉ C. Jaen 2 ☎ 95/450-2099 ⊕ www.citysightseeing-spain.com. **Sevilla Visión** ✉ Pl. Cristo de Burgos 9, Santa Catalina ☎ 95/422-4641. **Sevirama** ✉ Paseo de las Delicias, 2nd fl. on right, Edifico Cristina, Arenal ☎ 95/456-0693. **Sevilla Walking Tours** ☎ 902/158226 or 616/501100 ⊕ www.sevillawalkingtours.com.

DOÑANA NATIONAL PARK Jeep tours of the reserve depart twice daily (Tuesday–Sunday 8:30 and 3) from the park's Acebuche reception center, 2 km (1 mi) from Matalascañas. Tours are limited to 125 people and should be booked well in advance. Passengers can often be picked up from hotels in Matalascañas. **⑦ Parque Nacional de Doñana** ✉ Cooperativa Marisma del Rocío, Centro de Recepción, Matalascañas 21760 ☎ 959/430432 ⊕ www.donana.es.

SHERRY BODEGAS Winery tours can be arranged from Seville and Cádiz. In Jerez, most bodegas are open to visitors year-round. Tours, which include a tasting of brandy and sherry, should be reserved in advance; English-speaking guides are usually available. It's best to call the bodega and ask for Public Relations and book a time and language. To see a bodega in Puerto de Santa María, contact Osborne or Terry. In Sanlúcar de Barrameda, contact Barbadillo. **⑦ Barbadillo** ✉ Calle Luis de Eguilaz 11, Sanlúcar de Barrameda ☎ 956/385500 or 956/385521 ⊕ www.barbadillo.com ⌕€3 ⊙ Tours Mon.–Sat. at noon and 1 PM. **González Byass** ✉ Manuel María González 12, Jerez de la Frontera ☎ 956/357000 ⊕ www.gonzalezbyass.es ⌕€8 ⊙ Tours Mon.–Sat. at 11:30, 1:30, 3:30, and 5:30, in Aug. also at 6:30; Sun. between 11:30 and 1:30. **Harveys** ✉ Arcos 57, Jerez de la Frontera ☎ 956/346004 ⌕€4 ⊙ Tours weekdays at 10 and noon. **Osborne** ✉ Los Moros 7, Puerto de Santa María ☎ 956/869000 ⊕ www.osborne.es ⌕€5 ⊙ Tours in English weekdays at 10:30, in Spanish at 11 and noon. **Pedro Domecq** ✉ San Idelfonso 3, Jerez de la Frontera ☎ 956/151500 ⌕€6 ⊙ Weekdays 10–1. **Sandeman** ✉ Pizarro 10, Jerez de la Frontera ☎ 956/151700 ⊕ www.sandeman.com ⌕€5 ⊙ Visits by appointment only. **Terry** ✉ Santísima Trinidad s/n ☎ 956/857700 ⌕€3.60 ⊙ in English weekdays at 10 AM, in Spanish at 12:30, groups weekends only. **Williams and Humbert** ✉ NIV, Km 641.75, Jerez de la Frontera ☎ 956/353406 ⊕ www.williams-humbert.com ⌕€4 ⊙ Visits weekdays 9–3.

VISITOR INFORMATION
English is spoken in most hotels, top restaurants, and the main tourist sites but rarely in bars and rural destinations.

Seville has both regional and provincial tourist offices and also has branches at the Seville Airport and Santa Justa railway station. Tourist offices are generally open 9 to 2 and 3 to 7. Seville's provincial tourist office publishes a monthly events guide, *El Giraldillo*; it is in Spanish but is easy to understand for novice readers. Also in Seville you can pick up the free *Sevilla Welcome and Olé!*. It has both English and Spanish text, a map, and tourist information.

⑦ Andalusian Regional Tourist Offices Seville ✉ Av. de la Constitución 21 ☎ 95/422-1404, 95/421-8157, or 95/444-9128 ⊕ www.andalucia.org. **Cádiz** ✉ Av. Ramón de Carranza s/n ☎ 956/258646.

⑦ Provincial Tourist Offices Seville ✉ Pl. de Triunfo 1-3, by cathedral, Santa Cruz ☎ 95/421-0005 ⊕ www.turismosevilla.org. **Huelva** ✉ Av. Alemania 12 ☎ 959/257403. **Cádiz** ✉ Pl. de San Antonio 3, 2nd fl. ☎ 956/807061.

🖪 Local Tourist Offices **Almonte** ☒ Alonso Pérez 1 ☏ 959/450419. **Aracena** ☒ Pl. de San Pedro s/n ☏ 959/128825. **Arcos de la Frontera** ☒ Pl. del Cabildo s/n ☏ 956/702264. **Ayamonte** ☒ Ramón y Cajal s/n ☏ 959/502121. **Cádiz** ☒ Pl. San Juan de Dios 11 ☏ 956/241001 ⊕ www.cadizturismo.com. **Carmona** ☒ Arco de la Puerta de Sevilla ☏ 95/419-0955 ⊕ www.turismo.carmona.org. **El Rocío** ☒ La Canalieja s/n ☏ 959/443908 ⊕ www.parquenacionaldonana.com. **Isla Cristina** ☒ Ayamonte s/n ☏ 959/332694. ☒ **Islantilla** Av. de Riofrio s/n ☏ 959/646013. **Jerez de la Frontera** ☒ Larga 39 ☏ 956/331150 or 956/331162 ⊕ www.turismojerez.com. **La Rábida** ☒ Paraje de la Rábida s/n ☏ 959/531137. **Matalascañas** ☒ Av. las Adelfas s/n ☏ 959/430086. **Mazagón** ☒ Av. de los Conquistadores s/n ☏ 959/376300. **Moguer** ☒ Castillo s/n ☏ 959/371898 ⊕ www.aytomoguer.es. **Puerto de Santa María** ☒ Luna 22 ☏ 956/542413 ⊕ www.elpuertosm.es. **Rota** ☒ Castillo de Luna, Cuna 2 ☏ 956/846345. **Seville** ☒ Avenida de la Constitucíon 21, Arenal ☏ 95/422-1404 ⊕ www.sevilla.org ☒ Costurero de la Reina, Paseo de las Delicias 9, Arenal ☏ 95/423-4465.

Extremadura

WORD OF MOUTH

"Mérida is known for the Roman ruins that are still within the city. I was expecting these to be somewhere outside the city, but no. You turn a corner, and BAM! There is the Templo Diana mixed in with the shops!"

—Chele60

"The most extraordinary sight in [Cáceres's] old town, however, was not architectural, but natural. Atop every majestic spire and turret were massive cranes and storks (I think) tending their enormous nests. I met flocks of these birds several times during my visit."

—OReilly

Updated by
Mary McLean

THE VERY NAME *EXTREMADURA*—"the far end of the Duero"—suggests the wild, remote, and isolated character of this haunting region. With its poor soil and minimal industry, Extremadura has not experienced the kind of economic gains typical of other parts of Spain. However, tourism to the region *is* steadily increasing. Also, in recent decades a series of dams has brightened Extremadura's agricultural outlook. All the same, it's still hard to believe that, in the distant past, this area was one of Spain's most important and wealthy regions. No other place in Spain has as many Roman monuments as Mérida, the capital of the vast Roman province of Lusitania (the Iberian Peninsula); the town guarded the Vía de la Plata, the major Roman highway that crossed Extremadura from north to south, connecting Gijón with the port of Seville. The economy and the arts declined after the Romans left, but the region revived in the 16th century, when the surviving explorers and conquerors of the New World—from Francisco Pizarro and Hernán Cortés to Nuñez de Balboa and Francisco de Orellana, first navigator of the Amazon—returned to their birthplace. These men built the magnificent palaces that now glorify towns such as Cáceres and Trujillo, and they turned the remote monastery of Guadalupe—whose miraculous Virgin had inspired their exploits overseas—into one of the great artistic repositories of Spain.

Despite its strongly provincial character, Extremadura has long been influenced by its neighbors. Officially, Extremadura is made up of two provinces: Cáceres to the north and Badajoz to the south, divided by the Sierra de San Pedro (also called the Toledo Mountains). The villages and landscapes of Badajoz share much in common with neighboring Andalusia; Cáceres, with its wooded mountain valleys and half-timber, gray-stone houses, recalls both Castile and northern Spain. And Portugal, just over the western border, lends its accent to all of western Spain.

Exploring Extremadura

The rugged Extremadura is a boon for those who like the outdoors. The lush Jerte Valley and the craggy peaks of the Sierra de Gredos mark Upper Extremadura's fertile landscape. South of the Jerte Valley is the historical town of Plasencia and the 15th-century Yuste Monastery. In Extremadura's central interior is the provincial capital of Cáceres and the Monfrague Nature Park. Lower Extremadura's main towns—Mérida, Badajoz, Olivenza, and Zafra—lie near the Portuguese border, and have long exuded a Portuguese flavor, bolstered by the sizeable Portuguese population. The best way to explore is by car, as bus and train connections are not ideal for roaming such sparsely populated terrain.

Numbers in the text correspond to numbers in the margin and on the Extremadura map.

About the Restaurants

Extremaduran food reflects the austerity of the landscape: true peasant fare, with a strong character. In addition to fresh produce, Extremadurans rely on the pigs, of which every part is used, including the *criadillas* (testicles—don't confuse them with *criadillas de la tierra*, which are "earth testicles," also known as truffles). The dressed meats are outstand-

GREAT ITINERARIES

IF YOU HAVE 1 DAY

You can get a lightning impression of Extremadura in a day's drive from Madrid. Enter Extremadura through the Jerte Valley in the north (the scenic route). Take the N630 south to **Cáceres** ⑥, and then head east to **Trujillo** ⑦ on the N521. From here you can return to Madrid on the N-V. If you're pressed for time and don't mind missing one of the most breathtaking parts of Extremadura, enter the province by the N-V and go straight to Trujillo and Cáceres. For another day trip, enter the province from the Jerte Valley, then head down the N630 to Cáceres and **Mérida** ⑨. Lastly, a one-day trip can be made to the monastery of **Guadalupe** ⑧.

IF YOU HAVE 3 DAYS

From Madrid, take the slow and winding but highly scenic C501 to **Plasencia** ③ and wander through the *casco viejo* (old town). Drive next to the ▦ **Monasterio de Yuste** ④. On Day 2, head south to the provincial capital of **Cáceres** ⑥ and continue on to ▦ **Mérida** ⑨. On Day 3, travel back north by way of **Trujillo** ⑦ and **Guadalupe** ⑧.

IF YOU HAVE 5 DAYS

From Madrid, drive over the Tornavacas Pass (Puerto de Tornavacasa) on the N110 through the **Jerte Valley** ① to **Plasencia** ③. If you can, detour to the ancient Judería (Jewish Quarter) of **Hervás** ②. Spend the night at the parador in Jarandilla de la Vera—the fortified palace where Carlos V lived—before visiting the emperor's final home, the nearby **Monasterio de Yuste** ④. On Day 2, go south on the C524 to the **Parque Natural de Monfragüe** ⑤. Spend the night in ▦ **Trujillo** ⑦ and explore the town the next morning. Continue to **Cáceres** ⑥ for lunch and afternoon sightseeing. Spend your third night in ▦ **Mérida** ⑨, and take in its Roman monuments on Day 4. Head west to the provincial capital, **Badajoz** ⑩, with a side trip to the Spanish-Portuguese town of **Olivenza** ⑪. From here you can move on to Andalusia, stopping to see the castle-parador at **Zafra** ⑫, or drive back north on the N-V and turn off to admire the monastery of **Guadalupe** ⑧.

13

---

ing, most notably the sweetish cured hams from Montánchez; chorizo (spiced sausage); and *morcilla* (blood pudding), which is often made here with potatoes. The *caldereta de cordero* (lamb stew) is particularly tasty, as is the beef from the *retinto*, a local breed of long-horn cattle. Game is also common; *perdiz al modo de Alcántara,* partridge cooked with truffles, is a specialty. Local lake tench and river trout are also worth trying. Extremadurans make a gazpacho based on cucumbers, green peppers, and broth rather than tomatoes and water. A common accompaniment is *migas,* bread crumbs soaked in water and fried in olive oil with garlic, peppers, and sausage.

Local cheeses generally have a crumbly texture and strong flavors. If you have a chance, savor *tortas,* the round, semisoft cheeses of Cáceres; those from Casar and La Serena are especially prized. Favorite *ex-*

tremeño desserts include the *técula mécula* (an almond-flavor marzipan tart), which combines the flavors of Spain and Portugal. Marketed under the generic appellation "Ribera del Guadiana," Extremadura's little-known, light and fruity red wines are good values; try Lar de Lares. Typical digestifs include liqueurs made from cherries or acorns.

Dining out is not much of a tradition in Extremadura; some of the best food is served in modest bars. Reservations are generally unnecessary.

WHAT IT COSTS In Euros				
	$$$$	$$$	$$	$	¢
AT DINNER	over €20	€15–€20	€10–€15	€6–€10	under €6

Prices are per person for a main course at dinner.

About the Hotels

Extremadura's paradores are remarkable, occupying buildings of great historic or architectural interest in all major tourist areas. Reserve well in advance for a weekend stay. The Extremaduran government runs a few *hospederías,* a sort of regional version of the parador chain; some have historic quarters in scenic areas. Most other high-end hotels, with a few exceptions, are modern boxes with little character. Throughout Extremadura's countryside are a number of charming bed-and-breakfast inns (*hoteles rurales*) and 135 guesthouses (*casa rurales*). Despite their number, space in popular guesthouses is limited, so reservations are a must. Your best base for a series of day trips might be Cáceres—from there it's a just a hop to Trujillo, Mérida, and Plasencia.

WHAT IT COSTS In Euros				
	$$$$	$$$	$$	$	¢
FOR 2 PEOPLE	over €180	€100–€180	€60–€100	€40–€60	under €40

Prices are for two people in a standard double room in high season, excluding tax.

Timing

Summer is a good time to roam the nature parks or mountains, but note that southern Extremadura can get brutally hot. Spring and fall are ideal, as winter can be cold and rainy. The spectacle of cherry-blossom season in the Jerte Valley and the Vera erupts over two weeks around mid-March. Bird-watchers: visit in late February, after the migrating storks have arrived to nest and before the European cranes have returned to northern Europe.

UPPER EXTREMADURA

Extremadura stretches from Portugal to just west of Ciudad Real and from provinces Salamanca to Seville; it is crossed from east to west by the Tajo (Tagus) and Guadiana rivers. The Serena reservoir (fed by the Zújar River, which is fed by the Guadiana), is one of the largest in Europe. The province's fertile soil yields wheat, lamb, and pork, which has been exported to much of Europe for centuries.

IF YOU LIKE

FIESTAS

Extremadura is not a land of running bulls, except for the fiestas de **San Juan** in Coria, Cáceres, on the week of June 24, or the **Capeas,** in Segura de León, Badajoz, around September 14, when locals show off their bullfighting skills. Instead, the province of Cáceres has its share of colorful festivals commemorating past saints and sinners. January 20, the **Fiesta de San Estéban** (Feast of St. Stephen), inspires interesting folklore in several small towns. In Acehúche (near Garovillas), for example, *carantoñas* ("ugly mugs," men costumed in animal skins and frightening masks) bow before the statue of St. Stephen during his procession through town. In Piornal (near Plasencia), a *jaramplas* (a grotesquely costumed, masked jester) is pursued through the town and pelted with turnips. February 3 is the day to toast **San Blas** (St. Blaise), believed to heal sore throats, with hot cakes bearing his name, and multiple feasts. The second weekend in May brings the **WOMAD** (World of Music, Art and Dance) festival, attracting up to 75,000 spectators.

Semana Santa (Holy Week) is celebrated with rituals in cities throughout the region. One of the most dramatic, **Empalaos** ("impaled ones"), occurs on Holy Thursday in Valverde de la Vera. Young men's outstretched arms are tightly bound with rope tied to heavy logs across their backs for a procession recalling Christ's crucifixion. More savory is Trujillo's early May **Feria del Queso** (Cheese Festival). For Cáceres's September **Celebración del Cerdo y Vino** (Pig and Wine Celebration),

the area's innumerable pork products are prepared in public demonstrations, with free samples given afterward. For December's medieval **La Encamisá,** in Torrejoncillo (off the highway between Plasencia and Cáceres), white-robed riders brandish torches and thunder through the narrow streets on horseback in honor of the Immaculate Conception. On the same day, December 7, Jarandilla de la Vera fills the city with bonfires to celebrate **Los Escobazos,** when locals play-fight with torches made out of brooms.

In Badajoz the year opens on January 16 and 17 with **La Encamisá,** in Navalvillar de Pela. Horsemen re-create a medieval battle of the town's citizens against Arab invaders. During the **Carnival** celebration in Badajoz, parades of thousands wear extravagant costumes. Also colorful are the **Holy Week** celebrations at Oliva de la Frontera. Badajoz says *adios* to winter with the fiestas of **La Primavera** (Spring Festival) and **Los Mayos** (May Days), usually at the end of April and beginning of May. A significant date in Badajoz is May 3, **El Día de la Santa Cruz** (the Exaltation of the Holy Cross), celebrated in the villages of Corte de Peleas and Feria, where a local family is selected a month in advance to prepare a processional floral cross in its home. Some of these crosses become magnificent works of art and patience, tended to the point of depleting hard-earned savings. The crowd sings as a stone cross, the floral cross, and a statue of the Virgin Mary are paraded through town.

13

Valle del Jerte (Jerte Valley)

❶ *260 km (160 mi) west of Madrid. For a scenic route, follow N110 southwest from Ávila to Plasencia.*

There's no more striking introduction to Extremadura than the **Puerto de Tornavacas** (Tornavacas Pass)—literally, the "point where the cows turn back." Part of the N110 road northeast of Plasencia, the pass marks the border between Extremadura and the stark plateau of Castile. At 4,183 feet above sea level, it has a breathtaking view of the valley formed by the fast-flowing Jerte River. The valley's lower slopes are covered with a dense mantle of ash, chestnut, and cherry trees, whose richness contrasts with the granite cliffs of Castile's Sierra de Gredos. Cherries are the principal crop. To catch their brilliant blossoms, visit in the spring. Camping is popular in this region, and even the most experienced hikers can find some challenging trails. **Cabezuela del Valle,** full of half-timber stone houses, is one of the valley's best preserved villages. From the Jerte Valley, you can follow N110 to Plasencia or, if you have a taste for mountain scenery, detour from the village of Jerte to Hervás, traveling a narrow road that winds 35 km (22 mi) through forests of low-growing oak trees and over the Honduras Pass.

Where to Stay & Eat

$–$$ ✕🏨 **Valle del Jerte.** Service is always cheerful in this family-run inn just off the N110 in the village of Jerte. Specialties at the restaurant include gazpacho, *cabrito* (kid), and local trout. The homemade, regional desserts are outstanding, with many featuring the Jerte Valley's famed cherries; try the *tarta de cerezas* (cherry tart) or the *queso fresco de cabra con miel cerezo* (goat cheese topped with cherry-flavored honey). Ask to see the wonderful old wine cellar. The charming La Sotorriza *casa rural* upstairs has five comfortable guest rooms with chestnut furniture, cotton bedspreads, and beam ceilings. ✉ *Gargantilla 16, Jerte 10612* ☎ *927/470052* 🖷 *927/470448* ⊕ *www.donbellota.com* 🛏 *5 rooms* ⚐ *Restaurant, minibars, cable TV* ⊟ *MC, V.*

$$$$ 🏨 **El Molino del Sol.** A few miles past the town of Navaconcejo toward Cabezuela del Valle is this rural mill-turned-inn. The house is surrounded by cherry and fruit orchards, and just a few yards away is the Jerte (feel free to take a refreshing dip). The rooms are all decorated differently. The house is rented only in full (it accommodates as many as 12 people) for €200 daily, with a two-night minimum stay. ✉ *Camino la Barbara, Navaconcejo 10613* ☎ *927/470313* 🖷 *927/470313* ⊕ *www.alojamientorural.com* 🛏 *6 rooms* ⚐ *Restaurant, meeting room; no room TVs* ⊟ *AE, D, MC, V.*

$$$ 🏨 **Hospedería Valle del Jerte.** This turn-of-the-20th-century building is at the edge of the village, next to the Jerte River. The interior is modern and functional. Some rooms have river views, whereas others face the village; those on the top floor have sloped ceilings. Perks include a sitting room with fireplace and a pleasant Japanese garden. ✉ *Ramón Cepeda 118, Jerte 10612* ☎ *927/470403* 🖷 *927/470131* ⊕ *www.jertehotel.com* 🛏 *23 rooms* ⚐ *Restaurant, cafeteria, minibars, cable TV, library, meeting room* ⊟ *AE, D, MC, V.*

$$ 🏨 **Hotel Rural Finca El Carpintero.** In two adjacent stone buildings, this hotel has three types of rooms, the best of which has a fireplace, a sitting room (salon), and its own entrance. The simpler rooms are elegant and colorful, and have canopy wrought-iron beds. The restaurant has an €18 dinner menu. ✉ *N110, Km 360.5, Tornavacas 10611* ☎ *927/177089 or 659/732–8110* 🛏 *9 rooms* ⚐ *Restaurant, Wi-Fi, meeting room* ⊟ *AE, D, MC, V.*

$$ 🏨 **La Casería.** This rambling home is on a 120-acre working farm, once part of a 16th-century Franciscan convent. One of the first rural guesthouses established in Extremadura, it's run by a couple who also raise

---

MARY'S TOP 5

- Wandering around the medieval quarter of Cáceres at dusk.

- Impressing the folks back home with photos of the spectacular Jerte Valley cherry blossoms.

- Kicking back with a coffee or beer at one of the bars at Pizarro's magnificent main plaza.

- Splurging with a night's stay at Guadalupe's parador with a heady view of the monastery from your balcony.

- Absorbing the history of Mérida, with its incredible array of Roman buildings and artifacts.

13

sheep. This place is strictly for animal lovers, as the household includes lots of dogs and cats. Aside from the six rooms in the main lodge, there are three cottages, each of which can sleep two to four. Activities such as horseback riding, mountain biking, and paragliding can be arranged. It's wise to reserve in advance, and to keep your eyes peeled as you approach: The sign is easy to miss. ⊠ N110, Km 378.6, Navaconcejo 10613 ☎ 927/173141 🖷 927/177384 ⊕ www.lacaseria.net 🖙 6 rooms, 3 cottages ⌂ Pool; no a/c, no room TVs. ⊟ MC, V.

Hervás

➋ 63 km (39 mi) northeast of Plasencia, 142 km (88 mi) northeast of Cáceres, 25 km (16 mi) west of Cabezuela del Valle.

Surrounded by pine and chestnut groves, this charming, hilly village makes an interesting detour from either the Jerte Valley or Plasencia. Hervás, it's believed, grew into a predominantly Jewish settlement during the Middle Ages, populated by Jews escaping Christian and Muslim persecution in Spain's larger cities. In 1492, when the Jews were expelled from the country altogether during the Inquisition, their neighborhood was left intact but their possessions were ceded to the local nobility. Stripped of its wealth, the village lost its commercial reputation and was forgotten. Now fully restored, the **Judería** (Jewish Quarter) is among the best-preserved in Spain. It contains the 15th-century **Convento de los Trinitarios** (☎ 927/474828), part of which has been turned into a hospedería. At the top of the quarter there's a 16th- to 17th-century Renaissance church called the **Santa Maria de Aguas Vivas.**

Plasencia

➌ 270 km (169 mi) west of Madrid, 79 km (49 mi) north of Cáceres, 126 km (78 mi) northwest of Trujillo.

Rising dramatically from the banks of the narrow Jerte River and backed by the peaks of the Sierra de Gredos, this community was founded by Alfonso VIII in 1180, just after he captured the entire area from the Moors. The town's motto, *placeat Deo et hominibus* ("It pleases both God and men"), might well have been a ploy on Alfonso's part to attract settlers to this wild, isolated place on the southern border of the former kingdom of León. Badly damaged during the Peninsular War of 1808, Plasencia retains far less of its medieval quarter than other Extremaduran towns, but it still has extensive remains of its early walls and a smattering of fine old buildings. In addition to a site for visiting ruins, the city makes a good base for side trips to Hervás and the Jerte Valley, the Monasterio de Yuste and Monfragüe Nature Park, or, farther northwest, the wild Las Hurdes and Sierra de Gata.

Plasencia's **cathedral** was founded in 1189 and rebuilt after 1320 in an austere Gothic style that looks a bit incongruous looming over the town's red-tile roofs. In 1498 the great architect Enrique Egas designed a new structure, intending to complement or even overshadow the original, but despite the later efforts of other notable architects of the time, such as Juan de Alava and Francisco de Colonia, his plans were never fully realized. The entrance to this incomplete, curious, and not wholly satis-factory complex is through a door on the cathedral's ornate but somber north facade. The dark interior of the new cathedral is notable for the beauty of its pilasters, which sprout like trees into the ribs of the vault-ing. You enter the old cathedral through the Gothic cloister, which has four enormous lemon trees. Off the cloister stands the building's oldest surviving section, a 13th-century chapter house (now the chapel of **San Pablo**)—a late-Romanesque structure with an idiosyncratic, Moorish-in-spired dome. Inside are medieval hymnals and a 13th-century gilded wood sculpture of the Virgen del Perdón. The **museum** in the truncated nave of the old cathedral has ecclesiastical and archaeological objects. ☏ *927/ 414852* ⌹ *Old cathedral €2* ☉ *Oct.–Apr., Mon.–Sat. 9–12:30 and 4–5:30, Sun. 9–1; May–Sept., Mon.–Sat. 9–12:30 and 5–6:30, Sun. 9–1.*

13

The cloister of the elegant **Palacio Episcopal** (Bishop's Palace; ⌹ Pl. de la Catedral) is open weekdays from 9 AM to 2 PM. The **Casa del Deán** (Dean's House; ⌹ Pl. de la Catedral), a striking Renaissance building, is now a courthouse. The sober **Hospital de Santa María** serves as a cul-tural center.

The **Museo Etnográfico-Textil,** at the back of the Hospital de Santa María, has displays of colorful regional costumes. ⌹ *Enter on C. Plaza Mar-qués de la Puebla* ☏ *927/421843* ⌹ *Free* ☉ *Sept.–June, Wed.–Sat. 11–2 and 5–8, Sun. 11–2; July and Aug., Mon.–Sat. 9:30–2:30.*

Lined with orange trees, the narrow, carefully preserved **Plaza de San Vicente** is at the northwest end of the old medieval quarter. At one end is the 15th-century church of **San Vicente Ferrer,** with an adjoining con-vent that's now a parador. The north side of the square is dominated by the Renaissance **Palacio de Mirabel** (Palace of the Marquis of Mirabel; ☏ *927/410701*)—go through the central arch for a back view. The hours can be sporadic, but it's usually open daily 10 AM to 2 PM and 4 to 6 PM; tip the caretaker. East of the Plaza de San Vicente, at the other end of the Rúa Zapatería, is the **Plaza Mayor,** a cheerful, arcaded square where a market has been held every Tuesday morning since the 12th cen-tury. The mechanical figure clinging to the town-hall clock tower de-picts the clock maker himself and is called the **Mayorga** in honor of the craftsman's Castilian hometown. East of the Plaza de San Vicente you can find a large section of the town's **medieval wall**—on the other side of which is a heavily restored Roman aqueduct. Walk southeast from the Plaza de San Vicente to the **Parque de los Pinos,** home to wildlife that includes peacocks, cranes, swans, pheasants, and monkeys.

Where to Stay & Eat

$$–$$$ ✗⌹ **Hotel Alfonso VIII.** Grand but slightly past its prime, with undistin-guished modern rooms, this curious Franco-era relic is strangely agree-able. Its restaurant has long been regionally renowned for its food; the *ensalada de perdiz* (salad with partridge) makes for a tasty starter. There's parking in a garage in front. ⌹ *Alfonso VIII 32, 10600* ☏ *927/ 410250* ☎ *927/418042* ⊕ *www.hotelalfonsoviii.com* ⌨ *55 rooms, 2 suites* ⌹ *Restaurant, minibars, cable TV, in-room data ports, Wi-Fi, park-ing (fee)* ▭ *AE, DC, MC, V.*

$$$ 🏨 **Parador de Plasencia.** In a 15th-century Gothic convent, this parador cultivates a medieval environment. The common areas are majestic and somber, and the guest rooms are decorated with monastic motifs and heavy wood furniture. Rooms are spacious and comfortable with stylishly modern bathrooms; most have sitting rooms. The high-ceiling, stone-and-wood-beam restaurant—called The Refectory—is almost intimidating in its architectural magnificence. Parking adds a hefty €12 nightly. ✉ *Pl. de San Vicente Ferrer, 10600* 🕾 *927/425870* 🖷 *927/425872* ⊕ *www.parador.es* ⤳ *66 rooms* ⚹ *Restaurant, minibars, cable TV, in-room data ports, Wi-Fi, pool, bar, parking (fee)* ▭ *AE, D, MC, V.*

$ 🏨 **Rincón Extremeño.** Just off the Plaza Mayor in the heart of the old quarter, this property is basic and well maintained. The ground floor has a popular bar and restaurant, the latter serving regional dishes. You'll have nicer views—though more noise—in a guest room facing the narrow street. Twelve rooms have en-suite bathrooms. ✉ *Vidrieras 6, 10600* 🕾 *927/411150* 🖷 *927/420627* ⤳ *19 rooms* ⚹ *Restaurant, bar* ▭ *MC, V.*

Shopping

If you happen to be in Plasencia on a Tuesday morning, head for the Plaza Mayor and do what the locals have been doing since the 12th century: scout bargains in the weekly market. On the first Tuesday of every August the market is much larger, with vendors from all over the region. For local art and crafts, try **Bámbara de Artesanía** (✉ Sancho Polo 12 🕾 927/411766). Near the parador is **Artesanías Canillas** (✉ C. San Vicente Ferrer s/n 🕾 927/411668), which has regional costumes, pottery, and handmade straw hats. At **Casa del Jamón** (✉ C. Sol 18, east of Pl. Mayor 🕾 927/419328 ✉ C. Zapatería 17, between Pl. Mayor and parador 🕾 927/419328), stock up on sausages, *jamón ibérico* (Iberian ham), cheeses, Extremeño wines, and cherry liqueur from the valley.

Monasterio de Yuste & La Vera

❹ *17 km (11 mi) southeast of Jarandilla de la Vera, 45 km (28 mi) from Plasencia. Turn left off C501 at Cuacos and follow signs for the monastery (1 km [½ mi]).*

The **Monasterio de Yuste** (Yuste Monastery) was founded by Hieronymite monks in the early 15th century. Badly damaged in the Peninsular War, it was left to decay after the suppression of Spain's monasteries in 1835, but it has since been restored and taken over once more by the Hieronymites. Carlos V (1500–58), founder of Spain's vast 16th-century empire, spent his last two years in the Royal Chambers, enabling the emperor to attend Mass within a short stumble of his bed. The required guided tour also includes the church, the crypt where Carlos V was buried before being moved to El Escorial (near Madrid), and a glimpse of the monastery's cloisters. 🕾 *927/172130* ⊕ *www.yuste.org/monasterio* 🎫 *€2.50* ☉ *Oct.–May, daily 9:30–12:30 and 3–6; June–Sept., daily 9:30–12:30 and 3:30–6:30.*

The Yuste Monastery is in the heart of **La Vera,** a place of steep ravines (*gargantas*), rushing rivers, and villages. Following the road that climbs from the monastery into the mountains for 6 km (4 mi), you come to the delightful village of **Garganta La Olla**—as you approach, the road winds through cherry orchards and eventually dips into the village's narrow, twisting streets. If you're enchanted with the mountainous isolation and want to relax in the company of the villagers, a local gentleman, **El Abuelo Marciano** (Grandpa Marciano; ⊠ Ctra. Jaráiz-Garganta, Km 2.5 ☎ 927/460426), provides room and board, preferably to groups, in his sizeable six-bedroom house in the countryside.

Where to Stay & Eat

$$–$$$ ✕🖵 **Parador de Jarandilla de la Vera.** Nestled in the town of Jarandilla, this parador (sometimes called Parador Carlos V) was built in the early 16th century as a fortified palace. The emperor Carlos V stayed here for three months while he waited for his quarters at Yuste to be completed. The halls have stylish medieval furnishings, and

> **WORD OF MOUTH**
>
> "If you have ever dreamed of spending the night in a castle, look no further (than the Parador de Jarandilla de la Vera)."
>
> -ekscrunchy.

the regal dining room is the perfect place to indulge royal fantasies. In the restaurant, start with a humble classic, *huevos fritos con migas* (fried eggs with bread crumbs); then savor one of the house specialties: *caldereta de cordero* (lamb stew). ⊠ *Av. García Prieto 1, 59 km (36 mi) east of Plasencia, 17 km (11 mi) west of Monasterio de Yuste, 10450* ☎ *927/560117* 🖨 *927/560088* ⊕ *www.parador.es* 🛏 *53 rooms* ⚘ *Restaurant, in-room data ports, tennis court, pool, bar, playground* ▭ *AE, DC, MC, V.*

$$ 🖵 **Camino Real.** In a village in the highest valley of the Vera, this hotel is in a mansion. Rooms have exposed stone walls and wooden beam ceilings; most have hot tubs. The rate includes a lavish buffet breakfast. The owners organize local excursions. ⊠ *C. El Monje 27, Guijo de Santa Bárbara 10459* ☎ *927/561119* 🖨 *927/561119* ⊕ *www.casaruralcaminoreal. com* 🛏 *10 rooms* ⚘ *Restaurant* ▭ *MC, V* ⑪ *BP.*

$–$$ 🖵 **Antigua Casa del Heno.** This 150-year-old stone farmhouse is near a natural spring. With wood floors, stone walls, and sprightly fabrics, the rooms are cozy and cheerful; some have balconies or skylights, and all have unhindered views of the countryside. The inn is a favorite with stressed-out executives from Madrid, so reservations are essential. The restaurant, for guests only, serves Spanish dishes. Beware: the narrow, unpaved road uphill is challenging and remote. ⊠ *Finca Valdepimienta, Losar de la Vera, follow signs from village, Cáceres 10460* ☎🖨 *927/ 198077* ⊕ *www.antiguacasadelheno.com* 🛏 *7 rooms* ⚘ *Dining room; no a/c, no room TVs* ▭ *MC, V* ⑪ *BP.*

★ $ 🖵 **Posada de Pizarro.** In the village center, this posada may look ordinary from the outside, but step into any one of the guest rooms and you're greeted with some really stunning frescoes. The comfortable rooms, each with a small balcony, will suit most folks. The downstairs bar and breakfast room is decorated with antlers, and the corner TV is permanently set to the soccer channel. ⊠ *Cuesta de los Carrios, Jarandilla 10450* ☎ *927/560727* ⊕ *www.laposadadepizarro.com* 🛏 *10 rooms* ⚘ *breakfast room, bar* ▭ *MC, V* ⑪ *BP.*

13

Shopping

If you like to cook, pick up a tin or two of *pimentón de la Vera* (sweet paprika), made from the region's prized red peppers, in Jarandilla.

Parque Natural de Monfragüe

⑤ *20 km (12 mi) south of Plasencia on the Ex-208.*

At the junction of the rivers Tiétar and Tajo, between Plasencia and Trujillo, is the Monfragüe Nature Park. This rocky-mountain wilderness is known for its plant and animal life, including lynx, boar, deer, fox, black storks, imperial eagles, and the world's largest colony of black vultures. Bring binoculars and find the lookout point called **Salto del Gitano** (Gypsy's Leap), on the C524 just south of the Tajo River—this is where the vultures can often be spotted wheeling in the dozens at close range. The park's visitor center is in the hamlet of Villareal de San Carlos. ☎927/199134 ⊙ *May–Sept., daily 9–2:30 and 4:30–7:30; Oct.–Apr., daily 9–2:30 and 4–6; audiovisual show every hr on ½ hr.*

Where to Stay & Eat

$$$ ✕▦ **Hospedería Parque de Monfragüe.** On the main road, Ex-208, just south of the park, this hotel is in a trio of stark modern buildings. The interior, furnished with contemporary pieces, has been in several Spanish design magazines; in the guest rooms, neutral grays and browns are backed by natural stone walls. Rooms in the wing farthest from the road have the best mountain views. The light-flooded restaurant ($$$$) has large windows overlooking the park and serves top-notch regional cuisine, including locally produced sausages, cured hams, and cheeses. ⊠ *Ctra. Plasencia–Trujillo, Km 39.1, Torrejón el Rubio 10694* ☎ *927/455245* 🖷 *927/455016* ⊕ *www.hotelmonfrague.com* ⇦ *52 rooms, 4 suites, 4 apartments* ⌂ *Restaurant, cafeteria, in-room data ports, Wi-Fi, pool, meeting room* ▭ *AE, DC, MC, V.*

Cáceres

⑥ *307 km (190 mi) west of Madrid.*

Fodor'sChoice
★

Cáceres, the provincial capital, is a prosperous agricultural town whose vibrant nightlife draws villagers from the surrounding pueblos every weekend. One of Spain's oldest cities, Cáceres was first inhabited some 30,000 years ago, as the archaeological findings in the cave of Maltravieso 3 km (2 mi) south of the present city center confirm. The Roman colony called Norba Caesarina was founded in 35 BC, but when the Moors took over in the 8th century, they named the city Quazris, which eventually morphed into the Spanish Cáceres. It has been prosperous ever since noble families helped Alfonso IX expel the Moors in 1229, and the pristine condition of the city's medieval and Renaissance quarter is the result of the families' continued occupancy of the palaces first erected in the 15th century.

Cáceres Viejo (Old Cáceres), which begins just east of Plaza San Juan, is the best part of town to stay in and explore. On the long, inclined, arcaded **Plaza Mayor,** you can see several outdoor cafés, tourist offices, and—on breezy summer nights—nearly everyone in town. In the middle of the arcade opposite the old quarter is the entrance to the lively Calle General Ezponda, lined with tapas bars, student hangouts, and discos that keep the neighborhood awake and moving until dawn. On high ground on the eastern side of the Plaza Mayor, a portal beckons through the town's intact wall, which in turn surrounds one of the best-preserved old quarters in Spain. Literally packed with treasures, Cáceres's **Ciudad Monumental** (old town; also called the *casco antiguo*) is a marvel: small, but without a single modern building to distract from its aura. Virtually every tower and spire is topped by the nests of storks, which are quite common in the area. Crammed with somber, gray medieval and Renaissance palaces, the old town is virtually deserted in winter.

13

Once you pass through the gate leading to the old quarter, note the **Palacio de los Golfines de Arriba** (⊠ C. Adarve de Santa Ana), dominated by a soaring tower dating from 1515. The ground floor is a stylish restaurant. Check out the **Casa de Sanchez de Paredes** (⊠ C. Ancha), a 16th-century palace that now serves as a parador. On the Plaza San Mateo is the **San Mateo church** (⊠ C. Ancha). Built mainly in the 14th century, but with a 16th-century choir, it has an austere interior, the main decorative notes being the baroque high altar and some heraldic crests. The battlement tower of the **Palacio de Las Cigüeñas** (⊠ Pl. San Mateo) is officially named the Palacio del Capitán Diego but is also known as the Palace of the Storks for obvious reasons. It's now a military residence, but some rooms are occasionally opened up for exhibitions.

The **Casa de las Veletas** (House of the Weather Vanes) is a 12th-century Moorish mansion that is now the **Museo de Cáceres**. With archaeological finds, some dating as far back as the Neolithic era, this collection is an excellent way to acquaint yourself with the area's many inhabitants. One highlight is the eerie but superb Moorish cistern—the *aljibe*—with arches supported by moldy stone pillars. It's downhill from Plaza San Mateo. ⊠ *1 Pl. de las Veletas* ☎ *927/010877* ⊕ *www.museosextremadura.com/caceres* ⊠ *€1.20, free Sun. and for EU citizens* ☉ *Oct.–Apr., Tues.–Sat. 9–2:30 and 4–7, Sun. 10–2:30; May–Sept., 9–2:30 and 5–8, Sun. 10–2:30.*

The stony severity of the **Palacio de los Golfines de Abajo** (⊠ Cuesta de la Companía), with the finest exterior of any palace in Cáceres, is relieved by Mudejar and Renaissance decorative motifs. The Gothic church of **Santa María**, built mainly in the 16th century, is now the town cathedral. The elegantly carved high altar, dating from 1551, is barely visible in the gloom. A small museum displays religious objects. ⊠ *Cuesta de la Companía* ☎ *927/215313* ⊠ *Cathedral free, museum €2* ☉ *Mon.–Sat. 10–2 and 5–8, Sun. 9:30–2 and 5–7:30.*

Near the cathedral of Santa María is the elegant **Palacio de Carvajal,** the only old palace you can tour besides the Casa de las Veletas. It has an imposing granite facade and an arched doorway, and the interior has been restored, with period furnishings and art, to look as it did when the Carvajal family lived here in the 16th century. ⊠ *Pl. de Santa María* ⊠ *Free* ☉ *Weekdays 8 AM–9 PM, Sat. 9:30–2 and 5–8, Sun. 10–3.*

From Santa María cathedral, a 110-yard walk down Calle Tiendas takes you to Cáceres's northern wall. Don't miss the 16th-century **Palacio de los Moctezuma-Toledo** (now a public-records office), built by Juan Cano de Saavedra with the dowry provided by his wife, an Aztec princess who was the daughter of Montezuma (aka Moctezuma). ✉ *Pl. Conde de Canilleros 1* ☎ *927/249294* ⌾ *Free* ⊙ *Weekdays 8:30–2:30.*

The chief building of interest outside the wall of the old town is the church of **Santiago de los Caballeros** (✉ C. Villalobos), rebuilt in the 16th century by Rodrigo Gil de Hontañón, Spain's last great Gothic architect. Reach the church by exiting the old town on its west side, through the Socorro gate.

Just up the hill behind Cáceres's Ciudad Monumental is the **Santuario de la Virgen de la Montaña** (Sanctuary of the Virgin of the Mountain). Inside is a golden baroque altar and a statue of the patroness virgin. Each May the statue is paraded through town. On a clear day the view of old Cáceres from the front of the building is spectacular, well worth the 15-minute drive up the hill. ✉ *Follow C. Cervantes until it becomes Ctra. Miajadas; the sanctuary is just off town tourist map, which you can pick up from the local tourist office.* ☎ *927/220049* ⌾ *Donation suggested* ⊙ *Daily 8:30–2 and 4–8.*

OFF THE BEATEN PATH

GAROVILLAS AND MONASTERIO DEL PALANCAR – Garovillas, 10 km (6 mi) off the main road between Cáceres and Plasencia (turn left [northwest] onto the C522, 25 km [15 mi] north of Cáceres), is a perfectly preserved, though partially deserted, village. Its must-see square from the late 15th century has an impressive hospedería. East of Garovillas and near the Portuguese border, lies the Puente de Alcántara, a 2nd-century Roman bridge over the River Tajo that is one of Spain's prized architectural marvels. On the same road to Plasencia, past the Puerto de los Castañeos, is a detour to the **Monasterio del Palancar** (☎ 927/192023). In this Franciscan convent, San Pedro de Alcántara, an ascetic friar and saint, spent most of his life in a cell so tiny that he had to sleep sitting up. It's open Thursday through Tuesday 10 to 1 and 4:30 to 6:45.

Where to Stay & Eat

★ **$$$$** ✕ **Atrio.** On a side street off the southern end of Cáceres's leafy main boulevard, this elegant restaurant is the best in Extremadura, and possibly better than any in Andalusia, too. It specializes in highly refined modern cooking. The menu changes often, but you won't be disappointed with any of your selections, especially if they include venison, partridge, wild mushrooms, or truffles. ✉ *Av. de España 30* ☎ *927/242928* ▭ *AE, DC, MC, V* ⊙ *Closed Sept. 1–15. No dinner Sun.*

$$–$$$ ✕ **El Figón de Eustaquio.** A fixture on the quiet and pleasant Plaza San Juan, across from the Meliá hotel, Eustaquio is always busy, especially at lunch. In its jumble of small, old-fashioned dining rooms you'll be served mainly regional delicacies, including *venado de montería* (wild venison) or *perdiz estofada* (partridge stew). Fine Spanish wines are also available. ✉ *Pl. San Juan 12* ☎ *927/244362* ⌓ *Reservations essential* ▭ *AE, MC, V.*

$$–$$$ ✕ **Parador de Cáceres.** A 14th-century Renaissance palace provides a noble setting for this comfortable parador decorated in soft cream and ocher tones offset by exposed stone walls and wood beams. The rooms are cozy and comfortable, and the public spaces are ancient and elegant. The Torreorgaz restaurant (with tables in the patio terrace in summer) prepares local game specialties, including *lomo de venado a la Torta del Casar* (venison with the creamy Torta del Casar sheep cheese) or *cabrito asado al romero* (young goat roasted with rosemary). From Friday to Sunday, you can sample wines in the parador's wine cellar, Enoteca Torreorgaz. ⊠ *Ancha 6, 10003* ☎ *927/211759* 🖶 *927/211729* ⊕ *www. parador.es* ⋑ *32 rooms, 1 suite* ⚭ *Restaurant, minibars, in-room data ports, cable TV, meeting room, parking (fee)* ▤ *AE, DC, MC, V.*

★ **$$$** 🏨 **Meliá Cáceres.** This 16th-century palace built by the Marqueses de Oquendo is just outside the walls of the old town on the Plaza San Juan. The boutique hotel gracefully blends exposed brick and designer touches, with antique furniture. Rooms have ample bathrooms with ornate fittings. La Cava del Emperador, a street-level bar and restaurant with a vaulted brick ceiling, is a popular meeting place for the town's well heeled. ⊠ *Pl. San Juan 11–13, 10003* ☎ *927/215800* 🖶 *927/214070* ⊕ *www. solmelia.com* ⋑ *84 rooms, 2 suites* ⚭ *Restaurant, room service, cable TV, in-room data ports, bar, laundry service, meeting rooms, parking (fee)* ▤ *AE, DC, MC, V.*

★ **$** 🏨 **HotelIberia Plaza Mayor.** You don't have to shift your credit card into overdrive to stay in this 18th-century palace, which is furnished with antiques. The tastefully refurbished guest rooms have breezy blue tiled bathrooms and attractive dark-wood furniture. The location on a pedestrian shopping street just off Plaza Mayor is excellent but likely to be noisy—pack your earplugs. ⊠ *C. Pintores 2, 10003* ☎ *927/247634* ⊕ *www.iberiahotel.com* ⋑ *37 rooms* ▤ *MC, V.*

Nightlife & the Arts

Bars in Cáceres are lively until the wee hours. Nightlife centers on the **Plaza Mayor,** which fills after dinner with families out for a *paseo* (stroll) as well as students swigging *calimocho,* a mix of red wine and Coca-Cola. In the adjacent old town, you can take in some live music at **El Corral de las Cigueñas** (⊠ Cuesta de Aldana 6), which from October to April is open only Thursday to Sunday evenings. For livelier nightlife, head to nearby **Calle de Pizarro.** This block, south of Plaza de San Juan, is lined with cafés and bars, including **Mistura Brasileira,** at number 8, a Brazilian bar where you can perfect your hip-swinging steps with a live band beginning at 10:30 PM on Friday. The annual WOMAD (World of Music, Arts and Dance) festival is held in Cáceres center every May, attracting some 75,000 spectators. At the **Sala de Promoción de la Artisania** (⊠ San Antón 17 ☎ 927/220927), local artists and craftsmen sell their work. There's a weekly street market on Wednesday.

Trujillo

★ **❼** *48 km (30 mi) east of Cáceres, 250 km (155 mi) southwest of Madrid; at the junction of N521 and the A5.*

Trujillo rises up from the fertile fields around it like a great granite schooner under full sail. Up close, the rooftops and towers seem medieval; down below, Renaissance architecture flourishes in squares such as Plaza

Mayor, with its elegant San Martín church. The storks' nests that top many of the towers in and around the center of the old town have become a symbol of Trujillo. The city dates back at least to Roman times, when its castle was first constructed. The city was captured from the Moors in 1232 and colonized by a number of leading military families. It was only after Spain's discovery of the Americas in 1492, however, that the town's renown spread. Known today as the Cradle of the Conquistadors, Trujillo spawned some of the leading explorers and conquerors of the New World. The most famous of these was Francisco Pizarro, conqueror of Peru, born in Trujillo in 1475. Note that it's practical to see Trujillo only on foot, as the streets are mostly cobbled or crudely paved with stone. The two main roads into Trujillo leave you at the town's unattractive bottom. Things get progressively older the farther you climb, but even on the lower slopes—where most of the shops are concentrated—you need walk only a few yards to step into what seems like the Middle Ages.

Trujillo's large **Plaza Mayor,** one of the finest in Spain, is a superb Renaissance creation and the site of the local tourist office. At the foot of the stepped platform on the plaza's north side stands a large, bronze equestrian statue of conqueror Francisco Pizarro—the work, curiously, of a U.S. sculptor, Carlos Rumsey. The church behind the Pizarro statue, **San Martín** (⊠ Pl. Mayor), is a Gothic structure from the early 16th century, with Renaissance tombs and an old organ. Some of Spain's most prominent kings prayed there, including Carlos V, Felipe II, and Felipe V. If you visit at dusk, you may hear the men's choir rehearsing, adding a magical note to eventide.

The **Palacio de los Duques de San Carlos** (Palace of the Dukes of San Carlos) is next to the church of San Martín. The palace's majestically decorated facade dates from around 1600. The building is now a convent of Hieronymite nuns, who can occasionally be glimpsed on the balconies in full habit, hanging laundry or watering their flowers. To visit, ring the bell by pulling the chain in the foyer. The convent also produces and sells typical pastries, including *perrunillas* (small lard cakes) and *tocinillos del cielo* (custardlike egg-yolk sweets). ⊠ *Pl. Mayor* ☎ *927/320058* 🔊 *€1.20* ☉ *Mon.–Sat. 10–1 and 4:30–6, Sun. 10–12:30.*

NEED A BREAK?

If the intense summer sun leaves you parched and tired, revivify yourself at the **Bar Pillete Cafeteria** (⊠ Pl. Mayor 28 ☎ 927/321449). It sells fresh-squeezed juices, shakes, and other exotic fruit concoctions—a rarity in these remote parts.

The **Palacio del Marqués de la Conquista** (Palace of the Marquis of the Conquest; ⊠ Pl. Mayor) is the most dramatic building on the square. Built by Francisco Pizarro's half-brother Hernando, the stone palace is immediately recognizable by its rich covering of early Renaissance plateresque ornamentation. Flanking its corner balcony, around which most of the decoration is clustered, are lively, imaginative busts of the Pizarro family.

Adjacent to the Palacio de la Conquista is the arcaded former town hall, now a court of law; the alley that runs through its central arch takes you to the **Palacio de Orellana-Pizarro,** which functions as a school and has the most elegant Renaissance courtyard in town. Cervantes, on his way to thank the Virgin of Guadalupe for his release from prison, spent some time writing here. ⊠ *Free* ☉ *Weekdays 10–1 and 4–6, weekends 11–2 and 4:30–7.*

Trujillo's oldest section, known as **La Villa,** is entirely surrounded by its original, much restored, walls. Follow the wall along Calle Almenas, which runs west from the Palacio de Orellana-Pizarro, beneath the **Alcázar de Los Chaves,** a castle-fortress that was turned into a guest lodge in the 15th century and hosted visiting dignitaries, including Ferdinand and Isabella. The building has seen better days and is now a college. Passing the Alcázar, continue west along the wall to the **Puerta de San Andrés,** one of La Villa's four surviving gates (there were originally seven). Walk through and you're in a world inhabited by storks, who, in spring and early summer, hunker down in the many crumbling chimneys and towers of Trujillo's palaces and churches.

Attached to a Romanesque bell tower, the Gothic church of **Santa María Mayor** is occasionally used for masses, but its interior has been virtually untouched since the 16th century. The upper choir has an exquisitely carved balustrade; the coats of arms at each end indicate the seats Ferdinand and Isabella occupied when they attended mass here. Note the high altar, circa 1480, adorned with great 15th-century Spanish paintings; to see it properly illuminated, place a coin in the box next to the church entrance. Climb up the tower for stunning views of the town and surrounding vast plains stretching toward Cáceres and the Sierra de Gredos. ⊠ *Pl. de Santa María* ⊠ *€1.30* ☉ *Oct.–Apr., daily 10–2 and 4:30–7; May–Sept., daily 10–2 and 4–8.*

The Pizarro family home has been restored and is now a modest museum, the **Casa Museo de Pizarro,** dedicated to the links between Spain and Latin America. ⊠ *Pl. de Santa María* ⊠ *€1.30* ☉ *Oct.–Apr., daily 10–2 and 4–6; May–Sept., daily 10–2 and 4–8.*

Near the Puerta de la Coria, housed in a former Franciscan convent, is the **Museo de la Coria.** Its exhibits are similar to those in the Casa Museo de Pizarro, but they're more impressive, with an emphasis on the troops as well as other (non-Pizarro) conquistadors who led missions over the water. ☎ *927/321898* ⊠ *Free* ☉ *Weekends 11:30–2.*

Beyond the Casa Museo de Pizarro is the fortress of Trujillo's large **castle,** built by the Moors on Roman foundations. Climb to the top for spectacular views of the town and its surroundings, both modern and medieval: to the south are grain silos, warehouses, and residential neighborhoods; to the north are only green fields and flowers, partitioned by a maze of nearly leveled Roman stone walls. ⊠ *€1.30* ☉ *May–Sept., daily 10–2 and 5–8:30; Oct.–Apr., 10–2 and 4–7.*

Where to Stay & Eat

★ **$–$$$** ✕ **Pizarro.** Traditional Extremaduran home cooking is the draw of this friendly restaurant right on the main plaza in a small but quiet and elegant upstairs dining room. A house specialty is *gallina trufada,* an elaborately prepared chicken pâté with truffles. This was once a common

Christmas dish, but today few people know how to make it. ✉ *Pl. Mayor 13* ☎ *927/320255* 💳 *MC, V* ⏲ *Closed Tues.*

$–$$ ✕ **Mesón La Troya.** An institution in these parts, this restaurant is fronted by a noisy tapas bar papered with photos of celebrity diners happily posing aside the restaurant's ancient owner, Concha. The atmospheric dining room has a barrel-vaulted brick ceiling. If you choose the €20 prix-fixe meal, you're served a starter of *tortilla de patatas* (potato omelet), *chorizo ibérico* (pork sausage), and a salad. One notable main dish is the *prueba de cerdo* (pork casserole with garlic). Go here hungry—the portions are enormous. ✉ *Pl. Mayor 10* ☎ *927/321364* 💳 *MC, V.*

★ $$–$$$ ✕🏨 **Parador de Trujillo.** Originally the 16th-century Convent of Santa Clara, Trujillo's homey parador centers on a harmonious Renaissance courtyard. A living-museum quality is reflected in the furniture, paintings, and engravings, and, in this case, the knickknacks. The back wall of the vaulted dining room is lined with shelves of regional plates and copper ware as well as an exquisite mural painting. Go for the tomato soup spiced with cumin seeds or any of the *revueltos* (scrambled eggs) with asparagus or mushrooms. Carnivores may prefer one of the game dishes, including wild boar in an acorn-and-wine sauce. ✉ *C. Santa Beatriz de Silva 1, 10200* ☎ *927/321350* 📠 *927/321366* 🌐 *www.parador.es* 🛏 *45 rooms, 1 suite* ♿ *Restaurant, in-room broadband, Wi-Fi, bar, meeting room* 💳 *AE, DC, MC, V.*

$$ ✕🏨 **Soterraña.** Just 10 km (6 mi) away from Trujillo just off the N524 to Guadalupe, this cozy rural hotel is divided between two buildings. The rooms are neat and warm and look out onto the street or the courtyard, where barbecues are held in the summer. Even if you don't stay here, it's worth the trek from Trujillo just for dinner ($–$$, weekends only); Soterraña's dark-wood-panel-and-slate stable has been converted into a restaurant, especially pleasant in winter when you can enjoy the dining room's huge fireplace. For a starter, try the *embutidos,* various kinds of sausages. ✉ *C. Real 75, 10210* ☎ *927/334262* 📠 *927/319339* 🌐 *www.soterrana.com* 🛏 *21 rooms, 2 suites* ♿ *Restaurant, minibars, in-room data ports, pool, bar, meeting room* 💳 *MC, V* 🍽 *BP.*

★ $$$ 🏨 **Meliá Trujillo.** Once a 16th-century convent, this boutique hotel has a reddish-ocher color scheme on its facade, in its cloisters, and in its courtyard, where there's a swimming pool surrounded by wrought-iron furniture. The restaurant in the former refectory serves regional dishes such as wild boar. ✉ *Pl. del Campillo 1, 10200* ☎ *927/458900* 📠 *927/323046* 🌐 *www.solmelia.com* 🛏 *74 rooms, 3 suites* ♿ *Restaurant, pool, bar, meeting room* 💳 *AE, DC, MC, V* 🍽 *BP.*

$$–$$$ 🏨 **Finca Santa Marta.** Surrounded by 60 acres of olive, cherry, and almond trees, this ancient olive-oil mill and farm is run by a retired couple as a country refuge. Fourteen kilometers (9 mi) outside Trujillo on the road to Guadalupe (Ex-208), it's a relaxing alternative to staying in town. The restored living quarters have stone floors (rugs keep your feet warm), wood-beam ceilings, and fresh flowers. Breakfast is included; dinner is available for €28 if requested in advance. Be sure to make a reservation. ✉ *Pago de San Clemente, 10600* ☎ *927/319203* 📠 *927/334115* 🌐 *www.fincasantamarta.com* 🛏 *13 rooms, 1 suite* ♿ *Pool, bar, meeting room; no a/c, no room TVs* 💳 *MC, V* 🍽 *BP.*

Shopping

Trujillo sells more folk arts and crafts than almost any other place in Extremadura, among the most attractive of which are multicolor rugs, blankets, and embroideries. Several shops on the **Plaza Mayor** have enticing selections; the one just across from the tourist office displays a centuries-old loom along with the work of local craftswoman Maribel Vallar, though opening hours are erratic. **Eduardo Pablos Mateos** (⊠ Plazuela de San Judas 12 ☎ 927/321066) specializes in local wood carvings, basketwork, and furniture. For other stores selling pottery, glass, or iron crafts, ask at the tourist office.

13

Guadalupe

★ ⑧   *200 km (125 mi) southwest of Madrid, 143 km (88 mi) east of Cáceres, 96 km (60 mi) east of Trujillo, 200 km (125 mi) northeast of Mérida.*

The **Real Monasterio de Santa María de Guadalupe** (Royal Monastery of Our Lady of Guadalupe) is one of the most inspiring sights in Extremadura. Whether you come from Madrid, Trujillo, or Cáceres, the last stage of the ride takes you through wild, astonishingly beautiful mountain scenery. The monastery itself clings to the slopes, forming a profile that echoes the gaunt wall of mountains behind it. Pilgrims have been coming here since the 14th century, but for the past 10 years they have been joined by a growing number of tourists. Even so, the monastery's isolation—it's a good two-hour drive from the nearest town—has saved it from commercial excess. The story of Guadalupe goes back to around 1300, when a local shepherd uncovered a statue of the Virgin, supposedly carved by St. Luke. King Alfonso XI, who often hunted here, had a church built to house the statue and later vowed to found a monastery should he defeat the Moors at the battle of Salado in 1340. After his victory, he kept his promise. The greatest period in the monastery's history was between the 15th and 18th centuries, when, under the rule of the Hieronymites, it was turned into a pilgrimage center rivaling Santiago de Compostela in importance. Documents authorizing Columbus's first voyage to the Western Hemisphere were signed here. The Virgin of Guadalupe became the patroness of Latin America, honored by the dedication of thousands of churches and towns in the New World. The monastery's decline coincided with Spain's loss of overseas territories in the 19th century. Abandoned for 70 years and left to decay, it was restored after the civil war by Franciscan brothers.

On sale everywhere in Guadalupe is the copper ware that has been crafted here since the 16th century. In the middle of the tiny, irregularly shaped **Plaza Mayor** (also known as the Plaza de Santa María de Guadalupe, and transformed during festivals into a bullring) is a 15th-century **fountain,** where Columbus's two Native American servants were baptized in 1496. Looming in the background is the late-Gothic south facade of the **monastery church,** flanked by battlement towers.

The entrance to the monastery is to the left of the church. From the large Mudejar cloister, the required guided tour progresses to the **chapter house,** with hymnals, vestments, and paintings, including a series of small panels by Zurbarán. The ornate 17th-century **sacristy** has a series of eight Zurbarán paintings of 1638–47. These powerfully austere representations of monks of the Hieronymite order and scenes from the life of St. Jerome are the artist's only significant paintings still in the setting for which they were intended. The tour concludes with the garish, late-baroque **Camarín**, the chapel where the famous Virgen Morena (Black Virgin) is housed. The dark, mysterious wooden figure hides under a heavy veil and mantle of red and gold; painted panels tell the Virgin's life story. Each September 8, the Virgin is brought down from its altarpiece and a procession walks it around the cloister, with pilgrims following on their knees. Outside, the monastery's gardens have been restored to their original, geometric Moorish style. ⊠ *Entrance on Pl. Mayor* 🕾 *927/367000* 🖼 €3 ⊙ *Daily 9:30–1 and 3:30–6, guided tours every ½ hr.*

EN ROUTE Four kilometers (2½ mi) outside of Guadalupe toward Navalmoral de la Mata, there is a 15th-century Gothic hermitage, **Ermita del Humilladero.** On the same road immediately before it is a lookout point providing dramatic views of the monastery, with the small town of Guadalupe in the background.

Where to Stay & Eat

$–$$ ✕ **Extremadura.** For a hearty meal, particularly if you like mushrooms, try this restaurant just down the road from the monastery. The menu *de la casa* (of the house) includes migas, *sopa de ajo* (garlic soup), pork chops with green beans, and steak topped with mushrooms. ⊠ *Gregorio López 18* 🕾 *927/367351.*

$–$$ ✕ **Mesón el Cordero.** This relaxed and rustic dining room is known for fine regional dishes at good prices. Grab a table by the window for some stunning mountain views. Doña Antonia, chef and owner, is especially proud of her *escabeches de perdiz* (stewed partridge in preserves). ⊠ *Av. Alfonso el Onceno, 27* 🕾 *927/367131.*

★ $$–$$$ ✕🖸 **Parador de Guadalupe.** The first autopsy in Spain was performed in this building, a 15th-century hospital and pilgrim's hostel. Despite this prior use, the parador has an unusually luxurious feel, thanks to its Mudejar architecture, Moorish-style rooms, and exotic vegetation. The best rooms look out onto the monastery. The restaurant serves simple local dishes, such as *bacalao monacal* (cod with spinach and potatoes), migas, and *frite de cordero* (lamb stew). ⊠ *C. Marqués de la Romana 12, 10140* 🕾 *927/367075* 🖷 *927/367076* ⊕ *www.parador.es* 🛏 *41 rooms* ⟁ *Restaurant, in-room data ports, Wi-Fi, tennis court, pool, bar, meeting room* ⊟ *AE, DC, MC, V.*

$ ✕🖸 **Hospedería del Real Monasterio.** An excellent and considerably cheaper alternative to the parador, this inn was built around the 16th-century Gothic cloister of the monastery itself. The courtyard of the Gothic cloister is used as an outdoor café open to all from May to September. The simple, traditional rooms with wood-beam ceilings are exceptionally quiet. Fine local dishes include *caldereta de cabrito* (baby goat stew), *revuelto de cardillos* (scrambled eggs with thistle), and *morcilla de berza* (blood sausage with cabbage). ⊠ *Pl. Juan Carlos I s/n, 10140* 🕾 *927/367000* 🖷 *927/367177* 🛏 *46 rooms, 1 suite* ⟁ *Restaurant, bar* ⊟ *MC, V* ⊙ *Closed mid-Jan.–mid-Feb.*

Fodor'sChoice ★

★ **$$** ⌂ **La Clara.** Right in the center of town, across from the monastery, this small *casa rural* is decorated throughout with antiques. Friendly owner Maribel will welcome you with a shot of her homemade *cafe con puesto* (coffee liquor) in the small downstairs bar. The rooms have a homey appeal with flower-filled balconies overlooking the chairs on the square. ⊠ *Plaza Sta. Maria de Guadalupe 44, 10140* ☎ *927/154067* ⇆ *4 rooms* ⚬ *Bar* ⊟ *MC, V.*

Shopping
Guadalupe is the place to go for copper and tinware—the local metalwork industry is 400 years old.

LOWER EXTREMADURA

Extremadura's southern half sometimes seems more Andalusian or even Portuguese than classically Spanish. Long stretches of dusty farmland and a Portuguese-influenced Spanish dialect make it feel light-years away from Castile. Mérida was established in 25 BC as a settlement for Roman soldiers; it soon became the capital of the Roman province of Lusitania (the Iberian Peninsula), and its many ruins bear witness to its former splendor. Badajoz has also been a settlement since prehistoric times; Paleolithic remains have been found nearby. Minutes from the Portuguese border, it has long served as a gateway to Portugal and is home to many Portuguese as well as Portuguese descendants. Extremadura's links with Portugal come alive in Olivenza, whereas Zafra, near the southern end of the province, suggests an Andalusian town.

Mérida

❾ *70 km (43 mi) south of Cáceres, 66 km (40 mi) east of Badajoz, 250 km (155 mi) north of Seville.*

Strategically situated at the junction of major Roman roads from León to Seville and Toledo to Lisbon, Mérida was founded by the Romans in 25 BC on the banks of the River Guadiana. Then named Augusta Emerita, it became the capital of the vast Roman province of Lusitania soon after its founding. A bishopric in Visigothic times, Mérida never regained the importance that it had under the Romans, and as the administrative capital of Extremadura, it's now a rather plain large town—with the exception of its Roman monuments; they pop up all over town, surrounded by thoroughly modern buildings. The glass-and-steel bus station is in a modern district on the other side of the river from the town center. It commands a good view of the exceptionally long **Roman bridge,** which spans two forks of this sluggish river. On the farther bank is the Alcazaba fortress.

Some other Roman sites require a drive. Across the train tracks in a modern neighborhood is the **circo** (circus), where chariot races were held. Little remains of the grandstands, which seated 30,000, but the outline of the circus is clearly visible and impressive for its size: 1,312 feet long and 377 feet wide. Of the existing aqueduct remains, the most impressive is the **Acueducto de los Milagros** (Aqueduct of Miracles), north of

13

the train station. It carried water from the Roman dam of Proserpina, which still stands, 5 km (3 mi) away. If you're driving around Mérida, follow signs to the MUSEO DE ARTE ROMANO to reach Mérida's best-pre-

served **Roman monuments,** the **teatro** (theater) and **anfiteatro** (amphitheater), arranged in a verdant park. (The theater, the best-preserved in Spain, is used for a classical drama festival each July; it seats 6,000. The amphitheater, which holds 15,000 spectators, opened in 8 BC for gladiatorial contests.) Parking is usually easy to find here. Next to the entrance to the Roman ruins is the main tourist office, where you can pick up maps and brochures. You can buy a ticket to see only the Roman ruins or, for a slightly higher fee, an *entrada conjunta* (joint admission), which also grants access to the Basílica de Santa Eulalia and the Alcazaba. ☎ *924/ 312530 ▨ Theater and amphitheater €6.50; combined admission to Roman sites, basilica, and Alcazaba €9 ⊙ Oct.–Apr., daily 9:30–1:45 and 4–6:15; May–Sept., 9:30–1:45 and 5–7:15.*

★ Across the street from the entrance to the Roman sites, and connected by an underground passageway, is Mérida's superb, modern **Museo Nacional de Arte Romano** (National Museum of Roman Art), in a monumental building designed by the renowned Spanish architect Rafael Moneo. You walk through a series of passageways to the luminous, cathedral-like main exhibition hall, supported by arches the same proportion and size (50 feet) as the Roman arch in the center of Mérida, the Arco de Trajano (Trajan's Arch). The exhibits include mosaics, frescoes, jewelry, statues, pottery, household utensils, and other Roman works. Before leaving, be sure to visit the **crypt** beneath the museum—it houses the remains of several homes and a necropolis that were uncovered while the museum was built, in 1981, and were incorporated into the project as part of the exhibits. The museum is wheelchair accessible. ⊠ *José Ramón Mélida 2 ☎ 924/311690 ⊕ www.mnar.es ▨ €2.40, free Sat. afternoon and Sun. ⊙ Oct.–Apr., Tues.–Sat. 10–2 and 4–6, Sun. 10–2; May–Sept., Tues.–Sat. 10–2 and 5–7, Sun. 10–2.*

From the Museo Nacional de Arte Romano, make your way west down Suarez Somontes toward the river and the city center. Turn right at Calle Baños and you can see the towering columns of the **Templo de Diana,** the oldest of Mérida's Roman buildings. If you continue toward the river along Sagasta and Romera, you can come to the sturdy, square **Alcazaba** (fortress), built by the Romans and later strengthened by the Visigoths and Moors. To go inside, follow the fortress walls around to the side farthest from the river. Climb up to the battlements for sweeping river views. ☎ *924/317309 ▨ €7.20, includes Roman theater and amphitheater ⊙ May–Sept., daily 9:30–1:45, 5–7:15; Oct.–Apr., daily 9:30–1:45 and 4–6.*

Mérida's main square, the **Plaza de España,** adjoins the northwestern corner of the fortress and is highly animated both day and night. The plaza's oldest building is a 16th-century palace, now a Meliá hotel. Behind the palace stretches Mérida's most charming area, with Andalusian-style white houses shaded by palms—in the midst of which stands the **Arco de Trajano,** part of a Roman city gate.

The **Basílica de Santa Eulalia,** originally a Visigothic structure, marks both the site of a Roman temple and supposedly where the child martyr Eulalia was roasted alive in AD 304 for spitting in the face of a Roman magistrate. In 1990, excavations surrounding the tomb of the famous saint revealed layer upon layer of Paleolithic, Visigothic, Byzantine, and Roman settlements. ⌖ *Rambla Mártir Santa Eulalia* ☎ 924/303407 ⎙ €2.55 ☉ *Oct.–Apr., Mon.–Sat. 10–1:15 and 4–6:15; May–Sept., 10–1:15 and 5–7:15.*

OFF THE BEATEN PATH

SIBERIA EXTREMEÑA – For a taste of truly elemental Spain, drive to the "Extremaduran Siberia," between Mérida and the Castilian town of Ciudad Real (leave N430, which links the two towns, by following signs for Casas de Don Pedro, and continue south toward Talarrubias). This poor area of wild, rolling scrubland owes its nickname to the 12th duke of Osuna, a 19th-century Spanish ambassador to Russia who thought the terrain resembled the Siberian steppes. The oldest village is Puebla de Alcocer, which has an arcaded square. In nearby Peloche, to the north of Talarrubias, women still sit outside their front doors embroidering. Many people come to this region for water sports at its three reservoirs: Cíjara, García de Sola, and Orellana.

Where to Stay & Eat

$$–$$$ ✕ **Altair.** Under the same ownership as the renowned Atrio in Cáceres, Altair, on the bank of the river Guadiana, delivers high-quality regional food with a modern twist. The chef's specialties include *rollitos crujientes de prueba de ibérico* (crunchy pasta rolls stuffed with pork), *bacalo fresco con manitas de cerdo* (fresh cod with pig's trotters), and *patito asado con miel y higos* (roast duckling baked with honey and figs). Consider going for the menu degustáion if you can afford the 50 price tag. A translucent wall facing the river provides a silhouetted view of the Roman Bridge. ⌖ *Av. José Fernández López s/n* ☎ *924/304512* ▭ *AE, DC, MC, V* ☉ *Closed Sun.*

$$ ✕ **Casa Benito.** Famous for its tasty tapas and local *pitarra* wine, this atmospheric bar-restaurant hidden on a square off Calle Santa Eulalia also has a small, rustic dining area in the back with a reasonably priced daily set menu as well as decent à la carte options. The walls at Benito's are covered with pictures and memorabilia of matadors and bullfights. ⌖ *C. San Francisco 3* ☎ *924/330769* ▭ *AE, MC, V* ☉ *Closed Sun.*

$$ ✕ **Nicolás.** Mérida's best-known restaurant is in a distinctive house with yellow awnings, near the municipal market. There's a tavern serving tapas downstairs and a dining room upstairs. The regionally inspired food includes *perdiz en escabeche* (marinated partridge), lamb dishes, and frogs' legs. Desserts might include the traditional *tocino del cielo* made with honey and egg yolks, or creamy cheese from La Serena. The wine list is extensive, the service professional. ⌖ *Felix Valverde Lillo 13* ☎ *924/319610* ▭ *AE, DC, MC, V* ☉ *No dinner Sun.*

$$ ✕ **Rufino.** The dining room is above the popular bar, accessed by a separate door and a narrow flight of stairs. Tables are slightly cramped, but the food is authentic and tasty, and might include lamb stew, partridge, and *cochinillo frito* (fried suckling pig). It also has a fixed-price

13

menu and an excellent regional wine list. ⊠ *Pl. Santa Clara 2* 🕾 *924/312001* ⊟ *AE, DC, MC, V* ⊘ *Closed Sun. and Aug.*

★ **$$–$$$** ✕🖭 **Parador de Mérida.** Built over the remains of what was first a Roman temple, then a baroque convent, then a prison, this spacious white-washed building exudes an Andalusian cheerfulness, with hints at its Roman and Mudejar past. Also called Parador Via de la Plata, the hotel's guest rooms are bright, with traditional dark-wood furniture. The brilliant-white interior of the convent's former church has been turned into a restful lounge. Try the restaurant's *revuelto* (scrambled eggs) prepared in myriad ways, including *con aroma de pimentón* (in paprika sauce) and *cabrito al ajillo* (with baby goat fried with garlic). ⊠ *Pl. Constitución 3, 06800* 🕾 *924/313800* 🖶 *924/319208* ⊕ *www.parador.es* ➷ *80 rooms, 2 suites* △ *Restaurant, in-room data ports, Wi-Fi, pool, health club, bar, parking (fee)* ⊟ *AE, DC, MC, V.*

Nightlife & the Arts

The highlight of the cultural calendar is the annual **Festival de Teatro Clásico,** held in the Roman theater from early July to mid-August. Contact the tourist office in advance for information and tickets. The many cafés, tapas bars, and restaurants surrounding the Plaza España and in the Plaza de la Constitución fill with boisterous crowds late into the evening. Calle John Lennon, off the northwest corner of the plaza, is your best bet for late-night dance action, especially in summer. As you walk south on Santa Eulalia, the bars get cheaper, the music louder. Locals pack **Rafael II** (⊠ C. Santa Eulalia 13) for ham, cheese, and sausages; there's also a small, cork-lined dining room in the back.

Badajoz

 66 km (40 mi) west of Mérida, 90 km (59 mi) southwest of Cáceres.

A sprawling mass of concrete and glass in the midst of desolate terrain, Badajoz looks like an urban oasis on approach and is indeed modern and well stocked, relative to the surrounding towns. Hardly an aesthetic haven, however, the city has little to offer the traveler; it tries (not quite successfully) to make up for its lack of architectural interest with nighttime energy and the intellectual punch of its university. A mere 7 km (4 mi) from Portugal, this "border town" serves mainly as a suitable resting point on the way through Extremadura. The **Museo Extremeño e Iberoamericano de Arte Contemporáneo** is the main daytime incentive to spend a few hours here. Dedicated to contemporary Spanish and Latin American painting and sculpture, the museum is south of the city center in a striking circular building that was once the Badajoz prison. ⊠ *Nuestra Señora de Guadalupe s/n* 🕾 *924/013060* 🎫 *Free* ⊘ *Oct.–Apr., Tues.–Sat. 10:30–1:30 and 5–8, Sun. 10:30–1:30; May–Sept., Tues.–Sat. 10:30–1:30 and 6–9, Sun. 10:30–1:30.*

Make your way to the older section of town and wander down to the edge of the Guadiana River to admire the **Puerta de Palmas,** the 16th-century gateway to Badajoz and modern-day symbol of the city. Its two circular, crenellated towers are surrounded by decorative guard posts. The **Torre Espantaperros**—literally, Dog-Scarers' Tower; effectively a Christian-scarers' tower—is the watchtower of Badajoz's **Alcazaba.** Within the Alcazaba is the city's **Museo Arqueológico,** with lots of artifacts from the region. ⊠ *C. de San Juan* ☎ *924/222314* 🖾 *Free* ☉ *Tues.–Sun. 10–3.*

Where to Stay & Eat

$$$-$$$$ ✕ **Aldebarán.** Elegant touches, such as Bohemian glassware and embroidered tablecloths, set off this restaurant with a spacious interior. A former head chef of the renowned Arzak in San Sebastián runs the kitchen. Specialties include *merluza al aroma de romero* (hake infused with rosemary), *manitas de cerdo con judías verdes* (pig's feet with green beans), and a supremely delicious cheese-and-walnut tart. ⊠ *Av. de Elvas s/n, Urb. Guadiana, Las Terrazas* ☎ *924/274261* ▭ *AE, DC, MC, V* ☉ *Closed Sun.*

$$ ✕🔲 **Barceló Husa Zurbarán.** This large, modern building is near the River Guadiana and overlooks the Parque de Castelar. Although the exterior is bland, the rooms are large and modern and decorated in warm, earthy tones of cream and soft browns; service here is impeccable, and the elegant restaurant, Los Monjes, is one of the best in town. ⊠ *Paseo Castelar s/n, 06001* ☎ *924/001400* 🖾 *924/220142* ⊕ *www.barcelo.com* 🗗 *215 rooms* ⚐ *Restaurant, pool, Wi-Fi, bar, dance club, meeting room, parking (fee)* ▭ *AE, DC, MC, V.*

Nightlife & the Arts

Many of the bars and tapas places are around Plaza España, especially Calles Zurbarán and Muñoz y Torrero.

Olivenza

⓫ *22 km (14 mi) south of Badajoz.*

Olivenza is worth seeing for its curious double personality. Looking at the airy, elongated main square, with its patterned cobblestones and facades in the Portuguese *estilo manuelino,* an architectural style popular in Portugal during the reign of Manuel I (1469–1521), you might think you've inadvertently crossed the border into Portugal. In fact, this originally Spanish town was occupied by Portugal in 1297, recaptured by the Spanish duke of San Germán in 1657, recovered by Portugal in 1668, and definitively reclaimed for Spain again in 1801. Olivenza's Portuguese influence is most evident in the twisted *manuelina* columns and tiling in the **Iglesia de Santa María Magdalena** (Church of Mary Magdalene; ⊠ Pl. de la Constitución s/n). As befits a long-disputed border town, Olivenza has numerous fortifications, the largest of which is the castle, with its 15th-century **Torre del Homenaje** (Tower of Homage; ⊠ Pl. de Santa María). Adjoining the Torre del Homenaje is the **Museo Etnográfico González Santana,** surprisingly ambitious for a town this size. One room is devoted to archaeological finds (including a stele [commemorative stone slabs] from the 8th century BC), but the main thrust is recent history: exhibits cover traditional trades and crafts along with collections of musical instruments, toys, and other paraphernalia of daily rural life in the first half of the 20th century. ⊠ *Pl. de Santa María* ☎ *924/490222* 🖾 *Free* ☉ *Oct.–May, Tues.–Sun. 11–2 and 4–6; June–Sept., Tues.–Sun. 11–2 and 5–8.*

Where to Eat

$$–$$$ ✕ **Alcañices.** Refined cuisine with a Portuguese accent makes this a good choice for lunch or dinner. ✉ *Colon 3* ☎ *924/491570* ▤ *MC, V.*

Zafra

⑫ *62 km (38 mi) south of Mérida, 85 km (53 mi) southeast of Badajoz, 135 km (84 mi) north of Seville.*

Worth a stop on your way to or from Seville, Zafra is an attractive and lively town with a **Plaza Mayor** that's actually two contiguous squares, the 16th-century Plaza Chica (once a marketplace) and the 18th-century Plaza Grande (ringed by mansions flaunting their coats of arms). Connected by a graceful archway, both plazas make for enjoyable tapas crawls. There are several churches here, the finest being **Nuestra Señora de Candelaria** (✉ Conde de la Corte) a block west off the Plaza Mayor and a short walk from the parador—its *retablo* (altarpiece) has nine extraordinary panels by Zurbarán. The main reason travelers stop in Zafra, however, is the parador itself, otherwise known as the 15th-century **Alcázar de los Duques de Feria** (✉ Pl. Corazón de María 7). During the first week of October, Zafra is the site of one of Spain's oldest and largest livestock fairs, the **Feria Internacional Ganadera,** which dates back to 1417. Breeders and traders come from all over the country, and hotel rates rise accordingly; reserve well in advance.

Where to Stay & Eat

★ **$$$** ✕▦ **Rocamador.** Between Olivenza and Zafra, the hotel is a 16th-century monastery on top of a hill. You can stay in the former library, the kitchen, or the monks' cells, which have cavernous arches and wooden beam ceilings, brick-arch doorways, stone or clay tile floors, and rustic furniture. The monastery's chapel is a renowned restaurant run by two young, imaginative Basque chefs. It includes two fixed-price sampler menus. Reserve well in advance. ✉ *Ctra. Nacional Badajoz–Huelva, Km 41.1, Almendral 06160* ☎ *924/489000* 🖷 *924/489001* ⊕ *www.rocamador.com* ➘ *25 rooms, 5 suites* ⚐ *Restaurant, pool, bar, meeting rooms* ▤ *AE, DC, MC, V.*

★ **$$–$$$** ✕▦ **Parador Hernán Cortés.** This hotel is in the 15th-century castle where Cortés stayed before his voyage to Mexico. The military exterior conceals a refined elegant 16th-century courtyard attributed to Juan de Herrera. The suite and the chapel, which together now serve as a conference room, have an elaborate *artesonado* (coffered) ceiling. The rooms here are spacious and elegant, with high ceilings, antique furniture, and decorative ironwork. Try *pierna de cordero asado* (roasted leg of lamb). Local desserts include delicious marzipan-and-acorn cakes. The menu is in English as well as Spanish. ✉ *Pl. María Cristina 7, 06300* ☎ *924/554540* 🖷*924/551018* ⊕*www.parador.es* ➘*44 rooms, 1 suite* ⚐*Restaurant, in-room data ports, pool, meeting room* ▤ *AE, DC, MC, V.*

$$ ✕▦ **Huerta Honda.** Across a small square from the castle-parador, this gleaming-white Andalusian-style hotel has rooms painted in soothing pastel colors. Twelve luxurious "Gran Clase" rooms or suites have four-poster beds, sumptuous furnishings, and Jacuzzi baths; those on the ground floor, including one with wheelchair access, have patios. At

Barbacana, savor gazpacho *a la extremeña* (Extremeño-style) or local beef. The Huerta's lively Mesón cafeteria serves more modest fare. There's also an English-style pub. ☒ *Lopez Asme 30, 06300* ☎ *924/554100* 🖷 *924/552504* ⊕ *www.hotelhuertahonda.com* ⇰ *45 rooms, 3 suites* ⚐ *Restaurant, cafeteria, Wi-Fi, pool, pub* ▤ *AE, DC, MC, V.*

EXTREMADURA ESSENTIALS

To research prices, get advice from other travelers, and book travel arrangements, visit www.fodors.com.

13

Transportation

BY AIR

There are no airports in Extremadura. The nearest international airports are in Madrid and Seville.

BY BIKE

A good way to see Extremadura by bike is to follow the Ruta Vía de la Plata. It runs through Extremadura from north to south along N630, dividing it in two, and passes by such villages as Plasencia, Cáceres, Mérida, and Zafra. This route more or less follows the ancient Roman walkway Via de la Plata. Parts of the road are still preserved and walkable. Note that the region north of the province of Cáceres, including the Jerte Valley, the Vera, and the area surrounding Guadalupe, is mountainous and uneven. Be prepared for a bumpy and exhausting ride. The regional government has opened a Vía Verde, which goes from Logrosán (a couple of miles southwest of Guadalupe) to Villanueva de la Serena (east of Mérida and near Don Benito). This new path is a roughly cleared walkway, more like a nature walkway, and not for vehicles. Other options for bicyclists are the paved areas of the national parks of Monfragüe and Montalvo. Ask the local tourist offices about where to rent bikes. Rural lodgings also sometimes provide bikes for their guests.

BY BUS

Bus links between Extremadura and the other Spanish provinces are far more plentiful and reliable than train or plane services. Regular buses, some of them express, serve Extremadura's main cities from Madrid, Seville, Lisbon, Valladolid, Salamanca, and Barcelona. The first bus of the day on lesser routes tends to set off very early in the morning, so plan carefully to avoid getting stranded. Some examples of routes and frequency are Madrid to Badajoz (7 daily); to Cáceres (8 daily); to Guadalupe (2 daily); to Trujillo (10 daily); and to Mérida (8 daily).

Bus routes within the vicinity are similarly well serviced; the following routes run frequently: Badajoz to Cáceres (7 daily); to Caia, on the Portuguese border(4 daily); to Mérida (8 daily); to Olienza (12 daily); and to Zafra (8 daily). Cáceres to Guadalupe (2 daily); to Mérida (4 daily); and to Trujillo (8 daily). The main company involved in trips to and from Madrid is Auto Res, and its Web site, listed below, has an English-language option. Buses serve nearly every village in Extremadura, and you can generally pick up a detailed schedule from the respective local tourist office.

🚌 **Bus Stations Badajoz** ✉ José Rebollo López s/n, Badajoz ☎ 924/258661. **Cáceres** ✉ Crta. Gijó-Sevilla, Cáceres ☎ 927/232550.

🚌 **Bus Lines Auto Res** ✉ Pl. Conde de Casal 6, Madrid ☎ 91/551-7200 ⊕ www.autores.es ✉ Estación de Autobuses, Av. de la Libertad, Mérida ☎ 924/371955.

BY CAR

Locally, you can rent a car in Badajoz, Cáceres, or Mérida; however, it's best to reserve a car outside Extremadura, either in Madrid or Seville, or before you leave for Spain. Increasingly, it is more economical to rent a car through one of the numerous car-rental Web sites. (*See* Smart Travel Tips for details and contact information.)

Traffic moves quickly on the four-lane NV, the main highway from Madrid to Extremadura. The N630, or Vía de la Plata, which crosses Extremadura from north to south, is also effective. The fastest approach from Portugal is the A6 from Lisbon to Badajoz. If you're in any kind of a hurry, driving is the most feasible way to get around Extremadura. The main roads are well surfaced and not too congested. Side roads— particularly those that cross the wilder mountainous districts, such as the Sierra de Guadalupe—can be poorly paved and badly marked (though the Sierra de Guadalupe affords some of the most spectacular views in Extremadura. Head north of Guadalupe on Ex-118, heading toward the village of Navalmoral).

On major roads and motorways the speed limit is 120 kmph (75 mph), in urban areas it is 50 kmph (31 mph), and on other roads it is either 90 kmph (55 mph) or 100 kmph (62.5 mph). Severe fines are enforced throughout Spain for driving under the influence of alcohol. Spot breath checks are often carried out, and if the level of alcohol in your bloodstream is found to be 0.05 percent or above, you could have your driver's license confiscated and be fined as much as €600.

🚗 **National Agencies Avis** ✉ Hotel Barceló Zurbaran, Badajoz ☎ 924/224313 ⊕ www. avisworld.com. **EuropCar** ✉ Plus Ultra 1 Cáceres ☎ 927/212988 ⊕ www.europcar. com. **Hertz** ✉ Hotel Río, Badajoz ☎ 924/273510 ⊕ www.hertz.com.

🚗 **Local Agencies Albarran Rent a Car** ✉ Santa Ana 9 Badajoz ☎ 924/250353 ⊕ www.atesa.com. **Automoviles Palma** ✉ Poligrono Los Caños Badajoz ☎ 607/ 151888. **Lambea** ✉ Ctra. Gijón-Sevilla s/n Cáceres ☎ 927/629091. **Record Rent a Car** ✉ Poligrono Las Capellaniás 223 Cáceres ☎ 927/249097. **Rent a Car Extremadura** ✉ Avenida Reina Sofía 11 Merida ☎ 924/387562. **Sales Rent a Car** ✉ Ricardo Carapeto 97 Badajoz ☎ 924/260896 ⊕ www.carjet.com.

BY TAXI

Taxis are available at train or bus stations, most tourist sights, and on some commercial streets. Restaurants are usually obliging and will call you a taxi if required. Fares are reasonable, and meters are strictly used. There are extra charges for luggage. You are not required to tip taxi drivers, though locals generally round off the amount.

🚕 **Taxi Companies Radio Taxi Badajoz** ☎ 924/243101. **Radio Taxi Cáceres** ☎ 927/ 242424. **Radio Taxi Mérida** ☎ 924/371111. **Tele Taxi Mérida** ☎ 924/315756.

BY TRAIN

Trains from Madrid stop at Monfragüe, Plasencia, Cáceres, Mérida, Zafra, and Badajoz. They run as often as six times daily. From Seville there are daily trains to Zafra, Mérida, Cáceres, and Plasencia. The journey from Madrid to Cáceres takes about 5 hours; from Seville to Cáceres, 7½ hours. There is also a direct train from Lisbon to Badajoz, which takes five hours. Within the province there are services from Badajoz to Cáceres (2 daily, 1 hour 55 minutes) and to Mérida (7 daily, 1 hour); from Cáceres to Badajoz (3 daily, 2 hours), to Mérida (5 daily, 1 hour), to Plasencia (2 daily, 1 hour 20 minutes), and to Zafra (2 daily, 2 hours 10 minutes); from Plasencia to Badajoz (1 daily, 3 hours 30 minutes), to Cáceres (3 daily, 1 hour 20 minutes), and to Mérida (3 daily, 2 hours 20 minutes). Operators generally speak Spanish only, so check the RENFE Web site (www.renfe.es) for details in English. Note that train stations in Extremadura tend to be some distance from the town centers.

North Americans can purchase a Eurorail Spain Pass, available in both first- and second-class sections, which allows three days' unlimited travel within a two-month period for less than $200.

🚆 Train Information Eurorail ☎ 877/257-2887 from the United States, 800/361-7245 from Canada ⊕ www.raileurope.com/us. RENFE ☎ 902/240202 ⊕ www.renfe.es.

Sports & the Outdoors

OUTDOOR ADVENTURE

Peña del Aguila organizes hiking, horseback riding, cycling, kayaking, and quad rallies throughout Extremadura but particularly in the Sierra de Montánchez region; English is spoken. Valle Aventura arranges similar activities in the Jerte Valley; if you want to hike here, ask the tourist office near Cabezuela for its helpful maps, which describe each hike and detail the route. To visit the Cornalvo Nature Park, the second-largest park in the region next to Monfragüe, contact (in advance) the nature park's department at the Dirección General del Medio Ambiente. Most of the park is private land, and it's a good idea to take a guide. The regional government has set up a Centro de Interpretación, an information and permit center, in Trujillanos.

🚩 Centro de Interpretación ⊠ Ctra. Trujillanos-Embalse de Cornalvo, Trujillanos ☎ 924/002386. Dirección General del Medio Ambiente ⊠ Av. de Portugal s/n, Mérida ☎ 924/002520 or 924/002386 ⊕ www.juntaex.es. Peña del Aguila ⊠ 10170 Montánchez, Cáceres ☎ 626/712724 ⊕ www.pena-del-aguila.com/activities.htm. Valle Aventura ⊠ Av. de Plasencia, Cabezuela del Valle ☎ 927/472196 ⊕ www.valleaventura.com.

FISHING PERMITS

Trout fishing is popular in the Vera and Jerte districts, and tench, carp, royal carp, barbel, and pike abound in the Tajo and Guadiana rivers.

Non-EU residents can apply for one of two possible licenses to fish in public waters. You'll need to pick up a *Modelo 50* form, available from most banks in Extremadura. The licenses are called *especial*; the special granting permission to fish for trout for a one-year period is €6.49; the annual nontrout license is €4.25. Note that the licenses are mailed to your home address, so the Modelo form serves as proof of license for up to two months.

🚹 **Dirección General del Medio Ambiente** ✉ Av. de Portugal s/n, Mérida ☎ 924/002211 or 924/002467.

Contacts & Resources

BANKS & EXCHANGING SERVICES

Banks are generally in town and city centers, and the majority will have an ATM, enabling you to withdraw euros with your credit or debit card, providing you have a valid PIN. Your card issuer is likely to charge you a fee for using an ATM abroad. Banks are open from 8:30 AM to 2 PM weekdays plus on Saturday mornings, October to April. Currency-exchange offices are also common; however, in general, they charge a higher commission than the banks.

DISABILITIES & ACCESSIBILITY

Extremadura abounds with ancient buildings that do not easily accommodate travelers with disabilities. In Cáceres, visitors with disabilities have access to the old part of the city and, with some help, the Concatedral de Santa María. Plasencia's only accessible site is the Museo Etnográfico-Textil. Trujillo's celebrated main square was renovated in 2002 to provide, among other things, easier access for people with disabilities. From there, tourists can move into the old area and visit, with the help of a ramp, the Iglesia of Santa María. In Mérida, the Roman ruins and the Basílica de Santa Eulalia are accessible with accompaniment, unlike the Alcazaba; the Museo Nacional de Arte Romano is accessible. In Badajoz, only the Museo Extremeño e Iberoamericano de Arte Contemporáneo provides access for travelers with disabilities.

DISCOUNTS & DEALS

Trujillo has two different types of multisight passes. The first, at €4.50, provides access to Casa Museo Pizarro, the castle, the church of Santiago, and a guidebook (also sold separately). The second, at €6.50, grants access to the above plus Museo del Traje, Aljibe del Altamirano, and a guided tour. In Mérida, aside from the combined ticket for the Roman theater and amphitheater, there's a multisight pass for €7.20 that includes these sights plus Zona Arqueológica de Morerís, excavations of Basílica de Santa Eulalia, and Casa de Mitrea.

EMERGENCIES

The Hospital Infanta Cristina is a large hospital in Badajoz with a 24-hour emergency department. For nonemergencies, there are private medical clinics throughout Extremadura, some with English-speaking staff members.

Every town has at least one pharmacy open 24 hours; the address of the on-duty pharmacy is posted on the front door of all pharmacies. You can also dial Spain's general information number—11818—for the location of a doctor's office or pharmacy that's open nearest you.

⚡ Emergency Services Ambulance ☎ 061. **Guardia Civil** ☎ 062. **Hospital Infanta Cristina** (Hospital) ☎ 924/218199. **Insalud** (Public health service) ☎ 061. **Policía Local** (Local police) ☎ 092. **Police Nacional** (National police) ☎ 091.

INTERNET, MAIL & SHIPPING
⚡ Cybercafés Avalon ✉ C. Médico Sorapán 20, Cáceres ☎ 927/244488. **Cibercafe Ciberalia** ✉ C. Tienda 18, Trujillo ☎ 927/659087. **Locutorio Público Extrameño** ✉ Av. Fernando Calzadilla 2, Badajoz ☎ No phone. **⚡ Post Office** ✉ Paseo Primo de Rivera 2, Cáceres.

MEDIA
Extremadura's most popular local newspaper is *Diario Hoy*, which is published daily in Badajoz but also has sections on Cáceres, Merida, and Plasencia. The local television station is Telefrontera, and several radio stations provide a mix of commentary and music, including Radio Extremadura (1.008 AM) and Radio Forum, which is broadcast in Merida (107.4 FM). Tourist offices can provide information on bookshops that stock English-language books—to avoid disappointment, bring your leisure-reading material with you.

TOUR OPTIONS
There are many Web sites with information on tours of Extremadura. Riding enthusiasts can check out ⊕ www.hiddentrails.com, which offers weeklong riding tours of the Gredo Mountains on the border of Cáceres province. Extremadura is famous for its birdlife, and several companies offer bird-watching tours, including the U.K.-based ⊕ www.spainbirds.com. EuroAdventures Vacations, ⊕ www.euroadventures.net, also organizes specialized tours, including a half-day walking tour of the Cáceres Jewish quarter. With an office in town, Guías Turísticos de Cáceres offers tours around the city and information on accredited guides throughout Extremadura. In addition, several travel agencies can arrange custom-designed tours of the region. **⚡ Tour Operators Anibal Tours** ✉ Pl. de Portugal 18, Badajoz ☎ 924/221140. **CC Travel** ✉ Colon 10, Cáceres ☎ 927/217373. **Enjoy Travel** ✉ Antonio Cortes Lavado 2, Badajoz ☎ 924/242372. **Guías Turísticos de Cáceres** ✉ Pl. Mayor 2, Cáceres ☎ 927/217237. **Viajes Rutas del Suroeste de España** ✉ Av. Virgin de Guadalupe 27, Cáceres ☎ 927/240383.

VISITOR INFORMATION
⚡ Regional Tourist Offices Badajoz ✉ Pl. de la Libertad 3 ☎ 924/013659. **Cáceres** ✉ Pl. Mayor 3 ☎ 927/010834. **Mérida** ✉ Av. José Álvarez Saez de Buruaga s/n, at entrance to Roman theater ☎ 924/009730. **Plasencia** ✉ Plaza de Torre de Lucia s/n ☎ 927/017840. **Turismo Extremadura** ⊕ www.turismoextremadura.com.
⚡ Local Tourist Offices Badajoz ✉ Pasaje de San Juan s/n ☎ 924/224981. **Guadalupe** ✉ Pl. Mayor ☎ 927/154128. **Mérida** ✉ C. Santa Eulalia ☎ 924/330722. **Olivenza** ✉ Pl. de España s/n ☎ 924/490151. **Parque Nacional de Monfragüe** ✉ Vilarreal de San Carlos ☎ 927/199134. **Plasencia** ✉ El Rey 8 ☎ 927/423843. **Trujillo** ✉ Pl. Mayor s/n ☎ 927/322677. **Valle del Jerte (Jerte Valley)** ✉ Paraje de Peñas Alba, just off N110 north of Cabezuela ☎ 927/472122 or 927/472558. **Zafra** ✉ Pl. de España 30 ☎ 924/551036.

UNDERSTANDING SPAIN

A SHORT HISTORY

OVER THE FINAL QUARTER of the 20th century and the first years of the 21st, Spain's transformation from cloistered third-world dictatorship to booming high-tech European democracy must rank as the mother of all metamorphoses. A palpable sense of satisfaction bordering on exhilaration seems to electrify Spain today, from remote mountain villages to the slick, postmodern boulevards of Barcelona and Madrid. Naturally, there are dark spots in the picture—more homeless, more beggars, immigration overflow, petty larceny, and, most of all, Basque terrorism—yet it's difficult not to be infected by the overall optimism. Spain is undergoing a general sprucing up, which is evident in the newest designer bars and restaurants. Life is fiercely enjoyed and celebrated here; Spaniards have a huge capacity for living intensely and fully. Perhaps as a result of the ups and downs of a turbulent history and, in the past century, a bloody civil war, the Spanish embrace Horace's *carpe diem* (seize the day) so fervently they often appear to be trying to seize two at a time. Richard Wright, visiting in the 1950s, called it "pagan Spain"—but for 36 years of the 20th century, Spain labored under a repressive, ultraconservative, religious regime that ended only with the death of Francisco Franco in 1975. The renaissance that followed has been not only political but also cultural, artistic, social, and economic.

Spain's extraordinary heritage of history, art, and architecture begins with the ancient caves at Altamira, in which people wearing skins for warmth painted delicate pictures of animals on a rock ceiling. During the Age of Exploration, robust adventurers left Extremadura, Spain's poorest province, to probe the New World, and some returned to build great stone palaces on this stark, scrubby landscape. Stretched across northern Spain are the Romanesque churches of the Camino de Santiago (Way of St. James), Europe's most famous Christian pilgrimage in the Middle Ages, culminating at the soaring cathedral of Santiago de Compostela. Pre-Romanesque and cave churches built by the Visigoths (who were early Christians) are scattered across the north as a rough stone counterpoint to the opulent Moorish mosques and palaces of Andalusia. More than 10,000 castles are sprinkled across the Iberian Peninsula; some are merely ruins, others are in extraordinarily good shape. Villages of whitewashed buildings, harbors stuffed with brightly painted fishing boats, and majestic towns welded to craggy mountaintops are easy to find. Still washed by that subtle light that inspired Velázquez, the Spanish countryside remains mercifully unchanged.

More than any other country of its size—it's the second largest in Europe, after France—Spain is characterized by the distinctness of its many parts and peoples. The Galicians of the northwest are descended from the same Celtic tribes that colonized the British Isles. Bagpipes are a local instrument, kilts are not unknown, and the local language, Gallego, is closer to Portuguese than to Spanish. The Basque Country, which straddles the western end of Spain's border with France, also has its own language, Euskera, a non-Indoeuropean tongue so mysterious that linguists have never been able to agree on its origin. Local pride is fierce here: the Basque language and culture are purposefully celebrated, and nationalist sentiment is strong. Tragically, the terrorist group ETA (Euskadi Ta Askatasuna/Basque Homeland and Liberty) has killed almost 800 people since 1968. The 6 million Catalans who populate northeastern Spain around Barcelona are the speakers of Spain's most widely spoken regional language, Catalan, which is closer to Provençal French than to Castilian Spanish, while residents of the province of Valencia and the Balearic Islands speak and study in their own languages, generally considered dialects of Catalan. All of these areas suffered systematic cultural and linguistic repression under the totalitarian centralist pressure of the Franco regime.

The Iberian Peninsula's early peoples included Basques, Celts, Iberians, Phoenicians, Greeks, Romans, Visigoths, and (from 711 until 1492) Moors. By the end of the Middle Ages, Christians had intermarried widely with the Moorish and Jewish minorities, so while most Spaniards today see themselves as Christian Catholics, many have Muslim and/or Jewish ancestors.

Most of Spain transformed itself from an agrarian and largely feudal economy to a modern, industrialized one in remarkably little time, over the first half of the 20th century. Now, a lively economy and an optimistic outlook are giving modern Spain an anything-is-possible air, despite a high unemployment rate and the continuing scourge of terrorism. The 1992 Olympic Games, the Guggenheim Museum Bilbao, new freeways, high-speed trains, and state-of-the-art technology have radically transformed a country that was often described as borderline third-world in the '60s and '70s.

Modernity has come at a price. For generations, Spain was the travel destination of choice for the penniless artist or the adventurer willing to forego comfort for rugged romance, but all that has changed. After years of inflation, and a value-added tax imposed as a condition of entry into the European Union, Spain's cost of living compares to that of neighbors like France. The 1992 Summer Olympics in Barcelona and Universal Exposition in Seville further inflated hotel and restaurant prices in those cities. The rate of price increases slowed in the late 1990s, although with the advent of the euro a combination of "rounding up" and rampant inflation has brought about a new surge in the cost of life in Spain.

The Turning & Overturning of Civilizations

The story of this land, a romance-tinged tale of counts, caliphs, crusaders, and kings, begins long before written history. The Basques were among the first here, fiercely defending the green mountain valleys of the Pyrenees. The Iberians came next, apparently crossing the Mediterranean from North Africa around 3000 BC. The Celts arrived from the north about a thousand years later. The seafaring Phoenicians founded Gadir (now Cádiz) and several coastal cities in the south three millenniums ago. The parade continued with the Greeks, who settled parts of the east coast, and then the Carthaginians, who founded Cartagena around 225 BC— and who dubbed the then-wild, forested and game-rich country Ispania, after their word for rabbit: *span.*

Modern civilization began with the Romans, who expelled the Carthaginians and turned the peninsula into three imperial provinces. It took the Romans 200 years to subdue the fiercely resisting Iberians, but their influence was lasting. Evidence of the Roman epoch is left today in the great ruins at Mérida, Segovia, Tarragona, Barcelona, and other cities; in the peninsula's legal system; and in the Latin base of Spain's Romance languages and dialects. In the early 5th century, invading barbarians crossed the Pyrenees to attack the weakening Roman empire. The Visigoths became the dominant force in northern Spain by 419, establishing their kingdom at Toledo and eventually adopting Christianity.

But the Visigoths, too, were to fall before a wave of invaders. The Moors, an Arab-led Berber force, crossed the Strait of Gibraltar from North Africa in 711. The Moors swept through Spain in an astonishingly short time, meeting only token resistance and launching almost eight centuries of Muslim rule—a period that in many respects was the pinnacle of Spanish civilization. Unlike the semibarbaric

Visigoths, the Moors were extremely cultured. Arabs, Jews, and Christians lived together in peace during their reign, although many Christians did convert to Islam. The Moors also brought with them citrus fruits, rice, cotton, sugar, palm trees, glassmaking, and the complex irrigation system still used around Valencia. The influence of Arabic in modern Spanish includes words beginning with "al," such as *albóndiga* (meatball), *alcalde* (mayor), *almohada* (pillow), and *alcázar* (fortress), as well as prominent phonetic characteristics ranging from the fricative "j" to, in all probability, the lisping "c." Moorish culture is most spectacularly evident in Andalusia, derived from the Arabic name for the Moorish reign on the Iberian Peninsula, al-Andalus, which meant "western lands." The fairytale Alhambra palace overlooking Granada captures the refinement of the Moorish aesthetic, while the earlier, 9th-century mosque at Córdoba bears witness to the power of Islam in al-Andalus.

The Moors never managed to subdue Spain's northwest corner, and it was in Asturias that a minor Christian king, Pelayo, began the long crusade that came to be known as the *Reconquista* (Reconquest). By 1085, Alfonso VI of Castile had captured Toledo, giving the Christians a firm grip on the north. In the 13th century, Valencia, Seville, and finally Córdoba—the capital of the Muslim caliphate in Spain—fell to Christian forces, leaving only Granada in Moorish hands. Nearly two hundred years later, the so-called Catholic Monarchs—Ferdinand of Aragón and Isabella of Castile—were joined in a marriage that would change the world. Finally, on January 2, 1492, 244 years after the fall of Córdoba (longer than the entire history of the United States), Granada surrendered and the Moorish reign was over.

1492: A Turning Point

The year 1492 is a watershed in Spanish history, the beginning of the nation's political golden age: Christian forces conquered Granada and unified all of current-day Spain as a single kingdom; in what was, at the time, viewed as a peacekeeping measure promoting national unity, Jews and Muslims who did not convert to Christianity were expelled from the country; and Christopher Columbus, under the sponsorship of Isabella, landed in the Americas, initiating the Age of Exploration. Despite all of this, the departure from Spain of educated Muslims and Jews was a blow to the nation's agriculture, science, and economy that would require a bloody civil war and nearly 500 years to expiate. The colonies of the New World greatly enriched Spain at first, but massive shipments of Peruvian and Mexican gold later produced terrible inflation while inhibiting other kinds of economic development and placing most of Spain in the hands of the grandees and the church. The Catholic Monarchs and their centralizing successors maintained Spain's unity, but they sacrificed the spirit of international free trade that was beginning to bring prosperity to other parts of Europe.

Ferdinand and Isabella were succeeded by their grandson Carlos, who became the first Spanish Habsburg and one of the most powerful rulers in history. Cortés reached Mexico, and Pizarro conquered Peru under his rule. Carlos also inherited Austria and the Netherlands and in 1519, three years into his reign, became Holy Roman Emperor (as Charles V), wasting little time in annexing Naples and Milan. He championed the Counter-Reformation and saw the Jesuit order created to help defend Catholicism against European Protestantism. But Carlos V weakened Spain with his penchant for waging war, particularly against the Ottomans and German Lutherans. His son, Felipe II (Phillip II), followed in the same, expensive path, defeating the Turks at the Battle of Lepanto in 1571 but losing the "Invincible Spanish Armada" in the English Channel in 1588. Depressed by what he must have known was the turning of the tide for Spain's golden age, Felipe II dedicated the rest of his life to the construction of the somber Escorial monastery west of Madrid, where he died 10 years after losing the world's greatest fleet while attacking Protestant England.

From Empire to Civil War to Democracy

Under Felipes III and IV, the 17th century saw the full cultural flowering of Spain's golden age, even while the empire was crumbling under the weight of its own sprawling unmanageability. After a century of artistic brilliance and economic erosion, the War of the Spanish Succession was ignited by the death in 1700, without issue, of Charles II, the last Spanish Habsburg. After the 1700–14 War of the Spanish Succession between the Bourbons and Habsburgs, Philip of Anjou was crowned Philip V and inaugurated the Bourbon line in Spain (a representative of which sits on the throne today). The Bourbons of that era, a Frenchified lot, copied many of the attitudes and fashions of their northern neighbors, but the infatuation ended when Napoléon Bonaparte, on the pretext of crossing Spain to fight the English in Portugal, decided to stay after all, invited the Spanish monarchs Carlos IV and his son Fernando VII to abdicate and, in 1808, installed his brother Joseph Bonaparte on the throne. Mocked bitterly as "Pepe Botella" for his fondness for drink (*botella* means "bottle"), Bonaparte was widely despised, and an 1808 uprising against him in Madrid—chronicled harrowingly by the great painter Francisco de Goya y Lucientes (1746–1828)—began the War of Independence, known to foreigners as the Peninsular War. Britain, siding with Spain, sent the Duke of Wellington to the rescue. With the aid of Spanish guerillas, the French were finally expelled, but not before they had looted many of Spain's major churches, museums, and cathedrals. Fernando VII returned to the throne in 1814; in 19 catastrophic years he managed to alienate and embitter progressives with his autocratic regime and enrage reactionaries by overturning the Salic law in order to place his daughter Isabella II on the throne instead of his conservative brother Don Carlos. Meanwhile, many of Spain's American colonies took advantage of the war to claim their independence.

The rest of the 19th century was not a happy one for Spain, as conservative regimes grappled with civil wars and revolts inspired by the currents of European republicanism. The final blow came with the loss of Cuba, Puerto Rico, and the Philippines in 1898, a military disaster that ironically sparked a remarkable literary renaissance—the so-called Generation of '98, whose members included novelists Miguel de Unamuno and Pío Baroja, philosopher and essayist José Ortega y Gasset, and poet Antonio Machado. In 1902 Alfonso XIII, grandson of Isabella II, was restored to the throne, but a popular Republican mandate in the elections of 1931 resulted in his self-imposed exile. The Second Spanish Republic followed, to the delight of most Spaniards, but the 1936 election of a left-wing Popular Front government ignited bitter opposition from the right. In July 1936 the assassination of a monarchist leader gave the Spanish army the long-awaited opportunity to rise in revolt to restore law and order. A young general named Francisco Franco was soon named commander-in-chief of the anti-Republican rebels representing Spain's traditional right-wing alliance of church, feudal grandees, and army.

The Spanish civil war (1936–39) was the single most tragic episode in Spanish history. More than half a million people died in the conflict. Intellectuals and leftists the world over sympathized with the elected government, and the International Brigades with many American, British, and Canadian volunteers, took part in some of the worst fighting, including the storied defense of Madrid. But Franco, backed by the Catholic Church, got far more help from Nazi Germany, whose Condor legions destroyed the Basque town of Gernika (in a horror made infamous by

Picasso's monumental painting, Guernica), and from Fascist Italy. For three years, European governments stood quietly by as Franco's armies ground their way to victory. After the fall of Barcelona in January 1939, the Republican cause became hopeless and Franco's Nationalist forces entered Madrid on March 27, 1939.

Officially neutral during World War II but sympathetic to the Axis powers, Spain was largely shunned by the world until, in a 1953 agreement, the United States provided aid in exchange for land on which to build NATO bases. Gradually, the shattered economy began to pick up, especially with the late-1960s surge of a new sector: tourism. But when Franco announced in 1969 that his successor would be Juan Carlos, the grandson of Alfonso XIII and a prince whose militaristic education had been strictly overseen by the aging general, the hopes of a nation longing for democracy and progress sagged. Imagine the Spaniards' surprise when, six years later, Franco died and the young monarch revealed himself to be a closet democrat. Under his nurturing, a new constitution restoring civil liberties and freedom of expression was adopted in 1978. On February 23, 1981, the king proved his mettle once and for all, when a nostalgic Civil Guard colonel with visions of a return to Franco's authoritarian regime, along with a unit of would-be rebels, held the Spanish parliament—then center-right— captive for some 24 hours. Only the heroism of King Juan Carlos, who personally called military commanders across the country to ensure their loyalty to the Constitution and the elected government, quelled the coup attempt. The Socialists ruled Spain from 1982 until early 1996, when conservative José María Aznar was elected prime minister. In 2004, Socialist Workers' Party leader Jose Luis Rodriguez Zapatero won a surprise election victory over Aznar. The election was overshadowed by a series of terrorist explosions on Madrid commuter trains in which more than 200 people died just days beforehand.

In the arts, Spain seems to have picked up where it left off when the civil war and the ensuing 40-year cultural silence of the Franco regime intervened. Whereas the first third of the century produced such towering figures as poet Federico García Lorca, filmmaker Luis Buñuel, composer Manuel de Falla, and painters Pablo Picasso, Joan Miró, and Salvador Dalí, the final quarter (since Franco's death in 1975) will be known for novelist Camilo José Cela's 1989 Nobel Prize, Basque sculptor Eduardo Chillida's blocky forms, the conceptually challenging works of Catalan painter Antoni Tàpies, and filmmaker Pedro Almodóvar's postmodern Spanish films.

All in all, to experience the best from this diverse peninsula, take the country as the modern Spanish have learned to do, piece by piece. Spain at the turn of the 21st century is a patchwork of cultures and nationalities: Andalusia and Catalonia are as different as France and England, maybe more so. The miracle is that a common language and a central government have managed to bring these so-called Autonomous Communities as close together as they are. Castilians, Basques, Galicians, Asturians, Catalans, and Andalusians all contribute separately and equally to a Spain that begins the new millennium as one of the most vibrant nations in Europe.

—George Semler

CHRONOLOGY

ca. 12,000 BC	Paleolithic (Old Stone Age) settlement. Caves of Altamira painted.
ca. 2000 BC	Copper Age culture. Stone megaliths built.
ca. 1100 BC	Earliest Phoenician colonies, including Cádiz, Villaricos, Almuñecar, and Málaga. Native peoples include Iberians in south, Basques in Pyrenees, and Celts in northwest.
ca. 650 BC	Greeks begin to colonize east coast at Empuries, in northern Catalonia.
237 BC	Carthaginians land in Spain, found Cartagena circa 225 BC.
206 BC	Romans expel Carthaginians from Spain and gradually conquer peninsula over next two centuries. Spain becomes one of Rome's most important colonies.
AD 74	Roman citizenship extended to all Spaniards.
380	Christianity declared sole religion of Rome and her empire.
409	First Barbaric invasions.
419	Visigothic kingdom established in northern Spain, with capital at Toledo.

Moorish Spain

711–12	Christian Visigothic kingdom destroyed by invading Muslims (Moors) from northern Africa. Moors create emirate, with capital at Córdoba, of Ummayyad Caliphate at Damascus.
756	Independent Moorish Emirate established by Ummayyad heir Abd al-Rahman I at Córdoba.
778	Charlemagne establishes Frankish rule north of Ebro.
813	Discovery of remains of St. James, following which the cathedral of Santiago de Compostela is built and becomes a major pilgrimage site.
912–61	Reign of Abd al-Rahman III: height of Moorish culture (though it flourishes throughout Reconquest).

The Reconquest

1085	Alfonso VI of Castile captures Toledo.
1099	Death of Rodrigo Díaz de Vivar, known as El Cid, who served both Christian and Muslim kings; buried at Burgos Cathedral (completed 1126), first Gothic cathedral.
1137	Aragón unites with Catalonia through marriage.
1209	Moors found first Spanish university, in Valencia.
1212	Victory at Las Navas de Tolosa by united Christian armies: Moorish power crippled.

1236–48 Valencia, Córdoba, and Seville fall to Christians.

1270 End of main period of Reconquest. Portugal, Aragón, and Castile emerge as major powers.

1435 Alfonso V of Aragón and Sicily conquers Naples and southern Italy.

1469 Isabella, princess of Castile, marries Ferdinand, heir to the throne of Aragón.

1478 Spanish Inquisition established.

1479–1504 Isabella and Ferdinand rule jointly.

1492 Granada, last Moorish outpost, falls. Christopher Columbus, under the sponsorship of Isabella, "discovers" America, setting off a wave of Spanish exploration. Ferdinand and Isabella, also known as the Catholic Monarchs, expel Jews and Muslims from Spain.

1494 Treaty of Tordesillas: Portugal and Spain divide the known world between them.

1499 Publication of *La Celestina,* by Fernando de Rojas, considered most important literary precursor to *Don Quijote.*

1516 Death of Ferdinand. His grandson and heir, Charles I, inaugurates the Habsburg dynasty and Spain's golden age.

The Habsburg Dynasty

1519 Charles I is elected Holy Roman Emperor as Charles V. From his father, Philip of Habsburg, he inherits Austria, the Spanish Netherlands, Burgundy, and nearly continuous war with France. Hernán Cortés conquers the Aztec Empire in Mexico.

1519–22 First circumnavigation of the world by Ferdinand Magellan's ships completed by Basque navigator Juan Sebastián Elkano.

ca. 1520– 1700 Golden age. Funded by its empire, Spain's culture flourishes. Artists include El Greco (1541–1614), Velázquez (1599–1660), and Murillo (1617–82). In literature, the poet Quevedo (1580–1645), dramatists Lope de Vega (1562–1635) and Calderón (1600–81), and novelist Miguel de Cervantes (1547–1616) are known throughout Europe. Counter-Reformation Catholicism takes its lead from St. Ignatius of Loyola (1491–1556), founder of the Jesuit order (1540), and the mystic St. Teresa of Ávila (1515–82).

1531 Pizarro conquers the Inca empire in Peru.

1554 Charles's heir, Philip, marries Queen Mary of England ("Bloody Mary") circa 1558.

1556 Charles abdicates in favor of his son Philip II, who inherits Spain, Sicily, and the Netherlands. Holy Roman Empire goes to Charles's brother Ferdinand. Philip II leads cause of Counter-Reformation against Protestant states in Europe.

1561 Capital established at Madrid.

1571 Spanish fleet stops westward advance of Ottoman Empire in naval battle of Lepanto—afterward regarded as the high-water mark of the Spanish Empire.

1588 Philip attacks Protestant England with Spanish Armada, to no avail.

1598 Death of Philip II.

1605 Publication of first part of Miguel de Cervantes' masterpiece, *Don Quijote de la Mancha,* generally considered the first modern novel.

1609 Under Philip III, Moriscos (converted Muslims) expelled and independence of Netherlands recognized.

1618 Beginning of Thirty Years' War. Originally a religious dispute, it became a dynastic struggle between Habsburgs and Bourbons.

1621–65 Reign of Philip IV. Count-Duke Olivares reforms regime on absolutist model of France.

1640–59 Revolt in Catalonia; republic declared for a time.

1648 End of Thirty Years' War; Spanish Netherlands declared independent.

1659 Treaty of the Pyrenees ends war with France and Spanish ascendancy in Europe.

1665–1700 Reign of Charles II, last of the Spanish Habsburgs.

The Bourbon Dynasty

1701–14 War of the Spanish Succession: claimants to the throne are Louis XIV of France (on behalf of his eldest son Philip), Holy Roman Emperor Leopold I (on behalf of his son Archduke Carlos of Austria), and electoral prince Joseph Ferdinand of Bavaria. The Treaty of Utrecht, 1713, recognizes Philip as Philip V, first Bourbon king. By Treaty of Rastatt, 1714, Spain loses Flanders, Luxembourg, and Italy to Austrian Habsburgs; spends much of its energy in 18th century trying to regain them.

1756–63 Seven Years' War: Spain and France versus Great Britain. 1756: Spain regains Minorca, lost to Great Britain in 1709. 1762: Treaty of Paris in which Spain cedes Minorca and Florida to Great Britain and receives Louisiana from France in return.

1779 Spain supports rebels in American War of Independence, regains Florida and Minorca.

1793 Revolutionary France declares war.

1795 By Treaty of Basel, Spain allies with France against Great Britain.

Napoleonic Rule

1808 King Charles IV abdicates in favor of Joseph Bonaparte, Napoléon's brother. Napoléon takes Madrid in December.

The Peninsular War

1809–14 Napoleonic armies thrown out of Spain by a combination of Spanish resistance fighters and British and Portuguese troops under the command of Wellington.

Restoration of the Bourbons

1814 Bourbons restored under Ferdinand VII, son of Charles IV. Like other restored monarchs of the era, he was a reactionary and crushed all liberal movements.

1833 Ferdinand deprives brother Don Carlos of succession in favor of his infant daughter, Isabella; her mother, María Cristina, becomes regent.

1834–39 First Carlist War: Don Carlos contests the crown and begins an era of upheaval.

1840 Coup d'état: Gen. Baldomero Espartero becomes dictator, exiles María Cristina, and ushers in a series of weak and unpopular regimes.

1843 Espartero ousted; Isabella II restored to throne.

Period of Troubles

1868 Revolution, supported by liberals, topples Isabella II but ushers in the Period of Troubles: attempts to establish a republic and find an alternate monarch fail.

1873 First Spanish Republic declared; three-year Second Carlist War begins.

Restoration of the Bourbons

1874 Alfonso XII, son of Isabella, brought to throne.

1892 Peasant revolt, inspired by anarchist doctrine (to be repeated 1903).

1895 Revolution in Cuba, one of Spain's few remaining colonies. Spain moves to suppress it.

1898 Spanish-American War: United States annexes Spanish colonies of Puerto Rico and the Philippines. Cuba is declared independent.

1902–31 Reign of Alfonso XIII. Increasing instability and unrest.

1914 Spain declares neutrality in World War I.

1923 Coup d'état of Gen. Manuel Primo de Rivera, who models his government on Italian Fascism.

Republic, Civil War & Fascism

1930–31 Primo de Rivera is ousted. Republic is declared, and Alfonso XIII is deposed. Liberals attempt to redistribute land and diminish the power of the Church.

1936–39 Spanish Civil War: electoral victory of Popular Front (a coalition of the left) precipitates rightist military insurrection against the Republic, led by Gen. Francisco Franco. Europe declares neutrality, but Germany and Italy aid Franco, and the USSR and volunteer brigades aid (to a lesser extent) the Republic. More than 600,000 die, including the poet Federico García Lorca. Franco is victorious and rules Spain for the next 36 years.

1939 Fascist Spain declares neutrality in World War II.

1945 Spain is denied membership in the U.N. (but is admitted in 1950).

1953 NATO bases are established in Spain in return for aid.

1969 Franco names Prince Juan Carlos de Borbón, heir to the vacant throne, his successor.

1973 Franco's prime minister, Carrero Blanco, is assassinated by Basque separatists.

Restoration of the Bourbons

1975 Franco dies; Juan Carlos, grandson of Alfonso XIII, succeeds him.

1977 First democratic elections in 40 years are won by Center Democratic Union.

1978 New constitution restores civil liberties and freedom of the press.

1981 Attempted coup by Col. Antonio Tejero.

1982 Spain becomes a full member of NATO. Socialists win landslide victory in general election.

1985 Frontier with Gibraltar, closed since 1968, is reopened.

1986 Spain enters European Union. Socialists win for a second time.

1989 Camilo José Cela awarded Nobel Prize for Literature.

1992 Olympic Games held in Barcelona.

1993 Socialists win victory in general election.

1996 Popular Party, Spain's conservative party, wins general election, ending 14 years of Socialist rule.

1999 Popular Party reelected with a clear majority, curtailing the power of the Catalonian nationalist party.

2000 Juan Carlos celebrates 25 years as Spain's king.

2002 Nobel prize-winner Camilo José Cela dies.

2003 Socialists, led by José Luis Rodríguez Zapatero, win close victory overall in regional elections, buoyed by unpopularity of Aznar's support of Iraq war and mishandling of the Prestige oil spill.

2004 Terrorist bombs on packed, rush-hour trains in Madrid claim more than 200 lives on March 11. Socialists under Jose Luis Rodriguez Zapatero win a surprise victory in general elections a few days later.

SPANISH FOOD & WINE

SPAIN'S POST-FRANCO cultural Renaissance has encouraged richness and variety in everything from arts and letters to gastronomy. As with all things Iberian, food and wine take a great many forms. This is a country where each village takes pride in its unique way of preparing the simplest dishes, where a Pyrenean valley serves dishes whose very names are incomprehensible to fellow Catalans from the neighboring valley.

Each of Spain's Autonomous Communities has its own cuisine. While the only dishes that might be called universal are the *tortilla española de patatas* (potato and onion omelet), *gazpacho* (a cold Andalusian soup of ground vegetables, garlic, and bread in a tomato base), and *paella* (a Valencian feast of saffron-spiked rice and seafood), fresh vegetables, olive oil, and garlic are used in dishes throughout the country. Central Spain is known for roasts and stews, eastern Spain for rice and seafood, northern Spain for meat and fish, and southern Spain for deep-fried seafood.

Blessed with a geological diversity unusual for a country its size, Spain has been known since ancient times for rich wheat fields, vineyards, olive groves, and pig and sheep farming. The upper slopes of Andalusia's snowcapped Sierra Nevada, for example, have Alpine gentian, while the lower ones yield tropical produce unique to southern Europe, such as olives.

Nearly surrounded by a combination of the Atlantic and the Mediterranean, Spain is in large part a maritime nation. A statistic surprising to all but the Spanish themselves is that Spain ranks third in the world in per-capita fish and seafood consumption, closely behind Japan and Iceland. Moreover, those two islands have no population more than 200 km (120 mi) from the coast, whereas Spanish villagers in tiny Aranda de Duero, 500 km (300 mi)

inland, were cooking fish back in the 14th century. Madrid, at the dead center of the Iberian Peninsula, has long been considered a "first port" for the freshest fish in Spain. And, of course, the Mediterranean diet—high in fresh vegetables, fruit, virgin olive oil, fish, fowl, rabbit, garlic, onions, and wine; low in red meat, dairy products, and carbohydrates—is one of the healthiest of all regimes.

The almost 800-year Moorish presence on the Iberian Peninsula was a major influence on Spanish cuisine. The Moors brought exotic ingredients such as saffron, almonds, and peppers; introduced sweets and pastries; and created refreshing dishes, such as cold almond- and vegetable-based soups, still popular today. One of the world's culinary pioneers was Ziryab, a 10th-century Moorish chef who worked in Córdoba: he's credited with bringing to Europe the Arab fashion for eating a standard sequence of dishes, beginning with soup and ending with dessert.

Tapas
Another legacy of the Moorish taste for small and varied delicacies is Spain's best-known culinary innovation, the *tapa* (hors d'oeuvre; derived from the verb *tapar,* meaning "to cover"). Early tapas are said to have been pieces of ham or cheese laid across glasses of wine, both to keep flies out and to keep stagecoach drivers sober. It's said that as far back as the 13th century, ailing Spanish king Alfonso X El Sabio ("The Learned") took small morsels with wine by medical prescription and so enjoyed the cure that he made it a regular practice in his court. Even Cervantes refers to tapas as *llamativos* (attention getters), for their stimulating properties, in *Don Quijote*. Often miniature versions of classic Spanish dishes, tapas originated in Andalusia, where a combination of heat and poverty made nomadic grazing preferable to the formal meal. Today tapas are

generally taken as appetizers before lunch or dinner, but in the south they're often regarded as a meal in themselves. Eating tapas allows you to sample a variety of food and wine with minimal alcohol poisoning, especially on a *tapeo*—like a pub crawl but lower in alcohol and higher in protein. (You basically walk off your wine and tapas as you move around.)

In some of the more old-fashioned bars in Madrid and points south, you may be automatically served a tapa of the barman's choice upon ordering a drink—olives, a piece of cheese, sausages, or even a cup of hot broth. A few to watch for: *calamares fritos* (fried squid or cuttlefish, easily mistaken for onion rings), *pulpo feira* (octopus on slices of potato), *chopitos* (baby octopi), *angulas* (baby eels), *chistorra* (fried spicy sausage), *chorizo* (hard pork sausage), *champiñones* (mushrooms), *gambas al ajillo* (shrimp cooked in oil, garlic, and parsley), *langostinos* (jumbo shrimp or prawns), *patatas bravas* (potatoes in spicy sauce), *pimientos de Padrón* (hot peppers), *sardinas* (fresh sardines cooked in garlic and parsley), *chancletes* (whitebait cooked in oil and parsley), and *salmonetes* (small red mullet).

Just to complicate things, the generic term *tapas* covers various forms of small-scale nibbling. *Tentempiés* are small snacks designed to (literally) "keep you on your feet." *Pinchos* are bite-size offerings impaled on toothpicks, as are *banderillas,* the latter so called because the toothpick is wrapped in colorful paper resembling the barbed batons used in bullfights. *Montaditos* are canapés, innovative combinations of delicacies "mounted" on toast. *Raciones* (rations, or servings) are hot tapas served in small earthenware casseroles. You can often order a series of small dishes *para picar* (to pick at). A selection of *raciones* or *entretenimientos* (a platter of delicacies that might range from olives to nuts to cheese, ham, or sausage) makes a popular starter for those dining in a group. The modern gourmet *menú de degustación* (taster's menu) is essentially a succession of complex tapas.

Soups

A standard Spanish soup, especially in and around Madrid, is *sopa de ajo* (garlic soup), made with water, oil, garlic, paprika, bread, and cured ham. *Sopa de pescado* (fish soup) appears on many menus, concocted in many different ways. The classic gazpacho is a cold blend of tomatoes, water, garlic, bread, and vegetables. Though most gazpacho today is made in a blender, it tastes best when prepared by hand in an earthenware mortar. Gazpacho has several variations, including Córdoba's *salmorejo,* which has a denser texture, and *ajo blanco,* based on almonds rather than tomatoes and served with peeled muscatel grapes or slices of honeydew melon—another example of Moorish influence, combining sweet and spicy flavors.

Far more substantial are the heavy soups and bean stews of the central Castilian meseta and northern coast. *Cocido madrileño* is a hearty highland stew or thick soup of garbanzos, black sausage, cabbage, potatoes, carrots, pork, and chicken served in three courses, called *vuelcos* ("overturnings" of the pot): the broth, the vegetables and legumes, and finally the meat. *Escudella* is the Catalan version of cocido, using ground pork and no garbanzos. *Fabada asturiana* is the best-known Asturian dish, a powerful stew of white kidney beans, fatback, ham, black sausage, and hard pork sausage. *Judias estofadas,* made of white kidney beans with chorizo, black sausage, onion, tomato, and bacon, is a close cousin found across the north of Spain. Galicia's *caldo gallego* mixes white beans, turnip greens, chickpeas, cabbage, and potatoes. *Pisto manchego,* from La Mancha, is a stew of sausage and ham with onions, peppers, tomatoes, and squash. *Migas de pastor* (shepherd's crumbs) is a legendary Aragonese and Castilian specialty consisting of bread crumbs and bacon sautéed in garlic and olive oil. During one of the Basque country's frequent Atlantic storms, don't miss a chance to try *marmitako,* a hearty tuna and potato stew.

Meat Dishes

Carnivores can choose from thick and tender *txuletas de buey* or *solomillos* (beef steaks) in the Basque country and fragrant roasts in Castile. In Segovia, Burgos, and Madrid, the *cochinillo al horno* (roast suckling pig) and *cordero asado* (roast lamb) are cooked in wood ovens until at once crisp and tender enough to portion with the edge of a blunt plate.

Fish and seafood are prepared countless ways in Spain, but the Basques and the Andalusians are particular masters of the art. The Basque Country is especially known for *bacalao al pil-pil*—cod cooked in oil and garlic at a low temperature, generating a sauce of juice from the fish itself. (The dish is named for the popping sound that the oil makes as the fish cooks.) *Besugo* (sea bream), either *al horno* (roasted) or *a la brasa* (over coals), is another Basque classic. *Rape* (monkfish) in crayfish sauce; *merluza* (hake) in tomato, pepper, or green (olive oil, garlic, and parsley) sauce; and *dorada a la sal* (gilthead bream baked in salt) are also popular. Common all over Spain is *trucha a la Navarra,* trout wrapped in, or stuffed with, pieces of bacon or ham. In Andalusia most fish is deep-fried in batter, a practice requiring very fresh fish and the right kind of oil to achieve the proper counterpoint of crispness and succulence. *Chancletes* (whitebait) and *sardinas* (sardines) are especially good in Málaga, while the *salmonetes* (red mullet) and *acedías* (miniature sole) of the Cádiz coast are legendary. *Adobo,* also delicious, is fried fish marinated in wine.

Spain's ham and sausage products are renowned, particularly those derived from the *cerdo ibérico,* a remarkable breed of free-range pig that produces *jamón serrano*—roughly translatable as "ham from the sierra, or mountains." This term covers three levels of quality: *bellota* (the finest, from Iberian pigs fed exclusively acorns), *de recebo* (from pigs fed acorns but finished off with corn over the last three months), and simply *serrano* (from pigs fattened on feed pellets). Extremadura and the provinces of Salamanca and Huelva produce Spain's best cured hams; look for those of Guijuelo, Lasa, and Jabugo. The chorizo and *morcilla* (blood sausage) of Pamplona, Granada, and Burgos are known beyond Spain's borders. *Sobrasada* is a delicious pork-and-pepper paste from Majorca. *Fuet* (literally, "whip," named for its slender shape) is Catalonia's best sausage, though the *botifarra* is the most popular spicy sausage, usually consumed with *secas* or *mongetes* (white beans).

The most elaborate poultry dishes are prepared in the Catalan province of Girona. These include *pollastre amb llangosta* (chicken with lobster), *gall dindi amb panses, pinyones, i botifarra* (turkey stuffed with raisins, pine nuts, and sausage), and *oca (anec) amb naps* (goose, or duck, with turnips). *Pollo al ajillo,* fried chunks of chicken smothered in chips of garlic, is beloved all over Spain. Rabbit (*conejo*) is another standard light meat, prepared either *al ajillo* (in garlic), a la brasa, or in stews and ragouts with peppers and assorted vegetables.

Fish, meat, and seafood meet exuberantly in paella, a saffron-flavored rice dish widely considered the most emblematic of Spanish dishes. Paella is actually comparatively new, having originated in Valencia and the Levante, Spain's rice-growing eastern coastal plain, in the early 19th century. Cooked in a wide, flat, round pan, it comes in several versions, including *marinera* (seafood), *conejo* (rabbit), *pollo* (chicken), and *mixta* (mixed). Chosen from a *menú del día,* paella will always be disappointing, little more than rice with some saffron and a few ingredients mixed in. Prepared on the spot and in the pan, however, with a caramelized crust around its edges, paella is delicious. The archetypal version is *paella a la marinera,* a seafood anthology including shrimp, crayfish, monkfish, and mussels on a bed of saffron rice cooked in a seafood broth with peppers and tomatoes. Related dishes include *arroz a banda*, paella with the seafood pre-shelled; *fideuà*, paella based on pasta rather than rice; and *arroz negro* (black rice), paella that takes its color and flavor from cuttlefish ink instead of saffron.

Cheese & Wine

Iberian cheeses are many and varied. The sheep cheeses of La Mancha can be consumed *tierno* (soft and creamy, cured under three months), *semi-seco* (half-cured, for three to six months), or *seco* (dry, cured for more than six months). A mature *manchego seco* is nearly the equal of an Italian Parmesan. Cabrales, a powerful blue cheese from Asturias, makes Roquefort seem innocent. Other prominent northern cheeses include the soft and creamy breast-shape *tetilla gallega* and the sharper Asturian *pitu al' fuego*. The Basque Country's smoky *idiazábal* is like a cedar-flavored sharp cheddar. Extremadura's *Torta del Casar* is widely considered the best Spanish cheese of all, a creamy sheep cheese that never hardens and needs to be scooped by spoon.

Spanish wines are rapidly emerging from the long shadow cast by their neighbors to the north. La Rioja, traditionally Spain's finest wine-growing region, is known for the deep, woody flavor of its celebrated reds, the result of aging in casks of American oak, traditionally preferred over French oak for its superior porosity and faster oxidating properties. This aging technique was introduced by French vintners from Bordeaux and Burgundy who moved to the Rioja in the 19th century to escape a phylloxera epidemic that was destroying the vines in their own country. Among time-honored Rioja labels are Rioja Alta, Viña Ardanza, Imperial, Muga, Marqués de Murrieta, Pomal, Ramón Bilbao, Marqués de Riscal, and Viña Tondonia. In response to competition from other regions producing wines of more complex structure, La Rioja is now producing a series of new wines that break with the traditionally smooth and oaky Rioja reds. Roda, Artadi, Pujanza, Vina Ijalva, Palacios Remondo, Alma de TobÓa, Marqués de Riscal's Baron de Chivel, SeñorÓo de San Vicente, Sierra de Cantabria, Abel Mendoza, Ostatu, Solagüen, and Marqués de Vargas are among the leaders in this movement toward fruitier, more peppery brews.

The increasingly prestigious region of La Ribera del Duero, north of Madrid, produces fine bottles of both young wine and wine that will improve with age. Vega Sicilia is the most famous winery in La Ribera del Duero. Pesquera, Protos, and Viña Pedrosa are other fine labels, as are Pago de Carraovejas, Mauro, and Abadia Retuerto.

Southwest of Valladolid, the Rueda wine-growing district produces some of Spain's most distinguished white wines, and Huesca's Somontano wines, especially the Enate and Señorío de Lazán labels, are rapidly gaining respect. The Valdepeñas wine country, 200 km (120 mi) south of Madrid, remains Spain's prime producer of simple table wines in unabashedly greater quantity than quality. A pitcher of Valdepeñas with a meal or tapas in and around Castile is never disappointing.

Catalonia's Penedès region specializes in *cava* (sparkling white wine). The most famous cavas are Codorniu and Freixenet, but many smaller outfits, such as Juvé i Camps, Augustí Torelló, Mascaró, and Gramona, actually produce better bubbly. Along with the Torres reds and whites and the Raventós cavas and whites, the Penedès produces Spain's greatest variety of wines overall. New artisanal wines, however, are steadily emerging from such unlikely places as the rugged hills of the Priorat area, west of Tarragona, where the Costers de Siurana labels Clos de l'Obac and Miserere are standouts. The Raimat wines from Costers del Segre are excellent, as are the Gran Caus, the Castillo

Perelada, and the exciting new Oliver Conti wines from northern Catalonia's Ampurdán region.

Galicia's Ribeiro and Rías Baixas wines, especially the young green Albariños, are served in top restaurants throughout Spain with fish courses, and Albariño is gaining accolades overseas. The Basque country's *txakolí*, an even greener young white with a slight effervescence, has always been popular locally but is building a wider following as Basque restaurants and tapas bars flourish nationwide.

Sherry has always been popular abroad, especially with the British, who have dominated the sherry trade in Jerez de la Frontera since the 16th century. Indeed, many of the most famous labels are foreign—Domecq, Harvey, Sandeman. The classic dry sherry is the *fino*. *Amontillado* is deeper in color and flavor, and *oloroso* is really a sweet dessert wine, as are the even-sweeter creams. Another fortified Andalusian wine, often difficult for the inexperienced palate to distinguish from sherry, is *manzanilla*, from the coastal town of Sanlúcar de Barrameda. Manzanilla has a tangy, saline savor that comes from the cool Atlantic breezes at the mouth of the Guadalquivir River. With its faint taste of the sea, this wine does not travel well; there are even those who believe it tastes better in the lower part of Sanlúcar than in the upper town. Sherry and manzanilla are generally thought of as aperitif wines and are ideal with tapas—a Sanlúcar prawn with a glass of manzanilla is many a Spanish epicurean's idea of paradise. In England, sherry still has the genteel associations of an Oxbridge college, but Spain has a more robust attitude toward the beverage, especially during Sevilla's Feria de Abril, where more sherry and manzanilla are reputedly drunk in a week than in the whole of Spain the rest of the year.

Some of Spain's finest brandies, such as Osborne, Terry, Duque de Alba, and Carlos III, also come from Jerez. Málaga makes a sweet dessert wine that enjoyed a vogue with the English in the 19th century; look for the label Scholtz. *Aguardientes* (aquavits) are manufactured throughout Spain, with the most famous brands coming from Chinchón, near Madrid. A sweet and popular Jerez brandy, Ponche Caballero, is easy to identify by its silver-coated bottle, which looks like an amateur explosive. *Sangría*, a tourist potion imported from Mexico, is generally composed of cheap liquors and bad wine and should be avoided at all costs by those in search of Spanish delicacies.

Spain's top restaurants offer a selection of postprandial cheeses, but most meals end with dessert. Standard enticements are fresh fruit, such as strawberries with orange juice or vanilla ice cream, and *flan*, a caramel cream that comes close to being Spain's national dessert. In Catalonia, look for the ubiquitous *crema catalana*, a sort of crème brûlée, or the honey-and-fresh-cheese combination known as *mel i mató*.

Above and after all, Spain is the ultimate moveable feast.

— George Semler and Michael Jacobs

BOOKS & MOVIES

Ernest Hemingway is the novelist most responsible for the world's image of 20th-century Spain. Read *The Sun Also Rises* for a vicarious visit to Pamplona's running of the bulls. *For Whom the Bell Tolls* depicts the horrors of the Spanish civil war, and *Death in the Afternoon* explores the technical, artistic, and philosophical aspects of bullfighting.

James A. Michener's *Iberia: Spanish Travels and Reflections,* though a Franco regime–informed and occasionally inaccurate view of Spain, still covers a lot of ground, some of it superbly well. V. S. Pritchett (*The Spanish Temper*), H. V. Morton (*A Stranger in Spain*), George Orwell (*Homage to Catalonia*), and Washington Irving (*Tales of the Alhambra*) have all paid their respects to Spain. Gerald Brenan's works portray Spain before and during the Franco years: *The Face of Spain, The Spanish Labyrinth,* and *South from Granada,* released as a stunningly beautiful movie in 2003. *Moorish Spain,* by Richard Fletcher, details the cultural and intellectual riches of the Islamic era; *Farewell España,* by Howard M. Sacher, explores the lives of the Sephardim, the Spanish Jews who had to flee after the 1492 expulsion decree. Jane Gerber's *The Jews of Spain* deals with the history of Sephardic Jews, from their first Roman settlements to their expulsion from Spain.

Ian Gibson's biographies of Federico García Lorca (*Federico García Lorca: A Life*) and Salvador Dalí (*The Shameful Life of Salvador Dalí*) are richaccounts of the lives of two of Spain's great artists.

Among Spanish texts, the story of the errant knight *Don Quijote,* by Miguel de Cervantes, will always be Spain's towering classic. For more modern works, try translations of the realism-drenched novels of Galician Camilo José Cela, the 1989 recipient of the Nobel Prize for Literature: his best-known books are *The Beehive* and *The Family of Pascual Duarte.* One of Spain's great 20th-century novels is Mercé Rodoreda's *The Time of the Doves,* the story of a woman buffeted by the misfortunes of the civil war. Federico García Lorca's play *Blood Wedding* is a disturbing drama of Spain's repressed yet powerful women of the early 20th century. Novelist Javier Marías has been hugely successful in several countries; among his best works in translation are *A Heart So White* and *Tomorrow in the Battle Think on Me.* Arturo Pérez-Reverte has written several acclaimed mysteries.

The tragic bullfighting novel *Blood and Sand,* by Vicente Blasco Ibáñez, has three Hollywood adaptations: the first starring Rudolph Valentino; the second, Tyrone Power; the third, Sharon Stone. Carlos Saura has directed several beautifully crafted classic films consisting mostly of dance—*Carmen, Bodas de Sangre* (*Blood Wedding*), and *El Amor Brujo* (*Love, the Magician*). Luis Buñuel's *Un Chien Andalou* is a hallmark of surrealism. Orson Welles's film *Don Quixote* was painstakingly finished in 1992, after his death, by Jess Franco and Patxi Irigoyen. Set in 1930s Galicia, José Luis Cuerda's gorgeous *Butterfly* shows how the civil war divided communities before the first shots were fired.

VOCABULARY

	English	Spanish	Pronunciation
Basics			
	Yes/no	Sí/no	see/no
	Please	Por favor	pohr fah-**vohr**
	May I?	¿Me permite?	meh pehr-**mee**-teh
	Thank you (very much)	(Muchas) gracias	(**moo**-chas) **grah**-see-as
	You're welcome	De nada	deh **nah**-dah
	Excuse me	Con permiso/perdón	con pehr-**mee**-so/ pehr-**dohn**
	Pardon me/ what did you say?	¿Perdón?/Mande?	pehr-**dohn/mahn**-deh
	Could you tell me . . . ?	¿Podría decirme . . . ?	po-**dree**-ah deh-**seer**-meh
	I'm sorry	Lo siento	lo see-**en**-to
	Good morning!	¡Buenos días!	**bway**-nohs **dee**-ahs
	Good afternoon!	¡Buenas tardes!	**bway**-nahs **tar**-dess
	Good evening!	¡Buenas noches!	**bway**-nahs **no**-chess
	Goodbye!	¡Adiós!/ ¡Hasta luego!	ah-dee-**ohss/ ah**-stah-**lwe**-go
	Mr./Mrs.	Señor/Señora	sen-**yor**/sen-**yohr**-ah
	Miss	Señorita	sen-yo-**ree**-tah
	Pleased to meet you	Mucho gusto	**moo**-cho **goose**-to
	How are you?	¿Cómo está usted?	**ko**-mo es-**tah** oo-**sted**
	Very well, thank you.	Muy bien, gracias.	**moo**-ee bee-**en, grah**-see-as
	And you?	¿Y usted?	ee oos-**ted**
	Hello (on the phone)	Diga	**dee**-gah
Days of the Week			
	Sunday	domingo	doh-**meen**-goh
	Monday	lunes	**loo**-ness
	Tuesday	martes	**mahr**-tess
	Wednesday	miércoles	me-**air**-koh-less
	Thursday	jueves	hoo-**ev**-ess
	Friday	viernes	vee-**air**-ness
	Saturday	sábado	**sah**-bah-doh

Numbers

1	un, uno	oon, **oo**-no
2	dos	dohs
3	tres	tress
4	cuatro	**kwah**-tro
5	cinco	**sink**-oh
6	seis	saice
7	siete	see-**et**-eh
8	ocho	**o**-cho
9	nueve	new-**eh**-veh
10	diez	dee-**es**
11	once	**ohn**-seh
12	doce	**doh**-seh
13	trece	**treh**-seh
14	catorce	ka-**tohr**-seh
15	quince	**keen**-seh
16	dieciséis	dee-**es**-ee-**saice**
17	diecisiete	dee-**es**-ee-see-**et**-eh
18	dieciocho	dee-**es**-ee-**o**-cho
19	diecinueve	dee-**es**-ee-new-**ev**-eh
20	veinte	**vain**-teh
21	veinte y uno/ veintiuno	**vain**-te-oo-noh
30	treinta	**train**-tah
32	treinta y dos	train-tay-**dohs**
40	cuarenta	kwah-**ren**-tah
50	cincuenta	seen-**kwen**-tah
60	sesenta	sess-**en**-tah
70	setenta	set-**en**-tah
80	ochenta	oh-**chen**-tah
90	noventa	no-**ven**-tah
100	cien	see-**en**
200	doscientos	doh-see-**en**-tohss
500	quinientos	keen-**yen**-tohss
1,000	mil	meel
2,000	dos mil	dohs meel

Useful Phrases

Do you speak English?	¿Habla usted inglés?	**ah**-blah oos-**ted** in-**glehs**
I don't speak Spanish	No hablo español	no **ah**-bloh es-pahn-**yol**
I don't understand (you)	No entiendo	no en-tee-**en**-doh
I understand (you)	Entiendo	en-tee-**en**-doh
I don't know	No sé	no seh
I am American/ British	Soy americano (americana)/ inglés(a)	soy ah-meh-ree-**kah**-no (ah-meh-ree-**kah**-nah)/in-**glehs**(ah)
My name is . . .	Me llamo . . .	meh **yah**-moh
Yes, please/ No, thank you	Sí, por favor/ No, gracias	**see** pohr fah-**vor**/ no **grah**-see-ahs
Yesterday/today/ tomorrow	Ayer/hoy/mañana	ah-**yehr**/oy/mahn-**yah**-nah
This morning/ afternoon	Esta mañana/tarde	**es**-tah mahn-**yah**-nah/**tar**-deh
Tonight	Esta noche	**es**-tah **no**-cheh
This/Next week	Esta semana/ la semana que entra	**es**-tah seh-**mah**-nah/lah seh-**mah**-nah keh **en**-trah
This/Next month	Este mes/el próximo mes	**es**-teh mehs/el **prok**-see-moh mehs
How?	¿Cómo?	**koh**-mo
When?	¿Cuándo?	**kwahn**-doh
What?	¿Qué?	keh
What is this?	¿Qué es esto?	keh es **es**-toh
Why?	¿Por qué?	por **keh**
Who?	¿Quién?	kee-**yen**
Where is . . . ?	¿Dónde está . . . ?	**dohn**-deh es-**tah**
the train station?	la estación del tren?	la es-tah-see-**on** del **train**
the subway station?	la estación del metro?	la es-ta-see-**on** del **meh**-tro
the bus stop?	la parada del autobus?	la pah-**rah**-dah del oh-toh-**boos**
the bank?	el banco?	el **bahn**-koh
the hotel?	el hotel?	el oh-**tel**
the post office?	la oficina de correos?	la oh-fee-**see**-nah deh-koh-**reh**-os
the museum?	el museo?	el moo-**seh**-oh
the hospital?	el hospital?	el ohss-pee-**tal**
the bathroom?	el baño?	el **bahn**-yoh

Here/there	Aquí/allá	ah-**key**/ah-**yah**
Open/closed	Abierto/cerrado	ah-bee-**er**-toh/ ser-**ah**-doh
Left/right	Izquierda/derecha	iss-key-**er**-dah/ dare-**eh**-chah
Straight ahead	Todo recto	**toh**-doh-**rec**-toh
Is it near/far?	¿Está cerca/lejos?	es-**tah sehr**-kah/ **leh**-hoss
I'd like . . .	Quisiera . . .	kee-see-**ehr**-ah
a room	una habitación	**oo**-nah ah-bee-tah-see-**on**
the key	la llave	lah **yah**-veh
a newspaper	un periódico	oon pehr-ee-**oh**-dee-koh
a stamp	un sello	**say**-oh
How much is this?	¿Cuánto cuesta?	**kwahn**-toh **kwes**-tah
A little/a lot	Un poquito/ mucho	oon poh-**kee**-toh/ **moo**-choh
More/less	Más/menos	mahss/**men**-ohss
I am ill	Estoy enfermo(a)	es-**toy** en-**fehr**-moh(mah)
Please call a doctor	Por favor llame un médico	pohr fah-**vor ya**-meh oon **med**-ee-koh
Help!	¡Ayuda!	ah-**yoo**-dah

On the Road

Avenue	Avenida	ah-ven-**ee**-dah
Broad, tree-lined boulevard	Paseo	pah-**seh**-oh
Highway	Carretera	car-reh-**ter**-ah
Port; mountain pass	Puerto	poo-**ehr**-toh
Street	Calle	**cah**-yeh
Waterfront promenade	Paseo marítimo	pah-**seh**-oh mahr-**ee**-tee-moh

In Town

Cathedral	Catedral	cah-teh-**dral**
Church	Iglesia	**tem**-plo/ee-**glehs**-see-ah
City hall, town hall	Ayuntamiento	ah-yoon-tah-me-**yen**-toh
Door, gate	Puerta	poo-**ehr**-tah
Main square	Plaza Mayor	plah-thah mah-**yohr**
Market	Mercado	mer-**kah**-doh
Neighborhood	Barrio	**bahr**-ree-o

Tavern, rustic restaurant	Mesón	meh-**sohn**
Traffic circle, roundabout	Glorieta	glor-ee-**eh**-tah
Wine cellar, wine bar, wine shop	Bodega	boh-**deh**-gah

Dining Out

A bottle of . . .	Una botella de . . .	**oo**-nah bo-**teh**-yah deh
A glass of . . .	Un vaso de . . .	oon **vah**-so deh
Bill/check	La cuenta	lah **kwen**-tah
Breakfast	El desayuno	el deh-sah-**yoon**-oh
Dinner	La cena	lah **seh**-nah
Menu of the day	Menú del día	meh-**noo** del **dee**-ah
Fork	El tenedor	ehl ten-eh-**dor**
Is the tip included?	¿Está incluida la propina?	es-**tah** in-cloo-**ee**-dah lah pro-**pee**-nah
Knife	El cuchillo	el koo-**chee**-yo
Large portion of tapas	Ración	rah-see-**ohn**
Lunch	La comida	lah koh-**mee**-dah
Menu	La carta, el menú	lah **cart**-ah, el meh-**noo**
Napkin	La servilleta	lah sehr-vee-**yet**-ah
Please give me . . .	Por favor déme . . .	pohr fah-**vor deh**-meh
Spoon	Una cuchara	**oo**-nah koo-**chah**-rah

MENU GUIDE

Starters

aguacate con gambas avocado and prawns
caldo thick soup
champiñones al ajillo mushrooms in garlic
consomé clear soup
gazpacho chilled soup made with tomatoes, onions, peppers, cucumbers, and oil
huevos flamencos eggs with spicy sausage and tomato
judías con tomate/jamón green beans with tomato/ham
sopa soup
sopa de ajo garlic soup
sopa de garbanzos chickpea soup
sopa de lentejas lentil soup
sopa de mariscos shellfish soup
sopa sevillana soup made with mayonnaise, shellfish, asparagus, and peas

Omelets (Tortillas)

tortilla de champiñones mushroom omelet
tortilla de gambas prawn omelet
tortilla de mariscos seafood omelet
tortilla de patatas, tortilla española Spanish potato omelet
tortilla francesa plain omelet
tortilla sacromonte (in Granada) omelet with ham, sausage, and peas

Meats (Carnes)

beicón bacon
bistec steak
cerdo pork
lomo de cerdo pork tenderloin
cabrito roasted kid
chorizo seasoned sausage
chuleta chop, cutlet
cochinillo suckling pig
cordero lamb
filete steak
jamón ham
jamón de York cooked ham
jamón serrano cured raw ham
morcilla blood sausage
salchicha sausage
salchichón Spanish salami (cured pork sausage)
solomillo de ternera fillet of beef
ternera veal

Poultry (Aves) and Game (Caza)

conejo rabbit
cordonices quail
faisán pheasant
jabalí wild boar
oca, ganso goose
pato duck
pato salvaje wild duck
pavo turkey
perdiz partridge
pollo chicken

Organ Meats

callos tripe
criadillas bull's testicles (shown on Spanish menus as "unmentionables")
hígado liver
lengua tongue
mollejas sweetbreads
riñones kidneys
sesos brains

Fish (Pescados)

ahumados smoked fish (i.e. trout, eel, salmon)
anchoas anchovies
anguila eel
angulas baby eel
atún, bonito tuna
bacalao salt cod
besugo sea bream
boquerones fresh anchovies
lenguado sole
lubina sea bass
merluza hake, whitefish
mero grouper fish
pez espada, emperador swordfish
rape angler fish
raya skate
salmón salmon
salmonete red mullet
sardina sardine
trucha trout

Shellfish and Seafood (Mariscos)

almeja clam
calamares squid
cangrejo crab

centolla spider crab
chipirones, chopitos small squid
cigalas crayfish
concha scallops
gambas prawns, shrimp
langosta lobster
langostino prawn
mejillones mussels
ostra oyster
percebes barnacles
pulpo octopus
sepia cuttlefish
vieiras scallop (in Galicia)
zarzuela de mariscos shellfish casserole

Vegetables (Verduras)
aceituna olive
aguacate avocado
ajo garlic
alcachofa artichoke
apio celery
berenjena eggplant
berza green cabbage
brécol/bróculi broccoli
calabacín zucchini
cebollo onion
calabaza pumpkin
champiñon mushroom
col cabbage
coliflor cauliflower
endivia endive
escarola chicory
ensalada salad
ensaladilla rusa potato salad
espárragos asparagus
espinacas spinach
espinacas a la catalana spinach with garlic, rasins, and pine nuts
garbanzos chickpeas
guisantes peas
habas broad beans
judías dried beans
judías verdes green beans
lechuga lettuce
lenteja lentil
palmitos palm hearts
patata potato
pepinillo gherkin
pepino cucumber
pimientos green/red peppers

puerro leek
seta chanterelle
tomate tomato
verduras green vegetables
zanahoria carrot

Fruit (Frutas)
albaricoque apricot
ananás, piña pineapple
cereza cherry
chirimoya custard apple
ciruela plum
frambuesa raspberry
fresa strawberry
fresón large strawberry
grosella negra black currant
limón lemon
manzana apple
melocotón peach
melón melon
naranja orange
pera pear
plátano banana
sandía watermelon
uvas grapes
zarzamora blackberry

Desserts (Postres)
bizcocho, galleta biscuit
bizocho de chocolate chocolate cake
buñuelos warm, sugared, deep-fried doughnuts, sometimes cream-filled
con nata with cream
cuajada thick yogurt with honey
ensalada de frutas, macedonia fruit salad
flan caramel custard
fresas con nata strawberries and cream
helado de vainilla, fresa, café, chocolate vanilla, strawberry, coffee, chocolate ice cream
melocotón en almibar canned peaches
pastel cake
pera en almibar canned pears
pijama ice cream with fruit and syrup
piña en almibar canned pineapple
postre de músico dessert of dried fruit and nuts
la tarta de queso cheesecake
tarta helada ice-cream cake
la tartaleta de frutas fruit cake
yogur yogurt

Miscellaneous

a la brasa barbequed
a la parrilla grilled
a la plancha grilled
aceite de oliva olive oil
al horno roasted, baked
arroz rice
asado roast
azúcar sugar
carbonade pot roasted
churros: baton-shaped donuts for dipping in hot chocolate, typically eaten at breakfast.
crudo raw
espaguettis spaghetti
fideos noodles
frito fried
guisado stewed
huevo egg
mahonesa mayonnaise
mantequilla butter
mermelada jam
miel honey
mostaza mustard
pan bread
patatas fritas french fries
perejil parsley
poché poached
queso cheese
relleno filled, stuffed
sal salt
salsa sauce
salsa de tomate catsup
vinagre vinegar

Drinks (Bebidas)

agua water
agua con gas carbonated mineral water
agua sin gas still mineral water
blanco y negro cold black coffee with vanilla ice cream
café con leche coffee with cream
café solo black coffee (espresso)
caliente hot
caña small draught beer
cava, champán sparkling wine, champagne
cerveza beer
chocolate hot chocolate
cuba libre rum and coke
fino very dry sherry
frío/fría cold
gaseosa soda
granizado de limón (de café) lemon (or coffee) on crushed ice
hielo ice
horchata cold summer drink made from ground nuts
jerez sherry
jugo fruit juice
leche milk
limonada lemonade
manzanilla very dry sherry or camomile tea
sidra cider
té tea
con limón with lemon
con leche with milk
vaso glass
un vaso de agua a glass of water
vermut vermouth
vino wine
vino añejo vintage wine
vino blanco white wine
vino dulce sweet wine
vino espumoso sparkling wine
vino rosado rosé
vino seco dry wine
vino tinto red wine
zumo de naranja orange juice

SMART TRAVEL TIPS

Finding out about your destination before you leave home means you won't squander time organizing everyday minutiae once you've arrived. You'll be more streetwise when you hit the ground as well, better prepared to explore the aspects of Spain that drew you here in the first place. The organizations in this section can provide information to supplement this guide; contact them for up-to-the-minute details, and consult the Essentials sections that end each chapter for facts on the various topics as they relate to the country's many regions. Happy landings!

ADDRESSES

Apartment addresses in Spain include the street name, building number, floor level, and apartment number. For example, Calle Cervantes 15, 3°, 1a indicates that the apartment is on the *tercero* (third) floor, *primera* (first) door. In older buildings, the first floor is often called the *entresuelo*; one floor above it is *principal* and, then above this, the first floor. The top floor of a building is the *ático* (attic). More modern buildings often have no entresuelo or principal. Addresses with the abbreviation s/n are *sin numero,* or "without number."

If you see the word *bis* after an address, it means two buildings have the same street number, so the bis is given to one of them to clarify which building is being referred to. For example, in Madrid there's a Castellana 40 and a Castellana 40 bis.

AIR TRAVEL TO & FROM SPAIN

Regular nonstop flights serve Spain from the eastern United States; flying from other North American cities usually involves a stop. If you're coming from North America and would like to land in a city other than Madrid or Barcelona, consider flying a British or other European carrier, and know that you may have to stay overnight in London or another European city on your way home

Since 2004, there's been a revolution in cheap flights from the United Kingdom to Spain, with the emergence of scores of new carriers such as Monarch, Jet2, and Flybmi providing competition to the market's main players—easyJet and Ryanair. All these carriers offer frequent flights, cover small cities as well as large ones, and have very competitive fares.

There are no nonstop flights to Spain from Australia or New Zealand.

BOOKING

Look for nonstop flights and remember that "direct" flights stop at least once. Try to avoid connecting flights, which require a change of plane. Two airlines may operate a connecting flight jointly, so ask whether your airline operates every segment of the trip; you may find that the carrier you prefer flies you only part of the way. To find more booking tips, to check prices, and to make flight reservations, log on to www.fodors.com.

CARRIERS

From North America, Air Europa, Continental, Spanair, and US Airways fly to Madrid; American, Delta, and Iberia fly to Madrid and Barcelona. Within Spain, Iberia is the main domestic airline, but Air Europa and Spanair fly most domestic routes at lower prices. The budget airline Vueling.com heavily promotes its Internet bookings, which are often the country's cheapest domestic flight prices. The airline is servicing more and more major Spanish cities on and off the mainland and outside of Spain offers cheap flights to Amsterdam, Brussels, Berlin, Lisbon, Milan, Rome, and Paris. The earlier the ticket is bought online before your travel date, the more bargains you're likely to find. Air Europa and Spanair also travel both within Spain and to the rest of Europe.

Iberia runs a shuttle, the *puente aereo,* between Madrid and Barcelona from around 7 AM to 11 PM; planes depart hourly and around every 15 to 20 minutes during the morning and afternoon commute hours. You don't need to reserve ahead; you can buy your tickets at the airport ticket counter upon arriving or book online at Iberia.com. Passengers can now also use the newly installed self-service check-in counters to avoid queues. Terminal C in the Barcelona airport is used exclusively

by the shuttle; in Madrid, the shuttle departs from the newly opened Terminal 4.

🔂 **From North America** Air Europa ☎ 888/238-7672 ⊕ www.air-europa.com. **American** ☎ 800/433-7300 ⊕ www.aa.com. **Continental** ☎ 800/231-0856 ⊕ www.continental.com. **Delta** ☎ 800/221-1212 ⊕ www.delta.com. **Iberia** ☎ 800/772-4642 ⊕ www.iberia.com. **Spanair** ☎ 888/545-5757 ⊕ www.spanair.com. **US Airways** ☎ 800/622-1015 ⊕ www.usairways.com.

🔂 **From the U.K.** British Airways ☎ 0845/773-3377 ⊕ www.britishairways.com. **Buzzaway** ☎ 0870/240-7070 ⊕ www.buzzaway.com. **easyJet** ☎ 0870/600-0000 ⊕ www.easyjet.com. **Flybmi** ☎ 0870/607-0555 ⊕ www.flybmi.com. **Iberia** ☎ 0845/601-2854 ⊕ www.iberia.com. **Jet2** ☎ 0871/226-1737 ⊕ www.jet2.com. **Monarch Airlines** ☎ 0870/040-5040 ⊕ www.monarch-airlines.com. **Ryanair** ☎ 0871/246-0000 ⊕ www.ryanair.com. **Spanair** ☎ 888/545-5757 ⊕ www.spanair.com.

🔂 **Within Spain** Air Europa ☎ 902/401501 ⊕ www.air-europa.com. **Iberia** ☎ 902/400500 ⊕ www.iberia.com. **Spanair** ☎ 902/131415 ⊕ www.spanair.com. **Vueling** ☎ 902/333933 ⊕ www.vueling.com.

CHECK-IN & BOARDING

Always **find out your carrier's check-in policy.** Plan to arrive at the airport about 2 hours before your scheduled departure time for domestic flights and 2½ to 3 hours before international flights. You may need to arrive earlier if you're flying from one of the busier airports or during peak air-traffic times. To avoid delays at airport-security checkpoints, try not to wear any metal. Jewelry, steel-toe shoes, barrettes, underwire bras, and belt and other buckles are among the items that can set off detectors.

Assuming that not everyone with a ticket will show up, airlines routinely overbook planes. When everyone does, airlines ask for volunteers to give up their seats. In return, these volunteers usually get a several-hundred-dollar flight voucher, which can be used toward the purchase of another ticket, and are rebooked on the next flight out. If there are not enough volunteers, the airline must choose who will be denied boarding. The first to get bumped are passengers who checked in late and those flying on discounted tickets, so get to the gate and check in as early as possible, especially during peak periods.

Always **bring a government-issued photo ID** to the airport; even when it's not required, a passport is best.

CUTTING COSTS

The least expensive airfares to Spain are priced for round-trip travel and must usually be purchased in advance. Airlines generally allow you to change your return date for a fee; most low-fare tickets, however, are nonrefundable.

It's smart to call a number of airlines and check the Internet; when you are quoted a good price, book it on the spot—the same fare may not be available the next day, or even the next hour. Always check different routings, alternate airports, and off-peak flights, which may be significantly less expensive than others. Travel agents, especially low-fare specialists (⇨ Discounts & Deals), are helpful.

Consolidators are another good source. They buy tickets for scheduled flights at reduced rates from the airlines, then sell them at prices that beat the best fare available directly from the airlines. (Many also offer reduced car-rental and hotel rates.) Sometimes you can even get refundable tickets. Carefully read the fine print detailing penalties for changes and cancellations, purchase the ticket with a credit card, and confirm your consolidator reservation with the airline.

You can fly as a courier to Spain, though not within Spain. When you fly as a courier, you trade your checked-luggage space for a ticket deeply subsidized by a courier service. There are restrictions on when you can book and how long you can stay. Some courier companies list with membership organizations, such as the Air Courier Association and the International Association of Air Travel Couriers; these require you to become a member before you can book a flight.

Many airlines, singly or in collaboration, offer discount air passes that allow foreigners to travel economically in a particular country or region. These visitor passes usually must be reserved and purchased before you leave home. Information about passes often can be found on most airlines' international Web pages, which tend to be aimed at travelers from outside the carrier's home country. Also, try typing the name of the pass into a search engine, or search for "pass" within the carrier's Web site.

If you buy a round-trip transatlantic ticket on Iberia, you might want to purchase a **Visit Spain** Airpass, good for three or more domestic flights during your trip. The pass must be purchased before you arrive in Spain, and all flights must be booked in advance; the cost starts at $248. The maximum number of coupons you may purchase is nine, and the pass is valid for one year. On certain days of the week, Iberia also offers *minitarifas* (minifares), which can save you up to 40% on domestic flights. Tickets must be purchased at least two days in advance, and you must stay over Saturday night.

🔁 **Courier Resources Air Courier Association/ Cheaptrips.com** ☎ 800/461-8856 ⊕ www. aircourier.org or www.cheaptrips.com; $39 annual membership. **Courier Travel** ☎ 303/570-7586 ⊕ www.couriertravel.org; $40 onetime membership fee. **International Association of Air Travel Couriers** ☎ 308/632-3273 ⊕ www.courier.org; $45 annual membership. 🔁 **Online Consolidators AirlineConsolidator.com** ⊕ www.airlineconsolidator.com, for international tickets. **Best Fares** ⊕ www.bestfares.com; $59.90 annual membership. **Cheap Tickets** ⊕ www. cheaptickets.com. **Expedia** ⊕ www.expedia.com. **Hotwire** ⊕ www.hotwire.com. **lastminute.com** ⊕ www.lastminute.com specializes in last-minute travel; the main site is for the United Kingdom, but it has a link to a U.S. site. **Luxury Link** ⊕ www. luxurylink.com has auctions (surprisingly good deals) as well as offers at the high-end side of travel. **Onetravel.com** ⊕ www.onetravel.com. **Orbitz** ⊕ www.orbitz.com. **Priceline.com** ⊕ www. priceline.com. **Travelocity** ⊕ www.travelocity.com. 🔁 **Discount Passes FlightPass** ☎ 888/387-2479 **EuropebyAir** ⊕ www.europebyair.com. **Iberia** ☎ 800/772-4642 ⊕ www.iberia.com. **SAS Air Passes** ☎ 800/221-2350 Scandinavian Airlines, 0870/6072-7727 in U.K., 1300/727707 in Australia ⊕ www.scandinavian.net.

ENJOYING THE FLIGHT

State your seat preference when purchasing your ticket, and then repeat it when you confirm and when you check in. For more legroom, you can request one of the few emergency-aisle seats at check-in, if you're capable of moving obstacles comparable in weight to an airplane exit door (usually between 35 pounds and 60 pounds)—a Federal Aviation Administration requirement of passengers in these seats. Seats behind a bulkhead also offer more legroom, but they don't have underseat storage. Don't sit in the row in front of the emergency aisle or in front of a bulkhead, where seats may not recline.

Ask the airline whether a snack or meal is served on the flight. If you have dietary concerns, request special meals—vegetarian, low-cholesterol, or kosher, for example—when booking. It's a good idea to pack some healthful snacks and a small (plastic) bottle of water in your carry-on bag. On long flights, try to maintain a normal routine, to help fight jet lag. At night, get some sleep. By day, eat light meals, drink water (not alcohol), and **move around the cabin** to stretch your legs. For additional jet-lag tips, consult *Fodor's FYI: Travel Fit & Healthy* (available at bookstores everywhere).

Smoking policies vary from carrier to carrier. Many airlines prohibit smoking on all of their flights; others allow smoking only on certain routes or departures. There is no smoking on domestic flights in Spain.

FLYING TIMES

Flying time from New York is 7 hours; from London, just over 2; and from Sydney, 29 hours.

HOW TO COMPLAIN

If your baggage goes astray or your flight goes awry, complain right away. Most carriers require that you **file a claim immediately.** The Aviation Consumer Protection Division of the Department of Transportation publishes *Fly-Rights,* which discusses airlines and consumer issues and is available online. You can also find articles and information on www.mytravelrights.com, the Web site of the nonprofit Consumer Travel Rights Center.

⏳ Airline Complaints Aviation Consumer Protection Division ✉ U.S. Department of Transportation, Office of Aviation Enforcement and Proceedings, C-75, Room 4107, 400 7th St. SW, Washington, DC 20590 ☎ 202/366-2220 ⊕ airconsumer.ost.dot.gov. **Federal Aviation Administration Consumer Hotline** ✉ For inquiries: FAA, 800 Independence Ave. SW, Washington, DC 20591 ☎ 866/835-5322 ⊕ www.faa.gov.

RECONFIRMING

Check the status of your flight before you leave for the airport. You can do this on your carrier's Web site, by linking to a flight-status checker (many Web booking services offer these), or by calling your carrier or travel agent. Always confirm international flights at least 72 hours ahead of the scheduled departure time.

AIRPORTS

Most flights from the United States and Canada land in, or pass through, Madrid's Barajas (MAD). The other major gateway is Barcelona's El Prat de Llobregat (BCN). From England and elsewhere in Europe, regular flights also land in Málaga (AGP), Alicante (ALC), and Palma de Mallorca (PMI). Many of the new budget airlines flying from the United Kingdom to Barcelona land at the increasingly busy Girona airport, some 90 minutes north of Barcelona. The bus company Sagalés runs a shuttle service between Girona airport and Barcelona in conjunction with the departure and arrival times of Ryanair flights. Check the Web site (www.sagales.com) for timetables and fares.

⏳ Airport Information Madrid–Barajas ☎ 91/305-8343. **Barcelona–El Prat de Llobregat** ☎ 93/298-3838. **Girona–Girona** ☎ 972/186600. **Sagalés Buses** ☎ 93/231-2756 ⊕ www.sagales.com.

BIKE TRAVEL

Long distances, an abundance of hilly terrain, and unpleasant weather conditions (hot summers, rainy winters) make touring Spain by bike less than ideal for all but the fittest bikers. That said, Spain's numerous nature preserves are perfect for mountain biking, especially in spring and fall, and many have specially marked bike paths. It's usually better to rent a bike locally than deal with the logistics of bringing your own. Bikes are not usually allowed on trains, for instance; they must be packed and checked as luggage. At most nature preserves, at least one agency rents mountain bikes and, in many cases, leads guided bike tours. Check with the park's visitor center for details. In addition, rural hotels often make bikes available to guests, sometimes for free.

For general planning of cycle routes, Michelin maps are an excellent resource. The Michelin map (scale 1:100,000) of Spain and Portugal includes the Balearic and Canary Islands, and is detailed enough to include many minor roads. Michelin also has several Spain maps of a higher 1:200,000 to 1:400,000 scale. Also a good bet for cyclists are Kümmerly & Frey's detailed, 1:500,000-scale maps to Spain's different regions. Grupo Anaya's AA Road Map Spain and Portugal series includes 1:400,000-scale maps to all of Spain's regions. Higher-scale maps are considerably more detailed, so you may need more than one map per day if you are traveling long distances. You can find these maps in most large bookstores.

BIKES IN FLIGHT

Most airlines accommodate bikes as luggage, provided they are dismantled and boxed; check with individual airlines about packing requirements. Some airlines sell bike boxes for about $20 (bike bags can be considerably more expensive), but boxes are often free at bike shops. International travelers usually can substitute a bike for a piece of checked luggage at no charge; otherwise, the cost is about $100. Most U.S. and Canadian airlines charge $40 to $80 each way.

BOAT & FERRY TRAVEL

Regular car ferries connect the United Kingdom with northern Spain. Brittany Ferries sails from Plymouth to Santander, P&O European Ferries from Portsmouth to Bilbao. Trasmediterránea connects mainland Spain to the Balearic and Canary islands. If you want to drive from Spain to Morocco, you can take a car ferry from Málaga, Algeciras, or Tarifa, run by Trasmediterránea, which also offers a catamaran service that takes half the time

of the standard ferry. Buquebus runs ferries between Algeciras and Ceuta.

⚑ From the U.K. Brittany Ferries ☎ 0239/289-2200 ⊕ www.brittany-ferries.com. **P&O European Ferries** ☎ 0239/230-1000 ⊕ www.poferries.com. **⚑ In Spain** Buquebus ☎ 902/414242 ⊕ www.buquebus.es. **Trasmediterránea** ☎ 902/454645 ⊕ www.trasmediterranea.com.

BUSINESS HOURS

The ritual of a long afternoon siesta is no longer as ubiquitous as it once was. However, the tradition does remain, and many people take a post-lunch nap before returning to work or continuing on with their day. The two- to three-hour lunch makes it possible to eat and then snooze. Siestas generally begin at 1 or 2 and end between 4 and 5, depending on the city and the sort of business. The midafternoon siesta—often a half-hour power nap in front of the TV—fits naturally into the workday cycle, since Spaniards tend to work until 7 or 8 PM.

Traditionally, Spain's climate created the siesta as a time to preserve energy while afternoon temperatures spiked. After the sun began setting, Spaniards went back to working, shopping, and taking their leisurely *paseo*, or stroll. In the big cities—particularly with the advent of air-conditioning—the heat has less of an effect on the population; in the small towns in the south of Spain, however, many still use a siesta as a way to escape the heat.

Until a decade or so ago, it was common for many businesses to close for a month in the July/August period. Europeanization, changing trading hours, and a booming consumerism are gradually altering that custom. These days many small businesses are more likely to close down for two weeks only, maybe three. When open, they often run on a summer schedule, which can mean a longer-than-usual siesta break (sometimes up to four hours), a shorter working day (until 3 PM only), and no Saturday afternoon trading at all.

BANKS & OFFICES

Banks are generally open weekdays from 8:30 or 9 until 2 or 2:30. From October to May the major banks open on Saturday from 8:30 or 9 until 2 or 2:30, and savings banks are also open Thursday 4:30 to 8. Currency exchanges at airports, train stations, and in the city center stay open later; you can also cash traveler's checks at El Corte Inglés department stores until 10 PM (some branches close at 9 PM or 9:30 PM). Most government offices are open weekdays 9 to 2.

MUSEUMS & SIGHTS

Most museums are open from 9:30 to 2 and 4 to 7 six days a week, every day but Monday. Schedules are subject to change, particularly between the high and low seasons, so **confirm opening hours before you make plans.** A few large museums, such as Madrid's Prado and Reina Sofía and Barcelona's Picasso Museum, stay open all day, without a siesta.

PHARMACIES

Pharmacies keep normal business hours (9 to 1:30 and 5 to 8), but every midsize town (or city neighborhood) has a duty pharmacy that stays open 24 hours. The location of the duty pharmacy is usually posted on the front door of all pharmacies.

SHOPS

When planning a shopping trip, remember that **almost all shops in Spain close between 1 and 2 PM** for at least two hours. The only exceptions are large supermarkets and the department-store chain El Corte Inglés. Stores are generally open somewhere between 9 or 10 to 1:30 or 2 and from somewhere between 4 and 5 to 7:30 or 8. Most shops are closed on Sunday, and in Madrid and several other places they're also closed Saturday afternoon. Larger shops in tourist areas may stay open Sunday in summer and during the Christmas holiday.

BUS TRAVEL

Within Spain, a mix of private companies provide bus services that range from knee-crunchingly basic to luxurious. Fares are lower than the corresponding train fares, and service is more extensive: if you want to reach a town not served by train, you can be sure a bus goes there. Smaller towns don't usually have a central bus depot, so ask the tourist office where to

wait for the bus to your destination. Spain's major national long-haul bus line is **Alsa-Enatcar.** Note that service is less frequent on weekends. For a longer haul, you can travel to Spain by bus from London, Paris, Rome, Frankfurt, Prague, and other major European cities. It's a long journey, but the buses are modern. Although it may once have been the case that international bus travel was significantly cheaper than air travel, new budget airlines have changed the equation. For perhaps a little more money and a large saving of travel hours, flying is increasingly the better option. Smoking is prohibited on buses.

CLASSES

Most of Spain's larger bus companies have buses with comfortable seats and adequate legroom; on longer journeys (two hours or longer), a movie is shown on board, and earphones are provided. Except for smaller, regional buses that travel only short hops, all buses have a bathroom on board. Nonetheless, most long-haul buses usually stop at least once every two to three hours for a snack and bathroom break. Road and traffic conditions can make or break the journey; Spain's highways, particularly along major routes, are well maintained. That may not be the case in the country's more rural areas, where you could be in for a bumpy ride—sometimes exacerbated by older buses with worn shock absorbers. Alsa-Enatcar has two luxury classes in addition to its regular line. Supra Clase includes roomy leather seats and on-board meals; also, you have the option of *asientos individuales,* individual seats (with no other seat on either side) that line one side of the bus. The next class is the Eurobus, with comfortable seats and plenty of legroom. The Supra Clase and Eurobus usually cost, respectively, up to one-third and one-fourth more than the regular line.

CUTTING COSTS

If you plan to return to your initial destination, you can save by buying a round-trip ticket, instead of one-way. Also, some of Spain's smaller, regional bus lines offer multitrip bus passes, which are worthwhile if you plan to make multiple trips between two fixed destinations within the region. Generally, these tickets offer a savings of 20% per journey; you can buy these tickets only in the bus station (not on the bus). The general rule for children is that if they occupy a seat, they pay. Check the bus Web sites for deals (*ofertas*); you'll often find discounts for midweek and/or round-trip tickets to specific destinations.

FARES & SCHEDULES
In Spain's larger cities, you can pick up schedule and fare information at the bus station; smaller towns may not have a bus station but just a bus stop. Schedules are sometimes listed at the bus stop; otherwise, call the bus company directly or ask at the tourist office, which can usually supply all schedule and fare information.

PAYING
At bus station ticket counters, generally all major credit cards (except American Express) are accepted. If you buy your ticket on the bus, it's cash only. Traveler's checks are almost never accepted. Big lines such as Enatcar are now encouraging online purchasing. Once your ticket is booked, there's no need to go to the terminal sales desk—it's simply a matter of showing up at the bus with your ticket number and ID. The smaller regional services are increasingly providing online purchasing, too, but will often require that your ticket be picked up at the terminal sales desk.

RESERVATIONS
During peak travel times (Easter, August, and Christmas), it's a good idea to make a reservation at least a week in advance.
⚑ From the U.K. Eurolines/National Express ☎ 01582/404511 or 0990/143219 ⊕ www.eurolines. com.
⚑ In Spain Alsa-Enatcar ⊠ Estación Sur de Autobuses, Calle Méndez Álvaro, Madrid ☎ 902/422242 ⊕ www.enatcar.com.
⚑ Bus Tours Marsans ⊠ Gran Vía 59, Madrid ☎ 902/306090. **Pullmantur** ⊠ Plaza de Oriente 8, Madrid ☎ 91/541-1805 ⊕ www.pullmantur-spain.com.

CAMERAS & PHOTOGRAPHY
Spain is well served with places to have photos processed; such services are much cheaper than those at their European neighbors. The national chain Fotoprix is a one-stop shop for everything camera related, including processing and repairs. For digital camera users, Internet cafés are another option—some of the better ones have staff members who will assist with saving movies and stills.

All major brands of film are readily available in Spain, and at reasonable prices. Try to buy film in large stores or photography shops; film sold in smaller outlets may be out-of-date or stored in poor conditions. To have film developed, **look for shops displaying the Kodak Q-Lab sign,** a guarantee of quality. If you're in a real hurry and happen to be in a large town or resort, you will, of course, find shops that will process film in a few hours. X-ray machines in Spanish airports are said to be film-safe. The *Kodak Guide to Shooting Great Travel Pictures* (available at bookstores everywhere) is loaded with tips.
⚑ Photo Help Kodak Information Center ☎ 800/242-2424 ⊕ www.kodak.com.

CAR RENTAL
Alamo, Avis, Budget, Europcar, Hertz, and National (partnered in Spain with the Spanish agency Atesa) have branches at major Spanish airports and in large cities. Smaller, regional companies and wholesalers offer lower rates. All agencies have a range of models, but virtually all cars in Spain have a manual transmission—**if you don't want a stick shift, reserve weeks in advance and specify automatic transmission,** then call to reconfirm your automatic car before you leave for Spain. Rates in Madrid begin at the equivalents of U.S. $65 a day and $300 a week for an economy car with air-conditioning, manual transmission, and unlimited mileage. Add to this a 16% tax on car rentals. Although you should always rent the size car that makes you feel safest, a small car, aside from saving you money, is prudent for the tiny roads and parking spaces in many parts of Spain.
⚑ Rental Agencies Alamo ☎ 800/522-9696 ⊕ www.alamo.com. **Avis** ☎ 800/331-1084, 800/272-5871 in Canada, 0870/606-0100 in U.K., 02/9353-9000 in Australia, 09/526-2847 in New

Zealand, 902/135531 in Spain ⊕ www.avis.com.
Budget ☎ 800/527-0700, 800/268-8900 in
Canada, 0870/156-5656 in U.K., 13/0036-2848 in
Australia, 08/0028-3438 in New Zealand, 901/201212
in Spain ⊕ www.budget.com. **Europcar** ☎ 902/
105030 in Spain ⊕ www.europcar.es. **Hertz** ☎ 800/
654-3001, 800/263-0600 in Canada, 0870/844-8844
in U.K., 02/9669-2444 in Australia, 09/256-8690 in
New Zealand, 902/402405 in Spain ⊕ www.hertz.
com. **National Car Rental/Atesa** ☎ 800/227-7368,
0870/600-6666 in U.K., 902/100101 in Spain
⊕ www.nationalcar.com or www.atesa.es.

CUTTING COSTS

For a good deal, book through a travel
agent who will shop around. Do look into
wholesalers, companies that do not own
fleets but rent in bulk from those that do
and often offer better rates than traditional car-rental operations. Prices are best
during off-peak periods. Rentals booked
through wholesalers often must be paid
for before you leave home.

🔃 **Wholesalers** **Auto Europe** ☎ 207/842-2000 or
800/223-5555 ☐ 207/842-2222 ⊕ www.
autoeurope.com. **Europe by Car** ☎ 212/581-3040 or
800/223-1516 ☐ 212/246-1458 ⊕ www.europebycar.
com. **Kemwel** ☎ 877/820-0668 or 800/678-0678
☐ 207/842-2286 ⊕ www.kemwel.com.

INSURANCE

When driving a rented car you are generally responsible for any damage to or loss
of the vehicle. Collision policies that car-
rental companies sell for European rentals
typically do not cover stolen vehicles. Before you rent—and purchase collision or
theft coverage—see what coverage you already have under the terms of your own
auto-insurance policy and credit cards.

REQUIREMENTS & RESTRICTIONS

Anyone over 18 with a valid license can
drive in Spain, but some rental agencies
will not rent cars to drivers under 21.

SURCHARGES

Before you pick up a car in one city and
leave it in another, ask about drop-off
charges or one-way service fees, which
can be substantial. Also inquire about
early-return policies; some rental agencies
charge extra if you return the car before
the time specified in your contract,

whereas others give you a refund for the
days not used. To avoid a hefty refueling
fee, fill the tank just before you turn in
the car, but be aware that gas stations
near the rental outlet may overcharge. It's
almost never a deal to buy the tank of gas
that's in the car when you rent it; the understanding is that you'll return it empty,
but some fuel usually remains.

CAR TRAVEL

Your own driver's license is valid in Spain,
but you may want to get an International
Driver's Permit for extra assurance, as
having one may save you a problem with
local authorities. Permits are available
from the American or Canadian Automobile Association (AAA or CAA), or, in
the United Kingdom, from the Automobile
Association or Royal Automobile Club
(AA or RAC). These international permits,
valid only in conjunction with your regular driver's license (so have both on hand),
are universally recognized.

Driving is the best way to see Spain's rural
areas. The main cities are connected by a
network of excellent four-lane *autovías*
(freeways) and *autopistas* (toll freeways;
toll is *peaje*), which are designated with
the letter A and have speed limits of up to
120 km/h (74 mph). The letter N indicates
a *carretera nacional* (basic national route),
which may have four or two lanes. Smaller
towns and villages are connected by a network of secondary roads maintained by
regional, provincial, and local governments. Spain's major routes bear heavy
traffic, especially during holidays. Drive
with care: Spain has a yearly road toll that
is ghastly—most accidents are speed related. The roads are shared by a poten-
tially perilous mixture of local drivers and
non-Spanish vacationers, some of whom
are accustomed to driving on the left side
of the road. Be prepared, too, for heavy
truck traffic on national routes, which, in
the case of two-lane roads, can have you
creeping along for hours.

EMERGENCY SERVICES

The rental agencies Hertz and Avis have
24-hour breakdown service. If you belong
to an auto club (AAA, CAA, or AA), you

can get emergency assistance from the Spanish counterpart, RACE.

🚩 **RACE** ✉ José Abascal 10, Madrid ☎ 900/200093.

GASOLINE

Gas stations are plentiful, and most on major routes and in big cities are open 24 hours. On less-traveled routes, gas stations are usually open 7 AM to 11 PM. If a gas station is closed, it's required by law to post the address and directions to the nearest open station—but this is rarely adhered to, so plan your trip carefully. Most stations are self-service, though prices are the same as those at full-service stations. You punch in the amount of gas you want (in euros, not in liters), unhook the nozzle, pump the gas, and then pay. At night, however, you must pay before you fill up. Most pumps offer a choice of gas, including leaded, unleaded, and diesel, so **be careful to pick the right one** for your car. All newer cars in Spain use *gasolina sin plomo* (unleaded gas), which is available in two grades, 95 and 98 octane. *Super,* regular 97-octane leaded gas, is gradually being phased out. Prices vary little among stations and were at press time €1 a liter for leaded, 97 octane; €0.94 a liter for *sin plomo* (unleaded; 95 octane), and €1 a liter for unleaded, 98 octane. Credit cards are widely accepted.

ROAD CONDITIONS

Spain's highway system includes some 6,000 km (3,600 mi) of beautifully maintained superhighways. Still, you'll find some stretches of major national highways that are only two lanes wide, where traffic often backs up behind slow, heavy trucks. *Autopista* tolls are steep, but as a result, these highways are often less crowded than the free ones. If you're driving down through Catalonia, be aware that there are more tolls here than anywhere else in Spain. This can result in a quicker journey, but at a sizeable cost. If you spring for the autopistas, you'll find that many of the rest stops are nicely landscaped and have cafeterias with reasonable but overpriced food. Rather than ordering a plate of food, a cheese or ham *bocadillo* (baguette-style

sandwich) offers a much cheaper and often tastier alternative.

Most Spanish cities have notoriously long morning and evening rush hours. Traffic jams are especially bad in and around Barcelona and Madrid. If possible, **avoid the morning rush, which can last until noon, and the evening rush, which lasts from 7 to 9.** Also be aware that on the dates corresponding to the beginning, the middle, and the end of July and August, the country suffers its worst traffic jams (delays of six to eight hours are common) as millions of Spaniards embark on, or return from, their annual vacations.

ROAD MAPS

Detailed road maps are readily available at major bookstores, some *kioskos* (newsagents), and gas stations.

RULES OF THE ROAD

Spaniards drive on the right; they also pass on the right—so stay in the left-hand slow lane when not passing. Horns are banned in cities, but that doesn't keep people from blasting away. Children under 10 may not ride in the front seat, and seat belts are compulsory for both front and backseat riders. Speed limits are 50 km/h (31 mph) in cities, 100 km/h (62 mph) on N roads, 120 km/h (74 mph) on the *autopista* or *autovía,* and, unless otherwise signposted, 90 km/h (56 mph) on other roads.

Spanish highway police are increasingly vigilant about speeding and illegal passing. Fines start at €90, and police are empowered to demand payment from non-Spanish drivers on the spot. **It is an unfortunate reality that rental-car drivers are disproportionately targeted by police for speeding and illegal passing, so play it safe.**

Although local drivers, especially in cities such as Madrid, will park their cars just about anywhere, you should **park only in legal spots.** Parking fines are steep, and your car might well be towed, resulting in fines, hassles, and wasted time.

CHILDREN IN SPAIN

Children are greatly indulged in Spain. You can see kids accompanying their parents everywhere, including bars and restaurants. Shopkeepers often offer kids *caramelos* (sweets), and even the coldest waiters tend to be friendlier when you have a youngster with you, so you won't be shunted into a remote corner. However, you won't find high chairs or children's menus; kids are expected to eat what their parents do, so it's perfectly acceptable to ask for an extra plate and share your food. Be prepared for late bedtimes, especially in summer—it's common to see toddlers playing cheerfully outdoors until midnight.

Because children are expected to be with their parents at all times, few hotels provide babysitting services; but those that don't can often refer you to an independent babysitter (*canguro*). If you are renting a car, don't forget to arrange for a car seat when you reserve. For general advice about traveling with children, consult *Fodor's FYI: Travel with Your Baby* (available in bookstores everywhere).

FLYING

If your children are two or older, ask about children's airfares. As a general rule, infants under two not occupying a seat fly at greatly reduced fares or even for free. But if you want to guarantee a seat for an infant, you have to pay full fare. Consider flying during off-peak days and times; most airlines will grant an infant a seat without a ticket if there are available seats. When booking, confirm carry-on allowances if you're traveling with infants. In general, for babies charged 10% to 50% of the adult fare you are allowed one carry-on bag and a collapsible stroller; if the flight is full, the stroller may have to be checked or you may be limited to less.

Experts agree that it's a good idea to use safety seats aloft for children weighing less than 40 pounds. Airlines set their own policies: if you use a safety seat, U.S. carriers usually require that the child be ticketed, even if he or she is young enough to ride free, because the seats must be strapped into regular seats. And even if you pay the full adult fare for the seat, it may be worth it, especially on longer trips. **Docheck your airline's policy about using safety seats during takeoff and landing.** Safety seats are not allowed everywhere in the plane, so get your seat assignments as early as possible.

When reserving, request children's meals and a freestanding bassinet (not available with all airlines) if you need them. But note that bulkhead seats, where you must sit to use the bassinet, may lack an overhead bin or storage space on the floor.

FOOD

Visiting children may turn up their noses at some of Spain's regional specialties. Although kids seldom get their own menus, most restaurants are happy to provide them with simple dishes—plain grilled chicken, steak, or fried potatoes, for example. However, if a special request for food at lunchtime falls outside what is offered on the *menú del día* (the cheap three-course meal that most Spanish restaurants offer in the daytime), be prepared to pay extra. *Pescadito frito* (batter-fried fish) and *albondigas* (meatballs) are Spanish dishes that most kids seem to enjoy. If all else fails, chains such as McDonald's, Burger King, and Pizza Hut are well represented in the major cities and popular resorts. Spain's two leading fast-food chains, Pans y Company and Bocatta, have sandwiches, salads, and fries, and both offer specials and a kids' menu, sometimes with prizes and toys.

LODGING

Most hotels in Spain allow children under a certain age to stay in their parents' room at no extra charge, but others charge for them as extra adults; be sure to find out the cutoff age for children's discounts.

SIGHTS & ATTRACTIONS

Places that are especially appealing to children are indicated by a rubber-duckie icon (☺) in the margin. Museum admissions and bus and metro rides are generally free for children up to age five.

SUPPLIES & EQUIPMENT

Disposable diapers (*pañales*), formula (*leche maternizada*), and jars of baby food (*papillas*) are readily available at supermarkets and pharmacies.

CONSULATES & EMBASSIES

🇦🇺 Australia Madrid ⊠ Plaza del Descubridor Diego de Ordás 3, Chamberí ☎ 91/441-9300.

Seville ✉ Federico Rubio 14, Santa Cruz ☎ 95/422-0971 or 95/422-0240.
🇨🇦 Canada **Madrid** ✉ C. Nuñez de Balboa 35, Salamanca ☎ 91/423-3250. **Málaga** ✉ Pl. de la Malagueta 3 ☎ 952/223346.
🇳🇿 New Zealand **Madrid** ✉ Plaza de Lealtad 2, Centro ☎ 91/523-0226.
🇬🇧 United Kingdom **Madrid** ✉ C. Fernando el Santo 19, Chamberí ☎ 91/700-8200. **Málaga** ✉ Mauricio Moro 2 ☎ 952/352300.
🇺🇸 United States **Fuengirola** ✉ Av. Juan Goméz 8, Apt. 1c ☎ 952/474891. **Madrid** ✉ C. Serrano 75, Salamanca ☎ 91/587-2200. **Seville** ✉ Paseo de las Delicias 7, Arenal ☎ 95/423-1885.

COMPUTERS ON THE ROAD

The Internet boom came a bit late to Spain, with few or limited Internet cafés in the big cities at the turn of this century. But all that has changed, and the Internet is now in full swing. Huge increases in migration to the country's bigger cities means demand has skyrocketed for *locutorios* (cheap international phone centers), which double as places to get on the Internet. In addition to the locutorios, where Internet access is not always reliable, there are up-market cafés and bars that provide Internet service, often at faster speeds. The most you're likely to pay for Internet access is about €3 an hour.

Internet cafés are most common in tourist and student precincts. If you can't find one easily, ask at either the tourist office or a hotel's front desk. There's no perfect guide to the many cybercafés in Spain, but Ocio Latino's Web site (www.ociolatino.com) is probably the best. Click on "Guía Latina" and then "locutorios."

Internet access within Spanish hotels is not widespread and tends to be offered only in the more expensive hotels. (And those that do offer Internet access have varying services: Internet kiosks or rooms, in-room data ports or DSL, and/or Wi-Fi (either free or with a fee; sometimes in-room, sometimes in common areas).

CONSUMER PROTECTION

Credit-card fraud is common in Spain, so it's obligatory to show proof of ID when making purchases, no matter how small. ID must include a picture and signature. A passport is the most secure option—some shops will not accept alternatives. Be aware that although shops such as boutiques and major stores accept major credit cards, smaller businesses often do not. Large restaurants accept cards, but the typical local bar in many cases will not. Taxis may or may not accept cards; the post office does not.

Whether you're shopping for gifts or purchasing travel services, **pay with a major credit card** whenever possible, so you can cancel payment or get reimbursed if there's a problem (and you can provide documentation). Also, if you're buying a package or tour, always consider travel insurance that includes default coverage (⇨ Insurance).

CRUISE TRAVEL

Barcelona is the busiest cruise port in Spain and Europe. Other popular ports of call in the country are Gilbraltar, Málaga, Alicante, and Palma de Mallorca. Although cruise lines such as Silversea and Costa traditionally offer cruises that take in parts of Spain and other Mediterranean countries such as Italy and Greece, it is becoming increasingly common to package tours wholly within Spain. Two popular routes consist of island-hopping in the Balaerics or around the Canary Islands. Among the many cruise lines that call on Spain are Royal Caribbean, Holland America Line, Renaissance Cruises, the Norwegian Cruise Line, and Princess Cruises. To learn how to plan, choose, and book a cruise-ship voyage, consult *Fodor's FYI: Plan & Enjoy Your Cruise* (available in bookstores everywhere).

CUSTOMS & DUTIES

When shopping abroad, keep receipts for all purchases. Upon reentering the country, **be ready to show customs officials what you've bought.** Pack purchases together in an easily accessible place. If you think a duty is incorrect, appeal the assessment. If you object to the way your clearance was handled, note the inspector's badge number. In either case, first ask to see a supervisor. If the problem isn't resolved, write to the appropriate authorities, beginning with the port director at your point of entry.

IN AUSTRALIA

Australian residents who are 18 or older may bring home A$400 worth of souvenirs and gifts (including jewelry), 250 cigarettes or 250 grams of cigars or other tobacco products, and 1,125 ml of alcohol (including wine, beer, and spirits). Residents under 18 may bring back A$200 worth of goods. Members of the same family traveling together may pool their allowances. Prohibited items include meat products. Seeds, plants, and fruits need to be declared upon arrival.

🛃 **Australian Customs Service** 🗐 Regional Director, Box 8, Sydney, NSW 2001 ☎ 02/9213-2000 or 1300/363263, 02/9364-7222 or 1800/020-504 quarantine-inquiry line 📠 02/9213-4043 ⊕ www. customs.gov.au.

IN CANADA

Canadian residents who have been out of Canada for at least seven days may bring in C$750 worth of goods duty-free. If you've been away fewer than seven days but more than 48 hours, the duty-free allowance drops to C$200. If your trip lasts 24 to 48 hours, the allowance is C$50. You may not pool allowances with family members. Goods claimed under the C$750 exemption may follow you by mail; those claimed under the lesser exemptions must accompany you. Alcohol and tobacco products may be included in the seven-day and 48-hour exemptions but not in the 24-hour exemption. If you meet the age requirements of the province or territory through which you reenter Canada, you may bring in, duty-free, 1.5 liters of wine or 1.14 liters (40 imperial ounces) of liquor or 24 12-ounce cans or bottles of beer or ale. Also, if you meet the local age requirement for tobacco products, you may bring in, duty-free, 200 cigarettes and 50 cigars. Check ahead of time with the Canada Customs and Revenue Agency or the Department of Agriculture for policies regarding meat products, seeds, plants, and fruits.

You may send an unlimited number of gifts (only one gift per recipient, however) worth up to C$60 each duty-free to Canada. Label the package UNSOLICITED GIFT—VALUE UNDER $60. Alcohol and tobacco are excluded.

🛃 **Canada Customs and Revenue Agency** ✉ 2265 St. Laurent Blvd., Ottawa, Ontario K1G 4K3 ☎ 800/461-9999 in Canada, 204/983-3500, 506/636-5064 ⊕ www.ccra.gc.ca.

IN NEW ZEALAND

All homeward-bound residents may bring back NZ$700 worth of souvenirs and gifts; passengers may not pool their allowances, and children can claim only the concession on goods intended for their own use. For those 17 or older, the duty-free allowance also includes 4.5 liters of wine or beer; one 1,125-ml bottle of spirits; and either 200 cigarettes, 250 grams of tobacco, 50 cigars, *or* a combination of the three up to 250 grams. Meat products, seeds, plants, and fruits must be declared upon arrival to the Agricultural Services Department.

🛃 **New Zealand Customs** ✉ Head office: The Customhouse, 17-21 Whitmore St., Box 2218, Wellington ☎ 09/300-5399 or 0800/428-786 ⊕ www.customs.govt.nz.

IN THE U.K.

If you're a U.K. resident and your journey was wholly within the European Union, you probably won't have to pass through customs when you return to the United Kingdom. If you plan to bring back large quantities of alcohol or tobacco, check EU limits beforehand. In most cases, if you bring back more than 200 cigars, 3,200 cigarettes, 400 cigarillos, 10 liters of spirits, 110 liters of beer, 20 liters of fortified wine, and/or 90 liters of wine, you have to declare the goods upon return. Prohibited items include unpasteurized milk, regardless of country of origin.

🛃 **HM Customs and Excise** ✉ Portcullis House, 21 Cowbridge Rd. E, Cardiff CF11 9SS ☎ 0845/010-9000 or 0208/929-0152 advice service, 0208/929-6731 or 0208/910-3602 complaints ⊕ www.hmce.gov.uk.

IN THE U.S.

U.S. residents who have been out of the country for at least 48 hours may bring home, for personal use, $800 worth of foreign goods duty-free, as long as they haven't used the $800 allowance or any part of it in the past 30 days. This exemption may include 1 liter of alcohol (for travelers 21 and older), 200 cigarettes, and 100 non-Cuban cigars. Family members from the same household who are traveling together may pool their $800 personal exemptions. For fewer than 48 hours, the duty-free allowance drops to $200, which may include 50 cigarettes, 10 non-Cuban cigars, and 150 ml of alcohol (or 150 ml of perfume containing alcohol). The $200 allowance cannot be combined with other individuals' exemptions, and if you exceed it, the full value of all the goods will be taxed. Antiques, which U.S. Customs and Border Protection defines as objects more than 100 years old, enter duty-free, as do original works of art done entirely by hand, including paintings, drawings, and sculptures (but not including folk art or handicrafts.

You may send packages home duty-free, with a limit of one parcel per addressee per day (except alcohol or tobacco products or perfume worth more than $5). You can mail up to $200 worth of goods for personal use; label the package PERSONAL USE and attach a list of its contents and their retail value. If the package contains your used personal belongings, mark it AMERICAN GOODS RETURNED to avoid paying duties. You may send up to $100 worth of goods as a gift; mark the package UNSOLICITED GIFT. Mailed items do not affect your duty-free allowance on your return.

To avoid paying duty on foreign-made high-ticket items you already own and will take on your trip, register them with customs before you leave the country. Consider filing a Certificate of Registration for laptops, cameras, watches, and other digital devices identified with serial numbers or other permanent markings; you can keep the certificate for other trips. Otherwise, bring a sales receipt or insurance form to show that you owned the item before you left the United States.

For more about duties, restricted items, and other information about international travel, check out U.S. Customs and Border Protection's online brochure, *Know Before You Go.*

🛈 **U.S. Customs and Border Protection** ✉ For inquiries and equipment registration, 1300 Pennsylvania Ave. NW, Washington, DC 20229 ⊕ www.cbp. gov ☎ 877/287-8667 or 202/354-1000 ✉ For complaints, Customer Satisfaction Unit, 1300 Pennsylvania Ave. NW, Room 5.2C, Washington, DC 20229.

IN SPAIN

From countries that are not part of the European Union, visitors age 15 and over may *enter* Spain duty-free with up to 200 cigarettes or 50 cigars, up to 1 liter of alcohol over 22 proof, and up to 2 liters of wine. Dogs and cats are admitted as long as they have up-to-date vaccination records from their home country.

DISABILITIES & ACCESSIBILITY

Unfortunately, Spain has made only modest advances in making traveling easy for visitors with disabilities, but in cities such as Barcelona tighter laws are making major improvements in incorporating disabled access into new buildings both public and private. The Prado and some newer museums, such as Madrid's Reina Sofía and Thyssen-Bornemisza, have wheelchair-accessible entrances or elevators. In Granada, the palacios and most of the gardens of the Alhambra are wheelchair accessible. In Barcelona, the Institut Municipal de Persones amb Disminució provides a list of sights with wheelchair access and advice on getting around the city. Accessible Barcelona provides excellent information in English on everything from getting around to wheelchair-friendly tourist sites, bars, and restaurants, as well as a comprehensive list of emergency numbers. With four days' notice the organization will also coordinate transportation in wheelchair-accessible taxis. Note that most churches, castles, and monasteries on any group itinerary will involve a lot of walking, often on uneven terrain.

🛈 Local Resources If you're calling from outside Spain, you need to first dial country code 34. **Accessible Barcelona** ☎ 66/583-8424 ⊕ www. accessiblebarcelona.com **Institut Municipal de Persones amb Disminució** ✉ Av. Diagonal 233, Barcelona 08013 ☎ 93/413-2840 🖷 93/413-2800.

RESERVATIONS

When discussing accessibility with an operator or reservations agent, ask hard questions. Are there any stairs, inside *or* out? Are there grab bars next to the toilet *and* in the shower/tub? How wide is the doorway to the room? To the bathroom? For the most extensive facilities meeting the latest legal specifications, opt for newer accommodations. If you reserve through a toll-free number, consider also calling the hotel's local number to confirm the information from the central reservations office. Get confirmation in writing when you can.

TRANSPORTATION

🔊 Complaints **Aviation Consumer Protection Division** (⇨ Air Travel) for airline-related problems. **Departmental Office of Civil Rights** ✉ For general inquiries, U.S. Department of Transportation, S-30, 400 7th St. SW, Room 10215, Washington, DC 20590 ☎ 202/366-4648 🖷 202/366-9371 ⊕ www.dot. gov/ost/docr/index.htm. **Disability Rights Section** ✉ NYAV, U.S. Department of Justice, Civil Rights Division, 950 Pennsylvania Ave. NW, Washington, DC 20530 ☎ ADA information line 202/514-0301, 800/ 514-0301, 202/514-0383 TTY, 800/514-0383 TTY ⊕ www.ada.gov. **U.S. Department of Transportation Hotline** ☎ For disability-related air-travel problems, 800/778-4838 or 800/455-9880 TTY.

TRAVEL AGENCIES

In the United States, the Americans with Disabilities Act requires that travel firms serve the needs of all travelers; however, some agencies specialize in working with people who have disabilities.

🔊 Travelers with Mobility Problems **Access Adventures/B. Roberts Travel** ✉ 206 Chestnut Ridge Rd., Scottsville, NY 14624 ☎ 585/889-9096 ✍ dltravel@prodigy.net ⊕ www.brobertstravel.com, run by a former physical-rehabilitation counselor. **CareVacations** ✉ No. 5, 5110-50 Ave., Leduc, Alberta, Canada, T9E 6V4 ☎ 780/986-6404 or 877/478-7827 🖷 780/986-8332 ⊕ www.carevacations.com, for group tours and cruise vacations. **Flying Wheels Travel** ✉ 143 W. Bridge St., Box 382, Owatonna, MN 55060 ☎ 507/451-5005 🖷 507/451-1685 ⊕ www. flyingwheelstravel.com.

🔊 Travelers with Developmental Disabilities **Sprout** ✉ 893 Amsterdam Ave., New York, NY 10025 ☎ 212/222-9575 or 888/222-9575 🖷 212/222-9768 ⊕ www.gosprout.org.

EATING & DRINKING

Sitting around a table eating and talking is a huge part of Spanish culture, defining much of people's daily routines. Sitting in the middle of a typical bustling restaurant here goes a long way toward showing how fundamental food can be to Spanish lives.

Although Spain has always had an extraordinary range of regional cuisine, in the past decade or so its restaurants have won it international recognition at the highest levels. A new generation of Spanish chefs—led by the revolutionary Ferran Adrià—has transformed classic dishes to suit contemporary tastes, drawing on some of the freshest ingredients in Europe.

One of the major drawbacks of drinking and eating in Spanish bars and restaurants has been the unbridled smoking in almost all of them. The new antismoking laws introduced by the national government at the beginning of 2006 is changing all that. Establishments within shopping malls, theaters, and cinemas are now strictly nonsmoking. All establishments that measure 100 meters squared or more are obliged to provide a nonsmoking section. Children must eat in this space. However, establishments smaller than this size retain the option for the time being to permit smoking across the board or to ban it altogether. With a few exceptions, the proprietors of these establishments have maintained the status quo, presumably because of the fact that one in three Spaniards smoke, and they are fearful of losing clients. This may change over time as locals become more accustomed to the new regulations forbidding smoking in public places, shops, and places of work. All eating and drinking establishments are obliged to inform clients by posting a sign at the entrance. *Se permite fumar* means you can smoke, *No se permite fumar* means you can't, and *Sala habilitada para no fumadores* means a nonsmoking section is available.

The restaurants we list are the cream of the crop in each price category. Properties indicated by an ✕🏠 are lodging establishments whose restaurant warrants a special trip.

MEALS & SPECIALTIES

Most restaurants in Spain do not serve breakfast (*desayuno*); for coffee and carbs, head to a bar or *cafetería*. Outside major hotels, which serve morning buffets, breakfast in Spain is usually limited to coffee and toast or a roll. Lunch (*comida* or *almuerzo*) traditionally consists of an appetizer, a main course, and dessert, followed by coffee and perhaps a liqueur. Between lunch and dinner the best way to snack is to sample some tapas (appetizers) at a bar; normally you can choose from quite a variety. Dinner (*cena*) is somewhat lighter, with perhaps only one course. In addition to an à la carte menu, most restaurants offer a daily fixed-price menu (*menú del día*), consisting of two courses, wine, and dessert at a very attractive price (usually between €6 and €12). Coffee usually costs extra. If your waiter does not suggest the menú del día when you're seated, ask for it—"*Hay menú del día, por favor?*" Restaurants in many of the larger tourist areas will have the menú del día posted outside. The menú del día is traditionally offered only at lunch, but increasingly it's also offered at dinner in popular tourist destinations.

MEALTIMES

Mealtimes in Spain are later than elsewhere in Europe, and later still in Madrid and the southern region of Andalusia. Lunch starts around 2 or 2:30 (closer to 3 in Madrid), and dinner after 9 (later in Madrid). Weekend eating times, especially dinner, can begin upward of about an hour later. In areas with heavy tourist traffic, some restaurants open a bit earlier. Unless otherwise noted, the restaurants listed in this guide are open daily for lunch and dinner.

PAYING

Credit cards are widely accepted in Spanish restaurants, but beware that smaller establishments often do not take them. If you pay by credit card and you want to leave a small tip above and beyond the service charge, leave the tip in cash.

RESERVATIONS & DRESS

Reservations are always a good idea; we mention them only when they're essential or not accepted. Book as far ahead as you can, and reconfirm as soon as you arrive. (Large parties should always call ahead to check the reservations policy.) We mention dress only when men are required to wear a jacket or a jacket and tie.

WINE, BEER & SPIRITS

Apart from its famous wines, Spain produces many brands of lager, the most popular of which are San Miguel, Cruzcampo, Aguila, Mahou, and Estrella. Jerez de la Frontera is Europe's largest producer of brandy and is a major source of sherry. Catalonia produces most of the world's *cava* (sparkling wine). Spanish law prohibits the sale of alcohol to people under 18.

ELECTRICITY

To use electric-powered equipment purchased in the United States or Canada, **bring a converter and adapter.** Spain's electrical current is 220 volts, 50 cycles alternating current (AC); wall outlets take Continental-type plugs, with two round prongs. If your appliances are dual-voltage, you'll need only an adapter. Don't use 110-volt outlets marked FOR SHAVERS ONLY for high-wattage appliances such as blow dryers. Most laptops operate equally well on 110 and 220 volts and so require only an adapter.

EMERGENCIES

The pan-European **emergency phone number** (☎ 112) is operative in some parts of Spain, but not all. If it doesn't work, dial the emergency numbers below for the national police, local police, fire department, or medical services. On the road, there are emergency phones marked SOS at regular intervals on *autovías* (freeways) and *autopistas* (toll highways). If your documents are stolen, contact both the local police and your embassy. If you lose a credit card, phone the issuer immediately (⇨ Money Matters).

🆘 **National police** ☎ 091. **Local police** ☎ 092. **Fire department** ☎ 080. **Medical service** ☎ 061.

ENGLISH-LANGUAGE MEDIA

In cities and major resorts, you'll have no trouble finding newspapers and magazines in English. U.K. newspapers are available on the day of publication. You'll also see major news magazines, along with *USA*

Today and the *International Herald Tribune*. The *Tribune* includes a news section about Spain in English, provided by *El Pais*.

NEWSPAPERS & MAGAZINES

Several major cities and resorts in Spain have local English-language publications, including Madrid (the monthly *Broadsheet*); Barcelona (the monthly *Barcelona Metropolitan;* Alicante (the weekly *Costa Blanca News, Post,* and *Entertainer*); Málaga (the weekly *Sur, Entertainer,* and *Costa del Sol News* and the monthly magazines *Essential* and *Absolute Marbella*); Majorca (the *Majorca Daily Bulletin*); Ibiza (the *Ibiza Sun*); and the Canary Islands (the biweekly *Island Connections, Island Sun, Paper,* and *Tenerife News*). Distributed throughout the country are the U.K.–published monthly *Spain,* Spanish magazine, and *Everything Spanish,* with articles on travel, lifestyle, property, and gastronomy. The online English language site www.Spainmedia.com provides summaries and detailed analysis of daily news across Spain.

TELEVISION & RADIO

Spain is served by two state-owned national channels, two private networks, regional channels in some parts of Spain, and local channels serving individual towns. Many hotels have satellite service, which usually includes at least one news channel in English (CNN, BBC World, or Sky News). There are no national English-language radio stations; most of the English-language radio stations in Spain are in the south of Spain (Costa del Sol) and the Canaries, catering mostly to the British population.

ETIQUETTE & BEHAVIOR

The Spanish are very tolerant of foreigners and their different ways, but you should always behave with courtesy. In some cities there has been enormously politically charged debate about civil behavior—in Barcelona, for instance, many bars are putting their foot down and refusing to serve people entering in bathing suits; similarly, some town councils are cracking down on the wearing of such attire in public spaces. Use your common sense—it's

unlikely you'd be allowed entry in a bar or restaurant wearing swimming attire back home, so don't do it when overseas. Be respectful when visiting churches: casual dress is fine if it's not gaudy or unkempt. Spaniards object to men going bare-chested anywhere other than the beach or poolside and generally do not look kindly on public displays of drunkenness. When addressing Spaniards with whom you are not well acquainted or who are elderly, use the formal *usted* rather than the familiar *tu* (⇨ Language, *below*).

BUSINESS ETIQUETTE

Spanish office hours can be confusing to the uninitiated. Some offices stay open more or less continuously from 9 to 3, with a very short lunch break. Others open in the morning, break up the day with a long lunch break of two to three hours, then reopen at 4 or 5 until 7 or 8. Spaniards enjoy a certain notoriety for their lack of punctuality, but this has changed dramatically in recent years, and you are expected to show up for meetings on time. Smart dress is the norm.

Spaniards in international fields tend to conduct business with foreigners in English. If you speak Spanish, address new colleagues with the formal *usted* and the corresponding verb conjugations, then follow their lead in switching to the familiar *tu* once a working relationship has been established.

GAY & LESBIAN TRAVEL

In summer the beaches of the Balearics (especially Ibiza), the Costa Brava (Sitges and Lloret del Mar), the Costa Blanca (Benidorm), and the Costa del Sol (Torremolinos) are gay and lesbian hot spots. Bigger cities such as Barcelona, Madrid, and Valencia all have thriving gay and lesbian scenes. Violence against gays does occur, but it's generally restricted to the rougher areas of very large cities.

🏳 Gay- & Lesbian-Friendly Travel Agencies Different Roads Travel ✉ 155 Palm Colony Palm Springs, CA 92264 ☎ 310/289-6000 or 800/429-8747 📠 310/855-0323 📧 lgernert@tzell.com. Skylink Travel and Tour/Flying Dutchmen Travel ✉ 1455 N. Dutton Ave., Suite A, Santa Rosa, CA

95401 ☎ 707/546-9888 or 800/225-5759 🖷 707/636-0951; serving lesbian travelers.

HEALTH

Medical care is good in Spain, but nursing is perfunctory, as relatives are expected to stop by and look after patients' needs. In some popular destinations, such as the Costa del Sol, there are volunteer English interpreters on hand. In 2004, Spain was documented by the World Health Organization as having the highest number of cumulative AIDS cases in Europe, and like many European countries, it is once again experiencing increased rate of HIV infections. If you're applying for a work permit, you'll be asked for proof that you are HIV-negative.

OVER-THE-COUNTER REMEDIES

Over-the-counter remedies are available at any *farmacia* (pharmacy), recognizable by the large green crosses outside. Some will look familiar, such as *aspirina* (aspirin), and other medications are sold under various brand names. If you get traveler's diarrhea, ask for *un antidiarreico* (the general term for antidiarrheal medicine); Fortasec is a well-known brand. Mild cases may respond to Imodium (known generically as loperamide) or Pepto-Bismol. To keep from getting dehydrated, drink plenty of purified water or herbal tea. In severe cases, rehydrate yourself with a salt-sugar solution—½ teaspoon salt (*sal*) and 4 tablespoons sugar (*azúcar*) per quart of water.

If you regularly take a nonprescription medicine, take a sample box or bottle with you, and the Spanish pharmacist will provide you with its local equivalent.

MEDICAL PLANS

No one plans to get sick while traveling, but it happens, so consider signing up with a medical-assistance company. Members get doctor referrals, emergency evacuation or repatriation, hotlines for medical consultation, cash for emergencies, and other assistance.

🔒 **Medical-Assistance Companies International SOS Assistance** ⊕ www.internationalsos.com ✉ 8 Neshaminy Interplex, Suite 207, Trevose, PA 19053 ☎ 215/245-4707 or 800/523-6586 🖷 215/244-9617 ✉ Landmark House, Hammersmith Bridge Rd., 6th

fl., London, W6 9DP ☎ 20/8762-8008 🖷 20/8748-7744 ✉ 12 Chemin Riantbosson, 1217 Meyrin 1, Geneva, Switzerland ☎ 22/785-6464 🖷 22/785-6424 ✉ 331 N. Bridge Rd., 17-00, Odeon Towers, Singapore 188720 ☎ 6338-7800 🖷 6338-7611.

THE SUN & OTHER HAZARDS

In the summer, sunburn and sunstroke are real risks in Spain. On the hottest sunny days, even if you're not normally bothered by strong sun, you should cover yourself up, carry sunblock lotion (*protector solar*), drink plenty of fluids, and limit sun time for the first few days. If you require medical attention for any problem, ask your hotel's front desk for assistance or go to the nearest public **Centro de Salud** (day hospital); in serious cases, you'll be referred to the regional hospital.

HOLIDAYS

Spain's national holidays are January 1, January 6 (Epiphany), Good Friday, Easter, May 1 (May Day), August 15 (Assumption), October 12 (National Day), November 1 (All Saints' Day), December 6 (Constitution), December 8 (Immaculate Conception), and December 25.

In addition, each region, city, and town has its own holidays honoring political events and patron saints. Madrid holidays are May 2 (Madrid Day), May 15 (St. Isidro), and November 9 (Almudena). Barcelona celebrates April 23 (St. George), September 11 (Catalonia Day), and September 24 (Merce).

Many stores close during *Semana Santa* (Holy Week—also sometimes translated as Easter Week); it is the week that preceeds Easter.

If a public holiday falls on a Tuesday or Thursday, remember that **many businesses also close on the nearest Monday or Friday** for a long weekend, called a *puente* (bridge). If a major holiday falls on a Sunday, businesses close on Monday.

INSURANCE

The most useful travel-insurance plan is a comprehensive policy that includes coverage for trip cancellation and interruption, default, trip delay, and medical expenses (with a waiver for preexisting conditions).

Without insurance you'll lose all or most of your money if you cancel your trip, regardless of the reason. Default insurance covers you if your tour operator, airline, or cruise line goes out of business—the chances of which have been increasing. Trip-delay covers expenses that arise because of bad weather or mechanical delays. Study the fine print when comparing policies.

If you're traveling internationally, a key component of travel insurance is coverage for medical bills incurred if you get sick on the road. Such expenses aren't generally covered by Medicare or private policies. U.K. residents can buy a travel-insurance policy valid for most vacations taken during the year in which it's purchased (but check preexisting-condition coverage). British and Australian citizens need extra medical coverage when traveling overseas.

Always **buy travel policies directly from the insurance company**; if you buy them from a cruise line, airline, or tour operator that goes out of business, you probably won't be covered for the agency or operator's default, a major risk. Before making any purchase, review your existing health and home-owner's policies to find what they cover away from home.

🔢 In the U.S. **Access America** ✉ 2805 N. Parham Rd., Richmond, VA 23294 ☎ 800/729-6021 🖷 804/673-1491 or 800/346-9265 🌐 www.accessamerica. com. **Travel Guard International** ✉ 1145 Clark St., Stevens Point, WI 54481 🖷 715/345-1041 or 800/826-4919 🖷 800/955-8785 or 715/345-1990 🌐 www.travelguard.com.

🔢 In the U.K. **Association of British Insurers** ✉ 51 Gresham St., London EC2V 7HQ ☎ 020/7600-3333 🖷 020/7696-8999 🌐 www.abi.org.uk.

🔢 In Canada **RBC Insurance** ✉ 6880 Financial Dr., Mississauga, Ontario L5N 7Y5 ☎ 800/565-3129 or 905/816-2400 🖷 905/813-4704 🌐 www. rbcinsurance.com.

🔢 In Australia **Insurance Council of Australia** ✉ Level 3, 56 Pitt St., Sydney, NSW 2000 ☎ 02/9253-5100 🖷 02/9253-5111 🌐 www.ica.com.au.

🔢 In New Zealand **Insurance Council of New Zealand** ✉ Level 7, 111–115 Customhouse Quay, Box 474, Wellington ☎ 04/472-5230 🖷 04/473-3011 🌐 www.icnz.org.nz.

LANGUAGE

Although Spaniards exported their language to all of Central and South America, Spanish is not the principal language in all of Spain. Outside their big cities, the Basques speak Euskera. In Catalonia, you'll hear Catalan throughout the region, just as you'll hear Gallego in Galicia and Valenciano in Valencia (the latter, as with Mallorquín in Majorca and Menorquín in Menorca, are considered Catalan dialects). Although almost everyone in these regions also speaks and understands Spanish, local radio and television stations may broadcast in their respective languages, and road signs may be printed (or spray-painted over) with the preferred regional language. Spanish is referred to as Castellano, or Castilian.

Fortunately, **Spanish is fairly easy to pick up, and your efforts to speak it will be graciously received.** Learn at least the following basic phrases: *buenos días* (hello—until 2 PM), *buenas tardes* (good afternoon—until 8 PM), *buenas noches* (hello—after dark), *por favor* (please), *gracias* (thank you), *adiós* (good-bye), *sí* (yes), *no* (no), *los servicios* (the toilets), *la cuenta* (bill/check), and *habla inglés?* (do you speak English?), *no comprendo* (I don't understand) (⇨ Vocabulary, *in* the Understanding Spain chapter).

If your Spanish breaks down, you should have no trouble finding people who speak English in major cities and coastal resorts, but you won't necessarily be able to count on the bus driver or the passerby on the street. It's much more likely that you'll find an English-language speaker if you approach people under age 30. Those who do speak English may speak the British variety, so don't be surprised if you're told to queue (line up) or take the lift (elevator) to the loo (toilet). Many guided tours at museums and historic sites are in Spanish; ask which language will be spoken before you sign up. Alternatively, you can request a multilingual headset that guides you around a gallery or museum—these days they are fairly standard in the bigger establishments.

LANGUAGES FOR TRAVELERS

A phrase book and language tape set can help get you started. *Fodor's Spanish for Travelers* (available at bookstores everywhere) is excellent. Living Language sells comprehensive language programs: *Spanish Complete Course; Ultimate Spanish; All Audio Spanish;* and *Spanish Without the Fuss.*

LANGUAGE PROGRAMS

A number of private schools in Spain offer Spanish-language courses of various durations for foreigners, but be careful which one you choose. As is also the case with English-language schools in Spain, the quality of Spanish-language education can vary wildly in terms of quality and cost. It's safer to choose a reputable school that uses the latest teaching methods. The **International House** runs excellent Spanish departments in a number of cities. **Don Quijote** is another network with schools in several locations around Spain. Most Spanish universities, including Salamanca and Málaga, have longer-term Spanish programs, usually covering two months or more. **Instituto Cervantes,** devoted to promoting Spanish language and culture, teaches both in its offices worldwide and can advise you on other courses in Spain.

🚺 Language Programs Don Quijote ⊠ C. Placentinos 2, Salamanca 37998 ☎ 923/268860. Instituto Cervantes ⊠ 122 E. 42nd St., Suite 807, New York, NY 10168 ☎ 212/689-4232. International House Madrid ⊠ Zurbano, 8, Madrid 28010 ☎ 91/319-7224.

LODGING

Most of Spain's private hotels are modern high-rises, though more and more innkeepers are restoring historic properties. By law, hotel prices must be posted at the reception desk and should indicate whether or not the value-added tax (IVA; 7%) is included. Note that high-season rates prevail not only in summer but also during Holy Week and local fiestas. Like the restaurants, the lodgings we list are the cream of the crop in each price category. We always list the facilities that are available, but we don't specify whether they cost extra; when pricing accommodations,

always ask what's included and what costs extra. Properties are assigned price categories based on the range between their least and most expensive standard double rooms at high season (excluding holidays). Properties marked ✕🖾 are lodging establishments whose restaurants warrant a special trip.

In much of Spain, breakfast is normally *not* included. However, in the resort destinations, such as the Balearic Islands, and the Costa del Sol, a buffet breakfast is often included. Assume that hotels operate on the European Plan (EP, with no meals) unless we specify that they use either the Continental Plan (CP, with a continental breakfast), Breakfast Plan (BP, with a full breakfast), or the Modified American Plan (MAP, with breakfast and dinner) or are all-inclusive (including all meals and most activities).

APARTMENT & VILLA RENTALS

If you want a home base that's roomy enough for a family and comes with cooking facilities, consider a furnished rental. These can save you money, especially if you're traveling with a group. Home-exchange directories sometimes list rentals as well as exchanges.

🚺 International Agents Hideaways International ⊠ 767 Islington St., Portsmouth, NH 03801 ☎ 603/430-4433 or 800/843-4433 ⊟ 603/430-4444 ⊕ www.hideaways.com, annual membership $185. Hometours International ⊠ 1108 Scottie La., Knoxville, TN 37919 ☎ 865/690-8484 or 866/367-4668 ⊕ thor.he.net/~hometour. Interhome ⊠ 1990 N.E. 163rd St., Suite 110, North Miami Beach, FL 33162 ☎ 305/940-2299 or 800/882-6864 ⊟ 305/940-2911 ⊕ www.interhome.us. Villas and Apartments Abroad ⊠ 183 Madison Ave., Suite 201, New York, NY 10016 ☎ 212/213-6435 or 800/433-3020 ⊟ 212/213-8252 ⊕ www.vaanyc.com. Villas International ⊠ 4340 Redwood Hwy., Suite D309, San Rafael, CA 94903 ☎ 415/499-9490 or 800/221-2260 ⊟ 415/499-9491 ⊕ www.villasintl.com.

CAMPING

Camping in Spain is not a wilderness experience. The country has more than 500 campgrounds, and many have excellent facilities, including hot showers, restaurants, swimming pools, tennis courts, and even nightclubs. Also, no special camping pass is required. In summer, especially August, the best campgrounds fill with Spanish families, who move in with their entire households: pets, grandparents, even the kitchen sink and stove. You can pick up an official list of all Spanish campgrounds at the tourist office. It can be hard to find a site for independent camping outside established campgrounds. For safety reasons, you cannot camp next to roads, on riverbanks, or on the beach, nor can you set up house in urban areas, nature parks (outside designated camping areas), or within 1 km (½ mi) of any established campsite. And, of course, to camp on a private farm, seek the owner's permission.

HOME EXCHANGES

If you would like to exchange your home for someone else's, join a home-exchange organization, which will send you its updated listings of available exchanges for a year and will include your own listing in at least one of them. It's up to you to make specific arrangements.

🏠 **Exchange Clubs HomeLink International** ⌂ 2937 N.W. 9th Terr., Fort Lauderdale, FL 33311 ☎ 954/566-2687 or 800/638-3841 🖷 954/566-2783 ∰ www.homelink.org; $125 yearly for a listing, online access, and catalog; $80 without catalog. **Intervac U.S.** ✉ 30 Corte San Fernando, Tiburon, CA 94920 ☎ 800/756-4663 🖷 415/435-7440 ∰ www.intervacus.com; $126 yearly for a listing, online access, and directory; $78.88 without directory.

HOSTELS

No matter what your age, you can save on lodging costs by staying at hostels. Youth hostels (*albergue juvenil*) in Spain are usually large and impersonal (but clean) with dorm-style beds. Most are geared to students, though many have a few private rooms suitable for families and couples. These rooms fill up quickly, so book at least a month in advance. Other budget options are the university student dorms (*residencia estudiantil*), some of which offer accommodation in the summer months, when students are away. Note that dorm availability changes from year to year, so inquire at the tourist office when you arrive. The rooms are often small, basic, and sparsely furnished, but

the cost is low. Note that in Spain a *hostal* is a budget hotel.

In some 4,000 locations in more than 70 countries around the world, Hostelling International (HI), the umbrella group for a number of national youth-hostel associations, offers single-sex, dorm-style beds and, at many hostels, rooms for couples and family accommodations. Membership in any HI national hostel association, open to travelers of all ages, allows you to stay in HI-affiliated hostels at member rates; one-year membership is about $28 for adults (or $18 for those ages 55 and older) in the United States (C$35 for a two-year minimum membership in Canada, £15.95 in the United Kingdom, A$52 in Australia, and NZ$40 in New Zealand); hostels charge about $10 to $30 per night. Members have priority if the hostel is full; they're also eligible for discounts around the world, even on rail and bus travel in some countries.

🏠 **Organizations Hostelling International–USA** ✉ 8401 Colesville Rd., Suite 600, Silver Spring, MD 20910 ☎ 301/495-1240 🖷 301/495-6697 ∰ www.hiusa.org. **Hostelling International–Canada** ✉ 205 Catherine St., Suite 500, Ottawa, Ontario K2P 1C3 ☎ 613/237-7884 or 800/663-5777 🖷 613/237-7868 ∰ www.hihostels.ca. **YHA England and Wales** ✉ Trevelyan House, Dimple Rd., Matlock, Derbyshire DE4 3YH, U.K. ☎ 0870/870-8808, 0870/770-8868, or 01629/592-600 🖷 0870/770-6127 ∰ www.yha.org.uk. **YHA Australia** ✉ 422 Kent St., Sydney, NSW 2001 ☎ 02/9261-1111 🖷 02/9261-1969 ∰ www.yha.com.au. **YHA New Zealand** ✉ Level 1, Moorhouse City, 166 Moorhouse Ave., Box 436, Christchurch ☎ 03/379-9970 or 0800/278-299 🖷 03/365-4476 ∰ www.yha.org.nz.

HOTELS & BED-AND-BREAKFASTS

The Spanish government classifies hotels with one to five stars. Although quality is a factor, **the rating is technically only an indication of how many facilities the hotel offers.** For example, a three-star hotel may be just as comfortable as a four-star hotel but may lack a swimming pool. Similarly, Fodor's price categories (¢–$$$$) indicate room rates only, so you might find a well-kept $$$ inn more charming than the famous $$$$ property down the street.

All hotel entrances are marked with a blue plaque bearing the letter H and the number of stars. The letter R (standing for *residencia*) after the letter H indicates an establishment with no meal service. The designations *fonda* (F), *pensión* (P), *casa de huéspedes* (CH), and *hostal* (Hs) indicate budget accommodations. In most cases, especially in smaller villages, rooms in such buildings will be basic but clean; in large cities, these rooms can be downright dreary. Note that in Spain *hostales* are not the same as the dorm-style youth hostels common elsewhere in Europe—*hostales* are inexpensive hotels with individual rooms, not communal quarters.

All hotels listed have private bath and air-conditioning (*aire acondicionado*) unless otherwise noted. When inquiring in Spanish about whether a hotel has a private bath, ask if it's an *habitación con baño*.

Although a single room (*habitación sencilla*) is usually available, singles are often on the small side. Solo travelers might prefer to pay a bit extra for single occupancy of a double room (*habitación doble uso individual*.) Make sure you request a double bed if you want one—if you don't ask, you may end up with two singles placed together. Bear in mind, too, that a double bed in Spain is considerably smaller than a U.S. double. If you're tall, you might consider requesting a queen-size bed.

Spain's major private hotel groups include the Sol Meliá, Tryp, and Hotusa. The NH chain, which is concentrated in major cities, appeals to business travelers. Dozens of reasonably priced beachside high-rises along the various coasts cater to package tours.

There's a growing trend in Spain toward small country hotels and agrotourism. Estancias de España is an association of more than 40 independently owned hotels in restored palaces, monasteries, mills, and estates, generally in rural Spain; contact them for a free directory. Similar associations serve individual regions, and tourist offices also provide lists of establishments.

A number of *casas rurales* (country houses similar to bed-and-breakfasts) offer pastoral lodging either in guest rooms or in self-catering cottages. You may also come across the term *finca*, which is a country estate house. Many of the accommodations designated agroturismo are fincas that people have inherited and converted to upscale B&Bs. Comfort and conveniences vary widely; it's best to book these types of accommodation through one of the appropriate regional associations. Ask the local tourist office about casas rurales and fincas in the area.

🏨 **Small Hotels AHRA** (Andalusian Association of Rural Hotels) ☎ 95/237-8775 ⊕ www.ahra.es. **Estancias de España** ✉ Menéndez Pidal 31-bajo izq., Madrid 28036 ☎ 91/345-4141 ⊕ www.estancias. com. **Hosterías y Hospederías Reales** (Hotels in Castile–La Mancha) ✉ Frailes 1, Villanueva de los Infantes 13320, Ciudad Real ☎ 902/202010.

🏨 **Major Spanish Chains Hotusa** ☎ 93/268-1010 ⊕ www.hotusa.es. **NH Hoteles** ☎ 902/115116 ⊕ www.nh-hoteles.es. **Sol Meliá** ☎ 902/144444 ⊕ www.solmelia.com.

🏨 **International Chains Best Western** ☎ 800/780-7234, 900/993900 in Spain ⊕ www.bestwestern.com. **Choice** ☎ 877/424-6423 ⊕ www.choicehotels.com. **Hilton** ☎ 800/445-8667 ⊕ www.hilton.com or www.hilton.co.uk. **Holiday Inn** ☎ 800/465-4329 ⊕ www.holiday-inn.com. **Hyatt Hotels & Resorts** ☎ 800/233-1234 ⊕ www.hyatt.com. **InterContinental** ☎ 888/424-6835 ⊕ www.ichotelsgroup.com. **Marriott** ☎ 800/236-2427 ⊕ www.marriott.com. **Le Meridien** ☎ 800/543-4300 ⊕ www.lemeridien.com. **Radisson** ☎ 800/333-3333 ⊕ www.radisson.com. **Ritz-Carlton** ☎ 800/241-3333 ⊕ www.ritzcarlton.com. **Sheraton** ☎ 800/325-3535, 800/3253-5353 in Spain ⊕ www.starwood.com/sheraton. **Westin Hotels & Resorts** ☎ 800/228-3000 ⊕ www.starwood.com/westin.

DISCOUNT RESERVATIONS
🏨 **Hotel Rooms Accommodations Express** ☎ 800/444-7666 or 800/277-1064. **Hotels.com** ☎ 800/219-4606 or 800/364-0291 ⊕ www.hotels.com. **Turbotrip.com** ☎ 800/473-7829 ⊕ w3.turbotrip.com.

PARADORES
The Spanish government runs more than 80 paradores—upmarket hotels in historic buildings or near significant sites. Some are in castles on a hill with sweeping views; others are in monasteries or convents filled with artistic treasures; still others are in

modern buildings on choice beachfront, alpine, or pastoral property. Rates are reasonable, considering that most paradores have four- or five-star amenities; and the premises are invariably immaculate and tastefully furnished, often with antiques or reproductions. Each parador has a restaurant serving regional specialties, and you can stop in for a meal or a drink without spending the night. Breakfast, however, is an expensive buffet, so if you just want coffee and a roll, you'll do better to walk down the street to a local café.

Paradores are extremely popular with foreigners and Spaniards alike, so **make reservations well in advance.** If you plan to spend at least five nights in the paradores, the "five-night card" offers excellent savings. You can purchase and use the card at any parador within the valid calendar period; in most paradores, discounted nights aren't offered during the high-season summer months of June, July, and August, and are offered only Sunday through Thursday in spring. Note that you can still use the card during these periods, but you'll be paying the difference between the official and discounted rate. The card does not guarantee a room; you must make reservations in advance. The paradores offer 35% discounts to those 60 and over, usually in May and June, though the months may vary. Those 30 and under also qualify for special discounted deals (with the buffet breakfast included in the price), generally from May to December.

🚩 In Spain **Paradores de España** ✉ Central de Reservas, Requena 3, Madrid 28013 ☎ 91/516-6666 🌐 www.parador.es.

🚩 In the U.S. **Marketing Ahead** ✉ 433 5th Ave., New York, NY 10016 ☎ 212/686-9213 or 800/223-1356.

🚩 In the U.K. **Keytel International** ✉ 402 Edgeware Rd., London W2 1ED ☎ 0207/402-8182.

MAIL & SHIPPING

Spain's postal system, the *correos*, does work, but delivery times can vary widely. An airmail letter to the United States may take anywhere from four days to two weeks; delivery to other destinations is equally unpredictable. Sending your letters by priority mail (*urgente*) or the cheaper

registered mail *certificado* ensures speedier and safer arrival.

OVERNIGHT SERVICES

When time is of the essence, or when you're sending valuable items or documents overseas, you can use a courier (*mensajero*). The major international agencies, such as Federal Express, UPS, and DHL, have representatives in Spain; the biggest Spanish courier service is Seur. MRW is another local courier that provides express delivery worldwide.

🚩 Major Services **DHL** ☎ 902/122424. **Federal Express** ☎ 900/100871. **MRW** ☎ 900/300400. **Seur** ☎ 902/101010. **UPS** ☎ 902/888820.

POSTAL RATES

Airmail letters to the United States and Canada cost €0.78 up to 20 grams. Letters to the United Kingdom and other EU countries cost €0.57 up to 20 grams. Letters within Spain are €0.29. Postcards carry the same rates as letters. You can buy stamps at post offices and at licensed tobacco shops.

RECEIVING MAIL

Because mail delivery in Spain can often be slow and unreliable, it's best to have your mail sent to American Express. Mail can also be held at a Spanish post office; have it addressed to LISTA DE CORREOS (the equivalent of poste restante) in a town you'll be visiting. Postal addresses should include the name of the province in parentheses, for example, Marbella (Málaga).

🚩 **American Express** ✉ Pl. de las Cortes 2, Madrid 28014 ☎ 900/941413 ✉ La Rambla 74, Barcelona 08002 ☎ 93/342-7311 🌐 www.americanexpress.com.

MONEY MATTERS

Spain is no longer a budget destination, even less so in the expensive cities of Barcelona, San Sebastian, and Madrid. However, prices still compare slightly favorably with those elsewhere in Europe. Coffee (depending if it's a smaller espresso or a latte) in a bar generally costs anywhere from €0.80 to €2, again, depending on if you're standing or sitting at a bar, sitting at an inside table, or sitting at an outside terrace table. The latter is always the most expensive option—whether you're ordering coffee, a beer, or a packet of chips. Tap beer (regular size) in a bar: €1 standing or sitting at a bar, €1.50–€2 seated inside, and €1.50–€2.50 sitting outside. Small glass of wine in a bar: €1–€2.50. Soft drink: €1.20–€1.80 a bottle. Ham-and-cheese sandwich: €1.80–€2.70. Two-kilometer (1-mi) taxi ride: €2.40, but the meter keeps ticking in traffic jams. Local bus or subway ride: €0.90–€1.30. Movie ticket: €4–€6. Foreign newspaper: €2.

Prices throughout this guide are given for adults. Substantially reduced fees are almost always available for children, students, and senior citizens. (⇨ Taxes)

ATMS

You'll find ATMs in every major city in Spain, as well as most smaller cities. ATMs will be part of the Cirrus and/or Plus networks, and will allow you to withdraw euros with your credit or debit card, provided you have a valid PIN (pronounced *peen*). Make sure your PIN code is four digits, which is required in Spain. Also, if you go by a letter combination, know the numerical equivalents, because at some ATMs the keyboard is reverse from the American keyboard. For example, the 1, 2, 3, 4, etc., that you find on the keyboard will be 9, 8, 7, 6, etc., in Spain. Your card issuer is likely to charge you a fee for using an ATM abroad.

BANKS

The Spanish banking system has been hailed as Europe's most efficient on several occasions. Bank branches mushroom all over the country, especially in the cities. Banks are generally located in the town and city centers, and the majority will have an ATM. Major banks in Spain are Banco Popular (⊕ www.bancopopular.es), Banesto (⊕ www.banesto.es), BBVA (Banco Bilbao-Vizcaya Argentara ⊕ www.bbva.es), and BSCH (Banco Santander Central Hispano ⊕ www.gruposantander.com). *See* Business Hours, *above.*

CREDIT CARDS

Throughout this guide, the following abbreviations are used: **AE,** American Express; **DC,** Diners Club; **MC,** MasterCard; and **V,** Visa.

▣ Reporting Lost Cards Use these toll-free numbers in Spain. **American Express** ☎ 900/941413. **Diners Club** ☎ 901/101011. **MasterCard** ☎ 900/974445. **Visa** ☎ 900/971231.

CURRENCY

Since 2002, Spain has used the European monetary unit, the euro; other countries that also have adopted it are Austria, Belgium, Finland, France, Germany, Greece, Ireland, Italy, Luxembourg, the Netherlands, and Portugal. Euro notes come in denominations of 5, 10, 20, 50, 100, 200, and 500; coins are worth 1 cent of a euro, 2 cents, 5 cents, 10 cents, 20 cents, 50 cents, 1 euro, and 2 euros. **Forgery is quite commonplace in parts of Spain, especially with 50-euro notes.** You can generally tell a forgery by the feel of the paper: they tend to be smoother than the legal notes, and the metalic line down the middle is darker than those in real bills.

CURRENCY EXCHANGE

At this writing the euro is fairly strong against the U.S. dollar and other currencies: €0.84 to the U.S. dollar, €1.46 to the pound sterling, €0.72 to the Canadian dollar, €0.62 to the Australian dollar, €0.56 to the New Zealand dollar, and €0.14 to the South African rand.

For the most favorable rates, **change money through banks.** Although ATM transaction fees may be higher abroad than at home, ATM rates are excellent because they're based on wholesale rates offered only by major banks. You won't do as well at currency-exchange offices, exchange booths in airports or rail and bus stations, in hotels, in restaurants, or in stores. To avoid lines at airport exchange booths, and yet have money for a cab or bite to eat before you locate an ATM, get a bit of local currency (euros in most of Spain, pounds in Gibraltar) before you leave home, either from your bank or through an exchange service.

▣ Exchange Services **International Currency Express** ✉ 427 N. Camden Dr., Suite F, Beverly Hills, CA 90210 ☎ 888/278-6628 orders 🖶 310/278-6410 ⊕ www.foreignmoney.com. **Travel Ex Currency**

Services ☎ 800/287-7362 orders and retail locations ⊕ www.travelex.com.

PACKING

Pack light. Although baggage carts are free and plentiful in most Spanish airports, they're rare in train and bus stations.

Spaniards tend to dress up more than Americans or the British. Summer is hot nearly everywhere; visits in winter, fall, and spring call for warm clothing and, in winter, boots. It makes sense to wear casual, comfortable clothing and shoes for sightseeing, but you'll want to **dress up a bit in large cities, especially for fine restaurants and nightclubs.** American tourists are easily spotted for their sneakers—if you want to blend in, wear leather shoes. On the beach, anything goes; it's common to see females of all ages wearing only bikini bottoms, and many of the more remote beaches allow nude sunbathing. Regardless of your style, **bring a cover-up** to wear over your bathing suit when you leave the beach.

In your carry-on luggage, pack an extra pair of eyeglasses or contact lenses and enough of any medication you take to last a few days longer than the entire trip. You may also ask your doctor to write a spare prescription using the drug's generic name, as brand names may vary from country to country. In luggage to be checked, **never pack prescription drugs, valuables, or undeveloped film.** And don't forget to carry with you the addresses of offices that handle refunds of lost traveler's checks. Check *Fodor's How to Pack* (available at online retailers and bookstores everywhere) for more tips.

To avoid customs and security delays, carry medications in their original packaging. Don't pack any sharp objects in your carry-on luggage, including knives of any size or material, scissors, nail clippers, and corkscrews, or anything else that might arouse suspicion.

To avoid having your checked luggage chosen for hand inspection, don't cram bags full. The U.S. Transportation Security Administration suggests packing shoes on top and placing personal items you don't want touched in clear plastic bags.

CHECKING LUGGAGE

You're allowed to carry aboard one bag and one personal article, such as a purse or a laptop computer. Make sure what you carry on fits under your seat or in the overhead bin. Get to the gate early, so you can board as soon as possible, before the overhead bins fill up.

Baggage allowances vary by carrier, destination, and ticket class. On international flights from the United States, as of September 2005, you're allowed to check two bags weighing up to 50 pounds (23 kilograms) each, although a few airlines allow checked bags of up to 88 pounds (40 kilograms) in first class. Some international carriers don't allow more than 66 pounds (30 kilograms) per bag in business class and 44 pounds (20 kilograms) in economy. If you're flying to or through the United Kingdom, your luggage cannot exceed 70 pounds (32 kilograms) per bag. On domestic flights, the limit is usually 50 to 70 pounds (23 to 32 kilograms) per bag. Most airlines won't accept bags that weigh more than 100 pounds (45 kilograms) on domestic or international flights. Also, in general, carry-on bags shouldn't exceed 40 pounds (18 kilograms). Expect to pay a fee for baggage that exceeds weight limits. Check baggage restrictions with your carrier before you pack.

A word of warning on plane luggage. If you're flying a low-budget carrier such as Ryanair, be sure to check luggage restrictions before you book your flight—in many cases they are considerably more restrictive than other long-haul carriers. Ryanair, for example, permits only a day bag and 33 pounds of checked luggage—anything over that is charged at €8 a kilo—if you're not careful, your cheap budget flight could turn out to be an expensive one.

Airline liability for baggage is limited to $2,500 per person on flights within the United States. On international flights it amounts to $9.07 per pound or $20 per kilogram for checked baggage (roughly $540 per 50-pound bag), with a maximum of $634.90 per piece, and $400 per passenger for unchecked baggage. You can buy additional coverage at check-in for about $10 per $1,000 of coverage, but it often excludes a rather extensive list of items, shown on your airline ticket.

Before departure, itemize your bags' contents and their worth, and label the bags with your name, address, and phone number. (If you use your home address, cover it so potential thieves can't see it readily.) Include a label inside each bag and **pack a copy of your itinerary.** At check-in, make sure each bag is correctly tagged with the destination airport's three-letter code. Because some checked bags will be opened for hand inspection, the U.S. Transportation Security Administration recommends that you leave luggage unlocked or use the plastic locks offered at check-in. TSA screeners place an inspection notice inside searched bags, which are resealed with a special lock.

If your bag has been searched and contents are missing or damaged, file a claim with the TSA Consumer Response Center as soon as possible. If your bags arrive damaged or fail to arrive at all, file a written report with the airline before leaving the airport.

⚑ Complaints U.S. Transportation Security Administration Contact Center ☎ 866/289-9673 ⊕ www.tsa.gov.

PASSPORTS & VISAS

When traveling internationally, carry your passport—it's always the best form of ID—and **make two photocopies of the data page** (one for someone at home and another for you, carried separately from your passport). If you lose your passport, promptly call the nearest embassy or consulate and the local police.

U.S. passport applications for children under age 14 require consent from both parents or legal guardians; both parents must appear together to sign the application. If only one parent appears, he or she must submit a written statement from the other parent authorizing passport issuance

for the child. A parent with sole authority must present evidence of it when applying; acceptable documentation includes the child's certified birth certificate listing only the applying parent, a court order specifically permitting this parent's travel with the child, or a death certificate for the nonapplying parent. Application forms and instructions are available on the U.S. State Department's Bureau of Consular Affairs's Web site, www.travel.state.gov.

ENTERING SPAIN

Visitors from the United States, Australia, Canada, New Zealand, and the United Kingdom need a valid passport to enter Spain. Australians traveling on tourist visas can now stay up to three months in Spain without needing a visa before arrival. Under the European Union free movement of labor laws, U.K. citizens are entitled to stay in Spain indefinitely.

PASSPORT OFFICES

The best time to apply for a passport or to renew is in fall and winter. Before any trip, check your passport's expiration date; if necessary, renew it as soon as possible.

⚑ Australian Citizens Passports Australia ☎ 131-232 Australian Department of Foreign Affairs and Trade ⊕ www.passports.gov.au.
⚑ Canadian Citizens Passport Office ⊠ Apply by mail: Foreign Affairs Canada, Gatineau, Québec K1A 0G3 ☎ 800/567-6868 ⊕ www.ppt.gc.ca.
⚑ New Zealand Citizens New Zealand Passports Office ☎ 0800/22-5050 or 04/474-8100 ⊕ www.passports.govt.nz.
⚑ U.K. Citizens U.K. Passport Service ☎ 0870/521-0410 ⊕ www.passport.gov.uk.
⚑ U.S. Citizens National Passport Information Center ☎ 877/487-2778, 888/874-7793 TDD/TTY ⊕ www.travel.state.gov.

RELIGIOUS SERVICES

Most of Spain's residents are nominally Catholic, though what was one of Europe's most fervently religious countries in 1975 is now considered the most secular. Present-day religious practice in Spain includes Christian, Islamic, and Judaic services, among others. Churches are open during services, though tourism is limited to certain areas. Casual attire is acceptable as long as it's not gaudy, unkempt, or too revealing (women in sleeveless blouses may be denied entry to some churches and cathedrals). Taking pictures inside houses of worship is generally allowed only when services are not in session.

Spain's most important religious celebration is *Semana Santa* (Holy Week), a moveable feast held on the first Sunday after the full moon following the vernal equinox (dates range from late March to mid-to-late April), lasting a full week from Palm Sunday to Easter.

RESTROOMS

Spain has some public restrooms, including, in larger cities, small coin-operated booths, but they are few and far between. Your best option is to use the facilities in a bar or cafeteria, remembering that at the discretion of the establishment you may have to order something. Gas stations have restrooms (you usually have to request the key to use them), but they are more often than not in terrible condition.

SAFETY

Petty crime is a huge problem in Spain's most popular tourist destinations. The most frequent offenses are pickpocketing (particularly in Madrid and Barcelona) and theft from cars (all over the country). **Never leave anything valuable in a parked car,** no matter how friendly the area feels, how quickly you'll return, or how invisible the item seems once you lock it in the trunk. Thieves can spot rental cars a mile away, and they work very efficiently. In airports, laptop computers are choice prey. Except when traveling between the airport or train station and your hotel, don't wear a money belt or a waist pack, both of which peg you as a tourist. (If you do use a money belt while traveling, opt for a concealed one and don't reach into it once you're in public.) Distribute your cash and any valuables (including your credit cards and passport) between a deep front pocket or an inside jacket or vest pocket. When walking the streets, particularly in large cities, carry as little cash as possible. Men should carry their wallets in the front pocket; women who need to carry purses should strap them across the front of their bodies. Another alternative is to carry money or important documents in both your front pockets. Leave the rest of your valuables in the safe at your hotel. On the beach, in cafés, and restaurants (particularly in the well-touristed areas), and in Internet centers, always keep your belongings on your lap or tied to your person in some way.

It's not advisable to sleep on beaches—no matter how well you store your possessions, you are an easy target for those who prey there in the early morning. Additionally, be cautious of any odd or unnecessary human contact, verbal or physical, whether it's a tap on the shoulder, someone asking you for a light for their cigarette, someone spilling their drink at your table, and so on. Thieves often work in twos, so while one is attracting your attention, the other could be swiping your wallet.

LOCAL SCAMS

In the tourist areas of Madrid and Barcelona you'll sometimes see a raucous group standing around a makeshift cardboard table and cheering on a guy who appears to be playing the ancient game of hiding the seed under one of three walnut shells. He goads passersby to pick a shell, any shell, to see if they can guess where the seed is; someone takes the bait, and the con game has begun. You'll choose correctly and "win" at the beginning. The moment you start handing over betting money, it becomes noticeably more difficult—and all but impossible—to guess the right shell. This is a scam, through and through, and the people standing around cheering the guy on are his friends or paid accomplices. The whole thing is actually very entertaining to watch—but if you do so, stand at a distance, be aware of those around you, and continue on your way sooner rather than later. Also, be cautious when a group of gypsy women approaches you in tourist areas to sell flowers. While you're admiring the flowers and bargaining a price, they'll often be picking your pocket—or that of the person you're with. Alternatively they'll insist you pay them something for the flower even if you haven't asked for it.

WOMEN IN SPAIN

If you carry a purse, choose one with a zipper and a thick strap that you can drape across your body; adjust the length so that the purse sits in front of you at or above hip level. (Don't wear a money belt or a waist pack that is visible.) Store only enough money in the purse to cover casual spending. Distribute the rest of your cash and any valuables between deep front pockets, inside jacket or vest pockets, and a concealed money pouch.

SENIOR-CITIZEN TRAVEL

There are few early-bird specials or movie discounts in Spain for senior citizens, but older folks generally enjoy discounts at museums. Also, Spanish social life encompasses all ages—it's very common to see senior citizens next to young couples or families in late-night cafés.

To qualify for age-related discounts, mention your senior-citizen status up front when booking hotel reservations (not when checking out) and before you're seated in restaurants (not when paying the bill). Be sure to have identification on hand. When renting a car, ask about promotional car-rental discounts, which can be cheaper than senior-citizen rates.

🖪 Educational Programs **Elderhostel** ⊠ 11 Ave. de Lafayette, Boston, MA 02111-1746 ☎ 877/426– 8056, 978/323-4141 international callers, 877/426– 2167 TTY 🖶 877/426-2166 ⊕ www.elderhostel.org.

SHOPPING

Spain has plenty to tempt the shopper, from simple souvenirs to high-quality regional crafts. Clothing is highly fashionable, if expensive. Shoes and leather accessories are as chic as you'll find. Many of the best buys are food items; just check customs restrictions in your home country before purchasing edibles. Spanish wines make lovely souvenirs. Spain's major department store, El Corte Inglés, has branches in all major cities and towns. The store is considerably more expensive than smaller-scale specialty stores.

KEY DESTINATIONS

Every region in Spain has its souvenir specialties, from *damascene* (metalwork inlaid with gold or silver) from Toledo and kitchenware from Albacete to Modernisteinspired crafts and mementos from Barcelona.

Barcelona, Madrid, and Seville are the three cities that hold the most options for fashionable clothing, hosting established local and international designers as well as up-and-coming designers.

SMART SOUVENIRS

Spain's leather is highly esteemed for its top quality and reasonable prices. Shoe lovers, especially, are spoiled for choice in Spain, where there are many fashionable shoe stores with high-quality leather shoes at decent prices, particularly in Madrid and Barcelona. For more traditional footwear, pick up a pair of *alpargatas*, better known internationally by their French name, espadrilles. Originally farmers' shoes, these canvas shoes with rope soles come in many colors and are comfortable and cheap (you can pick up a basic pair for as little as €7). Spain's Riojan wines are world renowned—and one sip of a pungent Riojan red, you'll understand why. You can buy Riojan wines all over Spain, though the best prices are, of course, in the region of La Rioja itself. Spain's wines are matched by its superb cured ham (*jamón serrano*). Many ham shops sell vacuum-sealed packets of sliced, cured ham, which pack easily and make for tasty souvenirs to take home.

SPORTS & THE OUTDOORS

Spain's fair weather is conducive to outdoor sports virtually year-round, though in summer you should restrict physical activity to early morning or late afternoon. Spain has more golf courses than any other country in Europe and is also kind to hikers, water-sports enthusiasts, and, believe it or not, skiers. Spain's sports federations and local tourist offices can be helpful.

GOLF

Spain's best golf courses are on the Mediterranean coast, especially the Costa del Sol. Greens fees can be on the high side (they're cheaper in summer), but many hotels linked to golf courses offer all-inclusive deals.

fl Real Federación Española de Golf ⊠ Capitán Haya 9, Madrid 28020 ☎ 91/555-2682 ⊕ www. golfspainfederacion.com.

HIKING

Spain's national parks and regional nature preserves are perfect for hiking and rock climbing. The parks' visitor centers and local outing clubs usually have plenty of information.
fl Federación Española de Montañismo ⊠ C. Floridablanca 75, Barcelona 08015 ☎ 93/426-4267.

SKIING

Not everyone thinks of sunny Spain as a skier's destination, but it's the second-most mountainous country in Europe (after Switzerland) and has an impressive 28 ski centers. The best slopes are in the Pyrenees; there's also good skiing in the Sierra Nevada, near Granada.
fl Federación Española de Deportes de Invierno (Spanish Winter Sports Federation) ⊠ Arroyo Fresno 3A, Madrid 28035 ☎ 91/376-9930.
Recorded ski report ☎ 91/350-2020 in Spanish.

WATER SPORTS

With 1,900 km (1,200 mi) of coastline, Spain has no shortage of water sports. Yacht harbors dot the Mediterranean coast. The coast near Tarifa, on Spain's southernmost tip, constitutes the windsurfing capital of mainland Europe; surfing is good on the northern coast, and even better on the shores of the Canary Islands. Spain's best dive sites are Granada province and the Cabo de Gata (near Almería); regional tourist offices can direct you to the local diving clubs.
fl Federación de Actividades Subacuáticas (Underwater Activities Federation) ⊠ Santaló 15, Barcelona 08021 ☎ 93/200-6769. **Real Federación Española de Vela** (Royal Spanish Sailing Federation) ⊠ Luís de Salazar 9, Madrid 28002 ☎ 91/519-5008 ⊕ www.rfev.es.

STUDENTS IN SPAIN

Students can often get discounts on admission to museums and other sights, so bring your valid student ID with you.
fl IDs & Services **STA Travel** ⊠ 10 Downing St., New York, NY 10014 ☎ 212/627-3111, 800/781-4040 24-hr service center in U.S. ⊕ www.sta.com. **Travel Cuts** ⊠ 187 College St., Toronto, Ontario M5T 1P7,

Canada ☎ 800/592-2887 in U.S., 416/979-2406, 888/359-2887, and 888/359-2887 in Canada ⊕ www.travelcuts.com.

TAXES

VALUE-ADDED TAX

Value-added tax, similar to sales tax, is called IVA in Spain (pronounced "*ee*-vah," for *impuesto sobre el valor añadido*). It's levied on both products and services, such as hotel rooms and restaurant meals. When in doubt about whether tax is included, ask, "*Está incluido el IVA*"?

The IVA rate for hotels and restaurants is 7%, regardless of their number of stars or forks. A special tax law for the Canary Islands allows hotels and restaurants there to charge 4% IVA. Menus will generally say at the bottom whether tax is included (*IVA incluido*) or not (*más 7% IVA*).

Although food, pharmaceuticals, and household items are taxed at the lowest rate, most consumer goods are taxed at 16%. A number of shops participate in Global Refund (formerly Europe Tax-Free Shopping), a V.A.T. refund service that makes getting your money back relatively hassle-free. You cannot get a refund on the V.A.T. for such items as meals or services such as hotel accommodation, or taxi fares. There are also some taxable goods for which the refund doesn't apply, such as consumable items such as perfume.

When making a purchase, **ask for a V.A.T. refund form** and find out whether the merchant gives refunds—not all stores do, nor are they required to. Have the form stamped like any customs form by customs officials when you leave the country or, if you're visiting several European Union countries, when you leave the EU. Be ready to show customs officials what you've bought (pack purchases together, in your carry-on luggage); budget extra time for this. After you're through passport control, take the form to a refund-service counter for an on-the-spot refund, or mail it to the address on the form (or the envelope with it) after you arrive home.

A service processes refunds for most shops. You receive the total refund stated on the form. Global Refund is a Europe-wide service with 210,000 affiliated stores and more than 700 refund counters—at major airports and border crossings. Its refund form is called a Tax Free Check. The service issues refunds in the form of cash, check, or credit-card adjustment. If you don't have time to wait at the refund counter, you can mail in the form instead.

🚇 V.A.T. Refunds **Global Refund** ✉ In Canada: 2020 Clark Blvd., Brampton, Ontario L6T 5R4 ☎ 800/566–9828 or 800/993–4313. ✉ In Spain: Avada Llano Castellano 15, Madrid, 28034 ☎ 917/294380 ⊕ www.globalrefund.com.

TELEPHONES

Spain's phone system is perfectly efficient but can be expensive. Direct dialing is the norm. Most travelers buy phone cards, which for €5 or €6 allows for about three hours of calls nationally and internationally. Phone cards can be used on any hotel, bar, or public telephone. Although some phone cards from Australia, the United Kingdom, and the United States can be used in Spain, those with the best value are found in Spain itself. There are many cards that work for only certain regions of the country, but the all-encompassing *Fantastic* card works for anywhere in the world. Phone cards can be bought at any tobacco shop or at most Internet cafés. Such cafés also often provide phone booths that allow you to call at cheaper rates. If you do use coins, be aware that the public phones in the street are cheaper than the green and blue phones found inside most bars and restaurants. Spain's main telephone company is Telefónica.

Note that only cell phones conforming to the European GSM standard will work in Spain. Buying a cell phone without a contract (i.e., paying for your calls by adding money to your phone either via a cellphone card or at a cell-phone store) is popular in Spain. If you're going to be traveling in Spain for an extended period of time and plan on using a cell phone frequently to call within Spain, then buying a phone will often turn out to be a big money-saver. Using a Spanish cell phone means avoiding the hefty long-distance charges accrued when using your cell phone from home to call within

Spain. Prices fluctuate, but offers start at about €40 for a phone with about €30 worth of calls.

AREA & COUNTRY CODES

The country code for Spain is 34. The country code is 1 for the United States and Canada, 61 for Australia, 64 for New Zealand, and 44 for the United Kingdom.

DIRECTORY & OPERATOR ASSISTANCE

For general information in Spain, dial 1003. International operators, who generally speak English, are at 025.

INTERNATIONAL CALLS

International calls are awkward from coin-operated pay phones because of the many coins needed; and they can be expensive from hotels, as the hotel often adds a hefty surcharge. Your best bet is to use a public phone that accepts phone cards (⇨ Phone Cards, *below*) or go to the local telephone office, the *locutorio*: every town has one, and major cities have several. The locutorios near the center of town are generally more expensive; farther from the center, the rates are sometimes as much as one-third less. You converse in a quiet, private booth, and you're charged according to the meter. If the call ends up costing around €4 or more, you can usually pay with Visa or MasterCard.

To make an international call yourself, dial 00, then the country code, then the area code and number.

Madrid's main telephone office is at Gran Vía 28. There's another at the main post office, and a third at Paseo Recoletos 43, just off Plaza Colón. In Barcelona you can phone overseas from the office at Carrer de Fontanella 4, off Plaça de Catalunya.

Before you leave home, **find out your long-distance company's access code in Spain** (⇨ Access Codes, *below*).

LOCAL & LONG-DISTANCE CALLS

All area codes begin with a 9. To call within Spain—even locally—dial the area code first. Numbers preceded by a 900 code are no longer toll-free and often have long wait times, which can be expensive. Phone numbers starting with a 6 are going to a cellular phone. Note that when calling a cell phone, you do not need to dial the area code first; also, calls to cell phones are significantly more expensive than calls to regular phones.

LONG-DISTANCE SERVICES

AT&T, MCI, and Sprint access codes make calling long-distance relatively convenient, but you may find the local access number blocked in many hotel rooms. First ask the hotel operator to connect you. If the hotel operator balks, ask for an international operator, or dial the international operator yourself. One way to improve your odds of getting connected to your long-distance carrier is to travel with more than one company's calling card (a hotel may block Sprint, for example, but not MCI). If all else fails, call from a pay phone.

General Information AT&T ☎ 800/222-0300. MCI WorldCom ☎ 800/444-4444. Sprint ☎ 800/793-1153.

Access Codes AT&T Direct ☎ 900/990011. MCI WorldPhone ☎ 900/990014. Sprint International Access ☎ 900/990013.

PHONE CARDS

To use a newer pay phone you need a special phone card (*tarjeta telefónica*), which you can buy at any tobacco shop or newsstand, in various denominations. Some such phones also accept credit cards, but phone cards are more reliable.

PUBLIC PHONES

You'll find pay phones in individual booths, in special telephone offices (*locutorios*), and in many bars and restaurants. Most have a digital readout so you can see your money ticking away. If you're calling with coins, you need at least €0.15 to call locally and €0.45 to call another province. Simply insert the coins and wait for a dial tone. (With older models, you line coins up in a groove on top of the dial and they drop down as needed.) Note that rates are reduced on weekends and after 8 PM during the week.

TIME

Spain is on central European time, one hour ahead of Greenwich mean time, and six hours ahead of eastern standard time.

Like the rest of the European Union, Spain switches to daylight saving time on the last weekend in March and switches back on the last weekend in October.

TIPPING

Service staff expect to be tipped, and you can be sure that your contribution will be appreciated. On the other hand, if you experience bad or surly service, don't feel obligated to leave a tip.

Restaurant checks do not list a service charge on the bill, but consider the tip included. If you want to leave a small tip in addition to the bill, **do not tip more than 10% of the bill,** and leave less if you eat tapas or sandwiches at a bar—just enough to round out the bill to the nearest €1. Tip cocktail servers €0.30–€0.50 a drink, depending on the bar.

Tip taxi drivers about 10% of the total fare, plus a supplement to help with luggage. Note that rides from airports carry an official surcharge plus a small handling fee for each piece of luggage.

Tip hotel porters €0.50 a bag, and the bearer of room service €0.50. A doorman who calls a taxi for you gets €0.50. If you stay in a hotel for more than two nights, tip the maid about €0.50 per night. The concierge should receive a tip for any additional help he or she provides.

Tour guides should be tipped about €2, ushers in theaters or at bullfights €0.15–€0.20, barbers €0.50, and women's hairdressers at least €1 for a wash and style. Restroom attendants are tipped €0.15.

TOURS & PACKAGES

Because everything is prearranged on a prepackaged tour or independent vacation, you spend less time planning—and often get it all at a good price.

BOOKING WITH AN AGENT

Travel agents are excellent resources. But it's a good idea to collect brochures from several agencies, as some agents' suggestions may be influenced by relationships with tour and package firms that reward them for volume sales. If you have a special interest, find an agent with expertise in that area; the American Society of Travel Agents (ASTA; ⇨ Travel Agencies) has a database of specialists worldwide. You can log on to the group's Web site to find an ASTA travel agent in your neighborhood.

Make sure your travel agent knows the accommodations and other services of the place being recommended. Ask about the hotel's location, room size, beds, and whether it has a pool, room service, or children's programs, if you care about these. Something else to ask: has your agent been there in person, and if not, sent others whom you can contact?

Do some homework on your own, too: local tourism boards can provide information about lesser-known and small-niche operators, some of which may sell only direct.

BUYER BEWARE

Each year consumers are stranded or lose their money when tour operators—even large ones with excellent reputations—go out of business. So check out the operator. Ask several travel agents about its reputation, and try to **book with a company that has a consumer-protection program.** (Look for information in the company's brochure.) In the United States, members of the United States Tour Operators Association are required to set aside funds ($1 million) to help eligible customers cover payments and travel arrangements in the event that the company defaults. It's also a good idea to choose a company that participates in the American Society of Travel Agents' Tour Operator Program; ASTA will act as mediator in any disputes between you and your tour operator.

Remember that the more your package or tour includes, the better you can predict the ultimate cost of your vacation. Make sure you know exactly what is covered, and beware of hidden costs. Are taxes, tips, and transfers included? Entertainment and excursions? These can add up.

🔢 Tour-Operator Recommendations **American Society of Travel Agents** (⇨ Travel Agencies). **National Tour Association** (NTA) ✉ 546 E. Main St., Lexington, KY 40508 ☎ 859/226-4444 or 800/682-8886 🖷 859/226-4404 ⊕ www.ntaonline.com.

United States Tour Operators Association (USTOA) ✉ 275 Madison Ave., Suite 2014, New York, NY 10016 ☎ 212/599-6599 🖷 212/599-6744 ⊕ www. ustoa.com.

TRAIN TRAVEL

International overnight trains run from Madrid to Lisbon and from Barcelona and Madrid to Paris (both around 11½ hours). An overnight train also runs from Barcelona to Geneva (10 hours) and Zurich (13 hours).

Spain's wonderful high-speed train, the 290-km/h (180-mph) AVE, travels between Madrid and Seville (with a stop in Córdoba) in less than three hours at prices starting around €86 each way. The AVE also travels from Madrid to Lleida (with a stop in Zaragoza), and there are plans to extend it to Barcelona by 2007. The trip to Zaragoza is just under two hours, and starts at €63 each way; to Lleida, the trip is just under three hours and starts at €70 each way. The fast Talgo service is also efficient.

However, the rest of the state-run rail system—known as RENFE—remains below par by European standards. Local train travel within cities is efficient, but most long-distance trips run at night and are tediously slow. Although overnight trains have comfortable sleeper cars, first-class fares that include a sleeping compartment are comparable to, or more expensive than, airfares.

For shorter routes with convenient schedules, trains are the most economical way to go. First- and second-class seats are reasonably priced, and you can get a bunk in a compartment with five other people for a supplement of about €32.

Commuter trains and most long-distance trains forbid smoking, though some long-distance trains have smoking cars.

CUTTING COSTS

To save money, **look into rail passes.** But be aware that if you don't plan to cover many miles, you may come out ahead by buying individual tickets.

If you're coming from the United States or Canada and are planning extensive train travel throughout Europe, **check Rail Europe** for rail passes. Whichever of the many available passes you choose, remember that you must buy your pass before you leave for Europe.

Spain is one of 17 European countries in which you can use the Eurailpass, which buys you unlimited first-class rail travel in all participating countries for the duration of the pass. If you plan to rack up the miles, get a standard pass. These are available for 15 days ($605), 21 days ($785), one month ($975), two months ($1,378), and three months ($1,703). If your needs are more limited, look into a Europass, which costs less than a Eurailpass and buys you a limited number of travel days, in a limited number of countries (France, Germany, Italy, Spain, and Switzerland), during a specified time period.

In addition to the Eurailpass and Europass, Rail Europe sells the Eurail Youthpass (you must be younger than 26), the Eurail Saverpass (discount for two or more people traveling together), a Eurail Flexipass (a certain number of travel days within a set period), the Euraildrive Pass (four days of rail plus two days of car rentals), and the Eurail Selectpass Drive (three days of rail plus two days of car rentals).

If Spain is your only destination, check into Rail Europe's Spain passes. Consider a Spain Flexipass. Prices begin at $175 for three days of second-class travel within a two-month period and $225 for first class. Children between 4 and 11 travel half price. Other passes cover more days and longer periods. The Iberic Railpass offers three days of first-class travel over two months in Spain and Portugal for $259. The Iberic Saverpass, which offers a discount for two or more people traveling together in Spain and Portugal, starts at $229. The Spain 'n France Pass starts at $272 for four days of second-class travel within a two-month period and $312 for first class.

You should also **check for RENFE discounts** in Spain. If you purchase a round-trip ticket on AVE or any of RENFE's Grandes Lineas, which are its faster, long-distance trains (including the Talgo) while in Spain, you'll get a 20% discount. You have up to 60 days to use the return portion of your ticket. Passengers with international airline tickets who are traveling on the AVE within 48 hours of their arrival receive a 25% discount on their AVE ticket. This discount also applies to passengers with national airline tickets for travel to or from the Canary and Balearic Islands and Melilla. On regional trains, you receive a 10% discount on round-trip tickets, and you have up to 15 days to use the return portion. Children and students also receive good discounts. Note that even if you just buy a one-way ticket to your destination, you can still receive the round-trip discount if you present your ticket stub at the train station when buying your return (provided your return is within the allotted time frame, either 15 or 60 days).

🚈 Rail Passes **DER Tours** ☎ 800/782-2424. **Rail Europe** ☎ 877/456-7245 or 800/361-7245 ⊕ www.raileurope.com. **RENFE** ☎ 902/157507 ⊕ www.renfe.es.

FARES & SCHEDULES

Most Spaniards buy train tickets in advance at the train station's *taquilla* (ticket office). The lines can be long, so give yourself plenty of time. For popular train routes, you will need to reserve tickets more than a few days in advance and pick them up at least a day before traveling; call RENFE to inquire. The ticket clerks at the stations rarely speak English, so if you need help or advice in planning a more complex train journey, you may be better off going to a travel agency that displays the blue-and-yellow RENFE sign. The price is the same. For shorter, regional train trips, you can often buy your tickets directly from machines in the main train stations. Note that if your itinerary is set in stone and has little room for error, you can buy RENFE tickets through Rail Europe before you leave home.

🚈 Train Information **RENFE** ☎ 902/240202 ⊕ www.renfe.es.

PAYING

You can buy train tickets with a major credit card (except for American Express) at most city train stations. In the smaller towns and villages, it's cash only. Traveler's checks are no longer accepted.

RESERVATIONS

Seat reservations are required on some trains, particularly high-speed trains, and are wise on any train that might be crowded. You'll also need a reservation if you want a sleeping berth. Many travelers assume that rail passes guarantee them seats on the trains they wish to ride: not so. **Reserve seats in advance even if you're using a rail pass.**

The easiest way to make reservations is to use the TIKNET service on the RENFE Web site. TIKNET involves registering and providing your credit-card information. When you make the reservation, you'll be given a car and seat assignment and a *localizador* (translated as "localizer" on the English version of the site; it is similar to a confirmation number). Print out the reservations page or write down the car number, seat number, and localizer. When traveling, go to your assigned seat on the train. When the conductor comes around, give him the localizer, and he will issue the ticket on the spot. You'll need your passport and, in most cases, the credit card you used for the reservation (in Spain, credit cards are often used for an additional form of ID). The AVE trains check you in at the gate to the platform, where you provide the localizer. You can review your pending reservations online at any time.

Caveats: the first time you use TIKNET, you must pick up the tickets at a RENFE station (most major airports have a RENFE booth, so you can retrieve your tickets as soon as you get off your plane). A 15% cancellation fee is charged if you cancel more than two hours after making the reservation. You cannot buy tickets online for certain regional lines or for commuter lines (*cercanías*). Station agents cannot alter TIKNET reservations: you must do this yourself online. If a train is booked, the TIKNET process doesn't reveal this until the final stage of the reservation attempt—then it gives you a cryptic error message in a little box—but if you reserve a few days in advance, it's unlikely you'll encounter this problem except at Easter, Christmas, or during the first week of August.

There's no line per se at the train station for advance tickets (and often for information); you take a number and wait until it's called. Ticket clerks at stations rarely speak English, so if you need help or advice in planning a more complex train journey, you may be better off going to a travel agency that displays the blue-and-yellow RENFE sign. A small commission (American Express Viajes charges €3) should be expected.

FROM THE U.K.

Train services to Spain from the United Kingdom are not as frequent, fast, or affordable as flights, and you have to change trains—and stations—in Paris. Allow 2 hours for the changing process, then 13 hours for the trip from Paris to Madrid. It's worth paying extra for the Talgo or Puerta del Sol express trains to avoid changing trains again at the Spanish border. If you're under 26 years old, Eurotrain has excellent deals.

🚆 Eurotrain ✉ 52 Grosvenor Gardens, London SW1W 0AG, U.K. ☎ 0207/730-8832. **Transalpino** ✉ 71-75 Buckingham Palace Rd., London SW1W ORE, U.K. ☎ 0207/834-9656.

TRANSPORTATION AROUND SPAIN

After France, Spain is the largest country in western Europe, so seeing any more than a fraction of it involves considerable domestic travel. If you want the freedom of straying from your fixed itinerary to follow whims as they come, driving is the best choice. The roads are generally fine, although traffic can be heavy on major routes, trucks can clog minor routes, and parking is a problem in cities.

Spain is well served by domestic flights, though these cost more than ground options. However, it's well worth it to frequently check the Web sites of Vueling, Spanair, and Air Europa, all of which often offer low-fare flights that are competitive with train fares. Flying is also a big time-saver, especially if you're traveling long distances, such as from Barcelona to Seville. Train service between the largest cities is fast, efficient, and punctual, but trains on secondary regional routes can be slow and involve frequent transfers. In such cases, buses are far more convenient.

TRAVEL AGENCIES

A good travel agent puts your needs first. Look for an agency that has been in business at least five years, emphasizes customer service, and has someone on staff who specializes in your destination. In addition, **make sure the agency belongs to a professional trade organization.** The American Society of Travel Agents (ASTA)—the largest and most influential in the field with more than 20,000 members in some 140 countries—maintains and enforces a strict code of ethics and will step in to help mediate any agent-client disputes involving ASTA members if necessary. ASTA also maintains a Web site that includes a directory of agents. Additionally, ASTA's www.TravelSense.org, a trip-planning and travel-advice site, can help you locate a travel agent who caters to your needs. (If a travel agency is also acting as your tour operator, *see* Buyer Beware ⇨ Tours & Packages.)

⚠ Local Agent Referrals American Society of Travel Agents (ASTA) ⊠ 1101 King St., Suite 200, Alexandria, VA 22314 ☎ 703/739-2782, 800/965-2782 24-hr hotline 🖷 703/684-8319 ⊕ www. astanet.com and www.travelsense.org. **Association of British Travel Agents** ⊠ 68-71 Newman St., London W1T 3AH ☎ 0901/201-5050 ⊕ www.abta. com. **Association of Canadian Travel Agencies** ⊠ 350 Sparks St., Suite 510, Ottawa, Ontario K1R 7S8 ☎ 613/237-3657 🖷 613/237-7052 ⊕ www.acta. ca. **Australian Federation of Travel Agents** ⊠ Level 3, 309 Pitt St., Sydney, NSW 2000 ☎ 02/9264-3299 or 1300/363-416 🖷 02/9264-1085 ⊕ www.afta.com.au. **Travel Agents' Association of New Zealand** ⊠ Level 5, Tourism and Travel House, 79 Boulcott St., Box 1888, Wellington 6001 ☎ 04/499-0104 🖷 04/499-0786 ⊕ www.taanz.org.nz.

VISITOR INFORMATION

Learn more about foreign destinations by checking government-issued travel advisories and country information. For a broader picture, consider information from more than one country.

Before you go, consult the Tourist Office of Spain in your home country or on the World Wide Web. The site ⊕ www.

okspain.org provides a basic introduction; the Spain-based ⊕ www.tourspain.es is more sophisticated.

⚠ Tourist Offices Chicago ⊠ Water Tower Pl., 845 N. Michigan Ave., Suite 915-East, Chicago, IL 60611 ☎ 312/642-1992. **Los Angeles** ⊠ 8383 Wilshire Blvd., Suite 960, Beverly Hills, CA 90211 ☎ 213/658-7188. **Miami** ⊠ 1221 Brickell Ave., Suite 1850, Miami, FL 33131 ☎ 305/358-1992. **New York** ⊠ 666 5th Ave., 35th fl., New York, NY 10103 ☎ 212/265-8822. **Canada** ⊠ 2 Bloor St. W, Suite 3402, Toronto, Ontario M4W 3E2 ☎ 416/961-3131. **United Kingdom** ⊠ 22-23 Manchester Sq., London W1M 5AP, U.K. ☎ 0207/486-8077.

⚠ Government Advisories U.S. Department of State ⊠ Bureau of Consular Affairs, Overseas Citizens Services Office, 2201 C St. NW, Washington, DC 20520 ☎ 888/407-4747 or 202/647-5225 hotline from the U.S., or 202/501-4444 overseas ⊕ www. travel.state.gov. **Consular Affairs Bureau of Canada** ☎ 800/267-6788 in U.S. or 613/944-6788 overseas ⊕ www.voyage.gc.ca. **U.K. Foreign and Commonwealth Office** ⊠ Travel Advice Unit, Consular Division, Old Admiralty Bldg., London SW1A 2PA ☎ 0845/850-2829 or 020/7008-1500 ⊕ www. fco.gov.uk/travel. **Australian Department of Foreign Affairs and Trade** ☎ 300/139-281 travel advisories, 02/6261-3305 Consular Travel Advice ⊕ www.dfat.gov.au and www.smartraveller.gov.au. **New Zealand Ministry of Foreign Affairs and Trade** ☎ 04/439-8000 ⊕ www.mft.govt.nz.

WEB SITES

Do check out the World Wide Web when planning your trip. You'll find everything from weather forecasts to virtual tours of famous cities. Be sure to visit Fodors.com (⊕ www.fodors.com), a complete travel-planning site. You can research prices and book plane tickets, hotel rooms, rental cars, vacation packages, and more. In addition, you can post your pressing questions in the forums (Talk) section. Other planning tools include a currency converter and weather reports, and there are loads of links to travel resources.

For more information on Spain, visit the Tourist Office of Spain at ⊕ www. tourspain.es or ⊕ www.okspain.org. Also check out the sites ⊕ www.cyberspain. com and ⊕ www.red2000.com/spain. For a virtual brochure on Spain's paradores, go to ⊕ www.parador.es.

CONVERSIONS

DISTANCE

KILOMETERS/MILES

To change kilometers (km) to miles (mi), multiply km by .621. To change mi to km, multiply mi by 1.61.

km to mi	mi to km
1 = .62	1 = 1.6
2 = 1.2	2 = 3.2
3 = 1.9	3 = 4.8
4 = 2.5	4 = 6.4
5 = 3.1	5 = 8.1
6 = 3.7	6 = 9.7
7 = 4.3	7 = 11.3
8 = 5.0	8 = 12.9

METERS/FEET

To change meters (m) to feet (ft), multiply m by 3.28. To change ft to m, multiply ft by .305.

m to ft	ft to m
1 = 3.3	1 = .30
2 = 6.6	2 = .61
3 = 9.8	3 = .92
4 = 13.1	4 = 1.2
5 = 16.4	5 = 1.5
6 = 19.7	6 = 1.8
7 = 23.0	7 = 2.1
8 = 26.2	8 = 2.4

TEMPERATURE

METRIC CONVERSIONS

To change centigrade or Celsius (C) to Fahrenheit (F), multiply C by 1.8 and add 32. To change F to C, subtract 32 from F and multiply by .555.

°F	°C
0	-17.8
10	-12.2
20	-6.7
30	-1.1
32	0
40	+4.4
50	10.0
60	15.5
70	21.1
80	26.6
90	32.2
98.6	37.0
100	37.7

WEIGHT

KILOGRAMS/POUNDS

To change kilograms (kg) to pounds (lb), multiply kg by 2.20. To change lb to kg, multiply lb by .455.

kg to lb	lb to kg
1 = 2.2	1 = .45
2 = 4.4	2 = .91
3 = 6.6	3 = 1.4
4 = 8.8	4 = 1.8
5 = 11.0	5 = 2.3
6 = 13.2	6 = 2.7
7 = 15.4	7 = 3.2
8 = 17.6	8 = 3.6

GRAMS/OUNCES

To change grams (g) to ounces (oz), multiply g by .035. To change oz to g, multiply oz by 28.4.

g to oz	oz to g
1 = .04	1 = 28
2 = .07	2 = 57
3 = .11	3 = 85
4 = .14	4 = 114
5 = .18	5 = 142
6 = .21	6 = 170
7 = .25	7 = 199
8 = .28	8 = 227

LIQUID VOLUME

LITERS/U.S. GALLONS

To change liters (L) to U.S. gallons (gal), multiply L by .264. To change U.S. gal to L, multiply gal by 3.79.

L to gal	gal to L
1 = .26	1 = 3.8
2 = .53	2 = 7.6
3 = .79	3 = 11.4
4 = 1.1	4 = 15.2
5 = 1.3	5 = 19.0
6 = 1.6	6 = 22.7
7 = 1.8	7 = 26.5
8 = 2.1	8 = 30.3

CLOTHING SIZE

WOMEN'S CLOTHING

US	UK	EUR
4	6	34
6	8	36
8	10	38
10	12	40
12	14	42

WOMEN'S SHOES

US	UK	EUR
5	3	36
6	4	37
7	5	38
8	6	39
9	7	40

MEN'S SUITS

US	UK	EUR
34	34	44
36	36	46
38	38	48
40	40	50
42	42	52
44	44	54
46	46	56

MEN'S SHIRTS

US	UK	EUR
14½	14½	37
15	15	38
15½	15½	39
16	16	41
16½	16½	42
17	17	43
17½	17½	44

MEN'S SHOES

US	UK	EUR
7	6	39½
8	7	41
9	8	42
10	9	43
11	10	44½
12	11	46

INDEX

PHOTO CREDITS

ABOUT OUR WRITERS

Convinced that another dreary London winter might be the end of him, **Ben Curtis** escaped to Madrid seven years ago to pursue his passion for photography, languages and travel. He has since written about all aspects of living and traveling in Spain for guidebooks and travel websites, and is currently working with his Spanish wife on podcasts about Spain and Spanish cuisine.

Born and raised in Madrid, economist **Ignacio Gómez** spent three years living and working in New York and rode the online journalism wave in Madrid serving as a writer and editor for a Spanish technology and economy Web magazine. After completing a Masters in Comparative Literature, he now writes for both the online and paper version of *20 minutos* (a free Spanish newspaper) and is a frequent contributor for *OnMadrid* (the weekly entertainment and culture magazine for El País), Consumer as well as others.

Journalist **Michael Kessler** spent most of his childhood in Australia. He first arrived in Barcelona in the late 80s and stayed for a decade. He returned to Sydney, but his writing took him back to Spain continually, and he returned to Barcelona in 2003. Kessler writes almost exclusively on Spanish music, food, theater, film, travel, art, sports, and politics for the Australian press and a range of Spanish, American, and British magazines.

Jared Lubarsky is a university teacher and freelance journalist who has been writing for Fodor's since 1997, first on Japan, where he lived for 30 years, and more recently—having relocated, with unqualified delight, to Barcelona—on Spain. He contributes to a range of inflight and general interest magazines, guides, and newspapers, and is happiest exploring the myriad ways that the arts impact on social and economic affairs.

Journalist **Mary McLean** is from England and has worked in California, the Middle East, and, since 1990, Spain. Mary writes for many magazines and travel publications, including in-flight magazines and guidebooks. She has covered Portugal, Italy, and various regions of Spain and contributes to travel-related Web sites. In her spare time she likes nothing better than exploring the wilder regions of the Iberian peninsula, taking along a sketch pad as well her portable computer.

Norman Renouf was born in London and educated at Charlton Secondary School, Greenwich. Always interested in travel, he started writing travel guides, articles, and newspaper contributions in the early 1990s and has covered destinations throughout Europe. Now living in Spain, he has also written several guides about Washington, D.C., and the mid-Atlantic region.

Born and educated in Connecticut, writer and journalist **George Semler** has lived in Spain for the last 30-odd years. During that time he has written on Spain, France, Morocco, Cuba, and the Mediterranean region for *Forbes, Sky, Saveur,* the *International Herald Tribune,* and the *Los Angeles Times* and has published walking guides to Madrid and Barcelona. When not hiking, fly-fishing, skiing, or sampling Catalonia's hottest new restaurants, James Beard Journalism Awards Finalist Semler forges ahead on his magnum opus about the Pyrenees.

Kip Tobin is a freelance writer, journalist, music critic, English teacher, and DJ living in Madrid. Concerning Spain, he has written a handful of short stories, a slew of articles covering travel, music, film and human interest, several blogs, and (in his words) a poorly written novel. He currently is working on a collection of short stories based on Madrid and connected by Madrileño's zealousness to protest about anything at any time.